The
Golden Age
of Jewish
Achievement

The
Golden Age
of Jewish
Achievement

Steven L. Pease

DEUCALION

Sonoma, California

PICTURE CREDITS

Feynman image courtesy of Malcolm Kirk, www.malcolmkirk.com, p. 29.
Land image courtesy of Rowland Institute, with attribution to Jay Scarpenti, p. 40.
Friedman image courtesy of Friedman Foundation for Educational Choice, p. 64.
Koufax book cover courtesy of Harper Collins Publishers, p. 79.
Streisand image: Juergen Vollmer/Redferns/Getty Images, p. 114
Libeskind's World Trade Center rendering attribution to Silverstein Properties, p. 135.
Gehry's Guggenheim Bilbao courtesy of www.CreativeCommons.org, p. 135
Bunshaft's Lever House courtesy of GNU Licensing, p. 135
Grove image courtesy of Intel Corporation, p. 176
Chomsky image courtesy of Marcello Casal, Jr. Agência Brasil, p. 337

Other images are public domain or courtesy of private sources

First Edition 2009

ISBN: 978-0-9825168-0-5 hardcover
ISBN: 978-0-9825168-1-2 paperback
ISBN: 978-0-9825168-2-9 kindle ebook

Library of Congress Control Number: 2009935485

Design and production by Deborah Daly, Daly Design, deborahdaly.com

PRINTED IN THE UNITED STAES OF AMERICA

Table of Contents

"The suddenness with which Jews began to appear and make a mark in numerous…areas, of whose very existence their fathers had, in most cases no idea at all, is nothing short of astounding. It seemed as if a huge reservoir of Jewish talent, hitherto dammed up behind the wall of Talmudic learning were suddenly released to spill over into all fields of Gentile cultural activity. In…a few years after they were first allowed to sit on the benches of general secular schools Jews were found among the leaders of industry, of literature and journalism, of music and the performing arts of all fields of the sciences and even in painting and sculpture, two areas from which they had been most strictly debarred by their own religious tradition."

—Raphael Patai,
The Jewish Mind

A Summing Up — Achievements of Jews　　　　Table 1

Distinction	Relevant Geography	Total Recipients	Projected Jewish Recipients	Actual Jewish Recipients	Jews As A Multiple Of Projected	Jews As A Percent of all Recipients
The Greats of History						
Hart's Most Influential 100 in History	World[1]	100	0.2	8	35	8%
A&E's Millennium 100	World	100	0.2	8	35	8%
Time magazine's 100 of the 20th Century	U.S.[2]	67	1.4	13	9	19%
Intelliquest's World's Greatest 100	World	100	0.2	8	35	8%
Science						
Nobel Prize in Physics	World	181	0.4	48	116	27%
Nobel Prize in Physiology & Medicine	World	189	0.4	59	136	31%
Nobel Prize in Chemistry	World	151	0.3	30	87	20%
Total Nobels for Science	World	521	1.2	137	115	26%
Fields Medal (for mathematics)	World	48	0.1	12	109	25%
A. M. Turing Award (for computer science)	World	54	0.1	13	105	24%
Invention						
Encyclopedia Britannica's Great Inventors	World	267	0.6	13.7	22	5%
Education						
Enrollment in Ivy League Schools	U.S.	115,000	2,380	24,000	10	21%
Military and Aviation						
United States Astronauts	U.S.	268	5.5	9	2	3%
Economics						
Nobel Prize for Economics	World	61	0.1	22	157	36%
John Bates Clark Medal in Economics	U.S.	30	0.6	20	32	67%
Federal Reserve Chairmen	U.S.	14	0.3	4	14	29%
Politics and Law						
U.S. Senators (108th Congress)	U.S.	100	2.1	11	5	11%
U.S. Congressmen & Women (108th Congress)	U.S.	435	9.0	26	3	6%
Largest Political Donors (Mother Jones List)	U.S.	100	2.1	41	20	41%
United States Supreme Court Justices	U.S.	110	2.3	7	3	6%
Nobel Prize for Peace	World	95	0.2	9	41	9%
Sports and Games						
NFL Hall of Fame Inductees	U.S.	247	5.1	6	1	2%
NFL Team Owners (excludes "community owned" Green Bay)	U.S.	31	0.6	9	14	29%
MLB Prof. Baseball Team Owners (individually owned)	U.S.	26	0.5	5.5	10	21%
NBA Top 10 Coaches of All Time	U.S.	10	0.2	2	10	20%
NBA Basketball Team Owners	U.S.	30	0.6	10	16	33%
Naismith Basketball Hall of Fame Inductees	U.S.	285	5.9	20	3	7%
Olympics Medalists 1896 to date	see 5 below	16,167	66.9	231.74	3	1%
World Chess Champions - Years as Champion	see 5 below	122 yrs.	0.5	66 yrs.	131	54%
The Written Word						
Nobel Prize for Literature	World	104	0.2	13	55	13%
Pulitzer Prize for Fiction	U.S.	82	1.7	11	6	13%
Pulitzer Prize for Poetry	U.S.	89	1.8	17	9	19%
Pulitzer Prize for Non Fiction	U.S.	50	1.0	25.5	25	51%
Pulitzer Prize for Drama	U.S.	77	1.6	22	14	29%
Performing Arts and Comedy						
Kennedy Center Honorees	U.S.	157	3.2	41	13	26%
Conductors Major U.S. Symphony Orchestras	U.S.	202	4.2	66	16	33%
Composers "World's 50 Greatest" CD Collection	see 3 below	50	0.6	6	10	12%
Longest Running Broadway Musicals	U.S.	38	0.8	24	31	63%
Rock & Roll Hall of Fame Inductees	U.S.	238	4.9	29	6	12%

A Summing Up — Achievements of Jews   Table 1

Distinction	Relevant Geography	Total Recipients	Projected Jewish Recipients	Actual Jewish Recipients	Jews As A Multiple Of Projected	Jews As A Percent of all Recipients
Performing Arts and Comedy (cont.)						
Jazz Grammy Awards	U.S.	216	4.5	22	5	10%
Grammy Lifetime Achievement Winners (Indiv.)	U.S.	125	2.6	18	7	14%
Rate It All Ranking of Stand Up Comedians	U.S.	82	1.7	25	15	30%
Visual Arts and Architecture						
Phaidon's 500 Artists	see 3 below	500	6.3	37	6	7%
Combined Lists (7) of Great Photographers	see 4 below	587	7.4	153	21	26%
Combined Lists (6) of Master Architects	World	309	0.7	32	45	10%
Hollywood						
Academy Award Winning Directors	U.S.	83	1.7	31	18	37%
Greatest Movie Directors - Reel.com	U.S.	55	1.1	15	13	27%
Greatest Movie Directors - Filmsite.org	U.S.	75	1.6	27	17	36%
Star Power 500 Top Actors & Actresses	U.S.	500	10.3	75	7	15%
American Film Institute Lifetime Achievement Awards	U.S.	35	0.7	8	11	23%
American Film Institute Greatest American Screen Legends	U.S.	50	1.0	6	6	12%
Radio and Television						
Radio Hall of Fame Inductees	U.S.	108	2.2	19	8	18%
Television Hall of Fame Inductees	U.S.	108	2.2	39	17	36%
High Tech Entrepreneurs and CEOs						
Entrepreneurs (Fortune's Richest 40 Under 40)	U.S	27	0.6	6	11	22%
Forbes' 400 (November 2007)	U.S	400	8.3	126	15	31%
Fortune 500 CEOs						
CEOs of Major 1917 U.S. Corporations[5]	U.S.	153	4.7	7	1	5%
CEOs of Major 1997 U.S. Corporations	U.S.	72	1.5	16	11	22%
Fortune 100 CEOs	U.S.	100	2.1	15	7	15%
Fortune's 25 Most Powerful People in Business	U.S	25	0.5	6	12	24%
Finance						
Private Equity Hall of Fame	U.S.	26	0.5	8	15	24%
Real Estate						
Forbes' "25 Real Estate Fortunes Among Forbes' 400"	U.S.	25	0.5	18	35	72%
Social Activists						
Ladies Home Journal's "100 Most Important Women"	U.S.	100	2.1	20	10	20%
Philanthropy						
Business Week's 50 Leading Philanthropists	U.S.	50	1.0	19	19	38%
All Nobels						
Total - All Nobel Prizes	World	781	1.8	181	101	23%

1) As of 2002, there were an estimated 14.3 million Jews in a world of 6.23 billion people. Jews were .00207 percent of the World's population.

2) As of 2002, the United States population was 280,562,489. Of that number an estimated 5,807,000 were Jews (2.07 percent).

3) U.S., Canada, Europe, Australia, New Zealand and Israel.

4) Western Hemisphere, Europe, Australia and New Zealand Jews were .0126% of population.

5) Jewish percent of the world population has changed over the 112 years of the Olympics. For this exhibit, the current percent (.00207) was doubled to approximate the average.

Introduction

Asked why he, a Gentile, was donating $1 million to the Aish Ha Torah's World Outreach Center in Jerusalem, the successful American entrepreneur John Kluge responded:

"Last year I turned eighty....At my birthday party, I realized 85 percent of my friends are Jews. I have always admired the Jewish people and their contributions to humanity, to civilizing the world. What Aish Ha Torah is doing to reconnect Jews with their heritage, to strengthen their roots, to educate them about their values, is enabling the Jewish people to continue to be able to play their incredibly valuable role in history."[1]

What follows cannot compare with Kluge's generosity, but it arises from a similar impulse: recognition of many rich and rewarding friendships, appreciation for the immensely valuable role Jews have played over their 4,000-year history, and an effort to explore their achievements and the cultural influences behind them. Are Jews high achievers? If so, why is that so? And, are there lessons in those answers for all of us? That is what this book is about.

A Presbyterian by upbringing, of Scots-Irish, English, and German heritage, I do not claim Jewish genes. Nonetheless, Jews have played a long and important role in my life. Their vitality and determination has been as delightful as the warmth of their friendship and pleasure of their humor. In a later chapter, Gordon Gee, the Mormon president of Vanderbilt University at the time, is quoted as saying, Jews "by culture and by ability and by the very nature of their liveliness, make a university a much more habitable place in terms of intellectual life."[2] That has been my experience, and it was part of the motivation for this book.

Born in 1943 in Spokane, Washington, I was a kid when post-war television documentaries began to air. Together with books, magazines, and movies, they chronicled a tragic era. Pacific war atrocities were horrifying, but paled in comparison with those in Europe. Only Matthew Brady's pictures of thousands of Civil War dead could compare with images of what happened in Central and Eastern Europe between 1939 and 1945. Published in the United States in 1952, *The Diary of Anne Frank* personalized the terror in the account of a young Jewish girl in occupied Amsterdam who eventually died in Bergen-Belsen. To me it was horrifying and made no sense. How could anyone do this to other human beings?

It wasn't yet called the "Holocaust." William Shirer's 1959 Book, *The Rise and Fall of the Third Reich*, the first comprehensive history of what happened, does not use that term. Shirer and others called it the "genocide" or the "Jewish extermination." The expressions "Holocaust" and "Shoah" were first used in Israel and only later adopted worldwide. If Jews were but 0.7 percent of the world's population at the time, Hitler's evil made it impossible to be ignorant of the grisly way six million innocents were destroyed. That reality also taught most of us at least a smattering of the two-thousand-year history of anti-Semitism that led to the ovens. At about the same time, Leon Uris' book *Exodus* popularized the story of Israel's creation, and two years later it became a hit movie starring Paul Newman.

So I grew up sympathetic to Jews. In my life they were the underdogs, the victims who responded to their oppression by creating their own country and then defending it against countries with superior numbers.

There weren't many Jews in Spokane's grade schools and high schools. Nonetheless, curiosity led to a limited understanding of Jewish history and awareness that their Jewish Bible (or "*Tanakh*" in their parlance) was my Old Testament, a foundation of Christianity.

Elected class vice president at the University of Washington, I worked with a Jewish class president. A good student with a ready smile and a delightful sense of humor, Larry was one of perhaps five Jewish friends or close acquaintances I had before entering Harvard Business School. There I had a Jewish roommate, and of the eight of us sharing a common shower and lavatory, three were Jews. But at school it was classes, current events, sports, and dates we discussed. Jewish religion and culture were not taboo, they just rarely came up for conversation.

In 1965 James Michener's novel *The Source* used a fictional archaeological dig in Israel to reveal the long history of Jews in Palestine. Two years later, Chaim Potok's *The Chosen* depicted Hasidic and Orthodox Jewish life in Brooklyn. That same year, during six days in June, an outnumbered Israeli military won the most lopsided military victory since Agincourt. Over that six days, they quadrupled the territory under their control, including all of the Sinai. "Visit Israel, See the Pyramids!" was a popular joke of the times. My knowledge of Jewish history was growing, as was my respect for their spunk and skill.

After a stint at management consulting, my first opportunity to run a company came at the hands of a successful tough-minded Jewish entrepreneur. A college dropout, Dick taught me more than I had learned in two years at Harvard. When the company acquired our largest competitor, I began to work with an Israeli-born entrepreneur. David was the most technologically proficient businessman in our industry (real estate information). His friendship was matched by the efforts of our aggressive, mostly Jewish, sales force to test my leadership as their young Gentile boss. I haggled with Jewish competitors as we acquired ever more publishers around the country. Ted, my partner in those acquisitions, was a young Jewish attorney at a prominent New York firm who, like David, is now a friend of more than thirty-five years.

Concerned about the deterioration of the historic single-screen theater in downtown Sonoma, I formed a partnership with Ed, a Jewish entrepreneur. Our efforts led to a management change that restored that historic building. In time, I contributed money and served on the board of his Lifelong Learning Program. It pioneered senior adult education on the campus of Sonoma State University. And with financial support from Bernard Osher, it served as a model for today's Osher Lifelong Learning (OLLI) programs on nearly 120 college campuses around the United States.

Over the years, I have served with countless Jews on boards of directors, supervised Jewish employees, backed them as a venture capitalist, negotiated with them in various deals and competed with them often. If some were occasionally difficult, irascible, even obnoxious, (and matched by non-Jews of similar ilk), more often they were warm, open, thoughtful, and incredibly full of life. Ethnic jokes, though "politically incorrect" these days, contained grains of truth about Jewish mothers, rabbinic wisdom, and many other Jewish characteristics. Indeed, to this day one of my favorite Jewish jokes came from Danny, a close Jewish friend and neighbor.*

Through those and other experiences, two big questions grew in my mind.

First, it seemed to me that Jews were disproportionately high achievers (and contributors). Was that really true? I conjured up the idea of asking experts for lists of the 100 most important people in such fields as diplomacy, science, law, medicine, music, and a host of other domains. From those lists, I thought perhaps I could prove or disprove my instinctive sense that as a group Jews are disproportionately accomplished. Unfortunately, even if I could have found the experts and convinced them to prepare the lists, I lacked the time and resources to say, with confidence, which of those on each list were and were not Jews.

The second question was why virulent anti-Semitism has existed for more than two thousand years.

I knew Christians had reviled Jews as Christ's killers, but Christ's death and resurrection are at the core of the world's largest religion. The author of that drama was neither Judas nor the Pharisees. It was God. Christ's death presumably requites the sins of humanity. It was not the result of coins given to Judas nor Pharisees getting even with a rabble-rouser. And I thought it illogical that a loving God would use a people who failed to accept Christ as an eternally impoverished example of the price his "chosen" people would pay for disbelieving. It made no more sense than the charge that Jews killed infants for their blood or that they brought on the Black Plague.

But like Muhammad and Luther, both of whom tried unsuccessfully to convert Jews and became enraged when they could not, until quite recently most Christians and many Muslims found this small tribe of heretics a threat. And, of course, a tribe that used a different language, kept to themselves, dressed and ate differently, and followed their own Talmudic laws, could easily be made into scapegoats when anything went wrong. The temptation to vilify was exacerbated by the economic, academic, and cultural success of some Jews, which actually arose from the premium Jews placed on education and the historical circumstances of the Diaspora.

---

* A huge wave sweeps a young Jewish boy from his mother as they walk on an ocean beach. She raises her face to the heavens, shakes her fist and rails on and on, telling God she did not deserve this. How dare he? After nearly an hour of continuing harangue, God relents. The next wave brings her son back to the shore. He lands in an upright position with a smile on his face. His mother takes one look at her son before raising her face and fist to the skies shouting, "He had a hat!"

Later, there was *The Protocols of the Elders of Zion*, an early twentieth-century screed still in circulation today. It purportedly details a Jewish conspiracy to control the world. That it was, in fact, a work of propaganda fiction based on an 1864 book by a Frenchman, Maurice Joy, who was attacking the political ambitions of Napoleon III of France, is little known even today. Nonetheless, the Russian Cheka (secret police) spread the fabrication widely and in the United States, Henry Ford believed it was true and republished it. Even today, contemporary Middle Eastern television produces and airs "documentaries" suggesting the *Protocols* are established fact. They are not.

Greedy, outspoken, vile, conniving, and boorish. Yes, some Jews are all of those things and more. Bernie Madoff is just the most notorious recent example. And any reading of *Postville*, a contemporary account of the Kosher slaughterhouse in northeastern Iowa and its recent shutdown for unfair labor and contemptible business practices, is certain to create outrage among both Jews and Gentiles. But by any objective measure, Jews' behavior is no better or worse than that of any other tribe. And on the scale of atrocities, their behavior hardly moves the needle.

In the end, most historical anti-Semitic allegations fail rational justification. Jews did not kill Christ, kill infants for their blood, cause plagues, or any of the other allegations made against them. The two reasons that survive are equally wrong-headed. The first is "the other," the unique culture and isolation of Jews which allowed them to survive and avoid assimilation but which also engendered irrational fear and mistrust among those who did not understand the behavior and felt threatened by it. The second is resentment at Jewish success, and for some, an ignorant jealousy that sees conspiracy in their accomplishments. In other words, having done so well, they must be cheating. They aren't. And as this book argues, most of us can learn from them. Stated simply, culture matters. Many more of us could match the Jews' performance, but first we must understand it.

A few years ago, my mother's illness required that I be available on short notice and fly to Spokane frequently to provide for her. Through this period, I could not take on a full-time assignment. It gave me the time, and the Internet gave me the tool, to explore my interest in disproportionate Jewish achievement. An immense number of high-achiever rankings across many domains were available not only from books in my small library, but also from the ubiquitous sources of the Internet. Want to know the winners of the 1916 Winter Olympics? It is on the Internet. All of the Oscar winners, symphony conductors, or bridge champions, they are all there—and much, much more.

The Internet repository also complements published books in identifying prominent Jews. Some of those sites are wrong and some are anti-Semitic, but the Web provides tools never before so accessible. Annual Form 990 family foundation tax filings detail philanthropic donations. Jewish charities identify donors. Book, newspaper, and magazine articles provide authentication of ancestry. What was nearly impossible, and always time consuming, can now be accomplished very quickly at little or no cost.

In short, my mother's illness, my inability to take on a full-time assignment while I tended to her, and the enormous research capability unleashed by the Internet, gave me the time and the tools to explore disproportionate Jewish achievement.

It did not take long to confirm my instincts. But the more work I did, the more astonished I became. The performance went far beyond my expectations. Thirty-three percent of America's leading symphonic conductors, 23 percent of Nobel prize winners, and 38 percent of America's most generous philanthropists were Jews. My expectations were eclipsed by the magnitude of what they had done.

After sharing my findings with a few close friends, one of them passed a single page synopsis to Rabbi Harold S. Kushner, author of *When Bad Things Happen to Good People*. Rabbi Kushner took an interest, and in conversation raised the key question—"Why?" He knew better than I did what I would find as I finished up my research. But he posed for me the task of explaining why it had happened. Research that might have been completed in less than a year (simply measuring Jews' performance) now became a bigger task.

I needed to answer Rabbi Kushner's question. But to do that I had to learn much more about Jewish history and culture and compare it with other cultures. I had to read what others have said on the topic, develop my own thoughts and test them with feedback from Jews and non-Jews. In short I became something of a Gentile working toward a Ph.D. in Jewish Studies.

It was fascinating. I already knew more than most Gentiles about Jewish history, but digging in, studying, writing, and talking about it with Jews over time made me appreciate how incredible the story is. It is a four-thousand-year odyssey from which nearly all their early contemporary tribes have disappeared. And as I developed a better understanding of the religion and historical circumstances that drove the culture, I was complimented when Jewish friends told me I knew more of their history than they did.

I wish not to condense a rather large book into a few sentences that do not do justice to the full story, but a bit of foreshadowing may set the stage for those who might be aided by a preview.

Jews were the world's first people to believe in a single God. Their unique belief in monotheism led directly to Christianity and Islam, two religions now practiced by more than half the world's 6.7 billion people. It was a just God eclipsing the notion of multiple gods handing out capricious fates to individuals. The Jewish God was not fatalistic. Instead, his (or her) demand was for ethical behavior. If God's judgments were at times arbitrary, from Abraham on, Jews saw fit to challenge him. Timidity and acquiescence were not to become characteristics that describe most Jews. And if God had created an imperfect world, it was the Jew's duty (*tikkun olam*) as God's "chosen people" to help "heal the broken world." *Tzedakah* imposed a corresponding duty to work for justice, provide for the poor, and for one's family.

The Jewish God respected faith but demanded action. Unlike religions in which faith is what matters, in Judaism action trumps faith. And in Judaism, history is an arrow, not a circle as in Eastern faiths. Judaism starts with creation and thus inherently invokes the notion of progress and a future one can shape. There is no unceasing return, no reincarnation. Surrender is not cherished, nor is reaching out for the eternal harmony of acceptance, or pacifism. Talmudic Judaism is also pragmatic. The sages have constantly used reason to update the religious orthodoxy in light of changed circumstances. Hillel's revision to Biblical injunctions about loans (amending the requirement for all loans to be forgiven every seventh year) is but a small example of Jewish rationality, which over the two thousand years of rabbinic Judaism has reconciled Jewish Law with the ever-changing facts on the ground.

Circumstances also shaped the Jewish culture. Their rebellions against Roman rule led to the death of one million Jews and their dispersal (the Diaspora) to the four corners of the world. Over nearly all of the next two thousand years, Jews would exist as tiny minority enclaves within larger dominant populations. Earlier, ten of the twelve Jewish tribes had been lost forever following the Assyrian conquest of 722 B.C. In 586 B.C., the two remaining tribes were conquered by the Babylonians and most of the surviving Jews were forced into a Babylonian exile for a time.

Three times conquered, and already twice dispersed, having lost the ten tribes to the Assyrian dispersal, the sages of rabbinical Judaism (the surviving sect), deemed education mandatory for Jews. For the first time in human history, universal literacy was required of a people. The Jewish sages knew that if they were to preserve their religion, culture, and tribe over the years and across the thousands of miles, the religion and culture had to be committed to writing lest it dissipate over time through assimilation and diluted recall. The "Oral Law" could no longer be "oral." Jews had to codify their beliefs, be able to read what was written, discuss it, and write their questions, answers, and opinions down and communicate them to fellow Jews across the world.

No religion had ever made that demand on its followers. And it was a steep demand for a rural tribe of farmers. Literacy was expensive both in time and money, particularly before the arrival of printing. It served no purpose beyond religion and culture, did not put food on the table, nor help in growing the flock or the crops. It is thought the demand proved too steep for many Jews, who simply opted out of the religion. But those who remained taught their offspring. It became a cultural value which has endured nearly two thousand years.

If education was expensive, it was also a very portable form of investment in themselves, an investment with an enormous long-term return. As civilization advanced, as cities began to prosper, and as the needs of commerce demanded literacy for exchanging goods, buying and selling, keeping records, and hundreds of other tasks required in an ever more sophisticated world, no group was better able to fulfill those needs. And none had kin spread across the globe sharing a common language and a culture of trust, so vital to do business over long distances. Yeshivas flourished and Talmudic study sharpened the minds of Jewish students who debated complex, often arcane, issues from the Torah and Talmud.

Unique dress, rituals, diet, and other customs demanded by the sages were also vital to keep the culture and religion alive and to separate Jews from the host cultures that might otherwise assimilate them. But that separation made them "the other," a different people to be feared and vilified by non-Jews. The seemingly strange customs, the Jewish refusal to convert, and their commercial success arising from vital talents, their unique ability to lend money, and the demand of local royalty to use Jewish skills in ways (such as collecting taxes) that often served the ruler while oppressing the locals, bred hate and resentment.

Through it all, Jews were intellectual. The Talmud served the evolution of reason and rationalism. It was a text that constantly updated the religion and law in light of new circumstances. The Islamic Hadith is not nearly so progressive. That, and some Christians' views of a literal unchanging interpretation of the Bible as God's word, put both groups squarely into a more static orthodoxy than Talmudic Judaism.

In short, Jewish religion and culture became home to a determined people, a people who believed in the future, who were trained and accustomed to being different, and who were educated with rules (the Jewish laws and customs from the Torah, the Tanakh and the Talmud) that not only kept them together – and separate—but also evolved rational ways for Jews to function in ever-changing circumstances.

For the most part, from A.D. 70 to 1800, Jews were reviled, isolated, and put upon. Practically speaking, it was Napoleon who launched the Jewish Emancipation, and thereby began to break down most of the barriers against Jews. As the Emancipation spread from country to country, Jews experienced their own Enlightenment, and shortly thereafter, their Reform movement arose in Europe and the United States. The skills, intellectualism, and drive which previously focused on their religion and culture now shifted to the secular world. With that, disproportionate Jewish achievements in secular domains arose and grew over succeeding generations. It continues more than 200 years after the start of the Jewish Emancipation. This is their Golden Age.

While it can be argued that phenomenal rates of Jewish achievement arose from genes, second-generation immigrant status, or any number of other factors, in the end those arguments, while interesting, are not compelling. It was their culture, born of religion and circumstance that spurred exceptional rates of Jewish achievement.

That is the good news and a major reason for this book. The message is not that we should all become Jews. My heritage is Gentile, my upbringing Presbyterian. I am proud of my background and if I can rarely be found in church on Sunday mornings, I am not about to relegate Christ to the role of an interesting prophet.

The point is that culture matters, and all cultures are not equal, no matter how much we might wish it otherwise. Better understanding of the cultural values which induce positive behavior, outstanding rates of achievement, and undeniable contributions that have benefited us all, means Jewish success need not be unique. We need not have Jewish genes or convert to appreciate and learn from their performance.

As this book's author, I would hope every name, fact, and statement in *The Golden Age of Jewish Achievement* is accurate, properly spelled, and on point. But experience has taught me errors sometimes slip in. And while I would expect more errors of omission than commission in identifying those Jews who have accomplished much, any book with more than 600 pages, 4,000 index entries and sixty exhibits is likely to have mistakes. It would be very much appreciated if when you see one, you would consider e-mailing me care of the publisher, Deucalion@vom.com so I can make corrections for the next edition.

CHAPTER 1

The Measure of Their Achievements

"Properly, the Jew ought hardly to be heard of, but he is heard of, has always been heard of. He is as prominent on the planet as any other people, and his commercial importance is extravagantly out of proportion to the smallness of his bulk. His contributions to the world's list of great names in literature, science, art, music, finance, medicine, and abstruse learning are also away out of proportion to the weakness of his numbers...."

—MARK TWAIN
Harpers, 1899

Written more than 100 years ago, Twain's quote is prescient, even truer today than it was in 1899. No contemporary culture has achieved or contributed as much, relative to its scant population, as the Jews.

Perhaps the only eras in which small numbers of people have done as much in so many fields would be Renaissance Italy, the Golden Age of the Dutch, early Islam, Elizabethan England, the Scots between the 1700s and 1900, or Periclean Greece. No other contemporary culture has done anything like it.

There are, perhaps, thirteen to fifteen million Jews in a world of six billion people. Jews are so few in number that in a room of 1,000 people representing the world's population, only two would be Jewish. A comparable sample from the United States would count only twenty-two Jews among 1,000 representative Americans.

Jews have won 23 percent of all the Nobel Prizes ever awarded—27 percent since 1946—after the Holocaust destroyed a third of their numbers. Given their small population, Jews should have earned only one of the 521 Nobels awarded for physics, chemistry, medicine, and physiology through 2007. They have won 137.

The Fields Medal, awarded to the world's brightest mathematicians under age 40, is the honor non-Jew John Nash, of the book and movie *A Beautiful Mind,* had hoped to win. Instead, he took a Nobel Prize in economics as a consolation prize. One-fourth of the Fields Medal winners are Jews.

Encyclopædia Britannica provides its list of "Great Inventions." Of the 267 individual inventors, at least fifteen were Jews, including Zoll (the defibrillator and the pacemaker), Land (instant photography), Gabor (holography), and Ginsburg (videotape). Jews are represented on the list twenty-two times more than one would expect based on their population.

They are disproportionately counted in most of the arts. Since their respective dates of inception, America's leading symphony orchestras have been led by Jewish conductors one-third of the time. They have created nearly two-thirds of Broadway's longest-running musicals. Probably one-fourth of the greatest photographers of all time have been Jews, as have 10 percent of the world's great master architects. Of movie directors who earned Oscars, 37 percent were Jews. In broad artistic recognition, nearly 26 percent of the Kennedy Center Honors and 14 percent of the Grammy Lifetime Achievement Awards have gone to them.

As "People of the Book," the sobriquet Muhammad used to describe them, it is perhaps not surprising Jews have earned 13 percent of the Nobel Prizes for Literature and 51 percent of the Pulitzer Prizes for nonfiction. Their outpouring of books, screenplays, and newspaper and magazine articles is prodigious.

In education, it is difficult to name an academic discipline in which they have not played a leading role. Certainly Jews have been seminal thinkers in philosophy (Spinoza, Maimonides, Marx), deconstruction (Derrida), economics (Marx, Ricardo, Friedman, Samuelson, Becker, Kuznets), physics (Einstein, Bohr, Gell-Mann, Feynman, Szilard), mathematics (Von Neumann, Mandelbrot, Fefferman, Zelmanov, Erdös), chemistry (Heeger, Kohn, Kroto, Olah), linguistics (Chomsky), paleontology (Gould), medicine (Flexner, Chain, Goldstein and Brown, Salk, Sabin, Prusiner), law (Brandeis, Cardozo, Frankfurter, Tribe, Dershowitz), anthropology (Boas), psychiatry and psychology (Freud, Adler, Erikson, Fromm, Rapaport, Maslow), sociology (Riesman, Glazer, Lipset), and many other fields. Their research and teaching helped shape entire disciplines. They head two of the eight Ivy League schools (down from four several years ago), and Jewish students are 21 percent of all Ivy League students. Any review of the lists of faculty of most schools will evidence a disproportionate number of Jewish teachers. They are, for example, roughly 30 percent of the faculty of the Harvard, Stanford, and Yale law schools.

In politics, they were 11 percent of the United States Senate and 6 percent of the House of Representatives in the 108th Congress. They were 42 percent of the 100 largest political donors to the 2000 election cycle, and since 1917, when Judge Louis Brandeis was appointed, 16 percent of Supreme Court justices have been Jews. They now hold two of the nine positions.

As economists they are gifted. They have earned 36 percent of all Nobel Prizes for economics and 67 percent of the John Bates Clark Medals for promising economists under age 40. They were instrumental in the creation of the Federal Reserve System and have headed it for twenty-nine of the last thirty-eight years.

In philanthropy, a December 2007 *Business Week* listing of America's fifty most generous benefactors included at least nineteen Jewish families and individuals. Their charitable donations totaled more than $22 billion over the five years 2003 through 2007. More than 90 percent of their donations went to secular causes in support of education, health care and medicine, arts, culture, and the humanities.

Much of the wealth behind that philanthropy came from success as entrepreneurs. In that role, Jews created whole new industries. Increasingly, they also occupy the corner office as CEOs of some of America's largest and most important companies. Of the 2003 CEOs leading *Fortune*'s 100 largest companies, 10 to 15 percent were Jews. Of *Fortune*'s 2003 list of the twenty-five most powerful people in business, six (24 percent) were Jews. Of the entrepreneurs included in the 2004 *Fortune* "America's 40 Richest Under 40," six were Jews. Thirty-one percent of the 2007 *Forbes* 400 are Jews.

Jews pioneered the ready-to-wear garment industry and, in 1885, owned all but seven of New York's 241 garment factories. Names like Levi Strauss, Ralph Lauren, Calvin Klein, and Donna Karan are just a few contemporary representatives of that legacy. Of the four pioneers of prestige cosmetics—Helena Rubinstein, Elizabeth Arden, Estée Lauder, and Charles Revson—only Elizabeth Arden was not Jewish. More than half of America's department stores were started or run by Jews, including such greats as Macy's, Federated, May Company, Bloomingdale's, Filene's, Saks, Abraham & Straus, Neiman Marcus, Bergdorf Goodman, Sears, and, in London, Marks & Spencer.

In specialty retailing, major chains such as Gap Stores, Limited, Mervyns, Barneys, Men's Warehouse, Home Depot, Ritz Camera, Bed Bath & Beyond are just a few of the Jewish creations. In television retailing, both QVC and Home Shopping were largely shaped by Jews. The world's foremost demonstration salesman, Ron Popeil, used television to sell products he invented.

In diamonds, De Beers and the Lev Leviev Group are the dominant forces in the worldwide diamond trade, while Zales, Helzbergs, Whitehall, and Friedman's are among the leading diamond and jewelry retailers.

We drink our Starbucks coffee and have sipped Seagram's wines and distilled spirits. The Dove Bar, Häagen-Dazs, Ben & Jerry's and Baskin-Robbins ice cream lead to our later signing up for Weight Watchers, Jenny Craig, and NutriSystem programs or buying Slim-Fast in the supermarket. All these companies were founded by Jewish entrepreneurs.

We may lounge in our Fairmont, Loews, Hyatt, Helmsley, or Wynn hotel, or cruise on any of the eighty-five ships of Carnival or thirty-five of Royal Caribbean. These companies were founded or largely shaped by Jews.

Every major Hollywood studio was created or essentially shaped by Jews, as were NBC and CBS. Of the three original television networks, only ABC was not started by a Jew, but Leonard Goldenson bought it seven years after its founding and ran it for forty-five years. Viacom and Comcast were largely created by two Jewish families, while Steve Ross and Gerald Levin played critical roles at Time Warner.

In publishing, America's newspaper of record is *The New York Times*, and in the nation's capital, Katherine Meyer Graham's son, Donald, now heads *The Washington Post* Company. The Pulitzer Prize is the legacy of the family that still runs the *St. Louis Post Dispatch* and *Arizona Daily Star*. Reuters, Newhouse, Triangle, and Ziff Davis are just a few of our leading magazine publishers. Random House, Alfred A. Knopf, Simon & Schuster, and Farrar, Straus, and Giroux are but four of the major book publishers created and run by Jews.

In finance, the story is much the same. Premier names like Goldman Sachs,

Salomon Brothers, and Lazard Frères are just a few of the contemporary names of a legacy dating back to the Rothschilds, Warburgs, Kuhn-Loebs, and Seligmans. In private equity, names like Kohlberg Kravis Roberts, Thomas H. Lee Partners, Blackstone Group, Hellman & Friedman, Quantum Fund, Steinhardt Partners, Caxton, Arthur Rock, Alan Patricof, Gene Kleiner, and Ben Rosen are today's legends taking the place of Bernard Baruch and Henry Morgenthau Jr. Of the twenty-six individuals named to the Private Equity Hall of Fame, at least eight (31 percent), and perhaps as many as eleven, are Jewish.

Jews were often restricted from owning real estate outside the ghetto for the better part of 1,800 years. They have compensated by becoming a major force in development and management of property all over the world. Of the five largest Real Estate Investment Trusts listed by *Forbes* magazine in May 2002, four were headed by Jews. Of the twenty-five 2007 *Forbes* 400 entrepreneurs whose fortune was made in real estate, eighteen are Jews.

Today Michael Bloomberg is New York's mayor, but earlier, he created Bloomberg LP, the enterprise that gave him the wherewithal to take on a second career. It is the largest financial information company in the world.

Few people know that the shell of Shell Oil traces back to a London curio shop where the Samuel family featured seashells before two sons started trading kerosene. Nor would they know that the Amoco part of BP Amoco was the creation of the father and son team of Louis and Jacob Blaustein, who also invented the railroad tank car. Amerada Hess, Aurora Oil, Occidental Petroleum, and Kaiser-Francis are just a few more of the petroleum businesses started or principally shaped by Jews.

America's great legacy of the Guggenheim Museums and Smithsonian's Hirshhorn Museum and Sculpture Garden have their origins in the success of two great mining operations established by Jewish families.

In business services, Manpower is one of the world's largest temporary staffing companies, just as ADP is the largest payroll processing company and H & R Block is the largest preparer of tax returns. All were started by Jews.

And lest anyone think Jews are not on the leading edge of new technology, Jews:

Co-founded the world's most successful search engine (Google, Sergey Brin);
Head the world's largest software company (Microsoft, Steve Ballmer);
Co-founded and head the world's second largest software company (Oracle, Lawrence Ellison);
Created what was for years the world's largest and most valuable computer company (Dell, Michael Dell);
Co-founded, led and served as chairman of the world's dominant microprocessor and memory chip company (Intel, Andrew Grove);
Served as CEO or COO at three of the world's four most valuable Internet companies (Yahoo, Terry Semel; eBay, Jeff Skoll; and IAC, Barry Diller);
Co-founded and head the communications protocol/chip company whose chips are in most U.S. cell phones and are slated to be utilized in the next generation of cell phones to be used worldwide (Qualcomm, Irwin Jacobs).

And this does not consider Jews' vital role as labor leaders and advocates for the poor and the oppressed. While Jews were busy creating the garment industry, their fellow Jews, Bessie Abramowitz, Sidney Hillman, David Dubinsky, and others, were organizing that industry's labor force. In that same era, Samuel Gompers headed organized labor for much of the early twentieth century. Later, Saul Alinsky, Abbie Hoffman, Jerry Rubin, Betty Friedan, and Gloria Steinem were just a few of the Jews devoted to social change.

While there are not many prominent Jewish athletes in today's professional sports, most would be surprised to know they are two of the ten top NBA coaches of all time. Six of the 247 members in the NFL Hall of Fame are Jewish, and Jews own 29 percent of the NFL football teams and 40 percent of the NBA teams. Meanwhile, Jews served as commissioners of all five major professional sports: baseball, football, basketball, hockey, and soccer. And, where the games have more to do with brains than brawn, Jews have held the undisputed world chess championship title for 54 percent of the time since the title was established in 1886; and in bridge, the legend of the game, Charles Goren, was Jewish.

Charles Murray's book, *Human Accomplishment: The Pursuit of Excellence in the Arts and Sciences; 800 B.C. to 1950* looks at those who achieved excellence over nearly 3,000 years. He devotes part of that book to what he calls the "astounding" disproportionate representation of Jews among history's great figures. Following "the Jewish Emancipation," which he dates from 1790 to 1870, he measures the representation of Jews among the 1,277 great historical figures between 1870 and 1950. Based on their percentage of the population, he says twenty-eight should have been Jews. "The actual number was at least 158." His observation is corroborated in other listings of "history's greats." Michael Hart's book, *The 100: A Ranking of the Most Influential Persons in History*, counts eight Jews among the 100 (Jesus, St. Paul (Paul of Tarsus), Einstein, Marx, Moses, Freud, Pincus, and Bohr). This is thirty-five times what one would expect.

CHAPTER 2

History's Greats

Judging history's greatest people is difficult. We can say with certainty the gold medal winner of an Olympic high jump was the best in that competition. Judgment had no effect on the outcome. It was head-to-head competition with one winner and many losers. Conversely, when someone creates a list purporting to rank the "best" or "greatest" in a given field, the list's credibility is open to question because of the judgment involved.

As the twentieth century came to a close, we were barraged with lists of "The Greatest of the Millennium, of "All Time," the "Last 100 Years," and so on. Some were akin to Trivial Pursuit games created and publicized by those whose job it was to sell books, TV time, or magazines. As such, some of these lists must be taken with a grain of salt. Others were quite credible. Five efforts to rank the history's greats are covered below, and while some are more credible than others, collectively they yield a clear pattern— Jews are consistently included in disproportionate numbers among history's greatest.

Charles Murray's *Human Accomplishment*[3]

One recent effort is quite credible. Published in late 2003, Charles Murray's book, *Human Accomplishment* is the product of more than five years of research and analysis. In his work, Murray used an interesting, if controversial, technique called "historiometry" to measure greatness. The approach literally calculates the space devoted to major figures in 167 authoritative encyclopedias, biographic dictionaries, and other reference works published by leading experts in various fields of endeavor.

At first blush, the technique seems superficial in today's "fifteen minutes of fame" world where agents and publicists devote whole careers to spinning trivial events into press coverage measured in column inches.

But Murray distinguishes fame from eminence in explaining and defending his approach. In the sciences, for example, he utilized thirty-seven major reference works published since the 1960s including: *The Cambridge Illustrated History of the World's Science, Larousse Dictionary of Scientists, Histoire Générale des Sciences, Scienza e tecnica,* and thirty-three comparable publications. The premise is simply that experts devote more words to describe the achievements of the great than they do to lesser figures, and the collective wisdom of multiple experts provides the most credible approach known for identifying and ranking greatness.

Murray culled the data by excluding those written up by fewer than half the experts. This eliminated eccentric, outlying opinions and individual favorites that do not stand up to the collective wisdom of multiple experts. Potential Euro-centrism was dealt with by creating separate inventories, such as Chinese literature, Indian philosophy and Japanese art. National chauvinism was averted by drawing on experts from around the world and in literature, by not using write-ups by experts who live in the same country as a particular author. Cutting off the study at 1950 and focusing only on those who reached age forty or were dead by that year helped reduce "fashion" and any tendency to judge recent events and people disproportionately important versus earlier figures.

He goes to great lengths to demonstrate that different approaches to looking at the data would yield essentially the same people and rankings and he provides a solid defense for his analysis and conclusions.

Murray identified and ranked the 4,002 most important figures in: the sciences, literature, music, art, and philosophy from 800 B.C. to 1950. (In fact it was 3,869 individuals, since some were important in more than one domain.) Moreover, he surveyed the significant events that transpired in each field over the years and analyzed the circumstances that stimulated high levels of achievement.

His conclusions may generate controversy, just as some of his earlier efforts have, including *The Bell Curve.* Nonetheless, most knowledgeable readers will conclude that while one can disagree with this or that point or ranking, ultimately, Murray got the big picture right. Illustrating this is a small exchange on the Slate.com Web site, which was generally critical of Murray's work. Timothy Noah, a *Slate* columnist suggested Murray was biased ranking Marie Curie 14th among the great physicists, four places behind her husband, Pierre. "Foul" cried Noah citing Amazon's "Search Inside the Book" list which puts Marie 5th and Pierre 13th. Noah's conjecture about possible Murray prejudice is curious since the technique makes bias doubtful unless it represents a systematic bias by the thirty-seven science experts Murray drew upon. In any case, the telling counterpoint was made by a knowledgeable *Slate* reader who responded:

"...your Amazon method and high school method are misleading you. Marie Curie was one of the greatest 'chemists' of all time,...a great physicist,...the first woman to teach at the Sorbonne and justly, a hero to women researchers everywhere. None of that demands that as a physicist alone she be superior to Pierre, who although also a chemist devoted more of his research efforts to physics than did Marie. But it means that she will be cited more frequently in Amazon, and what she did...is easier for a high-schooler. Before meeting Marie, Pierre was co-discoverer...of piezoelectric materials....He explored the thermodynamics of magnetic materials ("Curie's Law" and the Curie temperature). He invented laboratory equipment that still bears his name. Most of his own (no Marie) research is just harder to state in a few words, and in many ways he was an established scientist, which Marie was not. That's why you're off base in this argument—he's not as memorable to non-physicists. I'll agree that Marie is a more important figure to science, just not necessarily to physics."

In short, Murray's technique yielded a more correct conclusion than his critic at Slate.com.

Perhaps because Murray looks only at the arts and sciences from 800 B.C. to 1950, but not political, commercial, military, religious, or other domains of accomplishment, his lists do not consider figures considered great by the others covered in this chapter. Jesus, Paul, and Moses are three of the most influential people of all time according to Michael Hart (see below). Hart's list suggests Jews have been disproportionately important for thousands of years. Murray's approach, however, yields only eleven important Jews before 1800. (All of the Jews identified by Murray are included as Exhibit 2a). Murray comments:

"In all those twenty-six centuries (800 B.C. to 1800), the roster of significant Western figures includes not one Jewish artist, scientist, physician or inventor and just one writer (Fernando Rojas), one composer (Salamone Rossi), and one mathematician (Paul Guldin). This sparse representation in European arts and sciences through the beginning of 19C reflects Jews' near-total exclusion from the arts and sciences. Jews were not merely discouraged from entering universities and the professions, they were often forbidden by law from doing so. Socially they were despised...In a practical sense, legal equality for Jews first occurred in the newly formed United States, where Jews were given full rights under federal law."

What Murray seems to take away in this lack of Jewish achievement before 1800 he promptly gives back in his analysis of what happened next. Again to quote him:

"Until nearly 1800, Jews were excluded. Then over about seventy years, the legal exclusions are lifted and the social exclusion eases. What happens? 'The suddenness with which Jews began to appear. . .is nothing short of astounding,' writes historian Raphael Patai. 'It seemed as if a huge reservoir of Jewish talent, hitherto dammed up behind the wall of Talmudic learning, were suddenly released to spill over into all fields of Gentile cultural activity.'"

Murray says that in the four decades from 1830 to 1870, sixteen Jews appeared on the list. Then, in the next four decades, the number grew to forty and between

1910 and 1950, it soared to 114. In fact, 20 percent of the great historical figures identified by Murray between 1910 and 1950 were Jews. He concludes that by rights there should have been twenty-eight Jews among the 1,277 great people over that eighty-year period; instead there were "at least 158." This is six times what he expected. Further, the consistent growth in the number of Jews on the list suggests that by 1950, the performance substantially exceeded the six-fold overrepresentation.

Murray goes beyond his basic 1950 cutoff date to make one further point. The prior chapter of this book noted Jews have won 23 percent of all Nobel Prizes awarded. Murray looks at the Nobel data differently. He breaks the award period into two halves. Looking first at the prizes awarded between 1901 and 1950, he finds Jews won 14 percent of the Nobels. Between 1950 and 2000, however, they won 27 per-cent—this after six million Jews, roughly one-third of their total population, were killed in the Holocaust.

By way of contrast, Murray notes that after 1950:

Japanese earned 2 percent of the scientific and 4 percent of the literature Nobels;
Indians earned 1 percent of the science and none of the literature Nobels;
Chinese won 2 percent of each category;
Arabs picked up 1 percent of the science and 2 percent of the literature Nobels; and
Africans earned 4 percent of the literature and none of the science Nobels.

Murray sees an accelerating trajectory for the Japanese and Chinese and opines they may soon grow to impressive numbers, but in the end, it is the Jews whose num-bers have simply dwarfed the rest.

Jewish achievement is not the principal thrust of Murray's book. Nonetheless, in his 2,750-year survey of 4,002 great figures in history, he singles out only one group—the Jews—for separate discussion.

Michael Hart's Most Influential[4]

An early contender among recent lists of "The Greatest" was Michael Hart's *The 100: A Ranking of the Most Influential Persons in History*. Copyrighted in 1978 by Hart and later republished in 1987, the book got good reviews in *The Wall Street Journal, the Los Angeles Times, Newsday, the London Daily*, and other publications. *The Wall Street Journal* said, "A fascinating book!...a concise and readable history of the world. Hart proves to be a clear writer and a fine teacher." The London *Daily Mail* said, "Hart's work is admirably un-chauvinistic, excluding mighty Americans and finding room for totally obscure names."

In the opening section of his book, Hart explained the book was his list of the 100 "most influential" persons in history, not the 100 "greatest" persons in history. He says that while Mother Cabrini might have made his list of the world's "greatest" persons, she would not make the list of the most "influential." Stalin, on the other hand, would not make his list of the greatest, but he was "honored" as No. 63 on Hart's list among the most influential. Stalin was not as influential as his mentor, Lenin (No.15), who, in turn was not as influential as Marx (No.11).

One can quibble with Hart's rankings and with some of the names he included as well as some he did not. Winston Churchill single-handedly held the small island nation of Great Britain together in defiance of Hitler through the darkest days of World War II. Had he not led the British after Chamberlain stepped down (Churchill was not first choice), Britain would almost certainly have capitulated or negotiated a very unsatisfactory peace with Hitler. Europe would be a very different place today had Churchill not steered the country, pulled in Roosevelt, and worked in harness with Roosevelt and Stalin to defeat Hitler. Churchill does not make Hart's list. Abraham Lincoln did not make the cut either, though few could reasonably argue the United States would have remained together had he not been elected president in 1861. On the other hand, in retrospect, few would put John F. Kennedy on the list. Kennedy handled the Cuban Missile Crisis well, but even in that success, with the later revealed U.S. concessions, his earlier efforts to assassinate Castro, the deaths of the Diems in Vietnam and the absence of other major accomplishments all suggest Kennedy does not deserve to be No. 80 on Hart's list. As noted previously, one should not take these lists as gospel.

Interestingly, Hart chose the Prophet Muhammad as No. 1, the most influential person of all time. Hart did so not because it was the politically correct thing to do in the 1980s, nor obviously because of events surrounding September 11, 2001—he compiled his list years earlier. He did it because while Christianity is larger in terms of numbers of followers, Muhammad had a greater personal influence on the formulation of the Moslem religion than Jesus did in building Christianity. One could say Christ shares the credit with St. Paul, and so Christians got two of the top ten slots, but Muhammad got No. 1.

Jesus made it onto the list, but as No. 3 behind No. 1 Muhammad and No. 2 Isaac Newton. Hart's entire list, including the honorable mentions, is provided in Exhibit 2b.

Toward the end of his book, Hart breaks out where his 100 most influential people were born (and where most of them lived their lives). It is worth noting—and as mentioned in the London *Daily Mail* review cited above—that despite being an American, Hart thought only seven Americans deserved to be on his list. There are seventy-one from Europe and eighteen from Asia. At seven, the United States comes in tied with China and western Asia (seven each) but behind Italy (eight), France (ten), Germany and Austria (fifteen), and Great Britain (eighteen).

One of Hart's most interesting observations is how important the Scots have been. To quote him:

> "It is interesting to note that, of the eighteen British on this list, no fewer than five came from Scotland. All five, in fact, are in the top half of the list. Since the Scots constitute about one-eighth of one percent of the world's population, this represents a truly astonishing concentration of talent and achievement."

Hart did not mention that Jews have eight names on the list—thirty-five times what we would expect. It would be nine if one were to count Lenin (No.15), but Lenin had only one Jewish grandparent.

The eight Jews and their rankings are:

Jesus Christ (No. 3)
St. Paul (No. 6)
Albert Einstein (No. 10)
Karl Marx (No. 11)
Moses (No. 16)
Sigmund Freud (No. 32)
Gregory Pincus (No. 81)
Niels Bohr (No. 100)

And, following Hart's lead in describing the Scots, six of the eight Jews are in the top half (five in the top quarter) of his ranking.

A&E's *Biographies of the Millennium*[5]

Narrowing the focus to just the last 1,000 years, the Arts & Entertainment Channel (A&E) took a stab at a similar listing as the millennium approached. The results are also included in Exhibit 2b. Authorship of this list is harder to discern, but with A&E's continuing job of producing videos for its *Biography* series, one expects the company has staff members capable of researching, writing, and producing good biographical material.

The A&E list has a good deal of overlap with the Hart book, and both lists use "influential" as the standard for choosing who belongs on the list. Of course, having not survived to the year 1,000, Muhammad, Jesus, St. Paul, Buddha, Confucius, Zoroaster, Aristotle, and a few others from Hart's list don't qualify for A&E's compilation.

Conversely, many make the A&E list that didn't qualify for Hart's list or only made "Honorable Mention." These include Churchill, Marco Polo, Leonardo da Vinci, Watson and Crick, and Saint Thomas Aquinas.

If Hart was a bit loose in giving John F. Kennedy the number 80 slot, A&E trumps him with Elvis Presley (No. 57), Walt Disney (No. 62), Princess Diana (No. 73), the Beatles (No. 76), Steven Spielberg (No. 91), Charlie Chaplin (No. 95), and Louis Armstrong (No. 98) counted among the 100 most influential persons of the last 1,000 years. Not surprisingly, one senses a tilt toward "entertainers" by the Arts & Entertainment judges.

Perhaps because of the overlaps between Hart's work and A&E's and their shared review of at least the last 1,000 years, it is not particularly surprising that the A&E list also contains eight Jews. It drops the three who died before the year 1,000 (Jesus, Moses, and St. Paul), but adds J. Robert Oppenheimer, Jonas Salk, and Steven Spielberg.

Despite a few questionable choices and a tilt towards Americans (31 of the 100 people honored are Americans versus 7 on Hart's list), the A&E list again represents a remarkable showing by the Jews. Eight Jews is thirty-five times what it should given that it encompasses all humanity over the last 1,000 years.

InteliQuest Learning Systems' *World's 100 Greatest People*[6]

InteliQuest publishes audiotapes. Its focus is tape compilations covering such topics as the great books, great composers, great thinkers, great investors, and great people. It was started by Steven DeVore who earlier founded Sybervision, a large company which developed sixty learning programs. InteliQuest does not provide the criteria for their selection of the "100 Greatest People," but when one reviews their list, many names are familiar. It will come as no surprise that 8 of the 100 are Jewish. The InteliQuest list is not sequenced in terms of importance. Instead, it groups similar careers together. The eight Jews include Karl Marx, Sigmund Freud, Albert Einstein, Jonas Salk, Abraham, Moses, Jesus Christ, and the Apostle Paul. All are highlighted as part of Exhibit 2b.

Time's 100 and Person of the Century[7]

Not about to miss out on a good thing, *Time* put together its own list of 100, in its case choosing "those individuals who—for better or worse—most influenced the last 100 years. They are organized into five categories with one singular distinction for the "Person of the Century."

We can end the suspense right now. The Person of the Century is Albert Einstein. What are the odds? Not bad for a Jewish professor who completely changed our understanding of the universe.

Time's categories (all included in Exhibit 2b) are:

Leaders and Revolutionaries
Artists & Entertainers
Builders & Titans
Scientists & Thinkers
Heroes & Icons

Included on *Time's* lists are fictional characters ("The American GI" and Bart Simpson), an unidentifiable person (the Chinese man who stood in front of the tanks in Tiananmen Square), and a family (The Kennedys). They also include partnerships: Wilbur and Orville Wright, Mary Louis and Richard Leakey, Rodgers and Hammerstein, Edmund Hilary and Tenzing Norgay and Watson and Crick. In the end, *Time's* "100" is really *Time's* "101 plus the Kennedys."

Like A&E's list, one can quibble with some selections. Princes Diana, Charlie Chaplin, the Beatles, Steven Spielberg, and Louis Armstrong all make it again. Bart Simpson is new to the list as are Pete Rozelle, Pele (the soccer player) and Aretha Franklin. Yet again the media appear incapable of resisting charismatic entertainers.Time will tell, but skeptics doubt some of *Time's* names will be little remembered in 2010, let alone 2100. *Time's* handling of John F. Kennedy is particularly interesting. As you will recall, Hart included him as No. 80 on his list of the most influential people of all time. *Time* magazine, aggregates the entire family (John, Bobby, Teddy, Joe, etc.) into a single entry. Thus, for *Time*, individually, John F. Kennedy doesn't even make the list of the most influential individuals of the twentieth century, let alone all of human history.

In any case, Jews take fourteen of *Time*'s 101+ slots (not counting Lenin who is one-quarter Jewish). Broken out by group, the Jews include:

Leaders & Revolutionaries: David Ben-Gurion
Artists & Entertainers: Richard Rodgers, Oscar Hammerstein, Bob Dylan, and Steven Spielberg
Builders & Titans: David Sarnoff, William Levitt, Louis B Mayer, and Estée Lauder
Scientists & Thinkers: Sigmund Freud, Albert Einstein, and Jonas Salk
Heroes & Icons: Anne Frank and Harvey Milk

Treating *Time*'s material as basically an American list (about two-thirds of those named are Americans), fourteen Jews is nine times what one would expect.

And, of course, Einstein was *Time*'s "Person of the Century."

While the names change from list to list, it deserves mention that many names end up on everyone's list. And while one can criticize any of the lists, taken together those individuals included on most or all of the rosters are genuinely deserving of being recognized among the greats. Moreover, their constant identification of large numbers of Jews establishes conclusively that Jews are disproportionately represented among history's greatest.

Chapter 3

Science

"Science is the belief in the ignorance of experts."
—*Richard Feynman*

"There are two types of genius. Ordinary geniuses do great things, but they leave you room to believe you could do the same if only you worked hard enough. Then there are magicians, and you can have no idea how they do it. Feynman was a magician." —*Hans Bethe*

"He is, by all odds, the most brilliant young physicist here (at Los Alamos) and everyone knows this." —*I. Robert Oppenheimer*

Richard Feynman[8]

His father, Melville, wanted a boy who would become a scientist. His mother, Lucille, wanted her child to have a sense of humor. Both got their wish. Richard Feynman won a Nobel Prize in Physics in 1965, and his quirky sense of humor would stay with him throughout his life and add to his legend.

Melville had emigrated from Minsk, Byelorussia, in 1895 when he was five. In 1917 he married Lucille, whose parents had come from Poland. Shortly after Richard was born on May 11, 1918, his father bought him puzzles and arranged colored tiles in front of his high chair to intrigue him with the patterns. Richard did not begin talking till he was two, but made up for the slow start by repairing radios before he was ten and devouring the *Encyclopædia Britannica* from cover to cover. Self-taught in so many fields, he learned elementary mathematics before he began school, and he won the New York University math championship when he was a high school senior.

He was accepted at MIT in 1935, earning grades in mathematics and physics that were among the highest ever recorded. After early resistance because of a de facto Jewish quota at Princeton, he was admitted in 1939 to pursue his Ph.D. After receiving it in 1942, he was offered a job on the Manhattan Project. At first, he rejected the offer, but after only a few minutes he realized Hitler might get an atomic bomb first, and he changed his mind.

At Los Alamos, he amazed his seniors, solving problems that had baffled them while also learning how to crack safes and pick locks, a talent he used to prove to the Army just how poor their security really was. Never taking anything, he left notes taunting officials with his breach of their systems.

Feynman had first met Arline Greenbaum when they were in high school. Over time, she became the most important person in his life and both felt star-crossed when they learned she was doomed with a diagnosis of tuberculosis. Streptomycin was not yet available as a cure and Feynman could not abide the prospect of leaving her behind when he moved to Los Alamos.

Instead, over his family's objections, they eloped. He took her West with him and found her a sanitorium in Albuquerque. Early on she had loved and supported his unique, fiercely independent personality.

For their wedding anniversary, she insisted he don a chef's hat and apron to grill steaks along Route 66, the highway which ran adjacent to the sanitorium. When he initially balked, she asked, "What do you care what other people think?" It was a line she had learned from him. He cooked the steaks and used the question as the title of his last memoir, a book about Arline and his work on the Challenger Commission.

They wrote each other nearly every day, and he drove the ninety-three miles from Los Alamos to Albuquerque to be with her nearly every weekend. He was with her when she died in July of 1945.

Following Arline's death, the bombing of Hiroshima and Nagasaki, and the end of the war, Feynman took a teaching position at Cornell, but ennui had set in. He became a notorious womanizer, partied and drank, and during his four years there he never moved into an apartment or a house. Over time, he found it increasingly hard to teach and he felt stale in his research efforts, though some of the work at Cornell helped him win the Nobel Prize.

While considering a teaching offer from Cal Tech, Feynman decided to take a sabbatical and teach in Rio de Janeiro. He also partied on the beach, learned to play bongo drums and the frigideira (a Brazilian rhythm instrument), and danced the samba. After ten months in Rio, he accepted the Cal Tech offer and headed to Pasadena.

The ennui behind him, he was simply brilliant. His work in those early years at Cal Tech might well have qualified him for three Nobels. The one he earned was"… for fundamental work in quantum electrodynamics, with deep-ploughing consequences for the physics of elementary particles." He had come up with a technique for calculating the probability of a quantum transitioning from one state to another subsequent state, and he adapted the approach to quantum electrodynamics to describe how atoms produce radiation.

When asked to explain in a few words what he had accomplished, he said, "Buddy, if I could tell you in a minute what I had done, it would not be worth the Nobel Prize."

He developed the so-called Feynman diagrams, which help in conceptualizing and calculating interactions between particles and space-time. They provide physicists with a clear, simple tool for envisioning atomic interactions and working with concepts that are otherwise hard to understand and use. The diagrams have since become a staple of today's physicists who work on string theory and M-branes.

Feynman also explained the physics of the superfluidity of supercooled liquid helium. He used an equation, created by fellow physicist Schrodinger in another context, to explain the phenomenon. His insight was a great help in understanding superconductivity.

With Murray Gell-Mann, he developed a theory involving the decay of a neutron into an electron, proton, and an anti-neutrino. The work ultimately resulted in the discovery of a new force of nature, the weak interaction.

Asked to help restructure the freshman physics course at Cal Tech, he devised the "Feynman Lectures" that are still listened to and read by students and professionals more than forty years after he first delivered them. The students loved him and vied for his attention. One solved an assigned problem and hastily dropped it into the mailbox at Feynman's home in the middle of the night. It woke Feynman from his sleep and he got up and read the answer. When a second student arrived with the answer during breakfast, Feynman told him he was too late.

Along the way, after a brief, failed second marriage, he met Gweneth Howard, a British woman sixteen years his junior. After a torturous romance, they married in 1960, staying together for the remaining twenty-eight years of his life. Always something of a prankster and clown, Feynman titled his first memoir: *Surely You Are Joking, Mr. Feynman!* It became a surprise hit and stayed on *The New York Times* best-seller list for fourteen weeks.

At Ronald Reagan's request, he served on the commission to investigate the Challenger space shuttle disaster. Unsatisfied with the emerging consensus that defended NASA from criticism, Feynman did experiments in his hotel room to test the theory that a lack of resilience in the rubber O-rings on the rocket boosters led to a leak of burning fuel, triggering the explosion. It was a fault NASA should have anticipated, but it was only because Feynman re-created his simple experiment during a televised hearing that people understood what happened and the bureaucratic failures behind it.

Feynman had battled cancer for eight years until he finally succumbed on February 17, 1988. Until two weeks before his death, he continued to teach. True to form, his last words were "I'd hate to die twice. It's so boring."

His friend from high school days, Julian Schwinger, was also a scientific competitor and a co-winner of the Nobel Prize. Schwinger provided an epitaph.

"An honest man, the outstanding intuitionalist of our age and a prime example of what may lie in store for anyone who dares to follow the beat of a different drummer."

The Nobel Prizes[9]

Each October, some of the world's greatest scientists sit by the phone hoping for the most exciting call of their life. The call may come from a representative of the Royal Swedish Academy of Sciences or, more likely, from a friend or family member who heard the news after the awards were announced at the Stockholm press conference.

For most of the rest of us, the annual award of the three Nobel Prizes for physics, physiology and medicine, and chemistry is news that stays with us for a day or so. These are prestigious prizes, and we get some personal insight to the fortunate winners through the bio-sketches provided by the media. Later, on December 10, the anniversary of Alfred Nobel's death, we are again reminded of the awards from news coverage of the dinner ceremony when the king of Sweden presents the Nobel medals to each laureate.

For most, receiving a Nobel is the most important recognition of their career. Certainly the money (a share of $1.4 million or so) is nice, but with it comes public confirmation of having reached the apex of one's chosen field. For the recipient and his or her peers, their work has been judged to be of great importance and will be considered so for as long as a Nobel Prize is the ultimate standard of recognition. For at least three awards—physics, physiology and medicine, and chemistry, if not for the literature, economics, and peace prizes, about which more will be said in later chapters – few questions have been raised over the years to question the overall excellence of the judge's decisions.

Interestingly, sometimes recognition arrives quickly. In physics, for example, roughly one in ten of the awards have been made within five years of the discovery that led to the award. But for others, it can be a very long wait. Einstein waited sixteen years, until 1921, to get a Nobel for work he did in 1905. Perhaps the longest to wait was Ernst Ruska, who got his Nobel in 1986—for work he did in 1933. The timing was fortunate, since the Nobel can only be awarded to a person who is still living. Ruska passed away in 1988.

The Nobel Prize for Physics

Physics is perhaps the most recognized of the three primary scientific disciplines. The prominent names include the likes of Albert Einstein, Marie and Pierre Curie, Niels Bohr, Enrico Fermi, Werner Heisenberg, Erwin Schrödinger (of "Schrödinger's Cat" fame), Max Planck, Felix Bloch, Arno Penzias, Murray Gell-Mann, and Richard Feynman, to name just a few. This is an elite group working in areas of great importance, too complex for most of us to fathom. Intellectually, the work is simply the leading edge. Ultimately, it touches our lives in the form of X-rays, electrons, color photography, wireless radio, relativity, quantum physics, nuclear power and weapons, the nature of light, nuclear magnetic resonance, transistors, lasers, and other discoveries and inventions too numerous to describe.

So, who gets the awards? How have the Jews and others done in the competition?

Chance would say that of 181 prizes awarded from 1901 through 2007, Jews should have gotten none, or at best one. That is, being 0.2 percent of the world's population, one might reasonably expect Jews to get 2 of every 1,000 prizes (1 of every 500). With 181 prizes awarded, the odds are that at best one Jew might have earned a Nobel for physics, but only if he (or she) beat the odds.

Actually, Jews have received forty-eight of the 181 awards. Among them are:

Albert Einstein, 1921, "for his services to theoretical physics, and especially for his discovery of the law of the photoelectric effect." (Interestingly, Einstein's Nobel was not for his immensely important theories of special relativity or general relativity.)

Niels Bohr, 1922, "for his services in the investigation of the structure of atoms and the radiation emanating from them."

Lev Landau, 1962, "for his pioneering theories for condensed matter, especially liquid helium."

Richard Feynman, 1965, "for...fundamental work in quantum electrodynamics."

Murray Gell-Mann, 1969, "for his contributions and discoveries concerning the classification of elementary particles and their interactions."

Dennis Gabor, 1971, "for his invention and development of the holographic method."

Leon Cooper, 1972, "for their [Cooper and non-Jews John Bardeen and John Schrieffer] jointly developed theory of superconductivity."

Arno Penzias, 1978, "for their [with non-Jew Robert Woodrow Wilson] discovery of cosmic microwave background radiation."

Frederick Reines, 1995, "for the detection of the neutrino."

Martin Perl, 1995, "for discovery of the tau lepton."

and thirty-eight more. All of the Nobel Prizes in Physics are shown in Exhibit 3a with the names of Jews highlighted.

If the Jews had been citizens of a single nation, that country would have come in second, behind the United States, in Nobel awards for physics. The United States has earned eighty-two versus the forty-eight earned by Jews. Germans would come in third with thirty-one, ten more than Britain's twenty-one. France has eleven, Russia ten and the Netherlands, nine.

Of the eighty-two U.S. recipients, twenty were native-born Jews, and another ten were Jews that lived in the United States and one or more other country during their lifetime (such as Hans Bethe who was born in Germany, but immigrated to the United States). Given that 2 percent of the U.S. population is Jewish, we should count ourselves grateful that Jews have helped us win 37 percent of our Nobels.

The Nobel Prize for Physiology or Medicine

Though declining reimbursement rates from HMOs, Medicare and other payers, bureaucratic interference in decisions, paperwork, and malpractice lawsuits have made practicing medicine a good deal less satisfying in recent years, it remains a career for the best and the brightest. At the leading edge of that field, though not necessarily in daily clinical practice, are the medical researchers for whom quintessential recognition comes with the Nobel Prize for Physiology or Medicine.

Over time, at the behest of the Karolinska Institute in Stockholm, which administers the award, the focus has shifted from physiology to medicine and the standard now used to determine the winners is "fundamental research in human health." In that assignment, the awards have gone to those whose discoveries and insights have changed our lives for the better. Immunization against tetanus and diphtheria won the first award in 1901. Since then, Nobels have gone for breakthroughs involving tuberculosis, malaria, chemotherapy, insulin, blood types, chromosomes, synthesis of vitamins, penicillin, DNA's double helix, cholesterol, monoclonal antibodies, and beta blockers, to name just a few. Like physics, medicine is vital. Those on the forefront have made enormous contributions to our world.

Since that first Nobel for physiology or medicine in 1901, 189 awards have been made. (For a variety of reasons, Nobels have not been awarded every year, and in some years more than one laureate has been honored.) Fifty-nine (31 percent) of those have gone to Jews. This is nearly two-thirds of the ninety-one Nobels for Physiology or Medicine earned by Americans and almost twice the thirty-two earned by Britains. Germany, with twenty-two, is the only other country with more than ten Nobel Prize laureates in physiology or medicine.

Among the fifty-nine Jewish winners those listed below.

> Karl Landsteiner, 1930, "for his discovery of human blood groups."
> Sir Ernst Boris Chain, 1945, "for the discovery [with non-Jews Alexander Fleming and Howard Walter Florey] of penicillin and its curative effects in various infectious diseases."
> Selman Waksman, 1952, "for his discovery of streptomycin, the first molecule effective against tuberculosis."
> Konrad Bloch, 1964, "for their discoveries [with non-Jew Feodor Lynen] concerning the mechanism and regulation of cholesterol and fatty acid metabolism."
> Joseph Goldstein and Michael Brown, 1985, "for their discoveries concerning the regulation of cholesterol metabolism." [Both Goldstein and Brown were later instrumental in the discovery of statins.]
> Stanley Prusiner, 1997, "for his discovery of Prions – a new biological principle of infection." [Prions were discovered to be involved in "mad cow disease."]

and fifty-two others, highlighted in the complete list of winners of the Nobel for Physiology or Medicine (Exhibit 3b).

Interestingly, neither Jonas Salk nor Albert Sabin, the two Jewish conquerors of polio, received Nobels for their important discoveries that brought an end to the polio scourge which lasted till the mid-1950s. With Salk and Sabin, the Nobel count for Jews in physiology or medicine would have been sixty-one.

The Albany Medical Center Prize and Other Medical Awards[10]

Five years ago, the Albany Medical Center announced the creation of a prestigious new prize to "be awarded each spring to a physician or scientist, or group, whose work has led to significant advances in the fields of health care and scientific research with demonstrated translational benefits applied to improved patient care." With its $500,000 award, the Albany Medical Center Prize in medicine and biomedical research was immediately recognized as the second richest prize in medicine and, after the Nobel, the most prestigious award in American medicine.

To date, there have been eleven awards. The first went to Dr. Arnold J. Levine, who co-discovered the p53 protein, described as perhaps the most important tumor suppressor gene in human cancer. (About 50 percent of all human cancers contain a mutation in p53.) The second award went to Dr. Anthony S. Fauci for his "pioneering work helping researchers understand how the AIDS virus destroys the body's defenses, his groundbreaking work in developing effective therapies for several once fatal rheumatic diseases, his efforts spearheading the drive for vaccines to prevent the HIV virus, smallpox, anthrax, and the Ebola virus, as well as his overall scientific leadership and public service." The third award went to Dr. Joseph Goldstein and Dr. Michael S. Brown. Goldstein and Brown are doubly recognized in that they also received the 1985 Nobel Prize for their discovery (cited above) that people with a common genetic predisposition to heart disease lacked receptors in their cells that transport LDL cholesterol out of the bloodstream causing it to accumulate on artery walls. The April/May 2003 Albany award was for subsequent work involving how a family of proteins regulates the amount of cholesterol by controlling LDL receptors (which led to the development of statins) and their joint discovery of an insulin-sensitive regulator that holds promise in treating a rare form of diabetes.

Stanley N. Cohen and Herbert W. Boyer won the 2004 Albany awards for their pioneering work in recombinant DNA (gene cloning), which paved the way for the modern biotechnology industry. They were the first to cut DNA and insert different genes into the DNA sequence, allowing the original cell to then reproduce the new DNA during cell division. This led to production of such products as human growth hormone and other pharmaceuticals to treat a wide range of ailments. Boyer went on to co-found Genentech Inc. and Cohen chaired Stanford's department of genetics.

Dr. Robert Langer won the award in 2005 for developing an implantable, biodegradable polymer that delivers chemotherapy directly to a tumor. In 2006 Seymour Benzer demonstrated that changes in a single gene can radically alter the behavior of a fruit fly. His work is important in the treatment of human neurological diseases. The 2007 award went to Dr. Robert J. Lefkowitz, Dr. Solomon H. Snyder, and Ronald M. Evans, Ph.D., for their work in discovering how cells communicate with their environment. Their work led to the development of drugs such as cortisone, antihistamines, antidepressants, and estrogens.

Goldstein and Brown are Jewish (see the Nobel list), as are Levine, Cohen, Langer, Benzer, Lefkowitz, and Snyder. Thus eight of the eleven Albany Medical Center Prizes awarded through 2007 have gone to Jews.

By way of filling out the picture, one credible Web site, www.jinfo.org, indicates that as of mid-2008, Jews have won 26 percent of the Gardner Foundation Awards, 41 percent of the Wolf Prizes in Medicine, 40 percent of the Louisa Gross Horwitz prizes, and 35 percent of the GM Cancer Research Foundation Alfred P. Sloan Jr. prizes.

The Nobel Prize for Chemistry

These days chemistry is not perceived as being nearly as glamorous as physics or medicine. Few laymen could recall a single Nobel Prize winner for chemistry in the way they could quickly cite Einstein, Fermi, or Heisenberg for physics.

For most of us, the two winners whose names we would immediately recognize, we would probably not associate with the Nobel Award for chemistry. Linus Pauling is most remembered for megadoses of vitamin C and his outspoken efforts on behalf of world peace. Few know he won a Nobel in 1954 for his 1928-30 creation of the valence bonding theory—and a second for peace in 1962.

There have only been three other double winners. One was Marie Curie who won a prize for physics in 1903 (for research on radioactivity) and one for chemistry in 1911 (for the discovery of radium and polonium). The other two are John Bardeen (physics, 1956 and 1972), and Frederick Sanger (chemistry, 1958 and 1980).

While some might say the zenith of chemical discovery passed in the nineteenth-century, there have been continuing major discoveries that affect on our daily lives in such fields as thermodynamics (1920), radioactive isotopes (1921), the synthesis of vitamins C and A (1937), sex hormones (1938), electrophoresis (1948), analysis of protein (1958), carbon-14 dating (1960), analysis of hemoglobin (1962), and base sequence of chromosomes (1980).

Chemical research remains important and, with the possible exception of failing to grant awards to Mendeleev (the creator of the periodic table), and Josiah Gibbs (developer of chemical thermodynamics), Nobel awards have gone to the world's leading chemists of the last century or so.

There have been 151 Nobel awards for chemistry since the first in 1901. Awards were made all but 8 of the 107 years. As before, given the statistic of 2 Jews per 1,000 in the world's population, Jews would be unlikely to have won even a single prize. In fact, they have received thirty (20 percent) of the prizes for chemistry. This is slightly more than half the fifty-six earned by U.S. citizens, equal to the thirty won by Germans. It is three more than the British (27) and twenty-two more than fourth-placed France with eight.

Among Jews who have won the Nobel for chemistry are:

Richard Willstatter, 1915, "for his researches on plant pigments, especially chlorophyll."
Fritz Haber, 1918, "for the synthesis of ammonia from its elements."
Walter Gilbert, 1980, "for their [with non-Jew Fredrich Sanger] contributions concerning the determination of base sequences in nucleic acids."
Paul Berg, 1980, "for his fundamental studies of the biochemistry of nucleic acids, with particular regard to recombinant DNA."

And twenty-six others, all included in Exhibit 3c.

The Fields Medal (for Mathematics)[11]

John Nash (not Jewish) received a Nobel Prize for Economics in 1994. He was immensely pleased with the recognition, and it probably contributed to his recovery from more than thirty years of schizophrenia. Ironically, the onset of his schizophrenia arose almost simultaneously with his immense disappointment at not winning the Fields Medal in 1958. To quote Sylvia Nasar, author of *A Beautiful Mind,* "to understand how deep the disappointment was, one must know that the Fields Medal is the Nobel Prize of mathematics, the ultimate distinction that a mathematician can be granted by his peers, the trophy of trophies." Nash's Nobel was for economics, but he thought of himself as a mathematician.

There is a fascinating, but groundless, bit of gossip suggesting the reason there is no Nobel for mathematics is because Gosta Mittag-Leffler, a mathematics professor at the University of Stockholm, had an affair with Nobel's wife, leading Nobel to damn all mathematicians. The problem is Nobel never married. But Nobel did know Mittag-Leffler, and disliked him. Moreover, Nobel preferred practical science to basic research. He thought mathematics was too theoretical to warrant a Nobel.

John Charles Fields was a Canadian, born in 1863. He devoted his career to mathematics, earning a Ph.D. from Johns Hopkins University. He taught and studied mathematics in the United States, Paris, and Berlin before returning to a professorship at the University of Toronto. As organizer and president of the 1924 International Congress of Mathematics, he attracted sponsors and money to establish an international award in mathematics. At his death in 1932, his estate went to help establish the prize.

The first awards were made in 1936, but because of World War II, no further awards were made until 1950. Awards have been made every four years since. Eligibility is restricted to mathematicians under the age of forty, and while the prize of $15,000 Canadian (about the same in U.S. dollars) won't go very far, the international recognition is immense, ensuring subsequent offers of full professorships that dwarf the prize money while providing career and financial security. The relatively young age (forty) by which one must be awarded the prize reflects both the notion that mathematicians do some of their best work at a very early age and the wish to encourage "further achievement by the recipients."

Selection of awards is intended to be truly international. Quoting from John Charles Fields' letter establishing the medal: "One would hear again emphasized the fact that the medals should be of a character as purely international and impersonal as possible. There should not be attached to them in any way the name of any country, institution or person."

Since 1966, up to four medals can be awarded every four years when the International Congress of Mathematicians meets. There have been forty-eight Fields Medals awarded through August of 2002. Those honored are included in Exhibit 3d with the names of the twelve Jewish winners highlighted.

Though Americans have won the most medals (fourteen), other countries have done well. France has had nine winners, the Soviet Union/Russia eight, the U.K. six, Japan three, and Belgium two.

When looking at the universities where the winners were teaching at the time of the award, one senses why John Nash, then at Princeton, was hopeful. Eleven of the forty-eight winners were at Princeton when they won the Fields Medal. Seven were at the Institut des Hautes Scientifiques (IHES) in Paris. Four each were at Cambridge and Harvard, and two each were at Oxford, MIT, and Moscow University.

Using the 2 in 1,000 proportion that Jews are of the world's population, and the fact that only forty-eight medals have been awarded, one would not expect any Jews to have won a Fields Medal. And in this domain, it is more difficult to know for sure who is and is not Jewish because little analysis has been done on the ethnic, religious, or cultural affiliation of winners. This is in sharp contrast to the Nobel, where fame has made the question of which winners were Jews a matter of more public discussion.

Nonetheless, the best estimate is that Jews have taken at least twelve (25 percent) of the forty-eight and perhaps as many as fifteen. This is roughly one hundred times more than one would expect.

Other Mathematical Awards[12]

Lest there be doubt whether the Fields Medal awards are representative of Jewish mathematical talent, three further prestigious mathematics awards, administered by the American Mathematical Society, plus the Wolf Prize deserve mention.

The Frank Nelson Cole Prizes in algebra and number theory honor Cole who served as secretary of the American Mathematical Society (AMS) and editor of the *Bulletin of the American Mathematical Society* until his death in 1926. Of the forty-six awards since 1928, twenty-one (46 percent) have gone to Jews. (See Exhibit 3e.)

The Bocher Memorial Prize honors Maxime Bocher for a notable research memoir in mathematical analysis. Of the twenty-seven awards made since 1923, eleven (41 percent) have gone to Jews (Exhibit 3e).

The Leroy P. Steele Lifetime Achievement Award, made under the auspices of the AMS, is granted "for the cumulative influence of the total mathematical work of the recipient...over a period of time." Of the nineteen awards since 1993, ten (53 percent) have gone to Jews (Exhibit 3e).

Perhaps less prestigious, the Wolf Prize in Mathematics was established by Dr. Ricardo Wolf, an inventor, diplomat, and philanthropist. It is awarded every year for outstanding achievements in the interest of mankind and friendly relations among people. The mathematics award is one of six Wolf Prizes (agriculture, chemistry, mathematics, medicine, physics, and arts). Of the forty-eight mathematics awards made since 1978, eighteen (37.5 percent) have gone to Jews. This award is not administered by the AMS, and because Wolf became an Israeli citizen, some might give this award less credence for our purposes than the other three awards and the Fields Medal. The results, however, are comparable (Exhibit 3e).

The A. M. Turing Award[13]

It seems every major award wants to be counted as the Nobel Prize of one thing or another. Computer science is no exception. The Association for Computing Machinery created the A. M. Turing Award in the 1960s to honor "the individual selected for contributions of a technical nature made to the computing community." As one might expect, a November 23, 1998, Microsoft press release honoring Jim Gray, as a winner of this $100,000 award, described the Turing as being "regarded in technical circles as the Nobel Prize of computer science."

To date, fifty-four Turing Awards have been made (Exhibit 3f). While the award could be considered "international" in character, the number of U.S. winners, the U.S. roots, the U.S. dominance in computers, and Intel's financial support to the award suggests the 2.1 percent standard (percent of the U.S. population that is Jewish) seems appropriate. It suggests that perhaps one Jew should have won a Turing Award. Instead, they have won thirteen. (Were the international standard used instead, the outcome would have been more than one hundred times greater than expected.)

CHAPTER 4

Invention

"An essential aspect of creativity is not being afraid to fail."   *—Edwin Land*

Edwin Land[14]

Jewish persecution in Tsarist Russia led Avram and Ella Salmonovitch to flee Odessa for the United States in the 1880s with their three sons, Harry, Sam, and Louis. Like millions of fellow immigrants, they left New York's Castle Garden emigrant processing station with new names. They were now Abraham and Ella Land. The five Lands were soon joined by two more brothers and three sisters and, in a fashion typical of striving immigrant Jews, they soon achieved what they could not in Russia. Among the siblings, two boys became lawyers, a third traded secondhand machinery, and Harry followed his father into the scrap-metal business. The three daughters married a lawyer, an architect, and a retailer.

Harry moved his business to Norwich, Connecticut, and began processing most of the scrap metal from the Electric Boat Company, which builds submarines. He married Matha Goldfaden, had a daughter, Helen, and four years later, on May 7, 1909, a son, Edwin Herbert. Helen soon nicknamed her little brother "Din." It was a nickname that would stick for the rest of his life.

As a child, kaleidoscopes and stereopticons fascinated Din. He read everything he could find on optics, including the leading technical treatise of the era, Robert Wood Johnson's *Physical Optics*. Land said he slept with it under his pillow and read it, "like a Bible." At thirteen, he became fascinated with the phenomenon of polarization when a camp counselor used a piece of Iceland spar (the mineral calcite) to extinguish the glare reflecting from a tabletop.

One evening's near collision of an automobile and a farmer's wagon made him realize the risk of headlight glare blinding oncoming drivers. This became the first in a lifetime of problems Land would concentrate his energies to solve.

He entered Harvard in 1926 but, intrigued with the potential of polarization to solve the glare problem, he dropped out after only a few months to read everything he could find on the problem. Like Thomas Edison before him, he studied the extensive material in the New York Public Library. His goal was to create an inexpensive, thin polarizer to filter light from auto headlamps.

If it worked, he knew there would be many other applications. He explored numerous techniques, including a failed effort to resolve problems that daunted an earlier expert, William B. Herapath. Ultimately Land came up with a new solution. He envisioned placing billions of needle-like light crystals, smaller than the wavelength of light, onto a sheet of film and using magnetic fields to align them so that only polarized light would pass through the film. By 1929 he had perfected the technique and his patent was filed.

Land then returned to Harvard where his work and knowledge so impressed the head of the physics laboratory that he was assigned his own lab. Three years later, he became the only Harvard undergraduate ever to deliver a seminar to the physics department. His topic was "A New Polarizer for Light in the Form of an Extensive Synthetic Sheet." Impatient as always, and this time joined by his physics instructor, George Wheelwright III, Land dropped out of Harvard for a second and last time in 1932.

Though Land could have gone to work in the laboratories of many of America's leading corporations, he opted instead for the autonomy of running his own show. Together, the two formed Land-Wheelwright Laboratories and began manufacturing and commercializing the new product. By 1934, Kodak had signed on as the first customer using the polarizing film in camera filters. American Optical followed a year later, incorporating the filters into sunglasses. Meanwhile, General Motors and General Electric were exploring other applications. Land was not yet twenty-four. In 1937 they renamed their company, Polaroid Corporation, and in 1939, their polarizers were used to view 3-D movies at the New York World's Fair.

Prospects for ever hotter, more intense headlamps and the heavy demands of wear from wind, rain, dust, and the sun caused Land to invent yet other new kinds of polarizers using dyes rather than crystals. With collaborator Joseph Mahler, he also created a new technology for making and viewing photographs in 3-D, which they named Vectographs.

Ironically, while Land's filters were incorporated into a huge number of profitable applications, they were never used in cars. After ten years of research on polarization, the industry chose to use headlight dimmers instead.

With the advent of World War II, Polaroid devoted its efforts to wartime production. Its vectographs were used for battlefield aerial surveys, including those for Normandy and Guadalcanal. Its polarizers helped reduce gun sight and tank telescope glare, and its goggles were for fighting day and night. The war also established Land as a leading scientist to be called on by Congress and the president to aid in America's defense.

In 1944 Land's three-year-old daughter became frustrated when she could not see the photograph immediately after her picture was taken. It spurred him to apply his energies to the intriguing problem of instant photography. In a technique that was his hallmark, once he recognized the problem, he quickly conceived a solution and then applied himself relentlessly to filling in the steps between the idea and the solution. "You always start with a fantasy," he said. "Part of the fantasy technique is to visualize something as perfect. Then with experiments, you work back from the fantasy to reality, hacking away at the components. Ever pragmatic, Land later said, "If you sense a deep human need, then you go back to...science....You make the system fulfill that need, rather than starting the other way around where you have something and wonder what to do with it."

By February 1947, he had demonstrated his new camera, and on November 26, 1948, the Polaroid Land camera was for sale in downtown Boston's Jordon Marsh for $89.75. He followed up with ever faster, smaller, single-lens reflex and color cameras that were continuously refined and improved.

During the early 1950s, Land began working directly with president Eisenhower as head of the Intelligence Section of Eisenhower's Technological Capabilities Panel. Their section conceived the U-2 program, using planes with cameras for spying and the subsequent satellite imaging systems, including the cameras and techniques used in high-altitude photography and intelligence gathering.

Ever charming and persuasive, Land helped golfer Eisenhower understand the benefits by telling him it would be akin to seeing a golf ball at 2,000 yards. Land's inventive talents were so ubiquitous that he even helped Kelly Johnson, head of Lockheed's famed Skunkworks, which secretly developed new aircraft, to design the U-2 wing. Together they conceived an elegant way to reduce heat on the wing's leading edge by funneling the fuel, chilled by the high altitude, past the wing's edge. The technique also warmed the fuel, thinning it to its required viscosity. In part for these efforts, Land received the Presidential Medal of Freedom in 1963. Akin to the Congressional Medal of Honor, it is the highest honor granted to a civilian.

Land continued his contributions to science, education, and defense for more than thirty years serving Presidents Eisenhower, Kennedy, Johnson, and later Nixon. Nixon was the only one Land came to despise. In a commencement address following the U-2 disaster, when one was shot down by the Soviets, Land revealed his passion for truth. He acknowledged Eisenhower's acceptance of full responsibility and for having told the truth.

In Land's view being truthful was something, "in our country, the leader must do at all cost despite the consequences and advantages our adversaries often gained by disinformation." As colleague and author James R. Killian Jr. put it, ". . . it was clear that absolute integrity underlay this man of genius and vision. I don't believe Din Land would have been happy with the lack of respect for truth in more recent administrations."

During Watergate, Land resigned his post as a presidential adviser. When told he had been listed as one of Nixon's 200 enemies, he responded that he was "particularly honored, as it was the only honor he had received without working for it."

Land's most famous failure was a product of his inventive genius and relentless determination. Seeing the need for instant movies, he invented Polaroid's instant movie process. It cost millions and was a huge technical success. What Land had not understood was that videotape (invented by Charles Ginsburg), arriving on the market at nearly the same time, was a cheaper and in some ways better product. The failure ultimately led to Land's resignation from Polaroid.

He went on to explore the phenomenon of light and vision. In the process, he developed his own theories of how color is perceived within the eye's retina and the brain's cortex. He coined the term "Retinex."

In the 1980s he showed his passion for individual contributions to progress by using personal funds to establish and endow the Rowland Institute for Science in Cambridge, Massachusetts. It still provides fellowships for young scientists to support their experiments. As he said in a 1957 MIT speech, group research must not take over. In a democracy one must cooperate, but democracy's "peculiar gift is to develop each individual into everything he might be." "If the dream of personal greatness died," he said, "democracy loses the real source of its future strength."

Land was devoted to the advancement of science and learning. In 1963 he said "Science…is a technique to keep you from kidding yourself." He personally endowed the building of the American Academy of Arts and Sciences. He also gave an anonymous $12.5 million grant to Harvard for its Science Center. His purpose was to give undergraduates access to better facilities to convince more of them to become interested in science.

Land died on March 1, 1991. In the end, he proved a Renaissance man of science. He is America's second most prolific inventor with 535 patents to his name. Only non-Jew Thomas Edison has more. Though Land never graduated from college, he received at least ten honorary doctorates, including one from Harvard where he had been a student.

He was admitted as a fellow of England's Royal Society, was a Fellow of the National Academy of Sciences, and served as president of the American Academy of Arts and Sciences. As a member of the Carnegie Commission, he helped establish public television. Taken together, Land was an exceptional achiever. He was a prolific inventor and scientist, a successful entrepreneur, an adviser to presidents and Congress, a benefactor of education, and a firm believer in truth.

Invention[15]

Inventing things is a domain where Jews are not generally recognized as having played a particularly significant role. Again, we would be surprised.

One source for identifying history's most significant inventions is the *Encyclopædia Britannica*. In its Almanac 2003, it lists 321 "Great Inventions" dating as far back as 13,000 B.C.

Who would have guessed the boomerang was the first "great invention," followed in 6000 B.C. by beer and in 4000 B.C., by wine. The most recent "great" invention, in 1997, is, of all things, Viagra.

While others could also provide excellent lists of great inventions, this one has the benefit of being from a credible source (*Encyclopædia Britannica*), which presumably used experts with no particular ax to grind.

Of the 321 inventions, a good many are so old that no individual inventor can be identified (beer, wine and the boomerang for example). In other cases, the inventor is an organization (such as General Electric Corporation, inventor of artificial diamonds). When all of the organizations and unidentifiable inventors are removed, there remain 267 great inventions, credited to one or more individuals.

Predicting how many of those should have been credited to Jews, gives rise to a question about the appropriate frame of reference. One could argue that since these are the world's greatest inventions, the proper reference frame should be the world's population. Another approach would draw only on the population of the Western hemisphere, Europe, all of Russia, western Asia and northern Africa. This approach involves the observation that nearly all of the great inventions have come from this, more limited, geography. And while the world population is probably the best standard, in this circumstance we provide both. Thus, if one projects the number of Jews that should be included on the list based on the world population, that number is .58 (less than one inventor). If instead, we use the more constrained geography, the number is 1.83. In fact, there are 13.7 Jews on the list. (The fractional number occurs because some inventions are attributed to more than one person. Note the fraction following some of the names shown below.) This is twenty-three times what one would expect based on the world's population and 7.5 times what would be expected if we considered only the more limited geography. In either case, Jews perform a multiple of what one would project based on their population. The Jewish inventors honored by *Encyclopædia Britannica* include those below.

Levi Strauss (1/2), Jeans, 1873
Maurice Levy (1), Lipstick, 1915
Lazlo Biro (1), Ballpoint Pen, 1938
J. Robert Oppenheimer, et al. (1), Atomic Bomb, 1945
Edwin Herbert Land (1), Instant Photography, 1947
Dennis Gabor (1), Holography, 1948
Peter Carl Goldmark (1), Long Playing Record, 1948
Robert Adler (1), Television Remote Control, 1950
Edward Teller, et al. (1), Thermonuclear Bomb, 1952
Paul M. Zoll (2), Defibrillator, 1952, and Cardiac Pacemaker, 1952
Gregory Pincus (1/3), Contraceptives, early 1950s
Charles Ginsburg (1), Videotape, 1950s
Gordon Gould (1/3), Laser, 1958
Stanley N. Cohen (1/2), Genetic Engineering, 1973
Jason Lanier (1), Virtual Reality, 1989

Though the *Britannica* list is published in alphabetical sequence based on the common name of the invention, it provides some very interesting insights when resorted chronologically. Both approaches are included in Exhibits 4a (alphabetical) and 4b (chronological).

Chronologically, the data show how clearly the Mideast and eastern Mediterranean dominated early history and early inventions. Namely, of the seventeen great inventions between prehistory and the Golden Age of Greece (roughly 450 B.C.), twelve or thirteen were invented in the Mideast or eastern Mediterranean. Interestingly, after the Golden Age of Greece, no further great inventions came from that part of the world.

From the Golden Age of Greece until 1200, China was the source of most inventions. Of the eleven inventions identified with that era, six came from China. This is two-thirds of the nine major Chinese inventions of which the last, the toothbrush, was invented in 1498. Nothing from China has made the list since.

The Dark and Middle Ages truly were a period of little change or invention. Of the 321 total inventions *Britannica* includes on their list, only ten arose in the 1,345 years between A.D. 105 and 1450. And of those ten, only five came from Europe.

The Renaissance marks the true beginning of the age of invention. Until 1450, when Gutenberg invented the printing press, there were only thirty-two noteworthy inventions. In the roughly 550 years since, there have been 289.

Once Isaac Newton and Leibniz invented the calculus, the U.K. and France flowered, creating twenty-three of the thirty-two inventions between the 1680s and the 1830s.

After the 1830s, the United States began to dominate. Of the 239 inventions since 1831, 151 came from Americans.

Of the 167 total U.S. inventions, 11.7 came from Jews. This is 2.5 times the 4.5 expected. Even more interesting, perhaps, is that both inventions credited to Hungarians came from Jews (holography by Gabor and the ballpoint pen by Biro). And that does not count Edward Teller, a U.S. emigrant from Hungary who is credited with inventing the thermonuclear bomb.

And last, the remarkable fact that the bulk of Jewish invention is so recent. Of the fifteen inventions by Jews, thirteen date from the end of World War II. In fact, the earliest Jewish inventor of note is Levi Strauss for his 1873 co-invention of jeans. Since World War II, *Britannica* counts seventy-two "Great Inventions," Jews were involved in thirteen of them, roughly one hundred times what one would expect. This point ultimately reinforces one of this book's main points. Namely, the Golden Age of Jewish Achievement arose over the past 200 or so years as Jews emerged into an Enlightenment and Emancipation-induced secular world.

CHAPTER 5

Education

Told by his daughter (the noted historian Gerda Kronstein Lerner), of the only "B" she ever received, her father, Robert Kronstein, replied angrily, "Jews don't get 'B's."[16]

A Little History of Jewish Enrollment in Higher Learning[17]

"In Effort to Lift Their Rankings, Colleges Recruit Jewish Students." That was the front-page headline from the April 29, 2002, *Wall Street Journal.* The article tells a marvelous tale of tantalizing ironies. "'Yes, we're targeting Jewish students,' Chancellor Gordon Gee told a March 17, 2002, board meeting of the Vanderbilt affiliate of Hillel, the nonprofit national Jewish campus organization. 'There's nothing wrong with that. That's not affirmative action. That's smart thinking.'" Later in the story, Gee, a Mormon who left Brown University to head Vanderbilt, indicated the effort was part of his "elite strategy" to move Vanderbilt into Ivy League status. "'Jewish students," he said, "by culture and by ability and by the very nature of their liveliness, make a university a much more habitable place in terms of intellectual life."

The irony arises from the Ivy League's historic efforts, from the 1920s until at least the end of World War II, to use "quotas" and other means to constrain the number of Jews attending Ivy League schools.

One delights at how interesting it would be if one could listen to a conversation between Chancellor Gee and A. Lawrence Lowell, Harvard's president in 1922. Eighty years earlier, Lowell's plans to establish a quota of 15 percent Jewish students at Harvard was derailed by Harry Starr, a second-generation Russian Jewish emigrant student. Starr learned of Lowell's plan and challenged it. He made the issue public and ultimately forced Lowell to back away from the quota. The retreat, however, was only tactical. Shortly thereafter, Harvard and other Ivy League schools introduced "geographic diversity," refined standards for reviewing applications, and in 1926 adopted the SAT tests, all steps intended, at least in part, to accomplish the same result, namely, reduce Jewish enrollment.

In one of the two recent Michigan cases before the U.S. Supreme Court, an issue for court consideration was whether awarding extra points to minorities during the college admission process was a de facto quota. In Michigan's case, the quota was used to enroll more minorities, rather than to exclude them as was Lowell's purpose eighty years earlier. One is struck by the shifting notions of "diversity" as a concept utilized in support of a "greater good." In 1922 it was "geographic diversity" to enhance the educational opportunity for all students. In the 1990s, "racial diversity" intends to serve the same purpose. Interestingly, some who opposed quotas to exclude Jews and considered "geographic diversity" to be code for "fewer Jews" would today jump through the required logical conundrums to encourage "racial diversity" and, perhaps, minority quotas in support of affirmative action.

To set the context for Vanderbilt's Jewish recruitment and Michigan's affirmative action, we must to go back in time. From the 1650s till about 1880, it is generally fair to say that the United States had two groups of Jews. The first were the early immigrants, mostly Sephardic Jews, whose roots traced back to the twenty-three Sephardics who arrived in New Amsterdam from Recife in 1654. Never large in numbers, between 1654 and the Revolution, the Jewish population in North America is estimated to have grown from twenty-three to 2,500 (out of 2,500,000 Americans). Particularly during the nineteenth century, a second group, the "Our Crowd" Jews of Western and Central Europe (many of them German Jews) arrived, set up businesses, and became successful and prosperous. (The term "Our Crowd" comes from Stephen Birmingham's book by that name which celebrates the lives of prominent nineteenth century New York Jewish families.) They brought with them a strong educational and cultural legacy from Europe, and they continued to demonstrate those values in their newly adopted country. By 1880 the United States had 250,000 Jews (0.5 percent of the country's fifty million people).

Between 1880 and 1920, everything changed. The pogroms of Russia and the open immigration policies of the United States brought millions of Eastern European Jews through Ellis Island and other ports of entry into the United States. By 1920, the United States had 3.6 million Jews representing 3.4 percent of the country's 106 million people. Thus, while the U.S. population more than doubled, the number of Jews had increased fourteen-fold. These new arrivals may have been "People of the Book," but many were illiterate, or nearly so. Opportunities for learning in areas now called Russia, Poland, Byelorussia, Ukraine, and the Baltic States were almost nonexistent for Jews. In that part of the world, so hard on Jews for so long, education may have been treasured, but only in an abstract "next year in Jerusalem" sort of way. With some exceptions, poverty, serfdom, and the kind of anti-Semitism that led to the pogroms afforded very limited opportunities for schools and schooling. When tested at Ellis Island upon arrival, most Jews performed poorly on what were then considered reliable measures of intelligence. And no group of people was more put off by the illiterate, pushy, difficult new group of Jews than the old-line "Our Crowd" German Jews of the Upper East Side.

But if the United States offered a modicum of safety for the oppressed and a chance to prosper, it also offered an opportunity for education. The newly arrived Jews grabbed it like water in the Sahara. First in the public grade schools and high schools, as well as the night schools one could attend while holding down a job, Jews went after whatever education they could get. Later, with the same zest, they pursued education in the Eastern colleges, many of them part of today's Ivy League. At Harvard, Jewish enrollment which had reached 6 percent by 1909 soared to 22 percent by 1922. At Columbia University, more convenient because of its New York location, Jewish enrollment climbed to 40 percent of the student body, and at Hunter College, it was 80 percent.

This was the "Jewish problem" facing Lowell at Harvard and his colleagues at other Ivy League schools. The flood of Jews was displacing old-line Gentile Americans. And it was all happening in the emerging era of eugenics, when tests, such as those administered earlier at Ellis Island and later on World War I Army recruits, were believed to have clearly established that people of Nordic, Alpine, and similar Western and Northern European backgrounds were intellectually superior to blacks, Jews, "Mediterraneans," and others of southern and eastern European origin. In the language of the times, admissions personnel, particularly at the Ivy League schools, would "reclaim the right to use social as well as academic criteria." "New application blanks would ask for personal background, including religious affiliation, father's name and place of birth…Columbia required a photograph, a personal interview, and three letters of recommendation." Prospective students were evaluated based on "character" and "background." Admissions staff would look favorably on the "boys of old American stock" and Gentile boys of "a desirable social type," while holding back on Jews whose energy and ambition was seen to outstrip their native IQ.

Lowell opted to face the issue more directly with a 15 percent quota, saying it would help Jews by mitigating resentment and anti-Semitism. Starr took the issue public and challenged the notion that a larger enrollment of "pure American stock" was a legitimate basis for restricting the entrance of Jews. The Boston press picked up on Starr's argument, criticized the quota and a thirteen member committee set up by Harvard's board of Overseers rejected the quota. Harvard, like the rest of the Ivy League schools, retreated to less obvious, but equally successful techniques to retain the white Anglo-Saxon Protestant (WASP) character of their schools (most of which were created by Christian denominations in the first place).

They added a couple of new twists. First, the Harvard Board of Overseers agreed to promote "geographic diversity" in its student body. The idea was that the Southern guy would have a better educational experience if he was exposed to a Midwestern farm kid, the son a Maine fisherman, and a Northwest logger. This "diversity" would "enhance the learning experience." Of course the downside was that it didn't leave much room for numerous otherwise qualified applicants from the Lower East Side.

Second, in 1926 Harvard and other Ivy League schools began using the Scholastic Aptitude Test (SAT) to replace the admissions test on which urban Jews had performed well. The SAT was grounded in the earlier Ellis Island and U.S. Army World War I tests in which Jews, among others, had performed poorly. That the poor test results were largely based on the lower literacy of the foreigners (on arrival), and their unfamiliarity with English and American terminology, was not yet understood. Here was a test that provided evidence Jews did not perform well; its use might help bring about the desired results. Moreover, the fact that some of the SAT questions were developed and tested on Princeton freshman and Cooper Union students (all scholarship recipients), demonstrated that smart Gentiles did well on the tests. Ironically, as time passed and Jews became literate, as they absorbed American terminology, and learned how to take such tests, the outcomes completely reversed. But that was in the future and not anticipated when SAT testing began in 1926.

With the revised processes for handling applications, the push for "geographic diversity," and the adoption of the SAT, the stage was set to bring Jewish enrollment back "in line." And some would say that Lowell helped it along by actually putting in place the quota the Board of Overseers had nixed. Selectivity, "geographic diversity," and SAT tests did, in fact, do the trick. Jewish enrollment fell, and by 1931, Jews were only 15 percent of Harvard's enrollment. (Still not bad, considering Jews were 3.4 percent of the U.S. population at the time.)

In the late 1930s, Lowell's successor, James Bryant Conant, completely changed the direction for Harvard admissions, and apparently did so for reasons that had little to do with Jews. According to Nicholas Lehman, author of *The Big Test—Secret History of the American Meritocracy:*

> "Conant believed that a narrow constricted group of wealthy descendants of the early settlers of America—people born into money, privately educated, often in New England boarding schools, especially Episcopalian—had formed a kind of club. They weren't especially able, to Conant's mind, and they kind of controlled everything…Conant's primary goal…was to break the hold of this old elite and put in its place, a new elite that would be made up of people from…all over the country, people selected on pure intelligence, not on their background."
>
> (Lehman *Frontline* interview)

Conant envisioned a pure meritocracy and worked with colleague Henry Chauncey to change the SAT, making it more of a pure IQ or aptitude test, rather than what he saw as an "achievement test" favoring the already privileged. At the same time, Conant dropped the emphasis on "geographic diversity." His pursuit of a pure meritocracy also shifted emphasis away from family background, religion, father's name and birthplace, and any standard giving a premium to "old American stock." This push for merit and de-emphasis of the old-line Anglican Ivy League legacy had the unforeseen consequence of reopening admission to Jews based on merit.

Particularly after World War II and the Holocaust, as attitudes in the United States changed, and as Jews continued to aspire to more and better education, their levels of enrollment at quality schools grew. In this same era it became easier for a Jewish professor to become tenured, and that resulted in an ever larger percentage of Jews in senior teaching positions at America's best universities.

Ironically, it was a Jew who saw an entrepreneurial opportunity in the SAT tests. Stanley Kaplan began his SAT test preparation company in 1946. It focused on training students to take the tests. While training students to take the test might have been considered "untoward," or sort of like cheating in the 1950s, it has evolved to become the standard. Now if one doesn't strive to learn how to take the SAT, you do yourself a grave disservice. Today Kaplan's company is a $2 billion a year enterprise owned by *The Washington Post*, and it is only the largest of a number of such companies.

After performing poorly on initial versions of such tests, Jews got ever better with the passage of time. The published results for the 2001 SAT (now called "SAT Reasoning Test") test place Jews second, behind only the small group of self-identified Unitarians. The Unitarians had average scores of 1209 (out of a maximum of 1,600) versus the Jews at 1,161 and the national average of 1,020.

Current Levels of Jewish Enrollment[18]

With the traditional Jewish emphasis on education, the reduced emphasis on geographic diversity, and outstanding SAT scores and high school grades, Jews have climbed to remarkable levels of enrollment at our best schools.

Exhibits 5a and 5b show what that means. Two caveats deserve mention before plowing into the numbers. First, realize the 2.1 percent estimate for Jews as a percent of the U.S. population is probably high for college-age students. This is because Jews are not reproducing at a replacement rate, and they have a median age of forty-one, six years higher than the U.S. average of thirty-five. Moreover, the percentage of Jews under age eighteen is only 21 percent of the Jewish population versus 26 percent for the overall U.S. population. The second caveat is that most of the enrollment numbers for Jews on the various campuses come from Hillel, the nonprofit association supporting Jewish students on campus. Hillel is not exactly a disinterested party, though they appear to be the single best source for such data, and both Jews and non-Jews draw on the data and regard them as credible.

In any case, Jews now are 21 percent of the enrollment at Ivy League schools (30 percent at Penn, 29 percent at Yale and 26 percent at Harvard). Perhaps now we now know why Bill Clinton had so many Jews in his administration. Like Lanny Davis, they were all his Yale classmates! Princeton and Dartmouth bring up the rear at 10 percent Jewish enrollment, and interestingly both have had something of a reputation for anti-Semitism despite until recently having had Jewish presidents. Even in the less prestigious but still excellent Big 10 and PAC 10 schools, enrollment numbers for Jews are impressive at 8 percent and 7 percent respectively. In that regard, since Big 10 and PAC 10 schools, unlike the Ivy League, tend to draw heavily from the local populations, it is instructive to compare the school-by-school averages with the percent of Jewish populations of the respective states. In that sense, the 8.4 percent Jewish enrollment at the University of Washington is even more impressive, since the state has a Jewish population of only 0.7 percent. The University of Michigan and Northwestern are similarly notable by that standard.

Jewish enrollment rates are even higher at the fifty small schools that *U.S. News and World Report* ranks among the "Top 50 Undergraduate Schools of 2003," That average is 12.3 percent with some schools like Sarah Lawrence, Vassar, Barnard and Skidmore showing 20 to 31 percent Jewish enrollment. (Exhibit 5b.)

This is an amazing accomplishment. For Ivy League schools, Jews are represented at least ten times more than one would expect. For individual schools, the range is five times at Dartmouth or Princeton to fifteen times at Pennsylvania, fourteen at Yale and thirteen at Harvard. And, mind you, the performance is really better than that. This outcome arises in competition with the United States' best students—and to some extent the world's best students—for the limited number of slots at the premier U.S. schools. Further, estimates say 80 to 90 percent of all college-age Jews go to college. This is dramatically above most other ethnic groups (though the Asians are closing fast). It is also much above the 1999 national average of 25.2 percent.

A final note on this topic. At Harvard, the current enrollment is 26 percent Jewish, 17 percent Asian, 7 percent black, 8 percent Hispanic and 1 percent American Indian/Alaskan native. In short, the minorities are the majority at Harvard (59 percent).

All of which brings us back to Vanderbilt. As reported in *The Wall Street Journal* story, Vanderbilt saw that its No. 21 ranking in *U.S. News and World Report's* annual survey of colleges and universities had placed it behind both Emory (No. 18) and Washington University in St. Louis (No. 14). Perhaps it had not missed Gee's attention that Vanderbilt's Jewish enrollment had dropped from an estimated 7 to 9 percent in the 1970s to only 2 to 4 percent in 2002. Washington University and Emory, on the other hand, had 35 percent and 30 percent Jewish enrollments, respectively. A 1996 study by Greg Perfetto, who by 2002 had become assistant provost at Vanderbilt, found that "Vanderbilt was competitive with Emory and Washington University on every demographic sector but one: Jewish students."

It is no coincidence that Vanderbilt faces competition in its efforts to recruit Jews. Similar efforts have also begun on other campuses, such as University of Southern California, and for the same reason. USC worked hard to improve its rating and perceived that cross-town rival UCLA, northern California's UC Berkeley, and the Ivy League schools were all better ranked and all had more Jews. As of 2002, USC had a recruiter, Jessica F. Pashkow, to specialize in recruiting Jews and a faculty that is one-third Jewish. USC now has 8.2 percent Jewish enrollment, up from 4.6 percent a decade ago. And in the rankings, they have climbed to thirty-one.

Joining Vanderbilt and USC (according to *The Wall Street Journal* story and the March 5, 1999, issue of *Jewish Times*) in Jewish recruitment are schools such as Southern Methodist, Texas Christian, and Duke. It may also not be coincidental that both Princeton and Dartmouth, which lagged the rest of the Ivy League in Jewish enrollment, recruited Jews to become their presidents, though both have since stepped down from that role.

The fact that Jews are now recruited openly has brought criticism from some Jewish quarters. In a July 18, 2002, *Baltimore Sun* editorial, "Jews Should Reject Preferences," Justin Shubow writes:

". . . it is not a stretch to imagine that having targeted Jews for admission, universities will be unable to resist selecting them over equally or even more qualified non Jews" Further, ". . .polls have consistently shown that Jews while vehemently rejecting all quotas, support affirmative action." And finally, "The majority of Jews care strongly about social justice and willingly support social engineering policies for the sake of that goal. But they hold dear the fundamental principle that people ought to be regarded and treated as individuals, not merely as members of a certain group."

How one squares affirmative action and bonus points for minorities as a group while regarding people as "individuals, not merely as members of a certain group" remains part of the mental jujitsu alluded to earlier in this chapter.

In the end, over a period of eighty years, Jews have gone from being discriminated against to being enticed. And both paradigms arise from the insatiable drive of Jews to be educated.

Achievement and Leadership in Academic Domains[19]

One cannot conceive of the study of economics without understanding its debt to Jews who have led the field. Whether it is Karl Marx, whose *Das Kapital* changed the world and is still studied as "gospel" by millions around the globe despite the failure of Soviet Communism; David Ricardo, who developed the theory of comparative advantage; Paul Samuelson, the MIT professor whose book was the leading college economics textbook for more than thirty years; or Milton Friedman, who almost single-handedly moved the discipline away from its love affair with John Maynard Keynes, Jews have played a seminal role in economic theory. Perhaps the clearest representation of their importance is measured in the 36 percent of Nobels for economics that have gone to Jews, most while serving as professors at major universities. For example:

> David Akerlof – UC Berkeley
> Kenneth Arrow – Stanford and Harvard
> Gary Becker – University of Chicago
> Robert Fogel – Harvard and University of Chicago
> Milton Friedman – University of Chicago and Hoover Institute at Stanford
> John C. Harsanyi – UC Berkeley
> Daniel Kahneman – Princeton University
> Lawrence Klein – University of Pennsylvania and Oxford
> Simon Kuznets – University of Pennsylvania, Harvard and Johns Hopkins
> Wassily Leontief – Harvard University and New York University
> Harry M. Markowitz – UCLA
> Merton H. Miller – Carnegie Institute and University of Chicago
> Franco Modigliani – New School and MIT
> Paul Samuelson – MIT
> Herbert A. Simon – Carnegie Mellon
> Robert M. Solow – MIT

On one of the most enduring questions of all time—What is the best economic system that brings the most benefit to the most people?—it is Jews, more than any other single group, who have helped lead the way in thinking through and debating the different economic theories and alternative courses of action.

Physics is another domain that explores enduring questions, in particular, "What is the nature of our universe?" In physics, as in economics, Jews have been prominent researchers and teachers. Much, if not most, of their work has been done in an academic environment. Einstein taught at Princeton after he immigrated to the United States. Leo Szilard (with Fermi, who was not Jewish), conducted the first controlled nuclear reaction at the University of Chicago. Felix Bloch taught at Stanford, Hans Bethe at MIT, Max Born at University of Edinburgh, Richard Feynman and Murray Gell-Mann at Cal Tech, Niels Bohr at the Niels Bohr Institute in Copenhagen. The list simply goes on and on. Nearly all of the forty-eight Jewish Nobel Prize winners in physics have done their research and taught in an academic environment, and therein stimulated succeeding generations of other young physicists.

By now, more than one hundred years later, we might well have finally stumbled onto relativity, the conversion of mass to energy, the nature of light and the relationship between the speed of light, mass, and energy, but it was Einstein who did it in 1905. More recently, it was Richard Feynman who used a glass of ice water to explain to the world how the freezing temperatures at Cape Canaveral (Kennedy) brought down the Challenger space shuttle in 1986. Again, our debt to this one group of people for their contributions is enormous.

Mathematics, like physics, is a largely academic domain. And like physics, Jews have played a huge role. The comments in Chapter 3 are on point. Of all winners of the Fields Medal for mathematics, at least twelve of the forty-eight medals (25 percent) have gone to Jews. Among them, Efim Zelmanov at the University of Wisconsin and Yale; Edward Witten at Princeton; Michael Freedman at the University of California, San Diego; Charles Fefferman at Princeton; Jesse Douglas at MIT; Paul Joseph Cohen at Stanford; and many, many more. And these are only those who won the Fields Medal. Felix Mandelbrot, who created fractal geometry, is the Sterling Professor of Mathematics at Yale. John Von Neuman, whose mathematical genius encompassed game theory, computers, and many other fields taught at Princeton. Marcel Grossman, who helped Einstein in the integration of mathematical and theoretical physics, was a professor of geometry at Eidgenoossische Technische Hochschule in Germany. Finally, Paul Erdös, one of the most brilliant mathematicians of the twentieth-century was another of the great mathematical minds teaching at Princeton.

Chemistry, in which Jews have won 20 percent of the Nobels, is another field in which the leadership of Jews is most demonstrated in academia. Alan Heeger, winner of the 2000 Nobel, spent twenty years at the University of Pennsylvania before moving to the University of California at Santa Barbara. Walter Kohn, the 1998 winner, taught at Harvard and Carnegie Mellon. Harold Kroto, the 1996 winner, taught at Sussex University. George Olah, 1994, taught at Western Reserve University in Cleveland. And on and on.

Franz Boas is often credited with being the "father of anthropology." While that might be considered excessive by some, the *Encyclopædia Britannica* does credit Boas with being the founder of the "relativistic, culture-centered school of anthropology that became dominant in the twentieth-century." Boas, who taught at Columbia University, inspired a succeeding generation of leading anthropologists including Edward Sapir and non-Jews Margaret Mead, Alfred L. Kroeber, and Ruth Benedict.

In the second half of the twentieth century, the field of linguistics was heavily influenced by Noam Chomsky, an MIT professor. Controversial both in his selected field—for his notion that humans have an innate capability to understand formal principles of language—as well as for his outspoken political views, Chomsky was the single most well-known linguist of the era. Interestingly, Esperanto, the "world language" which it was hoped would become a universal second language everyone could speak so we might reduce human misunderstanding, was created in 1887 by the Polish Jew Ludwig L. Zamenhof. An old joke says that one reason Esperanto never took off was because at meetings of the Esperanto Association, "Everyone was speaking Yiddish."

In philosophy, the debt is to Moses Maimonides, Baruch de Spinoza, Ludwig Wittgenstein, Henri Bergson, Jacques Derrida and others. The incidence of Jews is illustrated in a compilation of four lists: (1) The BBC Great Philosophers Series; (2) Chronological Map of the Great Philosophers; (3) Trinity College Philosopher's List; and (4) Fifty Major Philosophers. Combined, one-sixth of the major philosophers identified from the four lists are Jews.

Medical education in the United States and later in other parts of the world was fundamentally reshaped by Abraham Flexner, founder and director of a college-preparatory school in Louisville. Flexner received a commission to study medical education in the United States. He issued his report in 1910 calling for medicine to be treated as an academic study, rather than an apprenticeship organized for profit. He called for full-time faculties, laboratories, libraries, and access to hospitals for students and staff. After his report was issued, many of the schools he criticized were closed. Flexner went on to found the Institute for Advanced Study at Princeton, one of America's foremost academic havens.

And once again, in medicine, we find the Nobel winners working in academic environments and therein researching and teaching those who will follow them. Stanley Prusiner, the 1997 winner for his discovery of prions, is at the University of California San Francisco Medical Center. Sydney Brenner and H. Robert Horvitz, winners in 2002, are at the Molecular Sciences Institute in Berkeley, and MIT in Cambridge, respectively. Paul Greengard and Eric R. Kandel, the winners in 2000, are at Rockefeller University and Columbia. Going back, nearly all of the fifty-nine Jewish winners of Nobels in physiology or medicine have spent much of their careers at a university. Even Salk and Sabin who deserved, but did not get, Nobels, worked at the University of Pittsburgh and the University of Cincinnati, respectively.

Within the various specialties of medicine are areas where Jews have led the way, such as psychiatry and its siblings psychotherapy and psychology. Most prominent, perhaps, in these disciplines was Sigmund Freud, who felt indebted to Josef Breuer for his work with hysteria, and who passed along a father's guidance to his daughter, Anna, for her use in psychotherapy. Alfred Adler, Erik Erikson, Erich Fromm, Bruno Bettelheim, Frieda Fromm-Reichmann, and David Rapaport are but a few of the more prominent Jewish leaders in psychoanalysis. In psychology, the first doctorate ever awarded went to a Jew, Joseph Jastrow at Johns Hopkins in 1886 and two of the most influential psychologists of the "human potential" movement were Abraham Maslow and Erich Fromm.

In legal studies, political science, history, engineering and nearly any other field of academic endeavor, one could perform the kind of exercise written in the last few pages. Laurence Tribe, Harvard Law School, argued the case that Al Gore should have been awarded Florida's 2000 electoral votes before the U.S. Supreme Court. Mortimer Adler was a professor at Columbia and University of Chicago where he co-directed creation of the fifty-four volumes of the *Great Books of the Western World*. Allan Bloom, professor at the University of Chicago, Yale, and Cornell wrote the influential *Closing of the American Mind* about the "dumbing down" of American culture.

Daniel Boorstin was a professor of history at the University of Chicago for twenty-five years. Among others of his books, he wrote *The Discoverers, The Genius of American Politics,* and *The Lost World of Thomas Jefferson*. In 1975 he took over as head of the Library of Congress. Steven Jay Gould, paleontologist at Harvard was a prolific writer on evolution (and baseball). Nathan Glazer and David Riesman, both Harvard professors, wrote *The Lonely Crowd,* one of the seminal books of sociology of the 1950s and 1960s. Carl Sagan, who popularized astronomy, was a professor at Cornell, the University of California at Berkeley and Harvard.

In short, it is impossible to find an academic domain in which Jews have not played a disproportionate role. As John Derbyshire, a National Review contributing editor said in a November 2, 2000, piece, quoting Paul Johnson in *A History of the Jews:*

> "If you take almost anything, science, law, philosophy, literature, medicine, music— and track it back to its roots, you will find Jews there, or at least meet an awful lot of them along the way."

Jewish Faculty and Administration Roles[20]

If Jews have done well in college enrollment and research, they have mirrored the performance in serving on college and university faculties and in positions of leadership. Jews would not be shy in saying they have had to overcome much the same discrimination in those roles as students faced in the 1920s and 30s, really only breaking out of those constraints in a significant way after World War II.

The *American Jewish Desk Reference* notes that it was pretty tough sledding in the early days. Yale, for example, was reputed not to give tenure to any Jewish professor until the late 1940s. And even those who got teaching positions were required to have sponsors willing to "testify that the candidate did not 'push' his Jewish traits and was "courteous and quiet in disposition." In the 1920s, Arthur Schlesinger Sr. and Felix Frankfurter challenged Harvard in its prejudice. But with the growth of Jews in the student body, the end of World War II, the reactions to the Holocaust and the Civil Rights Act of 1964, which outlawed discrimination on the basis of ethnic background, race, and sex, things changed for the better. The *American Jewish Desk Reference* says that by the end of the 1960s, 12 percent of college teaching positions were filled by Jews, and that number was 20 percent at elite private universities. It goes further in saying that "at some institutions, the percentage of Jewish professors now approaches almost half the total faculty." Pinning the numbers down with precision is not easy because, unlike the domains of leadership where many Jewish winners are famous and thus easily identified as Jews, such recognition rarely filters down to the level of professors.

As such, two Exhibits may provide some limited insight. The first, Exhibit 5c, lists the faculties of the Stanford, Harvard, and Yale Law schools as of May 2003. The three schools were selected because they were the top-three-ranked law schools in the 2003 *U.S. News and World Report* ranking. Hence the effort is focused on the premier schools. The Law School Exhibit does not identify who among the faculty members are Jews. But a cursory review by the author and a software review done using so-called onomastic software that compares names to large lists (5,000 or more names) of Jews and non-Jews provides an indication or probability. In both the author's and the software review, the results were similar. Namely, that at Stanford, Harvard, and Yale law schools, Jews are probably between 23 percent and 34 percent of the faculty.

A second Exhibit (5d) shows similar information for the prestigious Princeton Institute for Advanced Study. This has been the academic home of some of the world's greatest scholars, among them Albert Einstein, John Von Neumann, J. Robert Oppenheimer, and many others. The institute consists of five programs: the School of Historical Studies, the School of Mathematics, the School of Natural Sciences, the School of Social Sciences, and the newest program in theoretical biology (from its Web site).

Nearly 5,000 members have spent time at the institute over the years since it was founded in 1933, and many will recall that this is where John Nash (of *A Beautiful Mind*) made his academic home. Of the roughly 5,000 "members," only eighty-five are considered "Present and Past Faculty." They are shown on Exhibit 5d. Again, no effort has been made to definitively confirm each identity, but the perusal and software review both end up saying that at least 15 percent of those listed are Jewish— and this from Princeton, which like Dartmouth, has long been regarded as a very difficult Ivy League school for Jewish admission and tenure. In this case, Jews are 7.5 times what they should be among this prestigious academic community.

Similar exercises done by others using onomastics software yielded additional data about likely Jewish representation on college faculties. Among its findings:

> Of the forty officers and national council members of the American Association of University Professors, 30 percent are Jewish.
>
> Of the 254 members of the psychology faculties at Texas, Emory, Yale, and Johns Hopkins, 24 percent are Jewish.
>
> Of the 146 cultural anthropologists at Northwestern, UCSD, UCSB, Southern Methodist and Duke, 18 percent are Jewish.
>
> Of the sixty-nine sociologists at Harvard, Yale, and Princeton, 28 percent are Jewish.
>
> Of the 150 professors of chemical engineering at the University of Akron, Ohio State, North Carolina State, University of Pennsylvania, Rensselaer, Rutgers, and USC, 7 percent are Jewish.
>
> Of the 208 professors of aeronautical engineering at the University of Illinois, University of Michigan, University of Cincinnati, UC Davis, and Rensselaer, 4.3 percent are Jewish.
>
> Interestingly, of the 246 names of mechanical engineering professors at the University of Illinois, Penn State, and the University of Maryland, only 2 percent are Jews. (Mechanical engineering appears to be one of few areas in which Jews merely match their proportion of the overall population!)

Rabbi Chaim Seidler-Feller, the executive director of the Hillel at UCLA, now estimates that Jews hold 50,000 to 60,000 professorships on American campuses, and he also assesses they are a third of the faculty at some of the best schools. Jews have much to be proud of.

Our final exercise is a quick look at Ivy League presidents:

School	Incumbent president	Predecessor
Princeton	Shirley M. Gilghman	**Harold T. Shapiro**
Harvard	Drew Gilpin Faust	**Lawrence H. Summers**
Yale	**Richard Charles Levin**	Benno Schmidt
Columbia	**Lee C. Bollinger**	George Rupp
Dartmouth	James Wright	**James O. Freedman**
Brown	Ruth J. Simmons	E. Gordon Gee
Penn	**Amy Gutmann**	**Judith Rodin**
Cornell	**David J. Skorton**	**Jeffrey Lehman**

As shown, four of eight current Ivy League presidents are Jewish (bold and underlined), as are five of their eight predecessors. Not shown on the listing are some of the Jewish presidents of other major universities including:

Lawrence S. Bacow, president of Tufts
Henry Bienen, president of Northwestern
Jared L. Cohon, president of Carnegie Mellon
Leon Botstein, president of Bard College

And with that, it seems realistic to say that Jews have broken down nearly all the anti-Semitic barriers of academia whether in terms of student enrollment, academic contribution to knowledge, representation on faculties, or leadership of our leading colleges and universities.

Chapter 6

Military and Aviation

The Six-Day War[21]

From April through early June of 1967, the world's media reported a dramatic escalation of Middle Eastern tensions. On April 7, the Israelis shot down six Syrian MiGs. On May 14, Syria claimed Israel was massing troops on its border. On May 15, the Egyptians moved troops into the Sinai while Nasser demanded the withdrawal of the 4,500-man United Nations Emergency Forces separating the Israelis from the Egyptians. On May 22, Nasser declared the Straits of Tiran closed, blocking all shipping to and from Israel's Red Sea port of Eilat. On May 25, Iraq and Saudi Arabia moved troops to Israel's border and on the 26th Nasser declared his intention to destroy Israel. On May 30, Jordan signed a pact with Egypt, essentially uniting the two forces and placing Egypt in overall command. On June 4, Iraq signed a similar agreement. Egyptian, Syrians, and Jordanians appeared to be massing for an attack on Israel. That same day, Israel was preparing to respond or mount a preemptive attack.

For the Israelis, the numbers were daunting.

The Israelis had roughly 275,000 men available, most of them reservists called up because of the crisis. This represented almost 10 percent of Israel's 2.9 million people. In addition, Israel had roughly 200 combat aircraft and 1,000 tanks.

Jordan had 56,000 men, twenty-four Hawker Hunter aircraft, and 270 modern tanks focused mostly on the narrow choke point where Israel's eastern border is only nine miles from the Mediterranean. The Syrians had 50,000 soldiers on the Golan Heights, 125 combat aircraft, 250 tanks, and as many field guns, soon to be reinforced with Iraqi tanks. The Egyptians had 130,000 men, 900 tanks, 1,100 guns, and 420 combat aircraft. In addition, troops and matériel were available or en route from Iraq, Saudi Arabia, Morocco, Libya, and Tunisia.

While the Egyptians, Jordanians, and Syrians were expected to be the principal fighters in any war with Israel, the combined Arab force available for action included up to 500,000 troops, 900 combat aircraft, and 5,000 tanks.

When war began on June 5, the pace was simply unbelievable. In just 132 hours—slightly less than six days—Israel destroyed its enemies' armies and quadrupled the territory under its control. The Egyptians lost 10,000 to 15,000 men, with another 5,000 missing. Jordan lost 700 men, with 6,000 wounded or missing. Syria lost 450 men and had 1,800 wounded. In contrast, Israel lost fewer than 800 men. The casualty ratio was an almost incredible twenty-five to one. Israel held 5,000 Egyptian POWs, 365 Syrians, and 550 Jordanians. In contrast, 15 Israeli soldiers were POWs.

All but 15 percent of Egypt's military hardware was destroyed or captured, including 700 of its 900 tanks, 286 of its 420 combat aircraft, and all of its bombers. Jordan lost 179 tanks, 1,062 guns, 3,166 vehicles, and nearly 20,000 assorted arms. Syria lost 118 tanks, 470 guns, and 1,200 vehicles, not counting the 40 tanks abandoned to the Israelis. Two-thirds of Syria's air force was destroyed. By contrast, Israel lost a total of thirty-six planes and eighteen pilots, roughly 20 percent of its air power.

The Israelis had captured all of the Golan Heights from Syria, the West Bank from Jordan and the Gaza Strip and Sinai from Egypt. From roughly 20,000 square kilometers of territory, the Israelis had expanded their control to more than 88,000 square kilometers. Moreover, the speed with which the Sinai fell led to the joke during mid-June that one should "Visit Israel to see the pyramids." In control of the eastern side of the Suez Canal, the Israeli army was less than 100 miles from Giza.

Up to that time, it was one of the most lopsided military victories ever. And for many, including the author, it was an early exposure to the remarkable accomplishments of one of the smallest groups of people on the planet.

Military[22]

Until Israel's War of Independence and the later Six-Day War, Jews were rarely thought to possess significant military talent. From A.D. 70, when Romans destroyed the Second Temple and later dispersed them, until 1948 when Israel came into existence, Jews had no country of their own requiring a military defense force. Further, until the Jewish Emancipation (1791 to 1874), they were typically proscribed from military service in most countries. If they served at all, they were generally excluded from the senior ranks.

The Holocaust further slandered their reputation as warriors. That so many seemed to have marched willingly to the gas chambers, together with their small physical stature as a people, tended to reinforce the view that Jews lacked the skills and temperament to be warriors.

In fact, that view would be wrong and the story is both more complex and more interesting than expected.

It is correct that from the time of Judah Maccabee, who led the rebellion that expelled the Syrian Greeks from Palestine, and the later (first- and second-century) revolts against the Romans, Jews were not prominent in warfare. But that began to change when they arrived in America in 1654. The next year Asser Levy led a successful protest demanding expanded rights for Jews, among them, the right to serve in New Amsterdam's militia.

When the Declaration of Independence was signed, the commencement of Europe's Jewish Emancipation was still fifteen years in the future. Though there were only an estimated 2,500 Jews—0.1 percent of the 2.5 million American population at the time—100 Jews served in the Continental Army. Francis Salvador, a Jew serving in the South Carolina provisional congress, was one of the war's first casualties when he was killed on August 1, 1776. Benjamin Nones served as aide-de-camp to the Marquis de Lafayette, and Colonel Solomon Bush saw his brother, Lewis, mortally wounded at Brandywine in an action for which Solomon was awarded a special citation by the Continental Army for bravery and distinguished service. And while not bearing arms, Haym Salomon was critical in securing the financing America required to fight a very long Revolutionary War.

The Civil War saw an estimated 8,500 to 10,000 Jewish soldiers fighting on both sides. Six of them, fighting for the North, were awarded the Congressional Medal of Honor. At the time, Jews were 0.5 percent of the population, and they earned roughly that same proportion of the war's 1522 Medals of Honor. One medal went to Edward Salomon at Gettysburg. He took command from his wounded general and became the regiment's commanding general for the balance of the war. He later became Governor the Washington Territory. Jews also served in the Confederate Army including David Camden De Leon, the Confederacy's surgeon general, and A.C. Myers, its quartermaster, for whom Ft. Myers, Florida, is named.

World War I saw Jews fighting for every country involved in that war. Herman Becker, William Frankel, and Fritz Beckhardt all served in the German Air Force, and Becker and Frankel both won the famed Blue Max, Germany's highest award for valor. During the war an inquiry, "the count" into the numbers of Jews serving in the German armed forces, proved that a disproportionate number of German Jews were fighting for the German cause.

Opposing them, Lt. General Louis Bernheim commanded a Belgian brigade that fought in the Battle of the Marne. Captain David Hirsch received England's Victoria Cross, Major General Emil Von Sommer was decorated for his service to Austria, Admiral Augusto Capon commanded an Italian frigate, and Amando Bachi, was awarded an Italian Military Cross and served as a lieutenant general in the Italian army until forced to resign his commission in 1943.

Lieutenant General Sir John Monash led an Australian brigade at Gallipoli and was the first general in 200 years to be knighted on the battlefield. Later he took command of all the Australian and New Zealand troops. Major General Sir Charles Rosenthal commanded the Australian and New Zealand artillery during the war. Also at Gallipoli, Private Leonard Keysor was awarded the Victoria Cross for bravery.

Canada saw almost 5,000 Jews in its World War I service and of them, 100 were killed and 84 received decorations for valor.

In the United States, an estimated 250,000 Jews served in World War I (roughly 10 percent of the Jewish population at the time) and 3,500 of them were killed. Jews received three of the 124 Medals of Honor awarded from that action.

World War II saw huge numbers of Jews fighting for the Allies. General Ivan D. Cheryakhovski led Russia's victories in retaking Vilna, Minsk, Frodno, and Kiev from the Germans. Darius Dassault commanded France's Fifth Army Corps and fought with the Resistance during the war. After liberation he was named Général d'Armée, the highest rank in the French army, and he was appointed governor of Paris. Mark Edelman led the Warsaw Ghetto uprising and, years later, he strongly supported Solidarity when it challenged Communist control of Poland. In Canada, 10 percent of the Jewish population of 170,000—roughly 20 percent of the male population—fought, and more than 500 were killed.

In the United States, estimates of Jews serving in the armed forces range from 4.3 to 8 percent. This contrasts with their 3.3 percent of the population at the time. In addition to the 550,000 serving in the armed forces, 340,000 women served as nurses or in other capacities. Major General Julius Ochs Adler commanded the 77th Infantry. General Mark Clark, born to a Jewish mother and Protestant father, commanded the Italian campaign (and later U.S. forces at the close of the Korean War). Admiral Ben Moreil commanded the U.S. Navy "Seabees." Colonel William F. Friedman served as the War Department's chief cryptologist until January 1941, and his group helped break the Japanese diplomatic code. Lieutenant Colonel Leon Hess headed logistics permitting Patton's Third Army to streak across Northern Europe. Major General Maurice Rose commanded the 3rd Armored Division and was the highest ranking American officer to be killed in combat during the war. Jacob Beser was the only person to serve on both the Enola Gay and Bock's Car, on the missions that dropped atom bombs on Hiroshima and Nagasaki. Lieutenant Frances Slanger was one of four nurses who waded ashore onto the D-Day beaches of Normandy and she died there. And, of course, Rabbi Alexander Goode was one of the four chaplains who gave their life vests to servicemen when the troopship Dorchester was torpedoed in the Atlantic.

In all, about 11,000 Jews died fighting in the U.S. forces during World War II. Another 40,000 were wounded and 52,000 received medals for bravery. Jews received three of the 464 Medals of Honor issued for service in World War II. One of those went to Dr. Ben Salomon, a dentist, whose aid station on Saipan was attacked. Before he died, he killed more than 100 attackers and was found with seventy-six bullet holes in his body.

A similar story concerns Marine Private First Class Leonard Kravitz (uncle of rock star Lenny Kravitz), who won the Distinguished Service Cross during the Korean War. When a large Chinese force attacked, Private Kravitz ordered the rest of his platoon to retreat, which they did with few casualties. He stayed behind to man the machine gun. When the Marines retook the position, Kravitz was dead. His machine gun had only six bullets left, and in the words of his citation, "numerous enemy dead lay in and around his emplacement."

Jews won two of the 245 Medals of Honor conferred during the Vietnam War. One went to John Lee Levitow. Severely wounded on a crippled aircraft, he threw himself atop a flare to save his comrades and the plane and then threw the flare from the aircraft. The other, Colonel Jack Jacobs, can be seen these days as a military analyst on television. A young lieutenant, Jacobs assumed command of a disorganized company when his superior officer was wounded. He organized withdrawal from the exposed perimeter and then, despite severe head wounds, made repeated trips across open rice paddies to retrieve wounded comrades. Including the company commander, he saved a U.S. adviser and thirteen soldiers, single handedly killing three Vietcong and wounding several others in the process. When asked why he had done it, he said that the words of Hillel kept running through his mind. "If not you, who? If not now, when?"

None of this counts others such as:

Abraham Wolfe who died in 1836 defending the Alamo;

Milton Wolff Commander of the "Abraham Lincoln Brigade" of American volunteers who, in the late 1930s, went to fight fascists in the Spanish Civil War;

Admiral Hyman Rickover, father of the U.S. nuclear submarine fleet;

Major General Eugene Fox, Jr., who headed up the Star Wars initiative under president Ronald Reagan;

Colonel Arthur "Bull" Simmons, a highly decorated WW II Army Ranger who served six tours in Vietnam, led a Special Forces raid on the Son Tay prison camp in North Vietnam, and led the raid, immortalized in Ken Follet's On Wings of Eagles, freeing three of Ross Perot's EDS employees who had been taken hostage following the Iranian Revolution.

In Israel:

Lieutenant Colonel "Yoni" Netanyahu, who led the spectacular 1976 raid to save ninety-nine Jewish passenger and Air France crew members from a flight high-jacked to the Entebbe airport in Uganda;

Uziel Gal, who at age twenty-seven won the competition to design a simple, reliable submachine gun (the "Uzi") and who later designed the "Galli" assault rifle.

Aviation[23]

Following the January 16; 2003, *Columbia* disaster, a few people might recall an Israeli (Ilan Ramon) among the seven astronauts who died that sad morning. Those who have followed the Apollo and Shuttle programs over a longer period might also remember that, in a tragic coincidence, Judith Resnik, an American Jewish astronaut, died in the January 28th 1986, *Challenger* disaster. If one thinks of the odds, the likelihood that two Jews would have died in the only two fatal shuttle tragedies simply defies the laws of chance.

Jews are not generally identified with aeronautics. Few would expect there to be very many Jews among the astronauts, nor for Jews to find any significant number of Jews among aviation's pioneers. Nobel prizes, perhaps, scads of attorneys and doctors, tons of Hollywood producers, certainly, but astronauts? Once more reality surprises. Among the 268 U.S. astronauts through 2004, nine were Jews. While not a dramatically disproportionate rate of achievement (roughly twice their percentage of the population), it is a surprise. The nine American Jewish astronauts included:

Jay Apt, a veteran of four missions	Ellen Baker, two missions
Martin Fettman, one mission	John Grunsfeld, four missions
Jeffrey Hoffman, three missions	Scott Horowitz, four missions
Marsh Ivins, three missions	Judith Resnik, one mission
David Wolf, three missions	

The list does not include Garrett Reisman who joined the astronaut program in 2000 but has yet to be assigned to a shuttle flight. Nor does it include Ilan Ramon who flew on that fateful *Challenger* U.S. mission, but was an Israeli, rather than an American. It also excludes Boris Volynov, a Russian Jewish cosmonaut veteran of two Soyuz missions. There may have been other Russian Jewish cosmonauts as well (a long-standing rumor had it that Yuri Gagarin, the world's first cosmonaut, was Jewish). Time has not corroborated that rumor and discerning who else among the Russian/Soviet cosmonauts might be Jewish is not nearly as easy as it is for Americans.

And, as is often the case in other fields, we find Jews in positions of administrative leadership as well as serving on the front lines. To date, there have been twelve NASA administrators. The odds say none would be Jewish. Daniel Goldin is. He was the longest serving Administrator ever. Appointed by George H.W. Bush, he served three presidents from April 1, 1992, to November 17, 2001. Goldin was also the leader who "saved the International Space Station program" when the Clinton administration proposed terminating it by incorporating capabilities of the Russian space program. More than half of all space shuttle flights occurred during his tenure and he coined the expression, "smaller, cheaper, faster and better" as the guiding expression of his philosophy about how to keep NASA alive and vital in an era of cost cutting and questions regarding the future of space flight.

Jews have played leading roles throughout the history of aviation.

Marcel Dassault, born Marcel Bloch (and brother of the earlier mentioned Général d'Armée Darius Dassault), founded and headed Dassault Aviation, the French company that produced the famous Mystère and Mirage aircraft;

Mikhail Gurevich, the Russian aircraft designer, was involved in the creation of every MiG aircraft, from the original propeller-driven models through the MiG 29 jet. The "G" in MiG stands for Gurevich;

Abraham Hyatt, an aerospace engineer, supervised the early development of the lunar landing program for NASA;

Ben Rich, who succeeded Kelly Johnson as head of Lockheed's incredible "Skunkworks." Rich was a designer of the SR-71 Blackbird and he led the Skunkworks in developing the F-117A Stealth fighter aircraft;

Jack Steiner, Boeing's chief designer, led design teams in the development of the 707, 727, 737 and 747 airplanes.

Taken together, history reveals that Jews have played a vital role as military warriors and as aviation and aerospace pioneers for a very long time.

Chapter 7

Economics

"There is no such thing as a free lunch."

"The Great Depression, like most other periods of severe unemployment, was produced by government mismanagement rather than by any inherent instability of the private economy."
—Milton Friedman

Milton Friedman[24]

In the 1890s, teenagers Jeno Saul Friedman and Sarah Ethel Landau left Berehovo in the Ukraine to immigrate to the United States. Jeno opened and ran a series of small businesses as a garment-maker, dry-goods retailer, ice cream parlor owner, and later, a jobber and petty trader. Sarah worked as a seamstress, and after they were married and had children, she ran a retail dry-goods store. Given the uncertainty of Jeno's income, they both needed to work to support themselves and their four children. Despite the economic insecurity, it was a warm and close family.

Milton, born July 31, 1912, was the youngest of the four and the only boy. As a youngster, he was a devout Orthodox Jew. He attended Hebrew School and followed every Orthodox practice until shortly before his bar mitzvah when he became an outspoken agnostic. Nonetheless, for his parent's sake he went through with his bar mitzvah.

An excellent student, he started college at fifteen. Though Rutgers gave him a partial scholarship, he worked as a part-time clerk, waiter, and entrepreneur—competing with the Rutgers bookstore in buying and reselling used textbooks—to earn the rest of his college expenses.

In summer, he sold Fourth of July fireworks and set up a school to teach failing high school students for fifty cents an hour. Perhaps it was his time as a waiter that led to his aphorism about "no free lunch," but his other endeavors to pay for his schooling also gave him firsthand experience with free enterprise.

He planned to become an actuary until he discovered economics, and with that was introduced to Arthur Burns and Homer Jones. Both later became well-known economists, and both mentored and inspired Friedman. They encouraged him to pursue postgraduate study at the University of Chicago and helped him get a scholarship.

From those first days at the University of Chicago in 1932, Friedman was exposed to not only some of the great economics teachers of the era, but also to brilliant fellow students with whom he had many free and open debates about economics. There, he also met Rose Director, his future wife and partner.

After getting his master's degree from Chicago, he took a year at Columbia University to supplement what he had learned about economic theory with an equivalent understanding of statistics. By then, Friedman had satisfied course requirements for a Ph.D. from Columbia. He returned to Chicago, did another year there and satisfied the University of Chicago's Ph.D. requirements as well.

The dearth of academic jobs during the Depression, and anti-Semitism at some schools where he might have taught, caused Friedman to spend the next two years in the New Deal administration of FDR. He followed that with three years at the National Bureau of Economic Research while teaching part time at Columbia, two years at the U.S. Treasury, two years in a statistical research job at Columbia, a year as a visiting professor at the University of Wisconsin, and a year at the University of Minnesota. While some have called these Friedman's "wilderness years," it was during these years that he completed his dissertation, received his Ph.D., and worked on several groundbreaking economic studies that helped establish him as one of the greatest economic minds of the century.

At the same time, in what he considered his worst intellectual mistake, he helped create the income tax withholding system. He believes it was ultimately the single most important cause for the rapid growth in government spending following its implementation.

But it was his research and resulting publications, typically challenging the economic orthodoxy of the times, that exposed Friedman's iconoclastic bent and his ability to forcefully and convincingly argue in favor of ideas for which he was typically the only visible advocate. In that sense, he demonstrated both his brilliance and his courage.

In 1946 Friedman returned to the University of Chicago where he spent the next thirty-one years until he retired in 1977, after which he became a Fellow at Stanford University's Hoover Institution. In 1951 he was the third recipient of the John Bates Clark medal, attesting to his status as one of the brightest young minds in economics.

He was an economic adviser to President Nixon, president of the American Economic Association (in 1967), and received the Nobel Prize in Economics in 1976. That Nobel became one of the most controversial ever awarded when four laureates, three of them American Jews (George Wald, Salvador Luria, and David Baltimore) plus non-Jew Gunnar Myrdal, a 1974 Nobel laureate for economics, protested and proposed the economics Nobel no longer be awarded.

Time has largely given Friedman and his supporters the last laugh. Though nearly always derided when he first proposed them, most of his theories have been validated by evidence and the passage of time. In fact, reading succeeding editions of Paul Samuelson's classic text, *Economics,* shows that although Friedman's theories in matters such as monetary policy were initially dismissed by Samuelson's text, they were later conditionally considered, and ultimately adopted in that textbook as the prevailing view in economics.

In the end, Friedman can take credit for a remarkable number of important changes to contemporary economic thinking. Almost single-handedly, he:

Established that the best standard for testing an economic theory is its ability to accurately predict results when applied. Once established, this doctrine allowed Friedman to disprove a number of commonly accepted, but fallacious theories, while helping establish the likely validity of others.

Challenged accepted Keynesian dogma that dominated economic thinking from the thirties through much of the eighties. It held that free markets were flawed, that only government intervention and spending could maximize social welfare while dampening or eliminating the boom and bust of the business cycle, and that government fiscal policy could be the ultimate "free lunch" of ever-increasing government deficit spending which would raise income levels and public benefits. Ultimately, much of the economic intelligentsia came around to Friedman's point of view that this was nonsense.

Challenged nearly a half century's common wisdom that the principal causes of the Great Depression were structural flaws in the free-enterprise system. Friedman showed the primary causes were mistakes made by the Federal Reserve, a view later borne out in the academic research of Ben Bernanke.

Demonstrated that Federal Reserve decisions were often ill-timed and thus exacerbated, rather than corrected, the business cycle.

Re-established monetary policy as more effective than government spending (fiscal policy) in managing the economy.

Promoted the importance of floating, rather than fixed, exchange rates between European currencies during the Marshall Plan. This notion has since come to prevail throughout most of the world economic order.

Demolished belief in the Phillips Curve (an accepted 1960s theory which held that unemployment and inflation involved an inherent trade-off in which lower unemployment meant higher inflation, and vice versa. Until Friedman proved it wrong, this mistaken theory drove U.S. political and economic decision-making.

Advocated free-market economic approaches to the Taiwanese and South Korean governments. Both have since been two of Asia's most successful "tiger economies," and both have prospered.

Counseled Chile, one of Latin America's few economic bright spots since the 1970s. Argentina, which ultimately adopted only his privatization suggestions, used the proceeds from sale of state-owned enterprises to finance enlarged government spending. Argentina has since faced continuing economic problems.

Ever the libertarian, Friedman was an early (1960s) advocate for school vouchers and the all-volunteer Army.

In books, articles, speeches, and even a ten-part PBS series with his wife, Rose, Friedman helped reestablish classical liberalism, the clear link between economic and political freedom and the importance of market-based approaches, rather than government planning and welfare state programs. Almost single-handedly he reestablished awareness that civilization's great advances rarely come from centralized government.

Finally worth noting was Friedman's courage in defending his ideas. Most often pitted against the prevailing views of the times, often defended by Jews such as Paul Samuelson, Robert Solow, Kenneth Arrow, and followers of Karl Marx, it was ultimately Friedman's views that won out.

The Sveriges Riksbank Prize in Economic Sciences in Memory of Alfred Nobel[25]

A mouthful, the formal name for this Nobel is so long it is typically shortened to the "Nobel Prize for Economics." It was not part of Alfred Nobel's original legacy. Instead, on the 300th anniversary of the founding of the Bank of Sweden, the chaps in charge of the bank offered to foot the bill for prize money if the Swedish Academy of Sciences would create and judge a new award for outstanding contributions in economics.

The academy agreed, but its decision was not without controversy since some Laureates, Murray Gell-Mann in particular, thought the importance of "the Nobels" would be cheapened if a lesser science (economics) was recognized with an award. What next, anthropology or sociology? Later, three laureates, Myrdal, Hayek, and Sen agreed with Gell-Mann and suggested its abolishment. This happened, of course, after they had already received their own Nobels. Their disdain arose because a prize was to be awarded to someone (Friedman) whose views differed sharply with their own.

Nonetheless, at its inception, those administering Nobels foresaw economics evolving into an ever more rigorous, mathematical/statistical field, and with that in mind, they decided to go ahead. Thus in October 1969, the Swedes began delivering annual announcements and invitations to attend the special December 10 dinner ceremony in Stockholm. The Bank of Sweden Prize in Economic Sciences in Memory of Alfred Nobel was born.

As noted in an earlier chapter, this is the award John Nash (not Jewish) won. Nash was the brilliant Princeton mathematician who hoped for a Fields Medal in mathematics, but took home a Nobel in economics as a consolation prize. His contributions to game theory were regarded as important, but he could not be recognized until he emerged from schizophrenia. In the mid-1980s he started recovering and by 1990, the Nobel committee began considering his nomination. In 1994 he was made an economics laureate.

While Nobels have gone to many brilliant economists, the awards have frequently triggered controversy. Many prizes have gone for work in esoteric, highly mathematical corners of the economic landscape, and those have generally been unchallenged. But some of the less quantitative, more "big picture," Nobels have gone for "discoveries" that challenged the theories of earlier laureates. Jews Friedman and Samuelson are a case in point. Samuelson's views appear to have shifted a bit to the right over the years, but when he first published his classic textbook, *Economics,* read by several generations of "Economics 101" college students, Samuelson's notions were decidedly Keynesian. They contrasted sharply with the ideas of the neoclassical Friedman, who received the same award just six years after Samuelson.

According to Burton Feldman, author of *The Nobel Prize,* since its founding, roughly two-thirds of the economic Nobels have gone to neoclassicists and one-third to the neo-Keynesians. In 1974 Nobels were awarded to Gunnar Myrdal and Friedrich August von Hayek (both non-Jews). Since Myrdal and Hayek saw the economic world in nearly opposing terms, some, (including both Myrdal and Hayek), found the awards curious. Their concerns were only later widely publicized when Myrdal took exception to Friedman's award.

How one squares the notion that economics is a science, while awarding Nobels to recipients with views so at odds that their prescriptions for solving any particular economic problem would be diametrically opposed, has yet to be explained by the academy. With the U.S. and world economy lingering between recession and expansion over the years, despite the input of thousands of economists, one might be inclined to think that perhaps Gell-Mann was right.

One cannot know if they anticipated how the selections would turn out, but since that first year, this Nobel has become largely U.S. property. Of the sixty-one prizes, forty-two have gone to Americans (Two of those forty-two, Daniel Kahneman and Robert Aumann, have dual U.S. and Israeli citizenship). The British are a distant second with eight Nobels. Norway and Canada each have three, and Sweden, France, Germany, Israel, and the Netherlands have two each.

If the United States holds preeminence, so too do the Jews. Through 2007, twenty-two (36 percent) of the sixty-one economics' Nobels have gone to them. (This includes two laureates, Selten and Merton, whose fathers were Jewish but whose mothers were not.) Of the forty-two U.S. Nobels, twenty were won by Jews (twenty-four times what one would expect). All of the laureates, with the Jewish winners highlighted, are shown in Exhibit 7a.

John Bates Clark Medal in Economics[26]

If anyone questions whether the 36 percent figure (Nobel prizes won by Jews) is a fluke, Jewish recipients of the John Bates Clark Medal confirm it is not.

This award is akin to the Fields Medal in Mathematics. It is given every two years to a young (under age 40) American economist conducting important, groundbreaking research. In part what makes the award so prestigious is its track record as a precursor to later Nobels—twelve of the thirty Clark medalists have later gone on to become Nobel laureates. The full list of recipients is shown as Exhibit 7b. Of the thirty medals awarded since inception, twenty (67 percent) have gone to Jews.

Other Great Economists[27]

Not every great economist receives a Nobel or John Bates Clark Medal. Some die too soon. (You must be alive—and sane—to receive a Nobel.) David Ricardo was a British Jew who began to study economics after making a fortune on the London Stock Exchange. He was among the first to peg inflation to excessive bank lending (too much money in circulation chasing too few goods), and that led to a book and an act of Parliament establishing England's Central Bank. It is similar to what we in the United States call the Federal Reserve.

Karl Marx might equally be classed a sociologist, historian, revolutionary, or economist. His *Communist Manifesto* (written with non-Jew Friedrich Engels) is his most famous work, and it involves all four domains. Marx has the distinction of being the spiritual father of Soviet Communism, which led over a billion people down the wrong road for a very long time. But, as an influential economist of the eighteenth and nineteenth centuries, non-Jew Adam Smith is Marx's only peer.

Some prominent economists did not die too soon, but they did not earn a Nobel. Robert Rubin may be considered a Wall Street financier by some, but as treasury secretary under Bill Clinton (and with help from fellow Jews, Fed chairman Alan Greenspan and Deputy Secretary Lawrence Summers), he drove U.S. economic policy to one of the longest sustained periods of economic growth ever. In its September 29, 2003 issue, *Fortune* magazine ranked him as one of the top three treasury secretaries of all time (out of seventy-two). To make it even more interesting, the other two were a non-Jew, Alexander Hamilton, and a Jew, Henry Morgenthau Jr. Two out of three "ain't bad!" Conversely, *Fortune's* three worst treasury secretaries, Roger B. Taney, William A. Richardson, and Ogden L. Mills were all non-Jews. Among prominent Jewish economists (and financiers) who have advised presidents over the years are Bernard Baruch, Martin Feldstein, Otto Eckstein, Herb Stein, Alan Blinder, Arthur Okun, Walter Rostow, Murray Weidenbaum, and many others.

Whenever you want to curse airline deregulation for your lack of leg room or "cattle-like" treatment in an airport or on an airplane, think of Alfred Kahn, the Carter administration economist, who pioneered airline deregulation—and who brought substantially lower ticket prices in the bargain. Robert Heilbroner wrote the classic *The Worldly Philosophers*, used as a basic economic history text in colleges for years. Julian Simon, a professor at the University of Maryland, made a famous $1,000 bet with fellow Jew, Paul R. Ehrlich, author of *The Population Bomb*, over future prices of commodities. The bet was a proxy for testing Ehrlich's pessimistic forecasts of gloom and doom versus Simon's optimism. Simon won the bet. David Landes a Harvard professor, wrote, *The Wealth and Poverty of Nations*, which among other topics, teaches the importance of culture in shaping successful versus failing political economies.

John von Neumann was a mathematician, chemist, computer scientist, and meteorologist, but his (and non-Jew Oskar Morgenstern's) *Theory of Games and Economic Theory Behavior* was the seminal work in game theory. It ultimately laid the foundation on which John Nash later built his own game theory, advancing the field beyond von Neumann's pioneering effort. Ludwig von Mises was the Austrian economist who challenged what he viewed as the elitist and totalitarian nature of socialist ideology in his books *Planned Chaos* and *The Anti-Capitalistic Mentality*.

Jeffrey Sachs, now at Columbia, has been a leading economist in the forefront of support to the poor and reforms in Bolivia, Poland, and Russia. And one should not close without mentioning *The New York Times* columnist, Nobel laureate, and John Clark Bates Medal winner, Paul Krugman. Finally, and as identified in the earlier chapter on education, Harvard's former president, former Clinton administration Treasury secretary, and expected Obama advisor, Lawrence Summers also won a John Bates Clark Medal in 1993. Perhaps in time Summers will replicate the success of his uncles, Paul Samuelson and Kenneth Arrow, who augmented their own John Bates Clark Medals with Nobel Prizes in Economics.

The Federal Reserve[28]

Occasionally, there is discussion about whether the chairman of the Federal Reserve Bank is the single most powerful man in the United States, or only second most powerful. Clearly the person heading the Fed is charged with keeping the U.S. economy heading in the right direction and hopefully averting a severe recession or a depression. And through much of post-World War II, despite a few bumps along the way, the United States has put in an excellent economic performance. With few exceptions, most financial sages would agree the Fed chairman has played a critical role in that performance.

There have only been fourteen Fed chairmen:

Charles S. Hamlin, 1914 to 1916
W.P.G. Harding, 1916 to 1922
Daniel Crissinger, 1923 to 1927
Roy A. Young, 1927 to 1930
Eugene Meyer, 1930 to 1933
Eugene R. Black, 1933 to 1934
Marriner Eccles, 1934 to 1948
Thomas McCabe, 1948 to 1951
William McChesney Martin, 1951 to 1970
Arthur Burns, 1970 to 1978
G. William Miller, 1978 to 1979
Paul Volker, 1979 to 1987
Alan Greenspan, 1987 to 2006
Ben Bernanke, 2006 to the present

Of the fourteen, at least four are Jews: Eugene Meyer (father of the now deceased *Washington Post* publisher, Kathryn Meyer Graham), Arthur Burns, Alan Greenspan, and Ben Bernanke. Eugene R. Black may also have been Jewish, but that is unconfirmed. Not counting Black, Jews have headed the Fed for thirty-two of its ninety-four years, including twenty-nine of the last thirty-eight.

Also important was Paul Warburg, an immigrant German Jew and a driving force behind creation of the Fed. Warburg also served, albeit reluctantly, as one of President Wilson's five initial appointments to the Fed board of Governors (from its 1914 inception until 1918). He was considered by some to be the de facto chairman. As noted on the Federal Reserve Bank of Minneapolis Web site, "Benjamin Strong, governor of the Federal Reserve Bank of New York, considered Warburg 'the real head of the board in Washington, so far as knowledge and ability go.'"

Arthur Burns ran the Fed from 1970 to 1978. It was perhaps the most challenging economic period since World War II. High inflation, arising from funding the 1960s federal poverty programs and the Vietnam War, was worsened by the economic chaos arising from OPEC's oil embargo and subsequent OPEC-induced oil shortages following the Yom Kippur War. A nearly "perfect storm" laid the stock market low for years, and with it came "stagflation" (simultaneous high unemployment and high inflation.) This, and perceived raw materials shortages, led president Jimmy Carter to discuss our "national malaise" on prime-time television. Perhaps Arthur Burns' happiest day at the Fed was the one when he walked out the door for the last time.

Alan Greenspan, whose eighteen-year term was chronicled by Bob Woodward in his book *Maestro,* receives praise for leading the Fed through one of the most remarkable periods of economic growth in U.S. history. It was a period of numerous crises including the stock market crash of 1987, the savings and loan meltdown, the Long Term Capital liquidity crises, the dot-com bust, September 11, and the ensuing recession, among others. Until recent questions arose about his policies, which may have encouraged the housing bust and a burst of inflation, both Republicans and Democrats sang his praises, including then Treasury Secretary James Baker, who said of him, "To my mind there is only one person we can turn to," and president Bill Clinton who said, "You've done a great job in a period when there was no rulebook to look to."

Only time will tell if Greenspan's reputation endures and Bernanke earns similar accolades.

CHAPTER 8

Politics and Law

"Toughness doesn't have to come in a pinstripe suit." —*Dianne Feinstein*

Dianne Feinstein[29]

For most San Franciscans over age 40, the memory of Dianne Feinstein's November 27, 1978, press conference announcing the assassinations of Mayor George Moscone and Supervisor Harvey Milk remains vivid. She was distressed but controlled. She heard the gunshots, had seen the killer, former Supervisor Dan White, in the moments between the two murders, and he had rebuffed her attempt to talk to him. She raced to Milk's office, saw the fatal wound, tried to take his pulse, but knew immediately he was dead.

Only nine days earlier, 913 people, mostly former Bay Area residents, had committed mass suicide with Reverend Jim Jones in Guyana. The same year, her second and much-loved husband, neurosurgeon Dr. Bertram Feinstein, had died of colon cancer. Though she had been contemplating retirement after returning the day before from a trip to the Mt. Everest area where she met the Dalai Lama, on that November day it fell to Dianne Feinstein not only to tell the world of the assassinations, but to step into Moscone's shoes as acting mayor. The very human and capable way in which she handled the situation and later restored confidence to the city, proved her abilities. She vaulted to the forefront among California's Democratic leadership.

She was born Dianne Goldman on June 23, 1933, the oldest of Betty (Russian Orthodox) and Leon Goldman's three daughters. She grew up in San Francisco's upscale Presidio Terrace neighborhood. Even today, when she is not in Washington, D.C., she lives in Presidio Terrace with her husband, Richard Blum.

Feinstein was confirmed in the Jewish faith at thirteen in a bat mitzvah, but attended a public grade school and, at her mother's insistence, a Roman Catholic high school. In *Dianne Feinstein: Never Let Them See You Cry,* biographer Jerry Roberts says she came from a dysfunctional home with an abusive mother, but her nationally renowned surgeon father doted on her.

She transformed her family difficulties into a steely, but velvet-gloved, determination that has manifested itself ever since. She was the first woman president of San Francisco's board of Supervisors, the city's first woman mayor, the first woman nominated by a major party to run for California's governor, the first woman to be considered a candidate for the vice presidential nomination and the first woman Senator from California.

She entered Stanford University in 1951 as a premed student, but soon shifted to political science and history. As a senior, she was elected student body vice president. She graduated in 1955, interned with San Francisco's Coro Foundation, which provided political experience for young people, and in late 1956, married San Francisco prosecutor Jack Berman. They had a daughter, but within three years, the marriage was over.

In 1960, when Feinstein was 27, Governor Edmund Brown appointed her to a seat on the California Women's Parole board. She was the nation's youngest parole board member. In 1962 she married well-known neurosurgeon Bertram Feinstein, and it was to spend more time with him and her daughter that she resigned from the Parole board in 1966. Shortly thereafter she was appointed chair of San Francisco's Advisory Committee for Adult Detention, and in 1969, was elected to San Francisco's board of Supervisors. As the leading vote-getter, she served as the board's president for five of her nine years on that board. Twice, in 1971 and 1975, she ran for mayor but was unsuccessful. Perhaps those losses led to her observation that "Winning may not be everything, but losing has little to recommend it."

Filling out Mayor Moscone's term, she earned great respect and was twice reelected. During her ten years as mayor, crime dropped 27 percent, she balanced nine budgets in a row, and she cleaned up what had become a dirty, graffiti-ridden city. In 1980 she married Richard Blum, a leading San Francisco financier who manages private equity partnerships.

In 1984 she was nearly nominated to run for vice president with Walter Mondale, but Geraldine Ferraro got the nod instead. Feinstein was nominated to run for California's governor in 1990, but lost to Republican Pete Wilson. Her determination would not let her quit, however, and she ran for and won the 1992 race taking the Senate seat Wilson had vacated to become governor. Two years later she defeated Michael Huffington, Ariana Huffington's then husband, to serve a full six-year term and she was reelected to the Senate in 2000 and 2006. When California Governor Gray Davis faced a recall in 2004, she wisely decided she preferred her senatorial job and removed herself as the only candidate who might have defeated Arnold Schwarzenegger.

As a Senator, she was appointed to the prestigious Judiciary and Appropriations committees, unprecedented for a freshman Senator in 1992. She has since added the Select Committee on Intelligence, the Energy and Natural Resources Committee, and the Rules and Administration Committee.

She has sponsored legislation no one expected to pass, got it through and signed into law. Her bills include: the Assault Weapons Ban, the Gun-Free Schools Act, the California Desert Protection Act, the Breast Cancer Research Stamp Act, the Lake Tahoe Restoration Act, the Headwaters Forest Agreement, the San Francisco Bay Wetlands Restoration Act, and others.

Her voting record is liberal but her reputation is that of a frequently bi-partisan legislator. There is about her a distinctive blend of quiet firmness, warmth, and common sense without the stridency typical of some of her peers. She is optimistic and cheerful, if at times humorless. Pragmatic, she carried a licensed concealed weapon while sponsoring the Assault Weapons Ban.

She strongly supports women's rights, but in 1993, she opposed President William Clinton's nomination of Zoe Baird for Attorney General because of Baird's improper employment of illegal aliens. Though she is a consistent advocate of minority rights, she helped avert construction of a tribal casino that would have been a blight in a wetland north of San Francisco Bay. Her successes have led to six honorary doctorate and law degrees, and she was awarded the French Légion d'Honneur by Pierre Mitterrand.

She remains an effective advocate for those causes in which she believes.

The U.S. Congress and the Administration[30]

The U.S. has yet to elect a Jewish president. One might say with forty-four presidents elected since George Washington, that matches expectations. With roughly 2 percent of today's U.S. population being Jewish, one in fifty should be a good rule of thumb. The time is coming. In 2000 staunch Democrats could argue that the popular vote did elect our first Jewish vice president. Joe Lieberman almost became the man "a heartbeat from the presidency." A thousand votes in Florida would have made it so. Perhaps in 2012?

The story was completely different in the U.S. Senate (108th Congress) where one would have logically expected to find two Jews. There were eleven.

Barbara Boxer (D-California)	Russ Feingold (D-Wisconsin)
Dianne Feinstein (D-California)	Herb Kohl (D-Wisconsin)
Frank Lautenberg (D-New Jersey)	Joseph Lieberman (D-Connecticut)
Carl Levin (D-Michigan)	Charles Schumer (D-New York)
Arlen Specter (R-Pennsylvania)	Norm Coleman (R-Minnesota)
Ron Wyden (D-Oregon)	

To these, one might also consider adding half of John Kerry since, as he recently discovered, he is half Jewish, rather than one-fourth as he had long suspected.

Eleven incumbent Jews in the Senate is five times what statistics would project.

To flesh things out, it is fair to note that the first Jew was not elected to the Senate until 1845 (David Levy Yulee), and Yulee had only Judah Benjamin as company for seven of the twelve years he served in the Congress. (For perspective, from 1790 to 1880 Jews were 0.5 percent of the population, or less, only rising to 1 percent around the turn of the century.) Between 1861 and 1879, no Jews served in the Senate. This was also true from 1913 to 1949 when anti-Semitism was a significant force in America, while at the same time, the U.S. Jewish population was approaching 4 percent. Nonetheless, until 1949, only six Jews had been elected to the Senate. After that, particularly in the mid-1950s, as anti-Semitism waned, Jews began to be elected ever more frequently and many of them became prominent figures including Jacob Javits, Abraham Ribicoff, Howard Metzenbaum, Warren Rudman, and Paul Wellstone.

Jews do not fare as well in the House as they do in the Senate. There they are only three times more likely to serve than one would expect. Again, using the 108th Congress, there were twenty-six (6 percent) elected Jews out of 435 seats. The Jews included:

Gary Ackerman (D-New York)	Shelly Berkley (D-Nevada)
Howard Berman (D-California)	Eric Cantor (R-Virginia)
Ben Cardin (D-Maryland)	Susan Davis (D-California)
Peter Deutsch (D-Florida)	Rahm Emanuel (D-Illinois)
Eliot Engel (D-New York)	Bob Filner (D-California)
Barney Frank (D-Massachusetts)	Martin Frost (D-Texas)
Jane Harman (D-California)	Steve Israel (D-New York)
Tom Lantos (D-California)	Sander Levin (D-Michigan)
Nita Lowey (D-New York)	Jerrold Nadler (D-New York)
Steve Rothman (D-New Jersey)	Bernie Sanders (I-Vermont)
Jan Schakowsky (D-Illinois)	Adam Schiff (D-California
Brad Sherman (D California)	Henry Waxman (D-California)
Anthony Weiner (D-New York)	Robert Wexler (D Florida)

Looking over these lists, one sees something that would not surprise an astute political observer. Of the thirty-seven names on both lists, thirty-three (89 percent) are Democrats. Only three (8 percent) are Republicans, and one (3 percent) is an Independent. In that makeup of the Senate, nine Jews represented nearly 20 percent of its Democrats, a large and important block. Conservative Republicans would like to do a better job of recruiting Jews, but since the Roosevelt administration, they have not. Instead, they often find themselves disagreeing with the strong liberal bent of many on the list. Barbara Boxer, Russ Feingold, Charles Schumer, Rahm Emanuel, Barney Frank, Jerrold Nadler, Henry Waxman, and Robert Wexler are not likely to get high ratings from the Americans for Conservative Action, but they are most assuredly strong and articulate leaders for their point of view.

There is also an interesting recent contrast in cabinet and senior administration posts between the Clinton and Bush (George W.) administrations, perhaps largely reflecting the strong tendency for Jews to be Democrats. While George W. is every bit as staunch in his support of Israel as Bill Clinton was, Bush has taken a different tack in his appointments. That is, in his first term, Bush appointed large numbers of women and minorities to senior posts including Colin Powell (black), Condoleezza

Rice (black and female), Rod Paige (black), Norman Mineta (Japanese-American), Spencer Abraham (Arab-American), Mel Martinez (Hispanic-American), Elaine Chao (Chinese-American and female) Gale Norton, Ann Veneman, and Christine Todd Whitman (all female). The number of prominent Jews was dramatically lower than for Clinton. Bush retained George Tenant as head of the CIA until Tenant's resignation, and Paul Wolfowitz was visible as the number two man in the Defense Department, but compared with Clinton's team, two prominent Jews was small potatoes.

Clinton's cabinets included Robert Rubin and Lawrence Summers as secretaries of the treasury, Robert Reich as secretary of labor, Dan Glickman as secretary of agriculture, Mickey Cantor as secretary of commerce. In addition, William Cohen, secretary of defense and Madeleine Albright, secretary of state, have Jewish backgrounds or heritage. Sandy Berger served as national security advisor, Richard Holbrooke was U.S. ambassador to the United Nations, and Charlene Barshefsky was U.S. trade representative. And who can forget Ann Lewis, White House communications director and Rahm Emanuel, senior advisor for policy and strategy (and chief of staff designate for Barack Obama) as outspoken supporters of Clinton in both the good and bad of that presidency—some of which arose from Clinton's relationship with… Monica Lewinsky.

While one can agree or disagree with the Democratic and liberal bent of many of the Jews that occupy (or have occupied) these important positions, it is undeniable that they have had an enormous impact. For a group that should be almost too small to matter (2 percent), they have achieved and contributed much.

Political Contributions[31]

If Jews have contributed much as elected and appointed holders of political office, their "contributions" of dollars to political campaigns is a virtual gusher. This is not exactly the sense in which the term Jewish "contributions" is generally used in this book, but "contributions" they most certainly were.

Mother Jones magazine reviewed the country's 400 largest political donors in a March 5, 2001, issue. (Exhibit 9a). And while the article began by noting the large number of dollars raised by the Bush campaign ($696 million) and the coincident question of what donors expected in exchange for their largess, Mother Jones seemed to miss the elephant in the room—namely, the large number of Jewish donors. Specifically, forty-one of the top one hundred donors were Jewish. What are the odds? Four of the top five (S. Daniel Abraham, Bernard Schwartz, David Gilo and Haim Saban) were Jewish Democrats, and each donated more than $1 million.

Law and the U.S. Supreme Court[32]

Nothing is more important in U.S. law than the Supreme Court. It is the ultimate arbiter of decisions made in all other courts and it alone can decide if a law passed by Congress or a decision made by the administration is "unconstitutional." Its importance is demonstrated by the constant fights in the U.S. Senate over the Senate's role to "advise and consent" on appointments to the federal bench, including the appeals courts, and ultimately, the Supreme Court.

As with the Senate, it took a long time for a Jew to be appointed to the Supreme Court. Louis Brandeis became the first Jewish associate justice when he was confirmed in 1916. This was 127 years after the first Supreme Court appointment (John Jay in 1789.) Since Brandeis was the sixty-seventh Supreme Court justice named in the history of the court, one might argue it was not really even overdue since Jews did not represent 2.2 percent of the population until 1910.

Nonetheless, after Brandeis' appointment, the pace changed dramatically. As of mid-2008, seven of the 110 justices (6.4 percent) have been Jewish. The 6.4 percent statistic exceeds the expected 2 percent but understates the magnitude of the change since Brandeis. That is, there have been forty-four appointments in the ninety-two years since Brandeis. Seven of those forty-two (16 percent) were Jews. In the forty-six years since Arthur Goldberg was appointed in 1962, four of fifteen appointments (27 percent) were Jews. And, two of the last four appointments (Ruth Bader Ginsburg, 1993, and Stephen G. Breyer, 1994) were Jews. That two of our nine Supreme Court Justices (22 percent or eleven times their percentage of the U.S. population) are now Jews indicates just how remarkable their achievement has been. All of the Supreme Court appointments are shown in Exhibit 8b.

The Nobel Prize for Peace[33]

No one can say for sure why the Nobel Prize for Peace is not selected by the Swedes, but it is clear that Alfred Nobel gave the job to the Norwegians. They make their announcement from Oslo at the same time the other Nobels are being announced from Stockholm. The Norwegian king awards the Nobel Prize for Peace in Oslo on December 10 at the same time that the Swedish king is awarding the other five prizes in Stockholm. One might think in the interests of peace between the Norwegians and the Swedes they would work out some kind of joint ceremony, but alas, the rupture between the Swedes and Norwegians that separated those two countries in 1905 remains.

If the Nobel Prizes for physics, chemistry and physiology or medicine are generally acknowledged to be excellent selections of the true greats in their respective fields, the Nobel Prize for Peace is more subjective and more controversial.

The 2003 award for Jimmy Carter may have been long overdue for what he accomplished in the Camp David Accords between Menachem Begin and Anwar Sadat, but the choice was not above criticism when the chair of the panel making the selection let it be known that he was influenced by Carter's position chiding the Bush White House stance on Iraq. At least he, as chair, seemed as interested in "sending a message" as he was in selecting the person most deserving recognition in the cause of peace. In 2003, the selection of Shirin Ebadi, an Iranian dissident, was considered well deserved. At the same time, ailing Pope John Paul II was eighty-three years old. He was determined in the cause of peace and had an immense impact on history over the last twenty-five years, including the peaceful resolution of the Cold War and the critical changes in Poland which helped end it. Nonetheless, the pope may have been deemed unsuitable by the panel because of the Church's position on such matters as birth control, abortion, the priesthood and homosexuality. A comparable series of observations could also be made about the selection of Al Gore in 2007, but alas....

This Nobel is also different in that eighteen times in the 106 years between 1901 and 2007, no prize was awarded. One can understand some reluctance during the two world wars (though prizes were awarded in 1917, 1943, and 1945), but awards were also not made in 1923, 1924, 1928, 1932, 1948, 1955, 1956, 1966, 1967, and 1972. One wonders if so few were worthy or if there was some difficulty in coming to a peaceful agreement among the Committee members. Unlike the other prizes, the peace prize often goes to entire organizations or groups of people—sometimes with the group's leader singled out for special recognition. Fourteen times organizations such as the Red Cross or Doctors Without Borders have received the award, and three times an organization and its leader have been selected (the United Nations and Kofi Annan, International Campaign to Ban Landmines and Jody Williams, and Pugwash Conferences on Science and World Affairs and Joseph Rotblat).

Including the leaders awarded prizes coincident with their organizations (above), ninety-five peace Nobel awards have been made to individuals in seventy-five of the 107 years since 1901. Unlike the Nobels for Chemistry, where few people would recognize more than a name or two, many recipients of the Peace prize are easily recognizable. Jimmy Carter, Kim Dae-jung, Yasser Arafat, Yitzhak Rabin, Anwar Sadat, Cordell Hull, Linus Pauling (his second), Dag Hammarskjold, Al Gore, and Lech Walesa, to name but a few. The large number of laureates who have held significant political office is both logical and the reason for including the Nobel for Peace in this chapter. All of the laureates are shown in Exhibit 8c.

Perhaps because the Middle East has been a powder keg since the Balfour Declaration, and particularly since the end of World War II, one might expect Jews to get a bit more than 0.2 percent of the awards. But again the numbers are startling. Nine of the ninety-five awards (9.5 percent) have gone to Jews. They are listed below.

Tobias Michael Carel Asser (1911)	Alfred Hermann Fried (1911)
Rene Cassin (1968)	Henry A. Kissinger (1973)
Menachem Begin (1978)	Elie Wiesel (1986)
Shimon Peres (1994)	Yitzhak Rabin (1994)
Joseph Rotblat (1995)	

The Norwegians have been notable in recognizing the contributions Jews have made to peace over the years. One hopes the Jews and Palestinians will soon find a way to share yet one more award for truly bringing lasting peace to that troubled part of the world.

Chapter 9

Sports and Games

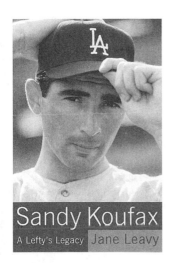

Sandy Koufax
A Lefty's Legacy   Jane Leavy

"Pitching is the art of instilling fear."

"Show me a guy who can't pitch inside and I'll show you a loser."   *—Sandy Koufax*

"She (Koufax biographer and Washington Post *sportswriter Jane Leavy) says she talked to 469 people and none had a bad word to say about him. 'Gentle' was the word she heard most often."*
—USA Today
Book Commentary
2/12/2003

Sandy Koufax[34]

Sandy Koufax came from a broken home in Brooklyn, New York. He was born on December 30, 1935, to Evelyn (Lichtenstein) and Jack Braun. When Sandy was three, his parents divorced and, for a while, he and his sister lived with their mother at his grandparents' home. When Sandy was nine, his mother married attorney Irving Koufax. For Sandy, Irving became his real father, a father who took the children to the Yiddish theater and who encouraged Sandy's athletic pursuits.

Sandy was a gifted athlete who often shot baskets and played team sports at the Jewish Community Center. He loved basketball and his aggressive style of play led some to consider him "an animal." Among his high school basketball teammates was Alan Dershowitz. Koufax also played first base at Brooklyn's Lafayette high school, occasionally pitching in the Baseball Ice Cream League. In 1953, when he entered the University of Cincinnati to study architecture, it was on a full basketball scholarship.

The University of Cincinnati baseball team was headed to New Orleans and Florida to play games over the spring break. To Sandy that sounded a lot better than heading home to Brooklyn, so he signed on to pitch for the road trip. In his first two games, he struck out thirty-four batters.

Sportswriter Jimmy Murphy saw him and encouraged Brooklyn Dodgers scouts to take a look. In 1954 they signed him for a $14,000 signing bonus and a salary of $6,000 a year. He was eighteen years old and in the words of Dodgers' owner, Walter O'Malley, Koufax was "the Great Jewish Hope of the franchise."

Because of professional baseball's rules at the time regarding his "large" signing bonus, the Dodgers could not start Koufax on a farm team. They had to keep him active on the Brooklyn roster for at least two years before he could play in the minor leagues. The result was probably bad for the Dodgers and for Koufax. He was simply erratic. In his first start, he lasted just four innings, striking out four but walking eight.

The next time out, more than a month later, he shut out the Cincinnati Reds on two hits with fourteen strikeouts. In his final two games that year, he lasted only one inning in the first game, and then, in the second, beat the Pittsburgh Pirates in a shutout on five hits with six strikeouts. Though the Dodgers won the World Series that year, Sandy warmed the bench. As Dodger executive Buzzie Bavasi told him, "You have one pitch – high."

Over his first six years as a Dodger, his record was thirty-six wins and forty losses. Nonetheless, in the process, he tied Bob Feller's record when he struck out eighteen batters in one game.

He almost quit in 1960, but showed up at spring training and asked to pitch more often, hoping it would improve his control. That was what everyone considered to be his problem—all speed and no control. About that time, Don Newcombe and Sandy's roommate, catcher Norm Sherry (also Jewish), suggested he "ease off a bit." Sherry told him he thought he was "overthrowing" and could be more effective if he tried not to pitch so hard. Koufax listened, changed, and in 1961, won eighteen games with 269 strikeouts for a league record.

The next year, he started out great, but a midseason blood clot led a physician to suggest he might need to amputate a finger. He did not. Anticoagulants did the trick and Koufax ended the year with fourteen wins, fourteen losses, 209 strikeouts and an earned run average (ERA) of 2.06 with one no-hitter.

In 1963 he was outstanding. He won twenty-five, lost five, struck out 306 batters and pitched a record eleven shutouts. His 1.88 ERA made him the league's best for a second year in a row. And, he won two of the four games it took the Los Angeles Dodgers to win the World Series. He was unanimously named the Cy Young Award winner (best pitcher in the major leagues) and the National League's Most Valuable Player.

In 1964 he went nineteen and five and in 1965, despite arthritis, he won twenty-six games, lost eight, and had an ERA of 2.04. He struck out 382 batters, breaking Bob Feller's record, and he pitched a perfect game, his fourth no hitter. He won the Cy Young Award once more.

But that is not the story that lingers more than forty years later. It was Koufax's decision not to pitch the first game of the 1965 World Series against the Minnesota Twins—because it fell on Yom Kippur—that baseball fans never forgot. Though he became an icon in the mind of most of his fellow Jews, there were also many uncomplimentary and snide comments, including some in the press.

Koufax lost when he pitched the next day, but he pitched and won two subsequent games, including the seventh game on two days' rest. His pitching made the

Dodgers world champions. He could take quiet satisfaction from the victories and from being named the World Series' Most Valuable Player.

The next year was a good one. He earned $135,000 and went twenty-seven and nine. His ERA was 1.75 and he won the Cy Young for a third time. But arthritis was becoming a major problem, and when the Dodgers lost the World Series in four straight, he retired.

Over that last six years of his career, he was, in the words of biographer Jane Leavy, "sublime." "His motion was bio-mechanically perfect." He had literally studied the physics and knew precisely why this was so. Famed Pittsburgh hitter, Willie Stargell, once said that hitting against Sandy Koufax was like "trying to drink coffee with a fork."

Leavy says that while his career was shorter than many other pitchers, in his prime "the beauty of his mechanics, what he could do with the ball, I'd say (and more to the point so does Willie Mays, Hank Aaron, and Ernie Banks), no one did it better."

But that is not the end of the story. When Koufax quit, he quit. Though he was a radio announcer for a few years following his retirement, he simply led a quiet, private life and never tried to milk his career. He never earned money from endorsements. He avoided celebrity, and he has stayed pretty much to himself as he has lived in Maine and now Florida. While he was willing to let Leavy write her book about him (published in 2002), allowing her to interview all but himself and close relatives, and agreed to verify facts, she doubts he has ever read the book and thinks that makes "perfect sense." "He is," she says, "a notoriously private person." "He is celebrity before celebrity became an entitlement."

Sandy Koufax was a remarkable mix. He was a fierce competitor on the basketball court ("the Animal of Bensonhurst") and on the pitching mound. His style of pitching was determined and aggressive. Yet "gentle" was the word most often used to describe him. He was unwilling to give up on himself in six frustrating years as a Dodger and he vindicated that determination in a subsequent record that made him, at 36, the youngest inductee in the Baseball Hall of Fame. He has remained modest and shy around people he does not know, but he's no hermit. He was never afraid of being different, whether that meant not pitching on Yom Kippur, walking away from baseball when he thought his arm had had enough, or living a quiet life ever since.

In the end, Leavy talks of the era in which he grew up. "Those post-war years were giddy with the can-do mentality…They were the children of their parents' expectations; anything that was imaginable was do-able. The time was pregnant with possibility." She talked to 469 people and not one of them had a bad thing to say about him.

Professional Football[35]

Anyone who lived in the Miami-Fort Lauderdale area during the 2002-03 football season might have told you the Miami Dolphins had two Jewish quarterbacks. Jay Fiedler was the starter and Sage Rosenfels, a backup. With two of the fifty-three players on the Dolphins' roster, you might have inferred Jews were reasonably well represented in the National Football League. Two was twice what one might expect.

Not so. Miami just happened to be the one place in the NFL where the sample was unrepresentative. In 2002–03 there were 1,699 players on the final NFL rosters of the thirty-two teams (fifty-three for all but the Houston Texans, the newest team, with fifty-six). Using the 2.1 percent benchmark, a total of thirty-four Jewish NFL players might have been projected. Instead, there were six, about one-sixth the projection. It turns out Miami was the fluke. In addition to Fiedler and Rosenfels, Hayden Epstein was a place kicker for Minnesota (and before that Jacksonville). Lennie Friedman was a guard for Denver. Josh Miller was a punter for Pittsburgh, and Mike Rosenthal was right tackle for the New York Giants.

Active Jewish players in recent years have included: Jeremy Bloom, Jay Fiedler, Lennie Friedman, Antonio Garay, Adam Goldberg, Josh Miller, Igor Olshansky, Sage Rosenfels, Mike Rosenthal, and Mike Seidman. Ten names is a far cry from thirty-four.

Offsetting their underrepresentation as players, Jews have beat the odds as NFL Hall of Fame inductees. Though it would have seemed unlikely to have more than a single Hall of Fame member among the 247 inductees, instead there are six.

Al Davis, general partner of the Oakland Raiders and a former coach.
Benny Friedman, the NFL's first great passer, who played for Cleveland, Detroit, New York (Giants) and Brooklyn.
Sid Gillman, coach of the Los Angeles Rams and Los Angeles/San Diego Chargers.
Marv Levy, coach of the Buffalo Bills and Kansas City Chiefs
Sid Luckman, quarterback of the Chicago Bears.
Ron Mix, offensive tackle for the Los Angeles/San Diego Chargers and the Oakland Raiders.

It is an interesting group: a tackle, two quarterbacks, two coaches, and a former coach, now general partner. For the most part, the Jews who made it into NFL's Hall of Fame have done so in leadership and executive roles.

Going back a few years, Harris Barton and John Frank of the San Francisco 49ers, Ben Davidson of the Oakland Raiders, Lyle Alzado of the Denver Broncos, Cleveland Browns and Raiders (LA and Oakland), and Ed Newman of the Miami Dolphins are also generally considered to have been outstanding Jewish NFL players, and All Pro Harris Barton may yet make it into the Hall of Fame.

The notion of leadership in professional football is further borne out in NFL team ownership. Among the teams with Jewish owners or managing partners are the Atlanta Falcons (Arthur Blank), Oakland Raiders (Al Davis), Tampa Bay Buccaneers (Malcolm Glazer), New England Patriots (Robert Kraft), Cleveland Browns (Randy Lerner), Philadelphia Eagles (Jeffrey Lurie), Washington Redskins (Dan Snyder), Minnesota Vikings (Zygi Wilf and partners), New York Giants (Steve Tisch half owner), and the Miami Dolphins (Stephen Ross half owner). Jews thus own or control nine (29 percent) of thirty-one teams. Green Bay, the NFL's thirty-second team, is excluded from the statistics because it is community owned.

To top it off, Paul Tagliabue was commissioner of the National Football League and Mark Cohon is Canadian football commissioner. And, to get just a bit ahead of our story, but fill out the picture, David Stern is commissioner of the National Basketball Association, Bud Selig is commissioner of Major League Baseball, Gary Bettman is commissioner of the National Hockey League and Don Garber is commissioner of Soccer.

Sports – Professional Baseball[36]

Anaheim, winner of the 2002 World Series, was the Miami Dolphins of Major League Baseball (MLB). They had two Jewish, pitchers Al Levine and Scott Schoeneweis. Levine did not play in the World Series, but he had four wins and four losses in regular season play with an ERA of 4.24. Not stellar, but not bad. Schoeneweis did play in the series, pitching the final two innings of a 10-4 Angels victory over San Francisco in game 3. While neither was the star of the team, an Anaheim fan might have been excused for expecting that with two Jews on their twenty-five-man roster, Jews were overrepresented (8 percent of the Angels' team) in Major Leagues.

Wrong again. Of the 750 major league players during the regular season, we might have expected fifteen Jews, but like Miami, Anaheim was a fluke. Eight Jews (1 percent) played regularly during 2002. They were:

Brad Ausmus of the Houston Astros (still playing in 2008)
Shawn Green of the Los Angeles Dodgers (retired Sept. 30, 2007)
Gabe Kapler of the Texas Rangers and Colorado Rockies (still playing)
Al Levine of the Anaheim Angels (played his last game June 5, 2005)
Mike Lieberthall of the Philadelphia Phillies (played last game Sept. 22, 2007)
Jason Marquis of the Atlanta Braves (still playing)
Scott Schoeneweis of the Anaheim Angels (still playing)
Justin Wayne of the Florida Marlins (Has not played since 2004)

A strange thing happened between 2002 and 2008. Somehow, somewhere, a crop of new Jewish baseball players emerged. At the start of the 2008 seasons, fourteen Jews were slated to play in the majors.

Brad Ausmus, a catcher still with the Houston Astros
Craig Breslow, a relief pitcher for the Minnesota Twins
Ryan Braun, a left fielder for the Milwaukee Brewers
Scott Feldman, a starting pitcher for the Texas Rangers
John Grabow, a relief pitcher for the Pittsburgh Pirates
Jason Hirsh, a starting pitcher for the Colorado Rockies
Brian Horwitz, an outfielder for the San Francisco Giants
Gabe Kapler, an outfielder with the Milwaukee Brewers
Ian Kinsler, a second baseman for the Texas Rangers
Mike Kaplove, a relief pitcher for the Los Angeles Dodgers
Jason Marquis, a starting pitcher for the Chicago Cubs
Scott Schoenweis, a relief pitcher for the New York Mets
Ryan Spilborghs, an outfielder with the Colorado Rockies
Kevin Youkilis, a first baseman with the Boston Red Sox.

Perhaps they and their successors will bump up the number of Jewish MLB Hall of

Famers. (After all, Kevin Youkilis and Ryan Braun were starters in the 2008 All Star game and Ian Kinsler was a reserve player.) As of 2008, with 286 total Hall of Fame inductees (228 players and fifty-eight managers, umpires, and executives), Jews might be expected to have five or six inductees. They are close with four. The three players are Hank Greenberg, Sandy Koufax, and Lou Boudreau. The owner/manager is Barney Dreyfus, a Pittsburgh Pirates' owner who created the World Series tradition. Some might argue that Al Rosen and Ken Holtzman also belong in the Hall of Fame as well, but....

Interestingly, some have argued Jews deserve more credit than they have gotten. They point out that between 1871 and 2003, 142 Jews played professional baseball. Collectively, their lifetime batting average of .265 is 3 percent higher than the league average over the same years. Moreover, they hit a disproportionate number of home runs (0.9 percent of all home runs from only 0.8 percent of all players). As pitchers, they were twenty games over a .500 winning percentage. (By definition, twenty games over the Major League pitching average for the same time frame.) And, their lifetime earned run average (ERA) of 3.66 is lower than the 3.77 for all pitchers.

There is the further consolation of team ownership. Among the Jewish owners and managing partners of MLB teams are Fred Wilpon of the New York Mets, Jerry Reinsdorf of the Chicago White Sox, Lewis Wolff of the Oakland A's, Stuart Sternberg of the Tampa Bay Rays, Theodore N. Lerner of the Washington Nationals, and Jamie McCourt, wife and partner of non-Jew Frank McCourt, owners of the Los Angeles Dodgers. Of the thirty teams, four are corporate owned, e.g. Liberty Media, owner of the Atlanta Braves. Thus 5.5 of the remaining twenty-six teams represents 21 percent Jewish ownership of Major League ball clubs.

None of this counts Sam Zell, who, at least for now, controls the *Chicago Tribune*, owner of the Chicago Cubs—till they sell them—or Bud Selig, MLB commissioner, who at one time owned the Milwaukee Brewers. Nor does it consider the San Francisco Giants, among whose partner owners are some of the city's most prominent Jews.

In addition, Mark Shapiro is (and Gabe Paul was) general manager (GM) of the Cleveland Indians, Larry Baer is chief operating officer of the San Francisco Giants, Paul Godfrey is CEO of the Toronto Blue Jays, and Theo Epstein is GM of the Boston Red Sox. Epstein led the Sox to overcome "the curse of the bambino," the eighty-seven-year World Series drought which, under Epstein's leadership, ended in 2004. He also led them back to win a second World Series in 2007.

Sports – Professional Basketball[37]

Surprising to most of us, in the 1920s and 1930s Jews were thought to have a genetic advantage in basketball. Though they were short, that supposedly conferred better balance and quicker foot speed. They were also believed to have better vision. Some felt the combination of balance, foot speed, and vision "explained" why the South Philadelphia Hebrew Association team (SPHAS or "Spas") was dominant in the semi-pro era which eventually morphed into the NBA. In twenty-two seasons between 1918 and 1940, the Spas played in eighteen championship series, winning thirteen of them. After World War II, however, Jews were overshadowed by the growing presence and superb talents of black players.

Suffice to say, Jews are not well represented among active players in today's National Basketball Association (NBA). As of the 2007/8 season, there was only one Jew (Jordon Farmar of the Los Angeles Lakers) among the 432 active NBA players. Today's Professional Basketball is just not their game. A measure of the recent drought is evidenced in the twenty-four basketball inductees into the International Jewish Sports Hall of Fame. Only two of the twenty-four were born after 1928: Tal Brody, born in 1943, who played in Israel, despite being drafted number two by Baltimore in 1965; and, Larry Brown, born in 1940, now coaching the Charlotte Bob Cats. Of the twenty-four inductees, most were coaches or players active between 1908 and 1949. Moreover, no Jews are listed on the NBA web site among the fifty greatest players of all time.

Offsetting that "drought" is the surprising representation of Jews in the James Naismith Basketball Hall of Fame (whose "members include NBA and NCAA players, coaches and other people who, in one way or another, have contributed in a very special way to the history of basketball.") Of its 285 inductees through 2008, twenty are Jews (7 percent). This is more than three times what we would expect based on their numbers. The twenty include:

William Davidson, as a contributor – NBA & WNBA owner/developer (2008)
Marvin (Mendy) Rudolph, as a referee (2007)
Larry Brown, as a head coach (2002)
Nancy Lieberman-Cline, as a player (1996)
Alexander Gomelsky, as a coach – the father of Soviet basketball (1995)
Earl Strom, as a referee (1995)
Lawrence Fleisher, as a contributor – he formed the Player Association (1991)
William "Red" Holzman, as a coach (1986)
Senda Berenson Abbott, as a contributor – womens' basketball founder (1985)
Harry Litwack, as a coach (1976)
Maurice Podoloff, as a contributor – the first basketball commissioner (1974)
Adolph Schayes, as a player (1973)
Max Friedman, as a player (1972)
Edward Gottlieb, as a contributor – organized SPHAs, and helped NBA (1972)
Abraham Saperstein, as a contributor – Harlem Globetrotters (1971)
Arnold J. "Red" Auerbach, as a coach (1969)
Nat Holman, as a player (1964)
Barney Sedran, as a player (1962)
Leonard D. Sachs, as a coach (1961)
David Tobey, as a referee (1961)

Interestingly, the breakout of the tallies shows Jews are five of the Hall of Fame's 134 players (3.7 percent), six of the seventy-nine coaches (7.6 percent), three of the thirteen referees (23 percent) and six of the fifty-six contributors (10.7 percent). Jews, particularly in the early era, were well represented among the players. More recently, they have been disproportionate achievers as coaches, referees, and executives.

Further, the NBA lists Jews as two of the top ten coaches in history. They are Red Auerbach, perhaps the greatest coach of all time, and Red Holzman. In addition, the Commissioner of Basketball since 1984 is David Stern. He has led the NBA through its most successful era in history.

To round out the story, twelve of the NBA's thirty teams (40 percent) have Jewish ownership or control. These include: (1) the Houston Rockets (Les Alexander), (2) Miami Heat (Micky Arison), (3) Atlanta Hawks (Steven Belkin), (4) Dallas Mavericks (Mark Cuban), (5) Detroit Pistons (William Davidson), (6) Milwaukee Bucks (Herb Kohl), (7) Washington Wizards (Abe Pollin), (8) New Jersey Nets (Bruce Ratner), (9) Chicago Bulls (Jerry Reinsdorf), (10) L.A. Clippers (Donald Sterling), (11) Indiana Pacers (Herbert and Melvin Simon), and (12) Cleveland Cavaliers (Dan Gilbert.)

And to add some final flavor, it was Abe Saperstein who created perhaps single most colorful basketball team of all time, the Harlem Globetrotters.

Sports Broadcasting[38]

Perhaps not surprising is the fact that the list of prominent Jews in professional sports broadcasting contains many familiar names. Among them, a few of the better known include:

Marv Albert	Kenny Albert	Mel Allen
Chris Berman	Len Berman	Al Bernstein
Bonnie Bernstein	Linda Cohn	Howard Cosell
Rich Eisen	Eddie Epstein	Roy Firestone
Hank Goldberg	Mike Greenberg	Bud Greenspan
Steve Levy	Josh Lewin	Al Michaels
Larry Merchant	Dick Schaap	Dick Stockton
Lesley Visser		

Other Sports[39]

The often surprising picture of Jewish involvement in professional football, baseball, and basketball is mirrored in other sports

Daniel Mendoza was England's bare knuckles heavyweight champion from 1792 to 1795. He invented the jab, and defeated Richard (The Gentleman) Humphries in sixty-five rounds. His contemporary, Samuel "Dutch Sam" Elias invented the uppercut and was another of the twenty, or so, prominent English Jews who boxed in that era.

The heyday for American Jewish boxing came in the early twentieth century, particularly the 1920s and '30s. Jews earned seventeen world championships, mostly in light-weight divisions (feather-weight, bantam-weight, etc.), though occasionally they also won as light-heavyweights. Benny Leonard, Louis "Kid" Kaplan, "Slapsie Maxie" Rosenbloom, Barney Ross, and Max Baer[†] (who wore a star of David on his trunks and called himself Jewish, though his Jewish legacy consisted solely of a paternal Jewish grandfather), are among the prominent Jewish fighters of that era. With

---

† The perhaps aprocryphal Max Baer Story has a reporter asking Baer why he is in a gym hitting a punching bag on Yom Kippur. "What are you doing?" asked the reporter. "Getting ready to fight Primo Carnera," Baer responded. "What about Yom Kippur?" asked the reporter." "I'll fight him next." Baer replied.

occasional exceptions, there were few major Jewish fighters in the years after World War II. One exception was Mike Rossman, who won the WBA Light Heavyweight title in 1978 wearing a star of David on his boxing trunks.

More recently there has been something of a rebirth of Jewish fighters. As of mid-2008, Yuri Foreman, a light middleweight, has an impressive twenty-five and 0 record and has been featured in several *New York Times* profiles. Dmitriy Salita, described as "a sensation" in a September 2002 *Washington Post* story, with a 25–0–1 record (twenty-five wins, no losses, and one draw) holds the light welterweight championship and is a contender for the junior welterweight crown. Roman Greenberg, a British based Israeli has a 27-0 record as a heavyweight and is currently the International Boxing Organization's Intercontinental heavyweight champion. And three New York brothers, Daniel (21–2–3), Josiah (9–1–1), and Zab Judah (36–5–0) all fight in different weight classes. Zab is the former welterweight champion.

Tennis legends Pete Sampras and Boris Becker both claim some Jewish heritage, but in both cases, the lineage is far from 100 percent. Sampras has one Jewish and three Greek Orthodox grandparents, and Becker says his mother was a Czech Jew, but the story is quite confusing. Anna Smashnova, who retired after the 2007 Wimbledon tourney, was among the world's top fifty female players, and Vic Seixas was top ranked some years ago, as were Harold Solomon, Eliot Teltscher, Brad Gilbert, and Tom Okker. And who could forget René Richards, the only professional player to play in both men's and women's professional tennis! Among the contemporary ranked players and up-and-comers are Audra Cohen, No. 1 collegiate female tennis player in 2007, Nicolas Massu, a Chilean Olympic gold medalist who was ranked No. 9, Shahar Pe'er, ranked No. 15 among female pros in January 2007, Andy Ram who was No. 9 in 2006, and Dudi Sela, currently Israel's top men's singles player, ranked No. 57 in 2008.

Corey Pavin (born Jewish, but reportedly a 1991 convert to Born Again Christian) and Amy Alcott are familiar names to golfers. Alcott is No. 14 on the LPGA list of all time money winners. Beyond those two, however, prominent Jewish golfers are few in numbers. A little digging yields: Bruce Fleisher, Monte Scheinblum, Jonathan Kaye, Skip Kendall, Cristie Kerr, Herman Barron, Morgan Pressel, and Emilee Klein among recently active professional golfers, but none are big money winners. Interestingly, some Jews cite anti-Semitic barring of Jews from tennis and golf clubs prior to World War II as one reason Jews have had few championship caliber players in either sport. Given the passage of three generations since 1945, the argument seems a bit thin.

Barry Asher, Marshall Holman and Mark Roth are members of the American Bowling Congress and Professional Bowlers Association Halls of Fame. With billiards, bowling shares the distinction that its principal early equipment maker was The Brunswick Company. Founded by John M. Brunswick who built the first perfect billiard table in 1845, the company also began making bowling equipment in 1888.

Vic Hershkowitz, James "Jimmy" Jacobs, and their Jewish contemporaries dominated handball from the 1950s through the '70s with Paul Haber and Fred Lewis holding the U.S. singles titles for all but two of the nine years from 1970 to 1978. And during the 1960s, Jews were said to be 35 percent of the United States Handball Association membership. Victor Niederhoffer was U.S. squash racquets champion from 1972 to 1975 and Stuart Goldstein held the World professional title in

1978. Racquetball's Marty Hogan is one of the greatest players ever to play that sport, and when he toured in the late '70s and early '80s with Benny Koltun and Jerry Hilecher, they were the most powerful trio in the sport. Mike Yellen dominated in the '80s and more recently, Sherman Greenfield, a Canadian Jew, was world singles' racquetball champion in 1996 and 1998.

Peter Revson, Steve Krisiloff, brothers Ian and Jody, and Jody's son Tomas Scheckter were all accomplished professional race car drivers.

Comparable data exist for ice hockey (three active Jewish players), roller skating (Scott Cohen, the only four time world free skating champion), professional wrestling (Bill Goldberg, at 6 feet four, 285 pounds, called "a David in Goliath's shoes"), and other sports. But generally, one can say across most of those sports, Jews are successful athletes, but they do not defy the odds in any significant way.

Olympic Sports

Olympic Sports, however, are another matter. In track and field, Harold Abrahams was immortalized in the movie *Chariots of Fire* for winnning the 1924 Olympic gold in the 100-yard dash and sharing a silver in the men's 4 x 100 relay. American Kerri Strug was a star in the 1996 Atlanta Olympics when she vaulted despite an ankle injury. The second greatest Olympic performance ever was turned in by Mark Spitz (right behind Michael Phelps' eight golds at the 2008 Beijing Olympics). Spitz won seven gold medals in 1972, in the process setting four individual and three relay-team world records. Together with his four medals from the 1968 Olympics, Spitz' eleven medals are 15 percent of the seventy-two total swimming medals Jews have won over the years.

Though Israel did not win an Olympic medal until 1992 (Yael Arad's silver in women's judo), Jews have won medals in every modern Olympics going back to their rebirth in 1896. That year, brothers Alfred and Gustav Flatow of Germany earned two individual and four team gymnastics medals, Alfred Hajos-Guttman of Hungary earned two individual swimming medals, and Paul Neumann and Otto Herschmann of Austria each won an individual swimming medal. Adjusting for the team events, (e.g. the gymnastics teams had eleven members each) Jews won 6.36 medals (5.1 percent) of the 125 medals awarded in that first modern Olympics. At the time, Jews were estimated to be .6 percent of the world's population.

The 2008 Olympics put Dara Torres, with twelve medals, one up on Spitz for total medals won by a Jew. While she has fewer golds, Torres already had nine medals from the 1984, 1988, 1992, and 2004 Olympics and she added three more in 2008 (one individual and two team silver medals). She began her career setting three world's records twenty-six years earlier, in 1982, and she is the first female swimmer to compete in five Olympics. At age 41, she is also the oldest Olympic female swimmer ever. Behind Torres and Spitz is ten-time medalist, Agnes Keleti, a Hungarian gymnast who competed in the 1952 and 1956 Olympics. Irina Kirszenstein-Szewinska won seven individual and team medals as a Polish swimmer in the 1964, 1968, 1972, and 1976 Olympics. And Lenny Krayzelburg, who immigrated to the United

States from Ukraine, won four gold medals swimming for the United States in the 1998 and 2002 Olympics.

Among the surprising aspects of Jewish Olympics performance is their strong record in fencing. Over the years, Jews have picked up seventy-one fencing medals (18 percent of all medals won by Jews). They have done this representing Hungary, Sweden, the United Kingdom, the Soviet Union, Russia, Denmark, Belgium, Austria, France, and the United States. Clearly it is not just their involvement with one particular school or culture of fencing that accounts for their success. Among the top Jewish fencing medalists:

> Jeno Fuchs, Hungary—four golds in 1908 and 1912
> Janos Garay, Hungary—a bronze and gold in 1924 and a gold in 1928
> Oskar Gerde, Hungary—golds in 1908 and 1912
> Endre Kabos, Hungary—four medals (three gold) in 1932 and 1936
> Gregory Kriss, USSR—a gold, two silver and a bronze in 1964, 1968 and 1972
> Alexandre Lippman, France—a gold and silver in 1908, silver and bronze in 1920 and a
> gold in 1924
> Mark Milder, USSR—two golds in 1960 and 1964
> Attila Petschauer, Hungary—golds in 1928 and 1932 and silver in 1928
> Mark Rakita, USSR—two golds and two silvers in 1964, 1968, and 1972
> Sergei Sharikov, Russia—two golds, a silver, and a bronze in 1996, 2000, and 2004
> Sada Jacobsen, United States with a silver and a bronze in 2008

Among other major Olympic sports in which Jews have solid records are swimming (72 medals), gymnastics (54 medals), track and field (42 medals) and various sailing and rowing events (31 medals).

As shown in Exhibit 9a, between 1896 and 2008, Jews have won a total of 401 Olympic medals. Of these, 187 were won in individual sports and 214 as members of Olympic teams. Adjusting the 401 total for team participation (e.g., one-fourth of a medal for being a member of a four-man relay team) yields a revised Jewish total of 231.7 medals. It represents 1.4 percent of the 16,167 Olympic medals awarded since 1896 and it is seven times their proportion of the world's population. Their performance was strongest in the pre-World War II years (the eleven Olympics staged between 1896 and 1936) when they earned 2.4 percent of the medals. Ironically, their second strongest performance (behind the 5.1 percent in 1896), was in 1932, just as Hitler was coming to power. That year they picked up 4.3 percent of the medals. In the seven post-World War II Olympics from 1948 through 1972, their performances were still excellent (2.2 percent) – and this was after the Holocaust had reduced their population by one-third. Since 1976, however, the performance has fallen off dramatically. In the most recent nine Olympics (through the 2008 Beijing Summer Olympics) Jews have won .7 percent of the medals. Though this is still three times their percent of the world's population, it is a drop of more than two-thirds from their average in the preceding eighty years. It is a significant and curious decline, only partially mitigated by the 2002/4 results when Jews picked up 1.3 percent of the medals. (See Exhibit 9a).

In the end, simple generalizations fail. In some sports, Jews beat the odds. In others they do not. In nearly every sport at least a few Jews stand out. Perhaps one can make a case that they perform better in amateur sports (as that term was classically defined) or that they do better in individual, rather than team sports—though 204 of their 387 Olympic medals were won in team sports. Much work might be done beyond the scope of this effort. One thing we can say with confidence is that in most sports, Jews play a prominent role. They may be athletic champions, team owners, coaches, broadcasters or league commissioners, but one way or another, they make a mark.

A review of Jews in sports would be incomplete without mentioning Sidney Franklin. Not a name that trips off the tongue of most sports buffs, he has a unique distinction. Ernest Hemingway befriended him and described him in *Death in the Afternoon*. Franklin was the only American matador to ever compete on equal terms with Latins. He was much admired during the 1930s and '40s, fighting in Mexico and Spain and earning, a then sizable $100,000 a year. He headlined the Madrid Plaza de Toros and Hemingway said of him. "Sidney Franklin is brave with a cold, serene, and intelligent valor. No history of bullfighting that is ever written can be complete unless it gives him the space he is entitled to." Of himself, Sydney said, "I didn't have the gracefulness or art of the Spaniards, but I was brave and that made me famous." And to be immortalized by Hemingway!

Chess[40]

Jews dominate chess. Jocks they may or may not be, but chess champions, they most certainly are.

Of eighteen recognized world chess champions since 1866, at least seven, and perhaps as many as ten, are of Jewish ancestry and of them, a surprising number are half Jewish.

William Steinitz, the first Jewish chess champion, broke onto the scene in 1866 and stayed there, unbeatable, for twenty-seven years. He lost the crown, in 1894, to another Jew, Emanuel Lasker, who also retained it for twenty-seven years. After Lasker lost to Cuban Jose Raul Capablanca in 1921, there was a long dry spell until 1948 when Jew, Mikhail Botvinnik of the USSR, won a championship match among the world's five strongest players. He kept the title, with two brief interruptions, until 1963. The two Soviets who interrupted Botvinnik's reign were half-Jew Vasily Smyslov (1957-58), and fellow Jew Mikhail Tal (1960-61).

In 1963 Armenian and non-Jew Tigran Petrosian, took the title and held it until 1969 when half-Jew Boris Spassky arrived on the scene. Bobby Fisher, who is either half or 100 percent Jewish (there is a question about his father), brought Spassky's reign to an end after three years. Fisher was beaten by Anatoly Karpov, three years later. Karpov's roots are a mystery, with some saying he certainly has Jewish ancestry and others expressing doubt. For our purposes, Karpov is not counted as Jewish. He lost the title to half-Jew Gary Kasparov, in 1985, and Kasparov, in turn, lost to Vladimir Kramnik in 2000. Like Karpov, Kramnik does not claim Jewish ancestry and the Jews in Sports Web site acknowledges they do not know. Nonetheless, a Web site devoted to the Kramnik family (www.eilatgordinlevitan.com/kurenets/k pages/kramnik.html) notes that Kramnik is a Russian Jewish name, it has a picture of Vladimir Kramnik playing chess, and it indicates that a number of family members have moved to Israel.

Not including Karpov or Kramnik, Jews have held the chess championship for sixty-six of the last 122 years. This represents 54 percent of the years between Steinitz formal designation as undisputed champion in 1886 and the present day. In that analysis, we have chosen to disregard a dispute between Kasparov/Kramnik and the International Chess Federation (FIDE). Kasparov broke with FIDE in 1993 and FIDE "installed" Anatoly Karpov as their champion. Kasparov, was nonetheless undefeated until he lost to Kramnik in 2000, and in 2006 Kramnik defeated the FIDE champion. Thus, the Karpov/Kramnik succession appears stronger than the FIDE designees. Kramnik finally lost the chess title in 2007 to an Indian, Viswanathan Anand.

Given their numbers, Jews should not count for much in chess. Until very recently, however, they have dominated the sport.

Bridge[41]

After Emanuel Lasker stopped playing championship chess, he took up bridge. He then led the German bridge team and became a life master. He was among the early prominent Jews in the game.

A generation later, Charles Goren's college girlfriend laughed at his ineptness in playing bridge. It drove him to become the best-known writer and player of his time. He gave up the practice of law to win the world championship in 1950, and his *Winning Bridge Made Easy* was just one of nearly forty books Goren wrote about the game. In his obituary, *The New York Times* estimated his books had sold more than ten million copies. In addition, he was a syndicated newspaper bridge columnist for decades. But, when asked how it felt to play with a great expert, his longtime Jewish partner, Helen Sobel Smith, is said to have replied, "Ask him."

Among contemporary Jewish championship players, authors and experts are Oswald (Ozzie) Jacoby with thirty national championships, Eddie Kantar, another author and world champion, and more recently, Bobby Wolff.

A measure of Jewish importance comes from the bridge bum Web site list of "Famous Players." Of the nine names listed, at least four are Jews (Charles Goren, Oswald Jacoby, Howard Schenken, and Helen Sobel Smith.) A second indicator is found at http://en.wikipedia.org/wiki/Category:American_bridge_players, the Wikipedia list of 52 prominent American bridge players. Roughly half are probably Jewish. Among the names are: Bergen, Bronstein, Cohen, Eisenberg, Gitelman, Goldman, Goren, Greenberg, Jacoby, Kantar, Kaplan, Rosen, Rosenberg, Rosenkranz, Roth, Rubin, Seligman, Sobel-Smith, Zeckhauser, and others. The British book on bridge, World Class by Marc Smith, provides interviews with twenty-six of the "world's best players." Of them, at least four are Jews (Larry Cohen of the U.S., Fred Gitelman of Canada, Eddie Kantar of the U.S. and Ron Klinger of Australia).

Chapter 10

The Written Word

"What a woman does for her children, what a man does for his family, what people most tenaciously cling to, these things are not adequately explained by Oedipus complexes, libidos, class struggle, or existential individualism—whatever you like. Now I know that psychoanalysis has found...the unconscious. A writer is supposed to go there and dig around like a truffle hound. He comes back with a truffle, a delicacy for the cultural world. Well I don't believe that...That's not the way it really is."

"The living man is preoccupied with such questions as who he is, what he lives for, what he is so keenly and interminably yearning for, what his human essence is." —Saul Bellow

Saul Bellow[42]

Saul Bellow was eighty when he nearly died. Poisoned eating toxic fish while visiting the Caribbean in 1995, he developed near fatal pneumonia. Only a lengthy, exhausting effort by his fifth wife, Janis, returned him to health. More than fifty years had passed since his first book and nineteen since he had earned the Nobel Prize for literature. For most, the advanced age, the near-death experience, and an extended recuperation would have signaled the end of a long and successful career as their energies and intellectual powers waned.

Not so for Bellow. He became recharged. He published *The Actual* in 1996 and *Ravelstein* in 2000—the later a major work based on the life of friend and colleague, Allan Bloom. In 1999, an eighty-four –year-old Bellow celebrated the birth of Naomi Rose, his fourth child and first daughter.

Abram and Lescha (Gorfin) Belo emigrated from St. Petersburg, Russia, in 1913. They first settled in Lachine, Quebec, an immigrant working-class suburb of Montreal. Abram started out importing Turkish figs and Egyptian onions before he became a bootlegger. Their fourth child, Saul, was born, June 15, 1915. When Saul was three, the family relocated to a mostly Jewish slum in Montreal where Lescha enrolled him in Hebrew school. She hoped he would grow up to become a rabbi or

Talmudic scholar. But watching neighbors die during the 1918 influenza plague, a bout with tuberculosis that landed him in a hospital ward for six months, his father's beating and near arrest for bootlegging, the family's 1924 escape from Canada to Humboldt Park Chicago, and his mother's death when he was seventeen, were all traumatic for the bookish, diminutive Saul.

His tonic was the rough-and-tumble atmosphere of 1920s Chicago. It honed and hardened him. There was vigor in the rich mixture of Jews, Poles, Germans, Italians, and Russians. Chicago combined meatpacking and heavy industry, railroads, Mafioso, innovative architecture, jazz, sin, wealth, and slums. The writing of Theodore Dreiser, Upton Sinclair, Willa Cather, Frank Norris, and other Chicago authors promoted a social realist atmosphere. Chicago's vitality helped shape Bellow into a young radical activist and intellectual.

Though interested in writing, a professor told him Jews would never understand English literary traditions. Bellow changed his aspirations. He studied anthropology and sociology, first at the University of Chicago, and later at Northwestern. He earned his degree with honors in 1937 and in 1938 entered graduate school at the University of Wisconsin. But over the Christmas break, he fell in love with fellow leftist Anita Goshkin, and he dropped out of school.

In 1940, after a stint at writing while working for *Encyclopædia Britannica* and the WPA, Saul and Anita traveled to Mexico to meet Leon Trotsky (Bellow's inspiration as a revolutionary socialist). Ill-fated, they arrived the day after Trotsky was murdered by Stalin's henchmen.

It was one of history's most wrenching eras. French existentialism, stoic pessimism, and Freudian theories were in vogue. Nihilism, alienation and a dour outlook arose from the havoc of World War I, the Russian Revolution, Leninist and Stalinist repression, the Great Depression, and the advent of World War II. Over the thirty-one years between 1914 and 1945, 100 million lives were destroyed, including six million Holocaust Jews. Nuclear weapons and the emerging Cold War after 1945 only exacerbated the pessimism. Avant-garde intellectuals scorned bourgeois middle-class American life and values. For a time at least, Bellow was engaged by Nietzschean philosophy, oedipal conflict, and the cultural views of *Paris Review* intellectuals.

His first book, *Dangling Man,* was published in 1944. It depicted a would-be author anticipating the World War II draft call-up. The protagonist sought isolation, intending to grow spiritually and intellectually as contemporary forces weighed on him. He studied Enlightenment writers and vacillated as he tried to cope with his anxieties. Ultimately in despair and alienating himself from everyone around him, the book's final scene had him standing naked amidst his fellow draftees in the real world of military induction. It was probably no coincidence that Bellow was inducted into the Merchant Marine in 1943.

His next book had a not dissimilar feel. *The Victim* published in 1947, involved post-World War II Jewish alienation and an occasionally self-critical view of anti-Semitism. It won Bellow a Guggenheim Fellowship.

The fellowship provided him with sufficient funds to move to Paris for two years. He lived with Ralph Ellison who was then writing *Invisible Man.* Somehow, in the midst of all this, and despite his earlier Trotskyite convictions, Bellow began to change. Striking evidence of the shift came in his third novel. Skeptical of the alienation expressed by his peers,

Bellow's book reverted to a semi-autobiographical world of Depression-era Chicago with its rogues ("picaresque" was the term most used by reviewers), matriarchs, and a coming-of-age to be experienced only in that time and place.

"I am an American, Chicago born…and go at things as I have taught myself, free style, and will make the record in my own way." These were the book's first words. It was a modern *Huck Finn*, or urban *Yearling*, more akin to J. D. Salinger than Marjorie Rawlings, in a story extending into early adulthood. *The Adventures of Augie March*, published in 1953, established Bellow with its rich characters, vivid images, and romantic relationships. This was a unique, gritty American voice, mostly set in Chicago. Often humorous, the book provided a completely different outlook from the one Bellow had depicted in the two earlier novels. It was breezy and if not "optimistic," it was certainly not despairing. And like Dickens, it was more fun to read.

The Adventures of Augie March won Bellow the National Book Award and praise from critics: "(Bellow's) body of work is more capacious of imagination and language than anyone else's …If there is a candidate for the Great American Novel, I think this *(Augie March)* is it." said Salman Rushdie in *The Sunday Times* (London). "The best postwar American novel, *The Adventures of Augie March* magnificently terminates and fulfills the line of Melville, Twain, and Whitman" said James Wood in *The New Republic*. "*The Adventures of Augie March* is the Great American Novel. Search no further," said Martin Amis in *The Atlantic Monthly*.

Bellow followed *Augie March* with a succession of mostly acclaimed books.

The Wreckers – 1954
Seize the Day – 1956, about failure and success in society that treasures only success
Henderson the Rain King – 1959, about an eccentric millionaire on an African quest
Herzog – 1964, a 1965 National Book Award winner, about the inner life of the cuck-
    olded professor Moses Herzog
The Last Analysis – 1965
The Arts and the Public – 1968
Mosby's Memoirs and Other Stories – 1968
Mr. Sammler's Planet – 1970, a 1971 National Book Award winner, reflecting Bellow's
    increasing disdain for the liberal establishment through the eyes of a Holocaust sur-
    vivor
Technology and the Frontiers of Knowledge – 1972
Humboldt's Gift – 1975, Pulitzer Prize-winner, a comic tragedy based on Bellow's rela-
    tionship with Delmore Schwartz

Bellow was increasingly anti-Freudian. He criticized the decline of Western humanism and the diminution of value authors and critics placed on the individual. Culture was deriding individualism, diminishing it and moving inexorably toward what today may be termed "Marxist deconstruction." Major social movements, rather than the individual, were ever more in vogue and viewed as determining behavior. Cultural equivalence and political correctness were arriving on the scene, and Bellow roiled against them both. He became politically incorrect. With the growing divergence between his views and those of the university culture, he became anathema to some of his colleagues and many students. Radical students booed him from the stage at San Francisco State College during the early 1970s. But he would not back down.

His 1976 Nobel Prize was a fitting riposte to his critics. It was a supreme accomplishment. In his acceptance speech, Bellow echoed his perspective. In the rich descriptive storytelling tradition of Joseph Conrad, he reveled against the pessimists.

Nonetheless, some wondered if the Nobel signaled the end of his greatness—as it had for Sinclair Lewis, Pearl S. Buck, Ernest Hemingway, and John Steinbeck before him. Was his career fated to decline? Even Bellow was worried.

In time, it became clear Bellow was not about to fade. After 1976, Bellow published roughly the same number of major works as before. Among them:

> *To Jerusalem and Back* – 1976, a non-fiction work involving Bellow's mixed feelings about Israel
> *The Dean's December* – 1982, contrasting Communist Romania with Capitalist America
> *Him With His Foot in His Mouth and Other Stories* – 1984
> *More Die of Heartbreak* – 1987, concerning modernity and its disconnectedness
> *A Theft: a Novella* – 1989, featuring Bellow's first female protagonist
> *The Bellarosa Connection* – 1989, created from a story overheard at a dinner, the protagonist attempts to repent a life of being aloof
> *Something to Remember Me By* – 1991
> *It All Adds Up: From the Dim Past to the Uncertain Future* – 1994
> *The Actual* – 1997, about reclaiming love in middle age
> *Ravelstein* – 2000, the semi-autobiographical story of Allan Bloom and Bellow

Along the way, Bellow went through four marriages and three offspring before Janis, his fifth wife arrived. It proved to be his most enduring, satisfying, and loving relationship—and the one that produced his daughter, Naomi Rose, in 1999. Bellow taught writing at the University of Minnesota, New York University, Princeton, the University of Chicago, Bard, and Boston University. He also received many honorary doctorates and France's highest literary distinction for non-citizens, the Croix de Chevalier des Arts et Lettres.

Still irascible in his late eighties, critics called him a narcissist, a racist, a profound political and literary conservative, a lifelong womanizer and raconteur, and prickly. He was, in the view of some, simply not very likable.

Bellow responded as always: determined, engaged, and informed. Though realistic about the potential for failure, he was positive and outspoken, often humorous, sometimes drawing on a wry, sarcastic wit. He derided categorization and the notion that all humans are merely representations of the groups to which they belong. Having grown up with views akin to his critics, he knew where he ultimately came down, and why. He rebelled against the "Wasteland" view of humanity and political correctness. Something of an Emersonian individualist, his themes typically encompassed personal quest and crises rather than action. His protagonists were often urban men, sometimes disaffected or discontent with society. Perhaps alienated, even threatened as they explored existential questions, they were not destroyed. Some were Jewish intellectuals reflecting and talking within themselves on deep, comic, occasionally absurd matters, but they remained in the real world, in touch both with the intellectual and the tangible. They combined cultural sophistication with street smarts.

His perspective made Bellow original. He affirmed life and the potential for individual human greatness. In his own words after surviving seafood poisoning and pneumonia, "When I opened my eyes eighty-two years ago I found myself suddenly here, in existence, which struck me as marvelous, tremendously moving and energizing. I'm here, this is my life!…You want to get a grip on that, to clutch that sense of what it is to be in the world."

Bellow died on April 5, 2005, a couple of months shy of his ninetieth birthday. A fitting epitaph came in his own words, "There is only one way to defeat the enemy, and that is to write as well as one can. The best argument is an undeniably good book."

Written Words[43]

Jewish written tradition begins with the Torah. Dating from 1,000 to 800 B.C. and likely put into final form by 500 B.C., after the Babylonian exile, it was taken to be the Word of God as dictated to Moses. Written onto a scroll, these five books became a Torah. In book form, they became a Pentateuch or Chumash. Augmented with the remaining thirty-four books, the Jewish Bible (or Tanakh) was reduced to writing, organized, and emerged as the official canon (list of books) sometime between 90 B.C. and A.D. 132. Later, Christians would adopt it, and with few changes, call it the "Old Testament."

The Pharisees are said to have been the first to proclaim the Oral Law. These were additional dictates from God to Moses that were not written into the Torah. Instead, they were handed down orally through the generations to supplement the Torah and provide specific guidance for Jews as to their Laws and traditions. For centuries, any effort to put the Oral Law into writing was prohibited. But the scholarly culture of the Pharisees, always open to debate and varying interpretations, led to growing disputes about the Oral Law.

Between 900 B.C. and A.D. 300, the Jews were dispersed three times. First, in 722 B.C. the Kingdom of Israel (northern Canaan) was defeated by the Assyrians, and its ten tribes were dispersed and lost to history. In 586 B.C., Nebuchadnezzar's Babylonians conquered Judah (southern Canaan), destroying the First Temple and exiling nearly all of the remaining Jews. In A.D. 70 the Romans destroyed the Second Temple and began what most now call the "Diaspora" or, dispersal of Jews to the four corners of the world.

Seeking to distill the cacophony of ever more diverse and divisive opinions about the-so called twofold Law, (the Pentateuch and the Oral Law), and to preserve Judaism, in the face of the Jewish Diaspora into minority enclaves around the world, the Pharisees, led by Judah Ha-Nasi, codified the Oral law into the Mishnah over the first to third centuries after Christ The Mishnah was intended to codify the evolving rabbinical interpretation of Jewish religion, and with that, the "Law" and culture of Jews.

Instead, by preserving the complete debates in writing, including the opposing arguments, the Mishnah ultimately encouraged a diversity of informed views. In Jerusalem and Babylon rabbinical scholars met, debated, and commented upon the Mishnah, adding their own "discourse, stories, legends, and pieces of sermons." Collected and organized in written form, these became the Gemara which, when combined with the Mishnah, became the Talmud. In the process, those words, first from memory and later in writing, became the vehicle that shaped Judaism and communicated it to fellow Jews over time and huge distances.

The Torah, the other books of the Jewish Bible, the Talmud, the Midrash, and the writings of Josephus, Hillel, and Shammai, Maimonides, Rabbi Joseph Caro, and others were the vital threads which transmitted Jewish religion, law, and culture across the 2,000 years of Diaspora. The complimentary requirement was literacy. Jews were the first to create a mandatory requirement that parents educate their offspring. Literacy was critical if Jews were to preserve their religion, tribe, and culture. These written words communicated, explained, and inspired. They ensured a cultural continuity which would otherwise almost certainly have been dissipated and swallowed up into the larger cultures surrounding the Jews.

In that sense the deep Jewish commitment to education, and to their written trove, was a survival skill for their people. Less apparent, that same commitment ultimately spurred a culture of high achievement. That was not the original purpose, but it clearly became a very positive, if unintended, consequence.

Jews became proficient with words, with their artistic use, with rhetorical flourish, description, debate, explanation, and analysis. When others let learning die out, as happened through much of the Dark and Middle Ages, Jews preserved their culture and their drive to learn.

Even when circumstances foreclosed literacy from them, as occurred in much of Eastern Europe before the Jewish Emancipation, Jews continued to place great value on words and education. The rabbi was typically the most scholarly man in each community and its leader. This high esteem for learning was later demonstrated in the voracious demand for education by Eastern European Jews arriving in the United States between 1880 and 1924.

The Nobel Prize for Literature[44]

If the Nobel Prize for Physics evidences consistently superb selections of those whose work has been the most important in physics over the last 100 years or so, the Nobel Prize for Literature holds much less esteem.

As Burton Feldman noted in his book, *The Nobel Prize,* the literature judges "blew it" until the later part of the twentieth century. One might think they were nominating candidates for a literary "witness protection program," making awards to authors such as: Romain Rolland, Frederic Mistral, Carl Spitteler, John Galsworthy, Grazia Deledda and J. V. Jensen. These six are but the tip of a large iceberg of writers whose works are largely unread, out of print, and otherwise lost despite the temporary accolade of a Nobel. In those same fifty years or so, the judges managed to miss: Leo Tolstoy, Joseph Conrad, Mark Twain, Henry James, Henrik Ibsen, Marcel Proust, D.H. Lawrence, Virginia Woolf, Theodore Dreiser, George Santanaya, and Willa Cather. All have survived, regarded as great writers despite having missed the December 10th awards dinner in Stockholm.

The judges' selections improved after World War II, though still leaving a good deal to be desired. They got Hemingway, T.S. Eliot, and Boris Pasternak, but missed Robert Frost, W. H. Auden, Bertolt Brecht, and Evelyn Waugh.

In the last thirty years or so, they seem to have gotten on track. Saul Bellow, Gunter Grass, V. S. Naipaul, Toni Morrison, Naguib Mahfouz, Samuel Beckett, and Doris Lessing all seem excellent selections as writers whose work deserves the award, and who will be read long after their titles drop from the best-seller lists.

The point is that over the full one hundred-plus years, the Nobel for Literature cannot be taken as the consistent gold standard for literary quality. It is an indicator of greatness, but not nearly so much so as the Nobels for physics, chemistry and physiology or medicine.

Here, though, the French can claim to lead the pack. Through 2007, they have picked up fourteen of the 104 Nobels versus twelve for the United States and the United Kingdom, nine for Germany, seven for Sweden, six for Italy, and five each for Poland, Russia, and Spain. Unfortunately for the French, half of their twelve were earned between 1901 and 1939, and, since 1965, they have only earned two (alors!), one of which went to Gao Xingjian, who is also Chinese. Since 1965 Americans and Brits have each picked up five, the Swedes, Germans and Poles three each, and the Italians, Spanish, Japanese, Russians, and South Africans two each.

How have the Jews done? They have earned thirteen (12.5 percent) of the 104 Nobels. Jewish laureates shown on Exhibit 10a include: Harold Pinter (2005); Elfriede Jelinek (2004), whose father was Jewish; Imre Kertesz (2002); Nadine Gordimer (1991); Joseph Brodsky (1987); Elias Canetti (1981); Isaac Bashevis Singer (1978); Saul Bellow (1976); Samuel Agnon and Nelly Sachs (1966); Boris Pasternak (1958); Henri Bergson (1927); and Paul Heyse (1910). With thirteen laureates, Jews are only one behind the French, and one ahead of the United States and the United Kingdom. In fact, three of the U.S. Nobels (Brodsky, Singer, and Bellow) were won by Jewish-Americans as were two of the U.K.'s (Pinter and Caenetti), two of the Germans (Hesse and Sachs) and one of the French (Bergson). When one considers there are sixty million French, 300 million Americans, sixty million British, and eighty-three million Germans, and perhaps fifteen million Jews, the overachievement becomes even clearer.

Two further points. None of the Jewish laureates was born in the United States, and only Brodsky, Singer, and Bellow emigrated. None of the other ten Jewish winners is American and only one is Israeli (Agnon). It is something of a reflection on the Diaspora that Jews, never more than .5 percent of the world's population, since the inception of the Nobels captured ten Nobels from the U.K., Austria, Hungary, South Africa, Germany, Israel, Sweden, Bulgaria, Russia, and France. This contrasts with the sciences where most Jewish laureates were born in, or now reside in, the United States, the world's most hospitable country for science over much of the twentieth century. Second, the incidence of Jewish laureates is greatest in the years since 1965, when, evidence suggests, judging quality was at its best, and Jewish proportion of the world's population smallest. As noted above, since then, Americans and English have won five Nobels, the Swedes, Poles, and Germans three each, and the Italians, Spanish, Japanese, Russians, and South Africans two each. In the same time period, Jews have won eight.

Pulitzer Prize for Fiction[45]

An American counterpart to the Nobel Prize for Literature is the Pulitzer Prize for Fiction (which is not limited to American authors). It was created from an endowment established by Joseph Pulitzer, an early twentieth-century Jewish journalist, who also endowed the Columbia School of Journalism.

The Pulitzer Prize for Fiction has been awarded eighty-two times between 1918 and 2008 (Exhibit 10b). Jews have won eleven (13.4 percent) of those Pulitzers: Edna Ferber (1925), Herman Wouk (1952), MacKinlay Kantor (1956), Bernard Malamud (1967), Saul Bellow (1976), Norman Mailer (1980), Alison Lurie (1985), Steven Millhauser (1997), Philip Roth (1998), Michael Chabon (2001), and Geraldine Brooks (2006).

And like the Nobels, the incidence of Jewish winners has been greatest in the years since 1965 when the Jews have earned seven of the forty awards.

A sense for the pivotal literary role of Jews in fiction writing can be gleaned from browsing the following table of selected "major" and "best-selling" Jewish novelists. The list does not attempt to be comprehensive, but it does provide a sense for the large number and importance of Jewish novelists.

Major Novelists:

Shmuel Yosef Agnon
(Nobel—with Sachs)
Isaac Asimov
Henri Bergson (Nobel)
Judy Blume (National Book
Foundation Medal)
Anita Brookner (Booker Prize)
Geraldine Brooks (Nobel)
Miguel de Cervantes (probable)
Paddy Chayefsky (Laurel Award
& Oscar)
Edna Ferber (Pulitzer)
Herbert Gold
Joseph Heller
Paul Heyse (Nobel)
Ruth Prawer Jhabvala (Booker Prize)
Roger Kahn
Imre Kertesz (Nobel)
Jamaica Kincaid – a convert
Jerzy Kosinski
Alison Lurie (Pulitzer)
Norman Mailer (Pulitzer)
Steven Millhauser (Pulitzer)
Amos Oz
Harold Pinter (Nobel)
Marcel Proust

Sholem Aleichem
Nelson Algren(National Book Award)
Isaac Emanuilovich Babel
Saul Bellow (Nobel & Pulitzer)
Harold Brodkey
Joseph Brodsky (Nobel & Poet
Laureate)
Elias Canetti (Nobel)
Michael Chabon (Pulitzer)
Benjamin Disraeli
E. L. Doctorow (Pulitzer)
Romain Gary
Nadine Gordimer (Nobel)
Mark Helprin
Elfriede Jelinek (Nobel)
Franz Kafka
MacKinley Kantor (Pulitzer Prize)
Joseph Kessel
Arthur Koestler
Carlo Levi
Primo Levi
Bernard Malamud (Pulitzer)
Michel de Montaigne
Boris Pasternak (Nobel)
Chaim Potok
Ayn Rand

Mordecai Richler
Philip Roth (Pulitzer and National
    Book Award)
Maurice Sendak
Isaac Bashevis Singer (Nobel)
Susan Sontag
Leon Uris
Nathanael West
Tobias Wolf (*LA Times* Book Award)

Henry Roth
Nelly Sachs (Nobel – with Agnon)
J. D. Salinger
Budd Schulberg
Muriel Spark
Gertrude Stein
Jerome Weidman (Pulitzer)
Elie Wiesel (Nobel for Peace)
Herman Wouk (Pulitzer)

Best-Selling Novelists:

Jackie Collins	Howard Fast	Erica Jong	Judith Krantz
Ira Levin	Ellery Queen	Harold Robbins	Erich Segal
Irwin Shaw	Sidney Sheldon	Danielle Steel	Irving Stone
Jacqueline Susann	Scott Turow	Irving Wallace	

One need not be a literary sophisticate to appreciate the debt owed to those who gave us the likes of Yossarian, Holden Caufield, Dr Zhivago, Captain Queeg, John Galt, "The Natural," and countless other characters and stories that taught so much and entertained so well.

Nonfiction Writers and Opinion/Political Columnists[46]

If Jews have done well as novelists, they have positively shined as nonfiction authors, and print journalists. Their Pulitzer Prizes for General Nonfiction tell the story. Of the fifty Pulitzers for Nonfiction awarded between 1962 and 2008, at least 25.5 (one was shared) went to Jews (Exhibit 10f). This is twenty-five times what one would expect and suggests at least half the most important works of American nonfiction since World War II have been the work of Jewish writers. In glancing through the following lists of selected, and certainly not all major Jewish nonfiction authors and print journalists, one is struck by the familiar names:

Nonfiction authors:

Match Albom
Shana Alexander
Ernest Becker (Pulitzer)
A Scott Berg (Pulitzer)
Harold Bloom
Robert Caro (Pulitzer)
Noam Chomsky
Robert Coles (Pulitzer)
David Brion Davis (Pulitzer)
Ariel Durant (Pulitzer)
Selby Foote

Anne Applebaum (Pulitzer)
Natalie Angier
Herbert Bix (Pulitzer)
Allan Bloom
Daniel Boorstin
Ron Chernow
Herbert Cohen
Alex Comfort
Jared Diamond (Pulitzer)
Dr. Dean Edell
Erik Erikson (Pulitzer)

Anne Frank
Saul Friedlander (Pulitzer)
Martin Gilbert
David Halberstam (Pulitzer)
Richard Hofstadter (Pulitzer)
Xavier Hollander
Flavius Josephus
Justin Kaplan (Pulitzer)
Richard Kluger (Pulitzer)
Michael Korda
J. Anthony Lukas (Pulitzer)
Norman Mailer (Pulitzer)
Dr. Sherwin Nuland
Tina Rosenberg (Pulitzer)
Oliver Sacks
Stacy Schiff (Pulitzer)
Sidney Schanberg
Julian Simon
Hebert B. Swope (Pulitzer)
Jacobo Timerman
Alvin Toffler
Rebecca Walker
Theodore White (Pulitzer)
Daniel Yergin (Pulitzer)

Alfred Fried (Nobel)
Josh Friedman (Pulitzer)
Steven Jay Gould
Douglas Hofstadter (Pulitzer)
Tony Horwitz (Pulitzer)
Irving Howe
Sebastian Junger
Robert Kaplan
Arthur Koestler
Joseph Lelyveld (Pulitzer)
Roger Lowenstein
Jonathan Miller
David Remnick (Pulitzer)
Leo Rosten
Carl Sagan (Pulitzer)
Carl E. Schorske (Pulitzer)
Susan Sheehan (Pulitzer)
Art Spiegelman (Pulitzer)
Studs Terkel (Pulitzer)
Lionel Trilling
Barbara Tuchman (2 Pulitzers)
Jonathan Weiner (Pulitzer)
Naomi Wolf

Print Journalists:

Elie Abel	Carl Bernstein	Phil Bronstein	Matt Drudge
Max Frankel	Linda Greenhouse	Seymour Hersh	Walter Lippman
Daniel Pearl	A.M. Rosenthal	Sidney Schanberg	

Similarly, when one browses a list of selected opinion commentators and political writers, one is struck by the large number of familiar names:

Opinion Commentators and Political Writers

Martin Agronsky	Saul Alinsky	David Broder
David Brooks	Elizabeth Drew	Andrea Dworkin
Ellen Goodman	Howard Fineman	Ari Fleischer
Glen Frankel (Pulitzer)	Max Frankel	Al Franken
Betty Friedan	Thomas Friedman	David Frum
David Horowitz	Michael Kinsley	Joel Klein
Charles Krauthammer	William Kristol	Irving Kristol
Paul Krugman	Max Lerner	Michael Lerner
Anthony Lewis	Flora Lewis	Seymour Martin Lipset
Walter Lippman	Robert Novak	Norman Orenstein
Norman Podhoretz	Frank Rich	Steven Roberts
Daniel Schorr	William Safire	Gloria Steinem
Bret Stephens	I. F. "Izzy" Stone	Theodore White (Pulitzer)
Mortimer Zuckerman	Ben Wattenberg	

Dramatists and Jewish Playwrights[47]

　　Both the Pulitzers and the Tony Awards have categories to recognize superb playwrights. While these artists might also be covered in chapters devoted to the performing arts, their skills are typically first expressed in writing. That, and the fact they also frequently display their talent in other written forms, such as novels, suggests treatment here is appropriate.

　　Jews have won twenty-two (29 percent) of the seventy-seven Pulitzer Prizes for Drama awarded since 1917 (Exhibit 10d). The Tony's results are even more striking, twenty-eight of the sixty-two awards (45 percent) as shown in Exhibit 10e. Among the more prominent Jewish playwrights and screenwriters:

Playwrights & Screenwriters:

David Auburn (Pulitzer & Tonys)
Michael Bennett (Pulitzer)
Abe Burrows (Tony & Pulitzer)
Harvey Fierstein (Tony)
Ira Gershwin (Pulitzer)
James Goldman (Oscar)
Oscar Hammerstein (Pulitzer)
Moss Hart (Pulitzer)
Lillian Hellman
Sidney Kingsley (Pulitzer)
Joseph Kramm (Pulitzer)
James Lapine (Pulitzer)
Frank Loesser (Pulitzer)
Donald Margulies (Pulitzer)
Arthur Miller (Pulitzer & Tonys)
Harold Pinter (Tony)
Yasmina Reza (Tony)
Richard Rodgers (Pulitzer)
Howard Sackler (Pulitzer & Tony)
Anthony Shaffer (Tony)
Neil Simon (Pulitzer & Tonys)
Tom Stoppard (Tonys & Oscars)
Paula Vogel (Pulitzer)
Jerome Weidman (Pulitzer)
Paul Zindel (Pulitzer)

George Axelrod
Jerry Bock (Pulitzer)
Eve Ensler
Herb Gardner (Tony)
William Goldman (Oscar)
Richard Greenberg (Tony)
Marvin Hamlisch (Pulitzer)
Sheldon Harnick (Pulitzer)
George S. Kaufman
Edward Kleban (Pulitzer)
Tony Kushner (Pulitzer & Tonys)
Jonathan Larson (Pulitzer)
David Mamet (Pulitzer)
Mark Medoff (Tony)
Clifford Odets
Bernard Pomerance (Tony)
Elmer Rice (Pulitzer)
Morrie Ryskind (Pulitzer)
Dore Schary (Tony)
Peter Shaffer (Tonys)
Stephen Sondheim (Pulitzer)
Alfred Uhry (Pulitzer & Tony)
Wendy Wasserstein (Pulitzer & Tony)
Peter Weiss (Tony)

　　Death of a Salesman, The Crucible, Driving Miss Daisy, Equus, The Elephant Man, Glengarry Glen Ross, The Odd Couple, Amadeus, and *Rent* are just a few of the dramas that helped shape the American stage over the twentieth century.

The Pulitzer Prize for Poetry and Jewish Poets[48]

Jews have also earned a disproportionate number of Pulitzer Prizes for Poetry since that award's inception in 1919. As shown in Exhibit 10c, of the eighty-nine prizes, Jews have won seventeen (19 percent). Among the important Jewish poets listed below, the seventeen Pulitzers Prize winners are noted.

Major Poets:

Carl Dennis (Pulitzer)

Jorie Graham (Pulitzer)

Anthony Hecht (Pulitzer)

Richard Howard (Pulitzer)

Stanley Kunitz (Pulitzer)

Philip Levine (Pulitzer)

Howard Nemerov
(Pulitzer & Poet Laureate)

Adrienne Rich

Louis Simpson (Pulitzer)

Mark Strand (Pulitzer)

Marya Zaturenska (Pulitzer)

Allen Ginsberg

Louise Glück (Pulitzer)

Heinrich Heine

Maxine Winokur Kumin (Pulitzer)

Emma Lazarus

Lisel Mueller (Pulitzer)

George Oppen (Pulitzer)

Robert Pinsky (Poet Laureate)

Karl Jay Shapiro (Pulitzer)

Philip Schultz (Pulitzer)

C. K. Williams (Pulitzer)

And as before, the prominence is greatest after 1965. Since then, Jews have won thirteen of forty-four (30 percent) Pulitzers for poetry.

She never won a Pulitzer, but for a nation of emigrants, it is worth noting that since 1883 new arrivals through the Port of New York have been greeted by the words of Emma Lazarus:

"…Give me your tired, your poor,
Your huddled masses yearning to breathe free,
The wretched refuse of your teeming shore.
Send these, the homeless, tempest-tost to me,
I lift my lamp beside the golden door!"

Humorist Writers and Cartoonists[49]

In *The Joys of Yiddish*, Leo Rosten noted, "In nothing is Jewish psychology so vividly revealed as in Jewish jokes." Plaintive, self-critical, anxious, and resigned are just a few of the words used to characterize the unique aspects of Jewish humor. For many it was their only antidote to terror. "Humor," Rosten said, "also serves the afflicted as compensation for suffering, a token victory of brain over fear." It can encourage a positive outlook even when so much else is going wrong.

If comedians perform mostly on stage or television, humorists more often write (or cartoon) for newspapers and books. The comic book industry could be said to be largely created by Jews, as were many of the more notable comic strips and comic characters. A few of the more notable humorists and cartoonists:

Jewish Humorists and Cartoonists:

> Otto Binder & C. C. Beck (Captain Marvel)
> Mel Blanc (Voice of a thousand characters)
> Art Buchwald (humor columnist)
> Herb Caen (San Francisco "three dot" columnist)
> Al Cap (Li'l Abner)
> Harry Donnenfeld & Jack Liebowitz (DC Comics)
> Max Fleisher (Popeye and Betty Boop)
> Isadore "Fritz" Freleng (Bugs Bunny, Daffy Duck)
> Max & Bill Gaines (Entertaining Comics)
> Rube Goldberg (goofy inventions)
> Martin Goodman (Marvel Comics)
> Bob Kane & Bill Finger (Batman)
> Jack Kirby & Joe Simon (Captain America)
> Harvey Kurtzman (*Mad Magazine*)
> Stan Lee (Spiderman & The Hulk)
> Dorothy Parker (The Round Table)
> S. J. Perlman
> Jerry Robinson (The Joker)
> Max Shulman
> Jerry Siegel & Joe Shuster (Superman)
> Shel Silverstein
> Art Spiegelman (*Maus*) – Pulitzer Prize
> Will Steig (cartoonist)
> Calvin Trillin (author/speaker)

In-Print Critics, Society and Advice Columnists[50]

From explaining good manners to suggesting which movies are worth seeing, and even educating us about sex, Jews are among America's foremost critics and advice columnists. God knows how many family problems have been solved, Hollywood careers made or lost, and crises averted because of advice proffered by Jewish critics, gossip, and advice columnists:

Critics, Society, and Advice Columnists

Clive Barnes	Harold Bloom	Judith Crist
Neal Gabler	Sheilah Graham	Pauline Kael
Alfred Kazin	Ann Landers	Jeffrey Lyons
Leonard Maltin	Michael Medved	Gerald Nachman
Louella Parsons	Sylvia Porter	Gene Shalit
Gene Siskel	Ruth Westheimer	Abigail (Abby) Van Buren
Walter Winchell		

Newspapers[51]

Among great U.S. newspapers, perhaps the three most prominent are: *The New York Times, The Washington Post,* and *The Wall Street Journal.* For many, these are authoritative sources of solid news and opinion and reading at least two of them, if not all three, is a daily routine. All three also share the distinction of having been started by non-Jews, but achieving great prominence under Jewish ownership or management.

The New York Times:[52] Adolph Simon Ochs, the son of Jewish emigrants, began as "printers devil" when he was fourteen. By age 20, he had founded one Chattanooga newspaper and purchased control of another. He combined them turning *The Chattanooga Times* into one of the South's best newspapers.

In 1896, *The New York Times* was in a losing battle with sensationalizing "yellow journalists," whose stories ran long on hyperbole and short on facts. Ochs bought the failing *Times,* announcing his commitment to objective, factually based news reporting. His slogan, "All the News That's Fit to Print," remains atop the masthead. Ochs dropped the newsstand price to a penny and turned The New York Times from a money loser into a viable, strong competitor.

He also created a family succession as strong as the paper itself. In 1935, Arthur Hays Sulzberger succeeded his father-in-law, Ochs, and was, in turn, briefly succeeded by his son-in-law, Orvil Dryfoos. Dryfoos died only a month later and was followed by thirty-seven –year-old Arthur Ochs Sulzberger, grandson of Adolph Simon Ochs. Sulzberger remained in charge until 1992 when his forty-year-old son, Arthur Sulzberger Jr. took over. More than twenty-five years later, Sulzberger Jr. remains publisher of what most people consider, America's "Newspaper of Record."

The Washington Post:[53] In 1933, Eugene Isaac Meyer bought *The Washington Post* for $825,000 at a bankruptcy auction. Started in 1877 by non-Jew Stilson Hutchins, the Post had fallen on hard times under its second owners, the McLean family (also not Jewish). Meyer was already an immensely successful financier. He had parlayed $600, earned from his father when he stopped smoking, into $50,000 shortly after graduating from Yale. Meyer went on to make an estimated $60 million fortune on Wall Street before he was 40.

Equally talented as an executive, Meyer was recruited by Woodrow Wilson to head the War Finance Corporation in 1918. Nine years later, in 1927, Calvin Coolidge brought him in to clean up the Federal Farm Loan board and, in 1930, Herbert Hoover appointed him governor of the Federal Reserve board. In 1946 Harry Truman named him the first president of what is now the World Bank (a position Meyer disliked so much he resigned after only six months).

Over time, Meyer turned the *Post* around, making it one of the foremost American newspapers. Philip L. Graham, his son-in-law, joined him in the business taking on ever increasing responsibility as they updated production facilities, acquired television stations, and bought out rivals. When Meyer died in 1959, Graham assumed complete control and acquired *Newsweek.*

Graham's 1963 suicide left his widow, and Meyer's daughter, Katherine Meyer Graham, in charge. Despite a self-effacing description of herself as a "housewife," Katherine Graham's handling of the Pentagon Papers, Watergate, the 1975 Pressman's Union strike, and numerous acquisitions, not only made the *Post* into the nations' second or third most prominent newspaper, it also generated a 3,315 percent increase in the value of Washington Post Group stock between 1971, when she took the company public, and 1991 when she stepped down.

She turned the job over to her son, Donald, who has proven equally capable. *Fortune* magazine's Andy Server called Graham: "Understated, underrated, and one hell of a CEO." Today, the Washington Post Group is still controlled by the family. Among its properties, the Washington Post Group includes: the *Post*, *The Everett Herald*, *Newsweek* magazine, a number of community and military newspapers and business publications, six network affiliated television stations, Cable One (serving much of the Midwest and Northwest), Newsweek Productions, Kaplan Educational Centers, and numerous other ventures.

The Wall Street Journal:[54] Peter Kann did not found Dow Jones or *The Wall Street Journal*, but after joining the *Journal* in 1963, and winning a Pulitzer Prize for his Indo-Pakistan War reporting, he rose to become its associate publisher in 1980, and publisher and editorial director of Dow Jones in 1989. From 1991 to 2007, he was chairman and chief executive officer of Dow Jones while his wife, non-Jew Karen Elliot House, for a time served as publisher of *The Wall Street Journal*. Kann won great respect for building and keeping the *Journal* perhaps the world's leading financial newspaper (only the *Financial Times* could be considered a peer), but he came in for criticism as a business executive. For some, he became the goat when Rupert Murdoch acquired control from the Gentile Bancroft family shortly after Kann retired.

Reuters:[55] Paul Julius Reuter (née, Israel Beer Josaphat, and later Joseph Josaphat), founded Reuters in London and built it into one of the world's first news agencies. In 1848 he established a carrier pigeon service linking Aachen, Germany, with Brussels, filling a gap in the telegraph lines operating between Berlin and Paris. Three years later, he started Reuters, to provide a telegram service for businesses operating near the London Stock Exchange. Later, he shifted its focus to providing news and information for those who had no reporters at distant locations where news was being made. His first hot exclusive came when he published the 1859 speech of the king of Sardinia, anticipating the "War of Italian Liberation." Later, Reuters scooped everyone once more with exclusive European reporting of Lincoln's assassination. Though born to a rabbi, Reuters changed his name and converted, becoming a Lutheran on November 16, 1845, just a week before he married Mary Elizabeth Clementine Magnus. He built Reuters into one of the world's foremost international press agencies before retiring in 1878 and turning the business over to his son, Herbert. In 1925 Great Britain's Press Association bought majority control of Reuters. Over the next few years, its ownership shifted to its subscribing newspapers until 1984, when it was taken public on the London Stock Exchange.

Pulitzer Inc.:[56] Joseph Pulitzer emigrated from Hungary to the United States in

1864 when he was seventeen. He immediately joined the Union Army, and at war's end, moved to St. Louis, where he took up politics and journalism. First, he won a seat in the Missouri legislature and, in 1878, he bought the *St. Louis Dispatch* and *The Post*. He merged the two and, by 1883, expanded, buying the *New York World*. At the time, the Gentile-owned Hearst papers pioneered what became known as "yellow journalism," promoting and sensationalizing causes such as the Spanish-American War. Pulitzer, a Hearst competitor, thus joined the "sensationalist" wave. He published exposés of corruption, promoted crusading investigative reporting, and carried out shameless self-promotion. This was the "yellow journalism" which Ochs disdained when he took control of *The New York Times*. Despite the history of flashy publications, when Pulitzer died in 1911, his estate endowed the country's first journalism school at Columbia University as well as the now famous Pulitzer Prizes. Joseph Pulitzer II took control when his father died and he was succeeded, in 1955, by Joseph Pulitzer III. One hundred twenty-five years since the founding, Michael E. Pulitzer continues as chairman of the board of Pulitzer Inc., and the family continues to control the company that publishes the *St. Louis Post Dispatch*, the *Arizona Daily Star*, twelve other daily, and sixty five weekly newspapers.

San Francisco Chronicle:[57] Brothers Charles and Michael de Young purchased the *Daily Dramatic Chronicle* in 1864 and transformed it into the San Francisco Chronicle. Though it is today owned by the Hearst Corporation, its longtime executive editor, from 1991 to 2008, was Phil Bronstein.

Magazines and Other Publications

Advance Publications Inc.:[58] Samuel Irving Newhouse (née Solomon Neuhaus) was a seventeen-year-old clerk for Judge Hyman Lazarus in 1911 when Lazarus took control of the money-losing *Bayonne Times*. He assigned young Newhouse the job of turning the paper around, which he did in a year. Four years later, Newhouse was being paid a remarkable (for the time) $30,000 a year. He began buying newspapers for his own account in 1922, starting with the *Staten Island Advance*. He made it profitable and parlayed it into a family of small New York and New Jersey newspapers. In 1950, he acquired the *Portland Oregonian* and later added the *St. Louis Globe-Democrat*, the *New Orleans Times Picayune*, and the *Cleveland Plain Dealer*. His 1959 acquisition of Condé Nast took him into magazines, radio, television stations, and cable television channels.

By 1979, when he died, he had created the third largest U.S. media chain. Along the way, he donated $15 million to establish the Newhouse School of Public Communications at Syracuse University. Today his sons, Samuel I. Jr. and Donald control Advance Publications as a private company whose annual sales exceed $5 billion. It publishes twenty-nine daily newspapers, forty-one local business journals, twenty-six Web sites, and forty-nine magazines including: *Parade, Vanity Fair, The New Yorker, GQ, Architectural Digest, Bon Appetit, Conde Nast Traveler, Vogue, W, Golf Digest, Home Furnishings News, Women's Wear Daily*, and *Supermarket News*.

Triangle Corporation:[59] Moses Annenberg, an East Prussian emigrant, was a salesman and later circulation manager for the Hearst organization before he took control of the *Daily Racing Form* and *The Philadelphia Inquirer.* When Annenberg died in 1942, after serving three years in jail for tax evasion and bribery, his holding company, Triangle Corporation, was deeply in debt. His thirty-two-year-old son, Walter, took on the job of turning it around. He succeeded beyond his wildest dreams, in the process building Triangle into the publisher of *TV Guide* and *Seventeen.*

Annenberg was also a savvy investor in the Pennsylvania Railroad and Campbell Soup Company. He sold *The Philadelphia Inquirer* to Knight-Ridder in 1970 and everything else to Rupert Murdoch in 1988, proclaiming he would devote the rest of his life to philanthropy and public service. Along the way, Annenberg also served as ambassador to the United Kingdom and his wife was chief of protocol for President Ronald Reagan.

His donation of impressionist paintings to the Metropolitan Museum of New York is valued at more than $1 billion. He also established the Annenberg School of Journalism at the University of Pennsylvania and a counterpart journalism school at the University of Southern California. He was a major supporter of the United Negro College Fund, the Corporation for Public Broadcasting, the state of Israel, and the rebuilding of black churches torched by arsonists. At his death in 1994, his Annenberg Foundation was worth $1.6 billion. It was one of the country's wealthiest charitable foundations, and that year, it announced plans to donate $500 million for reform of public schools.

Ziff Davis:[60] William Bernard Ziff and Bernard G. Davis created Ziff Davis in 1927. They started with Ziff's, a humor magazine, and later added other publications to build a family of magazines. When Ziff died in 1953, his son, William Jr., took over, bought out Davis, and expanded by adding *Car & Driver, Yachting, Popular Mechanics, Popular Photography, Stereo Review, Computer Gaming World,* and later *PC Magazine.*

In 1982, diagnosed with prostate cancer, William Jr. began selling off most of the magazines. Expecting to succumb to cancer, he established a family trust with his three sons as beneficiaries. Surprisingly, he regained his health, stepped back into the business and built an even more valuable enterprise. It became the dominant force in computer publications. In 1993 Ziff retired once more and the next year, he and his sons sold 95 percent of the remaining business to a leveraged buyout firm. The $1.4 billion in proceeds established an investment firm which continues to this day—along with the family's active support of conservation.

Hugo Gernsback[61] is an unfamiliar name to most of us. Born in Luxembourg in 1884, he immigrated to the United States in 1904, became an inventor (dry batteries), a writer *(Ralph 124C 41+),* and the publisher of numerous magazines. But it was his creation of the first science-fiction magazines that proved his entrepreneurial talent. He founded *Modern Electronics* magazine, the world's first radio magazine in 1908, *Science and Invention* in 1920 (covering hard science while debunking astrology, medical quackery, perpetual motion machines and spiritualism), and *Amazing*

Stories, in 1926. Later, he added six more science-fiction titles. His pioneering role in science fiction is memorialized today in the annual "Hugo" award for the best science-fiction novel.

Cahner's Publishing:[62] Norman Cahners first gained notoriety as a world class athlete in the hammer throw. He and Milton Green, then world record holder in the hurdles, chose to boycott the 1936 Olympics to protest Hitler and his persecution of Jews. (If they were joined by other Jews, the boycott helps explain the drop from twenty-five medals won by Jews in the 1932 Olympics to thirteen in 1936.) In 1946, after military service, Cahners created Cahner's Publishing. Its first publication was *Modern Materials,* a trade magazine that drew on a Navy publication he created while in the service to inform vendors how to best pack their shipments. He built Cahners into what became the largest trade-magazine publisher, with sixty-nine magazines ranging from *Variety* (started by Sime Silverman) to *Plastic Business News* and *Professional Builder.* Today Cahners is part of the $9 billion annual revenue British-Dutch publisher Reed Elsevier.

Rolling Stone:[63] Jann Wenner started *Rolling Stone* in 1967, later adding *US Weekly* and *Men's Journal* to his stable of publications. As of 2008, after more than forty years at the helm, Wenner shows no interest in selling out or stepping down.

The New Yorker[64] was founded by Harold Ross in 1925. A fixture for more than eighty years, it has grown into a national weekly magazine of sophisticated writing, humor, and a chronicler of major New York cultural events. Ross was a legend as was William Shawn, the editor from 1952 to 1987. Tina Brown served as editor from 1992 to 1998 and was followed by Pulitzer Prize-winner David Remnick. *The New Yorker* is currently owned by Advance Publications Inc., the Newhouse family's publishing company described above.

New York[65] magazine was founded by Clay Felker and Milton Glaser, who acquired it out of the failed *New York Tribune* newspaper. After a stint as part of Rupert Murdoch's media empire, *New York* was acquired by Bruce Wasserstein who, with hand-picked editor Adam Moss, has built it into a scrappy, highly regarded weekly.

The New York Review of Books:[66] In 1963 Robert Silvers and Barbara Epstein created this semi-monthly magazine which covers literature, culture, and current affairs, generally from a liberal perspective. (Non-Jew Tom Wolfe has called it "the chief theoretical organ of radical chic.") The two other founders, non-Jews A. Whitney Ellsworth and Elizabeth Hardwick, might be seen to have engendered a 50/50 Jewish/Gentile influence were it not for Hardwick's aspirations. In her *New York Times* obituary she is quoted as having said in 1979, "...my aim was to be a New York Jewish intellectual,...I say 'Jewish' because of their tradition of rational skepticism." For most of its forty-five years, the 140,000 circulation semimonthly was also known for the pen-and-ink drawings of David Levine. Following Epstein's death in 2006, Silvers continued on, age seventy-nine, as sole editor.

Books

In book publishing, the story is much the same.

Random House:[67] In 1925, a few years after earning his journalism degree from Columbia, Bennett Cerf and his friend, Donald Klopfer, bought Modern Library from the company Cerf had joined upon graduation. Though Modern Library focused on publishing "the world's best books," in 1927 Cerf and Klopfer decided they would also "publish a few books on the side at random." A Renaissance man, Cerf was a columnist, anthologist, author, lecturer, radio show host, joke collector, panelist (on the television show, *What's My Line?)* and a perennial judge of the Miss America Pageant. His skill in finding talented authors, charming them, and working with them as they wrote, and he published their books, built one of the strongest stables of twentieth-century authors. Among them: William Faulkner, James Joyce, Ralph Ellison, Isak Dinesen, Edgar Snow, Eudora Welty, Ayn Rand, John O'Hara, Eugene O'Neill, James Michener, Truman Capote, William Styron, Gertrude Stein, Robinson Jeffers, and Theodor Seuss Geisel. Cerf also built Random House by creating *American College Dictionary*. He took the company public in 1957, and then acquired other publishers such as Alfred A. Knopf, L.W. Singer, and Pantheon Books. In 1965 Cerf sold Random House to David Sarnoff's Radio Corporation of America (RCA). From 1980 to 1998, Random House was owned by Newhouse controlled Advance Publications Inc. They sold it to the German media giant, Bertelsmann AG, where it remains today.

Alfred Knopf[68] was considered something of a Jewish pioneer in 1912 when he entered publishing at the age of twenty. He had fallen in love with publishing while traveling in Europe and decided to pursue it rather than becoming the attorney his father had hoped for. At the time, publishing was said to be "overwhelmingly Gentile and conservative," Despite their difference of opinion, Knopf's father helped him get a junior accountant's job at Doubleday, which gave him his start.

In 1915 after a stint at Doubleday and at one other firm, and with strong encouragement from Blanche Wolf, his fiancée, he invested his $5,000 stake to start Alfred A. Knopf Inc. Over time, he built a cadre of great writers including: Willa Cather, Max Eastman, Kahlil Gibran, Ezra Pound, Thomas Mann, H.L. Mencken, Alfred Camus, Jean-Paul Sartre, Wallace Stevens, Langston Hughes, D. H. Lawrence, and Julian Huxley. Ultimately, after adding Vintage Books, which gave Knopf a paperback imprint, their son, Pat, left the firm in 1959 to establish Athenaeum, his own publishing firm. Shortly after, in April 1960, Knopf sold out to Random House, where his relationship with Bennett Cerf allowed him the autonomy he wanted.

The Book-of-the-Month Club:[69] Harry Scherman wanted to be a writer. He left Wharton, moved to New York and tried his hand at short stories and plays while earning a living as a journalist at a Jewish newspaper. Ultimately, he gave up creative writing to become a copywriter at J. Walter Thompson, Ruthrauff and Ryan, and other ad agencies.

Maxwell Sackheim, a Russian Jewish emigrant, worked with Scherman at J Walter Thompson, Ruthrauff and Ryan. In 1914 the two created a literary promotion partnership. They started Little Leather Library, offering a set of thirty classic books, bound in imitation leather and sold via direct mail for $2.98. Two years later, Scherman convinced Whitman Candy Company to include small copies of Shakespeare's plays with its packaged candy.

But it was 1926 when they came up with their most important innovation, the Book-of-the-Month Club. Scherman was credited with recruiting a prominent board of judges (Clifton Fadiman, John Marquand, Haywood Broun, and others) to provide credibility for the monthly book selections. Sackheim conceived of the so called negative option plan, sending a detailed description of each book two weeks in advance. That gave "members" a choice to "opt out" by returning a card to signal their decision not to purchase the book. Of course, many members did not return the card. The innovation triggered a stable, immense flow of books out the publisher's door each month. Within two years, the Club had 100,000 members.

Along the way, Scherman and Sackheim brought in publisher Robert K. Haas as a co-founder. Unlike Scherman and Sackheim, Haas had strong credentials as a publisher, a career he continued after leaving Book-of-the-Month Club. (Haas' next company, Harrison Smith and Robert Haas, Publishers, was purchased by Random House in 1936.)

The Book-of-the-Month Club would ultimately become an icon of American taste, helping middle-class Americans know about—and read—important books when they were first issued. Scherman's family retained control of the Club until 1977 when they sold it to Time-Life. Along the way, Scherman also created a family foundation which has since made charitable grants of more than $100 million.

Simon & Schuster:[70] Richard Leo Simon and Max Lincoln Schuster founded Simon & Schuster in 1924. Leon Shimkin, joined them that first year and was soon an equal partner, playing a critical role for more than fifty years. Simon, Schuster, and Shimkin pioneered crossword puzzle books (1924), the policy of allowing bookstores to return unsold books (1925), mass-market paperbacks (their 1939 introduction of Pocket Books), and "instant books" (The first, about Franklin Delano Roosevelt, was published six days after his death). They were known for aggressive marketing, often spending multiples of what competitors did to promote their titles.

In 1944 they sold the business to non-Jew Marshall Field, operating it with complete autonomy until 1957, when Field died and they promptly bought it back. Simon retired in 1956, and Schuster and Shimkin continued on together until 1966 when Schuster retired and Shimkin bought his shares. Shimkin then merged Simon & Schuster into his already public Pocket Book Company and continued expanding the business until he sold it to Charles Bluhdorn's Gulf+Western in 1975. Within Gulf+Western, Simon & Schuster continued to expand, acquiring sixty additional publishers including Prentice-Hall. Today Simon and Schuster operates as part of Sumner Redstone's Viacom.

Farrar, Straus, & Giroux:[71] Roger Straus never needed to work. He came from two very wealthy and prominent families. His grandfather was Oscar Straus of the R H Macy clan and his mother was Gladys Guggenheim. Nonetheless, he built one of

America's foremost late twentieth-century publishing houses. In 1945, with partner and non-Jew John Farrar, he started Farrar, Straus, & Company in New York.

After a few lean years (and numerous changes in the partners and the firm's name), Farrar and Straus recruited editor-in-chief and non-Jew Robert Giroux in 1955. In the process, they adopted the name that has lasted ever since. Before Giroux, the firm had published Carlo Levi's *Christ Stopped at Eboli* (1947), Gayelord Hauser's *Look Younger, Live Longer*, and other authors such as Edmund Wilson, Rabbi Philip S. Bernstein, and Robert Graves. Giroux brought along authors from Harcourt Brace including T.S. Eliot, Flannery O'Conner, Bernard Malamud, and fourteen more. Later, through acquisitions and clever marketing, Isaac Bashevis Singer, Robert Lowell, Philip Roth, Susan Sontag, Tom Wolfe, John McPhee, Alexander Solzhenitsyn, Nadine Gordimer, and Scott Turow joined this remarkable talent pool. Measures of the firm's quality and strength include its seven Pulitzer Prize-winning books and its twenty-one Nobel laureate authors. Farrar retired in 1972 and passed away two years later, but Straus, always the dominant partner, kept building the firm. Despite a wave of mergers and takeovers, Straus carried on as an independent publishing house until he became convinced his son would never take over the firm. He then sold it, in 1994, to the German firm Von Holtzbrinck. Even with that sale, however, Straus demanded, and got, autonomy within that huge publisher. Straus passed away in mid-2004.

Crown Publishers:[72] Nathan (Nat) Wartels and Bob Simon created Crown out of Outlet Book Company, which they bought in bankruptcy for a few hundred dollars in 1933. Outlet initially focused on marketing overstock and remaindered books. Later they shifted the focus to republishing back list and out of print nonfiction and fiction titles. That successful formula led to the 1936 creation of Crown to publish original titles. Wartels led the company for 52 years. By the early 1980s, he had built what was reputed to be the industry's third largest publishing house. In 1988, then eighty-six year old Wartels sold Crown to Random House.

Viking Press:[73] Harold K. Guinzburg founded Viking in 1925 and quickly established a top reputation, publishing authors such as Carl van Doren, Mohandas Gandhi, Bertrand Russell, and Thorsten Veblen. Guinzburg ran the firm till he died in 1961. His son Thomas took over, cofounded the *Paris Review* and sold Viking to Penguin in 1978.

Pantheon Books:[74] Kurt & Helen Wolf fled fascism and the Holocaust, immigrating to the United States in 1942. That year they formed Pantheon. Among their major titles were the *I Ching* and *Doctor Zhivago*. Pantheon became a prestigious brand which Random House acquired in 1961 and merged into Alfred A. Knopf. All are now part of the Bertelsmann AG, currently the United States largest book publisher.

Basic Books:[75] Arthur Rosenthal started Basic Books in 1952 and over the years built a stable of authors including Freud, Isaac Asimov, Lester Thurow, Orlando Patterson Niall Ferguson, Samantha Power, Richard Feynman, and others. Basic is currently owned by Perseus Books Group, controlled by the private equity firm which bought Basic from Harper Collins, an earlier acquirer. Perseus' president is David Steinberger.

Arthur Frommer[76] made himself into a one-man travel publishing conglomerate over a fifty-year period. Graduating with a Yale law degree, he joined Army Intelligence during the Korean War and was posted to Germany. Late in his enlistment, he created a travel guide for his fellow servicemen and, in 1956, he revised it, creating a civilian version which he published as *Europe on $5 a Day*. Back in the United States, Frommer practiced law for six years, all the while spending nights, weekends, and vacations creating new travel books covering other destinations such as: *Japan on $5 a Day, New York on $5 a Day*, and many more. He built the series over a period of years before selling it. It has since gone through various publishing hands including MacMillan U.S.A. and IDG (the *"For Dummies"* publishers). Today, it is part of John Wiley & Sons.

In 1961 Frommer created a wholesale travel operator, Arthur Frommer International Inc. and was its chairman and president for twenty years.

He has continued to publish new travel books, has a weekly radio program on CBS, appears regularly on such television programs as *Oprah,* and NBC's *Today,* writes a syndicated weekly travel column, operates an Internet site www.frommer.com and, most recently, produced a bi-monthly consumer travel magazine, *Arthur Frommer's Budget Travel*. It quickly grew to a circulation of 350,000 before Frommer sold it to Newsweek Inc. in 2000, together with his syndicated column, monthly newsletter and the Arthur Frommer's Budget Travel Club.

Jacob Kay Lasser[77] began writing tax guides in 1939. He published his books on taxes, financial planning, business record keeping and money management continuously until he died in 1954. Even today *J.K. Lasser Tax Guides* are consistently ranked among the best available. In 1952 his wife, Terese, who helped him publish his first edition of *Your Income Tax,* published her own book, *Reach to Recovery,* on breast cancer survival. The Reach to Recovery program she created is now operated by the American Cancer Society in forty-four countries. She is memorialized in their annual Terese Lasser Award. J.K. Lasser tax publications have gone through many hands since Lasser's death in 1954, including Prentice Hall, MacMillan USA, Simon & Schuster and IDG before becoming part of John Wiley in 1999.

Chapter 11

Performing Arts and Comedy

"I don't feel like a legend, I feel like a work in progress."

"I am simple, complex, generous, selfish, unattractive, beautiful, lazy and driven."
—Barbra Streisand

Barbra Streisand[78]

She was fifteen months old in July 1943 when her father, Emanuel Streisand, a respected teacher, died of a cerebral hemorrhage. Her mother, Diana, had to go to work to support them (Diana, Barbara, and her brother, Sheldon). Diana's bookkeeping wages were barely enough to keep the three out of poverty, and work demands left Diana with little time to bring up her children as she would have liked. When she remarried six years later, it was to a man Barbara would later describe as "allergic to children." It was neither a happy nor privileged childhood.

She attended grade school and high school in Brooklyn, graduating with an "A" average in 1959. But defying her mother's wishes that she go to college, Barbara instead headed to Manhattan to become an actress. She was rejected by the Actors Studio and at numerous auditions. Only after actor Alan Miller saw her potential, gave her acting lessons, and her boyfriend, Barry Dennen, suggested she sing and develop a nightclub act, was she able to get a start. At that point, she shortened her name to Barbra.

A talent contest at the Lion Club, a gay bar, was her first appearance. Her superb voice, humorous banter, and willingness to look and act different, made her an immediate favorite with gays, a fiercely loyal fan base ever since. Word-of-mouth filled the club for every performance, and her one-week run was extended to three. Next up was a three-week engagement (later extended to thirteen) at Bon Soir Club, where she earned twice the $108 she was paid at the Lion Club.

Jack Paar heard about her in 1961 and invited her to appear on his show. But the big break came in 1962. She was nineteen when she got the part of Miss Marmelstein in the Broadway musical, *I Can Get It for You Wholesale*. Her rendition of the eponymous song brought down the house each night, and because of her talent, the role was enlarged with more songs. The show ran for nine months leading to a New York Drama Critics Award, her first Tony nomination, and her 1963 marriage to Elliott Gould, the musical's male lead. Their marriage lasted eight years and from it came her son and only child, Jason.

But she was still considered "ethnic," eccentric, and unattractive. Her songs were thought too obscure and her style was seen as "homosexual." Columbia Records' executives weren't yet ready to sign her to a recording contract. She was too "Brooklyn" and too Jewish. In another indication of the determination she has shown throughout her career, Streisand persevered. In a few months, Columbia relented, and in 1963, *The Barbra Streisand Album* was finally released. For eighteen months, it was on the charts. It led to release of *The Second Barbra Streisand Album* later that same year and a second gold record. In 1963 she earned two Grammys. At age 22, she became, to that time, the youngest artist to receive a Grammy. At one point that year, and despite the huge popularity of rock 'n' roll and the Beatles, she had three albums on Billboard's Top Ten.

In 1964 she got the starring role as Fanny Brice in the Broadway play *Funny Girl*. It was an immense success. It ran for 1,348 performances, including a stint in London. She received her second Tony nomination and was voted the best female lead in a musical by the English critics. A memorable scene had her staring at herself in the mirror as she delivered the line, "Hello, gorgeous!" It was emblematic of her confidence and, some would say, her chutzpah.

The following year she was contracted to do five CBS television specials. Age 23, she demanded—and got—complete artistic control of her programs. This was a rare concession to any artist, yet alone someone so young and with so little experience. She was a phenomenon. Despite the unhappiness of some who found her "exhausting" and overbearing, she proved her talent when the first show, *My Name Is Barbra,* earned five Emmy awards and a Peabody.

She starred in the movie version of *Funny Girl* in 1968. It earned her an Academy Award (shared with Katharine Hepburn in the first-ever tie for Best Actress) and a Golden Globe, and she was named star of the year by the National Association of Theater Owners.

Though her records continued to do well, her next acting role proved a disappointment. She grabbed the lead role in *Hello, Dolly* away from Carol Channing, who had starred in the Broadway play. The film was a flop, and many felt Streisand deserved the ignominy. Her next movie, *On a Clear Day You Can See Forever* almost did not get released, and when it did, it was not a great success; nor was her subsequent movie, *The Owl and the Pussycat*.

It was with Ryan O'Neal in the 1972 film, *What's Up Doc?* that Streisand regained her stride. The pairing led to a second movie together, *The Main Event,* which was also popular. But it was the hit 1973 movie, *The Way We Were*, with Robert Redford, that clearly re-established her acting prominence and provided her with a number one song.

After starring in *Funny Lady*, she co-wrote the Academy Award-winning song, "Evergreen" for the 1976 remake of *A Star Is Born*. She produced and starred in the film and won six Golden Globes while the soundtrack topped the charts as a quadruple platinum album.

Yentl, released in 1983, was controversial. Isaac Bashevis Singer, who wrote the original short story, disliked the film saying it was unfaithful to his effort. Streisand who produced, directed, co-wrote the screen play, and starred in the movie, was lauded by some (Steven Spielberg said it was a masterpiece) but others disagreed. *Yentl* received a number of Academy Award nominations, but none for Streisand as director. Though she received a Golden Globe Award for Best Director and another for producing the Best Picture, she blamed male chauvinism for not receiving a Best Director Oscar nomination. Some said she was "crushed."

She rebounded with the movie *Nuts* in 1987, which she produced and in which she starred, and then *The Prince of Tides*, in 1991, for which she earned the respect of Pat Conroy, the book's author. *Prince of Tides* received much critical acclaim, and seven Academy Award nominations including Best Picture, but once more Hollywood did not honor Streisand with a Best Director nomination.

Over her entire Broadway, Hollywood, and live performance career, she kept recording songs. In the forty-two years between 1963 and 2005, Streisand released at least one album in all but five years, and she typically released two or more. Based on sales of her sixty albums (forty-nine of them gold, thirty platinum, eighteen multi-platinum), and her numerous hit singles, she is the second most popular recording artist of all time, behind only Elvis Presley, and ahead of the Beatles and the Rolling Stones.

In 2001 Hollywood finally saw fit to recognize her with an honor she may not have expected. The American Film Institute gave her its Lifetime Achievement Award for her combined work as an actress, director, producer, writer, and composer.

Through it all, Barbra Streisand has been proudly Jewish. She has played Jewish roles such as Fanny Brice, Dolly Levy, the Jewish psychiatrist in *Prince of Tides*, and a Jewish political activist in *The Way We Were*. She has chosen to produce movies with Jewish themes, such as *Yentl*, and she has turned characters in movies she produced into Jews, including the lead in *A Star Is Born*.

She has also been widely acknowledged as a demanding perfectionist, a diva who Hollywood considers arrogant and rude, and it reacts by snubbing her. Seemingly willing to be perceived that way, she responds with no apologies, "Of course I want utter and complete control over every product I do. You know, the audience buys my work because I control it, because I am a perfectionist, because I care deeply." But there is also an occasional trace of defensiveness, blaming sexism or other failings of those she believes to be judging her unfairly.

She has also been famously caricatured, with stories perhaps more apocryphal than true. Reportedly, she insists on being filmed from only one side. Tour guides in Beaufort, South Carolina, like to tell of her demand that Marine aviators stationed at a nearby airbase cease making early morning over flights of her rented house while she was in town making *Prince of Tides*. She supposedly demanded workers at the Las Vegas MGM Grand enter and leave her hotel room backward, so no one would be looking at her. And she requires peach-colored towels and toilet paper in her hotel rooms, because the color complements her peachy complexion.

Consistent with her perfectionist mentality is her stage fright, which first arose when she forgot the lines to a couple of songs during a 1968 Central Park concert before a crowd of 128,000. Stage fright is seen by many psychiatrists to arise in a perfectionist who is fearful of making mistakes.

And part of what drives her critics is her consistent, outspoken liberal Democrat party politics. She began by helping raise money for George McGovern's 1972 presidential run, and she was a strong supporter and fundraiser for Bill Clinton. She raised $5 million for the Gore-Lieberman campaign and keeps a tally of the number of candidates she has backed (194), and of them, how many have won political office (155). Her Web site featured a thirty-seven-page outspoken political polemic of her views criticizing the Bush administration, but she never followed through on her threat to leave the country if George W. Bush was re-elected to a second term.

If Barbra Streisand has been generous with her political opinions and fundraising, she has been equally philanthropic for causes in the United States and Israel. She funded the Streisand Chair in Cardiology at UCLA and the Streisand Chair on Intimacy and Sexuality at USC. She has donated her twenty-four-acre, five home Malibu property to the Santa Monica Mountains Conservancy. In addition, the Barbra Streisand Foundation has donated $15 million in support of environmental issues, women's issues, civil liberties and democratic values, civil rights, children's and youth-related issues, and AIDS research, advocacy, service, and litigation.

She has produced films and television shows devoted to advancing such causes as gun control, gay rights, Arab Jewish relations, and Gentiles who helped save Jews during the Holocaust. She has also performed at numerous charitable concerts that have raised more than $10 million for such causes as AIDS and women and children in jeopardy. She has donated money to Israeli causes (and in memory of her father) and has said she only works to earn more money which she will give away.

Following her divorce from Elliott Gould, Streisand briefly dated Canadian Prime Minister Pierre Trudeau and had longer-term relationships with Jon Peters (the hairdresser who became a movie producer), and tennis star Andre Agassi. In 1998 she married actor James Brolin.

In the end, Barbra Streisand is perhaps the most accomplished, versatile performing artist of the twentieth century. While her remarkable recording career, her live concerts, her stage, screen, and television acting career, her song and screen writing, her producing and directing of major films are each major accomplishments, together in one talented person, the combination is simply unequaled.

Two Academy Awards
Eight Grammys, plus the Grammy Legend Award, and the Grammy Lifetime
    Achievement Award
Six Emmy awards
The "Star of the Decade" Tony Award
Eleven Golden Globe Awards
Six People's Choice Awards

Two Peabody Awards
A New York Drama Critics Poll Award, and
The American Film Institute Life Achievement Award

Barbra Streisand manifests a stunning combination of huge talent matched with equally huge determination. She insists on making a difference.

Kennedy Center Honors[79]

One of the most prestigious artistic awards for an American performing artist is to be designated a Kennedy Center honoree. In the words of the Kennedy Center Web site, selection is "quintessential recognition for a lifetime's endeavor. This is America's equivalent of a British knighthood or the French Legion of Honor,"

Among the performing arts, Kennedy honorees cover the spectrum from opera to country-western, Hollywood to Broadway, and such points in between as folk, jazz, ballet, modern dance, and comedy. It is an immense palette recognizing American, and occasionally international, artistic achievement.

Nominations are put forward by a Committee of National Artists (twenty-nine members at this writing) plus all past honorees (now totaling 157). Final selections are made by the more than 150 members of the board of trustees, including various honorary chairs (seven), officers (nine), presidential appointees (thirty-five), congressional appointees (twenty-two), founding and emeritus chairmen (two), honorary trustees (five), emeritus trustees (seventy-five), and the board of the Kennedy Center Community and Friends. In true Washington, D.C., fashion, a cast of hundreds is required to select the five or six honorees. If nothing else, the number of dignitaries involved dispels any notion that a small clique controls the process.

The awards ceremony at the Kennedy Center is attended by the First Family and an entourage of artistic and political celebrities. Aired each year between Christmas and New Year's, the show is a perennial Emmy nominee.

As before, the Jewish representation is striking. Over a period of thirty years, 157 honorees have been selected (See Exhibit 11a). Of them, forty-one (26 percent) are Jews. This is thirteen times their proportion of the U.S. population. The talents for which Jews have been honored include symphony composer and conductor, violinist, pianist, opera soprano, movie, stage, and television producer, director, and actor, big band leader, comedian, playwrite, songwriter, and singer as well as choreographer and dancer. The range of talents honored makes a point demonstrated in the balance of this chapter; namely, Jews are counted among the greats in most areas of Western performing artistic achievement.

Music

Musical taste is largely cultural, shaped heavily by our geographic and ethnic roots, our age, and our current interests. Even our tonal preferences are influenced by where we grew up. The "do re mi" that sounds so natural to most Western ears can seem atonal and foreign to Asian sensibilities. From country-western to hip-hop, jazz to reggae, and rock 'n' roll to classical, our environment strongly influences our musical taste. Chinese opera will have few fans in Milan, and standing-room-only crowds are unlikely for a Puccini opera in Islamabad.

Moreover, musical forms exist with their own performance standards and, within any type of music, they draw upon different techniques for distinguishing the great from the mediocre. We expect Jews to dominate klezmer, and not rank high among the greats of reggae, but Jews have done well across a surprising range of musical genres. In classical, Broadway musicals, rock 'n' roll, and jazz they are prominent. But they have some distance to go in country-western.

Classical

The classical music form is sufficiently old (much of it dating to the Italian Renaissance and earlier) and so widely appreciated that nearly every Western country has at least one major symphony orchestra, and a coterie of composers, conductors, and artists that play the great halls. From present-day Italy, France, Germany and Austria, the genre spread throughout Europe and from there, on to the Western Hemisphere. From Moscow to Vienna and on to Los Angeles and Sydney, many consider classical music their favorite musical form, and for others it ranks high.

A telling measure of Jewish achievement in classical music is found among orchestra conductors. They lead their respective symphonies and are charged with selecting the songs to be played at concerts, and the artists to play them. And like most artistry, the ultimate test of talent is the caliber of the performance. Those conductors who are most gifted rise to lead the most important orchestras.

The University at Albany (of the State University of New York) provides helpful information about important conductors.[80] On a Web page, it listed every conductor of the nineteen major U.S. symphony orchestras from their respective dates of inception through 2002. The list is shown as Exhibit 11b. Among those symphonies, the oldest is the New York Philharmonic founded in 1842, while the youngest, the Atlanta Symphony Orchestra, was founded in 1945. Among the remaining orchestras are the Boston Symphony Orchestra, the Los Angeles Philharmonic, the San Francisco Symphony, the Cleveland Orchestra, Cincinnati Symphony, and twelve more. Those nineteen orchestras have had 202 conductors from inception to 2003, with some names appearing more than once as individual conductors have moved from one symphony to another over their career.

Among the 202 names, sixty-six (nearly a third) are Jews. This is sixteen times what we would expect. Among the major Jewish conductors are:[81]

Leonard Bernstein	Michael Tilson Thomas	Leon Botstein
Pierre Monteux	Lorin Mazel	Leonard Slatkin
Yoel Levi	Sir George Solti	James Levine
Gerhardt Zimmerman	Gerard Schwarz	Eugene Ormandy
George Szell	Daniel Barenboim	Andre Previn
Bruno Walter	Joseph Krips	Jeffrey Kahane

Five of these: Bernstein, Solti, Levine, Ormandy, and Previn are also Kennedy Center honorees.

If some believe the fact that a third of the great conductors are Jewish is a uniquely American phenomenon, consider the London Symphony. There, the outcome is even more disproportionate. Of the fourteen principal London Symphony conductors since 1904, five (36 percent) have been Jews. The U.K. has only 300,000 Jews (0.5 percent of its sixty million people). The incidence of Jewish conductors is thus seventy-two times greater than their proportion of the British population.

Another way to look at classical music is to consider favorite composers, the people who created the music. The American Symphony Orchestra League provides information about the pieces played by its member symphonies each year. As shown in Exhibit 11c, as measured by performances during the 2001–02 Season, the ten most frequently scheduled classical selections were composed by:[82]

Beethoven	Mozart
Brahms	Tchaikovsky
Straus, Richard	**Mahler**
Ravel	Haydn
Shostakovich	Prokofiev

One of the ten, Mahler, is Jewish.

The league also shows the most frequently performed works by Canadian and U.S. composers.

Barber	**Bernstein**
Copland	Adams
Gershwin (George)	Hindemith
Rouse	Schwantner
Ives	Corigliano & **Kernis**

Of the eleven, four—Bernstein, Copland, Gershwin and Kernis—are Jews.

A third approach is to look at the "World's 50 Greatest Composers CD Collection" offered by Knowledge Products, a company whose products are largely educational.[83] Those fifty composers are shown in Exhibit 11d. Of the 50, five (10 percent) are Jewish—Mahler, Gershwin, Mendelssohn, Schoenberg, and Copland. In this case, using the 1.3 percent that Jews are of the populations of the United States, Europe, Canada, Australia, New Zealand, and Israel, the outcome is nearly eight times what we would expect.

None of this considers great individual Jewish violinists, pianists, and other artists. Kennedy Center honorees have included Isaac Stern, Itzhak Perlman, Yehudi Menuhin, Rudolph Serkin, Nathan Milstein, and Arthur Rubenstein. It also does not take into account Jascha Heifetz, Vladimir Ashkenazy, and Vladimir Horowitz who many consider equally great.[84]

Grand opera counts Beverly Sills, Rise Stevens (both Kennedy Center honorees) and Roberta Peters among its divas and Jan Peerce and Robert Merrill among the great male baritones and tenors.[85] Even in a form thought dominated by Italians and Spaniards, Jews are among the top stars.

A final synopsis of the Jewish role in classical music comes from the Jinfo Web site, traditionally one of the most credible sources for such information.

"Of the one hundred leading virtuoso performers of the twentieth century listed at http://www.muzieklijstjes.nl/100players.htm, approximately two-thirds of the violinists, half the cellists, and forty percent of the pianists were, or are, Jews. Of the one hundred leading conductors of the twentieth century listed at www.muzieklijstjes.nl/100conductors.htm, approximately one-fourth were, or are, Jews. Among the leading classical composers, the Jewish representation is only about ten percent."

Broadway Musicals (and Popular Music)

If Jews are disproportionately accomplished as classical conductors, composers, and musicians, those accomplishments are not nearly so impressive as their near dominance of Broadway musicals. Names like Rodgers and Hammerstein, Rodgers and Hart, Lerner & Loewe, Stephen Sondheim, George and Ira Gershwin, Alain Boublil, Claude-Michel Schonberg, Herbert Kretzmer, Leonard Bernstein (who wrote *West Side Story* with Sondheim), and more recently Mel Brooks, produce a huge proportion of the hits.[86]

Jewish prominence in Broadway musicals recently received academic attention with the Harvard University Press publication of *Making Americans – Jews and the Broadway Musical* by Andrea Most, assistant professor at the University of Toronto. According to Harvard University Press, her book "examines two interwoven narratives crucial to understanding twentieth-century American culture: the stories of Jewish acculturation and the development of the American musical." Professor Most says that between 1925 and 1951:[87] "Jewish writers brought to the musical stage a powerfully appealing vision of America fashioned through song and dance. It was an optimistic meritocratic, selectively inclusive America in which Jews could at once lose and find themselves—assimilation enacted onstage and off."

The Wiesenthal Museum of Tolerance Multimedia Learning Center provides its own slant on how this all came to be. It notes the rapid increase in the population of Jews in New York during the formative Broadway period of the late 1800s and early 1900s. Jews developed Yiddish theater on Second Avenue, and it became a "training ground for actors." Similarly, the music hall, or variety theater "abounded in Jewish comedians and sent much of that talent to the 'real stage.'"[88]

From these roots, and in a fashion symbolized by Samson Raphaelson's 1925 Broadway play, *The Jazz Singer,* starring George Jessel, Jews moved on to Broadway. *The Jazz Singer* was later made into Hollywood's first popular "talking picture," with Al Jolson playing the lead.) The story, told at the beginning of Chapter 13 – "Hollywood," concerns "a Jewish boy who must choose between following in his father's footsteps to become a cantor or pursuing a career as a musical actor." That *The Jazz Singer* was a largely accurate portrayal of Al Jolson's life story made it all the more interesting. It was an apt dramatization of assimilation tensions and a metaphoric introduction to the rise of Jewish dominance of the Broadway musical.[89]

The Jazz Singer resonates with the "Golden Age" theme of this book. Following the Jewish Emancipation, Enlightenment, and reform movement, Jews transitioned their focus from traditional Orthodox Judaism to the secular world. Over generations, many musically inclined Jews migrated from the synagogue to popular musical forms and, ultimately, to the Great White Way and beyond. In the process, they shaped what would become a major American art form.

The lion's share of Broadway's longest-running shows are musicals. As of mid-2003, thirty-eight of the "50 Longest Running Broadway Shows" were musicals (see Exhibit 11e). Ranging from *Cats* with 7,485 performances to *How to Succeed in Business Without Really Trying* with 1,417. Twenty-four (63 percent) of the thirty-eight longest-running musicals were written by Jews. It is no coincidence that six of the top ten were as well. The six include:[90]

No. 2 *Les Misérables* by Alain Boublil, Claude-Michel Schonberg, and Herbert Kretzmer – 6,680 performances

No. 4 *A Chorus Line* by Marvin Hamlisch and Edward Kleban – 6,137 performances

No. 6 *Miss Saigon* by Alain Boublil, and Claude-Michel Schonberg – 4,092 performances

No. 7 *Beauty and the Beast* by Howard Ashman and Alan Menken – 3,812 performances

No. 8 *42nd Street* by Al Dubin and Harry Warren (who is not Jewish) – 3,486 performances

No. 10 Fiddler on the Roof by Sheldon Harnick and Jerry Bock – 3,242 performances

Interestingly, of the twelve "Top 50" Shows" that were not musicals, at least three were written by Jews, two by Neil Simon *(Barefoot in the Park and Same Time Next Year)* and one by Ira Levin, *(Deathtrap)*.

Because the musicals of earlier eras did not typically play for such long runs and were generally written in a different style (with more single hits and fewer numbers that repeat popular melodies throughout the show), it is useful to also look at what Chicago Critic.com (Tom Williams) ranks as "The 25 Broadway Musicals Everyone Should See".[91] Here, Jewish dominance is stronger still. As shown in Exhibit 11f, Jews wrote the words, music, or both, for twenty-one of Williams' twenty-five favored musicals.

Rock 'n' Roll[92]

The roots of rock 'n' roll are mostly in black southern blues, rhythm & blues, and gospel. Along the way, country made a contribution as did Tin Pan Alley. But as Buddy Holly reportedly said, it was Elvis that really got it going. In the 1950s he brought rock 'n' roll to America's white teenagers and from there, it flourished. It crossed the Atlantic where The Beatles and Rolling Stones helped Europeans develop the taste.

Today, it is popular nearly round the world. Travelers in Berlin, Tokyo, Buenos Aires and most other world capitals hear it on local radio stations and see their young dressed in the wild, colorful garb that began with rock stars like Kiss, The Grateful

Dead, early Elton John and others. In mid 2003, Paul McCartney played to a sold-out rock 'n' roll crowd in Moscow's Red Square. These days, when the Rolling Stones go on a "world tour," it really is a world tour.

After competing with efforts from several other cities, Cleveland, Ohio became home to the Rock 'n' Roll Museum. It commissioned Chinese architect, I. M. Pei, to design a home for its $84 million Museum which opened in late 1995.

The museum did not wait for the building's completion to begin honoring rock 'n' roll's greats. The first sixteen inductees were honored in 1986. To no one's surprise, non-Jews Elvis Presley, Chuck Berry, Little Richard, Jerry Lee Lewis, Buddy Holly, and Ray Charles were just a few of the greats from that initial group. There were no Jewish performers among the inductees, but Alan Freed was one of the sixteen honored. As a Cleveland DJ, it was Freed that gave "rock 'n' roll" its name, and he was an early promoter of "all-star" rock 'n' roll concerts in New York.

Over the twenty-three years through 2008, there have been 238 inductions into the Rock 'n' Roll Hall of Fame (see Exhibit 11g). Of the 238 awards, 160 have gone to individuals or duos and seventy-eight have gone to rock 'n' roll groups or bands of three or more musicians.

Over time, the honor has moved through the various genres of rock 'n' roll. It is no surprise that 34 percent of all the awards (82 Inductions) have gone to blacks, major originators of the form. More surprising, however, is that twenty-nine of the 160 individual/duo awards (12 percent) have gone to Jews. They include:

Alan Freed (1986) nonperformer	Leonard Chess (1987) nonperformer
Jerry Leiber (1987) nonperformer	Mike Stoller (1987) nonperformer
Jerry Wexler (1987) nonperformer	Bob Dylan (1988) performer
Phil Spector (1989) nonperformer	Simon & Garfunkel (1990) performers
Gerry Goffin (1990) nonperformer	Carole King (1990) nonperformer
Ralph Bass (1991) nonperformer	Bill Graham (1992) nonperformer
Doc Pomus (1992 nonperformer	Milt Gabler (1993) nonperformer
Paul Ackerman (1995) nonperformer	The Velvet Underground (1996) performer
Syd Nathan (1997) nonperformer	The Mamas and the Papas (1998) performers
Billy Joel (1999) performer	Clive Davis (2000) nonperformer
Paul Simon (2001) performer	Steely Dan (2001) performer
Ramones (2002) performers	Moe Ostin (2003) nonperformer
Jann Wenner (2004) lifetime achievement	Seymour Stein (2005) lifetime achievement
Herb Alpert (2006) lifetime achievement	Jerry Moss (2006) lifetime achievement
Leonard Cohen (2008) performer	

Jews are six times better represented in the Rock 'n' Roll Hall of Fame than their proportion of the U.S. population. It is important, though, to note that more than half the twenty-nine awards (sixteen) were earned by Jews not as performers, but as disc jockeys, promoters, songwriters, and founder/CEOs of the major record companies. As in professional sports, Jews have figured prominently in the business side of the art form. At the same time, they have earned six of the 159 performer awards and four of the seven lifetime achievement awards, still disproportionate to their numbers.

In the end, rock 'n' roll would be far poorer without Bob Dylan, Paul Simon, Billy Joel, the Ramones, and Mama Cass Elliot. Many would class Bob Dylan and

Paul Simon as two of the great songwriters and performers of the genre. But equally, without Alan Freed, Bill Graham, Clive Davis, Jann Wenner, and Phil Spector, rock 'n' roll would not have succeeded and survived as long, and as well as it has.

Jazz[93]

Like rock 'n' roll, the roots of jazz are in black culture. And like rock 'n' roll, the music that grew from those roots was strongly influenced by Jews. Consider some of the names: Benny Goodman, Buddy Rich, Eddie and Peter Duchin, Stan Getz, Art Hodges, Herbie Mann, Shelly Manne, Artie Shaw, Peter Nero, Dinah Shore, Eydie Gormé, Tony Martin, Mel Tormé and more recently, Harry Connick Jr., Michael Feinstein, Kenny G., and Flora Purim.

The list does not begin to consider the producers and promoters who influenced the form. The Newport Jazz Festival, New Orleans Jazz Festival, and Monterey Festival were early and popular forums promoting jazz to a wider audience. All were created by George Wein, a vital jazz figure for more than forty years. He also is the man behind the revival of Duke Ellington's career in 1956 and Miles Davis' career in 1981.

To date there is no acknowledged Jazz Hall of Fame like the one created for rock 'n' roll. To get a sense of Jewish incidence among jazz greats takes a bit more effort. (The Lincoln Center effort, Ertegun Jazz Hall of Fame, was begun in 2004 and has only twenty-six inductees, including Benny Goodman. Various cities' efforts appear largely parochial and some of the others seem focused on particular aspects of jazz.) For this book, two sources were used.

The first is the Grammys (Exhibit 11h). Jazz has been a Grammy category since 1958 when Count Basie and Ella Fitzgerald won the first two jazz awards. Over time, Grammy inflation, like "grade inflation" in academia, has set in and the numbers of annual awards have grown. By 1976 there were four jazz categories instead of just one. It grew to seven by 1981 before finally settling back to six where it has stayed since 1994. There have been 216 jazz Grammys (counting awards to jazz groups as a single award). Of those, twenty-two have gone to Jews—not counting the five Grammys won by the Manhattan Transfer (with two Jewish members) nor the 2002 Best Jazz Instrumental Album Award to Michael Brecker, Herbie Hancock and Roy Hargrove. (Brecker is Jewish.) At 10.2 percent, Jewish jazz artists have won jazz Grammys five times more often than expected.

Roughly corroborating the approximate 10 percent Jewish representation among jazz greats is the work of a group trying to create a Jazz Hall of Fame. They made their own nominations from 1978 through 2004 and mounted a Web site showing the names and soliciting donations. The list is shown in Exhibit 11i. Perusing it affords a basis for saying their effort was well done, at least in the early years, with most of the greats included. In later years, however, there was more room to question the effort, with seven duplications and some questionable nominees including Lawrence Welk, Perry Como, and Irving Berlin. Nonetheless, the 251 nominees include most of the big names in jazz. Of them, sixteen (6.4 percent) were Jews, roughly two-thirds the percentage of Jewish winners of jazz Grammys. Together the two sources provide a measure of confidence for saying Jews are three to five times more likely to be among jazz greats than their proportion of the U.S. population.

Country[94]

Most Americans realize Jews were not particularly prominent figures among Old West cowboys. They may have operated the local mercantile store, or made Levis and sold them to cowboys and miners, but Jews were not known for "riding the range," or leading the cavalry.

But, to challenge the perception just a bit, Broncho Billy Anderson was one of the first cowboy stars of the silver screen. (He made nearly 400 western "shorts" during the silent era.) His original name was Bill Aronson before being "anglicized." Later, of course, came Lorne Greene, head of the Bonanza Ranch and his Bonanza son, Michael Landon (Hoss was not Jewish!). But after that, it is a bit of a stretch to find many Jewish cowboys or cowboy movie stars.

The same is true for Country music. This is a musical domain where Jews do not figure prominently, at least among performers. Exhibit 11j shows the Country Music Hall of Fame Awards and Exhibit 11k is Country Music Television's lists of the forty top female and forty top male Country artists. The two lists have only one Jewish performer, K. D. Lange, who though only one-fourth Jewish (her grandmother), counts herself a practicing Jew. After that, no one else shown in the two exhibits is known to be a Jew. There is always the possibility that Minnie Pearl was really Minnie Pearlman, or that Fred and Wesley Rose, a father and son inducted into the Hall of Fame, were originally Rosens or Rosenthals (Fred Rose's "Tin Pan Alley" roots give reason to think that possible). Or perhaps Paul Cohen, admitted in 1976, or J.L. Frank, admitted in 1967, have some Jewish heritage, but that is conjecture.

Still, it seems appropriate to acknowledge credit to Steve Goodman, the country/folk entertainer who wrote "The City of New Orleans" among other hits he created before passing away much too young. Kinky Friedman, however, counts himself as "the first full-blooded Jew ever to appear on the Grand Ole Opry Stage" and he has his fans, including non-Jew Willie Nelson, who leads off Friedman's latest album with a "soulful rendition" of Friedman's "Ride 'em Jewboy." And Friedman also tried his hand at politics when he ran for governor of Texas (he lost). To add just a couple more, Ray Benson leads the Grammy-winning "Asleep at the Wheel" with fellow Jew Lucky Oceans (Reuben Gosfield) on the steel guitar. And, finally, there is Mickey Raphael, a superb harmonica player, who has backed up Willie Nelson for more than twenty-five years.

Musical Legends and Lifetime Achievement[95]

The Grammys make Special Merit Awards honoring Lifetime Musical Achievement and Legend Status. Both awards cover the gamut of recorded music and provide an excellent tool for assessing the overall breath of Jewish musical achievement.

There are only fifteen "Legend Award Winners" (Exhibit 111). Of those, two, Billy Joel and Barbra Streisand, are Jewish. The resulting 13 percent figure is mirrored almost exactly by the Grammy Lifetime Achievement Award Winners (also Exhibit 111). Of the 125 awards made to individuals 18 (14 percent) have gone to Jews.

Comedians[96]

In few areas of performing arts are Jews as important as they are in comedy. Books have detailed the chutzpah, tragedy, phobias, stereotypes, and other facets of the unique Jewish approach to humor. For many Jews, humor has been a way to cope with the tragic Jewish experience over much of their existence. Some would go further, suggesting it is a cultural value which has helped make them so successful. From any perspective, Jews are gifted humorists and comedians. From the turn of the twentieth century to today, many of the greatest names are Jews.

In burlesque it was Fanny Brice (discovered by Florenz Ziegfeld), Eddie Cantor, and George Jessel who stayed on top and went on to great success in the era of radio, early films, and later, television. They were joined during the era of radio and films by Jack Benny and Mary Livingstone, George Burns (Gracie was Irish Catholic from San Francisco), Groucho, Harpo, Chico, and Zeppo Marx, the Three Stooges, Joe E. Louis, and Bud Abbott (of Abbott & Costello).

More recently, it is Jon Stewart, Lewis Black, Bill Maher, Al Franken, Ben Stiller, and many more. The table below is not intended to be complete, but simply browsing the list, and its large number of familiar names, provides an indication of the debt we owe the Jewish comedians who have made us laugh.

Joey Adams	Marty Allen	Woody Allen
Morey Amsterdam	Tom Arnold	David Attell
Roseanne Barr	Jack Benny	Milton Berle
Shelly Berman	Sandra Bernhard	Joey Bishop
Lewis Black	Victor Borge	David Brenner
Fanny Brice	Albert Brooks	Mel Brooks
Lenny Bruce	George Burns	Red Buttons
Eddie Cantor	Sid Caesar	Andrew Dice Clay
Myron Cohen	Norman Crosby	"Professor" Irwin Corey
Billy Crystal	Rodney Dangerfield	Bill Dana ("Jose Jiminez")
Larry David	Marty Feldman	Larry Fine
Al Franken	Gilbert Gottfried	Shecky Greene
Charles Grodin	Buddy Hackett	Goldie Hawn
George Jessel	Al Jolson	Danny Kaye
Alan King	Pinky Lee	Tom Lehrer
Wendy Liebman	Jack E. Leonard	Oscar Levant
Jerry Lewis	Bill Maher	Howard Mandel
Marcel Marceau	Marx Brothers	Jackie Mason
Elaine May	Anne Meara	Lorne Michaels
Bette Midler	Larry Miller	Jan Murray
Louis Nye	Gilda Radner	Carl Reiner

Paul Reiser	Don Rickles	Paul Reubens
Ritz Brothers	Joan Rivers	(Peewee Herman)
Mort Sahl	Soupy Sales	Adam Sandler
Jerry Seinfeld	Garry Shandling	Allen Sherman
Phil Silvers	Yakov Smirnoff	Arnold Stang
Ben Stein	Jon Stewart	Ben Stiller
Jerry Stiller	Three Stooges	Rich Voss
Gene Wilder	Ed Wynn	Henny Youngman

At one point, Gentile comedian Steve Allen estimated 80 percent of the country's leading comics were Jews.[97] That figure is on the high side, but it reflects his experience and his perception in the era when he was performing with the very best comedians during the second half of the twentieth century.

"Rate It All" is a Web site that allows consumers to rank comedians based on their preferences. It is subjective, and by its nature tends to give emphasis to more current stars of comedy. Nonetheless, it still provides a snapshot of the importance of Jews in contemporary comedy. The list for August 13, 2003, is shown as Exhibit 11m. It counts eighty-two top-ranked comedians. Of them, 25 (30 percent) are Jews.

Two final points of reference, a few years ago, Gene Rayburn hosted a ninety-minute television tribute to "Television's Greatest Comedians." It featured fourteen acts which included seventeen comedians. They were:

Jack Benny	Steve Allen	Ed Wynn	**Sid Caesar**
Danny Thomas	Jackie Gleason	Lucille Ball	Martin and **Lewis**
Red Skelton	**Burns** and Allen	Bob Hope	**Allen** and Rossi
Milton Berle	**Groucho Marx**		

The seven highlighted Jews among the seventeen comedians are 41 percent of the group. Finally, in 1976, Bob Hope produced *Joys*, a television program spoofing the movie *Jaws*. Hope attempted to pull together fifty (it was actually thirty-nine) top comedians who would be swallowed up by what appeared to be a great white shark. (It was really Johnny Carson in costume.) Of Hope's thirty-nine top comedians, fourteen (36 percent) were Jews.

In the end, Steve Allen notwithstanding, it is safe to say the 30 to 40 percent of America's leading comedians are, or were, Jewish.

Magic[98]

Most of us cannot easily conjure up a list of the great magicians. One or two names perhaps, but not many come to mind. And for this book, no single reliable list of history's great magicians was discovered. Nonetheless, what is surprising is that for most of us, when someone provides a list of magicians, many of the names we recognize are Jewish. There was Harry Houdini and his brother, Theo Hardeen. The early "oriental" magician, Fu Manchu, was really David Bamberg. In the1950s, Dunninger and the Amazing Kreskin were prominent, while in the 1970s and '80s, it was Uri

Geller and David Copperfield. And more recently while we were entertained by Siegfried and Roy, who are not Jewish, we also laughed and were surprised by Teller (of Penn and Teller) who is. But when looking at the eleven names shown below from the "About.com" page for August 19, 2003, listing names for Magic and Illusion, six of the eleven are Jews.

Harry Blackstone, Jr.	Emile Brazeau	**David Blume**
Lance Burton	**David Copperfield**	**Harry Houdini**
Al Flosso	**Theo Hardeen**	**Shari Lewis**
Bob McAllister	Doug Henning	

Jews probably constitute something like half the great magicians of the last 100 years or more.

Chapter 12

Visual Arts and Architecture

"When...Chaim Soutine (1893-1943), the son of a poor Hasidic tailor, painted a portrait...his father flogged him. Chagall's father, who hauled herring barrels for a living, did not go so far when his son began to study with portraitist Yehuda Pen, but he flung the five-rouble fee violently to the ground as a gesture of disapproval."
—*Paul Johnson*, History of the Jews[99]

Charles Murray's book, *Human Accomplishment,*[100] lists the 479 great Western artists from 800 B.C. to A.D. 1950. They are not his selections, but consensus picks drawn from fifteen of the world's foremost art authorities, such as the thirty-four volumes of J. Turner's 1996 *Dictionary of Art, Encyclopædia Britannica,* and thirteen more. Based on their coverage of the individual artists, Murray took the implied rankings and compiled them into a single comprehensive list of the Western artists who have mattered most.

The fact that sixteen Jewish artists are included among the 479 (3.3 percent) seems only mildly interesting since, in the years Jews made the list, Murray calculates they were 2.1 to 2.2 percent of the West's population. Their representation among great artists was thus only slightly higher than their percentage of the relevant population. But, accurate as that observation is, it misses a key point. The Jewish Golden Age is of recent origin. Only in the last 125 years or so have Jews emerged as important figures in visual art. But once they arrived on the scene, they quickly rose to prominence. That story begins in biblical times.

Exodus 20:4 and Deuteronomy 5:8 in the King James Bible include among the Ten Commandments the familiar "Thou shalt not make unto thee any graven image, or any likeness of anything that is in the heaven above or that is in the earth beneath, or that is in the water underneath the earth."[101] More recent versions of the Jewish Bible slightly alter that text, saying, "You shall not make for yourself a sculptured image, any likeness of what is in the heavens above, or on the earth below, or in the waters below the earth."[102] Presumably, the Jewish Bible draws on more recent translations of Hebrew and Greek text than did the 1611 King James Version, and its prohibition of "sculptured" images seems to reduce the implication that the Bible proscribes drawn or painted images. Nonetheless, at different times and places, and at varying levels of intensity, that commandment's language has inhibited Jews from pursuing visual arts.[103]

But it was not always interpreted that way. The Jews who remained in Babylonia after their sixth-century B.C. exile made it into a cultural capital. They stimulated art in Jerusalem and, later, appear to have influenced the Byzantine school of painting.[104] Images of animals appear on carved capitals at Capernaum (Jesus' home in Galilee), as do owls, palms, and urns on early Jewish coins, and lions on early Torah curtains.[105] Visitors to Sepphoris (Zippori), the ancient "capital of the Galilee," can see mosaic images of people, animals, and an illustrated Zodiac in the remains of a fifth-century synagogue. Those images resemble earlier third-century (Dura-Europos) and fourth-century (Hammat Tiberias) synagogue mosaics.[106]

During the long period of Jewish interaction with Muslims, Jews created almost no art worthy of comment. This contrasts with important Jewish accomplishments in philosophy, medicine, science, mathematics, and linguistics over the same years.[107] Only during the Renaissance did Jews return to the arts in a significant way. They painted, sculpted, engraved, and served as purveyors and patrons of the arts, but in all of these, they were only minor figures. Italian artists and architects clearly surpassed them.[108]

But the Renaissance passed and the Inquisition arrived. Jewish involvement in visual art disappeared as Jews were forced into the ghettos. Sephardic populations declined while Ashkenazi populations grew. Many of those Ashkenazis chose to escape hostile Western European countries, moving east into what became the Pale‡ of Poland and Russia. There Orthodox, and later, Hasidic Judaism were the dominant theologies and they encompassed ever more of the world's Jews. Except in Vilnius, Lithuania where art flourished, for a time with sponsorship from a Russian patron, Orthodoxy and Hasidism discouraged Jewish visual artists.[109]

As in other domains, it was the Jewish Emancipation, Enlightenment and the Reform movement which stirred a Jewish golden age in visual art. Moses Mendelssohn (1729–1786), gained prominence in Germany and brought secular education to German Jews. He wrote critical essays on art, and helped open the possibilities for Jews in various secular fields, including art. Nonetheless, while Western European Jewish artists were emerging, the same was not true for Ashkenazis in the Russian/ Polish pale. Except in Vilnius, they were inhibited from sharing in the reawakening to visual art. That point is illustrated in this chapter's introductory quote, which tells of Jewish parental scorn towards the artistic aspirations of their offspring, Chaim Soutine and Marc Chagall.

---

‡ Catherine the Great created the "Pale of Settlement" in 1791. It encompassed much of present-day Poland, Ukraine, Belarus, Latvia, Lithuania, and Moldova (roughly 4 percent of Imperial Russia). Nearly all Russian Jews were consigned to live there in small villages ("shtetls"). Among the laws which discriminated against Jews in the Pale were double taxes and prohibitions against Jewish higher education, land ownership or leasing, and employment in certain trades. It was also the site of horrific pogroms in the late nineteenth century. The Pale lasted until 1917

Camille Pissarro is the first Jewish artist to appear on Murray's list in 1870. Said differently, over the 2,670 years between 800 B.C. and A.D. 1870, the consensus of art experts is that not a single Jewish artist was worthy of being considered "great."

But as the Jews were freed (Emancipation), as they explored Western arts and sciences (Enlightenment) migrated from an Orthodox to Reform mentality and began to interact with non-Jews in significant ways, some of them emerged as highly accomplished artists.

As suggested above, between 1800 and 1849, none of the twenty-two great artists identified by the experts was Jewish. Between 1850 and 1899, one Jew (Pissarro) made the list among the fifty-four great artists of that era. After 1900 Jews quickly rose to prominence. Of the 109 great Western artists named by the experts between 1900 and 1950, fifteen (13.8 percent) are Jewish. This is six times their percentage of the population. Those fifteen Jews include:

Max Beckmann	Laszlo Moholy-Nagy
Marc Chagall	Barnett Newman
Sonia Delaunay-Terk	Antoine Pevsner
Jacob Epstein	Man Ray
Adolph Gottlieb	Mark Rothko
Franz Kline	Ben Shahn
Jacques Lipchitz	Chaim Soutine
Amedeo Modigliani	

The Jews had arrived.

Phaidon's 500 Great Artists

London-based Phaidon first published *The Art Book* in 1994. Demand has been strong enough for it to be republished every year since. It is an excellent collection of representative work by important artists. Phaidon calls it "an A to Z guide of 500 great painters and sculptors from medieval to modern times."

A delightful collection to browse, it is also an excellent catalog of the best in Western art, from Ghiberti and Giotto to Picasso and Oldenburg. with Modigliani and Wyeth thrown in. The scope (500 artists) and a review of their selections encourage confidence that nearly all of the great Western artists since the Renaissance have been included. It also extends Murray's material by including 170 artists who are still alive or who died after 1950—Murray's cutoff date for inclusion.

The Phaidon list (see Exhibit 12a) corroborates Murray's list. While the simple tally includes just thirty-seven Jews among the 500, the real story only emerges when the list is broken down over time. Using the date of death as an index of when the artists were active, the analysis shows that:

Of Phaidon's 500 artists, 247 died before 1900. There were no Jews among them;
The first Jew to appear (and the earliest death among the thirty-seven) was Pissarro, who died in 1903;

Of the eighty-three great artists who died between 1900 and 1949, eight (9.6 percent) were Jews;

Of the 115 who died between 1950 and 2000, seventeen (14.7 percent) were Jews;

Of the fifty-five artists still alive when the volume was published, twelve (21.8 percent) were Jews.

The trend is unmistakable. The Murray and Phaidon data tell the same story. In roughly 125 years, Jews went from virtually no representation among world-class artists to become more than 20 percent—six to ten times more than their numbers would suggest.

Among the more prominent of the thirty-seven Jews in the Phaidon collection are:

Marc Chagall   Jim Dine
Frida Kahlo   Franz Kline
Roy Lichtenstein   Jacques Lipchitz
Man Ray   Amedeo Modigliani
Camille Pissarro   Mark Rothko
George Segal   Cindy Sherman
Chaim Soutine

Chagall   Modigliani   Pissarro

A completely different kind of index arises from "The Altahmazi Contemporary Art Gallery" owned by Khalid Al-Tahmazi, a Bahrain-based painter and an unlikely promoter of Jewish art. As noted on its Web site, in April 2002 Altahmazi did a survey of the world's fifty-three most popular painters, photographers, and sculptors.[110] "Popular" they are, including such names as Thomas Kinkade, Salvador Dali, and Andy Warhol (See Exhibit 12b.). Of the fifty-three, four are Jews including Chagall, Lichtenstein, Rothko, and Modigliani.

Photographers

Two World War II photographs came to symbolize the victory of the Allies over Germany and Japan.

Rosenthal   Khaldei

The first (on the left) is Joe Rosenthal's shot of five Marines raising the flag at Iwo Jima. That image is immortalized by a bronze statue not far from Arlington National Cemetery, symbolizing the determination and team spirit of the Marine Corps. The second photograph (on the right) is Yevgeny Khaldei's picture of a Russian soldier placing a Soviet flag atop the smoldering hulk of the Reichstag. Both photographers were Jews and Khaldei's photo became the iconic shot of the Soviet victory in what the Russians call "The Great Patriotic War" over the Nazis who had killed six million Jews.

According to George Gilbert, an author who has written about the history of photography and the role of Jews in that history, Jewish involvement in photography dates from the fourteenth century. At the time, Levi ben Gershom experimented with a camera obscura "to measure the apparent size of celestial bodies and safely observe an eclipse without looking directly at the sun."[111]

Within two years of the 1839 invention of daguerreotypes by Jacques Daguerre, Hermann Biouw, a Jewish artist, was offering improved plates, faster than those of Daguerre. Biouw went on to become one of the world's first news photographers with his photos of Hamburg's Great Fire. Shortly thereafter, Diaspora Jews opened photography studios in Australia, the United States, Venezuela, Warsaw, Ukraine, and other locations to which they had spread.

Images created by Jewish master photographers are indelible, particularly for anyone born in middle of the twentieth century or with anything more than a passing interest in photography. Stieglitz's 1893 photos of horse-drawn carriages traversing snow-covered Fifth Avenue, Eisenstaedt's August 1945 Times Square shot of a sailor leaning over to kiss a pretty girl on V-J day. The same is true for Steiglitz's shots of the Flatiron Building or his austere shots of Georgia O'Keeffe made around 1920.

Stieglitz   Eisenstaedt   Stieglitz

And, because Jews were involved from the inception of photography, it is no surprise they are disproportionately represented among the great photographers of all time.

Absent a single definitive source for identifying history's great photographers—and to reduce the effect of judgments by a single person—seven sources were pulled together. They include:

About.com's "Directory of Notable Photographers" – which includes sixty-four Jews (28 percent) among its 228 names.

Digital Camera HQ's "Masters of Photography" with seventeen Jews (28 percent) among its sixty-name list.

Fotoart magazine's "Short Biographies of Greatest Photographers," with thirty-four Jews (19 percent) among the 182 biographies.

Harry's Pro Shop list of "Some Great Photographers" with twenty Jews (42 percent) among the forty-eight profiles of "Great Master Photographers."

Photocamera 35's "The Great Photographers" with seven Jews (25 percent) among the twenty-eight names included

Riverman.fsbusiness, a U.K.-based list of "Great Photographers" with four Jews (18 percent) among its twenty-two names.

Here-ye.com, which includes seven Jews (37 percent) among its nineteen master photographers.

Taken together (see Exhibit 12c), the seven sites name 153 Jews (26 percent) out of the 587 great photographers.

Because the Islamic world discourages artistic images, such as art photography, and some other cultures fear pictures, the frame of reference for judging this performance is the West. Though it is a conservative definition (excluding Asia and Africa), it nonetheless provides a context for saying that Jews represent about 25 percent of the great master photographers.

Architects

Rebuilding the World Trade Center site will be one of the highest-profile architectural projects in the early years of the twenty-first century. After the horror of September 11, anything that arises from the ruin will be a national memorial both to the 3,000 innocent lives and to an event that changed the world. And, whatever is built there, it originated as the architectural conception of Daniel Libeskind, a Jewish immigrant from Poland who is now a U.S. citizen.

His selection symbolizes the importance of Jews in architecture, a conclusion amplified by the fact that one of two runners-up, the so called New York team, consisting of Peter Eisenman, Richard Meier, Charles Gwathmey, and Steven Holl included two Jewish master architects (Eisenman and Meier) among its four members. And the four principal partners of Think Design, the other runner-up, are: Shigeru Ban, Frederic Schwartz, Ken Smith, and Rafael Vinoly. Most likely, at least one of the four is Jewish.

The Guggenheim Museum in Bilbao, Spain, and the Getty Center in Los Angeles, both completed within the last ten years, are of similar importance to the World Trade Center site. Both projects were architectural trendsetters and both are important new buildings in their respective settings. Frank Gehry (née Goldberg) was the architect for Bilbao. Richard Meier did the Getty.

Going back to the 1950s, Manhattan's Lever House on Park Avenue (see below) became an early high-rise masterpiece helping to shape office design on one of the world's most prominent streets. Gordon Bunshaft, a Jew then working for Skidmore Owings and Merrill, designed Lever House. Only the Seagram's Building, a little further up Park Avenue and designed by non-Jew Ludwig Mies van der Rohe, could be considered as important in those influential few blocks that defined the twentieth-century high rise.

Libeskind	Gehry	Bunshaft

The shopping mall was the creation of Victor Gruen, an Austrian emigrant Jew, who designed the Northland Mall outside Detroit and Southdale, near Minneapolis. Southdale was the first completely enclosed mall. In 1967 Moshe Safdie designed the grounds for Expo 67, the World's Fair in Montreal. The names of Robert A. M. Stern, Lawrence Halprin, Morris Lapidus, Louis and Albert Kahn, Peter Eisenman and many others have become familiar to anyone with a continuing interest in architecture. All would be considered "masters", a preferred designation among architects.

There are many lists of great or master architects and a goodly number of awards. To set a context for Jewish achievement in architecture, six (shown in Exhibit 12d) were examined.

Logia's "List of Master Architects," where Jews are three (10.4 percent) of the nineteen designees

About.com's "List of Master Architects," where Jews are three (6.8) of the forty-four designees.

Indian architect's "List of Great Architects," with nine Jews (10.3 percent) among the eighty-seven designees.

Great Building's "List of Most Visited Architects," where Jews are four (13.8 percent) of the twenty-nine identified designees.

Pritzker Prize Laureates (1979 to 2002), of which there are three Jews (11.5 percent) among the twenty-six laureates.

Yahoo.com's "List of Master Architects," of which Jews are ten (9.6 percent) of the 104 designees.

Limited as they are to the greats of architecture, these lists provide solid grounds for talking about the representation of Jews among the great architects.

Of the 309 designees, laureates and other winners, thirty-two (ten percent) are Jews. This is a realistic estimate of the percent of great or master architects that are Jewish. Given the world as the context in which great architects practice (non-Jews I.M. Pei, Imhotep, Gaudi, Le Corbusier, Palladino, Christopher Wren, Brunelleschi, Hadrian, Arata Isozaki, Kisho Kurokawa, Kenzo Tange, and Leonardo Da Vinci are among other international figures on the six lists), the achievement is forty-five times what would be expected.

Chapter 13

Hollywood

"The chief difficulty of our home life was that Al and I had been absorbed by American customs, American freedom of thought, and the American way of life. My father still dwelt in the consciousness of the strict, orthodox teachings and customs of the old world."

—Harry Jolson, brother of Al Jolson

The Jazz Singer[112]

Not the first "talking motion picture," *The Jazz Singer* nonetheless revolutionized Hollywood. Its public acclaim and financial success forced the established old-line movie studios to hastily adopt sound, something they had not pursued with any urgency until then. Different techniques had been under development since 1890, before the upstart Warner brothers, Harry, Sam, Jack, and Albert, staked their company on Vitaphone, a new 1920s technology that synchronized sound and film.

The remarkable story richly echoes the life of the Warners and Al Jolson while also depicting the assimilation challenge facing so many recent Jewish immigrants.

Samson Raphaelson, a Jewish student at the University of Illinois, wrote a short story, *Day of Atonement,* after seeing Al Jolson perform in 1917. He recognized the cantor-like styling of Jolson's performance and may have known the perhaps apocryphal story of Jolson's early life. In 1894, when he was eight, Jolson had immigrated to the United States from Lithuania with his parents, Moshe Reuben Yeolson and Naomi Etta Cantor. Legend had it Jolson's father was a cantor who beat his son when Jolson performed popular songs in public and showed no interest in replacing his father as cantor. In short, Jolson was assimilating rather than following his religious and family traditions. Raphaelson's story seemingly paralleled Jolson's life.

138 THE GOLDEN AGE OF JEWISH ACHIEVEMENT

Jolson read *Day of Atonement* when it was published as a 1922 article in *Everybody's Magazine*. He approached Raphaelson and various movie producers hoping to convince them to adapt the story for the screen. The studios were not interested in a "Jewish story," and Raphaelson did not want his story to become the backdrop for a Jolson musical review. The notion appeared dead.

Instead, Raphaelson turned *Atonement* into a stage play. Renamed *The Jazz Singer*, it opened in September 1925 with George Jessel playing, Jack Robin (Jakie Rabinowitz), the lead. In the play, the father (Cantor Rabinowitz) and son (Jack Robin) are ultimately reconciled when Jack gives up his public career to take over as cantor for his dying father. In that version, the assimilation impulse and desire for secular achievement is overcome by a renewed commitment to Judaism. Over the course of its thirty-eight-week Broadway run, Jessel was so moved by the story, and his role playing Jack, that he reaffirmed his commitment to his own Jewish heritage.

Jolson followed a different course. He lived the assimilated lifestyle. His four wives were all Gentiles, and he performed publicly on Yom Kippur for nearly his entire career. He became one of the era's most popular entertainers. Among the genres in which he performed was "Jazz," a term with a somewhat different meaning today. In the "Jazz Age" 1920s, "Jazz" spoke to a free style of up-tempo, lively, and sometimes primitive music pioneered by Southern blacks. Its popularity caused Caucasian entertainers, such as Jolson, to sometimes adopt "blackface" when performing "jazz" before vaudeville audiences. Jolson's raw talent and his energetic and emotional (some would say "soulful") style was unique for the times and he was very popular. An international star, he was the first singer to sell more than ten million records. One *Billboard* archivist reckons Jolson had twenty-three No. 1 hits, over his twenty-nine-year (1911 to 1940) Broadway career. That would place him fourth, behind only Bing Crosby, Paul Whiteman, and Guy Lombardo for total No. 1 hits between 1890 and 1954.

Like many of the early Jewish entrepreneurs who helped found today's movie industry, the Warner brothers started small. Their father, a cobbler who barely made enough to keep the family fed and housed, could not stake them when son, Sam, wanted to buy a projector to show movies in different halls around Youngstown, Ohio. The brothers pooled their capital and eked out a living showing the occasional hot movie. After a time, they stopped moving from town to town and rented a single hall in Niles, Ohio. But before long, they decided they could make more money distributing movies (buying the movies and renting them to others) rather than just showing them. They also began producing their own movies. Both ventures had their ups and downs before the brothers bought the rights to *My Four Years in Germany,* a jingoistic anti-German documentary that sold well in post-World War I America. That movie established them as a small-time success. They set up a studio in Hollywood where Sam and Jack produced movies while Harry and Albert stayed in New York, helping finance the business and taking care of operations on the East Coast.

Times got dicey for the business in the mid-1920s, but Sam convinced his brothers to go after the Vitaphone opportunity. Vitaphone had been developed by Western Electric, then part of Bell Telephone. The Warners negotiated an exclusive license giving them control of the technology. They produced several shorts and a lengthier feature, *Don Juan,* in 1926. All were musicals. They also signed George Jessel to act in their productions and that contract was the reason *The Jazz Singer* ended its Broadway run. In its final weeks, the Warner brothers also bought rights to produce *The Jazz Singer* as a movie and everyone assumed Jessel would be the star.

Jessel's predispositions and family battles between the four Warner brothers would overturn that expectation. Older brothers Harry and Albert were devout Jews, serious about their religion and culture. They saw this movie as an opportunity to promote tolerance and understanding. Sam, and especially Jack, were not devout. Jack, in particular, wanted nothing to do with Judaism. He was constantly at war with Harry, and was as outrageous as Harry was dour and conventional. While all four had agreed to negotiate for the rights to *The Jazz Singer*, Harry and Albert were in New York while Sam and Jack were actually making the movies in Hollywood. Sam and Jack were the ones who would make *The Jazz Singer*, and they did it their way.

They changed the ending. Instead of Jack Robin giving up his public career to replace his father as cantor, they had Jack miss only the first night of his important Broadway debut, replacing his father that one night to sing Kol Nidre on Yom Kippur. The following night Jack returns to Broadway and scores a huge success. Jessel opposed the change. Reportedly, he wanted more money, and supposedly he wanted Harry to sign off on the arrangements. Sam and Jack would have none of it. For them, their version was not about the religious tolerance Harry envisioned, but instead, the tension they had experienced as Jews in their own family life and in America.

Thus, five years after his initial interest, Al Jolson got the opportunity to perform his semi-autobiographical role in the 1927 movie. And the story they told was thus one of assimilation and secular success, rather than reversion to family and religious orthodoxy.

The tragedy was that none of the four Warner brothers was at the October 6, 1927, premier. Sam, who had been ill for months, drove himself through production of *The Jazz Singer*. An abscess flared up and he died of an infection on October 5. He was buried on the eve of Yom Kippur.

If the movie was not a critical success, it was transformative for Hollywood. As Neal Gabler, author of *An Empire of Their Own* points out, "As a historic milestone, *The Jazz Singer* was incontrovertible. It more than revivified the sound movement. By ad-libbing a few lines, Jolson had made it the first feature film with speech and introduced a whole new set of possibilities." By May 1928, every Hollywood studio had licensed sound technology for making movies and in within fifteen months every studio was producing "talkies."

The Warners profited from their movies and from their share of the Vitaphone licensing revenues. By 1930, the company had $230 million in assets, had acquired more than 500 theaters to show its movies and was adding new theaters at the rate of one a day.

That the four brothers, warring among themselves about assimilation and Judaism, would produce a Jewish movie so reflective of their own lives and tensions (and those experienced by many other Jews) is as intriguing as the fact that Jolson, on whom the story was based, would play the lead rather than Jessel. *The Jazz Singer* revolutionized Hollywood and took the Warner brothers from parvenus to wealthy and important establishment figures. Ultimately, after the deaths of his siblings, it would be Jack who would head the studio until 1972. Today, of course, Warner Brothers is a major part of media powerhouse Time Warner.

The Hollywood Studios[113]

While Thomas Edison and the French Lumière brothers (non-Jews all) deserve credit for creating the first practical movie camera and projector, it was Jews that turned the new technology into today's movie industry. This is manifested in the studio logos audiences see at the beginning of nearly every major Hollywood release. More often than not, those logos symbolize eight prominent studios founded or led by Jews through much of their history.

For most, Hollywood's "major" studios include:

Paramount Pictures
Universal Studios
Twentieth Century Fox
Metro Goldwyn Mayer (MGM)
Columbia/TriStar - Sony Pictures Entertainment
Warner Brothers
United Artists (UA) now part of MGM
The Walt Disney Company

Jews created or had a critical role in shaping each of them. The importance of these eight studios is measured in the Oscars they have won. Of eighty-three Academy Awards for Best Picture since 1927, sixty-seven (81 percent) have gone to these eight studios. Further, if the three newer studios of Jewish origin (Miramax, Orion, and Dreamworks SKG) are added, the figure jumps to 94 percent.

Paramount Pictures:[114] Orphaned Hungarian Jew Adolph Zukor immigrated to the U.S. in 1888. He was fifteen and had only the $40 the Orphan's board had advanced him to help him get started. He began doing manual labor while attending night school. Before long, an acquaintance helped him get a job as a furrier's apprentice. Two years later, only nineteen, he was designing, producing and selling his own fur products. By 1892, he had saved enough to set up Zukor's Novelty Fur Company, in Chicago, with a partner. The vagaries of fashion in the fur business resulted in substantial profits and losses over a four-year period. But his reputation and integrity led to an invitation to form a second, very successful partnership with his future father-in-law. By age twenty-seven Zukor was wealthy. In one decision, he correctly forecast that red fox would become popular. That product line netted him a likely profit of $200,000.

By 1903, he could afford to make a speculative investment in the new form of entertainment, penny arcades (an amusement center where each device, such as a game or short peep show, cost a penny) and nickelodeons (small theaters featuring perhaps twenty minutes of short silent movies, and sometimes a brief live act, for five cents). Zukor's investment turned a quick profit and soon, though he did not need the money, he was entranced and embarked on a new career.

Marcus Loew, an American-born son of German and Austrian Jewish immigrants left school when he was nine to support his parents. In 1903, after ups and downs in the garment business and real estate investing, he met Zukor and the two invested in a nickelodeon. Each then built his own chain of nickelodeons, and Loew began combining live performances with short films. He did very well in that format which helped him grow even more quickly.

In 1910, after seeing an hour and a half film of the *Oberammergau Passion Play* (ironically, a notorious anti-Semitic tract), Zukor became convinced only quality feature-length films would convert the faddish, slightly disreputable business of short films and peep shows into a lasting industry. He merged his operation into Loew's on the condition that Loew run the business while Zukor explored the possibilities to produce and distribute feature films.

Zukor's first film distribution deal made him a small fortune. He bought rights to the French movie, *Queen Elizabeth,* starring Sarah Bernhardt, before it became a huge hit. He also formed Famous Players (with the motto, "Famous Players in Famous Plays") recruiting top actors and actresses, such as non-Jew Mary Pickford and one-half Jew Douglas Fairbanks to star in film versions of top theatrical productions including *The Count of Monte Cristo* and *Prisoner of Zenda.* To finance that venture, he sold his Loew's stock.

Born and raised in San Francisco, Jesse Lasky tried several failed ventures before pairing with his sister in a successful vaudeville act. When he tired of traveling on the road, he formed a booking agency. Before long he was producing movies and, like Zukor, licensing proven Broadway hits for some of those movies.

In 1916, Zukor approached Lasky about merging Famous Players and Lasky's studio. Zukor had realized the two studios represented 75 percent of the films distributed by Paramount, then the leading national distributor of movies. Before closing his deal with Lasky, Zukor began buying Paramount stock and talking with other shareholders. He led some of them to believe he might take his business elsewhere. Soon he owned or had allies with enough shares to replace the founding Paramount president, W.W. Hodkinson, a non-Jew from Utah who had picked a Wasatch Mountain peak to serve as the company's logo. Zukor installed his own candidate, Hiram Abrams.

Two weeks later, Famous Players and Lasky merged and three months after that, Famous Player-Lasky was merged into Paramount, with Zukor as president of the combined business.

When theater owners, wary of the power of strong studios and distributors, began pooling their resources to back movie stars in producing their own movies (United Artists), Zukor felt he must respond. Unable to come to an agreement with his former partner, Loew—this despite Zukor's much-loved daughter, Mildred, having married Loew's son—Zukor raised $10 million on Wall Street to build his own Paramount Theater chain. By 1921 Paramount owned 303 first run theaters. That size, and Paramount's ability to produce, distribute, and show films in hundreds of theaters, allowed Paramount to pay huge salaries, such as $1 million per year, to stars like Mary Pickford. Zukor then built a stable of leading actors and actresses, which only much later was eclipsed by the remarkable group assembled by MGM's Louis B. Mayer.

Zukor stayed on as Paramount's chairman, and later chairman emeritus, for an astonishing fifty-nine years (until 1976).

Over the years, many of Hollywood's leading Jewish figures worked at Paramount. In his 20s, Barney Balaban had introduced sloped floors, plush seats, balconies and air cooling to movie theaters. In 1936 he sold his theaters to Paramount, in the process becoming president, reporting to Zukor. Only later, in the 1940s, did the Justice Department intervene, forcing the division of movie production, distribution, and theater ownership into separate companies with different ownership. Nonetheless, that early strategic combination is the reason even today that one can still find Paramount theaters "downtown" in many American cities.

In 1966 Charles Bluhdorn's Gulf+Western, bought Paramount and with that, Robert Evans (née Shapera) became studio head, reporting to a still active Zukor. Evans led the company to great success with such classics as *The Godfather*. In the late '70s, it was Michael Eisner (reporting to Barry Diller) who headed the studio before Eisner left to head up Disney in 1984. Over the years, Stanley Jaffe, Jeffrey Katzenberg, Brandon Tartikoff, and Sherry Lansing were among the many prominent Jews who played senior roles at Paramount.

In 2005 Paramount's parent, Viacom, acquired David Geffen, Jeffrey Katzenberg and Steven Spielberg's Dreamworks (see more on that merger, below). And today, as a part of Sumner Redstone's Viacom, Paramount continues with Jewish control.

Universal Pictures:[115] Bavarian Jew Carl Laemmle promised his mother he would not immigrate to the United States so long as she was alive. When she died unexpectedly in 1883, sixteen year old Laemmle was released from his pledge. After his arrival, he moved from job to job (errand boy, office boy, farm hand, bookkeeper, and clerk) and place to place (New York, Chicago, and South Dakota) before settling in, first as bookkeeper, and later manager of the Oshkosh, Wisconsin, branch of a clothing chain. Over a twelve-year span from 1894 until 1906, he proved a good marketer for the store and a solid citizen. In 1905 he was selected as one of Oshkosh's fifteen outstanding citizens. The next year, after a quarrel with his wife's uncle—who was his boss—he was sacked.

Nearly forty years old, and with only $2,500 in savings, he was out of a job. He was scouting for something new when he "dropped into" one of Chicago's first nickelodeons. He was mesmerized. It made him laugh and he saw how the working class and new immigrants could enjoy this inexpensive entertainment. In February 1906, he put up about $1,000 of his savings to open his own Chicago nickelodeon. Within weeks he was taking in $180 a day. Two months later, he opened a second nickelodeon.

When he ran into difficulty with a film distributor who reneged on a deal, he began to buy movies and rent them to others after they had a "first run" in his own theaters. The Laemmle Film Service grew quickly. He opened offices in Minneapolis, Omaha, Salt Lake, Portland, Memphis, Des Moines, Winnipeg, and Toronto. By 1909, only three years after opening his first nickelodeon, he was the largest film distributor in the Midwest.

In 1908 Thomas Alva Edison and two others, who collectively held the dominant U.S. patents for cameras and projectors, created a trust. It was intended to monopolize all such equipment used by U.S. movie producers and theaters. The trust demanded a license fee for shooting movies or showing them using any of the patented equipment.

Laemmle led the charge against the WASP-dominated Trust. He told everyone he would get movies from Europe and produce his own films. His moves were very popular with independent theater owners. Soon the trust responded, filing nearly 300 lawsuits against Laemmle and his companies, costing them $300,000. Despite the cost, Laemmle's strategy worked and soon the independents had half the market.

In 1909 Laemmle began producing his own films, "presumably" using non-patented cameras. He named the company, Independent Motion Picture Company (IMP), using as its logo, an "imp" figure shown challenging the trust. Laemmle saw a need to upgrade the quality and length of films playing in his theaters, and his first film was a sixteen-minute version of Longfellow's *Hiawatha*.

After a first (1912) attempt at an alliance of independent producers and distributors was done in by squabbling among alliance members, he and five other producers formed what he named Universal Film Manufacturing Company. Following some in-fighting among its shareholders, Laemmle took control in 1915, and in March of that year, opened the gates of Universal's new 230-acre complex in North Hollywood. It was the world's first self-contained community devoted solely to filmmaking.

Universal's bread and butter through most of Laemmle's reign was low-budget, but popular "B" movies and movie serials, combined with occasional hits, such as Lon Chaney's 1923 *Hunchback of Notre Dame* and his 1925 *Phantom of the Opera* But in 1926, Laemmle became ill while shipboard en route to London. He nearly died of a ruptured appendix. Sensing his mortality and very much the doting father, he let his seventeen- year-old-son, Carl Laemmle Jr. write scripts and begin to produce movies. About the same time, Laemmle recruited Walter Lantz, creator of Woody Woodpecker, and director Erich von Stroheim.

To no one's surprise, on his twenty-first birthday in 1929, Junior took over the studio. Seeking to upgrade Universal's image, he began producing expensive films such as *All Quiet on the Western Front, Frankenstein* (1931), *Dracula* (1931) and *The Mummy (1932)*. Those higher costs collided with the Great Depression and by 1936, Universal, and the sixty-nine-year-old Laemmle Sr., were on the ropes. Overextended, mostly by Junior's spending, Laemmle lost control to the creditors. Father and son were out.

The studio languished for years, under a succession of different owners. Ultimately Decca Records acquired control in 1951. But it was in 1962 that Universal's fortunes improved. Music Corporation of America (MCA) bought Decca. MCA had been formed in 1924 by Jules Stein and William R. Goodheart. By 1962 MCA was headed by Lew Wasserman, who had joined the company when he was twenty-two (in 1936). Ten years later, Wasserman was president.

Universal prospered under Wasserman, producing television programs in addition to major films. Among its hits were *To Kill a Mockingbird, The Sting,* Steven Spielberg's *Jaws, The Deer Hunter,* and many more.

In 1991 Japan's Matsushita acquired MCA. Four years later, after some very public disagreements with Wasserman, they sold the bulk of it to Edgar Bronfman Jr.'s Seagram which later merged it into the French conglomerate Vivendi.

Subsequent problems at Vivendi led to Universal's sale to GE, where it now resides.

Twentieth Century Fox:[116] William Fox's (Fuchs) father was irresponsible. After bringing his wife and infant son to the United States from Tolcsva, Hungary, in 1879, he showed little ability to provide for them. When William was eight, he began working to support the family and by the time he was eleven, he dropped out of school, lied about his age, and took a foreman's job at a clothing firm. Fox's determination and workaholic behavior may have arisen from resentment of his father.

By the time he was twenty, he had saved enough to start his own business preparing bolts of cloth for garment companies. In two years he made $50,000. He dabbled in vaudeville and by 1903 (he was twenty-four), he and a friend acquired a penny arcade. On the floor above the arcade, they also installed a theater. Within six months, the partner had sold his interests to Fox, and in the first year, Fox made $40,000— on a $10,000 investment. Three years later, Fox bought a rundown theater in the Williamsburg section of Brooklyn. He fixed it up, used neighborhood pride as a marketing pitch for his theater (his upgrade and the publicity he generated gave the community a sense of self-esteem.) and soon made $100,000.

Like Laemmle, early on Fox decided that rather than simply renting movies, he should buy them and rent them to others after a first run with his audiences. He too challenged the Edison trust. Fox trapped them into contradictory offers and threats to buy out, or destroy, his company. He took that information to the U.S. attorney general, who went after the trust. Finally, like Laemmle, Fox concluded he had to begin producing his own movies to survive. In 1915 he started Fox Films.

Over the years, Fox built an assemblage of 1,100 Fox theaters to show his films. Some of the larger and more luxurious show places survive to this day. He introduced organ music to silent films and in 1925-26, purchased rights to a sound system developed by three Germans and another system for putting sound-on-film (rather than on disc, as the Warner Brothers Vitaphone system did). He named it Fox Movietone and ultimately that sound-on-film system and a counterpart developed by RCA Photophone won out as the prevailing sound technology still in use today, albeit in much refined form.

Through all of this, Fox became ever more imperious. He was patriarch to everyone in his family and generally intimidated them all. If Laemmle was loved for his kindness, Fox was feared and disliked. He was so demanding that both his daughters were forced to move to his estate after they were married and had given birth. The husbands were excluded, and one of them died of a heart attack shortly thereafter. Ultimately, Fox adopted his two grandsons. He was a powerhouse, but one with few friends.

His undoing came when he attempted to take over MGM and came up against Louis B. Mayer. Fox had cut a deal with MGM chairman Nicholas Schenck, but failed to reckon that CEO Mayer would fight. Fight Mayer did, taking his case to friends in the Hoover administration. An automobile accident which disabled Fox, prospective anti-trust action, the stock market crash and Depression, the cost of converting his 1,100 theaters to sound, and a lengthy dispute over sound system patents, all ended up in a seven-year legal struggle in which Fox lost out. The fight, the economy, and the costs he incurred over the seven years bankrupted him. He then made matters much worse by bribing his bankruptcy judge. In the end, he lost the studio to its creditors and he spent six months in jail. The creditors merged Fox Films into

Twentieth Century Pictures. And while Fox tried to get it all back, in the end those efforts were thwarted.

When he died in 1952, having built one of the industry's largest companies, pioneering its dominant sound system, and making more than 500 films, not one former industry colleague attended his funeral.

Following the 1936 Twentieth Century Fox merger, the studio was independent until Marvin Davis bought and controlled it from 1981 to 1985. In 1985 Davis sold it to non-Jew Rupert Murdoch's News Corporation, which still controls it and which has expanded the franchise to include Fox News and the Fox Television Network.

Metro Goldwyn Mayer:[118] July 4,1885, is the day Louis B. Mayer adopted as his birth date. He explained he did not know the real date, though recent biographers have nailed it down as July 12, 1884. Nonetheless, his dissembling choice of America's Independence Day marvelously captures the man.

Jacob and Sarah Mayer immigrated to St. John, New Brunswick, Canada, in 1888 when Louis was four. There was no love lost between father and son. A scrap-metal dealer, Jacob made Louis dive into the Bay of Fundy to retrieve metal from sunken ships. Louis brought the scraps to the surface and Jacob sold them. Louis formed a company, only to have his father put his own name on it. By the time Louis was a teenager, he was supervising two hundred men in salvaging operations. But Louis cherished his mother, Sarah. From her death in October, 1913 until his own in 1957, Louis kept her portrait over his bed.

With Sarah's blessing, Louis left St. John for Boston in January 1904. His daughter said he chose Boston because he had fallen in love with Margaret Shenberg after having seen only her picture. After overcoming the objections of her father (a cantor), Louis married Margaret before setting out for an entrepreneurial scrap-metal venture in New York. That venture failed in the 1907 recession. Returning to Boston, Mayer found a job in a theater. Its proprietor (also a film distributor) was impressed and helped Mayer find and lease a rundown 600-seat burlesque hall in Haverhill, Massachusetts Mayer fixed it up, renamed it, and began running family fare, including the combination of vaudeville performances and short movies. The New Orpheum was the only theater in working-class Haverhill and Mayer's formula was a huge hit. Soon he added a 1,600 seat theater and two smaller ones. He was Haverhill's impresario.

In 1913, he began distributing films as well as showing them and shortly thereafter, he joined in the creation of Metro Pictures. Its original purpose was to finance the production of feature films. Mayer was secretary and president of the New England branch.

D.W. Griffith's *Birth of a Nation* premiered on March 1, 1915. Startlingly racist and controversial by today's standards, Mayer, nonetheless, realized it would be a smash, and is said to have pawned his wife's wedding ring to help raise the $50,000 needed to buy distribution rights for New England. He made a fortune, by some accounts as much as $500,000 (in 1915 dollars), distributing *Birth of a Nation*.

Now wealthy, he began to produce his own fare. After some discord with the head of Metro, he briefly partnered with Ukrainian Jewish immigrant Lewis J. Selznick in 1917 before patching things up and going back to Metro. Shortly thereafter, the success of his Anita Stewart (not Jewish) movie, *Virtuous Wives,* led to his life-changing decision. He was moving to Hollywood.

When Mayer arrived in Hollywood, more than 80 percent of the world's movies were made there by roughly seventy production companies. They were in Los Angeles because its weather allowed year-round filming. Mayer began producing films in his own romantic, "good boy (or girl) wins out in the end" style. He was producing quality movies that emphasized moral behavior. Mayer and his films were well regarded, even if they were not yet first rank.

By 1919 Marcus Loew was first rank. His chain of theaters, his movie distribution companies, and his interest in production had led to his acquisition of Metro Pictures. But unhappy with its films and management, he was advised to add the Goldwyn Studios, named for its founders, Samuel Goldfish (brother-in-law of Jesse Lasky, and Paramount's president until Zukor fired him), and Edgar Selwyn. Impressed with Goldwyn's facilities, Loew nonetheless thought the studio, like Metro, lacked good management. Metro's attorney, J. Robert Rubin, knew Mayer from Metro's early days and was a partner in Mayer's new film studio. He recommended Mayer to Loew and introduced them at Mayer's studio in 1923. Loew was impressed. He bought both Goldwyn and Mayer, and hired Louis Mayer, in April 1924 to head the combined studios. Two years later it was all named Metro Goldwyn Mayer. Louis B. Mayer had arrived.

Or so he thought. Loew died in September 1927 and his Number 2, Nick Schenck, assumed control. But Schenck was insecure in the role, lacking the stock or power base to ensure he could keep the job. He cut a lucrative deal with William Fox to sell MGM, but purposely kept Mayer in the dark. As noted above in the Fox vignette, Mayer would have none of it. He fought tooth and nail and he won. MGM stayed independent. Schenck remained chairman, but it was Louis B. Mayer's studio, not Schenck's, at least for the next twenty years or so.

Mayer built MGM into the most powerful studio in Hollywood over the '30s, '40s and early '50s. His early partner was "boy wonder" Irving Thalberg. Son of German Jewish immigrants, Thalberg had been spotted while still in his teens by Carl Laemmle. By the time he was twenty, Laemmle had appointed Thalberg head of Universal's Hollywood Studio. Three years later, in early 1923, Thalberg left Universal to join Mayer as his second in command and close partner. Frail, with heart problems he knew would shorten his life, Thalberg was the quiet genius to Mayer's boisterous paternalism.

Thalberg's premature death from a heart attack at age thirty-seven in 1936, lost for Mayer a surrogate son, albeit one who in their later years disagreed strongly over who had contributed most to MGM's greatness. Thalberg's death also resulted in MGM's migration from his literary impulse in filmmaking to Mayer's more romantic Americana-styled pictures. After Thalberg's death, Mayer's son-in-law, David Selznick, was recruited as one of MGM's lead producers along with a so-called college of cardinals, a group of producers assembled around Mayer who created roughly fifty films a year. But whether it was Mayer or Thalberg, literary movies or romance, Selznick or the college of cardinals, MGM was simply the strongest force in Hollywood for nearly thirty years.

Mayer took Zukor's notion of a star system and trumped it. Even seventy years later, the names are impressive: Rudolph Valentino, Clark Gable, Spencer Tracy,

Katherine Hepburn, Mickey Rooney, Judy Garland, Lana Turner, Fred Astaire, Gene Kelly, Greer Garson, Ava Gardner, Norma Shearer, Robert Young, Greta Garbo, Jean Harlow, and more. They testify to MGM's ability to find and develop talent.

In films, MGM's list of huge hits is enormous. MGM had at least one Academy Award nominee for best picture in every year between 1924 and 1954. Among its hits were *Gone With the Wind, Ben Hur, Grand Hotel, The Good Earth, David Copperfield, Mutiny on the Bounty,* and other big films. Among MGM's popular series were: *Topper, The Thin Man, Andy Hardy, Our Gang, Lassie, and Dr. Kildare.* Its musicals were lavish and popular. *The Wizard of Oz* released in 1939, began a series of major hits, generally every other year from 1939 to 1948 including *Meet Me in St. Louis,* and *Easter Parade.* After 1949, as television began to pull audiences away from theaters, MGM hit musicals began to arrive once or twice each year including *Annie Get Your Gun, Show Boat, An American in Paris, Singin' in the Rain,* and others. Less well known was the studios' embrace of animation. Foremost in its stable of animators were William Hanna and Joseph Barbera, creators of Tom and Jerry.

As television took away ever more moviegoers, and as Mayer aged, MGM began losing its luster. Dore Schary was recruited in 1948 to be Mayer's Number 2. Schary was oriented toward "message" pictures, clearly different from Mayer's romantic storytelling. By 1951 MGM's sagging fortunes and Mayer's dissatisfaction with Schary led to a confrontation. Nick Schenck, still chairman, made his choice. Mayer was out and Schary was in charge. Six years later, after further losses, so too were Schary and Schenck. That same year (1957), Mayer died.

MGM drifted. In 1967 it was bought by Edgar Bronfman, who two years later sold it to non-Jew Kirk Kerkorian. The days of substantial Jewish ownership or control of MGM were over.

Kerkorian scaled it back, sold off valuable real estate and much of MGM's historical memorabilia. In 1981, Kerkorian bought United Artists (UA) and merged it into MGM. (See below.)

In 1985, after a failed attempt to take over CBS, Ted Turner purchased MGM/UA. Less than three months later, however, his bankers balked and he sold most of the assets back to Kerkorian. Turner retained much of UA's television programming and the MGM film library (all of MGM's pre-1986 films plus the pre-1948 Warner Brothers collection, the RKO collection and much of United Artists' backlist. They can all now be seen on Turner Classic Movies).

Then, in 1990, Italian financier Giancarlo Parretti acquired France's Pathe Freres movie production and MGM/UA. He soon defaulted on his loans leaving French bank, Credit Lyonnais, in control. After continuing losses in the mid-1990s the bank gave up. Kerkorian was the only bidder. For a third time he owned MGM. In 1997, Kerkorian added Orion Pictures (see below), the Samuel Goldwyn Company, and Motion Picture Corporation of America to the MGM stable. It represented a large film library as well as rights to the James Bond series.

Finally, in 2004, Time Warner offered to buy MGM. It soon became clear, however, that a syndicate of Sony Corporation, Comcast, the leveraged buyout firm Texas Pacific Group (now TPG Capital LP), and Providence Partners would pay more and they did. That syndicate now owns MGM though Kerkorian retains rights to the name and logo for use with his hotel properties.

Columbia Pictures:[118] Bella Cohn immigrated from the Pale and her husband, Joseph, from Germany. They had four sons, Max, Jack, Harry, and Nathan. All three siblings ultimately worked for Harry, but none enjoyed it. He thought them all weak. In An Empire of Their Own, Neal Gabler's classic tale of the Hollywood Jews, he describes Harry as "epitomizing the profane, vulgar, cruel, rapacious, philandering mogul." He was all that, but he was more.

Joseph Cohn tailored police uniforms and was a presence in the family, but it was Bella, his mother, that Harry adored. Fiercely independent, even when Harry was rich and wanted her to move to California, Bella stayed in New York and in her simple apartment.

Born in 1891, Harry dropped out of school when he was fourteen. After a brief time singing in a Broadway play, he took odd jobs including shipping clerk and trolley conductor. He also worked as a "song plugger" trying to convince leading singers to perform a songwriter's work. But through all that time, he was also a pool and bowling hustler, a scammer.

After six years at an ad agency, his brother Jack, also a school dropout, took a job in 1909 processing film for Carl Laemmle's IMP movie studio. Over the next few years as, Laemmle beat the Edison Trust and reorganized IMP into Universal Studios, Jack became an important part of that company. In 1913 a colleague came up with the idea for the movie *Traffic in White Souls* (about the white slave trade). The $5,000 budget was expensive and Universal said "No!" Jack then conspired with four colleagues who put up the cash and "borrowed" Universal facilities to make the movie. Though he was fired when he got caught, internal politics led to Universal paying Jack and his colleagues $25,000 for what turned out to be a huge 1913 hit.

Picking up on Jack's moviemaking, Harry conceived of the idea of using movies to plug songs. When the song plugging venture proved successful, he was hired by Universal and sent to their Hollywood studio.

In 1919–20, Jack Cohn, Joe Brandt—an attorney who had been Laemmle's executive secretary—and Harry Cohn formed C.B.C. movie studio (later embarrassingly referred to as Corn, Beef, and Cabbage). Jack and Joe Brandt headed up the business from New York, with Brandt serving as president, while Harry made movies on a shoestring in what was aptly named, Hollywood's Poverty Row. It was a group of motley buildings rented to equally motley movie studios and staff.

C.B.C. survived, mostly on Harry's hustle and his tough-guy style in lining up people and production. By 1924 Brandt had been bought out, Harry was in charge and he had changed the name to Columbia Pictures—in part to upgrade its image.

The turning point was a fluke. In 1928, Frank Capra, whose name came first on the alphabetical list of director prospects, got hired when Harry was too busy on another task to dispute Capra's generous contract demands. In his own way, Capra, a Sicilian immigrant and not Jewish, was as tough as Cohn. He made seven movies in his first year at Columbia. And if Cohn wanted respect from the Hollywood elite, Capra wanted an Oscar. Over time, Capra's films won recognition for his talent. In 1931 Capra's *Dirigible* opened in Grauman's Chinese Theater in Hollywood and his *Bitter Tea of General Yen* opened in New York's Radio City Music Hall. But, it was *It Happened One Night* in 1934 that put Columbia in the first rank. It won five

Oscars—for Best Picture, Best Director, Best Actor (Clark Gable), Best Actress (Claudette Colbert), and Best Writing.

From that point through *Mr. Deeds Goes to Town, You Can't Take It With You, Mr. Smith Goes to Washington,* and others, Capra and Columbia triumphed. Cohn, always jealous that Capra was getting more recognition than he was, nonetheless knew Capra was important, and when he challenged Capra, Cohn was smart enough to back down, buying time until they finally parted company in 1939.

By then, Columbia was established. It survived the loss of Capra with lead stars such as Rita Hayworth, Glen Ford, Jack Lemmon, William Holden, the Three Stooges, Lucille Ball, Judy Holliday, and Kim Novak. And without Capra, Cohn nonetheless had the judgment and skill to recruit other first-rate directors including Howard Hawks, George Cukor, Otto Preminger, Orson Welles, and others. And while MGM's fortunes sagged in the 1950s, Cohn, still in charge of Columbia, produced such hits as *From Here to Eternity, On the Waterfront,* and *The Bridge on the River Kwai.*

Cohn showed occasional touches of kindness. He was fiercely protective of his black chauffeur, Henry Martin, when Martin's livelihood was threatened and later, when Martin was ill.

In all, during his thirty-eight-year era at Columbia, with and without Capra, Cohn earned forty-five Academy Awards for films he produced. Nonetheless, when he was buried in 1958, Red Skelton, noting the huge crowd, spoke for many when he said, "Well, it only proves what they always say—give the public something they want to see, and they'll come out for it." Later, as if in rebuke, one of Cohn's two sons later reportedly converted to Roman Catholicism.

After Cohn's death, the studio languished for a time before Allen & Company's Herbert Allen (of Jewish heritage, but he does not consider himself a Jew) bought control, eventually selling it, in 1982, to Coca-Cola for a sizable gain. In 1989 Coke got out of the movie business and sold Columbia to Sony, which, after a difficult period of financial losses under Peter Guber and Jon Peters between1989 and 1995, remains its parent at this writing.

Warner Brothers:[119] As covered above, Harry, Albert, Samuel, and Jack Warner were Midwestern entrepreneurs who began by showing short silent movies using a projector they hauled from venue to venue around Youngstown, Ohio. They ended up having built one of Hollywood's great studios.

Following Sam's death in 1927, the studio was mostly a creature of Harry and Jack Warner, who loathed each other. Harry, the eldest and a devout Jew, operated from New York while Jack, irreverent and obnoxious, ran the studio in Hollywood. But their success, following *The Jazz Singer,* fueled Warner to generate hundreds of successful movies to run in their 360 U.S. and 400 foreign theaters. After Harry's retirement in 1956, it was all Jack's show. He headed Warner Brothers until selling his controlling shares in 1967.

In 1969 Warner was acquired by Steven J. Ross' (née Steven Jay Rechnitz) Kinney National Company. Three years later, it was spun off as Warner Communications with Ross as chairman and CEO. Ross controlled it for the next seventeen years until he merged it with Time to form Time Warner Communications in January 1989. Ross headed the combined business until his death in 1992, when Gerald Levin took over. Today Warner Brothers remains part of Time Warner.

United Artists:[120] In 1919 Douglas Fairbanks (one-half Jewish) and non-Jews Mary Pickford, Charlie Chaplin, D.W. Griffith, and their attorney, William McAdoo, formed United Artists (UA). They were alarmed by the emergence of the major studios and wanted to maintain their independence in creating and distributing their own work. Initially each star committed to producing five pictures a year, but by the time they were under way, movies were longer and cost more. None could afford to produce, let alone star in, five features a year. And they needed professional management.

They selected Hiram Abrams as their first managing director and when he stepped down in 1924, they replaced him with Joseph Schenck, brother of Nick Schenck, who became chairman of Metro Goldwyn Mayer. Joseph Schenck led United Artists until 1933 and was then replaced briefly by Al Lichtman. After Lichtman, the studio languished. Between 1919 and 1955, United Artists picked up only one Best Picture Oscar—for *Rebecca* in 1940. By the late 1940s the studio was moribund.

In 1951, Arthur Krim and Robert Benjamin offered to take over management of the studio for five years. If they could turn it around, they were to have an option to acquire it, which they did. Perhaps presaging Miramax (see below), they began with no physical studio at all, but they backed independents such as Sam Spiegel and non-Jew John Ford. Everything started to click. Between 1952 and 1967, United Artists, under Krim and Benjamin, won six Best Picture Oscars for: *Marty, Around the World in 80 Days, The Apartment, West Side Story, Tom Jones,* and *In the Heat of the Night.* United Artists became the dominant studio.

Krim and Benjamin sold out to non-Jew Kirk Kerkorian's Transamerica in 1967. For a while, the momentum (and involvement of Krim, Benjamin, and then CEO, Eric Pleskow) carried United Artists forward with hits like *Fiddler on the Roof,* and Best Picture awards for *Midnight Cowboy, One Flew Over the Cuckoo's Nest, Rocky,* and *Annie Hall.* But ultimately, the insurance company culture clashed with the Hollywood culture. Krim, Benjamin, and Pleskow left in 1978, and with the exception of *Rain Man* in 1988, United never won another Best Picture Oscar. Almost immediately after their departure, United Artists created *Heaven's Gate,* one of the biggest and most expensive bombs in Hollywood history. That artistic and financial disaster caused Transamerica to jettison United Artists.

By that point Kirk Kerkorian had left Transamerica, was head of MGM, and he once more acquired United Artists. But Kerkorian's financial talents did not extend to creating box-office success. Together with MGM, United Artists was sold to the partnership of Sony, Comcast, TPG, and Providence Partners in 2005, and in November 2006, it was announced that Scientologist Tom Cruise, and his partner, Paula Wagner, would take a small stake in United Artists and run the studio. It lasted till Lions for Lambs failed at the box office and Valkyrie became, at least for a time, an expensive mess. Wagner resigned in mid 2008. Only time will tell if worthy successors to Krim, Benjamin, and Pleskow can be found.

Disney Company:[121] Walt Disney was not Jewish. His father was Irish-Canadian and his mother German-American. But Disney was tagged as anti-Semitic. The charge is largely undermined in Neal Gabler's 2006 biography of Disney. Gabler, who also authored An *Empire of Their Own*, attributes most of the charge to Jews, unhappy with Disney's enormous antipathy to union organizers who organized his employees over his paternalistic wishes, and to Disney's strong early 1950s anti-Communist positions, when a disproportionate number of left-leaning industry figures were Jewish. Gabler notes Disney spent a good part of his life among Jews. When an employee who had changed his name from Teitelbaum to Tytle, to hide his ethnicity, told Disney he was half-Jewish, Walt replied that if he were all Jewish it would be better. Disney contributed to Jewish charities and was named Man of the Year by the Beverly Hills Lodge of B'nai Brith.

Walt founded his studio in 1928 and controlled it until his death thirty-eight years later in 1966. He was a remarkable, driven entrepreneur. His creation of Mickey Mouse after losing rights to his earlier creation, Oswald the Lucky Rabbit, to Universal was a classic of "pulling a mouse out of his hat." Mickey Mouse and *Silly Symphonies* sustained the Disney's animation studios through much of the Depression. Walt's determination to produce a full-length feature animation of humans (and dwarfs) overcame the vigorous objections of his wife, brother-partner Roy, and many others who forecast it would destroy the company. When *Snow White* opened in December 1937, it received a standing ovation. It went on to be the most successful movie of 1938, winning Walt one full-size and seven miniature Oscars.

Disney went on to produce hundreds of animated, conventional live action, and nature films. His studio was nominated for sixty-four Oscars and won twenty-six. He made a remarkably successful transition to television with his Disneyland and later Mickey Mouse Club TV programs. And he was equally driven in his pursuit of theme parks—over the objections of nearly everyone around him. In his own unique way, the Gentile Disney was a peer with the Jews who built Hollywood.

Following Disney's death in 1966, the company languished with the occasional hit, and its popular theme parks. But in 1984, Walt's nephew, Roy Disney, recruited Michael Eisner from Paramount to become CEO. Eisner recruited Jeffrey Katzenberg and Frank Wells (not Jewish) to form the triumvirate running the company.

Successful in turning around ABC's prime-time schedule, and then helping Paramount go from last to first among the major movie studios in the '80s, Eisner was eager to take on the Disney challenge after being passed over to become Paramount's CEO when Barry Diller left.

Eisner's notorious ambition, his intimidating, sometime vindictive style, and his lust for financial success (nearly $1 billion in stock and other compensation) has tinged his reputation, particularly since his September 2005 resignation and the publication of James B. Stewart's *Disney War,* which detailed many of the troubles at Disney including fights with Katzenberg, the botched recruitment of Michael Ovitz, and failed negotiations to acquire Pixar.

Still, Eisner's achievements are simply undeniable. A movie studio with a strong suit in animation, which also produced popular television programming and operated two large theme parks, was completely transformed by Eisner into one of the world's strongest media and entertainment companies. Under Eisner, the movie franchise was expanded with Touchstone, and Buena Vista studios, as well as the acquisition of Miramax. Theme parks were added outside the United States. Animated films, such as the *Lion King* became the basis for major Broadway and Las Vegas shows, and the Disney Cruise Line was created as well as eight Disney Vacation Club resorts. Disney Publishing Worldwide became the world's largest publisher of children's books and magazines, and with the acquisition of Capital Cities/ABC, the Walt Disney Company took over the ABC television network, ESPN, and expanded that franchise to include the Disney Channel, A&E Television Networks, Lifetime Entertainment Services, and others.

The Disney Company revenues grew from $1.7 billion when Eisner took over to $25.4 billion when he left. Profits grew from $291 million to $4.08 billion, and the market value of Disney went from $3 billion to $60 billion. Eisner doubtless felt he earned what he was paid.

Following Eisner's resignation, Robert Iger (also Jewish) took over. He resurrected and completed the Pixar acquisition, and he has gotten good marks for handling his major shareholders, the board, and his direct reports. Time will tell if he enhances the legacy created by Disney and Eisner.

The historical role of Jews heading Hollywood's major studios continues at this writing. Quoting from Joel Stein's December 19, 2008 *Los Angeles Times* story:

> "When the studio chiefs took out a full-page ad in the *Los Angeles Times* a few weeks ago...(it) was signed by News Corp. President Peter Chernin (Jewish), Paramount Pictures Chairman Brad Grey (Jewish), Walt Disney Co. Chief Executive Robert Iger (Jewish), Sony Pictures Chairman Michael Lynton (surprise, Dutch Jew), Warner Bros. Chairman Barry Meyer (Jewish), CBS Corp. Chief Executive Leslie Moonves (so Jewish his great uncle was the first prime minister of Israel), MGM Chairman Harry Sloan (Jewish), and NBC Universal Chief Executive Jeff Zucker (mega-Jewish). If either of the Weinstein brothers had signed, this group would have not only the power to shut down all film production but to form a minyan...."

Other Studios of Note

Miramax:[122] Miriam and Max Weinstein share honors for having a New York film studio and distribution company named to honor them by their sons, Harvey and Robert Weinstein, who founded Miramax in 1979. It quickly became be known for championing "independent" films such as *Sex, Lies and Videotape, The Crying Game,* and *Pulp Fiction.* Before long, the Weinsteins were so successful with their succession of late '80s and '90s hits, including *The Piano, Good Will Hunting,* and *Gangs of New York,* that Miramax was seen as more "mainstream" than independent. Then, over a seven year stretch between 1996 and 2002, their films *Chicago* (1996), *Shakespeare in Love* (1998), and *The English Patient* (2002), picked up three Oscars for Best Picture. In 2008 they followed that up with *No Country for Old Men.*

Tough and often controversial, the brothers came under fire for their aggressive style. When criticized for the slow release and editing of some foreign films, Harvey responded, "I'm cutting for the shit to work. All my life I served one master: the film. I love movies." When asked about bullying by the Weinsteins, one observer responded, "People just ignore it. They're good at what they do."

The brothers sold Miramax to Disney in 1993 and stayed with it until late 2005 when they left to form the Weinstein Company, an independent film producer.

Dreamworks SKG:[123] Steven Spielberg, Jeffrey Katzenberg, and David Geffen formed Dreamworks SKG in 1994, shortly after Katzenberg's very public falling out with Michael Eisner. The original idea was to develop, produce, and distribute films, music, interactive games, and television programming by drawing on the respective talents of the three prominent founders.

Over time, Dreamworks' music and interactive games fell by the wayside, while animated and live-action feature films became successful. Between 1999 and 2001, Dreamworks earned three consecutive Best Picture Oscars for *American Beauty, Gladiator,* and *A Beautiful Mind.* (As such, Miramax and Dreamworks won six of the seven Best Picture Oscars awarded between 1996 and 2002.) Animated features such as *Shrek 1, 2* and *3* were huge hits catapulting Dreamworks over Disney to compete directly with Pixar as the world's leading producer of animated films.

Despite great critical and artistic acclaim, financial success was more difficult. The animation studio was spun off as Dreamworks Animation SKG in 2004 and roughly a year later, Paramount bought the live action feature studio for $1.53 billion. This came after GE's NBC Universal had dropped the price of their earlier offer to buy the company, and then failed to meet the Viacom/Paramount price. For Paramount, the Dreamworks' library and films in the pipeline solved a number of problems including the small number of movies in production at Paramount. The Dreamworks' movies released after the merger returned Paramount to first place among major studios.

After a number of public disputes between Steven Spielberg and Paramount, Dreamworks and Paramount agreed to an amicable split in late 2008. As part of that arrangement, the Indian film group, Reliance ADA committed $1.2 billion to finance new projects created by Spielberg.

Orion Picture:[124] When Arthur Krim, Richard Benjamin, and Eric Pleskow left United Artists in 1978, they approached Warner Brothers. From that arose Orion Pictures, a joint venture of the three executives and Warner. Orion quickly moved to the first rank of Hollywood studios. In the eight years between 1984 and 1991, Orion won four Best Picture Oscars for *Amadeus, Platoon, Dancing With Wolves,* and *The Silence of the Lambs.*

By 1990 Krim's Gentile friend, John Kluge, and Kluge's Metromedia company were Orion's majority owner. With advancing age, Krim, (then eighty) and his partners were past their prime. The studio went through financial troubles before its assets were sold to Kerkorian's MGM.

Independent Film Producers

While most of the prominent Jewish producers mentioned previously, such as

Harry Cohn, Jack Warner, and Steven Spielberg, are generally identified with a single major studio, others have operated independent of those studios or have moved from studio to studio over the years. Among them are those listed below.

Joel and Ethan Coen:[125] Rena Coen was an art historian at St. Cloud State University. Edward, an observant Jew, was an economics professor at the University of Minnesota. Together, they raised sons, Joel and Ethan, in a suburb of Minneapolis. The Midwestern academic setting hardly suggests the immense early interest Joel and Ethan took in film (shooting their first movie before they were teenagers), nor their wide-ranging talent for writing, producing, editing, and directing some of Hollywood's most unique films of the last thirty years.

In every movie, their creativity, deep knowledge of films, and breadth of moviemaking skill are clear to critics and knowledgeable moviegoers. They have also proven willing to take huge artistic and commercial risks, resulting in occasional pans such as Wikipedia's critique, "a pastiche too far," for *The Hudsucker Proxy,* or Emanuel Levy's "...the Coens pull the viewers away from the actors to showcase their own virtuosity."

Nonetheless, from comedic to violent, and with startling combinations of both, their twelve films such as *O Brother Where Art Thou, No Country for Old Men,* and *Fargo* represent an important body of work. They have earned numerous Sundance, Cannes, and Independent Spirit film awards, plus nine Academy Awards nominations, just for their own work as directors, writers, and editors, plus many more nominations for their films. They won for Best Picture, Best Director, Best Adapted Screenplay, and Best Supporting Actor with *No Country for Old Men* and Best Screenplay for *Fargo*—which also earned a Best Actress Award for Joel's wife, Frances McDormand, who played the lead. The Coens are simply two of Hollywood's most creative and influential filmmakers.

Stanley Kubrick:[126] In July 1941, Stanley Kubrick's parents (Dr. Jacques Kubrick and Gertrude Perveler Kubrick) gave him a camera for his thirteenth birthday. He was fascinated. Named official high school photographer, he sold photos to *Look* magazine, and *Look* hired him while he was still in high school. Photography led him to film and, by 1953, when he was 25, he had made three short documentaries and a feature film *(Fear and Desire)*. He followed them with *Killer's Kiss,* in 1954, *The Killing* in 1956—which brought critical acclaim and access to MGM, and *Paths of Glory* in 1956—a critical and commercial success.

Kubrick demanded control. He and Brando fought over directorial control of *One-Eyed-Jacks.* Kubrick lost. The same thing happened with Kirk Douglas, the producer-star of *Spartacus,* but that time Kubrick won. The recognition Kubrick received for *Spartacus* positioned him as a major director in the eyes of the Hollywood elite. Nonetheless, his 1962 move to England was, in part, a protest of the studio system. He called it "film by fiat, film by frenzy." Though he liked the United States, he remained in England, rarely even traveling the forty minutes it took to get from his home to London.

In England, he began with Vladimir Nabokov's controversial *Lolita.* Despite the topic—pedophilia—it was a box-office success. He followed *Lolita* with the absurd black humor of *Dr. Strangelove*. Never intentionally commercial, Kubrick made enough from *Lolita* and *Strangelove* to be financially independent and their success provided access to funding for his subsequent films. By the time *Clockwork Orange* was released, his control was so complete he could demand that Warner Brothers pull the film from distribution in England after someone there copied the film's violence. Kubrick went on to make *Barry Lyndon, The Shining, Full Metal Jacket,* and *Eyes Wide Shut.*

Kubrick was simply a "filmmaker," an auteur whose talent encompassed nearly every aspect of moviemaking. Vladimir Nabokov observed that despite his screenwriting credit for *Lolita*, the bulk (80 percent) of the screenplay was Kubrick's. Sir Arthur C. Clarke said the same thing about *2001: A Space Odyssey*. Unhappy with Russell Metty's camera work in making *Spartacus*, Kubrick told him to "sit there and do nothing," Kubrick's cinematography won the Oscar for Metty. Kubrick was producer, screenwriter, special effects creator, cinematographer, editor, and director for most of his films. And for some of them, he also chose the score. Equally broad was his range of subject matter: from comic and political, to violent and horrific, from picaresque and lyrical, to protest and erotic. He was intentionally obscure, skeptical rather than romantic, and nearly always controversial. His movies often met with initial viewer complacency and critical disdain, but, weeks, months, or years later, nearly every film was critically acclaimed, popular, and seen as path breaking.

Between 1953's *Fear and Desire,* and 1999's *Eyes Wide Shut*—when he died just four days after screening the final cut—Kubrick made only thirteen films. Of them, ten were nominated for major British and American honors including twenty-seven Academy Award nominations and nine Oscars. But that understates Kubrick's impact. Of 100 Greatest American Films identified by the American Film Institute, three are Kubrick's *(2001: A Space Odyssey, Dr. Strangelove,* and *A Clockwork Orange)*. Only Sam Spiegel, with four, has more (see below). Steven Spielberg, Frank Capra, Billy Wilder, Stanley Kramer, and Samuel Goldwyn have two each. The Coen brothers and David Selznick have one.

David O. Selznick:[127] Son of Lewis J. Selznick, a Ukrainian Jewish silent film producer, David O. Selznick saw his father deplete the family fortune. It forced David to start out as an MGM script reader. He moved to Paramount as an associate director, to RKO as vice president production and back to MGM, helped by having earlier (1936) formed his own independent production company, Selznick International. He was only thirty-four and had already been recognized for his productions of *David Copperfield* and *Anna Karenina* as part of the studio system. Within three years on his own, he produced *Gone With the Wind* and hired Alfred Hitchcock (not Jewish). Later, Selznick produced *Spellbound, Since You Went Away, A Star Is Born,* and *A Tale of Two Cities,* all of which won Oscar nominations. He received the Irving Thalberg Award and Best Picture Oscars for *Gone With the Wind* and *Spellbound.*

Sam Spiegel:[128] Spiegel first came to the United States in 1927. He arrived as a bogus Austrian diplomat and wrote bad checks before heading (or being shipped) back to Europe. In 1933, he fled the Nazis and, in 1939, re-entered the United States. His checkered history forced him to adopt the pseudonym S. P. Eagle, which he kept until

1954, when his production of *On the Waterfront* was released. He was brilliant, charming, and roguish—his biographer, Natasha Fraser-Cavassoni, thought him a manipulative exaggerator, but also "the last of the great showmen." His talent was perhaps best reflected in three Oscars won in eight years for: *Bridge on the River Kwai, Lawrence of Arabia,* and *On the Waterfront.* He also received the Irving Thalberg Award.

Mike Todd:[129] He was born Abe (Avram) Hirsch Goldbogen on or about June 22, 1907, to a Bloomington, Minnesota, rabbi and his wife. His own son, Mike Jr., said his father was kicked out of school in the sixth grade for running a crap game and made and lost $1 million in a Chicago construction business by the time he was 19.

Todd became a Broadway producer, making and losing substantial sums on roughly thirty Broadway shows. Hollywood lured him and his promotional skills to invest in and develop the Cinerama wide-screen process. He and Mike Jr. helped promote Cinerama, but he was bought out when his bankruptcy from gambling losses became an embarrassment impeding Cinerama's public offering. His chagrin at being forced out of Cinerama led him to develop Todd-AO, a wide-screen sixty-five millimeter single-lens camera and projection system to compete with the three camera 35-millimeter system used by Cinerama. Todd-AO and its offspring, Dimension 150, were used by Hollywood studios until 1992.

Always promotional and always the risk taker, Todd bankrolled, produced, and at times directed *Around the World in 80 Days.* Notwithstanding his fractious relationship with Hollywood's most powerful, he won the 1956 Oscar for Best Picture. That same year, he met and wooed Elizabeth Taylor giving her a twenty-nine-and-a half carat diamond ring. "Thirty Carats," he observed, "would have been vulgar." A tragic plane crash en route to New York to accept the Friars' Club, Showman of the Year Award, ended his life at the pinnacle of his career.

Rob Reiner:[130] Meathead, the role for which he will forever be known, is the son of comedian and producer, Carl Reiner. Rob Reiner was born in 1947 and appeared on TV at age five when his father was featured on "This Is Your Life," When Rob was fifteen, he appeared in the first of his four episodes on the *Alfred Hitchcock Hour.* He was a veteran with more than sixteen television appearances before taking the role of Michael Stivic (Meathead) in *All in the Family.* That success led to appearances in more than fifty television programs and thirty movies. He has written nine movies or television series, composed for *Spinal Tap,* directed eleven movies and produced seventeen. Among his films are *This Is Spinal Tap, When Harry Met Sally, A Few Good Men, Misery,* and *Stand By Me.*

Movie Directors[131]

Studios and producers conceive films, identify and recruit actors, actresses and other key personnel, raise money to finance and promote their movies, get them distributed, and do the "bookkeeping," but directors are the ones who make ("make or break") the film. The movie is the director's artistic conception, and he or she guides the actors and crew to fulfill that conception. The importance of the director is symbolized in the Annual Academy Awards presentations with Best Director, Best Actress, Best Actor, and Best Film typically among the final awards made, letting the suspense build till the climax at the end of the evening. Directorial talent distinguishes a film masterpiece from an also ran. If there are hundreds of famous stars in Hollywood, there are far fewer great directors.

One approach to determining great directors is Oscar winners. Typically five directors are nominated each year, and members of the Academy (representing those most active in the industry) vote for their pick. The Best Directors since 1927-28 are listed in Exhibit 13a. Of the eighty-three winners, thirty-one (37 percent) are Jews including such greats as Steven Spielberg, Mike Nichols, George Cukor, Billy Wilder, Milos Forman, and Joel and Ethan Coen.

Another look at great directors comes from Reel.com and Filmsite.org (Exhibit 13b). Both identify their choices for history's great directors. Unlike the Oscars, in which some directors have received awards in more than one year (such as Spielberg and Wilder), duplicate names do not appear in these lists. Reel.com breaks their "Greatest Directors of the 20th Century" into two groups: the Classic Directors (25), and the Contemporary Directors (25). They also provide names for the five Great Silent Era Directors. Combining the lists of fifty five great directors yields fifteen Jews (five on the Classic list, nine on the Contemporary list and one from the Silent Era). Jews are thus 27 percent of Reel.com's "Great Directors. They include:

Stanley Kubrick	Woody Allen	Roman Polanski
Steven Spielberg	Joel & Ethan Coen	David Cronenberg
Oliver Stone	Milos Forman	Mike Leigh
Billy Wilder	François Truffaut	Fritz Lang
Ernst Lubitsch	George Cukor	Sergei Eisenstein

Filmsite.org is a seven-year old Web site that takes a similar approach to identifying its seventy-five Greatest Directors. While there is overlap with the Reel.com selections (such as Woody Allen and Billy Wilder), Filmsite.org adds Cecil B. De Mille, Stanley Kramer, Joseph L. Mankiewicz, Mike Nichols, Arthur Penn, and Otto Preminger. Others from Reel.com, such as François Truffaut, and Milos Forman do not make the Filmsite.org cut. Twenty-seven (36 percent) of Filmsite.org's "75 Greatest Directors" are Jewish.

A final ranking is the American Film Institute's "100 Greatest American Movies" (Exhibit 13c). One Web site, www.adherenets.com, lists all 100 films, names each director, and the religious affiliation of each director. Of those 100 "great" films, 39 percent were directed by Jews. Eliminating duplicates, where a director has more than one movie on the list, yields sixty-five individual directors of whom twenty-six (40 percent) are Jews.

Considering all the expert opinions and the Academy selections, clearly, a third or more of Hollywood's greatest directors have been Jews.

Movie Stars[132]

The *Hollywood Reporter* has periodically provided its fix on the "Star Power" of the industry's top 1,000 actors and actresses. The publication polled 114 industry executives at major studios and independent companies, financiers and various other industry players around the world. When the results were tallied, the stars were ranked in terms of "bankability," meaning each star's drawing power at the box office, which in turn meant the ease with which they command the best roles, attract large audiences, and bring in the financing needed to put an expensive production together.

The most recent (2002) Survey put Tom Cruise, Tom Hanks, and Julia Roberts (Gentiles all) on top of the list, each with the maximum score of 100. After that, 997 stars received ratings from 98.68 (No. 4 Mel Gibson) to 1.55 (No. 1,000 Erinn Bartlett). Focusing on just the top 500 (to make the analysis and presentation a bit easier), one finds seventy-five Jews (not counting Whoopi Goldberg who sometimes says she is a Jew, Steven Seagal who has some Jewish heritage but counts himself Buddhist, or Courtney Love, who defies any attempt to understand whether or not she is part Jewish). Excluding those three, Jews are 15 percent of the 500 top stars, roughly seven times what we would expect. Among them are many familiar names including Woody Allen, Billy Crystal, Michael Douglas, Barbra Streisand, Winona Ryder, Ben Stiller, James Caan, Richard Dreyfus, Jeff Goldblum, Bette Midler, Dustin Hoffman, and fifty-three others. The list of the 500 top stars, with the seventy-five Jews highlighted, is provided as Exhibit 13d.

One interesting facet of this list is its number of half-Jews and one-quarter Jews. That is, Jews with a mother or father of Jewish origin, but not both—or a grandparent. Among the half-Jews are Harrison Ford, Paul Newman, Michael Douglas, Adam Sandler, Gwyneth Paltrow, Goldie Hawn, Kevin Kline, Matthew Broderick and his wife, Sarah Jessica Parker. These are but nine of an estimated twenty-six who are half Jewish and four who are one-quarter Jewish among "Star Power's" top 500 stars.

By its nature, "Star Power" focuses on current stars—those who can draw an audience today. It misses great actors of years past. One way to add that perspective is to consider the American Film Institute's list of the "50 Greatest American Screen Legends," which includes twenty-five males and twenty-five females. (Exhibit 13e). That list yields "six" Jews—12 percent of the Great Legends including Kirk Douglas, the Marx Brothers, Edward G. Robinson, Marilyn Monroe, Elizabeth Taylor, and Lauren Bacall.

In this case the "six" is in quotation marks for several reasons. First, one could argue the Marx Brothers deserve to be counted as more than one since there were four of them. Second, two of the six were converts to Judaism (Monroe and Taylor), and last, we do not count Cary Grant, who, with Courtney Love, deserves a retrospective award for confusing the whole world as to any Jewish lineage. At different times he (and she) said entirely different things on this topic to close friends and acquaintances alike. It is easier to not count him.

Among other old-timers who were significant Jewish actors and actresses but not included on the two lists are Jeff Chandler, Danny Kaye, Walter Matthau, Shelley Winters, Jerry Lewis, Peter Lorre, Lee J. Cobb, Peter Falk, Douglas Fairbanks, John Garfield, and Judy Holliday.

Lifetime Achievements and Screen Legends[133]

Our final look at film is the American Film Institute list of Lifetime Award Winners, also included in Exhibit 13e. This list honors those whose talent has "in a fundamental way advanced the film art and been acknowledged by scholars, critics, professional peers and the general public and whose work has stood the test of time," Only one award has been given each year since 1973, and the list includes directors, producers, and movie stars, some dating back to the silent era. It is a distinguished bunch. Of the thirty-five recipients, eight (23 percent) are Jews.

If one wishes to be conservative and remove Harrison Ford as non-practicing and half Jewish, the numbers drop to seven and 20 percent. In either case, the conclusion remains the same, Jews have achieved and contributed in disproportionate measure to Hollywood's success.

Chapter 14

Radio and Television

"He was not an inventor, nor was he a scientist. But he was a man of astounding vision who was able to see with remarkable clarity the possibilities of harnessing the electron."
—New York Times *obituary of David Sarnoff*
December 13, 1971

David Sarnoff[134]

By today's standards, Sarnoff's youth was insufferable. Left by his father, his mother handed him off to a distant relative to teach him Hebrew, Aramaic and the Talmud somewhere in the vast expanses of the Russian Pale. Next, he was relocated to live among the polyglot, teeming masses of New York's lower East Side, where he had to work to support his family while learning English and attending school. He was not yet ten. Sarnoff simply never had a childhood. Today such trauma would be unthinkable. Counseling would be called for. But for Sarnoff, it helped spur the kind of dogged determination he demonstrated throughout his career as the leader behind two of the twentieth century's most influential media, radio and television.

Born February 27, 1891, in Uzlian, a Russian shtetl near Minsk, David Sarnoff was five when his father, Abraham, left to pursue opportunities in America. That same year, his mother, Leah, parceled him out to a granduncle to study the Talmud in hopes he would become a rabbi. Four years later, with his mother and younger brothers, he immigrated to America in the cheapest steerage available. It took them through Latvia, England, and Canada en route to New York, where months later, they would rejoin their ailing father.

160

Abraham's worsening tuberculosis would kill him ten years later, but in 1900, it meant David had to go to work immediately to help the family survive. Nine years old, he began selling Yiddish newspapers before and after school (and choir practice). He attended both day and night school and grabbed discarded English language newspapers to teach himself English. Ever the go-getter, by 1904, Sarnoff had saved $200, bought his own newspaper stand, and put his siblings to work with him.

His formal education ended in 1906 when his father's deteriorating health meant he had to work full-time. He wanted a job at a newspaper, but went through the wrong door and ended up as a messenger for an undersea cable company. Three months later, denied time off to sing in his choir for Rosh Hashanah and Yom Kippur, he either quit or was fired (sources vary). But by then he knew something about telegraphy. The possibility of becoming a telegraph operator drew him to the American Marconi Wireless Company, where he started as an office boy.

Only eleven years earlier, wireless communication had been invented by the non-Jew Guglielmo Marconi. Within four years, the British had formed the European parent, Marconi Company, and its American subsidiary, which Sarnoff joined in 1906. At inception, wireless was only seen as a technology for instant ship-to shore and overland Morse code telegraphy. Seven years passed before Lee De Forest, an American Gentile, came up with a way to use wireless to transmit voice as well as Morse code. With that new wrinkle, the potential for wireless exploded, but like many new technologies it took time for that potential to be understood.

In today's terms, it would be akin to a teenage immigrant starting in a promising Silicon Valley start-up just as the personal computer, Internet, cell phone and high-speed "broadband" communications arrived on the scene. The visionary Sarnoff recognized the opportunities.

As an office boy, Sarnoff was Marconi's personal assistant whenever the founder was in New York. Sarnoff ingratiated himself to Marconi, studied the technology, took night school and correspondence courses, and within a year was a "junior telegraph operator." The next year he was promoted to "full operator" and by 1910, the nineteen-year-old Sarnoff was the company's youngest station manager.

On April 12, 1912, working as a remote telegraph operator atop New York's John Wanamaker Department store, he was one of the few who heard and responded to the faint wireless signals coming from the sinking Titanic. Over the next seventy-two hours he received, and passed along to the anxious crowds outside, information from the ships trying to save passengers. His superiors were impressed.

He was made an equipment inspector and instructor, and by 1913 he was American Marconi's chief inspector and its assistant chief engineer. At age twenty-two, he was traveling to ships and trains to see wireless equipment in action, visiting all of Marconi's U.S. facilities, those of inventors, such as Lee De Forest, and those of Marconi's competitors.

His perceptiveness and vision are laid out in a 1916 memo to his boss, Marconi vice president and non-Jew Edward J. Nally. Sarnoff proposed that the company develop and market a "radio music box."

> "I have in mind a plan of development which would make radio a 'household utility' in the same way as a piano or phonograph. The idea is to bring music into the house

by wireless…(it) need not be limited to music (but could also be) a wireless class-room….Events of national importance can be simultaneously announced and received. Baseball scores transmitted….Farmers and others living at a distance could be greatly benefited…they could enjoy concerts, lectures, recitals, etc."

Sarnoff was not the first to conceive of radio. Since 1906 pioneers had been experimenting with De Forest's technology, but no one saw its potential as clearly as Sarnoff did, and no one was as committed to creating radio broadcasting as a commercial endeavor.

Nally did not pick up on Sarnoff's proposal. The company was satisfied selling wireless equipment for naval communications and equipment used to transmit signals from one person to another. "Broadcasting" signals to a large audience, as Sarnoff was suggesting, would be a diversion. But Nally was impressed. By 1917, twenty-six-year-old Sarnoff was supervising 725 employees in 582 Marconi installations. His task was so important that he was denied a U.S. Navy commission to fight in World War I. They needed him where he was.

At war's end, the U.S. government decided wireless technology was too vital for American security to be dependent on foreign ownership of American Marconi. Instead, General Electric (GE), United Fruit Company, Westinghouse, and later American Telephone and Telegraph, were encouraged to form a 1919 consortium to buy out the British interests, pool their patents and know-how and create what they renamed Radio Corporation of America (RCA). A GE vice president served as RCA's first chairman and Nally, by now also working at GE, became its part-time president. As Nally's right-hand man, twenty-eight-year-old Sarnoff was effectively RCA's chief operating officer.

A lengthy 1920 Sarnoff memo laid out his proposal for radio once more, and this time in greater detail. A copy went to GE, where money was set aside to build a prototype. Cross licenses were created between RCA, GE, AT&T (for Lee De Forest's inventions), and the inventor of a simple radio tuner. Around the same time, hobbyists began using crystal sets, and Westinghouse began broadcasting in Pittsburgh. In early 1921, thirty-year-old Sarnoff was formally named RCA's general manager and the next year, its vice president.

That same year, Sarnoff showed his promotional flair with a live July 21 broadcast of the Jack Dempsey-Georges Carpentier heavyweight championship fight. An estimated 300,000 people tuned in. His vision was proven as radio came on the scene. It was an immense success. Twenty-eight radio stations in 1921 became 576 stations the next year. Industry sales (GE, Westinghouse, RCA, and others) went from $60 million in 1922 to $358 million by 1924. RCA's $11 million of 1922 radio revenues climbed to $50 million by 1924 (all in 1922-24 dollars).Soon the pursuit of radio profits by the individual companies around RCA (GE, Westinghouse, and AT&T) found them competing with one another. Finally, in 1926, AT&T chose to sell its broadcasting network to RCA. Sarnoff combined it with RCA's, in the process creating the National Broadcasting Company (NBC), with two networks (NBC Red and NBC Blue), as a wholly owned subsidiary of RCA. Because of subsequent FCC anti-trust concerns, NBC had to sell NBC Blue and today it is known as the American Broadcasting Company (ABC).

Meanwhile, in the years 1910-19, Sarnoff had seen the potential for television.

By 1923 he was promoting it just as he earlier promoted radio. In five years, he had an experimental NBC television station up and operating. In one memo, he referred to television as "the technical name for seeing instead of hearing by radio." He anticipated viewers seeing events around the globe as they occurred, and he saw a linkage with movies. He said:

> "transmission and reception of motion pictures by radio...would result in current events or interesting dramatic presentations being literally broadcast...and, therefore, received in individual homes or auditorium...on a screen with much the appearance of present-day motion pictures."

His clairvoyance drove Sarnoff to pursue a broad palette of opportunities. In the 1920s and '30s, as RCA was producing and selling radio equipment, licensing its technology, and creating and broadcasting programs. He also:

created the national system of affiliated radio stations we now think of as a "network," first within RCA and later as part of NBC;
developed television;
acquired The Victor Talking Machine Company, (a leading phonograph company);
formed a union with Joseph Kennedy to create Radio-Keith-Orpheum (RKO) to produce movies and operate movie theaters;
acquired two large music publishers;
started a talent agency.

Sarnoff created a 1920s vision of today's entertainment conglomerate. He saw the "synergies" and turned them into reality. Today's Viacom, Time Warner, and Disney have nothing on 1920s RCA under David Sarnoff. Later, in the 1960s he was to add publishing to the mix with the acquisition of Random House, and he foresaw the development of videotape and the VCR.

The interconnections between RCA, GE, Westinghouse, and AT&T were not only troublesome at a competitive level, they also led to governmental antitrust intervention based on the exclusive patent-sharing relationships between the companies. The new Federal Communications Commission was beginning to investigate as well. It all worked to Sarnoff's benefit. AT&T stepped away when RCA bought out its broadcasting operation. Since then, Sarnoff had first been named acting president in 1928 and president in 1930. Two years later, GE and Westinghouse divested their RCA interests leaving forty-one year old Sarnoff on his own and in complete charge.

Though the Depression slowed down RCA, radio continued to grow as Sarnoff began to aggressively pursue the technology of television. He had already set up the experimental NBC studio, and in 1929 he underwrote the efforts of Vladimir Zworykin, the immigrant Russian inventor of the first TV camera. RCA also began to license or acquire patents from other inventors, and by 1939, Sarnoff was able to demonstrate RCA's first television at the New York World's Fair. At that event, Sarnoff said, "Now we add sight to sound....It is...the birth in this country of a new art, so important in its implications that it is bound to affect all society." By 1941 NBC launched commercial broadcasting from its station, WNBT, in New York.

World War II intervened and RCA focused on the war effort. It devoted the bulk of its resources to the Allies' needs for radio, sonar and other communications gear. Meanwhile, Sarnoff was recruited as a communications consultant to General Dwight Eisenhower. By war's end, he was a brigadier general, a title he coveted for the rest of his life.

The war over, Sarnoff was back developing commercial television. In 1946 RCA manufactured 10,000 television sets. By 1954 the number had grown to a million a year.

Along the way, Sarnoff fought and won a tragic victory over an old friend who had created FM radio. FM offered better-quality reception than AM, and non-Jew Edwin Armstrong was its inventor. Unfortunately, Sarnoff and RCA saw Armstrong's FM as a competitor both for its own AM and for the new FM technology RCA had developed to compete. Sarnoff succeeded in getting the FCC to change the licensable FM frequencies, in the process making Armstrong's equipment obsolete. In addition Sarnoff and RCA tied up Armstrong's commercial offerings in the courts until his patents had nearly run out. In the end Armstrong conceded by licensing his patents for little gain, but he later committed suicide. This time, Sarnoff's determination had tragic consequences.

He waged a similar war with non-Jew Philo Farnsworth, a major figure in the development of television. Farnsworth felt RCA and Zworykin had taken advantage of him. He won in the courts, but lost in the market. When he finally licensed his patents, they had nearly run out and he never earned the millions he thought he deserved. When Sarnoff was called "ruthless" for his aggressive style, he responded, "Competition brings out the best in products and the worst in men."

Sarnoff's next challenge was color. CBS was developing a unique technology for color television. By contrast RCA's was based on existing technology. Both companies needed FCC approval for their standards, but CBS got theirs first. Despite FCC delays in approving RCA's standards, Sarnoff had an advantage. His color sets and broadcasting technology were compatible with existing black-and-white sets. Fortune intervened in the form of the Korean War, which slowed the development and marketing of CBS' color equipment and televisions. Meanwhile, the numbers of less expensive black-and-white televisions grew as more and more Americans bought sets. By 1953, the presence of twenty million black-and-white televisions in consumer homes around the country led the FCC to conclude it could not afford to make them obsolete. It approved RCA's standards and, with that, Sarnoff had won. While CBS could also sell its color televisions, RCA had an unbeatable advantage, and within a year, CBS withdrew from the market.

Before he died, on December 12, 1971, Sarnoff was able to view digital photographs taken by RCA satellites, downloaded electronically to ground stations where they were reproduced and distributed.

A great visionary of immense personal drive, Sarnoff was the single most important figure behind the creation and development of radio and television. This was true in every aspect of both industries. In broadcasting equipment, broadcast networks, radio and television programming, and in-home consumer radio and television sets, Sarnoff set the path and the pace. No one since has replaced his force in shaping telecommunications. Twice on the cover of Time magazine they also recognized him as one of the "100 Most Important People of the Twentieth Century."

Radio and Broadcast Television[135]

Today radio and television are commonplace. We take them for granted as if they had been with us forever. In historic terms, they are relatively young. Radio did not arrive until the 1920s, and television, conceived shortly after radio, was not available to significant audiences until the late 1940s and early 1950s. Before them, only the telephone (1870s) and telegraph (1840s) allowed instant communications over long distances, and both were "point to point," enabling only one person to be in touch with one other person.

It was the application of "voice" to Marconi's wireless invention that allowed simultaneous communications to anyone who "tuned in" within range of the "broadcast." With that, everything changed. As suggested by his biography (above), the man who saw this most clearly was David Sarnoff. He was foremost among a number of Jews who largely developed the technologies, products, and organizations that made today's radio and television available to the public. In that sense, Jews were as disproportionately involved in radio and television as they were in motion pictures.

Two exhibits make this case. Exhibit 14a shows the inductees into the Radio Hall of Fame. Of its 108 members, at least nineteen (18 percent) are Jews. Representation is even higher in the Television Hall of Fame (Exhibit 14b), which includes thirty-nine Jews among its 108 members (36 percent.) In fact their importance in the early era of television is further demonstrated in the five Jews counted among the first seven inductees.

One way of looking at the growth of radio and television involves the creation of the major networks. They were the vehicle that made radio and television into national, and later international, media. Sarnoff realized that organizing local stations into a system of affiliates (a "network") allowed programming and advertising to benefit from economies of scale and the simultaneous transmission of programs to "coast-to-coast" audiences.

Over the first few years, there were only three significant networks: NBC Red, NBC Blue, and what we now call CBS. Later, in 1934, the Mutual Broadcasting System was created, followed by Dumont (1946) and the Liberty Broadcasting System (1946). In 1943, NBC was forced to sell NBC Blue and it became today's ABC Of those six, three (Mutual, Dumont, and Liberty) soon died out. Only NBC, CBS and ABC remained until the 1980s when cable and satellite facilitated the creation of CNN, Fox, Warner, and others. Of the three original networks, all three had Jewish roots.

National Broadcasting Corporation (NBC) As described above, NBC was David Sarnoff's creation. He was the first to see the benefits from establishing a national network. After the sale of NBC Blue, NBC (the "Red" designation disappeared), was a strong national radio network which carried its prominence over into television. For forty years, NBC was one of America's "big three" networks. And in one of those interesting ironies of Wall Street, NBC has recently returned to its roots. It is a subsidiary of GE, RCA's most important shareholder when RCA created NBC.

Columbia Broadcasting System (CBS): Arthur Judson, a leading talent agent, was miffed that David Sarnoff had failed to include any of his stars among the NBC roster. In 1927, with help from the Levy brothers of Philadelphia, Judson founded the Columbia Phonograph Broadcasting System. Within a year of its first broadcast, the company was nearly bankrupt with only sixteen affiliate radio stations. Judson sold out to Jerome Loucheim, Ike, and Leon Levy (who was engaged to William Paley's sister). Paley was the son of Ukrainian Jewish immigrants and a second-generation cigar-maker.

Twenty-seven years old, Paley discovered that radio advertising helped him sell cigars, and he was sufficiently well off that in January 1929, he bought majority control of the broadcaster for $400,000 and renamed it the Columbia Broadcasting System. Through the 1930s, Paley expanded CBS. He pioneered the offer of free programming to affiliate stations in exchange for an option to sell advertising, which he sold in huge chunks. He had an unerring eye for talent, signing up Bing Crosby, Kate Smith, Lucille Ball, and Ed Sullivan. He also showed his survival skills by cutting a Depression-era deal with Adolph Zukor of Paramount. It helped keep Columbia afloat through the tough times.

From 1955 on, Paley's talent and instincts for popular programming such as *I Love Lucy* and *The Ed Sullivan Show* made CBS the ratings leader for twenty-one years.

Paley also pioneered first-rate news coverage, encouraging the reporting of non-Jews Edward R. Murrow and historian William Shire during World War II. They, in turn, fathered a generation of excellent successors including Eric Sevareid, Howard K. Smith, and later, Walter Cronkite.

Despite the failure of the innovative CBS approach to color television, the same CBS inventor, Peter Goldmark, next created the long-playing 33 rpm record. It helped make CBS Records America's leading record company.

Until non-Jew Ted Turner arrived on the scene in 1986 and threatened a takeover, CBS was Paley's fiefdom. Responding to Turner's takeover attempt, Paley turned over control to Laurence Tisch, who had purchased 25 percent of CBS's stock. Tisch ran CBS until 1995 when Westinghouse bought it. A few years later, in a deal that brought Paramount and CBS back together as siblings, Sumner Redstone's Viacom took over CBS. For a time, Viacom's Mel Karmazin served as president. As such, CBS has remained under Jewish management in one form or another for nearly its entire existence.

American Broadcasting Corporation (ABC) As noted in the discussion of NBC, FCC pressure led to the $8 million sale of NBC Blue to the non-Jew, Edward J. Noble in 1943. He bought it with money earned from his Lifesavers Candy Company. Noble changed the name to American Broadcasting Systems, and later American Broadcasting Company (ABC).

Though ABC's radio network was profitable, by 1951 the costs of developing television were nearly bankrupting it. ABC had only forty of the country's 300 television stations as part of its network and NBC and CBS were dominant as Dumont slid out of existence. Noble sold ABC to Leonard Goldenson and his United Paramount theater chain for $25 million.

In 1954 Goldenson struck a deal that foreshadowed, in reverse, the Disney/ABC merger of 1996. In the 1950s, it was Walt Disney who approached ABC with his proposal for ABC to provide him with the financing he needed to complete the construction of Disneyland. From those negotiations arose a partnership in which, Goldenson/ABC sold its movie theaters and lent Disney $15 million for 35 percent of Disneyland. ABC also paid $35 million in license fees for *The Mickey Mouse Club* and *The Wonderful World of Disney* TV series. *The Mickey Mouse Club* became the daytime hit with children and Wonderful World did the same for children and adults at night.

Goldenson brought in non-Jew Roone Arledge in 1960, and within a year, ABC's *Wide World of Sports* began to transform sports programming into popular fare with ABC as its leading producer. Arledge followed *Wide World* up with *Monday Night Football* and superb coverage of major sporting events such as the Olympics.

Goldenson also brought in very popular Warner Brothers shows such as *Maverick* and *77 Sunset Strip* and in 1975, he recruited Fred Silverman from CBS where he had been a great success. Silverman developed such popular shows as *Starsky and Hutch, Rich Man, Poor Man,* and *Charlie's Angels.* The shows put ABC on top and Silverman on the cover of *Time* magazine. By the mid-1970s, ABC was consistently the Number 1 or Number 2 network.

The advent of cable and later satellite broadcasting began to hit ABC's rankings (and profits) and by 1986, the eighty-year-old Goldenson was ready to end his thirty-five-year reign. He accepted an offer to merge ABC into Capital Cities in a deal that valued ABC at $3.5 billion. Ten years later, Michael Eisner (a successful ABC executive from 1966 to 1976), reunited ABC with Disney in, what was, to its time, the second largest merger in American history. The difference was that this time it was Disney, not ABC, that ended up in control.

Newer Broadcast, Cable, Satellite, and Internet Networks[136]

Fox Broadcasting Company: Fox is the creation of non-Jew Rupert Murdoch, who acquired seven big-city Metromedia stations from another non-Jew, John Kluge. But it was Barry Diller, as Fox Broadcasting's CEO, who launched the infant fourth television network in 1987. In 1969, when he was only 27, Diller helped revive ABC's ratings by launching the hit *ABC's Movie of the Week* program. Within four years, he was ABC's vice president of Prime Time TV. At age 32, he left ABC to become chairman of Paramount Pictures. He led it for ten years until he joined Murdoch in 1985.

Diller's task for Murdoch was to create a fourth network, which he did by purchasing Metromedia Television from Kluge and building on that base. Diller began with only two nights of prime time broadcasting each week, but his success with low-budget shows like *America's Most Wanted, Married ...with Children* and *The Simpsons* made Fox into a significant force and that, plus programming directed at younger audiences, led to today's Fox network. Diller left Fox in 1992 and now leads IAC/Interactive Corp, a major Internet company covered in a later chapter.

Fox is part of Murdoch's huge News Corporation and through it, is affiliated with sibling Fox News (broadcast via cable and satellite). In 2005 Fox won the ratings race against NBC, ABC, and CBS. Fox News has matched it, leading ratings in the twenty-four-hour news format, consistently beating out CNN, MSNBC, and CNBC Among other parts of the News Corporation family are Twentieth Century Fox, Fox Searchlight, Fox Sports, DirecTV, *The Wall Street Journal,* and Harper Collins publishers. Serving as Murdoch's second in command is Peter Chernin. He is president and COO of News Corporation and Fox Entertainment, and he also serves as chairman and CEO of Fox Group (News Corporation's North American Operations).

Viacom: This is a company so diverse it could be included as a broadcast television and radio enterprise, movie production company, movie theater operator, book publisher, music publisher, video distributor, entertainment park operator, or outdoor advertising firm. Because of its strong presence in broadcast and cable TV (ownership of CBS, Viacom Television Group, and cable channels such as MTV, Nickelodeon, and others), its principal coverage is here.

Sumner Redstone, born Sumner Murray Rothstein, was first in his class from prep school. He graduated from Harvard in three years and was hand-picked to work in the World War II intelligence unit that cracked the Japanese code. After graduating from Harvard Law School in 1947, and several years in private practice, he began to work in his family's drive-in movie theater business.

He built the company from twelve theaters to 855. Already in his sixties, he then launched a major effort to expand and diversify through acquisitions. He bought control of Viacom, and that gave him the base from which he has further expanded to include:

CBS Television (discussed above)
Viacom Television Stations Group
Cable TV channels MTV, Nickelodeon BET, Nick at Nite, VH1, Spike TV, Noggin,
    CMT, Comedy Central, Showtime, Flix, The Movie Channel, Sundance Channel,
    TV Land, and Noggin.
Infinity Broadcasting, one of the largest radio operators in the United States
UPN (United Paramount Network)
Paramount Pictures, Paramount Television and Paramount Home Entertainment
Blockbuster
Viacom Outdoor, in outdoor advertising
Paramount Parks
Famous Players Theaters
Simon & Schuster
A host of Internet sites

Viacom has become a major American force in media, and as a result, Redstone became one of the country's most powerful business figures.

He is also benefactor of numerous charitable causes, including the Massachusetts General Hospital Burn Center, the Dana Farber Cancer Center, Children's Cancer Research, the American Cancer Crusade, and he actively supports the Boston Museum of Fine Arts and the Combined Jewish Philanthropies of Greater Boston.

Comcast: Ralph J. Roberts, Julian A. Brodsky, and Daniel Aaron founded Comcast in 1963 to buy a tiny, 1,200-subscriber, Tupelo, Mississippi, cable system. Ralph, the trio's leader, had prior success as the entrepreneur in a men's belt and jewelry business. With his two partners, he built the business, gave it a new name (Comcast) and, in 1972, took it public.

In 1986 Comcast began a series of purchases, sales, and joint ventures that ultimately made it the nation's largest cable operator. Along the way, in 1986, Comcast became a founding shareholder in QVC, the shopping channel. After expanding that stake and effectively running the business, they sold it to Liberty Media in 2003, netting $7.9 billion. For a time, they were in the cellular (wireless) telephone business. It was a venture they sold to SBC Communications for $1.7 billion. In addition, they acquired the NHL Philadelphia Flyers and NBA Philadelphia 76s; bought controlling interest in E!, Style, the Golf Channel, Outdoor Life and G4 (a gamers' channel), and accepted $1 billion from Microsoft for what is now Microsoft's 7.4 percent stake in Comcast Class A shares. In addition, Comcast bought AT&T's cable TV properties.

Comcast is now twice the size of its nearest rival, Time Warner Cable, and it owns 21 percent of Time Warner Cable. It is also the largest U.S. provider of high-speed Internet access.

Running all this is Brian Roberts, Ralph's son, a shy, late-forties CEO who has headed the company since being named its president in 1990 when he was 30. He began his career at the company in 1981, fresh out of Wharton, by climbing poles and hanging cable. Though he was a founder's son, his father insisted he begin at the bottom and he did.

With 2007 revenues of $29.3 billion and a market value north of $63 billion, Comcast is the biggest and strongest company in cable (24.1 million cable subscribers) and high-speed Internet (13.2 million subscribers), and in 2003 *Institutional Investor* magazine named Roberts one of America's best CEOs.

Suburban Cable: H.F. (Gerry) Lenfest was already a successful lawyer and executive with Walter Annenberg's Triangle Publications (he was running *Seventeen* magazine), when he decided to buy Suburban Cable in 1974. He borrowed $2.3 million and took over a 7,600-subscriber system serving Lebanon, Pennsylvania. When he finally sold it to Comcast in 2000, it served 1.2 million people in Pennsylvania, New Jersey, and Delaware. Lenfest and his wife, Marguerite, made $1.2 billion, which they are now in the process of giving away. They rejected a perpetual trust and intend for all the money to be donated to worthy causes within twenty years of their death. Mercersburg Academy, where Lenfest went to school, has already received $33 million. The Philadelphia Museum of Art, $17 million, the Barnes Foundation, $15 million, with lesser amounts going to such beneficiaries as Columbia University Law School, Temple University, and Washington and Lee University.

Time Warner: Like Viacom, Time Warner operates in so many different businesses that it could rightly be covered in several chapters. It is a leading publisher, moviemaker, cable network, Internet service provider, and a whole lot more. Because Steven J. Ross and Gerald Levin moved Time into cable and satellite television, its principal coverage is here.

Time magazine was created in 1923 by Henry Luce and Briton Hadden (both non-Jews). Hadden died six years later leaving Luce in sole charge of the company for nearly forty years. Luce launched *Fortune, Life,* and the *March of Time* newsreels in the 1930s. *Sports Illustrated* and *House and Home* came later (in the 50s) when Time also made its first television investment (KOB TV in Albuquerque, New Mexico). Before Luce died in 1967, he had expanded Time into book publishing.

Meanwhile, in 1979, Warner-Seven Arts was taken over by Kinney National, which had earlier combined the parking lot business of Caesar Kinney with the funeral-home operations of Steven J. Ross. Ross then became the head of Warner. Despite a résumé bereft of media experience, Ross restructured and diversified Warner. In his early years, he added computers (Atari), perfumes, cosmetics, and professional baseball and soccer. He later reversed course, refocusing Warner on the production and distribution of films, video and television, recorded music, and publishing.

In 1972 Time purchased Home Box Office (HBO) and Gerald Levin joined that division. In three years, he was HBO's chairman and in that post, he pioneered satellite distribution of premium cable channels and programming. His success with that decision revolutionized the business and led to a huge increase in the number of cable channels delivered to consumers via satellite. It also contributed to his becoming Time's vice chairman by 1988.

That same year, Time merged with Warner Communications and Steven J. Ross was soon Time Warner's CEO, with Levin as his Number 2. Ross immediately went after opportunities where Warner or Time properties could benefit from their new siblings. When Ross died unexpectedly in 1992, Levin became CEO.

In 1994, as Levin was expanding through acquisitions including Ted Turner's Turner Broadcasting, Edgar Bronfman Jr's Seagram Company bought 14.5 percent of Time Warner. Levin ran Time Warner until 2000, when he merged it with AOL and with that, non-Jew Steven Case, became chairman. Difficulties arising from the AOL merger ultimately caused Levin to step down as CEO in May 2002.

The combined Time Warner Business he left behind included:

Time Warner Cable.
Home Box Office.
Turner Broadcasting producing and distributing more than thirty leading cable channels such as CNN (co-founded by Maurice "Reese" Schonfeld in 1979), Turner Classic Movies, and Cartoon Network. Turner also owns the Atlanta Braves and the Atlanta Hawks.
Warner Brothers Entertainment, encompassing: Warner Bros. Pictures, Warner Bros. Television, Castle Rock Entertainment, DC Comics, Warner Home Video and other film and television production companies.
New Line Cinema.
Time Warner Book Group which includes Little Brown, Warner Books, Bullfinch Press, and other publishing operations.
Time Inc., publisher of more than 130 magazines.
AOL

Broadcast.com and HDNet: Mark Cuban grew up poor. He was the son of Russian Jewish emigrants in blue-collar Pittsburgh, but he had a native talent for salesmanship, selling garbage bags, greeting cards and magazines door-to-door, from the time he was twelve. He was also a bright student. At the University of Indiana, he started a chain letter and gave disco dancing lessons to pay for school. In 1983, after graduating, despite neither owning nor knowing much about computers, he started a computer consulting firm, MicroSolutions.

Self-taught from having to learn how to perform on the promises he made to customers, Cuban built MicroSolutions into a $30-million-a year company before selling it to Compuserve. With that sale, he was set for life and no longer needed to work. He kicked back for a few years, but returned, in 1995, with partner Todd R. Wagner (not known to be Jewish) to create a new business using the Internet as a broadcasting medium.

As the story goes, Cuban wanted a way to listen to Indiana basketball anywhere he traveled. He came up with a way to put a Dallas, Texas broadcast onto the Internet so anyone with an Internet connection could "tune in." His service was not the first. Internet radio had begun with Carl Malamud's 1993 "Talk Radio" and several other stations appeared in 1995. But it was Cuban and Wagner's effort (later named Broadcast.com) that caught on with its streaming audio and video. With that, today's Internet broadcasting was born.

Three years later, they took Broadcast.com public. It was a roaring success during those halcyon days for anything with a ".dot-com" in its name. A year later, Yahoo bought it for $5.7 billion. Cuban and Wagner were billionaires. Today Yahoo offers parts of the former Broadcast.com service as Yahoo Plus and other parts as SBC Yahoo DSL.

At first, Cuban focused his attention on his Dallas Mavericks basketball team. He is a brash, avid, courtside presence whose outbursts and antics have cost him more than $1 million in fines. At the same time, his savvy marketing and recruiting of top talent has converted the Mavericks from a perennial loser into a contender. He is still the charismatic leader of that team and at this writing is also courting the Chicago Cubs.

But ever at the forefront, Cuban has also launched two new media ventures. One, with Wagner, involves the purchase of Landmark Theaters, a large American chain of "art-house" movie theaters. The second, HDNet, is a leading independent provider of high-definition television programming. Its digital programs are transmitted to HD-ready television sets via cable, satellite, and conventional "over the air" broadcasts. To provide programming, Cuban has contracted with six major studios to convert selected movies from film to digital format so he can show them in Landmark Theaters or on HDNet. HDNet also produces its own high definition programs.

Even as traditional networks and providers expand into the digital age, it is clear that Cuban has now positioned himself as a leader in the new-era digital high definition. And with that, we "round the circle" from Sarnoff to Cuban. Jews continue to be leaders in the development of radio and television.

Content[137]

This chapter has told the story of Jewish leadership in radio and television from the perspective of the ways they are distributed to consumers via broadcast networks, cable, satellite, and now, in digital form, over those media and the Internet. That perspective misses the equally compelling story of their role in creating content. And while significant parts of those efforts overlap with the creation of content for movies and performing arts, it would be unfortunate to not at least identify some of the more prominent Jews among the leading writers, producers, and directors of radio and television fare.

Gertrude Berg was the quintessential "Jewish mother." She began in 1929 with a six-day-a-week radio series, *The Goldbergs,* which she wrote, produced, directed, and starred in. Five thousand radio and television episodes later, the series ended in 1954. She also wrote and appeared in movies and on the Broadway stage.

Herb Brodkin produced twenty-four television series, miniseries and movies over his forty years in television. His *Playhouse 90* and *Studio One* are classics of television's "Golden Age."

Himan Brown produced such radio fare as *Dick Tracy, Bulldog Drummond, Nero Wolfe, Grand Central Station, Inner Sanctum, CBS Radio Mystery Theater,* and the *Adventures of the Thin Man.*

Paddy Chayefsky began writing short stories and scripts for radio in the 1940s. He later transitioned to television, when he created four TV series and twelve TV plays. One of them, *Marty,* later won an Academy Award as a film. *Marty* and *Network* were only two of the twelve movies for which he wrote or co-wrote the screenplay.

Norman Corwin wrote hundreds of radio programs. He was the writer called when FDR wanted a special program to celebrate the Bill of Rights immediately after Pearl Harbor. *We Hold These Truths* was broadcast live on all four major radio networks on December 15, 1941.

John Frankenheimer directed such television series, miniseries and made-for-television movies as *You Are There, Playhouse 90,* and *Studio One,* in addition to his twenty-five films including *Manchurian Candidate* and *Birdman of Alcatraz.*

Fred Friendly began as a radio producer during the Depression. Starting with non-Jew Edward R. Murrow, he became one of televisions foremost news and documentary producers. It led to his 1960s role as president of CBS News.

Larry Gelbart wrote, or wrote and produced radio shows for Fanny Brice, Danny Thomas, Bob Hope, and others before moving on to television where he created *M*A*S*H*, The Red Buttons Show,* and eleven films.

Mark Goodson and partner **Bill Todman,** produced some of television's most popular game shows including *I've Got a Secret, What's My Line? To Tell the Truth, Concentration, Password,* and *The New Price Is Right.*

Karl Haas' program, *Adventures in Good Music,* won two Peabody awards for radio broadcasting.

Don Hewitt produced the first televised presidential debate between Richard Nixon and John F. Kennedy. He went on to produce CBS News for fourteen years before creating, and for more than thirty years, heading up *60 Minutes.*

Norman Lear created *All in the Family, Sanford and Son, Maude, One Day at a Time, Mary Hartman, Mary Hartman,* and numerous movies.

Sheldon Leonard was a writer, producer, director, and actor. Among the television series he produced were *I Spy, Gomer Pyle, The Dick Van Dyke Show, Andy Griffith,* and sixteen more. He acted in twenty-seven films.

Richard Levinson and **William Link** teamed up to write and produce sixteen television series, twenty-six made-for-TV movies, two films, and two stage plays. Among them, *Colombo, Mannix, The Fugitive, Murder She Wrote,* and *Hard Copy.*

Shari Lewis earned twelve Emmys and a Peabody for her children's programs featuring such hand-puppet characters as Lamb Chop and Charlie Horse.

Lorne Michaels is best known for *Saturday Night Live,* which he created in 1975 and has produced for twenty-seven of its thirty-three seasons. In addition, he has written or produced eleven other television series and fifteen movies.

Haim Saban created the Mighty Morphin Power Rangers and Marvel Comics characters as animated television fare. His early success led to a combination with Fox, which ultimately became the Fox Family Channel, seen in eighty-one million homes. The Walt Disney Company acquired the Fox Family Channel in 2002. (He now controls Univision.)

Rod Serling is best known for *The Twilight Zone,* which earned him one of his six Emmys. It was only one of the sixteen television plays and eight films that he wrote.

Fred Silverman was executive producer of such major 1980s series as *Matlock, In the Heat of the Night,* and the *Perry Mason* movies. He was also a major executive at CBS and ABC

Aaron Spelling created television programming for more than forty years. Among his major hits were *Johnny Ringo, The Mod Squad, Starsky and Hutch, Charlie's Angels, The Love Boat, Fantasy island, Dynasty, Beverly Hills 90210,* and *Melrose Place.*

David Susskind produced fifteen major television programs between 1947 and 1970, nine television movies, and eight films. From them, he earned a Peabody and forty-seven Emmys.

Brandon Tartikoff was president of NBC Entertainment for twelve years, conceived of *The Cosby Show* and shepherded *Hill Street Blues, Miami Vice* and others before leaving to head Paramount Pictures.

Ed Weinberger wrote or produced such hit shows as *Mary Tyler Moore Show*, *Taxi*, *The Betty White Show*, *The Cosby Show*, and nine more.

Tom Werner has been executive producer or producer for twenty-five television series such as *The Cosby Show*, *Roseanne*, *Cybil*, *3rd Rock from the Sun*, *That '70s Show*, *That '80s Show*, *Whoopi*, and others.

Ethel Winant became television's first female executive when she was named a CBS vice president in 1973. She began in casting for *Studio One* and *Playhouse 90*, but was soon developing such shows as *Hawaii Five-O*, *Green Acres*, *Hogan's Heroes* and *Lost in Space*. Such efforts won her two Emmys and a Peabody.

David Wolper was one of television's most successful and prolific producers. His eighteen television series and miniseries, sixty-three television specials and nineteen films made between 1958 and 1996 won him five Peabodys and forty Emmys.

Bud Yorkin produced or directed such hits as *Maude*, *Sanford and Son*, and *All in the Family*.

On-Air Talent[138]

As important as the writers, producers, and managers is the talent. Some of those shown on the following list have also appeared in films or in live performances. Moreover, many of them wrote their own material and produced their own shows. Were there space, each has a tale to tell. But by listing just some of the thousands of entertainers whose careers were mostly on radio or television, hopefully the material provides some sense of the significant Jewish contribution as on-air talent.

Dan Abrams	Martin Agronsky	Marv Albert	Mel Allen
Tim Allen	Jason Alexander	Shana Alexander	Linda Albin
Morey Amsterdam	Robert Arnot	Bea Arthur	Ed Asner
Barbara Bain	Roseanne Barr	Rona Barrett	Jules Bergman
Milton Berle	Jack Benny	Wolf Blitzer	Tom Bosley
David Brenner	Joyce Brothers	George Burns	Red Buttons
Eddie Cantor	Kitty Carlisle	Sid Caesar	Joan Collins
Howard Cosell	Larry David	Fran Drescher	Susan Estrich
Peter Falk	Michael Feldman	Eddie Fisher	Arlene Francis
Al Franken	Bonnie Franklin	Alan Freed	Stan Freberg
Jacob Freedman	Allen Funt	Estelle Getty	Hermione Gingold
Elliott Gould	Lee Grant	Teri Gross	Bettina Gregory
Lorne Greene	Jeff Greenfield	Charles Grodin	Bernard Goldberg
Jonah Goldberg	Steven Hill	Judd Hirsch	John Houseman
Clark Howard	Jackie Judd	Bernard Kalb	Marvin Kalb
Gabe Kaplan	Andy Kaufman	Murray Kaufman	Julie Kavner
Danny Kaye	Lesli Kay	Alan King	Larry King
Werner Klemperer	Jack Klugman	Andrea Koppel	Ted Koppel

Harvey Korman
Gypsy Rose Lee
Peggy Lipton
Elaine May
Bess Myerson
Leonard Nimoy
Sara Jessica Parker
Gilda Radner
Paul Reiser
Roseanne
Morley Safer
Dr. Laura Schlesinger
Dinah Shore
Jill St John
Mike Wallace
Ed Wynn

Michael Krasny
Irving R. Levine
Bill Maher
Michael Medved
Edwin Newman
Cynthia Nixon
Kenneth Pollack
Tony Randall
Geraldo Rivera
Roger Rosenblatt
Mort Sahl
Daniel Schorr
Phil Silvers
Lesley Stahl
Chris Wallace
Efrem Zimbalist Jr.

Michael Landon
Jerry Lewis
Groucho Marx
Henry Morgan
Lorraine Newman
Jerry Orbach
Maury Povich
Carl Reiner
Joan Rivers
John Rothmann
Michael Savage
Jerry Seinfeld
Lawrence Spivak
Bill Stern
Barbara Walters

Matt Lauer
Hal Linden
Jackie Mason
Debra Messing
Ron Nessen
Ronn Owens
Dennis Prager
Rob Reiner
Steven Roberts
Louis Rukeyser
Dick Schaap
William Shatner
Jerry Springer
Howard Stern
Henry Winkler

Chapter15

High Tech Entrepreneurs and CEOs

"Only the paranoid survive." —Andrew Grove

Andrew Grove

In September 1936, Hungarian Prime Minister Gyula Gömbös informed German officials he intended to establish a one-party Fascist state in Hungary. That same month, on September 2, András Grof was born in Budapest to secular Jewish parents. The first country to send a head of state to meet with Hitler, Hungary was dependent on the Germans for more than half its raw materials and markets. It would later send troops to the Eastern Front to fight alongside the Germans. The Soviets killed 40,000 of them and wounded 70,000 more. Later, German fears that Hungary might sign a separate peace with the Soviets or the West, led to a March 1944 German takeover of the country. With that began the full-scale deportation of Hungarian Jews to the death camps.[139]

In the end, despite Hungarian government efforts to avert those deportations, only 260,500 of Hungary's 725,000 Jews survived the war. Grof and his mother were among them. They had changed their names (Grof became András Malesevics) and were taken in by Christians. Grof's father survived as well (but just barely) in the Eastern labor camps. Grof was not yet nine. It was his second near-fatal experience. Five years earlier he almost died of scarlet fever.[140]

The Soviets, who took control after the war, were not anti-Semitic in the fashion

176

of Nazis but, as the Jewish son of a modestly successful capitalist dairyman, Grof experienced discrimination as "an enemy of the classes." Dismissed from a writing job in 1950 because a relative had been detained without trial, Grof is quoted as saying he "ran from writing to science." He said he "did not want to work in a profession where a totally subjective evaluation, easily colored by political considerations, could decide the merits of my work."[141]

Though Grof was not part of the failed 1956 Hungarian Revolution, rumors the invading Red Army was rounding up students led Grof and his best friend to bolt. As students, they were fearful they too would be picked up. It was a harrowing escape. They got their directions from a hunchback smuggler who could just as easily have deceived them and turned them over to the Soviets. Shouts of "Who is there?" yelled at Grof as he lay "face down in a muddy field," terrified him. His hesitant response, "Where are we?" brought the reassuring reply, "Austria." Once more, the twenty-year-old Grof had averted disaster.[142]

The International Rescue Committee helped him immigrate to the United States where an aunt and uncle, who had left Hungary in the 1930s, took him in. He became Andrew Grove, and he entered Manhattan's City College of New York to study chemistry. Perhaps it was the "C" he got in the English course on "Faulkner" (after speaking English for only three years) that kept him from being summa cum laude, but he received nearly straight "A"s. The New York Times wrote of his success and his freshman adviser is quoted as saying, "I was a little astonished by that kind of ambition. There's some advantage in being hungry."[143]

Meanwhile in 1957, while working as a busboy, Grove met Eva, a waitress and fellow refugee. By June 1958 they were married and in 1960, they headed for Berkeley, California, where Grove, an outstanding student, earned his chemistry Ph.D. in June 1963.[144]

His superb academic record, gave him his pick of prospective employers. He chose Fairchild Semiconductor. There, he would work with a legendary group of eight brilliant engineers whose efforts helped create what would later become known as "Silicon Valley." But in fact, it was Grove and two colleagues, whose solution to an "impurities problem" led to discovering silicon's practical usefulness as a component in integrated circuits.[145]

By the late 1960s, Fairchild was losing its edge. The parent company had bought out the eight founding engineers, and several had already left to start other companies. Robert Noyce and Gordon Moore placed a call to Arthur Rock to ask if he would help them secure financing to start Integrated Electronics (soon shortened to Intel). Rock responded "Yes," and Noyce and Moore then asked Grove to join them. They founded Intel in July 1968. (Grove is typically listed as Intel's employee No. 4—with Noyce and Moore No. 1 and No. 2 respectively. In fact, Grove's number and that of his fellow Hungarian émigré Les Vadasz were switched by mistake. Grove was No. 3.)[146]

Noyce was to lead sales and marketing, Moore, research and development, and Grove would run operations. Some characterized it as the "dream team," but smooth sailing it was not. Intel was to face a series of life threatening crises. In each case, the responses, typically championed by Grove, would overcome the threat and take Intel to new highs.[147]

Intel started out making dynamic random access memories (DRAMs), but soon pursued a separate opportunity. They could produce a small, general purpose device (a "chip") to replace twelve single-purpose chips being requested by a Japanese calculator company. The new chip could be "programmed" to carry out a variety of different tasks and thus perform all twelve functions. When the calculator company later asked for a cheaper price to respond to fierce competition within the calculator industry, Grove and the management team negotiated the right to sell the chip to any company that did not manufacture calculators. With that, the Intel 4004, the world's first microprocessor, became a proprietary Intel product.[148]

From 1976 on, Intel faced a series of crises in soft demand for memory, factory problems, Japanese "dumping," and other challenges. Grove led the responses. He made the decision to get Intel out of the memory (DRAM) business, to scale back, and to re-focus on microprocessors. He also played a key role in the IBM negotiations which led to Intel becoming the sole provider of microprocessors for the new IBM personal computer (PC). With that, Intel became the leading player in the booming PC business.

In 1994, after Intel had released millions of flawed Pentium chips, it was Grove who first had engineers tell customers the problem was nothing to be concerned about. Just as quickly, he realized he had made a horrible mistake. He reversed course and led a $475 million product recall. Incredibly expensive at the time, even for Intel, the decision ultimately convinced customers that Intel was committed to getting things right.[149]

Within two years of Intel's formation, Gordon Moore had already decided Grove was the future of the company. He told Grove "One day you'll run Intel." By 1979 Grove was president, and in 1987, when Moore stepped aside, Grove took his place as CEO. He remained in that role for the next eleven years until 1998, staying on as chairman for another six years until November 2004.[150]

Through his thirty years, first as head of operations and later, through his time as the CEO, Grove's personality and style were the dominant force shaping the culture of Intel. Noyce and Moore were vital to the company's success, but both were low key, not prone to confrontation, and the bulk of Intel's personnel reported to Grove. Subject to board approval, Grove made the critical decisions.[151]

One element of his style was coined "constructive confrontation." Anyone could—and did—challenge another's point of view and, at times, they did so with striking vehemence. As his successor Craig Barrett was to tell the *San Francisco Chronicle*, "He yells at you, and you accept it because he's usually right. Sometimes you yell back at him. It's give and take and anyone in the company can yell at him. He's not above it." Grove had set the tone. People were demanding of one another in a company that had a very low tolerance for mistakes. As one reporter indicated, it was a place of "ruthless intelligence." What mattered was not office politics, but the facts, intellectual honesty, merit, and performance.[152]

Grove was known for his intense focus, his concentration and his penetrating eyes. He had a "quick violent temper," which, in 1984, caused *Fortune* magazine to name him one of America's toughest bosses. On occasion, he went overboard as *Time* pointed out in its 1997 cover story. Once he became so heated that his later apology was not accepted. Another time, according to the book, *Inside Intel*, Grove berated a departing former star employee (Federico Fagin) saying, "You will fail in everything you do." Grove was high strung with an incredible sense of urgency and drive.[153]

And Grove was willing to take the same kind of grilling and demands he dished out to others. Arthur Rock, a Silicon Valley legend for his abrupt brilliance, was as intellectually demanding in his role as an Intel board member as Grove was of those working for him. Among other comments, Rock told Grove he did not think he could make it as chairman.[154]

But Grove was also courageous. He believed in tackling fear head on. In a Forbes interview, he said he regarded fear as a creative force, not an enemy: "It's fear that gets you out of comfortable equilibrium, that gets you to do the difficult tasks." Grove's life had so often placed him at risk, he developed remarkable survival skills. He believed crises arc inevitable and unpredictable. To survive, a company must simply detect them and respond to them. Though Intel's arena may have been tougher and more tumultuous than most, Grove felt the same rules applied to nearly every organization, and his thoughts in that regard led to his book, *Only the Paranoid Survive*. It described the threats, opportunities, need for vigilance, and tools one might use to spot and capitalize on such changes.[155]

At Intel, work began at 8 a.m., and there was no tolerance for arriving late to a meeting or for meetings that ran on and on with little being accomplished. Grove's office light was usually on late into the evening after everyone else had left. At the same time, Intel was egalitarian. Grove worked from the same 8-foot-by-9-foot cubicle as everyone else. He parked wherever there was a space. His work area was accessible to anyone who walked by.[156]

Those who have known Grove from the beginnings of Intel confirm that despite his success, and the wealth that came with it, he remains unchanged by everything he achieved. As Arthur Rock said, "He has no airs." He lives on a relatively modest scale, without his own jet or expensive cars.[157]

During his tenure as Intel's CEO, revenues grew from $1.9 billion per year to $25.1 billion. Employment doubled to 64,000 people. The company became a global force with more than half its revenues, and many of its products, generated offshore. Over those years, the value of Intel stock grew 24-fold. At 31.6 percent per year, it was twice the rate of the S&P 500 Index. In a world of high performance and accountability, Grove had delivered.[158]

If Grove was difficult at work, he was a loving family man at home. He has been married to Eva, the waitress he met in 1957, for more than fifty years. *Time* magazine noted, "He is still clearly nuts about her" and "she takes care of him." "There is a world-worn gentleness in their touch." His daughters think of their mother as a "saint" and their father as "wonderful." His younger daughter said, "Being Andy Grove's child is not for the faint of heart. But if you can roll with it, it's great." At Intel Grove worked to include his family in his business travels, but in a move some would find "typical," he expected his daughters to write reports on what they saw. And through it all his passion for physical fitness and his lifelong love of the opera remained a constant.[159]

In 1994 Grove faced yet another life-threatening crises. Told he had prostate cancer, he attacked the problem just as he had every other challenge in life. He schooled himself, obtained three expert opinions and then made a decision based on all the homework he had done. Fourteen years since he chose high-dose radiation, he appears, once again, to have made the right call.[160]

In leading and leaving Intel, he demonstrated his commitment to proper corporate governance, drawing on a majority of outside directors to guide the company and splitting the chairman's duties from those of the CEO. He practiced everything he preached as he stepped down in November 2004.[161]

Wealthy from his own efforts, Grove intends to give away the bulk of his fortune. Prostate cancer research is one beneficiary. Ten chemistry scholarships at CCNY is another. The International Rescue Fund, which brought Grove from Vienna to America, is yet another. It receives the profits from his memoir, *Swimming Across*. He also serves as chairman of the University of California San Francisco's $1.4 billion capital campaign to build a major medical campus and hospital in San Francisco's Mission Bay. Grove is committed to education and feels the United States is falling badly behind. In addition to his efforts to improve the educational infrastructure, he continues as an active lecturer at Stanford University. Meanwhile, over the years he has written forty technical papers, five books, and numerous articles and columns for *Fortune, The Wall Street Journal, The New York Times,* and others.[162]

Ultimately Grove, like other first- and second-generation immigrants described in this book, found America to be a country in which he could be successful and not be resented for it. One manifestation of that was his selection as *Time* magazine's 1997 "Man of the Year." But as with so many other of its immigrants, America got the better of the bargain.

Grove embodies many of the Jewish cultural values described earlier in this book. He is assertive and willing to be different, but he is tolerant, even inviting, of competing views. He stands for choice and accountability, and has been a tenacious hard worker for his entire life. Unwilling to place himself in a role where he might have to depend upon the subjective views of others, he chose science and is intellectually honest and rational. He has always been devoted to his wife and daughters. His commitment to education is manifested not only in his Ph.D. (and many honorary degrees) but in his own writing, teaching, and promoting of America's need to dramatically upgrade the quality of its educational programs and capabilities. And Grove is philanthropic. He might not use words like "heal a broken world," but in the end, he will devote the bulk of his wealth to benefit others.

Jews as High-Technology Entrepreneurs and Managers

Jews have traditionally been seen as prominent in such industries as finance, merchandising, apparel, textiles, entertainment, media, and publishing. And in most of those industries, Jews were true pioneers. They played leading roles as the industries emerged on the scene and as they matured.

Their disproportionate importance to the contemporary world of 24/7, competitive high technology is less well known, but they have flourished there as well. It plays to their strengths. High technology demands a solid grounding in the underlying science or engineering behind its products or services, and that typically calls for college, and sometimes a postgraduate education. Demographically, Jews are better educated than their peers. An earlier chapter pointed out the high levels of Jewish enrollment at leading public and private universities.

The National Jewish Population Survey 2000-2001 goes further. It points out:[163]

> More than half of all Jewish Adults (55 percent) received a college degree and a quarter (25 percent) earned a graduate degree. The Comparable figures for the total U.S. population are 29 percent and 6 percent. As a result,

> More than 60 percent of all employed Jews are in one of the three highest status job categories: professional or technical (41 percent), management and executive (13 percent) and business and finance (7 percent). In contrast, 46 percent of all Americans work in these three high status areas, 29 percent in professional or technical jobs, 12 percent in management and executive positions, and 5 percent in business and finance.

Jews also tend to be disproportionately entrepreneurial, working where they will succeed or fail based on their own efforts. Grove's decision to stop writing, and instead to pursue science, illustrates the point. Judgments about writers are often subjective while those about science are much less so. Grove wanted to work in a field where he would be judged on his own performance. He chose chemistry and got his Ph.D. After several years working with the best and brightest at Fairchild Semiconductor, he left to become one of the three founders of Intel.

Technology is a high-risk meritocracy. While even the most talented people sometimes fail, and fortune can obliterate the most brilliant of plans, technology is not political. Relationships and initial funding will carry a venture only so far. Ultimately it must succeed or fail on its own merits in a volatile, highly competitive arena. Such risky opportunities can be pursued in hospitable climates, such as the United States, and in such environments, Jewish entrepreneurs have done well. They:

> Created what became the world's largest and most valuable personal computer company (Michael Dell, Dell Computers);
>
> Co-founded the world's most successful search engine (Sergey Brin, Google);
>
> Head the world's largest software company (Steve Ballmer, Microsoft);
>
> Co-founded and head the world's second largest software company (Larry Ellison, Oracle);
>
> Co-founded, led and served as chairman of the dominant microprocessor and memory chip company whose products drive most of today's personal computers (Andrew Grove, Intel);
>
> Created the first "killer application" software which ignited demand for personal computers (Mitch Kapor, Lotus 1-2-3);
>
> Served as top or second in command person in three of the world's four most valuable Internet companies according to a May 2004 Fortune study (Terry Semmel at Yahoo, Jeff Skoll at eBay and Barry Diller at IAC);
>
> Co-founded and heads the communications protocol/chip company whose technology is the market leader in U.S. cell phones and is likely to be the world leader as the next generation cell phone technology (3G) is adopted worldwide (Irwin Jacobs, Qualcomm).

And that is only the barest overview.

Dell: Michael Dell and Larry Ellison (of Oracle) share the distinction of being two of the most successful college dropouts in history. (Non-Jew Bill Gates is a third.) Dell quit the University of Texas in 1985 when he was nineteen years old to start Dell Computer Corporation with a $1,000 stake. His idea was to "cut out the middle-man" by selling personal computers (PCs) directly to customers.

Dell's combination of custom built computers, excellent product quality, superb customer service, outstanding production efficiency, and low prices created the world's largest computer manufacturing company. In achieving that distinction, he took on IBM, Compaq, Hewlett Packard, Toshiba, and many other PC makers, most of them much bigger and better financed than Dell.

He is emblematic of the creative, determined nature of successful entrepreneurs. In the process, he made his company one of the most valuable in the world. In 1992, Dell became the youngest CEO in history to earn a spot on the Fortune 500 when his company had been in existence for only eight years. With fiscal year 2005 sales of $53 billion, Dell humbled most competitors. Despite the challenges of rapid growth and competitive success, Dell and its founder are consistently counted as among America's most respected.

The success has earned Dell a fortune, sufficient until just a few years ago, to consistently place him among *Fortune's* "40 under 40." These are all young entrepreneurs, athletes, and entertainers who have achieved stellar success before reaching age 40. With his wife, Dell has created the Michael & Susan Dell Foundation, endowing it with more than $1 billion. Its focus is the health, education, safety, care, and development of children. Among its recent commitments was $130 million to help boost high school graduation and college attendance rates in Texas.[164]

Google: Sergey Brin is the son of Russian Jewish emigrants who left the Soviet Union in 1979 to escape persecution. Sergey was six at the time. Mathematically inclined, he earned a computer science degree from the University of Maryland before entering Stanford as a postgraduate student. There he met non-Jew Larry Page, also studying for his doctorate. Together they developed a search engine—called BackRub before they renamed it Google.

They dropped out of Stanford, rounded up $1 million from friends, family and angel venture investors and on September 7, 1998, launched Google. More than ten years old, it is the most popular search engine on the Web with more than 100 million users each month accessing more than ten billion Web site pages. It employs more than 19,000 people and has had a spectacular run up in its stock price to a value of roughly $150 billion by mid 2008.[165]

Microsoft: Steve Ballmer did not found Microsoft. Non-Jews Bill Gates and Paul Allen did. They started the company in 1976, five years after they began programming together while attending Lakeside High School in Seattle where they had access to the school's computer. Gates went off to Harvard where he and Ballmer became good friends. Ballmer was a bright Jewish kid from Detroit who scored a perfect 800 on his math SATs and who took it upon himself to "socialize" Gates at Harvard—until Gates dropped out to start Microsoft. About the same time, Paul Allen dropped out of Washington State, and together Gates and Allen launched the company.

Gates tried to convince Ballmer to drop out as well, but instead, Ballmer stayed in school, going on to graduate magna cum laude from Harvard in 1977. He worked for Proctor and Gamble for two years and then entered Stanford Business School. Perhaps just to "fit in," he then dropped out of Stanford Business School in 1980 after Gates had made yet one more appeal for him to join Microsoft. Ballmer was the company's twenty-fourth employee.

Within three years Paul Allen was gone, the result of a bout with Hodgkin's Lymphoma. Ballmer served first as the company's financial disciplinarian and later became the number two guy, holding down every senior job in the company before being named president in 1998 and CEO in 2000. Known for his determination and salesmanship, Ballmer has been vital to Microsoft's success.[166]

Oracle: Larry Ellison is a University of Chicago dropout. He was one of the three (later four) partners who founded Oracle Corporation in 1977. Ellison, the leader, read an IBM article about a new kind of software termed a "relational database." Then commonly acknowledged as a revolutionary new way to build a database, no one, not even at IBM, thought it was commercially viable. Ellison disagreed and with $2,000, the partners began developing the software, using cash generated from consulting projects to augment the $2,000.

Of the four founders, two later left the company and one died. But from the start, it was Ellison that was, and still is, the driving force behind Oracle. "Relentless," "determined," and "ruthless" are among terms commonly used to describe him. He has been schooled in Japanese approaches to business where anything less than 100 percent market share is not enough.

His strong ego is characterized by the titles of two books about him. The first is titled, *The Difference Between God and Larry Ellison*. It is the first line of an old Silicon Valley joke for which the punch line is "God does not think he is Larry Ellison." The second book is *Everyone Else Must Fail,* for which the preamble is "It is not good enough that I should succeed."

Ellison was born to an unmarried Jewish teenage mother and an Italian-American Air Force pilot father, but he grew up with an aunt and an uncle who constantly put young Larry down saying he would never amount to anything. Harvard Business School's Entrepreneur of the Year in 1990, as of February 2008, Forbes ranked Ellison the fifteenth wealthiest person in the world.

Ellison has devoted roughly half a billion dollars to charities, particularly a medical foundation focused mostly on infectious diseases in the Third World and diseases of aging. In mid-2005, he also pledged $115 million to Harvard University.[167]

Intel: As noted in the Andrew Grove bio which opened this chapter, Intel was formed in 1968 by non-Jews Robert Noyce and Gordon Moore, who recruited Grove to be their co-founder and third employee. Their established reputations and ability to raise the needed $2.5 million from venture capitalist Arthur Rock financed the company, Noyce headed up sales and marketing, Moore R&D, while Grove headed manufacturing and product development. Grove disciplined the organization to set and reach goals and he made the critical decisions, such committing Intel to the microprocessors which made Intel the huge success it is.

Lotus: Mitch Kapor did not invent the spreadsheet, but his software program, Lotus 1-2-3, was the first application to spawn huge demand for personal computers. VisiCalc, an earlier spreadsheet program created by Jew Dan Bricklin and Bob Frankston in 1982, was available on several early computers including the Apple II a few years before Lotus 1-2-3 arrived. But Lotus 1-2-3 had many more features, was easier to use, and had far better graphics. It provided the compelling reason for consumers to buy personal computers and demand was so strong, Lotus grossed $53 million in its first year and $156 million by 1984. Kapor went on to create other major software programs including Lotus Agenda.[168]

eBay: Jeff Skoll did not create eBay, non-Jew Pierre Omidyar did in 1993. For Omidyar, born to French and Iranian parents, creating an online auction Web-site was a Labor Day weekend hobby project. For its first couple of years, it was simply a free Web-site Omidyar ran on his own home page along with several other of his Web page creations. During the early months, he tried to recruit Skoll, a Jewish French-Canadian he met through friends, to become his partner. Skoll turned him down, choosing to remain at Stanford Business School.

In early 1996, Omidyar's Internet service provider began charging him $250 a month to host the site. Omidyar was forced to start charging a fee, which he passed along to the site's users based on the sale price of auction items. As the checks started rolling in, Omidyar realized he needed help. Again, he approached Skoll. This time, after a few months of consulting for eBay, Skoll signed on as its first full-time employee and president.

Skoll grew up in Canada and showed early signs of being a driven entrepreneur. At twelve, he was selling Amway products door-to-door. After graduating from the University of Toronto with a 4.0 grade-point average, he set up two high-tech companies before moving to Palo Alto to enroll at Stanford Business School. Compensating for Omidyar's easygoing ways and enjoyment of programming, Skoll was the driven leader who planned the business and made things happen. He hired key people, established much of the culture, and constantly pushed to build the business.

The result is the number one auction Web site in the world. It grossed $7.7 billion in 2007 and was worth $34 billion in mid 2008. This has made both Omidyar and Skoll very wealthy. Skoll has since left eBay and now devotes the bulk of his time to philanthropic activities, particularly his Skoll Foundation to which he has donated $250 million. The foundation supports social entrepreneurs working to effect lasting positive social changes worldwide. In 2003 Skoll won recognition from *Business Week* magazine as "one of the most innovative philanthropists of the past decade."[169]

InterActive Corp. (IAC): Barry Diller has made a career of corporate transformations. He started in the mail room at the William Morris Agency in his early twenties, and at age twenty-four, moved to ABC TV. Within three years, he was vice president of Feature Films and Program Development. In that job he inaugurated *ABC's Movie of the Week*, the most popular movie series in television history. At ABC, Diller pioneered highly profitable "made-for-television" films that focused on social issues such as homosexuality, the Vietnam War, and drugs.

In 1974, following that success (and still only thirty-two), he was named president of Paramount Pictures. At Paramount, he oversaw creation of the hit television series *Cheers, Taxi,* and *Laverne and Shirley,* and hit movies including: *Raiders of the Lost Ark, Saturday Night Fever* and *Grease.* Ten years later he moved to Twentieth Century Fox where, in 1985, after Rupert Murdoch took over, he launched Fox as the fourth television network. By 1990 Diller had Fox producing five nights of prime time television with such popular shows as: *The Simpsons, Married With Children, Cops,* and *America's Most Wanted.*

Diller quit Fox to purchase a stake in QVC, the cable shopping network, and from there he launched an unsuccessful bid to take over Paramount. Sumner Redstone's Viacom beat him out. Shortly thereafter, in 1995, non-Jew John Malone recruited Diller to leave QVC, invest in and run Liberty Media's Silver King Communications, which was broadcasting the Home Shopping Network. Diller later merged Home Shopping into Silver King.

Through a blinding series of name changes, strategic redirections, and $8 billion worth of mergers, acquisitions, joint ventures, and investments in more than forty-five companies, Diller created what is now called Interactive Corp. (IAC), for a time the fifth major Internet company (behind Google, Amazon, eBay, and Yahoo). Little known to the general public, IAC controls such prominent Internet names as Ask.com, Citysearch, excite, and gifts.com. In 2005, Diller began to spin off industry specific businesses. Expedia.com, hotels.com and other travel related Web sites became a separate public company with Diller as its chairman. In August, 2008, he repeated the move, spinning off a number of prior acquisitions into four new public companies: HSN, (the former Home Shopping Network), Ticketmaster, Interval Leisure Group, and Tree.com, the former Lending Tree).

Over the years, Diller has served as a director of Coca-Cola and *The Washington Post,* trustee of New York University, member of the Executive Board for Medical Sciences at UCLA, member of the Board of Councilors of USC's School of Cinema-Television and a member of the board of the Museum of Television and Radio.[170]

Yahoo: Terry Semel did not create Yahoo. Non-Jews Jerry Yang and David Filo did in 1994, as a hobby, while pursuing their electrical engineering Ph.D.'s at Stanford. In those halcyon, "early bubble" days, Yahoo went public within two years. It was then, and still is today, regarded as one of the major Internet successes of all time, but along the way, it hit a bump in the road. In 2001, Yahoo lost $93 million on revenues of $717 million. The stock tanked and new talent was needed to avert a meltdown.

That is when Terry Semel arrived. Semel had twenty-four years at Warner Brothers, where he had been instrumental in building the company from $1 billion to $11 billion in annual revenues. Semel quickly pushed Yahoo's marketing, consumers' services, and acquisitions and by 2003, he had turned the company around. In 2004 Yahoo made $1.6 billion. But in mid-2007 Semel resigned under fire, in part because of the reported $500 million he made during his tenure, but also, in what might be seen to be an ironic observation by Wikipedia—because "while Yahoo's stock appreciated at 40 percent per year, …Google saw its stock grow 55 percent per year."[171]

Qualcomm: Irwin Jacobs is listed as one of seven Qualcomm founders, but by any measure, he has been the "essential man" from Qualcomm's 1985 inception till now.

Qualcomm created and controls Code Division Multiple Access (CDMA), a major wireless telecommunications technology. It is the most widely used wireless calling technology in the United States (47 percent market share) used by such carriers as Verizon, Cingular, and Sprint. Around the world, 212 million wireless phones already utilize Qualcomm technology and as 3G, the next generation of wireless, is deployed, Qualcomm is expected to become the international market leader as well.

Jacobs grew up in New Bedford, Massachusetts. He was a mediocre musician, but an excellent student earning a bachelor's degree from Cornell and a master's and a Doctor of Science degree from Massachusetts Institute of Technology (MIT). He taught at MIT and the University of California San Diego (UCSD) from 1959 to 1972.

While teaching, he wrote a still-used college text, *Principles of Communications Engineering,* and in 1969, co-founded Linkabit, a company he describes as his initial move toward becoming an "academic dropout." That finally happened in 1972 when he became Linkabit's full-time president and chairman. The company pioneered satellite TV receiver technology (VideoCipher) and was the first to commercially introduce Time Division Multiplex Access (TDMA), the predecessor technology to CDMA. Jacobs built Linkabit to 1,400 employees, before merging it with M/A-COM and he served on that board until 1985.

Initially, Qualcomm did research and development and some manufacturing for wireless companies while it built the largest satellite-based messaging service used by trucking companies to manage their fleets. That service was quickly overshadowed, however, by CDMA. By mid-2008, CDMA was generating over $8 billion in annual revenues and was worth $90 billion.

All of this has made Jacobs (and his fellow founders) quite wealthy. Jacobs has responded with major philanthropy. He and his wife have given $110 million to the San Diego Symphony (harkening back to his days as a mediocre musician), another $110 million went to the UCSD to "support the other faculty that are currently doing the teaching," $7 million went to the Salk Institute, and millions more have gone to support the San Diego Food Bank and historic New Bedford. Both he, and fellow Qualcomm founder (Italian Jew), Andrew Viterbi, now have schools of engineering named after them—Jacobs at UCSD and Viterbi at the University of Southern California.[172]

RealNetworks: Rob Glaser takes credit for creating the first technology to "stream" audio, video, and other digital content—such as music and games—to computers. He founded RealNetworks in 1994 to capitalize on the technology.

Fresh out of Yale with degrees in economics and computer sciences, Glaser joined Microsoft in 1983 where he rose, over his ten years there, to become vice president of multimedia and consumer systems. He left Microsoft in 1994, and shortly thereafter says he downloaded Mosaic, an early version of the Netscape Internet browser. He immediately saw the potential to augment the browser with "streaming." He founded RealNetworks and was soon able to take it public. It became a hot Internet stock, and for a time, Glaser was a billionaire.

Following the bursting of the Internet bubble and heightened competition with

Microsoft's Media Player and Apple's QuickTime, RealNetworks took a pounding for a number of years. Glaser decided to take on Microsoft in court. Like earlier federal and state lawsuits against Microsoft, Glaser's company claimed Microsoft was competing unfairly by bundling its media player into its software. The case settled with RealNetworks receiving more than $750 million in cash and services from Microsoft. As of mid-2008, Glaser was still in charge of a publicly traded Realsoft that was worth a tad less than $1 billion.[173]

Broadcast.com and HDNet: As described more fully in the prior chapter, Mark Cuban grew up poor, the son of Russian Jewish emigrants in blue-collar Pittsburgh. He was a bright student who was also considered something of a hustler with a native selling talent. After his 1983 graduation, he started a computer consulting firm, MicroSolutions, which he built it to $30 million of annual revenues before selling it to Compuserve. After "kicking back" for a couple years, he partnered with non-Jew Todd R. Wagner to create Broadcast.com. It was an early pioneer of radio and television broadcasting over the Internet. Cuban and Wagner took it public and, in 1999, sold it to Yahoo for $5.7 billion. Cuban then launched HDNet, a 24/7 high-definition television broadcast network available on satellite, cable, and selected over the air high definition broadcast stations. He and Wagner also purchased Landmark theaters, a fifty-seven theater chain of "art-house" movie theaters which air not only independent art films but also high-definition original movies.[174]

Measures of High-Tech Entrepreneurial Success

One measure of entrepreneurial success is provided by the *Fortune* "40 Under 40" annual list of the wealthiest young Americans, nearly all of them self-made. Though entrepreneurial success is not simply about wealth, it is one scorecard. The *Fortune's* list from 2004 is included as Exhibit 15a. While it includes thirteen athletes and entertainers, the remaining twenty-seven were all successful young entrepreneurs, mostly from high-technology companies they started or led. Of the twenty-seven, at least six are Jewish. Three of them are among the top five and five of them among the top ten. In order, the six include: No. 1 Michael Dell, No. 3 Jeff Skoll, No. 5 Sergey Brin, No. 9 Dan Snyder, No. 10 Marc Benioff, and No. 17 Jerry Greenberg. Statistically, at 2 percent of the U.S. population, Jews would be lucky if even one of the twenty-seven was Jewish. At 22 percent, the result is ten times what one would expect.

Chapter 16

Fortune 500 CEOs

*"Irv Shapiro led not only the DuPont company,...
his business sense and compassion were united as
he led other business leaders to join him in pursuit
of improving the lives of everyone he touched....
He was a statesman and a gentleman."[175]*
    *—Obituary Statement of Delaware Governor
        Ruth Ann Minner, September 11, 2001*

*"There are few business leaders recognized
throughout the country for probity and integrity in
the way such leaders as Edward Filene, who
headed the department store empire, Irving
Shapiro, the head of DuPont, Walter Wriston of
Citibank, and John Whitehead of Goldman Sachs,
were recognized as being spokespersons for a set
of realistic, intelligent, public-spirited values."[176]*
    —Arthur Levitt, former SEC chairman

Irving Shapiro

The selection of Irving Shapiro to head DuPont Corporation was a watershed moment in the history of Jews as CEOs of major U.S. Corporations. His appointment was seen to have broken a cultural logjam. It made *Wall Street Journal* headlines on December 14, 1973, and Shapiro was soon regarded as a prominent "business establishment" figure. For many, he was seen as "the first Jew to achieve such stature in a major corporation not founded or purchased by Jews."[177]

Shapiro's selection was remarkable on many counts. In the 171 years since its founding by French immigrant Eleuthère Irénée (E.I.) du Pont in 1802, the company had been headed only by succeeding generations of DuPont family members. Shapiro did not, as was common in post-World War II America, work his way up the organization chart through the rungs of operational, sales, and staff jobs. Further, he was not an entrepreneur, nor was he trained as a manager.

Instead, after graduating from the University of Minnesota Law School in 1941, he joined the U.S. Justice Department where he argued and won his first Supreme Court case in 1948. Three years later, he joined DuPont's legal staff and shortly thereafter, negotiated resolution of the General Motors-DuPont antitrust lawsuit. His skill in that important task earned him the trust of DuPont's senior management and board. By 1970 he was a member of the executive committee, and in July 1973, he became vice chairman. He was ready for the next step—to the chairmanship.[178]

Shapiro led DuPont in an era of regulation, recession, and mid-1970s energy crises that followed the Yom Kippur War. His diplomacy and skill in addressing those challenges gave him standing alongside such "white shoe" CEOs as non-Jews Walter Wriston, John Whitehead, David Rockefeller, and others. He was a leader of American industry.

For some, Shapiro's accession meant Jews had "arrived." Later, others would compare the notoriety surrounding his promotion to the relative quiet which greeted the naming of Michael Eisner to head Disney. They saw the quiescence of Eisner's accession as proof Jews were finally accepted as CEOs of major U.S. corporations.[179] That interpretation contains a good deal of truth, but the story is more interesting and more complex than that.

Conventional Thinking About Jewish CEOs

Over the 350 years following Peter Stuyvesant's failed attempt to keep Jews out of North America when they arrived from Brazil in 1654, the U.S. has been among the least discriminatory countries in the world for Jews. That history has, nonetheless, had its ups and downs. The generally benign period of most of the 1800s was interrupted in the late 1800s by a rise of anti-Semitism in Germany, which spread to the United States There was also discontent arising from the huge immigration of poor, often uneducated, Russian-Polish Jews between 1880 and 1924. Among them were anarchists, socialists, and communists, such as Emma Goldman, who soured many Americans on the recent immigrants. Certainly, controversy surrounding those emigrants contributed to anti-Jewish sentiment and the 1924 legislation which brought all immigration to a halt.[180]

The anti-Semitism of Henry Ford (who promoted the fraudulent *Protocols of the Elders of Zion* as proof of Jewish duplicity and ambitions) and General Robert Wood (who, in a remarkable irony, refused to hire Jewish buyers or senior executives at Sears, Roebuck from 1928 to 1954—after following Julius Rosenwald as Sears' CEO—were emblematic of the sometimes expressed, but often subtle, anti-Semitism which kept Jews from senior management positions and off boards of directors in selected industries and companies.

Mid-twentieth-century "conventional wisdom" held that Jews were unlikely to become chief executive officers (CEOs) of large U.S. companies. It was not considered their métier (after all, they were not seen to be "organization men" or "gray flannel suit" types). Some were seen as "pushy" or "loud."[181]

It was okay to have a Jew out there selling your products to fellow Jews, or to recruit a smart Jew for a professional staff job, such as corporate legal counsel or head of finance and accounting, but Jews were unlikely candidates for promotion to senior line management positions at corporate headquarters. This sentiment was empirically demonstrated by the long, difficult history of Jewish exclusion from the inner sanctum of companies and industries dominated by Gentiles. Moreover, they were often unwelcome in the halls of the exclusive golf and luncheon clubs where major customers were wooed, financiers and prospective new hires were wined and dined, and peers were entertained. And like much conventional wisdom of the times, it was self-fulfilling.

Jewish CEOs of Major Corporations in 1917

Harvard Business School Professor Richard S. Tedlow, and his associates Courtney Purrington and Kim Eric Bettcher recently summarized a business history project in their paper titled, *The American CEO in the Twentieth Century.*[182] Their work looked at the backgrounds of major U.S. company CEOs in 1917 and 1997. It sought to evaluate the demographic characteristics of the leaders in those two eras and the differences that arose over the intervening eighty years.

For the 1917 group, they identified who they believe were the CEOs of the 200 largest U.S. companies at the time. Of those 200, religion could be discerned for 153. Of them, Protestants dominated with two-thirds of the total. But Jews were a surprising and slightly disproportionate 4.5 percent of the executives at a time when Jews were 3.4 percent of the U.S. population. Further, as noted above, this was a time when Jews were subject to some measure of heightened anti-Semitism.

Tedlow's research suggests the years around 1917 represent an era when professional managers were taking over from the "robber barons" and larger-than-life figures of the late 1800s and early 1900s such as John D. Rockefeller, J.P. Morgan, Andrew Carnegie, Cornelius Vanderbilt, Jay Gould, and others. This profile does not apply, however, to the seven Jews. Their stories belie the notion they were second-generation professional managers. While it is difficult to know the backgrounds of all seven, we do know that:

Daniel Guggenheim, with his father, Meyer, and six brothers were entrepreneurs who emigrated from Switzerland. They began by importing embroideries, but later acquired interests in two successful Colorado copper mines. Eventually, the entire family fortune was invested in mining and smelters. Under Daniel, the Guggenheim mining interests were parlayed into control of the American Smelting and Refining Company (ASARCO). Under David, ASARCO became the world's dominant mining operation.[183] (See the more complete profile in Chapter 21 – Enterprise.)

Harry Hart, a German Jewish emigrant, began a Chicago clothing store with his brother Max in 1872. Fifteen years later, they brought aboard Marcus Marx and Joseph Schaffner to form Hart Schaffner and Marx. By 1917 it was one of America's foremost manufacturers of men's apparel.[184] (See Chapter 20 – Jewelry, Apparel and Cosmetics.)

Fred Hirschhorn was the founder and chief executive of General Cigar Co. Little biographical information is available on Hirschhorn but, like his contemporaries William Paley and Joseph Cullman, he was among the successful early twentieth-century Jews in the tobacco industry. In 1960 the Cullman family acquired control of

General Cigar, changed the name to Culbro Corporation, and as of 2005, they continue to lead the company, albeit with a Swedish partner.[185]

Jules (or Julius) Kessler was a Hungarian emigrant Jew who started out selling whiskey during Colorado's 1870s silver boom. He set up his own distilleries and began selling direct to retailers rather than through wholesalers. In the words of an August 26, 1935, *Time* magazine article, Kessler was so successful a distiller, salesman, and operator, that "Distillers Securities Corp. ('The Whiskey Trust') put itself and its surplus stocks in his hands." Prohibition ended Kessler's era and he retired, a wealthy man, to Vienna, Austria, returning only after Repeal. Kessler was later honored by Seagram when it formed a subsidiary and named it in his honor.[186]

Solomon Guedalia Rosenbaum was the 1917 CEO of the National Cloak & Suit Company. Though many pages from old National Cloak catalogues can be found, almost nothing is available on Rosenbaum. Nonetheless, as Thomas Sowell indicates in his book, Ethnic America, "By 1885, there were 241 garment factories in New York City – 234 of which were owned by Jews...As of 1890, about half of all Jews working in American Industry were clothing workers."[187] Thus, it is not surprising that in 1917, a "Rosenbaum" would have been CEO of one of America's foremost apparel companies.

Julius Rosenwald was already a successful manufacturer of men's summer clothing in 1895 when, with his brother-in law Aaron Nusbaum, he bought half of Sears, Roebuck for $75,000. Roebuck, a watchmaker, had left the business, as did Nusbaum after a few years. Rosenwald became CEO working with Sears, a gifted promoter, and it was Rosenwald who built Sears into the foremost retailer of the times.[188] (See the Rosenwald profile in Chapter 23 – Philanthropy.)

Adolph Zukor was a Hungarian Jewish emigrant who became a wealthy entrepreneur as a furrier. He took a "flier" on penny arcades and nickelodeons, made money, and then partnered with Marcus Loew to build a chain of theaters—and with Jesse Lasky—to build the Famous Players studio. In 1917 Famous Players acquired Paramount which Zukor then headed till 1936. He stayed on as a director, producer, and later chairman emeritus of Paramount until his death in 1976. His Paramount career spanned fifty-nine years.[189] (See Chapter 13 – "Hollywood").

The Jews leading seven of America's 200 largest companies in 1917 were not professional second-generation managers of established large corporations, nor did they "start at the bottom and work their way up." They were mostly first- or second-generation immigrants. They were successful entrepreneurs, running businesses they started or largely shaped. Some were involved in industries that traditionally had significant Jewish participation, such as retailing (Jews started more than half of American's department stores), tobacco, and spirits. And though one might not think of mining as a Jewish industry, by 1917 the Oppenheimers were becoming prominent in diamonds and, as noted above, Daniel Guggenheim was heading up the dominant U.S. mining company, having inherited the CEO mantle from his father.

Another facet deserves mention. The 1917 data, though anecdotal, tends to corroborate the notion of Jews as entrepreneurs who pursued opportunities that did not compete directly with established Gentile companies and industries. "Ready-to-wear" apparel did not exist as an industry before the invention of the Singer sewing machine and the mass migration of Jews from the Russian Pale. Many of the newly arrived Jews were tailors, and the inexpensive Singer sewing machine represented the opportunity to create a wholly new industry. Hart, Rosenwald, Rosenbaum, and Zukor all got their start that way. Later, Zukor, like others of the so-called Hollywood Jews, pursued a counterpart new opportunity in theaters and film.

In short, the seven Jews were mostly involved in new companies and new industries or industries in which Jews had long been engaged. None was a professional manager, promoted through the organization to become its CEO.

The Outsiders

In 1988 Professor Abraham Korman of Baruch College wrote *The Outsiders: Jews and Corporate America*.[190] His book supports the points made above but updates the analysis. Korman began by providing the historical business context, looking at different industries, such as commercial banking, insurance, shipping, and automobile production where there were relatively few Jews among senior executives. He contrasted that with retailing, entertainment, and apparel as examples of industries where Jews were numerous.

Korman cited a 1976 *Fortune* magazine article which estimated that 7 percent of CEOs at the 800 largest American corporations were Jews (versus their 2.75 percent of the U.S. population at that time.) He also described a 1985 *Fortune* study which found Jews to be 5 to 7 percent of the directors of large corporations and 7.6 percent of the CEOs. Still disproportionate overall, he nonetheless saw discrimination retarding Jews in selected industries.

He evaluated the 1985 data industry by industry, finding lowest Jewish penetration in upper ranks of the petroleum, chemical, food, glass, building materials, mining, and crude oil production businesses (all less than 4 percent). Highest Jewish penetration was found in apparel (26.7 percent), textiles and vinyl flooring (9.9 percent) and publishing/printing (9.5 percent). Korman also referenced a 1986 Korn-Ferry study showing that while 7.4 percent of top CEOs were Jews, of those CEOs under the age of forty, 13 percent were Jews.

A further study, not mentioned by Korman, but done in the same time frame, deserves mention. *Business Week* reported in its Oct. 20, 1989, issue that among the 1,000 most valuable U.S. companies at the time, 62 percent were headed by Protestants, 23 percent by Roman Catholics, and 13 percent by Jews. If those data were correct, Jews, then about 2.3 percent of the population, were overrepresented as CEOs of the 1,000 most valuable companies by a factor of six.

In short, things were improving, albeit slowly. Jews were a growing proportion of the senior management and boards of large corporations, and young Jews were doing even better. Many industries still favored old-line Gentiles, but others favored Jews and barriers appeared to be diminishing.

More Recent Studies of Jews as CEOs

A review of the CEOs of *Fortune's* 100 largest U.S. corporations in 2004 identified nine prominent Jewish CEOs:[191]

Maurice Greenberg – American International Group
Ivan Seidenberg – Verizon Communications
Michael Dell – Dell Computers
Robert Benmosche – MetLife
Steven Ballmer – Microsoft
Michael Eisner – Walt Disney
Sumner Redstone – Viacom
Seymour Sternberg – New York Life
Brian Roberts – Comcast

In addition, another eight CEOs may have been Jewish, or been of Jewish heritage, though they were not widely identified as such. It appears that today, Jews probably serve as CEOs of perhaps 15 percent of America's largest companies. This is seven times what one would expect.

In 2003 and 2004, *Fortune* magazine identified "The Power 25, The Most Powerful People in Business," the Warren Buffetts and Bill Gateses of corporate America. Of the 2003 group, six (24 percent) were Jews: Sandy Weill of Citigroup, Michael Dell of Dell Computer, Maurice Greenberg of AIG Insurance, Sumner Redstone of Viacom, Ivan Seidenberg of Verizon, and Brian Roberts of Comcast. Of the 2004 group, five (20 percent) were Jews. Weill, having resigned from Citicorp, was no longer included. The article also identified three "Lions in Winter," "business legends no longer running the show." Andy Grove and Weill were two of the three "Lions."[192]

That same year, Professor Tedlow and his Harvard colleagues released their paper (cited earlier) which looks at the demography of CEOs of America's 200 largest companies in 1917 and 1997. For the 1997 group, they used *Fortune* magazine's revenue-based rankings as the indicator of size. Their work provides an excellent tool for evaluating the contemporary circumstances of Jews as CEOs of major American companies and the changes that have occurred over time.

For the 1997 group, Tedlow et al. indicate that of the 200 CEOs, data on "religion" was available for only seventy-two, but of them, seventeen were Jewish. There is no assertion that the seventy-two were representative (though they felt most of those unaccounted for were likely to be Protestants). Nonetheless, it is surprising that 24 percent of those whose cultural or religious affiliation could be determined were Jews. Moreover, even if all of the remaining 128 CEOs, whose religious affiliation were unknown, were non-Jews, that would still leave Jews as CEOs of 8.5 percent of America's 200 largest companies in 1997. It is likely that the actual number is higher than 8.5 percent, and assuming some of those whose "religion" was not identified are Jewish, one may again surmise that today Jews are CEOs of 10 to 15 percent or more of major U.S. corporations.

Be that as it may, the seventeen corporate heads identified by Tedlow et al. provide useful insight into contemporary Jewish CEOs of major U.S. corporations and the basis for comparing their circumstances with those of the 1917 group.

Sanford I. Weill headed up Citicorp in 1997. A Cornell graduate, he began as a "runner" for Bear Stearns, became a broker, and soon, with three partners, started a stock brokerage firm. Weill, the leader, built the firm through fifteen acquisitions into the powerful Shearson brokerage. Later, after Weill had left Shearson, he began again in 1986, starting with Commercial Credit, a Control Data spinoff. He built it through acquisitions into Citicorp, then the world's largest financial services company.[193]

David H. Komansky headed Merrill, Lynch, Pierce, Fenner & Smith in 1997. Founded in 1917, Merrill Lynch was one of Wall Street's oldest and most powerful firms. It was run by founder, Charles Merrill, until 1956. Considered by many a Gentile brokerage firm, Merrill Lynch hired Komansky in 1968, shortly after he got out of the University of Miami. He served the firm in a wide range of positions over a twenty-seven-year career before being named COO in 1995 and CEO in 1996. Komansky led Merrill Lynch for seven tumultuous years. Since retiring, he has served on numerous boards including the New York Stock Exchange.[194]

Maurice R. Greenberg headed American International Group (AIG) in 1997. Founded by non-Jew Cornelius Vander Starr, in 1919 as a Shanghai-based offshore insurance company, Greenberg joined AIG in 1960 after two stints in the U.S. Army, one as an attorney, and eight years at Continental Casualty. Greenberg's early success in turning around AIG's failing North American operations led Starr to name him as his successor in 1967. Over the next thirty-eight years, Greenberg built AIG into the world's third largest insurance company, and the largest U.S. insurer. Before his 2005 troubles with New York's Attorney General Eliot Spitzer led to his retirement, Greenberg was regarded as one of America's foremost business leaders and philanthropists. Three years after Greenberg's departure, AIG became a "poster child" for the financial melt down of 2008. It had taken on too much risk insuring credit instruments, including pools of mortgages. He believes that had he stayed, it would never have happened. [195]

Andrew S. Grove was CEO of Intel in 1997. Grove escaped Hungary in 1956, graduated from NYU and earned a Ph.D. in engineering from Cal Berkeley before joining Fairchild Semiconductor. A few short years later, he was invited by Gordon Moore and Robert Noyce to join them in founding Intel. By 1979 he was president and he led and transformed Intel through its various challenges, being recognized for all he had done by being named *Time* magazine's 1997 Man of the Year.[196]

Laurence A. Tisch was head of Loews in 1997. At age 23, he purchased a 300-room winter resort in Lakewood, New Jersey. Later, joined by his brother Bob, the two bought other hotels before they took control of Loews Theaters (see Zukor above). They further diversified over the years, buying Lorillard, Bulova Watch Company, CNA Insurance Company, controlling interest in CBS, and other companies. Before his death in 2003, Tisch, like Weill and Greenberg, was counted among America's foremost business leaders and major philanthropists.[197]

Harvey Golub was CEO of American Express (AMEX) in 1997. Amex was then nearly 150 years old, having been started by non-Jews Henry Wells and William Fargo in 1850. During the 1980s, Golub's predecessor, James Robinson (not Jewish), made a failed attempt to build Amex into a financial conglomerate. In 1984 Golub, a senior partner at the prestigious management consulting firm of McKinsey & Company, was recruited by Amex. In 1993 Robinson's failures led to Golub's promotion to CEO. In a series of moves, Golub turned the company around and made it substantially more valuable. He retired in 2000, turning the reins over to Kenneth I. Chenault, a talented black executive mentored by Golub.[198] Golub now serves on a number of Boards, including his chairmanship of Campbell Soup Company.

Gerald M. Levin was CEO of Time Warner in 1997. Time was the 1922 creation of non-Jew Henry Luce while Warner was the Hollywood studio created by the four Warner Brothers. Levin joined Time's Home Box Office (HBO) in 1972 after brief stints with a law firm and one other business. He pioneered the distribution of HBO via satellite, a highly successful decision which transformed the industry, and he helped negotiate the 1990 merger with Warner (and later with Turner Broadcasting). Steven Ross became CEO after the Time-Warner merger and Levin was his protégé. When Ross died unexpectedly, Levin took over. Later, Levin's merger of Time Warner and AOL would prove a donnybrook and he stepped down in 2002.[199]

Michael S. Dell was CEO of Dell Computers in 1997. He started the company in his college dorm room in 1984 with an initial investment of $1,000. He soon dropped out of college to pursue his creation, and like fellow dropouts Bill Gates and Larry Ellison, he proved one could be very successful despite the absence of a sheepskin. In the ensuing twenty years, Dell built his company into what was for many years the world's largest, most profitable, and most valuable computer manufacturer.[200]

Michael Goldstein was CEO of Toys 'R' Us in 1997. Founded in 1948 by Charles Lazarus with $2,000 of borrowed money, Toys 'R' Us became the largest U.S. toy retailer. Michael Goldstein had begun his career as an accountant with a Jewish accounting firm. He joined Toys 'R' Us in the early 1980s, presumably in an accounting role. When Lazarus stepped down in 1994, Goldstein became CEO, a job he held until 1998, while retaining the chairmanship until 2001. Goldstein led the firm through seven challenging years as the Internet and discount retailers, such as Wal-Mart, began cannibalizing the toy industry.[201]

Leslie H. Wexner started The Limited in 1963 with $5,000 of borrowed money. The son of Russian emigrants, Wexner began with a single store in suburban Columbus, Ohio, and, by 1997, had built a huge chain of specialty women's apparel stores. He is now also a major philanthropist.[202]

Stephen P. Kaufman was CEO of Arrow Electronics in 1997. Arrow, founded in 1935, is the world's largest distributor of electronic components and computer products. Kaufman, who graduated from MIT and the Harvard Business School, worked for Midland-Ross Corporation and for ten years was an associate and then partner at McKinsey & Company. He joined Arrow in 1982 as president of the electronics distribution division. He became Arrow's COO in 1985 and its CEO in 1986, serving for fourteen years before retiring as CEO in 2000 and as chairman in 2002. He then became a senior lecturer at Harvard Business School, while also serving on several boards of directors.[203]

Lewis E. Platt was CEO of Hewlett-Packard (HP) in 1997. Platt joined HP in 1966 after graduating from the Wharton Business School. Two years earlier, he had earned a bachelor's degree in mechanical engineering from Cornell. Platt held a variety of positions at HP before becoming executive vice president in 1987 and CEO in 1993. Following David Packard's retirement in 1990, John Young served briefly as CEO before Platt took over. Platt then served as CEO until 1999. After retirement, Platt was CEO of Kendall Jackson Winery from 1999 to 2001 and was non-executive chairman of Boeing. Platt passed away in 2005.[204]

Harry P. Kamen was CEO of Metropolitan Life Insurance in 1997. Started in 1863, Metropolitan is America's second largest insurer. Kamen, a Penn undergraduate and Harvard Law School graduate, became CEO in April 1993 and served until mid-1998. He remained a Met Life director and was also a director of Pfizer and the NASD, and a regular attendee of Bill and Hillary Clinton's Renaissance Weekend events.[205]

Arthur M. Blank was CEO of Home Depot in 1997. Started by Blank and Bernard Marcus in 1979 after their storied firing from the Handy Dan home improvement chain, Home Depot began with three stores in Atlanta and built, what by 1997 was the world's largest home improvement store chain. Blank, since retired, has become a major philanthropist and the owner of the Atlanta Falcons football team.[206]

Seymour G. (Sy) Sternberg was CEO of New York Life Insurance Company in 1997. Founded in 1845, New York Life is the third largest U.S. insurance company. Sternberg became a Chartered Life Underwriter in 1976 after earning his master's degree in electrical engineering from Northeastern University in 1968. He spent thirteen years with Massachusetts Mutual Life Insurance Company before joining New York Life in 1989. He was promoted to COO in 1995 and CEO in 1997, a title he continues to hold in 2005 Sternberg has been involved in a large number of civic activities including board seats on the U.S. Chamber of Commerce, Big Brother Big Sisters of New York, the chairmanship of the CUNY Business Leadership Council and various appointments by the Clinton administration.[207]

Sumner M. Redstone was CEO of National Amusements (now Viacom) in 1997. It was his creation. Having graduated from Harvard University in less than three years, Redstone was recruited by Edwin Reischauer to work in the Army unit that cracked the Japanese code during World War II. At war's end, Redstone attended Harvard Law School and then practiced law, including an assignment as a special assistant to the U.S. attorney general. In 1954 he left the practice of law to join the family's small chain of outdoor movie theaters. Through internal growth and a dizzying array of acquisitions, Redstone built the company into today's Viacom.[208]

John B. Hess was CEO of Amerada Hess in 1997. It was the creation of his father, Leon, son of Hungarian Jewish emigrants. Leon began by selling heating oil from the back of a truck in Asbury Park, New Jersey. Initially with his father's help, Leon built Amerada Hess into a major oil company. John, a graduate of Harvard University and Harvard Business School, joined the family firm when he was 23. He became CEO in 1995, four years before his father died. John is active in support of Democratic Party politics and was a significant supporter of Moveon.org. He is also on the board of the USTA Tennis and Education Foundation.[209]

Comparing the industries and people described above with their counterparts in 1917 reveals the sea change which has occurred over the intervening eighty years. The sense of optimism surrounding Shapiro's 1973 accession to head DuPont has been realized, particularly from the 1990s on.

In part, this happened because the nature of American business changed. Heavy industries, such as steel, auto, and appliance manufacturing, and others, largely run by Gentiles over much of the twentieth century, declined in importance while industries in which Jews were long prominent, such as finance, retail, media, entertainment, and more recently high-tech startups became more important. But the 1990s also show evidence of growing Jewish leadership in companies and industries long considered to be the province of Gentiles.

As always for Jews there was the premium on education. All but one of the seventeen Jewish CEOs earned a bachelor's degree from schools such as NYU (3), Cornell (2), and Harvard (2). The only non-degree holder, Michael Dell, dropped out of college to start Dell Computers. Even more impressive, thirteen of the seventeen earned graduate degrees or participated in graduate education, four at Harvard Business School, three at Harvard Law School, plus an MBA from Wharton and a Ph.D. from Cal Berkeley.

As Jews have long been, some were entrepreneurial. These include Dell, Weill, Grove, Wexner, Blank, Redstone, and to some extent Greenberg. All of them were superb entrepreneurs.

But by 1997, some evidenced the more traditional temperament of CEOs who have worked their way up the organization chart, sometimes within companies whose long roots are considered to be quite Gentile. These include American Express, Merrill Lynch, Metropolitan Life, and New York Life. Golub and Kaufman both worked for McKinsey & Company and both worked their way up several non-Jewish organizations before being promoted to, or hired to, serve as CEOs of AMEX and Arrow Electronics, respectively. Komansky worked his way up Merrill Lynch after joining it in 1968 as a stockbroker. Grove, though entrepreneurial, worked for years as "Number 3" under two Gentiles before becoming Intel's CEO. Platt worked his way up Hewlett Packard for twenty-seven years before becoming its CEO.

In short, times have changed. Anti-Semitism has receded. Clubs discriminate less than they did even twenty-five or thirty years ago. Jews and Gentiles now work and play side by side more than ever before. Recently, non-Jew Bill Gates handed over Microsoft's CEO slot to Jew Steve Ballmer. Meanwhile, Sandy Weill, a Jew, turned Citicorp over to non-Jew Harold Prince. Goldman Sachs, which was created and long run by Jews, was for years headed by Treasury Secretary Henry Paulson, a Christian Scientist. And, of course, Ivan Seidenberg runs Verizon.

Jews are more assimilated and more accepted than ever. They have proven they perform well as CEOs of large organizations whether in industries and companies long considered Jewish havens or not. And, as has been proven true throughout this book, they are disproportionately successful in this role.

Chapter 17

Finance

Asked by a neighbor whether there would be war or peace, Gutele Rothschild, widow of Mayer Amschel Rothschild, replied, "War? Nonsense. My boys won't let them."

Mayer Amschel's five sons, clockwise from the top: Salomon, Amschel, Karl, James, and Nathan. There is no known likeness of their father.

The Rothschilds[210,211]

Before "globalization," before Goldman Sachs, Merrill Lynch, Morgan Stanley, or JP Morgan, there were the Rothschilds. Ten generations and more than 200 years later, they remain a force in international finance. If ever a family illustrated the consequences of Jewish Diaspora, when combined with intelligence, skill, and determination, it is revealed in the remarkable achievements of the Rothschilds.

The son of a small-time dealer in used merchandise, Mayer Amschel Rothschild (1744-1812) was orphaned at age twelve while studying to become a rabbi at a Nuremburg yeshiva. Lacking funds to continue his studies, he was apprenticed by relatives to an Oppenheimer banking house in Hanover. But when he was twenty, Mayer left Oppenheimer's, choosing to return home to the Frankfurt ghetto where he would work with his two brothers trading what some would call low-value antiques, others, classy junk. It was not an auspicious career move for Mayer. The family's lowly status was illustrated in its surname. Rothschild was not a Jewish name going back generations. It was simply a representation, in German, of the "red sign (or shield)" serving as the equivalent of a house number outside the family home.

In addition to their traditional merchandise, Mayer began collecting and trading old coins and medals. It was a hobby he shared with courtiers of Prince William IX of Hesse Hanau (Kassel), a small German principality. Initially Mayer traded and sold coins to a few of the courtiers he had met during his earlier days in Hanover. Later his elegant coin catalogs earned him an audience with the prince, who purchased some of his coins. As time passed and the relationship grew, Mayer became a trusted merchant to the court, and by 1769, he was designated a "Court Factor" (and later, "Superior Court Agent") to His Serene Highness Prince William of Hanau.

Mayer diversified. He began dealing in currencies, then dry goods, and later, wine and tobacco. Known for his integrity, his style was always gracious, low key, intellectual, and amiable. Mayer and his five sons provided ever more services to the prince in addition to trading coins and medals. At some point, one of the prince's key advisers became a partner in the very small bank Mayer had established.

On the death of his father in 1785, Prince William acceded to become Landgrave (a Holy Roman Empire title akin to "count."). From his own efforts, augmented by his inheritance, William became one of the wealthiest monarchs in Europe.

In 1798 Mayer's twenty-one-year-old son, Nathan Mayer Rothschild (1777–1836), moved to Manchester, England, where he set up shop trading cotton and other merchandise. Meanwhile back in present-day Germany, Mayer purchased English notes from William at a discount from face value. Before long, Mayer and Nathan combined the two activities into one, paying for Nathan's Manchester cotton with the discounted English notes purchased from William.

When the prince wished to make a loan to his impoverished uncle, the Danish monarch, discretion suggested that the use of an intermediary would help mitigate the sensitivities of revealing his own wealth. It would also avoid the uncle's embarrassment for accepting a loan from a nephew, and it reduced the risk of a "default" among family members. Mayer served as that trusted intermediary, shielding the role of William. In similar fashion, when the prince's son needed money, it was Rothschild who provided the loan.

But everything changed in 1806. Napoleon took over Hesse-Hanau and William fled to Denmark, leaving the stewardship of most of his loans and investments in trust with the Rothschilds. Neither Napoleon, nor any of his agents ever made the connection between William's presumed wealth and the Rothschilds' role in managing it during William's exile. Napoleon's agents attempted to nationalize and collect the debts, but Mayer's sons got there first.

With most of Europe swallowed up by Napoleon, William's ability to lend capital dried up. Mayer convinced him to have Nathan loan much of it to the British, buying consols (bonds) from which William would earn interest and the Rothschilds a commission. They agreed upon the price William would pay for the bonds, but as it turned out, Nathan's talent for anticipating price movements allowed him to purchase consols at an even lower price. He retained the spread and went on to successfully speculate in gold bullion. Rothschild delivered the promised returns and all of the capital to William, but they too profited handsomely.

Nathan also used his capital to acquire English goods which, in cooperation with his father and brothers, he smuggled into the continent in defiance of Napoleon's declarations that such goods were contraband. Through those early years, the family operated under the cover of being simple Frankfurt- and London-based dealers in merchandise. At the same time, they also served as William's agent while making their own successful investments and carrying out their smuggling operations.

By 1810, however, the family was no longer trading in merchandise. The days of smuggling were over as well. From now on the Rothschilds focused on only one commodity – money. No cotton, no whiskey or tobacco, no used coins (except for trading with William). Just money, or its equivalent in credit instruments, securities, or bullion.

Nathan was becoming a major force in England. When the British needed to transmit gold to Wellington in far-off Spain—to pay for troops and supplies fighting the French and their Spanish allies—it was the Rothschilds to whom they turned to move the bullion through France, and on to Wellington.

In 1811 Mayer's youngest son, James (Jacob) (1792-1868), moved to Paris to set up shop. His clever ruse—that the British would be harmed by the flow of gold from England—was the subterfuge which allowed the Rothschilds to import the gold into France. From that point they used various means to convert some of it to notes and to transmit those funds and the remainder of the bullion across France, the Pyrenees and on to Wellington. Their success led to further business for the Crown, including helping England finance its continental allies.

But the coup for which Nathan became most famous was the purported fortune he made from early knowledge of the outcome of the Battle of Waterloo. The battle was Napoleon's final downfall. It sealed England's role as the dominant world power for the next century up to World War I. It was also the culmination of Rothschild pre-eminence. From that point on, they were Europe's premier financiers until the later days of the nineteenth century.

But some legends surrounding the Rothschilds' success in the days immediately following Waterloo are false. No carrier pigeons transmitted the battle's outcome to Nathan Rothschild. Nor did he make a huge fortune from questionable transactions.

Nathan learned the battle's outcome from an early edition of a Dutch newspaper a Rothschild agent had sent to England by boat from Ostend, Holland. Nathan met the boat and learned the outcome a full twenty-four hours before Wellington's emissary arrived in England. Nathan immediately carried the news to the prime minister.

Only after that did he move to the floor of the stock exchange where he first sold consols (suggesting defeat) before later buying them. Reputedly he misled the market and made off with millions. Here too, however, the legend misrepresents the facts. During the days before and after the victory, consols fluctuated from a low of 69 $\frac{1}{16}$ to a high of 71 $\frac{1}{2}$ pounds. There was no sensational market manipulation, nor any colossal gain. Moreover, Nathan had expected the war to last much longer. Its quick end resulted in losses and a liquidity crisis for him after Waterloo.

But the successful stewardship for William, the transfer of gold to Wellington, the service as financial intermediaries for England, and their banking activities in England and on the continent, created an immense family fortune over time.

The brothers were operating from Europe's major financial centers. Nathan, who first set up shop in Manchester (1798), moved to London in 1809. In 1812 James established himself in Paris. In 1820 Salomon (1774–1855) went to Vienna, and later in the 1820s, Karl (1788–1855) opened his office in Naples. Meanwhile, following Mayer's death in 1812, Amschel (1773–1855) took over the Frankfurt operation.

Through the first half of the nineteenth century, the family served as bankers not only to William and the British Crown (in 1825–26 helping the Bank of England avert a liquidity crisis), but also to various post-Napoleonic governments in France, Hapsburg Austria, Italian City states, and German principalities. The brothers and their offspring founded or financed many of the Continent's early railroads and subways. They backed Cecil Rhodes' and DeBeers' gold and diamond mining operations in South Africa, financed Austria's Lloyd's steamship line, and Spain's Rio Tinto mines. They loaned Disraeli the funds England needed to purchase control of the Suez Canal, and they founded CreditAnstalt Bank of Austria and Sun Alliance Insurance Company. Nathan also pioneered the floating of foreign bonds denominated in the currency of the country where the bonds were sold, rather than that of the country doing the borrowing.

Measures of their nineteenth-century wealth are inexact at best, in no small measure because of the family's penchant for secrecy. But one estimate by Fredric Morton, a credible family biographer, puts the family's mid-nineteenth century worth at $40 billion (in today's money) or more. James, known to be the wealthiest man in France, was worth 600 million francs, 150 million more than all of France's other financiers combined. Biographer Niall Ferguson, who gained access to the family archives in the 1990s, says they became the richest family in the world. He estimates their banking resources at fourteen times those of Barings, then the world's second largest firm. Until the computer and Internet, such wealth had never been built so quickly, and all of it from a former yeshiva student who started trading used merchandise and brought his five sons into the family business.

But wealth was not the sole accomplishment of the family. Over the first hundred years, despite being Jewish, the family was honored with nobility (all five brothers were made Austrian barons). James acquired vineyards and developed one of France's best and most prestigious wines (Chateau Lafite Rothschild), while his nephew, Nathan, bought and developed Chateau Mouton Rothschild. They consulted with Metternich in Austria, with Bismarck in Germany, with all of the French royalty, the pope, as well as England's monarchs and prime ministers. Family members were elected to Parliament and knighted by the queen.

They were active in support of their fellow Jews. Mayer was instrumental in demanding relaxation of restrictions on Frankfurt Jews. Bismarck attributed Jewish emancipation in Austria to Rothschild efforts. The end of the Roman ghetto was attributed to Rothschilds lobbying the pope. Nathan's son, Lionel Nathan Rothschild, pushed for, and became, the first Jewish member of Parliament to take his oath as a Jew, and his son, Nathan Mayer, was the first Jew appointed to the House of Lords. It was Lionel Walter Rothschild to whom the letter from Lord Balfour was addressed declaring England's support for a Jewish state in Palestine. And Baron Edmond James de Rothschild made early purchases of land in Israel (125,000 acres by 1933) to support communities such as Rishon LeZion, where emigrants arriving from Eastern Europe would live. Israel's Knesset was built with funds donated by the son of the baron in his honor. Shimon Peres, Israel's former prime minster is quoted as saying, "Never has a family donated so much of its wealth to the making of history."

Today the Rothschild family institution continues. It is, perhaps, less prominent and less powerful in twenty-first-century finance than at its peak in the nineteenth century. (In 2004, Rothschild was ranked fourth among European merger and acquisition advisers and ninth globally, behind Goldman Sachs, number one in both markets.) But after ten generations, the mystique continues. Rothschild Inc. is a U.S.-based investment bank. N.M. Rothschild continues in London. La Compagnie Financière Edmond de Rothschild, initially a Swiss-based venture capital operation, has since become a full-fledged investment bank. After the French nationalized the Paris Rothschild operations in 1981, the family took a low profile for a number of years before re-establishing itself as Rothschild & Cie Banque, a leading Paris-based investment house. And in London, Rothschild Private Management Limited is a major asset management firm. The integrated operations function from forty countries.

The Rothschild story holds our attention for many reasons. Not least of these is the role of the Jewish Diaspora. Jews spread through much of Europe for the better part of a millennium before the Rothschilds. Always a tiny minority, many were merchants and financiers, often because other trades were foreclosed by law. But the great value they placed on education sharpened their minds and made the complex transactions of finance and merchandising something they did very well. These became careers in which they could and did excel.

The Rothschilds knew their extended family could be trusted to handle complex transactions over very long distances, particularly when all were handicapped by limited access to information. There was the family bond and Mayer Amschel taught all five sons that unity was vital. Rothschild family unity was a glue that was impossible to replicate in most business partnerships. A brother whom you saw rarely, operating in a foreign culture and speaking a foreign language, was still family. You knew him and you knew what he would do. Your interests and his were aligned. All of this was exacerbated by a remarkable tradition of intermarriage. Of the twelve marriages by the sons of Mayer's five boys, nine were to first cousins. And of Mayer's direct descendants, half of their fifty-eight marriages occurred between first cousins.

Though always a minority, Jews shared the benefit of not being seen as loyal to a competing, or enemy country. Stateless, Jews were disadvantaged, but not so much so as an Englishman doing business in France, or a French financier in England.

And the Rothschilds performed superbly. They provided services no one else could do nearly so well.

There is irony in the Rothschilds' success from Napoleon's downfall. Arguably, Napoleon was the only ruler to whom the Rothschilds showed no loyalty, perhaps because of their early ties to Prince William. In any case, England, Hesse-Hanau, Bismarck's Prussia, Hapsburg Austria, and Naples all found the Rothschilds loyal to their countries of residence. In each, they performed important and valuable service. England might well have lost to Napoleon without the Rothschilds, and it might never have gained control of the Suez Canal.

And while the Rothschilds could appreciate Cromwell's early role in letting Jews back into England in 1650 after a 360-year exile, it was Napoleon who deserves credit for pushing the Jewish Emancipation in Europe. After the French National Assembly voted emancipation for Jews on September 27, 1791, it was Napoleon who liberated many of the Italian ghettos and pressed for Jewish civil rights throughout present-day Germany. He also convened an 1806 "Sanhedrin" to dispel the issue of mixed Jewish loyalties. Napoleon's edicts ended many of the harsh restrictions on Jews in France, and later in other parts of the empire as well. Over time, with help from the Rothschilds, the Jewish Emancipation spread to the rest of Europe from its Napoleonic genesis. There is always the intriguing question of whether the family may have felt they did Napoleon a disservice. Should he have been classed as a righteous Gentile?

The Rothschilds also illustrate the critical value of good information, something we take for granted today. For Nathan, it was the Dutch newspaper that told him of Waterloo. Later the Rothschilds set up a network of carrier pigeons to move news quickly, and they augmented it with a network of couriers and agents to rapidly and securely move securities, cash, bullion—and information—around Europe and the rest of the world. They supplemented the information with a keen sense for human psychology and the impact the information would have on others and on the markets.

Mayer Amschel Rothschild created a culture that has endured. One can still visit any office of Rothschild, look at their publications, or go to their Web site to see the values he taught, and by which the firm still lives:

> "Strength in unity, which ensures that each part of the network, wherever in the world, can call upon the expertise and experience of the rest
> Active evolution to meet and respond to changing markets and circumstances
> Independence of spirit and structure, making for objective and sound advice and service to clients
> Integrity as a constant value, present in every transaction."

Some History of Jews and Finance

Clay shards from ancient Babylonian tablets prove loans were made—and interest earned on those loans—long before currency ever came into circulation.[212] This was well before Abraham left Ur for Canaan with his small flock of the "Chosen" and long before Moses received the Torah, or the Oral Law, from God. "Interest rates ranging from 10 to 25 percent for silver, and 20 to 35 percent for cereals" were common.[213] Ancient India had a similar history of charging interest for loans, with 15 percent being typical.[214] In his *History of the Jews,* Paul Johnson notes, "Most early religious systems in the ancient Near East, and the secular codes arising from them, did not forbid usury." [215]

The Torah changed all that. Exodus 22:25 says, "If thou lend money to any of my people that is poor…, thou shalt not be to him as a usurer, neither shalt thou lay upon him usury." Leviticus 25:36 went further: "Take thou no usury of (thy brother)…." So did Deuteronomy 23:24, "Unto a stranger thou mayest lend upon usury; but unto thy brother thou shalt not lend upon usury." In the context of the Torah, "usury" was any interest at all, no matter how small. The idea that at some level, interest was "fair" and therefore acceptable, but at a higher rate it was not and was "usurious," only came with the passage of time.

Further, Deuteronomy suggested that while a Jew could not charge or collect interest from a fellow Jew, no such prohibition existed against a Jew charging interest to non-Jews. Though there was disagreement, some Talmudic scholars felt this was not just a "permission," but an expression of God's will.[216,217] Jews should earn interest by making loans to non-Jews.

Further complicating matters was the fact that the prohibition against charging interest on loans to fellow Jews is said to have been honored more in the breach than in reality. Johnson says, "The Biblical record shows that the law was constantly evaded." [218]

As times changed, rabbinical commentators, including Maimonides, argued the admonition should be modified. To them, the Torah's prohibition of usury arose in a world of small farming communities. In that ancient agrarian culture, beset by non-Jews intent on destroying them, Jews felt it was imperative for them to help their "brothers." They should not profit from those who had to borrow to survive. But circumstances had changed. Commercial enterprises had evolved. Required capital could not be provided gratis, and as such, interest should be charged to fellow Jews needing loans to support their activities in trade and merchandising.[219,220]

While some commentators still saw the Torah as God's word—a command for all times—Johnson's sense is that, with exceptions, the pragmatic view prevailed. "Rabbinical Judaism," says Johnson, "is essentially a method whereby ancient laws are adapted to modern and differing conditions by a process of rationalization....This...in a worldly sense, was to turn Jews into methodical problem solving businessmen."[221]

The prohibition against charging interest to fellow Jews ebbed further in the sixteenth and seventeenth centuries with the commentaries of Farissol of Avignon and Isaac Abrabanel, and the seventeenth-century acceptance of *heter iskah,* a technique in which a "partnership" is created, or a "corporate intermediary" is used in transactions between individuals.[222] Money could thus be earned from the partnership, as compensation for funds advanced, or a loan could be made to an individual by a corporation, rather than as a direct loan from one person to another. Both techniques were tools for charging interest while complying with the Torah.

For most Jews, use of *heter iskah* has receded with time. Today most make loans or borrow from fellow Jews without using such techniques. But the issue has never completely disappeared, and even today some Orthodox Jews make sure each loan they make or receive is in accordance with *heter iskah.*[223]

For early Christians, acceptance of the Old Testament and creation of their own New Testament meant they inherited—and then expanded—the Torah's proscription against usury. In Matthew 25:27, Christ is seen to disapprove of "usury."[224] In 1179 the Catholic Church went further, saying Christians who charged interest would be excommunicated.[225] While some Christians continued to make loans for interest, it was generally uncommon until the Renaissance.

Sharing roots with Judaism going back to Abraham, Islam carried forth the prohibition against interest on loans as well. A Muslim is not to collect, or pay, interest ("riba" in Arabic), in connection with a loan.[226,227] It is a prohibition that remains in effect in the twenty-first century, with most of the world's Muslims having to utilize *heter iskah*-like techniques to make the loans *halal* (clean) when they borrow money to finance the purchase of a home or car.

Unlike Jews, and perhaps because of Matthew 25:27, Christians did not believe they had the option to charge interest on loans to non-Christians. The prohibition in Islam was equally absolute. (Of course, since Christians and Muslims were usually the dominant population where ever they lived, such an exception would have had little meaning before the late Middle Ages when Christian theology began to allow interest to be charged.)

In the centuries immediately following the death of Muhammad, Islam entered its own Golden Age. From the eighth through the fourteenth century, with intermittent ebbs and flows, Muslim countries were relatively progressive, prosperous, and commercially active, as compared with Christian Europe.[228] And while they sometimes treated Jews badly, on the whole Muslims were more tolerant and supportive of Jews than Christians.[229] And if Muslim rulers and tradesmen who needed financing could not get it from their fellow Muslims, there were always the Jews.

Only limited commerce and trade transpired in the largely agrarian feudal economies of Europe's Middle Ages. While there was a limited availability of capital, it was of no great consequence for most people. In those years, the bulk of the demand for loans came from sovereigns needing money to support armies or public projects.

Jews were in a unique position. Minorities in both the Christian and Islamic worlds, they were frequently persecuted and vilified. They were generally precluded from owning land, and thus were rarely farmers. Other trades and occupations were also foreclosed when dominant populations used guilds and laws to squelch competition, particularly from Jews. Jobs left open to them were typically those that Christians and Muslims could not, or would not, pursue.

Among those careers were merchandising and various "middleman" tasks required between those who made the goods and those who consumed them. Jews served as traders and merchants, sometimes on a global scale. Johnson notes, "The Jews carried with them certain basic skills: the ability to compute exchange rates, to write a business letter and, perhaps even more important, the ability to get it delivered along their wide-spun family and religious networks."[230] In short, Diaspora Jews had an advantage in their trusted extended families and networks of co-religionists operating in foreign countries.

Other Jews became doctors, Maimonides among them. It was a profession in which Jews remain prominent to this day.

Tax farming (collecting taxes for the sovereign) was another career, albeit one that created immense resentment among those who paid the taxes.[231] Tax farming typically involved discounted prepayment of the taxes (a form of factoring with the imputed interest built into the discount) before the tax farmer then collected the taxes from citizens.

And there was lending, a profitable, if precarious career.[232] By the tenth century, Jews were major lenders to the Moslem courts, a pattern repeated later in Christian Europe.[233] For those with sufficient capital and talent, this was a lucrative profession with the added possibility of becoming a favored courtier, sometimes later called a "Court Jew." But while favored for what you could provide the sovereign, Court Jews were also at the sovereign's mercy since the debt might later be repudiated (sometimes because it was found to be "usurious.") Marcus Meisel helped the Hapsburg emperor, Maximilian II, finance his late sixteenth-century war against the Turks, but on his death in 1601, all of Meisel's property was confiscated by Maximilian.[234]

Samuel Oppenheimer (1630-1703) helped finance Hapsburg fights against the French (1673-79) and Turks (1682), after which the state renounced his loans.[235]

Christians were not always true to prohibitions against lending for interest. Edward I of England apparently expelled Jews from England in 1290 only after the Knights Templar of Jerusalem and their European Commanderies became England's principal financiers; Edward I then concluded he could exile the Jews and confiscate their wealth.[236] But it was the emergence of Renaissance Italy which gave rise to the first great Christian financiers (such as the Medici, who encouraged and recruited Jewish financiers to join them in Florence.)[237,238, 239] Among major Jewish financial families in Italy, which emerged side by side with the Christian financiers, were the Jacobses, Finizis, Norzis, Wertheims, di Abramos, Spiras, and Carmis.

Lending and investing skill later migrated beyond Italy to present-day Germany, England, France, and other countries. Among the emergent non-Jewish houses were Barings, Fugger, later Morgan and many more. The great Jewish houses included such names as Rothschild, Oppenheimer, Wertheimer, Stern, Speyer, Seligman, Bischoffsheim, Goldsmid, de Hirsch, Strousberg, Cassel, Sassoon, Kuhn, and Loeb, among others. Most Jewish and non-Jewish houses first became known for their ability to finance large government projects. Later, those skills were extended to encompass private endeavors.

The Enlightenment, Industrial Revolution, and rise of the United States led to an explosion in the demand for ever more sophisticated international finance which, in turn, provided ever more opportunities.

Jews have long been disproportionately represented among the great financiers. In fact, finance, like medicine, is one of the fields in which that history of accomplishment predates their "Golden Age." Most likely this is because it was a career they practiced long before the Jewish Emancipation and Jewish Enlightenment opened up other possibilities for them. As a group, Jews have the world's longest cultural legacy in finance. Their talents have proven as fresh in the twenty-first century as they were in the tenth.

Contemporary finance defies simple distinctions. Practitioners serve both as principals and intermediaries. They provide services in one transaction and act as entrepreneurs in another. In the discussion which follows, less than perfect distinctions are employed to assist the description of Jewish institutions and financiers. The discussion is divided into three arbitrary groupings:

First, institutional intermediaries; these are service providers such as commercial and investment banks and brokers;

Second, financial investing firms that act as principals (typically, private equity partnerships and mutual funds) and that raise capital to invest in specific enterprises or strategies;

Third, individuals whose skills in finance have been instrumental in their success.

The material is intended to be illustrative rather than comprehensive. Some, but by no means all of the more prominent Jewish personalities and Jewish-founded enterprises are covered. Without being encyclopedic, the material thus intends to provide an overall demonstration of the disproportionate Jewish achievements and contributions in finance.

Investment, Merchant and Commercial Banks, Stock Brokerage and Trading Firms

The March 6, 2006 issue of *Fortune* magazine listed what it considered the six most highly respected "securities" firms. They were: Merrill Lynch, Lehman Brothers, Bear Stearns, Goldman Sachs, Franklin Resources and A.G. Edwards.[240] Three of the six firms were founded by Jews.

Thompson Financial ranked the top ten Global M&A (merger and acquisition) firms in 2005, by volume. They are listed below:[241]

Goldman Sachs
Citigroup
Morgan Stanley
JP Morgan
Merrill Lynch
Deutsche Bank
Lehman Brothers
CSFB
UBS
Rothschild

Bloomberg also ranks the top investment firms based on M&A volume. Its list for the first quarter of 2005 included the same firms as Thompson, but replaced Rothschild with Lazard.[242]

While mergers dilute the impact of any particular group of founders over time, it is clear Jews played major roles in half or more of these firms. Goldman Sachs, Lehman Brothers, Bear Stearns, Rothschild, and Lazard have (or had) mostly Jewish roots. Citigroup's move into investment banking was largely shaped by Sandy Weill, and Salomon Brothers was acquired by Weill as part of that effort. Warburg Pincus is important to Credit Suisse First Boston (CSFB), as is S.G. Warburg to UBS (Union Bank Switzerland).

Consider some of the more prominent firms with significant Jewish roots.

Goldman Sachs & Co.:[243] Samuel Sachs began his career as a merchant before joining his father-in-law, Marcus Goldman, in 1882, to create Goldman Sachs. As one would expect given Sach's background, the firm's initial client base came from retailing. Over the thirty-one years following Goldman's death, Sachs built the firm into one of Wall Street's premier investment banks, a position it still retains more than 125 years after its founding. The modern architect of Goldman Sachs culture was Sidney

Weinberg who started out as a porter's helper and retired fifty years later, in 1969, as managing partner.

Along the way, the firm has counted many prestigious partners including Robert Rubin, Clinton's treasury secretary; Jon Corzine, New Jersey's governor (and former Senator); Steve Friedman, Rubin's co-CEO and for a time, assistant to President George W. Bush for economic policy and director of the National Economic Council; Abby Joseph Cohen, a top Wall Street analyst; and many others. Perhaps symbolizing the end of ethnic domination of Wall Street, until several years ago, Goldman Sachs was headed by Henry Paulson, a Christian Scientist, who then became secretary of the treasury. Today the firm is headed by Lloyd Blankfein. In late 2008, Blankfein made two strategic decisions that will probably preserve Goldman Sachs' preeminence through the credit crises and recession which began that year. Non-Jew, Warren Buffett, became a major investor, and Goldman Sachs was converted into a regulated bank holding company. Together, the two steps afford access to capital in dangerous times that was denied to others and brought them down.

Lehman Brothers:[244] In 1844 Henry, Emanuel, and Mayer Lehman opened a Montgomery, Alabama general store. By 1850 they had begun trading cotton, a move necessitated by the fact that it was so often the "currency" they received in exchange for their merchandise. In 1858 they opened a New York office to facilitate their cotton trading and before long they were underwriting railroad expansion. By the early twentieth century, Lehman Brothers was financing Sears and Roebuck, R.H. Macys, and film studios such as Paramount. Heir Bobby Lehman ran the firm from the 1930s through the 1950s and kept it in the top ranks. (Meanwhile, his cousin Herbert served as governor and later United States Senator from New York.) The firm foundered when Bobby left, but was revived by non-Jew Peter Peterson. Lewis Glucksman then took over in 1983, selling out to American Express a year later. Earlier, in 1981, American Express had acquired Shearson Loeb Rhoades. In the bargain, they got Loeb Rhoades, the 1931 creation of Carl Loeb, which years earlier had swallowed the cash-starved Gentile firm, Rhoades & Co. In 1993, ten years after acquiring Lehman Brothers, American Express spun it off as a separate public company. For fifteen years, CEO Richard Fuld led Lehman Brothers to ever greater success till it all came crashing down in a September 2008 bankruptcy. Ever more aggressive use of leverage, short term borrowing to finance operations, and the rapid decline in the value of its real estate mortgage and securities portfolio wiped out Lehman Brothers' equity and left it insolvent. Its major operations were quickly sold off in months. Lehman is gone.

Kuhn, Loeb & Co.[245]: Abraham Kuhn and Solomon Loeb began as retailers operating general stores in Indianapolis and Cincinnati before moving to New York where they set up their banking firm in 1867. In its heyday, Kuhn, Loeb was the second most prominent U.S. investment bank, behind only the Gentile firm JP Morgan. In 1897 Otto Kahn joined Kuhn, Loeb and worked closely with non-Jew Edward Harriman to reorganize today's Union Pacific Railroad. A major philanthropist, Kahn was a large donor to both the Metropolitan Opera Company (he served as its CEO and president from 1903 to 1931) and efforts to restore the Parthenon in Athens.

Jacob Schiff joined the firm upon his arrival from Germany in 1865. Schiff later headed the firm and played a major role in its financing of U.S. railroads, the U.S government, and the Japanese (for whom he helped raise $200 million to finance their 1904-1905 war with Russia.) A generous benefactor, Schiff gave money to Barnard College and Montefiore Hospital, among other causes. His opposition to tsarist Russia and alleged support of Communism later made him controversial. Felix Warburg became a partner in 1897 and was ultimately named senior partner. He was joined by his son Freddy and by Paul Warburg. Like his predecessors. Felix was a major philanthropist giving generously to Hebrew Union College, Harvard's Fogg Museum, and other causes. In 1977 Kuhn, Loeb was merged into Lehman Brothers.

Bear Stearns & Co.:[246] Joseph Bear, Robert Stearns, and Harold Mayer launched Bear Stearns in 1923. In the ensuing eighty-three years up to 2007, it never had a losing year. No other major firm could make that claim. Bear Stearns was consistently ranked among the top investment banks, securities trading, and brokerage firms. It was probably best known for Salim "Cy" Lewis and Alan "Ace" Greenberg, two men who led the firm from 1938 until 1993. Under Lewis, Sanford Weill, Henry Kravis, George Roberts, and Jerome Kohlberg were all hired. And, after fifty years with the firm, Ace Greenberg's management style was as legendary as his willingness to take risks, his iron hand, stern quips, and infamous memos as CEO, many of which were captured in his 1996 book, *Memos from the Chairman*. Less well known was his requirement that employees donate 4 percent of their salaries to charity and his own considerable philanthropy. In March 2008, Bear Stearns failed. Greenberg's successors, Jews Alan Schwartz and James Cayne, proved incapable of managing the firm through the subprime mortgage crises. It was a painful and inglorious ending for what had been a consistently successful, important, and profitable firm for eighty-four of its eighty-five years.

Lazard:[247] After immigrating to the United States from the Lorraine in 1848, Simon, Alexandre, and Elie Lazard established Lazard Freres & Co., as a New Orleans dry- goods business. The next year they moved to San Francisco to pursue gold rush opportunities including exporting gold and importing goods. They opened a Paris office in 1852 to advise the French government on gold purchases and in 1870, they opened a London office as well. In 1880 Alexander Weill, a Lazard cousin and partner, took over, relocating headquarters to New York. Known as a genteel firm, Lazard has a long- standing reputation for strong, capable partners. Among them was non-family member Andre Meyer. He joined the Paris office in 1925, later relocated to New York, and then ran Lazard from the 1950s until 1977. Siegmund Warburg, a very demanding financier, was known to say that the only man who ever intimidated him was Andre Meyer.

Another partner, Marc Meyer (no relation to Andre) joined the firm in New York. His son, Eugene, served as Fed chairman from 1930 to 1933 and was father to Katherine Graham, publisher of *The Washington Post*. During Andre Meyers' tenure, Lazard grew into the world's leading M&A firm. In those years, Meyer was assisted by Felix Rohatyn, a French/Jewish immigrant who escaped the Nazis, orchestrated the mid-1970s bail out of New York City's finances, and served as President Clinton's ambassador to France. Another "friend of Bill's," non-Jew Vernon Jordan later joined the firm as well. Meyer was succeeded by Michel David-Weill (son of Alexander) in 1977. He consolidated the various international partnerships into a single firm under family control and in 2002, turned leadership over to Bruce Wasserstein. In 2005 Wasserstein took Lazard public.

Citigroup:[248] Founded in 1812 as the City Bank of New York with Samuel Osgood (not Jewish) as its first president, Citicorp was a white shoe, Waspish commercial bank for most of its history. Non-Jews like Walter Wriston (1967-1984) and more recently John Reed (1984-2000), led a bank consistently ranked one or two among the world's great commercial banks. That was before banking deregulation and Sanford Weill. Weill took over as CEO of Commercial Credit and in 1986, spun it off from Control Data Corporation as an independent public company with himself as CEO. Weill then built the company through a series of acquisitions into what would later become known as Travelers. It included: Travelers Insurance, Commercial Credit, Salomon Smith Barney, residual parts of Drexel Burnham, Dillon Reed, and Shearson Lehman. In 1998, anticipating deregulation, Weill and Reed saw the opportunity to create a huge financial services combination encompassing all of Citibank's U.S. and foreign commercial banking operations and Weill's Travelers. Reed retired in 2000 leaving Weill in sole charge. Under Weill, Citigroup then acquired European American Bank, Golden State Bancorp, California Federal Bank, Grupo Banamex, and Bank Handlowy w Warszawie S.A. By late 2005, Citigroup had roughly 300,000 employees and a market value of more than $230 billion. It was one of the world's largest financial institutions.

During 2003, in the face of pressure involving Jack Grubman, a former Solomon Smith Barney analyst, regulatory probes surrounding relationships with Enron and Worldcom, and a $440 million regulatory settlement, Weill turned over the reins to non-Jew Charles O. Prince, but stayed on as chairman until 2006. According to a *Forbes* July 16, 2003, story, a 1986 Commercial Credit shareholder, when Weill took it public, would have made a 3,488 percent compound return if he held that stock through July of 2003. Meanwhile, occupying the office next to Prince was former treasury secretary and former Goldman Sachs CEO, Robert Rubin. Like Bear Stearns, Lehman, AIG, and others, Citigroup struggled in the subprime and 2008 credit crises. Prince resigned and was replaced by Vikram Pandit, a devout Hindu who was working with Weill, Rubin, and Muslim, Prince Alwaleed Bin Talal Alsaud, to turn things around. At this writing, Citi's future is unclear.

Salomon Brothers:[249] Second-generation immigrants, Arthur, Percy, and Herbert Salomon started Salomon in 1910. Having little cachet on their own, they first merged with the firm of Morton Hutzler to gain a New York Stock Exchange seat and then found an opening in the Liberty Loan program to specialize in bonds. That move makes Salomon the oldest government bond brokerage firm in the United States. Second-generation Billy Salomon guided the firm through the 1960s, and in 1975, working with Felix Rohatyn of Lazard, Salomon helped bail out financially troubled New York City by selling its MAC bonds.

In 1978 Billy turned the CEO slot over to John Gutfreund who headed the firm through the halcyon 1980s, a period which included Salomon's acquisition by the huge commodities trading firm, Phillip Brothers (Phibro), and the colorful era described in Michael Lewis' book, *Liar's Poker*. The book immortalized Gutfreund, John Meriwether (not Jewish) and others. Later, with large losses arising from the 1987 crash, Gutfreund averted a takeover attempt by Ron Perelman who was backed by Drexel Burnham. Non-Jew Warren Buffett became Salomon's savior from Perelman and the 1987 losses.

In 1991 the firm ran into trouble once more when a key employee was discovered to have submitted illegal U.S. Government Bond bids. Buffett took over from Gutfreund and ultimately Salomon was merged into Smith Barney, which, in turn, became part of Sanford Weill's Citicorp (see above).

Warburg's:[250] There is no single Warburg or Warburg firm. This remarkably prolific family spawned at least five major investment firms. They began as German "Court Jews" about 1560 changing money and serving as pawnbrokers under the protection of the Prince Bishop of Paderborn. By 1798 the family evolved into the Hamburg firm of M.M. Warburg brokering bills (loans), trading precious metals, and later added banking to their services. In 1804 W. S. Warburg was formed by family members in a different part of Germany, and in 1929, Warburg & Company was established in Amsterdam. That company was a victim of the Nazis who grabbed it, changed its name, and demanded a large bribe before allowing most of the Warburgs living in Holland to leave. In 1938 Eric Warburg started E.M. Warburg in New York, and in 1970, its name was changed to E. M. Warburg, Pincus, when Eric returned to Germany to rebuild M. M. Warburg and a second-generation Polish Jew, Lionel Pincus, bought control. In 1946 S. G. Warburg was started in London by Siegmund Warburg.

Today M.M. Warburg continues as the second largest private bank in Germany. S. G. Warburg was acquired by Swiss Bank Corp in 1994 and, in turn, merged into UBS (Union Bank of Switzerland). Warburg Pincus was merged into CSFB (Crédit Suisse First Boston) in 1999. Through marriage and immigration, other family members were also heavily involved in other banks such as Kuhn, Loeb (above). As mentioned in Chapter 7 – "Economics," Paul Warburg was instrumental in creating the U.S. Federal Reserve and he served on its first board of governors. Ron Chernow made this illustrious family the subject of an excellent 1993 family biography, *The Warburgs*.

Wasserstein Perella:[251] Bruce Wasserstein and non-Jew Joseph Perella created this successful M&A shop in 1988 following their stint as co-heads of investment banking at First Boston (now part of CSFB). Wasserstein, a mover and shaker on Wall Street through much of the 1980s and 1990s, and major character in Kohlberg, Kravis and Roberts' takeover of RJR, was immortalized in *Barbarians at the Gate*. For a time he was labeled "Bid-em-up Bruce" by *Forbes* magazine for his knack at promoting inflated merger prices in the RJR leveraged buyout and the Campeau purchase of Federated Stores. In 1997 Wasserstein regained the spotlight and Wall Street cachet when he advised Dean Witter in its merger with Morgan Stanley & Co. Perella had left the firm in 1993 to go with Morgan Stanley, and thus the two partners were on opposite sides of the table for the Dean Witter-Morgan Stanley merger.

In 2001 Wasserstein sold the bulk of his firm (with its 600 employees based in New York, London, Paris, and Frankfurt) to Dresdner, Kleinwort Benson, the investment banking arm of Germany's Dresdner Bank, part of Allianz Group. In the transaction, he also spun out the firm's $2 billion private equity partnership (Wasserstein & Co.) into a stand-alone entity. Not long after the merger, Wasserstein had a falling out with Dresdner's senior management, and in late 2002 he left to become head of Lazard.

Oppenheimer:[252] In 1951, Max Oppenheimer started what have since become three separate businesses. The first, Oppenheimer & Co, grew into a major brokerage and money management firm, owned for a time by the Canadian Imperial Bank of Commerce (CIBC), and later sold to the Fahnstock brokerage firm in 2003. Fahnstock thereupon renamed itself Oppenheimer. The second business, The Oppenheimer Funds, was started by Oppenheimer & Co in 1960. It became part of Mercantile House Holdings, a British company in 1982, but subsequently bought out by its partners and Mass Mutual Insurance Company in 1990. The third business, Oppenheimer Capital, was formed in 1975. Today it is part of the Allianz Dresdner Pimco constellation of companies. Together the three firms manage more than $200 billion of capital. The original Oppenheimer was also home to two Wall Street legends, Leon Levy and Jack Nash. (See the discussion of Odyssey Partners, below.)

Cantor Fitzgerald:[253] Bernie Cantor and non-Jew John Fitzgerald, started this firm in 1945, but it was really only a creature of Cantor. (Fitzgerald, an insurance executive, was a minor partner.) Cantor had the foresight to shift from tax and investment advice to the bond market, and that change ultimately led to Cantor Fitzgerald's becoming the largest U.S. government bond dealer. Over its first fifty-six years, few people, apart from those in the bond market, even knew of it. September 11, 2001, changed all that. For a time, Cantor Fitzgerald became a household name as Americans learned that the firm, which occupied the top floors of the World Trade Center, had lost 658 of its 2,100 employees in the tragedy (more than 20 percent of all the September 11 victims).

The codicil to the September 11 tragedy is the role played by Bernie Cantor's successor, Howard Lutnick. Lutnick had joined Cantor when he was twenty-three and was named president when he was 30. When Cantor passed away in 1996, Lutnick became CEO. He was dropping his son off at school that morning when the planes struck the World Trade Center. The steps he took to save the business and preserve its jobs became the subject of much controversy as offices were shut, employees relocated, and wages terminated for those who had died. In the press and minds of some family members, Lutnick was seen as harsh and ruthless. To others, he was doing what had to be done for the firm to survive the crises. Ultimately, he and the firm received positive marks for setting aside 25 percent of its profits from 2001 to 2006 for the families and loved ones of the tragedy's victims. Today Cantor survives as a diversified financial services company with worldwide operations.

Drexel Burnham Lambert:[256] Michael Milken began as a part time operations consultant to the chairman of Drexel, Harriman, Ripley, a fading Waspish firm. Revived by a cash infusion from Firestone Tire and Rubber Company, it had been renamed Drexel, Firestone by the time Milken signed on full-time in 1970. Regarded by some of his Wharton professors as the smartest student they ever taught, Milken had discovered that bonds of riskier companies were not as risky as believed and were thus underpriced. In exploiting that mispricing, he created the "junk bond" industry as a huge new source of money for middle-market companies. Milken's concept of junk bond financing revolutionized the firm and brought him practical control (with Fred Joseph serving as CEO.) By the late 1980s, junk bonds made Drexel the most profitable firm on Wall Street ($545.5 million in 1986). Milken helped finance: MCI, Time Warner, Twentieth Century Fox, Viacom, and Turner Broadcasting, among others, before Ivan Boesky implicated Milken in the scandal that ultimately brought down Milken and Drexel. Milken's life since has been largely consumed with private investing and philanthropy.

Allen & Co.:[255] Herbert A. Allen does not consider himself Jewish. His Catholic mother had him baptized in the church, but these days, he largely eschews any formal religion. His father, Herbert, and uncle, Charles, however, were Jewish. They created the firm in 1922 and ran it for its first forty-four years until Herbert Jr. took over in 1966. He, in turn, ran it until late 2002 when he turned it over to his son, Herb. Allen & Co. is different. Though it is an investment bank, provides advice, brokers mergers, arranges financing, and works on initial public offerings (it was part of the Google offering), it is also a boutique "merchant bank" investing its own, mostly Allen family capital, in many of its deals. It is also one of the most entrepreneurial of firms with low salaries and high rewards for performance (Herbert A. Allen was once quoted, saying, "We have a welfare state for our employees and raw capitalism for the principals.")

Charles and Herbert Sr. made fortunes in Syntex and Benguet Consolidated. In Benguet, a Philippine mining company, the quintessential Allen & Co. story is told. Asked why they invested after Pearl Harbor, with the Philippines in Japanese hands, Charles responded, "If Japan won, it would not matter and if Japan lost, we would make a fortune." In Syntex, birth control pharmaceuticals invented in Catholic Mexico could best be developed and financed if Syntex was moved to Salt Lake City. Asked why they invested in a snap decision, while Lazard dithered, Charles answered, "Interesting product. Liked the people." Second-generation Herbert A. matched those deals with his own. Hollywood producer Ray Stark (whom Candice Bergen once called Herbert's father figure and "Jewish center") encouraged Allen to buy control of Columbia Pictures, which he did (over the objections of his father and uncle) for $1.5 million of his own and the firm's money. When Coca-Cola later bought Columbia, Allen received stock eventually worth 600 times what he had paid. The transaction also engendered a valuable relationship with Coca-Cola that endures to this day.

One report has it that the Allen's track record is among the best on Wall Street, earning more than 40 percent per year since the mid-1980s. Allen & Co. has stayed small (about 200 partners and staff) and very private, but its annual Sun Valley Conference is a prestigious event epitomizing the strong personal relationships on which Allen & Co is based.

Republic National Bank:[256] In 1966 Edmond Safra founded Republic National

Bank of New York City. At the time, he already controlled the Trade Development Bank of Geneva, which he set up in 1956, and Banco Safra S.A., a Brazilian bank he established in 1955. Safra was a Syrian Jew, born in 1932 to a family of bankers whose roots traced back to financing caravans of camels. What Safra built, and the tragedy that ended his life, are the stuff of novels. His sale of the Trade Development Bank to American Express in 1983 gave rise to a defamation lawsuit that ended when American Express apologized to him and paid $8 million to the charity of Safra's choice. That story was immortalized in the 1992 book, *Vendetta: American Express and the Smearing of Edmond Safra*. Safra built Republic to $51.2 billion of assets, the third largest bank in the New York area and the nineteenth largest bank in the United States., before selling it to Hong Kong Shanghai Bank (HSBC) in December 1999. Tragically, just before the deal closed, one of Safra's nurses—intending to be seen a hero—set fire to Safra's penthouse apartment in Monaco. He thought he could rescue Safra and impress him. He didn't. Safra died in the fire.

C.E. Unterberg Towbin:[257] Thomas Unterberg has spent a lifetime in investment banking, and this firm is only the most recent incarnation in which he has been a founding partner or principal. The firm is akin to the boutique investment banks of the 1970s and 1980s that focused on high-growth technology companies. It arranges financings, makes direct investments, makes markets in stocks, does research and manages partnerships in a fashion and on a scale of earlier non-Jewish firms such as Hambrecht and Quist and Robertson Stephens, both of which have since merged into larger firms. The Unterberg firm remains independent and was home to John Gutfreund after he left Salomon Brothers.

Bache & Company:[258] In 1892, thirty-year-old Jules Bache took over the firm his uncle had started and which he renamed J.S. Bache. Succeeding generations built and managed the firm through the end of World War II. It was prominent for much of the twentieth century, and at one point Bache vied with Merrill Lynch as one of the largest U.S. securities firms. In 1981, Bache was acquired by Prudential and renamed Pru-Bache Securities. Its reputation was destroyed, however, during the late 1980s by the management team that created a huge financial scandal (chronicled in the book *Serpent on the Rock*). Since 1991 Prudential Financial no longer uses Bache in its name. The legacy of Jules Bache, on the other hand, carries on in the sizable art collection he left to the Metropolitan Museum of Art in New York.

J. & W. Seligman:[259] Joseph Seligman started this firm in 1864 with his seven brothers. Early on it was involved in financing part of the North's Civil War debt (therein making a better bet than the Rothschilds, whose U.S. agent, August Belmont, chose to help finance the South.) An early member of the New York Stock Exchange (1869), the firm has migrated over the years into a successful manager of the Seligman Mutual Funds.

And, of course, there are the Rothschilds.

Private Equity Firms and Mutual Funds

More focused than investment banks and brokerages, private equity firms and mutual funds typically recruit institutional and individual limited partners to invest in, or with them, in pursuit of a particular kind of opportunity. Some specialize in leverage buy-outs, others venture capital, mezzanine financings, hedged stock market investments, derivatives, turnarounds, real estate (covered in a separate chapter), growth companies, selected industries, developing economies, and any of the numerous other such opportunities. These are professionals managing money for themselves and others. Here, performance is the measure. Generating profits builds net worth, reputations and an ever-growing pool of capital to pursue ever more and larger opportunities.

And again we find a domain in which Jews have been disproportionately successful in their financial results and in the recognition they have won from counterpart firms and professional associations.

Among the thirteen private equity firms elected to the Private Equity Hall of Fame through 2004, four (31 percent) have had at least one prominent Jewish partner: Matrix Group, Kohlberg, Kravis and Roberts, Blackstone Group, and Kleiner, Perkins, Caufield & Byers. Among the twenty-nine individuals named to the same Hall of Fame, at least eight (28 percent)—and perhaps as many as twelve—are Jewish. The eight include Thomas H. Lee, Arthur Rock, Robert Zobel, Alan Patricof, Stanley Golder, Ben Rosen, Jerome Kohlberg, and Stanley Rubel.[260]

Among prominent private equity and mutual funds with Jewish roots are those described below.

Kohlberg, Kravis, and Roberts (KKR):[261] Cy Lewis, then CEO of Bear Stearns, probably deserves blame for missing one of the great financial opportunities of the late twentieth century. In 1971, He ousted Henry Kravis, Kravis' cousin George Roberts, and their mentor Jerome Kohlberg in a very messy confrontation because Lewis did not like the threesome doing leveraged buyouts at Bear Stearns. They left, formed KKR and for eleven years the threesome worked together until 1987 when Kohlberg resigned after the firm had completed thirty buyouts. Following Kohlberg's departure, KKR continued on as dean of the LBO firms and they are still on top. As of mid-2008, they had done 160 buyouts involving $410 billion of financing. As noted above, in 1996 the firm was elected to the Private Equity Hall of Fame.

Thomas H. Lee Co.:[262] Thomas Lee set up a small fund to do "friendly" leveraged buyouts in 1974. He built it into a huge private firm, of which at one point he owned two-thirds, managing more than $13 billion of capital. The firm not only does leverage buyouts, but has also invested in start-up and prepublic offering companies. Despite an occasional controversy, Lee's record with such investments as Snapple, General Nutrition Company and others was sufficient to gain him a place in the Private Equity Hall of Fame in 2000. Lee is also notable for his $22 million gift to Harvard University, his trusteeship of Harvard and Brandeis universities, Lincoln Center for the Performing Arts, and the Whitney Museum of American Art. Lee gradually sold off parts of his interest in the firm, delegated management, and by 2006 had left Thomas H. Lee Company to start a new firm, Lee Equity Partners.

Blackstone Group:[263] Stephen Schwarzman and non-Jew Pete Peterson set up Blackstone in 1985 with two associates and $400,000 in invested capital. Both Peterson and Schwarzman came from Lehman Brothers where Schwarzman made partner at age 31. Earlier, Peterson served as Nixon's Assistant for Economic Affairs and as secretary of Commerce. Almost from the start, Peterson has been chairman and Schwarzman chief executive officer. Blackstone manages more than $110 billion for clients, investing it in a wide range of businesses, debt, real estate, and other kinds of assets. In addition, Blackstone does some M&A and some restructuring and reorganization advisory work for clients, and helps others raise money through its Park Hill Group. Blackstone was inducted into the Private Equity Hall of Fame in 2001 and went public in 2007.

Quantum Fund:[264] George Soros founded Quantum in 1969 and it quickly became a major Wall Street power. Soros is best known for the bets he made on the future value of the English pound, which reportedly netted his fund $1 billion and set him on his way to join the Forbes 400. A Hungarian Jew by birth, Soros has also become an important player in the Democratic Party and in Move-on.org. In addition, his Soros Foundation has been a major philanthropic organization supporting, among other endeavors, efforts directed at liberalizing and democratizing Eastern Europe and other former Soviet block countries.

Steinhardt Partners:[265] Michael Steinhardt and two partners formed Steinhardt, Fine, Berkowitz & Co. in 1968 when Michael was twenty-seven. This was after Steinhardt's graduation from Wharton at age nineteen and his short stints in the Army, at Loeb Rhoades, and at a small firm, Calvin Bullock. His hot hand, (99 percent returns in his first year, a correct call predicting the 1972 market downturn, and some great investments along the way) propelled Steinhart to early prominence. Nonetheless, he was torn by the stigma of his father, a pal of Meyer Lansky, who served time in Sing Sing for "fencing" stolen jewelry, before bankrolling his son through Wharton and some early investments.

Steinhardt's ego, passion for perfection, and demanding style took him through his two founding partners and many employees along the way toward managing a $5 billion fund. Controversy over a purported attempt to corner the market in short-term treasuries and a couple of investments that went south, led him to liquidate Steinhardt Partners in 1995. By that time, he had rolled up what one source says were 27 percent compound returns over a period of twenty years.

After he shut down the partnership, he moved on to philanthropy, which he approaches with the same passion. He and his wife donated $10 million to New York University's School of Education, and he is a member of Mega, a small but highly influential group of Jewish philanthropists described in Chapter 23 – "Philanthropy." He is also a major donor to Jewish causes and is the namesake of Steinhardt Hall, home to Hillel on the campus of the University of Pennsylvania.

Financial Trust Co. (née J. Epstein & Co.):[266] Jeffrey Epstein was the contemporary Jay Gatsby of wealth managers. He never graduated from college and yet was believed to manage $15 billion or more of private wealth for clients (only those whose net worth exceeded $1 billion). He was perhaps the most discrete and secret money manager around. While he enjoyed a luxurious lifestyle with multiple homes and numerous aircraft (he flew Bill Clinton all over Africa on his Boeing 727), he was also a generous benefactor to charitable causes. Among other projects, he is said to have spent $20 million a year supporting scientific research with the world's leading scientists, including Nobel Prize winners such as Gerald Edelman, Murray Gell-Mann, and others working at the Princeton Institute for Advanced Study.

In June 2008, Epstein pled guilty to a charge of felony solicitation of a prostitute and was given an eighteen-month jail sentence, a stiff probation, and he still has four civil lawsuits to follow. As an ironic footnote, following Epstein's 2006 indictment, but before his own problems surfaced, former Governor Eliot Spitzer returned Epstein's $50,000 campaign contribution.

Caxton Associates, LLC:[267] Bruce Kovner runs one of the world's larger hedge funds, estimated at more than $15 billion. Kovner dropped out of Harvard's John F. Kennedy School of Government in 1970, drove a cab, studied harpsichord, did some consulting, and then got interested in commodities. He quickly made and lost money before his 1977 move to the legendary Commodities Corp., established by Nobel laureate Paul Samuelson. He left Commodities Corp. in 1983 to set up Caxton. Reportedly delivering returns of 28 percent annually since inception, his track record helps explain why investors flocked to his fund. Kovner serves as chairman of the board of trustees of the Julliard School, chairman of School Choice Scholarships Foundation, chairman of the board of trustees of the American Enterprise Institute, and governor of the Israeli Philharmonic Orchestra International board of governors. In late 2007, Forbes ranked Kovner No. 91 on the Forbes 400 with a net worth of more than $3.5 billion.

Odyssey Partners:[268] Leon Levy and Jack Nash became partners at Oppenheimer before they sold it (see above) in 1982, after which they formed Odyssey Partners. At Odyssey, they hit another home run. When liquidated in 1998, it had grown to $3.3 billion returning an average of 22 percent per year over its sixteen years. In his later years, Levy gave away an estimated $140 million, $100 million of which went to Bard College and $20 million to the Museum of Modern Art. He was president of the Institute for Advanced Study at Princeton, and he sponsored an archaeological project in 1990 that discovered a Golden Calf in Israel (of the kind described in the Bible). In the end, Levy's New York Times obituary described him simply as a philanthropist. Nash did for Baruch University what Levy did for Bard. The Honors MBA program at Baruch is named for Jack Nash who passed away in 2008.

Third Avenue Funds and M.J. Whitman:[269] Martin J. Whitman is a fifty year Wall Street pioneer of value investing. A child of Polish Jewish immigrants, he grew up in the Bronx, served in World War II and returned to become a GI Bill graduate of Syracuse and the New School for Social Research, (a master's in economics, focused on the securities industry). After working for a number of investment firms, he set up M.J. Whitman & Company in 1974 as a bankruptcy advisory/stockholder litigation firm. In 1985 he took over Equity Strategies, a Security Pacific Bank mutual fund. He renamed it Third Avenue Fund and set up M. J. Whitman as a wholesale broker dealer/research firm specializing in distressed securities. With that Whitman had access to sufficient capital to pursue "distressed" opportunities such as Penn Central, Petro Lewis, and Public Service of New Hampshire where he already had, or would soon, make multiples on the dollars he invested.

Over time, he established an excellent record (consistently top ranked by Morningstar) and because of that success, Third Avenue manages more than $15 billion in assets. Along the way, Whitman was a Distinguished Management Fellow at the Yale School of Management for twenty-eight years, and an adjunct professor at Columbia Business School. He has authored two books and many articles. His "multimillion-dollar" 2003 gift to Syracuse University's Whitman School of Management is "one of the largest gifts in SU's history," and he and his wife, Lois, also provide MBA scholarships for minority students at Syracuse.

Neuberger Berman:[270] Roy R. Neuberger and Robert Berman founded their firm in 1939. It was one of the first no-load mutual funds. Over time, it has also become one of the largest. Today it manages more than $70 billion in assets, provides services of various kinds to investors, and employs 1,200 people. Roy Neuberger was already an avid art lover when he founded the firm, but the wealth he made as an investor (among other great calls, he started shorting RCA before the 1929 crash), and as founder of Neuberger Berman, allowed him to become both a great collector of modern art and a major benefactor. He donated art to the Metropolitan Museum of Art and the Museum of Modern Art and donated money in 1974 to create the Neuberger Museum of Art on the campus of the State University of New York. Neuberger Berman was sold to Lehman Brothers in 2003, and five years later, purchased by its management, following the September 2008 Lehman Brothers Chapter 11 filing.

Apollo Management, L.P., et al.:[271] Two years out of Harvard Business School in 1977, Leon Black joined Drexel Burnham Lambert. He spent the next thirteen years there. In 1990, after Drexel ran into problems, Black and a group of fellow Drexel alumni left to set up Apollo. They chose to specialize in what is generally termed "vulture investing." In 1993 they also established Apollo Real Estate Advisors to invest in real property. For a time, Black's firms were the subject of a good bit of controversy (mostly involving problems in California relating to the sale of junk bonds, and the business of a California insurance company to the French-owned bank, Crédit Lyonnais). Nonetheless, today the various Apollo Funds total more than $20 billion, and Black is active both on portfolio boards and as trustee of the Metropolitan Museum of Art, Mt. Sinai Hospital, Lincoln Center for the Performing arts, the Jewish Museum, and the Cardozo School of Law.

Hellman & Friedman:[272] Warren Hellman and Tully Friedman started this firm in 1984 some years after Hellman had become the youngest (age twenty-eight) partner in Lehman Brothers and later served as its president. In 1976 Hellman left

Lehman to co-found the venture capital firm of Hellman, Ferri, now Matrix Partners. He stayed with Matrix for eight years before organizing Hellman & Friedman. Tully Friedman came from Salomon Brothers where he founded the firm's West Coast Corporate Finance Department. After fourteen years together, Friedman left Hellman & Friedman in 1998 to start Friedman, Fleischer & Lowe, a comparable, but smaller (more than $1 billion) firm. Today, Hellman's firm is one of the most prominent names in Western U S finance and is reported to have delivered 30 percent annual returns on the more than $8 billion it has invested.

Hellman begins each day at 4 a.m. with a six-mile run before reading the Torah. He is quoted as saying this regime has the advantage of keeping him from having to attend cocktail parties. He and his wife fund the San Francisco Free Clinic, which provides health care to the needy. He is a trustee of the San Francisco Foundation, an advisory board member at the Walter A. Haas School of Business at the University of California Berkeley, and an honorary trustee of the somewhat liberal Brookings Institute. In contrast, his former partner, Tully Friedman, is a trustee and treasurer of the conservative American Enterprise Institute.

Blum Capital Partners:[273] Richard Blum started Blum Capital Partners in 1975. He came from Sutro & Co. (a San Francisco brokerage firm with Jewish roots) where Blum began when he was twenty-three and made partner before he was 30. At Sutro, Blum proved himself by buying Ringling Bros. & Barnum & Bailey Circus for $8 million and selling it to Mattel four years later for $40 million. Blum & Associates manages what was reported some years ago to be $4.5 billion. He is also co-chairman of Newbridge Capital, LLC and chairman of CB Richard Ellis. An avid mountain climber, in 1981, Blum organized the first modern expedition to scale the east face of Mt. Everest and since then, has founded the American Himalayan Foundation providing humanitarian assistance to Himalayans. He has been active in support of Tibet and the Himalayan culture.

As the husband of Senator Dianne Feinstein, he is very much the focus of criticism and controversy both for the success of some portfolio companies (for which he is vilified for supposedly using his political connections to personal advantage) and for his more than twenty-year relationship with the government of China (which granted permission for the Everest climb). Blum is also chairman of the Board of Regents of the University of California and a trustee and member of the executive committee of the Carter Center, founded by former President Jimmy Carter.

Arthur Rock & Co.:[274] If one person could be said to be the father of modern venture capital, many knowledgeable venture investors would give Arthur Rock the nod. He was the New York investment banker called on by Gene Kleiner's father (as discussed below) when "the traitorous eight" left Shockley Laboratories and needed someone to help find investors to finance their new "high-tech" venture. Rock is said to have received thirty-five "No, I won't invest" answers before he finally got a "Yes" from Sherman Fairchild. That financing launched Fairchild Semiconductor and led to Rock's later role as Intel's lead investor, a company that he also served as chairman of the board. Rock moved from New York to San Francisco, where he still maintains a modest office. But his importance is belied by those surroundings. He has been the lead or a major investor funding such important companies as Scientific Data Systems, Xerox, Apple Computer, Argonaut Insurance, Raychem, Teledyne, and AirTouch (now part of Verizon). He has also served as a director of the National Association of Securities Dealers (NASD). His partnership with non-Jew Tommy Davis led to Davis' later formation of Mayfield, another top ranked venture capital firm, after Rock and Davis had gone their separate ways.

Rock is also an active member of the partnership that owns the San Francisco Giants baseball team. His remarkable investment success has made Rock wealthy. He has donated $25 million to the Harvard Business School and is president of the BASIC Fund providing academic scholarships to inner-city children. Rock was inducted into the Private Equity Hall of Fame in 1999.

Kleiner, Perkins, Caufield & Byers (KPCB): Gene Kleiner[275] emigrated from Austria in 1938 following the Nazi occupation. He arrived in New York in 1941, served in the Army, earned a master's degree in industrial engineering from New York University, and was working for Western Electric in 1957 when Nobel laureate William Shockley recruited him to join Shockley Laboratories. Kleiner and seven others quickly found Shockley an extremely difficult man to work for and they, "the traitorous eight," left Shockley in 1958 to form Fairchild Semiconductor. Fairchild was the first company to mass-produce silicon chips with numerous transistors on them and thus, with Hewlett Packard, was part of the genesis of Silicon Valley, and the high-technology boom that followed.

A few years after leaving Fairchild, Kleiner met non-Jew Tom Perkins and together they formed what many believe is the world's premier venture firm, originally named Kleiner Perkins before non-Jews Brook Byers and Frank Caufield joined as partners. Later, KPCB proved its prowess in recruiting non-Jew John Doerr, who has since become another of the firm's legendary partners.

Among KPCB portfolio companies have been Google, Genentech, Amazon, Sun Microsystems, Compaq, Juniper Networks, AOL, Netscape, 3DO, Intuit, Travelocity, and many others. As the first firm ever inducted into the Private Equity Hall of Fame in 1995, Kleiner Perkins was credited with investing in 263 technology companies whose combined market value exceeded $63 billion. That was well before the successes with AOL, Amazon, Juniper, and Google.

Sevin-Rosen:[276] Ben Rosen and L. J. Sevin formed what became another of the top-tier venture capital firms, Sevin Rosen. Ben Rosen and his older brother, Harold, grew up during the 1930s and 1940s in a strict Jewish New Orleans household. Harold, with fifty patents to his name, pioneered the geostationary satellite for Hughes aerospace in 1963, but early on, while at Raytheon, recruited his brother Ben, who had recently gotten his electrical engineering degree from Cal Tech. Ben later earned a MBA from Columbia and went on to become a Wall Street security analyst. As a Morgan Stanley vice president, Rosen was credited with convincing the firm to take Apple Computer public in 1980. In 1982 he left Morgan Stanley to set up Sevin-Rosen with L.J. Sevin, principal founder of Mostek, another early high technology company. Together, Rosen and Sevin backed a stable of winners including Lotus, Silicon Graphics, Cypress Semiconductor and Compaq. Ben Rosen was inducted into the Private Equity Hall of Fame in 1995.

Sequoia Capital: Michael Moritz[277] did not start this top-tier venture firm, non-Jew Don Valentine did in the 1970s. But Moritz talked Valentine into hiring him in 1986, and he quickly made himself into a major figure at Sequoia. Despite a few busts along the way such as Webvan and eToys, this British immigrant (his Jewish parents were refugees who settled in Wales), has hit major home runs backing Google, Yahoo, and Paypal, (now part of eBay). Moritz was ranked No. 2 for his Midas touch in a January 2008 Forbes article right behind John Doerr of Kleiner Perkins. Perhaps in hopes he will soon return, in 2008, the BBC ranked Moritz as Wales' fourth richest man.

Apax Partners (née Patricof & Co. Ventures): Alan Patricof[278] started his partnership in 1969, at the time investing mostly family money in small public and private companies. Self-deprecating, he attributes a good deal of his early success to three lucky investments that all worked out well, one of which is today's *New York* magazine. Later, Patricof & Co. became a leading venture capital firm and was early in the move to raise money and invest in Europe.

Today Patricof has stepped down to invest in smaller deals, while Apax manages more than $12 billion. Patricof serves as trustee of Columbia University Graduate School of Business, Beth Israel Hospital, and Trickle Up (devoted to micro-lending to the poor). He also serves on the Council on Foreign Relations and the Commission on Financing Capital Flows to Africa. He is perhaps better known, however, for his strong support of Democratic Party candidates, including the Clintons. It was rumored that Patricof could have had any slot he wanted in the Clinton administration, including secretary of the treasury. He passed on that, but continues very actively supporting Democratic Party candidates. Patricof is a 1996 inductee into the Private Equity Hall of Fame.

Carlyle Group: David Rubenstein and non-Jew Stephen Norris created Carlyle in 1987. Later they hired three other "co-founders," of which two, non-Jews Daniel D'Aniello and William Conway, remain. In 1995, Norris left. Through it all, Rubenstein has been the public face of this manager of $81 billion in partnership assets. The money is invested and managed by 575 professionals based in twenty-one countries. Until recent problems with its mortgage-backed investment portfolio, Carlyle was well know for its consistently superb returns and its connections with numerous high-profile American and foreign politicians (such as James Baker, President George H.W. Bush, and former British prime minister, John Major). Its investors have been equally high profile, such as: Prince Al-Waleed bin Talal Al Saud, CalPers (the California Public Employees Retirement System), and Shafig bin Laden (Osama bin Laden's older brother).

Perry Capital:[279] In the mid-1970s, twenty year old Richard Cayne Perry learned investing as part of Robert Rubin's risk arbitrage desk at Goldman Sachs. Perry was a quick study becoming a Rubin protégé before Rubin moved up to co-chair Goldman Sachs, and later become Treasury secretary. In 1988, feeling he was not being fairly compensated, Perry moved on to form Perry Capital with partner, Paul Leff. Over the 20 years since, they have never had a losing year, earning 15 percent annually for their partners and themselves. Their portfolio now totals $14 billion. Perry, whose uncle, James Cayne's risk taking led Bear, Stearns into bankruptcy, has taken the opposite tack. Perry Capital uses almost no debt and was prescient in foreseeing the risks in subprime mortgages. The firm made $1 billion shorting subprime mortgages in 2006. Though known for being very private, Richard Perry is, nonetheless, well known for his cultural, athletic, and political interests. It was at his home that Barack Obama met Caroline Kennedy.

Notable Financiers and Financial Entrepreneurs

Often using their own money or family fortunes, but sometimes drawing on partners, or control of large companies, a number of prominent Jews have made and managed substantial fortunes. Typically they are actively involved with the companies they started, backed, turned around, or, on occasion, raided. And sometimes they have taken control of public companies and then used them as vehicles in their efforts. Others have followed a successful career in finance with service to important government financial institutions or as advisers to politicians. One of them was instrumental in financing the American Revolution.

Among the more notable are:

Baron Maurice de Hirsch[280] was born to a family of German court bankers in 1831. He began his career at Bischoffsheim & Goldschmidt in Brussels where he fell in love with, and married, Clara Bischoffsheim (daughter of the firm's head). Scrupulous about his affection, he refused to capitalize on her family fortune. Instead, he led his own efforts to build the Oriental Railway linking Constantinople (Istanbul) with Europe. That, and his other entrepreneurial efforts financing copper and sugar businesses, made him a fortune estimated at $100 million by 1890.

Ultimately much, if not all, of that fortune went to philanthropic efforts. When Russia refused his $10 million offer to finance better schools for Jews in Russia, he created and endowed the foundation that assisted immigration of Jews from Russia and Poland to North and South America, where he established colonies for them to live and work upon their arrival. His also provided training for immigrants and loaned money to farmers and displaced persons. His philanthropy extended beyond Jewish causes and when he died, it was estimated he had donated the $100 million to worthy causes.

Bernard Baruch:[281] This larger-than-life investor made a fortune before he was thirty from his early twentieth-century investments in railroads and other industries. That success brought him fame and he soon became a trusted adviser, first to Woodrow Wilson (chairman of the War Industries board) and later to Harding, Coolidge, Hoover, and Franklin Roosevelt. Truman made him the first U.S. representative to the U.N. Atomic Energy Commission, and still later he advised both Eisenhower and Kennedy.

Henry Morgenthau Jr.'s[282] grandfather arrived in the United States penniless in 1866 and stayed that way for the rest of his life. But his son, Henry Morgenthau Sr. gained admission to Columbia Law School and subsequently made a real estate fortune before serving as Woodrow Wilson's ambassador to Turkey. His son, Henry, Jr. then bought 1,000 acres in New York's Dutchess County, adjacent to Franklin Delano Roosevelt's Hyde Park estate. The two neighbors soon became friends and after Roosevelt's 1928 election as New York's governor, Roosevelt always asked Morgenthau to serve in his administrations. This included Morgenthau's 1934 to 1945 service as Roosevelt's treasury secretary. An immense sum of money (estimated at $200 billion) was raised during his tenure to finance efforts to stem the Depression and win World War II. Through it all, there was never a hint of scandal nor any question of Morgenthau's competence, this despite his lack of formal training in finance. Morgenthau was also instrumental in setting up the International Monetary Fund and what is today's World Bank. After he left the Treasury, the balance of his life was spent as a philanthropist and financial adviser to Israel.

Carl Icahn:[283] Though today he operates through High River Limited Partnership, most people think of him simply as Carl Icahn, one of the major "corporate raiders" of the late twentieth and early twenty-first century. He remains active at this writing, including recent runs at Time Warner and Yahoo. Along the way, has been involved in failed and successful takeover attempts against Trans World Airlines, Pennzoil, RJR Nabisco, Philips Petroleum, XO Communications, Morton's Restaurants, Marvel Comics, National Airlines, and countless others. Though he has not won every fight, he has amassed a large fortune and a reputation for shrewdness and paranoia. He is also a major benefactor, recently donating $10 million for a track and soccer field at Randalls Island Park.

McAndrews and Forbes:[284] A few years ago, Ron Perelman was dubbed a big, overgrown kid by a close business colleague. A man of remarkable energy and enthusiasms, Perelman started with the benefit of a family sheet metal business, in which his father had given him major responsibility at an early age. Perelman said that hands-on experience was a better education for him than the Wharton MBA he picked up in 1966. By 1979, he left the family business to strike out on his own. He began by taking over a small Jewelry business, Cohen Hatfield. He sold off its pieces, leaving him with the stake he then used to buy New York Stock Exchange-traded McAndrews and Forbes which he took private. He sold off its chocolate business leaving him with the rest of the company free and clear. Since then, he has used McAndrews and Forbes as his principal vehicle for taking over companies he believes will have better value under his leadership.

Over the years Perelman has had his share of ups and downs, both at the office and at home (where he has been through four marriages). Through it all, his drive and motivation have stayed strong. After a bruising battle with Carl Icahn over Marvel Entertainment—which ended in Marvel's bankruptcy—as well as the very public problems at Sunbeam, into which he had merged Coleman, Perelman still controls Revlon, Technicolor, Allied Security, and Panavision, among others. Along the way he has also bought and sold Consolidated Cigar twice and California's Golden State Bancorp.

Sir James Goldsmith:[285] Arguably the most interesting financier of his era, Sir James was a dual citizen, born to an English father and French mother. He dropped out of Eton and sustained early gambling and business losses before finally having success with Bovril, a product now owned by Unilever. His romantic life was legendary. Eloping with the daughter of a Bolivian tin magnate who said, "My family does not marry Jews," Goldsmith responded, "Normally, my family does not marry red Indians." At one time Goldsmith was simultaneously maintaining a weekend family in Paris with his second wife, Ginette, and a weekday one in London with Lady Annabel Birley. He also had two children by a third, Laure Boulay de la Meurthe, a reporter for *Paris Match*. To top it off, he was quoted saying, "If you marry your mistress, you create a job vacancy."

His business takeovers were best described as "swashbuckling." He moved to take over Goodyear and was repelled by a management group that ended up doing exactly what he would have done, but paid him $90 million to go away. Later he took control of Diamond International, Grand Union Supermarkets, and Crown Zellerbach, exiting his investments just before the 1987 crash. His biography was titled, *The Billionaire,* and when he died in July of 1997, he was leading a political effort in England to avoid monetary union and slow the pace of European integration.

Leucadia National Corp.:[286] Ian Cumming and Joseph Steinberg are as little known as Leucadia, the company they took over in 1978 (at the time it was named Talcott National) with $100,000 of their own money and $1.2 million invested by others. Their friendship began as Harvard Business School classmates and developed as employees at Carl Marks & Co. Inc., a New York brokerage and investment firm. Always low key, ("We don't talk to the press," said a lady answering the phone at Steinberg's offices), since 1978 Leucadia has been a huge success demonstrating their skill at buying and fixing up troubled companies. The split-adjusted eight cents per share Leucadia was worth in 1978 is now more than $44, and that is after a $13.58 cash dividend in 1999 plus the $.25 per share in annual dividends since. The returns are as good, or better than those of Warren Buffett—with whom they have partnered in several investments.

Along the way, they bought Colonial Penn Insurance for $128 million and sold it to GE, eight years later, for $1.5 billion. They bought Baldwin-United for $8.80 per share and sold it six years later for $32 per share. In the words of a July 14, 2004, *Wall Street Journal* story, "Leucadia, which typically keeps a low profile, is known as a savvy—and extremely patient—buyer of distressed assets." Today, after distributing roughly $1 billion in dividends since 1999, the company's market value is more than $10 billion. Leucadia controls a remarkably diversified portfolio from telecommunications (WilTel), to mining (MK Resources), as well as health care (Symphony), and with Berkshire Hathaway, a lending company (Finova), and many more. Meanwhile Steinberg is a trustee of New York University, YIVO Institute of Jewish Research, and the American Jewish Historical Society. He is also a co-founder of the *New York Sun* newspaper.

The Tisch Family:[287]In 1946 Laurence Tisch used money from the family's apparel business to purchase Laurel-in-the-Pines, a 300-room resort in Lakewood, New Jersey. Later, his brother Robert joined him, and together they built a chain of twelve hotels before diversifying into movie theaters. By 1961, they had gained control of the Loews theater chain. Later, they added CNA Financial (the insurance company), P. Lorillard (a tobacco company), Bulova Watches, and Diamond Offshore (an offshore drilling company). For nine years, Tisch also controlled CBS before he sold it to Westinghouse.

Since the deaths of Laurence (in 2003) and Robert (in 2005), their sons James S., Jonathan, and Andrew Tisch have provided second-generation leadership to this publicly traded (NYSE) company. In 2007 the combined businesses generated a $2.5 billion profit on revenues of $18.4 billion. In 2008 the tobacco interests were spun off as the second-generation Tisches focus increasingly on offshore drilling, High-Mount Exploration & Production (natural gas and petroleum), and Boardwalk Pipeline operations.

Among Laurence Tisch's philanthropic efforts in 2003 were donations to the Metropolitan Museum of Art, the NYU Medical Center, the Wildlife Conservation Society, New York University (which he served for twenty years as chairman of the board of trustees) and the Tisch's Children Zoo in Central Park. He also served for a time as president of the United Jewish Appeal. (Tisch is also briefly profiled in Chapter 21 – "Enterprise.")

The Pritzkers[288] family legacy began in the practice of law. Nicholas, the first American Pritzker, started a Chicago law firm in 1902 only twelve years after his arrival from Kiev. Second-generation Pritzkers practiced law like their father, but began the diversification (into real estate). In 1957 third-generation Jay Pritzker also practiced law, but diversified still further—building the chain of Hyatt Hotels. Today fourth- generation Thomas J. Pritzker is chairman of the $15 billion Pritzker Organization, but also still serves as a partner in the Pritzker and Pritzker law firm. Meanwhile, at one point, his brother, Robert, and an Israeli partner gained control of 51 percent of the stock of Royal Caribbean Cruise Lines. Along the way, they built one of the world's largest fleets of railroad tank cars (Union Tank Car) within their Marmon Group, which also owns TransUnion, one of the nation's largest credit information companies, and more than fifty other companies.

The 2006 settlement of a family dispute between fourth and fifth generation family members may well bring an end to the private family assemblage through the prospective series of public offerings, sales, and liquidations of portfolio companies. Meanwhile, the family's philanthropic efforts are as prolific as the Pritzker-owned companies. In the Chicago area alone there is: The Pritzker School of Medicine at the University of Chicago, the Pritzker Law Library at Northwestern University, the Pritzker Wing of the Art Institute of Chicago, the Pritzker Gallery of Cosmology at the Adler Planetarium, and the Pritzker Laboratory at the city's Field Museum. There is also the Pritzker Prize in Architecture and more recently, the *Pritzker Zohar*, a translation from Aramaic of this ancient Jewish manuscript. (The Pritzkers are also briefly profiled in Chapter 21.)

Henry Crown & Company:[289] Henry, Irving and Sol Crown, the three sons of Eastern European emigrants Arie and Ida Crown, started a construction materials supply firm, Material Service Corporation in 1919. Henry served as CEO from 1921 until leaving to join the military in 1941. He rose to the rank of Colonel and was decorated for his service in the Corps of Engineers. From first-year sales of $218,000, the Crowns built Material Service into the largest construction-material service company in the world. It had its own sand and gravel pits, mines, quarries, lime and cement plants, as well as fleets of the trucks, boats, and other equipment needed to handle and transport their inventory and products. As a vendor to major construction sites they also saw, and capitalized on, opportunities to invest in hotels, railroad, and real estate development projects including the Empire State Building. In 1959 Material Service was sold to General Dynamics and the family's fortunes shifted to financial investing.

Henry Crown & Company has interests in General Dynamics, the Chicago Bulls, the New York Yankees, Rockefeller Center, and a wide assortment of apartments, resorts, and skyscrapers. In 2008 Forbes estimated the family's worth at $4.5 billion. Today Henry's son, Lester, is chairman and grandson, James, is president. The family's charitable and civic involvements are diverse, including major support to the Aspen Institute, Northwestern University, Duke University, University of Chicago, and Children's Memorial Hospital. In addition, James is vice chairman of the University of Chicago's Trustees.

Bloomberg LP:[290]Over a period of twenty years, Michael Bloomberg created and built one of the world's leading financial information publishers. He started with $10 million earned when his Salomon Brothers' partnership stake was bought out in 1981. Later that year he founded Innovative Market Systems (subsequently renamed Bloomberg LP) to provide bond information to companies such as Merrill Lynch, his initial backer and 20 percent partner. Then Bloomberg expanded beyond bond data into all manner of securities and commodities data, financial news, and other information. All of it is delivered via computer terminals, television, radio, magazines, and the Web to 230,000 users around the world.

In November 2001, Michael Bloomberg stepped down, turning the keys over to non-Jew Lex Fenwick while Bloomberg took over as New York's mayor. He has donated an estimated $715 million to worthy causes, including $100 million to Johns Hopkins University. Despite having given up his post at Bloomberg LP, he reportedly still owns 68 percent of the company which grossed $4.7 billion in 2006. In early 2008, Forbes pegged Michael Bloomberg's net worth at $11.5 billion.

World Bank (and "Quartet Envoy to the Middle East"):[291] James Wolfensohn[291]did not create the World Bank. It was established in the ashes of World War II, and its first head was Eugene Meyer. But Wolfensohn led it for ten years until the end of his second five- year term in 2005, when he was appointed Quartet (U.S., EU, U.N., and Russia) Envoy to assist the Middle East peace process. An Australian by birth, Wolfensohn is a naturalized United States citizen. His history in finance dates back to a 1963 partnership in Ord Minnett, an Australian securities firm. Later he held positions with other firms in Australia, London, and New York, including Salomon Brothers, where he headed up investment banking. In 1981 he set up his own firm, Wolfensohn & Co. His success there and his solid reputation led to his 1995 appointment to the World Bank.

Louis Rukeyser:[292] Perhaps more media personality than financier, Rukeyser was a fixture of financial reporting for nearly thirty-five years. He moved from the Baltimore Sun to ABC News, where he pioneered the role of on-air economic commentator. In 1970 he began *Wall Street Week* on public television. It became the most popular TV program of its kind for thirty years until 2002, when public television, in a self-inflicted wound it was never able to heal, gave Rukeyser the boot. Ruykeyser passed away in 2006.

Haym Salomon:[293]Not well known today, Haym Salomon was a principal financier of the American Revolution, at a time when the U.S. government lacked the taxing power to pay its own expenses. An immigrant Polish Jew, Salomon sold bonds to France and Holland, loaned his personal funds, and even turned over his bond sales commissions to help his adopted country. In addition, he made personal loans to Thomas Jefferson, James Monroe and James Madison, refusing interest when the loans were repaid. In the end, the United States never repaid Salomon or his heirs the $600,000 (in 1784 dollars) shown as owed in the records of Robert Morris, U.S. superintendent of finance. If repaid with interest today, the United States would owe his heirs well over $1 trillion.

Alfred Lerner's[294] parents were Russian emigrants. His father, still a teen, had little schooling and went to work immediately upon arrival in America. His mother, already twenty when she arrived, was a college graduate. They quickly learned English and after their marriage, both read extensively for the rest of their lives. When their only child, Al, was born in 1933, it was the heart of the Depression. Family income from their soda fountain and candy store was meager despite eighteen-hour days with only three Jewish holidays off each year. But when not working, all three were reading in their rooms behind the store. Alfred passed the tough entrance exams for Brooklyn Technical high school and went on to study at Columbia, working summers to pay tuition. Upon graduation in 1955, Lerner became a Marine pilot and officer. He said the Marines taught him two lessons that stuck: One, you can do a lot more than you think you can; and two, a leader eats last. He takes care of the troops first.

After a stint as a furniture salesman and store owner, Lerner began investing in real estate. It became his career. A few years later, he sold the furniture stores, using the proceeds to invest in real estate. Over the years he built a portfolio of 15,000 apartments, mostly in the Mid-Atlantic states. He also made a small investment in the Cleveland Browns football team, which later moved to Baltimore. But it was in banking that Lerner had his greatest impact. With a partner, he took control of a Baltimore bank, and then rescued it from the early 1990s real estate loan crisis. He spun its credit card operations off into a separate public company, MBNA, which for a time was the world's largest credit card issuer. Next, he used some of his MBNA profits to bring professional football back to Cleveland. It made him a local hero.

But for many, the Lerner legacy is not the Cleveland Browns, the real estate empire, nor his.No. 36 ranking on the Forbes 400, but his decency and the money he gave away. Cleveland Clinic got $16 million in 1999 and another $100 million in

2002. Ten million went to University Hospitals of Cleveland, and $25 million to Columbia University for a student center. He also created, the Cleveland Browns Heroes Fund, which provided financial aid to survivors of rescuers killed in the World Trade Center. Lerner had only just begun his favorite career—philanthropy—when he died in 2002 at age sixty-nine.

Chapter 18

Real Estate

"Let me pay the price of the land...four hundred
shekels of silver at the going...rate."
            —*Abraham in Genesis 23: 13–16*

A Brief History of Judaism and Real Estate[295]

Four hundred shekels to buy the cave and the adjoining field of Machpelah, that's how much Abraham paid a Hittite landowner in history's first recorded real estate purchase by a Jew. When his wife, Sarah, died at the age of 127, Abraham bought the cave near the West Bank town of Hebron for her grave. Today roughly 3,700 years later, and despite restricted Jewish access, it remains one of Judaism's holiest sites. Revered as the Tomb of the Patriarchs, it is said to be the last resting place not only for Sarah, but also for Abraham, Isaac, Jacob, Rebecca, and Leah.[296]

In a sense, restricted Jewish access to the cave purchased by Abraham is a manifestation of the real estate difficulties Jews have faced for much of their history. But before that story is told, a second property transaction described in Genesis deserves attention. Less conventional, it is at the heart of Judaism and it remains at the center of today's news headlines.

Genesis describes the evolving "Covenant" between God and Abraham.[297]

Genesis 12: 1–3, recounts God's promise. In exchange for Abraham leaving his native land and going to Canaan, God will "make of you a great nation."

In Genesis 13: 14–15, the grant is made more specific. Near Bethel, in Canaan,

God tells Abraham, "Raise your eyes and look out from where you are to the north and south, to the east and west, for I give *all the land that you see* (emphasis added) to you and your offspring forever."

Still later, in Genesis 15, God promises Abraham many offspring, but forewarns him they will be "strangers in a strange land,…enslaved and oppressed four hundred years," before, on their return (presumably from Egypt), he will assign them all *"this land from the river of Egypt to the great river, the river Euphrates."*

Finally, in Genesis 17, God promises Abraham he will be "the father of a multitude of nations." "I assign the land you sojourn in to you and your offspring to come, *all the land of Canaan* as an everlasting holding." As part of that codicil, Abraham and his offspring must "keep My Covenant. …every male among you shall be circumcised."

The shifting scope of the Covenant's grant of land ("as far as the eye can see," "all of Canaan," "all the land from the Nile to the Euphrates") even if logically reconcilable by ancient biblical interpreters, remains confusing to the lay reader. Which is it? What land did God grant the Jews in the Covenant?

Disputes as to the validity of the Biblical grant and confusion as to its scope are at the heart of today's Arab-Israeli conflict as well as the wrangling between ultra-Orthodox Israelis and their less orthodox brethren. Controversies over Jewish rights to the state of Israel have been headline news for more than sixty years. Jewish settlements in the West Bank are a more recent cause of strife, but for ultra-Orthodox Jews, the settlements involve just a fraction of the grant God gave the Jews in Genesis. For them, legitimate Jewish claims extend all the way to the Euphrates on the east and Nile on the west.

———•———

The roughly 4,000-year history of the Jewish people has been so turbulent and their existence so long threatened that ownership or control of real estate, when not prohibited, could be so risky as to be unwise. Over those 4,000 years, Jews controlled their own country for fewer than 600 years (and most of that was before 586 B.C.). The rest of the time they were a colony of a controlling power such as Rome, or were dispersed to minority enclaves in other, often hostile countries such as the Pale of Russia.

While there have been peaceful interludes and occasional eras of political stability for Jews, the spans of time when they might have secure and unfettered ownership of land have been the exception—or of very recent origin. For most of Jewish history, life was sufficiently uncertain that wealth, when one had it, was best kept in concentrated form so it could be moved quickly if circumstances warranted. Real estate does not meet that standard.

The following brief history of the Jews is intended to provide insight to why their recent real estate achievements are so improbable in light of their history.

Egyptian Enslavement to the Temple's Destruction—1,600 Turbulent Years

Following the reputed Egyptian enslavement of 400 years or more (circa 1600

B.C. to 1200 B.C.), there was an interregnum after the conquest of Canaan by Joshua and his followers. The twelve Jewish tribes took over much of present-day Palestine and unified it into a single nation. That golden era culminated in the roughly ninety years (between 1029 B.C. and 938 B.C.) under the rule of Saul, David, and Solomon. But it was not to last.

After Solomon died, the northern and southern tribes split into two weakened nations. Between 750 B.C. and 722 B.C., the Assyrians defeated the ten northern tribes (Israel) and in the ensuing deportation, those ten tribes were annihilated or assimilated. They have completely vanished from history. No trace of them has ever been unearthed. The two remaining southern tribes (Judah) were later conquered by the Babylonians (598 - 586 B.C.) and nearly all were exiled to Babylon for sixty years or more.

The Persian Cyrus the Great was their savior. After defeating the Babylonians in battle (539 B.C.), the Jews were allowed to return to their homeland, but for those who did return, it was to a homeland ruled by Persians, not Jews. They remained a subject people. Two hundred years later, in 333 B.C., Alexander the Great defeated the Persians and for the next 167 years his successors, the Ptolemies and Seleucids, controlled Palestine. A successful revolt by the Jewish Maccabees against the Seleucid tyrant Antiochus IV resulted in a century of Jewish/Hellenistic independence before that "Hasmonean state" succumbed to the Romans.

Roman rule began with a promise of Jewish autonomy (albeit over a much reduced geography for the Hasmonean state), but it quickly devolved. Herod the Great, at least formally a Jew, was slavishly loyal to Rome. The Jewish rebellions in A.D. 66–73 and the Bar Kokhba revolt of A.D. 132–135 brought brutal Roman domination and absolute control over the Jews and their historical homeland.

Disastrous losses to Roman forces and the A.D. 70 destruction of the Temple in Jerusalem ended the first 2,000 years of Jewish history in a rout. Never willing to tolerate disloyalty, the Romans dispersed all but trace numbers of Jews from Palestine (the Diaspora) while also destroying Jewish communities throughout much of the Middle East. At the time of Christ, Jews are thought to have numbered 4.5 million (1.8 percent of the world's population). Two hundred years later, only 1.5 million Jews survived (.6 percent of the world's population.) Eighteen hundred years would pass before Jews would again total 4.5 million, and they have never gotten back to more than .8 percent of the world's population. Today they are just .2 percent.[298]

Early Diaspora

Jewish communities had existed outside Palestine for hundreds of years before the Diaspora, but with the Roman conquests of the first and second centuries, dispersal from Palestine to enclaves in foreign lands became the dominant life experience for Jews for the next 1,900 years. Many migrated to Babylon, beyond the control of the Romans. Others moved to communities around the Mediterranean and Black Sea, some to southern Egypt, Ethiopia, southern Africa, and Yemen, some east as far as India, and others into Europe as far north as today's Paris and the northern Rhine. Later, the dispersal went still further, into England, Eastern Europe, South and Central America, central Asia, and North America.

The Diaspora completely changed Judaism. With the destruction of the Temple in Jerusalem, synagogues became the center of worship. The priests and Sadducees were eclipsed by rabbis and Pharisees. Starting with the Torah, perhaps as early as 400 B.C., the Jewish Bible was canonized in pieces with the final books (commonly called The Writings) considered "closed" by A.D. 132. Over the ensuing centuries the "Oral Law" evolved into the Talmud. Some Judaic scholars attribute the existence of the Talmud, if not final canonization of the written Hebrew Bible, to the need to establish a common understanding of Judaism by a permanently dispersed people. A written Bible and Talmud were the only way to do that.[299]

The "wandering Jews" were once more described by the sobriquet "strangers in a strange land." For Christians, this was the price Jews were to pay for rejecting and murdering Jesus. For Romans it was the price of disloyalty and rebellion. With Diaspora and nearly unceasing discrimination came a life of near constant discomfort, risk, and uncertainty. Even when permitted, owning real estate in a foreign land was not something one could do with confidence.

For Diaspora Jews, in some areas and at some times, life was reasonably secure. Babylonia was hospitable under Parthian, and to a lesser extent, under Sassanian rule. But even then, a regime or policy change could quickly bring adverse consequences.[300]

Roman and later Byzantine Christian and Roman Catholic states, by way of contrast, were so consistently harsh that Jews initially welcomed the Islamic conquerors. Under Islam, Jews (and Christians) faced a variety of special taxes not levied against Muslims. Jews were never to act superior to Muslims. They could not construct buildings taller than a mosque, and, in general, they were second-class citizens. But if they "behaved," there was some level of protection, even if that arrangement was not always honored by the caliphate. In medieval Spain (A.D. 1090) the Almoravides expelled Jews from positions of influence, and later, the Almohads (successor rulers) demanded that Jews convert to Islam, forcing most of them to flee southern Spain.[301]

If Islam was usually stable though occasionally hostile, the reverse was true for Christianity. As Paul Johnson notes, "Late fourth and fifth century Jews living in Christian societies had most of their communal rights and all of their privileges withdrawn....The policy of the church was to allow small Jewish communities to survive in conditions of degradation and impotence."[302] Jews were often prohibited from owning land in Europe up to the time of the Jewish Emancipation (roughly 1790 to 1890), and when they could control land in Christian kingdoms, it was often in the form of a sovereign "trusteeship." In Aragon, a Jew might be able to sell property, but only to a fellow Jew, and the sovereign could confiscate the property at any time without compensation.[303]

The Middle Ages

In 1146-47, France's Louis VIII was advised to confiscate Jewish property to finance the Crusades. And with the Crusades came the slaughter and pillaging of Jews as Crusaders made their way to the Holy Land to fulfill their sacred duty.

Edward I of England needed money to ransom his cousin, Charles of Salerno.

To get it, he confiscated the property of his Gascony Jews and then, in 1290, he expelled them.[304] Jews were not allowed back into England for nearly 400 years.[305]

Jews were often invited into an area by a sovereign who wished to have an industrious people with special talents such as finance, or who could be compelled to do very unpopular tasks, such as tax farming (collection), but the invitation seemed always to end up in later Jewish expulsions.

Invited into Speyer in 1084, Jews were expelled in 1405, allowed to return in 1421, kicked out in 1430, readmitted in 1434, ejected again in 1435 and allowed back once more in 1465.[306] They were "expelled from Vienna and Linz in 1421, from Cologne in 1424, Augsburg in 1439, Bavaria in 1442 (and 1450), Moravia in 1454, Perugia in 1485, Vicenze in 1486, Parma in 1488, Milan and Lucca in 1489, and Tuscany in 1494.[307]

Among the most notorious of the Jewish persecutions was the Spanish Inquisition which commenced in 1480.[308] Spain had long been a haven for Jews, even in the early years of the Christian Reconquista, but circumstances deteriorated over the fourteenth and fifteenth centuries culminating in Ferdinand and Isabella's March 31, 1492, order expelling Jews from Spain.[309] Of the 200,000 Jews then in Spain, 100,000 left for Portugal—from which they would be expelled just four years later— 50,000 went to Northern Africa or present day Turkey, and the rest are thought to have converted to Christianity.[310] Over the life of the Inquisition, its victims totaled more than 340,000. Of them, 32,000, mostly Jews, were burned to death.[311]

Ultimately Spanish Jews spread out over much of Europe, the Middle East, and Northern Africa. A few ended up in present-day Holland where they found sanctuary. Others ended up in Venice. It was there, in 1515–16, that they became Europe's first Jews to be consigned to the ghetto.[312] Over the next 400 years, the ghetto, or its larger manifestation—the Pale of Settlement encompassing much of today's Eastern Poland, Byelorussia, the Ukraine and neighboring countries—became a common circumstance for many Jews up to the time of the Jewish Emancipation.

Jewish Emancipation, Dreyfus, Pogroms and the Birth of Zionism

In Europe, the first respite, the first opportunity to be treated as an equal, receive a secular education, serve in the military, pursue any career without qualification, and own property, commenced with the Jewish Emancipation. Arguably begun by Napoleon after he seized power in 1799, it was adopted, country by country, in Europe over the next 100 years.[313] It offered Jews full rights of citizenship essentially everywhere but in the Pale. In fact, however, the interlude of Emancipation rights and stability was only partial. The rights were diminished by anti-Semitism, of which the most notorious example was the 1890s Dreyfus affair in France.[314] As it became clear that allegations charging Dreyfus as a traitor were false, many Jews lost confidence they would ever be treated as equals in Europe, Asia, or colonial Africa. Today's Zionism was born in the Dreyfus courtroom.[315]

Theordor Herzl and others concluded Jews would never be safe until they had their own country. After considering other locations, Herzl and his compatriots decided Palestine was the most logical place for a Jewish homeland and the migration, controversial even then, began.

But worse than the discrimination Jews experienced in Western and Central Europe was the late nineteenth century treatment of Jews in the Pale of Eastern Europe. For a time, particularly in the late 1800s, life there was simply horrific for Jews. Whether by official Russian policy or not, the pogroms were brutal. Jews were murdered and communities ransacked. Ultimately the pogroms resulted in three major "migrations": one was to assimilate into what ultimately became the Communist Soviet Union; a second was the massive migration to the United States; the third was the migration of large numbers of Jews to Palestine.[316]

In Palestine those immigrants with money purchased their own land. For those who lacked money, it was the Rothschilds, the Schiffs, and other wealthy European and American Jews, as well as organized charities, such as the Jewish National Fund, that purchased large tracts from absentee Ottoman landowners for the Jewish immigrants.[317] Many Jews who migrated had become secularized. Politically many adopted socialism, Communism, anarchism, or other radical ideologies after giving up on their Jewish faith, perhaps because of persecution endured in the Pale and the apparent failure of a just God to intervene. The kibbutz was born. And while it represented collective ownership of land—essentially socialism—it was their land and their home.[318]

The Urban Culture of Diaspora Judaism and the Back to the Land Movement

If large numbers of Jews in pre-Roman Palestine were rural landowners and farmers, that was to change dramatically during the Diaspora. Restrictions and risks of property ownership, the need to live in enclaves for personal security, the existence of the ghetto (or Pale), and the limited careers open to Jews, such as finance, merchandising, tax collection, medicine and other professions, together consigned the Jewish culture to be almost totally urban for the better part of 1,900 years. For the most part, Jews became city dwellers.

Pogroms and the resulting immigrations of impoverished Jews to Israel, the United States, and other countries briefly triggered a remarkable "back to the land movement" that might have changed the highly urbanized character of Jewish society. The kibbutzim in Palestine, for example, were a manifestation of this return to the land and to efforts to restore an agricultural culture for at least some Jews.

The wealthy Bavarian, Baron Maurice de-Hirsch, among others, bought large tracts of land and sponsored new agricultural communities in North and South America and Asia Minor for Jewish immigrants who were expected to restore Jewish farming skills and provide food to meet their own needs and those of others. De-Hirsch hoped to found colonies of hundreds of thousands of Jews.[319] One small offshoot of that mentality is the interesting experience of the group of Jews who moved to Petaluma, California, in the early twentieth century to become chicken farmers. This group has been memorialized in a number of books and documentaries.[320]

But the farming move appears to have run out of steam in the second and third generations as sons, daughters, and grandchildren increasingly became absentee farmers returning to an urban lifestyle and leaving the farming to others. In particular, a number of studies of the American Jewish agricultural enclaves have told and retold of the emergence and decline of such communities. Though some of the communities still exist, generally the romance of farming soured within a generation or two.[321]

Some have said the literacy demanded by Judaism following publication of the Torah and Talmud, and the demands the culture places on educating children engendered a talent for occupations more interesting, more demanding, and more lucrative than farming. In turn, over many generations, Jews genetically self-selected for high IQs, which demanded more stimulation than could be had in conventional farming. In any case, by the end of World War II, and with some exceptions in South America and Israel, the "back to the land movement" was over.[322]

Nazism and the Creation of Israel

The rise of Nazism ended, for a time, the rights gained from the European Jewish Emancipation. Property of every kind was confiscated as six million Jews were systematically murdered. And while it was insufficient to save them, the Holocaust reaffirmed the need to keep one's wealth in transportable, concentrated form.

The loss of one-third of the World's Jews, historical claims dating to Genesis, the large numbers of Jews that had migrated to Palestine after the 1880s, British promises in the Balfour Declaration, passage of a 1947 United Nations resolution partitioning Palestine, and the 1947–48 War led to the establishment of today's state of Israel. Though its creation has resulted in the irony of a Palestinian Diaspora, and the expropriation of property owned by Palestinians, the Jews regained a homeland. Judaism's 1,900 stateless years were over.

America—The Exception

In 1654 twenty-three Ashkenazi and Sephardic Jews arrived in New Amsterdam (New York) from Recife, in present-day Brazil. They had been part of a Dutch colony recently recaptured by the Portuguese. Threatened by the ongoing Inquisition, the Jews sought asylum. Initially Governor Peter Stuyvesant was reluctant, but his decision was overturned by his superiors in Holland who ran the Dutch East India Company. This was the "Golden Age of the Dutch," a period in which unique Dutch tolerance provided protection for many Jews, including such notables as Spinoza. The Dutch told Stuyvesant to let the Jews in and he complied.[323] That legacy has continued unabated in North America since 1654.

While America has not been without its own history of anti-Semitism, on balance the United States was the world's most continuously hospitable place for Jews over the roughly 300 years from 1654 until the 1947-48 creation of Israel. The secure

---

§ Stephen Birmingham's 1967 classic book, *Our Crowd,* described the "aristocracy" of New York's German Jewish immigrants. They arrived poor in the mid-1800s, went on to start successful businesses, and became very wealthy. Their "high society," culture generally condescend to the poor, uneducated and ill-mannered eastern European Jews who immigrated a generation or two later.

position of Jews in America continues today, some seventy years later with anti-Semitism sufficiently minimal that Joseph Lieberman was nominated as the Democratic candidate for vice president in 2000.

Like nearly every immigrant group in America, including Irish, Italians, and others, Jews suffered demeaning treatment from those who preceded them. Like Catholics and blacks, they were sometimes threatened, had their property destroyed, and occasionally, though rarely, some were killed by bigots such as the Ku Klux Klan or southern rednecks. When waves of Jews arrived from the Pale (immigrating because the United States was perceived to be one of the only safe places for them, and a place with opportunities to succeed), most were initially looked down upon. Ironically, the condescension was perhaps greatest among the "Our Crowd"$ German Jews who preceded them, rather than in the White Anglo-Saxon Protestant community.

By the mid-1920s restrictions were placed on immigration, in no small part because of anti-Semitic reaction to immigrant activist Jews, such as Emma Goldman. Goldman's rumored involvement in the McKinley assassination and her espousal of anarchism, communism and socialism were perceived as a threat.[324] For a time, quotas restricting the numbers of Jews to be admitted to private colleges were proposed, but they were largely unsuccessful and, like the restrictive real estate covenants and conditions that were in place for a time, they have since been completely eliminated.

Through it all, American anti-Semitism was orders of magnitude less intense than Jews typically experienced anywhere else over their 4,000-year history. Jewish immigrants could and did become American citizens. With very few exceptions, they had full legal rights. They could vote, serve in the military, attend public schools, be elected to public office, and own real estate. In no small measure, the United States Constitution was based on Judeo Christian principles. Jews helped finance the Revolutionary War. Newly elected president George Washington wrote to the members of a Newport, Rhode Island, synagogue saying, "For happily the government of the United States, which gives to bigotry no sanction, to persecution no assistance, requires only that they who live free under its protections should demean [conduct] themselves as good citizens."[325] Jews fought on both sides during the Civil War. They were successful merchants, financiers and professionals, and by 1916, Louis Brandeis, a Jew, was appointed to the United States Supreme Court, where today two of the nine Justices are Jewish.

Over the later part of the nineteenth and early twentieth centuries, particularly as Jews increased from .5 percent of the population in 1880 to 3.4 percent by 1920, and as they became successful as merchants, financiers, bankers, entrepreneurs, entertainers, doctors, and lawyers, some of them began to own real estate, not just for their own residences, factories, and stores, but also in large portfolios of residential and commercial property which they developed and managed.

It is worth noting that substantial Jewish involvement in real estate has also been stimulated by the fact that Jews now have two homelands: Israel and the United States. The Diaspora is over. If "wandering Jews" were stateless for thousands of years, today, with 5.3 million Jews in Israel and 5.275 million in the United States, at least 81 percent of the world's 13.1 million Jews are citizens of just two countries, and in both they can safely own real estate and they do. They are as disproportionately accomplished in this domain as they are in many others.

Development, Ownership and Management of Real Estate

In 2007, Forbes named the top twenty-five individuals from among the Forbes 400 whose success largely arose from real estate. They included:

George Argyros	**Neil G. Bluhm**	**Donald Bren**
Eli Broad	**Matthew Bucksbaum**	**Alan I. Casden**
Edward DeBartolo Jr.	Archie Aldis Emerson	**Richard LeFrak**
Theodore Lerner	**Harry Macklowe**	**Paul Milstein**
Igor Olenicoff	George Perez	Edward Roski Jr.
Stephen Ross	**Melvin Simon**	John A. Sobrato
Sheldon Henry Solow	**Jerry Speyer**	**Leonard Stern**
Alfred Taubman	Donald Trump	**Sam Zell**
Mort Zuckerman		

More than two-thirds of the twenty-five (as least the eighteen in boldface) are Jews.

The balance of this chapter describes how these individuals, and others, most of them self-made, achieved so much.

Residential and Mixed Use Development

William J. Levitt – Levitt & Sons:[326]In 2000 *Time* magazine named William J. Levitt to its list of the 100 most important people of the twentieth century. In 2004 *Business Week* chronicled him as one of the greatest innovators of the past seventy-five years. A promoter, flashy dresser, and gambler, Levitt died broke in 1994, well before *Time* and *Business Week* made their selections. He was honored despite his problems.

Levitt revolutionized housing at precisely the moment it was most needed. A custom home builder before World War II, Levitt, his father Abraham, and brother Alfred contracted to build high-volume, low-cost Navy housing in 1942. They learned how to apply assembly-line production techniques to quickly build inexpensive quality housing within "planned communities," another notion pioneered by Levitt.

The United States had not built significant numbers of middle-class homes since the onset of the Great Depression, but by 1946–47, millions of returning GIs were starting families and wanted their own homes. The houses had to be inexpensive, since most ex-GIs were just entering the workforce and had little cash. To help them, the government offered mortgage guarantees while also guaranteeing loans for builders. Levitt saw a way to break production into twenty-seven steps allowing him to build and sell a typical house for $6,990 ($70,000 in today's dollars) while making a $1,000 profit. It was a huge opportunity. Levitt saw and acted on it before anyone else. (Today, those $6,990 homes sell for an average of $400,000.)

The first Levittown, on New York's Long Island, was a planned community on 1,200 acres. Today it includes 17,500 homes. After that project, others were built on Long Island, in New Jersey, Pennsylvania, Maryland, and Puerto Rico. They all had winding streets, good schools, nice parks, and were considered safer than the crowded apartments of Manhattan, Queens, and similar old-line communities. Many developers followed in Levitt's footsteps. The suburbs were born.

Levitt's pioneering changed residential real estate development from an industry of builders who completed only a few homes a year into an efficient mass-production business. In this, his contribution was akin to the Jews, conversion of the apparel industry from custom tailoring to "ready-to-wear." In total Levitt built more than 140,000 homes.

Fearing the taxes he would pay if he sold the ITT stock he received when he sold the company in 1968, Levitt rode ITT's stock all the way to the bottom. When the debts he incurred using ITT stock as collateral came due, he ended up broke, unable even to pay his hospital bills when he died in 1994. To add a further tragic dimension, after a succession of owners following ITT, Levitt Corporation went bankrupt in 2007.

Donald Bren – Irvine Ranch:[327] If William Levitt's homebuilding revolution began on 1,200 Long Island acres, Donald Bren's vision was realized on 93,000 acres (one-sixth of Orange County and three times the size of San Francisco). Bren's story is the antithesis of Levitt's. If Levitt drove down costs for returning GIs' housing, Bren drove for quality, eventually setting aside 50,000 of the 93,000 acres for open space and recreation. He did this, not as the manager of someone else's property, nor as CEO of a public company. No, this was all Bren's land, acreage he purchased between 1977 and 1996. If Levitt died broke, Bren is listed among America's richest on the *Forbes* 400 list, and as the ninth most generous on *Business Week's* 2007 list of "The 50 Most Generous Philanthropists."

Bren started small. In 1958, after three years in the Marine Corps, he set himself up as a small time builder of speculative homes on California's Lido Island. Successful, he moved on to develop Mission Viejo, selling out his interest there in 1967.

In 1977 a group of investors including Alfred Taubman, Max Fisher, and others joined Bren to buy the Irvine Company. By 1983 Bren owned all but 8 percent of the company, and by 1996 he bought out the remaining investor, Joan Irvine Smith.

As noted by the *Los Angeles Times,* "Simply put, Orange County looks like Orange County—much of it uniformly manicured and catering to the high life and high tech—because of the influence of Bren. UC Irvine, Fashion Island, the Irvine Spectrum, University Research Park, Newport Coast, Orange County's thousands of acres of wilderness and parkland and its enviable public school systems all bear Bren's imprint." Today Irvine Ranch houses more than 200,000 people and 250,000 jobs. Bren's holdings include "approximately 400 office buildings, ninety apartment communities, forty retail centers, two hotels, five marinas and three golf clubs."

Over the years, Bren has given away nearly $1 billion, of which $200 million went to public schools and to endow fifty chairs at UC Irvine, UC Santa Barbara and

Chapman University. An additional $50 million has gone to ensure the long-term restoration, preservation, and management of the 50,000 acres permanently set aside for open space and recreation on Irvine Ranch.

Donald Kaufman and Eli Broad – KB Home (née Kaufman & Broad):[328] In 1957 Eli Broad and Donald Kaufman (now deceased) started Kaufman & Broad in Detroit using $25,000 borrowed from Broad's father-in-law. Broad, then twenty-three and the youngest CPA in Michigan history, was the son of Lithuanian immigrants. While working as an accountant for Kaufman, his home-builder cousin, Broad perceived a major opportunity in building low-priced housing in volume. Kaufman and Broad's respective talents in home building and finance were perfect complements. Like Levitt, Kaufman & Broad went after the mass market and did it, in part by eliminating basements, letting buyers do their own landscaping, and drawing on purchasing and financing techniques developed by Broad. The company was profitable in its first year, went public in 1961, and was listed on the New York Stock Exchange shortly thereafter. By 1965, Kaufman had retired, leaving thirty-one year old Broad to take it from there.

Broad expanded beyond Michigan into Arizona, California, Chicago, New York and New Jersey and he moved corporate headquarters to Los Angeles. He diversified the company, forming a mortgage subsidiary in 1965, and expanded into France in 1967 and Canada by 1971. As noted in *Time* magazine, by 1972, Kaufman & Broad was second in size only to ITT Levitt. In 1971 Broad further diversified by acquiring Sun Life Insurance Company, which allowed Kaufman & Broad to market insurance and annuities to new homebuyers.

In 1972 Broad recruited Bruce Karatz and in 1986, when the company was split into two separate businesses, Karatz took over as president and CEO of Kaufman & Broad (now KB Home). After nearly thirty years in the business, Broad wanted to do something different, so he took over as CEO of the newly separate SunAmerica Insurance Company.

Karatz went on to successfully build and run KB Home for nearly twenty years until 2006, when he got caught up in a stock option backdating scandal and stepped down. By then, KB Home was ranked first among homebuilders in *Fortune* magazine's list of "Most Admired Companies." Since inception, KB home has built more than 500,000 homes and helped finance many of them.

Broad built SunAmerica into the fastest growing insurance company (in market value) during the 1990s before he sold it to AIG in 1998.

Broad has since gone on to become one of America's foremost philanthropists and civic activists. He has donated more than $2 billion to three Broad family foundations that focus on art, education, and scientific and medical initiatives. He and his wife, Edythe have donated $600 million to the Broad Institute of M.I.T. and Harvard to study genetic links and molecular causes for diseases, $20 million to UCLA for its arts complex, $60 million to the Los Angeles County Museum of Art, $60 million to create the nonprofit, Strong America School, and he was the leading donor to Caltech's $100 million Broad Center for Biological Sciences. As generous with his time as he is with his money, Broad was the driving force behind the new Los Angeles Walt Disney Concert Hall and the revitalization of downtown Los Angeles.

The New York Real Estate Families[329]

"All in the Families," was the title of a November 26, 2007, *Fortune* story noting that nine of the top twenty commercial property owners in New York were not Real Estate Investment Trusts (REITs) or private equity firms, but instead old line families, still private and still in control of substantial properties. Six families were featured in the story. They were:

LeFrak
Trump
Fisher
Durst
Silverstein
Rudin

Of the six, only Trump is not Jewish. Their stories, and those of other New York families, not mentioned by *Fortune,* typically involve three to five generations of immigrant families who started with next to nothing but built strong family real estate dynasties.

The LeFrak Family: The LeFrak Organization:[330] Harry LeFrak, a French glazier, immigrated to the United States in 1901. He did custom glazing for clients such as Tiffany, and his success eventually allowed him to buy a 120-acre farm in Williamsburg, Brooklyn. He split ten acres off from the farm to create his first residential development.

In 1948 his son, Samuel, took over. An energetic promoter of remarkable drive and vision, Samuel created one of America's foremost real estate companies. Initially the focus was on residential apartment buildings, including the signature LeFrak City of twenty 18-story apartment towers in Queens housing 5,000 residential units. Later he saw a huge opportunity in the rundown Jersey City rail warehouses across the Hudson River from lower Manhattan and the opportunity to build 1,800 apartments in Battery Park City.

He diversified by building LeFrak Oil and Gas and Lefrak Entertainment and Communications, which produces motion pictures and TV programs, owns cable and phone systems, and stages musicals and Broadway plays.

As much philanthropist as developer, Samuel gave away millions to the Guggenheim Museum, Barnard College, Michigan State, the University of Maryland, and Queens College while also picking up six international knighthoods. He served as a director of the Dana Farber Cancer Institute at Harvard Medical School and the Metropolitan Opera as well.

The LeFrak organization is now in the hands of Harry's grandson Richard, and his great-grandsons, Harrison and Jamie. The third- and fourth-generation LeFraks have expanded still further, into Los Angeles and London real estate.

After four generations LeFrak is still a family business, albeit one that owns and manages twenty-two million square feet of residential property (roughly 25,000 apartments) and twelve million feet of office space. In addition, LeFrak is developing a 600 acre, $10 billion, mixed-use project (Newport) on the New Jersey waterfront. Newport will include 9,000 apartments, seven million square feet of office space, two million square feet of retail space, a marina, and a number of entertainment and cultural venues.

The Silverstein Family – Silverstein Properties:[331] Compared to the other four real estate families featured by *Fortune,* Larry Silverstein is a new kid on the block. His is a three-generation business. His father, a Russian Jewish immigrant, was more real estate broker than developer, but working for his father was how Larry Silverstein paid his way through law school. After graduation, he returned to work with his father, and for a time with his brother-in-law.

In the late 1950s and 1960s, Silverstein migrated from brokering to buying, fixing up, and selling smaller properties. By the 1980s, he controlled ten million square feet of real estate.

Silverstein had the good—or bad—fortune to take over the World Trade Center property only months before the September 11 terrorist attack. After notable disputes and negotiations, he won $4.7 billion of insurance compensation to rebuild the ten million square feet of lost office and commercial space, and he overcame a wave of government and private objections about reuse and reconstruction on the original site.

A determined optimist, Silverstein takes counsel from Klara, his wife of more than fifty years, and he has brought his children, Roger and Lisa, into the business. At some point, a third generation will lead Silverstein properties.

Fisher Brothers:[332] Carl Fisher started the family in real estate in the early 1900s. His three sons, Martin, Larry, and Zachary founded Fisher Brothers in 1915 focusing mainly on residential property in and around New York City. By the 1950s, the family began to develop commercial space growing to eight million square feet by the 1980s. At that point, they had completely exited residential property.

Following the deaths of the three brothers, control has passed to the next generation, Larry's son Arnold, his sons, Steven and Kenneth, and his nephew, Winston.

The Fishers are now said to control a $4 billion portfolio. Every project is organized as a stand-alone investment with different family members and outside partners, including Morgan Stanley, involved from project to project. The Fishers have built and managed not only office space, but have diversified also into hotels in the United States and Mexico.

The family has also devoted huge amounts of time and money to philanthropic efforts. The Intrepid Air and Space Museum on the Hudson River is almost single-handedly the work of Zachary, who donated $25 million to the effort. Zachary also led efforts to establish a foundation that paid $10,000 to the families of servicemen lost in the Beirut, Lebanon, Marine barracks bombing. The Fisher House Program has constructed nearly forty homes to temporarily house visiting families of hospitalized servicemen and women, at little or no cost to the families. The Fisher Center for Alzheimer's Research at Rockefeller University is focused on the cause, care, and cure of Alzheimer's and those afflicted with it.

The Durst Family – The Durst Organization:[333] Joseph Durst is said to have arrived in the United States from Austria in 1915 with $3 sewed into his lapel. He built that trifling stake into a bank before shifting his focus to real estate, initially buying an office building on New York's 34th Street. Today a third and fourth generation of Dursts own and manage nine million square feet of prime real estate in eleven Manhattan buildings. They are also working to augment that portfolio with another huge project on Manhattan's West Side.

For some, the family is best known for the "Debt Clock," which Joseph's son, Seymour, erected. It is a huge electronic billboard on the side of a Sixth Avenue building in Manhattan tolling the growth of the national debt.

Two things have distinguished the family's real estate involvement. One is vision—the ability to foresee an opportunity and to shape it. Seymour Durst was among the first to see the potential to develop and improve midtown Manhattan's Third Avenue and Sixth Avenue when both were considered undesirable locations. He and his son, Douglas, saw the same kind of opportunity in buying and holding properties in the vicinity of Times Square when it was seedy and run down. Their Times Square developments, including the Conde Nast Building, have had a huge influence in revitalizing that part of Manhattan.

A second focus has been environmental consciousness. Their Bank of America building was expected to be the first skyscraper to earn a top environmental award when it opened in 2008. Reuse of wastewater and rainwater, close monitoring of air quality, under the floor (rather than overhead) ventilation, and technology to dissipate the sun's heat are among the novel innovations the Dursts have designed into the building.

The Rudin Family – Rudin Management Co.:[334] In 1902 Louis Rudinsky bought property at 153 East 54th Street in Manhattan. A native of Minsk (now in Byelorussia), the family's roots also trace to Volozhin, a legendary Conservative yeshiva near that city. In the 1880s Rudinsky fled the pogroms to immigrate to America. Later asked by his son Samuel why he bought the 54th Street property, Louis replied, "If it's good enough for the Rockefellers, it's good enough for me." (At the time, the Rockefellers owned a residence on 54th.)

Today, five generations later, 153 East 54th Street is still part of the family portfolio. In 1925 Samuel formed Rudin Management and incorporated his father's "buy and hold" philosophy as well as the family's independent, go-it-alone strategy. Today Rudin Management counts a portfolio of thirty-six New York City buildings totaling fifteen million square feet.

The family's philanthropy is legendary. The Samuel and May Rudin Foundation and the Louis and Rachel Rudin Foundation donate millions annually (roughly $10 million in 2006 alone) to medical, educational, cultural, and civic activities. Equally noteworthy has been their civic support. In New York's financial crises of the 1970s, it was Samuel and his sons, Jack and Lewis, who convinced many New York business and real estate owners to prepay their real estate taxes, thus helping avert the city's bankruptcy. The family also created and sponsored the first New York Marathon, and they were a principal force in keeping the U.S. Open Tennis Tournament in New York City. They also played key roles in "The Big Apple," and "I Love NY" publicity campaigns.

Among other notable New York real estate families not covered in the *Fortune* profile are those described below.

Sol and Irving Goldman – The Goldman Group, Building Management Company and Wembly Management Co.:[335] Their mother reportedly told her eldest son, Sol, "Never leave the store, Sol, it's a gold mine." She was referring to the family grocery business operated by Sol and Irving Goldman's father. Instead, at age eighteen and in the midst of the Depression, Sol left the store and started buying foreclosed New York property for cash (in one case for $500.) Later he, and Irving who had joined him, would use the appreciated value from earlier purchases as collateral for loans to buy still more properties. By the 1960s and early 1970s the Goldmans were considered the largest landlords in New York, in control of the Chrysler Building, among other properties.

It all began to crash during the very difficult 1970s, when national stagflation, recession, and particular problems unique to New York nearly bankrupted the city and caused hardship to its real estate mavens. Somehow, the Goldmans survived, losing some properties to default, selling others, and holding on to what they could. When the 1980s brought better times, the Goldmans prospered once more, and when Sol died in 1987, he, Irving, and their partners were said to control 600 properties, including the Stanhope and Hyde Park hotels and today's Peninsula Hotel on 55th Street and Fifth Avenue.

More recently Lloyd Goldman, Irving's son, has carried on the family tradition managing more than 400 properties, including more than 14,000 residential units and ten million square feet of commercial and industrial property. Always low key, the Goldmans were reportedly the principal source of equity capital used by Lawrence Silverstein in 2001 to take over the World Trade Center. They also control the Skydome Stadium in Toronto and many shopping centers around the United States.

Goldman family philanthropy is as notable as their real estate success. The Lillian Goldman Law Library at Yale University is a continuing beneficiary of their philanthropy as was the Goldman Jewish Community Center on 14th Street in Manhattan. In 2005 Johns Hopkins received $10 million for pancreatic research from the Sol Goldman Charitable Trust, and the Medical School at Ben Gurion University in Israel is named for Irving Goldman. Today the Sol Goldman Charitable Trust continues to dispense philanthropy from its assets of more than $100 million, while the Irving and Joyce Goldman Family Foundation does the same from its nearly $200 million.

The Tishman and Speyer Families – Tishman Realty and Construction, Tishman Speyer, and Tishman Management and Leasing:[336] Julius Tishman emigrated from Poland in 1885, starting out in the United States as a dry-goods merchant. In 1898 he sold that business to invest the proceeds building tenements on New York's lower East Side. By 1914 his first son, Louis, had joined the company, and together they began developing luxury apartments. By 1928 Tishman Realty and Construction was a publicly traded company headed up by a second son, David.

During the Depression, Tishman suspended developing new property, focusing instead on managing the existing portfolio. They resumed expansion in 1947, building 445 Park Avenue. It was the first Park Avenue office building north of Grand Central Station and New York's first new office building following World War II. Heading up the construction was Norman, another of Julius' five sons. By 1950 they had expanded to Los Angeles, and by 1958, they had thirty-one office and apartment buildings and three shopping centers in five cities. The next year they began constructing buildings for others, as well as for their own account. They also diversified into leasing factory and office equipment.

By 1967 grandson Robert was CEO, the company's expansion into Chicago had made them that city's largest landlord, they were in the process of building Detroit's Renaissance Center, and they had won the contract to build New York's World Trade Center.

Nonetheless, New York's mid-1970s real estate crunch was devastating. They had built a forty-four story office building (1166 Avenue of the Americas) on the strength of a letter of intent signed by a major corporation to lease much of the space. When the economy worsened, that company walked away leaving Tishman with an empty high-rise. Over the next two years the losses climbed to as much as $80 million. Those losses, coupled with family tensions, led to the decision to liquidate the company. It brought roughly $185 million. The proceeds were distributed to the investors, most of which went to Tishman family members as the largest shareholders.

Two new business plus Tishman Realty and Construction emerged. All were led by family members who preferred not to retire.

David's son, Alan V. Tishman, created Tishman Management and Leasing Company. It was a professional property management firm, counting among its clients, the second creation, Tishman-Speyer Properties. Tishman-Speyer, was created by Alan's brother, Robert V. Tishman, who partnered with his son-in-law, Jerry Speyer. Tishman-Speyer specialized in financing and developing real estate in partnership with others and for its own account. The third company, the original Tishman Realty and Construction, was owned by Rockefeller Center Corporation. It was headed by John L. Tishman, but in 1980, he and fifteen fellow executives bought the company back from Rockefeller. Nearly thirty years since, the same group and its successor executives still operate Tishman Realty & Construction as a privately owned business.

Robert V. Tishman remains founding chairman of Tishman-Speyer with Jerry Speyer as its chairman and CEO and Jerry's son, Rob Speyer, as president. The company's Web site indicates that since inception in 1978, Tishman-Speyer has owned, developed, syndicated, and managed 112 million square feet of property and more than 91,000 residential units in the United States, Europe, and Latin America. Together the properties are worth more than $74 billion.

John Tishman is still chairman and CEO of Tishman Realty & Construction Company, and his son, Daniel R. Tishman, is president and CEO. It is an international construction company and counts among its projects the original World Trade Center, Disney's Epcot Center, Madison Square Garden, Chicago's John Hancock Tower, and the rebuilt 7 World Trade Center (for Silverstein Properties). It is also slated to build the new Freedom Tower on the World Trade Center site. With 1,000 employees and reported annual revenues of $2.5 billion, Tishman Realty and Construction is a major builder and manager. In 2006 John Tishman was honored by *Buildings* magazine as one of four legendary real estate and construction industry leaders.

Among the family's civic and philanthropic endeavors are Robert Tishman's chairmanship of Montefiore Medical Center, Jerry Speyer's chairmanship of the Museum of Modern Art, his vice chairmanship of Presbyterian Hospital, chairmanship emeritus of Columbia University and board chairmanship of the Federal Reserve Bank of New York. John Tishman led the restoration of Carnegie Hall, and Alan Tishman was trustee of the American Museum of Natural History and president of the United Jewish Appeal-Federation of New York.

The Rose Family – Rose Associates Inc.:[337] David Rose and his brother Samuel were born in Jerusalem in 1892 and 1890 respectively. They immigrated to the United States, and by 1928 had built a 216-unit, six-story apartment house. From that start, Rose Associates has developed and managed more than thirty million square feet of office towers, retail, and residential property. Samuel's son Fredrick joined the business in the 1940s and led it till his death in 1999. His brother, Daniel, continues as chairman, and his son, Adam, is president. They are two of some twelve family members active in the business.

Fredrick gave away roughly $100 million to New York civic institutions and to Yale University. The Rose Center for Earth and Space at the Natural History Museum, Rose Hall, the Rose Building and Rose Rehearsal Studio at Lincoln Center, and the Rose Main Reading Room at the New York Public Library are among further beneficiaries of the family's philanthropy.

The Stern Family – Hartz Group:[338] In 1926 immigrant Max Stern brought 2,100 canaries from Germany to sell in the United States. Over the next thirty-three years, he built his Hartz Mountain Industries into a huge pet-supply business. It was further strengthened and turned into the industry's dominant company by his son, Leonard, who took over in 1959. (That story is more fully told in a Chapter 21 profile)

In 1966, while running Hartz Mountain, Leonard began buying New Jersey Meadowlands property for $20,000 an acre. By 1987 the land was worth $500,000 an acre. He began developing offices, retail malls, and industrial properties on it, and later developed office buildings and high-end hotels in Manhattan as well.

In 2000 Stern sold 85 percent of his pet-products company and, with his son Emmanuel, he focused entirely on real estate. Today the family real estate interests control 200 buildings in New York and New Jersey (thirty-eight million square feet of space). Stern's success in pet supplies and real estate made him 237th on the 2007 *Forbes* 400 Wealthiest Americans.

Though not without some controversy relating to operating practices in the pet-supply business before it was sold, his role as a Rite Aid director, and his son Edward's "late trading" of mutual funds, Stern has been an active philanthropist. He donated $30 million to New York University, where the business school is named in his honor, and in 1986, he founded Homes for the Homeless. Every day it serves 630 homeless families and 1,200 homeless children.

Other Prominent New York and New Jersey Real Estate Personalities

Sheldon Henry Solow – Solow Building Company:[339] Ivan Solovieff arrived from Byelorussia in 1905, married a second-generation American opera singer of Austrian descent, and worked his way up from cement mixer to brick layer to home builder. But he lost it all in the Great Depression. His second son, Sheldon, born in 1928, redeemed the family's fortunes. His first major success came with what was considered a high-risk building project, the Gordon Bunshaft high-rise at 9 West 57th Street. When completed in 1974, the United States was in recession and times were tough. Fortunately, Solow had leased enough space to Monsanto and Avon to weather the storm. Today, 9 West 57th is one of New York's best addresses. It made Solow's fortune and his early reputation.

Solow has followed up West 57th with other office and residential properties and is now regarded as a major builder and owner of commercial and residential New York space. His is current focus is a huge midtown Manhattan complex at ConEd's old East River site that may ultimately include 4,166 apartments (600 of them for low- and moderate-income residents), a forty-seven-story office tower, and a public school.

Known for his determination, Solow has made it to the *Forbes* 400, developed his talent and taste for fine art, and operates at least three foundations through which he has donated to the Metropolitan Museum, the Whitney Museum, the Benjamin Cardozo School of Law, the United Jewish Appeal, and numerous other charities. He has also developed a reputation for being litigious, having filed more than 200 lawsuits. Asked about his plans for succession, Solow points to his son, Stefan, as his heir apparent.

Uris Brothers:[340] Percy and Harold Uris were staked by their father, an 1892 Russian emigrant who built a successful ornamental ironworks factory. After college, their father helped them start developing residential properties. Percy handled the finances and Harold the construction. From the 1920s to the 1970s, the brothers developed more than thirteen million square feet of Manhattan property in eighteen buildings including the New York Hilton, the Colgate Palmolive Building, Paramount Plaza, 245 Park Avenue, and others.

After Percy's death in 1971, Harold decided to sell the publicly owned company. The timing of the 1973 sale was fortuitous, averting much of the financial maelstrom that hit New York later in that decade.

Earlier, in 1956, the brothers established the Uris Brothers Foundation. Over the forty-two years until its final distribution in 1998, it made $65 million in grants to the Metropolitan Museum of Art ($30 million), the New York Public Library, the Central Park Conservancy, Carnegie Hall, New York's public television channel (Thirteen/WNET), the New School for Social Research, and others.

Harry & Leona Helmsley – Helmsley-Spear:[341] Harry Helmsley was a contemporary of the Uris Brothers. He began as an office boy at age sixteen and rose to become a broker, then partner, then owner of the firm. He bought out a competitor, Spear and Company, in 1955, and for the rest of his life, Helmsley-Spear was Harry Helmsley. At his death, in 1997, Helmsley's properties were valued at $5.5 billion (later estimated at $5 to $8 billion), all of which went to his third wife, Leona. She had joined his company as a vice president in 1970 and become a public symbol, as the demanding boss of their high-end Helmsley Hotel chain (also see Chapter 21 – "Enterprise") until she was convicted of tax evasion and served nineteen months in prison. Following Leona Helmsley's death in August 2007, it was reported she intended that the bulk of her $5 to $8 billion estate go to the "care and welfare of dogs."

William Zeckendorf – Webb and Knapp:[342]William Zeckendorf built one of the most prominent real estate development empires in the post-World War II era. At one point, he owned the Chrysler Building, the Mile High Center in Denver and Place Ville Marie in Montreal, Canada, and he partnered with Alcoa to build Century City in Los Angeles. He also became known for the seventeen acres on New York's East River that he sold for a substantial profit to non-Jews John D. Rockefeller, Nelson Rockefeller, and Wallace Harrison, who, in turn, donated the land for the United Nations Building. Zeckendorf was undone by his failed (1963) Roosevelt Field project, which led to Web and Knapp's 1965 bankruptcy.

Macklowe Properties – Harry Macklowe:[343] "Audacious." In a word, that is the term many who have followed Harry Macklowe's career would use to describe him. Born to a Westchester County garment executive, Harry was a college dropout and, in the early 1960s, a real estate broker at an undistinguished firm. He was an unlikely candidate for his status for a number of years as a New York real estate superstar.

Macklowe went from broker to developer in the mid-1960s and by the mid-1980s was developing major office buildings. His controversial 1985 demolition of two single-room occupancy hotels near Times Square, just twenty-four hours before a demolition moratorium was to go into effect, made him a pariah. That controversy was followed by his construction of the Hotel Macklowe on the same property. But New York's early 1990s real estate turbulence undid that success. Hotel Macklowe was lost to its lenders. The build-boom-bust cycle is emblematic of Macklowe's history of controversy, success, failure, and resurrection.

Many thought Macklowe wildly "overpaid" when he purchased the General Motors Building for $1.4 billion in 2003 (reportedly using only $100 million of his own money). His renovations (including an Apple store in the front plaza) and a hot real estate market made him look like a genius when the building was estimated to be worth $3 billion or more in 2007. That success, together with his other holdings, placed him No. 239 on the 2006 *Forbes* 400.

He "doubled down" in February 2007, buying eight Equity Office properties in Manhattan as part of Blackstone's buyout of Sam Zell's Equity Office Properties (see below). Harry used short-term financing to complete the hasty purchase, put up the General Motors Building as collateral, and provided a $1.2 billion personal guarantee. It was a huge gamble, and he paid the price. As the subprime credit crunch rolled over into the broader real estate credit market, Macklowe defaulted on the short-term financing. As reported in a May 27, 2008, *Wall Street Journal* story, in order to resolve the default, the General Motors Building and three other Macklowe properties were sold to Boston Properties and Goldman Sachs. Macklowe also had to give up $1.4 billion of the cash made on the General Motors Building and other properties. While the family is still reportedly worth more than $500 million and in control of five to seven buildings and development sites, Harry has stepped down. The business is now run by his son, William, who blamed his father for making numerous mistakes. Yet, in the same interview, William went on, "He's my father. I'm his son. Life goes on."

The Related Companies, L.P.:[346] Stephen Ross, nephew of Max Fisher (profiled in Chapter 21 – Enterprise), started out in 1966 as a Detroit CPA. After stints at Laird Inc., and Bear Stearns, he created the Related Companies to develop New York real estate. Nearly bankrupted in the early 1990s real estate bust, he has since emerged to develop the Time Warner Center, Florida condominiums, and other projects estimated to be worth a total of $16 billion. It has made him very wealthy (No. 26 on the 2007 *Forbes* 400). He is also half owner of the Miami Dolphins and known for his philanthropy, including his $100 million donation to the University of Michigan.

Space does not permit treatment of the numerous other prominent Jewish families and individuals who have been active in New York real estate. Comparable coverage could also have been written on the Gural family, the Milstein family, the Benenson family, the Resnik family, the Wein/Malkin families, Charles B Kushner, Edward J. Miskoff, and many others.

Real Estate Investment Trusts (REITs)

In May 22, 2002, *Forbes* magazine listed the then five largest publicly traded real estate investment trusts. They were:

Equity Office Properties (EOP) $12.24 billion market value;
Equity Residential (EQR) $7.89 billion;
Plumb Creek Timber (PCL) $5.58 billion;
Simon Property Group (SPG) $5.71 billion;
Archstone Smith (ASN) $4.58 billion.

Of the five, only Plumb Creek was without Jewish roots.
Equity Office Properties and Equity Residential were both created by Sam Zell and his now deceased partner, Bob Lurie. Simon and Archstone-Smith were built respectively by the Simon brothers and Charles E. Smith, a Russian Jewish immigrant.
In another look at the same phenomenon, Morningstar.com provided its own list of major REITs in January 2004. Plumb Creek and Archstone-Smith were not on Morningstar's list. Instead they included Vornado Realty Trust and General Growth Properties. For more than twenty years, Vornado has been controlled by Steven Roth. General Growth was started by three brothers, Martin, Matthew, and Maurice Bucksbaum. The Morningstar list was five for five.

Sam Zell – Equity Office Properties and Equity Residential Properties:[345] Immediately outside his private office, Sam Zell has a lifesize wooden carving of a very fat, formally dressed character who looks like something from Charles Dickens or Thomas Nast. Wrapped around the statue in helter-skelter fashion is perhaps fifty feet of red tape. Labeled, "The Bureaucrat," the carving speaks volumes about this 5-foot 5- inch iconoclast who has long been able to spot value better than almost anyone. Often called "The Grave Dancer," the expression is a compliment to Zell's talent for seeing opportunity where others see only peril.

For a number of years, Zell was known as a corporate turnaround executive with his ability to solve problems at large troubled companies such as Anixter, ITEL, and others. Even before that, however, he was known for his talent in real estate, initially in residential properties and later in commercial/office properties as well.

Zell began in the mid-1960s with partner Robert Lurie (who passed away in 1990). While still in college they took control of distressed Ann Arbor apartment buildings and turned them around. Later, Zell expanded his real estate investing nationwide while also diversifying into containers, barges, insurance, cruise lines, drug-stores, communications products, professional sports, and numerous other businesses. But what Zell will likely be most remembered for is creating two of the world's largest REITs , Equity Office Properties and Equity Residential Properties.

In something of a partnership with Lurie's widow, Zell has continued to talk with Ann Lurie every day, just as he did with Bob for thirty years. With Bob gone, Sam just kept building the real estate empire, while Ann, with Sam's participation, gave away large sums to philanthropic causes including Wharton, the University of Michigan, and Northwestern University.

In early 2007, Zell decided the offer was too good to pass up. He agreed to sell Equity Office Properties, the country's largest office landlord, for a whopping $39 billion. The buyer, Blackstone Group, is headed by one of New York's most prominent financiers, Stephen Schwarzman. Control of the properties thus remains in Jewish hands – at least for now.

Zell's next foray was less successful. Using some of the proceeds from the Equity Office sale, he led the leveraged buy out of the Tribune Company in late 2007. Rapidly declining newspaper advertising revenues, falling circulation at the *Chicago Tribune* and *Los Angeles Times,* and the debt burden taken on to finance the buyout led to a Chapter 11 filing in late 2008. Asked why hadn't explored bankruptcy earlier, Zell responded, "There's this guy who was just elected president of the United States, and he wrote a book called, *The Audacity of Hope.*

Charles E. Smith – Archstone-Smith:[346] A particularly Waspish sounding name few would expect to be Jewish, Charles E. Smith immigrated to the United States from Russia in 1911 at age 10. Over time, he became the largest builder in the nation's capital. Ultimately, his Residential Realty Company was merged with Archstone Communities in 2001 to form Archstone-Smith. Both Charles' son, Robert H. Smith, and his grandson, David Bruce Smith, are active in Archstone-Smith. And, they continue the family tradition with philanthropic support for education (Tufts New England Medical Center and The Charles E. Smith Jewish Day School in Rockville, Maryland, among others) and the National Institute of Psychobiology in Israel.

Steven Roth – Vornado Realty Trust:[347] Steven Roth has run Vornado for more than twenty years. A March 20, 2002, *Wall Street Journal* story called him a "tough and demanding chairman." He narrowly avoided taking over the World Trade Center just six months before September 11, 2001. Instead, that deal was ultimately done by the Silverstein Group (see above). Conversely, commercial real estate from Charles

E. Smith's operation was merged into Vornado. With help from his second in command Michael Fascitelli (not Jewish), Roth has built an REIT worth more than $6
billion. He has also endowed a professorship, is principal donor to the Roth Center
for Jewish Life at Dartmouth, serves as a board member of the New York University
School of Medicine, and is a trustee of the Whitney Art Museum.

Mortimer Zuckerman – Boston Properties:[348] In 1970 Mortimer Zuckerman
co-founded Boston Properties with his partner Edward H. Linde. Together they built
it into one of the country's most prominent and successful REITs, taking it public in
1997. Boston Properties develops, manages, and owns Class A office buildings,
industrial space, and hotel properties in Boston, Washington, D.C., Manhattan, and
San Francisco. The company owns 139 properties totaling more than forty-three million square feet. With Goldman Sachs, Boston Properties was also involved in the
recent purchase of the General Motors Building and other properties from an imper-
iled Harry Macklowe.

Zuckerman is something of a Renaissance man. In addition to Boston Properties, he is also chairman and editor-in-chief of *U.S. News and World Report,* and chairman and publisher of the *New York Daily News.* He has appeared regularly on public
television's *The McLaughlin Report,* and was at one time an associate professor at
Harvard Graduate School of Design. He is past president of the board of trustees of
the Dana Farber Cancer Institute, and a trustee of Memorial Sloan-Kettering. He has
three honorary degrees.

Shopping Centers[349]

As noted in Chapter 12 – "Visual Arts and Architecture," Southdale, near Minneapolis, was the world's first shopping mall. It was the creation of Victor Gruen, a
Viennese Jew who fled the Nazis to practice architecture in the United States. His
enclosed, multilevel courtyard mall, with competing anchor tenants and a total of seventy-two retailers, revolutionized retailing and the America lifestyle following its
1956 opening. In subsequent years, Gruen continued designing malls across the
United States until, unsure his legacy was turning out as he originally intended, he
returned to his native Vienna in the mid-1970s.

Fifty-one years later, in July 2007, *National Retail Investor* listed "The Top 25
Shopping Center Owners." It counted Simon Property Group as the largest U.S.
shopping center owner (this even before Simon acquired the eleventh largest, Mills
Corporation). In second place was General Growth Properties. Both were also iden-
tified above among the nation's largest REITs. Looking at just the ten largest of the
shopping center owners, at least six appear to have been created, or are now led, by
Jews: Simon Property Group, General Growth Properties, Developers Diversified
Realty, CBL & Associates Properties, Inc., Westfield LLC, and Regency Centers.

Melvin, Herbert, Fred, and David Simon– Simon Property Group:[350]
Melvin, Herbert, and Fred Simon were born in Brooklyn in the late 1920s and early
1930s. Their father, Max, was a tailor. After graduating in 1949 with a degree in

accounting from City College, Melvin joined the Army and was posted to Fort Benjamin Harrison in Indianapolis, Indiana. Reportedly, he sold encyclopedias at least for a time, but when he got out of the Army, he stayed in Indianapolis, leasing property for an established real estate company. By 1959 he had formed his own company, and his brother Herb, who had worked with him at the leasing company, left to join him at Melvin Simon & Associates. Brother Fred also joined the company later, but left in 1983 to pursue other interests.

Melvin Simon & Associates started with strip centers, but soon expanded to shopping malls, first developing Southgate Plaza in Bloomington, Indiana. Before long the brothers were developing a million square feet of enclosed malls each year. Beyond Indiana, they expanded to Michigan, Illinois, Colorado, Kansas, New Jersey, and Virginia. They had become a national firm, and through the 1980s, Melvin Simon & Associates evolved into one of the larger U.S. shopping center developer/operators. Among other projects, they developed the Forum Shops at Caesar's Palace in Las Vegas, and with the Ghermezian family (Iranian Jews who immigrated to Canada where they had become major shopping center developers), they co-developed the Mall of America, the largest enclosed mall in the United States. But in the late 1980s the market tightened, credit became tight, and real estate became very illiquid. It became a very tough business.

In 1991 Melvin approached his son, David, asking him to leave Wasserstein-Perella to join the company. It was the perfect step. David, who earned his graduate business degree from Columbia in 1985, had been a standout student. Upon graduation, he became a protégé of non-Jew Joseph Perella, then of First Boston, a leading investment bank. In his years on Wall Street, David Simon learned investment banking and mergers and acquisitions. Though he was new to Wall Street, David so impressed his mentor that when Perella left First Boston to help form Wasserstein-Perella, he asked David to join him. Simon became a vice president in one of the world's top merger and acquisition firms.

When David Simon joined his father and uncle, he started out as chief financial officer. His task was to clean up the disorganized, undisciplined operation that was then Melvin Simon & Associates. He did that quickly and well. In a year or so, he had renegotiated financing with lenders, cleaned out the senior staff, and improved operating efficiency. Then his skills in strategy and mergers and acquisitions came to the fore. He was named president in 1993 about the same time the company (with its name changed to Simon Property Group) was taken public. It raised $1 billion. To its time, this was the largest real estate stock offering ever. By 1995 David was CEO. Instead of expanding one mall at a time, David began drawing on his mergers and acquisition expertise, using Simon's cash and public stock to make large strategic acquisitions of other mall operators including Corporate Property Investors, the Debartolo Realty Corporation, the Mills Corporation, and others. By early 2008, Simon had 286 United States, fifty-three European, and five Japanese centers, plus one in Mexico.

In 2007 Melvin Simon ranked 130 on the *Forbes* 400. His (and brother Herb's) ownership of the Indiana Pacers basketball team, his active support of Democratic political candidates, his philanthropy (including a recent $50 million grant to the University of Indiana School of Medicine Cancer Center), and his Simon board chairmanship, keep him active while son David runs the business.

Until 2008, the story of the Simons (above) bore an uncanny resemblance to the Bucksbaum family (below). Three first-generation brothers started shopping centers in the Midwest during the 1950s. They built their business through internal growth and acquisitions. In the 1990s, both families elevated a talented son of the CEO to take over and growth was accelerated through acquisitions made by the son. As a consequence, both families were ranked in the *Forbes* 400, and both were very philanthropic. Two different approaches to leverage, and the credit crisis of 2008, however, led to a very different outcome for the two family empires.

Martin, Matthew, Maurice, and John Bucksbaum – General Growth Properties:[351] In the early 1950s, the Bucksbaum family owned three grocery stores in Cedar Rapids, Iowa. During 1954, while planning a fourth store, three second-generation brothers, Martin (age 31), Matthew (26) and Maurice (29), saw the opportunity to become landlords, rather than tenants. They borrowed $1.2 million to build Iowa's first shopping center. They almost lost their shirt due to unnecessary costs incurred for constructing basements and a second story, but they survived. By 1964 they had five shopping centers. They kept expanding through the 1960s and by 1972, their company, General Growth Properties was a New York Stock Exchange-listed REIT.

Over the next decade or so, they developed additional centers and acquired other developer/operators, occasionally selling some properties for a profit, or entering into joint ventures. By the late 1980s they were among the largest U.S. shopping center owners.

Matthew's son, John, joined the company in 1979, and by 1999 he was CEO. Mergers and acquisitions became a top priority. Under him, General Growth acquired The Rouse Company (to its time, history's largest real estate acquisition), JP Realty Inc. and numerous individual malls.

By mid-2007, General Growth owned, had an interest in, or operated 200 regional malls in forty-five states. They were the nation's second largest shopping center owner/operator.

Like the Simons, the Bucksbaums own a large percentage of their company and because of that, the family was listed 105th on the 2007 Forbes 400.

And like the Simons the Bucksbaums became known for philanthropy. The Martin Bucksbaum Foundation, established before his death in 1995, endowed professorships at Harvard and Wharton, lectureships at Drake University, the Bucksbaum Award at the Whitney Museum for leading artists, and the Bucksbaum Center at Grinnell College. In 2000 the Martin Bucksbaum Family Foundation was Iowa's third largest foundation. Matthew has served as life trustee and chairman of the Aspen Music Festival and trustee of the Chicago Symphony. John is on the board of the University of Chicago Hospital.

In 2008, the two parallel threads of the Simon/Bucksbaum family stories diverged. After Martin Bucksbaum's death, a non-family member had been named chief financial officer and General Growth took on ever more debt—often very short term mortgages—to finance its rapid growth. By 2008, the company's debt soared to 83 percent of its asset values. Simon, by way of contrast was at 54 percent (and Taubman, 48 percent). With the world wide credit crises making refinancing difficult, $4 billion of debt coming due in late 2008 and 2009, an unfortunate family loan to the CFO – which was not disclosed to the Board and which led to John Bucksbaum's resignation as CEO—a stock price down 97 percent from its highs, and the prospect of bankruptcy on the horizon, the future of General Growth is very much in doubt.

Frank Lowy – The Westfield Group:[352] Frank Lowy is not a familiar name in the United States. Nor, unless one knows a good bit about shopping centers, is the Westfield Group. Nonetheless, Westfield is the world's largest shopping center developer and operator with 121 shopping centers in Australia, New Zealand, the United States, and the United Kingdom. At $40 billion, Westfield is valued at roughly twice the Simon Property Group.

Perhaps one project best symbolizes Westfield's prominence. Westfield was the operator of the retail shopping space at the World Trade Center on September 11, 2001. On January 16, 2008, it was announced that a $1.45 billion partnership of Westfield and the Port Authority of New York and New Jersey would develop and operate a new 500,000-square-foot complex of shops and restaurants at the rebuilt site.

Frank Lowy is a Slovakian Jew born in 1930. He survived the Holocaust, and though only fifteen at the time, immigrated to Israel in 1945. He joined the Haganah and fought in Israel's War of Independence. Seven years later, he traveled to Australia to see his mother, eldest brother, and sister who had emigrated directly from Slovakia. Lowy stayed in Australia.

While driving trucks delivering deli food, he met John Saunders, a Hungarian immigrant. The two set up their own deli. Though successful, they watched as a developer bought nearby land, built shops, and did very well. Lowy and Saunders were inspired. They sold the deli, bought land, subdivided it, sold some to homebuilders, developed the rest as a small hotel and retail center, and by 1959 they owned their first small shopping center. They named it Westfield, symbolizing the undeveloped land west of Sydney, Australia, they had chosen for the center. By 1960 Westfield was public on the Sydney Stock Exchange.

That same year, Lowy flew to California where he first saw American shopping centers. With a few variations dictated by local customs (grocery stores were anchor tenants in Australian shopping malls), Westfield quickly grew to be the dominant shopping center operator in Australia. It took only a few years for Westfield to tap the country's most significant opportunities. Still looking to grow, in 1977 Lowy bought a shopping center in Trumbull, Connecticut, his first offshore expansion. In 2000 Westfield expanded still further, into the United Kingdom

Saunders passed away some years ago after selling his interest. Lowy stayed on and has brought his three sons into the business. Westfield's value has increased tenfold over the last decade making Lowy *Forbes'* 222nd wealthiest person in the world in 2007.

Guilford Glazer, Guilford Glazer & Associates:[353] As a sophomore, Guilford Glazer left his engineering studies to join the Navy during World War II. At war's end, he returned to Knoxville, Tennessee, where his father's death required that he take over the family's two-employee steel business. Glazer built it quickly, and by 1951, when the U.S. Atomic Energy Commission decided to build a shopping center in Oak Ridge, Glazer was selected to build it.

He moved to Los Angeles and in the 1970s, developed what, at the time, was the world's largest shopping mall, Orange County's Del Amo Fashion Center. Its success led to his involvement in shopping centers all over the United States. In his early '80s, he began selling off his portfolio, including Del Amo. That sale and his other assets placed Glazer among the *Forbes* 400 for a number of years.

Glazer is now focused on philanthropy, much of it centered on assistance to Israel, in particular in helping create a successful Palestinian state. He has funded studies by the Rand Institute to determine the requirements for a viable Palestinian government and country.

Al Taubman – Taubman Centers Inc.:[354] Alfred Taubman borrowed $5,000 from his father, and used it to transform his father's small home-building operation into one of the United States' largest shopping center developers and owners. Along the way, he was mentored by Max Fisher, founder of Aurora Oil—later part of Marathon Oil (see his profile in Chapter 21—Enterprise). Fisher hired Taubman to build 200 gas stations and that launched Taubman as a major builder. As he prospered, Taubman transitioned from developing small retail strips into large shopping malls, culminating in today's thirty-one malls managed by the public Taubman Centers Inc.

Taubman's tragedy arose from his 2001 conviction for price fixing at Sotheby's and Christies. Though many believe he was victimized by Christies' British CEO, who was not subject to U.S. laws, and by Sotheby's president, Taubman was nonetheless convicted and sentenced to a year in jail. He resigned as chairman of Taubman Centers, turning the business over to his son, Robert.

If there was any consolation, it may have been averting the takeover attempt by Simon Property Group which, in the midst of the scandal, hoped to acquire Taubman Industries for $20 per share. The offer was rebuffed and Taubman shares have traded higher in the years since. Alfred Taubman was listed 271 among the 2007 *Forbes* 400.

Despite the scandal, Taubman is an active philanthropist. He has been the benefactor of the Taubman Center for State and Local Government at Harvard, the Taubman Center for Public Policy at Brown University, the Taubman College of Architecture and Planning at the University of Michigan, and other philanthropic projects.

Selected Other Jewish Real Estate Personalities

Robert A. Judelson, Judd Malkin and Neil Bluhm – JMB Realty & Walton Street Capital:[355] Judelson, Malkin and Bluhm, were the "J," "M," and "B" of JMB Realty when it was formed in 1968. Malkin and Bluhm were classmates at grammar school and fraternity brothers at the University of Illinois, where they graduated in 1959. They separated for nine years while Bluhm practiced law and Malkin distributed automobiles. But in 1968 they, and Robert Judelson, got together to form JMB Realty, a real estate brokerage.

In 1973 Judelson left to found Balcor, a real estate development syndicator, which subsequently became part of American Express. He continues developing property with Bojer Financial, but now spends a good deal of his time as a director of the Chicago White Sox and the Chicago Bulls. He also served as a trustee of the Utah Symphony, two prep schools, and the Moran Eye Institute at the University of Utah.

After Judelson's departure, Malkin and Bluhm built JMB into one of the country's largest real estate syndicator/managers with $20 billion of property under management. The real estate shakeout of the 1980s and 1990s did a good bit of damage to the value of their properties, but they stayed with it, each keeping a third of the private company. Patience and hard work has paid off. The portfolio now includes major properties in Chicago's Loop (such as Water Tower Place), in Century City, MGM Tower and Sun America Center, and in Niagara Falls, where they will develop a casino with the Pritzkers. In 2003 JMB and Malkin were honored as Century City's Citizen of the Year. Bluhm and Malkin have been honored for contributions to the University of Illinois, Urbana, and Bluhm is listed 220th among the 2007 *Forbes* 400.

Paul, Edward and Albert Reichmann – Olympia & York/Canary Wharf Group:[356] Paul Reichmann and his brothers Edward and Albert are Viennese Jews who fled Austria and the Nazis. They moved to Paris, London, and later Morocco, where Paul helped overhaul and establish schools for thousands of Jewish children— among them girls who attended the first-ever seminary open to women in Tangier. In the mid-1950s, Paul left for New York, and later Toronto, where the family eventually gathered. In 1964 they set up Olympia & York. Through it they became one of the world's foremost 1980s developers when they created New York's huge World Financial Center—an eight-million-square-foot office and retail complex built adjacent to the World Trade Center. They also developed England's tallest building, Canary Wharf, located east of downtown London on low cost property the British government was eager to see developed.

For the Reichmanns, the 1986 U.S. tax reform act, the ensuing real estate crash, the 1987 stock market crash, and the 1990-91 recession culminated with the 1992 bankruptcies of the Canary Wharf project and Olympia & York. Not until 1995 were the Reichmann Brothers able to regroup, recruit partners, and buy back control of Canary Wharf from its creditors under a new corporate vehicle named Canary Wharf Group. Four years later, they took that company public, leaving the Reichmanns with 9 percent of the stock. They lost control, however, in a 2004 a management buyout contest won by a Morgan Stanley-headed group.

Alan I. Casden – Casden Properties:[358] Alan Casden dropped out of UCLA after a disappointing freshman year. A few years later, he decided to give it another try, entered the University of Southern California as a sophomore and graduated cum laude in 1968. After seven years working as an accountant for a Los Angeles real estate developer, he struck out on his own, setting up Casden properties. His $10.6 million gift to USC in 2001 was both a small measure of his success and a "Thank You." Over the years he had built a complex of 90,000 apartments.

In 2001 he sold the bulk of his projects to Apartment Investment & Management Co, a Denver REIT. The sale landed him on the Forbes 400. He continues developing new projects and recently endowed the Institute for the Study of Jews in American Life as part of a $10.6 million gift to USC.

Carl Berg – Mission West Properties:[358]Carl Berg might be profiled either as a real estate maven or venture capitalist. In Silicon Valley he is well known for both. Taking some of his rent in stock, or stock options, and investing in high-tech start-ups, such as Sun Microsystems, Integrated Device Technology, and venture capital partnerships has made Berg very wealthy. In addition, however, he is one of Silicon Valley's most prominent developers. Very private, particularly after his wife and young daughter were kidnapped in 1982 (they escaped unharmed), Berg is also known as a demanding entrepreneur now worth well over $1 billion. With that, he is a *Forbes* 400 fixture.

Walter Shorenstein – The Shorenstein Company:[359] Walter H. Shorenstein is a huge presence in the San Francisco Bay Area and is one of the area's largest landlords. In 1946, after his discharge from the military, Shorenstein began working at Milton Meyer, a San Francisco commercial real estate brokerage firm. By 1951 he was a partner, and by 1960, he was president and sole owner. Renamed the Shorenstein Company, he proceeded to become the largest owner of Class A office buildings in San Francisco. After September 11, he expanded into Chicago and Washington, D.C., while others stayed on the sidelines waiting for more certain times. In recent years, Shorenstein has turned ever more of the day-to-day operations over to his son, Doug.

A major supporter of the Democratic Party, he is also one of the largest supporters of the United Way. Today, under his son Doug, the company owns twenty million square feet of prime office space in San Francisco, New York, Chicago, Philadelphia, Washington, D.C., and seven other U.S. cities.

Benjamin, Melvin, Richard, Kent Swig & Jack Weiler – Swig, Weiler, Swig Equities, The Swig Company:[360] By 1912, nineteen-year-old Ben Swig was already a bank treasurer. In the 1920s he shifted his focus to real estate and by the 1940s, he and his partner, Jack Weiler (a rabbi's son, who immigrated from the Ukraine in 1910 with his parents and eight siblings), were among top U.S. real estate developer-owners.

In 1946, as Weiler stayed in New York, Ben Swig moved from Boston to San Francisco where Swig, Weiler continued to expand their office and residential portfolio. They bought and sold the St. Francis Hotel before buying and operating the legendary Fairmont Hotel, a survivor of the 1906 earthquake. That same year, Ben's two sons moved to San Francisco, Melvin after completing his Army service, and Richard after his Navy service.

Melvin focused on the Swig, Weiler investment properties, ultimately taking over from his father and Weiler. He headed up that business until his death in 1993. Richard started out as a hotel steward. By 1953, he was CEO of the Fairmont Hotel, a job he held for forty-four years until his death in 1997. Over time, Richard built Fairmont into a chain of seven luxury hotels. Following the sale of half interest in the hotel operating business to a Saudi investor, the seven properties became the core of today's Fairmont Hotel chain. (See the Fairmont profile in Chapter 21)

After the passing of Ben Swig and Jack Weiler, the families ended their long partnership and, for a time, the Swig Company was run by outsiders. In recent years, however, Melvin's son, Kent (son-in-law of Harry Macklowe, and a partner with William Zeckendorf's two sons), has held the reins. The Swig Company now owns eleven million square feet of commercial office buildings and two of the fifty Fairmont Hotel properties. Kent is a principal of Swig Burris Equities, which owns and manages an additional 2.8 million square feet of commercial office properties and more than 1,100 residential units. Kent is also an owner and co-chairman of Terra Holdings, which owns two major New York real estate brokerage firms.

From Jack and Ben, through Melvin, Richard, and Kent, public service and philanthropy have been a constant. Ben Swig was knighted by the pope for his contributions to Catholic causes including Boys' Town in Italy. Melvin was active in Jewish Charities and was chairman of the University of San Francisco, a Catholic school. Richard received the Mahatma Gandhi Humanitarian Award and the Golda Meir Award while supporting and serving as chairman or board member of numerous charities, such as the Coast Guard Foundation, the Fromm Institute for Lifelong Learning, and others. Kent serves on the board of Business Executives for National Security and is president of the American Friends of Jaffa University.

Jack Weiler was as philanthropic as Ben Swig. The Einstein Hospital in the Bronx was renamed the Jack D. Weiler Hospital in 1985 in recognition of his work as chairman. He chaired the Bronx Lebanon Hospital and served on the board of Montefiore Hospital. He also led efforts to develop 14,000 homes and apartments that house 55,000 Israeli immigrants. In 1984 he was quoted, saying, "Philanthropy comes first, ahead of my business."

There are so many important Jews in real estate that it is simply impractical to profile them all. Max Karl single-handedly pioneered mortgage insurance with his company Mortgage Guarantee Insurance (MGIC). Richard First and David Nitka created the real estate information industry in the United States. Adolph Sutro pioneered real estate development in San Francisco in the late 1800s—at one point supposedly owning 12 percent of the city's land. Martin Selig and Jack Benaroya are a huge force in Seattle's real estate industry. Arthur Cohen built Arlen into one of America's largest developers. Robert Moses controlled public works real estate projects in New York for decades, the Ghermezian family, Francis Saul, and on and on. The list is endless. Jews have simply gone from limited involvement in real estate to disproportionate achievement over the space of roughly 100 years. Today they are among the world's most important real estate developers, managers, and owners.

Chapter 19

Retailing^361

The Jews were men who actually lived by commerce, and apart from a few Venetians they were almost the only people who did so.... Thanks to the contacts which they maintained among themselves, they constituted the only economic link which survived between Islam and Christendom.... (They) speak Persian, Roman, Arab, and the Frankish, Spanish, and Slav languages. They bring from the Occident eunuchs, women slaves, boys, silk, furs, and swords...to Sind, India, and China. On returning they are laden with musk, aloes, camphor, cinnamon...." — Henri Pirenne,
Mohammed and Charlemagne

Middlemen, merchants, and traders—for roughly 2,000 years, Jews have bought and resold goods. In this capacity, they have been gifted, but often also reviled by those who envied their success or saw no value in their middleman role of buying, transporting, inventorying, and merchandising goods for customers. How Jews came to their role as middlemen is shrouded in history, but some facts behind their long and disproportionate success as merchants are clear.

The Diaspora was key. The Romans' slaughter of an estimated 1 million Jews and the exile of millions more during and after the first- and second-century Jewish revolts changed Judaism forever. The Temple's destruction ended the Priestly Judaism of the Sadducees. It was eclipsed by the rabbinic Judaism of the Pharisees and the rise of the synagogue as the principal place of worship.

Dispersion and assimilation would probably have destroyed Judaism's two remaining tribes (as it had the ten lost tribes) were it not for canonization of the Hebrew Bible and conversion of the Oral Law into the written Talmud. To preserve a religion and culture, Judaism's most sacred works had to be canonized and reduced to writing. Differing texts of individual books of the Torah and complementary writings, such as the Psalms, had to be unified into the Hebrew Bible. The Oral Law, which helped interpret the Torah into tangible guides and laws for day to day Jewish living, could no longer be "oral." And as the Talmud changed over time, those

259

inquiries, debates, and responses (Responsa) had to be communicated in written form.

Said simply, the survival of Judaism as the religion and culture of a dispersed people could not rely on "word-of mouth" transmission of its most sacred beliefs over the generations and across a vast geography. Only through canonization and codification could the religion and culture be kept consistent and passed on through successive generations living as dispersed minority enclaves in outposts all over the world.

The written Hebrew Bible and Talmud demanded literacy, and even more, competence and fluency in reading, analyzing, and discussing these complex texts.

Rabbinic Judaism did not just encourage education, it demanded it. Educating one's children was made a solemn parental duty. It was a duty unique to Judaism. There was no equivalent requirement for Christians, Hellenic/Roman polytheists, Zoroastrians, Muslims, Hindus, Buddhists, or other religions of the time. Some scholars now say this demand for literacy, particularly at a time when most Jews were farmers, served to substantially reduce the numbers of Jews, especially when the investment in education served no economic purpose but was costly in time and money. Moreover, for some, reading, understanding, and discussing these works was simply too intellectually demanding. Millions of Jews opted out. They left the religion.

But for those who persevered and became educated, new avenues opened up. In any prospering economy, there were jobs, trades, and careers that could never be had by an illiterate farmer. And with a disproportionate number of Jews being educated, they took a disproportionate number of those more demanding—and rewarding—jobs.

Education helped Jews perform well as merchants. They could analyze the risks, buy wisely, do the math, keep the records, and market their wares. These were skills most others lacked. And Judaism's demand for—and the practical benefits of—educating one's children also meant necessary talents and learning were passed from generation to generation allowing growing families to build sizable enterprises sometimes networked with kin across multiple locations.

The Diaspora placed Jews in a unique position. Unlike other tribes or nations, they were not confined to a single geographic area. They were spread out and usually seen to be a neutral minority. They had fellow Jews residing in other countries and could thus trade with competing, or even warring, tribes and nations. Moreover, Jews typically wrote and spoke a common language (Hebrew), were usually conversant in the local languages and spoke others, such as Aramaic, Latin, and Greek. These were substantial advantages others did not have.

Jews were generally not burdened with usury, the prohibition on charging interest for the use of money. They could finance the purchase, transport, and inventory of merchandise in ways much simpler than techniques required of Christians and Muslims, particularly in the Dark and Middle Ages. They could provide or obtain such financing for their businesses.

And while Jews may not have been the only group with the combination of education, a dispersed population, kinsmen, language, and talent endowing them for success in trading, they were so successful that when local rulers determined middleman talents would benefit their own European or Middle Eastern community, Jews were the group most often recruited to immigrate.

That activity, the trading and retailing by a minority that typically did not assimilate, but stood aloof from the majority population and profited in their middleman role, often created resentments. But when that hate and anger led to evicting Jews, the local economy would typically suffer from their absence.

In short, the Diaspora and culture of education demanded by the religion stimulated an astonishing Jewish talent as merchants. Records show Jews trading goods along the Silk Road as early as the sixth century. Mayer Amschel Rothschild began as a small-time dealer in antiques. The peddler was a common fixture in nineteenth-century America, and many newly immigrant Jews began as peddlers before later setting up shop. Disproportionate achievement as Jewish merchants remains today. We see it in the retailing organizations that serve us.

Department Stores[362]

Department stores first appeared in the mid-nineteenth century. As in so many cases, the new industry represented an entrepreneurial opportunity for Jews. While Gentiles built many of the new department stores including John Wanamaker's, Strawbridge & Clothier, Jordon Marsh, Dayton Hudson, J.C. Penney, Marshall Field's, Dillard's, Nordstrom, Abercrombie & Fitch, Brooks Brothers, and others, Jews created a huge number, probably half or more of the leading stores and chains. Others such as Macys, were started by Gentiles, but were later acquired and run for most of their existence by Jews who built them into retail giants.

One way to gauge the role of Jews can be based on a January 11, 2008, *Wall Street Journal* story on retail sales at the major department store chains. *The Journal* listed what they regarded as the seven principal department store chains with their December 2007 sales. They included:

1. **Macy's:**	$4.6 billion
2. J.C. Penney:	$2.8 billion
3. **Kohl's:**	$2.7 billion
4. Nordstrom:	$1.2 billion
5. Dillard's:	$1.2 billion
6. **Neiman Marcus:**	$ .7 billion
7. **Saks:**	$ .4 billion

Of the seven, J.C. Penney, Dillard's, and Nordstrom were not created (or controlled for many years) by Jews. The other four were. The list tends to corroborate the notion that Jews, never more than 4 percent of the U.S. population (and now 2 percent), created roughly half, or more, of America's major department stores and chains.

It is impractical to profile all of the department stores started or acquired and then redirected by Jewish entrepreneurs and their offspring. Nonetheless, the following retailers (or chains) are among the more prominent. Most were created and run by great merchants—the Stanley Marcuses or Bernie Gimbels—with their superb knack for knowing what the customer would want, how to much to buy, what price to pay, how much to mark it up, and how to display, promote, and sell it. Jews are clearly among America's greatest merchants.

Macy's:[363] In 1848 Lazarus Straus immigrated to America from Germany, leaving behind his wife and four children. Unlike the impoverished Eastern European Jews of a later era, Lazarus was from a wealthy family and he came for political, not economic, reasons. He was leaving Germany's failed liberal reforms for America's democracy.

Despite his father's success, Lazarus brought no fortune and had to start over by peddling merchandise in Georgia when he was already forty. Within two years, he had his own dry-goods store, and four years later he was able to bring his wife, Sara, and the four children to America. All three sons worked in the business. The oldest, Isidor, planned to go to West Point, but the Civil War intervened. Unable to enter West Point, since he was from Georgia, and unwilling to tolerate hazing at the Georgia Military Academy, Isidor traveled to Europe where he sold (and traded) Confederate War Bonds and recruited blockade runners. Despite his financial losses when the Confederacy lost, Isidor returned to the United States at war's end with $10,000 in gold he had earned and saved while abroad. He used it to buy his parents a home.

Expecting Southern reconstruction to take decades, Isidor's father, Lazarus, moved the family to New York in 1865. He bought a wholesale glass and chinaware business, and in 1874, rented 2,500 square feet from non-Jew Rowland H. Macy for a retail operation. Macy had opened his New York store in 1858 and succeeded with a one-price (no haggling), cash-and carry-format.

In 1887 Isidor and Nathan Straus bought into Macy's business as partners, and when Macy died in 1896, they bought out his heirs. The brothers retained the Macy's name, continued the one-price, cash-and-carry policies, and used their purchasing skill and promotional talent to establish a dominant reputation for consistently selling merchandise at prices lower than those of competitors. They were so successful that in 1892 they were able to purchase half interest in a Brooklyn department store (Wechsler & Abraham) for $1.5 million. With Abraham's concurrence, the store was renamed Abraham and Straus.

The family's reputation for always paying their creditors was sufficiently strong that the brothers were able to borrow $4.5 million from New York banks in 1902 to build a new store at Herald Square. It would become the world's largest department store.

Though he was elected to Congress in 1893 and served one term, Isidor was always the principal merchant. His brother Nathan, though a partner in Macy's until 1914, became one of America's leading philanthropists. He gave away two-thirds of his fortune between 1914 when he sold his Macy's interests and 1931 when he died. In 1916 he sold his yacht, donating the proceeds to war orphans. He also set up an organization to provide pasteurized milk to New York's impoverished families. The third brother, Oscar, was never heavily involved in Macy's. Instead he became a political diplomat. In 1884, he was the first Jew to receive a presidential appointment when Grover Cleveland named him minister to Turkey. In 1906 Theodore Roosevelt named him secretary of commerce and labor, the first Jew to serve in the cabinet of a U.S. president.

On April 16, 1912, Isidor and his wife, Ida, died when the Titanic sank. Ida refused to enter a lifeboat without Isidor, and Isidor wouldn't enter one as long as there were younger men to be saved. When their behavior was chronicled by survivors, Isidor and Ida became American heroes. They left behind six children, three boys and three girls. To honor their mother and father, the children built Straus Hall in Harvard Yard. Shortly after their parents' death, Isidor's sons (Jesse, Percy, and Herbert), who together inherited half the business, bought out their uncle Nathan who owned the other half. The brothers continued to build Macy's New York while expanding into Toledo, Atlanta, and Newark.

Though ownership was evenly split among the three brothers, Jesse, like his father before him, was the eldest and more the merchant than his brothers. This was the generation that launched the Thanksgiving Day Parade in 1924, copying an idea originated by the Gimbels three years earlier in Philadelphia. Like his uncle Oscar, Jesse became active in government and served as FDR's ambassador to France. The three brothers also took Macy's public in 1922 and worked for the chain until their respective retirements between the late 1930s and early 1940s.

In the next generation, though Percy's son, Ralph, was active in the business, it was Jesse's eldest, Jack, who became the shopkeeper. He joined the firm in 1921, became CEO in 1940, chairman in 1956, and chairman of the executive committee from 1968 to 1976. During his tenure, Macy's grew from four stores to fifty-six. Jack and his brother Robert K. Straus endowed a professorship at Harvard Business School and he (Jack) was a member of the Harvard University board of overseers. Jack's son, Kenneth, joined the business in 1947 and was the last Straus (then in its fifth generation) to be active at Macy's. He was senior vice president when then CEO, Edward S. Finkelstein, engineered a leveraged buyout of the public company in 1985. By that time, the family tree had grown to roughly 200 Straus members, including merchants, diplomats, philanthropists, and publishers.

In 1994 Macy's became part of Federated Department Stores, then the largest department store chain in America. (See the Federated coverage below, including its 2007 name change to Macy's Inc.)

Filene's:[364]Eighteen-year-old William Filene emigrated from Germany in 1848 and eight years later, he opened his first retail store in Salem, Massachusetts. Despite great early success he was wiped out in the infamous 1868 Black Friday financial panic. Nearly penniless, he started over in Lynn, Massachusetts, expanded to Boston with two stores and then to Bath, Maine. When he had a stroke in 1880, his twenty-year-old son, Edward (E.A.) set aside plans to go to Harvard, stepped in and ran the business. In 1891, and after his recovery, William turned the business over to E.A. and E.A.'s younger brother, Lincoln. Together they built Filene's into one of the world's foremost department stores.

Both E.A. and Lincoln were innovators. E.A. created the "automatic markdown" system that made Filene's Basement world famous. He introduced credit unions to the United States, founded the United States Chamber of Commerce, and co-invented a simultaneous translation system later used in the Nuremberg war crimes trials and at the United Nations. A lifelong liberal Democrat, E.A. was one of the few prominent businessmen to support Franklin Delano Roosevelt. Lincoln introduced employee profit sharing in 1903, set up an employee-run organization for arbitrating disputes, an employee health clinic, and employee retirement plans. He was a co-founder of the Boston Symphony Orchestra, supported women's suffrage, funded

Boston's first educational television station, and his daughter, Catherine, donated the land and helped fund Virginia's Wolf Trap National Park for the Performing Arts near Washington, D.C.

In 1929 Filene's merged with Abraham & Straus and F & R. Lazarus, in what became Federated Stores, now called Macy's Inc. (see below). At that point, though Fred Lazarus Jr. was Federated's president and CEO, Lincoln became chairman, a post he held till his death in 1957. Because E.A. was a lifelong bachelor and Lincoln had three daughters but no sons, neither brother had an heir to take over Filene's. With that in mind, they recruited Lou Kirstein in 1911 and when Lincoln became Federated's chairman, Kirstein took over as Filene's' CEO, a post he held till his death in 1942.

Abraham & Straus:[365] In 1865 Abraham Abraham, the twenty-two-year-old son of Bavarian immigrant Judah Abraham, partnered with Joseph Wechsler to form Wechsler & Abraham a Brooklyn dry-goods store. Twenty-eight years later, in 1893, when Wechsler retired, Abraham's son-in-law, Simon F. Rothschild, partnered with Isidor and Nathan Straus to buy out Wechsler's half interest. They then changed the name to Abraham & Straus. By 1900 the firm had nearly 5,000 employees, covered seven acres, and augmented its in-store sales with a major catalog operation serving Long Island.

Following the death of Isidor Straus in 1912, his three sons gave up their interest in Abraham & Straus as partial payment for their Uncle Nathan's half interest in Macy's. Nathan thus became a major partner in Abraham & Straus. Nonetheless, three years later, in an example of the fascinating "Our Crowd" family and industry ties, Abraham's daughter, Edith, married Isidor Straus' son, Percy. Earlier Percy had given up his Abraham & Straus interests but retained a one-third interest in Macy's. Through marriage, Percy thus became competitor to his father-in-law as well as his uncle.

Nathan Straus and Simon Rothschild expanded Abraham & Straus, and in a prescient 1929 move, they merged it with Filene's, and F. & R. Lazarus to form Federated Stores. The merger helped all three stores—plus Bloomingdale's, which joined in 1930—weather the Great Depression. Though part of Federated, Abraham family members continued to head up Abraham & Straus. Simon Rothschild was CEO till 1937 and his son, Walter, led it from 1937 to 1955 when the first non-family member, Sidney Solomon took over. At the time, Abraham & Straus had 12,000 employees. Today, because of Federated control, the Abraham and Straus stores now display the Macy's name over their door.

Gimbels:[366] Adam Gimbel emigrated from Bavaria in 1835 when he was 18. He opened his first store (a trading post) in Vincennes, Indiana in 1842. His marriage to Fridolyn Kahnweiler, daughter of a Philadelphia dry-goods merchant, produced seven sons of their own, plus an eighth who they adopted. In 1887 the family moved to Milwaukee, establishing the city's third Jewish department store. Business was good. By 1894 they expanded to Philadelphia, buying out Granville B. Haines and Company to compete with Jewish-owned Snellenburgs and successful Gentile merchants Wanamaker's and Strawbridge & Clothier.

Because Adam's second son, Isaac, was more talented than Jacob, his first, when Adam died in 1894 Isaac became CEO (and Jacob was named chairman.) Despite strong competition from the other merchants, Gimbels did very well. In part this was because other brothers were pitching in. Ellis, for example, originated the Gimbels' Thanksgiving Day Parade in 1921, and in 1915 he launched the annual handout of free circus tickets to orphans.

In 1909 Gimbels' success prompted the opening of a new store in New York. Leading it was Isaac's son (and third-generation Gimbel), Bernie, who moved to New York to build and run it. A Wharton graduate, a sports fan, always affable, and always down to earth, Bernie Gimbel was a "natural." He found a location a block from Macy's and his showmanship and talents as a New York "booster" made the store a huge success. He was another in a large family of great merchants. In 1922 he took Gimbels public, and in 1923, using the public stock, he acquired Saks and its proposed Fifth Avenue location. Later he installed his cousin, Adam Long Gimbel, to run Saks. It was a wise move. Under Adam Gimbel's leadership, Saks' profits kept Gimbels afloat during the darkest days of the Great Depression. Ultimately Bernie built Gimbels into Macy's' foremost (and carefully cultivated) competitor.

Gimbels was a family affair into its fourth generation. Bruce Gimbel, a decorated WWII Air Transport Command pilot and a major patron of Yale, took over the business in 1973. Ultimately Gimbels was sold to B.A.T. Industries in the 1970s. B.A.T. proved to be a lousy merchant, and the last Gimbels store was closed in 1987, 100 years after the first had opened.

Saks:[367] In 1867, twenty-year-old Andrew Saks, born and raised in Baltimore, set up a men's dry-goods store in Washington, D.C. In 1902 he added a New York store at Herald Square, near what would later become the location for both Macy's and Gimbels. On Andrew's death in 1912, his son, Horace, took over. Sensing a more "upscale" opportunity on Fifth Avenue, Horace merged his company with Gimbels. As a publicly traded company, Gimbels had the capital to finance the expansion to Fifth Avenue.

When Horace died in 1926, Bernie Gimbel's cousin, Adam, took the reins. He ran Saks Fifth Avenue until 1969. He added new stores in Palm Beach, Southampton, Beverly Hills, Chicago, and other high end locations and he constantly worked to build Saks reputation for exclusive high-end merchandise. After Gimbels' sale to B.A.T. Industries, Saks Fifth Avenue was expanded to roughly thirty stores.

Over the decade of the 1990s, Saks went through a dizzying series of changes. In 1990 it was "taken private" in a leveraged buyout. In 1995 it was taken public as a stand-alone company, and then in 1998, it was acquired by Proffitt's, a Birmingham- based retailer. Today, with most of the Proffitt's stores and others of the Proffitt's acquisitions divested, Saks is once more the heart of a publicly traded premium retailer. It retains two small subsidiaries, "Off 5th" outlet stores and Club Libby, a specialty chain focused on merchandising to young girls. It is counted seventh among major department store chains in *The Wall Street Journal* list provided at the beginning of this section on "Department Stores."

Bergdorf Goodman:[368] Alsatian Jew Harman Bergdorf founded what became Bergdorf Goodman in 1899. He recruited Edwin Goodman to head the tailoring department, but found Goodman so capable, he soon turned the store's management over to him. By 1906 Edwin Goodman bought out Bergdorf and adopted the name now used for more than 100 years. Goodman was a superb merchant who "lived above the store" in a sixteen-room penthouse he used to entertain the high society to which Bergdorf's catered.

Edwin's son Andrew took over from his father and ran the store until 1953. In 1972 Bergdorf was acquired by the chain of Carter Hawley Hale, which made it part of Neiman Marcus in 1987. Today Bergdorf remains a subsidiary of privately owned Neiman Marcus.

Bloomingdale's:[369] Lyman and Joseph Bloomingdale, sons of a Bavarian Jewish immigrant, began by selling hoop skirts in the notions shop they opened in 1861. By 1872 they broadened the line and moved to Third Avenue and 56th Street. Fourteen years later they moved once more to 59th and Lexington, their primary location for more than 120 years. After Joseph retired in 1896, Lyman and his son Samuel were in charge with Samuel's brothers, Hiram and Irving, also helping out in the family store, but not nearly as active as Samuel or their father. On Lyman's death in 1905, Samuel took charge. Among other initiatives, he was a major promoter of the Queensborough Bridge, which provided a direct link from Queens to Manhattan (and, of course, directly to the Bloomingdale's store).

It was Samuel who agreed to merge Bloomingdale's into Federated Stores in 1930. He then stepped down as CEO to become a Federated director, a position he held until 1962. With no sons of his own, Samuel did not pass the baton to a family member. Instead, Fred Lazarus Jr. would become instrumental in selecting the store's CEOs from then on until Lazarus himself retired.) Samuel's famous nephew (and Hiram's son), Alfred S. Bloomingdale, worked only briefly in the store before deciding not to follow in his uncle's footsteps. Instead Alfred, like his father before him, pursued theatrical interests as a producer and director of Broadway plays. Later, he was instrumental in creating the Diners Club card. His inheritance together with his Diners Club profits made him prominent and wealthy.

"Bloomies," as it came to be known—because of the name stamped on ladies panties during a 1973 promotion—was later run for fourteen years by Marvin Traub, considered by many the contemporary "godfather" of the New York department store business. Traub built Bloomingdale's into one of the most important department store chains in the country. Today it is the premium brand name used for the thirty-six high-end stores in the Macy's Inc., chain around the United States. Meanwhile, Traub, at age eighty-three, is logging more than 200,000 air miles a year consulting to retailing clients all over the globe.

B. Altman:[370] A son of Bavarian immigrant Jews who arrived in the United States in 1835, Benjamin Altman opened his department store in 1865 when he was twenty-five. By the turn of the century, it was said New Yorkers preferred B. Altman's to the Metropolitan Museum of Art. This because "Altman's merchandise was of higher quality—and you could buy it!" B. Altman set the standard for high-end New York retailing.

In a nice touch, Altman donated his $20 million art collection to the Met when he died in 1913, while also establishing a $30 million charitable foundation. Though he left no heirs, earlier he had recruited Michael Friedsam, a very capable merchant, to run the business. Altman's stock was left to his own foundation, which controlled what by then was a chain with stores in Short Hills, New Jersey, and White Plains and Manhasset, New York.

In 1985 the foundation sold the stores to a group which included members of the Gucci family (not Jewish). They, in turn, sold it to an Australian real estate development company which envisioned B. Altman stores as anchor tenants in new shopping centers. Knowing nothing about how to operate the stores, the chain went bankrupt in 1989 and closed all the B. Altman stores in 1990.

Bamberger's:[371] In 1892 Louis Bamberger, son of German Jewish immigrants, and his brother-in-law, Felix Fuld, founded the L. Bamberger and Company department store in downtown Newark, New Jersey. By 1928 they had built it into the fourth highest grossing department store in the United States. When he sold it to Macy's in 1928, after thirty-seven years at the helm, Bamberger felt he should share the proceeds with his employees. He allotted $1 million to be apportioned among the 240 employees. Later he and his sister provided $5 million to help establish the renowned Princeton University Institute for Advanced Study.

Stern's (originally Stern Brothers):[372] Louis Stern was born in February 1847 to German Jewish watchmaker, M.A. Stern and his wife, Sophia. After the family immigrated to the United States in the 1850s, M.A. moved to Albany to set up a jewelry and watchmaking business, taking along his three youngest sons, Isaac, Bernard, and Benjamin. Louis, the eldest, was sent to Petersburg, West Virginia, to learn how to be a merchant in his uncle's small store. When the four brothers completed their respective internships, Louis proposed they set up a dry-goods and novelties store in Manhattan. In March of 1867, Louis and Isaac opened the store. A few years later, Bernard and Benjamin joined them.

Isaac retired in 1910 and Louis' sons, Melville and Irving, became active, as, for a time, was Irving's father-in-law, Arthur Brandeis, owner of the largest department store west of Chicago. The family expanded in New York, New Jersey, and Pennsylvania and ran the business until 1951 when they sold to Federated Stores. In 2001 all the remaining Stern's stores were converted to Macy's or Bloomingdale's.

Sears, Roebuck and Company:[373] Non-Jew Richard Warren Sears, a "marketer," started Sears in 1887–88. He recruited self-taught watchmaker Alvah Curtis Roebuck (also not Jewish) as his partner after Sears had proved to himself he could sell Roebuck's watches by mail. Seven years later, to finance his expansion, Sears sold half interest to Aaron Nusbaum for $75,000. Nusbaum's brother-in-law, Julius Rosenwald, a successful garment entrepreneur, took half of Nusbaum's position (one-fourth of Sears, Roebuck stock) and became Sears, Roebuck's head of operations. In 1901 Sears and Rosenwald bought out Nusbaum for $1.25 million after Sears and Nusbaum concluded they could not work together. (Later, when Sears proved hugely successful, Nusbaum had second thoughts about the deal he had cut.)

On Sears' retirement in 1909, Rosenwald assumed sole control of the company, and led it till his death in 1932. Rosenwald deserves credit for leading Sears' explosive growth into a huge nationwide mail-order and retail store business. By the mid-1970s, Sears, the Wal-Mart of its day, was the largest retailer in the world. Rosenwald introduced the "money-back guarantee," established procedures to quickly fill catalog orders, reduced returns, instituted quality control, and took numerous other steps to improve efficiency.

A major philanthropist, Rosenwald was the catalyst in building YMCAs in twenty-five communities. He became a trustee of Tuskegee Institute and then offered to contribute up to half the cost of building new black schools throughout the South. Ultimately his $4,366,519 helped generate another $28,408,520, which, in turn, built 5,357 schools for blacks in fifteen Southern states. Two million more went for educational fellowships for Southerners and $2 million went to the University of Chicago's Museum of Science and Industry. (A more complete discussion of Rosenwald's philanthropy and his remarkable leadership of Sears, Roebuck is told as the introduction to Chapter 24 – "Philanthropy.")

Kaufmann's:[374] In 1871 three years after emigrating from the Rhenish (German) village of Viernheim, Jacob Kaufmann and his brother, Isaac, founded Pittsburgh-based Kaufmann's Department Store. They were soon joined by siblings Morris and Henry. Kaufmann's was not the first store in Pittsburgh. Horne's, which served the carriage trade, predated it by twenty-two years. But second-generation Edgar Kaufmann, son of Morris and Betty Kaufmann, was a larger-than-life figure whose philandering and philanthropy were legendary in Pittsburgh. Edgar built Kaufmann's reputation and power as a Pittsburgh-based chain with stores in New York, Ohio, West Virginia, and Pennsylvania.

Edgar also commissioned non-Jew Frank Lloyd Wright, to build the famous "Fallingwater" residence. (Fallingwater has been judged, by the American Institute of Architects, one of the most important architectural buildings in American history.) Edgar was also a major benefactor who enhanced downtown Pittsburgh.

When none of the third-generation Kaufmann's was interested in continuing the business, the department stores were sold to the May Company in 1946. When he died in April, 1955, Edgar Kaufmann left half his estate to charity. More recently May Company became part of Federated, and with the consolidation of brands, the Kaufmann's stores have now been renamed Macy's.

Hecht's:[375] Samuel Hecht emigrated from Hesse, Germany, in 1847 when he was seventeen. After ten years of peddling, he opened a used-furniture store in Baltimore. It was one of what would become three major Jewish-owned department stores in that city— Hecht's, Huntzler's, and Hochschild Kohns. By 1879 Samuel added clothing to his line of merchandise, and the next year, Emmanuel the first of four sons, would join in the business. Over time, carpeting and other items were added to the product offering.

When Samuel died in 1907, his sons and grandsons continued to lead the firm. They expanded, adding stores in New York City, Easton, and Annapolis, Maryland, and Washington, D.C. Later, in the 1950s, they expanded to the suburbs of Washington, D.C., and Baltimore. In 1959, May Company bought Hecht's and expanded it to sixty stores operating across the mid-Atlantic from Pennsylvania to North Carolina and Tennessee. Today the remaining Hecht's stores operate as Macy's.

Garfinckel's:[376] In 1872 Julius Garfinckel was born in Syracuse, New York, the fifth of six children born to Harris and Hannah Harrzon Garfinkel, Bavarian Jewish emigrants. Harris was an itinerant peddler who, over the years, traded goods in New Orleans, Syracuse, and Texas. Julius reportedly moved from Denver to Washington, D.C., in 1899 where he opened his first store.

Julius built Garfinckel's into one of the country's premier high-end stores. By the time of his death in 1936, it had 500 employees. A bachelor, he left an estate of $6 million to charity and his employees. After his death, the firm continued to expand, and by 1946, Garfinckel's consisted of a chain of stores, including the Miller Stores in Tennessee and Georgia. That year, it also bought the quintessential WASP chain, Brooks Brothers. Over the next thirty-four years, Garfinckel's expanded Brooks Brothers into a nationwide chain of ten stores before selling the chain to Allied Stores in 1980. Then, in 1988, Allied, sold Brooks Brothers to the British chain Marks & Spenser—profiled below.

Ultimately, Garfinckel's overexpanded. In 1990, then chairman George Kelly, (likely not Jewish) placed the firm in bankruptcy and it was liquidated.

Goldsmith's:[377] Louis Ottenheimer emigrated from Germany before the Civil War. He operated an Arkansas trading post, saving enough from its profits to later open a store in Memphis. In 1867 he brought his two nephews, Isaac and Jacob Goldsmith, to America to work in the Beale Street store. When Jacob fell in love with Louis' daughter (and Jacob's cousin), Dora, Louis fired him. Isaac followed Jacob out the door. The $500 the brothers had saved while working for Ottenheimer staked them to open their own store.

Five years later, Louis allowed the twenty-five-year-old Jacob to marry Dora, and in 1881, Jacob and Isaac bought out Dora's father. After Isaac's death, Jacob's three sons, Fred, Elias, and Leo, all worked in the business with Fred taking over as CEO when Jacob died in 1931. Fred and the Goldsmith's store were major forces as Memphis community benefactors. Among other civic acts, in 1926, Fred Goldsmith and Abe Plough (later of Schering Plough) helped save the Christmas deposits of small depositors at the failing American Savings Bank in Memphis. The bank's president had committed suicide over bank shortages, and Goldsmith and Plough provided $232,000 from their own funds to cover depositor's accounts.

Third-generation Jack Goldsmith affiliated with Federated Stores in 1959 and then sold out to them in 1969.

Rich's:[378] Hungarian Jews Morris and William Rich immigrated to the United States from Czechoslovakia in 1859. Twelve-year-old Morris peddled notions in Ohio for his first six years and then moved to Atlanta, where in 1867, using $500 borrowed from William, he opened his first store. Rich's Department Store was to become synonymous with the notion "The customer is always right." It pioneered accepting returned merchandise with no questions asked (even as late as ten years after the merchandise was purchased). and Morris Rich adopted a remarkably liberal and widely appreciated credit policy in the difficult years following the Civil War.

Over time, Rich's became an Atlanta institution. Among its publicly recognized acts were accepting Liberty Bonds at par in 1918 as payment for merchandise, subsidizing the city's teachers' payroll when Atlanta was virtually bankrupt in 1930, and supplying sports equipment, musical instruments, and other items for local schools and teams.

When no one in the Rich family was prepared to take over the store in 1924, the family hired Frank Neely, a Gentile who had converted to Judaism years earlier when he married the Jewess Rae Schlesinger. But when it was time for Neely to pass the baton, Morris' grandson Richard Rich took over and continued the traditions started by his grandfather.

In 1976, after 109 years of family control, Richard's son, Michael, was forced by his board of directors to sell out to Federated Department Stores.

Neiman Marcus:[379] Al Neiman, Herbert Marcus, and Carrie Neiman (Al's wife and Herbert's sister) founded Neiman Marcus in 1907. Neiman Marcus lore says Herbert's wife, Minnie, was pregnant with their first son, Stanley, at the time. Feeling the raise offered by Sanger Brothers (a major Jewish-owned department store in Dallas) was too small to support his wife and expected child, Herbert quit Sanger Brothers and later started his own store with his sister and brother-in-law. Carrie was Herbert's equal as a talented saleswoman and merchandise buyer, and Al was good at promotion. Together they created what would become Dallas', and later the Southwest's, premier high-end department store. It has since grown to become a national chain. Not long after its founding, Neiman Marcus outdistanced the much older Sanger Brothers, whose Dallas store predated it by thirty-five years.

Neiman Marcus' greatest fame came under the leadership of Herbert's son, Stanley, a tireless merchant and promoter who cultivated an image for exclusive high- end merchandise, superb treatment of customers, and great promotional flare. Stanley, like his father and aunt before him, was a superb salesman. In 1946 while in France, he was introduced to General Dwight Eisenhower. Suspecting Ike might later run for president, Stanley pitched him to buy Mamie's inaugural gown at Neiman Marcus. Six years later, Ike did just that. Stanley Marcus came up with many clever merchandising innovations, of which perhaps the best known was the unique and very expensive "his and hers gifts" touted in the Christmas catalog.

In 1969 Neiman Marcus sold out to Carter Hawley Hale, which tried, with mixed results, to clone the Neiman Marcus brand in new stores all over the United States. Following the failure of Carter Hawley Hale, Neiman Marcus emerged as a separate public company with thirty-nine Neiman Marcus stores, two Bergdorf Goodman stores, twenty-two Last Call clearance centers, and Neiman Marcus Direct, marketing online and through catalogs under the Neiman Marcus, Bergdorf Goodman, and Horchow brand names.

Thirty years after selling his company, ninety-four-year-old Stanley Marcus was still active with his own retail consulting practice and still driven. That year he did a consulting assignment for Jeff Bezos at Amazon.com. Marcus died in 2002.

Harris & Company and Sanger Brothers:[380] In 1887 Adolphus Harris, a Prussian emigrant Jew, opened his department store in Dallas. Later he added a second in Galveston. By 1961 after three generations of family ownership and management, A. Harris & Company was sold to Federated, which subsequently merged it with Sanger Brothers, a Dallas competitor. Earlier, Sanger Brothers, had been established by Bavarian Jews who immigrated in 1851, predating Harris. They opened their first store in McKinney, Texas, in 1858 and their Dallas store in 1872. At the end of the nineteenth century, Sanger Brothers was the largest dry-goods company west of the Mississippi. But by 1925, Sanger family members had lost their touch. With little talent for merchandising, they were forced to sell out. Those buyers, in turn, sold Sanger Brothers to Federated in 1951. The combined Sanger-Harris brand lasted until 1990 when Foleys, which had been started in Houston by Irish immigrants, bought the Sanger-Harris stores from Federated. Sixteen years later the sale was reversed when Federated bought Foleys. In 2006, Foleys' remaining stores, including those originally operated as A. Harris & Company and Sanger Brothers, were all converted to Macy's.

Goldwater's:[381]"Big (6'3") Mike" Goldwater ("Goldwasser") immigrated from Konin, Poland, via London, where he met and married the English Jewess Sarah Nathan. In 1852, when Mike was thirty-one, he moved to California. Two years later, his savings from peddling were sufficient to bring Sarah and his first two children, Morris and Carrie, to join him. In 1862, after ventures in Sonora, Los Angeles, and San Francisco, Mike moved to La Paz, Arizona, to work for, and later buy out, the adobe store of his friend, Bernard Cohn. Wanting nothing to do with the violence she associated with Arizona, Sarah instead moved to San Francisco where their remaining six children were born, presumably conceived during Big Mike's frequent buying trips. As Arizona towns sprung up, and flourished or died, Mike and his sons set up, and occasionally shut down, Goldwater's stores in Prescott, Parker, Seymour, Lynx Creek, Phoenix, Bisbee, Fairbank, Contention, Tombstone, Benson, and Crittenden. By 1877, their Prescott store was considered "mammoth" and according to the *Weekly Miner,* "certainly the finest in Arizona."

Mike's eldest son, Morris, ran some of the family stores, while also serving as Prescott's elected mayor for forty-eight years. His youngest son, Baron Goldwater, re-opened the Phoenix store, which would later eclipse Prescott as the flagship of the Goldwater's chain. For a time the Phoenix store was headed by Baron's sons, Bob and Barry—that is until Barry followed in Uncle Morris' footsteps, first being elected to the Phoenix city council in 1949, and then to the United States Senate in 1952. He retained his Senate seat for the next thirty-five years and was the Republican nominee for U.S. president in 1964.

In 1963 the family sold their department store chain to Associated Dry Goods. Later Associated was absorbed by the May Company, which in turn was absorbed by Federated. Today the Goldwater's stores still in operation have been rebranded as Macy's.

Gump's:[382] In 1850, seventeen-year-old Solomon Gump emigrated from Heidelberg to New York. Thirteen years later, he moved to California to work for his brother-in-law. After a few years, he bought him out. Solomon renamed the store and then built Gump's into a San Francisco institution. Always a specialty retailer, Solomon focused on high-end luxury goods. His fourth son, Abraham, took over from Solomon, and added Asian art and furnishings. For well over 100 years, Gump's was internationally known for its unique, eclectic mix of high-quality merchandise sold from stores in San Francisco, Beverly Hills, Houston, and Dallas.

Third-generation Gump brothers Richard and Robert sold the business to the conglomerate, Macmillan Inc., in the late 1960s, after which Gump's went through a succession of ownership changes and managers, all of which demonstrated that without the family running the store, Gump's wasn't the same. Currently a syndicate led by Art Berliner, a longtime San Francisco venture capitalist, owns and operates Gump's, its Web site and direct-mail operation.

I. Magnin and Joseph Magnin:[383] After emigrating from Holland in 1876 with his wife, Mary Ann, Isaac Magnin began his career at Gump's. Isaac's craft was the application of gilt during San Francisco's "gilded age." Meanwhile, Mary Ann made and marketed women's clothing from their modest home. By 1888 her talent and success led to the creation of what became the prestigious Market Street retailer I. Magnin. By 1910 they also had shops in six luxury hotels. Their Union Square store in San Francisco and Wilshire Boulevard store in Los Angeles, which opened in 1939, were among the most elegant retail stores in mid-twentieth-century America.

When passed over by his mother to run the business, Mary and Isaac's third son, Joseph, set up his own shop in 1913. Joseph Magnin stores went after popular-priced garments for young ladies. It too was successful. In 1940 Joseph named his son, Cyril, president, and over the next forty-eight years until he died, Cyril Magnin evolved into a San Francisco icon.

A few weeks after Mary's death in 1943, I. Magnin was sold to Bullock's, which expanded the chain to more than sixty locations in California, Arizona, Illinois, Maryland, Washington, and Oregon. In the department store shakeout of the early 1990s, control of I. Magnin passed to Macy's which shut it down after more than 100 years in business.

In 1969 Cyril Magnin sold his firm to the Hawaii-based conglomerate AMFAC. Despite expanding to twenty-four Joseph Magnin (and seven Gucci stores), AMFAC lacked the Magnin family's talent for merchandising. In September 1984, Joseph Magnin filed for bankruptcy and was liquidated.

Meier & Frank:[384] Twenty-four-year-old Aaron Meier immigrated from Ellerstadt, Bavaria, in 1855 to work in his brothers' Downieville, California, store. Two years later, he moved to the small village of Portland, Oregon, then with a population of only 1,000, to open his own store. By 1863 he had saved enough to return to Germany and marry Jeannette ("Shannet") Hirsch. Once in Portland, and over the next sixty-two years until she died in 1925, Shannet became a driving force behind the store's success. She carefully vetted her prospective son-in-law, Sigmund Frank, when Aaron brought him home from a San Francisco buying trip. After the marriage, the store was renamed Meier & Frank, and on Aaron's death, in 1889, Sigmund became president. When Sigmund died in 1910, his brother-in-law, Julius Frank, took over (though, for family's sake the honorific title of president went to Julius' older brother, Abe.)

Julius proved a superb merchant, becoming prominent for his civic efforts to promote Portland. He also received accolades for using his own money to save depositors of the failing Pacific Bancorporation when, at the outset of the Great Depression, he thought it his duty as chairman to do so. He was so well thought of that, in 1931, he was elected Oregon's first Jewish governor. But when he died in 1937, his nephew, the ever-difficult Aaron, took control. Because of Aaron's imperious and vengeful style, Julius' son Jack finally led a rebellion against Aaron which ultimately led to the 1966 sale of Meier and Franks to the May Company. May Company operated and expanded the franchise to seventeen stores in Oregon, Washington, and Utah, before May was acquired by Federated in 2005. In 2006 the stores were all converted to Macy's.

The May Company Department Stores:[385] David May, a German Jewish immigrant began as a Leadville, Colorado, merchant in 1877. In 1892, with his three brothers-in-law, he acquired the Famous Clothing store in St. Louis, followed six years later by the purchase of another store in Cleveland. In 1905 May moved corporate headquarters from Leadville to St. Louis, where it remained for the next 100 years.

David May was succeeded by his son, Morton J. May, and later his grandson, Morton "Buster" David May. Named president in 1951, Buster served as chairman until 1972 and stayed on the board until 1982, a year before he died.

Taken public on the New York Stock Exchange in 1911, May Company public stock was used by three generations of family members to build the company into the nation's second largest department store chain. By 2004 May Company owned 491 stores grossing $14.4 billion a year. Among prominent stores and chains May acquired were Lord & Taylor, Famous-Barr, Foley's, Hecht's, Filene's, Kaufmann, L.S. Ayres, Meier & Frank, Robinsons, Thalheimer's Woodward & Lothrup, Strawbridge & Clothier, Goldwater's, Zion Co-operative Mercantile Institutions (ZCMI) and The Jones Store, as well as specialty stores chains After Hours Formalwear, David's Bridal, Gary's Tux Shop, Gingiss Formalwear, Modern Tuxedo, and Priscilla of Boston. Following the 2005 Federated purchase of May, most of the stores were rebranded as Macy's, and others were shuttered.

City Stores:[386] Unlike the German Jewish immigrants who created most of the department stores profiled so far, Avrum Moishe Grunfeld (who would become Albert M. Greenfield), was a first-generation Russian Jew, born in 1887 near Kiev, in the Pale of Russia. If the Strauses, Filenes, Gimbels, Sakses, Rothschilds, and others were the elite "Our Crowd" Jews, Greenfield typified everything those old-line Jews came to despise about their Eastern European brethren, most of whom arrived after 1880. Greenfield was, in words quoted by Leon Harris (of A. Harris & Company) in his classic book *Merchant Princes,* "short, ugly, brilliant, devious, and vengeful. If anyone could give anti-Semitism a good name, it would be Albert M. Greenfield." And though he is deservedly covered in this chapter, in fact his role was more that of financier than merchant. He assembled a large group of department stores and oversaw them, but the job of "running the stores" was left to others.

Greenfield immigrated as a small boy, started a real estate brokerage when he was 18, and quickly built a successful business. He married well and by the early 1920s had a large portfolio of properties and control of twenty-seven building and loan associations. He parleyed that into control of a small Philadelphia commercial bank which he took public and used to acquire nine more banks.

The crash of 1929 destroyed his company, but Greenfield had retained control of a single investment, Bankers Securities Company, which had purchased control of Lit Brothers department store and shortly after that, City Stores. At the time, City Stores controlled a number of department stores in six states. If Federated (see below) always bought the leading department store in each market, Greenfield bought whatever he could get at a bargain basement price. Eventually, Greenfield was able to acquire control of more than forty-five stores in nineteen states. Among the major acquisitions were Bonwit Teller, Tiffany's, W&J Sloane, Maison Blanc in New Orleans, Lowensteins in Memphis, and Loveman's in Birmingham. Along the way, Greenfield also acquired control of many of Philadelphia's major hotel properties.

Greenfield was a hard driving, difficult personality who tried to get the best of every deal. When he died in 1967, one person among 1,400 funeral attendees was heard to say that he came, "to make certain the son-of-a-bitch is dead." At the same time, there were accolades from Lyndon Johnson, Hubert Humphrey and leaders of Philadelphia society, as well as a moving tribute from Mildred Custin, president of Bonwit Teller who, while acknowledging Greenfield's reputation for being "difficult" noted, "...he taught me a lot and I always thought I owed him a lot. Then when he lay dying of cancer—his weight had fallen from 275 or so to ninety pounds—he called me down from New York to his home.... He handed me an envelope and said: 'I want to give you this $25,000. You did a great deal for Bonwit's and for me.'"

He was also a major benefactor to the University of Pennsylvania, was honored with the rank of Commander of the Order of Pius IX by the Pope, and was a Trustee of Temple University, and the American Heritage Foundation, among others.

Following his death, City Stores went downhill. The pieces were sold off to various buyers with some, such as Tiffany's, still prominent today. Yet in Philadelphia, his Alfred J. Greenfield, the original real estate brokerage company he started, continues in business more than 100 years after its founding.

F & R Lazarus & Company, Federated Department Stores, and Macy's Inc.:[387] Rabbi Simon Lazarus emigrated from Germany in 1830. His first store was in Cincinnati, but by 1850 he had moved to Columbus, Ohio, and, in 1851, he opened a Lazarus store there. At 1,000 square feet (20 feet by 50 feet), it was a far cry from what it would later become. Simon was an early pioneer of "one low price" (non-negotiable) pricing and was the first merchant in Columbus to anticipate that returning Civil War soldiers would not want to wait for new clothes to be custom tailored. He ordered 200 ready-to-wear men's suits and sold them out in no time. It was but one of many innovations he and succeeding generations of "Lazari" would pioneer, making them one of America's dominant retailing families over five generations, spanning more than 125 years.

When Simon died, his widow, Amelia, and sons Fred and Ralph took over and substantially expanded the small store into seven buildings covering an entire city block. On Amelia's death in 1899, the store was renamed F & R Lazarus.

Fred's sons Simon and Fred Jr. took over in 1917. Of the two, five-foot-tall Fred Jr. became the dominant figure. He would completely transform the business over his fifty years at the helm. Among other innovations, he noticed some Paris stores organized garments by size, rather than price, the standard practice of U.S. merchants at the time. His proposal was initially opposed, but in weeks it proved very popular with customers and substantially improved sales. Fred expanded to Cincinnati, acquiring Shillito's, a department store founded in 1830. Lazarus also pioneered the use of escalators and air conditioning in Lazarus department stores.

But Fred Lazarus Jr.'s most important innovation was the 1929 creation of Federated Department stores when he combined his company with Filene's and Abraham and Straus. The move converted what had been a buying cooperative—to help merchants purchase overseas merchandise—into a single organization (Federated). Two months later, Bloomingdales joined what became Cincinnati-based Federated Stores with Fred Jr. as chairman. Under his leadership, Federated began a sustained program to acquire the strongest department stores in each market. He added Burdines in Florida, Bullocks and I Magnin's in California, Goldsmiths in Memphis, Sanger Brothers and A. Harris & Company in Dallas, and others.

In 1939 Fred Jr. convinced FDR to set the Thanksgiving holiday as the fourth Thursday of November, thereby guaranteeing an extended Christmas holiday shopping season.

In 1967 he was succeeded as chairman and CEO by his son, Ralph, who continued building the chain. By the time Fred Jr. died in 1973, Federated was the largest department store chain in the world. Its $5 billion of annual sales was twice as large as Dayton Hudson, May Company, Allied Stores, Carter Hawley Hale, Macy's, Marshall Field, Associated Dry Goods, or Garfields. Only Sears, with sales of $17 billion, was larger.

Ralph Lazarus led Federated until 1981 when he was succeeded by Howard Goldfeder of Bloomingdale's. And while not in the CEO slot, other Lazarus family members continued to work at Federated until 2002 (Robert Lazarus Jr. was Assistant to Ron Klein, chairman of Federated's Rich's/Lazarus/Goldsmith division).

In 1988 Federated was bought out in a botched takeover by Canadian-based Campeau, which had earlier (1986) acquired Allied Stores. By 1990 the debt associated with Campeau's overreaching led to Federated's (and Allied's) bankruptcy. Federated emerged from the bankruptcy in 1992 without Campeau, but with all of what had been the Allied department stores. Two years later, Federated took over Macy's—which in 1992 had also filed for bankruptcy. In 2005, the industry consolidation continued with Federated acquiring the May Company—while divesting some its stores to resolve various anti-trust issues. Shortly thereafter, in 2006, Federated decided to cease operating the large number of legacy names (brands) it had acquired. Only the Macy's and Bloomingdales names were to be retained. As part of that shift, in 2007 shareholders approved changing the parent company name from Federated to Macy's Inc.

On May 14, 2007, Charles Lazarus died. He was the last of four generations of family members to have run the Lazarus chain. Stuart Lazarus, his son, reported his father was "crushed" when the family name was replaced with Macy's. The "Lazari" were all gone.

Kohl's:[388] Max Kohl emigrated from Poland in the 1920s. In the United States, he met and married Russian Jewish immigrant Mary Hiken. In 1929, when he was 28, they opened their first grocery store on the south side of Milwaukee. Seventeen years later, they opened their first "supermarket." Over time, and with help from their three sons, Herb, Sidney, and Allen, the firm grew to forty-eight supermarkets. It was the largest grocery store chain in Wisconsin, and in 1962, the family "diversified," opening their first department store.

By 1970 sons Herb and Allen were both active in the business, with Herb serving as president and CEO. When the family sold the business to BATUS (British American Tobacco Company U.S.) in 1972, Herb and Allen stayed on—until 1979 when they left, reportedly over differences of business philosophy with BATUS.

In 1983 BATUS sold the grocery store business to A&P, which then experienced its own problems and adapted poorly to changes in the Wisconsin market. The 43 percent market share Kohl's supermarkets had under family management dropped to ten percent under A&P. The chain was shut down by A&P in 2003.

In 1986 the Kohl's department stores' management team bought out BATUS, and four years later, took Kohl's public. Kohl's management and board (apparently mostly Gentiles with some Jews) have done a superb job in the years since. At the end of 2007, Kohl's was operating 929 department stores in forty-seven states with total 2006 gross revenues of $15.5 billion.

Max Kohl died in 1981 and Mary died in 2000 (at ninety-five.). Son Herb went on to buy the Milwaukee Bucks basketball team, become one of Wisconsin's leading philanthropists—with the largest single donation ever to the University of Wisconsin ($25 million). He created the Herb Kohl Education Foundation which makes annual grants of $100,000 to 100 graduating seniors, 100 teachers, and 100 schools in Wisconsin. In 1988, he ran for the United States Senate. He won and has since been re-elected three times by ever larger margins over his Republican opponents.

To wrap up this commentary on Jewish founded or run department stores, we should mention just a couple more.

Marks & Spencer:[389] Born in Slonin, Belarus, in 1859, Michael Marks immigrated to England where he set up a market stall in 1884. Ten years later, he was joined by non-Jew Tom Spencer in co-founding Marks & Spencer. Marks ran the business as chairman until 1907. After an interim nine years under William Chapman, Michael's son, Simon, took the reins in 1916. Except for a brief World War I service interruption, Simon ran the firm for a remarkable forty-eight years until 1964. Knighted in 1944, he was honored as Lord Marks of Broughton in 1961. As CEO, Simon was followed by Israel, Edward, and Marcus Sieff, all Marks' family members by marriage. Together, family members led the firm until 1984.

Publicly traded since 1926, Marks & Spencer now grosses more than $16 billion annually from stores operating in thirty-eight countries (560 stores in the United Kingdom alone). Stuart Rose is CEO. He was recruited back to Marks & Spencer, (he worked there earlier for seventeen years), to respond to an unsolicited takeover offer from Philip Green, owner of Arcadia Group (see below). Rose was CEO of Arcadia before Green bought it, and he left shortly after Green took over.

When Green made his offer, Marks & Spencer was seen as vulnerable, bureaucratic, and slow to respond to the rapidly changing preferences of young shoppers. While Green was known to be Jewish, most sources referred to Rose as a "White Russian," whose family fled Russia during the Revolution. During the takeover attempt, however, Robert Peston, a Jewish reporter covering the story for the *Daily Telegraph*, called it "a battle of Jewish egos" (and) "the best entertainment in town." Rose rejected Green's offer and succeeded both in fending him off and in substantially rebuilding the Marks & Spencer franchise and its value. In early 2008, in recognition of his success, Rose was promoted to chairman of the board.

Arcadia and BHS:[390] In 1952 Philip Green was born in North London to a middle-class Jewish family. When he was twelve and attending boarding school, his father died. At fifteen, he dropped out of school to apprentice with an importer of shoes. He then traveled to the Far East, the United States, and Europe. By age twenty-seven, he returned to England, borrowed £20,000 and imported jeans which he resold to retailers netting him $30,000. Four years later, his second foray netted him $3 million when he bought, turned around, and then sold the Jean-Jeanie jeans franchise. Then, with partners, he bought, turned around, and three years later (1998) sold Olympus Sports, netting him $73 million. His next deal was the purchase and sale—only six months later—of Sears Group (not related to Sears in the United States). That sale made him $340 million.

After his initial unsuccessful attempt to buy Marks & Spencer in 2000, he bought floundering British Home Stores (BHS), Britain's fifth largest retail chain. Here Green returned to month after month of fifteen-hour days of detailed, demanding, and sometimes abrasive work as an operating retailer. Nothing was too small for his attention either on the buying or selling side of the business. BHS was transformed and made much more profitable. By 2007 Green had already received BHS dividends worth twice what he paid to buy the company. In 2002 he bought Arcadia, a group of retail chains, for $1.6 billion, $131 million of which was his own money. Following the purchase, Stuart Rose, who had been running Arcadia, left. At Arcadia, Green doubled operating profits by focusing on better merchandising, faster decisions, and cost cutting.

Despite his second rejection by Marks & Spencer in mid-2004, Green is still left with 2,502 retail stores and an estimated $8.6 billion net worth, ranking him fourth on the annual *Sunday London Times* list of Britain's wealthiest people. Green was knighted in 2006.

Specialty Retailers, Discounters and Apparel Stores

The Jan. 11, 2008, *Wall Street Journal* article listing major department stores (above) also listed the major discount and apparel stores and their December 2007 sales.

Discounters

Wal-Mart	$46.6 billion
Target	$ 9.3 billion
Costco	$ 7.6 billion

Apparel

TJX	$ 2.5 billion
Gap	$ 2.2 billion
Ann Taylor	$ .3 billion

Though something of an overlap, CNNMoney.com[391]provided its own list of Fortune 500 "Specialty Retailers" based on 2005 results. The ten largest included:

Home Depot	$81.5 billion
Costco Wholesale	$52.9 billion
Lowe's	$42.2 billion
Best Buy	$27.4 billion
Staples	$16.1 billion
TJX	$16.1 billion
Gap	$16.0 billion
Office Depot	$14.3 billion
Toys "R" Us	$11.2 billion
Circuit City Stores	$10.5 billion

As with department stores, at least half the companies (those in boldface) have Jewish roots or a significant history of Jewish leadership.

Profiling all the prominent specialty chains with Jewish roots is an impossible task given the space limitations of this book. Nonetheless, among the more prominent (or interesting) are:

Home Depot:[392] In retrospect, Bernard Marcus and Arthur Blank think being unfairly fired from their jobs as president and CFO of Handy Dan Stores in 1979 was a blessing. It motivated them to start Home Depot. They built a huge chain and stayed on for twenty-one years until 2000 when they had 1,123 stores and $45.7 billion in sales. That year Home Depot was one of *Fortune* magazine's "Global Most Admired Companies" and was ranked first in social responsibility in a Harris Interactive survey. Blank is now focused on the Atlanta Falcons, which he owns, and his family foundation, which has donated over $220 million to various causes. Bernard Marcus was named Georgia philanthropist of the year in 2002. He donated $200 million to fund the Georgia Aquarium—his thank-you to the state where Home Depot was founded. He also donated $3.9 million to fund anthrax research at the Centers for Disease Control, and he created the Israel Democracy Institute.

Costco/Price Clubs: [393] In 1976 Sol Price and his son, Robert, raised $2.3 million from prospective small-business customers, employees, and their own funds to start the first warehouse club featuring narrow selections of a broad range of high-quality merchandise. Costs and prices were kept low with products sold "in bulk" to "club members." By 1983 Price Club's success spawned competitors, including Wal-Mart's Sam's Clubs, Kmart's Pace, and Costco—founded in 1983 by non-Jew James D. Sinegal, a former Price Club executive vice president, and his partner, Jeffrey Brotman. In 1993, after a fair amount of Sturm und Drang, the two companies, both of which had become very large, merged, with Robert Price as chairman and Sinegal as CEO. In 1997 the name PriceCostco, was changed to Costco Wholesale. By 2006 Costco was No. 32 on the Fortune 500, generating $1.1 billion in annual profits from $60.2 billion in revenues.

TJX Companies/Zayre:[394] In 1956 Russian immigrant Jews, Max and Morris Feldberg, and Max's son Stanley planned to name their start-up discount store "Zayre Gut," meaning "very good" in Yiddish. Reportedly lacking funds to put both words on their signs, they settled for Zayre. It was one of the world's first self-service discount department stores, an idea they built into a chain of more than 1,100 stores. After Max retired, Stanley served as president and later chairman. In 1988 then President Maurice Segall announced the sale of the Zayre stores to Ames Department Stores for $200 million less than book value.

While the sale appeared to acknowledge failure, in fact, it did not. What was not sold was TJX, a subsidiary Stanley had created and which Zayre had taken public two years before. It was Ames' purchase of the Zayre stores that was a mistake. Ames later failed and the Zayre brand is gone. But TJX, on whose board Stanley served until 1996, has grown into the world's largest off-price apparel and home fashion chain. Its 2007 revenues totaled $18.6 billion from its T.J. Maxx, Marshalls, Winners, HomeSense, T.K. Maxx, HomeGoods, A.J. Wright, and Bob's Stores. Max, Morris, and Stanley were all major donors and trustees of Brandeis University, and the Feldberg Library at Dartmouth is named for the family.

Gap Stores:[395] In 1969 Donald and Doris Fisher began Gap with a single store in San Francisco. Since then their chain has grown to 3,100 Gap, Banana Republic, and Old Navy stores generating more than $16 billion in annual revenues. For many years, Gap's spectacular growth was led by CEO Mickey Drexler, son of Jewish immigrants whose father was a button and piece goods buyer. Among his actions at Gap, Drexler, now CEO of J. Crew, bought Banana Republic, founded years earlier by Mel Ziegler. Donald Fisher, a Founding board member of San Francisco's Presidio Trust, is working to build a major public gallery on Presidio grounds for his valuable collection of contemporary art. After donating a substantial sum to Princeton in 2006, Fisher Hall Dormitory was named for him. He is also a major contributor to KIPP charter schools.

Toys "R" Us: [396]In 1948 twenty-five-year-old Charles Lazarus began selling baby furniture in his father's bicycle shop. New parents bought the furniture and encouraged him to add toys. Considered by some the father of the "Category Killer" big-box concept, Lazarus built a four-store chain of "toy supermarkets" which he named Toys "R" Us in 1957. In 1966, he sold out, but by 1974 the buyers had bankrupted Toys "R" Us. Lazarus stepped back in, led a buyout, and by 1978 had the company out of bankruptcy. Over the next sixteen years he built Toys "R" Us into one of the most profitable, fastest-growing specialty retailers in the world. It spawned Kids "R" Us, in 1983 (focused on children's clothes), Babies "R" Us, in 1996 (offering everything for new parents), and other spin-offs. In 2005 a consortium of Kohlberg, Kravis & Roberts, Bain Capital, and Vornado Realty Trust took Toys "R" Us private. As described elsewhere in this book, two of those three buyers (Kohlberg and Vornado) have strong Jewish roots. Today the toy-store chain generates roughly $11 billion annually from more than 550 U.S. and 700 foreign stores.

Limited Brands:[397] In 1929 Les Wexner's mother, Bella Cabakoff Wexner, then twenty-one, was the youngest buyer at F. & R. Lazarus. Earlier, in 1912, she and her parents had emigrated from Russia to the United States. Bella and her husband, Harry, opened their own women's clothing store in 1951. Named after their son, Leslie, it became his training ground. After a few years, and a disagreement with his father, in 1963 Leslie borrowed $5,000 from an aunt to open his own store. Today Wexner heads an $11 billion retailer operating 2,900 stores including Victoria's Secret, Bath & Body Works, the White Barn Candle Co., Henri Bendel, C.O. Bigelow, and La Senza. In 1989 Wexner and his mother were the first people to donate $1 million each to the United Way. He was a major donor to the Harry Wexner Center for the Arts at Ohio State University (honoring his father), and earlier, Bella donated $3 million to build the Wexner Center for Pediatric Research at Ohio State.

Mervyns:[398] During the gold rush, Mervin Morris' great-grandparents had their own store in Columbia, California. Later, his parents owned the Morris Department Store in Delano, California. When he was twenty-nine, Mervin hired two employees to open his own "little junior department store" in San Lorenzo, California. He built Mervyns into a major chain before selling it, in 1978, to Dayton Hudson (later renamed Target). In 2004 Mervyn's was purchased from Target by a private investment group. Following the purchase, Mervyns was operating 177 stores in seven states, but began struggling in early 2008 and was forced to file for bankruptcy in July of that year after the private equity group had stripped the valuable real estate from the company, leaving only the retail chain leasing space it could not afford. Mervin Morris, no longer active in the business, who serves on the board of the U.S. Holocaust Museum, which he helped finance, the Boys & Girls Clubs of America, the Jewish Home for the Aged, and Mount Zion hospital visited the corporate headquarters one last time on October 23, 2008. Seventy workers, many of whom worked for him when he owned the company, gave him a standing ovation. He walked out in tears. Emily Thornton's *Business Week's* story about Mervin Morris and the Mervyn's failure was aptly titled "What Have You Done to My Company?"

Barneys New York:[399] In 1923 Barney Pressman started a cut-rate clothier in New York. He was a superb, if shameless, promoter. His son, Fred, wanted to upgrade the business and clientele by shifting to luxury clothing. All went well until the third-generation Pressman brothers overextended the business, moving into expensive "uptown" Madison Avenue quarters and opening new stores around the United States and overseas, including Tokyo. It ended in a Shakespearean tragedy involving multiple acrimonious lawsuits between the two brothers and their two sisters, plus two divorces, and the 1996 bankruptcy of Barneys.

The company emerged from the bankruptcy in 1999, a slimmer publicly traded retailer of men's, women's, and children's apparel, accessories, and items for the home. In 2004 Jones Apparel bought Barneys for $400 million and, in September 2007, sold it to Dubai-owned investment firm Istithmar PJSC for $942 million. At the time, Barneys New York had thirty-eight stores in the Barneys (nine), Barneys Outlet (thirteen) and Barneys CO-OP (sixteen) operations.

Men's Warehouse:[400] In early 1973, a few years out of Washington University, George Zimmer got into a fight with his father. Robert Zimmer owned a coat factory and George sold coats for his father's business out of his Buick. When a customer promised to place a large order later if he could return some unsold coats, Robert said, "No!" and George said, "Yes!" George took the coats back, but his father was right. No "large order" ever materialized. Nonetheless, later that year, his father staked him $300,000 to open George's first Men's Warehouse store in Houston. Thirty-five years later, Zimmer runs a $1.9 billion per year retail chain of 1,269 stores.

Burlington Coat Factory:[401] Born in 1927 to a Russian Jewish immigrant father and a Jewish American mother, Monroe Milstein and his wife, Henrietta, started Burlington as a coat factory and outlet store in 1972. Henrietta helped finance the business with savings from her salary as a teacher and librarian. Thirteen years later, they had a publicly traded, New York Stock Exchange company. In 2006 Bain Capital bought out the Milsteins (owners of 62 percent of the company's stock) and the public shareholders for $2.1 billion. In 2004 Burlington grossed $2.8 billion from 360 stores in forty-two states. Under Milstein, Burlington was lauded for its charitable donations to the United Way, the Leukemia and Lymphoma Society, and the YMCA located near Burlington's headquarters in Burlington, New Jersey

Jones Apparel Group:[402] In 1970 Sydney Kimmel started Jones Apparel as a division of W.R. Grace. Five years later, he and a partner bought it from Grace and proceeded to build a $4 billion revenue designer, wholesaler, and retailer of such brands as Nine West, Evan-Picone, Bandolino, Gloria Vanderbilt, Jones New York, and others. Jones operates more than 400 retail outlets. This does not count Barneys New York which was sold in 2007, netting a $542 million gain for Jones Apparel. Kimmel has been a major philanthropist committing more than $495 million to a wide range of causes including Cancer Centers at Memorial Sloan-Kettering, Johns Hopkins, Thomas Jefferson University, and in San Diego. He was also lead donor to the Kimmel Center for Performing Arts in Philadelphia and a major donor to the U.S. Holocaust Museum and the National Museum of Jewish History.

Ross Stores:[403] Ross Dress for Less was a tiny six-store operation in 1982 when Mervin Morris joined with a group of investors to bring in experienced retailer and venture capitalist Stuart Moldaw, and his partner, non-Jew Don Rowlett. They proceeded to buy out and then build what has since become a $5.5 billion revenue chain of 771 Ross Dress for Less and twenty-six dd's Discount stores.

Lillian Vernon:[404] Just before World War II, Lillian Vernon (née Menasche) and her family fled from Leipzig, Germany, where Lillian was born. An early catalog entrepreneur, she started Lillian Vernon in 1951 to "to help pay the bills and keep busy while awaiting the birth of her first child." She built it into a $260 million a year catalog business. In 2003 she sold it to an investment firm that had planned to substantially expand its Internet and television home-shopping presence. The company passed through several buyers with none able to successfully execute the strategy and keep costs in line. Marc Leder and Roger Krause's Sun Capital Partners, a private equity firm specializing in retail turnarounds, put Lillian Vernon in bankruptcy in February 2008.

Loehmann's:[405] In 1921 Frieda Loehmann began by buying overstocks to sell in her first New York store. In Loehmann's famous "Back Room," designer tags were discretely "obliterated, but not quite cut off." Between 1921 and 1962 when Frieda died, Loehmann's approach, selling high-quality designer fashions at 30 to 65 percent off, built Loehmann's into the largest "off-price" women's apparel retailer of its era. Shortly after Frieda's death, the company was taken public. It then went through a series of private buyers and public offerings before its 1999 bankruptcy. In 2006, Istithmar, the Dubai state-owned investment firm that bought Barneys New York, also bought Loehmann's. They now operate a fifty-five store, sixteen-state chain.

Petrie Stores:[406] In 1932 Milton Petrie, son of a Russian Jewish immigrant, created what became a huge 1,700-store, forty-nine-state chain of women's clothing stores operating under such names as Petrie, Marianne's, Jean Nicole, Winkelman's, and others. Petrie Stores also owned a 23 percent stake in Charles Lazarus' Toys "R" Us. Milton and his wife, Carroll, were huge benefactors of numerous charities across a broad spectrum of giving, including Memorial Sloan-Kettering, the Metropolitan Museum of Art, and needy individuals, such as the family of fallen police officer Anthony Venditti, who was killed by mobsters. When he died in 1994, Milton Petrie left no one capable of running the business. Times had changed, and in 1995 Petrie's filed for bankruptcy. Unlike what happens in most bankruptcies, however, Petrie's shareholders ultimately came out well. Over the next eleven years, they received more than $100 million in cash and thirty-three million shares of Toys "R" Us stock. The total payout to shareholders probably approached $1 billion.

Sharper Image:[407] Richard Thalheimer's great-grandparents were German Jewish immigrants who, in the 1850s, operated a Little Rock, Arkansas, livery stable. His father's family later developed a statewide chain of department stores that they merged into Dillard's. While in law school, Richard began an office supply business he named Sharper Image—for the quality of copier paper he was selling. In 1977 Thalheimer found a shock-resistant watch for joggers, which he marketed with great success. Next it was a cordless phone. For thirty years, his remarkable talent for finding, developing, and marketing high-tech gadgets was successful. It made him wealthy and famous. By 2006, Sharper Image reached annual sales of more than $650 million.

In the end, problems with his Ionic Breeze air purifier brought it all down. In May

2007, Thalheimer sold the last 20 percent of his Sharper Image stock to Sun Capital. (See Lillian Vernon above.) Despite their efforts to turn it around, in early 2008, after a disappointing 2007 holiday season, Sun placed Sharper Image into Chapter 11 bankruptcy. Thalheimer has gone on to start an Internet-based retailer, Richardsolo.com, to market similar items. The Sharper Image buyer hopes to revive the Sharper Image brand name on products to be marketed using infomercials, catalogs and the Internet.

Brentano's:[408] In 1852 twenty-four-year-old Austrian Jewish immigrant, August Brentano, founded his newsstand in Manhattan. August and his three nephews (he was a lifelong bachelor) built the newsstand into an international boutique bookseller with stores in Paris, Chicago, San Francisco, Boston, and Washington, D.C. For three generations it was a family business (albeit owned for some of those years by an absentee non-family member). For a time it was the world's largest bookstore chain and the publisher of such authors as George Bernard Shaw. In 1985 Walden Books bought the company and later merged it into Borders. But, in the mid-1990s Brentano's emerged once more as an independent company with stores around the United States. Tragically, however, Brentano's beautiful Fifth Avenue flagship store failed after Barnes and Noble opened a megastore nearby and siphoned off its customer base.

E. J. Korvette (later Korvette's):[409] An apocryphal story has it that E. J. Korvette stood for "eight Jewish Korean War veterans." It is not true. Eugene Ferkauf and Joe Zwillenberg were World War II vets who started the company in 1948, three years before the Korean War began. E.J. Korvette was a pioneer discount department store. It was one of the very first to use a membership format allowing it to avoid "suggested retail pricing" provisions of the Robinson-Patman Act that prohibited price discounting. Korvette's was the model for later twentieth century discount chains such as Costco. At its peak, Korvette's had fifty-eight stores in eight states. It thrived into the 1960s, began to lose ground in the 1970s, and was closed in 1980.

Ritz Camera, Brooks Camera, and Wolf Camera:[410] Benjamin Ritz started a portrait studio on Atlantic City's boardwalk in 1918, occasionally selling photographic equipment on the side. Later he expanded to New York City and Philadelphia. In 1936, his younger brother, Edward, joined him, opening a store in Washington, D.C., and adding a photo-finishing service. In the late 1960s, Edward brought his nephew, Chuck Wolf, into the business. A few years later when Edward's son, David, appeared likely to become president, Wolf traded his Ritz Camera stock for nine stores in Atlanta and Charlotte. He renamed them Wolf Camera stores. By 1978, David Ritz, then president of Ritz Cameras, was aggressively adding stores and buying out competitors. Among others, he bought Brooks Camera, a twenty-one store chain founded by Julius Bloch, a German Jew who fled that country in 1936 after the owner of the camera store where he worked forewarned him of Hitler's plans. Meanwhile, Wolf added photo finishing and, like his cousin David, quickly built new stores and made numerous acquisitions.

Throughout the 1990s, the cousins pushed each other in a heated competition.

They became the two largest U.S. camera store chains. Then Wolf stumbled. He acquired Eastman Kodak's Fox Photo chain of 449 film labs leaving him with 790 stores, only twenty fewer than Ritz. But there was too much debt, too many expensive leases, and not enough revenue. After shuttering 300 stores, he took Wolf Camera into bankruptcy and then sold out to David.

Today the combined privately owned business has 900 stores in thirty-nine states. David and other investors have also set up Ritz Interactive, a sister e-commerce business allied with Amazon.com. Though its figures are private, several years ago Ritz Camera's annual sales were estimated at $1.4 billion, making it the largest company of its kind. Meanwhile David has diversified. He also operates Boater's World Marine Centers, with 125 stores selling boating supplies.

Television Retailing (Home Shopping)

Its early roots are in "demonstration selling" at shows and fairs. Later, in the 1950s and 1960s, televised sales pitches (infomercials) were shown on non-prime-time television featuring such products as Veg-O-Matic. With the advent of cable and satellite channels, home shopping emerged as a major retailing force. Again, Jews were pioneers.

Ronco:[411] Ron Popeil wasn't the first "pitchman" in the United States, not even the first in his family. But he was the best, defeating family members and anyone else who thought they could outsell him head to head.

Popeil's grandparents, Isidor and Mary Popeil, emigrated from Poland. Isidor worked in the garment district, but Mary's family included "pitchmen" initially selling goods on New Jersey's Asbury Park boardwalk. Ron's father, Samuel, began by filling in for his uncle, Nathan Morris, doing kitchen appliance demonstrations in Macy's. Samuel proved not only an excellent salesman, but also a talented inventor. He created many of the devices he later sold.

A far cry from a warm, loving father, Samuel nonetheless gave his teenage son an opportunity to hawk some of his merchandise in the 1950s. In no time, Ron was pulling down $1,000 a week, this at a time when the average U.S. salary was $500 a month. Like his father, Ron proved a gifted inventor, creating new kitchenware items as well as pitching them. The two Popeils created the Showtime Rotisserie, the Electric Food Dehydrator, Veg-O-Matic, Dial-O-Matic, Mince-O-Matic, the Popeil Pocket Fisherman, the GLH hair system, and many other consumer products.

Ron Popeil also merits distinction as the first person to use television to sell products requiring demonstration and an aggressive sales pitch to close the sale. His success is legendary. He sold merchandise worth more than $1 billion on television, including a QVC stint in 2000, memorialized in a *New Yorker* article, when, in his first hour on the air, he sold $1 million of merchandise. In 2005, seventy-one–year-old Popeil sold his company for $55 million. Two years later, perhaps once more proving how vital he was, Ronco was bankrupt. The buyers could reproduce neither his genius for new inventions nor his unique television selling skills.

QVC:[412] In 1986 Joseph Segel started QVC (an acronym for "Quality, Value, Convenience"). A serial entrepreneur, Segel founded seventeen other companies before QVC (and five after). Among his smart entrepreneurial moves, Segal brought in Ralph Roberts of Comcast (see above) as a founding shareholder. In 1992 Barry Diller, fascinated by what he called "the fastest link between action and reaction I've ever seen," bought 3 percent of QVC for $25 million. When Segal retired in 1993, Diller became QVC's chairman. He stayed only two years. In 1995, the QVC board turned down Diller's proposed acquisition of CBS, and Diller resigned. Comcast then increased its ownership to 57 percent and assumed management responsibility. They kept QVC under their wing until 2003, when they sold their stake in the $4.4 billion revenue, 11,000-employee company to John Malone's (not Jewish) Liberty Media for $7.9 billion. By 2006 QVC's revenues climbed to $7.1 billion with operating income of $1.1 billion. That year the channel was broadcast on networks reaching ninety-one million U.S. and seventy-six million European homes

Home Shopping Network (HSN):[413] Gentile Lowell (Bud) Paxson was the principal founder of Home Shopping Network. It began as a fluke in 1977 when a Clearwater, Florida, radio advertiser could not pay his bill. The Paxson-controlled station took 112 electric can openers in payment and decided to sell them over the air. They sold quickly. By 1981 a Tampa, Florida, TV station was airing Paxson's television selling program and by 1985 a twenty-four-hour nationwide cable channel had been launched. The next year, Home Shopping Network went public. But in the early 1990s, it languished until Barry Diller, fresh from his QVC stint, bought control in 1995 and took over as chairman. HSN grew dramatically as part of Diller's Interactive Corporation (IAC), profiled in Chapter 23, and in 2008, Diller spun it off as a $3 billion a year publicly traded retailer.

Chapter 20

Jewelry, Apparel, and Cosmetics

"As a boy, they used to make us stand at attention and salute the statue of Lenin...I'd curse him and the other Communists under my breath. They sent my grandfather to Siberia. They wouldn't let us keep the Sabbath—we had to go to school on Saturday's. Just being Jewish was dangerous."

—Lev Leviev,
The New York Times,
September 16, 2007

Lev Leviev and the Soviet Jews[414]

He was born in Soviet Tashkent, Uzbekistan, in July 1956. Only three years had passed since Stalin's death and the end of the "Doctor's Plot." In his last months, Stalin had accused Jewish doctors of attempting to poison the Soviet leadership, and following a show trial, Stalin planned a pogrom and the exile of all Soviet Jews to Siberia.

Lev Leviev spent his first fifteen years in Tashkent, before his prominent Jewish family was allowed to leave for Israel in 1971. His father, Avner, was an underground rabbi. While Tashkent was mostly Muslim, the threat to Jews was not intolerant Islam, but Stalin's ever more paranoid attitude about Jews, particularly after the 1947-48 creation of Israel. Many of Stalin's anti-Semitic policies survived his death.

Yuri Slezkine's *The Jewish Century* chronicles the Soviet Jewish experience. Before the turn of the twentieth century, more than 5.2 million of Europe's 8.7 million Jews lived in the Russian Pale. Between 1880 and 1924, roughly 2 million of them left for the United States. Another 200,000 went to England and 75,000 immigrated to Palestine. All were fleeing the pogroms and Russian tsarist policies which encouraged them to leave, convert, or starve. Ironically, nearly all of those who chose to stay and remained in Poland or western Ukraine were later decimated, not by the Russians but by the Nazi Holocaust.

Pre-Revolutionary tsarist restrictions resulted in only a very small number of mostly urban Jews living within Russia proper (outside the Pale). In 1897 this Russian Jewish population was estimated at 315,000, many of them illegal. Moscow's Jewish population was estimated at 9,000 in 1910. St Petersburg had 21,000. Despite their small numbers—and as detailed repeatedly in this book—they were disproportionately accomplished. In 1886, when Jews were less than 0.4 percent of the seventy million Russians living outside the Pale, 14.5 percent of university students were Jews as were 10.9 percent of Russian gymnasium students. In 1889, of 264 apprentice lawyers in St. Petersburg, 104 were Jews. In 1913, when Jews were 2 percent of the St. Petersburg population, 17 percent of the doctors and 52 percent of the dentists were Jewish. Jascha Heifetz, Chaim Soutine, Marc Chagall, and Boris Pasternak (whose father, Leonid Pasternak, was a prominent painter and professor at the Moscow School of Painting, Sculpture and Architecture, and whose mother, Rosa Kaufman, was a concert pianist) are but a few of the many prominent Jewish artists of the times. In short, though small in numbers and severely repressed, Jews were disproportionate high achievers even in tsarist times.

With the creation of the Soviet Union, the attraction of Jews to the United States and Palestine was matched by the appeal of Soviet Communism. Tsarist restrictions were gone and Communism promised equality for all. It was to be a "utopian" society. For many Jews of the Pale, dispirited and disillusioned by the long history of Jewish persecution, false messiahs, and recent pogroms, as well as for Jews rebelling against the religion of their fathers, the atheistic and egalitarian appeal of Communism was essentially that of a new "religion." Many Jews became secular party members. Large numbers of Jews, not already living in the Ukraine or Belarus (Byelorussia)—two countries incorporated into the Soviet Union—moved there or to Russia to become Soviet citizens. Still others, who remained Orthodox Jews, found practicing Judaism in secret a small price to pay for life in a country that generally did not discriminate against them. At the end of the Russian Revolution, Jews were just one of the Soviet Union's 182 "nationalities."

The 1926 a Soviet census counted 2.6 million Jews (1.8 percent) in a country of 150 million people (roughly the same percentage as in today's United States). Unlike the United States, however, Soviet identification documents identified them as Jews. That was their nationality, albeit a nationality without a nation. And the Communists were incredibly bureaucratic at keeping records. The names and the statistics were catalogued in huge files.

Lenin had a Jewish grandmother—though some believe he did not know it, suggesting it was only discovered by his sister after his death. It is well known that Jews were disproportionately represented among early Bolshevik leaders. Trotsky was of Jewish descent, as were three of the seven Politburo members who led the October Revolution (Trotsky, Zinoviev, and Sokolnikov). At the July 1917 Sixth (Bolshevik) Party Congress, 16 percent of the congress was Jewish, as was 24 percent of the Central Committee. A huge body of data demonstrates the disproportionate role of Jews at senior levels in early Soviet Communism.

Less well known is the astonishing later rise of Soviet Jews to disproportionate levels of achievement in nearly every walk of Soviet society. Quoting from Slezkine:

"In 1939 in Leningrad, Jews made up 69.4 percent of all dentists; 58.6 percent of all pharmacists; 45 percent of all defense lawyers; 38.6 percent of all doctors; 34.7 percent of all legal consultants; 31.3 percent of all writers, journalists, and editors; 24.6 percent of all musicians; 18.5 percent of all librarians; 18.4 percent of all scientists and university professors; 11.7 percent of all artists; and 11.6 percent of all actors and directors. In Moscow, the numbers were very similar.... At the First Congress of Soviet Writers in 1934, Jews made up 19.4 percent of all delegates .... In the OGPU, the secret police successor to the Cheka, Jews were 15.5 percent of the leading officials and four of the eight members of the Collegium Secretariat which ran the OGPU."

This is not to say Jews did not suffer from terrorism under Lenin and Stalin, nor that they did not suffer disproportionately. When caught practicing Judaism, the price could be very high indeed. But the same fate was typical for those practicing Christianity or Islam. And those in the upper reaches of Soviet society were all disproportionately victimized and terrorized, particularly by Stalinism. Those closest to Stalin or with the greatest power were always at greatest risk. Because Jews were disproportionately represented among senior government officials, writers, leaders, artists, and other groups targeted by Stalin's paranoia, and State sponsored terrorism, Jews appear to have suffered proportionate to their representation in those reaches of society, but not just because they were Jews.

The beginning of the end of Soviet egalitarian treatment for Jews commenced with the August 1939 Ribbentrop Pact between Stalin and Hitler. Stalin could hardly make peace with Hitler (and divide Poland and the Baltic states) without everyone within and outside the Soviet state realizing his new ally was history's most prominent anti-Semite. Crystal Night happened in 1938. Nazi concentration camps already existed. Those Jews who could leave Germany were getting out. The decimation of Polish Jewry began within weeks of the pact. After the signing, Stalin ordered Molotov to "get rid of the Jews" from the External Affairs Commissariat. Equally important, Soviet Jews knew a pact had been reached with the devil.

Nonetheless, when Hitler invaded the Soviet Union in June of 1941, Stalin's needs and those of the world's Jews were immediately realigned. Jews in Soviet and Allied uniforms fought bravely and aggressively against the Germans.

And at the end of the war, Jews and non-Jews alike were appalled by what they learned of the Holocaust. Jews worldwide regained or heightened their sense of Jewish identity from the loss of 6 million of their brethren. For Soviet Jews, many were pulled back to an identity they had foresworn and thought they had left behind.

But what most dramatically altered the Soviet/Jewish rapprochement was the creation of Israel. Ironically, Stalin had supported it and done so more readily than the United States. But once established, and perhaps worsened by Stalin's advancing age and growing paranoia, Jews were no longer seen as a "nation-less nationality." Stalin had trusted them because they seemingly had no divided loyalty—to their religion, their people, or their own country. They were Soviet Communists and loyal only to that ideology and country. Now they had their own homeland. They were prospective traitors.

In 1948 Solomon Mikhoels, the Jewish chairman of the Anti-Fascist Committee, died in a questionable accident. His death was followed by mass arrests of important Jews. In 1952, Stalin ordered the execution of thirteen prominent Jewish intellectuals, including writers, actors and poets. This same mentality gave rise to the Doctors' Plot (Stalin's delusion that Jewish Doctors were scheming to poison the Soviet leadership). Soviet policy targeted Jews, and Jews realized they could no longer trust Soviet society to treat them as equals. The romantic utopian notion of Soviet Communism was dead.

Anti-Israel and anti-Semitic policies survived Stalin's death. And with that, Jews began to immigrate to the West and Palestine. The 1974 Jackson-Vanik Amendment put U.S. policy squarely behind the right of Jews to leave the Soviet Union, and with the fall of the Berlin Wall, and of Communism, the stream became a torrent. Over 1 million Russian Jews left for Israel. Though figures range widely, as of 2001, Jews in the former Soviet Union were reckoned to total only 462,000. (Chabad, the Hasidic sect to which Lev Leviev belongs, claims the numbers are much higher with 1 million Jews still in Russia.) Indisputable, in any case, is the fact that there was a massive exodus of Jews from the Soviet Union between 1948 and 2001.

In 1971, after a seven-year wait, the Leviev family left the Soviet Union for Israel. In addition to serving as an underground rabbi, Lev's father was a successful textile merchant and collector of Persian carpets. Before the family's exit, he converted his accumulated wealth into what he believed was $1 million of raw diamonds to smuggle out of Soviet Uzbekistan. In Israel the diamonds fetched only $200,000, supposedly because of their inferior quality. The family believed they were cheated by those controlling the diamond trade and fifteen year old Lev vowed to right that wrong.

His father enrolled him in an Israeli yeshiva, but after a short time Lev quit to begin his career. As he told a *New York Times Magazine* writer, since age six he felt "destined to be a millionaire." Perhaps that perception and his need to redeem the family fortune helps explain the incredible drive Leviev has shown since.

Through family friends, he was apprenticed as a diamond cutter. He quickly determined that he was gifted, with a talent for understanding the nature of the stones he was cutting. Not satisfied to learn the single task for which he apprenticed, he ignored industry practice and paid his fellow workers to show him how to perform the other ten "secret" steps in diamond cutting.

After mandatory military service, he began as a diamond polisher and in 1977 opened his own diamond-cutting factory. Later, after a boom in diamond prices lured many small diamond processors to buy and hold large diamond inventories on credit, the ensuing bust in diamond prices wiped them out. Leviev eschewed leverage. For him, the bust became an opportunity to buy out twelve failed operators. By 1986, with $23 million of annual export sales, thirty-year-old Leviev was named Israel's Exporter of the Year. He was invited to become one of only 100 De Beers' "sightholders." It was a distinction allowing him to buy "lots" of uncut diamonds directly from the company. Sightholders were an exclusive group through which De

Beers then controlled 80 to 90 percent of the world's diamond sales. De Beers, in turn, was run by the Oppenheimer family, which took control shortly after World War I. (See their story below.)

While Leviev appreciated the recognition and practical benefits of being a sightholder, he formed an intense dislike for the controlling behavior of the cartel. If one did not buy the allocated De Beers diamonds sight unseen, the sightholder lost the right to purchase from De Beers. Over the next eight years, Leviev's sales grew more than ten-fold to $250 million by 1994.

But the event that changed his life was the failure of the Soviet Union. In 1989 Gorbachev's Ministry of Energy asked Leviev to help set up a diamond cutting factory. Like Leviev, the Russians were grating at the De Beers' monopoly and wanted to loosen its grip by processing Russian diamonds in Russia without going through De Beers. They thought (and later Leviev confirmed) that De Beers was taking advantage of them.

Leviev's father cautioned his son against going back to Russia. Because of that concern, Leviev, who had been raised a Lubavitcher Hassidic Jew, flew to New York to ask rebbe Menachem Mendel Schneerson for advice. Schneerson blessed the trip. He told Leviev, "Go. Go to Russia and do business, but don't forget to help the Jews. Remember your family tradition."

Leviev's initial efforts in Russia led to a joint venture between Alrosa, Russia's diamond mining and selling entity, and Leviev, which ended De Beers' exclusive relationship to market Russian diamonds. Some Russian stones would be sold to Russian cutters, polishers, and marketers. As part of that arrangement, Leviev became a partner in Ruis, Russia's oldest jewelry factory. He invested his own money to update the business with state-of-the-art computer-driven laser technology, and he substantially expanded its labor force. Still later, Leviev acquired 100 percent of the Ruis stock. By 2003 Ruis was grossing $140 million per year while employing 2,000 Russians. A few years later, Leviev also bought control of a Russian diamond mine.

For a time, rumors circulated that Leviev had also helped Russia sell its hoard of diamonds when the country had economic difficulties in the mid-1990s. He denies it. What is clear is that Leviev developed superb relations with important Russians and was trusted by the Russian power structure. In 1992, he planned to use his own money to build a Jewish school in St. Petersburg. The mayor hesitated, but his deputy did not. Vladimir Putin gave Leviev the go-ahead. They remain friends to this day. Later, when Putin wanted to meet with Ariel Sharon, it was Leviev who made the arrangements.

By 1995 De Beers had had enough of Leviev's efforts in Russia, which damaged their market control. They booted him as a sightholder.

In the mid-1990s, Leviev's Russian connections introduced him to Angola's president, José Eduardo Dos Santos, a Russian ally who had studied engineering in the U.S.S.R. Angola was under attack by Jonas Savimbi's Unita rebels who had grabbed some of Angola's diamond mines and the waterways in which diamonds were found. Unita was flooding the market with $1.2 billion of Angolan "blood diamonds" annually. To retain market control and keep prices high, De Beers was buying the blood diamonds. When the United Nations slapped sanctions on blood diamonds, De Beers closed down its operation. Meanwhile Leviev had suggested Dos

Santos form a company to serve as the exclusive buyer (and reseller) of all Angolan diamonds. Angola Selling Corp. (Ascorp) was formed with 50 percent Angolan government ownership and the balance held essentially 25 percent each by Omega Diamonds of Antwerp, Belgium, and Leviev. As Unita failed and Santos retook control of its mines and waterways, Angola's diamond tax revenues climbed from $10 million in 1998 to more than $60 million in 2003.

In 1996, when Alrosa, the Russian government entity, could not come up with cash, Leviev paid $60 million to buy 16 percent of Catoca, Angola's largest diamond mine. In the years since, Leviev and a Brazilian partner have taken an even larger position with Leviev now holding the majority. He also set up a diamond processing factory in Luanda.

Next Leviev went to Namibia, investing $30 million to buy 37 percent of Namibian Minerals Corp (Namco). In 2004, as part of that deal, he set up a diamond polishing factory, something others had told the Namibian government was impossible. When his partners refused to provide capital to pay off $50 million of Namco debt and make needed repairs to Namco equipment, Leviev forced Namco into bankruptcy. He then acquired 100 percent control for a reported $3 million and he invested $47 million to make the required improvements. His polishing factory employs 500 Namibians. De Beers had been unwilling to set up the factory, and they suffered as Leviev's relationship with Namibia strengthened.

After Leviev successfully built his facilities and relationships in Namibia, he offered to build a factory in Botswana. Over the years, he has built diamond factories in the Ukraine, Armenia, India, and other countries.

In 1996 Leviev began to diversify. For $400 million, he bought control (75 percent) of Africa Israel Investments (AFI) from Israel's Bank Leumi. Today publicly traded AFI is a holding company with a market value of roughly $5 billion. Among its holdings and those of its subsidiaries and affiliates are: AFI Development, the largest property developer/owner in Russia; Alon Israel Oil company, Israel's largest fuel company; Dany Cebus Ltd., Israel's largest construction company; Dorgas, and Dor Energy which operate gas stations and convenience stores in Israel; Alon Gas which owns 1,700 Fina brand gas stations and more than 200 7-11 convenience stores in the southwestern United States; Africa Israel Hotels, Israel's largest hotel chain with 2,500 rooms in ten hotels; Packer Plada, Israel's leading steel company; and Israel Plus, a Russian-language television station in Israel. African Israel also develops and owns property in Holland, the Czech Republic, Serbia, Romania, Bulgaria, the Philippines, Canada, and Israel and it plans to expand to India, China, Poland, Latvia, Slovakia and Hungary. In the United States, Africa Israel owns the former *New York Times* building and other major properties totaling more than 900 million square feet in New York, Miami, Las Vegas, Los Angeles, San Francisco, Phoenix, and North and South Carolina. The JP Morgan building, purchased in 2002 for an estimated $100 million, was sold in 2007 for $325 million. None of this counts Leviev's diamond and gold mining interests in Russia, Israel, Angola, Namibia, Kazakhstan, the Ukraine, Armenia, India, and other countries. In 2007 Forbes estimated his net worth at $4.5 billion. Others place it between $6 and $8 billion.

Leviev never forgot his promise to rebbe Schneerson. A September 2007 *New York Times Magazine* feature story on Leviev written by Zev Chafets estimated

Leviev's philanthropic giving at $50 million per year. As noted above, his first meeting with St. Petersburg's deputy mayor Vladimir Putin in 1992 arose from Leviev's plan to open the city's first new Jewish school in fifty years. In 2000 President Putin was guest of honor at the opening of the Moscow Jewish Community Center, which Leviev helped finance. Most saw Putin's attendance as a goodwill gesture toward Leviev, as well as toward Russia's Jews.

Also behind Putin's attendance is the remarkable story of how, with assistance from Russian Oligarch Roman Abromovich, Leviev arranged for an Italian-born Lubavitcher rabbi, Berel Lazar, to be recognized by Putin as Russia's chief rabbi. It was a confluence of interest. Lazar's predecessor, Rabbi Adolf Shayevich, had backed a prominent Putin critic and Russian oligarch, Vladimir Gusinsky. After Lazar was elected chief rabbi by his Russian Lubavitcher peers, he reportedly received a Russian passport in record time. Next, he was recognized by Putin as head of the Russian Jewish community. On the day of Lazar's election, Gusinsky was jailed, and a few days later, exiled from Russia. Shayevich, Gusinsky's supporter was immediately persona non grata within the Kremlin. An Italian Lubavitcher had become the chief spokesman for the Russian Jews. (Ironically, Lazar was later induced to lobby the United States to overturn Jackson-Vanik, the law which had facilitated the emigration of so many Russian Jews during the late Soviet era.)

Among other pictures on Leviev's office desk is Putin's. Zev Chafets' *New York Times Magazine* story went on to note Leviev's underwriting of "Jewish day schools, synagogues, orphanages, social centers, and soup kitchens in more than 500 communities" and his subsidy to "an army of some 10,000 Jewish functionaries from Ukraine to Azerbaijan, including 300 rabbis." Natan Sharansky, a prominent former Soviet dissident and Israeli political leader is quoted saying, "When it comes to contributing to the Jewish people, Lev Leviev is in a class by himself."

In 2003 Leviev restored Kiev's only remaining synagogue after the Nazis had converted it to an armory, and the Communists used it as a cinema. When Azerbaijan threatened to close all religious schools over fear that Islamic madrassas would inflame its youth, Leviev single-handedly convinced President Heydar Aliyev to keep the Jewish school in Baku open. In 1999 Leviev convinced Narsultan Nazarbayev, then president of Kazakhstan, to open a Jewish school in that country. In December 2001, he convinced then Ukrainian president, Leonid Kuchma, to return twelve buildings that belonged to the Jewish community. In 2002 he introduced the Birthright Israel program into Russia and spent $1 million to pay for young Russian Jews to visit Israel. In 2003 he set up a school in Dresden, Germany, to educate secular immigrant Jews about Judaism. His Ohr Avner Foundation (named for his father) has created more than sixty Jewish schools and summer camps. When told of concern that Bukharan Jewish children were being poorly educated in New York's public schools, Leviev established a private school in Elmhurst and has since paid annual tuition for 800 students at roughly $18,000 each.

A guiding principle for Leviev is reintroducing Judaism to Jews who became (or were forced to become) secular during the Soviet era. The Jewish Telegraph Agency quotes him: "When you have Jews who have been under Soviet conquest for seventy years, who had everything erased—their religion, their nationality—I think the most important thing is education." "My dream is that every Jew will know he's a Jew and that every Jew can get the things connected to Judaism that he wasn't able to receive in the last eighty years." In short Leviev intends to overcome the secular atheistic religion of Soviet Communism. In that sense, he has triumphed over Lenin and Stalin.

In producing and selling diamonds and jewelry, Jews have played the leading role for a very long time. In part, this arose from their history of persecution. Diamonds and jewelry are a compact store of wealth. Unlike real estate, a family business, or a certificate of stock ownership that may or may not be negotiable at a moment's notice, diamonds and jewelry can be carried or quickly sold if anti-Semitic fervor necessitates quick relocation.

Further, as internationally recognized commodities of great value, gems and precious metals were and are tradable among dispersed Jewish merchants all over the world, where historical ties and shared religion and culture facilitate trust. And because Islam and early Christianity prohibited adherents from charging interest on loans, while Jews generally could earn interest, some Jews became lenders. In that role, they often required collateral, sometimes in the form of precious metals or gems. If one was to know the value of the collateral, knowledge about precious metals or gems and their marketability was critical.

Edward Jay Epstein's book, *The Diamond Invention*, notes, "For a thousand years, diamonds had been almost entirely a Jewish business."

De Beers:[415] The Oppenheimer family has controlled De Beers for approximately eighty of its more than 125 years. It is the world's largest diamond miner, producing about 40 percent of the world's gem diamonds. Its trading company, DTC, sorts, values, and sells about half of the world's annual supply of rough diamonds.

De Beers was created by non-Jew Cecil Rhodes in 1880. Earlier, Rhodes had made a fortune providing pumps to miners, often taking mine shares in payment. After consolidating his holdings into De Beers, Rhodes engineered the takeover of the Kimberley Central Mine, the other major African diamond mining company, controlled until then by Barney Barnato (née Barney Isaacs). By 1890 Rhodes' De Beers ownership position gave him control of 95 percent of the world's diamond production.

In 1902, when he was only forty-eight, Rhodes died. He was single, wealthy, and he left the bulk of his estate to establish the Rhodes Scholarship.

After 1893 all De Beers' diamonds were sold to a London syndicate of ten Jewish buyers, the forerunner of what is today called the "Central Selling Organization." They, in turn, owned shares in De Beers. An apprentice in the London syndicate, Ernest Oppenheimer, moved to Africa in 1902. During World War I, he created Anglo American Corporation as a vehicle to help German gold mine owners combine their interests and, with his involvement, reduce the risk of British expropriation. Over time, Oppenheimer gained control of Anglo American, and through it he acquired the Namibian diamond properties that became Consolidated Diamond Mines. De Beers badly wanted Consolidated, and Oppenheimer/Anglo American sold it to them in 1919. In the process, he accepted De Beers stock in exchange for

Consolidated. Anglo American, (and thus Oppenheimer) became De Beers' controlling shareholder.

Now in its third generation, Ernest's grandson, Nicky F. Oppenheimer, a graduate of Harrow and Oxford, and a member of a Johannesburg Anglican church, now heads the family business. His son, fourth-generation Jonathan, is next in line.

De Beers was taken private in 2001. Today 15 percent of it is owned by the government of Botswana. Its other two shareholders are Central Holdings Group, the Oppenheimer family holding company which has 40 percent, and Anglo American PLC, the publicly traded minerals company which owns 45 percent. Because the Oppenheimer family also owns approximately 7 percent of Anglo American, they control De Beers. In 2007 De Beers grossed $6.8 billion netting $483 million.

Nicky Oppenheimer may still have a small edge on Lev Leviev. A 2007 *Forbes* listing which estimated Leviev's fortune at $4.5 billion, put Oppenheimer's at $5.2 billion. Both estimates, however, are most likely understated.

Diamond and Jewelry Retailing

Two of the three largest jewelry store operators were created by Jewish families. Of the three, only Tiffany & Co., the second largest by sales volume, was not.

Zales:[416] Jewelry's third largest retail chain was started by Morris and William Zale with the 1924 opening of their Wichita Falls, Texas, store. Today, after going public in 1957, being taken private again in a 1986 leveraged buyout and then going through an early 1990s bankruptcy, Zales is once more public. It is headed by Neil Goldberg and grosses $2.4 billion annually from 2,200 stores that trade under such names as Zales, Gordon's Jewelers, Peoples Jewelers, Mappins Jewelers, and Piercing Pagoda. Until early 2008, when they sold it, Zales also owned Bailey, Banks and Biddle.

Signet Group Plc:[417] The world's largest jewelry retail chain (by sales volume) is Signet. It began in 1957 as a family business operating a small number of Ratner's stores. In 1966 second-generation scion Gerald Ratner joined the family business and by 1982 was CEO. In 1984 he embarked on a six-year string of acquisitions that turned Ratner's into the world's largest jewelry chain. Among his acquisitions were Terry's (U.K.) 1984, H. Samuels (U.K.) 1986, Ernest Jones (U.K.) 1987, Westhall (U.S.) 1987, Sterling (U.S.) 1987, Osterman's (U.S.) 1988, Time Ltd. (Jersey) 1988, Stephens Jewelers Ltd. (U.K.) 1988, Zales Ltd. (U.K.) 1988, Weisfield's (U.S.) 1989, and Kays (U.S.) 1990.

Then, having built the world's largest jewelry chain, Ratner gave an unfortunate speech in which, as an aside, he intended to make a joke about the quality of two products he did not like in the H. Samuels stores. The joke backfired. It was picked up by the press, customers stayed away, and the company's public value took a substantial pounding. Gerald Ratner left in 1992. Only one significant acquisition has been made in the years since he left and in 1993, the corporate name was changed to Signet. Today Signet grosses $3.6 billion annually from nearly 2,000 stores operating under the Kays, Jared The Galleria of Jewelry, H. Samuel, Ernest Jones, Leslie Davis, and various other regional names.

Among the smaller chains and stores not acquired by Signet or Zales are three that caught the eye of legendary Gentile investor Warren Buffett.

Borsheim's:[418] Louis Borsheim opened his Omaha, Nebraska, store in 1870. While little is known of his background, his legacy is an immense 62,500-square-foot jewelry store, one of the nation's largest. It was chronicled in a 2001 *New York Times* column by Maureen Dowd, noting Hillary Clinton's "bridal registry" listing at Borsheim's. The list identified gifts Hillary hoped to receive for the Washington, D.C. home she would occupy after leaving the White House.

Louis Friedman and his son, Ike, bought the business in 1947. In part, Ike's talent as a merchant is what attracted Warren Buffett to buy Borsheim's in 1989. Six years earlier, Buffett had purchased 90 percent of Rose Blumkin's Nebraska Furniture Mart. Rose was Friedman's aunt, and Omaha is not a large city. Buffett knew the family and he knew their character. It contributed not only to his decision to buy Borsheim's, but also to his aphorism, still in use by Borsheim's, "If you don't know jewelry, know your jeweler."

Helzberg Diamond:[419] Morris Helzberg opened the first Helzberg jewelry store in 1915. When he fell sick, his fourteen-year-old son, Barnett, took over until Barnett's older brother, Gilbert, returned from World War I. Together, they built a chain of stores before passing the baton to twenty-nine-year-old Barnett Jr. in 1963. He, in turn, recruited CEO Jeffrey W. Comment (not Jewish) in 1987, and in 1995, Barnett Jr. sold the chain to Berkshire Hathaway. Today Helzberg Diamond operates 270 stores under an apparently non-Jewish CEO, Marvin Beasley.

Ben Bridge:[420] In 1912 Polish émigré Samuel Silverman set up shop in Seattle, Washington, as "a combination watchmaker, jeweler, and optician." The store did well, but when he became ill in 1927, he decided to move to California. He sold the business to his son-in-law, Ben Bridge (Bryczkowski), a 1906 Polish émigré who had married his daughter, Sally. Ben operated the business for twenty-eight years before turning it over to his sons Herb and Bob in 1955. They met the challenge to downtown Seattle merchants arising from the growth of suburbs and malls by expanding Ben Bridge into today's chain of seventy-eight stores in twelve states. In 2000 Berkshire Hathaway bought the business. As he has done so often, Warren Buffett left existing management in place. Herb and Bob Bridge are co-chairmen and their sons, Ed and Jon, run the business.

It has remained a family operation for nearly 100 years, during which the Bridges have built a long record of civic involvement. Herb Bridge, who earned the sobriquet "Mr. Downtown," has been lauded for his efforts on behalf of Seattle and the homeless as well as his chairmanship of the United Way. When asked, he explained it was "tzedakah," his duty, his obligation to justice. More recently, Jon's wife, Bobbe Bridge, resigned her post as a Washington State Supreme Court Justice to take over as head of the new $10 million MacArthur Foundation funded Center for Children and Youth Justice.

Apparel[421]

Today names such as: Ralph Lauren, Calvin Klein, Donna Karan, and Liz Claiborne are synonymous with high-fashion apparel and, in the case of Lauren and others, a franchise extending well beyond garments to a wide range of merchandise capitalizing on Lauren and Polo-like images of sophisticated luxury.

The story goes back well more than 100 years. Economist Thomas Sowell's book *Ethnic America,* and this book's previous chapter on retailing, explained that many Jews, particularly German Jews in nineteenth-century America, were peddlers. It was dry-goods merchandising that drew Levi Strauss to the gold fields of California. Once there, he saw even greater opportunity in Levis, a product he and his partner created to meet the demand for durable work pants for California and Nevada miners.

In the late 1800s, roughly half the emigrant Jews from Russia and Poland brought tailoring skills to the United States. They arrived as Isaac M. Singer was introducing the first practical sewing machine, a machine that could produce garments on a massive, and relatively inexpensive scale. Until the late 1800s, most clothing purchased in the United States had been custom-made for the buyer or produced at home by a family member.

In only a few years, the largely "homemade" or "tailor-made" approach to producing clothing was transformed into today's "ready-to-wear" apparel industry. It was Jews who pioneered and pursued the opportunity—often with German Jews as the owners and Eastern European Jews as factory workers. In Sowell's words, "By 1885, there were 241 garment factories in New York City, 234 of which were owned by Jews." In fact, so successful were Jews in developing the market for ready-to-wear clothing that, according to Sowell, by 1890 half the Jews working in American industry were employed in the garment industry.

Among prominent Jewish apparel and footwear entrepreneurs are those described below.

Levi Strauss:[422] Levi (Loeb) Strauss was born in Buttenheim, Bavaria on February 26, 1829. Eighteen years later, in 1847, he immigrated to the United States to join his brothers in a New York dry-goods business. By 1853 he had moved to San Francisco and the gold rush. There, as a dry-goods merchant, he made canvas pants (later blue dyed denim) as part of his dry-goods line. In 1872 Jacob Davis, who became his partner, conceived the idea of using rivets to secure the pants pockets, and together Strauss and Davis shared the patent (See Chapter 4 – "Invention"). Single when he died, Strauss left millions to Jewish and non-Jewish charities, and his nephews took the reins.

At its February 2008 annual stockholders' meeting, chairman Robert Haas, the fifth-generation family member to run the company over its 153 years, reported Levi Strauss & Co. annual revenues of $4.4 billion. At that same meeting he stepped down as chairman, turning the job over to non-Jew Gary Rogers, a Haas colleague from the days both worked as McKinsey & Co., consultants. Before taking over as Levi Strauss chairman, Rogers built Dreyers Grand into the world's largest ice cream company.

Hattie Carnegie:[423] Almost forgotten today, Hattie Carnegie (née Henrietta Kanengeiser) was fourteen years old in 1900 when she arrived in New York from Austria. The diminutive (4'9", 90-pound) Hattie began as a Macy's model and hat designer—hence the nickname "Hattie." In 1909 she set up the store that would ultimately establish her as one of the foremost women's fashion designers over her thirty-seven-year career. When she opened the store, she changed her last name to Carnegie, choosing, for good luck, the name of the wealthiest man in the United States. Her clientele included the Duchess of Windsor, Joan Crawford, and the Carmelite Sisters.

Among her charitable acts was a 1928 intervention to take to the hospital, pay the medical bills, and create a special job for her disabled model, non-Jew Lucille Ball. The impoverished Ball had fallen during a show and was diagnosed with an extremely painful form of rheumatoid arthritis. It left Ball unable to stand and model clothing. Carnegie chose to use her as a "sitting" model until she recovered. Ball celebrated Carnegie in her own biography, *Love Lucy*. In 1951 Carnegie received the Congressional Medal of Freedom for her work designing the Women's Army Corp uniform and for her other charitable and patriotic contributions. When she died in 1956, Hattie Carnegie left behind a fashion empire of 1,000 employees.

Calvin Klein:[424] In November 1942, Calvin Klein was born to Hungarian Jewish immigrants. Among his childhood memories, he recalls pleasant afternoons in his grandmother Molly's dress and alteration shop. Molly had worked for Hattie Carnegie and his mother, Flo, enjoyed sketching fashions as the three of them talked.

At age five, Klein met Barry Schwartz, who would be his close friend and then business partner over the next fifty-six years until they sold the business in 2003. Schwartz loaned Klein $10,000, and later another $25,000 to help him launch his first line of coats. When riots following the April, 4, 1968, assassination of Martin Luther King destroyed Schwartz' Harlem grocery store, the $35,000 loan became his "equity" in their thirty-five-year business partnership.

They landed their first substantial order from Bonwit Teller and were on their way. Klein built an image of clean lines and spare shapes, moved into designer jeans and later men's underwear and other accessories. Through spectacular success and occasional failures, both commercial and personal, Klein was an icon. In 1996 *Time* magazine named him one of the "25 Most Influential People," but by 2003, he felt burned out. He and Schwartz sold the business to Phillips-Van Heusen.

Ralph Lauren:[425] Ralph Lauren (née Lifshitz) was born on October 14, 1939, in the same Bronx neighborhood as Calvin Klein. His parents were Belarus immigrants, and his father was a housepainter, reportedly descended from a long line of rabbis. Lauren began his career selling sweaters at Brooks Brothers. In 1967 he opened a small store offering his own designer ties. Over the years since, he has made himself into one of the world's foremost designers promoting an image of taste, Old-World luxury and elegance. Along the way, the business almost failed more than once, but today, Lauren owns 88 percent of his publicly traded company which grossed $4.3 billion in 2007. Success landed him as No. 243 on the 2007 *Forbes* 400 list.

Anne Klein:[426] Hannah Golofski was one of the first to create elegant, casual women's clothing that could be worn to work or out for the evening. She began as a "sketcher" in 1938 when she was only fifteen years old. In 1968, with her husband, Matthew (Chip) Rubenstein, she founded her own company, Anne Klein. For the brand, she chose the last name from her first marriage to Ben Klein, and Anne, a first name she preferred to Hannah. Her superb styling and use of interchangeable clothing items that could be assembled in a variety of ways, won her a huge following. The tragedy was her 1974 death to breast cancer at age 50. The brand has continued and is still considered highly fashionable, and her company is now part of Jones Apparel Group.

Donna Karan:[427]Donna Karan was twenty-six when the 1974 death of Anne Klein resulted in her being named Klein's chief designer. She stayed on for ten years, building the Klein franchise. When she left in 1984, she received backing from Klein's financiers to set up her own company. Her distinctive line of garments was simple, including "seven essential pieces every woman should have in her closet." They could be worn "interchangeably throughout the day or evening." Later, she added the DKNY brand of modern, moderately priced garments for younger customers. For fifteen years, Karan was one of the world's top designers. The illness of her husband, Stephan Weiss, with lung cancer, ultimately coincided with the sale of the business to LMVH, the French luxury goods company, five months after his death in June 2001.

Liz Claiborne:[428] Born in 1929 to American parents living in Belgium, Liz Claiborne's family fled the Nazis ten years later. After the war, she returned to Belgium and France to study art. She won a *Harper's Bazaar* fashion design contest in 1950, and that prompted her to return to New York to start out as a model, sketcher, and design assistant at two New York firms. In 1960 she joined Joshua Logan as a chief designer. She left Logan in 1976 to set up her own company. Five years later it was public, and after five more years, and numerous entrepreneurial awards, hers was the first Fortune 500 company started by a woman. It grew phenomenally, grossing $1.2 billion in 1988, her last full year at the helm. Its growth has continued. In 2007 Liz Claiborne's revenues were $5 billion.

After she retired in 1989, Claiborne and her husband's foundation distributed millions of dollars to environmental causes. They helped fund the *Nature* series on public television and backed programs aimed at curbing domestic violence and helping women become self-sufficient.

Guess:[429] Paul, Maurice, and Armand Marciano are not names one would instantly recognize as either French or Jewish, but the three brothers grew up in Marseille as sons, grandsons and great-grandsons of rabbis. In partnership with the Nakash Brothers (see Jordache below), the three sold their first pair of Guess jeans to Bloomingdale's in 1981. Bloomingdale's thought denim jeans were a dated product but bought two dozen pairs of Marilyn 3-zip jeans as a favor. They sold out within hours. From that beginning, the Marcianos have built a publicly traded company that grosses $1.7 billion designing and marketing trendy upscale apparel and accessories. The brothers continue to own more than 40 percent of the company.

Jordache:[430] Israeli-born Joe, Ralph, and Avi Nakash used their respective first and last names to create the Jordache brand when they founded the company in 1977. They pioneered the "tight sexy" European look in jeans marketed in the United States and then expanded into a full line of denim apparel and accessories under the Jordache, Earl Jean, U.S. Polo Association, and other brand names. Jordache also manufactures denim products for companies such as Gap, Levi's, Tommy Hilfiger, Abercrombie & Fitch, and others. For a time, Jordache owned 51 percent of Guess before they sold the shares back to the Marcianos in 1989. With success, the Nakash brothers have diversified into a substantial portfolio of U.S. and Israeli real estate, aviation and food-processing businesses. Based in New York, Jordache produces and sells more than thirty million garments a year from factories in sixteen countries, and it licenses its brand to sixty companies.

Hart Schaffner & Marx/Hartmarx:[431] In 1858 brothers Harry and Max Hart emigrated from Germany. By 1872 they had their own men's clothing store on Chicago's State Street. Seven years later, their brother-in-law, Marcus Marx, joined them as an investor, and in 1889 a distant cousin, Joseph Schaffner, brought his accounting and business skills to the venture. They later adopted what would become America's foremost name in men's clothing.

Hart Schaffner & Marx was the first apparel company to do national advertising, the first to abolish contract work in the home, the first to sign a union contract, the first to offer zippered pants, and the first to guarantee colorfast garments. For most of 100 years it was also America's largest men's clothing company. But the 1990s move to casual styles took its toll. The company shuttered its retail stores. Today it remains America's largest suitmaker, and all of its garments are manufactured in the United States. Among its brands are Hickey Freeman, Burberry men's tailored clothing, Austin Reed, Tommy Hilfiger, Perry Ellis, Pierre Cardin, Jack Nicklaus, and Claiborne.

Phillips-Van Heusen:[432] In 1881 Polish Jewish emigrants Moses Phillips and his wife, Endel, began hand-making flannel shirts and selling them to Pennsylvania miners from his pushcart. By 1889 they had relocated to Manhattan's Lower East Side where their son, Isaac, would later take over the business. In 1919 Isaac met non-Jew John M. Van Heusen, a Dutch immigrant who had created a patented, comfortable, self-folding shirt collar. They formed what would later become Phillips-Van Heusen and introduced the first collar-attached dress shirts. The Phillips family ran the business while Van Heusen earned royalties. Subsequent generations of Phillips family members built the company, finally selling their last remaining shares and stepping down from the chairmanship in 1995.

They created what has become the world's largest shirt manufacturer. It owns the Calvin Klein, Van Heusen, Izod, and Arrow brands, and it licenses others such as Geoffrey Beene, Max Azaria, Chaps, Kenneth Cole New York, and Joseph Abboud.

In 1987 the company also acquired the Bass Shoe Company. Revenues in 2007 were $2.4 billion.

The family's commitment to civic philanthropy dates back to Moses Phillips. When he discovered new immigrants did not meet New York residency requirements for hospital admission, he led the effort to set up the Henry Street Clinic. It has since grown into today's Beth Israel Medical Center. In 1994 his great-grandson Lawrence, then president of Phillips-Van Heusen, donated $5 million to support the hospital while his mother added $1 million more to renovate the family-practice unit. In 1985 Lawrence also created the American Jewish World Service to provide offshore charity in South America and Africa, and under him, Phillips-Van Heusen contributed to building six schools in Guatemala where the company operated three plants.

Warnaco:[433]Linda Wachner took over this apparel company in 1986 as part of her plan to turn it around. Self-made, she had studied economics and business and worked in a variety of companies. The hostile takeover she led ended with her as Warnaco CEO, and for years she was considered superb in that role. At one point she was the only female CEO in the *Fortune* 500. Wachner and Warnaco faced tough times in 2001, partly as the result of a dispute with Calvin Klein. Wachner resigned when Warnaco entered the bankruptcy from which it emerged without her in early 2003.

Reebok/Adidas:[434] In 1979 American entrepreneur, Paul Fireman, saw some British- made running shoes at an international trade show. He negotiated rights for the North American market and began building what is today a $3.1 billion company. He ran the business himself till 1987 when he brought in a new CEO. But Reebok languished, and in 1999 Fireman returned. He got the company back on track and sold it in 2006 to Adidas for $3.8 billion. The Adidas story is similar. Almost bankrupt in the early 1990s, Robert Louis Dreyfus, scion of a legendary French Jewish family, acquired control in 1993 after having already successfully turned around Saatchi & Saatchi, the huge advertising agency, and IMS, the world's leading pharmaceutical information company. Dreyfus saved Adidas, took it public in 1996, and after eight years, with 2001 annual sales of $5.8 billion and pre-tax profits of $347 million, Dreyfus stepped down.

Timberland:[435] In the mid-1950s, Nathan Swartz, a Boston shoemaker, bought a local shoe company that mostly produced shoes for others under contract. He brought his sons into the business, and in 1960 they pioneered use of a new technology to completely waterproof boots. Their proprietary Timberland brand was launched in 1973, and following its success, the company was renamed Timberland. Today Nathan's son, Sidney, is chairman and his grandson, Jeffrey, is CEO. Timberland is a $1.4 billion revenue producer of shoes and apparel geared for those "who value the outdoors and their time in it." Among other programs directed at corporate social responsibility, the company provides employees with forty hours of annual paid leave to work in local community-service activities.

Florsheim:[436] With help from his father Sigmund, Milton Florsheim began producing high quality shoes in 1892. He pioneered "branding" shoes by putting the company name on the sole and later retailing them through Florsheim stores. For sixty-one years, it was a family-owned business until 1953, when control was sold to International Shoe company, then the world's largest shoe manufacturer. After the sale, the family stayed on to run the Florsheim subsidiary. By 1963 Florsheim represented 25 percent of International's sales and nearly 60 percent of its profits. Second-generation Harold Florsheim was named chairman of International Shoe and served from 1966 to 1969. Ultimately International Shoe went bankrupt in 1994, spun off Florsheim, and after surviving difficult times in the late 1990s, was bought, in 2002, by fifth-generation Florsheim family members who now run the company.

Dexter Shoes:[437] Harold Alfond started Dexter Shoes in 1957 using $10,000 made from a prior success with Norrwock Shoe Company. Alfond repeated his success at Dexter, this time in casual men's and women's shoes, with a particularly strong franchise in golf and bowling shoes. Warren Buffett liked the company so much he bought it in 1993, leaving Alfond with enough Berkshire Hathaway stock to place him among the *Forbes* 400. The next generation of Alfonds have once again become footwear entrepreneurs, this time by buying Etonic shoes out of the Spaulding bankruptcy.

Maidenform:[438] In 1922 Enid Bissett and Ida Rosenthal created the modern brassiere. They modified the boyish "bandeaux"-style bra, then in vogue, to create a style more complimentary to a woman's natural shape. Ida's husband added straps and by 1925, they had a manufacturing plant in Bayonne, New Jersey. A clever advertising program, "I dreamed I...[words describing some typical activity such as 'walked my dog']...in my Maidenform Bra," was a huge twenty-year marketing success building annual sales to $250 million by 1992. Maidenform remained family owned and managed for seventy-five years until 1990s problems led to a lengthy restructuring. It emerged as a public company in 2005 with Ares Management (a private equity firm) partner David Kaplan as chairman of the board.

Cosmetics[439]

For many, the modern pioneers of prestige cosmetics include Helena Rubinstein, Elizabeth Arden, Estée Lauder, Revlon, L'Oreal, and Max Factor. They are also the companies identified by Wikipedia as today's six major cosmetics businesses. Of them, four were created by Jews.

Helena Rubinstein:[440] Born in Krakow, Poland, in 1871, Helena Rubinstein immigrated to Melbourne, Australia, when she was 18. There, locals were intrigued by the "family formula" facial cream she brought with her. At 20, she set up her own shop and nine years later she expanded, first to London, four years later to Paris, and in 1912, to New York. In 1928 she sold the business to Lehman Brothers, but bought it back in 1929 for about one-fifth of her 1928 selling price. She continued building the business until she died in 1965, at age ninety-four. She left behind a foundation that to date has made grants totaling more than $100 million in support of women's education, community service, the arts, art education, and health. Today her brand is part of the French cosmetics giant L'Oreal.

Estée Lauder:[441] Josephine Esther Mentzer was born in Queens, New York, to Hungarian Jewish immigrants sometime between 1906 and 1908. (Family members dispute the voter registration records.) Influenced by a chemist uncle who created skin creams, and having learned merchandising and salesmanship in her father's hardware store, Esther began selling cosmetics to beauty salons from her home in the 1930s. Earlier, she had married Joseph H. Lauter (who changed his last name back to the original Austrian "Lauder" while she adopted the first name "Estée").

Her big break came in a small order from Saks Fifth Avenue, after which she began selling mostly to department stores. She built her cosmetics empire by producing high-quality products, selecting and carefully photographing models for print ads, providing samples to customers, and placing products in only the best stores.

Though she died in 1994, Estée Lauder remains a family business, albeit one with a non-family member now serving as chief operating officer. The Lauder family controls more than 70 percent of the voting power of the publicly traded company's stock. Her son, Leonard, is chairman; his brother Ron is chairman of the Clinique subsidiary; Leonard's son, William is CEO; and his wife, Evelyn, is a senior vice president. Ronald's oldest daughter, Aerin, is a director, and his youngest daughter, Anne, is active in management. Annual revenues total $7.5 billion.

Revlon:[442] Boston-born Charles Revson was the son of a cigar maker. He began as a dress salesman, but, in 1932, when passed over for a promotion, the twenty-six-year-old Revson partnered with his brother and a chemist, Charles Lachman, to form Revlon (Lachman was the "L" in Revlon). They created a company based on pigment, rather than dye-based fingernail polish, and within six years, the $300 start-up capital had become a multimillion dollar international company selling nail polish, lipstick, and manicure products. It was the first cosmetic company to market matching lipsticks and nail polish. After World War II, Revlon developed a full line of cosmetics and women's care products. Revson gave them exotic names and advertised heavily. He coined the now famous expression, "We don't sell products, we sell hope" and was a demanding perfectionist acknowledged to be the creative, persuasive advertiser and promoter who turned Revlon into a household name.

Fierce as the rivalries were between Rubinstein, Arden, Lauder, and Revson, it was Revson who bought Rubinstein's huge twenty-six room triplex on New York's Park Avenue when she died. He used it, as she had, to entertain famous clients and run his empire. Like Rubinstein, Revlon left behind a foundation that has disbursed well over $100 million in grants. Revson died in 1975. Today his legacy, Revlon, generates $1.4 billion of revenues and is controlled by Ronald O. Perelman.

Max Factor:[443] Max Factorowitz's father, a rabbi, could not afford a yeshiva education for his son. Instead Max was apprenticed to a pharmacist/dentist. A traveling theater troupe bought cosmetics from Max's small Moscow cosmetics and wig shop, and after they performed for Russian nobility, Max was appointed as make-up artist to the Russian royal family and the Russian Grand Opera.

In 1904, then twenty-seven years old, "Max Factor" immigrated through Ellis Island and set up a small perfume and hair products shop at the St. Louis World's Fair. Five years later, he moved to Hollywood where he opened a small cosmetics company. He quickly became the movie industry's "Makeup artist to the stars." Judy Garland, Jean Harlow, Claudette Colbert, and Joan Crawford are just a few of his famous clients, some of whom appeared for free in his advertisements. He pioneered movie makeup (earning him a 1928 Oscar), invented pancake makeup, lip gloss, false eyelashes, and numerous other products.

When he died in 1938, his son Max Jr. took over with his siblings and a brother-in-law. Over the next thirty-five years, they continued to serve the movie industry while building a major international cosmetics company. In 1973 they sold it to Norton Simon which, in 1986, sold it to Ron Perlman. Perlman made a reported $1 billion profit five years later when he, in turn, sold it to Proctor & Gamble.

In addition to Rubinstein, Lauder, Revson, and Max Factor, three more cosmetics entrepreneurs deserve mention. At age 18, **Adrien Arpel**[444] started her women's skin-care business and, over the years, she built it into a 500-salon company. **Samuel Rubin** created Fabergé Inc.,[445] the perfume and cosmetics company (not the Russian creator of the Fabergé egg), and in 1954, twenty-six-year-old hair stylist **Vidal Sassoon**[446] opened his first salon on London's Bond Street. In the 1960s he became prominent and capitalized on the notoriety by opening salons, which carried a full line of his own hair-care products, in the United Kingdom, United States and Canada.

Chapter 21

Enterprise

"Gottex was started in 1949 by Leah and Armin Gottlieb, who arrived in Tel Aviv with their two daughters.... Mr. Gottlieb had been a raincoat manufacturer in his native Budapest and set up a similar business in Israel. There was not too much rain, however, and the couple next tried baby clothes. When they made their first swimsuits, they clicked."
— The New York Times, *June 4, 1991*

A career making raincoats in Hungary was useless in Israel. And while an influx of young Jews to post-World War II Israel made baby clothes a better bet, what really "clicked" was swimsuits. Leah and Amin Gottlieb built what Bernadine Morris' *New York Times* story called, "the world's largest swimsuit manufacturer." Gottex is now part of Lev Leviev's Africa Israel Investments Inc.[447]

The achievements of Jews as entrepreneurs are dazzling—as good, perhaps even better, than their success in winning Nobel Prizes. In the high wire act of seeing or creating an opportunity, implementing a novel idea to start a new business from scratch, dealing with inevitable adversity (or taking over something that is not meeting its potential and completely changing its character for the better), the results are spectacular. Such skill is not unique to Jews, but by any measure Jews are disproportionately accomplished as entrepreneurs. Previous chapters have already told that story in high-tech start-ups, retailing, apparel, real estate, and other fields. This chapter rounds out that picture.

The *Forbes* 400

The *Forbes* 400 includes many fortunate family members whose substantial net worth arose from the work of others. In that sense, it is more a measure of wealth than accomplishment. But mostly it is a list of self-made men and women who started, substantially shaped, or turned around one or more enterprises. It is the most widely known report of its type, and recently *Forbes* began to supplement it with equivalent information about international success.

Exhibit 21a summarizes the 2007 *Forbes* 400. All 400 names are shown with the Jews highlighted. We would expect perhaps eight Jews among the 400. The actual figure is 126 (31 percent). It is a remarkable figure, up 6 percent from the 2004 *Forbes* 400 list. Akin to winning 23 percent of the Nobel Prizes, 26 percent of the Kennedy Center honors, and 37 percent of the Best Director Oscars, it shows us once more how striking and diverse the Golden Age achievements of Jews have been.

Jews have played a pioneering role in so many industries this book can only highlight some of the more notable. End notes and the Bibliography point readers to more extensive coverage elsewhere. In premium ice cream, food and beverages, weight-loss programs, toys and games, cruise ship tourism, hotels, petroleum, mining, management consulting, payroll services, and countless other areas, Jews have been the indisputable leaders who created or importantly shaped whole industries or the leading companies in those industries.

Premium Ice Cream and Ice Cream Novelties

America's major premium ice cream brands ("super-premium" in the lexicon of some) and the world's largest chain of ice cream stores were created by Jewish entrepreneurs.

Häagen-Dazs:[448] Reuben Mattus immigrated to the Bronx from Poland with his parents after World War I. He met and married Rose Vesel, whose parents were also Polish immigrants. Mattus' father established a small ice cream company and Reuben sold and distributed its products. By the late 1950s the business was being squeezed by the decline of independent corner grocery stores. America was migrating to supermarket chains and with that, large dairy-products companies were selling cheap low-quality ice cream in volume through the chains.

In 1959 Reuben Mattus decided to do precisely the opposite. He created the world's first "premium ice cream" brand. Made with egg yolks, butterfat, and cream, it was rich, dense, textured, and very tasty. At the time, Americans wrongly thought Europeans made higher quality ice cream. Mattus chose to capitalize on the misperception. He created the name, Häagen-Dazs, intending a "sort of Scandinavian sound" and he put a map of Denmark on the cap. (Rose Mattus later indicated the Danish connection arose from Reuben's respect for Denmark's protection of Jews during the Holocaust.) Mattus was the first to use round pint-size containers. Before Häagen-Dazs, ice cream was sold in rectangular cartons. Mattus reasoned that small, round pint containers, in varying colors (for the different flavors), would reinforce an image of superior quality.

In the early 1960s, his distribution was limited to New York, and marketing was mostly by word of mouth. It caught on. By the 1970s, Häagen-Dazs became the first super-premium ice cream brand distributed nationally. Its commercial success created the super-premium "category." In an appropriately foreign sequel, after selling the brand to Pillsbury in 1983, Häagen-Dazs was sold to Swiss-based Nestle in 2002.

Ben & Jerry's:[449] In 1978 Ben Cohen and Jerry Greenfield started one of the world's wackiest and most delightful companies. Friends since the seventh grade, they took a $5 ice-cream-making correspondence course from Penn State before moving to Burlington, Vermont, to set up shop in a renovated gas station. Among their numerous slightly loopy efforts they created the world's largest (27,102-pound) ice cream sundae, fed their ice cream to pigs at Stowe, Vermont, took a national tour in their modified mobile-home "cowmobile," which burned to the ground four months later outside Cleveland—"The world's largest baked Alaska." said Ben—and they conducted a national CEO search featuring a "Yo! I'm Your CEO" contest inviting 100 word essays from candidates applying for the slot. First prize was the CEO job! Second prize was a lifetime supply of ice cream. Over 22,000 applications (many of them bizarre) flooded the company's headquarters in Waterbury, Vermont.

What has always distinguished Ben & Jerry's is its constant stream of unique flavors, "Phish Food," "Cherry Garcia," "Chunky Monkey," "Willie Nelson's Country Peach Cobbler," etc. (mostly associated with rock 'n' roll and country stars), the founders' distinctive brand of hippy and liberal social activism, and Ben & Jerry's wacky, often self-deprecating humor. In the last year before its 2001 sale to Anglo-Dutch giant, Unilever, Ben & Jerry's had sales of $237 million. It was purchased for $326 million, a rather nice bump up from the original $12,000 in start-up capital.

Baskin-Robbins:[450] In 1916 Irvine Robbins was born in Winnipeg, Manitoba, to Jewish immigrants from Russia and Poland. As a child, his family moved to Tacoma, Washington, where his father became a partner in a dairy. As a teen, Irv worked in a retail store connected with the dairy. He proved his marketing prowess early with clever signage. He changed "Three Scoops of Ice Cream, a Slice of Banana, Two Kinds of Topping," into "Super Banana Treat!" Sales of banana splits doubled.

In late 1945, when ice cream cones and sundaes were mostly dispensed from soda fountains in drugstores, Irv Robbins set up a store devoted solely to twenty-one flavors of ice cream. Three years later, his brother-in-law, Burt Baskin, joined him. They added stores—and flavors—until 1953 when, at eight stores, they decided to focus on making and distributing ice cream to licensees rather than building more stores. The eight stores were sold to their managers and, as Robbins later told *The New York Times*, "without realizing it we were in the franchise business."

"Thirty-one flavors" became the brand's signature, but when Fidel Castro tried to "one up" the United States saying Cuba's ice cream stores would soon offer forty-two flavors, Robbins responded that Baskin-Robbins already made 290 flavors. They simply featured thirty-one at a time (actually thirty-four counting vanilla, strawberry, and chocolate).

In 1967 with more than 650 Baskin-Robbins stores in operation, they sold out to United Fruit. Over the years since, Baskin-Robbins has gone through a succession of owners. Today it is part of Dunkin Brands owned by Thomas Lee, the Carlyle

Group, and Bain Capital. Its 5,800 stores serve 300 million customers a year. It is the world's largest chain of ice cream stores (and so far, it has created more than 1,000 flavors).

Dove Bar:[451] After playing eighteen holes at a Deerfield, Illinois, country club, golfers sometimes enjoyed hand-dipped ice cream bars in the men's locker room. Richard Zacharias, a member, thought the bars were delicious. In the early 1980s his brother-in-law, Ed Stolman, running a hospital company in Nashville, also owned commercial property in Franklin, Tennessee. Ed wanted to put a small ice cream soda fountain into one of his rental properties, and he mentioned the idea to his brother-in-law. Richard suggested Ed try a Dove Bar. He did and was as impressed as Richard.

The bars were made in a small room at a Chicago confectionery owned by Greeks, Leo Stefanos, and his son, Mike. Ed and Richard visited the confectionary store to explore the family's interest in distributing Dove Bars beyond Chicago. After a number of conversations, the Stefanos family agreed. A 50/50 partnership was formed. The Stefanos family owned half, while Ed, his sister "Bubbles," Richard, his brother James, and a few others shared the other half.

The partners agreed to introduce the bars at a fancy food show in Washington, D.C., (By coincidence, the same show that launched Ben & Jerry's beyond its Burlington, Vermont roots.). The partners arranged for a fancy decorated pushcart to occupy a well located booth while they passed out free hand-dipped samples to the show's attendees from silver trays. The bars were a huge hit, and a stranger approached the partners. He had pushcart vending rights in Manhattan for sixty refrigerated carts manufactured for another ice cream company that went bust. A deal was struck.

The retail launch featured a small parade in Manhattan and the release of perhaps fifty doves as part of the festivities. Sales took off and additional capital was raised to expand production and distribution facilities to meet the growing demand.

A couple of years later, and facing yet another round of fundraising to finance the growing business, Stolman, the Zacharias brothers, and the Stefanos family decided the venture would best be pursued by a marketer with deeper pockets. Their legal counsel set up a meeting with a pleasant, unshaven man wearing a leather jacket to the attorney's office. Forrest Mars Jr. introduced himself and announced he thought the Bars were superb. He had done extensive research and he wanted to buy the company. He offered a price well beyond their expectations, added a seven-year employment contract for Mike Stefanos, and an earn-out—on top of the purchase price—for the partners. The deal was struck that day and closed within two weeks. Thus was the Dove Bar opportunity identified by Jewish entrepreneurs, successfully pursued and, in 1986, sold to the Mars Corporation.

Beverages and Food

Sara Lee:[452] Her full name was Sara Lee Lubin. In 1949 she was eight years old when her father, Charlie Lubin, named his cream cheesecake and his company after her. By 1953 Sara Lee products were so popular Charlie had to come up with a special process to freeze them for distribution beyond Chicago. His was the first high-quality frozen line of baked goods, and he pioneered the use of a single container to package, cook, freeze, and distribute them. Capitalizing on the technology, by 1955 Sara Lee was distributed in forty-eight states.

Two years later Consolidated Foods created and, for three decades, run by Charlie's friend Nathan Cummings, bought Sara Lee and retained Charlie as its CEO. In the 1960s, Charlie began extensive use of television advertising. (He coined the now familiar slogan, "Nobody doesn't like Sara Lee.") His marketing prowess so established the Sara Lee brand that in 1985, Consolidated Foods changed its name to Sara Lee. (In one of those "small-world" coincidences, Richard Zacharias—see the Dove Bar above—was a close friend of Charlie's and asked his advice when the Dove Bar partnership was formed. It was Charlie who told the partners they must attend a fancy food show to test whether or not the bar would be successful.)

Over time, Consolidated/Sara Lee has continued to expand through acquisitions of numerous brands and products. Today it is a $12 billion revenue international company producing and selling an extensive line of food, household, and body-care products. It is led by a decidedly "ecumenical" board of directors and management team.

Starbucks:[453] Howard Schultz grew up poor in a tough Brooklyn public housing project. He shared a small bedroom with his siblings. Smart, he was a determined if not gifted athlete, and that earned him a football scholarship to Northern Michigan University. Upon graduation, Schultz took a sales job at Xerox, later leaving to work for a kitchenware importing company. He made a sales call on Starbucks, a tiny company selling coffee beans from four Seattle stores. He was enthralled. In 1982, he left the importing company to sign on for lower pay as Starbucks' retail sales director.

In Italy a few years later, he visited a coffee bar and conceived his notion to reshape Starbucks into a retail coffeehouse chain. But the three founders preferred to stay small, and Schultz moved on to form his own small coffeehouse chain in Seattle and Vancouver. Several years later the Starbucks founders had a change of heart. With legal help from Bill Gates Sr. (of the Seattle law firm Preston Gates), Schultz borrowed $3.8 million to buy Starbucks. From that, he built what is today the world's largest coffee-house chain. At the end of fiscal year 2008, it operated more than 16,000 coffeehouses in forty-four countries, grossed more than $10 billion in revenues and had operating earnings of more than $300 million.

The Seagram Company:[454] Born in Bessarabia in 1889, Samuel Bronfman's family immigrated to Western Canada shortly after his birth. They farmed and sold horses, firewood, and frozen fish, and may have operated a small hotel. Legend has it Sam told his father that since the hotel bar was the most profitable part of their businesses, he would pursue opportunities in distributing liquor. (Ironically, in Yiddish, "bronfn" can mean "strong spirits" or "whiskey man.")

In 1924 Sam established Distillers Corporation and four years later, he acquired then seventy-one-year old Joseph E. Seagram & Sons Ltd. Sam had a superb sense of the U.S. and Canadian liquor markets, and he insisted on top quality and strong brand names. Throughout Prohibition, he operated within Canadian and U.S. law selling large quantities of liquor to bootleggers who smuggled it into the United States. At Prohibition's end, he was in a superb position. Seagram had large inventories of aged, high-quality liquor. No one else did.

By 1965, headquartered in both Montreal and Manhattan, Seagram controlled the world's top brands. Its sales were 20 percent of United States liquor market, and it was grossing over $1 billion per year. It was Sam's daughter, Phyllis Lambert, who urged her father to commission non-Jew Mies van der Rohe to design the architectural classic, Seagram's Building on Park Avenue, which opened in 1958. Sam's sons Charles and Edgar took over Seagram when Sam passed away in 1971.

In 1966 Edgar began the family's involvement with movies, purchasing 820,000 shares of MGM which he briefly served as chairman.

In the end, with help from his brother, Charles, Edgar built Seagram into a $5.2 billion revenue company before turning it over to his son, Edgar Jr., in 1994. Edgar Jr. took Seagram on a tortured path into entertainment and a roller-coaster merger with the French conglomerate Vivendi. Initially, the move tripled the value of the Seagram stock before Vivendi crashed, destroying 80 percent of that value. In the subsequent breakup of Vivendi, Seagram's liquor properties went to Pernod Ricard, the French spirits company, and Diago, a British counterpart. Edgar Jr.'s brother, Samuel II, now operates the wine properties acquired by Diago.

Through all of this, Samuel, Edgar Sr., Charles and Samuel II, were active philanthropists and social activists. Edgar Sr. was awarded the Presidential Medal of Freedom by President Clinton. He held six honorary doctorate degrees and was awarded the Chevalier de la Legion D'Honneur by the Government of France. He has also been president of the World Jewish Restitution Organization, seeking recovery of Jewish property stolen during the Holocaust, and he was president of the World Jewish Congress.

Welch's Grape Juice:[455] Jacob Merrill Kaplan was born in Lowell, Massachusetts, in 1891, the son of a Russian Orthodox rabbi. Around the turn of the century, he moved to Latin America to work in the sugarcane fields. Soon he was helping organize the cane growers into a cooperative and by the early 1920s, he was president of Oldetyme Molasses Company.

In the mid-1920s he and his brother owned a seat on the stock exchange which they sold after the crash of 1929. Instead of stock, Jacob then invested in real estate, particularly grape-growing acreage and grape processing plants, including the Welch's operation, which he acquired in 1945. During the 1940s, he also encouraged and then sponsored the creation of the National Grape Cooperative Association, bringing growers together to better manage their farms and sell their products.

Kaplan modernized Welch's operations, pioneered frozen juice, and sponsored early television programs, such as *Howdy Doody*. In the seven years he owned Welch's, he more than tripled sales, from $8 million to $26 million. In 1952 he sold Welch's to the cooperative, and today it boasts sales of $550 million.

Much of the proceeds from his sale of Welch's went into the J.M. Kaplan Fund, which today continues under Kaplan's grandchildren, making grants from a $168 million endowment. The foundation played an active role in establishing New York's

New School, which Kaplan served as chairman for twenty years. It was also active in the restoration of Carnegie Hall and Gracie Mansion, home to New York's mayor. It has also worked to encourage and promote union democracy, human rights, and environmental preservation.

Hunt Foods:[456] Norton Simon graduated from San Francisco's Lowell High School at age sixteen. Admitted to UC Berkeley, he dropped out within six weeks, moved to Los Angeles, and when he was eighteen, set up a sheet-metal distribution company. Four years later, in 1929, he bought a bankrupt Fullerton juice bottler for $7,000, turned it around and parlayed a merger of the bottler into control of Hunt Foods. Simon focused Hunt's on tomato sauce and aggressively marketed Hunt products using recipes, full-color print ads in top women's magazines, and a consumer education program touting the "great taste" of tomato paste. He followed that up with new-product introductions and a series of mergers and acquisitions.

He built Hunt Foods into a diversified conglomerate consisting of Hunt-Wesson, Canada Dry, Avis Car Rental, McCall's Publishing Corp., Saturday Review of Literature, Max Factor, and other properties, which together represented a 1960s billion-dollar conglomerate. At the time, Hunt Foods was among the 100 largest U.S. corporations. After his 1969 resignation, Simon devoted himself to art with the same passion he showed in developing Hunt Foods. His 12,000 piece art collection, ranging from Asian art to Old Masters, with Impressionists and rare Indian art thrown in, form the core of what is now the Norton Simon Art Museum in Pasadena. California.

Weight Loss Products and Programs

If Häagen-Dazs, Sara Lee, and Frappuccinos have added to our waistline, Jewish entrepreneurs have also built companies to remove the extra inches.

Slim-Fast:[457] S. Daniel Abraham introduced Slim-Fast in 1977 as a new Thompson Medical Company product. He had purchased Thompson in 1947 for $5,000 after returning from World War II and serving a brief stint with a small drug company owned by his uncle. Abraham built Thompson from a tiny single-product company (San Cura skin ointment) into a sizable business which netted him $200 million when he sold it in 1998. But if Thompson was a "double," Slim Fast was the "home run". After his late 1950s launch of Slim-Mint gum, which supposedly quelled hunger, and 1976 introduction of Dexatrim, a daily diet pill, Abraham created and began marketing Slim-Fast. Successful, Abraham spun it off as a stand-alone company a year before he sold Thompson. Two years later, Abraham sold Slim-Fast to Unilever for $2.3 billion. The Thompson and Slim-Fast sales landed him on the Forbes 400 with an estimated $1.8 billion net worth.

The Slim-Fast sale to Unilever closed on the same day as Unilever's purchase of Ben & Jerry's. Slim-Fast sold for 3.8 times its 1999 sales of $611 million. Ben & Jerry's went for 1.4 times sales. The difference spoke to the high margins, large market share (45 percent) and rapid growth of Slim-Fast under Abraham.

Over the years, Abraham has been a huge contributor to the Democratic party, but more important to him has been his support of Birthright Israel, his founding and continuing chairmanship of the Center for Middle East Peace and Economic Cooperation—devoted to helping bring peace in the Middle East—and his support of the Mayo Clinic, among other philanthropic efforts.

Weight Watchers:[458] Overweight from childhood, thirty-eight-year-old Jean Nidetch loved cookies and was fearful she would regain the twenty pounds she lost after so much effort. She invited six overweight friends to her Queens, New York, apartment in 1961 to talk about the problem. They began meeting weekly. Two months later, the group had grown to forty women meeting to support and reinforce one another in a fashion akin to Alcoholics Anonymous. By October 1962, Nidetch had shed seventy-two pounds. Her success in taking and keeping off the pounds led to her 1963 creation of Weight Watchers. By 1968 it was operating nationwide.

After fifteen years, Nidetch sold the company to H. J. Heinz, staying on as a consultant until 1998 when she retired. Today publicly traded Weight Watchers hosts 50,000 meetings a week attended by one million people in thirty countries around the world. It grosses roughly $1.5 billion annually. Nidetch was honored by the Horatio Alger Association and named by *Ladies Home Journal* as one of "The Most Important Women in the United States." Her Jean Nidetch Foundation benefits economically disadvantaged teenagers as did her donation to create the Jean Nidetch Women's Center at the University of Nevada, Las Vegas.

NutriSystem:[459] Harold Katz founded NutriSystem in 1971. His inspiration was his mother's frequent weight gains and losses. He envisioned a combination of behavioral counseling, medical supervision, and low-calorie meals to achieve permanent weight loss. He invested $40,000, half of it borrowed, to set up two weight-loss centers designed to look like medical offices. After success with both, he decided to franchise most future outlets. That approach allowed rapid growth and sizable profits from the sale of the meals through franchisees to dieters. After early problems with low-calorie, high-protein liquid diets, Katz hired Jay Satz. He was a Pennsylvania State Department of Health Ph.D., and Katz retained him to formulate nutritionally sound prepackaged and shelf-stable meals made up of small portions of real food.

The business did extremely well, and Katz took NutriSystem public in 1981—at which point he was worth roughly $300 million. An unfortunate series of subsequent acquisitions and the ensuing fights with franchisees ultimately led to Katz' selling the business in 1986 to a group led by a CEO he recruited to end the disputes. The company then soared (to $1.2 billion in 1990 sales) before false allegations of gallstone problems led to a 1993 bankruptcy and the subsequent closing of nearly all the outlets.

It only got worse until December 2002, when non-Jew Michael Hagan took control. He terminated the remaining franchise agreements and rehired Dr. Jay Satz to reformulate the diets around the "glycemic index" (ranking carbohydrates based on their effect on blood sugar). Hagan also began direct-response Internet, QVC, and cable TV marketing featuring celebrities such as Marie Osmond, Dan Marino, and Don Shula. First-year sales under Hagan (in 2003) were only $22.6 million. But as the reformulated diets and direct-response marketing caught hold, sales soared, totaling $776 million by 2007.

Katz, a former owner of the Philadelphia 76ers basketball team, moved on to become chairman of L.A. Weight Loss Centers, reportedly operating 450 centers in the United States and Canada.

Jenny Craig:[460] In the 1970s, after selling his five Arthur Murray franchises, Sid Craig bought a stake in Body Contour Inc. and helped build it into a chain of 200 women's figure salons. While attending the opening of new salons in New Orleans, he met Genevieve "Jenny" Guidroz Bourcq. Born in 1932, she had a family history of obesity. Her mother died of an obesity related stroke at age forty-nine, and when Jenny gained forty-five pounds during pregnancy, she decided to change her life through a combination of diet and exercise. Craig hired her, later named her Body Contour's national director of operations, and in 1979, they married. In 1982 Body Contour was sold to Harold Katz' NutriSystem (see above). For Katz it was a mistake, and it led to his 1986 sale of the business. (NutriSystem franchisees took great exception to having to compete with the Body Contour salons.)

Following the 1982 Body Contour's sale to Katz, Sid and Jenny Craig moved to Melbourne, Australia, where they opened their first Jenny Craig Weight Loss Center in 1983. When their non-compete agreement expired in 1985, they expanded to the United States, opening twelve Centers in Los Angeles. Over the next few years they built a network of 621 centers, took the company public, and, in 2002, sold control to a group of private equity investors, retaining 20 percent for themselves. Five years later, Nestle bought Jenny Craig for five times the 2002 price.

Sid and Jenny Craig had a long history of active philanthropy. They donated $10 million to the Fresno State University School of Business and $10 million to the University of San Diego, $7 million of which was used to build the Jenny Craig multi-use sports pavilion. Additional money went to the Susan G. Komen Breast Cancer Foundation, San Diego Hospice, Easter Seals, United Way, educational scholarships, and various other causes. Sid Craig died in mid-2008.

Toys and Games

Lionel Trains:[461] Joshua Lionel Cowen was born in New York on Aug. 25, 1877. Shortly after the Civil War, his parents had immigrated, via England, from Suvalk, a shtetl in the Eastern Pale. With the $1,000 his father had saved from a successful business as an English hatmaker, a yeshiva education, and the family's fluency in English, the Cowens had more in common with German Jews who arrived about the same time than with the later massive wave of immigrants from the Pale. Joshua was twenty-three in 1900 when he organized his toy train company. He built Lionel Trains into the dominant producer of toy trains, ultimately acquiring both Ives and American Flyer, the other two significant toy train companies. The business peaked in the mid-1950s, after which toy cars became more popular. Cowen's grand-nephew

Roy Cohn (of McCarthy- era fame) bought the business in 1959 and proved a disaster as a businessman. Today's surviving business is controlled by Guggenheim Corporate Funding and the Estate of Marvin Davis, former chairman of Paramount, who is profiled later in this chapter. As such, Lionel retains its Jewish endowment.

Mattel Toys:[462] Though named for Harold "Matt" Matson (likely not Jewish) and Elliot Handler (hence the company's name, Matt-el), the person most responsible for creating the world's largest toy company was Elliot's wife, Ruth (Mosko) Handler. The youngest of ten children born to Polish immigrants, in 1945 she encouraged her husband to partner with Matson in making picture frames. She was the one who sold them while also handling the day-to-day administration. Picture frames were soon replaced by doll-house furniture, and the company made $30,000 on first-year sales of $100,000. By 1947 it was ukuleles. About that time, Matson sold his shares and left the business.

Each year, new toys were introduced, but in 1955 the Handlers took a huge risk. They launched their Burp Gun (an automatic cap gun) in conjunction with the exclusive (and very expensive) sponsorship of the new *Mickey Mouse Club* television program. Sales shot through the roof. A year later, while vacationing in Switzerland, Ruth Handler saw a three-dimensional adult doll. She took it home, insisting Mattel's designers create the "Barbie" doll, named for her daughter, Barbara. (Ken was named after her son). Mattel sold 351,000 Barbies in 1959, and went public the next year. Sales rocketed from $18.3 million in 1960 (when the stock was $10 per share) to $211 million in 1969. The stock peaked at $522.50 in 1971.

The Handlers ran Mattel till 1975 when new product and acquisition stumbles led to their resignations. In the 1990s, they were followed by Jill Barad, another talented, determined CEO who dramatically built sales before her failed acquisition of the Learning Company led to her 2000 resignation, after twenty years with the company. Mattel's $6 billion revenues in 2007 made it the world's largest toy company. In addition to Barbie, its operations also encompass, Hot Wheels, Tyco, American Girl, Sesame Street, Fisher Price Toys, and numerous other brands.

Hasbro:[463] In 1920 brothers Henry & Helal Hassenfeld founded their business selling textile remnants. Left with a large inventory of book-binding cloth, Henry decided to convert it to pencil boxes for students. Subsequent large orders from Woolworth and Kresge led to their diversification into pencils and school supplies. In 1923 Hassenfeld Brothers was incorporated and, in 1985, renamed Hasbro Inc.

Over the years Hasbro migrated from crayons and paint into junior doctor kits and, later, other toys and games. Over nearly ninety years and three generations of Hassenfelds, the family built the world's second largest toy company. Among their acquisitions were the major assets of Coleco, including the Cabbage Patch doll. (Coleco was the 1932 creation of Maurice Greenberg.) Included in Hasbro's huge current lineup of products and brands are: Parker Brothers, Milton Bradley, Clue, Monopoly, Scrabble, Yahtzee, Mr. Potato Head, Play-Doh, Tinkertoy, Tonka, Playskool, and many others. As of mid-2008, third-generation, Alan Hassenfeld is chairman of a $3.8 billion annual revenue business.

Hotels and Cruise Lines

Grossinger's:[464] In 1900 Asher Selig Grossinger, his wife, Malka, and their daughter, Jennie, immigrated from Galacia in what was then part of the Austro-Hungarian Empire. After business failures in New York, Grossinger moved his family to the Catskills in 1914. He intended to become a farmer. Once there Jennie's idea to rent out rooms to visitors seeking escape from New York's summer heat quickly proved more lucrative than farming. In 1919 Asher sold the original farm, purchasing 100 acres for a new hotel to be headed by Jennie with a spotless kosher kitchen to be run by Malka. It was the start of the famed Borscht Belt with the Concord, Brown, Flagler, and perhaps 300 other hotels which became the training ground for Jewish comedians such as Jerry Lewis, Mel Brooks, George Burns, Woody Allen, and many others.

Jennie's talent for running the business built Grossinger's into a huge success, serving 150,000 guests a year. The property had thirty-five buildings on its 1,200 acres, its own airstrip, golf course, and post office. In 1952 Grossinger's featured the first use of artificial snow for winter skiing. By the time Jennie died in 1972, the advent of Las Vegas, relatively inexpensive international travel, the beginnings of Atlantic City, and changing Jewish-American taste, brought hard times on the Borscht Belt hotels. Grossinger's closed in 1986 and the buildings were later demolished. In the late 1990s, the property re-emerged as a golf resort and spa.

Fairmont Hotels and Resorts:[465] Fairmont is the most "ecumenical" of major hotel chains. San Francisco's Fairmont was built by Catholic silver heiresses Tessie (Fair) Oelrichs and her sister Virginia (Fair) Vanderbilt. They named it to honor their father, Senator James G. Fair, an Irish immigrant who developed America's richest silver mine in Nevada's Comstock Lode. He left his daughters $40 million when he died in 1894. In 1902 they began construction at a site atop Nob Hill (hence the suffix, "mont"). Damaged before completion by the 1906 earthquake, it was repaired, completed, and opened for business in 1907.

Tessie, who, with Virginia, had sold the hotel just before the earthquake, repurchased it in 1908 and owned it until 1924. She sold it to D.M. Linnard who, in turn, sold it to Ben Swig in 1945. (See the Swig family profile in Chapter 18 – Real Estate.) Upon returning from World War II U.S. Naval service, Ben's son, Richard, began work as a hotel steward. By 1953 he was CEO, a job he held for the next forty-four years as he built Fairmont into a national chain of seven major luxury hotels, including New York's famed Plaza. In 1994 the Swigs sold half interest to Saudi Prince Alwaleed bin Tatal. Five years later, the prince and his partners combined the bulk of their Fairmont management company interests with those of Canadian Pacific Hotels. In 2006, Alwaleed partnered with Colony Capital, owner of Raffles Hotels and Resorts, in taking the Fairmont chain private. Today Fairmont Hotels and Resorts operates fifty-seven luxury hotels and resorts around the world with twenty more slated to open over the next several years.

Loews Hotels:[466] In 1946 twenty-three-year-old Laurence Tisch bought a 300-room summer camp at Lakewood, New Jersey. Two years later his younger brother,

Preston Robert, joined him. Together, they built what is today an eighteen-hotel luxury chain operating in the United States and Canada. The properties include the prestigious Regency Hotel in New York, the Madison in Washington, D.C., and sixteen more in Maryland, Canada, Florida, Louisiana, Arizona, Illinois, Pennsylvania, Colorado, Tennessee, and California. (Also see the Tisch profile in Chapter 16 – "Finance.")

Hyatt Hotels:[467] One day in 1957, Jay Pritzker flew into Los Angeles on a business trip. He noticed a new hotel, built by non-Jews Hyatt R. von Dehn and his partner, Jack Crouch. It was nicer—and busier—than other hotels near the L.A. airport. Almost on a whim, he decided to buy out von Dehn, and eight years later, he also bought out Crouch. Jay put his younger brother, Don, in charge and they began building a chain of hotels modeled on that first one. In 1967, they introduced the first atrium style hotel as the Hyatt Regency Atlanta. By 1969 they owned thirteen Hyatt hotels and built their first international hotel in Hong Kong. In the 1980s Hyatt began developing resort properties and, in 1989, Don's daughter, Penny Pritzker, led the creation of Hyatt Classic Residences, luxury retirement properties for seniors. In 2004 and 2005, Hyatt acquired AmeriSuites and Summerfield Suites from the Blackstone Group.

Though a minority position was sold in 2007 to Goldman Sachs Capital Partners and Madrone Capital Partners—an affiliate of Wal-Mart Stores' non-Jewish chairman, S. Robson Walton—Hyatt is still controlled by the Pritzker family. As of 2007, it is one of the world's largest premium hotel companies, operating 735 hotels and resorts in forty-four countries. (Also see the Pritzker profile in Chapter 16 – "Finance," and the Royal Caribbean comments below.)

Helmsley Hotels:[468] Harry and Leona Helmsley created what, in the 1980s, was one of the world's best-known boutique chains of luxury hotels. Harry was a prominent New York real estate owner, manager, and broker. He controlled the Empire State Building, the Flatiron Building, the Helmsley Building, and many others. And while his portfolio of office and residential properties was huge, he also owned thirty Helmsley and Harley hotels, including the prestigious Carlton House. He began acquiring residential apartment buildings in San Francisco and New York with an eye to converting them into condominiums and cooperatives.

In 1969 Leona Roberts (originally Lena Rosenthal) joined his firm to sell the converted residential units and by April 1972, they were married. When residential conversions became difficult, Leona and Harry focused instead on expanding his luxury hotel chain, featuring Leona as the demanding CEO who wanted everything to be "perfect" for their guests. The keystone property was the new Helmsley Palace in mid-town Manhattan, a 1,143-room fifty-story building just off Madison Avenue. It opened in 1981 as New York's top hotel.

The difficult times began in 1988 when Harry and Leona were indicted for tax fraud. Ultimately Harry was unable to stand trial, but Leona did, and after being convicted, she served eighteen months in jail. Disputes with partners, Harry's death in January 1997, and Leona's failing health led to the sale of more than half of the properties by the time of Leona's death in August 2007. The Helmsley Palace became the

New York Palace when a private limited partnership took over its ownership and management.

While the Leona M. and Harry B. Helmsley Charitable Trust has made substantial donations, including a $10 million 2006 grant to New York Presbyterian Hospital, a July 2, 2008, front-page story in *The New York Times,* indicated that Leona Helmsley intended that the bulk of her $5 to $8 billion estate be used for the care and welfare of dogs. At her death, five Helmsley hotels remained, four in Manhattan and one in Sarasota, Florida. (Also see the Helmsley material in Chapter 18 – Real Estate.)

Wynn Resorts and Mirage Resorts:[469] If Bugsy Siegel and his Flamingo Hotel could be said to have introduced big-time Las Vegas casino gambling to post World War II America, Steve Wynn transformed the glitzy X-rated hotel and casino scene into one featuring large first-class hotels catering to a family audience.

Wynn moved to Las Vegas in 1967. He first invested the small stake, derived from his deceased father's bingo parlors, buying a piece of the Frontier Hotel. He was subsequently bought out, reportedly for no profit, by Howard Hughes. In the process, Wynn became friends with a local banker, E. Parry Thomas, who provided invaluable help in later deals. In one, Wynn and Thomas bought an option on a piece of property Howard Hughes wanted. Then they exchanged the option with Hughes for a small parcel of land needed by Caesars Palace. When they sold that parcel to Caesars, Wynn and Thomas pocketed $1 million.

Wynn used that stake and his knowledge of management malfeasance to take control of the Golden Nugget. He quadrupled its profits the first year and later increased them by a factor of twelve. He turned that success into another, building a sister Golden Nugget in Atlantic City. A few years later he sold it, making enough to expand the Las Vegas Golden Nugget and develop the new 3,000-room Mirage Hotel. The Mirage, designed to create an impression of a South Seas paradise, started a trend, copied by Caesars Palace, MGM Grand, and Circus Circus, of behemoth family-oriented attractions built around a particular theme. Next Wynn added the successful Treasure Island Hotel. But it was his 1998 opening of the 3,000-room Bellagio that transformed the image of Las Vegas. For the first time, Las Vegas had a major resort destination, a truly high-end hotel with world-class art galleries, lavish public rooms, and first-class dining. Some consider Bellagio among the world's finest hotels. Wynn followed up Bellagio with the 1,780-room Beau Rivage in Biloxi, Mississippi.

Mirage Resorts, the public company through which Wynn had performed his magic, was bought out by Kirk Kerkorian in 2000 for $6.6 billion. Wynn used part of the $500 million he made from the sale to buy the site of the old Desert Inn and, in 2002, he created a new public company, Wynn Resorts. It has since financed a new casino on that site, the $2.7 billion Wynn Hotel, which opened in 2005, and a sister hotel, the Wynn Macau, which opened in 2006. Wynn followed those two up with Encore, a 2,500-room extension of Wynn Las Vegas, which opened in December 2008. In 2006 Time magazine listed Wynn as one of the "World's Most Influential People," and *Forbes* now ranks him 277th among the world's billionaires with $3.9 billion.

The Venetian Hotel:[470] His mother's family came from the Ukraine, his father's from Lithuania. Growing up, Sheldon Adelson's dad was a Boston cab driver. When he was twelve, Sheldon had to borrow $200 from his uncle to become a newspaper distributor. He was a college dropout and a late bloomer. He worked in a variety of jobs and businesses until 1979 when, at age forty-six, he opened his first COMDEX consumer electronics trade show. It was inspired and it proved his entrepreneurial talent. He liked to say he was "enthralled by the idea of renting convention space for twenty-five cents a foot and selling it to vendors $25 or more." The annual COMDEX trade show featured all the hot new consumer electronics products slated for introduction the following year. At its peak, 200,000 people walked the aisles to see and demonstrate the products shown by 2,200 companies in 1.2 million square feet of exhibition space. By 1989, he and his partners had decided to forego renting convention space. They bought the Sands Hotel in Las Vegas and the next year, on that site they built the largest U.S. privately owned and operated convention center. In 1995 Adelson decided to sell COMDEX. In Softbank, he found a hot Japanese Internet conglomerate that would pay him $860 million in cash. (Ultimately, it was a disaster for Softbank. COMDEX began losing money, was spun off, went through bankruptcy, and when it finally emerged from the bankruptcy in 2004, it was canceled.)

Inspired by a trip to Italy, Adelson tore down the Sands and built the Venetian. When it opened in 1999, Adelson, like Wynn, had broken all the rules. His $1.5 billion, 4,000-room resort focused on convention business, an approach that all the old-timers said would never work in Las Vegas. It did. When the holding company, Las Vegas Sands Corp., went public in December 2004, Adelson's 86 percent stake was worth $15 billion. He was the eleventh richest person in the United States. And then he "doubled down." He expanded to Asia. He currently operates two hotel casinos in Macau and has thirteen more in various stages of development. He has also expanded the Las Vegas Venetian complex to 7,200 rooms. It is the world's largest hotel.

The run-up and meltdown of the Chinese stock market, together with the 2008 credit crises, resulted in the fastest gain and loss to one individual's net worth in history. Adelson shot from a $15 billion net worth in 2005 to $34 billion by early 2007 (a gain of $1 million an hour). By mid 2008, it was back to $15 billion only to be reduced by another $4 billion by early October, 2008.

To date, Adelson has given away well more than $50 million to such causes as Birthright Israel, the M.I.S. Hebrew Academy in Las Vegas, the Miriam and Sheldon G. Adelson Medical Research Foundation, and others. As might be expected, Wynn and Adelson are fierce competitors.

Carnival Cruise Lines:[471] Ted Arison was a third-generation Israeli whose grandparents emigrated from Romania in 1882. He fought as a lieutenant colonel in Israel's 1948 War of Independence before immigrating to the United States in 1952 because he believed Israel opposed free enterprise. In 1972 he created Carnival Cruise Lines. He purchased a former Atlantic liner, *Empress of Canada* renamed it the *Mardi Gras,* and launched it. With 300 journalists aboard, it ran aground within hours of departing on its maiden voyage. Some very lean years followed that inauspicious start before Arison's vision of less formal, more relaxed cruising caught on.

In 1987 Carnival went public, providing Arison with publicly tradable stock to use for acquisitions. Carnival has since acquired Holland America Line, Seabourn Cruise Lines, Costa Cruises, Cunard P&O Princess, Princess Cruises, AIDA, Ocean Village, Iberocruceros, and Costa. Today its combined fleet includes eighty-five ships with twenty-two more on order.

After returning to Israel in 1990 (it had become decidedly less Socialist), Arison acquired control of Israel's largest bank, Bank Hapoalim, and Shikun Ufituah, Israel's largest construction firm. When he died in 1999, Arison left his son, Micky, as Carnival's chairman and his daughter, Shari, as Israel's then richest resident. With 2007 revenues of $13.5 billion, income of $2.4 billion and a market value of $29.7 billion, Carnival dwarfed the comparable hotel and cruise gaming operators profiled in this section. According to Morningstar.com, the second most valuable of the hotel and cruise gaming stocks was Adelson's Las Vegas Sands Inc. at $19.5 billion. Wynn Resorts Ltd., was fourth at $9.9 billion.

Royal Caribbean:[472] It was founded in 1969 by Norwegians, Arne Wilhelmsen and Sigurd Skaugen, Englishman Harry Larsen's Gotaas-Larsen shipping company, and American Gentile Edwin Stephan. As such, Royal Caribbean preceded Carnival by several years. Though it did not fail, the partnership sputtered while Arison's Carnival grew.

In 1988 Arne Wilhelmsen approached Jay Pritzker about buying out Gotaas Larsen and Skaugen, who had already offered their shares to Arison. Pritzker, in turn, asked Israel's largest ship owner—and shipping savvy—Samuel Ofer to participate. (Previously Pritzker had acquired businesses that owned ships and retained Ofer to manage them. A strong friendship had developed from that experience.) When the transaction closed, Wilhelmsen was the largest shareholder with 49.5 percent, but the Pritzker family owned 40.5 percent, and Samuel Ofer, 10 percent, giving Pritzker and Ofer effective control.

Pritzker, Wilhelmsen, and Ofer, working with Stephan, and Richard Fain, who soon became CEO, then built Royal Caribbean into the world's second largest cruise line with thirty-five cruise ships operating under the Royal Caribbean, Celebrity Cruises, Azamara, and CDF Croisières de France brands. In recent years the next generation of each of the major shareholder groups has taken over with Thomas Pritzker (Jay's son), Arne Alexander Wilhelmsen (Arne's son), and Eyal Ofer (Samuel's son) all now holding board seats. In 2007 Royal Caribbean's revenues were $6.4 billion.

Other Consumer Products and Services

Hartz Mountain:[473] Legend has it Willie Odenwald could only repay the loan from his twenty-six year old friend, Max Stern, with merchandise—5,000 singing canaries. Stern then cut a deal with Hamburg-American Steamship line. He paid the freight cost to ship the canaries to New York and the steamship line provided him free passage to accompany and care for the birds. Stern struggled after his 1926 New York arrival until he was able to sell the canaries to John Wanamaker's department store. Building on that first success, he repeated the trip many times over, bringing ever more canaries to the United States. By 1932 Stern was the largest U.S. importer of livestock (Odenwald eventually also immigrated and worked with Stern in the business). Max diversified into packaged bird food and an ever growing array of complementary products as he expanded his distribution to include R.H. Macy, Sears, Roebuck, F.W. Woolworth, and others.

In 1959 Max's son, Leonard, joined him. Leonard took the business far beyond its avian roots into goldfish, tropical fish, dog and cat remedies and accessories. By 1973 Hartz Mountain was the dominant U.S pet-supply company with an estimated 75 percent market share. Leonard also diversified into publishing (*Village Voice, Harmon Homes,* and weekly newspapers in major cities), commercial real estate development and management, and other endeavors. In the late 1990s, when sons Emanuel and Edward became involved in the business, the Stern family decided to focus on real estate and investments. (See Chapter 18 – Real Estate.) After more than seventy-five years, the family's legacy pet business was sold to a leveraged buyout firm and four years later, in 2004, it was bought by Sumitomo Corporation of America.

Max Stern is honored by the Stern College for Women at Yeshiva University named in recognition of his 1954 generosity in establishing the school. Leonard is similarly honored: the New York University Stern School of Business recognizes his generosity in donating $30 million to the school.

Polaroid:[474] In 1926, as a seventeen-year-old Harvard freshman, Edwin Land took a leave of absence to develop a new, inexpensive, polarizer (orienting light rays in a plane with respect to its source thus reducing glare). The inventions would later be used in photographic filters, sunglasses, and airplane windows. After a two-year return to Harvard, he left again in his senior year, to start his own lab (taking his professor with him!) By 1937 twenty-eight-year-old Land had founded Polaroid Corporation to make and market his polarizing material. In 1941 he invented a process for three-dimensional motion pictures and during World War II he used his polarizing technology to create military equipment. But it was in 1944 that an impatient question from his daughter wishing to "instantly" see a photograph, led to his 1947 introduction of the Polaroid Land camera. It produced finished photographs in sixty seconds. By 1958 Polaroid was the third largest photographic company behind Eastman Kodak and General Aniline and Film. (Also see the Land profile at the beginning of Chapter 6 – Invention.)

U.S. Healthcare:[475] Leonard Abramson drove cabs while attending Penn State and Nova University, earning degrees in pharmacology and public administration. He worked for Parke-Davis selling pharmaceuticals, but quit when he was passed over for a promotion.

In the early 1970s, he conceived of an opportunity to create one of the nation's first health maintenance organizations (HMOs). Congress had passed legislation in 1973 intending to help rein in rising health-care costs. Abramson realized he could use the legislation to create an efficient health-care network. Unlike prior HMO approaches in which patients met with a staff of medical personnel in a sterile clinic-like setting, Abramson contracted with doctors practicing in groups (Independent Practice Associations) and with hospitals. In Abramson's model, patients could select their own doctors rather than being forced to use only those in the HMO's facilities. At the same time, employers and others who paid for health care would benefit from the lower cost of HMO styled "managed care," as compared with expensive "preferred provider" plans. Abramson's initial approach, in 1975, was "nonprofit," but seven years later, he converted to a "for profit" HMO and changed its name to U.S. Healthcare.

Over the next fourteen years, he built U.S. Healthcare into one of the largest managed care organizations in the country. When he sold it to Aetna for $8.3 billion in 1996, it covered roughly one in every twelve Americans. *Forbes* indicated the sale netted him $760 million, placing him on the *Forbes* 400 for a number of years.

He and his wife subsequently donated $100 million to establish the Madlyn and Leonard Abramson Family Cancer Research Institute at the University of Pennsylvania where he is a trustee. In addition, he has served on the boards of Aetna, Johns Hopkins, Children's Hospital of Philadelphia, the Brookings Institution, the Republican Jewish Coalition, and Friends of Joe Lieberman. The Madlyn and Leonard Abramson Family Foundation also supports a center providing compassionate care for the aged and a program (EMET) intended to bring the facts about the Middle East crises to students.

Ex-Lax:[476] In 1890 Israel Matz was twenty-one when he immigrated to the United States from Kalvarija, Lithuania. Though he began as an accountant, by 1906 Matz entered the drug business founding the Ex-Lax company (now part of the Swiss pharmaceutical giant, Novartis).

For 100 years, Ex-Lax has been part of the American culture. In 2005, referring to Congressional inaction, New Orleans mayor, Ray Nagin said, "Everyone knows there's a certain amount of constipation in Washington. We need to be the Ex-Lax to bust through that."

Matz success led to his role as a patron of Hebrew literature, and philanthropist. He purchased a large tract of land in Palestine for Jews who wished to move there, supported efforts to make Hebrew a living language, and actively supported the creation of a Jewish state. Today the Hebrew University of Jerusalem is the home of the Israel Matz Institute for Research in Jewish Law, and New York University is home to the Sidney Matz Teaching Fellowship, established by Israel Matz in 1947 to honor his son who died in a plane crash. The Weizmann Institute of Science is home to the Israel Matz Chair of Organic Chemistry, and the Israel Matz Fund was established to support Hebrew writers. Indeed, one of the more eloquent memoirs of Jewish life in Lithuania, the cultural premium Jews placed on education, and the reasons they chose to immigrate to America are told in Matz's, "My Home Town, Kalvarija," which Matz wrote in 1948. It can be found at www.jewishgen.org/Yizkor/lita/lit1499.html.

Hertz:[477] Motor-vehicle leasing began when Leon C. Greenbaum created Metropolitan Distributors to lease trucks during World War I. A few years later, in 1918, twenty-two-year-old Walter Jacobs set up the first automobile rental company (His fleet consisted of a dozen Model T Fords). When he sold it to John Hertz, president of Yellow Cab and Yellow Truck, and Coach Manufacturing in 1923, the company was renamed Hertz-Rent-a-Car. Jacobs stayed on as head of operations and administration. General Motors bought the business from Hertz in 1926 and operated it until 1953 when it was first sold and then taken public in 1954. The early era of vehicle renting/leasing culminated that same year when Hertz bought Greenbaum's Metropolitan Distributors. Initially, Greenbaum, the father of vehicle leasing, served as Hertz's vice chairman. He became chairman and CEO when Jacobs retired in 1960.

In the mid-1980s, Ford Motor Company began a long period of intermittent minority/majority stock ownership. That involvement culminated in late 2005, when Ford sold Hertz to a consortium of private equity firms, which took it public once more in late 2006.

Arthur Murray Dance Studios:[478] Born in 1895 to Austro-Hungarian (Galacian) Jewish parents, Moses Teichman and his family immigrated to the United States in 1897. By 1912, seventeen-year-old Teichman was moonlighting as a dance instructor while working days as a draftsman. It was at the outbreak of World War I that Teichman became Arthur Murray, adopting a name that sounded less German. In 1920, while a student at Georgia Tech, he arranged the first "radio dance," broadcasting band music from the college campus to a group of dancers in downtown Atlanta. He tried to start a mail-order dance instruction business using a "kinetoscope" (a precursor to today's movie projectors), but it failed. His next idea did work. It was a mail-order dancing correspondence course, selling "footprints" one could place on the floor to learn various dance steps.

But his big success—in fact two successes—commenced in 1925 when he married Kathryn Kohnfelder and opened Arthur Murray Studio of Dancing in Manhattan. In 1938 he began franchising (only the second company—after A&W Root Beer—to do so). His first franchisee opened an Arthur Murray Studio in Minneapolis. Always an intensive advertiser and promoter, Arthur Murray wrote his best-selling book, *How to Become a Good Dancer,* in 1938, and in 1950, created a network television program, *The Arthur Murray Dance Party,* hosted by Kathryn Murray. It was a smash. It ran until 1961 and generated substantial interest in learning how to dance.

By 1964, when he sold the business to a group of franchisees and stepped down as president, there were 356 franchised studios in fifty countries. He then moved to Hawaii where he ran an investment fund for his family and friends and lived till he was ninety-six. At this writing, approximately 190 franchisees continue to operate as part of Arthur Murray International.

Simplicity Pattern Company:[479] In 1927 Joseph Shapiro and his son, James (both Russian immigrants), founded what would become the world's largest sewing pattern company. It is a quintessential entrepreneurial story. At the time, sewing patterns were only sold through magazines, such as McCall's. Customers were forced to buy the magazine and then send off for a pattern from the limited selection featured in the publication. The pattern might cost a quarter.

Simplicity, instead, distributed patterns directly to stores such as Woolworth's, which also sold fabric and sewing supplies. The patterns were marketed in open boxes through which one could browse to find the particular pattern one liked. The pattern might cost a dime. At its peak in the early 1970s, Simplicity sold 150 million patterns a year, had 4,000 employees, owned its own paper mill and printing operations, was public, and was considered a so-called Nifty Fifty stock—a high-quality company whose stock you could buy and hold forever. Joseph was considered a superb entrepreneur and James a marketing genius.

After James and his brother Robert retired in 1976, Simplicity went downhill. Women were flooding the workforce rather than staying home and sewing. The company had $100 million in cash, and financiers, such as Victor Posner, Charles Hurwitz, Carl Icahn, and others raided the cash and the Pension Fund's surplus reserves. Today Simplicity still exists, but as part of Conso, a small private company marketing the patterns with Conso's trim, ribbons, quilting, and related products.

Fisher Radio:[480] In 1906 Avery Fisher was born in Brooklyn, New York, to immigrants from Kiev. His father had a large record collection and everyone in the family, including his five siblings, played a musical instrument. Graduating from NYU in 1929, his first job was at an ad agency serving publishers. Three years later, he left the agency to work for G.P. Putnam's Sons publishers. A year after that, he joined the publisher Dodd, Mead & Company, where he worked for ten years (until 1943) as a graphic artist and book designer. (Among the books he designed was Winston Churchill's *A History of the English-Speaking Peoples.*) Designing books was his career and he enjoyed it so much that he moonlighted as a book designer years after leaving Dodd, Mead to work in his own companies.

An avid amateur violinist, in the mid-1930s he became interested in the reproduction of high-quality sound. He began building his own high-end radios and before long, friends asked him to make radios for them—this in his spare time. In 1937 while still at Dodd Mead, he started the Philharmonic Radio Company. It made major improvements in the design of speakers, tuners, and amplifiers. But not until 1943 did he leave Dodd, Mead to work full time at his own company.

He sold it in 1945 to start a new company, Fisher Radio, focused on audio components for advanced stereo and hi-fi systems. He recruited some of Europe's finest engineers and with them created new technology that he incorporated into the company's unique products. In 1956 he invented the first transistorized amplifier and in 1958, the first stereo-radio phonograph combination. Later he improved AM-FM stereo tuner design and the sensitivity and power of his radio's components.

He sold Fisher Radio in 1969 for $31 million. Within four years, he had donated $10.5 million to help rescue the acoustically flawed Philharmonic Hall. In his honor, it was renamed Avery Fisher Hall at New York's Lincoln Center. In addition, he endowed the Avery Fisher Listening Room at NYU and grant programs for musicians. He also served as a board member of the New York Philharmonic and the Chamber Music Society of Lincoln Center. In 2000 he was posthumously inducted in the inaugural group of the Consumer Electronics Hall of Fame.

H&R Block:[481] Born in 1922, Henry Bloch was the second of three sons of a prominent Kansas City attorney. Henry returned from World War II a decorated B-17 navigator, having flown thirty-one combat missions over Germany. At Harvard Business School, he read the transcript of Professor Sumner Schlicter's speech about the growing need for professional services (such as accounting and staffing) to support small businesses. It inspired him to partner with his older brother, Leon, in establishing an accounting firm to serve small businesses in Kansas City. It grew slowly from its inception in 1946 to a staff of only twelve by 1955. Along the way, Leon left to pursue a law degree and Henry's younger brother, Richard, replaced him.

The twelve-hour days and seven-day work week were exhausting and in 1955, before tax season, Henry and Richard decided to stop offering tax preparation services. An advertising agency client talked them out of it. He offered, instead, to create a newspaper ad that they reluctantly agreed to run twice. The response was simply astonishing. Henry and Richard had not known the ad would appear just as the IRS was ending its free tax preparation service in Kansas City. Demand was enormous. The IRS had also slated a shut down of free tax preparation services in New York the following year. In 1956 the renamed H&R Block ("Block" to avoid confusion about pronunciation of their last name) opened seven offices there. By 1962 the company was publicly traded, and in 1978, one of every nine United States tax returns was prepared by H&R Block. They were the world's largest tax preparation and financial services company.

Richard retired in 1982 after surviving both lung and colon cancer, and Henry retired in 2000. By 2007 H&R Block's revenues were $6.8 billion as it served twenty-two million customers. The brothers' philanthropy is legendary. Richard, who died in 2004, established the National Cancer Hotline, which his R.A. Bloch Foundation continues to fund. He also created the R.A. Bloch Cancer Support Center and the Cancer Management Center at the University of Missouri-Kansas City. The latter provides free second opinions and treatment advice to Kansas City citizens. It serves as the model for at least 125 other centers nationwide. For his unceasing efforts, the National Cancer Center Institute named its Bethesda, Maryland, building after him. Henry's philanthropy led to the creation of the Henry W. Bloch School of Business and Public Administration at the University of Missouri–Kansas City, and he continues to fund scholarships and endow faculty chairs. The Bloch Building at Kansas City's Nelson-Atkins Museum of Art arose from another of his gifts.

Jacoby & Meyers:[482] Len Jacoby and Stephen Meyers revolutionized the practice and marketing of consumer law when they launched their law firm in 1972. Both felt the average person was poorly served by high-priced, intimidating, and inefficient law firms. They conceived the idea of a national firm of neighborhood offices networked with legal specialists in fields such as bankruptcy, divorce, estate planning, and other fields. Television advertising would attract clients and efficient operations and large volumes would allow low fees. They offered a $15 consultation fee and posted prices for other legal services in their ads.

It was all highly controversial, and seemingly violated bar association codes of legal ethics. Their 1972 press conference announcing the planned opening of their first office led to a California State Bar action and lawsuit. Five years later, the California Supreme Court ruled in their favor. Meanwhile their opening had led to the creation of a counterpart firm in Arizona. Its advertising led to a federal case. One month after the Jacoby and Meyers decision in the California case, the U.S. Supreme Court found in favor of the Arizona firm. That decision freed not only lawyers, but also doctors, accountants, and other professionals to "inform the public of their services through paid commercial advertising."

In one sense, the court victories were pyrrhic. They spawned huge numbers of competitors. The overhead of 150 offices and national advertising was unworkable against thousands of lawyers advertising their services locally. Jacoby and Meyers transitioned to a smaller firm specializing in personal injury. In what some might call sweet irony, the partners became embroiled in their own legal wrangle in 1995. Jacoby sued Meyers and another partner, Gail Koff. Tragically, just months after an amicable settlement was reached, Meyers was killed in a traffic accident. As of 2007, the firm survives, and its Web site links Jacoby and Koff, with Jacoby heading a Southern California practice while Koff practices in New York.

Oil, Gas, and Petrochemicals

Not an industry typically associated with Jews, they have nonetheless played a vital role in petroleum and petrochemicals.

Shell Oil Company:[483] In 1897 Marcus Samuel, and his brother Samuel, founded the Shell Transport and Trading Company in London. Its roots trace to 1833 when their father began a curio shop in London's East End featuring imported seashells and boxes encrusted with shells. The brothers inherited the business in 1870.

Eight years later they began trading kerosene, then the world's top-selling fuel oil. In 1890 they saw an opportunity to export Russian kerosene to the Far East and placed an order to build eight uniquely designed oil tankers, the first ever to ply the Suez. That routing gave them a substantial cost advantage over Standard Oil. Soon, they were also competing with a new (1890) Dutch company (later named Royal Dutch Petroleum Company), which had developed an oil field in Sumatra. By 1907 the two companies merged with Marcus Samuel as chairman. Royal Dutch Shell then expanded by exploring, developing, and acquiring oil reserves in Rumania, Russia, Egypt, Venezuela, and later the United States. It also built refineries and international marketing facilities, including gas stations. Shell became one of the world's foremost oil companies with an internationally known brand name and logo.

Marcus was knighted by the British Crown in 1898, served as lord mayor of London, and was made the first Viscount Bearsted of Maidstone in 1925. During World War I, Samuel refused to accept any inflationary price increases for Shell Oil, holding prices to pre-war levels. He also expanded Shell into petrochemicals, and by 1917 was providing England with 80 percent of the explosives used by its army and navy.

Amoco (American Oil Company—now part of BP):[484] Sixteen-year-old Louis

Blaustein emigrated from Lithuania in 1883. He began work in a Philadelphia tannery but was soon peddling merchandise to farmers in eastern Pennsylvania. In 1891 he opened a small wholesale grocery business in Baltimore and sold kerosene (coal oil). Observing problems with leakage from the wooden barrels used to transport the oil, Blaustein invented the galvanized tank (later to be used in tank trucks and railroad tank cars) and he sold kerosene from his horse-drawn tank wagon.

In 1910, with his eighteen year old son, Jacob, he started the American Oil Company, dispensing gasoline from his tank wagon. The Blausteins were pioneer innovators. Quoting from Jacob Blaustein's *New York Times* obituary, "Thanks to numerous innovations, the company (Amoco) grew quickly. It opened the first drive-in gasoline station in the United States on Cathedral Street in Baltimore. Then, a gasoline pump complete with meter reading in dollars and gallons. And finally, its greatest innovation—anti knock gasoline." They named the new "high-test" gasoline "Amoco," later adopting it as the company name.

Though they competed with the Rockefeller's Standard Oil Companies from inception (both in the market place and in the courts), in 1954, they merged Amoco with Standard Oil of Indiana, after which the combined companies adopted the Amoco name. Then, in 1998, America's twenty-second largest company, Amoco, merged into British Petroleum to form BP Amoco, later shortened to BP.

The Blaustein family has long been remarkably active in politics and philanthropy. Jacob Blaustein helped convince V.M. Molotov, Russian foreign minister, to accept the human rights article in the United Nations Charter. He helped talk David Ben-Gurion into the 1948 Palestine partition, and he negotiated with Konrad Adenauer to obtain $10 billion in reparations for Holocaust survivors. He counseled every president from Franklin Roosevelt to Lyndon Johnson. Blaustein family foundations have donated hundreds of millions to support education, health, human rights, arts and culture, Israeli democracy, Jewish life, and other causes. As of 2006, grants continued to be made from more than $250 million of the foundations' assets. Among the huge number of beneficiaries are the Jacob Blaustein Institute for Desert Research at Ben Gurion University of the Negev—a leading solar energy research center. Another $10 million went to assist construction of a cancer research building at Johns Hopkins University, and the Blaustein Graduate School of Public Policy at Rutgers. These are but a smattering of the hundred or more grants made each year.

Amerada Hess:[485] Leon Hess grew up poor in Asbury Park, New Jersey. His father, a trained kosher butcher, emigrated from Lithuania and started a small fuel-delivery business. It went bankrupt in 1933 when Leon was nineteen. Leon took over and reorganized it. He bought scrap residual fuels from the back of his 1929 Dodge truck. He also traded oil, buying it during the slow summer season and selling for a profit in the winter.

Called up for World War II service, he ended up as head of logistics for Patton's Third Army. For his work in helping move the Third Army across northern Europe at lightning speed, he was promoted to lieutenant colonel. He returned from the war to take up where he left off. He re-assumed the CEO slot from his future father-in-law, whom he had left in charge while he was away. Hess kept expanding the volume and scope of his business, adding refineries, gas stations, and supporting facilities. In 1969 he acquired British-owned Amerada oil and changed the company name to Amerada Hess.

A football fan, he bought into the New York Jets and assembled the 1969 Super Bowl winners. When Hurricane Allen destroyed much of Saint Lucia, Hess set up a fund that rebuilt seventy schools on the island for its 30,000 students. He was also active in providing scholarships for Mississippi students, among others. The Hess Center for Interventional Radiology and Leon Hess Medical Research Fund were named in his honor, and he was a major backer of the Opera House at Lincoln Center. He resigned as CEO of Amerada Hess in 1995, turning the job over to his son, John. Leon Hess died in 1999.

Occidental Petroleum:[486] Armand Hammer did not start Occidental Petroleum. When Occidental was established in 1920, Hammer was finishing medical school and heading for an adventure in Russia. But in 1956, Occidental, reportedly worth $34,000 at the time, was a tiny, nearly bankrupt company. Hammer invested $100,000 and shortly thereafter two newly drilled "wildcat" wells struck oil. Hammer bought more stock and took control. Then came major natural gas discoveries in California and a 1966 Libyan concession to drill for what proved to be a billion-barrel oil field. When Qaddafi took over Libya, Hammer sold 51 percent of its production to the Libyan government and used the proceeds for successful North Sea and Latin American exploration. In the 1980s some of Occidental's foreign operations were sold to buy Cities Service. Over thirty-four years Hammer built Occidental into one of the largest U.S.- based petroleum exploration, production, refining, and marketing companies. Today, it is the fourth largest U.S. oil and gas company.

As successful as he was at building Occidental, Hammer was uniquely controversial. His father named him Armand, because of his own Communist sympathies (the arm and hammer being important Soviet symbols). Jailed in 1920 as an abortion doctor, his father was also linked to the founding of the U.S. Communist Party. In 1921 shortly after getting his own M.D., Armand headed for Ekaterinberg, Russia, where he set up a field hospital to treat a typhus epidemic. It brought him to Lenin's attention. Hammer and Lenin then created a unique trading partnership involving asbestos, wheat, furs, pencils, and Romanov crown jewels. During and after his nine years in Russia, Hammer helped run a family pharmaceutical business. When he returned to the United States, he traded works of art, controlled a television network (Mutual Broadcasting System), and bought and sold a whiskey distillery (J.W. Dant) before taking over Occidental.

Hammer remained an enigma throughout his life and was involved in Soviet-United States relations until his death in 1990, just as the Soviet Union was coming apart. He won the Soviet Union's "Order of Friendship of People" award, the U.S. National Arts Medal, the French Legion of Honor, Italy's Grand Order of Merit and numerous other honors. An avid art collector, Hammer donated millions to Columbia University, the Metropolitan Museum, and other organizations, and left the bulk of his impressionist and post-impressionist paintings to form the core of the permanent art collection at the UCLA's Hammer Museum.

Kaiser-Francis Oil Co:[487] George B. Kaiser is little known outside Tulsa, Oklahoma. He prefers it that way. His parents and an uncle began a small family owned oil company in Oklahoma after arriving as refugees from Nazi Germany in 1938. They made a living and had ten employees when George graduated from Harvard Business School in 1966 and joined the business. By 1969, he was CEO.

In the years since, he has turned Kaiser-Francis into a major oil and gas company, now producing twelve million barrels of oil and natural gas equivalents annually. He is considered particularly skilled at buying during tough times when prices are low. He has also successfully invested in venture capital and banks, among them, the Bank of Oklahoma, which he bought as a distressed asset from the Federal Deposit Insurance Corp. He now owns 70 percent of BOK Financial (which owns the bank) and that stake is valued at more than $2 billion. His newest major project is the so-called land bridge, purchased from then distressed El Paso Corp. and completed by Kaiser. Liquid natural gas (LNG) tanker ships deliver natural gas to platforms 100 miles offshore in the Gulf of Mexico. The gas is then piped underwater to the mainland. The approach allows the United States to import needed gas without requiring construction of onshore unloading facilities that some might see as high risk or environmentally undesirable. Kaiser's entrepreneurial acumen has created a net worth estimated at $11 billion.

These days, however, his top priority is philanthropy. As of 2006, the George Kaiser Family Foundation assets totaled $2.9 billion. While it makes grants to the Tulsa community, to the Oklahoma Jewish community, and to support the arts and other worthy projects, Kaiser's principal focus is early-childhood education for low-income kids, and complementary programs that manifest his commitment to support equal opportunity and end poverty. Though very private, Kaiser is quite public and passionate is this work. Asked in an interview for his definition of success, he responded, "I won't be a success unless I leave something…that truly intervenes in the cycle of poverty in ways that change the lives of subsequent generations." Among recent donations was $60 million to redevelop a blighted Arkansas River community and $50 million to the University of Oklahoma to endow thirty-five professorships, fill those chairs, and provide scholarships, all of this part of a new program to improve community-based medicine, particularly for the poor.

Aurora Oil:[488] Shortly after his 1908 birth in Pittsburgh to Byelorussian immigrant parents, Max Fisher's family moved to Salem, Ohio. There, his father owned a clothing store. Max played center on the high school football team earning him a scholarship to Ohio State. While Max was in college, his family moved to Detroit where his father started Keystone Oil, a small oil reclamation business. Graduating in 1930, Max began his career just as the United States entered the Great Depression. He started out as a $15-a-week salesman for his father. Three years later, approached by two businessmen who wanted to build a refinery, Max tried but failed to get his father to back him. Instead, Max then proposed that Aurora Oil, a venture owned by the two businessmen, kick in $38,000 and his father deed over some of Keystone's land to form a joint venture, Aurora Gas. Together Keystone and Aurora would build the Aurora Gas refinery. For his creativity and hard work, his father gave him half of the Keystone stock. At age 25, Max was now chairman of Aurora Gas. Over the next twenty-six years, Fisher built Aurora Gas. He added a chain of 680 Speedway Gas stations and made Aurora into one of the Midwest's largest independent oil companies. In 1959 he merged it into Marathon Oil.

He then turned to real estate, including ownership of Detroit's Fisher Building (named for the GM Body by Fisher family, not Max), Irvine Ranch in California, Detroit's Renaissance Center, and a number of other projects. His investing acumen put him on the *Forbes* 400 List in 1982. He remained there until his death in 2005.

Fisher made his first notable philanthropic donation when he was twenty-four. From that day on, he remained philanthropic and politically active until he died. He counseled every Republican president from Eisenhower to George W. Bush. And when a 1975 rift developed between Israel and the United States over relations with Egypt, it was Max Fisher that Henry Kissinger and Gerald Ford called to help patch things up. He did and his contribution was acknowledged by Kissinger, Ford, and Yitzhak Rabin. Fisher donated $20 million to endow Ohio State University's Max M. Fisher College of Business (and later added another $5 million), $10 million to the Detroit Symphony Orchestra, and he was instrumental in efforts to revitalize downtown Detroit including creation of the Detroit Renaissance. When Rosa Parks was assaulted in August 1994, it was Fisher who offered her an apartment in his Riverfront apartment complex, sent a check to help her over the hump, and offered her more if she needed it.

Marvin Davis:[489] Arguably, Davis could be discussed in conjunction with oil and gas, real estate, Hollywood, or corporate takeovers. He did them all. But his roots, and much of his fortune, arose from oil and gas "wildcatting" in the Rocky Mountain West, followed by comparable success in Texas and the Gulf of Mexico. Davis' parents emigrated from London. His father, Jack, began by selling ready-to-wear dresses in New York. Marvin was born in Newark on Aug. 31, 1925, and later, in the early 1940s, the family moved to Colorado where they got into oil and gas. Marvin joined the business in 1947 upon graduating from NYU. He pioneered the technique of financing his wildcatting hunches by selling one-fourth interests in new drilling ventures for one-third of their cost. It made him a fortune.

In 1981 he sold the bulk of his petroleum interests and partnered with Marc Rich to buy Twentieth Century Fox for $725 million. When he sold it to Rupert Murdoch four years later, he made $325 million. He repeated the success with his 1990 sale of Pebble Beach for $841 million. Along the way, he also owned the Beverly Hills Hotel, Aspen Skiing Company, the Denver Broncos, and various other properties. His reported $5.8 billion net worth in 2004 made him one of Los Angeles' wealthiest men, and he was a major supporter and fundraiser for Democratic Party causes. He died in September 2004, leaving his son Gregg (one of five siblings) as head of Davis Offshore and a scaled-down Davis Petroleum that went through Chapter 11 reorganization in 2006.

Mining

American Smelting and Refining Company (ASARCO), Kennecott Copper, Chilean Copper Company, and Others:[490] In 1847 nineteen-year-old Meyer

Guggenheim immigrated to the United States from Switzerland. He met his wife, Barbara, on the boat, and together, they and their eleven children spawned a dynasty comparable only to the Rothschild's (at least for two generations). After early years selling and producing commodities such as glue and stove polish, Meyer began selling Swiss embroideries and lace. Demand was so strong he sent several of his seven sons to Europe both for their education and to run the European operations. The family became wealthy.

When Meyer felt the embroidery opportunity had matured, he looked for something new. In 1879 he bought half interest in two Colorado silver mines. Intrigued, he bought additional silver, lead, and copper mines, and, in Pueblo, Colorado, he built one of America's largest smelters to process ore. Soon everything Guggenheim had was invested in mining, smelting, and refining. He brought all seven sons into the business, with son Daniel as first among equals. The family built an enormous, far-flung enterprise. In 1899, when the Rockefellers tried to take control of America's mining industry through the American Smelting and Refining Trust (ASARCO), it was Daniel who not only blocked them, but in 1901, merged Guggenheim's smelting operations into ASARCO. In the process he obtained public stock worth $90 million (in 1901 dollars) for the family and became ASARCO's CEO. He would remain CEO or chairman for nearly twenty years. Quoting *Encyclopædia Britannica,* following the ASARCO merger, Meyer and Daniel Guggenheim "dominated the (mining) industry for the next three decades and laid the foundation for today's U.S. mining industry. ASARCO was only part of the Guggenheim colossus. In addition, they developed copper in Chile, Utah, and Arizona, nitrate in Chile, silver in Mexico, tin in Bolivia, gold in Alaska, diamonds in Angola, rubber in the Congo, plus railroads to serve the mines and smelters, and banks to help finance it all.

The family's philanthropic efforts, particularly in support of the arts, are as legendary as their mining and smelting enterprises. The Solomon R. Guggenheim Foundation supports the Guggenheim Museum in Manhattan, the Guggenheim Museum, SoHo (also in Manhattan), the Guggenheim Museum in Bilbao, Spain, the Deutsche Guggenheim Berlin, and the Peggy Guggenheim Collection in Venice. All of them arose from bequests of Meyer's fourth son, Solomon, and Solomon's niece (and Ben's daughter), Peggy. Sixth son, Simon, established a memorial foundation in honor of his own son to award fellowships to aid artists and scholars studying abroad and he served as U.S. Senator from Colorado. Daniel, set up the Daniel and Florence Guggenheim Foundation and the Daniel Guggenheim Foundation for the Promotion of Aeronautics. Through it, he and his son, Harry, supported Charles Lindbergh, Robert Goddard, aeronautic science and education, and the development and safety of commercial aviation.

Hirshhorn:[491] Joseph H. Hirshhorn was born in 1899, the twelfth of thirteen children in a Mitau, Latvian Jewish family. In 1905, after his father's death, Joseph's mother moved the family to Brooklyn, New York. She took a job in a purse factory and worked twelve hour days, six days a week to support them. Among her expenditures were premiums on an insurance policy. Each year the insurance company sent a calendar featuring reproductions of great art. Joseph cut out the images and pinned them to the wall by his bed.

He left school when he was twelve, selling newspapers to help support the family. At fourteen, he became an office boy at what became the American Stock Exchange. By the time he was seventeen, he invested his $255 savings to become a stockbroker. He made $168,000 his first year (and moved his mother to Long Island). In 1924 he became a broker-dealer in bank stocks and unlisted securities and made $1 million. Two months before the 1929 crash, Hirshhorn thought the market overpriced and sold out, netting $4 million. He was thirty years old.

When gold prices rose in 1932, he was intrigued. The next year he placed a full-page ad in the *Toronto Miner* seeking partners. He scored in 1936 when he invested $25,000 to drill a new shaft in a gold mine everyone thought had played out. Digging a few feet from an old shaft he found a new vein. He invested $2,000 in another mine and later sold the shares for $500,000. There were other such hits. In the 1940s, he began looking for uranium, bought 56,000 acres, and developed two huge mines. Just one, the Algoma, could produce more uranium than all 600 U.S. uranium mines put together. When he sold his uranium interests in the late 1950s, he reportedly made $100 million. Then, he went on to develop oil in western Canada.

In 1917, his first year as a stockbroker, he had purchased two Albrecht Durer etchings for $75. Over all of the years on Wall Street and while prospecting and mining in Canada, he had collected art. He amassed one of the world's largest private art collections and almost no one knew he had it. Finally, in 1962, a show featuring a selection of his paintings was arranged at a Manhattan gallery. In addition, drawings of sculptures were displayed in a second gallery, and sculptures were featured in the Guggenheim Museum. There were pieces by Rodin, Picasso, Degas, Giacometti, Rivers, Cassatt, Kline, O'Keefe, Warhol, Eakins, de Kooning, Pollack, Matisse, Calder, Daumier, Gauguin, and many others. It was a sensation. Museums and galleries all over the world were after him.

But it was the 6 foot, 3-inch president Lyndon Johnson heaping Texas charm on the 5-foot, 4-inch Hirshhorn that won out. Hirshhorn donated 6,000 sculptures, paintings and other artwork (valued at more than $100 million) plus $1 million in cash to create Smithsonian's Hirshhorn Gallery on the Washington, D.C., Mall. It opened in 1974. Then, to the Smithsonian's surprise, Hirshhorn left another 6,000 pieces plus $5 million when he died in 1981. His wife, similarly generous, left her $10 million art collection to Washington, D.C.'s Corcoran Gallery, on whose board she served for nearly twenty years.

Engelhard:[492] In 1891 twenty-four-year-old Charles Engelhard Sr. emigrated from Germany via London (where he was a jewelry salesman). He began as an agent, selling platinum for a German company. In 1902 he began acquiring and establishing a series of companies to produce, refine, and fabricate platinum, and later silver, silver alloys, gold, and liquid gold as well. In time, the companies would be combined to form Engelhard Industries. Platinum's unique properties—resistance to chemical corrosion and heat, and its compatibility with a range of catalysts—made it valuable for uses beyond jewelry and dentistry. But, until the discovery in the 1920s of a way to make platinum as a by-product of mining nickel, scarcity constrained these uses. When the new sources arose, Charles Engelhard's unique position as a platinum specialist allowed him to capitalize on them. He built Engelhard into the world's leading precious metals fabricator.

But it was his son, Charles Jr., who would make Engelhard huge, prominent, and controversial. A World War II bomber pilot, he returned from the War, joined his father and capitalized on the ever-expanding range of applications for platinum. His unique style and determination built the company. When Engelhard needed a supply of gold, Charles Jr., moved to South Africa. When he learned that except in art form, gold was not legally exportable from South Africa without a permit which was nearly impossible to obtain, he produced gold religious art, shipped it to Hong Kong, and melted it down into bullion. In 1949 he retained the services of London's Robert Fleming & Co. In the process, he met Ian Fleming. Fleming would immortalize the gold caper in his 1959 James Bond book, *Goldfinger*, which was later made into the movie.

In South Africa, Charles Jr., became a close friend of Henry Oppenheimer. Both shared second-generation German-Jewish roots, substantial inherited wealth, and a passion for horse racing. They formed a number of business partnerships, some controversial, but all successful. By the time of Charles Jr.'s premature death of a heart attack in 1971, at age fifty-four, Engelhard Corporation was a $2 billion a year behemoth. Two years later, it was worth $5 billion, all from minerals, chemicals, and commodities trading.

Though the Engelhard family owned 10 percent of the company's stock, plus the value of numerous successful South African investments, there was no third-generation Engelhard to carry on. While the family's wealth was sustained after Charles Jr.'s death, control of the business shifted. The Oppenheimer family, with 30 percent of the stock, was in charge. Over the years after 1980, most of the pieces of Engelhard were spun off or sold. By 2006 a smaller ($3.7 billion per year) residual chemicals business with no ties to the either the Engelhard or Oppenheimer families was sold to BASF, the German chemical giant.

Before his death, Charles Engelhard Jr. and his wife established a charitable foundation to support education, medical research, culture, wildlife, and conservation, Among its bequests were the funds to build the library at the Kennedy School of Government at Harvard, the Charles Engelhard Court at the Metropolitan Museum, the Christmas crèche used each year at the White House, academic programs at the University of Montana, and numerous other beneficiaries such as the Natural Resources Defense Council, the National Fish and Wildlife Foundation, and other environmental causes. After thirty-five years of bequests, the endowment still had more than $125 million at the end of 2006.

Anglo American:[493] As noted in the discussion of diamond giant De Beers in Chapter 20 – Jewelry, Apparel and Cosmetics, Ernest Oppenheimer was originally a member of the London-based De Beers, diamond buying syndicate. He moved to South Africa in 1902 and during World War I, conceived of Anglo American as a consortium to pool the ownership of German-owned mines into a single company. Presumably the combination and Oppenheimer's British roots would mitigate the risk of British expropriation. Over time, Oppenheimer became the controlling shareholder of Anglo American. Later De Beers' interest in owning Anglo American's Namibian Consolidated Diamond mine led to the merger of De Beers and Anglo American. As the largest shareholder of the merged business, Oppenheimer became controlling shareholder.

Today, nearly 100 years and three generations later, and despite the separation of De Beers and Anglo American, the family still retains approximately 7 percent of publicly traded Anglo American stock, and Nicky Oppenheimer serves on its board. The company's mines produce platinum, gold, diamonds, coal, base metals (such as copper, zinc, and nickel) construction materials (such as crushed rock, sand, gravel, and lime), and ferrous metals, (such as manganese and carbon steel). It is huge, with 2006 annual revenues of $26 billion and an early 2008 market value of $85 billion. In March 2007, it became the industry's first large company to hire a female CEO, Cynthia Carroll (née Blum). Her performance, following a brief stock price drop after the hiring was announced, led to a substantial stock price rise.

Business Services and Products

Manpower:[494] Elmer Winter and his brother-in-law and law partner, Aaron Scheinfeld, started Manpower in 1948. Scheinfeld had clients who needed temporary employees and both Winter and Scheinfeld knew firsthand the value of quickly retaining "temps" when under pressure to complete legal briefs. Though Kelly Services predated Manpower by a year or more, Manpower was first to provide temporary employees for industrial positions as well as clerical and administrative jobs. Winter became Manpower's first CEO. He built it into a New York Stock Exchange company with offices in thirty countries before retiring in 1976. He passed the reins to Mitchell Fromstein who served until 1999. (Between them, they served as CEO for fifty-five years.)

Today Manpower is the world's second largest temporary staffing company (Kelly is much smaller. Number one, Adecco, became largest because of its European base and the rise of the Euro against the dollar.) Grossing $21 billion per year, in 2007 Manpower placed five million people through its 4,500 offices in eighty countries.

Still active in 2007 at age ninety-five, Winter was an accomplished painter and sculptor, had written thirteen books, received a Horatio Alger Award, and created the Committee for Economic Growth of Israel (acknowledged by Yitzhak Rabin at the time as "an important economic tool for building and economically stable and secure Israel").He was also honored by his hometown—Milwaukee—for heading up a program providing computers to inner-city schools, helping renovate a failing neighborhood, and efforts to reduce dropout rates and student delinquency.

Automatic Data Processing (ADP):[495] Morris Taub was a junk peddler. He emigrated from Lodz, Poland, in the 1920s after World War I service in the German army. Laid off as a weaver, he peddled with a horse and cart on the streets of Paterson, New Jersey, all through the Great Depression and into the late 1960s.

His oldest son, Henry, was a quick study. He skipped two grades to enter NYU at age sixteen. Three years later he had his bachelor's degree in accounting. After two years as a CPA, with two partners he set up Automatic Payrolls, a payroll processing firm in 1949. Thinking the business was growing too slowly, one of the partners quit and Henry borrowed $6,000 to buy out the other. The next year, he recruited his younger brother, Joe, to help him run the business. In 1952, when they moved to new offices in the basement of a hotel, a life insurance salesman (Frank Lautenberg—son of Polish and Russian immigrants), who had an office in the same building, talked them into letting him become their first salesman.

The threesome built the world's foremost payroll services company. It was highly complex work, particularly for large client companies operating in numerous states and countries. And it was not an easy sell. Convincing companies to part with payroll information and trust that ADP would process it perfectly, confidentially, and more cheaply than they could themselves, required sales skill and a superb reputation built over the years. In time ADP would add specialized services for stock brokerages and automobile dealers. Henry Taub stepped down as CEO in 1975, turning the job over to Lautenberg, who served until 1982 when he ran for, and won, a U.S. Senate seat from New Jersey.

Today, after spinning off the brokerage service business, ADP is a $7.8 billion a year publicly traded company with Henry still serving as honorary chair while Lautenberg is back in the U.S. Senate. For twenty years, Henry and Joe were members of the "Secaucus Seven," owners of the New Jersey Nets. In addition, Henry and his wife, Marilyn, retain a $160 million family foundation from which they have been generous benefactors to many causes. Among them, $10 million went to Columbia University for Alzheimer's research. A 2003 gift established the Taub Center for Israel Studies at New York University—where Henry has been a trustee since 1976 and where he served as an adjunct professor at the Stern (Business) School. Even the removal of land mines in Bosnia and Herzegovina was a beneficiary of Taub's generosity. His brother Joseph has been a benefactor to the redevelopment of Paterson, New Jersey, to college scholarships for disadvantaged students, and to support of women's health issues.

Peter Drucker:[496] He was born to an upper-middle-class Viennese family of intellectuals in 1909. Peter Drucker met Sigmund Freud when he was eight, studied under non-Jews John Maynard Keynes and Joseph Schumpeter, and earned his doctorate of international and public law in 1931 from Frankfurt University. After Drucker worked as a securities analyst and writer-journalist, Hitler's rise to power (two of Drucker's publications were banned and burned by the Nazis) led to his immigration, first to England in 1933 where he worked as an economist and then to the United States in 1937. He started out as a correspondent for a group of European newspapers while also advising British banks operating in the United States. His 1939 book, *The End of Economic Man,* was a favorite of Winston Churchill's, as was his 1942 book, *The Future of Industrial Man.*

The second book also caught the eye of General Motors. Though he was teaching political science and philosophy at Bennington College, GM retained him (in his first and, at the time, somewhat novel role) as a management consultant. It was after the war that the field of management consulting began to emerge. The assignment lasted three years, from 1943 to 1946. Over its course, Drucker had access to every GM employee from Alfred P. Sloan (not Jewish) on down and to every board meeting, decision-making process, and production technique. The engagement was the basis for his 1946 classic, *The Concept of the Corporation,* which defined the "scientific discipline of management."

Over the next fifty-nine years until his death in late 2005, Drucker consulted for an astonishing list of major corporations and institutions including GE, Intel, Coca-Cola, Citicorp, the Salvation Army, Reverend Rick Warren, the Girl Scouts, and many others.

Always the loner, he refused to hire people to work for him. Ken Witty, who produced a CNBC documentary on Drucker in 2002, noted: "He could have been the McKinsey & Co of the century...but he chose to work alone." Andrew Grove of Intel said, "Drucker is a hero of mine. He writes and thinks with such exquisite clarity—a standout among a bunch of muddled fad mongers." Drucker deserves credit for GE's strategy to focus on companies that were No. 1 or No. 2 in their respective industries. His thirty-eight books created entirely new management disciplines, such as "Management by Objectives," and he pioneered the view that employees were resources to be respected and developed, rather than expenses to be cut. He fathered the notion of decentralized operations and saw his approach adopted throughout industry in the years following his 1946 formulation of its importance. He was first to anticipate the huge influence pension plans would have on financial markets and institutional stock ownership. He championed privatization, but was highly critical of excessive executive compensation. A professor of management at New York University from 1950 to 1972, he then moved to Claremont University, which named its Graduate Management Center after him in 1987. In July 2002, President George W. Bush awarded Drucker the Presidential Medal of Freedom.

Kroll Associates:[497] Jules Kroll was born in 1941, the son of a Brooklyn, New York, printing company owner. After graduating from Georgetown University Law School in 1966, he served as an assistant district attorney in Manhattan. Six years later, a failed campaign to be elected councilman-at-large in Queens led to his 1972 creation of Kroll Associates. His first client, Curtis Publishing, drew on his family background in printing. They asked him to consult to their purchasing department by reviewing the operations and making recommendations to cut costs. By 1974 the scope of Kroll's consulting had expanded to include the investigation of white-collar crime for corporate clients.

As mergers swept Wall Street in the 1980s, Kroll became the preferred firm to check out prospective acquirers, financiers, executives, and others involved in take-overs. Wall Street's leading attorneys, investment banks, and financiers made Kroll the firm of choice. By 1985, the U.S. House of Representatives Foreign Affairs Committee retained Kroll to investigate allegations of embezzlement by Ferdinand and Imelda Marcos. The next year, Kroll traced the millions stashed away by Haiti's Jean-Claude "Baby Doc" Duvalier. Success in these investigations and a growing international reputation led to other high-profile assignments. The government of Kuwait asked Kroll to track down Saddam Hussein's $10 billion of missing oil profits. The

Port Authority of New York and New Jersey hired Kroll after the 1993 bombing of the World Trade Center. Kroll's security advice for the Port Authority is credited with the rapid evacuation of the center after the first plane hit the North Tower on September 11, 2001.

Kroll went public in 1997 through what would later prove an unworkable combination with a publicly traded armored-car manufacturer. Following the merger, Kroll made a series of acquisitions until 2001, when the armored-car business was sold and Kroll then refocused on its traditional investigation, intelligence, and security work. In July 2004, the professional services firm Marsh & McLennan approached Kroll seeking to acquire the business. Kroll acquiesced and was purchased for $1.9 billion in cash. Today, with 3,000 employees, the firm maintains sixty-five offices in thirty-three countries around the globe. Despite the competitors spawned from its success, Kroll remains the world's foremost firm in what is today called "risk consulting."

Jules Kroll, who retired in June 2008, is chairman of the John Jay College of Criminal Justice Foundation and is a former regent of Georgetown University and Trustee of Cornell. He and his wife are also honored by the Lynn and Jules Kroll Fund for Jewish Documentary Film.

Snyder Communications:[498] Dan Snyder lost $3 million in his second failed start-up. His first, bus-trip packages allowing Washington Capitals hockey fans to attend away games, was a loser as well. But three years later in 1985 when he was 20, Snyder dropped out of college to fly students to beaches for spring break—using leased jets. It was a winner. Next, he started *Campus USA,* a magazine for college students. He was bankrolled, to the tune of $3 million, by Mortimer Zuckerman (profiled Chapter 18 – "Real Estate") and a partner, Fred Drasner. Snyder worked hard to pitch Zuckerman, who was also CEO of *Newsweek* magazine. Unfortunately he was less successful in selling advertisers. Two years later, *Campus USA* failed.

Undaunted, in 1988 he set up Snyder Communications, a marketing services company to provide wallboard advertising and distribute product samples for client companies. Snyder was not the first Jew to work in advertising and marketing. Albert Lasker built Lord & Thomas, one of the most successful ad agencies of the early twentieth century. Arthur Fatt and Larry Valenstein made Grey Advertising one of the great ad agencies of the post World War II era. And Grey alumni, William Bernbach, founded Doyle Dane Bernbach (DDB) whose Volkswagen, Levy's Jewish Rye, Polaroid, and other ads in the '60s and '70s set industry standards for unique classy advertising that worked. But for sheer impact, for quickly building a huge marketing and advertising organization, none of them, not Lord & Thomas, not Grey, not Bernbach, nor for that matter any of the traditional Gentile ad agencies, such as: BBDO, J. Walter Thompson, McCann Erickson, Leo Burnett, or Saatchi & Saatchi ever did as much as fast as Snyder.

From his 1989 start with its very narrow focus, Snyder expanded into direct marketing, sponsored information displays, telemarketing, database marketing and numerous other marketing and advertising services for clients. Some he built from scratch, but mostly, he acquired (some thirty or so existing businesses over a period of ten years). The company grew quickly: $2.7 million in 1991, $4.1 million in 1992, and $9 million in 1993. By 1996, with $82 million in revenues, he took Snyder Communications public. At 32, he was, to that time, the youngest CEO of a New York Stock Exchange listed company. The next year, he acquired Arnold Communications, a full-service ad agency with revenues of $865 million. When Snyder finally sold his company to Havas, the international marketing/advertising conglomerate in April 2000, his shareholders netted $2.1 billion. Along the way, Snyder set aside shares for Zuckerman and Drasner. Their earlier $3 million loss was eclipsed by the $500 million they realized in Snyder Communications shares.

Dan Snyder has since gone on to acquire control of the Washington Redskins (a mixed scorecard on that deal so far), Dick Clark Productions, Six Flags amusement parks and Johnny Rockets, the dinner chain. Among other priorities, his Family Foundation is active in its support of youth, education, health, and cultural programs.

Chapter 22

Social Activists and Union Leaders

"Language is a process of free creation; its laws and principles are fixed, but the manner in which the principles of generation are used is free and infinitely varied. Even the interpretation and use of words involves a process of free creation."

"If the Nuremberg laws were applied, every post-war American president would have been hanged."

"Propaganda is to democracy what the bludgeon is to a totalitarian state." —Noam Chomsky

Noam Chomsky[499]

To avoid being drafted, William (Zev) Chomsky fled tsarist Russia in 1913. William first found work in a Baltimore sweatshop, but self educated in Russia, he was soon hired to teach in Baltimore's Hebrew elementary schools. While teaching he worked his way through Johns Hopkins, earning a Ph.D. in Hebrew. It was to become the focus for the rest of his career.

In Baltimore, he met Elsie Simonofsky, a Lithuanian emigrant, whose interest and talents in Hebrew matched his own. They married, and after his graduation, moved to Philadelphia where they taught at the Mikveh Israel congregation religious school. On December 7, 1928, Elsie gave birth to Avram Noam Chomsky, the first of two sons.

His *New York Times* obituary said, "William became one of the world's foremost Hebrew grammarians." He was a warm and outgoing personality, influential in his field of expertise, and his enthusiasm drew Noam into a shared love of intellectual matters, academia, and language. By age twelve, Noam was already reviewing one of his father's five books. Late in life, William said his life's major objective had been educating "individuals who are well integrated, free and independent in their thinking, concerned about improving and enhancing the world, and eager to participate

337

in making life more meaningful and worthwhile for all." It was a telling description of both his aspirations and his effect on Noam.

Chomsky's mother, Elsie, matched William as an intellectual and teacher. More austere, she was also more outwardly political and leftist in her thinking. Noam was shaped by a family life centered on active involvement in Jewish issues, including the revival of Hebrew, Zionism, and Jewish cultural activities. In the end, Chomsky was a product of both parents. His interest in language and his warmth and humor came from his father. His lifelong anarchist, libertarian, and socialist political orientation came from his mother, and both parents contributed to his intellectual talent and willingness to speak out vigorously in support of his academic and political views.

At school Noam often led class discussions and it was there, when he was five, that he met three-year-old Carol Doris Schatz. In 1949 she became his lifelong wife, partner, and later, the mother to their three children.

A family friend sought to make conversation with the bright, competitive young Noam, asking if he had looked through any of the volumes of Compton encyclopedias in the Chomsky home. Seven-year-old Noam replied he had read only half of them. By the time he was ten, he was writing editorials on the Spanish Civil War for the school newspaper, and by twelve, he became an avowed anarchist who rejected Marxism.

Chomsky entered the University of Pennsylvania in 1940 to study linguistics under Zellig S. Harris, a charismatic leftist whose political views attracted the sixteen year old as much as his reputation in linguistics. Noam, of course, was already well grounded in linguistics from his family upbringing. While Harris had substantial influence on his protégé, Chomsky's linguistic insights ultimately far exceeded those of his mentor. Earning his Ph.D. in 1955, Chomsky started teaching modern languages and linguistics at Massachusetts Institute of Technology (MIT), becoming a full professor in 1961. He remains at MIT to this day, having also served as a visiting professor on other campuses over the years.

Chomsky's 1955 doctoral dissertation and lecture outline served as the basis for his 1957 book, *Syntactic Structures*. In the words of *Encyclopædia Britannica*, that book "revolutionized the development of theoretical linguistics." Not bad for a twenty-nine year-old, newly minted Ph.D.

Before Chomsky, linguistics was something of a dry, esoteric field. It basically considered language to be a system of phonetic, grammatical, and syntax habits one learns through training and experience. Linguistics was basically a discipline devoted to naming and describing the different parts and features of languages, and it attached significance to the meaning (semantics) of the utterances. At the time, most academics believed language was learned through behavioral conditioning, the Pavlovian stimulus/response notion wherein subjects were "trained" by rewarding good, and penalizing bad, behavior. Behavioral conditioning was championed by Harvard's psychology professor B.F. Skinner, who, among other proofs, used his technique to teach pigeons to play Ping-Pong. In 1959 Skinner wrote *Verbal Behavior*, saying that language was simply learned by conditioning. That same year, Chomsky wrote a critique of Skinner's book.

In part Chomsky's insight came from his study of the way mathematicians derive an infinite number of proofs from a limited number of postulates, principles, and inferences. Chomsky thought perhaps our limitless ways of expressing a single idea involved something similar. He posed a simple question in challenging the behaviorists. If language is learned from conditioning, how can a child who has just begun speaking devise such an astonishing variety of utterances? The child could not possibly have been exposed to all the combinations of words it so easily demonstrates in everyday speech. Chomsky theorized instead that the human capability for language is innate.

His argument was supported by the ability of young children, particularly between ages three and ten, to quickly and easily learn language (even multiple languages) in ways most adults cannot. Moreover, research has also shown children learn almost unaided, or if aided, derive little incremental benefit from the training. Further, attempts by adults to correct grammatical mistakes generally have little effect until children mature, at which point they gravitate to the correct grammatical form.

Said differently, if behaviorists conceived the mind and its language skills as something of a "blank slate" (a software program with only a few initial instructions), Chomsky's formulation was of humans born with innate language capability. Our software is "hard-wired" in the brain, so to speak, and it is ready to be fired up for use at the appropriate point in our maturation.

Chomsky convinced many people that his explanations were more viable than conditioning, and in the process he changed linguistics and behavioral psychology. It was perhaps not coincidental that early work in sociobiology was arriving on the Harvard scene about the same time that Chomsky was developing his theories. Sociobiology shared Chomsky's skepticism of conditioning ("nurture") as the dominant explanation for behavior. Sociobiology explored the effect of genes (or "nature") on behavior, personality, and orientation. Both approaches convincingly challenged the "blank slate" proposition that humans can be programmed to think, believe, and act in particular ways.

Encyclopædia Britannica notes that "Chomsky's work virtually defined the methods of linguistic analysis used in the second half of the twentieth century." His approach revolutionized the stale discipline of linguistics and extended its scope to encompass the underlying thought and meaning of utterances. In the process, he expanded linguistics to draw upon and influence biology, psychology, philosophy, computer programming, and other fields. As but one example, the 1984 Nobel Prize for Medicine and Physiology went to non-Jew Niels K. Jerne, who freely acknowledged his use of Chomsky's "generative model" to help explain the human immune system.

While some of Chomsky's theories have been challenged over the years by his peers, many of his seminal insights remain widely accepted. And nearly everyone agrees it was Chomsky who revolutionized linguistics.

A few years after receiving tenure in 1961, Chomsky's outspoken views on politics and economics began to emerge. From 1964 on Chomsky criticized U.S. involvement in Vietnam, culminating in his 1969 publication of *American Power and the New Mandarins*. With the book and his public pronouncements and articles, Chomsky became a cult figure of the American, and later European, left. He began to publicly espouse the anarchist and socialist views developed in early childhood, and they became an ever larger focus of his work and public commentary. It was as though Chomsky created a second endowed chair for himself as a full professor of anarchist, libertarian socialism.

In Chomsky's paradigm, anarchy did not encompass violent acts to destroy government. Instead, all government, corporate, and other forms of power and authority should be viewed as suspect, and only those most essential should be accepted. As the world's most powerful government, the United States thus serves, in his view, as his principal perpetrator of evil and his whipping boy.

A second element of his worldview is a belief in socialism and rejection of capitalism, which he sees as authoritarian and repressive of individual freedoms. At the same time, he rejects Marxism and Leninism. (It is as though he learned from the shattering experiences of his parents' contemporaries, Emma Goldman and Alexander Berkman, two anarchists deported to Russia who became utterly disillusioned by what they saw there.) Chomsky openly criticized the Soviet Union, albeit with substantially less vehemence than his criticisms of the United States.

Democratic capitalism came in for particular contempt. In interviews, Chomsky was quoted as saying, "American democracy was founded on the principle...that the primary function of government is to protect the opulent minority from the majority."

Chomsky's worldview seems to envision humans as naturally cooperative and sharing. It is power—and the powerful—that inhibit our innate libertarian socialistic impulses. Humans can have the political and economic world they deserve if only the nefarious groups and individuals who control power are moved aside. Once that coercion is eliminated, human beings will naturally work together and cooperate in a socialistic economy for everyone's benefit. ("From each according to his ability, to each according to his need.")

While Chomsky has said he does not wish to create the impression he completely understands human nature, his political/economic paradigm involves a Rousseau-like belief in something akin to "the noble savage," popularized by Franz Boas and Margaret Mead. In that view, left untouched by a corrupting civilization, the "noble savage" is pure, innocent, and happy. Chomsky has said the purest model for the kind of political and economic culture he envisions was 1930s Spain after the Republicans took power. His description also harkens back to Tito's Yugoslavia, where each factory was to be democratically run by its workers. It is also reminiscent of the kibbutzim of the 1940s and 1950s which Chomsky contemplated joining as a teen.

For Chomsky, Third-World citizens are the purest remaining representation of innocents who continue being devastated by an evil United States and its capitalist power (with Western Europe occasionally thrown in for good measure). When challenged by those who say he has been unwilling to equally criticize other countries, institutions and individuals whose behavior is as bad or worse, Chomsky's consistent defense is that his duty is to focus on the one country he is most capable of influencing. Presumably he would have limited impact on the others and must focus his energies on the country of which he is a citizen.

A chronicle of Chomsky campaigns and criticisms include:

Christopher Columbus' "discovery" of America: which Chomsky says may have led to 100 million deaths as the Spanish, and others, plundered the Americas, destroying, in the process, the indigenous population. In one interview, Chomsky said, "Columbus was one of the main specialists in genocide during that period." (Presumably 1492 to the early 1500s.)

Vietnam: where Chomsky first unleashed his attacks on the escalating American involvement and resulting carnage. Never particularly critical of the North Vietnamese or of their Russian backers, Chomsky defended the National Liberation Front, and to some extent justified its terror tactics as necessary to lift Vietnamese peasantry.

Cambodia: wherein Chomsky blamed United States bombing of areas adjacent to the Vietnam border for the subsequent death of perhaps two million people before and during Pol Pot's regime. For the most part, Chomsky defended Pol Pot and the Khmer Rouge, including his justification of some Khmer atrocities as necessary in support of a revolution for the 'greater good.'

Maoist China: defending its forced collectivization in pursuit of a "new society."

East Timor: in which he blamed the United State for supporting 1970s massacres.

Chile: where he alleged the United States had instigated the overthrow of a legitimate government in support of an illegitimate one.

Central America: Guatemala, Nicaragua, Grenada, where he held the United States responsible for the deaths of hundreds of thousands. Chomsky defended the Sandinistas and their counterparts within the region.

Castro's Cuba: where Chomsky has strongly defended Castro, including his signing a May 2003 petition supporting Cuba against imperialist Yankees. His publisher notes that Chomsky's 2004 book, *Hegemony or Survival*, criticizes the United States for "being willing, as in the Cuban Missile Crisis, to follow the dreams of dominance no matter how high the risk."

Serbia: where Chomsky attacked the Clinton administration's war of aerial bombardment in defense of Kosovo.

Sudan: for which Chomsky alleged Clinton's nighttime missile strike on a chemical and pharmaceutical plant, which perhaps caused one immediate fatality, was a terrorist act equivalent or worse than September 11 because "tens of thousands" would die when the factory's loss curtailed access to life saving drugs.

Israel: as the vicious oppressor of Palestinians. Chomsky believes Jews should have an ethnic homeland in Palestine, not a Jewish state. Chomsky would combine Muslim Arab Palestine with Jewish Israel into a single socialist Arab-Jewish country. Several years ago Chomsky was a leading advocate for forcing all university endowments to divest of any investment they may have in Israel.

Robert Faurisson, a Holocaust denier: Chomsky supported Faurisson in an essay defending his freedom of speech and "findings." Chomsky found no hint of anti-Semitic implications in Faurisson's work, and a Chomsky essay later became the introduction to a Faurisson book.

September 11: which, in various interviews and writings, Chomsky minimized, in part by characterizing the United States as the leading terrorist state of modern times. Chomsky first used the Sudan missile strike as a point of comparison suggesting the United States should focus on what it did to cause the attack.

Afghanistan and the Taliban: which Chomsky feels were unfairly victimized by the United States' war of aggression. He anticipates up to three to four million deaths in a "silent genocide" arising from the invasion, speaks of U.S. intentions to retain permanent bases there, and he expects formal trappings of democracy to mask de facto United States control of the country.

Osama bin Laden and al-Qaeda: which Chomsky feels have been victimized and unfairly characterized since their primary purpose was to oppose the United States behavior as the principal oppressor of Arabs and Islam.

Iraq: in which Chomsky has been a vehement critic of both U.S. wars. He has blamed the attacks not only on U.S. greed for oil, but also U.S. insistence on dominating the region with strategically located military bases.

Chomsky and his colleague, Edward Herman, have also developed theories of "propaganda," a tool they see being used by those in power to control public thinking in supposed democracies. Not necessarily an outright conspiracy directed by individuals, instead they theorize there is an institutionalized system of filters involving:

1. concentration of media ownership;
2. adverse effects arising from advertising—as the principal source of income;
3. media reliance on business, government and experts to provide information;
4. the use of "flak" to discipline recalcitrant media; and
5. in the 1970s and 1980s, reliance on anti-Communism as a constant theme to determine the content and orientation of programming.

Together the five filters control the media, limit content, and shape the programming "spin." Since that is all the filters allow through, the filters ultimately inhibit the free expression of truth, and instead condition the populace to the views of a powerful elite. As a consequence, even though we think of ourselves as a democracy, in fact, powerful corporate and government interests control our very thinking and attitudes, thereby keeping themselves in power. Citizens are simply entertained and manipulated, in a manner akin to a Roman circus.

Astonishingly outspoken and acerbic, even acid in his comments, Chomsky has invited a hail of critics who respond to his views with matching vitriol. Among them is Arthur Schlessinger, who said, "One can only conclude that Chomsky's idea of the responsibility of an intellectual is to forswear reasoned analysis, indulge in moralistic declamation, fabricate evidence when necessary and shout, always at the top of one's voice." Anthony Lewis, retired opinion columnist at *The New York Times,* criticized Chomsky for his defense of Pol Pot, and former supporter and non-Jew Christopher Hitchens finally broke with Chomsky after Chomsky likened September 11 to the Sudan missile strike. Chomsky has elicited particularly harsh criticism from fellow Jews, some of whom now characterize him as a "self-hating Jew" or "no longer Jewish." Among his prominent Jewish critics are Alan Dershowitz and David Horowitz, both of whom challenge Chomsky on a range of fronts.

Interestingly, Chomsky has recently criticized deconstruction and postmodern dogma. He has called much of deconstruction: "truism, error or gibberish" and says he finds deconstructionist criticism of "white male science," akin to pre-World War II German criticism of "Jewish physics." For Chomsky, science is valid or wrong, but its origin is only incidental to that truth. Chomsky also supports the notion that there is such a thing as a scientific fact, which is independent of the person who discovers or proves it.

Despite the controversies, Chomsky has earned more than twenty honorary degrees from the likes of Cambridge University, Harvard, Swarthmore, Delhi University, Amherst, the University of London, Georgetown, and others. He has written more than seventy books and a thousand articles. The measure of his influence is characterized in the comments of non-Jew Paul Robinson in a *New York Times* book review saying, "Judged in terms of the power, range, novelty and influence of his thought, Noam Chomsky is arguably the most important intellectual alive today." London's *Times* named Chomsky "one of the thousand makers of the twentieth century." Similarly, in *The New York Times,* non-Jew Christopher Lehmann-Haupt called him "the foremost gadfly of our national conscience."

Jewish Activism

"When it comes to helping someone in need, do not rely on prayer alone. Let the person in need pray, not you, your task is to help."   —Elie Wiesel,
Somewhere a Master (1981)[500]

Abraham protested God's seeming indifference to the destruction of innocents in Sodom and Gomorrah.[501] Moses protested the Pharaoh's treatment of Jews, unleashed Ten Plagues on Egypt, and led the Jews to the Promised Land. Elijah, Isaiah, Jeremiah, and other prophets protested the backsliding of kings and fellow Jews, railed at their failures to properly honor Yahweh, and demanded that Jews dedicate themselves to righteousness and justice.

In focusing on deeds rather than beliefs, Judaism makes demands. Not only are there duties *(mitzvot)*, but also an obligation to pursue justice and charity (tzedakah), and to work to heal the broken world *(tikkun olam)*.[502] There is the presumption that by design or accident, the world was made imperfect and Jews were "chosen," or have otherwise inherited a duty to be proactive in correcting those imperfections and inequities.

If some Christians believe faith trumps action and deeds don't count, and some secularists prefer leisure in their spare time, Jewish activists, instead, will be at a rally or a protest. And while only a minority of Jews are outspoken public activists, a substantial percentage of outspoken public activists are Jewish. Perhaps apocryphal, Ernest Van den Haag is quoted in *The Jewish Mystique* as saying, "out of one hundred Jews, five may be radicals, but out of ten radicals, five are likely to be Jewish."[503]

Paul Johnson notes in his *A History of the Jews*, that so-called non-Jewish Jews (who rejected characterization as "Jews" because they considered it an archaic vestige of outmoded economic and political systems), "were prominent in every revolutionary party, in virtually every European country, just before, during, and immediately after the First World War."[504]

While there is no authoritative listing of the most important progressive, radical, and utopian causes over the last 150 years, any discussion of the better-known movements reveals Jews to be prominent in nearly every one.

Socialism:[505] Modern Socialism was conceived in the early nineteenth century by non-Jews Comte Henri de Saint-Simon and François-Marie-Charles Fourier. With the Jewish Emancipation and Enlightenment then under way, it is not surprising that Jewish intellectuals and financiers were among their early supporters. In 1863 Jews Moses Hess and Ferdinand Lassalle formed the first German Workers' (Socialist) party and in 1897, the Bund (General Jewish Workers' Union of Lithuania, Poland and Russia), was formed. It became a socialist political movement and in its time, the Bund was the most effective socialist organization in Russia. Later it allied itself with Russia's Mensheviks and after the Bolshevik Revolution, most of its members became Communists.

Never a widely popular movement in the United States, Socialism attained notoriety in 1890, when Daniel De Leon, a Jewish Marxist joined the Socialist Labor Party and brought the movement to public attention in his work to build and shape it with elements from Marxism. Eventually, U.S. Socialist leadership went to non-Jews, Eugene Debs, and later, Norman Thomas. De Leon moved on to help found the International Workers of the World, more popularly known as the "Wobblies."

Kurt Eisner, a German Jew and member of the German Social Democrat Party, led a November 1918 overthrow of the Bavarian government declaring Bavaria a Socialist republic. He was assassinated less than four months later.

Socialism was always part of Zionist planning for Israel. Over its first thirty years, Socialism dominated the Israeli economy until the Likud party took control from Labor in 1977 and began moving economic policy to the right. Even today, however, as much as 40 to 50 percent of Israel's economy is state-owned or run by cooperatives affiliated with Histadrut, the Israeli trade union organization. Perhaps, the best-known manifestation of Socialist Zionism is the kibbutz, which remains part of Israel's farming landscape to this day.

Communism:[506] Karl Marx has had an enormous impact on world history with his (and non-Jew Frederick Engels') 1840s conception of Communism. Their views were reportedly influenced by Moses Hess (see above), who converted them to the concept of historical materialism, a critical underpinning of communism.

Communism became a force throughout Europe, but particularly in Russia where, in the late nineteenth and early twentieth centuries, it competed with the socialist Bund and other movements for influence. Many Jews were counted as members of the competing Menshevik (democratic Communism) and Bolshevik (professional revolutionaries) parties. Jews were the clear majority of the Menshevik party and were prominent among the Bolsheviks, albeit as a minority.

Leon Trotsky was effectively second in command when Lenin was in power, many leading Bolsheviks were Jews (Kamenev, Yaroslavsky, Sverdlov, Kaganovich, Zinoviev, etc.), and Jews held senior positions in the post-revolutionary Soviet Union leadership and in the Cheka (secret police). Their prominence, however, was short-lived. After Stalin took charge in 1924, he systematically purged nearly every one of them.

In Germany the first prominent Jewish Communist was the Russian, Rosa Luxemburg, who moved to Berlin to co-found and lead the Spartacus League. It was a Social Democratic Party offshoot that became a revolutionary Communist movement. Luxemburg was murdered in January 1919 in the midst of the Spartacus Revolt.

Bela Kun was briefly the Communist dictator of Hungary until he too was murdered in 1918.

In the United States, the heyday of Communism was the 1930s, when the U.S. economy was weak, Hitler was in control of Germany, and the Soviet Union was ascendant. Many experts have noted that at the time, a third or more of the membership of the Communist Party of the United States (CPUSA) was Jewish. But Communism was never widely accepted by Americans, and for Jews, the Aug. 23, 1939, Nonaggression Pact between Hitler and Stalin marked the beginning of their disaffection with Communism. Later, when Stalin's anti-Semitism became known, Jewish participation in CPUSA plummeted, as did that of non-Jews with the advent of the Cold War.

Finally, there was Joe Slovo, the Lithuanian-born Jew who headed the South African Communist Party and was active in the African National Congress.

Anarchism:[507] Not particularly well known or popular today, this was a utopian vision of a human reasonableness so self-capable that government would be unnecessary. Its roots date back to classical antiquity, but it became a contemporary movement after 1840 when the French non-Jew Pierre-Joseph Proudhon named and described it. Though its early promoters (such as Proudhon, William Godwin, Robert Owen, Mikhail Bakunin, and Peter Kropotkin) were not Jewish, in Europe and the United States emigrant Jews soon became forceful anarchist leaders.

By the late nineteenth to early twentieth century, however, anarchism was no longer "reasonable." It became radical and violent. Anarchists carried out numerous assassinations including King Umberto I of Italy, Empress Elizabeth of Austria, president Carnot of France, President William McKinley of the United States, General Simon Petliura, a former leader of Ukraine, and Antonio del Castillo of Spain. The assassinations were purportedly necessary to "inspire and unleash the masses." Among the assassins, Bessarabian-French Jew Sholom Schwartzbard was directly responsible for the death of General Simon Petliura.

London's East End was home to the Federation of Jewish Anarchists, a group larger than England's native anarchist movement. In the United States, Emma Goldman and Alexander Berkman were driving figures in a movement with many Jewish members. Berkman attempted to assassinate Henry Frick (Andrew Carnegie's manager) and was sent to jail. Later, Goldman was indirectly implicated in McKinley's death when the assassin told authorities that she was the last person he spoke with before he shot McKinley. Finally, in late 1919, Goldman, Berkman, and other Jewish anarchists were deported to Russia (which they soon discovered was not the "worker's paradise" they had hoped).

Never particularly popular in the United States, anarchism had to grapple with the inherent problem of "how one organizes a group of anarchists." And in Europe the movement essentially died out after 1920 when the Communists, Nazis, and Fascists took power. Today a few prominent anarchists remain (such as Noam Chomsky), but they are a marginal group on the world stage.

Labor unions:[508] Jews have been at the forefront of the U.S. labor movement for more than a century. They were a particularly vital force during the early years (from 1880 to 1950) when many unions openly espoused progressive political ideologies such as socialism, communism, and anarchy.

The first great Jewish labor leader, however, was a pragmatist who focused on improving wages and working conditions. Born in England to Dutch Jewish parents, Samuel Gompers was not interested in the Jewish religion, nor was he steeped in the tsarist oppression of the Russian Pales—a historical phenomenon that shaped most early twentieth-century Jewish labor leaders. Only twelve years after his 1863 emigration to the United States at age thirteen, Gompers was president of a cigar maker's local. By 1881 he was president of the Federation of Organized Trades and Labor Unions, and by 1886 he was head of its successor, the American Federation of labor (AFL). Except for one year (1895), Gompers headed the two unions for forty-two consecutive years until 1924, when he retired from the then three million member AFL.

It was during Gompers' early years as an American labor leader that millions of Eastern European Jews entered the United States. Most arrived with a fervent hatred for the oppressive racist political and economic system they left behind in tsarist Russia. Many were (or would soon become) radical socialists, communists, or anarchists. Moreover, most who immigrated between 1880 and 1924 began life in America as laborers. It would be a generation or more before their offspring gravitated into the professions and entrepreneurial roles that leave very few Jews as union members today.

While the United States provided a freedom they had never experienced before, that did not keep them from spotting inequities, promoting their ideologies and organizing their fellow workers. And in that era of child labor, unsafe working conditions, enforced thirteen- to fourteen-hour work days, and low wages, there was plenty to be angry about, organize against and strike for. The 1911 Triangle Shirtwaist Factory fire, which killed 146 workers, most of them young Jewish women, was but one notorious example of the horrific unsafe conditions of the times. Rose Schneiderman, a young radical dubbed by her critics the "Red Rose of Anarchy," memorialized those deaths in a speech to the Women's Trade Union League, saying,

> "I would be a traitor to these poor burned bodies if I came here to talk good fellowship...I can't talk fellowship ...Too much blood has been spilled. I know from my experience it is up to the working people to save themselves. The only way they can save themselves is by a strong working class movement."

An ardent suffragist, she was an organizer for the United Cloth Hat and Cap Makers Union, served as president of the Women's Trade Union League, and New York Women's Trade Union League, became a close friend of Eleanor, and later Franklin Roosevelt, and served on that Administration's Labor Advisory board.

Clara Lemlich (Shavelson) agitated for a 1909 strike that grew to 20,000 female shirtwaist makers. The strike was followed a year later by another of 60,000 cloakmakers. Together the two strikes established the struggling International Ladies Garment Workers Union (ILGWU), earned (with help from Louis Brandeis and Jacob Schiff) ILGWU recognition, and won higher wages for its members. Even in retirement at the Jewish Home for the Aged in Los Angeles, Lemlich helped unionize the orderlies and arranged for the home to honor the United Farm Workers boycott of grapes and lettuce.

Pauline Newman organized New York's largest rent strike in 1907-08, ran on the Socialist ticket for New York's secretary of state, campaigned for women's suffrage, and became the first female organizer for the ILGWU, where she worked for seventy years.

Morris Hillquit, a leader of the American Socialist Party and member of the Socialist Labor Party, ran twice for Congress, helped organize the United Hebrew Trades and took on the International Workers of the World, arguing the socialist base should be established within the existing AFL trade union rather than as part of the more radical, Communist-oriented "Wobblies."

Ben Gold, an avowed Communist and organizer for the Fur and Leather Workers Union, became its president in the late 1920s and ran the union for forty years.

Bessie Abramowitz led a 1910 walkout from Hart Schaffner & Marx which grew into a strike of some 8,000 workers, resulting in union recognition and higher wages. She then helped lead her fellow workers to bolt from the conservative United Garment Workers and join the Amalgamated Clothing Workers, on whose executive board she later served.

Abramowitz married Sidney Hillman, a Lithuanian with roots in the social democratic and Russian Jewish Bund movements. Hillman helped organize the union at Hart Schaffner & Marx and shortly thereafter became president of the Amalgamated Clothing Workers. He was a close associate of Franklin Roosevelt and, with David Dubinsky, and Max Zaritsky, he organized the Congress of Industrial Organizations (CIO).

In 1909 then seventeen-year-old David Dubinsky escaped from a train taking him to a Siberian prison. He found his way to the United States, began as a clothing cutter and rose to become president of the ILGWU in 1932. In that job, he followed two Jews, Benjamin Schlesinger and Morris Sigman. They had led the ILGWU through a tumultuous 1920s power struggle when Communist-run New York ILGWU locals forced a disastrous and failed strike which called in local gangsters (Arnold Rothstein), lasted seven months, and nearly bankrupted the union. Sigman ousted the Communists, and then, at Dubinsky's suggestion, returned the reins to Schlesinger. When Schlesinger died in 1932, Dubinsky was left in charge.

Despite his Socialist roots, Dubinsky was strongly opposed to Communist efforts to take over the U.S. labor movement. In the late 1930s, when he saw renewed Communist involvement in the CIO, he pulled the ILGWU out, returning it to the AFL. Meanwhile, he formed the strongly anti-Communist Liberal Party and supported the United Auto Workers' efforts to keep Communists out of that union as well. Dubinsky finally stepped down as head of the ILGWU in 1966.

Over last fifty years, nearly all U.S. unions, including those headed by Jews, have returned to Gompers' more pragmatic approach. The politics may be Democratic, or occasionally Republican, but there is less focus on radical ideologies and more energy devoted to improving wages and working conditions.

Since Dubinsky, the ILGWU has merged with the Amalgamated Clothing and Textile Workers Union (headed for a time by Murray Finley) and the Hotel Employees and Restaurant Employees Union. Today it operates as "Unite Here," represents 450,000 workers and 400,000 retirees, and is headed by Bruce Raynor.

In 1983 Jackie Presser took over as president of the Teamsters. Earlier, in 1966, he had formed a Teamsters local and built it to 6,000 members. His five years as Teamster's president are a mixed record. He garnered substantial political capital from the Union's endorsement of Ronald Reagan, and he followed that up by leading the Teamsters back into the AFL-CIO. But it was later revealed his effort to become Teamsters president had been supported by New York's Genovese crime family and an out-of-court settlement, after his 1988 death, resolved federal charges of corruption against him.

In 1985, Morton Bahr headed up the 700,000-member United Communications Workers of America (CWA) from 1985 to 2005 when he was succeeded by CWA executive vice president, Larry Cohen. Albert Shanker served as president of the American Federation of Teachers (AFT) and as head of the New York local for the United Federation of teachers (UFT). In 1997, he was succeeded at the AFT by Sandra Feldman, who led the 1.3 million-member union until 2004. Meanwhile, Randi Weingarten is UFT president. Victor Gotbaum was head of the State and Local Government Employees Union from the late 1960s to the early 1980s and Andrew Stern now heads the 1.8 million-member Service Employees International Union.

Jews are but a small fraction of today's unionized labor force in America, but they continue to be a major part of its leadership.

The National Association for the Advancement of Colored People (NAACP):[509] In 1909 the NAACP was founded in the home of Joel Elias Spingarn (a Jewish Columbia University professor of comparative literature who was also a founder of publisher Harcourt Brace). Among the NAACP's six to eight founders (sources vary) was also Henry Moscowitz. Joel Spingarn served as NAACP's chairman of the board from 1913 to 1939 and as its president from 1929 to 1939. He also established the Spingarn medal for outstanding achievement by an African-American.

Following Spingarn in office was Arthur Spring, who served as the NAACP president from 1939 to 1966. He, in turn, was succeeded by Kivie Kaplan, president from 1966 to 1975. Jews thus headed up the NAACP for nearly all of its first sixty-six years. Since 1975 the NAACP presidency has been held by blacks.

Blacks Schools in the South: As covered more fully in Chapter 24 – Philanthropy, over 5,000 schools for blacks were built throughout the southern United States at the behest of Julius Rosenwald.

Black Voting Rights in the South:[510] The commitment of young Jews to the cause of black civil and voting rights was manifested in the murder of Michael Schwerner and Andrew Goodman, both members of the Congress of Racial Equality (CORE). They lost their lives along with James Chaney, a black, on June 21, 1964. The three were looking into the bombing of a Meridian, Mississippi, church that was to be used for voter registration when, after trumped up charges of involvement in the bombing, they were grabbed and taken to awaiting Ku Klux Klan members, who then beat and murdered them.

Native American rights:[511] Winona LaDuke was born to a Jewish mother and Chippewa father. After graduation from Harvard, she became a Native American rights activist, particularly in the cause of lands taken unfairly from the tribes. She has written two books on Native American rights, appeared in numerous documentaries on the subject, was named 1997 Woman of the Year by Ms. magazine, and ran as Ralph Nader's vice presidential running mate on the 2000 ticket.

Peruvian Indian (Sendero Luminoso) rights:[512] One of South America's most controversial and dangerous political movements of the 1980s and early 1990s was the Sendero Luminoso (Shining Path). A Maoist guerrilla faction of perhaps 10,000 militants, it was responsible for an estimated 30,000 deaths before its founder, and probable non-Jew, Manuel Ruben Abimael Guzman Reynoso, was captured in 1992.

In 1995 Lori Berenson was arrested and tried for complicity in Shining Path and for heading a counterpart insurgency called MRTA. After two trials, she is now serving a twenty-year sentence in a Peruvian jail. On the Web site of the Committee to Free Lori Berenson, they write "Lori Berenson is a social activist...a firm believer in the need to work for a better world for all, for a world in which everyone's fundamental human rights are respected."

The American Civil Liberties Union (ACLU):[513] The ACLU is prominent in a wide range of progressive or liberal causes. Among them: free speech, racial justice, reproductive freedom, lesbian and gay rights, drug policy, disability rights, the death penalty, women's rights, voter rights, police practices, and many others.

ACLU has a long history of strong Jewish presence. Among those instrumental in its 1920 creation were co-founder Stephen Wise (who also co-founded the NAACP) and Felix Frankfurter. For twenty-three years, from 1978 until September 2001, Ira Glasser led the ACLU, and during his tenure he tripled the organization from a staff of thirty-five attorneys to one with one hundred. Following his resignation, the executive director slot was turned over to Anthony D. Romero, a non-Jewish openly gay Latino who reported to President, Nadine Strossen (one-fourth Jewish). Strossen's bios typically describe her as the granddaughter of a Buchenwald survivor. Among the other six "Staff and Leaders" listed on the ACLU Web site are Geri E. Rozanski, Dorothy M. Ehrlich, and Steven Shapiro. For fifteen years, from 1985 to 2000, the New York ACLU was headed by Norman Siegal and a few years ago, an ACLU poll reportedly found 21 percent of its membership and 27 percent of its leadership were Jewish.

Student protests and the Free Speech movement:[514]The Students for a Democratic Society (SDS) was America's most strident student movement of the 1960s and 1970s. It spawned an even more radical sibling, the violent Weather Underground. In 1979 Arthur Liebman wrote his influential *Jews and the Left*, one of several scholarly books written by Jews to explore the disproportionate representation of Jews among leftist student activists. Liebman concluded that Jews were 46 percent of the delegates at the 1966 SDS convention. They were equally important in the movement's leadership, including Richard Flacks, Al Haber, Robb Ross, Steve Max, Mike Spiegal, Mike Klonsky, Todd Gitlin, Kathy Boudin, Bettina Aptheker, and Mark Rudd (who came to national prominence as leader of the student takeover of the president's office at Columbia University). Between 1960 and 1970, five of the nine SDS presidents were Jewish—Haber, Gitlin, Spiegel, Klonsky, and Rudd.

Liebman also concluded that the majority of the Free Speech Movement steering committee at University of California, Berkeley, was Jewish, as were 50 percent of the California Peace and Freedom party, according to David R. Schweitzer and James Eden.

The most radical group was the Weathermen, so named for Bob Dylan's line "You don't have to be a weatherman to know which way the wind is blowing." The name was later changed to Weather Underground. In today's terms the Weather Underground would be classed as "terrorist." Frustrated by the Vietnam War, disaffected by failures in the civil rights movement, and opposed to capitalism, the group intended to take over the government. They freed Timothy Leary (not Jewish) from jail, bombed two dozen public buildings, including the Capitol Building and Penta-gon, and lost three of their members to a premature bomb explosion in Greenwich Village. One member was also later implicated in the death of two police officers as the result of a Brinks truck robbery. Among its leaders were Mark Rudd, Bernadine Dohrn, Naomi Jaffe, David Gilbert, Laura Whitehorn and Brian Flanagan, and Bill Ayers. Of the seven, only Ayers (whose association with Barack Obama became part of the 2008 presidential campaign) and Flanagan are not Jewish.

Meanwhile, in France, a similar level of Jewish activist leadership led to the 1968 takeover of the Consistory building in Paris, "a symbol of traditional French political culture."

Today student activism is much less inflamed, but typing the words "Jewish stu-dent activism" into a Google search will yield 347,000 hits, many with references to *tikkun olam* and the goal of "healing and repairing the world."

The Chicago Seven:[515] One high water mark of the tumultuous late 1960s was the riot at Chicago's 1968 Democratic National Convention. It came after the Viet-cong had mounted the Tet offensive, draft cards were being burned, Martin Luther King and Robert F. Kennedy had been assassinated, and the Democrats were poised to nominate Hubert Humphrey to succeed Lyndon Johnson—this despite the peace movement's efforts to have Eugene McCarthy nominated instead.

Two groups, the National Mobilization to End the War (MOBE) and Youth International Party (YIPPIES), organized joint demonstrations to effect the nomina-tion. What may have begun as peaceful and fun ended up violent, with almost 25,000 police, Army and National Guardsmen trying to control thousands of demonstrators. Curfews were violated, the police used force, and the demonstration's leaders made public comments, such as non-Jew Tom Hayden's, "Make sure that if blood is going to flow, let it flow all over the city," and Jerry Rubin's "Kill the pigs! Kill the cops!"

After the riots, a Chicago grand jury indicted eight rioters and eight police offi-cers. The rioters included: Abbie Hoffman, Jerry Rubin, David Dellinger, Tom Hay-den, Rennie Davis, John Froines, Lee Weiner, and Bobby Seale. Seale was later removed from the case, and it became the Chicago Seven. Through it all, there was a decidedly disproportionate Jewish involvement. Of the seven defendants, three—Abbie Hoffman, Jerry Rubin, and Lee Weiner were Jewish, as was the presiding judge, Julius Hoffman, and two of the lead defense attorneys, William Kunstler and Leonard Weinglass (both of whom received multiple contempt citations from Hoffman).

Together with the 159 contempt citations issued by Hoffman, the jury found five of the seven defendants guilty. Ultimately, however, every one of those verdicts was overturned on appeal and all of the police officers were acquitted or had their charges dismissed.

Gay, Lesbian, and Transgender rights:[516] Harvey Milk was named one of *Time's* "100 Most Important People of the Twentieth Century." He was the first self-acknowledged homosexual to win high local office in the United States when he was elected to the San Francisco Board of Supervisors in 1977. His first piece of legisla-tion was a gay rights bill which San Francisco adopted and which, in its passage, led tragically to Milk's assassination by former supervisor, non-Jew Dan White.

Two years earlier, Bella Abzug had sponsored the first gay rights bill in the U.S. Congress, and that, together with Milk's opening of the closet door, led to a string of Jewish lesbian and gay activists. Barney Frank was elected to Congress from Massachusetts. Larry Kramer, an Academy Award nominee for his screenplay of D.H. Lawrence's *Women in Love* was a co-founder of both the Gay Men's Health Crises and ACT UP. After her election to the San Francisco Board of Supervisors, Roberta Achtenberg moved on to serve the Clinton administration as assistant secretary of Fair Housing and Equal Opportunity, and as senior advisor to HUD Secretary Henry Cisneros (neither Gay nor Jewish).

Leslie Feinberg was the editor of the *Marxist Workers World* and is a leading transgender activist and author of *Transgender Liberation* and *Stone Butch Blues*. Among the founders of the Gay and Lesbian Alliance Against Defamation (GLAAD) was Arnie Kantrowitz. Its treasurer is William Weinberger, its secretary, Judy Gluckstern, general counsel, David Huebner and at least three of the twenty directors are also Jewish. The Human Rights Campaign, which bills itself as the largest gay and lesbian organization, is similar with a likely five Jews of thirty-seven directors Jewish. Finally, the gay magazine Advocate was owned by David Goodstein from 1975 to 1985 and it is now led by senior vice president and Corporate Editorial Director, Judy Wieder.

Women's suffrage and feminism:[517]Though Jews such as Rose Schneiderman, Ernestine Rose, and Aletta Jacobs were leaders in the early twentieth-century suffrage and women's rights movements in Europe and in the United States, it is in the contemporary feminist movement, starting in the 1970s, where Jews have been the most prominent leaders. Nearly any article chronicling that history will identify Bella Abzug, Betty Friedan, and Gloria Steinem as seminal figures.

Bella Abzug first showed her independence by reciting Kaddish (something only men were supposed to do in her Orthodox temple) for a year after her father's death in 1933. She went on to practice civil rights law before becoming the first Jewish woman elected to the U.S. House of Representatives. Friedan wrote *The Feminine Mystique* and co-founded and served as first president of the National Organization for Women (NOW). Gloria Steinem founded *Ms.* magazine, wrote four books and helped found the National Women's Political Caucus.

Among other leading feminists, Robin Morgan served as editor of *Ms.* magazine. Andrea Dworkin was an outspoken, often vehement lesbian feminist, Naomi Wolf wrote *The Beauty Myth* and was active in the 2000 Gore campaign, Rebecca Walker (half Jewish) founded Third Wave Direct Action Corporation, and Susan Faludi won a National Book Critics Circle Award for her essay, "The Undeclared War Against Women."

One further measure of the role of Jews as leaders among women is found in the *Ladies Home Journal's* "100 Most Important Women of the 20th Century" (Exhibit 22a). Twenty of the one hundred women are of Jewish heritage.

Greenpeace:[518]Non-Jew Rex Wyler is credited by Greenpeace for writing the "definitive book on Greenpeace." Though they were not the only founders, Wyler begins his story with Irving and Dorothy Stowe. They are "Jewish-American Quaker pacifists (who) moved to Vancouver in 1966, and co-founded the "Don't Make a Wave Committee," which later became Greenpeace. Wyler then tells of the 1970 meeting where plans were made to send a boat to protest nuclear tests off Amchitka Island. At that meeting, "Stowe flashed the 'V' sign and said 'Peace,' Bill Darnell (presumably not Jewish), who had been recruited by Stowe, replied, "Make it green peace." Though Irving Stowe has since passed away, 1960s Jewish student revolutionary Todd Gitlin now serves as one of the six Greenpeace directors.

Earth First!:[519] One of the more radical environmentalist groups is Earth First! and among its seven founders, acknowledged in Susan Zakin's book, *Coyotes and Town Dogs: Earth First! and the Environmental Movement,* is Judi Bari, also credited with leading the campaigns against redwood logging and the use of tree spiking as a tactic. Bari died of breast cancer in 1997, but to this day, she is the subject of an unresolved mystery concerning the identity of the party who placed the pipe bomb, which exploded on May 24, 1990, under the seat of her car.

Community Organizing:[520] Saul Alinsky created the idea of community activism in 1930s Chicago. Originally focused on neighborhood action, he took it to black neighborhoods and was an inspiration for the mid-1960s Community Action Agencies (CAA's) established as part of Lyndon Johnson's Poverty Program. Ever the radical, Alinsky found the CAAs to be too "establishment," and he advocated more direct action to get results. He also decried mainstream liberals, feeling they were impotent pacifists. So influential was Alinsky in his prime that non-Jew Hillary Clinton wrote her undergraduate thesis on him.

Other Activists: Among other Jewish activists in service to other causes:

Henry Spira founded Animal Rights International;
Daniel Ellsberg protested the Vietnam war by releasing the Pentagon Papers;
Bernard Lown and non-Jew Dr. Evgueni Chazov of the Soviet Union earned a Nobel
    Prize on behalf of the International Physicians for the Prevention of Nuclear War
    for their role in establishing that organization..

Kahanist/settler movement:[521] Perhaps the single most controversial and radical movement in Israel involves followers of the assassinated father, Rabbi Meir David Kahane, and son, Binyamin Kahane. They, and others with a similar outlook, have used violent means to promote not just more settlements, but also the expansion of Israel. In their view, Israel must include land from the Nile to the Euphrates rivers, encompassing Jordon, Lebanon, and parts of Egypt and Iraq. These radicals see such expansion, and the creation of a theocratic state, as a religious duty under the Covenant. Many of them see war as necessary to expel the Arabs and expand Israel so Jews can be "redeemed" with the coming of the Messiah. For them, the plans of Yitzhak Rabin, Ehud Barak, Ariel Sharon, Ehud Olmert, and the majority of Israelis (whom Kahanists derisively call Hellenized Jews), to permit a Palestinian state and to return most or all of the West Bank and Gaza to the Palestinians, must be halted at any cost.

Among the terrorist acts committed by this group are Dr. Baruch Goldstein's massacre of twenty-nine praying Muslims on February 25, 1994, Yigal Amir's assassination of Yitzhak Rabin, various murders of Palestinians, and a failed attempt to bomb a Muslim girl's school and hospital. Like Al-Qaeda, Hezbolah, Hamas, Islamic Jihad, and other Islamic terrorist groups, these people believe they have a religious duty to God to be violent.

Anti-Zionism and Palestinian rights:[522] Perhaps fitting, this chapter ends where it began. Noam Chomsky, Tim Wise, and other prominent Jews, not only decry the settlers' movement, they are activists against the way Palestinians have been treated by the Israeli government. Some, such as Chomsky, are completely opposed to the existence of the state of Israel. They harken back to the early debates before Israel's founding and believe the only proper form of Zionism would be one in which Palestinians and Jews share political power in a combined state.

Chapter 23

Bad Guys (and Gals)

Judas Iscariot betrayed Christ. He nodded or otherwise gave the signal leading to Jesus' arrest, trial, and crucifixion. And for that, Judas paid the ultimate price. He committed suicide by hanging himself. That he had no choice in what he did, and in what transpired after, did not matter. God, not Judas, was the author of the drama. In that sense, Judas was a victim. But his conscience led him to suicide, and for the 2,000 years since, history has seen him as a traitor whose first name alone lives as a symbol of deceit and betrayal.

For many Christians, Judas is the ultimate Jewish bad guy and a core reason for anti-Semitism. But he is not the only Jew to have committed a nefarious deed. And this book would not do justice to the topic of Jewish achievement without discussing the other side of the coin. On occasion the remarkable achievements of Jews have been negative.

Marxism, Communism, and Stalin[523]

Karl Marx remains a controversial political figure more than 120 years after his death. Considered a "bad guy" by many, others continue to see him as a "genius" and believe strongly in the notions he fathered. Marxist philosophy still draws millions of followers around the world and on college campuses. Though Marx was descended from long lines of rabbis on both sides of his family, his parents converted to Lutheranism. Marx, instead, chose to become atheist. He never considered himself a Jew, and he spoke of Jews in the third person. Nonetheless, his genetic origins were Jewish.

An outgrowth of Marxism, Communism is the major political movement in which Jews have played the most significant role. As a movement, Communism lost most of its credibility in its failed seventy-five-year Soviet experiment. It simply did not work. It brutalized and impoverished its own people and because of Communism, millions died unnecessarily. It created an environmental mess in Russia that will take generations to clean up. It led to an incredible waste of time, money, and lives for those who experienced its evils or had to respond to its challenges.

Lenin sometimes gets tagged as a Jew. In fact, it is believed one grandparent on his mother's side was Jewish and Lenin married a Jewess. So there is a connection, but it is tenuous, and by most traditional definitions Lenin is not Jewish, nor did he consider himself one. (He wanted Jews to assimilate.)

Not tenuous, however, is the fact that Leon Trotsky was a Jew (He considered himself a "non-Jewish Jew.") Trotsky was a vital figure in the early revolution, and he led the fight to preserve the Soviet Union against the White Army and its counterrevolution.

Among other Jewish members of the Bolshevik inner circle were Lev Kamenev, a leader in the Politburo and chairman of the Moscow Soviet; Grigori Zinoviev, head of the Petrograd (St. Petersburg) Soviet; Adolf Yoffe, who served in ambassadorial roles to the United Kingdom, China, Austria, and Japan; Karl Radek, who was a member of the Central Committee and the Executive Committee of the Comintern; and Yakov Sverdlov, chairman of the Bolshevik Party Central Committee. These were all brutal men living in brutal times. The stories of how Bolsheviks seized power from the democratically oriented Mensheviks, the nastiness with which they fought to survive, and the regime of terror that commenced during Lenin's rule and was only made orders of magnitude worse by Stalin, leave no question that this group truly belongs on the "bad guy" side of the ledger.

What this listing of Bolshevik Jews neglects, however, is that by Stalin's reckoning, Jews were more important to the Mensheviks than to the Bolsheviks. In *Stalin and the Jews,* Arno Lustiger quotes Stalin as saying,

> "Statistics show that Jews are a majority within the Menshevik faction …followed by the Georgians and then by the Russians. In contrast to the overpowering majority of Russians in the Bolshevik faction, followed by the Jews…and then the Georgians, etc."

Statistics cited by Lustiger show the Bolshevik party had 964 Jewish members before the revolution. This was 4 percent of its 23,600 membership. These data are corroborated in Yuri Slezkine's, *The Jewish Century,* which points out the Soviet Union considered Jewish status to be a nationality, akin to being a Russian or a Georgian. Jewish nationality was stamped on every Jew's identity papers. That, and the Soviet's bureaucratic penchant for maintaining detailed records, means statistics about numbers of Jews at various levels in different organizations (and their disproportionate level of achievements in Soviet society) are not in dispute.

More important, however, is the simple fact that the villain of the piece was Stalin, and Stalin was a Georgian who, early in life, studied for the Orthodox priesthood. He was not Jewish. Lenin lasted for only a few years after the revolution. Stalin grabbed power in 1924 and held onto it for nearly thirty years. The true horrors of Communism occurred during his paranoid leadership.

In that paranoia, Stalin killed nearly every other founder of Soviet Communism, Jew and non-Jew alike. Sverdlov died early (1919) and thus didn't have to be dealt with by Stalin. But Stalin had Trotsky murdered with a pickax to the back of the head. He arranged for Kirov (a charismatic non-Jew and potential challenger) to be assassinated. He put Kamenev and Zinoviev on trial for treason (as "enemies of the people") and extracted phony confessions from them, having promised he would spare their families. Then he had them executed for complicity in the Kirov murder (among other crimes). Radek was probably shot in 1939 for having been sympathetic to Trotsky. Yoffe was also associated with Trotsky and reportedly committed suicide. These are but a small tip of the horrific iceberg of what Stalin did to those close to him or those he thought might become a threat. Only one prominent Jewish Bolshevik from the founding cadre, Lazar Kaganovich, survived Stalin.

Robert Conquest, perhaps the foremost Stalin biographer, estimates Stalin's leadership caused eighteen million deaths from famines, imprisonments, and executions carried out in conjunction with forced collectivization, purges, show trials, and other acts of terror between 1930 and 1939. In his 1946 memoir, *I Choose Freedom*, defector Victor Kravchenko said, "From 1 January 1935 to 22 June 1941, 19,840,000 enemies of the people were arrested. Of these, 7 million were shot in prison and a majority of the others died in camp." Stalin purged (killed) virtually his entire inner circle and much of the Soviet military officer corps. He launched an anti-Semitic campaign in 1948 and was ready to conduct show trials, mostly against Jewish doctors, when he died in 1953.

So we can place some blame on Jews for helping father a failed, very nasty system (Soviet Communism), but Stalin, the Georgian, was the evil genius behind Communism's worst excesses.

Spies and Traitors[524]

The story of how Stalin got the atomic bomb cannot be told without discussing the Jews who helped him get it. That spies, mostly Jews, were involved, is no longer in question. As recently as 2008, revelations by the spy, Morton Sobel, finally convinced Julius and Ethel Rosenberg's sons that, at least, their father was guilty as charged.

Earlier, the Venona documents—secret Soviet cable traffic from the 1940s—augmented by the Mitrokhin Archive—a trove of documents smuggled out of Russia by a veteran KGB officer—plus access to the long closed KGB files, definitively proved the case. Allegations of revealing atomic secrets and other acts of betrayal were made against Julius and Ethel Rosenberg, Harry Gold, David Greenglass, Theodore Hall,

Morton Sobell, Elizabeth Bentley, George Koval, and William Perl, all Jews, as well as non-Jews Klaus Fuchs, Guy Burgess, Donald MacLean, Harry Dexter White, and Kim Philby. Ultimately, the cables also proved Alger Hiss, Harry Hopkins, (both non-Jews) and J. Robert Oppenheimer were providing information to the Soviets. That the Venona data could not be used during the resulting trials was an unfortunate casualty of not wanting to reveal FBI tradecraft. But when the Venona data was finally made available in 1995 and could be corroborated from then open archives of the KGB, all doubt was erased. Mitrokhin's archive, and a 2007 Russian ceremony honoring Koval, further corroborated the facts.

And while the Soviets had brilliant nuclear physicists and would doubtless have ultimately built a bomb, there is no question their efforts were substantially accelerated by the information the traitors provided. And as many sources have reported, one ironic result of the spies' efforts was that Stalin knew all about the Manhattan Project. Truman, on the other hand, only found out about it on the day he was sworn in as president.

One cannot minimize the damage done, nor the betrayal. At the same time, it is important to consider that, despite the 1939 Ribbentrop pact, until 1948, Stalin was not known to be particularly anti-Semitic, and his antagonism toward Jews was not widely understood until after his death in 1953. (Please see the Lev Leviev biosketch at the beginning of Chapter 20.) Moreover, the scale of Stalin's crimes, though occasionally rumored, was not conclusively laid out for the world until Khrushchev made his famous February 1956 revelations to the Communist Party Conference and still later, in 1969, when Robert Conquest's book, *The Great Terror,* was published to document the horrors of Stalin and the Soviet system.

Communism and the Soviet Union arrived on the world scene with the October revolution of 1917. For most of the early 1920s it was on the defensive, but with Stalin's accession, and the Party's series of five-year plans, which forced industrialization and the collectivization of agriculture, the Communists began to bring a backward Russian culture into the twentieth century. The effort began to bear fruit, and the Communists aggressively propagandized the Soviet Union as a "worker's paradise." This happened while Germany was falling apart and dramatic labor unrest fomented in much of the West. The Crash of 1929 and ensuing worldwide Depression destroyed hope and confidence.

For many who matured in that era, Communism appeared to work while the democracies and capitalism did not. And while Hitler's fascism might also work, it was viewed as evil by anyone with left-wing sentiments. For many idealists, intellectuals and others with liberal views, Communism's successes and the fear of Western decline created sympathy and strong support for Communism. And once their allegiances were compromised, there was simply no turning back.

Interestingly, once the facts about Stalin and Communism became more widely understood, the age of ideological spying for the Soviet Union closed, and with that, the era in which Jews were Communism's principal spies ended. Only Gus Hall and the U.S Communist Party persisted, having already made their bed. But once Stalin's excesses became known, the motivation for spying changed. Treason became essentially economic (a nice "payday" in the cases of Aldrich Ames, the Walkers, Edward Lee Howard, and others) or pathological and economic (as in the case of Robert

Hansen). With few exceptions, after the 1950s, U.S. traitors were generally not political and not Jewish. As noted in his *Economist* magazine obituary, the last great Soviet spy catcher, Rem Krassilnikov, caught every single CIA spy in the Soviet Union by the end of the 1980s. He did this not because ideological traitors in the United States revealed their identities, but because non-Jews Edward Lee Howard, and Aldrich Ames (both CIA employees), and Robert Hansen (an FBI employee) were working for the Soviets—for money.

So in the end, the Jewish traitors did the West a huge disservice. Their naiveté helps explain why they did it, but that is an inadequate defense. One can call it an achievement to spirit atomic weapons secrets to the Soviets, thereby changing the balance of power. But it was a pyrrhic achievement. The Soviet Union was never the worker's paradise it promised. It was a murderous, bureaucratic mess. A further measure of the ill-fated efforts by the Jewish traitors was demonstrated in the reversal of the Soviet position on Israel. After having been an early supporter, Stalin's Soviet Union became an opponent of Israel and stayed opposed to the Jewish state until the Soviet Union fell apart.

Ironically, the only other major Jewish traitor was again ideological. Jonathon Pollard was an ideological spy for Israel. He felt that U.S. secrets should not be secrets from Israel, and he revealed those secrets to them. He was caught and has stayed in jail despite continuing efforts from Israel and American Jewish supporters to have him freed. The odds are he will stay in jail till he dies, or, at best, is a very old man.

Court TV maintains a "Crime Library" on their Web site listing the major criminals of various kinds. One of their lists is shown in Exhibit 23a. Of the fifteen major spies they identify, three—Pollard, and both Rosenbergs—mean Jews are three of the fifteen names, well above what one would expect. At the same time, two of the three were involved in the atomic spying scandal.

Oligarchs[525]

Russia's oligarchs are a topic suitable for either of two chapters in this book, Chapter 21 – "Enterprise," or this chapter. That the oligarchs are very shrewd and have accumulated great wealth and power is indisputable. In that sense, they would fit nicely with the entrepreneurs. Nonetheless, the rich irony of their contemporary role in Russia (as contrasted with the pogroms of the tsars and the anti-Semitism of Stalinism), coupled with the questionable ways in which they (at least the original oligarchs) amassed their fortunes, makes it more fitting that we discuss them here.

So first, what is an oligarch? As generally used, the word "oligarch" means one of a very small number of men who have taken over major state enterprises and assets of the former Soviet Union. Oligarchs are most often Russian or Ukrainian, but there are oligarchs in other former Soviet republics and Warsaw Pact countries as well. And in fact, the term "oligarch" has been so popularized that it has begun to have currency in countries that were never part of the Soviet Union. For our purposes, however, only the Russians matter. They are the original and most important of the oligarchs.

Oligarchs acquired wealth and power in a variety of ways, more often than not "questionable." On occasion, they used relationships with Russian government officials to buy state assets for a pittance, often paying bribes back to the officials handling the sale. In other cases, oligarchs acquired control of shares originally distributed free to employees of the enterprise. In those instances, the oligarchs bought the shares for pennies on the dollar from poor Russians who had little sense of their value or were desperate for cash to survive the early days after the breakup of the Soviet Union. In other cases, oligarchs borrowed money from companies they controlled, then loaned it back to the companies in exchange for huge numbers of additional shares. Those additional shares locked in the oligarch's control while diluting the ownership of the rest of the shareholders. This wiped out the value of the investment owned by the other shareholders and eliminated any influence they might have had.

Perhaps the most fascinating and questionable tactic was the "loans for shares" program. This scheme arose from the fact that Boris Yeltsin was facing re-election in 1996 and was likely to lose. His poll numbers were so abysmal, his popularity could be measured in single digits. The odds of his winning re-election were trivial. Many expected the Communists to win big, take over the presidency, hold onto the Duma (legislature) and return to complete power. At one infamous dinner, Yeltsin met with a group of wealthy oligarchs. They had access to sufficient cash to give him a shot at winning re-election. He would use it to retain Western political consultants, purchase huge amounts of media time, and generally portray himself as a youthful and vigorous leader while depicting his opponents as representing a demonstrably failed ideology.

The oligarchs loaned the money to the Yeltsin government. The loans were collateralized by Russian state-owned assets (businesses and natural resources). Yeltsin used the money to get re-elected, and when the loans were not repaid (and the plan never was for them to be repaid), the oligarchs grabbed the collateral. In short, in exchange for loans representing but a small fraction of the value of the collateral, a few Russian oligarchs took control of major sectors of the Russian economy and made themselves more powerful and much wealthier than they had been. After re election, but before his term ended, Yeltsin turned the presidency over to Vladimir Putin, a former KGB officer, who was subsequently elected in his own right. Since then, Putin has proven popular with the Russian electorate and has evolved a different, often strident strategy to attack a number of the oligarchs, in particular, those who have challenged him.

By nearly everyone's analysis, these chaps have simply not played the game according to the "Rules of the Marquis of Queensberry."

So how many "original oligarchs" are there? The answer to that question depends upon who provides the list and how many names they wish to include. The San Jose State economics department lists "The original seven oligarchs," the California National Guard in the International Section of its Web site lists the top ten. David E. Hoffman, *The Washington Post's* foreign editor, lists six in his book, *The Oligarchs: Wealth and Power in the New Russia*. The lists share mostly the same names, but for our purposes, Hoffman's list is authoritative and it makes the point. His list includes:

Boris Berezovsky	**Vladimir Gusinsky**
Alexander Smolensky	**Mikhail Khodorkovsky**
Yury Luzhkov	Anatoly Chubais

Berezovsky began by reselling Russian Ladas (automobiles), which he bought at artificially low prices because of his cozy relationship with the bureaucrats running the state-owned manufacturer. He resold the cars at a huge markup and pocketed the profits. Later he opened his own dealerships and controlled a major share of the Moscow automobile market. For a time he had effective operating control of Aeroflot, the Russian airline, several newspapers and magazines, and ORT, the country's state-owned and largest television network. He is now on the outs with Putin, has been exiled, and is in the United Kingdom where that government has refused to extradite him to Russia to stand trial for corruption.

Gusinsky began by buying copper wire on the black market, converting it into bracelets, selling them and making a small fortune in the process. Later, he spent time in the United States at the University of Virginia where he did some work for Ted Turner and his Goodwill Games. Upon his return to Moscow, he became a Russian consultant and then a property renovator and construction contractor. Still later, he opened Most Bank, bringing to it deposits from Moscow city government, which he got because of the relationship he had developed with Moscow's mayor (Yury Luzhkov) from his property renovation and construction business. Gusinsky did not have to make interest payments to Moscow for those deposits, but he was able to use them for his own benefit, mostly profiting from foreign exchange trades and purchases of state securities. Ultimately, he purchased media properties and came to control major radio, TV, newspaper, and magazine enterprises. Like Berezovsky, Gusinsky ran afoul of Putin. Gusinsky is now in exile and was arrested and later released on bail by the Greek government, pending possible extradition to Russia. If nothing else, Putin has demonstrated his concern over control of the Russian media, and it is in that realm that he has frequently challenged the oligarchs.

Smolensky was arrested by the KGB in 1981 for publishing a Bible using government presses and ink. Under Gorbachev in 1987, he had formed a cooperative supplying materials to Moscow tradesmen. The enterprise was so profitable, Smolensky decided to create his own bank, Stolichny Bank, which, for a time, was one of Moscow's largest. In addition, he has developed media properties including two newspapers and part ownership of the ORT television network. He is also a shareholder in the Sibneft Oil Company. Though Stolichny bank failed and wiped out many depositors, Smolensky remains in Russia and he is powerful.

Mikhail Khodorkovsky controlled Yukos, one of Russia's largest petroleum companies. In addition, he controlled MENATEP, a major holding company formed in 1982 when he was a member of the Young Communist League. MENATEP became a major trader and market maker in shares of privatized state-owned enterprises and through MENATEP, Khodorkovsky came to control large companies in the chemical, construction, textile, consumer goods, mining and oil industries. His takeover of Yukos for a pittance relative to its value, his dilution of other shareholders, his consolidation of control, and his participation in the loans for shares program gave Khodorkovsky great notoriety in Russia. It has also made him one of the world's wealthiest men. His life appeared assured until those around Putin saw Khodorkovsky as a potential threat. The FSB (successor to the KGB) surrounded his plane one night when it landed in Siberia. He was arrested, tried, found guilty of fraud, and given an eight year jail sentence. The most valuable parts of Yukos were grabbed and later bought by Russian state owned oil company, Rosneft. Khodorkovsky may well face additional charges and may spend a very long time in prison beyond the current 2012 end of his current jail sentence.

Yury Luzhkov is the mayor of Moscow. Luzhkov is a larger than life figure, a Mayor Richard Daly writ even larger in Russia's most important city. That he is effective is without question. Ultimately, however, it is his second wife, Yelena Baturina, Russia's wealthiest woman, who has proven to be the family's most significant oligarch.

Anatoly Chubais headed the early privatization program of Russian state property and later served as head of UES, Russia's electric power monopoly. Many view Chubais as the single person most responsible for the ascendancy of the oligarchs. His willingness to cut deals and hastily distribute shares representing about one-third of the Soviet economy to citizens who had no sense of their value was probably dictated by a fear that if he failed to move quickly, the Communists would return and undo the privatization process. Nonetheless, together with Yeltsin's "loans for shares" program, the consequence was the ascendancy of the oligarchs. Chubais, the subject of a 2005 assassination attempt now heads RUSNANO, a state-sponsored effort to develop nanotechnology in Russia.

What is interesting about these six oligarchs is that four of them are of Jewish extraction (Chubais and Luzhkov are not). Further, Berezovsky now counts himself a Christian—a conversion some say is intended only to avert anti-Semitic criticism. In addition, Khodorkovsky and Smolensky are of mixed parentage.

If we were to compare the Hoffman list to the one from San Jose State, we would remove Luzhkov and Chubais but add Vladimir Potanin, Vladimir Vinogradov, and Mikhail Friedman. The San Jose State grouping results in five of its seven oligarchs being of Jewish extraction. Other lists would yield similar outcomes. By any count, Jews have been the dominant oligarchs. When one considers that there are supposedly only 550,000 Jews among Russia's 145 million people (0.38 percent of the population versus 2.1 percent in the United States), it is simply amazing that Jews represent roughly two-thirds or more of the country's oligarchs, therein controlling a huge part of the wealth of the country in which they were reviled both in tsarist and late Stalinist times.

Mobsters[526]

Meyer Lansky (Meyer Suchowljansky) was not, as commonly believed, just a clever financier for the mob. Nor was he an isolated case of Jewish involvement during the heyday of American organized crime.

In fact, if anyone could be said to have "organized" crime, it was Meyer Lansky—working with his close friend, non-Jew Charles "Lucky" Luciano (Salvatore Luciana). Together they created the modern syndicate, set up Murder Incorporated, established huge and profitable bootlegging operations and developed much of the gambling industry in the United States and Cuba.

But Lansky and Luciano really belong to the third generation of American Jewish mobsters, not the first. The story properly begins with Monk Eastman (Edward Osterman). Eastman was born in Brooklyn in 1873. By the time he was in his early twenties, he was the leader of all the Jewish thugs on the East Side of New York. According to Rich Cohen, author of *Tough Jews,* Monk Eastman "could call out over a thousand soldiers," all of them Jewish. They were all part of the "Gangs of New York," largely ethnic groupings of tough guys who, when not fighting each other, stole from the poor and weak while shaking down merchants "needing protection." Thomas Sowell, in his book, *Ethnic America,* noted that in 1909, 3,000 Jewish youngsters were brought before the juvenile court in New York. It was neither pretty nor sophisticated.

It was Arnold Rothstein who deserves credit for converting the unruly Jewish mob into a smart, well-organized, highly profitable criminal business. He became the ultimate boss of the New York underworld. Rothstein is most remembered, perhaps apocryphally, as the "fixer" behind the 1919 World Series "Black Sox" scandal. (In fact, he was never indicted for anything having to do with the scandal.) Rothstein was a very smart, very dapper fellow, a remarkable gambler, a champion pool player, and the scion of a wealthy Jewish family that owned a dry-goods store and a cotton-processing plant. Unlike others who saw crime as part of their immigrant legacy from the violent gangs of Odessa or Bucharest, or as a reaction to the poverty and discrimination of the Lower East Side ghettos, Rothstein was apparently drawn by the excitement and drama of the lifestyle. And he was so good at it that before he was killed in 1928, he had far surpassed his father's fortune, and in fact, anonymously arranged to bail out his father when he had fallen on hard times.

Rothstein truly was the original Jewish Godfather. He was among the very first to see the enormous money to be made from bootlegging and drugs, and he set up organizations to go after those profits. He also recruited some of the best criminal talent in history, including Meyer Lansky, Benjamin "Bugsy" Siegel, Lucky Luciano, Frank Costello (Francesco Castiglia), Legs Diamond, Waxy Gordon, Dutch Schultz, Louis Lepke, and Gurrah Shapiro. It is doubtful that even a legend like Jack Welch of GE could claim such a remarkable recruiting history. And through it all, until his death over a dispute about a relatively small sum of money, Rothstein dressed immaculately, gambled successfully, and wined and dined with the likes of Governor Al Smith and Justice Louis Brandeis. F. Scott Fitzgerald depicted Rothstein as the character Meyer Wolfshiem in *The Great Gatsby,* and in Rich Cohen's words, Rothstein was "the Moses of the underworld."

In the hiatus between Rothstein's death in 1928 and the ascendancy of Lansky and Luciano, two Italians, Giuseppe "Joe" Masseria and Salvatore Maranzano took over as joint kingpins of New York crime. Both were old-school Sicilians, and each of them wanted Lucky Luciano to ditch Meyer Lansky and come work solely for them.

Luciano had other plans. He knew that Maranzano intended to destroy Masseria and thereby control all crime in the eastern United States. It was an opportunity for Lansky and Luciano to change the game. First they orchestrated Masseria's classic mob-style execution over lunch (shot immediately after Luciano left the table to go to the men's room). Maranzano thanked Luciano and immediately declared himself "boss of all bosses." That lasted less than six months. Lansky and Luciano set up Maranzano and had him killed. Together, they then took over. They organized the five crime families in New York into a "syndicate" with no "boss of all bosses." The five families would be independent but act in concert. To enforce discipline, and with support from the families, Lansky and Luciano established Murder Incorporated. Its job was to kill all the "mutually agreed upon" renegades who defied the power of any family or otherwise insulted key players in the syndicate. To make it work, they assigned the job as co-heads of Murder Incorporated to Louis "Lepke" Buchalter (Jew) and Albert Anastasia (non-Jew), two very nasty fellows. Together they invented "contract killing" and recruited mostly Jews to do the work, including Abraham "Kid Twist" Reles, Harry Strauss, Bugsy Goldstein, and others.

Meanwhile, in 1927, Lepke and Jacob "Gurrah" Shapiro killed Augie Orgen. In the process, they took over the business of shaking down labor unions and the companies those unions were trying to organize. It did not take Lepke and Gurrah long to decide that working on a "payment-for-services" basis was not nearly as profitable as taking over the unions themselves. Soon they controlled thousands of workers in trucking, motion pictures, and painting, and with that, mob control of unions—and their pension funds—had begun.

From their early days under Rothstein, Lansky, Luciano, Frank Costello and Bugsy Siegel honed their skills in casino gambling and hotel operations starting originally with hotels in Saratoga Springs in upstate New York. They learned both how to pay off cops and other officials and to operate clean, high-quality casinos and hotels where customers got good value and were not cheated. This followed the earlier pattern set by Rothstein in which their bootleg booze was always of the best quality and never watered down. Customers liked the quality Lansky and his cronies provided, and they came back for more. As Prohibition ended, gambling became the vehicle to replace the lost profits—and profit they did.

Working with Lansky, Bugsy Siegel is said to have "pioneered" large-scale Las Vegas hotels and casinos just as America's GIs were returning from World War II. This move ultimately led to his execution for being overbudget and behind schedule with the Flamingo Hotel and Casino, and perhaps for diverting some funds to a girlfriend.

Lansky paid off Governor Huey Long for rights to operate in New Orleans and he set up operations in Hot Springs, Arkansas, as well as Kentucky and South Florida. Lansky's most notorious operation, however, was in Havana, Cuba, in a partnership with Dictator Fulgencio Batista. Those operations were later popularized in Francis Ford Coppola's movie, *Godfather II* wherein Michael Corleone has to come to grips with Hyman Roth, the fictional characterization of Meyer Lansky. In the movie, Michael has Roth killed. In real life, however, the ending was much different. After a drawn out and ultimately unsuccessful effort to immigrate to Israel (or anyplace else that would have him), Lansky was returned to the United States, where he faced three separate charges. He defeated the first in court, had a preliminary conviction on the second overturned, and saw the third charge dismissed. In fact, through his entire life, Lansky never spent significant time in jail. He died of old age (eighty-two) at his home in Miami.

In the end, Lansky's death coincides with the demise of prominent Jewish involvement in organized crime. Rich Cohen's take on the fact that Italians continue to lead organized crime while Jews pulled out is interesting. He quotes John Cusack, a retired thirty-six-year agent of the Federal Bureau of Narcotics, as saying "The Jewish Mafia was never passed on like the Italian Mob. Jews didn't recruit. The old-timers did what they felt they had to do; but they did not want the younger generation of Jews mixed up in it."

Throughout his long life, Lansky was involved with so many other Jews in organized crime that they are simply too numerous to mention. Among them were Dutch Schultz (Arthur Flegenheimer), Mickey Cohen, Charlie Workman, Albert Tannenbaum, Detroit's Bernstein Brothers (the "Purple Gang"), Kidd Cann, Moe Dalitz, Motche Goldberg, Abner "Longy" Zwillman, Louis Amberg, Abe Greenthal, and the Sheeny Gang and many, many others. It simply does not wash to say that there were very few Jews in organized crime. There were many.

Major Jewish involvement in organized crime really came to an end well before Lansky's death. The era culminated between 1935 and 1945. Dutch Schultz was taken out by Murder Incorporated in October of 1935 because he refused to go along with a mob decision not to kill prosecutor Thomas E. Dewey. Abe "Kid Twist" Reles, tired of serving jail time, began to rat on his former colleagues in March of 1940, providing information on seventy unsolved Murder Incorporated "contract" murders. Charlie Workman was sentenced to life in jail. Harry Strauss and Bugsy Goldstein were tried and executed for murder during 1941. On August 24, 1940, Louis Lepke turned himself in to newspaper columnist Walter Winchell—of all people—who in turn handed him over to non-Jew, J. Edgar Hoover. Lepke was later tried and executed on the same night as Mendy Weiss and Louis Capone, based in part on Reles' information. Reles either jumped, or was shoved, from the window of the room where he was being watched over by eighteen cops during the trials of his former friends. Many other Jewish mobsters were sentenced to long terms or went to death row during this time period. Bugsy Siegel lasted till June 1947, when he was executed by the mob.

In the end, it is fair to say that between 1900 and 1945, organized crime in the United States was mostly a product of two cultures, Italians and Jews—with a few Irish and others thrown in. Further, though the story of Jewish involvement is fascinating, the dominant players were always the Italians. Jews were critical players with a vital role, but the big numbers were with the Italians. Court TV's "Library of Crime" describes at least sixty-three leading "Mob Bosses," "Crime Family Leaders," and heads of "Unique Gang Organizations." Of the sixty-three (See Exhibit 23b), one is Japanese (representing Japan's Yakuza), two are English (the Kray Bothers), three are Irish (James Burke of the Lufthansa Heist, Willie Egan, and Bugs Moran) and nine are Jewish. The rest (forty-eight), are Italian. Out of the sixty-three, sixty are American and thus, based on population we might have projected there to be 1.2 Jews on the list. Instead we get eight times that number.

Today most would say there is no significant Jewish involvement in residual organized crime in America, and that appears to be the case. Less well documented, however, is the extent to which the so-called Russian Mafia has significant Jewish involvement. That topic will wait for a later edition of this book.

Jewish Pirates[527]

Who knew? Seeking refuge from the Inquisition, Spanish and Portuguese Jews fled to the New World (including some who reportedly served on Columbus' voyages). Though vilified, Catholic rulers and locals initially set aside their religious intolerance when Jews proved useful in setting up trade networks for commodities such as tea, coffee, grains, sugar, gold, and silver. But when the Inquisition reached the Americas, Jews in Mexico and Peru were burned and their property confiscated. To survive, and to exact revenge, they and fellow Jews from Holland (a Spanish enemy at the time), carved out a swashbuckling niche, sometimes from a base in British controlled Jamaica that lasted into the 1600s.

Violent Crime and Assassins[528]

David Berkowitz ("Son of Sam") makes everybody's list as one of the most notorious criminals of all time. He terrorized New York for more than a year between July 29, 1976, and August 10, 1977. He killed five young women and one man, and he wounded at least seven more. His was the rampage of a probable paranoid schizophrenic who had lost his mother to breast cancer when he was fourteen. Son of Sam was national news as the story played out during that year and later over the course of his trial. Berkowitz is still in jail, has converted to Christianity, and acknowledges that he is unlikely to ever be paroled.

Berkowitz is one of only six Jews to make the Court TV Library's lists of Serial Killers, Notorious Murderers, Outlaws, Terrorists, and Assassins. The other five are: Ira Einhorn, Nathan Leopold, Richard Loeb, Joel Steinberg, and Otto Sanhuber. All but Sanhuber are well-known names, and Sanhuber was not really certain that he was Jewish, but he thought that he was. There are 200 American names included on these lists and seventy-eight foreigners (Exhibit 23c). None of the six Jews is foreign. Perhaps the incidence of violent crime by Jews outside the United States is extremely rare, but there are insufficient data to make a definitive statement. The U.S. data is clear. Of 200 violent U.S. criminals, one could project there to be a bit more than four Jews. Instead, at six, the incidence is roughly 50 percent more than expected. And while our sample may be off—missing some violent criminals who did not make Court TV's lists or missing Jews whom we did not identify—those errors would not likely change the overall observation that Jews are involved in violent crime only somewhat more than would be expected. Violent crime (not counting the heyday of organized crime) is not an area in which Jews represent disproportionately high numbers. They do their share, but not that much more or less than others. Interestingly, none of the seventy listed sexual predators is Jewish.

One omission from the Court TV list deserves a passing mention. That is Yigal Amir. Amir is Israeli. He will go down in history as having committed a notorious political assassination that changed the course of Middle East history. He shot and killed Yitzhak Rabin, the Israeli prime minister who signed the Oslo Peace Accords with the Palestinians. That breath of hope was intentionally destroyed by Amir. His purpose was to set back any compromise agreement that would have resolved the fifty-year dispute between the Jews and Palestinians. That the assassin was a conservative Jew rather than a Palestinian has been a source of shame and embarrassment to many Jews, both in Israel and abroad. Deservedly so, it was and is a tragedy.

Financial Crime, Frauds, and Scams[529]

In a matter of days in late 2008, Bernard Madoff, a name all but unknown outside his limited circles in Manhattan, the Hamptons, and the Florida Gold Coast, became notorious as history's greatest scam artist. Trusted, low key, a *macher* (a big hearted big shot), he refused to take money from some who wanted to invest with him. He was seen as a uniquely capable manager of other peoples' money, wealthy from that endeavor, generous in his philanthropy, and active in various Jewish causes. He was the embodiment of Jewish financial success and integrity.

With a single phone call, some learned their life savings had evaporated. Major charities were shut down. A respected French money manager slit his wrists. As one of the author's Jewish friends observed, Bernie Madoff did far more damage to Jews than Osama bin Lauden ever could. He destroyed more Jewish family fortunes than non Jews and more Jewish charities as well. He decimated the sense of confidence, pride and contentment Jews have enjoyed in recent decades as anti-Semitism, at least in the United States, had waned. As Edgar Bronfman noted just two months before in a *New York Times* interview, he knew anti-Semitism was no longer a threat when Al Gore lost the 2000 election and no one blamed his selection of Joe Lieberman as a running mate.

At Yeshiva University, on whose board Madoff had served and whose endowment was out $110 million, the $50 billion scandal became a teaching moment about trust, Judaism, anti-Semitism, materialism, and Jewish values. Rabbi Benjamin Blech spoke for many when he noted, "If you cheat and steal, you cannot claim you are a good Jew."

In Los Angeles, it was Rabbi David Wolpe who observed that within the communal bonds of the Jewish family, "your family can embarrass you as no one else can." Going further he noted that a Jew who comes before God after death is asked a series of questions. The first, said Wolpe, is "Were you honest in your business dealings?" The last, 'Did you hope for redemption?' Rabbi Wolpe said he believes Madoff can never make amends. "It is not possible for him to atone for all the damage he did and I don't even think that there is a punishment that is commensurate with the crime, for the wreckage of lives he's left behind. The only thing he could do, for the rest of his life, is work for redemption that he would never achieve."

If there are relatively few Jews among street criminals and murderers, many people feel the reverse is true for financial crimes. Those who follow the financial news sense that Jews commit more than their share of financial misdeeds. Names like Bernard Madoff, Michael Milken, Marc Rich, Ivan Boesky, Andrew Fastow, and others are just too well known and too often discussed in the media to avoid a sense that as active players in money and finance, Jews commit a significant number of financial crimes. In fact, that conclusion is wrong, but it takes some history and some context to explain why.

No one source gathers all financial scandals through time into a single frame of reference for this evaluation. In its absence the author has compiled one list which is provided in Exhibit 23d. It includes eighty major financial scandals involving 120 individuals. It was developed from sources such as the March 3, 2002, *Fortune* magazine list of white-collar criminals (Exhibit 23e), the New York Chapter of the Institute of Financial Auditors "Million-Dollar Frauds," the University of Exeter list of "Classic Financial Scandals," and others. And while it cannot claim to be comprehensive, it is reasonably representative.

The companies listed and the individual names bring to mind some of the more notorious scandals over time including such well-known fiascos as Enron, the insider trading scandals of the 1980s, the Clinton pardons of Marc Rich and Pincus Green, the Mississippi Company, which fleeced thousands of French citizens of their savings, and the counterpart South Seas Bubble, which did the same thing to the British.

Browsing the list is a bit of a walk down the Memory Lane of financial scandals for anyone who has followed such shenanigans over the last forty years or so.

A review of the entire list shows that of the 120 names, twenty-five (21 percent) are Jewish. Because the scandals generally arose in the United States, Canada, Western Europe, Australia, and New Zealand, those populations form the basis for saying, we would have expected two Jews on the list rather than the twenty-five shown.

Culled to include only the seventy-five names involved in predominantly U.S. scandals, we would expect 1.5 Jews. Instead there are eighteen. Both approaches suggest Jews have been involved in financial scandals at a rate twelve times their proportion of the population. Corroboration comes in the shorter 2002 "White Collar Criminals" list from *Fortune* magazine. It includes twenty-three individuals, mostly from the United States. Of the twenty-three, only .5 should have been Jewish. Instead, there were six: Bernie Cornfield, Marc Rich, Ivan Boesky, Michael Milken, Martin Frankel, and Al Taubman—again, twelve times what we would expect based solely on population.

The problem is the frame of reference. That is, Jews have significantly higher levels of education, hold disproportionate numbers of white-collar jobs, and are disproportionately counted among entrepreneurs, financiers, and attorneys. The appropriate frame of reference for measuring the incidence of Jewish financial fraud is not their percentage of the overall population, but their percentage of those in a position to commit such crimes. Consider:

23 percent of *Fortune's* "40 Richest Under 40" were Jews (Exhibit 15a).
24 percent of *Fortune* magazine's "25 Most Powerful People in Business" were Jews (Chapter 16).
Half or more of the major Wall Street investment firms were created by Jews (Chapter 17) and,
31 percent of 2007 *Forbes* 400 were Jews (Exhibit 21a).

Given that context, the analysis showing Jews were involved in 21 percent of the major financial scandals means Jews commit financial crimes roughly in proportion to their numbers, but not substantially more, nor less.

Finally, while some Jews are "high achievers" in financial scandals, that conclusion must be matched with the corollary observation that non-Jews are still the predominant actors in such scandals. That twenty-five of 120 financial criminals were Jews means ninety-five were not. This obvious point deserves being made explicit because those who dislike Jews, or are otherwise anti-Semitic, suggest Jews commit the bulk of the world's financial crimes. That view is ignorant or disingenuous. Ken Lay and Jeffrey Skilling (Enron), Billie Sol Estes, Joseph Jett (Kidder Peabody), Nicholas Leeson

(Barings Bank), Bernie Ebbers and Scott Sullivan (Worldcom), "Chainsaw" Al Dunlap (Sunbeam), Albert B. Fall (Teapot Dome) Charles Ponzi (Ponzi Scheme), and many others are (or were) not Jewish. Jews do their share, but that is all.

Embarrassments[530]

Jews also have their share of embarrassments. Among them:

Kevin Mitnik was the compulsive computer hacker who could not stop himself. He just had to prove to himself and others that he could crack their computers no matter what they thought. And crack them he did till a guy smarter than he was used computers to get one up on him, tracing him to the apartment he was using. That led to five years in the slammer at Lompoc and three years of probation during which he was not allowed to use computers. One hopes Kevin stays on the straight and narrow now that his probation is over and he can promote his consulting business and his books on computer security.

Jack Ruby killed Lee Harvey Oswald in front of the world's television cameras a few days after Oswald had assassinated John F. Kennedy. Why Ruby did it and the consequence of silencing any explanation from Oswald for his actions gave rise to more than forty-five years of conspiracy theories, books, movies, and careers literally built on what happened and why, during those fateful days in Dallas. An incoherent Dallas nightclub owner, Ruby used his friendship with a local police official to gain entry to the jail where Oswald was being transferred from one location to another. In those days, before metal detection equipment was used routinely in jails and courthouses, Ruby was able to enter with the loaded gun he used as he stepped from the crowd to shoot Oswald. When it was over, Ruby was unable to explain why he had done it. He went on trial, defended by non-Jew Melvin Belli, and through the trial, and the guilty verdict which followed, there was never a plausible explanation for Ruby's act. For most, Ruby was simply angry and deranged. For others, he was a tool of those behind the Kennedy assassination to eliminate any possibility for Oswald to point a finger at them. For many Jews, Ruby was simply an embarrassment, and he remains so to this day.

Vladimir Zhirinovsky is a buffoon. He gained great notoriety as an anti-Semitic member of the Russian Duma who hoped to be elected president. He emerged in those hectic days after the fall of the Soviet Union as a right-wing demagogue. He was outrageous. He would shout down anyone else in the Duma, and he slugged some with whom he disagreed. He made vehement criticisms of Jews from the Duma floor and in the forums where he often spoke in the tumultuous days in the early 1990s. That he had early credibility was eclipsed a few years later when he was found (despite his earlier denials) to be half Jewish. After Yeltsin won re-election and later, as power shifted to Putin, Zhirinovsky was increasingly marginalized. Little is heard about him these days.

While other names could easily be added to the above profiles, clearly embarrassments happen—even in the best of families.

Chapter 24

Philanthropy

"Shall we devote the few precious days of our existence to buying and selling....My Friends, it is the unselfish effort, helpfulness to others that ennobles life, not because of what it does for others, but more what it does for ourselves."
—*Julius Rosenwald*

Julius Rosenwald[531]

Julius Rosenwald may qualify as the original "compassionate conservative." A successful Republican, Rosenwald opposed FDR's New Deal politics and his approach to welfare. Nonetheless, Rosenwald alone was responsible for the construction of more than 5,000 black schools built throughout the South between 1916 and 1932. Although as a Jew he could not serve on any local or national YMCA board of directors, he was also the driving force behind the building of twenty-five YMCAs.

Rosenwald was born August 12, 1862, at the family home, about a block from Abraham Lincoln's Springfield, Illinois, residence. His father, Samuel, had emigrated from Germany, beginning as a door-to-door peddler and working his way up to a horse- drawn cart before he married Augusta Hammerslough in 1857. Augusta's brothers were very successful retailers and they put Samuel in charge of several of their stores.

Julius was an outgoing, affable young man who left high school after his sophomore year to work for his uncles in their New York store. There he became boyhood friends with Henry Goldman, a future leader of Goldman Sachs, and Henry Morgenthau, father of FDR's treasury secretary. At 23, after five years with his uncles and with their support, Julius started his own clothing store.

He soon realized there was an even bigger opportunity in manufacturing men's summer clothing and, once more, with support from his uncles and his father, he started the new business in Chicago. It was a hit from the start. Five years later, in 1890, he married Augusta Nusbaum, and by 1895, he had sold that business to invest in and operate Sears, Roebuck.

Non-Jew Richard Warren Sears, a gifted promoter, had started Sears, Roebuck in 1887. He recruited self-taught watchmaker Alvah Curtis Roebuck (also not Jewish) as a partner after Sears had proved he could sell watches by mail.

In 1895, to finance expansion, and raise funds to buy out a by-then-disgruntled Roebuck, Sears sold half the business to Aaron Nusbaum for $75,000. Nusbaum approached his brother-in-law, Rosenwald, with the idea of taking half his position— a 25 percent ownership interest in Sears, Roebuck—and serving as co-head of operations. Sears was a superb copywriter and promoter, but a poor businessman with little operational ability. Rosenwald's management skills were critical, and the partnership was an immense success.

In 1901 Sears and Rosenwald bought out Nusbaum for $1.25 million after Sears and Nusbaum concluded they could not work together. When Sears sold his shares to Goldman Sachs in 1909 and retired, Rosenwald assumed sole control and led the company until his death in 1932.

Rosenwald deserves the credit for running Sears and managing its explosive growth into the huge nationwide mail-order and retail store operation it became. By the mid-1970s, Sears, the Wal-Mart of its day, was the largest retailer in the world. Rosenwald introduced the "money-back guarantee," filled catalog orders quickly, reduced returns, and instituted quality control.

Long before Rosenwald had invested in Sears, when he was still a struggling clothing manufacturer, he and his wife, Augusta, had proved their commitment to philanthropy. After attending a meeting about the immense difficulties faced by Jews in tsarist Russia, they pledged $2,500 at a time when it was a very large sum of money, and when they were still struggling to make their own small business a success. Though he opposed Zionism, Rosenwald later committed to donate 10 percent of every million dollars raised to help one million World War I Jewish refugees trying to leave Galacia and Russia.

But the act for which Rosenwald will be longest remembered was his creation of the "Rosenwald Schools." In 1912 he had joined the board of Booker T. Washington's Tuskegee Institute. At the time, average annual education spending was $21.14 per pupil. The South averaged only $4.92 for white students and less than half that ($2.21) for blacks. Conditions were abysmal. Serving on the Tuskegee board, Rosenwald became aware of the problem and he felt compelled to act.

His style was instructive. He began by having Tuskegee draw up plans for an inexpensive one-room school building that could be built anywhere in the South. Plans in hand, he then approached parents in black communities throughout the South. He offered to match their volunteer contributions of time, materials, and money, dollar for dollar, to build new schools for their children. They had to do their part. He was willing to provide 50 percent, but the rest was us up to them.

He wanted to avoid the dependence of welfare, and create pride, self-respect, and commitment. The parents did their part, and Rosenwald pointed out that their sacrifice was greater than his. In proportion to their means, they had given much more than he had. His approach also roused two other groups of supporters. Other whites kicked in with donations. And, uncomfortable with their own failure, local governments soon found a way to preserve their dignity by raising substantial tax funds. In the end, 5,357 Rosenwald schools were built at a cost of $28.4 million (in 1932 dollars). Of that, Rosenwald provided $4.4 million. Cash and in-kind contributions from blacks totaled $4.8 million. Other whites had donated $1.1 million, and the balance came from local taxes. At the time, only the 2,509 libraries built by Andrew Carnegie's philanthropy could compare. A few Rosenwald schools remain as part of the National Trust for Historic Preservation. For more information, visit the www.rosenwaldschools.com Web site.

Black schools were only part of Rosenwald's legacy. Despite being a Jew who could not serve on a local or national board of the Young Men's Christian Association, he did much the same for YMCA's. Twenty-five YMCA buildings were constructed because he offered to pay 25 percent of the cost if the local people who would benefit from the housing, fellowship, and exercise that would come up with the other 75 percent.

He did more. He funded $2 million in university fellowships for southerners. Another $2 million went to the University of Chicago, and $3 million helped build Chicago's Museum of Science and Industry.

He opposed establishing a lasting foundation, stipulating that all of his money be spent for good works within twenty-five years of his death. And it was. By 1948 it was all gone. In total, he had given away $63 million—in today's terms, more than $750 million.

Philanthropy in America

In visiting France—or most of Europe for that matter—it is striking that most institutions, most hospitals, museums, schools, or similar public facilities are either public or private. Few "not-for-profit" institutions are established by French citizens. Unlike most of our Ivy League schools, the Sorbonne is run by the Ministry of Education. Unlike New York's St. Patrick's cathedral, Notre Dame, and Chartres cathedrals are supported by French taxes. Unlike the Metropolitan Museum of Art, the Louvre is an organ of the Ministry of Culture.

In October 2001, Daniel Boorstin wrote an essay "From Charity to Philanthropy."[532] It drew on an earlier essay of the same name from his book *Hidden History*.[533] Boorstin's essays made the point that, dating back to the Mayflower Compact, America's history has consistently generated independent, vigorous individuals who, upon seeing need for a new institution or service, established a voluntary organization to plan, fund, and run it. America has no hereditary monarchy that might see meeting such needs as its duty; nor is there a government or monarch that might find such independent acts threatening.

Boorstin thought of non-Jew Ben Franklin as America's "patron saint of philanthropy." Franklin saw the need for, and helped establish, the Philadelphia police. He promoted paving, cleaning, and lighting of city streets. He organized the circulating library and arranged an Academy for the Education of Youth—later to become the University of Pennsylvania. He also helped set up the volunteer fire department.

Citizen activism, seeing a need, organizing for it and getting it funded, is a peculiarly American phenomenon. It may arise from our revolutionary history, the lack of government on the frontier, or the independent spirit and self-reliance we think of as part of the American character. Alex de Tocqueville saw and commented on it in the 1830s when he visited the United States. He was fascinated by the remarkable number of voluntary associations he found in the United States. But, no matter the source, voluntary non-profit organizations to meet society's needs are an American reality.

Daniel Gross, in reviewing the new book *The Greater Good: How Philanthropy Drives the American Economy and Can Save Capitalism,* by Claire Gaudiani,[534] noted that "In the U.S., where 89 percent of Americans made voluntary contributions in 2001, and more citizens give than vote, we collectively give about 2 percent of our Gross Domestic Product (GDP) to charity; the parsimonious Brits give just 0.7 percent." Jonathan Freedland, a British citizen, made a similar point in his July 3, 1998, article for the *New Statesman,* "Lessons from America (Citizen Power in the U.S.)."[535] In it he cited comparable donation statistics from 1993 ($880 per average American family, versus $300 for the Brits) and then went on to note that "more than half of all Americans—54 percent—volunteer for charitable or social service activities involving the poor, the sick or the elderly. The average volunteer gives up four hours per week."

Since 1928 when $2.5 billion was donated to U.S. charities, charitable giving has grown more than one hundred fold.[536] Between 2000 and 2003, despite September 11 and a recession, donations averaged nearly $250 billion a year, and by 2007, that number had climbed to $306 billion. Of that, roughly three-fourths came from individuals, 7.5 percent from bequests, 12 percent from foundations, and 5 percent from corporations.

Counterpart data from the American Association of Fundraising Councils puts the 2002 overall U.S. rate of charitable giving at 2.06 percent. It also indicates that over a forty-year period from 1963 to 2002, the rate has ranged from a high of 2.3 percent in 1963 to a low of 1.5 percent in 1995. The November 2006 Charities Aid Foundation report, which put the American charity rate at 1.7 percent of Gross National Product (GNP), noted that comparable rates of giving were .73 percent for Britain, .72 for Canada, .69 for Australia and .64 for South Africa. All other countries were below .5 percent.

It was Andrew Carnegie who coined the phrase, "He who dies wealthy, dies disgraced." Americans have generally taken that message to heart and with the maturing of the baby boomers, the wealth and attendant philanthropy will only grow.

Tzedakah, Kuppah, and *Tikkun Olam*[537]

Tzedakah and *kuppah* are unfamiliar words to most non-Jews. And those who have heard them sometimes incorrectly think of them as meaning "charity." It is true that charity has a relationship to *tzedakah* and *kuppah,* but they are cousins, not siblings. The distinction is at the core of the Jewish approach to helping those in need.

Tzedakah, derives not from "being magnanimous," or "helping out" but, as Rabbi Joseph Telushkin points out in his book, *Jewish Literacy*, *tzedakah* comes from the Hebrew root of a word that means "justice." Others tie it to the Hebrew *tzade-dalet-Qof*, meaning "righteous," "justice," or "fairness." These are not matters of the kind heart, the discretionary choice, nor of the privileged few, willing to help the less fortunate. No, *tzedakah* is a duty, a form of self-taxation. One simply must do this. It is a *mitzvah*, a commandment rather than a good deed or a voluntary act of kindness. The idea is manifested in the way some Jewish friends budget for charity just as they do for food or housing. It is also demonstrated in paying dues to synagogues and buying tickets for services on religious holidays, rather than relying on the collection plate or pledges. *Tzedakah* may also be a kindness, but it is first an obligation. Not doing so would be unfair, unjust, even unrighteous.

In his *History of the Jews*, Paul Johnson writes of the *kuppah*:

> "From Temple times, the *kuppah* or collecting box was a pivot around which the Jewish welfare-community revolved, Maimonides stated: 'We have never seen or heard of a Jewish community which does not have a *kuppah*. There were three trustees, solid citizens for each *kuppah* and, charity being mandatory in Jewish law, they had the power to seize goods from non-contributors.... The notion of 'from each according to his ability, to each according to his need' was one the Jews adopted before the birth of Christ and practiced even when the community as a whole was distressed. A solvent Jew had to give to the *kuppah* once he had resided in the community a month; to the soup-kitchen fund after three, the clothing fund after six, and the burial fund after nine."

Johnson went on to note that the duty to give also involved a reciprocal duty of the recipient.

> "The Jews hated welfare dependence. They quoted the Bible: 'You must help the poor man in proportion to his needs' but added, 'you are not obligated to make him rich.' The Bible, Mishnah, Talmud, and the commentaries were full of injunctions to work, to achieve independence."

The Jewish Web site "Judaism 101" makes the point:

> "We have an obligation to avoid becoming in need of *tzedakah*. A person should take any work that is available, even if he thinks it is beneath his dignity, to avoid becoming a public charge. However, if a person is truly in need and has no way to obtain money on his own he should not feel embarrassed to accept *tzedakah*."

The spirit of *tzedakah* is the subject of a ranking system created by Maimonides nearly 800 years ago that survives today in the Talmud. The hierarchy identifies eight levels of *tzedakah* extending from the least meritorious to the most. They are:

Giving begrudgingly.
Giving less than you should, but cheerfully.
Giving after being asked.
Giving before being asked.

Giving when you do not know the recipient's identity, but the recipient knows yours.
Giving when you know the recipient's identify but the recipient does not know yours.
Giving when neither party knows the other's identity.
Giving in a way that enables the recipient to become self-reliant. This may involve making a loan rather than a gift, providing a job or training, or similar acts that engender self-reliance and self-respect.

For Jews, whether their spirit of giving arises from level one or level eight, the point is to give. The Jewish community will serve to reinforce the duty. Telushkin also comments on the notion inherent in the public listing of donors.

"The Jewish community regards publicizing donors' gifts in the same spirit as the American practice of asking political candidates to release their tax returns. In both cases, public scrutiny causes people to act more justly."

Tikkun Olam is another vital Jewish notion. Generally considered to mean the "repair or mending of a broken world," for some it draws on concepts relating to removal from the Garden of Eden and a response to Original Sin. For others it involves the mystical view that in making the world, vessels of light, into which God was pouring Divine Light, were catastrophically shattered. This left countless shards, which entrapped sparks of Divine Light. Humanity must help free and reunite this light to restore a broken world. For some, this is the role of "the Chosen." Namely, Jews are "Chosen" not in the sense of being favored by God, but chosen for the duty of *tikkun olam*. And in this sense, their duty is to all of humanity, not just to their fellow Jews. While Jews have a long tradition of taking care of their own, they have a duty to others as well. Historically, Jewish loan societies, and other works of charity and philanthropy, focused not solely on Jews, but on benefiting all of humanity. As pointed out by Gary Tobin in his 2001 study: "The Transition of Communal Values and Behavior in Jewish Philanthropy:"

"*Tzedakah* is also dedicated to serving the world-at-large, non-Jews as well as Jews. The need to "repair a broken world" *(Tikkun Olam)*, is deeply embedded in community values and norms. A strong universalistic component characterizes Jewish philanthropy. The interest in social justice and volunteering evolves constantly. It continues to take new forms, such as the Jewish Service Corps, which is designed to serve the secular rather than Jewish World."

Pinning Down Rates of Jewish Philanthropy[538]

There appear to be no definitive estimates for overall rates of Jewish philanthropy. Experts disagree and the available data are complex. Nonetheless, it appears that, in no small part driven by the bequests of the very wealthy, Jewish philanthropy is probably three or more times the U.S. average of approximately 2 percent of annual income.

As background, it is useful to know that the January 2004 National Jewish Population Survey 2000-2001 estimated the U.S. Jewish population at 5.3 million individuals living in 2.9 million households. Annual Jewish household income averaged

$54,000 making aggregate Jewish household income $156.6 billion. At double the national average (4 percent of income), Jewish philanthropy would have totaled $6.3 billion per year in 2000-2001. At triple, it would have been $9.4 billion. Thus, one way to approach the question is to examine whether Jewish philanthropy totals $9.4 billion per year, or more.

At the low end of the range, Julia Duin's *Philanthropy* magazine cites Gary Tobin, of the Institute for Jewish and Community Research, who estimated Jewish charitable donations at 1.5 to 2.9 percent of annual income. At Tobin's 2.9 percent figure, total Jewish philanthropy would have been $4.5 billion.

At the high end, four experts (Hoge, Zech, McNamara and Donohue), who researched rates of charitable giving by different religious groups, came up with much higher figures. Without citing data, they indicated Jewish giving rivals Mormons, who they say give something approaching 7.5 percent of annual income.

In 1997 Jack Wertheimer, provost of the Jewish Theological Seminary of New York, said in the *1997 American Jewish Year Book*, that "American Jews...raised as much as $4.5 billion annually *for Jewish causes...*" (emphasis added). Of that, $1.6 billion went to Jewish federations, $1.4 billion to religious institutions, $700 million to other Jewish charities, $250 to $300 million to Jewish cultural, educational, religious and community relations institutions, and $425 million through the United Way, other government funding agencies under Jewish auspices, or as direct funding of Jewish community centers.

As covered later in this chapter's analysis of *Business Week's* list of the 50 most generous philanthropists, nineteen wealthy Jews made bequests averaging $4.5 billion per year between 2003 and 2007 to mostly non-Jewish causes. This pattern of bequests to non-Jewish causes was also commented on in a June 14, 2002, issue of *Jewish Week*, where Tobin noted, "Many Jewish foundations give little or nothing to Jewish causes, and most give a minority of their dollars to Jewish causes." His 2003 study, "Mega Gifts in American Philanthropy", looked at 865 philanthropic gifts of $10 million or more made between 1995 and 2000. Of those, the 188 made by Jews totaled $5.3 billion. He said only 6 percent of that money went to Jewish organizations or institutions. Most of it went to education (49 percent), arts/culture, and humanities (21 percent) and health (6 percent).

Taking a conservative approach, we can say, Jewish philanthropy almost certainly exceeds 6 percent of annual income. Wertheimer's $4.5 billion (Jewish giving to Jewish causes) and *Business Week's* $4.5 billion (wealthy Jewish giving to mostly non Jewish causes) involve almost no overlap and total nearly 6 percent of Jewish family income. Neither figure includes Jewish giving to non-Jewish causes by those not included in the Business Week list. While we do not have an estimate of that giving, we can, nonetheless, say Jewish philanthropy totals more than 6 percent of annual income, and is thus more than three times the national average.

Declines in Giving to Israel and to Jewish Causes[539]

As noted above, recent decades have seen declining Jewish philanthropy (as a percent of total giving) directed to Israel and Jewish causes.

Exhibit 24a shows total funds raised by the Jewish Federation, United Jewish Appeal and the United Israel Appeal, and of that, the amount allocated to Israel. While these are not the only sources of U.S. Jewish financial support to Israel, they are a significant part. The exhibit shows the large early support when Israel's survival was in question ($147 million of the $200 million raised in 1948), a second spike at the time of the 1967 Six-Day War ($237 million of the $302 million raised) and a third spike when the Yom Kippur War spurred donations of $488 million from the $684 million raised. Since then, the dollars allocated to Israel have stayed in the $300 to $375 million range, while the percentage allocated to Israel has dropped from 73 percent in 1948 to 36 percent in 1999.

Mirroring this is the ever growing support for secular causes, the subject of many articles in the Jewish press. Tobin's 2003 publication analyzing gifts larger than $10 million (see above) made the case in stark terms. His review of 188 Jewish philanthropic gifts of $10 million or more between 1995 and 2000 showed that 94 percent of the money went to non-Jewish causes. Tobin suggested some of the reasons, saying, "*tzedakah* has taken more of a character of American philanthropy, and will continue to do so, representing less the religious tradition of Jews and more the civil tradition of philanthropy in the United States." Some of this he attributes to assimilation, some to an ecumenical view of *tikkun olam*, some to the need to give back to the country that afforded the opportunity to earn such wealth, some to the desire to be a positive ambassador of the Jewish community, and some because the non-Jewish causes are "more compelling."

In the press coverage of Tobin's data, concern was expressed about ever present, perhaps growing, assimilation and the alienation of some Reform and Conservative Jews by the increasingly Orthodox orientation of the Israeli government that may be "turning off" their less orthodox American brethren.

Mega[540]

If there is one group working hard, albeit quietly, to sustain philanthropy directed to Israel and Jewish causes, it is Mega.

On December 21, 2001, Forward, a leading Jewish publication, did a story titled "Moneyed 'Study Group' Is Engine for Charity Revolution." It provided historical background and an inside look at the goals of "mega-group," more commonly called Mega. It followed by more than two years, a May 4, 1998, *Wall Street Journal* story, "Titans of Industry Join Forces To Work for Jewish Philanthropy," the first significant mainstream press reporting on Mega.

Mega is probably the single most powerful and influential group of philanthropists to support Jewish causes and Israel. As described in the *Forward* story, Rabbi Brian Lurie, former chief executive of the United Jewish Appeal (UJA), first assembled what would become the original Mega group in 1991. His purpose was to arrange financial support for Operation Exodus, the UJA program to bring Jews from the Soviet Union to Israel as the Soviet Union collapsed. Rabbi Lurie arranged for a small group ("a dozen or so") of very wealthy Jews to provide the needed support, operating under the leadership of Charles Bronfman and Leslie Wexner. The group soon took on the flavor of a "9-1-1" service, ready to organize and fund efforts required to respond to any major crises threatening Jews.

Over time, Mega's scope broadened. The "study group" has since become a forum for discussing perspectives on philanthropy and Jewishness. As assimilation, marriages outside the faith, and other forces have weaned Jews from their religion and culture, Mega has attempted to respond by encouraging a certain pride and commitment to retaining Jewish heritage. Edgar Bronfman is quoted saying "We want it to be cool to be Jewish." Steven Spielberg spoke about his "personal religious journey" when he attended the April 1998 meeting.

Members share their perspectives on philanthropy and how to have the greatest impact from their sometimes entrepreneurial approaches to practicing it. They also promote their own high-priority projects and attempt to enlist support from fellow members. Thus, in Mega, the talk is not about funding a new hospital or library, unless it is one needed in Israel, or in some part of the world where Jews are poorly served. There is also a commitment to helping Israel in a wide-ranging series of projects.

Among major projects that members have singly, or jointly pursued are:

Hillel - support of its on-campus Jewish chaplaincy.

STAR - Synagogue Transformation and Renewal.

Partnership for Jewish Education - an $18 million project to provide matching grants for Jewish day schools.

Birthright Israel - helping to send any young Jew, who wishes to go, to Israel; as of December 2001, 22,000 young people had already gone.

Jewish Campus Service Corps - allowing recent college graduates to provide at least a year's service supporting "Jewish life" on college campuses.

Partnership for Excellence in Jewish Education.

Bronfman Curriculum Initiative - intended to help private high schools teach Jewish ethics and philosophy (an early program not considered particularly successful).

Foundation for Jewish camping (and summer camps).

Foundation for the Defense of Democracies (FDD) - formerly called Emet and occasionally called "Truth," a controversial "think tank" intended to provide education about terrorism and to better communicate the Israeli perspective to the American public. One project brought 52 undergraduates, nineteen professors and a journalist to Israel to see, firsthand, the effects of terrorists. Another organized a conference for Iraqi women in conjunction with the U.S. Agency for International Development.

Mega reportedly meets twice a year, typically over dinner the night before with a session the next day. Often there are presentations by nonmembers and sometimes spouses attend. Members pay annual dues ($30,000 per year in 1998) to cover costs of "research, speakers and incidentals."

Mega does not release a membership list, but among those who are said to be or have been members are some of America's wealthiest and most prominent Jews: Charles and Edgar Bronfman, Leslie Wexner, Michael Steinhardt, Howard "Bud" Meyerhoff, Leonard Abramson, Lester Crown, Marvin Lender, and Richard Goldman. Charles Schusterman, Laurence Tisch, and Max Fisher (all now deceased), were early members of Mega. At the time of the May 1998 meeting, Steven Spielberg was reportedly considering membership.

Mega's initial success led to formation of other mega-like groups whose members reportedly include Bernard Marcus and Peter May. An international group may include the Arison family, the Bronfmans, and others, including members of the Rothschild family.

Mega's members work to keep the group private and low-profile. Should one wonder why, a Google search of the word "mega" together with the name of any prominent member will yield a case study of Web-based suspicion, hate, and anti-Semitism.

Business Week's "50 Most Generous Philanthropists"[541]

A *Business Week* November 2007 feature article "The Greatest Givers" provided a list of "The 50 Most Generous Philanthropists." It focused on amounts given or pledged over the five years 2003 through 2007. Some names were no surprise. Non-Jews Bill and Melinda Gates and Warren Buffett topped the list having pledged or given away nearly $69 billion. Among other prominent non-Jews were Gordon and Betty Moore, the Walton family, David Rockefeller, John Templeton, T. Boone Pickens, Ted Turner, and Kirk Kerkorian.

But perhaps most striking is the fact that at least nineteen of the fifty "Givers"are Jews. As such, they were 38 percent of America's fifty most generous philanthropists.

The nineteen names are highlighted on Exhibit 24b. They donated nearly $23 billion over the five years—a bit more than $4.5 billion a year—to philanthropic causes. Lest the 2007 data be thought a fluke, the same *Business Week* feature three years earlier (2000 to 2004) resulted in the same 38 percent statistic. Six of the nineteen Jews on the 2004 list lost ground or disappeared and were replaced by six new Jewish benefactors.

This disproportionate level of Jewish philanthropy is corroborated by data from other sources. Nathaniel Popper wrote a story for *Forward's* March 2, 2007, issue indicating that twenty-one of the sixty largest 2006 charitable donations (35 percent) were made by Jews. Gary Tobin's 2003 study of Mega-gifts (gifts of more than $10 million) indicated 22 percent of the large donations between 1995 and 2000 were given by Jews. Tobin also cited another study, "Charity Begins at Home: Generosity and Self-Interest Among the Philanthropic Elite." In that study, 28.5 percent of the sample of philanthropists interviewed were Jews.

Several further aspects deserve mention.

We know 31 percent of the 2007 *Forbes* 400 are Jews (Exhibit 21a) as are 38 percent of *Business Week's* most generous philanthropists. Taken together the data suggest that among the very wealthy, Jews are probably somewhat more generous than non-Jews (that is, the proper frame of reference is not 38 percent versus the 2 percent that Jews are of the population, but the 38 percent that Jews are of the major philanthropists versus the 31 percent that Jews are of the very wealthy. Finally, a review of the causes to which the nineteen *Business Week* donors have made grants (see Exhibit 24b) as well as the work done by Tobin, demonstrates the bulk of Jewish philanthropy goes not to religious or Israeli recipients but, instead, to secular causes such as education, health, environment, and culture.

Synopsis

Taken together, the previous material suggests the following conclusions about the philanthropy of American Jews.

American Jews are very philanthropic, as disproportionately generous as they are accomplished.

Even with the efforts of Mega and others to encourage support of Israel and Jewish causes, American Jews devote the bulk of their philanthropy to secular causes.

The large and sustained Jewish bequests in support of education, medical research, the arts, and other secular causes confirms that we all would be substantially poorer if Jews did not contribute such significant amounts to these projects and institutions.

Chapter 25

Why?

The preceding chapters demonstrate stunning levels of Jewish achievement and contribution relative to their small numbers. This one delves into possible reasons behind the phenomenon. It does not presume to provide the definitive explanation. Instead, by identifying likely causes it intends to stimulate discussion in hopes the ensuing dialogue will yield insights beneficial to us all.

As noted in the book's introduction, if an equivalent performance happened in a major organization or corporation, pressures would arise to "benchmark" it. There would be a hue and cry to identify and learn the lessons which might be replicated so others could do as well.

So, why has it happened? What is behind the talent and drive that led to such disproportionate performance?

Consider…

Chance

The notion that Jewish achievements might simply be attributable to good fortune can be dismissed out of hand. Were they disproportionately accomplished in one or two fields, perhaps, but across the range described by this book, it is simply impossible. While anomalies do occur, it is statistically and logically impossible to conclude that the disproportionate achievements of Jews arose from chance. It would be akin to explaining the thousands of years of Diaspora, anti-Semitism, and Holocaust as simply "bad luck." It did not happen that way.

God's Chosen People

The conception of Jews as "God's chosen people" is an explanation some might find plausible. Abraham entered into a "Covenant" with God, who promised to protect and revere his people if they obeyed his commandments. "'Now Adonai' (the Lord) said to Avram (Abraham), 'Get...out of your country, away from your kinsmen...and go to the land that I will show you. I will make of you a great nation. I will bless you and ...make your name great.'"[542]

The Covenant with Abraham was reaffirmed in B'resheet (Genesis) 17:2-7, and with Moses in Sh'mot (Exodus) 19:5. "Now if you will...keep my Covenant, then you will be my own treasure from among all peoples."

Being "chosen" might explain Jewish achievement were it not for the unbelievable hardships Jews have endured. For 2,534 years until Israel was created in 1948, Jews were forced to live as minorities in widely dispersed enclaves over much of the world.[543] With notable, generally brief exceptions, wherever they lived they were persecuted, particularly in the Second Millennium. And while some Jews may have believed their hardships arose from the collective failure of Jews to keep up their end of the Covenant (and was thus the retribution by a just God for their failings), for most Jews, the advent of the Jewish Emancipation and Enlightenment in the late eighteenth century, the growth of reform movements, and the horror of the Holocaust—which called into question the very notion that six million deaths could be the work of a just God—eroded the traditional sense of being "chosen."

But a further notion of "chosen" deserves mention, one which in recent years has become more mainstream. This view of "chosen" marries it to the concept of *tikkun olam,* which is generally taken to mean chosen by God for the special responsibility of helping "repair a broken world." For some, the obligation of *tikkun olam* arises from the Jewish response to original sin. For others, it involves a mystical conception of the need to reunite sparks of divine light which were shattered when God created the world. In either conception, Jews must help heal the broken world for the benefit of all mankind. In essence Jews are "chosen" to fulfill this duty.

Second-Generation Immigrants

It is impossible to read the preceding chapters and not be struck by the incidence of second-generation immigrant Jews among the high achievers: Milton Friedman, Saul Bellow, Richard Feynman, Edwin Land, and on and on. All were sons of immigrants. For some commentators this became the simple and accepted explanation for disproportionate Jewish achievement. In essence the performance was a predictable response to a history of oppression before immigration, a reaction against the mild to moderate level of American anti-Semitism (much lower than in other countries, but still present), and an ambition to move beyond the tenement, and sometimes perhaps beyond one's parents whose language and behavior might be a source of embarrassment. Such were the driving forces in a country that functioned mostly as a meritocracy. Need met opportunity, prompting disproportionate levels of achievement.

Clearly the perspective has appeal. It is not, however, compelling, nor for the author is it a complete explanation. It suffers from what logicians call the fallacy of *post hoc proctor hoc* (namely, "after this, therefore because of this"). Because it is common among many high achievers to have been second-generation immigrant Jews does not make that the cause. It may be a contributing factor, but there is much more to it than that.

Realize, Jews were high achievers well before the American immigration. Jesus, St. Paul, Moses, Sigmund Freud, Karl Marx, Albert Einstein, and Maimonides are typically counted among the most influential people of all time. None were second-generation immigrants.

Further, in his book *The Jewish Mind,* Raphael Patai noted the disproportionate number of Jewish scientists in Europe during the Middle Ages.[544] That is, between 1150 and 1300, when 2.7 percent of Spain's population was Jewish, 41.2 percent of its pre-eminent scientists were Jews. In France, 25.4 percent of the scientists were Jews and in Germany, they were 21.4 percent. Jews did not have to be second-generation immigrants to be disproportionate achievers in those countries.

An earlier chapter of this book described the emergence of great Jewish visual artists. Charles Murray's book, *Human Accomplishment* identified them.[545] The first important Jewish artist (in 1870) was the French Jew Camille Pissarro. Of the other fifteen listed by Murray, only five were born in the United States. Six were Russian and the other four were Ukrainian, German, Hungarian, and Italian.

If second-generation immigrants are high achievers, why have comparable performances not been turned in by Italians, Irish, Germans, French, and other immigrant groups. The Irish and Italians were similarly discriminated against and looked down upon. Presumably, their next generations were also motivated to get ahead. After all, Jews were only about 10 percent of the huge 1880 to 1924 immigration. But other immigrant populations never touched the Jewish levels of achievement. One clue that something else was involved comes from Michael Barone's book, *The New Americans.*[546] In 1910, among first-generation Jews ages fourteen to eighteen, 56 percent were in school. For Italians, the number was 31 percent.

There is also the experience of the offshore Chinese. In every locale where Chinese have been a minority, they have been disproportionately successful. Perhaps apocryphal, it is said the reason Singapore was carved out of Malaysia to become a separate island nation was that the Chinese were much more successful than the native Malays. The only practical solution to the resulting anger of the majority Malays was to carve out a separate country for the Chinese. Like the Jews, the Chinese have long placed a premium on education and hard work, suggesting their culture, rather second-generation status, drove their performance.

High levels of Jewish achievement also arose in nineteenth and early twentieth century Austria, Germany, and Switzerland. As the Jewish Emancipation and Enlightenment unfolded, the likes of Mendelssohn, Einstein, Freud, and others arrived on the secular scene making impressive contributions.

And both before and after the Russian Revolution, Jews were disproportionate achievers. Yuri Slezkine's book, *The Jewish Century,* delineates just how influential a relatively small number of Jews were in the Communist Party, the Soviet government, and among leading lawyers, educators, scientists, and artists.[547]

Finally, when one looks at Nobel prizes over the decades, it is striking that while Jews have won 23 percent of all the individual Nobels awarded, the rate since 1990 has climbed to 30 percent. The higher percentage of Nobel prizes going to Jews over the last two decades hardly sustains the second generation theory.

In the end, second-generation immigrant status may have contributed to disproportionate Jewish achievement, but its influence is likely dwarfed by other factors.

Genes

Might genetics or natural selection help explain the phenomenon? An interesting theory arose some years ago bearing on that question. It noted that in feudal Europe, where most were born to their station for life, the Roman Catholic priesthood was the one meritocracy. There, a person of talent could rise to a position of power in the one institution unsullied by nepotism. The downside was that some of Europe's best and brightest were choosing a career in which their genes would not be passed on.

Jews had a different arrangement. They selected rabbis for their knowledge and intelligence, but generally required them to have a wife and children. Unlike priests, rabbis could multiply, and they did.[548]

Perhaps this "natural selection" made a difference, but celibacy did not exist in the Eastern Orthodox Church, nor in the cultures of Asia or Africa (and some have suggested it was "more honored in the breach" within Catholic Europe as well).[549] In any case, following the Reformation, celibacy had ever less effect on Protestant Europe, and it was never significant in North America. Further, some commentators have observed the greatest flowering of Jewish achievement commenced well after the Reformation. Thus, while interesting, the theory is not yet compelling.

Others suggest a different form of natural selection. Namely, over the thousands of years Jews have endured, the weak have been culled while the strong survived. Esther Rantzen, a prominent British (BBC) personality says: "The slow often got wiped out. You always had to be a jump ahead of the pogrom. I am casting no aspersions on those who died, but, if you are persecuted for thousands of years, it is a very tough form of the survival of the fittest."[550] One would be hard-pressed to imagine circumstances more challenging and more likely to distill the best from the rest than what Jews have been through.

Others respond that natural selection for survival skills and intelligence, though helpful, were hardly sufficient to explain the phenomenon. They point to the survival of the Roma (or Gypsies), one of the few cultures or tribes to last as long as the Jews. Its longevity can hardly be attributed to high levels of identifiable survival skills arising from natural selection. Conversely, the accomplishments of high achievers would be more likely to make them targets, rather than survivors of, pogroms and the Holocaust.

Going a step further, with today's greater scientific understanding of genes and chromosomes, is there evidence pointing to a Jewish genetic predisposition for achievement? The answer is "not yet," but recent studies raise intriguing, if controversial, ideas about how the interaction of natural selection, Jewish culture and talents may have yielded higher IQs for some Jews.[551] Before elaborating on that notion, some context may be helpful. Apart from distinctive DNA sequences of the Cohanim and perhaps the Levites,[552] there are many different strains of Jewish DNA, some of which are very common among Middle Eastern Arabs including Palestinians, Syrians, Greeks, and other ancient Mediterranean lines.[553,554] In the words of Dr. Robert Pollack, professor of biological sciences at Columbia University, "There are no DNA sequences common to all (Ashkenazi) Jews and absent from all non-Jews."[555] Jews are genetically close to many other cultures, including those whose accomplishments pale by comparison.

But three recent papers have added much to the debate.

In December 2005, Maristella Botticini and Zvi Eckstein weighed in with an article in the *Journal of Economic History*.[556] They were among the first to document the unique demand for literacy by Rabbinical Judaism. They pointed out that over a period commencing before the Roman destruction of the Second Temple in A.D. 70, the Pharisees had begun to develop schools and academies and promote education so all Jews could study the Torah and the Oral Law. With the destruction of the Temple and the disappearance of the Sadducees, the Pharisees and Rabbinical Judaism became dominant. Their synagogues became schools, and they made education a mandatory duty for parents and communities.

Other commentators have added that the move to literacy was also motivated by remembrance of the lost ten tribes, presumably to assimilation. Hopefully, literacy would avert a repeat for the two remaining tribes in the dispersal (Diaspora) of most Jews from Palestine. To sustain the culture and religion of a dispersed population, indeed to retain familial and other ties across a broad geography, literacy was mandatory. The religious trove had to be written down and Jews needed to be able to read, discuss, and understand it if their common religion and culture were to survive across the great distances. Only written tracts and literacy kept Judaism alive.

Judaism was transformed. Education flourished and by the time of the Muslim ascendency after A.D. 638, "basic literacy among male Jews was almost universal."[557] And as urban centers arose within the Muslim world, Jews were uniquely able to migrate to these communities where their education afforded them unique advantages in pursuing careers other than farming. A tribe that was 80 to 90 percent farmers in the years between 0 and A.D. 400 was transformed to only 5 to 30 percent farmers by 638 to A.D. 1170. They were now predominantly artisans, craftsmen, merchants, doctors, and moneylenders.[558] The imperative for education had dramatically changed the culture of Judaism.

A year after Botticini and Eckstein's paper, Cochran, Hardy and Harpending published "Natural History of Ashkenazi Intelligence" in the *Journal of Biosocial Sci-*

ence.[559] It posited that from A.D. 800 to 1700, many Ashkenazi Jews worked in intellectually challenging trades, such as money lending and various other managerial and financial careers. These careers required higher levels of intelligence than farming and the other careers generally pursed by non-Jews. The attendant success and prosperity arising from these more lucrative careers led to larger Jewish families. A process of "natural selection" thus resulted in disproportionately high IQ levels for Ashkenazi Jews—as compared with other groups of people. The study also correlated the high IQ levels with substantially greater risks of genetic ailments such as Tay Sachs, Gaucher, and others; presumably the genetics were somehow linked.[560]

Cochran, Hardy, and Harpending's conclusions were later joined in a "concurring" though somewhat "dissenting" opinion by the Scots-Irish Charles Murray in an April 2007 article in *Commentary* magazine.[561] Murray said the intellectual challenges of reading, understanding, and debating the Torah and Talmud, coupled with other demands of Rabbinic Judaism, resulted in self selection for Jewish intelligence well before the 800 to 1700 time frame focused upon by Cochran, et al.

Murray noted the sharp decline in the numbers of Jews following the Roman conquest and Diaspora that he said could not be explained simply from deaths in the Jewish revolt against the Romans, nor by any natural phenomenon, such as a plague. In Murray's view, it was the educational demands (to read, discuss, and debate the Torah and Talmud) led to a diminished population. These skills were useless for farmers. As a result, many of the less talented (lower IQ) and less motivated Jews opted out. In this way, natural selection resulted in fewer but smarter Jews in succeeding generations.

And while high IQ does not automatically ensure high achievement, Murray figures it substantially alters the odds. In short, genetic self-selection accounted for higher IQs, which facilitated disproportionate levels of achievement. Murray would certainly acknowledge that, if his surmise is accurate, it was the culture of Judaism the premium placed on literacy and the demands of the religion—that led to the genetic selection, but for him, given enough generations, it was the genetic selection and higher IQ that mattered.

One further aspect of this topic deserves mention. In the Middle Ages, the gifted Jews were not the Ashkenazi, but the Sephardics, such as Maimonides. They were the high achievers of Jewry. Today the reverse is true. In Israel, the Sephardics are generally seen to be the underperformers in academic and achievement circles. And for the Sephardics, the argument works in reverse. That is, a number of commentators have observed that over the centuries, as Sephardics interacted with the dominant Arab/Islamic cultures around the Mediterranean, they have adopted elements of those cultures, such as low literacy, low levels of educational attainment, low income and substandard housing, high levels of poverty and disease, high fertility and mortality, a subordinated role for women, a fatalistic religious outlook, and similar attributes.[562] Once again we have the question. Is the current Sephardic situation genetic? Over the last 800 to 1,000 years, did they self-select for low IQs and underperformance, or have they unconsciously adopted a pattern of cultural values that are self-defeating?

In the end, what we have are correlations that may or may not be causes. To date, no one has linked individual genes or groups of genes to behavior. The hope and optimism of 1980s and 1990s geneticists for definitive links, as for example to aggression, drive, talent, or other behaviors, have yet to be borne out. Today's DNA claims by geneticists are becoming ever more modest, and there is growing recognition that the genetics of behavior are highly complex and they are constantly at play with environmental and cultural factors.[563]

All of which leads us to consider the role of culture.

Culture

Random House Dictionary provides two useful definitions for "culture":

5. the behaviors and beliefs characteristic of a particular social, ethnic or age group....and 6. Anthropol. The sum total of ways of living built up by a group of human beings and transmitted from one generation to another.[564]

In his book *The Wealth and Poverty of Nations,* Professor David Landes of Harvard defines culture as "inner values and attitudes that guide a population."[565] He says, "If we learn anything from the history of economic development, it is that culture makes all the difference."[566]

Jews are not monolithic. Generally in Judaism, differences in beliefs are not just tolerated, but seen as healthy."[567] Followers of Orthodox, Conservative, Reform, Hasidic, Reconstructionist, Kabbalist, and other Jewish denominations disagree, sometimes vehemently, but they have a family of shared views derived over a 4,000-year heritage. Generally they agree on much more than they disagree about. In the same way that individual American Indian tribes have differences from tribe to tribe but share a common culture, so do "mainstream" Jews.

And while Jews share some values and beliefs with other cultures, they embrace a unique and distinctive combination.

What follows are the author's views on elements of Jewish culture that have contributed to their "need to achieve."

Ethical Monotheism: Jews were the first to believe in a single God. Their conception of ethical monotheism is a unique Jewish contribution to us all. From it came the Old Testament and much of Western civilization. Today Christianity and Islam encompass half the world's more than six billion people, but they both began with Judaism.

David S. Ariel, president of Cleveland College of Jewish Studies, says: "There is no one authoritative Jewish conception of God, although all Jewish thinkers agree that God is one and indivisible....Judaism presents two interconnected sacred myths....The first presents God as transcendent...a fearsome God who judges the world....The other...views God as an accessible personal being...a nurturing and comforting parent...."[568]

Whether transcendent or personal, both conceptions imply an absolute connection between ethical behavior and divine action. For Babylonians, Greeks, Romans, and other pagans, the "gods" were capricious, dealing a random, arbitrary fate to humans. As Ariel says, "The moral God of the universe is the fundamental axiom of Jewish belief."[569] Humans' lives are not shaped by unpredictable, mercurial gods, but by their own actions. In Judaism, actions have consequences.

Progress: "In the beginning..."[570] These are the first three words in the Bible. They envision a single point (perhaps a "big bang") from which history began. Time is an arrow, not a circle. History does not repeat for Jews as it does for Hindus and Buddhists. Eastern passivity is transcended. Islam ("submission") and Inshah Allah ("God willing") involve theistic determinism most Jews reject. As Paul Johnson wrote in, *A History of the Jews*, "No people has ever insisted more firmly than the Jews that history has a purpose and humanity a destiny."[571] Jews believe in a future different from, and better than, the past, and that God has given them a role in shaping that future.[572]

Choice, Action, and Accountability: Faith and action are cherished in Jewish culture, but faith does not trump action.[573] Admission to heaven is not based on faith as in some religions. Choice and action are what counts. In the words of the ancient rabbis, "Everything is foreseen, yet freedom of choice is given."[574] God creates options, but does not direct responses. From this flows freedom and accountability, a linkage that both ennobles and inspires as it mitigates victimhood. Almost no culture has more basis for feeling persecuted—and Jews do not forget their tortured history—but they rarely demonstrate the propensity of some cultures to see themselves as victims. They take responsibility for themselves.

Rationality, Modernism, and Verges: Though some Jewish denominations are traditional, even backward-looking, mainstream Judaism, particularly since the Jewish Emancipation, has been pragmatic and forward-looking. "What works?" "What makes sense?" "How can this problem be solved?" As Johnson said in *A History of the Jews*, "The Jews were the first rationalizers in world history. This...was to turn Jews into problem solving businessmen."[575] "Above all, the Jews taught us how to rationalize the unknown."[576] Great Jewish thinkers from the Middle Ages to the age of Jewish Enlightenment, Maimonides, Spinoza, and Mendelssohn, were all rationalists. And in some senses, the Talmud is the ever-changing application of Jewish Law to new circumstances as they arise. The commentary and the responses are the rational process of great Talmudic scholars integrating differing points of view, debating them and thinking through the best way to deal with new circumstances. In that sense the Talmud is a body of work that will never be final, but will serve to help Judaism deal with the future.

A small example—Jews rationalized charging interest for loans among themselves (usury) long before Christians did. Islam still struggles with the issue. Thus Jews could practice finance while others could not. Dispersed from Argentina to India and North America to China, they had networks of family and "landsmen" around the world they could work with and trust. This was a huge advantage in international trade.

Throughout the Diaspora, Jews lived on what former Pulitzer Prize-winning historian Daniel Boorstin called "verges."[577] He attributed much American creativity and success to the country's being a place where different cultures, technologies, and political views encountered one another (at "verges"). Each experienced interactions impossible in their own insular worlds. Those encounters challenged their thinking, and therein stimulated change and growth. "In ancient, more settled nations, uniformity was idealized.... The American situation was different. The creativity, the hope of the nation was in its verges."[578]

No culture has experienced more verges than Jews. They traversed the world. Thomas Sowell's book, *Migrations and Cultures*, speaks of Jews during Spain's Golden Age "standing at the crossroads of two great civilizations (the Moorish Islamic and Spanish Catholic worlds), Jews were peculiarly well situated to deal in the ideas and cultures of both the Islamic and Christian worlds...to advance themselves culturally and materially.... They received knowledge from different directions (which)...stimulated their own thinking and (the) development of...Jewish culture.... Maimonides, was a product of such cultural crosscurrents."[579]

Jews processed new ideas by integrating dissimilar facts and cultures and developing new insights that added to their collective knowledge and capabilities.

Tolerance for Competing Views: As the title of a collection of Jewish quotations says, Two Jews, Three Opinions.[580] In his book *What Is a Jew*, Rabbi Morris N. Kertzer notes, "The most distinctive feature of the Jewish religion has been its hospitality to differences. In all of Jewish law will be found both an austere interpretation and a liberal one—and the rabbis have ruled 'both opinions are the word of the living God.'"[581] Hillel the Elder (70 B.C. to 10 B.C.) and his contemporary Shammai (50 B.C. to A.D. 10) disagreed strongly about Judaism.[582] And though many prefer Hillel's views, Shammai's are also accepted as correct. And the Talmud itself, in its commentary represents something of a debate with different commentators offering up differing views.

One further aspect of this phenomenon deserves comment. This is the frequent role of Jews as leaders on different, often opposing, sides of major issues. Nobel laureate Paul Samuelson was a leading Keynesian when he wrote his classic college textbook *Economics*. It was fellow Jew Milton Friedman, also a Nobel laureate, who became the foremost economist to discredit much of the Keynesian dogma. Paul Ehrlich made his reputation forecasting a dismal Malthusian future as the world became overwhelmed by its burgeoning population. Ehrlich lost his famous $1,000 bet in a ten-year test of his hypothesis to economist and fellow Jew Julian Simon, whose outlook was decidedly more optimistic. Marx and Trotsky were among prominent Jews to theorize and devote their lives to Communism. Yet among their fellow Jews are some of the most successful capitalist entrepreneurs of all time. Noam Chomsky is a shrill critic of nearly everything done by the Israeli government. Two of his constant adversaries are Alan Dershowitz and David Horowitz. At *The New York Times*, Paul Krugman and Thomas Friedman were strident critics of President George W. Bush. William Kristol and David Brooks often countered their arguments, presenting their own strong case for a more conservative view. J. Robert Oppenheimer ultimately opposed nuclear weapons, while his former colleague, Edward Teller, developed the hydrogen bomb and supported the Star Wars missile defense program. Herbert Marcuse, I.F. Stone, Noam Chomsky, and many fellow Jews strongly criticized the United States, often defending Socialism, while Norman Podhoretz, Charles Krauthammer, and other conservatives defended America and argued for a more muscular approach to the threats it faces.

Such contrasts could fill a book. In the end, they demolish simple-minded anti-Semitic stereotypes of Jews as monolithic, single-issue advocates of one dogma or another. On the contrary, what seems to engage them is an energetic involvement in all sides of most issues. The debates and differences of opinion are often vigorous, sometimes even verbally aggressive, but such differences are rarely physically violent such as those which occur, for example, between Sunni and Shiite Muslims. Jews acknowledge there may be more than one right answer, and thus they are often more tolerant of opposing views than many of us.

Assertiveness and Verbal Skills: Abraham challenged God.[583] God said he would destroy Sodom and Gomorrah for their wickedness. Abraham responded: "Will you actually sweep away the righteous with the wicked? Maybe there are fifty righteous people in the city.... Shouldn't the judge of all the earth do what is just?"[584] Heresy in most religions, such "chutzpah" began with the first Jew.

For most Jews, standing up and speaking out is valued. To see a wrong and not work to change it is irresponsible. Jews have a sense of duty and confidence about sticking up for their beliefs.

Such assertiveness is complemented by the premium placed on verbal skills and verbal self-confidence. One must be capable of thinking and reaching conclusions, and that skill must be coupled with a willingness to air those views, have them challenged, and challenge others in return. Yeshivas and Talmudic education stress thought and debate. Such skills were seen by some classmates to confer an unfair advantage on Scott Turow when he was a student at Harvard Law School.[585]

Bar mitzvahs and bat mitzvahs transition boys and girls from childhood to adulthood. In both, the thirteen-year-old must stand before family and friends to publicly assert, "Today, I am a man" or "woman."

Speaking out and speaking well is important in Jewish culture. And in the significant numbers of Jews who practice in major law firms, hold political office, work in journalism, literature, the media, and entertainment, we see those skills manifested every day.

Education: By the time Muhammad called Jews "The People of the Book,"[586] the books in question already included all thirty-nine books of the Hebrew Bible, plus much of the "Oral Law," written into the numerous volumes of Talmud and Midrash. As noted earlier in this, and other chapters, after Romans destroyed the Temple, killed a million Jews, and dispersed most of the rest into small scattered enclaves around the world, the need to write down, and the ability to read and understand this trove became fundamental to keeping the religion and culture alive. Jews thus became the first to demand that parents educate their children. Made when most were still farmers and well before the invention of the printing press, this was an expensive and time-consuming requirement for something—literacy—of little benefit to farmers. But over the centuries that followed, as Jews became urban, and as their brethren moved to distant points, literacy took on ever more importance while conferring the capability to work in careers substantially more challenging and lucrative than farming.

The duty to educate and be educated was absolute. In the twelfth century, Maimonides, the Jewish philosopher, said, "Appoint teachers for the children in every country, province and city. In any city that does not have a school, excommunicate the people...until they get teachers for the children."[587] This value was reinforced with the smartest and best educated Jews serving as rabbis. For much of 2,000 years, rabbis were more than simply religious leaders, in most communities rabbis were the local civil authority and the revered head of the community. Intellectual, more than physical skill, conferred prominence.

Though circumstances made education difficult in Eastern Europe in the 1700s and 1800s, a relatively illiterate Jewish population still craved learning. Thomas Sowell's book, *Ethnic America*, notes that roughly half the Eastern European Jews were illiterate when they arrived in the United States.[588] Once here, however, they "seized upon free schools, libraries and settlement houses in America with a tenacity...seldom approached by others. They not only crowded into public schools, but adult night schools as well (after long days of work)....And still, the Jewish daily newspaper, *Forward*, castigated them for not doing enough."[589]

Though destitute and testing poorly on IQ tests when they arrived from Eastern Europe, "Jews rose to have not only higher incomes than other Americans, but also more education and higher IQs. By (the 1950s), more than one-fourth of Jewish males had four or more years of college, while less than 10 percent of the U.S. population...had that much education."[590] "As of 1990, more than half of all Jews over age twenty-five were college graduates with 30 percent also completing postgraduate study. By contrast, 21 percent of the corresponding...(U.S.) white population had completed college with 9 percent completing postgraduate studies.[591] Further, Jews not only have more education, but better education—from higher quality colleges in more demanding and remunerative fields such as law, medicine and science."[592]

The same happened wherever Jews had the opportunity. In Australia, "Among young people between the ages of sixteen and twenty-two, nearly three-quarters of the Jews were full-time students, compared to about 20 percent of...the general population."[593] In Argentina, "While Jews were only about 1 percent of the...population in 1980, they were 20 percent of the university student body."[594] In early twentieth-century Germany, "one fourth of all law students and medical students...were Jews, though Jews were only 1 percent of the population."[595] And in the Prussia of 1911–12, where five of every 10,000 male Catholics were university students, (and thirteen of 10,000 Protestants), sixty-seven of every 10,000 Jews were in university.[596]

These high levels of education, including advanced degrees from the best of schools allowed Jews to practice demanding scientific, literary, education, artistic, professional, and entrepreneurial careers. It facilitated their high achievement.

Family: Marriage and family have long been indispensable in Jewish life. A man without a wife was seen to be "without joy, without blessing, and without good."[597] In Ethnic America, Sowell said, "Jews are more likely to marry...than others and less likely to divorce."[598] Jewish fathers were also less likely to desert their families.[599]

Fathers have a duty to support their children, educate them and teach them a trade, and children have a duty to honor their parents.[600] Scores of Jewish family rites link religious duties to love of home. These traditions strengthen both home and religion.[601] Family support was critical in an environment where discrimination reinforced the need to take care of one's own. And traditions, such as Shabbat kept the family close, while high expectations encouraged and pushed children to study, and defer immediate gratification for longer term goals. While the author may have been out partying with friends on a Friday night, his Jewish friends were home with their families engaged in a spirited intellectual conversation over dinner.

Jewish families also inculcated a drive to succeed into their young. Both "Italians and Jews," notes Sowell, "have had highly stable families, but the values of the Jewish family drive the individual toward upward mobility."[602]

In many Jewish families, the day-to-day job of raising kids, instilling values, and encouraging academic performance has been the job of a loving—even demanding— Jewish mother. In a recent biography, Sherwin Nuland, author of *How We Die*, reflected on how vitally important his mother was. He perceived that she lived only for him.[603] Even Meyer Lansky found his mother critically important in his life. She was the one person he did not want to disappoint.[604]

Moderation in Diet and Drink: Traditional Jewish culture follows kosher dietary practices arising from Biblical injunctions about what Jews should eat and drink and how food should be prepared and served. All vegetables are kosher. Pork is prohibited, as are certain kinds of seafood. Blood must be removed, and dairy products must not be served with meats. Because they are creatures of God, animals must be killed in a humane fashion. Their death should not be taken lightly.

For many non-Jews, some kosher practices seem strange. Presumably, even if there were safety concerns about eating pork and shellfish 2,000 years ago, those concerns are no longer justified.[605]

Orthodox Jews would respond that today's safer food is irrelevant. The Torah calls for kosher. Kosher "disciplines Jews toward holiness" in satisfying a basic need— for food.[606] It cultivates respect for the distinctive requirements of being Jewish, and once more we are drawn back to the Covenant. God requires it, and being Jewish means being different.

Many have observed that most Jews enjoy wine and some alcohol, but they avoid excess. Recent research suggests there may be a genetic basis for that restraint.[607] Drinking only in moderation is also both healthy and a survival skill. Michael Barone has noted that among all immigrant groups, the rates of both violent crime and alcoholism were lowest among Jews.[608] In his book *Ethnic America*, Sowell notes, "Like the Italians, Jews served wine with meals but seldom became drunkards. Drunkenness, boisterousness, or recklessness induced by drink could easily have become fatal in the precarious situation of most European Jews."[609] He goes further in *Migrations and Culture*, noting, "...the unusually low rates of alcoholism...found in studies of Jews in Poland, Canada, Prussia, Australia, and the United States."[610]

Skills, Autonomy, and Independence: Diaspora Jews were rarely farmers or landlords, and they were unwelcome in many established trades and industries controlled by locals. Still, they had to survive. If they were to provide for their families in a hostile world, skills were vital, even doubly important for Jews since those who dislike you will pay for your services if what you do is valuable, you do it very well, and they have no better choices.

Historically Jews shied away from large organizations. Anti-Semitism made it unwise to trust the goodwill of others or serve an institution where a change in sentiment could put you at risk. Better to control your own destiny and succeed or fail based on your own performance.[611]

The major paths open to Jews were the professions (such as doctor, lawyer, scientist, or entertainer) and working as merchants, financiers, and entrepreneurs. In each such field, skills are distinguishable and excellence is valued. Professions typically allow one to function outside large organizations and to relocate if threats arise. Merchant and middleman skills were viewed as "beneath" most locals, while finance and lending were needed, but prohibited by some religions. Jewelry and precious metals had the further advantage of being quite compact in relation to their value. They could be moved quickly and quietly if circumstances warranted.

Jews created new industries where there were no established barriers. Their European legacy in the clothing industry had no peer in early nineteenth-century America where they created the "ready-to-wear" industry from scratch.[612] The feature-motion-picture business never existed before they started or shaped every major studio.[613] More recently, they have created a huge number of new high-tech companies. When banks and law firms were already staffed by old-line, white-shoe Gentiles, Jews started their own firms—and later started their own country clubs as well when they found those doors closed to them.[614]

Even the religion embodies autonomy. There is no pope, Christ, or priest serving as a religious intervenor[615] between the individual Jew and God, and each synagogue selects its own rabbi.[616]

Hard Work, Tenacity, and Excellence: Jews rarely had family wealth to fall back on. Parents had to instill awareness that life was serious, play was not a priority, and determination mattered. Tenacity and superior talent made you valuable and discrimination costly. As Johnson has noted in his *History of the Jews*, "Where are the Edomites? Where are the ancient Hellenes and the Romans, the Byzantines, the Franks, the Mamlukes and the Ottomans? They have vanished into time, irrevocably. But the Jews are still in Hebron[617].. Hebron reflects the long, tragic history of the Jews and their unrivaled capacity to survive their misfortunes."[618] He goes further: "The Jews are the most tenacious people in history."[619]

Determination and hard work were complemented with superior skills, and such excellence provided a sense of achievement. Financially rewarding, it was also a ticket to respect. But more, it was psychological compensation for the world's false view that you might be unworthy. In any meritocracy, Jews excelled.

Willingness to Be Different: Judaism began with Abraham's willingness to be different. In the Covenant, "...the Lord had said unto Abraham, Get thee out of thy country and from thy kindred, and from thy father's house, unto a land that I will shew thee."[620] It was an astonishing thing for a person to do 4,000 years ago. Abraham packed up and left virtually everything he knew. He had confidence in his God and in himself, enough to leave his home and go where God directed him.

Later Moses defied the comfort and security of the Pharaoh's household to champion slaves and lead them from Egypt. Most prophets defied conventionality. Jesus and Paul demonstrated remarkable tenacity at standing apart, dedicated to their beliefs despite the humiliation and risks involved.

From inception, Jews have followed seemingly strange religious practices. They dressed and ate differently, spoke their own languages, kept to themselves, performed work no one else was willing to do, and generally refused to assimilate. This was not so much an accident of taste as a code of religious mandates which kept the tribe together—and apart from others. It lessened the likelihood of assimilation for a dispersed people. And while there was a price to be paid, the code survived for thousands of years. It only began to slacken with the growth of the Reform movement in Europe and the United States and the subsequent shift to secularism. Meanwhile, among some of the ultra-Orthodox, separateness, if anything, has grown. Stephan G. Bloom's *Postville*, written in 2000, provides a recent illustration in Postville, Iowa.[621]

Being perceived as "different" can be as liberating as it is uncomfortable. While the comfort of being in tune with the larger society may be absent, being different conditions Jews to stand apart and to live by their principles and their wits. They may as well "get over it," since conforming is impossible. Being viewed as an outsider only spurs a compulsion to demonstrate superiority, thereby overcoming negative stereotypes through superior performance.

In 1905, when Einstein proposed that the speed of light is constant, and because of that, both time and motion are relative (to the observer), the concept was so revolutionary, so remarkably different from conventional wisdom, that years passed before his notions were accepted. $E=mc2$ was equally revolutionary and hard to comprehend in the Isaac Newton paradigm of the times. Indeed, though Einstein developed four papers in 1905 and completed his general theory of relativity by 1916, it wasn't until 1922 that he received a Nobel Prize, and that was principally for his work on the photoelectric effect.[622] Indeed, virtually every Nobel is an award for being different, for having thought through a problem in a new way that yields dazzling new insights. Two-tenths of 1 percent of the world's population, Jews have won 181 (23 percent) of the 781 Nobels awarded to individuals through 2007.

Money: Jewish culture comes in for a good deal of both respect and derision when the subject is money. While a Scot may be kidded about being frugal in a charming sort of way, Jews come in for a rather more broad-brush, often pejorative, treatment. To some, Jews are miserly or hoarding. Others see them as ostentatious. Still others see them using money as an instrument of control. Envy and anti-Semitic stereotypes come into play.

In a meritocracy, however, money is the reward for success, the scorecard of achievement, a proxy for status, and an insurance policy for survival. It goes to those with talent who work hard to earn it. It also provides the means to survive if, as in the 1930s, there is risk to you and your family. Threatened for as long as Jews have been, wealth may be seen as insurance. Money helps compensate for discrimination.

You can do business on a mutually beneficial basis with those who dislike you if you have something they want and the means to say no.

Finally, money is the tool for providing charity. Many Jews feel a special duty to help those in need. Wealth provides the means to fulfill that responsibility, and they do.

In the end, money is important in Jewish culture in ways less true for other cultures.

Justice and Charity: In 1987, Thomas Sowell wrote a remarkable book titled *Conflict of Visions*.[623] In it he posited the notion of two prevailing social or political visions. Both want the best for everyone but differ sharply in their view of how the world works and how best to effect change. The "unconstrained view" sees a world where people can intervene directly to bring about desired social goals. That view believes results can be directly prescribed. If you see an injustice, you can and should intervene to make things better.

The "constrained view" sees a nuanced world complex beyond comprehension. It shares the unconstrained view's value for what is being sought, but sees most interventions as counterproductive, yielding unintended consequences that typically make things worse rather than better.

For those in the constrained camp, the unconstrained view is well-meaning, but flawed and elitist. It attempts to manipulate levers that don't work the way they are thought to work. For them, the world is both more complex and often self-corrective (Adam Smith's "invisible hand," the body's natural healing process, etc.). Intervention, if drawn upon at all, should complement the natural order rather than challenge it.

For the unconstrained, the constrained view is uncaring and aloof, ignorant of what can be achieved and, in not intervening, irresponsible in abdicating responsibility. While the analogy may do a grave disservice to Sowell, the unconstrained would find and give fish to the poor because they are starving; the constrained would help them make a fishing rod.

Perhaps arising from the long history of anti-Semitism, Jewish culture strongly identifies with the underdog. Even more, many Jews believe they have a duty to care for, and demand justice for, others as much as for themselves.[624] And in *tikkun olam*, they were "chosen" to take action. The world and injustice will not heal themselves.

Jews are remarkably generous. As noted earlier, only 2 percent of the U.S. population, they were nineteen (38 percent) of *Business Week's* 2007 list of the fifty most generous philanthropists. Those nineteen donated almost $23 billion over five years to mostly secular causes.[625] Since "Temple times," the *kuppah*, or collection box, has been the community welfare box to which Jews were obligated to donate.[626] Many Jews think of charity as an item to budget, just as they would the mortgage payment. It is an obligation (*tzedakah*), not an afterthought. One reason for accumulating great wealth is to help those in need.

In short, one sees in the activist liberal orientation of many Jews the consequence of long-standing cultural values akin to Sowell's "unconstrained view." By intervening, they established trade unions, helped get blacks the right to vote, cured polio, created birth control pills, split the atom, created Israel and thousands of other interventions that benefit us all. They act.

Enlightenment, Emancipation, and the Golden Age

Jews have long been disproportionate high achievers, but this book has focused mostly on their Golden Age. It commenced roughly 200 years ago and continues to the present day.

The eighteenth-century Enlightenment opened Europe to an age of reason, and tolerance. Religious wars generally came to an end and religious intolerance came to be seen as evil.[627] Spinoza's view of the unity of God and nature gained currency, and Europeans, though still somewhat anti-Semitic, were more open to considering Jews as equals. Europeans pursued science, were less dogmatic and more secular, and Jews were not pressed to convert and assimilate.[628] No longer seen as guilty of Deicide, instead, they could remain Jewish while participating in the secular flowering of science, literature, politics, and the arts. Rather than compulsion, there was encouragement.

In this context, the French Assembly granted Jews the rights of citizenship in 1791. They were to be denied everything as a nation, but granted everything as individuals. As it turned out, true equality had to wait for Napoleon to organize a Sanhedrin and pass the Civil Code of 1804, but Jews first realized equality in France.[629] Then, over the next seventy years the Jewish Emancipation extended to encompass the rest of Western Europe. Meanwhile, of course, equivalent rights and freedoms had long existed in the United States, though the American Jewish population was quite small until the German Jewish emigration of the 1830s.

The European Enlightenment was complemented with a Jewish Enlightenment (*Haskalah*). Beginning with Moses Mendelssohn in Germany, intellectual Jews responded to the Enlightenment notion of tolerance by seeking to engage the German culture (and later other European cultures as well), and that opening led to the birth of the Jewish Reform movement in Germany.[630] Enlightenment values began to infuse Jewry and Jews became ever more engaged in the secular world. As noted earlier in this book, Charles Murray synthesized these events very well in his book, *Human Accomplishment*.

> "Until nearly 1800, Jews were excluded. Then over about seventy years, the legal exclusions were lifted and the social exclusion eases. What happens? 'The suddenness with which Jews begin to appear...is nothing short of astounding' writes Raphael Patai. 'It seemed as if a huge reservoir of Jewish talent, hitherto dammed up behind the wall of Talmudic learning were suddenly released to spill over into all fields of Gentile cultural activity.'"[631]

What was a long, interesting, and impressive performance by Jews exploded into an era of phenomenal achievement. Whether it arose from predominantly cultural or genetic origins, or some mix of both, there is simply no question that following the Enlightenment and Emancipation, Jews moved from being an interesting footnote in the history of high achievers to center stage. Over the last 200 years, no group has accomplished as much relative to its numbers.

———•———

In the end, luck had nothing to do with Jewish achievement. A self-perception of being "chosen" and perhaps second-generation drive may have contributed somewhat. Natural selection or some other as yet not understood aspect of genetic predisposition may have also played a role. More likely, however, and certainly over time, it has been the unique, remarkable, and ever-evolving 4,000-year-old Judaic culture that has driven, and continues to drive, the extraordinary performance.

Chapter 26

A Fading Golden Age?

"The main thrust of Jewish demographic change over the...post-World War II period, and more intensely since the 1990s, included overall quantitative stagnation at the global level, considerable aging due to comparatively low fertility rates...and a dramatic migration...from Muslim countries and Eastern Europe to Israel, and to...western countries. In turn...negative balances of...births and deaths, and of weak propensities to raise (as Jews)...the children of intermarriages, further impacted Jewish population size and distribution....Entire Jewish communities dried up completely...and others shrank significantly....Israel, from a relatively small and marginal Jewish community at the end of World War II, emerged (with the United States) as one of the two leading centers of world Jewish population....In the US, however, much because of the same reasons...the historical momentum of Jewish population growth reached a standstill at the end of the 20th century."[632]
—*Prof. Sergio DellaPergola, Nov. 2003*

In his book, *Jewish Literacy*, Rabbi Joseph Telushkin tells of the 1964 *Look* magazine cover story titled, "The Vanishing American Jew." Its demographic observations paralleled those of DellaPergola (above) in painting a bleak picture for the future. Commenting on the story, Telushkin offered up a quote from his friend, Michael Medved, who said, "It is now more than thirty-five years later. Look at the Jewish people, and look at *Look* magazine."[633]

DellaPergola, *Look* magazine, and Medved frame a long-running debate about the future of Judaism, a future which inherently reflects on the prospects for continuing high levels of Jewish Achievement. Is the Golden Age secure or endangered? Will it continue or fade? Many pick up on Telushkin's implied perspective, expressing confidence about the future while others are alarmed. To explore this topic, first consider the reasons some expect Jews to continue to thrive. Then contemplate the threats which may bring the Golden Age to an end.

The Optimistic Perspective

It seems foolish to forecast a fading "Golden Age" just now when Jews are so disproportionately accomplished. Their 4,000-year history demonstrates nothing if not a unique ability to withstand greater challenges and persecutions than those which destroyed so many other civilizations and cultures along the way. Through all the hardship, Jews not only survived, they developed their religion and cultural values in ways that led to their Golden Age.

Judaism and Jews have shown a stunning ability to respond to challenges.[634] Time after time they have transformed themselves whether in reaction to internal disruptions or external threats, some of which would have annihilated the Jewish people while others would have enveloped them into the surrounding cultures. Each time, their response sustained them, often taking them to new highs.

The monarchy and First Temple brought together the twelve tribes in response to the Philistine threat, while offsetting the absolute power of kings with the priesthood and Temple.[635,636] After Ten Tribes were lost in the Assyrian Diaspora, promulgation of the book of Deuteronomy, in circa 621 B.C., helped unify differing views within the religion and codified the Mosaic Code (the Law.)[637] That step also served to dilute the disparate views of prophets, while further unifying the religion. Around 450 B.C., Babylonian Jews fused various versions of the Five Books of Moses into a single written Pentateuch.[*,638] That step enhanced and clarified the common religion of a dispersed people and laid the early foundation for the premium Jews place on literacy. Still later, the entire Hebrew Bible (the Tanach), was canonized.

Rome's destruction of the Second Temple and dispersal of Jews to the four corners of the world, served as an impetus for the Pharisees' establishment of rabbinical Judaism, institutionalization of the synagogue, and the writing down of the "Oral Law" and commentary (Mishnah and Gemara) to form the Talmud.[639] When distributed to Diaspora Jews, the Jewish Bible and Talmud permitted a stateless people to have a compendium of universal "Jewish Laws" to govern their day-to-day existence wherever they lived throughout the Diaspora.

The Talmud reinforced the premium on literacy (one had to be literate to read and understand the Torah and Talmud.), and it stimulated yet more Talmudic debate and interest in yeshiva-styled education. All of this encouraged the immense value Jews place on learning and treasuring the "best and brightest." Stateless and relatively powerless, Jews had no political or aristocratic hierarchy. Instead, they established a religious and intellectual meritocracy.

Jews are one of history's great representations of the aphorism, "Whatever doesn't kill me, makes me stronger." Somehow, no matter how grave the threat or extreme the circumstance, Judaism came up with an appropriate response to sustain and improve itself. Critical challenges often served to reinforce and sustain Judaism.

In more recent times, even when large numbers of Jews have been secular, comparable challenges and occasional events have stimulated a resurgent commitment to Judaism. The late nineteenth century "Jewish Awakening" drew Jews back to a more conservative faith in response to German anti-Semitism which had spread to the United States. That anti-Semitism discredited the liberal orthodoxy of the times and discouraged assimilation. Conservative Judaism became strong, Reform Judaism enacted changes, and secular and Zionist Jews responded to anti-Semitism by turning inward toward their own culture and people. Around the same time, the Dreyfus Affair in France drove Theodor Herzl to champion Zionism, and that doctrine began to gain strength in the United States.[640]

After World War II, the horror of the Holocaust brought Jews together once more, and still later, the creation of Israel and the Israeli victories in 1948 and 1967 reinforced Jewish pride in their heritage.

More recently, the failure of the August 2000 Camp David talks, the second Intifada, increased anti-Israeli sentiment in many countries, and continued threats to Israel—including prospects for a nuclear-armed Iran—have served to reinforce the commitment of Jews to religious and secular Judaism and to Israel.

In keeping the religion of Judaism vital, one can also appreciate the resurgent interest in ultra-Orthodox Judaism. This is the only group of Jews whose numbers are significantly increasing through reproduction. There has also been a corresponding growth of interest in Kabbalah and other mystical and spiritual elements of Judaism. The Reform Movement reportedly continues to integrate traditional elements into its services, and both in the 1960s (the havurah movement) and today, many younger Jews have developed a heightened interest in their religion (occasionally, pulling their more assimilated parents back to the fold with them).

At the same time, significant numbers of Jews are reportedly "branching out" into new approaches, some blending Judaism and Buddhism, as described in Rodger Kamenetz's 1994 book, *The Jew in the Lotus.*[641]

Going still further, some believe the threatened demographic decline in Judaism is overstated. They challenge the population projections of experts such as DellaPergola,[642] (see above) and particularly those developed for the 2001–2002 National Jewish Population Survey. In their view, a substantial number of Jews have been missed in the census and the situation is not nearly as bleak as the pessimists portray. Some express the view that a "crisis" is being manufactured to encourage fears which will stimulate prodigals to return to the fold. Others feel the facts have been manipulated to promote fundraising. A few even see the current high intermarriage rate as a positive force which will bring new children to Judaism—when the offspring are raised Jewish within a mixed family.[643]

Some believe that even if the challenges are real, appropriate responses are being framed in programs such as "Birthright Israel," which sends to Israel any young Jew who wishes to go. They note that forty-five years ago, there was only one professionally staffed museum in the United States focused on Judaica and Jewish culture. Now, there are sixty or more. Back then, there were no Holocaust monuments. Now there are more than 100. In 1962 there were no annual Jewish film festivals. Today there are more than thirty.[644] There is the Synagogue Transformation and Renewal (STAR) Program, the Partnership for Jewish Education, a Hillel project to support on-campus activities, and countless similar efforts to encourage awareness, involvement, and commitment to the religion, history, and culture of Judaism. In addition, there was the immense and successful effort to bring most of the Soviet Jews to Israel, the United States, and other Western countries.

In short, the Jews are a tiny people who have survived 4,000 difficult years. They remain vital today and will cope with whatever challenges come their way.[645, 646]

Threats to Judaism and the Golden Age

The preceding arguments have merit but do not tell the whole story. Absent a tragedy akin to the Holocaust, or a material rise in U.S. anti-Semitism, it will be a challenge for Jews to cope with the magnitude of the current demographic and cultural tides which threaten to dilute the "Golden Age" over the next fifty years or more.[647] Demography, apathy, and dissipation of cultural values are all serious threats. Even noted columnist William Safire has recently been on the stump citing the need for a determined proactive effort to bring more converts to Judaism.[648]

Perhaps just over the horizon lies a powerful "transformation" in Judaism which we lack sufficient foresight to perceive. Or perhaps the numerous new "outreach" programs, such as Birthright Israel, will collectively renew the people, reinforce the culture, and turn the tide, but if so, it will not be because anyone who analyzed the trends in the early twenty-first century could easily see it coming. In fact, the momentum is headed in the wrong direction. Jews will become an ever smaller proportion of the world's people, and the religion shows some signs of fragmenting at the extremes of religiosity and secularity. The solid core values that arose from the religion and Judaism's response to challenges are at risk of dissipating over time. And in some quarters, apathy is seen as a growing problem. Such evolutions would almost certainly dilute the impetus that drove the Jews to achieve so much.

First, consider the raw demographics.

Only twice since the beginnings of Judaism, nearly 4,000 years ago, have Jews been as small a proportion of the world's population as they are today.[649]

From 1.7 percent of the world population in 1000 B.C., their numbers fell to 0.2 percent between 500 and 200 B.C. following the Assyrian conquest, loss of the Ten Tribes and the subsequent Babylonian conquest and Diaspora. By the time of Christ, however, Jews had renewed themselves. They had grown to perhaps 1.8 percent of the world population and are thought to have been 5 percent to 10 percent of the Roman population before the Jewish revolts and ensuing Roman Diaspora reduced them to 0.4 percent, still twice today's level.

In the roughly 250 years between 1492, when the Inquisition commenced, and 1750, Jews were once again reduced to the 0.2 percent figure. Yet from that low, they grew to 16.6 million people (roughly 0.7 percent of the world's population) by 1940. The Holocaust then destroyed a third of them, but still, in 1946 the remaining eleven million Jews were twice the proportion of the world's population that they are today. And at war's end, they were 4 percent of the U.S. population, also twice today's figure.

Some tallies indicate that since World War II, there have never been more than thirteen million Jews, and since reaching that post-war peak, their numbers have stayed flat or declined.[650] Other tallies put the figures somewhat higher (fourteen or fifteen million) but still with declines since World War II rather than growth or stability. In the United States, despite a net growth in migration, mostly from Europe and the former Soviet Union, Jews are now only about 2 percent of the population.

**The Pentateuch encompasses the first five books of the Jewish Bible. It is typically called the Torah when written on parchment as a single scroll. For Christians, with only minor differences, these are the first five books of the "Old Testament."

A July 12, 2005, projection by the Jewish People Policy Planning Institute of Jerusalem, says that by 2020, the world's Jews will total 13.5 million.[651] By then, the earth's population will have grown to 7.58 billion.[652] At that point, Jews will be only 0.18 percent of the world's people. Should the trend continue, they will fall below 0.1 percent before the end of the twenty-first century.

In the United States the phenomenon is driven by:[653]

The low Jewish birth rate (1.8 children per family versus a replacement rate of 2.1). Jewish women tend to have no more than two children, and of Jewish women thirty to thirty-four years of age, 52 percent are childless. This compares with 27 percent for all American women. Many believe high levels of Jewish education and affluence have stimulated the shift to smaller families started later in life.

The average age of Jews is now forty-one years old versus thirty-seven just ten years ago. The U.S. average is thirty-five. Children are now only 19 percent of the Jewish population, down from 21 percent just ten years ago. The U.S. average is 26 percent;

The rate of intermarriage to non-Jews is perhaps as high as 52 percent, with only one child in three of interfaith marriage being raised Jewish. In the 1930s the intermarriage rate was estimated to be 5 to 9 percent. By the 1950s and 1960s, it was 8 percent in New York and 37 percent in Marin County, California.[654] It has climbed steadily. Unabated, this will prove a huge force behind a decline in Judaism.

In Israel the numbers are somewhat better. Immigrants, particularly from the former Soviet Union, have substantially increased the population on a "one-time" basis. This cannot continue, however, since relatively few Diaspora Jews are left to move to Israel. (Eighty percent of the world's Jews already live in the United States or Israel.) Further, even if more did move to Israel, there is no evidence that Jewish communities outside Israel or the United States are growing more quickly than their contemporaries.

Further, though Israel's Jewish birth rate is somewhat higher than that of U.S. Jews (driven heavily by high rates of reproduction among the ultra-Orthodox), the higher rate of reproduction is substantially below that of the Palestinians and their Arab/Muslim neighbors.

In the end, Jewish population demography is daunting.

But the "head count" tells only part of the story. One thesis of this book has been that the Jewish religion and people have functioned for the better part of 4,000 years in often hostile environments which at times threatened their existence. In responding to those challenges, Judaism evolved a culture of shared values that were remarkably effective. Those values "fit" in the Darwinian sense that they were "appropriate" to the circumstances. They allowed Judaism not just to survive, but to evolve—to develop.

Moreover, despite doctrinal disputes about the theology of Judaism, and occasional periods when many Jews went astray (in pursuit of false Messiahs for example), mainstream Judaism, where the bulk of Jews functioned, had strong shared values. Whether guided by the thinking of Hillel, Ben Zakkai, Maimonides, Caro, Bal Shem Tov, Mendelssohn, or countless others, Jews were committed to each other and their shared cultural values and they lived their lives accordingly. Oppressed by frequent anti-Semitism and restrictions on their ways of living, they focused their talents and energies on their religion, community, and the limited number of careers and lifestyles open to them, such as international trade, finance, and merchandising.

The Jewish Emancipation and Enlightenment changed all that. The United States was nearly always a hospitable environment, but it was unique, at least in the period following commencement of the Spanish Inquisition in 1492. The Emancipation and Enlightenment removed restrictions and opened up physical and intellectual opportunities which did not exist before, while the Reform movement changed both the theology and behavior of Jews. They became less "the other" and thus more part of the secular world. It was a world of art and science, rather than just theology and commerce.

As Paul Johnson said,

"Quite suddenly, around the year 1800, this ancient and highly efficient social machine for the production of intellectuals began to shift its output. Instead of pouring all of its products into the closed circuit of rabbinical studies, where they remained completely isolated from general society, it unleashed a significant and ever growing proportion of them into secular life. This was an event of shattering importance in world history.[655]

An incipient talent required only a hospitable environment to liberate Jews and ignite them to explore and master the secular world around them.

Looking forward, that dynamic is at risk. Apart from the damning demographics, there are threats to the qualitative and cultural factors which contributed to high rates of Jewish achievement. The underpinnings which brought about "The Golden Age" are less secure.

Historically, life as a Jew was difficult and sometimes dangerous. Among the major cultures that tried, at one point or another, to destroy or change Jews in fundamental ways were the Assyrians, Greeks, Romans, early Christians, Muslims, Crusaders, Spanish, Russians, and Germans. Jews were "the other," practicing strange customs while living among the various dominant foreign cultures.

Even within Judaism, tension arose from different interpretations of the Torah, Talmud, Kabbalah, and other texts. In biblical times, the Sadducees disputed the Pharisees, and the Essenes disputed them both. Eighth century Karaites dismissed the authenticity of the Talmud and eighteenth century Hasid's preached mysticism and spirituality rather than rabbinical pragmatism. Secularists even derided the very idea of God, and many Jews chose to simply assimilate.

Being Jewish has involved persistent challenges, but the tensions spurred them. They did not cower.

In *Human Accomplishment*, Charles Murray points out that tension has been common to many periods of great accomplishment.

"The first and most famous golden age of them all, in Athens…took place against a backdrop of civil and military strife…. Life in Renaissance Florence was not quite as harrowing as in Athens, but it was not tranquil…. Florence had just ousted its ruler, was invaded by the French…would spend the next five years as a theocratic republic under the religious radical Savonarola…The Dutch golden age…gathered strength in the middle of the Thirty Years' War."[656]

Israel exists and to date has withstood every challenge. In major confrontations, it has consistently defeated overwhelming numbers in defending the country. America remains supportive of both its Jews and of Israel.

There is still anti-Semitism, and in recent years it has grown in Europe and other parts of the world. Even so, its effect is small in comparison with most of Jewish history. And of course there is none in Israel, and in the United States it is nominal. Between them, Israel and the United States hold 80 percent of the world's Jews.

The war on terror, prospects for a nuclear-armed Iran, and the potential for Hamas, Hezbollah or Al Qaeda-inspired WMD terrorist attacks on Tel Aviv or New York are real, but the magnitude of those threats is certainly no greater, and is arguably smaller, than the Holocaust, the Spanish Inquisition, the Roman destruction of the Temple and Palestine's Jews, and the massed Egyptian, Syrian, Jordanian, and Iraqi forces that fought against Israel intending to destroy it in 1948 and 1967.

Today Jews have more power and they have an alliance with the United States to help them respond to threats. Today Egypt and Jordan are at peace with Israel; it is hoped Iraq is moving toward democracy; the Saudis are promoting a two-state solution; Syria, though backed by Iran, is apparently willing to talk peace if the right deal can be cut for the Golan Heights; and Libya has renounced nuclear weapons and its historical advocacy of terrorism.

Economic affluence is another solvent with potential to dilute their drive. High levels of achievement have often brought financial rewards and security in an otherwise insecure world. Wealth provides the means to protect one's lifestyle, and the capability to move quickly if circumstances warrant. Jews are financially successful. Their median income levels are high and they are disproportionately represented among the rich. Life is good. Life is comfortable. A week at a Tuscan Villa is more pleasant than a week in the lab, at the desk, or rehearsing for a big show.

Said more succinctly, over time, the consequences of reduced threats and greater comfort may diminish the motivation of Jews in succeeding generations.

Further, for all practical purposes the Diaspora is over. The Israeli "right of return" and American immigration have caused the ever greater concentration of Jews in just two countries. For two thousand years the Diaspora was a vital force in shaping Jewish values, talents, and outlook. It will soon be a memory. For all its negative aspects, Jews enveloped as tiny colonies within often hostile communities around the world were exposed to the knowledge, art, and philosophies of those foreign cultures. They were on the "verges" of those cultures and they learned from them. The Diaspora helped shape them into superb traders with fellow Jews and non-Jews across the globe. No other culture had outposts in so many places with family and fellow Jews who could be trusted to perform mercantile tasks at great distances and over long periods of time.

Today the plaintiff cry "Next year in Jerusalem" is more likely to be heard from a twelve-year-old Jew in New York than a denizen of the Diaspora. Israel and America offer Jews security and opportunity, but ever less exposure to the influences of other countries and cultures. Jews are evolving toward an ever more insular, and perhaps more chauvinistic, outlook. "Be careful what you wish for" may be an apt aphorism when increased comfort and security, and the joys of being surrounded "by your own kind" mean a substantially narrowed experience and frame of reference. Lost as well may be the motivation for proving oneself to the larger culture so willing to perceive Jews as unworthy.

A different kind of risk involves a decline in the number of Jews committed to mainstream values of Jewish culture, a culture which helped drive the high rates of achievement.[657] The concern is that Judaism may be fragmenting. At one edge, the ultra-Orthodox are the only group of Jews whose population is growing. At the other edge are Jews who assimilate completely, or whose "à la carte" combining of elements of Judaism with elements from other religions and philosophies dilutes their commitment to their own tribe and culture.

Mainstream Judaism involves varying levels of religious dedication coupled with a commitment to living in (and for some, repairing) the real world. Rarely monastic, and heavily mystical (Hasidic mysticism) only for the 100 years between the mid-eighteenth century and mid-nineteenth century, today's mainstream Judaism is rooted in historic Torah and Talmudic scholarship, cultural values and traditions which largely arose from the religion and pragmatic engagement with life in this world.[658]

The ultra-Orthodox are committed to the religious heritage of Judaism, but some are doctrinaire and focused more on the mystical than rational elements of Judaism. The orientation is inward, toward the individual, the family, and the Orthodox community rather than outward toward the secular world. They may reach new heights of spiritual attainment, but they are unlikely to be committed to or concerned with the less Orthodox world. They harken back to a form of orthodoxy Jews practiced hundreds of years ago, well before the Jewish Emancipation, Enlightenment, and Golden Age. And for many ultra Orthodox, their commitment to scholarship is focused almost entirely on the Religion and it constrains the education and intellectual involvement of its women. There are exceptions, but ultra-Orthodox Jews are much less likely to be high achievers in the secular world. Like radical Islam, the orientation is more toward a return to the past than a focus on the future.

At the other end of the spectrum are Jews, particularly among the young, who select among Jewish values they will believe in, and others who totally assimilate, pulling away from any association with Judaism and its shared values.

It is important to point out this book's distinction between "secular Jews," "fully assimilated Jews" and "à la carte" Jews. The first have played a vital role in the Golden Age. The second and third are likely to dilute it over time.

The last 200 years have seen a substantial increase in the numbers of secular Jews.[660] One might even think of them as a movement (or denomination) all their own. From the mid-nineteenth century through the end of World War II, the United States Jewish community was largely secular. Whether that was because the United States was generally hospitable to Jews and many preferred something of an assimilated lifestyle, or because increased anti-Semitism from the late nineteenth century through World War II made it wise to keep a low profile, the fact is that there is a long history of secularism and humanism among those who do not count themselves as religious, but who are strong in their commitment to being Jewish.

From inception, the Zionist movement was also largely secular. At least in part, because Orthodox Jews predated Zionists in Palestine and outnumbered any other denomination, Israel has Orthodox Judaism as the state religion, but the Zionists who fought to create and defend the country, and who were a significant part of the early population, were mostly secular. Even today, after huge numbers have immigrated, 51 percent of Israel's Jews refer to themselves as secular.[660]

While most secular Jews no longer believe in God, or are essentially agnostic when compared with their more religious brethren, they still share a commitment to the culture of Judaism, its core values, and their fellow Jews. Most retain pride and belief in such essential Jewish values as ethical behavior, accountability, hard work, loyalty to community and family, education, excellence, assertiveness, tolerance, tzedakah—a duty to justice while assisting the underprivileged—and healing the broken world. They are proud of their people and their history, and some follow many of the religion's traditions, whether or not they belong to or are active in a synagogue

There is legitimate concern that over the long run, the cultural values which evolved from the religion may wither if ever fewer people are committed to the religion itself. Presumably commitment to those values might wane, diluting the motivation for high levels of achievement. While this may yet occur, certainly the last 150 years have not seen a reduced commitment to those values. Moreover, if anything, the rates of secular achievement have been consistently remarkable and in some domains, have advanced rather than receded. The rate at which Jews earn Nobels is higher today (27 percent) than before the Holocaust (14 percent) when their proportion of the population was greater.

Compared with secular Jews, their assimilated "brethren" reject being Jewish, or simply do not care. They may or may not share the values of mainstream Jews, but if they do, it is not because of their commitment and pride in being Jewish. They may continue to be high achievers, but over time, they and their offspring will become ever more a part of the culture into which they have assimilated. They will increasingly function in ways compatible with whatever values are then treasured by that group.

"A la carte" Jews are attracted by some parts of Judaism and repelled by others. They live by the parts they like and combine those with parts from other religions and philosophies they find attractive. In that sense, à la carte Judaism is individualistic. Each person picks and chooses what he or she likes without reference to the core beliefs of Judaism and any sense of how the parts relate to the whole.

An illustration of "à la carte" Judaism might be seen in Rodger Kamenetz's book, *The Lotus in the Jew*. He describes the JUBUs (Jewish Buddhists) who reject aspects of Judaism and its culture and go on to combine elements of Judaism and Buddhism into a practice compatible with their own beliefs. This book has not explored the question but is skeptical that Buddhists have won a disproportionate number of Nobels.

Variations on this "à la carte" sense of values arise in Israel as well. Notwithstanding the country's impressive programs to educate its youth about Jewish and Israeli history and culture, the mandatory three year stint in the Israeli military during which every recruit is taken to Masada to pledge his or her life and honor to defend Israel, and the organized educational trips armed soldiers take to historic sites all over the country, two knowledgeable Israelis employed at senior levels at one university, profess concern for the future of their culture. 'Our young people are becoming too American,' are the words. By this they mean the strong ties to their own history and culture are being supplanted by the MTV, Gameboy, *USA Today* mentality, the short attention spans, the superficial and materialistic values, and a selfish individualism that neglects the common good and the underprivileged. It may be simply a normal generational gap, but one suspects it is real, and the culture of Israel is changing.

Another frame of reference is the kibbutz. A lifestyle dating back nearly 100 years is endangered. In part, Israel's youth find the collective mentality and life style of the kibbutz inhospitable. There is more to it than just the lack of interest by the young, but the individualistic outlook by young Israelis has contributed to an average age for kibbutz members in their fifties. Only thirty-five to fifty of the 267 kibbutzim are reported to be doing well, and the rest are experiencing financial and membership difficulties.[661]

In the end, three forces threaten the culture of disproportionate Jewish achievement. The first is the raw numbers and the seemingly inevitable reduced Jewish presence on the planet relative to others. The second is apathy and a narrower life experience arising from fewer challenges, greater affluence, and less exposure to the world's diversity. And third, a dissipation of mainstream Jewish cultural values as some gravitate to the extremes of ultra-Orthodox (focused inward and backward), or assimilation (a loss of commitment to the Jewish people—the tribe and its values), while others adopt an eclectic-styled Judeo-spiritualism. Collectively these trends may leave an ever smaller number of people who believe in Judaism's core values and go on to accomplish great things.

Let us hope the Jews rise, once more, to the challenges.

———•———

At the beginning of this book, there was an effort to make the point that the author may be wrong in his analysis of the causes behind *The Golden Age of Jewish Achievement*. That is, the book has always presumed two questions. First are the Jews uniquely disproportionate high achievers? And second, if so, why has that happened? To the first question, any reasonable response is almost certain to be "yes." Unless one believes their achievements have not been earned from merit (which some do believe, though their arguments cannot withstand serious scrutiny), one must conclude Jews are the most disproportionately accomplished group of the last 125 years and perhaps much longer. We have all benefited from those contributions.

As to the second question, this book has laid out ideas in hopes further thought and debate will yield better and more complete understanding of the phenomenon. In the end, the task has to do with learning what we can so that those lessons can be applied elsewhere. As noted in the prior chapter, if Jews were a corporation, their practices would be "benchmarked" and copied. If they were a pharmaceutical, we would strive to learn the "method of action" in hopes those lessons would help us develop other beneficial pharmaceuticals. The risk of envy will be ever present, but the benefits from knowing what led to such high achievement and how those lessons can be utilized elsewhere offers rewards much greater than the prospective risks.

Afterword

One of the more interesting aspects of writing this book was the remarkable ambivalence of so many Jews about the notion of discussing their disproportionate performance. Almost the first time I raised the subject with Charles, a longtime friend, he was complimented by my interest, but skeptical about my pursuit of the topic. In an early brief presentation of the book's premise to a small mixed audience, one Jewish attendee was impressed and grateful for my interest. Another accused me of anti-Semitism.

The author of an excellent book on a related topic told me of the difficulties on his book tour when, at the last minute, he was canceled from an interview on National Public Radio (NPR). Reportedly, the cancellation arose from fears NPR would lose the sponsorship of some prominent Jews. The same author told me of his conversation with one very wealthy and prominent Jew who said he would do anything he could to squelch the book's publicity and success. Certainly, my long-suffering literary agent saw the same phenomenon firsthand as publishing houses expressed reluctance, not just about the work of an unpublished author, but also about the book's chosen topic.

There is justification for such concern. If there has been one powerful lesson for Jews over the last two thousand years, it is to keep your head down. In so many civilizations, when times were good, the small Jewish minority was well respected and they prospered from contributions to their country of residence. But when things began to go badly in war, the economy, or some other maelstrom, Jews were typically the first scapegoat. Germany was the most enlightened home for Jews in the late nineteenth century. In less than twenty years, following Germany's loss in World War I and the later economic meltdown, it became history's most horrible embodiment of Jewish hatred. "Be cautious," is a message Jews have learned very well. Even when things are going well, circumstances can quickly turn dangerous. Envy of your success can become a powerful driver of your undoing.

There is an intellectually interesting second aspect to this conundrum. That is, singling out one culture for such recognition not only flies in the face of today's politically correct notion that "all cultures are equal," it also stimulates concern that it may demonstrate a "racist" perspective akin to the Aryan superiority gospel of the Nazis, with all the subsequent tragedy that racial theory inspired.

Third, there is the understandable, if occasional, reaction of, "Who is this non-Jew to think he understands us and is competent to write about us? He is neither a published author nor a scholar of Judaism or Jewish history."

In the end, I acknowledge all three points. There is risk such public recognition of their achievements can backfire. And yes, I do dispute the politically correct notion that all cultures are equal, but my views are simply not racist. They are precisely the opposite. They represent an optimistic message. Unlike the determinism of genetics, culture, which is malleable and open to conscious shaping, is seen as a driving force behind the remarkable Jewish performance. It should be similarly possible for other groups to become overachievers as well.

As to chutzpah, I confess. After all, though I hardly compare, it was Daniel Boorstin, the Jewish Pulitzer Prize-winning historian and former head of the Library of Congress, who acknowledged historians' debt to amateur historians such as Edward Gibbon, Winston Churchill, and Henry Adams.[662]

In an era where anti-Semitism is on the rise in Europe and at the United Nations, when a world of six billion people seems to increasingly vilify Jews, perhaps it can be helpful to lay some irrefutable facts on the table to help non-Jews understand what Jews have contributed. In the process, hopefully some anti-Semitic myths about their historic role and values can be proven wrong. This book raises the notion that Jewish culture provides some lessons from which others can learn.

One late evening conversation with a mildly anti-Semitic Ukrainian friend was instructive. After the discussion and his review of a prospective magazine article on the topic, he became interested in exploring publication of the article in Russia. I took this as positive evidence that while extremists are unreachable, facts, presented in the right way, can influence the attitudes of the open-minded. I hope this effort can make that kind of contribution.

A logical question arises from this Afterword and the chapters which preceded it. Am I saying Jews are superior? The answer is no, I am not. There is much to be learned from Jewish history and culture, but this book does not propose Jews are superior. Yes, they are disproportionately accomplished. The book clearly makes that case. And it goes further, suggesting why that may have happened. But it never says, nor does it intend to suggest, that Jews are genetically or in any other way superior to the rest of us.

If it was possible to array all Jews statistically in terms of their achievements and contributions, that distribution would be shaped like a bell (normal) curve. There would be many Jews in the middle and at the bottom of the curve and their combined achievements and contributions would be modest. Compared with other groups, similarly arrayed, two things would be clear. First, the total number of Jews depicted in their bell curve would be small, almost trivial compared to the other groups. Most of the other bell curves would be much larger, representing many more people. (Realize that in a sample of 1,000 of the world's people, only two would be Jews.) Second, most other groups would have members whose achievements and contributions are as important as those of the most accomplished Jews.

By the standards of "greatness" in Michael Hart's *The 100: A Ranking of the Most Influential Persons in History,* ninety-two of history's one hundred most influential people were not Jews,[663] and Muhammad and Isaac Newton were ranked one and two respectively. While Jews have done phenomenally well in winning Nobel prizes, 77 percent of the Nobels have gone to non-Jews. And, as is discussed earlier in the book, Jews have their share of villains, some of them very nasty (Meyer Lansky and Dutch Schultz), others criminally insane (David Berkowitz) and some unethical (Ivan Boesky). Jews have had their share of con men, idiots, and embarrassments. The normal curve applies. They are not racially superior. But their achievements and contributions are disproportionate to their numbers and, in the popular expression of a few years ago, as a group they are "overachievers."

———•———

Without the interest of many supportive friends, this book would never have happened. Danny, Barbara and Linda Kaplan took an early interest, read drafts, made suggestions and introductions. They were often as surprised as I was by the reticence of some Jews. Ed and Carolyn Stolman and Nancy Conrad were similarly helpful in commenting on the book. Ed introduced my work to Dr. Robert Butler who reviewed a draft, and to Rabbi Harold Kushner, who was kind enough to talk with his agent and publisher about my efforts and helped in other ways as well. Michael Sonnenfeldt was vital in reviewing draft chapters, introducing me to people interested in the topic, and hosting an event at New York's Upper West Side Jewish Community Center. Les Vadasz was always there with suggestions and critiques. He proved once more to be the world's best "nudger." Charles Kremer, Ted Kozloff, Jeffrey Hirschberg, Fred Perry, John and Libby Brady, Robert Nicholas, Elsa and Gary Nelson, Alycia and Elvin Case, Barbara Thomas and Roger Wright, Toby and Steve Rosenblatt, David Auerbach, Kevin Calhoun, Andy Weinberger and Dr. Nelson Schiller read drafts and made many helpful comments. Stan Cohn convened a small group—Peggy Lipson, Sy Lenz and Henry Lasky—for me in Sonoma, and for the price of lunch, they provided helpful insights and suggestions. Howard Metzenberg shared his thoughts and his library. Kathleen Gurney provided encouragement and suggestions about "getting published" as did April Eberhardt. Frank Caufield was very helpful with his comments on the "Hollywood" chapter, Steven Dobbs became interested, introduced me to colleagues and suggested many ways to get the material in front of key people and publications. Dr. John Stace provided his constant support, reading the manuscript and exchanging e-mails as he traversed Western Australia treating his patients. Charles Murray was willing to share his data and review a chapter which discusses his book *Human Accomplishment*. Thomas Sowell responded warmly to my inquiry and provided inspiration on many key points.

In the end, six others deserve great thanks. Deborah Daly did a superb job designing the book and its cover, Alex Carlin helped me develop the book's original Web site. Janet Volkman spent countless hours reading and editing the material. My original literary agent, Michael Larsen, spent even more hours seeking out a publisher and counseling me on ways to best develop the manuscript and market it. And to seasoned, professional editor, Michael Denneny, a very special thanks for the long hours he spent reading the manuscript, advising me on the book proposal, and providing his invaluable suggestions and continuing encouragement.

But it was my long-suffering wife, Joyce, who had to read and re-read the material, put up with my writing at all hours, and through it all she provided continuing love and support for a project that became much more consuming than either she or I ever envisioned when it began.

Appendix: Exhibits

*Please note: Exhibit numbers
correspond to chapter numbers.*

A Summing Up — Achievements of Jews   Table 1

Distinction	Relevant Geography	Total Recipients	Projected Jewish Recipients	Actual Jewish Recipients	Jews As A Multiple Of Projected	Jews As A Percent of all Recipients
The Greats of History						
Hart's Most Influential 100 in History	World[1]	100	0.2	8	35	8%
A&E's Millennium 100	World	100	0.2	8	35	8%
Time magazine's 100 of the 20th Century	U.S.[2]	67	1.4	13	9	19%
Intelliquest's World's Greatest 100	World	100	0.2	8	35	8%
Science						
Nobel Prize in Physics	World	181	0.4	48	116	27%
Nobel Prize in Physiology & Medicine	World	189	0.4	59	136	31%
Nobel Prize in Chemistry	World	151	0.3	30	87	20%
Total Nobels for Science	World	521	1.2	137	115	26%
Fields Medal (for mathematics)	World	48	0.1	12	109	25%
A. M. Turing Award (for computer science)	World	54	0.1	13	105	24%
Invention						
Encyclopedia Britannica's Great Inventors	World	267	0.6	13.7	22	5%
Education						
Enrollment in Ivy League Schools	U.S.	115,000	2,380	24,000	10	21%
Military and Aviation						
United States Astronauts	U.S.	268	5.5	9	2	3%
Economics						
Nobel Prize for Economics	World	61	0.1	22	157	36%
John Bates Clark Medal in Economics	U.S.	30	0.6	20	32	67%
Federal Reserve Chairmen	U.S.	14	0.3	4	14	29%
Politics and Law						
U.S. Senators (108th Congress)	U.S.	100	2.1	11	5	11%
U.S. Congressmen & Women (108th Congress)	U.S.	435	9.0	26	3	6%
Largest Political Donors (Mother Jones List)	U.S.	100	2.1	41	20	41%
United States Supreme Court Justices	U.S.	110	2.3	7	3	6%
Nobel Prize for Peace	World	95	0.2	9	41	9%
Sports and Games						
NFL Hall of Fame Inductees	U.S.	247	5.1	6	1	2%
NFL Team Owners (excludes "community owned" Green Bay)	U.S.	31	0.6	9	14	29%
MLB Prof. Baseball Team Owners (individually owned)	U.S.	26	0.5	5.5	10	21%
NBA Top 10 Coaches of All Time	U.S.	10	0.2	2	10	20%
NBA Basketball Team Owners	U.S.	30	0.6	10	16	33%
Naismith Basketball Hall of Fame Inductees	U.S.	285	5.9	20	3	7%
Olympics Medalists 1896 to date	see 5 below	16,167	66.9	231.74	3	1%
World Chess Champions - Years as Champion	see 5 below	122 yrs.	0.5	66 yrs.	131	54%
The Written Word						
Nobel Prize for Literature	World	104	0.2	13	55	13%
Pulitzer Prize for Fiction	U.S.	82	1.7	11	6	13%
Pulitzer Prize for Poetry	U.S.	89	1.8	17	9	19%
Pulitzer Prize for Non Fiction	U.S.	50	1.0	25.5	25	51%
Pulitzer Prize for Drama	U.S.	77	1.6	22	14	29%
Performing Arts and Comedy						
Kennedy Center Honorees	U.S.	157	3.2	41	13	26%
Conductors Major U.S. Symphony Orchestras	U.S.	202	4.2	66	16	33%
Composers "World's 50 Greatest" CD Collection	see 3 below	50	0.6	6	10	12%
Longest Running Broadway Musicals	U.S.	38	0.8	24	31	63%
Rock & Roll Hall of Fame Inductees	U.S.	238	4.9	29	6	12%

A Summing Up — Achievements of Jews   Table 1

Distinction	Relevant Geography	Total Recipients	Projected Jewish Recipients	Actual Jewish Recipients	Jews As A Multiple Of Projected	Jews As A Percent of all Recipients
Performing Arts and Comedy (cont.)						
Jazz Grammy Awards	U.S.	216	4.5	22	5	10%
Grammy Lifetime Achievement Winners (Indiv.)	U.S.	125	2.6	18	7	14%
Rate It All Ranking of Stand Up Comedians	U.S.	82	1.7	25	15	30%
Visual Arts and Architecture						
Phaidon's 500 Artists	see 3 below	500	6.3	37	6	7%
Combined Lists (7) of Great Photographers	see 4 below	587	7.4	153	21	26%
Combined Lists (6) of Master Architects	World	309	0.7	32	45	10%
Hollywood						
Academy Award Winning Directors	U.S.	83	1.7	31	18	37%
Greatest Movie Directors - Reel.com	U.S.	55	1.1	15	13	27%
Greatest Movie Directors - Filmsite.org	U.S.	75	1.6	27	17	36%
Star Power 500 Top Actors & Actresses	U.S.	500	10.3	75	7	15%
American Film Institute Lifetime Achievement Awards	U.S.	35	0.7	8	11	23%
American Film Institute Greatest American Screen Legends	U.S.	50	1.0	6	6	12%
Radio and Television						
Radio Hall of Fame Inductees	U.S.	108	2.2	19	8	18%
Television Hall of Fame Inductees	U.S.	108	2.2	39	17	36%
High Tech Entrepreneurs and CEOs						
Entrepreneurs (Fortune's Richest 40 Under 40)	U.S	27	0.6	6	11	22%
Forbes' 400 (November 2007)	U.S	400	8.3	126	15	31%
Fortune 500 CEOs						
CEOs of Major 1917 U.S. Corporations[5]	U.S.	153	4.7	7	1	5%
CEOs of Major 1997 U.S. Corporations	U.S.	72	1.5	16	11	22%
Fortune 100 CEOs	U.S.	100	2.1	15	7	15%
Fortune's 25 Most Powerful People In Business	U.S	25	0.5	6	12	24%
Finance						
Private Equity Hall of Fame	U.S.	26	0.5	8	15	24%
Real Estate						
Forbes' "25 Real Estate Fortunes Among Forbes' 400"	U.S.	25	0.5	18	35	72%
Social Activists						
Ladies Home Journal's "100 Most Important Women"	U.S.	100	2.1	20	10	20%
Philanthropy						
Business Week's 50 Leading Philanthropists	U.S.	50	1.0	19	19	38%
All Nobels						
Total - All Nobel Prizes	World	781	1.8	181	101	23%

1) As of 2002, there were an estimated 14.3 million Jews in a world of 6.23 billion people. Jews were .00207 percent of the World's population.

2) As of 2002, the United States population was 280,562,489. Of that number an estimated 5,807,000 were Jews (2.07 percent).

3) U.S., Canada, Europe, Australia, New Zealand and Israel.

4) Western Hemisphere, Europe, Australia and New Zealand Jews were .0126% of population.

5) Jewish percent of the world population has changed over the 112 years of the Olympics. For this exhibit, the current percent (.00207) was doubled to approximate the average.

Charles Murray's List of Great Historical Jewish Figures (chronological) Exhibit 2a

	Name	Year Born	Year Died	Primary Domain	Relative Importance
1	Philo Judaeus	-25	54	Phil.West	7.55
2	Avicebron (ibn Solomon Gabirol)	1021	1058	Phil.West	1.76
3	Maimonides, Moses	1135	1204	Phil.West	6.45
4	Rojas, Fernando de	1465	1541	Lit.West	1.50
5	Sachs, Hans	1494	1576	Lit.West	4.44
6	Montaigne, Michel de	1533	1592	Lit.West	15.72
7	Montaigne, Michel de	1533	1592	Phil.West	2.89
8	Rossi, Salamone	1570	1630	Music.West	1.50
9	Guldin, Paul	1577	1643	Scientific	5.56
10	Spinoza, Benedict	1632	1677	Phil.West	27.39
11	Mendelssohn, Moses	1729	1786	Phil.West	1.77
12	Herder, Johann	1744	1803	Phil.West	3.83
13	Meyerbeer, Giacomo	1791	1864	Music.West	14.14
14	Heine, Heinrich	1797	1856	Lit.West	22.20
15	Halévy, Fromental	1799	1862	Music.West	4.38
16	Adam, Adolphe	1803	1856	Music.West	2.73
17	Jacobi, Carl	1804	1851	Scientific	16.61
18	Henle, Friedrich	1809	1885	Scientific	16.17
19	Mendelssohn, Felix	1809	1847	Music.West	29.85
20	Gutzkow, Karl	1811	1878	Lit.West	2.58
21	Singer, Isaac	1811	1875	Scientific	10.46
22	Auerbach, Berthold	1812	1882	Lit.West	2.08
23	Sylvester, James	1814	1897	Scientific	9.40
24	Remak, Robert	1815	1865	Scientific	8.83
25	Offenbach, Jacques	1819	1880	Music.West	5.70
26	Kronecker, Leopold	1823	1891	Scientific	9.82
27	Cohn, Ferdinand	1828	1898	Scientific	14.93
28	Gottschalk, Louis	1829	1869	Music.West	1.14
29	Heyse, Paul	1830	1914	Lit.West	1.94
30	Pissarro, Camille	1830	1903	Art.West	18.55
31	Suess, Eduard	1831	1914	Scientific	24.21
32	Halevy, Ludovic	1834	1908	Lit.West	2.05
33	Baeyer, Johann von	1835	1917	Scientific	7.52
34	Cohnheim, Julius	1839	1884	Scientific	5.45
35	Breuer, Josef	1842	1925	Scientific	24.76
36	Pasch, Moritz	1843	1930	Scientific	3.20
37	Strasburger, Eduard	1844	1912	Scientific	11.93
38	Cantor, Georg	1845	1918	Scientific	49.98
39	Wallach, Otto	1847	1931	Scientific	2.21
40	Lilienthal, Otto	1848	1896	Scientific	13.87
41	Meyer, Viktor	1848	1897	Scientific	4.52
42	Goldstein, Eugen	1850	1930	Scientific	17.86
43	Michelson, Albert	1852	1931	Scientific	24.97
44	Moissan, Ferdinand	1852	1907	Scientific	4.47
45	Moissan, Ferdinand	1852	1907	Scientific	6.63
46	Ehrlich, Paul	1854	1915	Scientific	59.26
47	Neisser, Albert	1855	1916	Scientific	7.28
48	Freud, Sigmund	1856	1939	Scientific	34.46
49	Hertz, Heinrich	1857	1894	Scientific	30.14
50	Koller, Carl	1857	1944	Scientific	11.44
51	Bergson, Henri	1859	1941	Phil.West	9.56
52	Husserl, Edmund	1859	1938	Phil.West	7.61
53	Mahler, Gustave	1860	1911	Music.West	23.15
54	Volterra, Vito	1860	1940	Scientific	5.31
55	Svevo, Italo (Schmitz)	1861	1928	Lit.West	5.72
56	Schnitzler, Arthur	1862	1931	Lit.West	3.81

Charles Murray's List of Great Historical Jewish Figures (chronological)   Exhibit 2a

	Name	Year Born	Year Died	Primary Domain	Relative Importance
57	Flexner, Simon	1863	1946	Scientific	3.51
58	Minkowski, Hermann	1864	1909	Scientific	11.98
59	Dukas, Paul	1865	1935	Music.West	3.96
60	Hadamard, Jacques	1865	1963	Scientific	10.94
61	Steinmetz, Charles	1865	1923	Scientific	1.00
62	Gomberg, Moses	1866	1947	Scientific	3.82
63	Wassermann, August von	1866	1925	Scientific	6.90
64	Curie, Marie [sic]	1867	1934	Scientific	40.78
65	Haber, Fritz	1868	1934	Scientific	11.18
66	Hausdorff, Felix	1868	1942	Scientific	5.49
67	Landsteiner, Karl	1868	1943	Scientific	24.35
68	Levene, Phoebus	1869	1940	Scientific	16.13
69	Proust, Marcel	1871	1922	Lit.West	22.25
70	Willstätter, Richard	1872	1942	Scientific	14.25
71	Levi-Civita, Tullio	1873	1941	Scientific	3.98
72	Loewi, Otto	1873	1961	Scientific	6.09
73	Schwarzschild, Karl	1873	1916	Scientific	19.04
74	Wassermann, Jakob	1873	1934	Lit.West	2.69
75	Goldberger, Joseph	1874	1929	Scientific	16.09
76	Hofmannsthal, Hugo von	1874	1929	Lit.West	14.06
77	Schönberg, Arnold	1874	1951	Music.West	39.00
78	Stein, Gertrude	1874	1946	Lit.West	3.48
79	Glier, Reinhold	1875	1956	Music.West	1.06
80	Jacob, Max	1876	1944	Lit.West	3.11
81	Buber, Martin	1878	1965	Phil.West	1.53
82	Meitner, Lise	1878	1968	Scientific	15.83
83	Schreker, Franz	1878	1934	Music.West	2.32
84	Einstein, Albert	1879	1955	Scientific	98.47
85	Bloch, Ernest	1880	1959	Music.West	3.18
86	Epstein, Jacob	1880	1959	Art.West	1.35
87	Zweig, Stefan	1881	1942	Lit.West	3.52
88	Born, Max	1882	1970	Scientific	20.18
89	Franck, James	1882	1964	Scientific	4.70
90	Neurath, Otto	1882	1945	Phil.West	2.20
91	Noether, Emmy	1882	1935	Scientific	10.05
92	Schlick, Moritz	1882	1936	Phil.West	3.80
93	Kafka, Franz	1883	1924	Lit.West	21.82
94	Mises, Richard von	1883	1953	Scientific	1.18
95	Warburg, Otto	1883	1970	Scientific	21.63
96	Beckmann, Max	1884	1950	Art.West	7.11
97	Brod, Max	1884	1968	Lit.West	2.62
98	Funk, Casimir	1884	1967	Scientific	23.54
99	Meyerhof, Otto	1884	1951	Scientific	5.99
100	Modigliani, Amedeo	1884	1920	Art.West	6.90
101	Bohr, Niels	1885	1962	Scientific	51.66
102	Delaunay-Terk, Sonia	1885	1979	Art.West	3.72
103	Hevesy, György	1885	1966	Scientific	13.26
104	Kern, Jerome	1885	1945	Music.West	1.00
105	Broch, Hermann	1886	1951	Lit.West	3.77
106	Pevsner, Antoine	1886	1962	Art.West	3.23
107	Fajans, Kasimir	1887	1975	Scientific	13.31
108	Paneth, Friedrich	1887	1958	Scientific	6.44
109	Berlin, Irving	1888	1989	Music.West	1.46
110	Goldschmidt, Victor	1888	1947	Scientific	7.68
111	Stern, Otto	1888	1969	Scientific	8.68
112	Waksman, Selman	1888	1973	Scientific	21.68

Charles Murray's List of Great Historical Jewish Figures (chronological)   Exhibit 2a

	Name	Year Born	Year Died	Primary Domain	Relative Importance
113	Chagall, Marc	1889	1985	Art.West	11.97
114	Gutenberg, Beno	1889	1960	Scientific	13.94
115	Wittgenstein, Ludwig	1889	1951	Phil.West	12.83
116	Müller, Hermann	1890	1967	Scientific	32.95
117	Pasternak, Boris	1890	1960	Lit.West	11.76
118	Ray, Man	1890	1976	Art.West	7.06
119	Werfel, Franz	1890	1945	Lit.West	4.48
120	Ehrenberg, Ilya	1891	1967	Lit.West	5.00
121	Lipchitz, Jacques	1891	1973	Art.West	7.23
122	Reichenbach, Hans	1891	1953	Phil.West	1.97
123	Mandelstam, Osip	1892	1938	Lit.West	2.29
124	Milhaud, Darius	1892	1974	Music.West	12.81
125	Schulz, Bruno	1892	1942	Lit.West	0.96
126	Soutine, Chaim	1893	1943	Art.West	4.44
127	Toller, Ernst	1893	1939	Lit.West	3.18
128	Babel, Isaak	1894	1941	Lit.West	4.33
129	Kapitsa, Pyotr	1894	1984	Scientific	4.77
130	Wiener, Norbert	1894	1964	Scientific	7.18
131	Moholy-Nagy, Laszlo	1895	1946	Art.West	7.27
132	Tamm, Igor	1895	1971	Scientific	9.44
133	Cori, Gerty	1896	1957	Scientific	7.26
134	Tzara, Tristan	1896	1963	Lit.West	4.15
135	Reichstein, Tadeus	1897	1996	Scientific	10.14
136	Gershwin, George	1898	1937	Music.West	6.18
137	Rabi, Isidor Isaac	1898	1988	Scientific	6.76
138	Schoenheimer, Rudolf	1898	1941	Scientific	9.69
139	Shahn, Ben	1898	1969	Art.West	2.16
140	Szilard, Leo	1898	1964	Scientific	6.77
141	Taussig, Helen	1898	1986	Scientific	7.46
142	Lipmann, Fritz	1899	1986	Scientific	13.81
143	Copland, Aaron	1900	1990	Music.West	7.19
144	Gabor, Dennis	1900	1979	Scientific	10.81
145	Krebs, Hans	1900	1981	Scientific	20.85
146	Levine, Philip	1900	1987	Scientific	12.17
147	London, Fritz	1900	1954	Scientific	8.67
148	Pauli, Wolfgang	1900	1958	Scientific	31.64
149	Seghers, Anna (Radvanyi)	1900	1983	Lit.West	2.46
150	Weill, Kurt	1900	1950	Music.West	5.27
151	Loewe, Frederick	1901	1988	Music.West	1.00
152	Goudsmit, Samuel	1902	1978	Scientific	4.89
153	Lwoff, André	1902	1994	Scientific	4.73
154	Morgenstern, Oskar	1902	1977	Scientific	6.94
155	Wigner, Eugene	1902	1995	Scientific	6.33
156	Beadle, George	1903	1989	Scientific	14.48
157	Gottlieb, Adolph	1903	1973	Art.West	2.48
158	Pincus, Gregory	1903	1967	Scientific	16.88
159	Pincus, Gregory	1903	1967	Scientific	15.49
160	Rothko, Mark	1903	1970	Art.West	10.53
161	Von Neumann, John	1903	1957	Scientific	18.52
162	Von Neumann, John	1903	1957	Scientific	26.07
163	West, Nathanael	1903	1940	Lit.West	0.83
164	Frisch, Otto	1904	1979	Scientific	3.08
165	Heitler, Walter	1904	1981	Scientific	6.60
166	Oppenheimer, Robert	1904	1967	Scientific	4.98
167	Bloch, Felix	1905	1983	Scientific	14.30
168	Newman, Barnett	1905	1970	Art.West	7.64

Charles Murray's List of Great Historical Jewish Figures (chronological)   Exhibit 2a

	Name	Year Born	Year Died	Primary Domain	Relative Importance
169	Segrè, Emilio	1905	1989	Scientific	21.56
170	Bethe, Hans	1906		Scientific	11.83
171	Chain, Ernst	1906	1979	Scientific	26.42
172	Gelfond, Aleksander	1906	1968	Scientific	6.82
173	Goldmark, Peter	1906	1977	Scientific	14.68
174	Odets, Clifford	1906	1963	Lit.West	0.92
175	Sabin, Albert	1906	1993	Scientific	4.37
176	London, Heinz	1907	1970	Scientific	5.41
177	Moravia, Alberto (Pincherle)	1907	1990	Lit.West	7.56
178	Frank, Ilya	1908	1990	Scientific	7.60
179	Land, Edwin	1909	1991	Scientific	18.29
180	Levi-Montalcini, Rita	1909		Scientific	8.15
181	Ayer, Alfred	1910	1989	Phil.West	3.55
182	Kline, Franz	1910	1962	Art.West	6.03
183	Schuman, William	1910	1992	Music.West	2.28
184	Biro Brothers	c 1900		Scientific	9.74

The Greatest - A Comparative Appendix

Four Lists of The Greatest, Most Influential, or Most Important

Hart's "The 100 – A Ranking of the Most Influential Persons in History		A&E's "Biography of the Millennium"		Time Magazine's "Time 100 – The Most Important People of the 20th Century"	InteliQuest's "The World's 100 Greatest People"	
1	Muhammad	1	Johann Gutenberg	*Scientists & Thinkers*	1	Socrates
2	Isaac Newton	2	Isaac Newton	**Sigmund Freud**	2	Plato
3	**Jesus Christ**	3	Martin Luther	Leo Bekeland	3	Aristotle
4	Buddha	4	Charles Darwin	Wilbur & Orville Wright	4	Francis Bacon
5	Confucius	5	William Shakespeare	**Albert Einstein**	5	Rene Descartes
6	**St. Paul**	6	Christopher Columbus	Alexander Fleming	6	John Locke
7	Ts'ai Lun	7	**Karl Marx**	Robert Goddard	7	Voltaire
8	Johann Gutenberg	8	**Albert Einstein**	**Jonas Salk**	8	Jean Jacques Rosseau
9	Christopher Columbus	9	Nicolaus Copernicus	Edwin Hubble	9	Adam Smith
10	**Albert Einstein**	10	Galileo Galilei	Ludwig Wittgenstein	10	Immanuel Kant
11	**Karl Marx**	11	Leonardo Da Vinci	Jean Piaget	11	**Karl Marx**
12	Louis Pasteur	12	**Sigmund Freud**	Enrico Fermi	12	Freidrich Nietzsche
13	Galileo Galilei	13	Louis Pasteur	Mary Louis & Richard Leakey	13	Marco Polo
14	Aristotle	14	Thomas Edison	Philo Farnsworth	14	Christopher Columbus
15	Vladimir Lenin	15	Thomas Jefferson	Kurt Godel	15	Vasco da Gama
16	**Moses**	16	Adolf Hitler	Rachel Carson	16	Ferdinand Magellan
17	Charles Darwin	17	Mahatma Gandhi	William Shockley	17	James Cook
18	Shih Huang Ti	18	John Locke	Alan Turning	18	Roald Amundsen
19	Augustus Ceasar	19	Michaelangelo	John Maynard Keynes	19	Archimedes
20	Mao Tse-tung	20	Adam Smith	James Watson & Francis Creek	20	Johan Gutenberg
21	Genghis Kahn	21	George Washington	Tim Berners-Lee	21	Eli Whitney
22	Euclid	22	Genghis Kahn	*Heroes and Icons*	22	Thomas Edison
23	Martin Luther	23	Abraham Lincoln	Emmeline Pankhurst	23	Alexander Graham Bell
24	Nicolaus Copernicus	24	St. Thomas Aquinas	Helen Keller	24	Henry Ford
25	James Watt	25	James Watt	Charles Lindbergh	25	The Wright Brothers
26	Constantine the Great	26	Wofgang Amadeus Mozart	Bill Wilson	26	Gugliemlmo Marconi
27	George Washington	27	Napoleon Bonaparte	The American G.I.	27	Galen
28	Michael Faraday	28	Johann Sebastian Bach	Jackie Robinson	28	Nicolas Copernicus
29	James Clark Maxwell	29	Henry Ford	**Anne Frank**	29	Galileo
30	Wilbur & Orville Wright	30	Ludwig von Beethoven	Billy Graham	30	Issac Newton
31	Antoine Laurent Lavoisier	31	James Watson & Francis Crick	Edmund Hillary & Tenzing Norgay	31	Charles Darwin
32	**Sigmund Freud**	32	Rene Descartes	Rosa Parks	32	Louis Pasteur
33	Alexander the Great	33	Martin Luther King, Jr.	Che Guevara	33	Gregor Mendel
34	Napoleon Bonaparte	34	Jean-Jacques Rousseau	Marilyn Monroe	34	Joseph Lister
35	Adolf Hitler	35	Vladimir Lenin	The Kennedys	35	**Sigmund Freud**
36	William Shakespeare	36	Alexander Fleming	Muhammad Ali	36	Marie Curie
37	Adam Smith	37	Voltaire	Bruce Lee	37	**Albert Einstein**
38	Thomas Edison	38	Francis Bacon	Pele	38	Alexander Fleming
39	Antony van Leewenhoek	39	Dante Alighieri	**Harvey Milk**	39	**Jonas Salk**
40	Plato	40	Wilbur & Orville Wright	Mother Teresa	40	Sophocles
41	Guglielmo Marconi	41	Bill Gates	Diana, Princess of Wales	41	Virgil
42	Ludwig von Beethoven	42	Gregor Mendel	Andrei Sakharov	42	Dante Alighieri
43	Werner Heisenberg	43	Mao Tse-tung	*Leaders and Revolutionaries*	43	Geoffrey Chaucer
44	Alexander Graham Bell	44	Alexander Graham Bell	Theodore Roosevelt	44	William Shakespeare
45	Alexander Fleming	45	Willaim the Conqueror	Vladimir Lenin	45	John Milton
46	Simon Bolivar	46	Niccolo Machiavelli	Margaret Sanger	46	Charles Dickens
47	Oliver Cromwell	47	Charles Babbage	Mao Tse-tung	47	George Eliot
48	John Locke	48	Mary Wollstonecraft	Winston Churchill	48	Leo Tolstoy
49	Michaelangelo	49	Mikhail Gorbachev	Franklin Delano Roosevelt	49	Emily Dickenson
50	Pope Urban II	50	Margaret Sanger	Eleanor Roosevelt	50	Mark Twain
51	Umar ibn al-Khattab	51	Edward Jenner	Adolf Hitler	51	Leonarlo dia Vinci
52	Asoka	52	Winston Churchill	Mahatma Gandhi	52	Raphael
53	St. Augustine				53	Michelangelo

The Greatest - A Comparative Appendix   Exhibit 2b

Four Lists of The Greatest, Most Influential, or Most Important

Hart's "The 100 – A Ranking of the Most Influential Persons in History	A&E's "Biography of the Millennium"	Time Magazine's "Time 100 – The Most Important People of the 20th Century"	InteliQuest's "The World's 100 Greatest People"
54 Max Planck	53 Marie Curie	**David Ben-Gurion**	54 Rembrandt
55 John Calvin	54 Marco Polo	Ho Chi Minh	55 Claude Monet
56 William T. G. Morton	55 Ferdinand Magellan	Martin Luther King	56 Vincent Van Gogh
57 William Harvey	56 Elizabeth Stanton	Ayatulla Ruhollah Khomeini	57 Pablo Picasso
58 Antoine Henri Becquerel	57 Elvis Presley	Margaret Thatcher	58 Johann Sebastian Bach
59 Gregor Mendel	58 Joan of Arc	Lech Walesa	59 George Frideric Handel
60 Joseph Lister	59 Immanuel Kant	Ronald Reagan	60 Wolfgang Amadeus Mozart
61 Nikolaus August Otto	60 Franklin D Roosevelt	Mikhail Gorbachev	61 Ludwig van Beethoven
62 Louis Daguerre	61 Michael Faraday	Pope John Paul II	62 Frederic Chopin
63 Joseph Stalin	62 Walt Disney	The Unknown Rebel	63 Richard Wagner
64 Rene Descartes	63 Jane Austen	Nelson Mandella	64 Johannes Brahms
65 Julius Ceasar	64 Pablo Picasso	*Artists and Entertainers*	65 Peter Tchaikovsky
66 Francisco Pizarro	65 Werner Heisenberg	Pablo Picasso	66 Claude Debussy
67 Hernando Cortes	66 D.W. Griffith	Martha Graham	67 **Abraham**
68 Queen Isabella I	67 Vladimir Zworykin	Le Corbusier	68 **Moses**
69 William the Conqueror	68 Benjamin Franklin	Igor Stravinsky	69 Lao-tzu
70 Thomas Jefferson	69 Willan Harvey	Coco Chanel	70 Buddha
71 Jean Jacques Rousseau	70 Pope Gregory VII	James Joyce	71 Confucius
72 Edward Jenner	71 Harriet Tubman	T.S. Eliot	72 **Jesus Christ**
73 Wilhelm Conrad Rontgen	72 Simon Bolivar	Louis Armstrong	73 **The Apostle Paul**
74 Johann Sebastian Bach	73 Diana, Princess of Wales	Charlie Chaplin	74 Saint Augustine
75 Lao Tzu	74 Enrico Fermi	Marlon Brando	75 Muhammad
76 Enrico Fermi	75 **Gregory Pincus**	**Rodgers & Hammerstein**	76 Thomas Aquinas
77 Thomas Malthus	76 The Beatles	Frank Sinatra	77 Martin Luther
78 Francis Bacon	77 Thomas Hobbs	Lucille Ball	78 John Calvin
79 Voltaire	78 Queen Isabella I	The Beatles	79 Joseph Smith
80 John F. Kennedy	79 Joseph Stalin	**Bob Dylan**	80 Constantine the Great
81 **Gregory Pincus**	80 Queen Elizabeth I	Aretha Franklin	81 Charlemagne
82 Sui Wen Ti	81 Nelson Mandela	Jim Henson	82 Queen Elizabeth I
83 Mani	82 **Neils Bohr**	**Steven Spielberg**	83 Oliver Cromwell
84 Vasco da Gama	83 Peter the Great	Bart Simpson	84 Benjamin Franklin
85 Charlemagne	84 Guglielmo Marconi	Oprah Winfrey	85 Catherine the Great
86 Cyrus the Great	85 Ronald Reagan	*Builders and Titans*	86 George Washington
87 Leonhard Euler	86 James Joyce	Henry Ford	87 Thomas Jefferson
88 Niccolo Machiavelli	87 Rachel Carson	**David Sarnoff**	88 Abraham Lincoln
89 Zoroaster	88 **Robert J. Oppenheimer**	Charles Merrill	89 Susan B. Anthony
90 Menes	89 Susan B. Anthony	Willis Carrier	90 Mahatma Gandhi
91 Peter the Great	90 Souis Daguerre	Lucky Luciano	91 Winston Churchill
92 Mencius	91 **Steven Spielberg**	**William Levitt**	92 Franklin D. Roosevelt
93 John Dalton	92 Florence Nightingale	Leo Burnett	93 Martin Luther King
94 Homer	93 Eleanor Roosevelt	Ray Kroc	94 Alexander the Great
95 Queen Elizabeth	94 Patient Zero	Pete Rozelle	95 Julius Ceasar
96 Justinian I	95 Charlie Chaplin	Sam Walton	96 William the Conqueror
97 Johannes Kepler	96 Enrico Caruso	**Louis B. Mayer**	97 Genghis Khan
98 Pablo Picasso	97 **Jonas Salk**	Amadeo Giannini	98 Napoleon Bonaparte
99 Mahavira	98 Louis Armstrong	Stephen Bechtel	99 Robert E. Lee
100 **Niels Bohr**	99 Vasco Da Gama	Walt Disney	100 Dwight D. Eisenhower
	100 Suleiman I	Juan Trippe	
		Walter Reuther	
		Thomas Watson, Jr.	
		Estee Lauder	
		Akio Morita	
		Bill Gates	

The Nobel Prize in Physics – Laureates   Exhibit 3a

2007   Albert Fert, Peter Grünberg
2006   John C. Mather, George F. Smoot
2005   **Roy J. Glauber**[6,7,10] John L. Hall, Theodor W. Hänsch
2004   **David J. Gross**[6,7,10] **H. David Politzer**[6,7,10] Frank Wilczek
2003   **Alexei A. Abrikosov**[6,7,9,10] **Vitaly L. Ginzburg**[6,7,9,10] Anthony J. Leggett
2002   Raymond Davis Jr., Masatoshi Koshiba, Riccardo Giacconi
2001   Eric A. Cornell, Wolfgang Ketterle, Carl E. Wieman
2000   **Zhores I. Alferov**[3,6,7,9,10] Herbert Kroemer, Jack S. Kilby
1999   Gerardus 't Hooft, Martinus J.G. Veltman
1998   Robert B. Laughlin, Horst L. Störmer, Daniel C. Tsui
1997   Steven Chu, **Claude Cohen-Tannoudji**[1,2,3,4,5,6,7,9,10] William D. Phillips
1996   **David M. Lee**[1,3,4,5,6,7,9,10] **Douglas D. Osheroff**[1,3,4,5,6,7,9] Robert C. Richardson
1995   **Martin L. Perl**[1,2,3,4,5,6,7,8,9,10] **Frederick Reines**1994[1,2,3,5,6,7,9,10]
1994   Bertram N. Brockhouse, Clifford G. Shull
1993   Russell A. Hulse, Joseph H. Taylor Jr.
1992   **Georges Charpak**[1,2,3,4,6,7,9,10]
1991   Pierre-Gilles de Gennes
1990   **Jerome I. Friedman**[2,3,5,6,7,9,10] Henry W. Kendall, Richard E. Taylor
1989   Norman F. Ramsey, Hans G. Dehmelt, Wolfgang Paul
1988   **Leon M. Lederman**[1,2,3,4,6,7,8,9,10] **Melvin Schwartz**[1,3,6,7,8,9,10] **Jack Steinberger**[1,3,4,5,6,7,8,9,10]
1987   J. Georg Bednorz, K. Alex Müller
1986   Ernst Ruska, Gerd Binnig, Heinrich Rohrer
1985   Klaus von Klitzing
1984   Carlo Rubbia, Simon van der Meer
1983   Subramanyan Chandrasekhar, William A. Fowler
1982   Kenneth G. Wilson
1981   Nicolaas Bloembergen, **Arthur L. Schawlow**[1,6] Kai M. Siegbahn
1980   James Cronin, Val Fitch
1979   **Sheldon Glashow**[1,2,3,5,6,7,8,9,10] Abdus Salam, **Steven Weinberg**
1978   **Pyotr Kapitsa**[1,3,5,7,8,9] **Arno Penzias**[1,2,3,4,5,6,7,8,9,10] Robert W. Wilson
1977   Philip W. Anderson, Sir Nevill F. Mott, John H. van Vleck
1976   **Burton Richter**[1,2,3,5,6,7,8,9,10] Samuel C. C. Ting
1975   Aage N. Bohr[1,5,6] (1/4th Jew), **Ben R. Mottelson**[1,2,3,5,6,7,8,9,10] James Rainwater
1974   Martin Ryle, Antony Hewish
1973   Leo Esaki, Ivar Giaever, **Brian D. Josephson**[1,2,3,5,6,7,8,9,10]
1972   John Bardeen, **Leon N. Cooper**[3,6,7,9,10] Robert Schrieffer
1971   **Dennis Gabor**[1,2,3,5,6,7,8,9,10]
1970   Hannes Alfvén, Louis Néel
1969   **Murray Gell-Mann**[1,2,3,4,5,6,7,8,9,10]
1968   Luis Alvarez
1967   **Hans Bethe**[1,2,3,4,5,6,7,9,10]
1966   Alfred Kastler
1965   Sin-Itiro Tomonaga, **Julian Schwinger**[1,2,5,6,7,8,9,10] **Richard P. Feynman**[1,2,3,4,5,6,7,8,9,10]
1964   Charles H. Townes, Nicolay G. Basov, Aleksandr M. Prokhorov
1963   **Eugene Wigner**[1,2,3,5,6,7,9,10] Maria Goeppert-Mayer, J. Hans D. Jensen
1962   **Lev Landau**[1,2,3,4,5,6,7,8,9,10]
1961   **Robert Hofstadter**[1,2,3,5,6,7,8,9,10] Rudolf Mössbauer
1960   **Donald A. Glaser**[1,2,3,5,6,7,8,9,10]
1959   **Emilio Segrè**[1,2,3,5,6,7,8,9,10] Owen Chamberlain
1958   Pavel A. Cherenkov, **Il'ja M. Frank**[2,3,6,7,10] **Igor Y. Tamm**[2,3,5,6,7,8,9,10]
1957   Chen Ning Yang, Tsung-Dao Lee
1956   William B. Shockley, John Bardeen, Walter H. Brattain
1955   Willis E. Lamb, Polykarp Kusch
1954   **Max Born**[1,2,3,5,6,7,8,9,10] Walther Bothe
1953   Frits Zernike
1952   **Felix Bloch**[1,2,3,5,6,7,8,9,10] E. M. Purcell
1951   John Cockcroft, Ernest T. S. Walton
1950   Cecil Powell
1949   Hideki Yukawa

The Nobel Prize in Physics – Laureates

1948   Patrick M. S. Blackett
1947   Edward V. Appleton
1946   Percy W. Bridgman
1945   **Wolfgang Pauli** [1,2,3,4,6,7,9,10]
1944   **Isidor Isaac Rabi** [1,2,3,4,5,6,7,8,10]
1943   **Otto Stern** [1,2,3,5,6,7,8,10]
1942   Prize money was allocated 1/3 to Main Fund & 2/3 to Special Fund of this prize section
1941   Prize money was allocated 1/3 to Main Fund & 2/3 to Special Fund of this prize section
1940   Prize money was allocated 1/3 to Main Fund & 2/3 to Special Fund of this prize section
1939   Ernest Lawrence
1938   Enrico Fermi
1937   Clinton Davisson, George Paget Thomson
1936   Victor F. Hess, Carl D. Anderson
1935   James Chadwick
1934   Prize money was allocated 1/3 to Main Fund & 2/3 to Special Fund of this prize section
1933   Erwin Schrödinger, Paul A. M. Dirac
1932   Werner Heisenberg
1931   The prize money was allocated to the Special Fund of this prize section
1930   Venkata Raman
1929   Louis de Broglie
1928   Owen Willans Richardson
1927   Arthur H. Compton, C. T. R. Wilson
1926   Jean Baptiste Perrin
1925   **James Franck** [1,2,3,5,6,7,8,9,10] **Gustav Hertz** [1,2,3,5,7,8,9]
1924   Manne Siegbahn
1923   Robert A. Millikan
1922   **Niels Bohr** [1,2,3,4,5,67,8,9,10]
1921   **Albert Einstein** [1,2,3,4,5,6,7,8,9,10]
1920   Charles Edouard Guillaume
1919   Johannes Stark
1918   Max Planck
1917   Charles Glover Barkla
1916   The prize money was allocated to the Special Fund of this prize section
1915   William Bragg, Lawrence Bragg
1914   Max von Laue
1913   Heike Kamerlingh Onnes
1912   Gustaf Dalén
1911   Wilhelm Wien
1910   Johannes Diderik van der Waals
1909   Guglielmo Marconi, Ferdinand Braun
1908   **Gabriel Lippmann** [1,2,3,5,6,7,8,9,10]
1907   **Albert A. Michelson** [1,2,3,4,5,6,7,8,9,10]
1906   J. J. Thomson
1905   Philipp Lenard
1904   Lord Rayleigh
1903   Henri Becquerel, Pierre Curie, Marie Curie
1902   Hendrik A. Lorentz, Pieter Zeeman
1901   Wilhelm Conrad Röntgen

Notes: For Jewish Laureates, the parenthetical numbers after the underlined/bolded name indicate the source: (1) is the website "jewho.com" section on Nobels for 2002 and pages devoted to Physics. (2) is the book "The Nobel Prize" by Burton Feldman. (3) is the "us-israel.org" web site. (4) is the web site "yahoodi.com". (5) is the book "Nobel Laureates 1901-2000" by Alan Symons. (6) is the web site www.jinfo.org; 7) is www.jewishvirtuallibrary.com; 8) is www.about.com; 9) is www.jewishmag.com; 10) is www.science.co.il.

For purposes of statistics, Maria Goeppert Mayer (1963) is not counted as Jewish even though jinfo.org notes that Edward Teller identified her as such on page 119 of his Memoirs. The same is true of Aage Bohr (1975) who was 1/4th Jewish.

The Nobel Prize in Physiology or Medicine – Laureates   Exhibit 3b

2007   Mario R. Capecchi, Sir Martin J. Evans, Oliver Smithies
2006   **Andrew Z. Fire,**[6] Craig C. Mello
2005   Barry J. Marshall, J. Robin Warren
2004   **Richard Axel,**[6] Linda B. Buck
2003   Paul C. Lauterbur, Sir Peter Mansfield
2002   **Sydney Brenner**[1,3,6,7,9] **H. Robert Horvitz**[1,3,6,7,9] John E. Sulston
2001   Leland H. Hartwell, R. Timothy (Tim) Hunt, Sir Paul M. Nurse
2000   Arvid Carlsson, **Paul Greengard**[1,3,6,7] **Eric R. Kandel**[1,6,7,9]
1999   Günter Blobel
1998   **Robert F. Furchgott**[3,6,7,9] Louis J. Ignarro, Ferid Murad
1997   **Stanley B. Prusiner**[1,2,3,4,5,6,7,8,9]
1996   Peter C. Doherty, Rolf M. Zinkernagel
1995   **Edward B. Lewis**[3,8,9] Christiane Nüsslein-Volhard, Eric F. Wieschaus
1994   **Alfred G. Gilman**[2,3,6,8,9] **Martin Rodbell**[1,2,3,5,6,9]
1993   **Richard J. Roberts**[3,8,9] **Phillip A. Sharp**[3,8,9]
1992   **Edmond H. Fischer**[6] Edwin G. Krebs
1991   **Erwin Neher**[3,9] **Bert Sakmann**[3,7,8,9]
1990   Joseph E. Murray, E. Donnall Thomas
1989   J. Michael Bishop, **Harold E. Varmus**[1,3,6,7,9]
1988   Sir James W. Black, **Gertrude B. Elion**[1,2,3,5,6,7] George H. Hitchings
1987   Susumu Tonegawa
1986   **Stanley Cohen**[1,2,3,4,6,7] **Rita Levi-Montalcini**[1,2,3,4,5,6,7]
1985   **Michael S. Brown**[1,3,5,6,7] **Joseph L. Goldstein**[1,2,3,4,5,6,7]
1984   Niels K. Jerne, Georges J.F. Köhler, **César Milstein**[1,2,3,4,5,6,7]
1983   Barbara McClintock
1982   Sune K. Bergström, Bengt I. Samuelsson, **John R. Vane**[6]
1981   Roger W. Sperry, David H. Hubel, Torsten N. Wiesel
1980   **Baruj Benacerraf**[1,2,3,5,6,7] Jean Dausset, George D. Snell
1979   Allan M. Cormack, Godfrey N. Hounsfield
1978   Werner Arber, **Daniel Nathans**[1,2,3,4,5,6,7] Hamilton O. Smith
1977   Roger Guillemin, **Andrew V. Schally**[3,4,5,6,7] **Rosalyn Yalow**[1,2,3,5,6,7]
1976   **Baruch S. Blumberg**[1,2,3,4,5,6,7] D. Carleton Gajdusek
1975   **David Baltimore**[1,2,3,4,5,6,7] Renato Dulbecco, **Howard M. Temin**[1,2,3,4,5,6,7]
1974   Albert Claude, Christian de Duve, George E. Palade
1973   Karl von Frisch, Konrad Lorenz, Nikolaas Tinbergen
1972   **Gerald M. Edelman**[1,2,3,5,6,7], Rodney R. Porter
1971   Earl W. Sutherland, Jr.
1970   **Sir Bernard Katz**[1,2,3,4,5,6,7] Ulf von Euler, **Julius Axelrod**[1,2,3,5,6,7]
1969   Max Delbrück, Alfred D. Hershey, **Salvador E. Luria**[1,2,3,5,6,7]
1968   Robert W. Holley, Har Gobind Khorana, **Marshall W. Nirenberg**[1,2,3,5,6,7]
1967   Ragnar Granit, Haldan Keffer Hartline, **George Wald**[1,2,3,4,5,6,7]
1966   Peyton Rous, Charles Brenton Huggins
1965   **François Jacob**[1,2,3,5,6,7] **André Lwoff**[1,2,3,5,6,7] Jacques Monod
1964   **Konrad Bloch**[1,3,5,6,7] Feodor Lynen
1963   Sir John Carew Eccles, Alan Lloyd Hodgkin, Andrew Fielding Huxley
1962   Francis Harry Compton Crick, James Dewey Watson, Maurice Hugh Frederick Wilkins
1961   Georg von Békésy
1960   Sir Frank Macfarlane Burnet, Peter Brian Medawar
1959   Severo Ochoa, **Arthur Kornberg**[1,2,3,5,6,7]
1958   George Wells Beadle, Edward Lawrie Tatum, **Joshua Lederberg**[1,2,3,4,5,6,7]
1957   Daniel Bovet
1956   André Frédéric Cournand, Werner Forssmann, Dickinson W. Richards
1955   Axel Hugo Theodor Theorell
1954   John Franklin Enders, Thomas Huckle Weller, Frederick Chapman Robbins
1953   **Hans Adolf Krebs**[1,2,3,4,5,6,7] **Fritz Albert Lipmann**[1,2,3,5,6,7]
1952   **Selman Abraham Waksman**[1,2,3,4,5,6,7]
1951   Max Theiler
1950   Edward Calvin Kendall, **Tadeus Reichstein**[1,2,3,4,7] Philip Showalter Hench
1949   Walter Rudolf Hess, Antonio Caetano de Abreu Freire Egas Moniz

The Nobel Prize in Physiology or Medicine – Laureates

1948   Paul Hermann Müller
1947   Carl Ferdinand Cori, **Gerty Theresa Cori, née Radnitz** [3,5,6,7] Bernardo Alberto Houssay
1946   **Hermann Joseph Muller** [1,2,3,4,5,6,7]
1945   Sir Alexander Fleming, **Ernst Boris Chain** [1,2,3,5,6,7] Sir Howard Walter Florey
1944   **Joseph Erlanger** [1,2,3,5,6,7] **Herbert Spencer Gasser** [1,3,5,6,7]
1943   Henrik Carl Peter Dam, Edward Adelbert Doisy
1942   Prize money was 1/3 allocated to the Main Fund, 2/3 to the Special Fund of this prize section
1941   Prize money was 1/3 allocated to the Main Fund , 2/3 to the Special Fund of this prize section
1940   Prize money was 1/3 allocated to the Main Fund , 2/3 to the Special Fund of this prize section
1939   Gerhard Domagk
1938   Corneille Jean François Heymans
1937   Albert von Szent-Györgyi Nagyrapolt
1936   Sir Henry Hallett Dale, **Otto Loewi** [1,2,3,5,6,7]
1935   Hans Spemann
1934   George Hoyt Whipple, George Richards Minot, William Parry Murphy
1933   Thomas Hunt Morgan
1932   Sir Charles Scott Sherrington, Edgar Douglas Adrian
1931   **Otto Heinrich Warburg** [1,2,3,5,6,7]
1930   **Karl Landsteiner** [1,2,3,5,6,7]
1929   Christiaan Eijkman, Sir Frederick Gowland Hopkins
1928   Charles Jules Henri Nicolle
1927   Julius Wagner-Jauregg
1926   Johannes Andreas Grib Fibiger
1925   The prize money was allocated to the Special Fund of this prize section
1924   **Willem Einthoven** [2]
1923   Frederick Grant Banting, John James Richard Macleod
1922   Archibald Vivian Hill, **Otto Fritz Meyerhof** [1,2,3,6,7]
1921   The prize money was allocated to the Special Fund of this prize section
1920   Schack August Steenberg Krogh
1919   Jules Bordet
1918   The prize money was allocated to the Special Fund of this prize section
1917   The prize money was allocated to the Special Fund of this prize section
1916   The prize money was allocated to the Special Fund of this prize section
1915   The prize money was allocated to the Special Fund of this prize section
1914   **Robert Bárány** [1,2,3,5,6,7]
1913   Charles Robert Richet
1912   Alexis Carrel
1911   Allvar Gullstrand
1910   Albrecht Kossel
1909   Emil Theodor Kocher
1908   **Ilya Ilyich Mechnikov** [1,2,3,4,5,6,7] **Paul Ehrlich** [1,2,3,4,5,6,7]
1907   Charles Louis Alphonse Laveran
1906   Camillo Golgi, Santiago Ramón y Cajal
1905   Robert Koch
1904   Ivan Petrovich Pavlov
1903   Niels Ryberg Finsen
1902   Ronald Ross
1901   Emil Adolf von Behring

Notes: For Laureates identified as Jewish, the superscript numbers after their name indicates the source: 1) is the website www.jewho.com section on Nobels for 2002 and the pages devoted to Medicine. 2) is the book "The Nobel Prize" by Burton Feldman. 3) is the www.us-israel.org Web site. 4) is the Web site www.yahoodi.com. 5) is the book "Nobel Laureates 1901 – 2000" by Alan Symons. 6) is the Web site www.jinfo.org. 7) is www.jewishvirtuallibrary.org. 8) is www.about.com: 9) is www.jewishmag.com.

Nobel Prize Winners In Chemistry   Exhibit 3c

2007	Gerhard Ertl
2006	**Roger D. Kornberg** [6,7,8,10]
2005	Yves Chauvin, Robert H. Grubbs, Richard R. Schrock
2004	**Aaron Ciechanover** [6,7,8,9,10] **Avram Hershko** [6,7,8,9,10] **Irwin Rose** [6,7,8,9,10]
2003	Peter Agre, Roderick MacKinnon
2002	John B. Fenn, Koichi Tanaka, Kurt Wüthrich
2001	William S. Knowles, Ryoji Noyori, K. Barry Sharpless
2000	**Alan J. Heeger** [1,3,6,9,10] Alan G. MacDiarmid, Hideki Shirakawa
1999	Ahmed H. Zewail
1998	**Walter Kohn** [1,2,5,6,9,10] John A. Pople
1997	Paul D. Boyer, John E. Walker, Jens C. Skou
1996	Robert F. Curl Jr., **Sir Harold W. Kroto** [1,4,5,6] Richard E. Smalley
1995	Paul J. Crutzen, Mario J. Molina, F. Sherwood Rowland
1994	**George A. Olah** [6,10]
1993	Kary B. Mullis, Michael Smith
1992	**Rudolph A. Marcus** [1,2,3,5,6,7,8,9,10]
1991	Richard R. Ernst
1990	Elias James Corey
1989	**Sidney Altman** [1,2,3,5,6,7,8,9,10] Thomas R. Cech
1988	Johann Deisenhofer, Robert Huber (3), Hartmut Michel
1987	Donald J. Cram, Jean-Marie Lehn, Charles J. Pedersen
1986	**Dudley R. Herschbach** [3,9] Yuan T. Lee, **John C. Polanyi** [6]
1985	**Herbert A. Hauptman** [1,2,3,5,6,7,8,9,10] **Jerome Karle** [1,2,3,6,7,8,9,10]
1984	Robert Bruce Merrifield
1983	Henry Taube
1982	**Aaron Klug** [1,2,3,4,5,6,7,8,9,10]
1981	Kenichi Fukui, **Roald Hoffmann** [1,2,3,4,5,6,7,8,9,10]
1980	**Paul Berg** [1,2,3,5,6,7,8,9,10] **Walter Gilbert** [1,2,3,5,6,7,8,9,10] Frederick Sanger
1979	**Herbert C. Brown** [1,2,3,4,5,6,7,8,9,10] Georg Wittig
1978	Peter D. Mitchell
1977	**Ilya Prigogine** [1,2,3,6,7,8,9,10]
1976	William N. Lipscomb
1975	John Warcup Cornforth, Vladimir Prelog
1974	Paul J. Flory
1973	Ernst Otto Fischer, Geoffrey Wilkinson
1972	**Christian B. Anfinsen**[1] [1,6,9,10] Stanford Moore, **William H. Stein** [2,3,5,6,7,8,9,10]
1971	Gerhard Herzberg [(2)(5)] but disclaimed by Herzberg per [(6)]
1970	Luis F. Leloir
1969	Derek H. R. Barton, Odd Hassel
1968	Lars Onsager
1967	Manfred Eigen, Ronald George Wreyford Norrish, George Porter
1966	Robert S. Mulliken
1965	Robert Burns Woodward
1964	Dorothy Crowfoot Hodgkin
1963	Karl Ziegler, Giulio Natta
1962	**Max Ferdinand Perutz** [1,2,3,5,6,,8,9,10] John Cowdery Kendrew
1961	**Melvin Calvin** [1,2,3,5,6,7,8,9,10]
1960	Willard Frank Libby
1959	Jaroslav Heyrovsky
1958	Frederick Sanger
1957	Lord (Alexander R.) Todd
1956	Sir Cyril Norman Hinshelwood, Nikolay Nikolaevich Semenov
1955	Vincent du Vigneaud
1954	Linus Carl Pauling
1953	Hermann Staudinger
1952	Archer John Porter Martin, Richard Laurence Millington Synge
1951	Edwin Mattison McMillan, Glenn Theodore Seaborg

[1] Per the Jewhoo web site, Anfinsen converted to Judaism in 1978 on the occasion of marring a religious Jewish woman

Nobel Prize Winners In Chemistry   Exhibit 3c

1950	Otto Paul Hermann Diels, Kurt Alder
1949	William Francis Giauque
1948	Arne Wilhelm Kaurin Tiselius
1947	Sir Robert Robinson
1946	James Batcheller Sumner, John Howard Northrop, Wendell Meredith Stanley
1945	Artturi Ilmari Virtanen
1944	Otto Hahn
1943	**George de Hevesy** [1,2,3,5,6,7,8,9,10]
1942	Prize money was 1/3 allocated to the Main Fund and 2/3 to the Special Fund of this prize section
1941	Prize money was 1/3 allocated to the Main Fund and 2/3 to the Special Fund of this prize section
1940	Prize money was 1/3 allocated to the Main Fund and 2/3 to the Special Fund of this prize section
1939	Adolf Friedrich Johann Butenandt, Leopold Ruzicka
1938	Richard Kuhn
1937	Walter Norman Haworth, Paul Karrer
1936	Petrus (Peter) Josephus Wilhelmus Debye
1935	Frédéric Joliot, Irène Joliot-Curie
1934	Harold Clayton Urey
1933	Prize money was 1/3 allocated to the Main Fund and 2/3 to the Special Fund of this prize section
1932	Irving Langmuir
1931	Carl Bosch, Friedrich Bergius
1930	Hans Fischer
1929	Arthur Harden, Hans Karl August Simon von Euler-Chelpin
1928	Adolf Otto Reinhold Windaus
1927	Heinrich Otto Wieland
1926	The (Theodor) Svedberg
1925	Richard Adolf Zsigmondy
1924	The prize money was allocated to the Special Fund of this prize section
1923	Fritz Pregl
1922	Francis William Aston
1921	Frederick Soddy
1920	Walther Hermann Nernst
1919	The prize money was allocated to the Special Fund of this prize section
1918	**Fritz Haber** [1,2,3,4,5,6,7,8,9,10]
1917	The prize money was allocated to the Special Fund of this prize section
1916	The prize money was allocated to the Special Fund of this prize section
1915	**Richard Martin Willstätter** [1,2,3,5,6,7,8,9,10]
1914	Theodore William Richards
1913	Alfred Werner
1912	Victor Grignard, Paul Sabatier
1911	Marie Curie
1910	**Otto Wallach** [1,2,3,5,6,7,8,9,10]
1909	Wilhelm Ostwald
1908	Ernest Rutherford
1907	Eduard Buchner
1906	**Henri Moissan** [1,2,3,5,6,7,8,9,10]
1905	**Johann Friedrich Wilhelm Adolf von Baeyer** [2,3,5,6,7,8,9,10]
1904	Sir William Ramsay
1903	Svante August Arrhenius
1902	Hermann Emil Fischer
1901	Jacobus Henricus van 't Hoff

Notes: For Laureates identified as Jewish, the parenthetical numbers after their name indicates the source: (1) is the web-site www.jewho.com section on Nobels for 2002 or the pages devoted to Chemistry. (2) is the book "The Nobel Prize" by Burton Feldman. (3) is the www.US-Israel.org web site. (4) is the web site www.yahoodi.com. (5) is the book "Nobel Laureates 1901 – 2000" by Alan Symons, 6) is the Web site www.jinfo.org; 7) is the www.jewishvirtuallibrary.org; 8) is www.about.com; 9) is www.jewishmag.com 10) is www.science.co.

For purposes of this book, the tally used in the text and tables includes only Jews identified as such by more than one source. Thus, of the above list, Robert Huber was identified only by a single Web source that has since discontinued. He is thus not included in the statistics as a Jew.

Fields Medal Winners: Inception to 2006   Exhibit 3d

1936   Lars Valerian Ahlfors (Harvard University)
        Jesse Douglas (Massachusetts Institute of Technology)

1950   **Laurent Schwartz** (Université de Nancy)
        Atle Selberg (IAS, Princeton)

1954   Kunihiko Kodaira (Princeton University)
        Jean-Pierre Serre (College de France)

1958   **Klaus Friedrich Roth** (University of London)
        René Thom (Université de Strasbourg, IHÉS since 1964)

1962   Lars V. Hormander (University of Stockholm)
        John Willard Milnor (Princeton University)

1966   Michael Francis Atiyah (Oxford University)
        Paul Joseph Cohen (Stanford University)
        Alexander Gröthendieck (University of Paris)
        Stephen Smale (University of California, Berkeley)

1970   Alan Baker (Cambridge University)
        Heisuke Hironaka (Harvard University)
        Serge P. Novikov - perhaps (Moscow University)
        John Griggs Thompson (University of Chicago)

1974   Enrico Bombieri (University of Pisa)
        David Bryant Mumford (Harvard University)

1978   Pierre René Deligne (IHÉS)
        Charles Louis Fefferman (Princeton University)
        Gregori Alexandrovitch Margulis (Moscow University)
        Daniel G. Quillen (Massachusetts Institute of Technology)

1982   *Alain Connes* - perhaps (Collège de France and IHÉS)
        William P. Thurston (Princeton, University)
        Shing-Tung Yau (IAS, Princeton)

1986   Simon Donaldson (Oxford University)
        Gerd Faltings (Princeton University)
        Michael Freedman (University of Califomia, San Diego)

1990   **Vladimir Drinfeld** (Physics Institute Kharkov)
        Vaughan Jones (Univ. of California, Berkeley)
        Shigefumi Mori (University of Kyoto)
        Edward Witten (LAS, Princeton)

1994   Pierre-Louis Lions (Université de Paris-Dauphine)
        Jean-Christophe Yoccoz (Université de Paris-Sud)
        Jean Bourgain - perhaps (IHÉS and IAS, Princeton)
        Efim Zelmanov (University of Wisconsin)

1998   Richard E. Borcherds (Cambridge University)
        W. Timothy Gowers (Cambridge University)
        Maxim Kontsevich - perhaps (IHÉS) Curtis T. McMullen (Harvard University)
        Curtis T. McMullen (Harvard University)

Fields Medal Winners: Inception to 2006   **Exhibit 3d**

2002   Laurent Lafforgue (IHÉS)
        Vladimir Voevodsky (IAS, Princeton)

2006   Andrei Okounkov (Princeton University)
        Grigori Perelman (St. Petersburg, Russia)
        Terence Tao (University of California)
        Wendelin Werner - perhaps (University of Paris-South)

428   APPENDIX

Cole, Bocher, Steele and Wolf Mathematical Prizes   Exhibit 3e

Frank Nelson Cole Prize of the American Mathematical Society

1928	Leonard E. Dickson (Algebra)	1977	Goro Shimura (Number Theory)
1931	Harry S. Vandiver (Number Theory)	1980	M Aschbacher, **Melvin Hochster** (Algebra)
1939	**A Adrian Albert** (Algebra)	1982	Robert P Langlands, **Barry Mazur** (Number Theory)
1941	Claude Chevalley (Number Theory)	1985	**George Lusztig** (Algebra)
1944	**Oscar Zariski** (Algebra)	1987	**Dorian M Goldfeld, B. H. Gross, Don B Zagier**
1946	**H B Mann** (Number Theory)		(Number Theory)
1949	**Richard Brauer** (Algebra)	1990	Shigefumi Mori (Algebra)
1951	**Paul Erdös** (Number Theory)	1992	**Karl Rubin**, Paul Vojta (Number Theory)
1954	Harish-Chandra (Algebra)	1995	**David Harbater**, & Michel Raynaud (Algebra)
1956	John T. Tate (Number Theory)	1997	Andrew J. Wiles (Number Theory)
1960	**Serge Lang & Maxwell A. Rosenlicht** (Algebra)	2000	Andrei Suslin, Aise Johan de Jong (Algebra)
1962	Kenkichi Iwasawa , **Bernard Dwork** (Number Theory)	2002	Henryk Iwaniec, Richard Taylor (Number Theory)
1965	**Walter Feit** & John G. Thompson, & (Algebra)	2003	Hiraku Nakajima (Algebra)
1967	**James B. Ax, Simon B. Kochen** (Number Theory)	2005	**Peter Sarnak** (Number Theory)
1970	John R. Stallings, Richard G. Swan (Algebra)	2006	János Kollár (Algebra)
1972	Wolfgang M. Schmidt (Number Theory)	2008	Manjul Bhargava (Number Theory)
1975	**Hyman Bass**, Daniel G. Quillen, (Algebra)		

The Bocher Memorial Prize

1923	George D. Birkhoff	1969	**Isadore. M. Singer**
1924	Eric Temple Bell	1974	**Donald S. Ornstein**
1924	**Solomon Lefschetz**	1979	Alberto P. Calderón
1928	James W. Alexander	1984	Luis A. Caffarelli
1933	Marston Morse	1984	Richard B. Melrose
1933	**Norbert Wiener**	1989	Richard M. Schoen
1938	**John von Neumann**	1994	**Leon Simon**
1943	**Jesse Douglas**	1999	Demetrios Christodoulou, **Sergiu Klainerman**,
1948	A.C. Schaeffer & D.C. Spencer		Thomas Wolff
1953	**Norman Levinson**	2002	Daniel Tataru, Terence Tao, Fanghua Lin
1959	**Louis Nirenberg**	2005	Frank Merle
1964	**Paul J. Cohen**	2008	Alberto Bressan

LeRoy P. Steele Lifetime Achievement Awards (since 1993)

1993	**Eugene B Dynkin**	2001	**Harry Kesten**
1994	**Louis Nirenberg**	2002	Michael Artin, **Elias Stein**
1995	John T. Tate	2003	Ron Graham, Victor Guillemin
1996	Goro Shimura	2004	Cathleen Synge Morawetz
1997	**Ralph S. Phillips**	2005	**Israel M Gelfand**
1998	**Nathan Jacobson**	2006	Frederick W. Gehring, Dennis P. Sullivan
1999	**Richard V. Kadison**	2007	Henry P. McKean
2000	**Isadore M. Singer**	2008	**George Lusztig**

Wolf Prize in Mathematics

1978	**Israel Gelfand**, Carl L. Siegel	1992	Lennart Carleson, John G. Thompson
1979	Jean Leray, **André Weil**	1993	**Mikhail Gromov**, Jacques Tits,
1980	Henri Cartan, Andrey Kolmogorov	1994/5	Jürgen Moser
1981	Lars Ahlfors, **Oscar Zariski**	1995/6	Robert Langlands, Andrew Wiles
1982	Hassler Whitney, **Mark Grigoryevich Krein**	996/7	**Joseph B. Keller, Yakov G. Sinai**
1983/4	Shiin-Shen Chern, **Paul Erdös**	1999	László Lovász, **Elias Stein**
1984/5	Kunihiko Kodaira, **Hans Lewy**	2000	**Raoul Bott**, Jean-Pierre Serre
1986	**Samuel Eilenberg**, Atle Selberg	2001	**Vladimir Arnold, Saharon Shelah**
1987	**Peter Lax**, Kiyoshi Ito	2002/3	Mikio Sato, John Tate
1988	Friedrich Hirzebruch, Lars Hörmander	2005	**Gregory Margulis**, Sergei Petrovich Novikov
1989	Alberto Calderón, John Milnor	2006/7	Stephen Smale, **Hillel Furstenberg**
1990	Ennio de Giorgi, **Ilya Piatetski-Shapiro**	2008	Pierre Deligne, Phillip A. Griffiths, David B. Mumford

Sources: American Mathematical Society Web site at www.ams.org/prizes, Jewish listings at www.jinfo.org/mathematics, the Wikipedia site at http://en.wikipedia.org

A.M. Turing Award[1]

1966	**A.J. Perlis**	1989	**William (Velvel) Kahan**
1967	Maurice V. Wilkes	1990	Fernando J. Corbato
1968	Richard Hamming	1991	Robin Milner
1969	**Marvin Minsky**	1992	Butler W. Lampson
1970	J.H. Wilkinson	1993	Juris Hartmanis
1971	**John McCarthy**	1993	Richard E. Stearns
1972	E.W. Dijkstra	1994	**Edward Feigenbaum**
1973	Charles W. Bachman	1994	Raj Reddy
1974	Donald E. Knuth	1995	**Manuel Blum**
1975	Allen Newell	1996	**Amir Pnueli**
1975	**Herbert A. Simon**	1997	Douglas Engelbart
1976	**Michael O. Rabin**	1998	James Gray
1976	Dana S. Scott	1999	Frederick P. Brooks, Jr.
1977	John Backus	2000	Andrew Chi-Chih Yao
1978	Robert W. Floyd	2001	Ole-Johan Dahl
1979	Kenneth E. Iverson	2001	Kristen Nygaard
1980	C. Antony R. Hoare	2002	Ronald L. Rivest
1981	Edgar F. Codd	2002	**Adi Shamir**
1982	Stephen A. Cook	2003	**Leonard M. Adleman**
1983	Kenneth Lane Thompson	2003	Alan Kay
1983	Dennis M. Ritchie	2004	Vinton G. Cerf
1984	Niklaus E. Wirth	2004	**Robert E. Kahn**
1985	**Richard M. Karp**	2005	Peter Naur
1986	John E. Hopcroft	2006	Frances E. Allen
1986	Robert E. Tarjan	2007	Joseph Sifakis
1987	John Cocke	2007	E. Allen Emerson
1988	Ivan Sutherland	2007	Edmund M. Clarke

1. The Association for Computing Machinery (ACM)'s most prestigious technical award is accompanied by a prize of $100,000. It is given to an individual selected for contributions of a technical nature made to the computing community. The contributions should be of lasting and major technical importance to the computer field. Financial support of the Turing Award is provided by Intel Inc.

Alphabetical List of Encyclopædia Britannica's Great Inventions

Exhibit 4a

From the Encyclopædia Britannica Almanac 2003

INVENTION	YEAR	INVENTOR	COUNTRY
aerosol can	1926	Erik Rotheim	Norway
air conditioning	1902	Willis Haviland Carrier	US
airbag, automotive	1952	John Hetrick	US
airplane, engine-powered	1903	Wilbur & Orville Wright	US
airship	1852	Henri Giffard	France
alphabet	c. 1700–1500 BC	Semitic-speaking peoples	east coast Mediterranean
American Sign Language	1817	Thomas H. Gallaudet	US
animation, motion-picture	1906	J. Stuart Blackton	US
answering machine, telephone	1898	Valdemar Poulsen	Denmark
aspartame	1965	James Schlatter	US
aspirin	1897	Felix Hoffmann (Bayer)	Germany
assembly line	1913	Henry Ford	US
astrolabe	c. 2nd century	—	—
AstroTurf	1965	James M. Faria, Robert T. Wright	US
audiotape	1928	Fritz Pfleumer	Germany
automated teller machine (ATM)	1968	Don Wetzel	US
automobile	1889	Gottlieb Daimler	Germany
baby food, prepared	1927	Dorothy Gerber	US
bag, flat-bottomed paper	1870	Margaret Knight	US
Bakelite	1907	Leo Hendrik Baekeland	US
ball bearing	1794	Philip Vaughan	England
balloon, hot-air	1783	Joseph & Étienne Montgolfier	France
bandage, adhesive	1921	Earle Dickson	US
bar code	1952	Joseph Woodland	US
barbed wire	1874	Joseph Glidden	US
barometer	1643	Evangelista Torricelli	Italy
battery, electric storage	1800	Alessandro Volta	Italy
beer	before 6000 BC	Sumerians, Babylonians	Mesopotamia
bicycle	1818	Baron Karl de Drais de Sauerbrun	Germany
bifocal lens	1784	Benjamin Franklin	US
bikini	1946	Louis Réard	France
blood bank	late 1930s	Charles Richard Drew	US
blow-dryer	1920	Racine Universal Motor Co., Hamilton Beach Manufacturing Co.	US
bomb, atomic	1945	**J. Robert Oppenheimer**, et al.	US
bomb, thermonuclear (hydrogen)	1952	**Edward Teller**, et al.	US
boomerang	c. 15,000 years ago	Aboriginal peoples	Australia
Braille system	1824	Louis Braille	France
brassiere (bra)	1913	Mary Phelps Jacob	US
bread, sliced (bread-slicing machine)	1928	Otto Frederick Rohwedder	US
button	c. 700 BC	Greeks, Etruscans	Greece, Italy
buttonhole	13th century	—	Europe
calculator, electronic hand-held	1967	Jack S. Kilby	US
calculus	1680s	Sir Isaac Newton & Gottfried Wilhelm Leibniz (separately)	England and Germany
calendar, modern (Gregorian)	1582	Pope Gregory XIII	Italy
camcorder	1982	Sony Corp.	Japan
camera, motion picture	1891	Thomas Alva Edison, William K.L. Dickson	US
camera, portable photographic	1888	George Eastman	US
can, metal beverage	1933	American Can Co.	US
can opener	1858	Ezra J. Warner	US
candle	c. 3000 BC	—	Egypt, Crete
canning, food	1809	Nicolas Appert	France
carbon-14 dating	1946	Willard F. Libby	US
cardboard, corrugated	1871	Albert Jones	US

Alphabetical List of Encyclopædia Britannica's Great Inventions   Exhibit 4a
From the Encyclopædia Britannica Almanac 2003

INVENTION	YEAR	INVENTOR	COUNTRY
cards, playing	c. 10th century	—	China
cash register	1879	James Ritty	US
cat litter	1947	Edward Lowe	US
catalog, mail-order	1872	Aaron Montgomery Ward	US
cellophane	1911	Jacques E. Brandenberger	Switzerland
celluloid	1869	John Wesley Hyatt	US
cement, portland	1824	Joseph Aspdin	England
cereal flakes, breakfast	1894	John Harvey Kellogg	US
chewing gum (modern)	c. 1870	Thomas Adams	US
chocolate	c. 3rd–10th century	Maya, Aztecs	Central America, Mexico
chronometer	1762	John Harrison	England
clock, pendulum	1656	Christiaan Huygens	The Netherlands
clock, quartz	1927	Warren A. Marrison	Canada/US
cloning, animal	1970	John B. Gurdon	UK
coffee, drip	1908	Melitta Bentz	Germany
coffee, decaffeinated	1905	Ludwig Roselius	Germany
coins	c. 650 BC	Lydians	Turkey
compact disc (CD)	1980	Philips Electronics, Sony Corp.	The Netherlands, Japan
compass, magnetic	c. 12th century	—	China, Europe
computed tomography (CT scan, CAT scan)	1972	Godfrey Hounsfield, Allan Cormack	UK, US
computer, electronic digital	1939	John V. Atanasoff, Clifford E. Berry	US
computer, laptop	1983	Radio Shack Corp.	US
computer, personal	1974	MITS (Micro Instrumentation Telemetry Systems)	US
concrete, reinforced	1867	Joseph Monier	France
condom, latex	c. 1930	—	—
contact lenses	1887	Adolf Fick	Germany
contraceptives, oral	early 1950s	**Gregory Pincus**, John Rock, Min Chueh Chang	US
corn, hybrid	1917	Donald F. Jones	US
correction fluid, white	1951	Bette Nesmith	US
cotton gin	1793	Eli Whitney	US
coupon, grocery	1894	Asa Candler	US
crayons, children's wax	1903	Edwin Binney, C. Harold Smith	US
cream separator (dairy processing)	1878	Carl Gustaf Patrik de Laval	Sweden
credit card	1950	Frank McNamara, Ralph Schneider (Diners' Club)	US
crossword puzzles	1913	Arthur Wynne	US
DDT	1874	Othmar Zeidler	Germany
defibrillator	1952	**Paul M. Zoll**	US
dentures	c. 700 BC	Etruscans	Italy
detector, metal	late 1920s	Gerhard Fisher	Germany/US
detector, home smoke	1969	Randolph Smith, Kenneth House	US
diamond, artificial	1955	General Electric Co.	US
diapers, disposable	1950	Marion Donovan	US
digital videodisc (DVD)	1995	consortium of international electronics companies	Japan, US, The Netherlands
dishwasher	1886	Josephine Cochrane	US
DNA fingerprinting	1984	Alec Jeffreys	UK
doughnut, ring-shaped	1847	Hanson Crockett Gregory	US
door, revolving	1888	Theophilus von Kannel	US
drinking fountain	c. 1905–1912	Luther Haws, Halsey W. Taylor (invented separately)	US
dry cleaning	1855	Jean Baptiste Jolly	France

Alphabetical List of Encyclopædia Britannica's Great Inventions   Exhibit 4a
From the Encyclopædia Britannica Almanac 2003

INVENTION	YEAR	INVENTOR	COUNTRY
dynamite	1867	Alfred Nobel	Sweden
elastic, fabric	c. 1830	Thomas Hancock	UK
electric chair	1888	Harold P. Brown, Arthur E. Kennelly	US
electrocardiogram (ECG, EKG)	1903	Willem Einthoven	The Netherlands
electroencephalogram (EEG)	1929	Hans Berger	Germany
electronic mail (e-mail)	1971	Ray Tomlinson	US
elevator, passenger	1852	Elisha Graves Otis	US
encyclopedia	c. 4th century BC or 77 AD	Speusippus (compliation of Plato's teachings) or Pliny the Elder (comprehensive work)	Greece or Rome
engine, internal-combustion	1859	Étienne Lenoir	France
engine, jet	1930	Sir Frank Whittle	UK
engine, liquid-fueled rocket	1926	Robert H. Goddard	US
engine, steam	1698	Thomas Savery	England
escalator	1891	Jesse W. Reno	US
eyeglasses	1280s	Salvino degli Armati or Alessandro di Spina	Italy
facsimile (fax)	1842	Alexander Bain	Scotland
fiber optics	1955	Narinder S. Kapany	India
fiberglass	1938	Owens Corning (corp.)	US
film, photographic	1884	George Eastman	US
flashlight, battery-operated portable	1899	Conrad Hubert	Russia/US
flask, vacuum (Thermos)	1892	Sir James Dewar	Scotland
food processor	1971	Pierre Verdon	France
foods, freeze-dried	1946	Earl W. Flosdorf	US
foods, frozen	c. 1924	Clarence Birdseye	US
Fresnel lens	1820	Augustin-Jean Fresnel	France
fuel cell	1839	William R. Grove	UK
genetic engineering	1973	**Stanley N. Cohen**, Herbert W. Boyer	US
Geiger counter	1908	Hans Geiger	Germany
glass	c. 2500 BC	Egyptians or Phoenicians	Egypt or Lebanon
glass, safety	1909	Édouard Bénédictus	France
greeting card, Christmas	1843	John Callcott Horsley	England
guillotine	1792	Joseph-Ignace Guillotin	France
guitar, electric	1941	Les Paul	US
gunpowder	c. 10th century	—	China or Arabia
hanger, wire coat	1903	Albert J. Parkhouse	US
helicopter	1939	Igor Sikorsky	Russia/US
holography	1948	**Dennis Gabor**	Hungary
hypodermic syringe	1853	Charles Gabriel Pravaz	France
in vitro fertilization (IVF), human	1978	Patrick Steptoe, Robert Edwards	UK
ink	c. 2500 BC	—	Egypt, China
insulin, extraction and preparation of	1921	Sir Frederick Grant Banting, Charles H. Best	Canada
integrated circuit	1958	Jack S. Kilby	US
Internet	1969	Dept. of Defense Advanced Research Projects Agency (ARPA)	US
iron, electric	1882	Henry W. Seely	US
irradiation, food	1905	—	US/UK
jeans	1873	**Levi Strauss**, Jacob Davis	US
JELL-O (gelatin dessert)	1897	Pearle B. Wait	US
jukebox	1889	Louis Glass	US
Kevlar	1965	Stephanie Kwolek	US
Kool-Aid (fruit drink mix)	1927	Edwin E. Perkins	US

Alphabetical List of Encyclopædia Britannica's Great Inventions
From the Encyclopædia Britannica Almanac 2003

Exhibit 4a

INVENTION	YEAR	INVENTOR	COUNTRY
laser	1958	**Gordon Gould** and Charles Hard Townes, Arthur L. Schawlow (invented separately)	US
laundromat	1934	J.F. Cantrell	US
lawn mower, gasoline-powered	c. 1940	Leonard Goodall	US
Lego	late 1940s	Ole Kirk Christiansen	Denmark
light bulb, incandescent	1879	Thomas Alva Edison	US
light bulb, fluorescent	1934	Arthur Compton	US
light-emitting diode (LED)	1962	Nick Holonyak, Jr.	US
linoleum	1860	Frederick Walton	UK
lipstick, tube	1915	**Maurice Levy**	US
liquid crystal display (LCD)	1963	George Heilmeier	US
lock and key	c. 2000 BC	Assyrians	Mesopotamia
locomotive	1829	George Stephenson	England
longbow	c. 1000	—	Wales
loudspeaker	1924	Chester W. Rice, Edward W. Kellogg	US
magnetic resonance imaging (MRI)	early 1970s	Raymond Damadian, Paul Lauterbur	US
margarine	1869	Hippolyte Mège-Mouriès	France
matches, friction	1827	John Walker	England
metric system of measurement	1795	French Academy of Sciences	France
microphone	1878	David E. Hughes	UK/US
microscope, compound optical	c. 1600	Hans & Zacharias Jansen	The Netherlands
microscope, electron	1933	Ernst Ruska	Germany
microwave oven	1945	Percy L. Spencer	US
miniature golf	c. 1930	Garnet Carter	US
mirror, glass	c. 1200	Venetians	Italy
missile, guided	1942	Wernher von Braun	Germany
mobile home	1919	Glenn H. Curtiss	US
money, paper	late 900s	—	China
Monopoly (board game)	1934	Charles B. Darrow	US
Morse code	1838	Samuel F.B. Morse	US
motor, electric	1834	Thomas Davenport	US
motor, outboard	1907	Ole Evinrude	Norway/US
motorcycle	1885	Gottlieb Daimler, Wilhelm Maybach	Germany
mouse, computer	1963–64	Douglas Engelbart	US
Muzak	1922	George Owen Squier	US
nail, construction	c. 3300 BC	Sumerians	Mesopotamia
necktie	17th century	—	Croatia
neon lighting	1910	Georges Claude	France
nuclear reactor	1942	Enrico Fermi	US
nylon	1937	Wallace H. Carothers	US
oil lamp	1784	Aimé Argand	Switzerland
oil well	1859	Edwin Laurentine Drake	US
pacemaker, cardiac	1952	**Paul M. Zoll**	US
paper	c. 105	Ts'ai Lun	China
paper clip	1899	Johan Vaaler	Norway
paper towel	1931	Arthur Scott	US
parachute, modern	1797	André-Jacques Garnerin	France
parking meter	1932	Carl C. Magee	US
particle accelerator	1929	Sir John Douglas Cockcroft, Ernest Thomas Sinton Walton	Ireland/UK
pasteurization	1864	Louis Pasteur	France
pen, ballpoint	1938	**Lazlo Biro**	Hungary

Alphabetical List of Encyclopædia Britannica's Great Inventions   Exhibit 4a
From the Encyclopædia Britannica Almanac 2003

INVENTION	YEAR	INVENTOR	COUNTRY
pencil	1565	Conrad Gesner	Switzerland
periodic table	1871	Dmitry Ivanovich Mendeleyev	Russia
personal watercraft, motorized	1968	Bombardier, Inc.	Canada
petroleum jelly	1870s	Robert Chesebrough	US
phonograph	1877	Thomas Alva Edison	US
photocopying (xerography)	1937	Chester F. Carlson	US
photography	1837	Louis-Jacques-Mandé Daguerre	France
photography, instant	1947	**Edwin Herbert Land**	US
Play-Doh	1956	Noah W. & Joseph S. McVicker	US
plow, steel	1836	John Deere	US
pocket watch	c. 1500	Peter Henlein	Germany
polyethylene	1935	Eric Fawcett, Reginald Gibson	UK
polygraph (lie detector)	1921	John A. Larson	US
polyvinyl chloride (PVC)	1872	Eugen Baumann	Germany
Post-it Notes	mid-1970s	Arthur Fry (3M)	US
potato chips	1853	George Crum	US
printing press, movable type	c. 1450	Johannes Gutenberg	Germany
Prozac	1972	Ray W. Fuller, Bryan B. Molloy, David T. Wong	US
radar	c. 1904	Christian Hülsmeyer	Germany
radio	1896	Guglielmo Marconi	Italy
radio, car	early 1920s	William P. Lear	US
rayon	1884	Louis-Marie-Hilaire Bernigaud, count of Chardonnet	France
razor, electric	1928	Jacob Schick	US
razor, safety	c. 1900	King Camp Gillette	US
reaper, mechanical	1831	Cyrus Hall McCormick	US
record, long-playing (LP)	1948	**Peter Carl Goldmark**	US
refrigerator	1842	John Gorrie	US
remote control, television	1950	**Robert Adler**	US
respirator	c. 1955	Forrest M. Bird	US
revolver	1835–36	Samuel Colt	US
Richter scale	1935	Charles Francis Richter, Beno Gutenberg	US
rifle, assault	1944	Hugo Schmeisser	Germany
roller coaster	1884	LeMarcus A. Thompson	US
rubber, vulcanized	1839	Charles Goodyear	US
rubber band	1845	Stephen Perry	UK
saccharin	1879	Ira Remsen, Constantin Fahlberg	US, Germany
saddle	c. 200 BC	—	China
safety pin	1849	Walter Hunt	US
satellite, successful artificial earth	1957	Sergey Korolyov, et al.	USSR
satellite, communications	1960	John Robinson Pierce	US
saxophone	1846	Antoine-Joseph Sax	Belgium
Scotch tape	1930	Richard Drew (3M)	US
scuba gear	1943	Jacques Cousteau, Émile Gagnan	France
seat belt, automotive shoulder	1959	Nils Bohlin (Volvo)	Sweden
sewing machine	1841	Barthélemy Thimonnier	France
shoelaces	1790	—	England
silicone	1904	Frederic Stanley Kipping	UK
skateboard	1958	Bill & Mark Richards	US
skates, ice	1000 BC	—	Scandinavia
skates, roller	1760s	Joseph Merlin	Belgium
ski, snow	c. 2000–3000 BC	—	Sweden, Finland, Norway
skyscraper, steel-frame	1884	William Le Baron Jenney	US
slot machine	1890s	Charles Fey	US

Alphabetical List of Encyclopædia Britannica's Great Inventions   Exhibit 4a
From the Encyclopædia Britannica Almanac 2003

INVENTION	YEAR	INVENTOR	COUNTRY
snowmobile	1922	Joseph-Armand Bombardier	Canada
soap	600 BC	Phoenicians	Lebanon
soft drinks, carbonated	1772	Joseph Priestley	UK
sonar	1915	Paul Langevin	France
stamps, postage	1840	Sir Rowland Hill	UK
stapler	1866	George W. McGill	US
steamboat, successful	1807	Robert Fulton	US
steel, mass-production	1856	Henry Bessemer	UK
steel, stainless	1914	Harry Brearley	UK
stereo, personal	1979	Sony Corp.	Japan
stereophonic sound recording	1931	Alan Dower Blumlein	UK
stethoscope	1819	René-Théophile-Hyacinthe Laënnec	France
stock ticker	1867	Edward A. Calahan	US
stove, electric	1896	William Hadaway	US
stove, gas	1826	James Sharp	UK
straw, drinking	1888	Marvin Stone	US
submarine	1620	Cornelis Drebbel	The Netherlands
sunglasses	1752	James Ayscough	UK
sunscreen	1944	Benjamin Green	US
supermarket	1930	Michael Cullen	US
synthesizer, music	1955	Harry Olson, Herbert Belar	US
synthetic skin	1981	Ioannis V. Yannas, John F. Burke	US
tampon, cotton	1931	Earle Cleveland Haas	US
tank, military	1915	Admiralty Landships Committee	UK
tea bag	early 1900s	Thomas Sullivan	US
teddy bear	1902	Morris Michtom	US
Teflon	1938	Roy Plunkett	US
telegraph	1832–35	Samuel F.B. Morse	US
telephone, wired-line	1876	Alexander Graham Bell	Scotland/US
telephone, mobile	1946	Bell Laboratories	US
telescope, optical	1608	Hans Lippershey	The Netherlands
television	1923, 1927	Vladimir Kosma Zworykin, Philo Taylor Farnsworth	Russia/US, US
thermometer	1592	Galileo	Italy
thermostat	1830	Andrew Ure	UK
threshing machine	1778	Andrew Meikle	Scotland
tire, pneumatic	1888	John Boyd Dunlop	UK
tissue, disposable facial	1924	Kimberly-Clark Co.	US
tissue, toilet	1857	Joseph Gayetty	US
toaster, electric	1893	Crompton Co.	UK
toilet, flush	c. 1591	Sir John Harington	England
toothbrush	1498	—	China
tractor	1892	John Froehlich	US
traffic lights, automatic	1923	Garrett A. Morgan	US
transistor	1947	John Bardeen, Walter H. Brattain, William B. Shockley	US
typewriter	1868	Christopher Latham Sholes	US
ultrasound imaging, obstetric	1958	Ian Donald	UK
vaccination	1796	Edward Jenner	England
vacuum cleaner, electric	1901	Herbert Cecil Booth	UK
Velcro	1948	George de Mestral	Switzerland
vending machine	c. 100–200 BC	—	Egypt
Viagra	1997	Pfizer Inc.	US
video games	1972	Nolan Bushnell	US
videocassette recorder	1969	Sony Corp.	Japan
videotape	1950s	**Charles Ginsburg**	US

Alphabetical List of Encyclopædia Britannica's Great Inventions   Exhibit 4a
From the Encyclopædia Britannica Almanac 2003

INVENTION	YEAR	INVENTOR	COUNTRY
virtual reality	1989	**Jaron Lanier**	US
vision correction, laser	1987	Stephen Trokel	US
washing machine, electric	1907	Alva J. Fisher	US
wheel	about 3500 BC	proto-Aryan people or Sumerians	Russia/Kazakhstan or
wheelbarrow	1st century BC	—	China
wheelchair	1590s	—	Spain
windmill	644	—	Persia
wine	before 4000 BC	—	Middle East
World Wide Web	1989	Tim Berners-Lee	UK
wristwatch, digital	1970	John M. Bergey	US
X-ray imaging	1895	Wilhelm Conrad Röntgen	Germany
Zamboni (ice resurfacing machine)	1949	Frank J. Zamboni	US
zipper	1893	Whitcomb L. Judson	US

Chronological List of Encyclopædia Britannica's Great Inventions   **Exhibit 4b**
From the Encyclopædia Britannica Almanac 2003

INVENTION	YEAR	INVENTOR	COUNTRY
boomerang	c. 15,000 years ago	Aboriginal peoples	Australia
beer	before 6000 BC	Sumerians, Babylonians	Mesopotamia
wine	before 4000 BC	—	Middle East
wheel	about 3500 BC	proto-Aryan people or Sumerians	Russia/Kazakhstan or Mesopotamia
nail, construction	c. 3300 BC	Sumerians	Mesopotamia
candle	c. 3000 BC	—	Egypt, Crete
glass	c. 2500 BC	Egyptians or Phoenicians	Egypt or Lebanon
ink	c. 2500 BC	—	Egypt, China
ski, snow	c. 2000–3000 BC	—	Sweden, Finland, Norway
lock and key	c. 2000 BC	Assyrians	Mesopotamia
alphabet	c. 1700–1500 BC	Semitic-speaking peoples	east coast Mediterranean
skates, ice	c. 1000 BC	—	Scandinavia
button	c. 700 BC	Greeks, Etruscans	Greece, Italy
dentures	c. 700 BC	Etruscans	Italy
coins	c. 650 BC	Lydians	Turkey
soap	c. 600 BC	Phoenicians	Lebanon
encyclopedia	c. 4th century BC or 77 AD	Speusippus (compliation of Plato's teachings) or Pliny the Elder (comprehensive work)	Greece or Rome
saddle	c. 200 BC	—	China
vending machine	c. 100–200 BC	—	Egypt
wheelbarrow	c. 100-200 BC	—	China
paper	c. 105	Ts'ai Lun	China
astrolabe	c. 2nd century		—
chocolate	c. 3rd–10th century	Maya, Aztecs	Central America, Mexico
windmill	644	—	Persia
money, paper	late 900s	—	China
longbow	c. 1000	—	Wales
cards, playing	c. 10th century		China
gunpowder	c. 10th century	—	China or Arabia
mirror, glass	c. 1200	Venetians	Italy
eyeglasses	c. 1280s	Salvino degli Armati or Alessandro di Spina	Italy
compass, magnetic	c. 12th century	—	China, Europe
buttonhole	c. 13th century	—	Europe
printing press, movable type	c. 1450	Johannes Gutenberg	Germany
toothbrush	1498	—	China
pocket watch	c. 1500	Peter Henlein	Germany
pencil	1565	Conrad Gesner	Switzerland
calendar, modern (Gregorian)	1582	Pope Gregory XIII	Italy
toilet, flush	c. 1591	Sir John Harington	England
thermometer	1592	Galileo	Italy
wheelchair	1590s	—	Spain
microscope, compound optical	c. 1600	Hans & Zacharias Jansen	The Netherlands
telescope, optical	1608	Hans Lippershey	The Netherlands
submarine	1620	Cornelis Drebbel	The Netherlands
barometer	1643	Evangelista Torricelli	Italy
clock, pendulum	1656	Christiaan Huygens	The Netherlands
calculus	1680s	Sir Isaac Newton and Gottfried Wilhelm Leibniz (separately)	England and Germany (respectively)
engine, steam	1698	Thomas Savery	England
necktie	17th century	—	Croatia
sunglasses	1752	James Ayscough	UK
chronometer	1762	John Harrison	England

Chronological List of Encyclopædia Britannica's Great Inventions   Exhibit 4b
From the Encyclopædia Britannica Almanac 2003

INVENTION	YEAR	INVENTOR	COUNTRY
skates, roller	1760s	Joseph Merlin	Belgium
soft drinks, carbonated	1772	Joseph Priestley	UK
threshing machine	1778	Andrew Meikle	Scotland
balloon, hot-air	1783	Joseph & Étienne Montgolfier	France
bifocal lens	1784	Benjamin Franklin	US
oil lamp	1784	Aimé Argand	Switzerland
shoelaces	1790	—	England
guillotine	1792	Joseph-Ignace Guillotin	France
cotton gin	1793	Eli Whitney	US
ball bearing	1794	Philip Vaughan	England
metric system of measurement	1795	French Academy of Sciences	France
vaccination	1796	Edward Jenner	England
parachute, modern	1797	André-Jacques Garnerin	France
battery, electric storage	1800	Alessandro Volta	Italy
steamboat, successful	1807	Robert Fulton	US
canning, food	1809	Nicolas Appert	France
American Sign Language	1817	Thomas H. Gallaudet	US
bicycle	1818	Baron Karl de Drais de Sauerbrun	Germany
stethoscope	1819	René-Théophile-Hyacinthe Laënnec	France
Fresnel lens	1820	Augustin-Jean Fresnel	France
Braille system	1824	Louis Braille	France
cement, portland	1824	Joseph Aspdin	England
stove, gas	1826	James Sharp	UK
matches, friction	1827	John Walker	England
locomotive	1829	George Stephenson	England
thermostat	1830	Andrew Ure	UK
elastic, fabric	c. 1830	Thomas Hancock	UK
reaper, mechanical	1831	Cyrus Hall McCormick	US
telegraph	1832–35	Samuel F.B. Morse	US
motor, electric	1834	Thomas Davenport	US
revolver	1835–36	Samuel Colt	US
plow, steel	1836	John Deere	US
photography	1837	Louis-Jacques-Mandé Daguerre	France
Morse code	1838	Samuel F.B. Morse	US
fuel cell	1839	William R. Grove	UK
rubber, vulcanized	1839	Charles Goodyear	US
stamps, postage	1840	Sir Rowland Hill	UK
sewing machine	1841	Barthélemy Thimonnier	France
facsimile (fax)	1842	Alexander Bain	Scotland
refrigerator	1842	John Gorrie	US
greeting card, Christmas	1843	John Callcott Horsley	England
rubber band	1845	Stephen Perry	UK
saxophone	1846	Antoine-Joseph Sax	Belgium
doughnut, ring-shaped	1847	Hanson Crockett Gregory	US
safety pin	1849	Walter Hunt	US
airship	1852	Henri Giffard	France
elevator, passenger	1852	Elisha Graves Otis	US
hypodermic syringe	1853	Charles Gabriel Pravaz	France
potato chips	1853	George Crum	US
dry cleaning	1855	Jean Baptiste Jolly	France
steel, mass-production	1856	Henry Bessemer	UK
tissue, toilet	1857	Joseph Gayetty	US
can opener	1858	Ezra J. Warner	US
engine, internal-combustion	1859	Étienne Lenoir	France
oil well	1859	Edwin Laurentine Drake	US
linoleum	1860	Frederick Walton	UK

Chronological List of Encyclopædia Britannica's Great Inventions   Exhibit 4b
From the Encyclopædia Britannica Almanac 2003

INVENTION	YEAR	INVENTOR	COUNTRY
pasteurization	1864	Louis Pasteur	France
stapler	1866	George W. McGill	US
concrete, reinforced	1867	Joseph Monier	France
dynamite	1867	Alfred Nobel	Sweden
stock ticker	1867	Edward A. Calahan	US
typewriter	1868	Christopher Latham Sholes	US
celluloid	1869	John Wesley Hyatt	US
margarine	1869	Hippolyte Mège-Mouriès	France
bag, flat-bottomed paper	1870	Margaret Knight	US
chewing gum (modern)	c. 1870	Thomas Adams	US
cardboard, corrugated	1871	Albert Jones	US
periodic table	1871	Dmitry Ivanovich Mendeleyev	Russia
catalog, mail-order	1872	Aaron Montgomery Ward	US
polyvinyl chloride (PVC)	1872	Eugen Baumann	Germany
jeans	1873	**Levi Strauss**, Jacob Davis	US
barbed wire	1874	Joseph Glidden	US
DDT	1874	Othmar Zeidler	Germany
petroleum jelly	1870s	Robert Chesebrough	US
telephone, wired-line	1876	Alexander Graham Bell	Scotland/US
phonograph	1877	Thomas Alva Edison	US
cream separator (dairy	1878	Carl Gustaf Patrik de Laval	Sweden
microphone	1878	David E. Hughes	UK/US
cash register	1879	James Ritty	US
light bulb, incandescent	1879	Thomas Alva Edison	US
saccharin	1879	Ira Remsen, Constantin Fahlberg	US, Germany
iron, electric	1882	Henry W. Seely	US
film, photographic	1884	George Eastman	US
rayon	1884	Louis-Marie-Hilaire Bernigaud, count of Chardonnet	France
roller coaster	1884	LeMarcus A. Thompson	US
skyscraper, steel-frame	1884	William Le Baron Jenney	US
motorcycle	1885	Gottlieb Daimler, Wilhelm Maybach	Germany
dishwasher	1886	Josephine Cochrane	US
contact lenses	1887	Adolf Fick	Germany
camera, portable photographic	1888	George Eastman	US
door, revolving	1888	Theophilus von Kannel	US
electric chair	1888	Harold P. Brown, Arthur E. Kennelly	US
straw, drinking	1888	Marvin Stone	US
tire, pneumatic	1888	John Boyd Dunlop	UK
automobile	1889	Gottlieb Daimler	Germany
jukebox	1889	Louis Glass	US
camera, motion picture	1891	Thomas Alva Edison, William K.L. Dickson	US
escalator	1891	Jesse W. Reno	US
flask, vacuum (Thermos)	1892	Sir James Dewar	Scotland
tractor	1892	John Froehlich	US
toaster, electric	1893	Crompton Co.	UK
zipper	1893	Whitcomb L. Judson	US
cereal flakes, breakfast	1894	John Harvey Kellogg	US
coupon, grocery	1894	Asa Candler	US
slot machine	1890s	Charles Fey	US
X-ray imaging	1895	Wilhelm Conrad Röntgen	Germany
radio	1896	Guglielmo Marconi	Italy
stove, electric	1896	William Hadaway	US

Chronological List of Encyclopædia Britannica's Great Inventions   Exhibit 4b
From the Encyclopædia Britannica Almanac 2003

INVENTION	YEAR	INVENTOR	COUNTRY
aspirin	1897	Felix Hoffmann (Bayer)	Germany
JELL-O (gelatin dessert)	1897	Pearle B. Wait	US
answering machine, telephone	1898	Valdemar Poulsen	Denmark
flashlight, battery-operated	1899	Conrad Hubert	Russia/US
paper clip	1899	Johan Vaaler	Norway
razor, safety	c. 1900	King Camp Gillette	US
vacuum cleaner, electric	1901	Herbert Cecil Booth	UK
air conditioning	1902	Willis Haviland Carrier	US
teddy bear	1902	Morris Michtom	US
airplane, engine-powered	1903	Wilbur & Orville Wright	US
crayons, children's wax	1903	Edwin Binney, C. Harold Smith	US
electrocardiogram (ECG, EKG)	1903	Willem Einthoven	The Netherlands
hanger, wire coat	1903	Albert J. Parkhouse	US
silicone	1904	Frederic Stanley Kipping	UK
radar	c. 1904	Christian Hülsmeyer	Germany
coffee, decaffeinated	1905	Ludwig Roselius	Germany
irradiation, food	1905	—	US/UK
tea bag	early 1900s	Thomas Sullivan	US
animation, motion-picture	1906	J. Stuart Blackton	US
Bakelite	1907	Leo Hendrik Baekeland	US
motor, outboard	1907	Ole Evinrude	Norway/US
washing machine, electric	1907	Alva J. Fisher	US
drinking fountain	c. 1905–1912	Luther Haws, Halsey W. Taylor (invented separately)	US
coffee, drip	1908	Melitta Bentz	Germany
Geiger counter	1908	Hans Geiger	Germany
glass, safety	1909	Édouard Bénédictus	France
neon lighting	1910	Georges Claude	France
cellophane	1911	Jacques E. Brandenberger	Switzerland
assembly line	1913	Henry Ford	US
brassiere (bra)	1913	Mary Phelps Jacob	US
crossword puzzles	1913	Arthur Wynne	US
steel, stainless	1914	Harry Brearley	UK
lipstick, tube	1915	**Maurice Levy**	US
sonar	1915	Paul Langevin	France
tank, military	1915	Admiralty Landships Committee	UK
corn, hybrid	1917	Donald F. Jones	US
mobile home	1919	Glenn H. Curtiss	US
blow-dryer	1920	Racine Universal Motor Co., Hamilton Beach Mfg. Co.	US
bandage, adhesive	1921	Earle Dickson	US
insulin, extraction and	1921	Sir Frederick Grant Banting, Charles H. Best	Canada
polygraph (lie detector)	1921	John A. Larson	US
Muzak	1922	George Owen Squier	US
snowmobile	1922	Joseph-Armand Bombardier	Canada
radio, car	early 1920s	William P. Lear	US
traffic lights, automatic	1923	Garrett A. Morgan	US
loudspeaker	1924	Chester W. Rice, Edward W. Kellogg	US
tissue, disposable facial	1924	Kimberly-Clark Co.	US
foods, frozen	c. 1924	Clarence Birdseye	US
television	1923, 1927	Vladimir Kosma Zworykin, Philo Taylor Farnsworth	Russia/US, US
aerosol can	1926	Erik Rotheim	Norway
engine, liquid-fueled rocket	1926	Robert H. Goddard	US

Chronological List of Encyclopædia Britannica's Great Inventions   **Exhibit 4b**
From the Encyclopædia Britannica Almanac 2003

INVENTION	YEAR	INVENTOR	COUNTRY
baby food, prepared	1927	Dorothy Gerber	US
clock, quartz	1927	Warren A. Marrison	Canada/US
Kool-Aid (fruit drink mix)	1927	Edwin E. Perkins	US
detector, metal	late 1920s	Gerhard Fisher	Germany/US
audiotape	1928	Fritz Pfleumer	Germany
bread, sliced (bread-slicing	1928	Otto Frederick Rohwedder	US
razor, electric	1928	Jacob Schick	US
electroencephalogram (EEG)	1929	Hans Berger	Germany
particle accelerator	1929	Sir John Douglas Cockcroft, Ernest Thomas Sinton Walton	Ireland/UK
engine, jet	1930	Sir Frank Whittle	UK
Scotch tape	1930	Richard Drew (3M)	US
supermarket	1930	Michael Cullen	US
condom, latex	c. 1930	—	—
miniature golf	c. 1930	Garnet Carter	US
paper towel	1931	Arthur Scott	US
stereophonic sound recording	1931	Alan Dower Blumlein	UK
tampon, cotton	1931	Earle Cleveland Haas	US
parking meter	1932	Carl C. Magee	US
can, metal beverage	1933	American Can Co.	US
microscope, electron	1933	Ernst Ruska	Germany
laundromat	1934	J.F. Cantrell	US
light bulb, fluorescent	1934	Arthur Compton	US
Monopoly (board game)	1934	Charles B. Darrow	US
polyethylene	1935	Eric Fawcett, Reginald Gibson	UK
Richter scale	1935	Charles Francis Richter, Beno Gutenberg	US
nylon	1937	Wallace H. Carothers	US
photocopying (xerography)	1937	Chester F. Carlson	US
blood bank	late 1930s	Charles Richard Drew	US
fiberglass	1938	Owens Corning (corp.)	US
pen, ballpoint	1938	**Lazlo Biro**	Hungary
Teflon	1938	Roy Plunkett	US
computer, electronic digital	1939	John V. Atanasoff, Clifford E. Berry	US
helicopter	1939	Igor Sikorsky	Russia/US
lawn mower, gasoline-powered	c. 1940	Leonard Goodall	US
guitar, electric	1941	Les Paul	US
missile, guided	1942	Wernher von Braun	Germany
nuclear reactor	1942	Enrico Fermi	US
scuba gear	1943	Jacques Cousteau, Émile Gagnan	France
rifle, assault	1944	Hugo Schmeisser	Germany
sunscreen	1944	Benjamin Green	US
bomb, atomic	1945	**J. Robert Oppenheimer**, et al.	US
microwave oven	1945	Percy L. Spencer	US
bikini	1946	Louis Réard	France
carbon-14 dating	1946	Willard F. Libby	US
foods, freeze-dried	1946	Earl W. Flosdorf	US
telephone, mobile	1946	Bell Laboratories	US
cat litter	1947	Edward Lowe	US
photography, instant	1947	**Edwin Herbert Land**	US
transistor	1947	John Bardeen, Walter H. Brattain, William B. Shockley	US
Lego	late 1940s	Ole Kirk Christiansen	Denmark
holography	1948	**Dennis Gabor**	Hungary
record, long-playing (LP)	1948	**Peter Carl Goldmark**	US
Velcro	1948	George de Mestral	Switzerland

Chronological List of Encyclopædia Britannica's Great Inventions   Exhibit 4b
From the Encyclopædia Britannica Almanac 2003

INVENTION	YEAR	INVENTOR	COUNTRY
Zamboni (ice resurfacing	1949	Frank J. Zamboni	US
credit card	1950	Frank McNamara, Ralph Schneider (Diners' Club)	US
diapers, disposable	1950	Marion Donovan	US
remote control, television	1950	**Robert Adler**	US
correction fluid, white	1951	Bette Nesmith	US
airbag, automotive	1952	John Hetrick	US
bar code	1952	Joseph Woodland	US
bomb, thermonuclear (hydrogen)	1952	**Edward Teller**, et al.	US
defibrillator	1952	**Paul M. Zoll**	US
pacemaker, cardiac	1952	**Paul M. Zoll**	US
contraceptives, oral	early 1950s	**Gregory Pincus**, John Rock, Min Chueh Chang	US
diamond, artificial	1955	General Electric Co.	US
fiber optics	1955	Narinder S. Kapany	India
synthesizer, music	1955	Harry Olson, Herbert Belar	US
videotape	1950s	**Charles Ginsburg**	US
respirator	c. 1955	Forrest M. Bird	US
Play-Doh	1956	Noah W. & Joseph S. McVicker	US
satellite, successful artificial	1957	Sergey Korolyov, et al.	USSR
integrated circuit	1958	Jack S. Kilby	US
laser	1958	**Gordon Gould** and Charles Hard Townes, Arthur L. Schawlow (invented separately)	US
skateboard	1958	Bill & Mark Richards	US
ultrasound imaging, obstetric	1958	Ian Donald	UK
seat belt, automotive shoulder	1959	Nils Bohlin (Volvo)	Sweden
satellite, communications	1960	John Robinson Pierce	US
light-emitting diode (LED)	1962	Nick Holonyak, Jr.	US
liquid crystal display (LCD)	1963	George Heilmeier	US
mouse, computer	1963–64	Douglas Engelbart	US
aspartame	1965	James Schlatter	US
AstroTurf	1965	James M. Faria, Robert T. Wright	US
Kevlar	1965	Stephanie Kwolek	US
calculator, electronic hand-held	1967	Jack S. Kilby	US
automated teller machine (ATM)	1968	Don Wetzel	US
personal watercraft, motorized	1968	Bombardier, Inc.	Canada
detector, home smoke	1969	Randolph Smith, Kenneth House	US
Internet	1969	Advanced Research Projects Agency (ARPA) at the Dept. of	US
videocassette recorder	1969	Sony Corp.	Japan
cloning, animal	1970	John B. Gurdon	UK
wristwatch, digital	1970	John M. Bergey	US
electronic mail (e-mail)	1971	Ray Tomlinson	US
food processor	1971	Pierre Verdon	France
computed tomography (CT scan,	1972	Godfrey Hounsfield, Allan Cormack	UK, US
Prozac	1972	Ray W. Fuller, Bryan B. Molloy, David T. Wong	US
video games	1972	Nolan Bushnell	US
magnetic resonance imaging	early 1970s	Raymond Damadian, Paul Lauterbur	US
genetic engineering	1973	**Stanley N. Cohen**, Herbert W. Boyer	US
computer, personal	1974	MITS (Micro Instrumentation Telemetry Systems)	US

Chronological List of Encyclopædia Britannica's Great Inventions   **Exhibit 4b**
From the Encyclopædia Britannica Almanac 2003

INVENTION	YEAR	INVENTOR	COUNTRY
Post-it Notes	mid-1970s	Arthur Fry (3M)	US
in vitro fertilization (IVF), human	1978	Patrick Steptoe, Robert Edwards	UK
stereo, personal	1979	Sony Corp.	Japan
compact disc (CD)	1980	Philips Electronics, Sony Corp.	The Netherlands, Japan
synthetic skin	1981	Ioannis V. Yannas, John F. Burke	US
camcorder	1982	Sony Corp.	Japan
computer, laptop	1983	Radio Shack Corp.	US
DNA fingerprinting	1984	Alec Jeffreys	UK
vision correction, laser	1987	Stephen Trokel	US
virtual reality	1989	**Jaron Lanier**	US
World Wide Web	1989	Tim Berners-Lee	UK
digital videodisc (DVD)	1995	consortium of international electronics companies	Japan, US, The Netherlands
Viagra	1997	Pfizer Inc.	US

Ivy League, Big 10 and PAC 10 Student and Jewish Enrollment Figures — Exhibit 5a

Ivy Leage School	Undergrad Enrollment	Undergrad Jewish Enr.	Jews %	Grad Enrollment	Jews Grad Enrollment	Jews %	Total Enrollment	Total Jews Enrolled	Jews % of Total	Jews % of State
Princeton	4,611	490	10.6%	1,853	150	8.1%	6,464	640	9.9%	5.6%
Harvard	6,748	2,000	29.6%	10,351	2,500	24.2%	17,099	4,500	26.3%	4.3%
Yale	5,253	1,400	26.7%	4,485	1,400	31.2%	9,738	2,800	28.8%	3.2%
Columbia & Barnard	8,000	2,000	25.0%	21,000	2,500	11.9%	29,000	4,500	15.5%	8.7%
Dartmouth	4,118	440	10.7%	1,377	100	7.3%	5,495	540	9.8%	0.8%
Brown	5,999	1,400	23.3%	1,775	300	16.9%	7,774	1,700	21.9%	1.5%
Pennsylvania	9,730	3,000	30.8%	10,283	3,000	29.2%	20,013	6,000	30.0%	2.3%
Cornell	13,801	3,000	21.7%	5,619	500	8.9%	19,420	3,500	18.0%	8.7%
Total	58,260	13,730	23.6%	56,743	10,450	18.4%	115,003	24,180	21.0%	21.0%

Source: Hillel 5/27/03

Big 10 Conference	Undergrad Enrollment	Undergrad Jewish Enr.	Jews %	Grad Enrollment	Jews Grad Enrollment	Jews %	Total Enrollment	Total Jews Enrolled	Jews % of Total	Jews % of State
University of Illinois	28,746	2,500	8.7%	8,952	500	5.6%	37,698	3,000	8.0%	2.2%
Indiana University	30,157	3,000	9.9%	6,908	500	7.2%	37,065	3,500	9.4%	0.3%
University of Iowa	19,603	600	3.1%	9,165	200	2.2%	28,768	800	2.8%	0.2%
University of Michigan	24,547	4,000	16.3%	13,701	2,000	14.6%	38,248	6,000	15.7%	1.1%
Michigan State University	34,880	1,800	5.2%	9,353	110	1.2%	44,233	1,910	4.3%	1.1%
University of Minnesota	30,142	1,200	4.0%	14,462	400	2.8%	44,604	1,600	3.6%	0.9%
Northwestern University	7,816	1,200	15.4%	6,474	800	12.4%	14,290	2,000	14.0%	2.2%
Ohio State University	36,049	2,800	7.8%	9,452	900	9.5%	45,501	3,700	8.1%	1.3%
Penn State University	34,510	3,500	10.1%	6,115	500	8.2%	40,625	4,000	9.8%	2.3%
Purdue University	30,900	420	1.4%	6,300	80	1.3%	37,200	500	1.3%	0.3%
University of Wisconsin	28,677	4,000	13.9%	10,000	1,000	10.0%	38,677	5,000	12.9%	0.5%
Total	306,027	25,020	8.2%	100,882	6,990	6.9%	406,909	32,010	7.9%	

Source: Hillel 5/27/03

Big 10 Conference	Undergrad Enrollment	Undergrad Jewish Enr.	Jews %	Grad Enrollment	Jews Grad Enrollment	Jews %	Total Enrollment	Total Jews Enrolled	Jews % of Total	Jews % of State
Arizona State	35,191	2,200	6.3%	10,502	200	1.9%	45,693	200	0.4%	1.6%
University of Arizona	26,878	3,000	11.2%	6,074	500	8.2%	32,952	3,500	10.6%	1.6%
USC	16,020	1,500	9.4%	13,793	1,500	10.9%	29,813	3,000	10.1%	2.9%
UCLA	25,328	2,500	9.9%	12,166	1,200	9.9%	37,494	3,700	9.9%	2.9%
UC Berkeley	23,835	2,200	9.2%	9,310	1,300	14.0%	33,145	3,500	10.6%	2.9%
Stanford University	6,443	750	11.6%	11,312	1,300	11.5%	17,755	2,050	11.5%	2.9%
University of Oregon	15,113	1,200	7.9%	3,843	200	5.2%	18,956	1,400	7.4%	0.9%
Oregon State University	n/a	n/a		n/a	n/a		15,000	250	1.7%	0.9%
University of Washington	25,660	2,000	7.8%	9,950	1,000	10.1%	35,610	3,000	8.4%	0.7%
Washington State Univ.	n/a	n/a		n/a	n/a		17,000	375	2.2%	0.7%
Total	174,468	15,350	8.8%	76,950	7,200	9.4%	283,418	20,975	7.4%	

Source: Hillel 5/27/03 and US-Israel 1/27/03 for state populations; also note Wash. State's 375 is average of 250-500 shown on Hillel web site

Total Undergraduate and Jewish Enrollment at 50 Top Colleges   Exhibit 5b

U.S. News & World Report Top 50 Undergraduate School 2003	Total Enrollment	Total Jewish Enrollment	Jewish % of Total
Amherst College (MA)	1600	250	15.6%
Swarthmore College (PA)	1500	300	20.0%
Williams College (MA)	2000	240	12.0%
Wellesley College (MA)	2100	180	8.6%
Carleton College (MN)	1800	200	11.1%
Pomona College (CA)	1580	140	8.9%
Bowdoin College (ME)	1521	150	9.9%
Middlebury College (VT)	2200	220	10.0%
Davidson College (NC)	1600	25	1.6%
Haverford College (PA)	1100	300	27.3%
Wesleyan University (CT)	2700	700	25.9%
Grinnell College (IA)	1300	160	12.3%
Claremont McKenna College (CA)	1082	115	10.6%
Smith College (MA)	2800	230	8.2%
Harvey Mudd College (CA)	702	85	12.1%
Vassar College (NY)	2200	600	27.3%
Washington and Lee University (VA)	1900	30	1.6%
Colby College (ME)	1800	180	10.0%
Colgate University (NY)	2870	500	17.4%
Hamilton College (NY)	1760	150	8.5%
Bryn Mawr College (PA)	1200	200	16.7%
Bates College (ME)	1700	150	8.8%
Mount Holyoke College (MA)	2000	80	4.0%
Oberlin College (OH)	2840	694	24.4%
Trinity College (CT)	2000	200	10.0%
College of the Holy Cross (MA)	n/a	n/a	n/a
Macalester College (MN)	1600	100	6.3%
Barnard College (NY) affil Columbia	2297	574	25.0%
Bucknell University (PA)	3300	200	6.1%
Colorado College	1900	150	7.9%
Connecticut College	1600	180	11.3%
Kenyon College (OH)	1500	100	6.7%
Lafayette College (PA)	2000	250	12.5%
Scripps College (CA)	786	100	12.7%
University of the South (TN)	n/a	n/a	n/a
Bard College (NY)	1100	175	15.9%
Franklin and Marshall College (PA)	1800	220	12.2%
Union College (NY)	2050	360	17.6%
DePauw University (IN)	2090	35	1.7%
Whitman College (WA)	1350	75	5.6%
Furman University (SC)	n/a	n/a	na/
Rhodes College (TN)	1400	20	1.4%
Skidmore College (NY)	2200	450	20.5%
Centre College (KY)	n/a	n/a	n/a
Dickinson College (PA)	2065	200	9.7%
Gettysburg College (PA)	2200	45	2.0%
Occidental College (CA)	1600	160	10.0%
Wabash College (IN)	n/a	n/a	n/a
Sarah Lawrence College (NY)	1050	325	31.0%
Illinois Wesleyan University	Est 1829	n/a	n/a
Lawrence University (WI)	n/a	n/a	n/a
Willamette University (OR)	n/a	n/a	n/a
Total	79743	9798	12.3%

Source: U.S. News & World Report web site & Hillel web site May 26, 2003

Barnard	2297	574.25
Columbia	5703	1425.75
Total	8000	2000

Law School Faculties: Exhibit 5c
Stanford, Harvard and Yale (May, 2003)

Stanford Law School

1	Janet Cooper Alexander	20	Barbara H. Fried	39	John Henry Merryman
2	Michelle Alexander	21	Lawrence M. Friedman	40	David Mills
3	Barbara Allen Babcock	22	Ronald J. Gilson	41	Maude Pervere
4	Joseph Bankman	23	Paul Goldstein	42	A. Mitchell Polinsky
5	R. Richard Banks	24	William B. Gould IV	43	Robert L. Rabin
6	John H. Barton	25	Henry T. Greely	44	Margaret Jane Radin
7	Bernard S. Black	26	Thomas C. Grey	45	Deborah L. Rhode
8	Paul Brest	27	Joseph A. Grundfest	46	David Rosenhan
9	Gerhard Casper	28	Thomas C. Heller	47	Kenneth E. Scott
10	William Cohen	29	Deborah R. Hensler	48	Byron Sher
11	G. Marcus Cole	30	J. Myron Jacobstein	49	William H. Simon
12	Richard Craswell	31	Pamela S. Karlan	50	James Frank Strnad II
13	Mariano-Florentino Cuéllar	32	Mark G. Kelman	51	Kathleen M. Sullivan
14	Michele Landis Dauber	33	Michael Klausner	52	Barton H. Thompson, Jr.
15	Lance E. Dickson	34	William Koski	53	Michael S. Wald
16	John J. Donohue III	35	William C. Lazier	54	Robert Weisberg
17	George Fisher	36	Lawrence Lessig	55	Howard R. Williams
18	Richard Thompson Ford	37	J. Keith Mann		
19	Marc A. Franklin	38	Miguel A. Méndez		

Harvard Law School

1	Alford, William P.	35	Cratsley, John C.	69	Hay, Bruce L.
2	An-Na'im, Abdullahi Ahmed	36	Darwin, Florrie	70	Heen, Sheila
3	Anaya, S. James	37	Dershowitz, Alan M.	71	Hersch, Joni
4	Ancheta, Angelo	38	Desan, Christine	72	Herwitz, David Richard
5	Andrews, William D.	39	Dixon, Megan	73	Heymann, Philip B.
6	Bagenstos, Samuel	40	Donahue, Charles	74	Horwitz, Morton J.
7	Ball, Carol	41	Donohue, John J.	75	Hutt, Peter Barton
8	Barron, David	42	Edley, Christopher F.	76	Jackson, Howell
9	Bartholet, Elizabeth	43	Elhauge, Einer R.	77	Jolls, Christine M.
10	Basile, Mary Beth	44	Fallon, Richard H.	78	Jones-Pauly, Christina
11	Bebchuk, Lucian A.	45	Farber, Hillary	79	Juliar, Diane
12	Ben-Menahem, Hanina	46	Ferrell, Allen	80	Kagan, Elena
13	Benkler, Yochai	47	Ferrey, Steven	81	Kaplan, Benjamin
14	Berman, Harold J.	48	Field, Martha A.	82	Kaplow, Louis
15	Bienenstock, Martin J.	49	Fisher, Roger	83	Katyal, Neal Kumar
16	Bird, Richard M.	50	Fisher, William W.	84	Kaufman, Andrew L.
17	Bordone, Robert C.	51	Fried, Charles	85	Keeton, Robert E.
18	Brennan, Troyen	52	Friedman, Lawrence	86	Kennedy, David W.
19	Brewer, Scott	53	Frug, Gerald E.	87	Kennedy, Duncan
20	Bright, Stephen	54	Frumkin, Elizabeth	88	Kennedy, Randall L.
21	Bromberg, Howard	55	Geradin, Damien	89	Knebel, Jack
22	Brudney, Victor	56	Gerken, Heather K.	90	Kowal, Jennifer Meir
23	Burbank, Stephen B.	57	Glendon, Mary Ann	91	Kraakman, Reinier H.
24	Byse, Clark	58	Goodman, Ryan	92	Lempereur, Alain
25	Charn, Jeanne	59	Gordon, Jeffrey N.	93	Mack, Kenneth
26	Cheffins, Brian R.	60	Greene, Edward F.	94	Manning, John F.
27	Clark, Robert C.	61	Grossman, David	95	Mansfield, John H.
28	Coates, John C.	62	Guinier, Lani	96	Margalioth, Yoram
29	Collier, Paul R.	63	Haar, Charles M.	97	Martin, Harry S.
30	Cooper, Graeme S.	64	Halley, Janet	98	Meltsner, Michael
31	Cope, David	65	Halperin, Daniel	99	Meltzer, Daniel J.
32	Coquillette, Daniel Robert	66	Hamilton, Eugene N.	100	Michelman, Frank I.
33	Cossman, Brenda	67	Hanson, Jon	101	Miller, Arthur R.
34	Cox, Archibald	68	Hart, Oliver	102	Minow, Martha L.

Law School Faculties:
Stanford, Harvard and Yale (May, 2003)

Harvard Law School (continued)

103 Mnookin, Robert H.	126 Sander, Frank E. A.	149 Susskind, Lawrence
104 Murray, Peter L.	127 Sargentich, Lewis D.	150 Taranto, Richard G.
105 Musgrave, Richard A.	128 Schlanger, Margo	151 Todd, Gillien
106 Nesson, Charles R.	129 Scott, Hal S.	152 Trachtman, Joel
107 Netsch, Linda	130 Shalakany, Amr A.	153 Tribe, Laurence H.
108 Ocampo, Luis Moreno	131 Shapiro, Daniel L.	154 Trubek, Louise
109 Ogletree, Charles J.	132 Shapiro, David L.	155 Unger, Roberto Mangabeira
110 Ohlin, Lloyd E.	133 Shavell, Steven M.	156 Vagts, Detlev F.
111 Oldman, Oliver	134 Simon, William H.	157 Viscusi, W. Kip
112 Parker, Richard D.	135 Singer, Joseph	158 Vogel, Frank E.
113 Pearlman, Ronald A.	136 Smalley, Kathleen	159 von Mehren, Arthur T.
114 Polinsky, A. Mitchell	137 Sohn, Louis B.	160 Warren, Alvin C.
115 Pozen, Robert C.	138 Song, Sang Hyun	161 Warren, Elizabeth
116 Rakoff, Todd D.	139 Spencer, Shaun	162 Weiler, Paul C.
117 Ramseyer, J. Mark	140 Steiker, Carol	163 Weinreb, Lloyd L.
118 Ring, Diane M.	141 Steiker, Jordan M.	164 Westfall, David
119 Rivkin, Dean Hill	142 Steiner, Henry J.	165 White, Lucie E.
120 Roberts, Michele	143 Stern, Donald K.	166 Wilkins, David B.
121 Roe, Mark J.	144 Stone, Alan A.	167 Williams, Robert A.
122 Rosenbaum, Jay D.	145 Stone, Douglas	168 Wise, Virginia
123 Rosenberg, David	146 Stuntz, William J.	169 Wolfman, Bernard
124 Rosenblum, Peter J.	147 Styles-Anderson, Sharon	170 Zittrain, Jonathan
125 Sandel, Michael	148 Subramanian, Guhan	171 Zolt, Eric M.

Yale Law School

1 Bruce Ackerman	25 E. Donald Elliott	49 J. L. Pottenger, Jr.
2 Anne L. Alstott	26 William Eskridge, Jr	50 George L. Priest
3 Akhil Reed Amar	27 Daniel C. Esty	51 W Michael Reisman
4 Ian Ayres	28 Owen M. Fiss	52 Judith Resnik
5 Jack M. Balkin	29 Daniel J. Freed	53 Roberta Romano
6 Boris I. Bittker	30 Paul Gewirtz	54 Carol M. Rose
7 Lea Brilmayer	31 Abraham S. Goldstein	55 Susan Rose-Ackerman
8 Robert A. Burt	32 Robert W. Gordon	56 Peter H. Schuck
9 Guido Calabresi	33 Michael J. Graetz	57 Vicki Schultz
10 Stephen L. Carter	34 Henry B. Hansmann	58 Alan Schwartz
11 Marvin A. Chirelstein	35 Oona A. Hathaway	59 Reva Siegel
12 Amy L. Chua	36 Quintin Johnstone	60 John G. Simon
13 Elias Clark	37 Dan M. Kahan	61 Henry E. Smith
14 Morris L. Cohen	38 Paul W. Kahn	62 Robert A. Solomon
15 Jules L. Coleman	39 Jay Katz	63 Kate Stith
16 Dennis E. Curtis	40 Alvin K. Klevorick	64 Harry H. Wellington
17 Harlon L. Dalton	41 Harold Hongju Koh	65 Stanton Wheeler
18 Mirjan R. Damaska	42 John H. Langbein	66 James Q. Whitman
19 Drew Days, III	43 Michael E. Levine	67 Ralph Winter, Jr
20 Jan Ginter Deutsch	44 Carroll L. Lucht	68 Stephen Wizner
21 Brett Dignam	45 Daniel Markovits	69 Kenji Yoshino
22 Francis X. Dineen	46 Burke Marshall	70 Howard V. Zonana
23 Steven B. Duke	47 Jerry L. Mashaw	
24 Robert C. Ellickson	48 Jean Koh Peters	

Present and Past Faculty of the Princeton Instutue for Advanced Study   **Exhibit 5d**

1	Stephen L. Adler	44	Juan Maldacena
2	James W. Alexander	45	Eric S. Maskin
3	Andrew E. Z. Alfoldi	46	Jack F. Matlock, Jr.
4	Michael F. Atiyah	47	Millard Meiss
5	John N. Bahcall	48	Benjamin D. Meritt
6	Arne K. A. Beurling	49	John W. Milnor
7	Enrico Bombieri	50	David Mitrany
8	Armand Borel	51	Deane Montgomery
9	Jean Bourgain	52	Marston Morse
10	Glen W. Bowersock	53	J. Robert Oppenheimer
11	Caroline Walker Bynum	54	Abraham Pais
12	Luis A. Caffarelli	55	Erwin Panofsky
13	Harold F. Cherniss	56	Peter Paret
14	Marshall Clagett	57	Tullio E. Regge
15	Giles Constable	58	Winfield W. Riefler
16	Patricia Crone	59	Marshall N. Rosenbluth
17	José Cutileiro	60	Joan Wallach Scott
18	Roger F. Dashen	61	Nathan Seiberg
19	Pierre Deligne	62	Atle Selberg
20	Freeman J. Dyson	63	Kenneth M. Setton
21	Edward M. Earle	64	Carl L. Siegel
22	Albert Einstein	65	Thomas Spencer
23	John H. Elliott	66	Walter W. Stewart
24	Clifford Geertz	67	Bengt G. D. Strömgren
25	Felix Gilbert	68	Homer A. Thompson
26	James F. Gilliam	69	Kirk Varnedoe
27	Kurt Gödel	70	Oswald Veblen
28	Hetty Goldman	71	Vladimir Voevodsky
29	Oleg Grabar	72	John Von Neumann
30	Christian Habicht	73	Heinrich Von Staden
31	Harish-chandra	74	Michael Walzer
32	Ernst Herzfeld	75	Robert B. Warren
33	Albert O. Hirschman	76	André Weil
34	Lars V. Hörmander	77	Hermann Weyl
35	Piet Hut	78	Morton White
36	Jonathan Israel	79	Hassler Whitney
37	Ernst H. Kantorowicz	80	Avi Wigderson
38	George F. Kennan	81	Frank Wilczek
39	Robert P. Langlands	82	Edward Witten
40	Irving Lavin	83	Ernest Llewellyn Woodward
41	T. D. Lee	84	C. N. Yang
42	Elias A. Lowe	85	Shing-tung Yau
43	Robert D. Macpherson		

The Sveriges Riksbank Prize in Economic Sciences   Exhibit 7a
in Memory of Alfred Nobel – Laureates

2007	**Leonid Hurwicz**[6,7] **Eric S. Maskin**[6,7] **Roger B. Meyerson**[6,7]
2006	Edmund S. Phelps
2005	**Robert J. Aumann**[6,7] Thomas C. Schelling
2004	Finn E. Kydland, Edward C. Prescott
2003	Robert F. Engle III, Clive W. J. Granger
2002	**Daniel Kahneman**[1,3,6,7] Vernon L. Smith
2001	**George A. Akerlof**[1,3,6,7] A. Michael Spence, **Joseph E. Stiglitz**[3,6,7]
2000	James J. Heckman, Daniel L. McFadden
1999	Robert A. Mundell 1998 Amartya Sen
1997	**Robert C. Merton**[6] **Myron S. Scholes**[2,3,6,7]
1996	James A. Mirrlees, William Vickrey
1995	Robert E. Lucas Jr.
1994	**John C. Harsanyi**[1,3,4,5,6,7] John F. Nash Jr., **Reinhard Selten**[1,4,5,6]
1993	**Robert W. Fogel**[1,2,3,5,6,7] Douglass C. North
1992	**Gary S. Becker**[1,2,3,5,6,7]
1991	Ronald H. Coase
1990	**Harry M. Markowitz**[1,2,3,5,6,7] **Merton H. Miller**[1,3,6,7] William F. Sharpe
1989	Trygve Haavelmo
1988	Maurice Allais
1987	**Robert M. Solow**[1,2,3,5,6,7]
1986	James M. Buchanan Jr.
1985	**Franco Modigliani**[1,2,3,4,5,6,7]
1984	Richard Stone
1983	Gerard Debreu
1982	George J. Stigler
1981	James Tobin
1980	**Lawrence R. Klein**[1,3,5,6,7]
1979	Theodore W. Schultz, Sir Arthur Lewis
1978	**Herbert A. Simon**[1,2,3,4,6,7]
1977	Bertil Ohlin, James E. Meade
1976	**Milton Friedman**[2,3,4,6,7]
1975	**Leonid Vitaliyevich Kantorovich**[1,2,3,5,6,7] Tjalling C. Koopmans
1974	Gunnar Myrdal, Friedrich August von Hayek
1973	**Wassily Leontief**[1,3,6,7]
1972	John R. Hicks, **Kenneth J. Arrow**[1,2,3,6,7]
1971	**Simon Kuznets**[1,2,3,4,5,6,7]
1970	**Paul A. Samuelson**[1,2,3,5,6,7]
1969	Ragnar Frisch (2), Jan Tinbergen

Notes: For Laureates identified as Jewish, the superscript numbers after their name indicates the source: (1) is the website "jewho.com" section on Nobels for 2002 or the pages devoted to Economics. (2) is the book "The Nobel Prize" by Burton Feldman. (3) is the US-Israel.org web site (4) is the web site "yahoodi.com". (5) is the book "Nobel Laureates 1901 – 2000 by Alan Symons and (6) is the web site "jinfo.org" (7) is the Jewish Virtual Library at www.jewishvirtuallibrary.org.

The John Bates Clark Medal   Exhibit 7b

Year of Award	Winner	Nobel	Wait Time (in yrs)
1947	**Paul A. Samuelson**	1970	23
1949	Kenneth E. Boulding		out
1951	**Milton Friedman**	1976	25
1953	No Award		n/a
1955	James Tobin	1981	26
1957	**Kenneth J. Arrow**	1972	15
1959	**Lawrence R. Klein**	1980	21
1961	**Robert M. Solow**	1987	26
1963	**Hendrik S. Houthakker**		
1965	**Zvi Griliches**		out
1967	**Gary S. Becker**	1992	25
1969	**Marc Leon Nerlove**		
1971	Dale W. Jorgenson		
1973	**Franklin M. Fisher**		
1975	Daniel McFadden	2000	25
1977	**Martin S. Feldstein**		
1979	**Joseph E. Stiglitz**	2001	22
1981	A. Michael Spence	2001	20
1983	James J. Heckman	2000	17
1985	**Jerry A. Hausman**		
1987	**Sanford J. Grossman**		
1989	**David M. Kreps**		
1991	**Paul R. Krugman**	2008	17
1993	**Lawrence H. Summers**		
1995	David Card		
1997	Kevin M. Murphy		
1999	**Andrei Shleifer**		
2001	**Matthew Rabin**		
2003	**Steven Levitt**		
2005	Daron Acemoglu		
2007	Susan C. Athey		

The 100 Largest 2000 Donors from the Mother Jones 400

Rank	Name	Primary Title	Primary Company	City	State	Industry	Party	Amount
1	S. Daniel Abraham (with Ewa)	Former Chairman	Slim Fast Foods	Palm Beach	FL	Healt & Diet	Demo	$1,518,500
2	Bernard L. Schwartz (with Irene)	CEO	Loral Space & Communications	New York	NY	Communications	Demo	$1,317,000
3	Davidi Gilo (with Shamaya)	Chairman	Vyyo, Inc.	Cupertino	CA	Communications	Demo	$1,311,000
4	Petter L. Buttenwieser (with Terry A. Marek)	Owner	Peter L. Buttenwieser & Assoc.	Philadelphia	PA	Single Issue & Other	Demo	$1,304,700
5	Haim Saban (with Cheryl)	Chairman & CEO	Fox Family Worldwide, Inc.	Los Angeles	CA	Communications	Demo	$1,250,500
6	Carl H. Lindner (with Edyth)	Chairman & CEO	American Financial Group	Cincinnati	OH	Finance	Both	$1,216,000
7	Peter G. Angelos (with Georgia K.)	President	Law Offices Peter G. Angelos	Baltimore	MD	Lawyers & Lobbyists	Demo	$959,500
8	Fred Eychaner	Owner	Newsweb Corp.	Chicago	IL	Communications	Demo	$946,000
9	Constance Milstein	Principal	Milstein Properties	New York	NY	Finance	Demo	$932,515
10	John M. O'Quinn	Partner	O'Quinn & Laminack	Houston	TX	Lawyers & Lobbyists	Demo	$840,250
11	Finn M.W. Casperson (with Barbara)	Chairman & CEO	Knickerbocker Management	Gladstone	NJ	Finance	Both	$807,000
12	Richard M. DeVos Sr. (with Helen)	Founder	Amway, Inc.	Grand Rapids	MI	Manufacturing & Retail	Republican	$764,500
13	Stephen L. Bing	Screenwriter & Producer		Los Angeles	CA	Communications	Demo	$759,000
14	David J. Shimmon	President	Kinetics Group, Inc.	Los Altos Hills	CA	High Tech	Demo	$727,000
15	Richard T. Farmer (with Joyce E.)	Chairman	Cintas Corp.	Cincinnati	OH	Manufacturing & Retail	Republican	$721,000
16	Terrance Watanabe	Chairman	Oriental Trading Co.	Omaha	NE	Manufacturing & Retail	Demo	$704,700
17	John W. Childs (with Marlene)	President	J.W. Childs Associates	Boston	MA	Finance	Republican	$670,000
18	Walter H. Shorenstein	Chairman Emeritus	The Shorenstein Co.	San Francisco	CA	Finance	Demo	$664,148
19	Steven T. Kirsch (with Michele)	Founder & Former Chrmn.	Infoseek	Los Altos Hills	CA	High Tech	Demo	$655,000
20	David S. Steiner (with Sylvia)	Chairman	Steiner Equities	West Orange	NJ	Finance	Demo	$651,150
21	Michael J. Perik (with Elizabeth Beretta Perik)	Cofounder	The Learning Company	Wellesley	MA	High Tech	Demo	$643,000
22	Ian M. Cumming (with Annette P.)	Chairman	Leucadia National Corp	Salt Lake City	UT	Finance	Demo	$632,300
23	Sam Fox (with Marilyn)	Chairman & CEO	The Harbour Group	Clayton	MO	Manufacturing & Retail	Republican	$626,700
24	John Eddie Williams, Jr.	Partner	Williams & Bailey Law Firm	Houston	TX	Lawyers & Lobbyists	Demo	$621,000
25	Kenneth A. Eldred (with Roberta E.)	Founder	Ariba, Inc.	Portola Valley	CA	Finance	Republican	$617,500
26	David Bohnett	Founder	GeoCities	Los Angeles	CA	High Tech	Demo	$601,900
27	Larry Addington (with Kathy)	Chairman & CEO	AEI Resources	Ashland	KY	Energy	Republican	$598,000
28	Alex G. Spanos (with Faye)	President & CEO	A. C. Spanos Companies	Stockton	CA	Finance	Republican	$593,000
29	Leo J. Hindery, Jr. (with Deborah)	Chairman & CEO	GlobalCenter, Inc.	Sunnyvale	CA	Communications	Demo	$591,902
30	Joseph C. Canizaro (with Sue Ellen)	President	Columbus Properties	New Orleans	LA	Finance	Republican	$587,250
31	John T. Chambers (with Elaine)	President & CEO	Cisco Systems	Los Altos	CA	High Tech	Republican	$582,933
32	Bernard Daines (with Marsha)	Chairman & CEO	World Wide Packets	Spokane	WA	High Tech	Republican	$568,000
33	Vance K. Opperman (with Darin B.)	President	Key Investment, Inc.	Minneapolis	MN	Finance	Demo	$561,250
34	Dr. John M. Templeton, Jr. (with Josephine)	President	John Templeton Foundation	Bryn Mawr	PA	Single Issue & Other	Republican	$555,950
35	Thomas E. McInerney (with Paula G.)	General Partner	Welsh, Carson, Anderson & Stowe	New York	NY	Finance	Republican	$544,500
36	A. Jerrold Perenchio (with Margaret)	Chairman & CEO	Univision Communications, Inc.	Los Angeles	CA	Communications	Republican	$541,500
37	Philip Levine	President	Onboard Media, Inc.	Miami Beach	FL	Communications	Demo	$538,000
38	Lawrence Kadish (with Susan)	Real Estate Broker	First Fiscal Fund Corp.	Westbury	NY	Finance	Republican	$532,900
39	Jeffrey Levy-Hinte (with Jeanne)	Film Producer	Post 391, Inc.	New York	NY	Communications	Demo	$527,000
40	Barbara Stephenson (with Thomas F.)	Homemaker (Genl Part.)	Sequoia Capital	Atherton	CA	Finance	Republican	$519,200
41	Alfred Lerner (with Norma)	Chairman & CEO	MBNA Corp	Shaker Heights	OH	Finance	Republican	$516,000
42	David I. Saperstein (with Suzanne)	Founder	Metro Networks	Houston	TX	Communications	Republican	$514,000

The 100 Largest 2000 Donors from the Mother Jones 400

Exhibit 8a

Rank/Name	Primary Title	Primary Company	City	State	Industry	Party	Amount
43 David E. Shaw (with Beth K.)	Chairman & CEO	D.E. Shaw & Co.	New York	NY	Finance	Demo	$512,568
44 Charles W. Ergen (with Cantey M.)	Chairman & CEO	Echostar	Littleton	CO	Communications	Both	$511,250
45 Ronald A. Kapche	President	International Partners, Inc.	Houston	TX	Single Issue & Other	Republican	$508,834
46 David Liniger (with Gail)	Chairman	RE/MAX International, Inc.	Castle Rock	CO	Finance	Republican	$506,000
47 John A. Kaneb (with Virginia M.)	CEO	Gulf Oil	Chelsea	MA	Energy	Republican	$502,600
48 Thomas M. Siebel	Chairman & CEO	Siebel Systems, Inc.	San Mateo	CA	High Tech	Republican	$500,000
49 Jon S. Corzine (with Joanne)	U.S. Senator		Summit	NJ	Single Issue & Other	Demo	$498,075
50 S. Donald Sussman	Chairman & CEO	Paloma Partners Management Co.	Greenwich	CT	Finance	Demo	$498,000
51 David H. Koch (with Julia)	Executive Vice Pres.	Koch Industries	Witchita	KS	Energy	Republican	$487,500
51 Robert F. Green (with Giner)	Investor		Amarillo	TX	Finance	Demo	$487,500
53 DR. Phillip Frost (with Patricia)	Chairman & CEO	Ivax Corp	Miami	FL	Healt & Diet	Demo	$485,000
54 Marc B.Nathanson (with Jane)	Vice Chair & Dir.	Charter Communications, Inc.	Los Angeles	CA	Communications	Demo	$484,000
55 John Doerr (with Ann)	Partner	Kleiner, Perkins, Caufield & Byers	Woodside	CA	Finance	Demo	$477,500
56 Meyer A. Berman (with Patricia N.)	President	M.A. Berman Co.	Boca Raton	FL	Finance	Demo	$471,250
57 John Price (with Marcia)	Chairman & CEO	JP Realty Group	Salt Lake City	UT	Finance	Republican	$467,550
58 Jeffrey Katzenberg (with Marilyn)	Partner	Dreamworks SKG	Los Angeles	CA	Communications	Demo	$460,000
59 Jonathan M. Tisch	President & CEO	Loews Hotels	New York	NY	Finance	Demo	$453,500
60 Harold Snyder	Principal	HBJ Investments	Cliffside Park	NJ	Finance	Demo	$449,500
61 Michael King (with Jena)	Consultant	King World Productions	Los Angeles	CA	Communications	Demo	$448,000
62 C. Cary Patterson (with Lois)	Partner	Nix, Patterson & Roach	Daingerfield	TX	Lawyers & Lobbyists	Demo	$443,000
63 Marvin Davis	Owner	Davis Companies	Los Angeles	CA	Energy	Demo	$426,500
64 William R. Hambrecht (with Sally)	Chairman & CEO	WR Hambrecht & Co.	San Francisco	CA	Finance	Demo	$423,000
65 Louis Weisbach (with Ruth)	Chairman	Halo Branded Solutions	Chicago	IL	Manufacturing & Retail	Demo	$412,914
66 Alan D. Solomont (with Susan L.)	Chairman	Solomont Ballis Ventures	Weston	MA	Healt & Diet	Demo	$411,500
67 Tim Gill	Founder	Quark, Inc.	Denver	CO	High Tech	Demo	$410,750
68 Leonard A. Lauder (with Evelyn H.)	Chairman	Estee Lauder Companies	New York	NY	Manufacturing & Retail	Demo	$408,000
69 James V. Kimsey	Chairman Emeritus	America Online, Inc.	Washington	DC	High Tech	Republican	$406,350
70 Max M. Fisher (with Marjorie S.)	Director	Comerica, Inc.	Franklin	MI	Finance	Republican	$405,500
71 Bernard D. Bergreen (with Barbara)	Chairman	Gilman Co.	New York	NY	Agribusiness	Demo	$404,000
71 Marc L. Andreessen	Co-founder	Netscape	Los Gatos	CA	High Tech	Demo	$404,000
73 Charles R. Schwab (with Helen O.)	Chairman & CEO	The Charles Schwab Corp.	San Francisco	CA	Finance	Republican	$393,500
74 Denise Rich	Songwriter		New York	NY	Communications	Demo	$391,500
75 Bren Simon (with Melvin)	President & Owner	MBS Associates	Indianapolis	IN	Finance	Demo	$390,350
76 Kenneth L. Lay (with Linda P.)	Chairman	Enron Corp.	Houston	TX	Energy	Republican	$387,500
77 Philip D. Murphy (with Tammy S.)	Managing Director	Golman Sachs & Co.	New York	NY	Finance	Demo	$384,500
78 Bert Boeckmann (with Jane)	Owner & President	Galpin Motors	North Hills	CA	Transportation	Republican	$384,000
79 Samuel J. Heyman (with Ronnie)	Former Chairman	GAF Corp.	Westport	CT	Manufacturing & Retail	Republican	$382,970
80 Berry Gordy	Chairman	West Grand Media	Los Angeles	CA	Communications	Demo	$381,250
81 David C. Pratt (with Kathleen)	Chairman	United Industries Corp.	St. Louis	MO	Agribusiness	Republican	$378,500
82 John H. McConnell (with Peggy)	Founder & Chrmn Em.	Worthington Industries	Columbus	OH	Manufacturing & Retail	Republican	$372,500
83 Roland E. Arnall	Chairman	Ameriquest Capital	Orange	CA	Finance	Demo	$371,000
84 Garu Winnick (with Karen B.)	Chairman	Global Crossing, Ltd.	Beverly Hills	CA	Finance	Both	$363,750

The 100 Largest 2000 Donors from the Mother Jones 400

Rank/Name	Primary Title	Primary Company	City	State	Industry	Party	Amount
85 Lodwrick Cook (with Carole D.)	Co-chairman	Global Crossing, Ltd.	Beverly Hills	CA	Communications	Republican	$361,500
86 Norman Pattiz (with Mary)	Chairman	Westwood One	Los Angeles	CA	Communications	Demo	$360,000
87 Eve Weinstein (with Harvey)	Vice President	Elegant Films	New York	NY	Communications	Demo	$359,742
88 Bernard Marcus (with Wilma)	Co-founder & Chrmn.	Home Depot, Inc.	Atlanta	GA	Manufacturing & Retail	Republican	$353,500
89 Lew R. Wasserman (with Edith)	Chairman	Universal Studios	Beverly Hills	CA	Communications	Demo	$352,597
90 Gerhard R. Andlinger (with Jeanne D.)	Chairman	Andlinger & Co.	Vero Beach	FL	Finance	Republican	$352,000
91 Donald L. Saunders	President	D.L. Saunders Companies	Boston	MA	Finance	Demo	$351,875
92 Jack Thompson (with Vicki)	Co-founder	J.D. Edwards & Co.	Larkspur	CO	High Tech	Republican	$345,200
93 Fredric Mack (with Tami)	Partner	The Mack Co.	Rochelle Park	NJ	Finance	Demo	$344,850
94 John Galbraith (with Rosemary)	Director	Templeton Emerging Markets Fund	St. Petersburg	FL	Finance	Republican	$343,250
95 Robert E. McDonough (with Simone)	President	Remedy Intelligent Staffing	Capistrano	CA	Manufacturing & Retail	Demo	$338,000
96 Heinz C. Prechter (with Waltraud E.)	Chairman	ASC, Inc.	Southgate	MI	Transportation	Republican	$335,775
97 Ira Lipman (with Barbara)	Chrmn, CEO & Pres.	Guardsmark	Memphis	TN	Manufacturing & Retail	Demo	$335,000
97 Marsh B. Belden	President	McBel Trust	Canton	OH	Energy	Natural Law	$335,000
99 Darlyn Davenport (with Charles)	Vice President	Sea/West Wincpower, Inc.	San Diego	CA	Energy	Demo	$334,000
100 Irwin M. Jacobs (with Joan Klein Jacobs)	CEO	Qualcomm, Inc.	La Jolla	CA	Communications	Demo	$333,000

U.S. Supreme Court Justices Chronologically by Appointment

Exhibit 8b

1. John Jay (Chief: 1789–1795)
2. John Rutledge (Associate: 1790–1791, Chief: 1795–1795)
3. William Cushing (Associate: 1790–1810)
4. James Wilson (Associate: 1789–1798)
5. John Blair (Associate: 1790–1795)
6. James Iredell (Associate: 1790–1799)
7. Thomas Johnson (Associate: 1792–1793)
8. William Paterson (Associate: 1793–1806)
9. Samuel Chase (Associate: 1796–1811)
10. Oliver Ellsworth (Chief: 1796–1800)
11. Bushrod Washington (Associate: 1799–1829)
12. Alfred Moore (Associate: 1800–1804)
13. John Marshall (Chief: 1801–1835)
14. William Johnson (Associate: 1804–1834)
15. Brockholst Livingston (Associate: 1807–1823)
16. Thomas Todd (Associate: 1807–1826)
17. Gabriel Duvall (Associate: 1811–1835)
18. Joseph Story (Associate: 1812–1845)
19. Smith Thompson (Associate: 1823–1843)
20. Robert Trimble (Associate: 1826–1828)
21. John McLean (Associate: 1830–1861)
22. Henry Baldwin (Associate: 1830–1844)
23. James M. Wayne (Associate: 1835–1867)
24. Roger B. Taney (Chief: 1836–1864)
25. Philip P. Barbour (Associate: 1836–1841)
26. John Catron (Associate: 1837–1865)
27. John McKinley (Associate: 1838–1852)
28. Peter V. Daniel (Associate: 1842–1860)
29. Samuel Nelson (Associate: 1845–1872)
30. Levi Woodbury (Associate: 1845–1851)
31. Robert C. Grier (Associate: 1846–1870)
32. Benjamin R. Curtis (Associate: 1851–1857)
33. John A. Campbell (Associate: 1853–1861)
34. Nathan Clifford (Associate: 1858–1881)
35. Noah Swayne (Associate: 1862–1881)
36. Samuel F. Miller (Associate: 1862–1890)
37. David Davis (Associate: 1862–1877)
38. Stephen J. Field (Associate: 1863–1897)
39. Salmon P. Chase (Chief: 1864–1873)
40. William Strong (Associate: 1870–1880)
41. Joseph P. Bradley (Associate: 1870–1892)
42. Ward Hunt (Associate: 1873–1882)
43. Morrison R. Waite (Chief: 1874–1888)
44. John M. Harlan (Associate: 1877–1911)
45. William B. Woods (Associate: 1881–1887)
46. Stanley Matthews (Associate: 1881–1889)
47. Horace Gray (Associate: 1882–1902)
48. Samuel Blatchford (Associate: 1882–1893)
49. Lucius Q.C. Lamar (Associate: 1888–1893)
50. Melville W. Fuller (Chief: 1888–1910)
51. David J. Brewer (Associate: 1890–1910)
52. Henry B. Brown (Associate: 1891–1906)
53. George Shiras, Jr. (Associate: 1892–1903)
54. Howell E. Jackson (Associate: 1893–1895)
55. Edward D. White (Associate: 1894–1910, Chief: 1910–1921)
56. Rufus Peckham (Associate: 1896–1909)
57. Joseph McKenna (Associate: 1898–1925)
59. William R. Day (Associate: 1903–1922)
60. William H. Moody (Associate: 1906–1910)

U.S. Supreme Court Justices Chronologically by Appointment

61. Horace H. Lurton (Associate: 1910–1914)
62. Charles E. Hughes (Associate: 1910–1916, Chief: 1930–1941)
63. Willis Van Devanter (Associate: 1911–1937)
64. Joseph R. Lamar (Associate: 1911–1916)
65. Mahlon Pitney (Associate: 1912–1922)
66. James C. McReynolds (Associate: 1914–1941)
67. **Louis D. Brandeis** (Associate: 1916–1939)
68. John H. Clarke (Associate: 1916–1922)
69. William Howard Taft (Chief: 1921–1930)
70. George Sutherland (Associate: 1922–1938)
71. Pierce Butler (Associate: 1923–1939)
72. Edward T. Sanford (Associate: 1923–1930)
73. Harlan Fiske Stone (Associate: 1925–1941, Chief: 1941–1946)
74. Owen J. Roberts (Associate: 1930–1945)
75. **Benjamin N. Cardozo** (Associate: 1932–1938)
76. Hugo L. Black (Associate: 1937 1971)
77. Stanley Reed (Associate: 1938 1957)
78. **Felix Frankfurter** (Associate: 1939–1962)
79. William O. Douglas (Associate: 1939–1975)
80. Frank Murphy (Associate: 1940–1949)
81. James F. Byrnes (Associate: 1941–1942)
82. Robert H. Jackson (Associate: 1941–1954)
83. Wiley B. Rutledge (Associate: 1943 1949)
84. Harold Burton (Associate: 1945–1958)
85. Fred M. Vinson (Chief: 1946–1953)
86. Tom C. Clark (Associate: 1949–1967)
87. Sherman Minton (Associate: 1949–1956)
88. Earl Warren (Chief: 1953–1969)
89. John M. Harlan (Associate: 1955–1971)
90. William J. Brennan, Jr. (Associate: 1956–1990)
91. Charles E. Whittaker (Associate: 1957–1962)
92. Potter Stewart (Associate: 1958–1981)
93. Byron R. White (Associate: 1962–1993)
94. **Arthur J. Goldberg** (Associate: 1962–1965)
95. **Abe Fortas** (Associate: 1965–1969)
96. Thurgood Marshall (Associate: 1967–1991)
97. Warren E. Burger (Chief: 1969–1986)
98. Harry A. Blackmun (Associate: 1970–1994)
99. Lewis F. Powell, Jr. (Associate: 1972–1987)
100. William H. Rehnquist (Associate: 1972–1986, Chief: 1986–)
101. John Paul Stevens (Associate: 1975–)
102. Sandra Day O'Connor (Associate: 1981–)
103. Antonin Scalia (Associate: 1986–)
104. Anthony Kennedy (Associate: 1988–)
105. David H. Souter (Associate: 1990–)
106. Clarence Thomas (Associate: 1991–)
107. **Ruth Bader Ginsburg** (Associate: 1993–)
108. **Stephen G. Breyer** (Associate: 1994–)
109. John Glover Roberts, Jr. (Chief (2005–)
110. Samuel Alito (Associate: 2006–)

The Nobel Peace Prize – Laureates   Exhibit 8c

2007   Intergovernmental Panel on Climate Change, Al Gore
2006   Muhannad Yunus, Grameen Bank
2005   International Atomic Energy Agency, Mohamed ElBaradei
2004   Wangari Maathai 2003 Shirin Ebadi
2002   Jimmy Carter
2001   United Nations (U.N.), Kofi Annan
2000   Kim Dae-jung
1999   Médecins Sans Frontières
1998   John Hume, David Trimble
1997   International Campaign to Ban Landmines (ICBL), Jody Williams
1996   Carlos Filipe Ximenes Belo, José Ramos-Horta
1995   **Joseph Rotblat** [1,2,5,6] Pugwash Conferences on Science and World Affairs
1994   Yasser Arafat, **Shimon Peres** [2,3,5,6] **Yitzhak Rabin** [2,3,4,5,6]
1993   Nelson Mandela, Frederik Willem de Klerk
1992   Rigoberta Menchú Tum
1991   Aung San Suu Kyi
1990   Mikhail Sergeyevich Gorbachev
1989   The 14th Dalai Lama (Tenzin Gyatso)
1988   United Nations Peace-keeping Forces
1987   Oscar Arias Sanchez
1986   **Elie Wiesel** [2,3,4,5,6]
1985   International Physicians for the Prevention of Nuclear War
1984   Desmond Mpilo Tutu
1983   Lech Walesa
1982   Alva Myrdal, Alfonso García Robles
1981   Office of the United Nations High Commissioner for Refugees (UNHCR)
1980   Adolfo Pérez Esquivel
1979   Mother Teresa
1978   Mohamed Anwar al-Sadat, **Menachem Begin** [2,3,5,6]
1977   Amnesty International
1976   Betty Williams, Mairead Corrigan
1975   Andrei Dmitrievich Sakharov
1974   Seán MacBride, Eisaku Sato
1973   **Henry A. Kissinger** [2,3,5,6] Le Duc Tho
1972   The prize money for 1972 was allocated to the Main Fund
1971   Willy Brandt
1970   Norman E. Borlaug
1969   International Labour Organization (I.L.O.)
1968   **René Cassin** [3,5,6]
1967   Prize money was 1/3 allocated to the Main Fund and 2/3 to the Special Fund of this prize section
1966   The prize money was allocated to the Special Fund of this prize section
1965   United Nations Children's Fund (UNICEF)
1964   Martin Luther King Jr.
1963   Comité international de la Croix Rouge (International Committee of the Red Cross)
1962   Linus Carl Pauling
1961   Dag Hjalmar Agne Carl Hammarskjöld
1960   Albert John Lutuli
1959   Philip J. Noel-Baker
1958   Georges Pire
1957   Lester Bowles Pearson
1956   Prize money was 1/3 allocated to the Main Fund and 2/3 to the Special Fund of this prize section
1955   The prize money was allocated to the Special Fund of this prize section
1954   Office of the United Nations High Commissioner for Refugees (UNHCR)
1953   George Catlett Marshall
1952   Albert Schweitzer
1951   Léon Jouhaux
1950   Ralph Bunche
1949   Lord (John) Boyd Orr of Brechin

The Nobel Peace Prize – Laureates   **Exhibit 8c**

1948   Prize money was 1/3 allocated to the Main Fund and 2/3 to the Special Fund of this prize section
1947   Friends Service Council (The Quakers), American Friends Service Committee (The Quakers)
1946   Emily Greene Balch, John Raleigh Mott
1945   Cordell Hull
1944   Comité international de la Croix Rouge (International Committee of the Red Cross)
1943   Prize money was 1/3 allocated to the Main Fund and 2/3 to the Special Fund of this prize section
1942   Prize money was 1/3 allocated to the Main Fund and 2/3 to the Special Fund of this prize section
1941   Prize money was 1/3 allocated to the Main Fund and 2/3 to the Special Fund of this prize section
1940   Prize money was 1/3 allocated to the Main Fund and 2/3 to the Special Fund of this prize section
1939   Prize money was 1/3 allocated to the Main Fund and 2/3 to the Special Fund of this prize section
1938   Office international Nansen pour les Réfugiés (Nansen International Office for Refugees)
1937   Cecil of Chelwood, Viscount (Lord Edgar Algernon Robert Gascoyne Cecil)
1936   Carlos Saavedra Lamas
1935   Carl von Ossietzky
1934   Arthur Henderson
1933   Sir Norman Angell (Ralph Lane)
1932   The prize money was allocated to the Special Fund of this prize section
1931   Jane Addams, Nicholas Murray Butler
1930   Lars Olof Nathan (Jonathan) Söderblom
1929   Frank Billings Kellogg
1928   The prize money was allocated to the Special Fund of this prize section
1927   Ferdinand Buisson, Ludwig Quidde
1926   Aristide Briand, Gustav Stresemann
1925   Sir Austen Chamberlain, Charles Gates Dawes
1924   The prize money was allocated to the Special Fund of this prize section
1923   The prize money was allocated to the Special Fund of this prize section
1922   Fridtjof Nansen
1921   Karl Hjalmar Branting, Christian Lous Lange
1920   Léon Victor Auguste Bourgeois
1919   Thomas Woodrow Wilson
1918   The prize money was allocated to the Special Fund of this prize section
1917   Comité international de la Croix Rouge (International Committee of the Red Cross)
1916   The prize money was allocated to the Special Fund of this prize section
1915   The prize money was allocated to the Special Fund of this prize section
1914   The prize money was allocated to the Special Fund of this prize section
1913   Henri La Fontaine
1912   Elihu Root
1911   **Tobias Michael Carel Asser** [3,5,6] **Alfred Hermann Fried** [2,3,5,6]
1910   Bureau international permanent de la Paix (Permanent International Peace Bureau)
1909   Auguste M. F. Beernaert, Paul H. B. d'Estournelles de Constant
1908   Klas Pontus Arnoldson, Fredrik Bajer
1907   Ernesto Teodoro Moneta, Louis Renault
1906   Theodore Roosevelt
1905   Baroness Bertha Sophie Felicita von Suttner
1904   Institut de droit international (Institute of International Law)
1903   William Randal Cremer
1902   Élie Ducommun, Charles Albert Gobat 1901 Jean Henri Dunant, Frédéric Passy

Notes: For Laureates identified as Jewish, the superscript numbers after the names indicates the source: 1) is the website www.jewho.com section on Nobels for 2002 and any other pages devoted to Economics and world leaders. 2) is the book "The Nobel Prize" by Burton Feldman. 3) is the www.us-israel.org Web site. 4) is the web site www.yahoodi.com. 5) is the book "Nobel Laureates 1901 – 2000" by Alan Symons. 6) is the Web site www.jinfo.org

Olympics Medals Awarded to Jews

Year	Jews Winning Medals	Adjusted Jewish Total	Total Medals Awarded	Percent Won By Jews	Major Sports In Which Jews Won Medals
1896	10	6.36	125	5.1%	Gymnastics (6), Swimming (4)
1900	7	5.22	254	2.1%	Swimming (2), Track & Field (2)
1904	7	5.17	259	2.0%	Track & Field (3), Lacrosse (2)
1906	6	5.25	236	2.2%	Swimming (3), Track & Field (2)
1908	19	8.71	302	2.9%	Fencing (9), Swimming (3), Rugby & Track & Field (2)
1912	19	6.40	309	2.1%	Fencing (11), Swimming (3), Gymnastics & Track & Field (2)
1920	9	6.39	419	1.5%	Fencing (2), Water Polo (2), Boxing (2), Wresting (2)
1924	15	8.48	421	2.0%	Track & Field (5), Fencing (3), Water Polo & Stadium Design (2)
1928	19	9.56	371	2.6%	Gymnastics (5), Fencing & Track & Field (4), Boxing (2)
1932	25	16.73	388	4.3%	Wrestling (4) Fencing, Swimming & Water Polo (3), Gymnastics & Speed Skating (2)
1936	13	6.10	439	1.4%	Figure Skating & Water Polo (3), Fenciing & Basketball (2)
1948	6	5.17	480	1.1%	Track & Field (2)
1952	26	17.12	526	3.3%	Gymnastics (12), Swimming &Wrestling (3)
1956	23	13.08	540	2.4%	Gymnastics (8), Fencing & Boats (4), Weighlifting (2)
1960	23	14.92	542	2.8%	Boats (7), Fencing, Track & Field (4), Gymnastics (2)
1964	21	12.12	607	2.0%	Track & Field (7), Fencing (5), Volleyball & Judo (2)
1968	22	12.03	632	1.9%	Fencing & Swimming (6), Track & Field, Figure Skating, Boats & Volleyball (2)
1972	21	12.61	707	1.8%	Swimming (9), Fencing (3), Track & Field, Boats, Equestrian (2)
1976	12	5.43	724	0.8%	Volleyball & Basketball (2)
1980	4	3.00	745	0.4%	
1984	10	5.90	805	0.7%	Gymnastics (4), Judo (2)
1988	10	4.78	883	0.5%	Gymnastics (4), Swimming (2)
1992	12	6.42	987	0.7%	Gymnastics (6), Volleyball & Judo (2)
1994/96	7	4.81	964	0.5%	Fencing (3), Gymnastics & Boats (2)
1998/00	14	7.30	1129	0.6%	Swimming (7), Fencing (2)
2002/04	24	14.79	1163	1.3%	Swimming (11), Figure Skating (3), Fencing & Tennis (2)
2006/08	17	7.89	1210	0.7%	Swimming (9), Figure Skating (3), Fencing (2)
Totals	**401**	**231.74**	**16167**	**1.4%**	**Fencing (69), Swimming (63), Gymnastics (54), Track & Field (42)**

The Nobel Prize in Literature – Laureates

2007   Doris Lessing
2006   Orhan Pamuk
2005   **Harold Pinter**[6]
2004   **Elfriede Jelinek**[6]
2003   J. M. Coetzee
2002   **Imre Kertész**[1,3,6]
2001   V.S. Naipaul
2000   Gao Xingjian
1999   Günter Grass
1998   José Saramago
1997   Dario Fo
1996   Wislawa Szymborska
1995   Seamus Heaney
1994   Kenzaburo Oe
1993   Toni Morrison
1992   Derek Walcott
1991   **Nadine Gordimer**[1,2,3,4,5,6]
1990   Octavio Paz 1989 Camilo José Cela
1988   Naguib Mahfouz
1987   **Joseph Brodsky**[1,2,3,4,5,6]
1986   Wole Soyinka
1985   Claude Simon
1984   Jaroslav Seifert
1983   William Golding
1982   Gabriel García Márquez
1981   **Elias Canetti**[1,2,3,4,5,6]
1980   Czeslaw Milosz
1979   Odysseus Elytis
1978   **Isaac Bashevis Singer**[1,2,3,4,5,6]
1977   Vicente Aleixandre
1976   **Saul Bellow**[1,2,3,4,5,6]
1975   Eugenio Montale
1974   Eyvind Johnson, Harry Martinson
1973   Patrick White
1972   Heinrich Böll
1971   Pablo Neruda
1970   Alexander Solzhenitsyn
1969   Samuel Beckett
1968   Yasunari Kawabata
1967   Miguel Angel Asturias
1966   **Samuel (Shmuel) Agnon**[1,2,3,4,5,6] **& Nelly Sachs**[1,2,3,4,5,6]
1965   Michail Sholokhov
1964   Jean-Paul Sartre
1963   Giorgos Seferis
1962   John Steinbeck
1961   Ivo Andric
1960   Saint-John Perse
1959   Salvatore Quasimodo
1958   **Boris Pasternak**[1,2,3,5,6]
1957   Albert Camus
1956   Juan Ramón Jiménez
1955   Halldór Kiljan Laxness
1954   Ernest Hemingway
1953   Winston Churchill
1952   François Mauriac
1951   Pär Lagerkvist
1950   Bertrand Russell
1949   William Faulkner

The Nobel Prize in Literature – Laureates   Exhibit 10a

1948	Thomas Stearns Eliot
1947	André Gide
1946	Hermann Hesse
1945	Gabriela Mistral
1944	Johannes V. Jensen
1943	Prize money was 1/3 allocated to the Main Fund and 2/3 to the Special Fund of this prize section
1942	Prize money was 1/3 allocated to the Main Fund and 2/3 to the Special Fund of this prize section
1941	Prize money was 1/3 allocated to the Main Fund and 2/3 to the Special Fund of this prize section
1940	Prize money was 1/3 allocated to the Main Fund and 2/3 to the Special Fund of this prize section
1939	Frans Eemil Sillanpää
1938	Pearl Buck
1937	Roger Martin du Gard
1936	Eugene O'Neill
1935	Prize money was 1/3 allocated to the Main Fund and 2/3 to the Special Fund of this prize section
1934	Luigi Pirandello
1933	Ivan Bunin
1932	John Galsworthy
1931	Erik Axel Karlfeldt
1930	Sinclair Lewis
1929	Thomas Mann
1928	Sigrid Undset
1927	**Henri Bergson** [1,2,3,4,5,6]
1926	Grazia Deledda
1925	George Bernard Shaw
1924	Wladyslaw Reymont
1923	William Butler Yeats
1922	Jacinto Benavente
1921	Anatole France
1920	Knut Hamsun
1919	Carl Spitteler
1918	The prize money was allocated to the Special Fund of this prize section
1917	Karl Gjellerup, Henrik Pontoppidan
1916	Verner von Heidenstam
1915	Romain Rolland
1914	The prize money was allocated to the Special Fund of this prize section
1913	Rabindranath Tagore
1912	Gerhart Hauptmann
1911	Maurice Maeterlinck
1910	**Paul Heyse** [1,2,3,4,6]
1909	Selma Lagerlöf
1908	Rudolf Eucken
1907	Rudyard Kipling
1906	Giosuè Carducci
1905	Henryk Sienkiewicz
1904	Frédéric Mistral, José Echegaray
1903	Bjørnstjerne Bjørnson
1902	Theodor Mommsen
1901	Sully Prudhomme

Notes: For Jewish Laureates, superscript numbers after the names indicates the source is: 1) the Website www.jewho.com section on Nobels for 2002 and the pages devoted to Authors and Literature. 2) the book "The Nobel Prize" by Burton Feldman. 3) the www.us-israel.org Web site. 4) Web site www.yahoodi.com. 5) the book "Nobel Laureates 1901 – 2000" by Alan Svmons. 6) Web site www.iinfo.org 7) and www.iewishvirtuallibrarv.org.

Pulitzer Prize for Fiction: 1918 – 2008   Exhibit 10b

2008	Junot Diaz	1962	Edwin O'Connor
2007	Cormac McCarthy	1961	Harper Lee
2006	**Geraldine Brooks**	1960	Allen Drury
2005	Marilynne Robinson	1959	Robert Lewis Taylor
2004	Edward P. Jones	1958	James Agee
2003	Jeffrey Eugenides	1957	No Award
2002	Richard Russo	1956	**MacKinlay Kantor**
2001	**Michael Chabon**	1955	William Faulkner
2000	Jhumpa Lahiri	1954	No Award
1999	Michael Cunningham	1953	Ernest Hemmingway
1998	**Philip Roth**	1952	**Herman Wouk**
1997	**Steven Millhauser**	1951	Conrad Richter
1996	Richard Ford	1950	Alfred Bertram Guthrie, Jr.
1995	Carol Shields	1949	James Gould Cozzens
1994	E. Annie Proulx	1948	James A. Michener
1993	Robert Olen Butler	1947	Robert Penn Warren
1992	Jane Smiley	1946	No Award
1991	John Updike	1945	John Hersey
1990	Oscar Hijuelos	1944	Martin Flavin
1989	Anne Tyler	1943	Upton Sinclair
1988	Toni Morrison	1942	Ellen Grasgow
1987	Peter Hillsman Taylor	1941	No Award
1986	Larry McMurtry	1940	John Steinbeck
1985	**Alison Lurie**	1939	Marjorie Kinnan Rawlings
1984	William Kennedy	1938	John Phillips Marquand
1983	Alice Walker	1937	Margaret Mitchell
1982	John Updike	1936	Harold L. Davis
1981	John Kennedy O'Toole	1935	Josephine Winslow Johnson
1980	**Norman Mailer**	1934	Caroline Miller
1979	John Cheever	1933	T.S. Stribling
1978	James Alan McPherson	1932	Pearl S. Buck
1977	No Award	1931	Margaret Ayer Barnes
1976	**Saul Bellow**	1930	Oliver La Farge
1975	Michael Shaara	1929	Julia Peterkin
1974	No Award	1928	Thornton Wilder
1973	Eudora Welty	1927	Louis Bromfield
1972	Wallace Stegner	1926	Sinclair Lewis
1971	No Award	1925	**Edna Ferber**
1970	Jean Stafford	1924	Margaret Wilson
1969	N. Scott Momaday	1923	Willa Cather
1968	William Styron	1922	Booth Tarkington
1967	**Bernard Malamud**	1921	Edith Wharton
1966	Katherine Anne Porter	1920	No Award
1965	Shirley Ann Grau	1919	Booth Tarkington
1964	No Award	1918	Ernest Poole
1963	William Faulkner		

Pulitzer Prize for Nonfiction: 1962 – 2008   Exhibit 10c

2008   **Saul Friedlander, The Years of Extermination: Nazi Germany and the Jews 1939-1945**
2007   Lawrence Wright, The Looming Tower: Al-Qaeda and the Road to 9/11
2006   Caroline Elkins, Imperial Reckoning: The Untold Story of Britain's Gulag in Kenya
2005   Steve Coll, Ghost Wars: The Secret History of the CIA, Afghanistan, and Bin Laden From the Soviet
        Invasion to September 10, 2001
2004   **Anne Applebaum, Gulag, A History**
2003   Samantha Power, A Problem From Hell: America and the Age of Genocide
2002   Diane McWhorter, Carry Me Home: Birmingham, Alabama, the Climactic Battle of the Civil Rights Revolution
2001   **Herbert P. Bix, Hirohito and the Making of Modern Japan**
2000   John W. Dower, Embracing Defeat: Japan in the Wake of World War II
1999   John McPhee, Annals of the Former World
1998   **Jared Diamond, Guns, Germs and Steel: The Fates of Human Societies**
1997   **Richard Kluger, Ashes to Ashes: America's Hundred-Year Cigarette War, the Public Health, and the
        Unabashed Triumph of Philip Morris**
1996   **Tina Rosenberg, The Haunted Land: Facing Europe's Ghosts After Communism**
1995   **Jonathan Weiner, The Beak of the Finch: A Story of Evolution in Our Time**
1994   **David Remnick, Lenin's Tomb: The Last Days of the Soviet Empire**
1993   Garry Willis, Lincoln at Gettysburg: The Words That Remade America
1992   **Daniel Yergin, The Prize: The Epic Quest for Oil, Money and Power**
1991   Edward O. Wilson, The Ants
1990   Michael Williamson, And Their Children After Them
1989   Neil Sheehan, A Bright Shining Lie, John Paul Vann and America in Vietnam
1988   Richard Rhodes, The Making of the Atomic Bomb
1987   David K. Shipler, Arab and Jew: Wounded Spirits in a Promised Land
1986   **Joseph Lelyveld, Move Your Shadow: South Africa, Black and White**
1986   **J. Anthony Lukas, Common Ground: A Turbulent Decade in the Lives of Three American Families**
1985   **Studs Terkel, The Good War: An Oral History of World War Two**
1984   **Paul Starr, The Social Transformation of American Medicine**
1983   **Susan Margulies Sheehan, Is There No Place on Earth for Me?**
1982   Tracy Kidder, The Soul of a New Machine
1981   **Carl E. Schorske, Fin-De-Siecle Vienna: Politics And Cure**
1980   **Douglas R. Hofstadter, Godel, Escher, Bach: An Eternal Golden Braid**
1979   Edward O. Wilson, On Human Nature
1978   **Carl Sagan, The Dragons of Eden**
1977   William W. Warner, Beautiful Swimmers
1976   Robert N. Butler, Why Survive? Being Old In America
1975   Annie Dillard, Pilgrim at Tinker Creek
1974   **Ernest Becker, The Denial of Death**
1973   **Robert Coles, Children of Crisis, Volumes II and III**
1973   Frances Fitzgerald, Fire in the Lake: The Vietnamese and the Americans in Vietnam
1972   **Barbara W. Tuchman, Stilwell and the American Experience in China, 1911-1945**
1971   John Toland, The Rising Sun
1970   **Erik H. Erikson, Gandhi's Truth**
1969   **Norman Mailer, The Armies of the Night**
1969   Rene Jules Dubos, So Human An Animal
1968   Will & **Ariel Durant, Rosseau And Revolution (The Story of Civilization: Voume 10)**
1967   **David Brion Davis, The Problem of Slavery in Western Culture**
1966   Edwin Way Teale, Wanding Through Winter
1965   Howard Mumford Jones, O Strange New World
1964   **Richard Hofstadter, Anti-Intellectualism in American Life**
1963   **Barbara W. Tuchman, The Guns of August**
1962   **Theodore H. White, The Making of the President, 1960**

Pulitzer Prizes for Drama: 1917 – 2008   Exhibit 10d

1917 (No Award)
1918 *Why Marry?* by Jesse Lynch Williams
1919 (No Award)
1920 *Beyond the Horizon* by Eugene O'Neill
1921 *Miss Lulu Bett* by Zona Gale
1922 *Anna Christie* by Eugene O'Neill
1923 *Icebound* by Owen Davis
1924 *Hell-Bent Fer Heaven* by Hatcher Hughes
1925 *They Knew What They Wanted* by Sidney Howard
1926 *Craig's Wife* by George Kelly
1927 *In Abraham's Bosom* by Paul Green
1928 *Strange Interlude* by Eugene O'Neill
1929 **Street Scene by Elmer L. Rice**
1930 *The Green Pastures* by Marc Connelly
1931 *Alison's House* by Susan Glaspell
1932 **Of Thee I Sing by George S. Kaufman, Morrie Ryskind and Ira Gershwin**
1933 *Both Your Houses* by Maxwell Anderson
1934 **Men in White by Sidney Kingsley**
1935 *The Old Maid* by Zoe Akins
1936 *Idiots Delight* by Robert E. Sherwood
1937 **You Can't Take It With You by Moss Hart and George S. Kaufman**
1938 *Our Town* by Thornton Wilder
1939 *Abe Lincoln in Illinois* by Robert E. Sherwood
1940 *The Time of Your Life* by William Saroyan
1941 *There Shall Be No Night* by Robert E. Sherwood
1942 (No Award)
1943 *The Skin of Our Teeth* by Thornton Wilder
1944 (No Award)
1945 *Harvey* by Mary Chase
1946 *State of the Union* by Russel Crouse and Howard Lindsay
1947 (No Award)
1948 *A Streetcar Named Desire* by Tennessee Williams
1949 **Death of a Salesman by Arthur Miller**
1950 **South Pacific by Richard Rodgers, Oscar Hammerstein**, and Joshua Logan
1951 (No Award)
1952 **The Shrike by Joseph Kramm**
1953 *Picnic* by William Inge
1954 *The Teahouse of the August Moon* by John Patrick
1955 *Cat on A Hot Tin Roof* by Tennessee Williams
1956 *Diary of Anne Frank* by Albert Hackett and Frances Goodrich
1957 *Long Day's Journey Into Night* by Eugene O'Neill
1958 *Look Homeward, Angel* by Ketti Frings
1959 *J. B.* by Archibald Macleish
1960 **Fiorello! by Book by Jerome Weidman** and George Abbott, **Music by Jerry Bock and Lyrics by Sheldon Harnick**
1961 *All The Way Home* by Tad Mosel
1962 **How To Succeed In Business Without Really Trying by Frank Loesser and Abe Burrows**

1963 (No Award)
1964 (No Award)
1965 *The Subject Was Roses* by Frank D. Gilroy
1966 (No Award)
1967 *A Delicate Balance* by Edward Albee
1968 (No Award)
1969 **The Great White Hope by Howard Sackler**
1970 *No Place To Be Somebody* by Charles Gordone
1971 **The Effect of Gamma Rays on Man-In-The-Moon Marigolds by Paul Zindel**
1972 (No Award)
1973 *That Championship Season* by Jason Miller
1974 (No Award)
1975 *Seascape* by Edward Albee
1976 **A Chorus Line by Michael Bennett**, book by James Kirkwood & Nicholas Dante, **music by Marvin Hamlisch, lyrics by Edward Kleban**
1977 *The Shadow Box* by Michael Cristofer
1978 *The Gin Game* by Donald L. Coburn
1979 *Buried Child* by Sam Shepard
1980 *Talley's Folly* by Lanford Wilson
1981 *Crimes of the Heart* by Beth Henley
1982 *A Soldier's Play* by Charles Fuller
1983 *'Night, Mother* by Marsha Norman
1984 **Glengarry Glen Ross by David Mamet**
1985 **Sunday in the Park With George by Music and lyrics by Stephen Sondheim**, book by **James Lapine**
1986 (No Award)
1987 *Fences* by August Wilson
1988 **Driving Miss Daisy by Alfred Uhry**
1989 **The Heidi Chronicles by Wendy Wasserstein**
1990 *The Piano Lesson* by August Wilson
1991 **Lost in Yonkers by Neil Simon**
1992 *The Kentucky Cycle* by Robert Schenkkan
1993 **Angels in America: Millennium Approaches by Tony Kushner**
1994 *Three Tall Women* by Edward Albee
1995 *The Young Man From Atlanta* by Horton Foote
1996 **Rent by the late Jonathan Larson**
1997 (No Award)
1998 **How I Learned to Drive by Paula Vogel**
1999 *Wit* by Margaret Edson
2000 **Dinner With Friends by Donald Margulies**
2001 **Proof by David Auburn**
2002 *Topdog/Underdog* by Suzan-Lori Parks
2003 *Anna in the Tropics* by Nilo Cruz
2004 *I Am My Own Wife* by Doug Wright
2005 *Doubt, a parable* by John Patrick Shanley
2006 (No Award)
2007 *Rabbit Hole* by David Lindsay-Abaire
2008 *August: Osage County* by Tracy Letts

Tony Awards Author/Play: 1947 – 2008

Year	Author	Play
1947	**Arthur Miller**	**All My Sons**
1948	Thomas Heggen & Joshua Logan	Mr. Roberts
1949	**Arthur Miller**	**Death of a Salesman**
1950	T.S. Eliot	The Cocktail Party
1951	Tennessee Williams	The Rose Tattoo
1952	Jan de Hartog	The Fourposter
1953	**Arthur Miller**	**The Crucible**
1954	John Patrick	The Teahouse of the August Moon
1955	Joseph Hayes	The Desperate Hours
1956	Francis Goodrich & Albert Hackett	The Diary of **Anne Frank**
1957	Eugene O'Neill	Long Days Journey Into Night
1958	**Dory Schary**	**Sunrise At Campobello**
1959	Archibald MacLeish	J.B.
1960	William Gibson	The Miracle Worker
1961	Jean Anouilh	Beckett
1962	Robert Bolt	A Man for All Seasons
1963	Edward Albee	Who's Afraid of Virginia Wolf
1964	John Osborne	Luther
1965	**Neil Simon**	**The Odd Couple**
1966	**Peter Weiss**	**Marat/Sade**
1967	**Harold Pinter**	**The Homecoming**
1968	**Tom Stoppard**	**Rosencrantz and Guildenstern Are Dead**
1969	**Howard Sackler**	**The Great White Hope**
1970	Frank McMahon	Borstal Boy
1971	**Anthony Shaffer**	**Sleuth**
1972	David Rabe	Sticks and Bones
1973	Jason Miller	That Championship Season
1974	Joseph A. Walker	The River Niger
1975	**Peter Shaffer**	**Equus**
1976	**Tom Stoppard**	**Travesties**
1977	Michael Cristofer	The Shadow Box
1978	Hugh Leonard	Da
1979	**Bernard Pomerance**	**The Elephant Man**
1980	**Mark Medoff**	**Children of a Lesser God**
1981	**Peter Shaffer**	**Amadeus**
1982	David Edgar	The Life and Adventures of Nicholas Nickleby
1983	**Harvey Fierstein**	**Angels Fall**
1984	**Tom Stoppard**	**The Real Thing**
1985	**Neil Simon**	**Biloxi Blues**
1986	**Herb Gardner**	**I'm Not Rappaport**
1987	August Wilson	Fences
1988	David Henry Hwang	M. Butterfly
1989	**Wendy Wasserstein**	**The Heidi Chronicles**
1990	Frank Galati	The Grapes of Wrath
1991	**Neil Simon**	**Lost in Yonkers**
1992	Brian Friel	Dancing at Lughnasa
1993	**Tony Kushner**	**Angels in America: Millennium Approaches**
1994	**Tony Kushner**	**Angels in America: Perestroika**
1995	Terrence McNally	Love! Valour! Compassion!
1996	Terrence McNally	Master Class
1997	**Alfred Uhry**	**The Last Night of Ballyhoo**
1998	**Yasmina Reza**	**Art**
1999	Warren Leight	Side Man
2000	Michael Frayn	Copenhagen
2001	**David Auburn**	**Proof**
2002	Edward Albee	The Goat or Who Is Sylvia
2003	**Richard Greenberg**	**Take Me Out**
2004	Doug Wright	I Am My Own Wife

Tony Awards Author/Play: 1947 – 2008

2005	John Patrick Shanley	Doubt: A Parable
2006	Alan Bennett	The History Boys
2007	**Tom Stoppard**	**The Coast of Utopia**
2008	Tracy Letts	August: Orange County

Pulitzer Prize for Poetry: 1919 – 2008

Exhibit 10f

2008	Robert Hass & **Philip Schultz**	1962	Alan Dugan
2007	Natasha Trethewey	1961	Phyllis McGinley
2006	Claudia Emerson	1960	William Snodgrass
2005	Ted Kooser	1959	**Stanley Kunitz**
2004	Franz Wright	1958	Robert Penn Warren
2003	Paul Muldoon	1957	Richard Wilbur
2002	**Carl Dennis**	1956	Elizabeth Bishop
2001	Stephen Dunn	1955	Wallace Stevens
2000	**C. K. Williams**	1954	Theodore Roethke
1999	**Mark Strand**	1953	Archibald MacLeish
1998	Charles Wright	1952	Marianne Moore
1997	**Lise Mueller**	1951	Carl Sandburg
1996	**Jorie Graham**	1950	Gwendolyn Brooks
1995	**Philip Levine**	1949	Peter Viereck
1994	Yusef Komunyakaa	1948	W.H. Auden
1993	**Louise Gluck**	1947	Robert Lowell
1992	James Tata	1946	**Karl Shapiro**
1991	Mona Van Duyn	1945	No Award
1990	Charles Simic	1944	Stephen Vincent Benet
1989	Richard Wilbur	1943	Robert Frost
1988	William Meredith	1942	WilliamRose Benet
1987	Rita Dove	1941	Leonard Bacon
1986	Henry Taylor	1940	Mark Van Doren
1985	Carolyn Kizer	1939	John Gould Fletcher
1984	Mary Oliver	1938	**Marya Zaturenska**
1983	Galway Kinnell	1937	Robert Frost
1982	Sylvia Plath	1936	Robert P.T. Coffin
1981	James Schuyler	1935	Audrey Wurdemann
1980	Donald Rodney Justice	1934	Robert Hillyer
1979	Robert Penn Warren	1933	Archibald MacLeish
1978	**Howard Nemerov**	1932	George Dillon
1977	James Merril	1931	Robert Frost
1976	John Asbery	1930	Conrad Aiken
1975	Gary Snyder	1929	Stephen Vincent Benet
1974	Robert Lowell	1928	Edwin Arlington Robinson
1973	**Maxine Winokur Kumin**	1927	Leonara Speyer
1972	James Wright	1926	Amy Lowell
1971	William S. Merwin	1925	Edwin Arlington Robinson
1970	**Richard Howard**	1924	Robert Frost
1969	**George Oppen**	1923	Edna St. Vincent Millay
1968	**Anthony Hecht**	1922	Edwin Arlington Robinson
1967	Anne Sexton	1921	No Award
1966	Richard Eberhart	1920	No Award
1965	John Berryman	1919	Magaret Widdemer
1964	**Louis Simpson**	1919	Carl Sandburg
1963	William Carlos Williams		

Kennedy Center Honorees

2007
Leon Fleisher
Steve Martin
Diana Ross
Martin Scorsese
Brian Wilson

2006
Zubin Mehta
Dolly Parton
Smokey Robinson
Steven Spielberg
Andrew Lloyd Webber

2005
Tony Bennett
Suzanne Farrell
Julie Harris
Robert Redford
Tina Turner

2004
Warren Beatty
Sir Elton John
Ossie Davis
Ruby Dee
Dame Joan Sutherland
John Williams

2003
James Brown
Carol Burnett
Loretta Lynn
Mike Nichols
Itzhak Perlman

2002
James Earl Jones
James Levine
Chita Rivera
Paul Simon
Elizabeth Taylor

2001
Julie Andrews
Van Cliburn
Quincy Jones
Jack Nicholson
Luciano Pavarotti

2000
Mikhail Baryshnikov
Chuck Berry
Plácido Domingo
Clint Eastwood
Angela Lansbury

1999
Victor Borge
Sean Connery
Judith Jamison
Jason Robards
Stevie Wonder

1998
Bill Cosby
Fred Ebb & John Kander
Willie Nelson
André Previn
Shirley Temple Black

1997
Lauren Bacall
Bob Dylan
Charlton Heston
Jessye Norman
Edward Villella

1996
Edward Albee
Benny Carter
Johnny Cash
Jack Lemmon
Maria Tallchief

1995
Jacques d'Amboise
Marilyn Horne
Riley B.B. King
Sidney Poitier
Neil Simon

1994
Kirk Douglas
Aretha Franklin
Morton Gould
Harold Prince
Pete Seeger

1993
Johnny Carson
Arthur Mitchell
George Solti
Stephen Sondheim
Marion Williams

1992
Lionel Hampton
Paul Newman
Joanne Woodward
Ginger Rogers
Mstislav Rostropovich
Paul Taylor

1991
Roy Acuff
Betty Comden
Adolph Green
Fayard Nicholas
Harold Nicholas
Gregory Peck
Robert Shaw

1990
Dizzy Gillespie
Katharine Hepburn
Rise Stevens
Jule Styne
Billy Wilder

1989
Harry Belafonte
Claudette Colbert
Alexandra Danilova
Mary Martin
William Schuman

1988
Alvin Ailey
George Burns
Myrna Loy
Alexander Schneider
Roger L. Stevens

1987
Perry Como
Bette Davis
Sammy Davis, Jr.
Nathan Milstein
Alwin Nikolais

1986
Lucille Ball
Ray Charles
Hume Cronyn
Jessica Tandy
Yehudi Menuhin
Antony Tudor

1985
Merce Cunningham
Irene Dunne
Bob Hope
Alan Jay Lerner
Frederick Loewe
Beverly Sills

1984
Lena Horne
Danny Kaye
Gian Carlo Menotti
Arthur Miller
Isaac Stern

1983
Katherine Dunham
Elia Kazan
Frank Sinatra
James Stewart
Virgil Thomson

1982
George Abbott
Lillian Gish
Benny Goodman
Gene Kelly
Eugene Ormandy

1981
Count Basie
Cary Grant
Helen Hayes
Jerome Robbins
Rudolf Serkin

1980
Leonard Bernstein
James Cagney
Agnes deMille
Lynn Fontanne
Leontyne Price

1979
Aaron Copland
Ella Fitzgerald
Henry Fonda
Martha Graham
Tennessee Williams

1978
Marian Anderson
Fred Astaire
George Balanchine
Richard Rodgers
Arthur Rubenstein

Conductors of Major American Orchestras   Exhibit 11b

Atlanta Symphony Orchestra (founded 1945)
Henry Sopkin (1945-1966)
Robert Shaw (1967-88)
Yoel Levi (1988-2000)
Robert Spano (2001-present)

Baltimore Symphony Orchestra (founded 1916)
Gustav Strube (1917-1930)
George Siemonn (1930 – 1935)
Ernest Schelling (1935-1937)
Werner Janssen (1937–1939)
Howard Barlow (1939-1942)
Reginald Stewart (1942-1952)
Massimo Freccia (1952-1959)
Peter Herman Adler (1959-1968)
Sergiu Comissiona (1968-1984)
David Zinman (1985-1998)
Yuri Temirkanov (1999-present)

Boston Symphony Orchestra (founded 1881)
Sir George Henschel (1881-84)
Wilhelm Gericke (1884-89)
Artur Nikisch (1889-93)
Emil Paur (1893-98)
Wilhelm Gericke (1898-1906)
Karl Muck (1906-08)
Max Fiedler (1908-12)
Karl Muck (1912-18)
Henri Rabaud (1918-19)
Pierre Monteux (1919-24)
Serge Koussevitzky (1924-49)
Charles Munch (1949-62)
Erich Leinsdorf (1962-69)
William Steinberg (1969-72)
Seiji Ozawa (1973-present)
James Levine (beginning 2002)

Buffalo Philharmonic (founded 1936)
Franco Autori (1936-45)
William Steinberg (1945-63)
Josef Krips (1953-63)
Lukas Foss (1963-70)
Michael Tilson Thomas (1971-78)
Julius Rudel (1979-84)
Semyon Bychkov (1984-89)
Maximiano Valdes (1989-98)
JoAnn Falletta (1998-present)

Chicago Symphony Orchestra (founded 1891)
Theodore Thomas (1891-1905)
Frederick Stock (1905-1942)
Désiré Defauw (1943-1947)
Artur Rodzinski (1947-1948)
Rafael Kubelík (1950-1953)
Fritz Reiner (1953-1962), Musical Advisor 1962-1963
Jean Martinon (1963-1968)
Irwin Hoffman (1968-1969, Acting)
Sir Georg Solti (1969-1991, Music Dir.Laureate 1991-1997)
Daniel Barenboim (1991-present)

Cincinatti Symphony (founded 1895)
Frank Van der Stucken (1895-1907)
Leopold Stokowski (1909-12)
Ernst Kunwald (1912-18)
Eugène Ysaÿe (1918-22)
Fritz Reiner (1922-31)
Eugene Goossens (1931-47)
Thor Johnson (1947-58)

Los Angeles Philharmonic (founded 1919)
Walter Henry Rothwell (1919-27)
Georg Schnéevoigt (1927 -1929)
Artur Rodzinski (1929 -1933)
Otto Klemperer (1933 -1939)
Alfred Wallenstein (1943 -1956)
Eduard van Beinum (1956 -1959)
Zubin Mehta (1962 -1978)
Carlo Maria Giulini (1978 -1984)
André Previn (1985 -1989)
Esa-Pekka Salonen (1992 -present)

Minnesota Orchestra (founded 1903)
Emil Oberhoffer (1903-1922)
Henri Verbrugghen (1923-1931)
Eugene Ormandy (1931-1936)
Dimitri Mitropoulos (1937-1949)
Antal Dorati (1949-1960)
Stanislaw Skrowaczewski (1960-1979)
Sir Neville Marriner (1979-1986)
Edo de Waart (1986-1995)
Eiji Oue (1995-present)

National Symphony Orchestra (founded 1931)
Hans Kindler (1931-49)
Howard Mitchell (1950-69)
Antal Dorati (1970-76)
Mstislav Rostropovich (1977-94)
Leonard Slatkin (1996-present)

New York Philharmonic (founded 1842)
Ureli Corelli Hill (1842-1847)
Theodore Eisfeld (1848-1865)
Carl Bergmann (1855-1876)
Leopold Damrosch (1876-1877)
Theodore Thomas (1877-1891)
Anton Seidl (1891-1898)
Emil Paur (1898-1902)
Walter Damrosch (1902-1903)
Wassily Safonoff (1906-1909)
Gustav Mahler (1909-1911)
Josef Stransky (1911-1923)
Willem Mengelberg (1922-1930)
Arturo Toscanini (1928-1936)
John Barbirolli (1936-1941)
Artur Rodzinski (1943-1947)
Bruno Walter (1947-1949)
Leopold Stokowski (1949-1950)
Dimitri Mitropoulos (1949-1958)
Leonard Bernstein (1958-1969)

Conductors of Major American Orchestras   Exhibit 11b

New York Philharmonic (continued)
George Szell (1969-1970)
Pierre Boulez (1971-1977)
Zubin Mehta (1978-1991)
Kurt Masur (1991-present)
Lorin Maazel (beginning 2002)

Philadelphia Orchestra (founded 1900)
Fritz Scheel (1900-07)
Carl Pohlig (1907-12)
Leopold Stokowski, (1912-38)
Eugene Ormandy (1936-1980)
Riccardo Muti (1980-1992)
Wolfgang Sawallisch (1993-present)
Christoph Eschenbach (beginning 2002)

Pittsburgh Symphony Orchestra (founded 1895)
Frederic Asker (1895-98)
Victor Herbert (1898-1904)
Max Rudolf (1958-70)
Thomas Schippers (1970-77)
Walter Susskind (1978-80)
Michael Gielen (1980-86)
Jesus Lopez-Cobos (1986-2001)
Paavo Jarvi (beginning 2001-present)

Cleveland Orchestra (founded 1918)
Nikolai Sokoloff (1918-33)
Artur Rodzinski (1933-43)
Erich Leinsdorf (1943-46)
Georg Szell (1946-70)
Lorin Maazel (1972-80)
Christoph von Dohnányi (1981-present)
Franz Welser-Most (beginning 2002)

Dallas Symphony Orchestra (founded 1900)
Hans Kreissig (1900-05)
Walter J. Fried, Carl Venth, Paul Van Katwijk
and Jacques Singer
Antal Dorati (1945-49)
Walter Hendl (1949-58)
Paul Kletzki (1958-61)
Donald Johanos, Anshel Brusilow, **Max Rudolf**
and Louis Lane Eduardo Mata (1977-93)
Andrew Litton (1994-present)

Detroit Symphony Orchestra (founded 1914)
Weston Gales (1914-17)
Ossip Gabrilowitsch (1918-36)
Franco Ghione (1936-40)
Victor Kolar (1940-42)
Karl Krueger (1944-49)
(Orch. disbanded 1949-51)
Paul Paray (1951-62)
Sixten Ehrling (1963-73)
Aldo Ceccato (1973-77)
Antal Dorati (1977-81)
Gunther Herbig (1984-90)
Neeme Jarvi (1990-present)

Houston Symphony Orchestra (founded 1913)
Julian Paul Blitz (1913-16)
Paul Berge (1916-17)
Orch. reorganized 1930.
Frank St Leger (1931-35)
Ernst Hoffman (1936-47)
Efrem Kurtz (1948-54)
Ferenc Fricsay (1954)
Leopold Stokowski (1955-61)
Sir John Barbirolli (1961-67)
Andre Previn (1967-69)
Lawrence Foster (1971-78)
Sergiu Comissiona (1979-88)
Christoph Eschenbach (1988-99, Conductor Laureate)
Hans Graf (2002-present)
Emil Paur (1904-10)
Disbanded 1910, reorganized 1926
Antonio Modarelli (1930-37)
Otto Klemperer (1937)
Fritz Reiner (1938-48)
William Steinberg (1952-76)
Andre Previn (1976-1984)
Lorin Maazel (1984-96)
Mariss Jansons (1996-present)

Rochester Philharmonic (founded 1922)
Eugene Goossens (1923-31)
Coates
Jose Iturbi (1935-44)
Erich Leinsdorf (1947-56)
Theodore Bloomfield (1959-63)
Laszlo Somogyi
David Zinman (1977-85)
Jerzy Semkow (1985-89)
Christopher Seaman (1998 -present)

Saint Louis Symphony Orchestra (founded 1880)
Joseph Otten (1880 – 1894)
Alfred Ernst (1894 – 1907)
Max Zach (1907 – 1921)
Rudolph Ganz (1921 – 1927)
Vladimir Golschmann (1931 – 1958)
Edouard van Remoortel (1958 – 1962)
Elazar de Carvalho (1963 – 1968)
Walter Susskind (1968 – 1975)
Jerzy Semkow (1975 – 1979)
Leonard Slatkin (1979 – 1995)
Hans Vonk (1996 –present)

San Francisco Symphony (founded 1911)
Henry Hadley (1911-15)
Alfred Hertz (1915-29)
Basil Cameron and **Issay Dobrowen** (1929-31)
Pierre Monteux (1935-52)
Enrique Jorda (1954-63)
Josef Krips (1963-70)
Seiji Ozawa (1970-76)
Herbert Blomstedt (1985-95, Conductor Laureate)
Michael Tilson Thomas (1995-present)

Conductors of Major American Orchestras   Exhibit 11b

London Symphony Orchestra
Hans Richter (1904-11)
Sir Edward Elgar (1911-12)
Artur Nikish (1921-14)
Sir Thomas Beecham (1915-17)
Albert Coates (1919-22)
Willem Mengelberg (1930-31)
Sir Hamilton Harty (1932-35)
Josef Krips (1951-54)
Pierre Monteux (1960-64)
Istvan Kertesz (1965-68)
André Previn (1968-79)
Claudio Abbado (1979-87)
Michael Tilson Thomas (1987-95)
Sir Colin Davis (1995-present)

This list was compiled by the University at Albany, part of the State Univeristy of New York and is available at its web site. Jews were identified using a list of Jewish conductors from the "jinfo.org" web site as well as information from "iewhoo.com".

American Symphony Orchestra League: 2001 – 2002 Season   Exhibit 11c
Orchestra Repertoire Report

A: Composers With Most Works Scheduled (3432 performances of 1737 compositions by 475 composers)

	Composer	Performances
1	Beethoven, Ludwig Van	566
2	Mozart, Wofgang Amadeus	540
3	Brahms, Johannes	394
4	Tchaikovsky, Piotr Ilyich	321
5	Strauss, Richard	262
6	**Mahler, Gustav**	227
7	Ravel Maurice	204
8	Haydn, Franz Joseph	203
9	Shostakovich, Dmitri	187
10	Prokofiev, Sergei	183

B: Most Frequently Performed U.S. & Canadian Composers

	Composer	Performances
1	Barber, Samuel	133
2	**Bernstein, Leonard**	101
3	**Copland, Aaron**	66
4	Adams, John	52
5	**Gershwin, George**	47
6	Hindemith, Paul	43
7	Rouse, Christopher	42
8	Schwantner, Joseph	33
9	Ives, Charles	29
10	Corigliano, John & Kernis, Aaron Jay	26

Source: "Symphony.org" web site 3/4/03

The World's 50 Greatest Composers CD Collection   Exhibit 11d

1	Giovanni da Palestrina	26	Camile Saint-Saens
2	Claudio Monteverdi	27	Georges Bizet
3	Henry Purcell	28	Modest Mussorgsy
4	Antonio Vivaldi	29	Peter Tchaikovsky
5	Jean-Philipe Rameau	30	Antonin Dvorak
6	Johann Sebastian Bach	31	Edvard Grieg
7	George Frideric Handel	32	Nikolay Rimsky-Korsakov
8	Christoph Gluck	33	Gabriel Faure
9	Franz Joseph Haydn	34	Giacomo Puccini
10	Wolfgang Amadeus Mozart	35	**Gustav Mahler**
11	Ludwig van Beethoven	36	Richard Strauss
12	Franz Schubert	37	Leos Janacek
13	Karl Maria von Weber	38	Claude Debussy
14	Gioacchino Rossini	39	Jean Sibelius
15	Gaetano Donizetti	40	Ralph Vaughan Williams
16	Hector Berilioz	41	Sergei Rachmaninoff
17	**Felix Mendelssohn**	42	**Arnold Schoenberg**
18	Frederic Chopin	43	Maurice Ravel
19	Robert Schumann	44	Manuel de Falla
20	Franz Liszt	45	Bela Bartok
21	Richard Wagner	46	Igor Stravinsky
22	Giuseppe Verdi	47	Sergei Prokofiev
23	Cesar Franck	48	**George Gershwin**
24	Johann Strauss	49	**Aaron Copland**
25	Johanes Brahms	50	Dmitrie Shostakovich

On fifty 60-minute compact disks that detail the lives, times and music of history's greatest composers. Each CD consists of a detailed biography of a master composer, selections of his music, and a discussion of each of his featured works - its form, style and contribution to the development and evolution of classical music. Over 300 musical selections are included in the collection.

This collection is designed to provide a clear understanding of classical music - its history, development and evolutions - through the lives, times, and music of selected composers listed below.

50 Longest Running Broadway Shows   Exhibt 11e

Rank / Broadway Show	Musical	Performances	Writers - Words (w) and Music (m)
1 Cats	X	7,485	T.S. Eliot (w) Andrew Lloyd Weber (m)
2 **Les Miserables**	X	6,680	**Alain Boublil/Herbert Kretzmer (w) & Claude-Michel Schonberg (m)**
3 The Phantom of the Opera	X	6,485	Charles Hart (w) Andrew Lloyd Weber (m)
4 **A Chorus Line**	X	6,137	**Edward Kleban (w) and Marvin Hamlisch (m)**
5 Oh Calcutta (1976 Revival)	X	5,959	Robert Dennis, Peter Schickele & Stanley Walden (w & m)
6 **Miss Saigon**	X	4,092	**Alain Boublil (w) & Claude-Michel Schonberg (m)**
7 **Beauty and the Beast**	X	3,812	**Howard Ashman (w) and Alan Menken (m)**
8 **42nd Street**	X	3,486	**Al Dubin (w)** Harry Warren (m) Warren is not Jewish
9 Grease	X	3,388	Jim Jacobs and Warren Casey (w & m)
10 **Fiddler on the Roof**	X	3,242	**Sheldon Harnick (w) and Jerry Bock (m)**
11 Life With Father		3,224	Howard Lindsey, Russel Crouse & Clarence Day (playwrites)
12 Tobacco Road		3,182	Jack Kirkland (playwrite) based on Erskine Caldwell nov
13 **Rent**	X	3,040	**Jonathan Larson (w & m)**
14 **Hello Dolly**	X	2,844	**Jerry Herman (w & m)**
15 **Chicago**	X	2,811	**Fred Ebb (w) and John Kander (m)**
16 **My Fair Lady**	X	2,717	**Alan Jay Lerner (w) and Frederick Loewe (m)**
17 The Lion King	X	2,403	Tim Rice (w), Elton John (m) and others
18 **Annie**	X	2,377	**Martin Charnin (w) and Charles Strouse (m)**
19 **Man of La Mancha**	X	2,328	**Joe Darion (w) and Mitch Leigh (m)**
20 Abbie's Irish Rose		2,327	Anne Nichols (playwrite)
21 **Cabaret (1998 Revival)**	X	2,217	**Fred Ebb (w) and John Kander (m)**
22 **Oklahoma**	X	2,212	**Richard Rogers(m) & Oscar Hammerstin, II (w)**
23 **Smokey Joe's Café**	X	2,037	**Jerry Leiber and Mike Stoller (w & m)**
24 **Pippin**	X	1,944	**Stephen Schwartz (w & m)**
25 **South Pacific**	X	1,925	**Richard Rogers(m) & Oscar Hammerstin, II (w)**
26 **The Magic Show**	X	1,920	**Stephen Schwartz (w & m)**
27 Gemini		1,819	Albert Innaurato (playwrite)
28 **Deathtrap**		1,793	**Ira Levin (playwrite)**
29 Harvey		1,775	Mary Chase (playwrite)
30 Dancin	X	1,774	Various songwriters including Neil Diamond and other
31 **La Cage aux Folles**	X	1,761	**Jerry Herman (w & m)**
32 Hair	X	1,750	Gerome Ragni & James Rado (w) and Galt MacDermot (
33 The Wiz	X	1,672	Charlie Smalls (w & m)
34 Born Yesterday		1,642	Garson Kanin (playwrite)
35 **Crazy for You**	X	1,638	**Ira Gershwin (w) and George Gershwin (m)**
36 The Best Little Whorehouse in Texas	X	1,584	Carol Hal (w & m)
37 Mary, Mary		1,572	Jean Kerr (playwrite)
38 Evita	X	1,567	Tim Rice (w) and Andrew Lloyd Weber (m)
39 Ain't Misbehavin'	X	1,565	Mostly Fats Waller plus others
40 The Voice of the Turtle		1,557	John Van Druten (playwrite)
41 **Jekyll & Hyde**	X	1,543	**Leslie Bricusse (w?) and Frank Wildhorn (m)**
42 **Barefoot in the Park**		1,530	**Neil Simon (playwrite)**
43 Dreamgirls	X	1,521	Tom Eyen (w) and Henry Krieger (m)
44 **Mame**	X	1,508	**Jerry Herman (w & m)**
45 Grease (1994 Revival)	X	1,505	Jim Jacobs and Warren Casey (w & m)
46 **Same Time, Next Year**		1,453	**Neil Simon (playwrite)**
47 Arsenic and Old Lace		1,444	Joseph Kesselring (playwrite)
48 **The Sound of Music**	X	1,443	**Richard Rogers(m) & Oscar Hammerstin, II (w)**
49 Me and My Girl	X	1,420	L. Arthur Rose & Douglas Furber (w) and Noel Gay (m
50 **How to Succeed in Business Without Really Trying**	X	1,417	**Frank Loesser (w & m)**

Sources: Geocities and The League of American Theatres and Producers August 20, 2003 and
www.iinfo.org/musicals.html. 8/20/03

Chicago Critic.com's (Tom Williams) List of: Exhibit 11f
"The 25 Broadway Musicals Everyone Should See"

Musical	Words and Music By
1	My Fair Lady	Alan Jay Lerner and Fredrick Loewe
2	Les Miserables	Alain Boublil, Claude-Michel Schonberg and Herbert Kretzmer
3	Show Boat	Jerome Kern & Oscar Hammerstein, II
4	Gypsy	Jule Styne & Stephen Sondheim
5	Oklahoma	Richard Rogers and Oscar Hammerstein, II
6	Crazy for You	George and Ira Gershwin
7	The Sound of Music	Richard Rogers and Oscar Hammerstein, II
8	Carousel	Richard Rogers and Oscar Hammerstein, II
9	The Fantastiks	Harvey Schmidt and Tom Jones
10	Hello Dolly	Jerry Herman
11	A Chorus Line	Marvin Hamlish and Edward Kleban
12	Anything Goes	Cole Porter
13	The Producers	Mel Brooks
14	42nd Street	Harry Warren (not Jewish) and Al Dubin
15	Company	Stephen Sondheim and George Furth
16	The Secret Garden	Lucy Simon and Marsha Norman
17	Fiddler on the Roof	Jerry Bock, Sheldon Harnick and Joseph Stein
18	West Side Story	Leonard Bernstein and Stephen Sondheim
19	Annie Get Your Gun	Irving Berlin
20	A Little Night Music	Stephen Sondheim and Hugh Wheeler
21	The Music Man	Meredith Wilson
22	The King and I	Richard Rogers and Oscar Hammerstein, II
23	Sweeney Todd	Stephen Sondheim and Hugh Wheeler
24	Cabaret	John Kander and Fred Ebb
25	Oliver	Lionel Bart

Rock 'n' Roll Hall of Fame Inductees   Exhibit 11g

1986
performers
Chuck Berry
James Brown
Ray Charles
Sam Cooke
Fats Domino
The Everly Brothers
Buddy Holly
Jerry Lee Lewis
Elvis Presley
Little Richard

early influences
Robert Johnson
Jimmie Rodgers
Jimmy Yancey

lifetime achievement
John Hammond

non-performers
Alan Freed
Sam Phillips

1987
performers
The Coasters
Eddie Cochran
Bo Diddley
Aretha Franklin
Marvin Gaye
Bill Haley
B. B. King
Clyde McPhatter
Ricky Nelson
Roy Orbison
Carl Perkins
Smokey Robinson
Big Joe Turner
Muddy Waters
Jackie Wilson

early influences
Louis Jordan
T-Bone Walker
Hank Williams

non-performers
Leonard Chess
Ahmet Ertegun
Jerry Leiber and Mike Stoller
Jerry Wexler

1988
performers
The Beach Boys
The Beatles
The Drifters
Bob Dylan
The Supremes

early influences
Woody Guthrie
Lead Belly
Les Paul

non-performers
Berry Gordy, Jr

1989
early influences
Dion
Santana
Otis Redding
The Rolling Stones
The Temptations
Stevie Wonder

early influences
The Inkspots
Bessie Smith
The Soul Stirrers

non-performers
Phil Spector

1990
performers
Hank Ballard
Bobby Darin
The Four Seasons
The Four Tops
The Kinks
The Platters
Simon and Garfunkel
The Who

early influences
Louis Armstrong
Charlie Christian
Ma Rainey

non-performers
Gerry Goffin & Carole King
Holland, Dozier and Holland

1991
performers
LaVern Baker
The Byrds
John Lee Hooker
The Impressions
Wilson Pickett
Jimmy Reed
Ike and Tina Turner

early influences
Howlin' Wolf

lifetime achievement
Nesuhi Ertegun

non-performers
Dave Bartholomew
Ralph Bass

1992
performers
Bobby "Blue" Bland
Booker T. and the M.G.'s
Johnny Cash
The Isley Brothers
The Jimi Hendrix Experience
Sam and Dave
The Yardbirds

early influences
Elmore James
Professor Longhair

non-performers
Leo Fender
Bill Graham
Doc Pomus

1993
performers
Ruth Brown
Cream
Creedence Clearwater Revival
The Doors
Frankie Lymon
  and the Teenagers
Etta James
Van Morrison
Sly and the Family Stone

early influences
Dinah Washington

non-performers
Dick Clark
Milt Gabler

1994
performers
The Animals
The Band
Duane Eddy
The Grateful Dead
Elton John
John Lennon
Bob Marley
Rod Stewart

early influences
Willie Dixon

non-performers
Johnny Otis

1995
performers
The Allman Brothers Band
Al Green
Janis Joplin
Led Zeppelin
Martha and the Vandellas
Neil Young
Frank Zappa

early influences
The Orioles

non-performers
Paul Ackerman

1996
performers
David Bowie
Gladys Knight and the Pips
Jefferson Airplane
Little Willie John
Pink Floyd
The Shirelles
The Velvet Underground

early influences
Pete Seeger

non-performers
Tom Donahue

Rock 'n' Roll Hall of Fame Inductees   Exhibit 11g

1997
performers
The (Young) Rascals
The Bee Gees
Buffalo Springfield
Crosby, Stills and Nash
The Jackson Five
Joni Mitchell
Parliament-Funkadelic

early influences
Mahalia Jackson
Bill Monroe

non-performers
Syd Nathan

1988
performers
The Eagles
Fleetwood Mac
The Mamas and the Papas
Lloyd Price
Santana
Gene Vincent

early influences
Jelly Roll Morton

non-performers
Allen Toussaint

1999
performers
Billy Joel
Curtis Mayfield
Paul McCartney
Del Shannon
Dusty Springfield
Bruce Springsteen
The Staple Singers

early influences
Bob Wills and His
   Texas Playboys
Charles Brown

non-performers
George Martin

2000
performers
Eric Clapton
Earth, Wind & Fire
Lovin' Spoonful
The Moonglows
Bonnie Raitt
James Taylor

early influences
Nat "King" Cole
Billie Holiday

sidemen
Hal Blaine
King Curtis
James Jamerson
Scotty Moore
Earl Palmer

non-performers
Clive Davis

2001
performers
Aerosmith
Solomon Burke
The Flamingos
Michael Jackson
Queen
Paul Simon
Steely Dan
Ritchie Valens

sidemen
James Burton
Johnnie Johnson

non-performers
Chris Blackwell

2002
performers
Isaac Hayes
Brenda Lee
Tom Petty and
   the Heartbreakers
Gene Pitney
Ramones
Talking Heads

sidemen
Chet Atkins

non-performers
Jim Stewart

2003
performers
AC/DC
The Clash
Elvis Costello &
   the Attractions
The Police
Righteous Brothers

sidemen
Benny Benjamin
Floyd Cramer
Steve Douglas

non-performers
Mo Ostin

2004
performers
Jackson Browne
The Dolls
George Harrison
Prince
Bob Seger
Traffic
ZZ Top

lifetime achievement
Jann Wenner

2005
performers
Buddy Guy
The O'Jays
The Pretenders
Percy Sledge
U2

lifetime achievement
Frank Barsalona
Seymour Stein

2006
performers
Black Sabbath
Blondie
Miles Davis
Lynyrd Skynrd
Sex Pistols

lifetime achievement
Herb Alpert and Jerry
Moss

2007
performers
Grandmaster Flash
   and the Furious Five
R.E.M.
The Ronettes
Patti Smith
Van Halen

2008
performers
The Dave Clark Five
Leonard Cohen
Madonna
John Mellancamp
The Ventures

non-performers
Kenny Gamble
Leon Huff

sidemen
Little Walker

Grammy Awards for Jazz

	Best Jazz Performance, Group (or Instrumental Performance, Group)	Best Jazz Performance Large Group (or Big Band, Soloist with a Group, Large Group or Large Jazz Ensemble)	Best Jazz Performance Small Group (or Soloist with Group, later, Small Group of Soloist with Small Group	Best Jazz Individual (or Vocal Performance, later Vocal Album)	Best Jazz Vocal Performance, Male
1958	Count Basie			Ella Fitzgerald	
1959	Jonah Jones			Ella Fitzgerald	
1960		Henry Mancini	**Andre Previn**		
1961		Stan Kenton	**Andre Previn**		
1962		Stan Kenton	**Stan Getz**		
1963		Woody Herman	Bill Evans		
1964		Laurinda Almeida	**Stan Getz**		
1965		Duke Ellington	Ramsey Lewis		
1966			Wes Montgomery		
1967		Duke Ellington**	Cannonball Adderly		
1968		Duke Ellington**	Bill Evans		
1969		Quincy Jones**	Wes Montgomery		
1970		Miles Davis	Bill Evans		
1971	Bill Evans	Duke Ellington			
1972	Freddie Hubbard	Duke Ellington			
1973	Supersax	Woody Herman			
1974	Joe Pass, Niels Pedersen & Oscar Peterson	Woody Herman			
1975	Chick Corea & Return To Forever	Michel LeGrand & Phil Woods			
1976	Chick Corea	Duke Ellington		Ella Fitzgerald	
1977	Phil Woods	Count Basie		Al Jarreau	
1978	Chick Corea	Mel Lewis & Thad Jones		Al Jarreau	
1979	Chick Corea & Gary Burton	Duke Ellington		Ella Fitzgerald	
1980	Bill Evans	Count Basie			George Benson
1981	Chick Corea & Gary Burton	Gerry Mulligan			Al Jarreau
1982	Phil Woods	Count Basie			**Mel Torme**
1983	Phil Woods	Rob McConnell			**Mel Torme**
1984	Art Blakey	Count Basie		Joe Williams	
1985	Wynton Marsalis	Bob Wilber & John Barry			Bobby McFerrin & Jon Hendricks
1986	Wynton Marsalis	Doc Severinsen			Bobby McFerrin
1987	Wynton Marsalis	Mercer Ellington			Bobby McFerrin
1988	Cecil McBee, David Murray, McCoy Tyner, Pharoah Sanders & Roy Haynes	Gil Evans			Bobby McFerrin
1989	Chick Corea Akoustic Band	Miles Davis			Harry Connick, J
1990	Oscar Peterson Trio	Frank Foster			Harry Connick, J
1991	Oscar Peterson Trio	Dizzy Gillespie		Take 6	
1992	Branford Marsalis	McCoy Tyner		Bobby McFerrin	
1993		Miles Davis & Quincy Jones		Natalie Cole	
1994		McCoy Tyner		Etta James	
1995		Tom Scott		Lena Horne	
1996		Grover Mitchell		Cassandra Wilson	
1997		Joe Henderson		Dee Dee Bridgewater	
1998		Grover Mitchell		Shirley Horn	
1999		Bob Florence		Diana Krall	
2000		Joe Levano & James Farber		Dianne Reeves, et, al	
2001		Bob Minter Big Band Artist		Dianne Reeves, et, al	
2002		Dave Holland Big Band		Diana Krall	
2003		**Michel Brecker Quindectet**		Dianne Reeves	
2004		Maria Schneider		Nancy Wilson	
2005		Dave Holland Big Band		Dianne Reeves	
2006		John Beard, Dmarcio octor, Michael Brecker, Peter Erskine, Randy Brecker, Vince Mendoza, WDR Big Band & Will Lee		Nancy Wilson	
2007		Terence Blanchard		Parri Austin	

Grammy Awards for Jazz   Exhibit 11h

	Best Jazz Vocal Performance, Female	Best Jazz Performance, by a Soloist (or Instrumentalist Solo)	Best Jazz Instrumental Performance, Individual or Group, and later, Album	Best Jazz Composition over 5 minutes
1958				
1959				
1960				Miles Davis & Gill Evans
1961				
1962				
1963				
1964				
1965				
1966				
1967				
1968				
1969				
1970				
1971		Bill Evans		
1972		Gary Burton		
1973		Art Tatum		
1974		Charlie Parker		
1975		Dizzie Gillespie		
1976		Count Basie		
1977		Oscar Peterson		
1978		Oscar Peterson		
1979		Oscar Peterson		
1980	Ella Fitzgerald	Bill Evans		
1981	Ella Fitzgerald	John Coltrane		
1982	Sarah Vaughn	Miles Davis		
1983	Ella Fitzgerald	Wynton Marsalis		
1984		Wynton Marsalis		
1985	Cleo Lane	Wynton Marsalis		
1986	Diane Schuur	Miles Davis		
1987	Diane Schuur	Dexter Gordon		
1988	Betty Carter	Michael Brecker		
1989	Ruth Brown	Miles Davis		
1990	Ella Fitzgerald	Oscar Peterson		
1991		Stan Getz		
1992		Joe Henderson		
1993		Joe Henderson	Joe Henderson	
1994		Benny Carter	Herbie Hancock, Ron Carter, Tony Williams, Wallace Roney & Wayne Shorter	
1995		**Michael Brecker**	McCoy Tyner Trio	
1996		**Michael Brecker**	**Michael Brecker**	
1997		Doc Cheatham & Nicholas Payton	Charlie Haden & Pat Methany	
1998		Chick Corea & Gary Burton	Herbie Hancock	
1999		Wayne Shorter	Chick Corea, Dave Holland, Gary Burton, Pat Methany & Roy Haynes	
2000		Pat Methany	Bradford Marsalis Quartet	
2001		**Michael Brecker**	Sonny Rollins, et al	
2002		Herbie Hancock	Herbie Hancock, **Michael Brecker**, Roy Hargrove, et, al	
2003		Chick Corea	Wayne Shorter	
2004		Herbie Hancock	Christian McBride, Gary Bartz, Lewis Nash, McCoy Tyner & Terence Blanchard	
2005		Sonny Rollins	Wayne Shorter, Brian Blade, John Patitucci, Danilo Perez	
2006		**Michael Brecker**	Chick Corea	
2007		**Michael Brecker**	**Michael Brecker**	

Grammy Awards for Jazz

	Best Original Jazz Composition	Best Jazz Fusion Performance, Vocal or Instrumental	Best Jazz Performance, Duo or Group, (or Best Contemprary Jazz Performance)	Best Latin Jazz Perfomance
1958				
1959				
1960				
1961	Galt McDermott			
1962	Vince Guaraldi			
1963	Ray Brown & Steve Allen			
1964	Lalo Schifrin			
1965	Lalo Schifrin			
1966	Duke Ellington			
1967				
1968				
1969				
1970				
1971				
1972				
1973				
1974				
1975				
1976				
1977				
1978				
1979		Weather Report		
1980		Manhattan Transfer		
1981		Grover Washinton, Jr.	Manhattan Transfer	
1982		Pat Metheny	Manhattan Transfer	
1983		Pat Metheny	Manhattan Transfer	
1984		Pat Metheny		
1985		David Sanborn	Manhattan Transfer	
1986		David Sanborn & Bob James	2+2	
1987		Pat Metheny Group		
1988		Yellowjackets	Take 6	
1989		Pat Metheny Group	Dr. John & Rickie Lee Jones	
1990		Quincy Jones		
1991			Manhattan Transfer	
1992			Pat Methany	
1993			Pat Metheny Group	
1994			**Brecker Brothers**	Arturo Sandoval
1995			Pat Metheny Group	Jobim
1996			Wayne Shorter	Paquito D'Rivera
1997			**Randy Brecker**	Roy Hargrove's Crisol
1998			Pat Metheny Group	Arturo Sandoval
1999			David Sanborn	Poncho Sanchez
2000			**Bela Fleck & The Flecktones**	Chucho Valdes
2001			Marcus Miller, et al	Charlie Haden, et Al
2002			Pat Metheny Group	Caribbean Jazz Project
2003			**Randy Brecker**	Michael Camilo, Charles Flores & Horacio Hernandez
2004			William Frisell	Charlie Haden
2005			Pat Metheny Group	Eddie Palmieri, Sr.
2006			**Bela Fleck & The Flecktones**	Brian Lynch & Eddie Palmieri, Sr.
2007			Herbie Hancock	Paquito D'Rivera Quintet

Jazz Hall of Fame   Exhibit 11i

	1978		**1979**		**1980**		**1981**
1	Louis Armstrong	6	Charlie Parker	11	John Coltrane	17	Count Basie
2	Duke Ellington	7	Bix Beiderbecke	12	James P. Johnson	18	Tommy Dorsey
3	**Benny Goodman**	8	Fletcher Henderson	13	Thelonious Monk	19	Charlie Christian
4	Glenn Miller	9	Miles Davis	14	Earl Hines	20	Woody Herman
5	Ella Fitzgerald	10	Billie Holiday	15	Lester Young	21	**Buddy Rich**
				16	Frank Sinatra	22	Billy Strayhorn
						23	W. C. Handy
						24	Bessie Smith

	1982		**1983**		**1984**		**1985**
25	Jelly Roll Morton	33	Sidney Bechet	43	King Oliver	53	Art Tatum
26	Stan Kenton	34	Ben Webster	44	Charlie Barnet	54	Roy Eldridge
27	Art Blakey	35	Wes Montgomery	45	Claude Thornhill	55	Mary Lou Williams
28	Charles Mingus	36	Harry James	46	Eric Dolphy	56	C. Adderley
29	Coleman Hawkins	37	**Stan Getz**	47	Chu Berry	56	Bunny Berigan
30	Dizzy Gillespie	38	Gene Krupa	48	Gerry Mulligan	58	Jay McShann
31	Bill Evans	39	Eddie Condon	49	Django Reinhardt	59	Clifford Brown
32	Sarah Vaughan	40	Jimmy Dorsey	50	Fats Navarro	60	Jack Teagarden
		41	Eubie Blake	51	Chick Webb	61	Illinois Jacquet
		42	Ma Rainey	52	Carmen McRae	62	Billy Eckstine

	1986		**1987**		**1988**		**1989**
63	Red Nichols	73	Pee Wee Russell	84	Quincy Jones	93	Ornette Coleman
64	Bunk Johnson	74	**Willie Smith**	85	J. J. Johnson	94	Fats Waller
65	Lil Armstrong	75	Bennie Moten	86	Dexter Gordon	95	Frankie Carle
66	Dave Brubeck	76	Cab Calloway	87	Johnny Dodds	96	Milt Jackson
67	Kenny Clarke	77	Ray Noble	88	Buddy Tate	97	**Shorty Rogers**
68	Kid Ory	78	Sun Ra	89	Billy May	98	Sonny Stitt
69	Gil Evans	79	Chet Baker	90	Buddy Bolden	99	Isham Jones
70	Eddie Lang	80	Jimmie Lunceford	91	Benny Carter	100	Lawrence Welk
71	Lionel Hampton	81	Scott Joplin	92	Jimmy Rushing	101	Mildred Bailey
72	Johnny Hartman	82	Jimmie Noone				
		83	Dinah Washington				

	1990		**1991**		**1992**		**1993**
102	**Artie Shaw**	110	Horace Silver	119	**Ben Pollack**	129	James Moody
103	Buck Clayton	111	Clarence Williams	120	Jimmy McPartland	130	Budd Johnson
104	Kenny Burrell	112	Paul Desmond	121	Hal Kemp	131	Louie Bellson
105	Johnny Hodges	113	Andy Kirk	122	Bud Freeman	132	Meade Lux Lewis
106	Don Redman	114	Baby Dodds	123	Zoot Sims	133	Paul Whiteman
107	Jo Jones	115	Bud Powell	124	Oscar Pettiford	134	John Kirby
108	Les Paul	116	Max Roach	125	Pops Foster	135	Cootie Williams
109	**Mel Torme**	117	Red Norvo	126	Sammy Kaye	136	Erroll Garner
		118	Lena Horne	127	Guy Lombardo	137	Louis Prima
				128	Peggy Lee	138	Teddy Wilson
						139	Nat King Cole

	1994		**1995**		**1996**		**1997**
140	Clark Terry	150	Don Cherry	159	Wynton Marsalis	169	Wild Bill Davison
141	Freddie Hubbard	151	Oscar Peterson	160	Tal Farlow	170	Bobby Hackett
142	Sweets Edison	152	Herbie Hancock	161	Doc Cheatham	171	Pete Fountain
143	Paul Chambers	153	Red Allen	162	Sid Catlett	172	Ray Brown
144	Stuff Smith	154	Thad Jones	163	Tex Beneke	173	Tony Williams
145	Raymond Scott	155	Joe Pass	164	Lucky Millinder	174	Freddie Keppard
146	Jimmy Blanton	156	Tito Puete	165	**Al Cohn**	175	Mel Powell
147	Wynton Kelly	157	Stephane Grappelli	166	Jess Stacy	176	Muggsy Spanier
148	Rex Stewart	158	Joe Williams	167	Milt Hinton	177	Charlie Shavers
149	Betty Carter			168	Alberta Hunter	178	Tony Bennett

	1998		**1999**		**2000**		**2001**
179	Eddie Miller	189	Sonny Rollins	199	Joe Venuti	209	Art Farmer
180	Dorothy Donegan	190	Barney Kessel	200	Harry Carney	210	Lawrence Brown
181	Wayne Shorter	191	Billy Taylor	201	Dave Tough	211	Lennie Tristano
182	Yank Lawson	192	Jonah Jones	202	Sy Oliver	212	Tadd Dameron
183	Claude Hopkins	193	Tommy Flanagan	203	Hank Jones	213	Jimmy Rowles
184	Adrian Rollini	194	Barry Harris	204	Freddie Green	214	John Lewis
185	**Art Hodges**	195	Marian McPartland	205	Chubby Jackson	215	**Terry Gibbs**
186	Will Bradley	196	Nancy Wilson	206	McCoy Tyner	216	Toshiko Akiyoshi
187	Louis Jordan	197	Les Brown	207	Ron Carter	217	Gerald
188	Maxine Sullivan	198	Stanley Dance	208	Shirley Horn	218	**Helen Forrest Wilson**

	2002		**2003**		**2004**
219	John Lewis	228	Bob Brookmeyer	240	Mundell Lowe
	Buddy DeFranco	229	Jim Hall	241	Specs Powell
	Lennie Tristano		Toshiko Akiyoshi	242	Paul Tanner
	Lawrence Brown		Jimmy Rowles		Gerald Wilson
220	Ralph Sutton	230	Ray Nance		Terry Gibbs
221	**Shelly Manne**	231	Scott LaFaro		Tadd Dameron
222	Art Pepper	232	Howard McGhee	243	Paul Gonsalves
223	Bing Crosby	233	JC Higginbotham	244	Trummy Young
224	Nina Simone	234	Bob Eberly	245	Perry Como
225	T-Bone Walker	235	Jo Stafford	246	Martha Tilton
226	Gray's Casa Loma Orche	236	Eddie Sauder	247	Sammy Nestico
227	George T. Simon	237	B. B. King	248	Ray Charles
		238	Ted Weems	249	William McKinney
		239	**Norman Granz**	250	Helen Dance
				251	**Irving Berlin**

Members of the Country Music Hall of Fame   **Exhibit 11j**

1961	Jimmie Rodgers	1981	Grant Turner	1999	Dolly Parton
1961	Fred Rose	1982	Lefty Frizzell	1999	Conway Twitty
1961	Hank Williams	1982	Marty Robbins	2000	Charley Pride
1962	Roy Acuff	1982	Roy Horton	2000	Faron Young
1964	Tex Ritter	1983	Little Jimmy Dickens	2001	Bill Anderson
1965	Ernest Tubb	1984	Ralph S. Peer	2001	The Delmore Brothers
1966	Eddy Arnold	1984	Floyd Tillman	2001	The Everly Brothers
1966	James R. Denny	1985	Lester Flatt & Earl Scruggs	2001	Don Gibson
1966	George D. Hay	1986	Wesley H. Rose	2001	Homer & Jethro
1966	Uncle Dave Macon	1986	Whitey Ford	2001	Waylon Jennings
1967	Red Foley	1987	Rod Brasfield	2001	The Jordanaires
1967	J. L. Frank	1988	Roy Rogers	2001	Don Law
1967	Jim Reeves	1988	Loretta Lynn	2001	The Louvin Brothers
1967	Stephen H. Sholes	1989	Cliffie Stone	2001	Ken Nelson
1968	Bob Wills	1989	Hank Thompson	2001	Webb Pierce
1969	Gene Autry	1989	Jack Stapp	2001	Sam Phillips
1970	Bill Monroe	1990	Tennessee Ernie Ford	2002	Bill Carlisle
1970	Original Carter Family	1991	Felice and Boudleaux Bryant	2002	Porter Wagoner
1971	Arthur Edward Satherley	1992	Frances Williams Preston	2003	Floyd Cramer
1972	Jimmie H. Davis	1992	George Jones	2003	Carl Smith
1973	Chet Atkins	1993	Willie Nelson	2004	Jim Fogelsong
1973	Patsy Cline	1994	Merle Haggard	2004	Kris Kristofferson
1974	Owen Bradley	1995	Jo Walker-Meador	2005	Alabama
1974	Frank "Pee Wee" King	1995	Roger Miller	2005	DeFord Bailey
1975	Minnie Pearl	1996	Patsy Montana	2005	Glen Campbell
1976	Kitty Wells	1996	Buck Owens	2006	Harold Bradley
1976	Paul Cohen	1996	Ray Price	2006	Sony James
1977	Merle Travis	1997	Harlan Howard	2006	George Strait
1978	Grandpa Jones	1997	Brenda Lee	2007	Ralph Emery
1979	Hubert Long	1997	Cindy Walker	2007	Vince Gill
1979	Hank Snow	1998	George Morgan	2007	Mel Tillis
1980	Connie B. Gay	1998	Elvis Presley	2008	Tom T. Hall
1980	Original Sons of the Pioneers	1998	E.W. "Bud" Wendell	2008	Emmylou Harris
1980	Johnny Cash	1998	Tammy Wynette	2008	The Statler Brothers
1981	Vernon Dalhart	1999	Johnny Bond	2008	Ernest "Pop" Stoneman

Election to the Country Music Hall of Fame is the highest honor in country music. The Hall of Fame award was created in 1961 by the Country Music Association (CMA), the country music industry's leading trade organization. The award recognizes persons who have made outstanding contributions to country music over the length of their careers.

The Hall of Fame honors performers, promoters, music publishing and recording leaders, broadcasters and others in the music industry, reflecting country music's stature as both art and enterprise. Hall of Fame members are selected annually by an anonymous panel of 200 electors, each of whom has been an active participant in the country music business for at least 15 years and has made a major contribution to the industry. The CMA conducts the election, with winners honored during the CMA Awards Show each fall.

The first Hall of Fame members -- Jimmie Rodgers, Fred Rose and Hank Williams -- were elected in 1961. Hall of Fame plaques were displayed at the Tennessee State Museum in Nashville until 1967, when the first Country Music Hall of Fame and Museum building was opened on Music Row in Nashville. The plaques are now housed in the new Country Music Hall of Fame and Museum in downtown Nashville.

Country Music Television's 80 Greatest Men & Women of Country Music   **Exhibit 11k**

40 Greatest Women of Country Music		**40 Greatest Men of Country Music**	
1	Patsy Cline	1	Johnny Cash
2	Tammy Wynette	2	Hank Williams
3	Loretta Lynn	3	George Jones
4	Dolly Parton	4	Willie Nelson
5	Emmylou Harris	5	Waylon Jennings
6	Reba McEntire	6	Merle Haggard
7	Shania Twain	7	Garth Brooks
8.	Maybelle Carter	8	Conway Twitty
9	Connie Smith	9	George Strait
10.	Trisha Yearwood	10	Alan Jackson
11.	The Judds	11	Alabama
12	Alison Krauss	12	Buck Owens
13	Dixie Chicks	13	Randy Travis
14	Minnie Pearl	14	Roy Acuff
15	Kitty Wells	15	Elvis Presley
16	Patty Loveless	16	Bill Monroe
17	Lee Ann Womack	17	Vince Gill
18	Patsy Montana	18	Charley Pride
19	Faith Hill	19	Kenny Rogers
20	Tanya Tucker	20	Hank Williams Jr.
21	Mary Chapin Carpenter	21	Ernest Tubb
22	Rosanne Cash	22	Eddy Arnold
23	Dottie West	23	Roger Miller
24	Anne Murray	24	Flatt & Scruggs
25	Martina McBride	25	Brooks & Dunn
26	**k.d. lang**	26	Tim McGraw
27	Lorrie Morgan	27	Bob Wills
28	Brenda Lee	28	Chet Atkins
29	Lynn Anderson	29	Glen Campbell
30	Pam Tillis	30	Ronnie Milsap
31	June Carter Cash	31	Lefty Frizzell
32	Cindy Walker	32	Charlie Daniels
33	Crystal Gayle	33	Jimmie Rodgers
34	Dale Evans	34	Eagles
35	Wanda Jackson	35	Mel Tillis
36	Lucinda Williams	36	Toby Keith
37	K.T. Oslin	37	Ricky Skaggs
38	Barbara Mandrell	38	Gene Autry
39	LeAnn Rimes	39	Dwight Yoakam
40	Linda Ronstadt	40	Travis Tritt

Grammy Legend and Lifetime Achievement Awards Winners   Exhibit 111

Grammy Legend Award Winners

1	Bee Gees	6	Elton John	11	Lucinao Pavarotti
2	Johnny Cash	7	Quincy Jones	12	Smokey Robinson
3	Aretha Franklin	8	Curtis Mayfield	13	Frank Sinatra
4	Michael Jackson	9	Liza Minnelli	14	**Barbra Streisand**
5	**Billy Joel**	10	Willie Nelson	15	Andrew Lloyd Webber

Grammy Lifetime Achievement Award Winners

1	Roy Acuff	48	Bill Evans	95	Willie Nelson
2	Marian Anderson	49	Everly Brothers	96	Jessye Norman
3	Louis Armstrong	50	Ella Fitzgerald	97	Roy Orbison
4	Eddy Arnold	51	Aretha Franklin	98	Charlie Parker
5	Fred Astaire	52	The Funk Brothers	99	Joe Willie "Pinetop" Perkins
6	Chet Atkins	53	Judy Garland	100	**Itzhak Perlman**
7	**Burt Bacharach**	54	Marvin Gaye	101	Oscar Peterson
8	Joan Baez	55	Dizzy Gillespie	102	Elvis Presley
9	The Band	56	**Benny Goodman**	103	Leontyne Price
10	Count Basie	57	**Morton Gould**	104	Richard Pryor
11	Beach Boys	58	Stephen Grappelli	105	Tito Puente
12	Harry Belafonte	59	The Grateful Dead	106	Otis Redding
13	Tony Bennett	60	Al Green	107	Paul Robeson
14	**Irving Berlin**	61	Woody Guthrie	108	Smokey Robinson
15	**Leonard Bernstein**	62	Merle Haggard	109	The Staple Singers
16	Chuck Berry	63	**Jascha Heifetz**	110	Rolling Stones
17	Art Blakey	64	Jimi Hendrix	111	Max Roach
18	Bobby "Blue" Bland	65	Woody Herman	112	Sonny Rollins
19	Booker T. & The MG's	66	Billie Holiday	113	**Artur Rubenstein**
20	David Bowie	67	Buddy Holly	114	Earl Scruggs
21	James Brown	68	John Lee Hooker	115	Pete Seger
22	Dave Brubeck	69	Lena Horne	116	Andres Segovia
23	Maria Callas	70	**Vladimir Horowitz**	117	**Artie Shaw**
24	Cab Calloway	71	Mahalia Jackson	118	**Simon & Garfunkel**
25	Benny Carter	72	Etta James	119	Frank Sinatra
26	The Carter Family	73	Ellen Jenkins	120	Bessie Smith
27	Enrico Caruso	74	Robert Johnson	121	**Georg Solti**
28	Pablo Casals	75	Janis Joplin	122	**Isaac Stern**
29	Johnny Cash	76	B.B. King	123	Igor Stravinsky
30	Ray Charles	77	Led Zeplin	124	**Barbra Streisand**
31	Patsy Cline	78	Peggy Lee	125	Art Tatum
32	Rosemary Clooney	79	John Lenon	126	**Mel Torme**
33	Nat "King" Cole	80	Jerry Lee Lewis	127	Arturo Toscanini
34	Ornette Coleman	81	Little Richard	128	Van Cliburn
35	John Coltrane	82	Henry Mancini	129	Sarah Vaughan
36	Perry Como	83	Bob Marley	130	Fats Waller
37	Sam Cooke	84	Johnny Mathis	131	Muddy Waters
38	Cream	85	Curtis Mayfield	132	Doc Watson
39	Bing Crosby	86	Paul McCartney	133	The Weavers
40	**Sammy Davis, Jr.**	87	Glenn Miller	134	Kitty Wells
41	Miles Davis	88	**Mitch Miller**	135	The Who
42	Doris Day	89	Mills Brothers	136	Hank Williams, Sr.
43	Bo Diddley	90	Charles Migus	137	Bob Wills
44	Fats Domino	91	Joni Mitchell	138	Stevie Wonder
45	The Doors	92	Thelonious Monk	139	Frank Zappa
46	**Bob Dylan**	93	Jelly Roll Morton		
47	Duke Ellington	94	Bill Monroe		

Rate it All - The Opinion Network

Rating of Stand-up Comedians August 13, 2003

#	Comedian	Rating	#	Comedian	Rating
1.	Robin Williams	★ ★ ★ ★ ☆	42.	Bill Hicks	★ ★ ★ ☆ ☆
2.	John Cleese	★ ★ ★ ★ ☆	43.	Damon Wayans	★ ★ ★ ☆ ☆
3.	Bill Cosby	★ ★ ★ ★ ☆	44.	**Wendy Liebman**	★ ★ ★ ☆ ☆
4.	**Gilda Radner**	★ ★ ★ ★ ☆	45.	**Gene Wilder**	★ ★ ★ ☆ ☆
5.	Eddie Izzard	★ ★ ★ ★ ☆	46.	Janeane Garofalo	★ ★ ★ ☆ ☆
6.	Steve Martin	★ ★ ★ ★ ☆	47.	Sinbad	★ ★ ★ ☆ ☆
7.	Bill Murray	★ ★ ★ ★ ☆	48.	David Spade	★ ★ ★ ☆ ☆
8.	**Lewis Black**	★ ★ ★ ★ ☆	49.	**Milton Berle**	★ ★ ★ ☆ ☆
9.	Eddie Murphy	★ ★ ★ ★ ☆	50.	**George Burns**	★ ★ ★ ☆ ☆
10.	**Jack Benny**	★ ★ ★ ★ ☆	51.	Dennis Miller	★ ★ ★ ☆ ☆
11.	**Dave Attell**	★ ★ ★ ★ ☆	52.	Tracey Ullman	★ ★ ★ ☆ ☆
12.	John Candy	★ ★ ★ ★ ☆	53.	Denis Leary	★ ★ ★ ☆ ☆
13.	**Jon Stewart**	★ ★ ★ ★ ☆	54.	Benny Hill	★ ★ ★ ☆ ☆
14.	Dana Carvey	★ ★ ★ ★ ☆	55.	**Tim Allen**	★ ★ ★ ☆ ☆
15.	Greg Proops	★ ★ ★ ★ ☆	56.	Bob Hope	★ ★ ★ ☆ ☆
16.	Mike Myers	★ ★ ★ ★ ☆	57.	Margaret Cho	★ ★ ★ ☆ ☆
17.	Richard Pryor	★ ★ ★ ★ ☆	58.	Jeff Foxworthy	★ ★ ★ ☆ ☆
18.	George Carlin	★ ★ ★ ★ ☆	59.	Dave Chapelle	★ ★ ★ ☆ ☆
19.	John Belushi	★ ★ ★ ★ ☆	60.	**Howie Mandel**	★ ★ ★ ☆ ☆
20.	Steven Wright	★ ★ ★ ★ ☆	61.	Tom Green	★ ★ ★ ☆ ☆
21.	**Jerry Seinfeld**	★ ★ ★ ☆ ☆	62.	**Lenny Bruce**	★ ★ ★ ☆ ☆
22.	Lucille Ball	★ ★ ★ ☆ ☆	63.	Jay Leno	★ ★ ★ ☆ ☆
23.	Steve Allen	★ ★ ★ ★ ☆	64.	Martin Lawrence	★ ★ ★ ☆ ☆
24.	Charlie Chaplin	★ ★ ★ ★ ☆	65.	Caroline Rhea	★ ★ ★ ☆ ☆
25.	Richard Jeni	★ ★ ★ ★ ☆	66.	**Paul Reiser**	★ ★ ★ ☆ ☆
26.	Carol Burnett	★ ★ ★ ★ ☆	67.	Kevin Nealon	★ ★ ★ ☆ ☆
27.	Chris Rock	★ ★ ★ ★ ☆	68.	Chris Elliott	★ ★ ★ ☆ ☆
28.	Norm MacDonald	★ ★ ★ ★ ☆	69.	D.L. Hughley	★ ★ ★ ☆ ☆
29.	David Letterman	★ ★ ★ ★ ☆	70.	**Jerry Lewis**	★ ★ ★ ☆ ☆
30.	Jim Carrey	★ ★ ★ ★ ☆	71.	Bob Goldthwait	★ ★ ★ ☆ ☆
31.	Michael Palin	★ ★ ★ ★ ☆	72.	Paula Poundstone	★ ★ ★ ☆ ☆
32.	Eric Idle	★ ★ ★ ★ ☆	73.	**Jackie Mason**	★ ★ ★ ☆ ☆
33.	Chris Farley	★ ★ ★ ★ ☆	74.	Ellen DeGeneres	★ ★ ★ ☆ ☆
34.	Martin Short	★ ★ ★ ★ ☆	75.	**Gary Shandling**	★ ★ ☆ ☆ ☆
35.	Chris Tucker	★ ★ ★ ★ ☆	76.	Sam Kinison	★ ★ ☆ ☆ ☆
36.	**Rodney Dangerfield**	★ ★ ★ ★ ☆	77.	**Gilbert Gottfried**	★ ★ ☆ ☆ ☆
37.	Christopher Titus	★ ★ ★ ★ ☆	78.	**Sandra Bernhard**	★ ★ ☆ ☆ ☆
38.	Drew Carey	★ ★ ★ ★ ☆	79.	**Roseanne**	★ ★ ☆ ☆ ☆
39.	**Adam Sandler**	★ ★ ★ ★ ☆	80.	**Andrew Dice Clay**	★ ★ ☆ ☆ ☆
40.	**Andy Kaufman**	★ ★ ★ ★ ☆	81.	Carrot Top	★ ★ ★ ☆ ☆
41.	**Billy Crystal**	★ ★ ★ ★ ☆	82.	Rosie O'Donnell	★ ★ ☆ ☆ ☆

The Art Book, Phaidon's 500 Great Painters and Sculptors   Exhibit 12a

Agasse, Jacques-Laurent (1848)
Albers, Josef (1976)
Algardi, Alessandro* (1654)
Allston, Washington (1843)
Alma-Tadema, Sir Lawrence (1912)
Altdorfer, Albrecht*(1538)
Amigoni, Jacopo* (1752)
Andre, Carl (alive 2001)
Andrea del Sarto* (1530)
Fra Angelico* (1455)
Anguissola, Sofonisba* (1625)
Antonello da Messina* (1479)
Appel, Karel (alive 2001)
Archipenko, Alexander (1964)
Arcimboldo, Giuseppe* (1593)
Arp, Jean (1966)
Audubon, John James (1851)
Auerbach, Frank (alive 2001)
Avercamp,Hendrick* (1634)
Bacon, Francis (1992)
Baldung, Hans* 1545)
Balla, Giacomo (1958)
Balthus (alive 2001)
Fra Bartolommeo* (1517)
Baselitz, Georg (alive 2001)
Basquiat, Jean-Michel (1986)
Bassano, Jacopo* (1592)
Batoni, Pompeo* (1787)
Baumeister, Willi (1955)
Bazille, Frederic (1870)
Beauneveu, Andre* (1402)
Beccafumi, Domenico* (1551)
Beckmann, Max (1950)
Bellini, Gentile* (1507)
Bellini, Giovanni* (1516)
Bellmer, Hans (1975)
Bellotto, Bernardo * (1780)
Bellows, George (1926)
Bernini, Gianlorenzo* (1680)
Beuys, Josef (1986)
Bierstadt, Albert (1902)
Bingham, George Caleb (1879)
Blake, Peter (alive 2001)
Blake, William (1827)
Boccioni, Umberto (1916)
Bocklin, Arnold (1901)
Boltanski, Christian (alive 2001)
Bomberg, David (1957)
Bonington, Richard Parkes (1828)
Bonnard, Pierre (1947)
Bordone, Paris* (1571)
Bosch, Hieronymus* (1516)
Botero, Fernando (1932)
Botticelli, Sandro* (1510)
Boucher, Fracois* (1770)
Boudin, Eugene (1898)
Bourdelle, Antoine (1929)
Bourgeois, Louise (alive 2001)

Bouts, Dieric* (1475)
Boyd, Arthur (alive 2001)
Brancusi, Constantin (1956)
Braque, Georges (1963)
Brauner, Victor (1966)
Bronzino, Agnolo* (1572)
Broodthaers, Marcel (1976)
Brown, Ford Madox (1893)
Bruegel, Jan* (1625)
Bruegel, Pieter* (1569)
Buren, Daniel (alive 2001)
Burne-Jones, Sir Edward (1898)
Burra, Edward (1976)
Burri, Alberto (1995)
Caillebotte, Gustave (1894)
Calder, Alexander (1975)
Campin, Robert* (1444)
Canaletto* (1768)
Canova, Antonio (1822)
Caravaggio* (1610)
Caro, Sir Anthony (alive 2001)
Carpaccio, Vittore* 1526)
Carra, Carlo (1966)
Carracci, Annibale* (1609)
Cassatt, Mary (1926)
Castagno, Andrea del* (1457)
Catena, Vincenzo* (1531)
Catlin, George (1872)
Cellini, Benvenuto* (1571)
Cezanne, Paul (1906)
Chagall, Marc (1985)
Champaigne, Philippe de* (1674)
Chardin, Jean-Baptiste-Simeon* (1779)
Chase, William Merritt (1916)
De Chirico, Giorgio (1978)
Christo & Jean-Claude (alive 2001)
Church, Frederick (1900)
Cimabue* (1302)
Claesz, Pieter*1661)
Claude Lorrain* (1682)
Clemente, Francesco (1952)
Clout, Francois* 1572)
Cole, Thomas (1848)
Constable, John (1837)
Copley, John Singleton (1815)
Cornell, Joseph (1972)
Corot, Jean-Baptiste-Camille (1875)
Correggio* (1534)
Del Cossa, Francesco* (1478)
Courbet, Gustave (1877)
Cozens, John Robert* (1797)
Cragg, Tony(1949)
Cranach, Lucas the Elder* (1553)
Cuyp, Aelbert* (1691)
Dali, Salvador (1989)
Daubigny, Charles-Francois (1878)
Daumier, Honore (1879)
David, Gerard* (1523)

David, Jacques-Louis (1825)
Davis, Stuart (1964)
Deacon, Richard (alive 2001)
Degas, Edgar (1917)
Delacroix, Eugene (1863)
Delaunay, Robert (1941)
Delvaux, Paul (1994)
Denis, Maurice (1943)
Derain,Andre (1954)
Diebenkorn, Richard (1994)
Dine, Jim (alive 2001)
Dix, Otto (1969)
Dobson, William* (1646)
Van Doesburg, Theo (1931)
Domenichino* (1641)
Donatello* (1466)
Van Dongen, Dees (1968)
Dossi, Dosso* (1542)
Dou, Gerrard* (1675)
Dove, Arthur (1946)
Dubuffet, Jean (1985)
Duccio* (1319)
Duchamp, Marcel (1968)
Dufy, Raoul (1953)
Durer, Albrecht* (1528)
Van Dyck, Sir Anthony* (1641)
Eakins, Thomas (1916)
Elsheimer, Adam* (1610)
Ensor, James (1949)
Epstein, Sir Jacob (1959)
Ernst, Max (1976)
Estes, Richard (alive 2001)
Etty, William (1849)
Van Eyck, Jan* (1441)
Fabritius, Carel* 1654)
Fantin-Latour, Henri (1904)
Fautrier, Jean (1964)
Feininger, Lyonel (1956)
Flavin, Dan (alive 2001)
Fontana, Lucio (1968)
Foujita, Tsugouharu (1968)
Fouquet, Jean* (1481)
Fragonard, Jean-Honore (1806)
Francis, Sam (1994)
Frankenthaler, Helen (1928)
Freud, Lucian (1922)
Freidrich, Caspar David (1840)
Frink, Dame Elisabeth (1993)
Froment, Nicolas* (1490)
Gabo, Naum (1977)
Gainsborough, Thomas* (1788)
Gaudier-Brzeska, Henri (1915)
Gaugin, Paul (1903)
Gentile da Fabriano* (1427)
Gentileschi, Artemisia* (1652)
Gericault, Theodore (1824)
Gertler, Mark (1939)
Ghiberti, Lorenzo* (1455)

The Art Book, Phaidon's 500 Great Painters and Sculptors

Ghirlandaio, Domenico* (1494)
Giacometti, Alberto (1966)
Giambologna* (1608)
Gilbert and George (alive 2001)
Gilman, Harold (1919)
Giordano, Luca* (1705)
Giorgione* (1510)
Giotto* (1337)
Giulio Romano* (1545)
Van der Goes, Hugo* (1482)
Van Gogh, Vincent (1890)
Gontcharova, Natalia (1962)
Gorky, Arshile (1948)
Goya, Francisco (1828)
Van Goyen, Jan* (1656)
Gozzoli, Benozzo* (1497)
El Greco* (1614)
Greuze, Jean-Baptiste (1805)
Grimshaw, Atkinson (1893)
Gris, Juan (1927)
Gros, Antoine-Jean, Baron (1835)
Grosz, George (1959)
Grunewald, Matthais* (1528)
Guardi, Francesco* (1780)
Guercino* (1666)
Gunston, Philip (1980)
Hals, Frans* (1666)
Hamilton, Richard (alive 2001)
Hammershoi, Wilhelm (1916)
Hartung, Hans (1992)
Hassam, Childe (1935)
Hausmann, Raoul (1971)
Hayter, Stanley William (1988)
Heckel, Erich (1944)
De Heem, Jan Davidsz* (1384/4)
Hepworth, Barbara (1975)
Heron, Patrick (alive 2001)
Hicks, Edward (1849)
Hilliard, Nicholas* (1619)
Hiroshige, Ando (1858)
Hobbema, Meindert* (1706)
Hockney, David (alive 2001)
Hodgkin, Howard (alive 2001)
Hodler, Ferdinand (1918)
Hofmann, Hans (1966)
Hogarth, William* (1764)
Hokusai, Katsushika (1849)
Holbein, Hans* (1543)
Homer, Winslow (1910)
Honthorst, Gerrit van* (1656)
De Hooch, Pieter* (1684)
Hopper, Edward (1967)
Houdon, Jean-Antoine (1828)
Hunt, William Holman (1910)
Ingres, Jean Auguste Dominique (1867)
Ivanov, Alexander (1858)
Jawlensky, Alexei von (1941)
John, Gwen (1939)

Johns, Jasper (alive 2001)
Jones, Allen (alive 2001)
Jordaens, Jacob* (1678)
Judd, Donald (1994)
Kahlo, Frida (1954)
Kalf, Willem* (1693)
Kandinsky, Wassily (1944)
Kapoor, Anish (1954)
Kauffmann, Angelica (1807)
Kelly, Ellsworth (alive 2001)
Kiefer, Anselm (alive 1945)
Kirchner, Ernst Ludwig (1938)
Kitaj R B ((alive 2001)
Klee, Paul (1940)
Klein, Yves (1962)
Klimt, Gustav (1918)
Kline, Franz (1962)
Kneller, Sir Godfrey* (1723)
Kokoschka, Oskar (1980)
De Kooning, Willem (alive 2001)
Koons, Jeff (alive 2001)
Kossoff, Leon (alive 2001)
Kroyer, Peter Severin (1900)
Kupka, Frantisek (1957)
Lam, Wilfredo (1982)
Lancret, Nicolas* (1743)
Landseer, Sir Edwin (1843)
Lanyon, Peter (1964)
La Tour, Georges de* (1652)
Laurencin, Marie (1956)
Lawrence, Sir Thomas (1830)
Leger, Fernand (1955)
Leighton, Frederic, Lord (1896)
Lely, Sir Peter* (1680)
Leonardo da Vinci* (1519)
Lewis, Wyndham (1957)
LeWitt, Sol (alive 2001)
Lichtenstein, Roy (1997)
Limbourg, Jean and Paul* (1416)
Liotard Jean-Etienne* (1789)
Lipchitz, Jacques (1973)
Lippi, Filippino* (1504)
Lippi, Fra Filippo* (1469)
Lissitzky, El (1941)
Lochner, Stefan* (1451)
Long, Richard (alive 2001)
Longhi, Pietro* (1785)
Lorenzetti, Ambrogio* (1348)
Lorenzo Monaco* (1424)
Lotto, Lorenzo* (1556)
Louis, Morris (1962)
Lowry, L S (1973)
Lucas van Leyden* (1533)
Luini, Bernardino* (1532)
Mabuse* (1532)
Magritte, Rene (1967)
Maillol, Aristide (1944)
Malevich, Kasimir (1935)

Man Ray (1976)
Manet, Edouard (1883)
Mangold, Robert (alive 2001)
Mantegna, Andrea* (1506)
Manzu, Giacomo (1991)
Marc, Franz (1916)
Marin, John (1953)
Marini, Marino (1980)
Martin, John (1854)
Martini, Simone* (1344)
Masaccio* (1428)
Masolino* (1433)
Massys, Quentin* (1530)
Matisse, Henri (1954)
Matta, Roberto Sebastian Echaurren (1
Memling, Hans* (1494)
Mengs, Anton Raphael* (1779)
Mertz, Mario (alive 2001)
Metsu, Gabriel* (1667)
Michelangelo* (1564)
Millais, Sir John Everett (1896)
Millet, Jean-Francois (1875)
Miro, Joan (1983)
Modersohn-Becker, Paula (1907)
Modigliani, Amedeo (1920)
Moholy-Nagy, Laszlo (1946)
Mondrian, Piet (1944)
Monet, Claude (1926)
Moore, Henry (1986)
Morandi, Giorgio (1964)
Moreau, Gustave (1898)
Morisot, Berthe (1895)
Moroni, Giovanni Battista* (1578)
Motherwell, Robert (1991)
Moulins, Master of * (c1500)
Mucha, Alphonse (1939)
Munch, Edvard (1944)
Murillo, Bartolome Esteban* (1682
Nash, Paul (1946)
Nauman, Bruce (alive 2001)
Newman, Barnett (1970)
Nicholson, Ben (1982)
Noguchi, Isamu (1988)
Nolan, Sir Sidney (1992)
Noland, Kenneth (alive 2001)
Nolde, Emil (1956)
O'Keeffe, Georgia (1986)
Oldenburg, Claes (alive 2001)
Orcagna* (1368)
Organ, Bryan (1935)
Orozco, Jose Clemente (1949)
Orpen, Sir William (1931)
Van Ostade, Adriaen* (1685)
Overbeck, Johann Friedrich (1869)
Palma Vecchio* (1528)
Pannini, Giovanni Paolo* (1765)
Parmigianino* (1540)
Patenier, Joachim* (1524)

488 APPENDIX

The Art Book, Phaidon's 500 Great Painters and Sculptors   Exhibit 12a

Pechstein, Max Hermann (1955)
Perugino* (1523)
Picabia, Francis (1953)
Picasso, Pablo (1973)
Piero della Francesca* (1492)
Piero di Cosimo* (1521)
Pietro da Cortona* (1669)
Piper, John (1992)
Pisanello* (1455)
Pisano, Andrea* (1348)
Pissarro, Camille (1903)
Poliakoff, Segre (1969)
Polke, Sigmar (alive 2001)
Pollaiuolo, Antonio* (1498)
Pollock, Jackson (1956)
Pontormo,Jacopo* (1556)
Popova Ljubov (1924)
Poussin, Nicolas* (1665)
Powers, Hiram (1873)
Primaticcio, Francesco* (1570)
Prud'hon, Pierre-Paul (1823)
Della Quercia, Jacopo* (1438)
Raeburn, Sir Henry (1823)
Ramsay, Allan* (1784)
Raphael* (1520)
Rauschenberg, Robert (alive 2001)
Redon, Odilon (1916)
Rego, Paula (alive 2001)
Reinhardt, Ad (1967)
Rembrandt* (1669)
Reni, Guido* (1642)
Renoir, Pierre Auguste (1919)
Reynolds, Sir Joshua* (1792)
Ribera, Jusepe* (1652)
Richter, Gerhard (alive 2001)
Riley, Bridget (alive 2001)
Riopelle, Jean-Paul (alive 2001)
Rivera, Diego (1957)
Della Robbia Luca* (1482)
Rodchenko, Alexander (1956)
Rodin, Auguste (1917)
Romney, George (1802)
Rosa, Salvator* (1673)
Rosenquist, James (1933)
Rosselli, Cosimo* (1507)
Rossetti, Dante Gabriel (1882)
Rosso Fiorentino* (1540)
Rothko, Mark (1970)
Rouault, Georges (1958)
Roubiliac, Louis-Francois* (1762)
Rousseau, Henri (1940)
Rousseau, Theodore (1867)
Rubens, Sir Peter Paul* (1640)
Ruisdael, Jacob van* (1682)
Ruysch, Rachel* (1750)
Ryman, Robert (alive 2001)
Salviati, Francesco* (1563)
Sanchez-Cotan, Juan* (1637)

Sargent, John Singer (1925)
Sassetta* (1450)
Savery, Roelandt* (1639)
Schad, Christian (1982)
Schiele, Egon (1918)
Schmidt-Rottluff, Karl (1976)
Schnabel, Julian (alive 2001)
Schongauer, Martin* (1491)
Schwitters, Kurt (1948)
Van Scorel, Jan* (1562)
Sebastiano del Piombo* (1547)
Segal, George (alive 2001)
Serra, Richard (alive 2001)
Seurat, Georges (1891)
Severini, Gino (1966)
Sheeler, Charles (1965)
Sherman, Cindy (alive 2001)
Siberechts, Jan* (1703)
Sickert, Walter (1942)
Signac, Paul (1935)
Signorelli, Luca* (1523)
Siqueiros, David Alfaro (1974)
Sisley, Alfred (1899)
Sittow, Michiel* (1525/6)
Sluter, Claus* (1405)
Smith, David (1965)
Snyders, Frans* (1657)
Sodoma* (1548)
Soulages, Pierre (alive 2001)
Soutine, Chaim (1943)
Spencer, Sir Stanley (1959)
Spilliaert, Leon (1946)
De Stael, Nicolas (1955)
Steen, Jan* (1679)
Stella, Frank (alive 2001)
Still, Clyfford (alive 2001)
Stuart, Gilbert (1828)
Stubbs, George (1806)
Sutherland, Graham (1980)
Tamayo, Rufino (1991)
Tanguy, Yves (1955)
Tapies, Antoni (alive 2001)
Tatlin, Vladimir (1953)
Teniers, David* (1690)
Ter Borch, Gerard* (1681)
Terbrugghen, Hendrick* (1629)
Thiebaud, Wayne (alive 2001)
Tiepolo,Giovanni Battista* (1770)
Tinguely, Jean (1991)
Tintoretto, Jacopo* (1594)
Tissot, James (1902)
Titian* (1576)
Tobey, Mark (1976)
Talouse-Lautrec, Henri de (1901)
De Troy, Jean-Francois* (1752)
Turner, J M W (1850)
Twombly, Cy (alive 2001)
Uccello, Paolo* (1475)

Utamaro, Kitagawa (1806)
Utrillo, Maurice (1955)
Vallotton, Felix (1925)
Vasarely, Victor (alive 2001)
Velazquez, Diego de Silva y* (1660)
Vermeer, Jan* (1675)
Veronese* (1588)
Verrocchio, Andrea del* (1488)
Vieira da Silva, Maria Elena (1992)
Vigeee-Lebrun, Marie-
    Louise-Elisabeth (1842)
Violoa, Bill (alive 2001)
Vlaminck, Maurice de (1958)
Vouet, Simon* (1649)
Vuillard, Edouard (1940)
Wadsworth, Edward (1949)
Wallis, Alfred (1942)
Warhol, Andy (1987)
Waterhouse, John William (1917)
Watteau, Antoine* (1721)
Weight, Carel (1997)
Wesselmann, Tom (1931)
West, Benjamin (1820)
Van der Weyden, Rogier* (1464)
Whistler, James Abbot McNeill
(1903)
Wilkie, Sir David (1841)
Wilson, Richard* (1782)
Witz, Konrad* (1446)
Wood, Grant (1942)
Wright of Derby, Joseph* (1797)
Wyeth, Andrew (alive 2001)
Yeats, Jack Butler (1957)
Zoffany, Johann (1810)
Zorn, Anders (1920)
Zuccareli, Franceso* (1788)
Zurbaran,Francisco de* (1664)

Altahmazi Contemporary Art's - Top Famous Artists   Exhibit 12b

Leonardo DaVinci
Thomas Kinkade
Salvador Dali
Pablo Picasso
Vincent Van Gogh
Andy Warhol
Diego Rivera
Claude Monet
Ansel Adams
Kim Anderson
M.C. Escher
Rembrandt
Pierre-Auguste Renoir
Jacob Lawrence
Jackson Pollock
Henri Matisse
Georgia O'Keeffe
Roy Lichtenstein
Edgar Degas
Joan Miro
Edvard Munch
Mary Cassatt
Edward Hopper
Paul Klee
Wolf Kahn
Marc Chagall
Rene Magritte

Edouard Manet
Paul Cezanne
Paul Colin
Paul Gaugin
Gustav Klimt
Robert Johnson
Henri de Toulouse Lautrec
Andrew Wyeth
Romare Bearden
Alexander Calder
David Hockney
Keith Haring
Jasper Johns
Fernando Botero
Piet Mondrian
Robert Batemen
Maxfield Parrish
Jack Vettriano
Sandro Botticelli
Wassily Kandinsky
John Singer Sargent
Robert Mapplethorpe
Mark Rothko
Amadeo Modigliani
Steve Hanks
Franz Marc

Combined Lists of Master Photographers   Exhibit 12c

Riverman's
Great Photographers
1   **Werner Bischof**
2   Bill Brandt
3   **Margaret Bourke-White**
4   **Brassai**
5   Julia Cameron
6   Henri Cartier-Bresson
7   Larry Clark
8   Imogen Cunningham
9   Terence Donovan
10 Roger Fenton
11 **Robert Frank**
12 Horst P. Horst
13 Yousuf Karsh
14 **Andre Kertesz**
15 Josef Koudelka
16 Dorethea Lange
17 Sally Mann
18 Lee Miller
19 Alexander Rodchenko
20 Edward Steichen
21 Josef Sudek
22 Edward Weston

Here-ye's 2nd Floor Lobby
1   Ansel Adams
2   Edward Steichen
3   Dorthea Lange
4   Walker Evans
5   Yousuf Karsh
6   **Andre Kertesz**
7   **Alfred Eisenstaedt**
8   Gordon Parks
9   Imogene Cunningham
10 Eugene Smith
11 Lennart Nilsson
12 **Margaret Bourke-White**
13 **Phillipe Halsmann**
14 **Irving Penn**
15 **Diane Arbus**
16 Edward Curtis
17 Matthew Brady
18 Edward Maybridge
19 **Alfred Stieglitz**

Harry's Photo Shop
Some Great Photographers
1   Abbott, Berenice
2   Adams, Ansel
3   **Arbus, Dianne**
4   Atget, Eugene
5   **Avedon, Richard**
6   Brady, Matthew
7   **Bourke-"White, Margaret**
8   Brandt, Bill
9   **Brassai, Gyula**
10 Bravo, Alvarez
11 Bulloch, Wynn

12 Callahan, Harry Morey
13 Cameron, Julia Margaret
14 **Capa, Robert**
15 Cartier-Bresson, Henri
16 Coburn, Alvin Langdon
17 Cunningham, Imogen
18 **Eisendstaedt, Alfred**
19 Evans, Walker
20 **Frank, Robert**
21 **Friedlander, Lee**
22 Hine, Lewis
23 Karsh, Yousef
24 **Kertesz, Andre**
25 **Klein, William**
26 Lange, Dorthea
27 Livick, Stephen
28 **Man Ray**
29 Mapplethorpe, Robert
30 **Michals, Duane**
31 **Moholy-Nagy, Laszlo**
32 Muybridge, Eadweard
33 O'Sullivan, Timothy
34 Outerbridge, Paul
35 **Penn, Irving**
36 Porter, Eliot
37 Riis, Jacob
38 **Sander, August**
39 Smith, W. Eugene
40 Steichen, Edward
41 **Stieglitz, Alfred**
42 **Strand, Paul**
43 Sudek, Josef
44 **Talbot, W.H. Fox**
45 Warhal, Andy
46 **Weegee (Arthur Fellig)**
47 Weston, Edward
48 **Winogrand, Gary**

Photocamera 35's
The Great Photographers
1   Eugene Atget
2   Ansel Adams
3   **Margaret Bourke-White**
4   Henri Cartier-Bresson
5   **Sebastiao Salgado**
6   Edward Steichen
7   **Alfred Stieglitz**
8   Bill Brandt
9   Cecil Beaton
10 **Robert Capa**
11 Jaques-Henri Lartigue
12 Nadar
13 **David Seymour "Chim"**
14 William Eugene Smith
15 **Paul Strand**
16 Edward Weston
17 Minor White
18 Fulvio Roiter
19 Franco Fontana

20 Luigi Ghirri
21 Gianni Barengo-Gardin
22 Mario Giacomelli
23 Luciano Bovina
24 Steve Mc Curry
25 Niepce
26 Louis-Jacques Mande Daguerre
27 **William Henri Fox-Talbot**
28 Hippolyte Bayard

Digital Camera's
Masters of Photography
1   Abbott
2   Ansel Adams
3   Robert Adams
4   Alvarez Bravo
5   **Arbus**
6   Atget
7   Bellocq
8   Blossfeldt
9   **Bourke-white**
10 Brandt
11 **Brassaï**
12 Callahan
13 Cameron
14 Coburn
15 Cunningham
16 Decarava
17 Doisneau
18 Eggleston
19 Evans
20 **Friedlander**
21 Gowin
22 Gutmann
23 Hine
24 Karsh
25 **Kertész**
26 **Klein**
27 Koudelka
28 Lange
29 Lartigue
30 Laughlin
31 **Levitt**
32 Mapplethorpe
33 Meatyard
34 **Model**
35 Modotti
36 Muybridge
37 Nadar
38 **Newman**
39 O'sullivan
40 Outerbridge
41 **Penn**
42 Riis
43 Rodchenko
44 **Salgado**
45 **Sherman**
46 Shore
47 Smith

Combined Lists of Master Photographers

**Digital Camera's
Masters of Photography
(continued)**
48 Sommer
49 Steichen
50 **Stieglitz**
51 **Strand**
52 **Talbot**
53 **Uelsmann**
54 Waldman
55 Watkins
56 **Weegee**
57 Weston
58 White
59 **Winogrand**
60 Wolleh

**About.com's Directory
of Notable Photographers**
1 Abbott, Berenice
2 Ansel Adams
3 Adams, Robert
4 Alinari Brothers
5 Alpert, Max
6 Araki, Nobuyoshi
7 **Arbus, Diane**
8 Atget, Eugene
9 **Avedon, Richard**
10 Bailey, David
11 Baldessari, John
12 **Baltz, Lewis**
13 Bayer, Herbert
14 Beato, Felice (and Antonio)
15 Beaton, Cecil
16 Bellocq, E J
17 Becher, Bernt and Hilla
18 Berry, Ian
19 **Bischof, Werner**
20 Blakemore, John
21 Blossfeldt, Karl
22 Boubat, Edouard
23 **Bourke-White, Margaret**
24 Brady, Matthew
25 Brandt, Bill
26 **Brassai**
27 Bravo, Manuel Alvarez
28 Bullock, Wynn
29 Cabado, Pablo
30 Callahan, Harry
31 Cameron, Julia Margaret
32 **Capa, Cornell**
33 **Capa, Robert**
34 Caponigro, Paul
35 Cartier-Bresson, Henri
36 Chim (David Seymour)
37 Christenberry, William
38 Clark, Larry
39 Close, Chuck
40 Coburn, Alvin Langdon

41 Connor, Linda
42 Cravo Neto, Mario
43 Cruz, Valdir
44 Cunningham, Imogen
45 Curtis, Edward S
46 Cypriano, Andre
47 Daguerre, Louis M
48 Dahl-Wolfe, Louise
49 **Dater, Judy**
50 **Davidson, Bruce**
51 Davies, John
52 de Barros, Geraldo
53 De Meyer, Baron Adolf
54 Deal, Joe
55 Decarava, Roy
56 Demachy, Robert
57 Depardon, Raymond
58 Doisneau, Robert
59 Echague, Jose Ortiz
60 Edgerton, Harold
61 Eggleston, William
62 **Eisenstadt, Alfred**
63 Elksen, Ed van der
64 Emerson, Peter H
65 Epstein, Mitch
66 **Erwitt, Elliot**
67 Evans, Frederick
68 Evans, Walker
69 Ewald, Wendy
70 Faurer, Louis
71 **Feininger, Andreas**
72 Fellig, Arthur (Weegee)
73 Fenton, Roger
74 **Fink, Larry**
75 **Fox Talbot - see Talbot**
76 Franck, Martine
77 **Frank, Robert**
78 **Freed, Leonard**
79 Freedman, Jill
80 **Friedlander, Lee**
81 Funke, Jaromir
82 Gardner, Alexander
83 **Gibson, Ralph**
84 Gilpin, Laura
85 Goldblatt, David
86 **Goldin, Nan**
87 Gowin, Emmet
88 Griffiths, Philip Jones
89 Groover, Jan
90 **Haas, Ernst**
91 Hahn, Betty
92 **Halsman, Phillipe**
93 Harbutt, Charles
94 Hardy, Bert
95 Hare, Chauncey
96 **Heartfield, John**
97 Henri, Florence
98 **Heyman, Abigail**
99 Hill, David Octavius

100 Hill, Paul
101 Hine, Lewis
102 Hopkins, Thurston
103 Hoppe, E Otto
104 Hosoe, Eikoh
105 Hurn, David
106 Hutton, Kurt
107 Ikko (Ikko Narahara)
108 Ishimoto, Yasuhiro
109 Iturbide, Graciela
110 Izis (Israel Bidermanas)
111 Jackson, William H
112 **Jacobi, Lotte**
113 Jenshel, Len
114 **Josephson, Kenneth**
115 Karsh, Yousuf
116 Kasebier, Gertrude
117 **Kertesz, Andre**
118 Killip, Chris
119 **Klein, William**
120 Koudelka, Josef
121 **Krims, Les**
122 Kruger, Barbara
123 **Land, Edwin H**
124 Lange, Dorothea
125 Lartigue, Jacques H
126 Laughlin, Clarence John
127 **Levitt, Helen**
128 Lestido, Adriana
129 **Lyon, Danny**
130 **Man Ray - see Ray**
131 Mann, Sally
132 Manos, Constantine
133 Mapplethorpe, Robert
134 Mark, Mary Ellen
135 Marlow, Peter
136 Mascaro, Cristiano
137 McCullin, Donald
138 Meatyard, Ralph Eugene
139 **Meisalas, Susan**
140 **Metzker, Ray**
141 Metzner, Sheila
142 Meyer, Pedro
143 **Meyerowitz, Joel**
144 **Michals, Duane**
145 Miller, Lee
146 **Model, Lisette**
147 Modotti, Tina
148 **Moholy-Nagy, Lazlo & Lucia**
149 Moore, Ray
150 Morris, Wright
151 Mortenson, Ray
152 **Newman, Arnold**
153 **Newton, Helmut**
154 Nixon, Nicholas
155 O'Sullivan, Timothy
156 **Orkin, Ruth**
157 Outerbridge, Paul
158 Owens, Bill

Combined Lists of Master Photographers   Exhibit 12c

About.com's Directory
of Notable Photographers
(continued)
159 Papageorge, Todd
160 Parker, Olivia
161 **Penn, Irving**
162 Peress, Gilles
163 Petersen, Anders
164 Plossu, Bernard
165 Plowden, David
166 Porter, Eliot
167 Post Wolcott, Marion
168 Ray, Man
169 Rejlander, Oscar G
170 Renger-Patsch, Albert
171 Rheims, Bettina
172 Riboud, Mark
173 **Ritts, Herb**
174 Rio Branco, Miguel
175 Robinson, Henry P
176 Rodchenko, Alexander
177 Rodger, George
178 Ronis, Willy
179 **Rosenblum, Walter**
180 **Rothstein, Arthur**

181 **Salgado, Sebastião**
182 **Saloman, Erich**
183 **Sander, August**
184 Saudek, Jan
185 **Seymour, David**
186 Shahn, Ben
187 **Sherman, Cindy**
188 Shore, Stephen
189 Sieff, Jeanloup
190 **Siskind, Aaron**
191 Smith, Edwin
192 Smith, W Eugene
193 Snelson, Kenneth
194 Sommer, Frederick
195 Spence, Jo
196 Steichen, Edouard
197 Steinert, Otto
198 Steiner, Ralph
199 **Stern, Bert**
200 Stern, Grete
201 **Sternfield, Joel**
202 **Stieglitz, Alfred**
203 Stoumen, Lou
204 **Strand, Paul**
205 Suda, Issei

206 Sudek, Josef
207 Sutcliffe, Frank M
208 Tenneson, Joyce
209 Thomson, John
210 Tice, George A
211 **Tress, Arthur**
212 **Uelsmann, Jerry N**
213 **Ulmann, Doris**
214 Umbo (Otto Umbehr)
215 Uzzle, Burk
216 Walker, Todd
217 Waplington, Nick
218 Watkins, Carleton E
219 Webb, John
220 **Weegee**
221 **Wegmann, William**
222 Weston, Brett
223 Weston, Edward
224 White, Clarence
225 White, Minor
226 **Winogrand, Gary**
227 **Witkin, Joel-Peter**
228 Yavno, Max

Foto Art's Greatest Photographers
1   Abbot Berenice (1898-1991)
2   Adams Ansel (1902-1984)
3   Adamson Robert (1821-1848)
4   Adams Robert (1937-)
5   Anschutz Ottomar (1846-1907)
6   **Arbus Diane** (1923-1971)
7   Atget Jean Eugene Auguste (1857-1927)
8   Atkins Anna (1799-1871)
9   **Avedon Richard** (1923-.....)
10 Baldus, Edouard-denis (1815-1882)
11 Baltermants, Dmitri (1912-1990)
12 Barnard, George N. (1819-1902)
13 Bayard Hippolyte (1801-1887)
14 Bayer-hecht, Irene (1898-1991)
15 Beard, Richard (1802-1885)
16 Beato Felice A. (1825-1907)
17 Yannis Behrakis (1960-)
18 Bedford, Francis (1816-1894)
19 Bell, William H. (1830-1910)
20 Bennett, Henry Hamilton (1843-1908)
21 Bentley, Wilson A. (1865-1931)
22 Bergmann-michel, Ella (1896-1971)
23 Bisson, Louis (1814-1876)
24 Bisson, Auguste-rosalie (1826-1900)
25 **Bischof Werner** (1916-1954)
26 Black, James Wallace (1825-1896)
27 Blanchard, Valentine (1831-1901)
28 Blanquart-evrard, Louis-desire (1802-1872)
29 Blossfeldt, Karl (1865-1932)
30 Boissonnas Fred (1858-1946)

31 **Bourke-white, Margaret** (1904-1971)
32 Bourne, Samuel (1834-1912)
33 Brady, Mathew B. (1823-1896)
34 Bragaglia Antonio Giulio (1889-1963)
35 Brancusi, Constantin (1876-1957)
36 Brandt, Bill (1904-1983)
37 **Brassai (Gyula Halasz** 1899-1984)
38 Braun, Adolphe (1811-1877)
39 Bravo, Manuel Alvarez (1902-)
40 Bresson Cartier Henri (1908-.......)
41 Bridges George (1788-1863)
42 Brigman, Anne W. (1869-1950)
43 Bruguiere, Francis (1880-1945)
44 Bullock, Wynn (1902-75)
45 Burrows, Larry (1926-71)
46 Callahan, Harry (1912-)
47 Cameron Julia Margaret (1815-1879)
48 Camp Du Maxime (1822-1894)
49 **Capa, Robert** (1913-1954)
50 Caponigro Paul (1932-.....)
51 Carter Kevin (1961-1994)
52 Carroll, Lewis (1832-1898)
53 Cartier-bresson, Henri (1908-)
54 Claudet, Jean Francois Antoine (1797-1867)
55 Clifford, Charles (1819-1863)
56 Coburn, Alvin Langdon (1882-1966)
57 Croner, Ted
58 Cunningham, Imogen (1883-1976)
59 Curtis, Edward Sheriff (1868-1952)
60 Daguerre Louis Jacques Mande (1787-1851)
61 Davidson, George

Combined Lists of Master Photographers

Foto Art's Greatest Photographers
(Continued)

62 Day, Fred Holland (1864-1933)
63 De Meyer, Baron Adolf Gayne (1868-1949)
64 Decarava, Roy (1919-)
65 Delaroche, Paul (1797-1859)
66 Demachy, Leon Robert (1859-1937)
67 Diamond, Dr Hugh Welch (1809-1886)
68 Disd_ri, Andre Adolphe Eugene (1819-1890)
69 Dodgson, Rev. Charles Lutwidge (1832-1898)
70 Doisneau, Robert (1912-1994)
71 Ducos Du Hauron Louis (1837-1920)
72 **Duane Michals** (1932-....)
73 Eggleston, William (1937-)
74 Einzig, Richard (1932-1980)
75 **Eisenstaedt, Alfred** (1898-1995)
76 Emerson, Dr Peter Henry (1856-1936)
77 Erfurth, Hugo (1874-1948)
78 Eugene, Frank (1865-1936)
79 Evans, Walker (1903-1975)
80 Evans, Frederick Henry (1852-1943)
81 Fellig, Arthur (1899-1968)
82 Fenton, Roger (1819-1869)
83 **Feininger, Andreas** (1906 ...)
84 **Frank Robert Louis** (1924-.....)
85 **Friedlander, Lee** (1934-)
86 Frith, Francis (1822-1898)
87 Gardner Alexander (1821 1882)
88 Gros Jean Baptiste Louis (1793-1870)
89 **Gibson Ralph** (1939-....)
90 Gray Le Gustave (1820-1862)
91 Greene, John Beasley (1832-1856)
92 Gutmann, John (1905)
93 Gutierrez Alberto Diaz Or Korda (1929 -2001)
94 **Haas Ernst** (1921-....)
95 Hal_sz, Gyula (1899-1984)
96 Harisiadis Dimitris
97 Hawarden, Lady Clementina (1822-1865)
98 Herscel Sir John F.W. (1792-1871)
99 Hill David Octavius (1802-1870)
100 Hine, Lewis Wickes (1874-1940)
101 Hockney, David (1937-)
102 Howlett, Robert (1831-1858)
103 Jackson William Henry (1843-1942)
104 Kardiakidis George (1883 - 1958)
105 Keetman Peter (1916-....)
106 **Kertesz Andre** (1894-1985)
107 Korda Or Alberto Diaz Gutierrez (1929 -2001)
108 Koudelka Josef
109 Lange, Dorothea (1895-1965)
110 Lartigue, Jacques-henri (1894-1986)
111 Laughlin, Clarence John (1905-1985)
112 Le Gray, Gustave (1820-1882)
113 Le Secq, Henri (1818-1882)
114 **Leibovitz, Annie** (1949)
115 **Levitt, Clarence Helen** (1907-)
116 List Herbert (1903-1975)
117 Lewelyn, John Dillwyn (1810-1882)

118 Magritte, Ren_ (1898-1967)
119 Manos Konstantinos
120 Mann, Sally (1951)
121 Mapplethorpe, Robert (1946-1989)
122 Margaritis Filiposs (1810-1892)
123 Marey Etienne Jules (1830-1904)
124 Martin, Paul Augustus (1864-1944)
125 Megalokonomou Manolis
126 Meletzhs Spyros
127 Miller, Lee (1907-1977)
128 Modotti, Tina (1896-1942)
129 **Moholy-nagy, Laszlo** (1895-1946)
130 Mpalafas Kostas
131 Mortimer, Francis James (1874-1944)
132 Muybridge Eadweard (1830-1904)
133 Nadar (Gaspard Felix Tournachon) (1820-1910)
134 Negre Charles (1820-1880)
135 **Newman Arnold** (1918-...)
136 Niepce Joseph Nicephore (1765-1833)
137 Nelly's (Ellh Seraidari)
138 O'sullivan Timothy H. (1840-1882)
139 Outerbridge, Paul (1896-1958)
140 Papaioannoy Boula
141 **Penn Irving** (1917-...)
142 Poitevin Alphonse Louis (1819-1882)
143 Porter, Eliot (1901-1990)
144 **Ray Man** (1890-1976)
145 Rejlander Oscar (1813-1875)
146 Riis, Jacob (1849-1914)
147 Robinson Henry Peach (1830-1901)
148 Rodchenko Alexander (1891-1956)
149 **Rothstein, Arthur** (1915-1985)
150 **Salgado Sebastiao** (1944-...
151 **Salomon, Erich** (1886-1944)
152 Samaras Loukas (1936-...)
153 **Sander August** (1876-1964)
154 Seeley, George Henry (1880-1955)
155 Shaw, George Bernard (1856-1950)
156 **Sherman, Cindy** (1954-)
157 **Seymour David** (1911-1956)
158 **Siskind Aaron** (1903-1991)
159 Smaragdis Adreas (1947-...)
160 Smith, William Eugene (1918-1978)
161 Snelling, Henry H.
162 Sommer, Frederick (1905)
163 Steichen Edward (1879-1973)
164 **Stieglitz Alfred** (1864-1946)
165 **Strand, Paul** (1890-1976)
166 Sudek, Josef (1896-1976)
167 Sutcliffe, Frank Meadow (1853-1941)
168 **Talbot William Henry Fox** (1800-1877)
169 Thomson, John (1837-1921)
170 Tripe, Linnaeus (1822-1902)
171 Tloupas Takis
172 **Uelsman Jerry** (1934-...)
173 **Weegee (Arthur Fellig** 1899-1968)
174 Weston Edward (1886-1958)

Combined Lists of Master Photographers   Exhibit 12c

Foto Art's Greatest Photographers
(Continued)
175 White Charence (1871-1925)
176 White Minor (1908-1976)
177 Wilson, Edward L. (1838-1903)
178 Wilson, George Washington (1823-1893)
179 **Winogrand, Garry** (1928-1984)
180 **Witkin, Joel-Peter** (? 1939)
181 Wolcott, Alexander (1804-1844)
182 Zografos, Nicos (1881-1967)

Combined Lists of Master Architects

Logia.com's
Master Architects
1   Alvar Aalto
2   **Marcel Breuer**
3   Le Corbusier
4   Antoni Gaudi
5   Walter Gropius
6   **Louis I. Kahn**
7   Charles Rennie Mackintosh
8   Bernard Maybeck
9   Ludwig Mies van der Rohe
10 **Richard Neutra**
11 Andrea Palladio
12 A.W.N. Pugin
13 H. H. Richardson
14 Gerrit Rietveld
15 Eliel and Eero Saarinen
16 Carlo Scarpa
17 R. M. Schindler
18 Louis Sullivan
19 Sir Christopher Wren

About.com's
Master Architects
1   Alvar Aalto
2   Denise Scott Brown
3   Le Corbusier
4   Pierre de Meuron
5   Peter Dominick
6   Sir Norman Foster
7   R. Buckminster Fuller
8   Antoni Gaudí
9   Cass Gilbert
10 Bertram Goodhue
11 Bruce Graham
12 Michael Graves
13 Walter Gropius
14 Charles Gwathmey
15 Jacques Herzog
16 William Holabird
17 Arata Isozaki
18 William Le Baron Jenney
19 Philip Johnson
20 Rem Koolhaas
21 Theodore Link
22 Adolf Loos
23 Bernard Maybeck
24 **Richard Meier**
25 Mies van der Rohe
26 Addison Mizner
27 Julia Morgan
28 William Morris
29 Glenn Murcutt
30 **Richard Neutra**
31 Frederick Law Olmsted
32 Andrea Palladio
33 I.M. Pei
34 Cesar Pelli
35 John Ruskin

36 Robert Siegel
37 **Robert A. M. Stern**
38 Louis Sullivan
39 Susana Torre
40 Robert Venturi
41 Philip Webb
42 Paul Williams
43 Sir Clough Williams-Ellis
44 Frank Lloyd Wright

Indian Architects
Great Architects
1   Aalto, Alvar
2   Ain, Gregory
3   Alberti, Leon Battista
4   Albini Franco
5   Alexander, Christopher
6   Ando, Tadao
7   Bernini, Gian Lorenzo
8   Bofill, Ricardo
9   Borromini, Francesco
10 Botta, Mario
11 Bramante, Donato
12 Brunelleschi, Filippo
13 Calatrava, Santiago
14 Candela, Felix
15 Costa, Lucio
16 Croci Antonio
17 Domenico da Cortona
18 Eames, Charles
19 **Eisenman, Peter**
20 Fathy Hassan
21 Foster, Sir Norman
22 Fuller, Richard Buckminster
23 Gaudi, Antoni
24 **Gehry O. Frank**
25 Graves Michael
26 Garnier Tony
27 Gropius Walter
28 Hadid Zaha
29 Hoffman Josef
30 Hopkins Michael
31 Hadrian
32 Isozaki Arata
33 **Israel Frank**
34 Johnson Philips Cortelyou
35 Jenny William Le Baron
36 **Jocobsen Arne**
37 Kurokawa Kisho
38 **Kahn Louis Isadore**
39 **Kahn Albert**
40 Kollhoff Hans
41 Leonardo Da Vinci
42 Le Corbusier
43 Loos Adolf
44 Mackintosh, Charles Rennie
45 Maki, Fumihiko
46 **Meier, Richard**
47 Mendini, Alessandro

48 Michelangelo, Buonarroti
49 Mies van der Rohe, Ludwig
50 Michelucci Giovanni
51 Moneo, Raffael
52 **Moos, Eric Owen**
53 Niemeyer Oscar
54 Nouvel Jean
55 Nash John
56 Nervi Pier Luigi
57 Neumann Balthasar Johann
58 Otto Frey
59 Owen Robert
60 Oud Jacobus Johannes Pieter
61 Pei, I.M.
62 Pelli Cesar
63 Ponti, Gio
64 Quaroni Ludovico
65 Richardson, Henry Hobson
66 Roche, Kevin
67 Rogers Richard
68 Rossi, Aldo
69 Soane, Sir John
70 Soleri, Paolo
71 **Stern, Robert A. M.**
72 Stirling, James
73 Sullivan, Louis H.
74 Tange, Kenzo
75 Trezzini Domenico
76 Tschumi Bernard
77 Utzon Jorn
78 Vasari Giorgio
79 Venturi, Robert
80 Scott Brown, Denise
81 Wagner Otto
82 Wood John
83 Wren, Christopher
84 Wright, Frank Lloyd
85 Wurster, William Wilson
86 Zanuso, Marco
87 Zumthor, Peter

Great Building's.com's
Most Visited
1   Antonio Gaudi
2   Le Corbusier
3   **Frank Gehry**
4   Ludwig Mies van der Rohe
5   Frank Lloyd Wright
6   Tadao Ando
7   Norman Foster
8   I.M. Pei
9   Alvar Aalto
10 Rem Koolhaas
11 Santiago Calatrava
12 Mario Botta
13 Walter Gropius
14 **Peter Eisenman**
15 **Richard Meier**
16 Gustave Eiffel

Combined Lists of Master Architects   Exhibit 12d

Great Building's.com's
Most Visited (continued)
17 Renzo Piano
18 Imhotep
19 Phillip Johnson
20 Richard Rogers
21 Carles Rennie Mackintosh
22 Eero Saarinen
23 Jean Nouvel
24 Robert Venturi
25 **Louis I. Kahn**
26 Luis Barragan
27 Andrea Palladio
28 Aldo Rossi
29 Oscar Niemeyer

Pritzker Laureates
1   Philip Johnson 1979
2   Luis Barragan 1980
3   James Stirling 1981
4   Kevin Roche 1982
5   Ieoh Ming Pei 1983
6   **Richard Meier 1984**
7   Hans Hollein 1985
8   Gottfried Boehm 1986
9   Kenzo Tange 1987
10 **Gordon Bunshaft 1988**
11 Oscar Niemeyer 1988
12 **Frank Gehry 1989**
13 Aldo Rossi 1990
14 Robert Venturi 1991

15 Alvaro Siza 1992
16 Fumihiko Maki 1993
17 Christian de Portzamparc 1994
18 Tadao Ando 1995
19 Rafael Moneo 1996
20 Sverre Fehn 1997
21 Renzo Piano 1998
22 Sir Norman Foster 1999
23 Rem Koolhaas 2000
24 Jacques Herzog 2001
25 Pierre de Meuron 2001
26 Glenn Murcutt 2002

Yahoo.com's
Master Architects
1   Aalto, Alvar (1898–1976)
2   Ain, Gregory (1908–1988)
3   Alberti, Leon Battista (1404–1472)
4   Alexander, Christopher (b. 1936)
5   Ando, Tadao (b. 1941)
6   Artigas, João Batista Villanova (1915–1984)
7   Asplund, Erik Gunnar (1885–1940)
8   Barragán, Luis (1902–1988)
9   Belluschi, Pietro (1899–1994)
10 Botta, Mario (b. 1943)
11 Burnham, Daniel Hudson (1846–1912)
12 Calatrava, Santiago (b. 1951)
13 Calthorpe, Peter
14 Codussi, Mauro (1440–1504)
15 Colter, Mary Elizabeth Jane (1869–1958)
16 Diller, Elizabeth & Ricardo Scofidio
17 Duany, Andres and Elizabeth Plater-Zyberk
18 Eames, Charles (1907–1978) & Ray (1912–1988)
19 **Eisenman, Peter (b. 1932)**
20 Ellwood, Craig (b. 1922)
21 Emberton, Joseph (1889–1956)
22 Foster, Norman (b. 1935)
23 Frey, Albert (1903–1998)
24 Fuller, Richard Buckminster (1895–1983)
25 Furness, Frank (1839–1912)
26 Gaudí, Antoni (1852–1926)
27 **Gehry, Frank (b. 1929)**
28 Gerber, Arthur U. (1878–1960)
29 Gilbert, Cass (1859–1934)
30 Gill, Irving J. (1870–1936)
31 Goff, Bruce (1904–1982)
32 Graves, Michael (b. 1934)
33 Gray, Eileen (1878–1976)
34 Greene, Charles Sumner (1868–1957)
35 Greenway, Frances (1777–1837)
36 Griffin, Walter Burley (1876–1937)
37 Gropius, Walter (1883–1969)
38 Hadid, Zaha (b. 1950)

39 Haertling, Charles A. (1928–1984)
40 Harris, Harwell Hamilton (1903–1990)
41 Hejduk, John (1929–2000)
42 Holabird, William (1854–1923)
43 Hood, Raymond (1881–1934)
44 Horta, Victor (1861–1947)
45 **Hundertwasser, Friedensreich (1928–2000)**
46 **Israel, Frank (1945–1996)**
47 **Jacobsen, Arne (1902–1971)**
48 Jeanneret, Charles Edouard 'Le Corbusier' (1887–1965)
49 Jerde, Jon
50 Johnson, Philip (b. 1906)
51 Jones, Inigo (1573–1652)
52 **Kahn, Albert (1869–1942)**
53 **Kahn, Louis I. (1901–1974)**
54 Koenig, Pierre (b. 1925)
55 Koolhaas, Rem (b. 1944)
56 Koulermos, Panos (1933–1999)
57 Larry, Everett Nicholas (1891–1926)
58 Lautner, John (1911–1994)
59 **Libeskind, Daniel (b. 1946)**
60 Lin, Maya (b. 1959)
61 Lissitzky, El (Lazar) (1890–1941)
62 Loos, Adolf (1870–1933)
63 Lutyens, Edwin (1869–1944)
64 Mackintosh, Charles Rennie (1868–1928)
65 Maybeck, Bernard (1862–1957)
66 **Meier, Richard (b. 1934)**
67 Mies van der Rohe, Ludwig (1886–1969)
68 Mockbee, Samuel (1944–2001)
69 Moneo, Jose Rafael (b. 1937)
70 Moore, Charles W. (1925–1993)
71 Morgan, Julia (1872–1957)
72 Murcutt, Glenn (b. 1936)
73 **Neutra, Richard (1892–1970)**
74 Niemeyer, Oscar (b. 1907)
75 Palladio, Andrea (1508–1580)
76 Pei, I. M. (b. 1917)
77 Pelli, Cesar (b. 1926)
78 Piano, Renzo (b. 1937)

Combined Lists of Master Architects

Yahoo.com's
Master Architects (continued)

79 Plecnik, Joze (1872–1957)
80 Portzamparc, Christian de (b. 1944)
81 Prince, Bart (b. 1947)
82 Pugin, Augustus Welby Northmore (1812–1852)
83 Richardson, Henry Hobson (1838–1881)
84 Rietveld, Gerrit (1888–1964)
85 Rossi, Aldo (1931–1997)
86 Saarinen, Eero (1910–1961)
87 Scarpa, Carlo (1906–1978)
88 Schindler, Rudolph M. (1887–1953)
89 Seidler, Harry (b.1923)
90 Smirke, Robert (1781–1867)
91 Speer, Albert (1905–1981)

92 Starck, Philippe (b.1949)
93 Stevens, John Calvin (1855–1940)
94 Stirling, James (1926–1992)
95 Sullivan, Louis (1856–1924)
96 Taniguchi, Yoshio (b. 1937)
97 Utzon, Jørn (b. 1918)
98 van Eyck, Aldo (1918–1999)
99 Venturi, Robert (b. 1925)
100 Wren, Sir Christopher (1632–1723)
101 Wright, Frank Lloyd (1867–1959)
102 Wurster, William Wilson (1895–1973)
103 Yamasaki, Minoru (1912–1986)
104 Zumthor, Peter (b. 1943)

Academy Award Winning Directors: 1929 – 2007   Exhibit 13a

Award Date	Film	Recipient(s)
2007	No Country for Old Men	**Joel & Ethan Coen**
2006	The Departed	Martin Scorsese
2005	Brokeback Mountain	Ang Lee
2004	Million Dollar Baby	Clint Eastwood
2003	The Pianist	**Roman Polanski**
2002	A Beautiful Mind	Ron Howard
2001	Traffic	Steven Soderbergh
2000	American Beauty	**Sam Mendes**
1999	Saving Private Ryan	**Steven Spielberg**
1998	Titanic	James Cameron
1997	English Patient, The	Anthony Minghella
1996	Braveheart	Mel Gibson
1995	Forrest Gump	Robert Zemeckis
1994	Schindler's List	**Steven Spielberg**
1993	Unforgiven	Clint Eastwood
1992	Silence of the Lambs, The	Jonathan Demme
1991	Dances with Wolves	Kevin Costner
1990	Born on the Fourth of July	**Oliver Stone**
1989	Rain Man	**Barry Levinson**
1988	Last Emperor, The	Bernardo Bertolucci
1987	Platoon	**Oliver Stone**
1986	Out of Africa	**Sydney Pollack**
1985	Amadeus	**Milos Forman**
1984	Terms of Endearment	**James L. Brooks**
1983	Gandhi	Richard Attenborough
1982	Reds	Warren Beatty
1981	Ordinary People	Robert Redford
1980	Kramer vs. Kramer	Robert Benton
1979	Deer Hunter, The	Michael Cimino
1978	Annie Hall	**Woody Allen**
1977	Rocky	John G. Avildsen
1976	One Flew Over the Cuckoo's Nest	**Milos Forman**
1975	Godfather: Part II, The	Francis Coppola
1974	Sting, The	George Roy Hill
1973	Cabaret	Bob Fosse
1972	French Connection, The	**William Friedkin**
1971	Patton	Franklin J. Schaffner
1970	Midnight Cowboy	**John Schlesinger**
1969	Oliver!	Carol Reed
1968	Graduate, The	**Mike Nichols**
1967	Man for All Seasons	Fred Zinnemann
1966	Sound of Music	Robert Wise
1965	My Fair Lady (1964)	**George Cukor**
1964	Tom Jones (1963)	Tony Richardson
1963	Lawrence of Arabia (1962)	David Lean
1962	West Side Story (1961)	Robert Wise, **Jerome Robbins**
1961	Apartment, The (1960)	**Billy Wilder**
1960	Ben-Hur (1959)	**William Wyler**
1959	Gigi (1958)	Vincente Minnelli
1958	Bridge on the River Kwai, The	Norman Taurog
1957	Giant	George Stevens
1956	Marty	Delbert Mann
1955	On the Waterfront	Elia Kazan
1954	From Here to Eternity	**Fred Zinnemann**
1953	Quiet Man, The	John Ford
1952	Place in the Sun, A	George Stevens
1951	All About Eve	**Joseph L. Mankiewicz**
1950	Letter to Three Wives, A	**Joseph L. Mankiewicz**

Academy Award Winning Directors: 1929 – 2007   Exhibit 13a

Award Date	Film	Recipient(s)
1949	Treasure of the Sierra Madre, The	John Huston
1948	Gentleman's Agreement	Elia Kazan
1947	Best Years of Our Lives, The	**William Wyler**
1946	Lost Weekend, The	**Billy Wilder**
1945	Going My Way	Leo McCarey
1944	Casablanca	**Michael Curtiz**
1943	Mrs. Miniver	**William Wyler**
1942	How Green Was My Valley	John Ford
1941	Grapes of Wrath, The	John Ford
1940	Gone with the Wind	Victor Fleming
1939	You Can't Take It with You	Frank Capra
1938	Awful Truth, The	Leo McCarey
1937	Mr. Deeds Goes to Town	Frank Capra
1936	Informer, The	John Ford
1935	It Happened One Night	Frank Capra
1934	Cavalcade	Frank Lloyd
1933	Bad Girl	Frank Borzage
1932	Skippy	Norman Taurog
1931	All Quiet on the Western Front	**Lewis Milestone**
1930	Divine Lady, The	Frank Lloyd
1929	Two Arabian Knights (1927)	**Lewis Milestone**
1927/8	Seventh Heaven (1927)	Frank Borzage

List Provided from the Academy of Motion Picture Arts and Sciences web site "oscars.org"
Jewish Directors identified from information provided on web site of "jewhoo.com" as well as "yahoodi.com" and the book "Jewish Contributions to the American Way of Life" by Asher B. Etkes

Great Directors selected by Reel.com and Filmsite.org	Exhibit 13b

Reel.com

Classic

1   Alfred Hitchcock
2   Orson Welles
3   **Billy Wilder**
4   Ingmar Bergman
5   Federico Fellini
6   Akira Kurosawa
7   **Francois Truffaut**
8   Luis Bunuel
9   John Huston
10 John Ford
11 **Fritz Lang**
12 David Lean
13 Howard Hawks
14 Jean Renoir
15 John Cassavetes
16 Preston Sturges
17 Elia Kazan
18 Vittorio De Sica
19 Sergio Leone
20 **Ernst Lubitsch**
21 Frank Capra
22 Sam Peckinpah
23 Nicholas Ray
24 **George Cukor**
25 Vincente Minnelli

Silent Era

1   D. W. Griffith
2   **Sergei Eisenstein**
3   F.W. Murnau
4   Erich von Stroheim
5   Buster Keaton

Contemporary

1   Martin Scorsese
2   **Stanley Kubrick**
3   **Woody Allen**
4   Robert Altman
5   Francis Ford Coppola
6   **Roman Polanski**
7   Peter Weir
8   **Steven Spielberg**
9   David Lynch
10 Jean-Luc Godard
11 Terry Gilliam
12 Bernardo Bertolucci
13 **Joel and Ethan Coen**
14 **David Cronenberg**
15 John Sayles
16 **Oliver Stone**
17 Spike Lee
18 **Milos Forman**
19 Tim Burton
20 Krzystof Kieslowski
21 Peter Greenaway
22 Ridley Scott
23 James Ivory
24 **Mike Leigh**
25 Jane Campion

Filmsite.org

Greatest 75 (in alphabetical order)

1   **Woody Allen**
2   Robert Altman
3   Busby Berkeley
4   Frank Borzage
5   Clarence Brown
6   Tim Burton
7   James Cameron
8   John Cassavetes
9   John Cassavetes
10 Charles Chaplin
11 **Joel and Ethan Coen**
12 Francis Ford Coppola
13 Roger Corman
14 **George Cukor**
15 **Michael Curtiz**
16 **Cecil B. De Mille**
17 Walt Disney
18 Victor Fleming
19 John Ford
20 D.W. Griffith
21 Howard Hawks
22 Alfred Hitchcock
23 John Huston
24 Elia Kazan
25 Buster Keaton
26 Henry King
27 **Stanley Kramer**
28 **Stanley Kubrick**
29 **Fritz Lang**
30 David Lean
31 Spike Lee
32 **Ernst Lubitsch**
33 George Lucas
34 David Lynch
35 **Sidney Lumet**
36 Louis Malle
37 Rouben Mamoulian
38 **Joseph Mankiewicz**
39 Leo McCarey
40 **Lewis Milestone**
41 Vincente Minnelli
42 F.W. Murnau
43 **Mike Nichols**
44 **Max Ophuls**
45 Ssm Peckinpah
46 **Arthur Penn**
47 **Roman Polanski**
48 **Sydney Pollack**
49 Michael Powell
50 **Otto Preminger**
51 Nicholas Ray
52 Ken Russell
53 **John Schlesinger**
54 Martin Scorsese
55 Ridley Scott
56 Mack Sennett
57 **Don Siegel**
58 Douglas Sirk
59 **Steven Spielberg**
60 George Stevens
61 **Oliver Stone**
62 Preston Sturges
63 King Vidor
64 **Josef von Sternberg**
65 **Erich von Stroheim**
66 Raoul Walsh
67 Peter Weir
68 Orson Welles
69 William A. Wellman
70 **Billy Wilder**
71 Robert Wise
72 Sam Wood
73 **William Wyler**
74 Robert Zemeckis
75 **Fred Zinnemann**

American Film Institute 100 Greatest American Movies -   Exhibit 13c
Religious Affiliation Identified by www.adherents. Com

1.	Citizen Kane (1941)	Orson Welles	Protestant Christian
2.	Casablanca (1942)	**Michael Curtiz**	Jewish
3.	The Godfather (1972)	Francis Ford Coppola	Catholic (non-practicing)
4.	Gone With the Wind (1939)	Victor Fleming	Christianity
5.	Lawrence of Arabia (1962)	David Lean	Quaker
6.	The Wizard of Oz (1939)	Victor Fleming	Christianity
7.	The Graduate (1967)	**Mike Nichols**	Jewish
8.	On the Waterfront (1954)	Elia Kazan	Greek Orthodox (lapsed); Communist
9.	Schindler's List (1993)	**Steven Spielberg**	Judaism
10.	Singin' In the Rain (1952)	**Stanley Donen**	Reform Judaism (lapsed)
11.	It's a Wonderful Life (1946)	Frank Capra	Catholic; Christian Science
12.	Sunset Boulevard (1950)	**Billy Wilder**	Jewish
13.	The Bridge On the River Kwai (1957)	David Lean	Quaker
14.	Some Like It Hot (1959)	**Billy Wilder**	Jewish
15.	Star Wars (1977)	George Lucas	Buddhist Methodist
16.	All About Eve (1950)	**Joseph L. Mankiewicz**	Jewish parents; atheist father
17.	The African Queen (1951)	John Huston	Episcopalian (lapsed)
18.	Psycho (1960)	Alfred Hitchcock	Catholic
19.	Chinatown (1974)	**Roman Polanski**	Jewish Catholic (lapsed)
20.	One Flew Over the Cuckoo's Nest (1975)	**Milos Forman**	Jewish father; Protestant mother
21.	The Grapes of Wrath (1940)	John Ford	Catholic
22.	2001: A Space Odyssey (1968)	**Stanley Kubrick**	Jewish
23.	The Maltese Falcon (1941)	John Huston	Episcopalian (lapsed)
24.	Raging Bull (1980)	Martin Scorsese	Catholic (lapsed former seminarian)
25.	E.T. The Extra-Terrestrial (1982)	**Steven Spielberg**	Judaism
26.	Dr. Strangelove (1964)	**Stanley Kubrick**	Jewish
27.	Bonnie and Clyde (1967)	Arthur Penn	
28.	Apocalypse Now (1979)	Francis Ford Coppola	Catholic (non-practicing)
29.	Mr. Smith Goes To Washington (1939)	Frank Capra	Catholic; Christian Science
30.	The Treasure of the Sierra Madre (1948)	John Huston	Episcopalian (lapsed)
31.	Annie Hall (1977)	**Woody Allen**	Jewish (raised Orthodox); agnostic
32.	The Godfather, Part II (1974)	Francis Ford Coppola	Catholic (non-practicing)
33.	High Noon (1952)	**Fred Zinnemann**	Jewish
34.	To Kill a Mockingbird (1962)	Robert Mulligan	Catholic
35.	It Happened One Night (1934)	Frank Capra	Catholic; Christian Science
36.	Midnight Cowboy (1969)	**John Schlesinger**	Jewish
37.	The Best Years of Our Lives (1946)	**William Wyler**	Jewish
38.	Double Indemnity (1944)	**Billy Wilder**	Jewish
39.	Doctor Zhivago (1965)	David Lean	Quaker
40.	North By Northwest (1959)	Alfred Hitchcock	Catholic
41.	West Side Story (1961)	Robert Wise	
		Jerome Robbins	Jewish
42.	Rear Window (1954)	Alfred Hitchcock	Catholic
43.	King Kong (1933)	Merian C. Cooper	Protestant
44.	The Birth of a Nation (1915)	D. W. Griffith	Methodist
45.	A Streetcar Named Desire (1951)	Elia Kazan	Greek Orthodox (lapsed); Communist
46.	A Clockwork Orange (1971)	**Stanley Kubrick**	Jewish
47.	Taxi Driver (1976)	Martin Scorsese	Catholic (lapsed former seminarian)
48.	Jaws (1975)	**Steven Spielberg**	Judaism
49.	Snow White and the Seven Dwarfs (1937)	David Hand, et al.	
50.	Butch Cassidy and the Sundance Kid (1969)	George Roy Hill	
51.	The Philadelphia Story (1940)	**George Cukor**	Jewish
52.	From Here To Eternity (1953)	**Fred Zinnemann**	Jewish
53.	Amadeus (1984)	**Milos Forman**	Jewish father; Protestant mother
54.	All Quiet On the Western Front (1930)	**Lewis Milestone**	Jewish
55.	The Sound of Music (1965)	Robert Wise	
56.	M*A*S*H (1970)	Robert Altman	Catholic (lapsed)

American Film Institute 100 Greatest American Movies -   **Exibit 13c**
Religious Affiliation Identified by www.adherents. Com

57.	The Third Man (1949)	Carol Reed
58.	Fantasia (1940)	Joe Grant
		Dick Huemer
59.	Rebel Without a Cause (1955)	Nicholas Ray
60.	Raiders of the Lost Ark (1981)	**Steven Spielberg** Judaism
61.	Vertigo (1958)	Alfred Hitchcock Catholic
62.	Tootsie (1982)	**Sydney Pollack** Jewish
63.	Stagecoach (1939)	John Ford Catholic
64.	Close Encounters of the Third Kind (1977)	**Steven Spielberg** Judaism
65.	The Silence of the Lambs (1991)	Jonathan Demme
66.	Network (1976)	**Sidney Lumet** Jewish
67.	The Manchurian Candidate (1962)	**John Frankenheimer** Jewish
68.	An American In Paris (1951)	Vincente Minnelli Catholic
69.	Shane (1953)	George Stevens
70.	The French Connection (1971)	**William Friedkin** Jewish
71.	Forrest Gump (1994)	**Robert Zemeckis** Jewish
72.	Ben-Hur (1959)	**William Wyler** Jewish
73.	Wuthering Heights (1939)	**William Wyler** Jewish
74.	The Gold Rush (1925)	Charlie Chaplin Anglican; agnostic
75.	Dances With Wolves (1990)	Kevin Costner Baptist
76.	City Lights (1931)	Charlie Chaplin Anglican; agnostic
77.	American Graffiti (1973)	George Lucas Buddhist Methodist
78.	Rocky (1976)	John Avildsen
79.	The Deer Hunter (1978)	Michael Cimino Catholic
80.	The Wild Bunch (1969)	Sam Peckinpah Protestant
81.	Modern Times (1936)	Charlie Chaplin Anglican; agnostic
82.	Giant (1956)	George Stevens
83.	Platoon (1986)	**Oliver Stone** Jewish father; Catholic mother; raised Episcopalian; Tibetan Buddhism (convert)
84.	Fargo (1996)	**Joel & Ethan Coen** Jewish
85.	Duck Soup (1933)	Leo McCarey Catholic
86.	Mutiny On the Bounty (1935)	Frank Lloyd
87.	Frankenstein (1931)	James Whale
88.	Easy Rider (1969)	Dennis Hopper
89.	Patton (1970)	Franklin Schaffner
90.	The Jazz Singer (1927)	Alan Crosland
91.	My Fair Lady (1964)	**George Cukor** Jewish
92.	A Place In the Sun (1951)	George Stevens
93.	The Apartment (1960)	**Billy Wilder** Jewish
94.	Goodfellas (1990	Martin Scorsese Catholic (lapsed former seminarian)
95.	Pulp Fiction (1994)	Quentin Tarantino Communist
96.	The Searchers (1956)	John Ford Catholic
97.	Bringing Up Baby (1938)	Howard Hawks Christian Science
98.	Unforgiven (1992)	Clint Eastwood raised Protestant; agnostic
99.	Guess Who's Coming to Dinner (1967)	**Stanley Kramer** Jewish
100.	Yankee Doodle Dandy (1942)	**Michael Curtiz** Jewish

Although there are 100 movies on the AFI list of the greatest American films of the last century, there are only 65 directors represented on the list because many directors have more than one film on the list. Jewish director Steven Spielberg has 5 movies on the list. Alfred Hitchcock (Catholic) and Billy Wilder (Jewish) have 4 films each. 10 directors have 3 films on the list. 8 directors have 2 films on the list. The rest of the directors have only one film on the AFI list.

Hollywood Reporter Star Power 2002

1	Tom Cruise 100.00	60	Gene Hackman 68.30	119	Michael J. Fox 54.82
2	Tom Hanks 100.00	61	Tommy Lee Jones 68.14	120	Haley Joel Osment 54.82
3	Julia Roberts 100.00	62	Cate Blanchett 66.59	121	**Joaquin Phoenix 54.65**
4	Mel Gibson 98.68	63	Ashley Judd 66.01	122	**Kate Hudson 54.61**
5	Jim Carrey 98.46	64	**Sean Penn 66.01**	123	Rene Russo 54.42
6	George Clooney 95.18	65	Reese Witherspoon 66.01	124	Demi Moore 54.39
7	Russell Crowe 94.74	66	**Winona Ryder 65.79**	125	**Helena Bonham Carter 54.17 (1/**
8	***Harrison Ford 94.74***	67	Meryl Streep 65.79	126	Vin Diesel 54.17
9	Bruce Willis 94.30	68	John Cusack 65.35	127	**Goldie Hawn 54.17**
10	Brad Pitt 92.98	69	**Barbra Streisand 65.13**	128	**Claire Danes 53.95**
11	Nicolas Cage 91.23	70	Wesley Snipes 64.91	129	Liam Neeson 53.95
12	Leonardo Dicaprio 91.01	71	Danny Devito 64.69	130	Kim Basinger 53.29
13	Will Smith 89.91	72	Chris Tucker 63.60	131	Heather Graham 53.07
14	Denzel Washington 89.04	73	Warren Beatty 63.39	132	Hugh Jackman 53.07
15	Sandra Bullock 87.28	74	**Billy Crystal 63.38**	133	Ethan Hawke 52.90
16	Robert De Niro 87.17	75	Sylvester Stallone 63.38	134	Woody Harrelson 52.85
17	Jackie Chan 86.84	76	Benicio Del Toro 62.94	135	Laurence Fishburne 52.63
18	Jack Nicholson 86.84	77	**Woody Allen 62.83**	136	Kevin Bacon 52.41
19	Sean Connery 86.40	78	**Paul Newman 62.72**	137	Jennifer Love Hewitt 51.97
20	Eddie Murphy 86.40	79	Penelope Cruz 62.28	138	Tobey Maguire 51.97
21	Cameron Diaz 84.87	80	Madonna 61.95	139	Holly Hunter 51.54
22	**Michael Douglas 84.87**	81	Jude Law 61.84	140	Val Kilmer 51.54
23	Nicole Kidman 84.65	82	Martin Lawrence 61.84	141	***Whoopi Goldberg 51.10***
24	Clint Eastwood 83.85	83	**Tim Allen 61.28**	142	Emma Thompson 51.10
25	Meg Ryan 83.77	84	Ewan Mcgregor 60.96	143	Kenneth Branagh 50.88
26	Mike Myers 83.55	85	Annette Bening 60.53	144	**Robert Downey Jr. 50.88 (1/4)**
27	Al Pacino 82.89	86	Julianne Moore 59.65	145	**David Duchovny 50.88**
28	Keanu Reeves 82.02	87	Jennifer Aniston 59.43	146	Salma Hayek 50.88
29	Jodie Foster 81.80	88	**Daniel Day-lewis 59.43**	147	Britney Spears 50.88
30	John Travolta 81.80	89	Uma Thurman 59.43	148	**Matthew Broderick 50.44**
31	Anthony Hopkins 81.58	90	Steve Martin 59.21	149	Gerard Depardieu 50.44
32	**Adam Sandler 80.70**	91	Sharon Stone 59.21	150	Nick Nolte 50.44
33	Ben Affleck 80.48	92	Chris Rock 58.99	151	Geoffrey Rush 50.00
34	Arnold Schwarzenegger 79.61	93	Chow Yun-fat 58.99	152	Josh Hartnett 49.56
35	Kevin Spacey 79.61	94	Susan Sarandon 58.77	153	**Harvey Keitel 49.56**
36	Angelina Jolie 79.39	95	Ralph Fiennes 58.63	154	Liv Tyler 49.12
37	Johnny Depp 77.19	96	Kurt Russell 58.49	155	Judi Dench 48.90
38	**Gwyneth Paltrow 76.97**	97	Billy Bob Thornton 58.33	156	Matt Dillon 48.90
39	Matt Damon 76.10	98	Kate Winslet 58.33	157	**Sarah Michelle Gellar 48.90**
40	Robin Williams 75.88	99	Marlon Brando 58.11	158	**Natalie Portman 48.90**
41	Robert Redford 75.66	100	Glenn Close 58.11	159	Andy Garcia 48.68
42	Richard Gere 75.22	101	Matthew Mcconaughey 57.89	160	Danny Glover 48.68
43	Michelle Pfeiffer 75.00	102	Tim Robbins 57.89	161	Gary Oldman 48.68
44	Drew Barrymore 74.78	103	Charlize Theron 57.89	162	Christina Ricci 48.46
45	Catherine Zeta-jones 74.78	104	Heath Ledger 57.68	163	Hilary Swank 48.46
46	Jennifer Lopez 73.68	105	Jet Li 57.68	164	Halle Berry 48.45
47	Pierce Brosnan 73.67	106	John Malkovich 57.68	165	Kate Beckinsale 48.03
48	Kevin Costner 72.81	107	Roberto Benigni 57.30	166	Joseph Fiennes 48.03
49	**Dustin Hoffman 72.81**	108	Jeff Bridges 57.02	167	Whitney Houston 48.03
50	Hugh Grant 72.15	109	Cuba Gooding Jr. 57.02	168	Dennis Quaid 48.03
51	**Helen Hunt 71.88**	110	Bill Murray 56.80	169	Elizabeth Hurley 47.81
52	Antonio Banderas 71.49	111	Kirsten Dunst 56.58	170	**Sarah Jessica Parker 47.59**
53	Mark Wahlberg 71.49	112	Ed Harris 56.58	171	**Richard Dreyfuss 47.37**
54	Samuel L. Jackson 69.96	113	Robert Duvall 56.36	172	Guy Pearce 47.37
55	Renee Zellweger 69.96	114	Sigourney Weaver 55.92	173	Julia Stiles 47.37
56	Morgan Freeman 69.30	115	Juliette Binoche 55.70	174	James Gandolfini 47.15
57	Brendan Fraser 69.08	116	Michael Caine 55.70	175	Jessica Lange 47.15
58	Edward Norton 69.08	117	**Kevin Kline 55.70**	176	Lucy Liu 47.15
59	**Ben Stiller 68.64**	118	Alec Baldwin 55.04	177	Jeremy Irons 46.93

Hollywood Reporter Star Power 2002

(continued)

178 Frances Mcdormand 46.43	237 Leslie Nielsen 40.79	296 Tom Selleck 35.75
179 Ice Cube 46.27	238 Julie Andrews 40.57	297 Patrick Swayze 35.75
180 Oprah Winfrey 46.27	239 **Patricia Arquette 40.57**	298 **Thora Birch 35.53 (1/4)**
181 Michael Keaton 46.05	240 Albert Finney 40.57	299 Anna Paquin 35.53
182 **Bette Midler 46.05**	241 Mira Sorvino 40.57	300 Kiefer Sutherland 35.53
183 Willem Dafoe 45.83	242 Keenen Ivory Wayans 40.57	301 Don Cheadle 35.31
184 Greg Kinnear 45.83	243 Anjelica Huston 40.35	302 Burt Reynolds 35.31
185 Melanie Griffith 45.61	244 Vince Vaughn 40.35	303 Martin Short 35.18
186 **Freddie Prinze Jr. 45.61**	245 Ray Liotta 40.13	304 Javier Bardem 35.09
187 **Jamie Lee Curtis 45.58**	246 **Rob Schneider 40.13**	305 Alan Rickman 35.09
188 Janet Jackson 45.39	247 **Jennifer Jason Leigh 39.91**	306 **Albert Brooks 34.87**
189 Jane Fonda 45.18	248 Joe Pesci 39.69	307 Ll Cool J 34.87
190 John Goodman 45.18	249 Bill Pullman 39.69	308 Paul Hogan 34.87
191 Joan Allen 45.13	250 James Woods 39.69	309 Denis Leary 34.87
192 Ed Burns 45.13	251 Jean Reno 39.60	310 Ian Mckellen 34.87
193 Geena Davis 44.96	252 Dan Aykroyd 39.47	311 Jimmy Smits 34.87
194 **Jeff Goldblum 44.96**	253 **James Caan 39.47**	312 **Elizabeth Taylor 34.87**
195 Cher 44.74	254 Sophia Loren 39.47	313 Owen Wilson 34.87
196 Dennis Hopper 44.74	255 Matthew Perry 39.25	314 Matt Leblanc 34.73
197 Diane Keaton 44.74	256 Charlie Sheen 39.25	315 Jenna Elfman 34.65
198 **Neve Campbell 44.52**	257 **Alicia Silverstone 39.25**	316 Diane Lane 34.65
199 Rupert Everett 44.52	258 Steve Buscemi 39.04	317 Carrie-anne Moss 34.65
200 Minnie Driver 44.30	259 Philip Seymour Hoffman 39.04	318 Forest Whitaker 34.65
201 Tim Roth 44.08	260 Mariah Carey 38.94	319 Stanley Tucci 34.43
202 William H. Macy 43.81	261 Joan Cusack 38.82	320 Mick Jagger 34.21
203 Courteney Cox Arquette 43.64	262 Anne Heche 38.82	321 Dylan Mcdermott 33.85
204 Kelsey Grammer 43.64	263 Bill Paxton 38.82	322 Ellen Burstyn 33.77
205 Nathan Lane 43.64	264 **David Arquette 38.38**	323 Robert Carlyle 33.77
206 **Ben Kingsley 43.42**	265 Laura Linney 38.38	324 Jeff Daniels 33.77
207 Robin Wright Penn 43.36	266 Elisabeth Shue 38.38	325 Bob Hoskins 33.77
208 **Mel Brooks 43.20**	267 Mena Suvari 38.38	326 **David Schwimmer 33.77**
209 Billy Crudup 43.14	268 Patrick Stewart 37.94	327 Chevy Chase 33.55
210 Martin Sheen 42.98	269 Emily Watson 37.94	328 Julia Ormond 33.55
211 Christian Slater 42.98	270 Gillian Anderson 37.72	329 Marisa Tomei 33.33
212 Rowan Atkinson 42.76	271 Donald Sutherland 37.61	330 James Coburn 33.11
213 Bridget Fonda 42.76	272 Pamela Anderson 37.28	331 Colin Farrell 33.11
214 Andie Macdowell 42.76	273 Gabriel Byrne 37.06	332 John Leguizamo 33.11
215 William Hurt 42.54	274 Marlon Wayans 37.06	333 John Lithgow 33.11
216 **Lisa Kudrow 42.54**	275 Jason Biggs 36.84	334 Rachael Leigh Cook 32.89
217 Chris O'donnell 42.54	276 Rob Lowe 36.84	335 Janeane Garofalo 32.89
218 Jean-claude Van Damme 42.54	277 **Leelee Sobieski 36.62**	336 Juliette Lewis 32.89
219 Christopher Walken 42.54	278 Colin Firth 36.61	337 Ice T 32.89
220 Ryan Phillippe 42.32	279 Brenda Blethyn 36.50	338 Toni Collette 32.68
221 Dwayne "The Rock" Johnson 42.12	280 Katie Holmes 36.40	339 Laura Dern 32.68
222 Angela Bassett 42.11	281 Vanessa Redgrave 36.40	340 Marcia Gay Harden 32.46
223 Kathy Bates 42.11	282 Ving Rhames 36.40	341 Nastassja Kinski 32.46
224 Catherine Deneuve 42.11	283 **Harry Connick Jr. 36.18**	342 Jared Leto 32.46
225 Christian Bale 42.04	284 James Earl Jones 36.18	343 Aaron Eckhart 32.37
226 Wes Bentley 42.04	285 Milla Jovovich 36.18	344 **Jon Lovitz 32.30**
227 David Spade 41.89	286 Shirley Maclaine 36.18	345 Claire Forlani 32.24
228 Sally Field 41.67	287 John Turturro 36.18	346 Denise Richards 32.24
229 Gary Sinise 41.67	288 Eminem 35.96	347 Elijah Wood 32.24
230 Damon Wayans 41.67	289 Peter Fonda 35.96	348 Chris Klein 31.92
231 ***Steven Seagal 41.45***	290 Jamie Foxx 35.96	349 Lynn Redgrave 31.86
232 John Cleese 41.23	291 Sidney Poitier 35.96	350 Chloe Sevigny 31.86
233 Kristin Scott Thomas 41.23	292 Jon Voight 35.84	351 **Lauren Bacall 31.80**
234 Sam Neill 41.15	293 Michelle Yeoh 35.84	352 Tom Green 31.80
235 **Courtney Love 41.01**	294 Benjamin Bratt 35.75	353 Sophie Marceau 31.80
236 Tea Leoni 40.79	295 Daryl Hannah 35.75	354 Giovanni Ribisi 31.80

Hollywood Reporter Star Power 2002   Exhibit 13d
(continued)

355 Jim Caviezel 31.64	404 Natasha Richardson 29.17	453 Rebecca Romijn-stamos 26.32
356 Linda Fiorentino 31.64	405 Candice Bergen 28.95	454 Stephen Baldwin 26.10
357 Judy Davis 31.58	406 Snoop Doggy Dogg 28.95	455 Tyra Banks 26.10
358 Isabella Rossellini 31.58	407 Faye Dunaway 28.95	456 James Belushi 26.10
359 James Spader 31.58	408 Jon Bon Jovi 28.95	457 David Bowie 26.10
360 Tracey Ullman 31.58	409 Isabelle Adjani 28.76	458 Ben Chaplin 26.10
361 James Van Der Beek 31.58	410 **Jack Black 28.73**	459 **Stephen Dorff 26.10**
362 Madeleine Stowe 31.19	411 Helen Mirren 28.73	460 Stephen Rea 26.10
363 Bjork 31.14	412 Richard Harris 28.64	461 **Noah Wyle 26.10**
364 Randy Quaid 31.14	413 Christopher Lambert 28.57	462 Joan Chen 25.88
365 Kathleen Turner 31.14	414 **Gina Gershon 28.54**	463 Julie Christie 25.88
366 **Jason Alexander 31.03**	415 **Rosanna Arquette 28.51**	464 Julie Delpy 25.88
367 Michael Clarke Duncan 30.92	416 Shannon Elizabeth 28.51	465 Keri Russell 25.88
368 Viggo Mortensen 30.92	417 Peter O'toole 28.51	466 Dianne Wiest 25.88
369 Dmx 30.75	418 Jada Pinkett-smith 28.51	467 Edward Furlong 25.66
370 Lena Olin 30.70	419 Sissy Spacek 28.51	468 Mark Ruffalo 25.66
371 Taye Diggs 30.48	420 Alan Alda 28.29	469 Danny Aiello 25.45
372 Charlton Heston 30.48	421 Vivica A. Fox 28.29	470 Christina Applegate 25.44
373 Shawn Wayans 30.48	422 **Amanda Peet 28.29**	471 Armand Assante 25.44
374 Elle Macpherson 30.31	423 **Rachel Weisz 28.29**	472 Kim Cattrall 25.44
375 Parker Posey 30.31	424 Brian Dennehy 28.10	473 Joshua Jackson 25.44
376 Rachel Griffiths 30.26	425 Anne Bancroft 28.07	474 Jeremy Northam 25.44
377 Terence Stamp 30.26	426 Joe Pantoliano 28.07	475 Louis Gossett Jr. 25.22
378 **Jon Favreau 30.09**	427 Emilio Estevez 27.85	476 Alyssa Milano 25.22
379 Anthony Edwards 30.04	428 Ian Holm 27.85	477 David Hyde Pierce 25.00
380 Timothy Hutton 30.04	429 Jason Patric 27.85	478 **Peter Falk 24.78**
381 Brooke Shields 30.04	430 Zhang Ziyi 27.85	479 **Seth Green 24.78**
382 Jeanne Tripplehorn 30.04	431 Lauren Holly 27.63	480 Gregory Hines 24.78
383 Luke Wilson 30.04	432 Kyle Maclachlan 27.63	481 Isabelle Huppert 24.78
384 John Hurt 29.87	433 Aidan Quinn 27.63	482 Lili Taylor 24.78
385 **Julianna Margulies 29.82**	434 Beau Bridges 27.41	483 Anne Archer 24.56
386 **Hank Azaria 29.65**	435 Matthew Modine 27.41	484 Mia Farrow 24.56
387 **Ellen Barkin 29.61**	436 Edward James Olmos 27.41	485 Linda Hamilton 24.56
388 Tom Berenger 29.61	437 Chazz Palminteri 27.41	486 Joe Mantegna 24.56
389 Lara Flynn Boyle 29.61	438 Paul Walker 27.41	487 Catherine Mccormack 24.56
390 Vincent D'onofrio 29.61	439 **Garry Shandling 27.21**	488 **Scott Glenn 24.55**
391 Natasha Henstridge 29.61	440 Stockard Channing 27.19	489 James Cromwell 24.34
392 Jason Lee 29.61	441 Will Ferrell 27.19	490 Ann-margret 24.34
393 Miranda Richardson 29.61	442 Roger Moore 27.19	491 **Mary Tyler Moore 24.34 (1/4)**
394 Vanessa L. Williams 29.61	443 Thandie Newton 27.19	492 Gena Rowlands 24.34
395 **Debra Winger 29.61**	444 William Baldwin 26.97	493 Paul Sorvino 24.34
396 Dana Carvey 29.39	445 Rebecca Demornay 26.97	494 Alfre Woodard 24.34
397 Famke Janssen 29.39	446 Tara Reid 26.97	495 Alan Cumming 24.12
398 **Martin Landau 29.39**	447 Eric Stoltz 26.97	496 Kelly Preston 24.12
399 Sam Shepard 29.39	448 Oliver Platt 26.77	497 Tom Sizemore 24.12
400 Billy Zane 29.39	449 Dermot Mulroney 26.54	498 Steve Zahn 24.12
401 **Christopher Guest 29.24**	450 **Jennifer Connelly 26.32**	499 Tim Curry 23.90
402 Sean Combs 29.20	451 Timothy Dalton 26.32	500 Hector Elizondo 23.90
403 Brandy 29.17	452 Christopher Lloyd 26.32	

The Hollywood Reporter. John Burman, editor of The Hollywood Reporter's International Edition said the survey polled 114 executives at both major studios and independent companies, financiers and various industry players from around the world. It measured not only the star's box office drawing power, but also the ability to get films funded and obtain wide distribution in multiple countries based on the strength of their names. The poll scored 1,000 actors on their "bankability" with a top score of 100. Hanks, Cruise and Roberts all reached that mark. Here is the list ranked numerically 1 to 500 of the top stars.

American Film Institute Awards   Exhibit 13e

Lifetime Achievement Award Winners

Recipient	Year	Recipient	Year
Al Pacino	2007	Gregory Peck	1989
Sean Connery	2006	Jack Lemmon	1988
George Lucas	2005	Barbara Stanwyck	1987
Meryl Streep	2004	**Billy Wilder**	1986
Robert De Niro	2003	Gene Kelly	1985
Tom Hanks	2002	Lillian Gish	1984
Barbra Streisand	2001	John Huston	1983
Harrison Ford	2000	Frank Capra	1982
Dustin Hoffman	1999	Fred Astaire	1981
Robert Wise	1998	James Stewart	1980
Martin Scorsese	1997	Alfred Hitchcock	1979
Clint Eastwood	1996	Henry Fonda	1978
Steven Spielberg	1995	Bette Davis	1977
Jack Nicholson	1994	**William Wyler**	1976
Elizabeth Taylor	1993	Orson Welles	1975
Sidney Poitier	1992	James Cagney	1974
Kirk Douglas	1991	John Ford	1973
David Lean	1990		

When AFI was founded in 1967, one of its purposes was to ensure that "great accomplishments of the past are recognized to the end that masters of film may take their deserved place in history beside leaders in other arts. The criteria stated that "the recipient should be one whose talent has in a fundamental way advanced the film art; whose accomplishment has been acknowledged by scholars, critics, professional peers and the general public; and whose work has stood the test of time."

Greatest American Screen Legends (50)s

Recipient	Recipient
1. Humphrey Bogart	1. Katharine Hepburn
2. **Cary Grant** ???	2. Bette Davis
3. James Stewart	3. Audrey Hepburn
4. Marlon Brando	4. Ingrid Bergman
5. Fred Astaire	5. Greta Garbo
6. Henry Fonda	6. **Marilyn Monroe**
7. Clark Gable	7. **Elizabeth Taylor**
8. James Cagney	8. Judy Garland
9. Spencer Tracy	9. Marlene Dietrich
10. Charlie Chaplin	10. Joan Crawford
11. Gary Cooper	11. Barbara Stanwyck
12. Gregory Peck	12. Claudette Colbert
13. John Wayne	13. Grace Kelly
14. Laurence Olivier	14. Ginger Rogers
15. Gene Kelly	15. Mae West
16. Orson Welles	16. Vivien Leigh
17. **Kirk Douglas**	17. Lillian Gish
18. James Dean	18. Shirley Temple
19. Burt Lancaster	19. Rita Hayworth
20. **The Marx Brothers**	20. **Lauren Bacall**
21. Buster Keaton	21. Sophia Loren
22. Sidney Poitier	22. Jean Harlow
23. Robert Mitchum	23. Carole Lombard
24. **Edward G. Robinson**	24. Mary Pickford
25. William Holden	25. Ava Gardner

"This is the American Film Institute's list of the 50 Greatest American Screen Legends, the top 25 male and top 25 female leends selected by more than 1,800 leaders from across the film community from the list of 500."

Radio Hall of Fame

Goodman & Jane Ace	Bob Edwards	**Groucho Marx**
Fred Allen	Ralph Edwards	L. Lowry Mays
Mel Allen	Fred Foy	J.P. McCarthy
Don Ameche	**Stan Freberg**	Edward F. McLaughlin
Eddie Anderson	**Alan Freed**	Gordon McLendon
Eve Arden	John A. Gambling	Robert W. Morgan
Edwin H. Armstrong	Arthur Godfrey	Bruce Morrow
Gene Autry	**Leonard Goldenson**	Edward R. Murrow
Red Barber	**Benny Goodman**	Charles Osgood
Dick Bartley	Gale Gordon	Gary Owens
Jack Benny	Freeman Gosden	**William S. Paley**
Gertrude Berg	Ralph Guild	Edward Pate, Jr.
Edgar Bergen	**Karl Haas**	Virginia Payne
Jesse B. Blayton, Sr.	Milo Hamilton	Wally Phillips
Martin Block	Lynne "Angel" Harvey	Dick Purtan
Dick Biondi	Paul Harvey	James H. Quello
Jim Bohannon	Paul Harvey Aurandt	Orion Samuelson
Dr. Amar G. Bose	Ernie Harwell	**David Sarnoff**
Jack Brickhouse	Gordon Hinkley	Chuck Schaden
Himan Brown	Bob Hope	Vin Scully
Jack Buck	Don Imus	Red Skelton
Eddie Cantor	Hal Jackson	Rick Sklar
Harry Caray	Michael Jackson	Kate Smith
Jack Carney	Jim & Marian Jordan	**Susan Stamberg**
Andrew Carter	Tom Joyner	Frank Stanton
Dick Clark	**Mel Karmazin**	Bob Steele
William Conrad	Casey Kasem	**Bill Stern**
Charles Correll	**Murray "the K" Kaufman**	Fran Striker
Norman Corwin	Garrison Keillor	Lowell Thomas
Bing Crosby	Herb Kent	Les Tremayne
Yvonne Daniels	**Larry King**	Bob Uecker
Rick Dees	Kay Kyser	Orson Welles
Lee DeForest	Rush Limbaugh	Bruce Williams
Tommy Dorsey	Larry Lujack	Jerry Williams
Jim Dunbar	Tom & Ray Magliozzi	Walter Winchell
Don Dunphy	Guglielmo Marconi	Wolfman Jack

Television Hall of Fame

16th Awards
Bob Barker
Art Carney
Katie Couric
Dan Rather
Brandon Tartikoff
Charles Cappleman

15th Awards
Tim Conway and **Harvey Korman**
John Frankenheimer
Bob Mackie
Jean Stapleton
Bud Yorkin

14th Awards
Herb Brodkin
MacNeil/Lehrer
Lorne Michaels
Carl Reiner
Fred Rogers
Fred Silverman
Ethel Winant

13th Awards
James L. Brooks
Garry Marshall
Diane Sawyer
Grant Tinker
Quinn Martin

12th Awards
Ed Asner
Angela Lansbury
Aaron Spelling
Lew Wasserman
Marcy Carsey
Tom Werner
Charles Kuralt
Steven Bochco

11th Awards
Michael Landon
Richard Levinson and William Link
Jim McKay
Bill Moyers
Dick Van Dyke
Betty White

10th Awards
Alan Alda
Howard Cosell
Barry Diller
Fred Friendly
Bill Hanna and Joseph Barbera
Oprah Winfrey

9th Awards
Dick Clark
John Chancellor
Phil Donahue
Mark Goodson
Bob Newhart
Agnes Nixon
Jack Webb

8th Awards
Bill Cosby
Andy Griffith
Ted Koppel
Sheldon Leonard
Dinah Shore
Ted Turner

7th Awards
Desi Arnaz
Leonard Bernstein
James Garner
I Love Lucy - Not counted
Danny Thomas
Mike Wallace

6th Awards
Roone Arledge
Fred Astaire
Perry Como
Joan Ganz Cooney
Don Hewitt
Carroll O'Connor
Barbara Walters

5th Awards
Jack Benny
George Burns and Gracie Allen
Chet Huntley and David Brinkley
Red Skelton
David Susskind
David Wolper

4th Awards
Johnny Carson
Jacques-Yves Cousteau
Leonard Goldenson
Jim Henson
Bob Hope
Ernie Kovacs
Eric Sevareid

3rd Awards
Steve Allen
Fred Coe
Walt Disney
Jackie Gleason
Mary Tyler Moore
Frank Stanton
Burr Tillstrom

2nd Awards
Carol Burnett
Sid Caesar
Walter Cronkite
Joyce Hall
Rod Serling
Ed Sullivan
Sylvester (Pat) Weaver

1st Awards
Lucille Ball
Milton Berle
Paddy Chayefsky
Norman Lear
Edward R. Murrow
William S. Paley
David Sarnoff

Fortune America's 40 Richest Under 40 (Sept. 20, 2004)   Exhibit 15a

Rank / Name	Age	Company	Wealth
1 **Michael Dell**	39	Dell Computer	$17.95 billion
2 Pierre Omidyar	37	eBay	$10.05 billion
3 **Jeff Skoll**	37	eBay, Skoll Foundation	$4.69 billion
4 Larry Page	31	Google	$4.19 billion
5 **Sergey Brin**	31	Google	$4.17 billion
6 Jerry Yang	35	Yahoo	$2,81 billion
7 David Filo	38	Yahoo	$2.57 billion
8 Ken Griffin	35	Citadell Investment Group	$1.00 billion
9 **Dan Snyder**	39	Synder Communications, Wash Redskins	$823 million
10 **Marc Benioff**	39	Salesforce.com	$376 million
11 Jeffrey Citron	34	Vonage	$346 million
12 Elon Musk	33	Pay Pal, CTO Space Exploration	$328 million
13 *Sean Combs (P. Diddy)*	34	*Bad Boy Entertainment*	*$315 million*
14 ***Tiger Woods***	28	*Golf*	*$295 million*
15 Halsey Minor	39	Cnet, Grand Central Communications	$286 million
16 *Shawn Carter (Jay-Z)*	34	*Roc-a-Fella Enterprises*	*$286 million*
17 **Jerry Greenberg**	38	Sapient	$278 million
18 Raul Fernandez	38	ObjectVideo	$263 million
19 *Jennifer Lopez*	35	*Actress*	*$255 million*
20 Marc Andreessen	33	Netscape, Opsware	$253 million
21 Joe Liemandt	36	Trilogy	$234 million
22 ***Shaquille O'Neal***	32	*Basketball*	*$222 million*
23 Michael Robertson	37	MP3.com, Linspire	$220 million
24 Marc Ewing	35	Red Hat, Alpinist Magazine	$217 million
25 *Julia Roberts*	36	*Actress*	*$212 million*
26 *Will Smith*	35	*Actor*	*$188 million*
27 ***Andre Agassi***	34	*Tennis*	*$162 million*
28 Jared Polls	29	Bluemountain.com, Provide-Commerce	$160 million
29 ***Jeff Gordon***	33	*Nascar Driver*	*$155 million*
30 Sudhakar Ravi	39	SonicWALL, retired	$137 million
31 *Ashley Olsen*	18	*Actress*	*$137 million*
32 *Mary-Kate Olsen*	18	*Actress*	*$137 million*
33 John MacFarlane	38	Sonos.com	$136 million
34 Jeffrey Zients	37	Advisory Board, Portfolio Logic	$132 million
35 Sreekanth Ravi	37	SonicWall	$131 million
36 Paul Gauthier	32	Inktomi	$129 million
37 W. Glen Boyd	37	Net analytics	$125 million
38 *Britney Spears*	22	*Entertainer*	*$123 million*
39 Michale Saylor	39	MicroStrategy	$113 million
40 ***Kevin Garnett***	28	*Basketball*	*$106 million*

Indented names in *italicized* font are entertainment figures.
Indented names in ***bold italicized*** font are sports figures.

Forbes 400 (September 2007)   Exhibit 21a

Rank / Name	Net Worth ($bill)	Rank / Name	Net Worth ($bil
1 William Gates III	$59.0	57 **Henry Kravis**	$5.5
2 Warren Buffett	$52.0	57 **George Roberts**	$5.5
3 **Sheldon Adelson**	$28.0	57 Charles Schwab	$5.5
4 **Lawrence Ellison**	$26.0	57 **James Simons**	$5.5
5 **Sergey Brin**	$18.5	62 Rupert Johnson Jr.	$5.2
6 Larry Page	$18.5	63 Robert Holding	$5.0
7 Kirk Kerkorian	$18.0	64 Min Kao	$4.7
8 **Michael Dell**	$17.2	64 **Ralph Lauren**	$4.7
9 Charles Koch	$17.0	64 Patrick McGovern	$4.7
9 David Koch	$17.0	64 David Murdock	$4.7
11 Paul Allen	$16.8	68 William Cook	$4.5
12 Christy Walton & family	$16.3	68 **Lester Crown & family**	$4.5
12 Jim Walton	$16.3	68 **William Davidson**	$4.5
14 S Robson Walton	$16.3	68 **Edward Lampert**	$4.5
15 Alice Walton	$16.1	68 **Paul Milstein & family**	$4.5
16 **Steven Ballmer**	$15.2	68 Gordon Moore	$4.5
17 Abigail Johnson	$15.0	68 **Stephen Ross**	$4.5
18 **Carl Icahn**	$14.5	68 James Sorenson	$4.5
19 Forrest Mars Jr	$14.0	76 Henry Ross Perot	$4.4
19 Jacqueline Mars	$14.0	76 John Sall	$4.4
19 John Mars	$14.0	78 **Joan Tisch**	$4.2
19 Jack Taylor & family	$14.0	79 **Leonard Stern**	$4.1
23 **Donald Bren**	$13.0	79 Steven Udvar-Hazy	$4.1
24 Anne Cox Chambers	$12.6	79 Ty Warner	$4.1
25 **Michael Bloomberg**	$11.5	82 **Leon Black**	$4.0
26 **George Kaiser**	$11.0	83 Ray Dalio	$4.0
27 Charles Ergen	$10.2	84 Ray Hunt	$4.0
28 Edward Johnson III	$10.0	85 Herbert Kohler & family	$4.0
28 **Ronald Perelman**	$10.0	86 George Lucas	$3.9
30 Philip Knight	$9.8	87 **Stephen Wynn**	$3.9
31 John Kluge	$9.5	88 Bradley Hughes	$3.7
32 Pierre Omidyar	$8.9	89 Richard DeVos	$3.6
33 Rupert Murdoch	$8.8	90 John Simplot & family	$3.6
33 **George Soros**	$8.8	91 Riley Bechtel	$3.5
35 Jeffrey Bezos	$8.7	91 Stephen Bechtel Jr	$3.5
35 James Goodnight	$8.7	91 Ronald Burkle	$3.5
37 **Donald Newhouse**	$8.5	91 Stanley Druckenmiller	$3.5
37 **Samuel Newhouse Jr**	$8.5	91 Kenneth Hendricks	$3.5
39 Dan Duncan	$8.2	91 **Bruce Kovner**	$3.5
40 **Stephen Schwarzman**	$7.8	91 Richard Rainwater	$3.5
41 Philip Anschutz	$7.6	91 **Ira Rennert**	$3.5
41 **Sumner Redstone**	$7.6	91 **Daniel Ziff**	$3.5
43 Harold Simmons	$7.6	91 **Dirk Ziff**	$3.5
44 John Menard Jr.	$7.4	91 **Robert Ziff**	$3.5
45 **Leonard Blavatnik**	$7.3	102 **Haim Saban**	$3.4
46 **Eli Broad**	$7.2	102 Richard Schulze	$3.4
47 **Steven Cohen**	$7.0	102 Dennis Washington	$3.4
48 Eric Schmidt	$6.8	105 David Bonderman	$3.3
49 Robert Rowling	$6.5	105 **Matthew Bucksbaum & family**	$3.3
50 James Kennedy	$6.4	105 Paul Tudor Jones	$3.3
51 Blair Parry-Okedon	$6.3	108 **Edgar Bronfman Sr**	$3.2
52 **David Geffen**	$6.0	108 Charles Dolan & family	$3.2
52 Charles Johnson	$6.0	108 Harold Hamm	$3.2
52 **Samuel Zell**	$6.0	108 Pater Kellogg	$3.2
55 **Micky Arison**	$5.8	108 **Leonard Lauder**	$3.2
56 Steven Jobs	$5.7	108 **Ronald Lauder**	$3.2
57 Robert Bass	$5.5	114 Gary Burrell	$3.1

Forbes 400 (September 2007)   Exhibit 21a

Rank / Name	Net Worth ($bill)	Rank / Name	Net Worth ($bil
114	A Jerrold Perenchino	$3.1	165	**David Gottesman**	$2.5
114	Carl Pohlad	$3.1	165	H. Wayne Huizengs	$2.5
117	Lee Bass	$3.0	165	Ann Walton Kroenke	$2.5
117	Sid Bass	$3.0	165	**Theodore Lerner**	$2.5
117	Kenneth Griffin	$3.0	165	Mary Alice Dorrance Malone	$2.5
117	Henry Hillman	$3.0	165	**Michael Milken**	$2.5
117	**Richard LeFrak & family**	$3.0	165	**John Paulson**	$2.5
117	T Boone Pickens	$3.0	165	Peter Peterson	$2.5
117	**Thomas Pritzker**	$3.0	165	Robert Rich Jr	$2.5
117	Mitchell Rales	$3.0	165	**David Rubenstein**	$2.5
117	Donald Schneider	$3.0	165	**Lynn Schusterman**	$2.5
117	John Sobrato & family	$3.0	165	David Shaw	$2.5
117	Patrick Soon-Shiong	$3.0	165	**Evgeny (Eugene) Shvidler**	$2.5
117	**Steven Spielberg**	$3.0	165	David Sun	$2.5
117	Donald Trump	$3.0	165	John Tu	$2.5
130	Victor Fung	$2.9	165	Oprah Winfrey	$2.5
130	Richard Kinder	$2.9	188	Bennett Dorrance	$2.4
130	**Melvin Simon**	$2.9	188	Gordon Getty	$2.4
130	Clemmie Spangler Jr	$2.9	188	William Randolph Heart III	$2.4
130	Ronda Stryker	$2.9	188	Martha Ingram & family	$2.4
135	James Coulter	$2.8	188	John Malone	$2.4
135	**Maurice Greenberg**	$2.8	188	Fredrick Smith	$2.4
135	Amos Hostetter Jr	$2.8	188	**Mortimer Zuckerman**	$2.4
135	Pauline MacMillan Keinath	$2.8	188	Thomas Barrack	$2.3
135	Cargill MacMillan Jr	$2.8	188	Charles Butt & family	$2.3
135	John MacMillan III	$2.8	188	William Hilton	$2.3
135	Whitney MacMillan	$2.8	188	Carl Lindner Jr. & family	$2.3
135	Craig McCaw	$2.8	188	Henry Nicholas III	$2.3
135	George Mitchell	$2.8	188	**Nicholas Pritzker II**	$2.3
135	Marion MacMillan Pictet	$2.8	201	Edward Roski Jr	$2.3
135	**Penny Pritzker**	$2.8	202	**Henry Samueli**	$2.3
135	Steven Rales	$2.8	203	Robert E. "Ted" Turner	$2.3
135	T Denny Sanford	$2.8	204	Franklin Booth Jr	$2.2
135	**Leslie Wexner**	$2.8	204	**Phillip Frost, MD**	$2.2
149	Ray Dolby	$2.7	204	Barbara Carlson Gage & family	$2.2
149	Barbara Piasecka Johnson	$2.7	204	**Tom Gores**	$2.2
149	Roger Penske	$2.7	204	Jess Jackson	$2.2
149	**Anthony Pritzker**	$2.7	204	H. Fisk Johnson	$2.2
149	**Daniel Pritzker**	$2.7	204	Imogene Powers Johnson	$2.2
149	**James Pritzker**	$2.7	204	S. Curtis Johnson	$2.2
149	**Jay Robert (JB) Pritzker**	$2.7	204	Helen Johnson-Leipold	$2.2
149	**Jean (Gigi) Pritzker**	$2.7	204	Winnie Johnson-Marquart	$2.2
149	**Karen Pritzker**	$2.7	204	Omid Kordestani	$2.2
149	**Linda Pritzker**	$2.7	204	E Stanley Kroenke	$2.2
149	David Rockefeller Sr	$2.7	204	Nancy Walton Laurie	$2.2
149	Glen Taylor	$2.7	204	**Alfred Mann**	$2.2
161	**Mark Cuban**	$2.6	204	John Marriott Jr	$2.2
161	**John Pritzker**	$2.6	204	Marily Carlson Nelson & family	$2.2
161	J Joseph Ricketts & family	$2.6	220	**S Daniel Abraham**	$2.1
161	**Wilama Tisch**	$2.6	220	John Anderson	$2.1
165	**Leonore Annenberg**	$2.5	220	**Neil Bluhm**	$2.1
165	Edward Bass	$2.5	220	John Catsimatidis	$2.1
165	Charles Brandes	$2.5	220	Phoebe Hearst Cooke	$2.1
165	William Conway Jr	$2.5	220	Archie Aldis "Red" Emmerson	$2.1
165	Daniel D'Aniello	$2.5	220	Austin Hearst	$2.1
165	Jim Davis & family	$2.5	220	David Hearst Jr	$2.1
165	**Malcolm Glazer & family**	$2.5	220	George Hearst Jr	$2.1

Forbes 400 (September 2007)   Exhibit 21a

Rank / Name		Net Worth ($bill)	Rank / Name		Net Worth ($bil
229	James Laprino	$2.1	286	**Edmund Ansin**	$1.7
229	Richard Marriott	$2.1	286	Louis Bacon	$1.7
229	Clayton Mathile	$2.1	286	Bharat Desai & family	$1.7
229	Aubrey McClendon	$2.1	286	**Louis Gonda**	$1.7
229	John Morgridge	$2.1	286	**Michael Krasny**	$1.7
229	**Ernest Rady**	$2.1	286	Igor Olenicoff	$1.7
229	Phillip Ruffin	$2.1	286	**Stewart Rahr**	$1.7
229	Jon Stryker	$2.1	286	Wilbur Ross Jr	$1.7
229	Tom Ward	$2.1	286	Walter Scott Jr	$1.7
229	William Wrigley Jr	$2.1	286	Ernest Stempel	$1.7
239	**Herbert Alllen Jr & family**	$2.0	286	Dean White	$1.7
239	Frank Batten Sr	$2.0	297	John Abele	$1.6
239	**Alan Casden**	$2.0	297	Peter Buck	$1.6
239	David Filo	$2.0	297	Robert Day	$1.6
239	J Christopher Flowers	$2.0	297	Fred DeLuca	$1.6
239	B Thomas Golisano	$2.0	297	Wesley Edens	$1.6
239	**Joshua Harris**	$2.0	297	Thomas Friedkin	$1.6
239	James Jannard	$2.0	297	Alan Gerry	$1.6
239	James Kim & family	$2.0	297	Marguerite Harbert	$1.6
239	William Koch	$2.0	297	Stanley Stub Hubbard	$1.6
239	Leslie Lampton	$2.0	297	**Michael Ilitch**	$1.6
239	**Thomas Lee**	$2.0	297	**Irwin Jacobs**	$1.6
239	**Henry Macklowe**	$2.0	297	Brad Kelley	$1.6
239	Margaret Magerko	$2.0	297	Randal Kirk	$1.6
239	Joseph Mansueto	$2.0	297	**Nancy Lerner**	$1.6
239	**Bernard Marcus**	$2.0	297	**Norma Lerner**	$1.6
239	Frederik GH Meijer & family	$2.0	297	**Randolph Lerner**	$1.6
239	Charles Munger	$2.0	297	Billy Joe "Red" McCombs	$1.6
239	**Sheldon Solow**	$2.0	297	Richard Peery	$1.6
239	**Jerry Speyer**	$2.0	297	Bernard Saul II	$1.6
239	R Allen Stanford	$2.0	297	Phyllis Taylor	$1.6
239	**David Tepper**	$2.0	317	Dennis Albaugh	$1.5
261	John Calamos & family	$1.9	317	**Roland Arnall**	$1.5
261	Paul Foster	$1.9	317	John Arnold	$1.5
261	Thomas Frist Jr & family	$1.9	317	John Arrillaga	$1.5
261	Donald Hall	$1.9	317	**Ronald Baron**	$1.5
261	Jon Huntsman	$1.9	317	Andrew Beal	$1.5
261	Michael Jaharis	$1.9	317	**Carl Berg**	$1.5
261	George Lindemann & family	$1.9	317	**Arthur Blank**	$1.5
261	Thomas Siebel	$1.9	317	Peter Briger Jr	$1.5
261	Albert Ueltschi	$1.9	317	**Barry Diller**	$1.5
261	Jerry Yang	$1.9	317	**Israel Englander**	$1.5
271	George Argyros	$1.8	317	John J. Fisher	$1.5
271	Armar Bose	$1.8	317	Gerald J Ford	$1.5
271	William Connor II	$1.8	317	James France	$1.5
271	Edward Debartolo Jr	$1.8	317	Robert Friedland	$1.5
271	L John Doerr	$1.8	317	Christopher Goldsbury	$1.5
271	Kenneth Fisher	$1.8	317	**Alec Gores**	$1.5
271	David Green	$1.8	317	Timothy Headington	$1.5
271	Jorge Perez	$1.8	317	Jeffrey Hildebrand	$1.5
271	**Michael Price**	$1.8	317	Jeremy Jacobs Sr	$1.5
271	Kavitark Shriram	$1.8	317	Joseph Jamail Jr	$1.5
271	Pat Stryker	$1.8	317	Hamilton James	$1.5
271	**A Alfred Taubman**	$1.8	317	Jerral Jones	$1.5
271	Theodore Waitt	$1.8	317	Vinod Khosla	$1.5
271	**Sanford Weill**	$1.8	317	**Jerome Kohlberg Jr**	$1.5
271	Arthur Williams Jr	$1.8	317	**Marc Lasry**	$1.5

Forbes 400 (September 2007)   Exhibit 21a

Rank / Name		Net Worth ($bill)	Rank / Name		Net Worth ($bil
317	Thomas Marsico	$1.5	361	**Robert Naify**	$1.4
317	Robert McNair	$1.5	361	**Nelson Peltz**	$1.4
317	Gary Michelson	$1.5	361	Leandro Rizzuto	$1.4
317	William Moncrief Jr	$1.5	361	Patrick Ryan	$1.4
317	Michael Novogratz	$1.5	361	John Sperling	$1.4
317	Daniel Och	$1.5	361	Hope Hill van Beuren	$1.4
317	Trevor Rees-Jones	$1.5	361	Charlotte Colket Weber	$1.4
317	David Rich	$1.5	361	Margaret Whitman	$1.4
317	**Marc Rich**	$1.5	380	Stephen Bisciotti	$1.3
317	**Steven Roth**	$1.5	380	Timothy Blixseth	$1.3
317	**Marc Rowan**	$1.5	380	John Brown	$1.3
317	**Tamir Sapir**	$1.5	380	S Truett Cathy	$1.3
317	Fayez Sarofim	$1.5	380	**Glenn Dubin**	$1.3
317	**Herbert Simon**	$1.5	380	Frank Fertitta III	$1.3
317	O Bruton Smith	$1.5	380	Lorenzo Fertitta	$1.3
317	Peter Sperling	$1.5	380	William Gross	$1.3
317	**Joseph Steinberg**	$1.5	380	Michael Heisley Sr	$1.3
317	Todd Wagner	$1.5	380	Thomas Hicks	$1.3
361	James Clark	$1.4	380	William Kellogg	$1.3
361	James Dinan	$1.4	380	Michael Moritz	$1.3
361	Roy Disney	$1.4	380	Julian Robertson Jr	$1.3
361	Richard Egan	$1.4	380	**Barry Rosenstein**	$1.3
361	**Robert Fisher**	$1.4	380	Richard Scaife	$1.3
361	**William Fisher**	$1.4	380	**Walter Shorenstein & family**	$1.3
361	**Leslie Gonda**	$1.4	380	**Herbert Siegel**	$1.3
361	Bruce Karsh	$1.4	380	George Steinbrenner III	$1.3
361	**Robert Kraft**	$1.4	380	**Henry Swieca**	$1.3
361	Anne Windfohr Marion	$1.4	380	Kenny Troutt	$1.3
361	Howard Marks	$1.4	380	Roger Wang	$1.3

The Ladies Home Journal's 100 Most Important Women of the 20th Century		Exhibit 22a

Activists & Politicians
Jane Addams
Madeleine Albright
Mary McCleod Bethune
Carrie Chapman Catt
Hillary Rodham Clinton
Marian Wright Edelman
Indira Gandhi
Ruth Bader Ginsburg
Emma Goldman
Anita Hill
Dolores Huerta
Maggie Kuhn
Golda Meir
Rigoberta Menchú
Sandra Day O'Connor
Jacqueline Kennedy Onassis
Rosa Parks
Alice Paul
Frances Perkins
Eva Per_n
Jiang Qing
Eleanor Roosevelt
Phyllis Schlafly
Gloria Steinem
Daw Aung San Suu Kyi
Mother Teresa
Margaret Thatcher

Doctors & Scientists
Virginia Apgar
Helen Caldicott
Marie Curie
Rosalind Franklin
Jane Goodall
Grace Hopper
Melanie Klein
Mary Leakey
Barbara McClintock
Lise Meitner

Writers & Journalists
Maya Angelou
Hannah Arendt
Rachel Carson
Agatha Christie
Simone de Beauvoir
Anne Frank
Betty Friedan
Ann Landers
Margaret Mead
Margaret Mitchell
Toni Morrison
Dorthy Parker
Sylvia Plath
Gertrude Stein
Barbara Walters
Laura Ingalls Wilder
Virginia Woolf

Entrepreneurs
Coco Chanel
Julia Child
Elsie de Wolfe
Katharine Graham
Ruth Handler
Estée Lauder
Jean Nidetch
Mary Quant
Martha Steward
Oprah Winfrey

Athletes
Nadia Comaneci
Babe Didrikson
Gertrude Ederle
Sonja Henie
Billie Jean King
Suzanne Lenglen
Wilma Rudolph

Artists & Entertainers
Marian Anderson
Lucille Ball
Margaret Bourke-White
Maria Callas
Isadora Duncan
Ella Fitzgerald
Jane Fonda
Greta Garbo
Martha Graham
Katharine Hepburn
Billie Holiday
Janis Joplin
Frida Kahlo
Dorothea Lange
Madonna
Marilyn Monroe
Georgia O'Keeffe
Mary Pickford
Leni Riefenstahl

Pioneers & Adventurers
Nancy Brinker
Helen Gurley Brown
Diana, Princess of Wales
Amelia Earhart
Betty Ford
Helen Keller
Maria Montessori
Jane Roe (Norma McCorvey)
Margaret Sanger
Valentina Tereshkova

Court TV's Spies (August 2008)

	Spies	Country
1	Ames, Aldrich	
2	Boyce, Christopher	
3	Lee, Andrew Daulton	
4	Philby, Kim	United Kingdom
5	Burgess, Guy	United Kingdom
6	McLean, Donald	United Kingdom
7	Blunt, Anthony	United Kingdom
8	Fuchs, Klaus	
9	Hanssen, Robert	
10	Zelle, Margaretha "Mata Hari"	France
11	Hiss, Alger	
12	**Pollard, Jonathon**	
13	**Rosenberg, Julius**	
14	**Rosenberg, Ethel**	
15	Walker, John	

**Court TV's Mob Bosses, Crime Family Leaders   Exhibit 23b
& Unique Gang Leaders (April 2003)**

	Mob Bosses	Foreign Country	Foreign Tally
1	Capone, Al		
2	**Cohen, Mickey**		
3	DeMeo, Roy		
4	Giancana, Sam		
5	Gotti, John		
6	Gravano, Sammy "The Bull"		
7	Kray, Reggie	United Kingdom	1
8	Kray, Ronnie	United Kingdom	2
9	**Lansky, Meyer**		
10	Luciano, Lucky		
11	Moran, George "Bugs"		
12	O'Banion, Dion		
13	**Rothstein, Arnold**		
14	**Schultz, Dutch**		
15	**Siegel, Bugsy**		
16	DeCavalcantes, Sam		
17	Taccetta, Michael		
18	Riccardi, Tommy		
19	Scarfo, Nicky Jr.		
20	Sodano, Joey		
21	Valachi, Joseph		

	Crime Family Epics
22	Galante, Carmine
23	Bonanno, Joeseph
24	Bonanno, Bill
25	Garofolo, Frank
26	Barbara, Joseph
27	Di Gregorio, Jasper
28	Rastelli, Philip
29	Massino, Joseph C. "Big Joey"
30	Profaci, Joe
31	Mangano, Vincent
32	Mangano, Philip
33	Anastasio, Albert
34	**Lepke (Buchalter), Louis**
35	**Reles, Abe "Kid Twist"**
36	Gambino, Carlo
37	Columbo, Joseph
38	Castellano Paul
39	Gotti, Peter
40	Costello, Frank
41	Genovese, Vito
42	Eboli, Tommy
43	Gallo, Joey
44	Gallo, Vincent
45	Gigante, Vincent "The Chin"
46	Salerno, Anthony
47	Tieri, Alphonse
48	Cirillo, Dominic
49	Gagliano, Gaetano, "Tom"
50	Lucchese, Tommy
51	Trafficante, Santo
52	Corallo, Antonino "Tony Ducks"
53	Luongo, Anthony "Buddy"
54	Amuso, Vittorio
55	D'Arco, Alphonso

Court TV's Mob Bosses, Crime Family Leaders **Exhibit 23b**
& Unique Gang Leaders (April 2003)

	Crime Family Epics (continued)	**Foreign Country**	**Foreign Tally**
56	Crea, Steven L.		
57	Marcello, Carlos		
58	Patriarca, Raymond L.S.		
59	Egan, Willie		
	Unique Gang Organizations		
60	Burke, James		
61	**Strauss, Harry "Pittsburgh Phil"**		
62	**Bernstein, Abe**		
63	Kodama, Yoshio	Japan	3

Crime TV's Library of Violent Criminals (April 2003)   Exhibit 23c

Serial Killers

Most Notorious	**Foreign**
1 **Berkowitz, David** ¡	
2 Bernardo, Paul	
3 Homolka, Karla	
4 De Salvo, Albert	
5 Bundy, Ted	
6 Chikatilo, Andrei	Russia
7 Dahmer, Jeffrey	
8 Fish, Albert	
9 Gacy, John Wayne	
10 Gein, Eddie	
11 Genovese, Kitty	
12 Lopez, Pedro	South America
13 Manson, Charles	
14 McVeigh, Timothy	
15 Ramirez, Richard	
16 Onoprienko, Anatoly	Ukraine
17 Resendez, Angel	
18 Shipman, Dr. Harold	U.K.
19 Sobraj, Charles	Asia

Sexual Predators

20 Armstrong, John Eric	Worldwide
21 Bathory, Elizabeth	Hungary
23 Bittaker, Lawrence	
24 Norris, Roy	
25 Cole, Carroll Edward	
26 Collins, John Norman	
27 DeBardeleben, Mike	
28 Denyer, Paul	Australia
29 Francois, Kendall	
30 Garrow, Robert	
31 Carlton, Gary	
32 Gaskins, Doland, "Pee Wee"	
33 Glatman, Harvey Murray	
34 Glover, John Wayne	
35 Heirens, William	
36 Buono, Angelo	
37 Bianchi, Ken	
38 Jesperson, Keith Hunter	
39 Kallinger, Joseph	
40 Kemper, Edmund	
41 Kiss, Bela	Hungary
42 Long, Bobby Joe	
43 Lucas, Henry Lee	
44 Milat, Ivan	Australia
45 O'Neall, Darren	
46 Ng, Charles	
47 Pickton, Robert	Canada
48 Rogers, Dayton Leroy	
49 Rolling, Danny	
50 Russell, George	
51 Schaefer, Gerard	
52 Schmid, Charles	
53 Rifkin, Joel	
54 Shawcross, Arthur	
55 Speck, Richard	
56 Staniak, Lucian	Poland

57 Stayner, Cary	
58 Sutcliffe, Peter	U.K.
59 Wallace, Henry Louis	
60 Worrell, Christopher	Australia
61 Miller, James	Australia
62 Yates, Robert Lee	
63 Baumeister, Herb	
64 Berdella, Bob	
65 Bonin, William	
66 Conahan, Daniel Jr.	
67 Dillon, Thomas	
68 Eyler, Larry	
69 Ireland, Colin	U.K.
70 Kraft, Randy	
71 MacDonald, William	Australia
"the Mutilator"	
72 Nilsen, Dennis	U.K.
73 Bishop, Arthur Gary	
74 Black, Robert	U.K.
75 Coril, Dean	
76 Davis,Richard Allen	
77 de Rais, Gilles	France
78 Dodd, Westley Allan	
79 Dutroux, Marc	Belgium
80 Iqbal, Javed	Pakistan
81 Kanka, Megan	
82 Luckman, Paul	Australia
83 Reid, Robin	Australia
84 Brady, Ian	U.K.
85 Hindley, Myra	U.K.
86 Olson, Clifford	Canada
87 Panzram, Carl	
88 Porter, Father James	
89 Williams, Wayne	

Truly Weird & Shocking

90 Allitt, Beverly	U.K.
91 Ball, Joe	
92 Burke, William	U.K.
93 Hare, William	U.K.
94 Chase, Richard Trenton	
95 Clark, Hadden	
96 Claux, Nico	France
97 Costanzo, Adolfo	Mexico
98 Cooke, Eric Edgar	Australia
99 DeMeo, Roy	
100 Ford, Dr. Larry C.	
101 Haigh, John George	U.K.
102 Bennett, Robert Leigh	
103 Harvey Donald	
104 Heidnik, Gary	
105 Jones, Genene	
106 Mullin, Herb	
107 Pandy, Andras	Belgium
108 Sagawa, Issei	Japan
109 Saldivar, Efren	
110 Sappingon, Marc	
111 Seda, Heriberto "Eddie"	
112 Swango, Michael	

Crime TV's Library of Violent Criminals (April 2003)   Exhibit 23c

**Truly Weird & Shocking
(continued)**

		Foreign
113	West, Fred	U.K.
114	West, Rose	U.K.

Partners In Crime

115	Beck, Martha	
116	Fernandez, Raymond	
117	Birnie, David	Australia
118	Birnie, Catherine	Australia
119	Clark, Doug	
120	Bundy, Carol	
121	Coleman, Alton	
122	Brown, Debra	
123	Gallego, Gerald	
124	Gallego, Charlene	
125	Lewingdon, Gary	
126	Lewingdon, Thaddeus	
127	McCafferty, Archibald Beattie	Australia

Killers From History

128	Makin, John	Australia
129	Makin, Sarah	Australia
130	Francis Knorr	Australia
131	Mitchell, Alice	Australia
132	Christie, John	U.K.
133	Cream, Dr. Thomas Neill	Canada
134	Deeming, Frederick	Australia
135	Gunness, Belle	
136	Haarmann, Fritz	Germany
137	Holmes, H.H.	
138	Kurten, Peter	Germany
139	Landru, Henri	France
140	Lynch, John	Australia
141	Mengele, Dr. Josef	Germany
142	Nelson, Earle Leonard	
143	Petiot, Dr. Marcel	France
144	Pomeroy, Jesse	
145	Prince Vlad	Romania

**Notorious Murders
Most Famous**

146	Bell, Mary	U.K.
147	Binion, Ted	
148	Borden, Lizzie	
149	Downs, Diane	
150	**Einhorn, Ira**	
151	Graham, Barbara	
152	Hauptman, Richard	
153	**Leopold, Nathan**	
154	**Loeb, Richard**	
155	List, John	
156	de Sade, the Marquis	France
157	Menendez, Lyle	
158	Menendez, Erik	
159	Skakel, Michael	
160	Smith, Susan	
161	Taylor, William Desmond	
162	Turner, Cheryl	

Mass & Spree Killers

		Foreign
163	Crump, Kevin	Australia
164	Baker, Allan	Australia
165	Banks, George	
166	Kehoe, Andrew	
167	Bryant, Martin	Australia
168	Crowley, Francis	
169	Cunanan, Andrew	
170	Gilmore, Gary	
171	Jones, Jim	
172	Harris, Eric	
173	Kiebold, Dylan	
174	Lundgren, Jeffrey	
175	Kuklinski, Richard	
176	Cowan, Frederick W.	
177	Gonzalez, Julio	
178	Starkweather, Charles	
179	Whitman, Charles	

**Angels of Death
Young Killers**

180	Bosket, Willie	
181	Bulger, James	
182	Stinney, George Junius, Jr.	
183	Travers, John Raymond	Australia
184	Murdoch, Michael James	Australia
185	Murphy, Gary Steven	Australia
186	Murphy, Leslie Joseph	Australia
187	Murphy, Michael Patrick	Australia
188	Parker, Jim	
189	Tulloch, Robert	
190	Hunt, Joe	
191	Sharer, Shanda	
192	Zamora, Diane	
193	Graham, Diane	

Women Who Kill

194	Barfield, Velma	
195	Bembenek, Bambi	
196	Cotton, Mary Ann	U.K.
197	Doss, Nannie	
198	Ellis, Ruth	U.K.
199	Harris, Jean	
200	Hilley, Marie	
201	Judd, Wiinnie Ruth	
202	Kimes, Sante	
203	Kimes, Kenny	
204	Likens, Sylvia	
205	Neelley, Judith Ann	
206	Nelson, Leslie	
207	Puente, Dorthea	
208	Routier, Darlie	
209	Smith, Madeleine	U.K.
210	Snyder, Ruth	
211	Gray, Judd	
212	Tucker, Karla Faye	
213	Warmus, Carolyn	
214	Wuornos, Aileen	

Crime TV's Library of Violent Criminals (April 2003)   Exhibit 23c

Death In The Family

	Foreign
215 Abequa, Mohammed	Jordon
216 Brando, Christian	
217 Crimmins, Alice	
218 Douglas, Scott	
219 Broderick, Betty	
220 Smith, Perry	
221 Hickock, Dick	
222 Gingerich, Edward D.	
223 Crippen, Dr. Hawley, Harvey	U.K.
224 Durst, Robert	
225 Fletcher, Michael	
226 Gluzman, Rita	
227 Hightower, Christopher	
228 Lucan, Lord	U.K.
229 Macdonald, Dr. Jeffrey	
230 Rossum, Kristen	
231 Smart, Pam	
232 **Steinberg, Joel**	
233 Wilson, Garrett	
234 Crafts, Richard	

Celebrity Crimes

	Foreign
235 Arbuckle, Fatty	
236 Aude, Eric	Pakistan
237 Brach, Helen	
238 Bailey, Richard	
239 George, Barry	U.K.

Timeless Classics

240 Capano, Thomas
241 Chapman, Mark David
242 Chessman, Caryl
243 Parkman, Dr.
244 Webster, John
245 **Sanhuber, Otto**
246 Willis, Howard Hawk

Not Guilty

247 Hinkley, John Jr.

Outlaws

248 Barrow, Clyde
249 Parker, Bonnie
250 Dillinger, John
251 Floyd, Charles Arthur "Pretty Boy"
252 Karpis, Alvin
253 Barker, Ma
254 Kelly, George "Machine Gun"
255 Gillis, Lester "Baby Face Nelson"
256 Casidy, Butch
257 Longbaugh, Harry "Sundance Kid"
258 James, Jesse
259 McCarty, Henry "Billy the Kid"

Terrorists

	Foreign
260 Matsumoto, Chizuo (Shoko Asahara)	Japan
261 Baader, Andreas	Germany
262 Meinhof, Ulrike	Germany
263 bin Laden, Osama	Saudi Arabia
264 Sanchez, Ilich Ramirez (Carlos the Jackal)	Eur/Mid-East
265 Ford, Dr. Larry C.	
266 DeFreeze, Donald (Field Marshall Cinque Mtume)	
267 Kaczynski, Ted	
268 McVeigh, Timothy	
269 Metesky, George	
270 Nosair, El-Sayid	
271 Padilla, Jose	
272 Rudolph, Eric	
273 Gilbert, David	
274 Boudin, Kathy	

Assassins

	Foreign
275 Booth, John Wilkes	
276 Chapman, Mark David	
277 Hinkley, John	
278 Oswald, Lee Harvey	
279 Sirhan, Sirhan	
280 Czolgosz, Leon	
281 Ray, James Earl	
282 **Amir, Yigal**	Israel

Major Financial Scandals & Key Principals Involved

Company or Scandal Name	Venue		Key Figures	US #
Adelphia	U.S.	1	Rigas, John & family	1
Allied Irish Bank	U.S.	2	Rusnak, John	2
Archer Daniels Midland	U.S.	3	Michael Andreas	3
	U.S.	4	Mark Whitacre	4
Bank of Credit & Commerce Intl (BCCI)	Intl	5	Abedi Agha Hasan	
	Intl	6	Gokal, Abbas	
Bankers Trust	U.S.	7	Shanks, Gene	5
Barings Bank	Intl	8	Leeson, Nicholas	
Billy Sol Estes	U.S.	9	Estes, Billie Sol	6
Bond Corporation	Australia	10	Bond, Alan	
Bre-X	Intl	11	de Guzman, Michael	
	Intl	12	Felderhof, John B.	
	Intl	13	Walsh, David G.	
Browning Ferris	U.S.	14	Phillips, Harry	7
Cendant	U.S.	15	Forbes, Walter	8
Chase Wiggin Scandal	U.S.	16	Wiggin, Albert	9
Citibank	U.S.	17	Elliott, Amy	10
	U.S.	18	Giraldi, Antonio	11
Citigroup	U.S.	19	**Weill, Sanford**	12
	U.S.	20	**Grubman, Jack**	13
Columbia/HCA	U.S.	21	Whiteside, Robert	14
	U.S.	22	Jarrell, Jay	15
Credit Lyonnais	Europe (Fr)	23	Trichet, Jean-Claude	
	Europe (Fr)	24	Parretti, Giancarlo	
	Europe (Fr)	25	Fiorini, Florio	
	Europe (Fr)	26	Vigon, Georges	
Credit Mobilier	U.S.	27	Ames, Oakes	16
Daewoo	S. Korea	28	Kim Woo-Choong	
Daiwa Bank	Japan	29	Iguchi, Toshihide	
	Japan	30	Akira, Fujita	
Darien Scandal	Europe	31	Patterson, William	
Flf Acquitaine	Europe (Fr)	32	Dumas, Roland	
	Europe (Fr)	33	Sirven, Alfred	
	Europe (Fr)	34	Le Floch-Prigent, Loik	
Enron & Arthur Anderson	U.S.	35	Lay, Kenneth	17
	U.S.	36	Skilling, Jeffrey	18
	U.S.	37	**Fastow, Andrew**	19
	U.S.	38	Bernardino, Joseph	20
	U.S.	39	Duncan, David	21
Equity Funding	U.S.	40	**Goldblum, Stanley**	22
First Jersey Securities	U.S.	41	Brennan, Robert	23
Flaming Ferraris	Europe (UK)	42	Archer, James	
Frankel, Martin	U.S.	43	**Frankel, Martin**	24
Franklin National	U.S.	44	Sindona, Michele	25
GE/Westinghouse & Others Price Fixing Scandal	U.S.	26		
	U.S.	27		
Gold Scandal of 1869	U.S.	45	Gould, Jay	28
	U.S.	46	Fisk, James	29
Griffin Trading	Europe (UK)	47	Park, John Ho	
Guinness Four	Europe (UK)	48	**Ronson, Gerald**	
	Europe (UK)	49	**Saunders, Ernest**	
Health South	U.S.	50	Scrushy, Richard M.	30
Helmsley Tax Fraud	U.S.	51	**Helmsley, Leona**	31
Imclone stock trading	U.S.	52	**Waksal, Samuel**	32
	U.S.	53	Stewart, Martha	33
Insull	U.S.	54	Insull, Sam	34

Major Financial Scandals & Key Principals Involved   **Exhibit 23d**

Company or Scandal Name	Venue		Key Figures	US #
Insider Trading Scandal of 1980s	U.S.	55	**Milkin, Michael**	35
	U.S.	56	**Boesky, Ivan F.**	36
	U.S.	57	**Levine, Dennis**	37
	U.S.	58	**Siegel, Martin**	38
Investors Overseas Services	Europe	59	**Cornfield, Bernie**	
	Europe	60	**Vesco, Robert**	
Jarding Fleming	Intl	61	Armstrong, Colin	
	Intl	62	Thomas, Robert	
Kidder Peabody	U.S.	63	Joseph Jett	39
Kreuger - Match King Scandal	U.S.	64	Kreuger, Ivar	40
Lernout & Hauspie	Europe	65	Bastiaens, Gaston	
	Europe	66	Lernout, Jo	
	Europe	67	Hauspie, Pol	
Lincoln Savings & Saving & Loan Scandals	U.S.	68	Keating, Charles	41
Lloyds of London Asbestos & Names Scandal	Europe (UK)	69	Green, Peter	
	Europe (UK)	70	Middleton, Peter	
Madoff, Bernard	U.S.	71	**Madoff, Bernard**	42
Maritime Phantom Cargo	Intl	72	Patel, Madhav	
Metallgesellschaft	Europe	73	Davila Silva, Juan Pablo	
	Europe	74	Schimmelbusch, Heinz	
Mississippi Company	Europe (Fr)	75	Law, John	
Morgan Greenfell	Europe (UK)	76	Young, Peter	
National Student Marketing	U.S.	77	Randall, Cortes Wesley	43
NatWest Markets	Europe (UK)	78	Gaskelll, Ian	
"Network Capacity" Telecom and "	U.S.	79	Watson, Chuck	44
"Round Trip" Energy Trades	U.S.	80	McCormick, William T. Jr.	45
Including: CMS Energy, Duke Energy,	U.S.	81	**Winnick, Gary**	46
Dynergy, El Paso Global Crossing,	U.S.	82	Naeve, Steve	47
Qwest, Reliant and others	U.S.	83	Nacchio, Joseph	48
Nigerian 419	Intl		Various Nigerians	
Occidental Petroleum & Armand Hammer	Intl	84	**Hammer, Armand**	
Orange County	U.S.	85	Citron, Robert	49
Polly Peck	Europe	86	Nadir, Asil	
Ponzi Scheme	U.S.	87	Ponzi, Charles	50
Prudential Bache	U.S.	88	Ball, George	51
	U.S.	89	Darr, James	52
Rich, Marc & Pincus Green	Intl	90	**Rich, Marc**	
	Intl	91	**Pincus Green**	
Robert Maxwell	Europe	92	**Maxwell, Robert**	
Salad Oil Scandal	U.S.	93	De Angelis, Anthony	53
Salomon Brothers	U.S.	94	Mozer, Paul	54
Sotheby's	Intl	95	**Taubman, Al**	
South Sea Bubble	Europe (UK)	96	Craggs, James	
	Europe (UK)	97	Sunderland, Charles Spencer	
Sumitomo Trading Scandal	Japan	98	Hamanaka, Yasuo	
Sunbeam	U.S.	99	Dunlap, Al	55
Teapot Dome	U.S.	100	Fall, Albert B.	56
	U.S.	101	Sinclair, Harry F.	57
	U.S.	102	Doheney, Edward L.	58
Tulip Mania	Europe		No key figure named	
Tweed Ring and Whiskey Ring	U.S.	103	Tweed, William Macy	59
Tyco	U.S.	104	Kozlowski, L. Dennis	60
	U.S.	105	**Swartz, Mark H.**	61
	U.S.	106	Belnick, Mark A.	62
United American Bank	U.S.	107	Butcher, Jake	63
	U.S.	108	Butcher, C.H.	64

Major Financial Scandals & Key Principals Involved   **Exhibit 23d**

Company or Scandal Name	Venue		Key Figures	US #
Vatican Bank & Banco Ambrosiano	Europe	109	Calvi, Roberto	
Viviendi	Europe (Fr)	110	Messier, John-Marie	
Waste Management	U.S.	111	Buntrock, Dean	65
	U.S.	112	Rooney, Phillip	66
Wedtech	U.S.	113	Wallach, E. Bob	67
Whitney Scandal	U.S.	114	Whitney, Richard	68
World Com	U.S.	115	Ebbers, Bernie	69
	U.S.	116	Sulivan, Scott	70
Xerox Accounting	U.S.	117	Allaire, Paul	71
	U.S.	118	Romeril, Barry	72
	U.S.	119	Thoman, Rick	73
Yazoo Land Scandal	U.S.		No key figure named	
Wolfson Stock Scams	U.S.	120	**Wolfson, Alan Z**	74
ZZZ Best	U.S.	121	**Minkow, Barry**	75

Fortune Magazine's List of "White Collar Criminals" Exhibit 23e
(Sunday, March 3, 2002 by Ellan Florian)

1. 1929: The Ponzi Scheme – Charles Ponzi
2. 1929: Albert Wiggen's shorting of Chase National stock while serving as CEO
3. 1930: Ivar Krueger, the Match King whose match empire collapsed
4. 1938: Richard Whitney who stole from Trusts and assets he managed
5. 1961: The Electric Cartel of GE, Westinghouse and others that fixed prices
6. 1962: Billie Sol Estes who mortgaged nonexistent farm gear
7. 1970: **Bernie Cornfield** and **Robert Vesco** and their IOS scam
8. 1983: **Marc Rich** and hisillegal and tax evasion dealings
9. 1986: **Ivan Boesky**, **Mike Milken** and Drexel insider trading scandal
10. 1989: Charles Keating and the collapse of Lincoln S&L
11. 1991: BCCI – the Bank of Credit & Commerce and it money laundering
12. 1991: Solomon Brothers Paul Mozer who violated Treasury Auction rules
13. 1995: Nick Leeson and Barings Bank, trading losses that destroyed the Bank
14. 1995: Bankers Trust misled clients about derivatives and lost $200 million+
15. 1997: Walter Forbes who cooked the books at CUC before selling to Cendant
16. 1997: Columbia/HCA involved in major Medicare fraud
17. 1998: Waste Management and its cooking of its books
18. 1998: Al Dunlap, the "Chainsaw Al" who destroyed Sunbeam
19. 1999: **Martin Frankel** who siphoned $200 million from insurance companies
20. 2000: Sotheby's and **Al Taubman** who fixed prices with Christies

Note that the 20 scandals identify 23 significant names

UJA Fund Raising and Allocation to Israel   Exhibit 24a

	Total Raised (in 000s)	Total Allocated to Israel (in 000s)	Total Allocated to other than Israel (in 000s)	Percent Sent to Israel
1948	$200,700	$146,926	$53,774	73%
1949	161,000	101,954	$59,046	63%
1950	142,200	86,639	$55,561	61%
1951	136,000	79,311	$56,689	58%
1952	121,200	66,902	$54,298	55%
1953	117,200	63,694	$53,506	54%
1954	109,300	56,753	$52,547	52%
1955	110,100	56,101	$53,999	51%
1956	130,500	74,302	$56,198	57%
1957	138,100	80,119	$57,981	58%
1958	123,300	64,606	$58,694	52%
1959	130,700	66,058	$64,642	51%
1960	127,700	64,661	$63,039	51%
1961	126,000	64,785	$61,215	51%
1962	129,400	53,539	$75,861	41%
1963	124,700	59,799	$64,901	48%
1964	126,700	58,890	$67,810	46%
1965	131,300	61,601	$69,699	47%
1966	136,500	64,257	$72,243	47%
1967	301,674	236,515	$65,159	78%
1968	215,677	144,495	$71,182	67%
1969	243,336	163,754	$79,582	67%
1970	275,394	191,940	$83,454	70%
1971	334,213	230,449	$103,764	69%
1972	349,649	228,497	$121,152	65%
1973	362,282	236,440	$125,842	65%
1974	683,527	488,032	$195,495	71%
1975	465,631	295,416	$170,215	63%
1976	448,759	259,318	$189,441	58%
1977	450,760	263,609	$187,151	50%
1978	470,590	266,588	$204,002	57%
1979	474,697	265,077	$209,620	56%
1980	502,773	288,081	$214,692	57%
1981	538,164	304,766	$233,398	57%
1982	558,164	322,698	$235,466	58%
1983	583,270	302,975	$280,295	52%
1984	634,738	322,496	$312,242	51%
1985	656,491	345,500	$310,991	53%
1986	687,959	249,485	$438,474	36%
1987	724,725	361,583	$363,142	50%
1988	738,593	352,797	$385,796	48%
1989	757,620	366,374	$391,246	48%
1990	756,281	357,391	$398,890	47%
1991	738,607	327,458	$411,149	44%
1992	732,850	322,004	$410,846	44%
1993	722,363	317,593	$404,770	44%
1994	726,644	299,368	$427,276	41%
1995	732,960	297,368	$435,592	41%
1996	751,723	305,044	$446,679	41%
1997	760,117	287,608	$472,509	38%
1998	804,887	305,000	$499,887	38%
1999	837,800	300,000	$537,800	36%
Total	$21,545,518	$10,976,616	$10,568,902	51%

UJA Fund Raising and Allocation to Israel

Jewish Giving to Israel Versus Other Causes

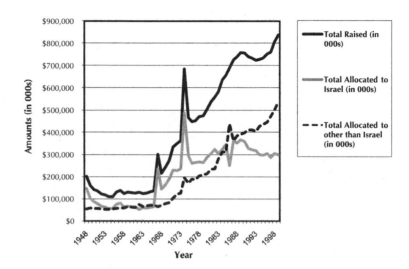

Percent Sent to Israel

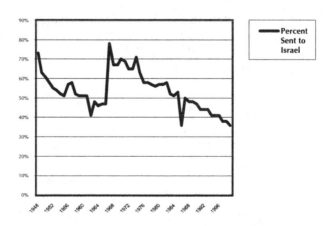

Business Week 50 Most Generous Philanthropists: 2003 – 2007   Exhibit 24b

Rank	Name	Background	2003 to 2007 Given or Pledged in Millions	Causes	Est Lifetime Giving in Millions	Net Worth	Giving as % of Net Worth
1	Warren Buffett	Berkshire Hathaway CEO	$40,650	Health, education, humanitarian causes	$ 40,780	$52,000	78
2	Bill and Melinda Gates	Microsoft co-founder	3,519	Global health and development, education	28,144	59,000	48
3	George Kaiser	Oil and gas, banking, real estate	2,271	Poverty in Oklahoma	2,522	11,000	23
4	George Soros	Investor	2,109	Open and democratic societies	6,401	8,800	73
5	Gordon and Betty Moore	Intel co-founder	2,067	Environment, science, San Fran. Bay area	7,404	4,500	165
6	Walton Family	Family of Wal-Mart founder	1,475	Education	2,015	82,500	2
7	Herbert and Marion Sandler	Golden West co-founders	1,358	Medical research, education, social reform	1,389	2,400	58
8	Eli and Edythe Broad	SunAmerica, KB Home founder	1,216	Public educ., arts, scientific and medical research	2,286	7,000	33
9	Donald Bren	Real estate developer	915	Education, conservation, research	1,326	13,000	10
10	Jon Huntsman	Huntsman chairman	830	Cancer, business education	1,233	1,900	65
11	Bernard Osher	Banking, investments	730	Arts, education, social services	805	900	89
12	Alfred Mann	Medical devices	638	Biomedical education and research	1,735	2,200	79
13	Michael and Susan Dell	Dell founder	674	Children's health, education	1,200	17,200	7
14	Michael Bloomberg	Bloomberg founder, NYC mayor	534	Health, education, arts, social services	1,045	11,500	9
15	David Rockefeller	Standard Oil heir, banking	552	Biomed research, global development, arts	937	2,700	35
16	Jeff Skoll	Founding president of eBay	560	Social entrepreneurs	744	3,500	21
17	T. Denny Sanford	Banking and credit cards	539	Science education, medical research	559	2,800	20
18	Veronica Atkins	Widow of Dr. Robert Atkins	519	Eradication of obesity and diabetes	519	60	865
19	John Templeton	Investor	514	Science about life's big questions	1,003	2,000	50
20	Robert Wilson	Investor	508	Environment	541	600	90
21	Pierre and Pam Omidyar	eBay chairman and founder	493	Unleashing human potential	657	8,900	7
22	T. Boone Pickens	Energy and investing	445	Higher education and athletics, health	445	3,000	15
23	Sandy and Joan Weill	Former Citigroup chairman, CEO	435	Education, healthcare, arts, social causes	800	1,800	44
24	John Kluge	Metromedia founder	401	Library of Congress, higher education	751	9,500	8
25	Ted Turner	CNN founder	389	Environment, global security	1,500	2,300	65
26	Lorry Lokey	Business Wire founder, chairman	373	Education, libraries, and culture	415	NA	NA
27	Kirk Kerkorian**	Investor	365	Humanitarian and Armenian causes	696	18,000	4
28	Shelby White**	Widow of investor Leon Levy	365	Ancient studies, arts, humanities	525	600	88
29	David Koch	Koch Industries EVP	364	Medical care, cancer, education	500	17,000	3
30	Bernard Marcus	Home Depot co-founder	351	Jewish causes, health, free enterprise, children	700	2,000	35
31	Irwin and Joan Jacobs	Qualcomm co-founder	330	Education, arts	627	1,600	39
32	Frank and Jane Batten	Landmark Comm. founder	314	Education, early childhood development	510	2,000	26
33	Robert Meyerhoff	Real estate developer	300	Arts, higher education	305	NA	NA
34	Paul Allen	Microsoft co-founder	283	Arts, health/human services, science	937	16,800	6
35	Oprah Winfrey	Harpo chairman	263	Education; women, children, and families	303	2,500	12
36	Robert Day	Trust Company of the West CEO	262	Education, health and arts	305	1,600	19

Business Week 50 Most Generous Philanthropists: 2003 – 2007   Exhibit 24b

Rank	Name	Background	2003 to 2007 Given or Pledged in Millions	Causes	Est Lifetime Giving in Millions	Net Worth	Giving as % of Net Worth
37	Ted and Vada Stanley	MBI founder	254	Mental illness, crisis relief	568	NA	NA
38	David and Cheryl Duffield	PeopleSoft co-founder	244	Animals, humane society, education	331	1,200	28
39	James Simons	Investor	243	Math, science, education, autism	267	5,500	5
40	Dan Duncan and family	Enterprise Products Ptnrs. co-founder	230	Medical research, education, youth	300	8,200	4
41	Frances Comer	Widow of Lands' End founder	228	Environment, education, youth	268	1,000	27
42	Ira and Mary Lou Fulton	Fulton Homes CEO	224	Higher education, community	266	410	65
43	**Dawn Greene**	Widow of lawyer Jerome Greene	200	Education, medicine, arts	**260**	NA	NA
44	Marguerite Hoffman	Widow of investor Robert Hoffman	199	Dallas arts and social services, science	208	NA	NA
45	George Lucas	Lucasfilm founder	196	Education, arts, health, civil rights	213	3,900	5
46	**Larry Ellison**	Oracle CEO	193	Research on aging and diseases	**808**	26,000	3
47	Thomas Siebel	Siebel Systems founder	189	Education, meth prevention, community	386	1,900	20
48	**Peter Lewis**	Progressive chairman	188	Arts, environment, youth, social reform	**426**	NA	NA
49	Leo and Kay Drey	Schram Glass heir, silviculture	180	Conservation	180	NA	NA
50	**Haim and Cheryl Saban**	Saban Capital Group CEO, Chairman	176	Children's healthcare, U.S. and Israeli charities	195	3,400	6
Total Jewish Giving					$22,779		

Source: Business Week, November 26, 2007

Select Bibliography

American Jewish Historical Society. *American Jewish Desk Reference*, New York, New York: The Philip Lief Group, Inc. Random House, 1999

Ariel, David S. *What Do Jews Believe: The Spiritual Foundation of Judaism*, New York, New York: Schocken Books, 1995

Armstrong, Karen. *A History of God: The 4,000 Year Quest of Judaism, Christianity and Islam*, New York, New York: Ballantine Books, a division of Random House, 1993

Asa-El, Amotz. *The Diaspora and the Lost Tribes of Israel*, Hugh Lauter Levin Associates, Inc. 2004

Barnavi, Eli and Denis Charbit, *A Historical Atlas of the Jewish People*, New York, NY: Schocken Books, 2002

Barone, Michael. *The New Americans: How the Melting Pot Can Work Again*, Washington D.C.: Regnery Publishing, Inc., an Eagle Publishing Company, 2001

Bellow, Saul. *The Adventures of Augie March*, Penguin Books, New York, 1996

Biale, David. *Cultures of the Jews: A New History*, Schocken Books, New York, 2002

Ben Ami, Shlomo, *Scars of War, Wounds of Peace: The Israeli-Arab Tragedy*, Oxford University Press, Oxford, New York, 2006

Benbassa, Esther & Aron Rodrigue. *Sephardi Jewry: A History of the Judeo-Spanish Community, 14th–20th Centuries*, University of California Press, Berkeley and Los Angeles, California 2000

Bergsman, Steve. *Maverick Real Estate Investing*, John Wiley & Sons, Hoboken, New Jersey, 2004

Bickerman, Elias J. *The Jews in the Greek Age*, Harvard University Press, Cambridge Massachusetts, 1988

Birmingham, Stephen. *Our Crowd: The Great Jewish Families of New York*, Syracuse, New York: Syracuse University Press, 1967

Birmingham, Stephen. *The Grandees: The Story of America's Sephardic Elite*, New York, New York: Dell Publishing Company, Inc. 1971

Bloom, Stephen G. *Postville: A Clash of Cultures in Heartland America*, A Harvest Book: Harcourt, Inc. San Diego, New York, London, 2000

Boorstin, Daniel J. *Hidden History: Exploring Our Secret Past*, New York, New York: Vintage Books, a Division of Random House, 1989

Boorstin, Daniel J. *The Daniel J. Boorstin Reader*, New York, New York: The Modern Library, a Division of Random House, 1995

Brawarsky, Sandee and Deborah Mark. *Two Jews, Three Opinions: A Collection of Twentieth-Century American Jewish Quotations*, New York, New York: A Perigee Book, Berkley Publishing Group, a Division of Penguin Putnam, Inc., 1998

Brzezinski, Matthew. *Casino Moscow: A Tale of Greed and Adventure on Capitalism's Wildest Frontier*, The Free Press, Simon & Schuster, New York, 2001

Bullock, Alan. *Hitler and Stalin: Parallel Lives*, New York, New York: Vintage Books, a Division of Random House, Inc. 1993

Cahill, Thomas. *The Gift of the Jews: How a Tribe of Desert Nomads Changed the Way Everyone Thinks and Feels*, New York, New York: Nan A. Talese/Anchor Books, Imprints of Doubleday, a Division of Random House, Inc., 1998

Chernow, Ron. *The Warburgs: The Twentieth-Century Odyssey of a Remarkable Jewish Family*, New York, New York: Random House, 1993

Chetkin, Len, *Guess Who's Jewish (you'll never guess)* Norfolk/Virginia Beach: The Donning Company/ Publishers 1985

Cohen, Abraham. *Everyman's Talmud: The Major Teachings of the Rabbinic Sages*, New York, New York: Schocken Books, 1995 Reprint of the 1949 edition published by E.P. Dutton

Cohen, Rich. *Tough Jews: Fathers, Sons and Gangster Dreams*, New York, New York: Vintage Books, A Division of Random House, Inc., 1999

D'Epiro, Peter and Mary Desmond Pinkowish. *Sprezzatura: 50 Ways Italian Genius Shaped the World*. Anchor Books, Random House, 2001

Dershowitz, Alan. *The Case for Israel*, John Wiley & Sons, Inc. Hoboken, New Jersey, 2003

Dimont, Max I. *Jews God and History*, New American Library, New York, 1994

Diner, Hasia R., *The Jews of the United States: 1654 to 2000*, University of California Press, Berkeley and Los Angeles, California, 2004

Dobbs, Stephen Mark, *The Koret Foundation: 25 Years as a Catalyst to Positive Change*, Western Jewish History Center, Berkeley, California, 2004

Duke, David. *My Awakening: A Path to Racial Understanding*, Free Speech Press, Mandeville, Louisiana, 1998

Economist, *The Pocket World in Figures: 2002 Edition*. London, England, 2002

Encyclopædia Britannica. *The New Encyclopædia Britannica: Volume 22 Macropedia*, Chicago, Illinois: Encyclopædia Britannica, Inc., University of Chicago: 1988

Etkes, Asher B and Saul Stadtmauer, *Jewish Contributions to the American Way of Life*, Long Island City, NY: Northside Publishing Inc. 1995

Falcon, Rabbi Ted, Ph.D. and David Blatner, *Judaism for Dummies*, New York, New York: Hungry Minds, Inc., 2001

Felder, Deborah G. and Diana Rosen, *Fifty Jewish Women Who Changed the World*, New York, NY: Citadel Press, Kensington Publishing Company, 2003

Feldman, Burton. The *Nobel Prize: A History of Genius, Controversy and Prestige*. New York, New York: Arcade Publishing, 2000

Fox, John G and Julian Krainin, Heritage: *Civilization and the Jews*, New York, New York: Thirteen/ WNET, 1994 & 1998, (A DVD video)

Gabler, Neal. *An Empire of Their Own: How the Jews Invented Hollywood*, New York, New York: Anchor Books, Random House, 1988

Gilbert, Martin, *The Jews in the Twentieth Century: An Illustrated History*, New York, New York: Schocken Books, a Division of Random House, 2001

Gilbert, Martin, *The Routledge Atlas of Jewish History, Sixth Edition*, Routledge, New York & London: 2003

Harris, Leon. *Merchant Princes: An Intimate History of the Jewish Families Who Built Great Department Stores*, New York, New York: Harper & Row 1979 and Kodansha America, 1994.

Harrison, Lawrence E. and Huntington, Samuel P. *Culture Matters: How Values Shape Human Progress*, New York, New York: Basic Books, A Subsidiary of Perseus Books, LLC, 2000

Harrison, Lawrence E., *The Central Liberal Truth: How Politics Can Change a Culture and Save It From Itself*, Oxford University Press, Oxford, New York, 2006

Hart, Michael H. *The 100: A Ranking of the Most Influential Persons in History*. Secaucus, New Jersey: Citadel Press, 1987

Herman, Arthur, *How the Scots Invented the Modern World*, Random House, New York, 2001

Hyman, Paula E. and Moore, Deborah Dash, *Jewish Women in America: An Historical Encyclopedia*, Volumes I & II, Routledge, New York, 1998

Jewish Publication Society, *Tanakh: The Holy Scriptures*. Philadelphia, Pennsylvania: The Jewish Publication Society, 1985

Johnson, Paul. *A History of the Jews* New York, New York: Harper Perennial, A Division of Harper Collins Publishers, 1988

Kamenetz, Rodger. *The Jew in the Lotus*, Harper Collins, New York, 1995

Keter Publishing House, Ltd., *Encyclopedia Judaica*, New York, NY: Lambda Publishers, Inc.

Kertzer, Rabbi Morris N. *What Is A Jew?* New York, New York: Collier Books, A Division of Macmillan Publishing Co., Inc. Fourth Edition, 1978

King James Version. *The Holy Bible: Containing the Old and New Testaments*, Nashville, Tenn.: Memorial Bibles International, Inc., 1976

Kleiman, Rabbi Yaakov. *DNA & Tradition: The Genetic Link to the Ancient Hebrews*, Jerusalem, Israel, Devora Publishing Company, 2004

Konner, Melvin. *Unsettled: An Anthropology of the Jews*, Penguin Group, New York, 2003

Korman, Abraham K. *The Outsiders: Jews and Corporate America.* Lexington, Mass.: D.C Heath and Company, Lexington Books, 1988

Kugel, James L. *How to Read the Bible: A Guide to Scripture Then and Now,* Free Press, New York, London, Toronto, Sydney, 2007

Kushner, Harold S. *When Bad Things Happen To Good People*, New York, New York. Avon Books, Harper Collins, 1981

Kushner, Harold S. *The Lord is My Shepherd: Healing Wisdom of the Twenty-Third Psalm*, New York, New York. Alfred A. Knopf, 2003

Landes, David S. *The Wealth and Poverty of Nations: Why Some Are So Rich and Some So Poor.* New York, New York: W. W. Norton & Company, 1998

Lebrecht, Norman, *The Song of Names*, Anchor Books, New York, Random House, 2002

Lustiger, Arno. *Stalin and the Jews*, New York, New York: Enigma Books by arrangement with Aufbau Verlag GMBH, 2003

Lyman, Darryl. *Jewish Heroes and Heroines*, Middle Village, New York: Jonathan David Publishers, Inc., 1996

Marsden, Victor E. (translator), *Protocols of the Learned Elders of Zion*, Briton Publishing Society, London, circa 1923

Michner, James A. *The Source*, New York, New York: Random House, 1965

Menchin, Robert. *101 Classic Jewish Jokes: Jewish Humor From Groucho Marx to Jerry Seinfeld*, Memphis, Tennessee Mustang Publishing Company, Inc., 1997

Mearsheimer, John J. and Walt, Stephen M., *The Israel Lobby and U.S. Foreign Policy*, Farrar, Straus and Giroux, New York, 2007

Milton, Joyce. *The Road to Malpsychia: Humanistic Psychology and Our Discontents*, San Francisco, California: Encounter Books, 2002

Moorehead, Alan. *The Russian Revolution*, New York, New York: Bantam Books, Time, Inc., 1959

Morton, Frederic. *The Rothschilds*, Greenwich, Connecticut: Fawcett Crest Publications, Inc.,1961

Murray, Charles. *Human Accomplishment: The Pursuit of Excellence in the Arts and Sciences; 800 B.C. to 1950.* New York, New York: HarperCollins, 2003

Nasar, Sylvia. *A Beautiful Mind: The Life of Mathematical Genius and Nobel Laureate John Nash.* New York, New York: Touchstone Books, Simon & Schuster, 1998

Nusseibeh, Sari with David, Anthony, *Once Upon a Country: A Palestinian Life*, Farrar, Straus and Giroux, New York, 2007

Olson, Steve. *Mapping Human History: Discovering the Past Through Our Genes*, Houghton Mifflin Company, Boston, Massachusetts, 2002

Oren, Michael B. *Six Days of War: June 1967 and the Making of the Modern Middle East.* New York, New York: Oxford University Press, 2002

Patai, Raphael. *The Jewish Mind*, Detroit, Michigan, Wayne State University Press, 1977

Phaidon. *The Art Book*, London, England: Phaidon Press, Ltd., 2001

Pilkington, C. M. *Judaism*, Lincolnwood (Chicago), Illinois: NTC Publishing Group, 1995

Potok, Chaim. *The Chosen*, New York, New York: Fawcett World Library, 1968

Prager, Dennis and Rabbi Joseph Telushkin. *Why The Jews? The Reason for Antisemitism*, New York, New York: Touchstone, Simon & Schuster, Inc, 1983, 2003.

Rhodes, Richard. *Dark Sun: The Making of the Hydrogen Bomb*, New York, New York: Touchstone, Simon & Schuster, 1995

Rivkin, Ellis. *The Unity Principle: The Shaping of Jewish History*, Behrman House, Springfield, New Jersey, 2003

Rosten, Leo. The *Joys of Yiddish*, New York, New York: Pocket Books, a Division of Simon & Schuster, 1970

Ruderman, David B. *Jewish Intellectual History: 16th to 20th Century*, (transcript and DVD video), The Teaching Company, Chantilly, VA, 2002

Salfati, *Talmud*, the Video, Arte France Developpement, Paris 2007

Shapiro, Michael. *The Jewish 100: A Ranking of the Most Influential Jews of All Times*, New York, New York: Citadel Press, Published by Kensington Publishing Corp., 1994

Schmemann, Serge, *Echoes of a Native Land: Two Centuries of a Russian Village*, Vintage Books, Random House, New York, 1997

Silbiger, Steven. *The Jewish Phenomenon: Seven Keys to the Enduring Wealth of a People*, Marietta Georgia: Longstreet Press, 2000

Singer, Isaac Bashevis, *The Slave*, Farrar, Straus, Giroux, New York, 1962

Slater, Robert, *Great Jews in Sports*, Middle Village, New York: Jonathan David Publishers, Inc., 2000 edition

Slezkine, Yuri. *The Jewish Century*, Princeton, New Jersey: Princeton University Press, 2004

Sowell, Thomas. A *Conflict of Visions: Ideological Origins of Political Struggles*, New York, New York: Quill, William Morrow and Company, 1987

Sowell, Thomas. *Conquest and Cultures: An International History*, New York, New York: Basic Books, A Subsidiary of Perseus Books, LLC, 1998

Sowell, Thomas. *Ethnic America*, New York, New York: Basic Books, A subsidiary of Perseus Books, LLC, 1981

Sowell, Thomas. *Migrations and Cultures: A World View*, New York, New York: Basic Books, A subsidiary of Perseus Books, LLC, 1996

Sowell, Thomas. *Race and Culture*, New York, New York: Basic Books, A subsidiary of Perseus Books, LLC, 1994

Steinsaltz, Adin. *The Essential Talmud*, Basic Books, 1976

Stern, David H. (translator) *Complete Jewish Bible: An English Version of the Tanakh (Old Testament)* and B'rit Hadashah (New Testament), Clarksville, Maryland: Jewish New Testament Publications, Inc. 1998

Stewart, James B. *Den of Thieves*, Touchstone, Simon & Schuster, New York, 1992

Symons, Alan. *The Jewish Contribution to the 20th Century*, Hampton, Middlesex, England, Polo Publishing, 1997

Symons, Alan. *Nobel Laureates: 1901–2000*, Hampton, Middlesex, England: Polo Publishing, 2000

Teller, Edward with Judith Shoolery, . *Memoirs: A Twentieth–Century Journey in Science and Politics*, Cambridge, Massachusetts: Perseus Publishing, 2001

Telushkin, Rabbi Joseph. *Jewish Humor: What the Best Jewish Jokes Say About the Jews*, New York, New York: William Morrow, 1992 and HarperCollins Perennial 2002

Telushkin, Rabbi Joseph. *Jewish Literacy: The Most Important Things To Know About the Jewish Religion, Its People, and Its History*, New York, New York. William Morrow & Company, 1991, reissued 2001

Thomas, Baylis. *How Israel Was Won: A Concise History of the Arab-Israeli Conflict*, Lanham, Maryland: Lexington Books, 1999.

Uris, Leon. *Exodus*, New York, New York: Bantam Books, 1958

Van Den Haag, Ernest. *The Jewish Mystique*. New York, New York: Stein & Day, 1969

Wechsberg, Joseph. *The Merchant Bankers*, New York, New York: Pocket Books, a Simon & Schuster Division of Gulf & Western, 1966

Zavatto, Amy. *Judaism: The Pocket Idiot's Guide to*, Indianapolis, Indiana: Alpha Books, a Pearson Publishing Company, 2003

End Notes

1. Rabbi Kalman Packouz, *Shabbat Shalom Weekly*, May 15, 1999, at www.aish.com/torahportion/ shalomweekly/ Bamidbar_5759.asp.

2. Daniel Golden, "In Effort to Lift Their Rankings, Colleges Recruit Jewish Students," The *Wall Street Journal*, April 29, 2002, available at www.wsj.com.

3. The two primary sources for this Section: 1) Charles Murray, *Human Accomplishment : The Pursuit of Excellence in the Arts and Sciences, 800 B.C. to 1950*, Harper Collins Publishers, New York, 2003, 59 86, 275–281, 605–07, and 2) Timothy Noah, *Slate*, "Battle of the Genius-rankers, Oct. 30, 2003 at www.slate.msn.com/id/2090555/ with the posting "Remarks from the Fray" immediately after the Noah article.

4. Among sources: Michael H. Hart, *The 100: A Ranking of the Most Influential Persons in History*, Citadel Press, Secaucus, New Jersey, 1987; For the importance of Churchill and his selection as Prime Minister, see: John Lukacs, *Five Days in London: May 1940*, Yale University Press, New Haven 1999 or, John Lukacs, *The Duel, 10 May–31 July 1940, The Eighty-Day Struggle Between Churchill and Hitler*, Ticknor & Fields, New York, 1991. Most biographies of Lincoln will establish his critical role in holding the Union together. Among them, an excellent source is: William Lee Miller, *Lincoln's Virtues: An Ethical Biography*, Alfred A. Knopf, New York, 2002.

5. A&E Television Networks, *Biography of the Millennium*, ran on the A&E Network, was produced into a four video-tape collection (AAE –17448 to 17561) and is available at www.biography.com/features/ millennium/topten.html.

6. IntelliQuest Learning Systems, *The World's 100 Greatest People, Audio Knowledge Mastery Collection*, is covered on the Web site: www.4iq.com/people1.htm.

7. *Time Magazine, "Time* 100 – *The Most Important People of the 20th Century*, were the subject of five issues that ran from April 13, 1998 to June 14, 1999, culminating in the *Person of the Century* on January 3, 2000. The choices are also at www.time.com/time/time100 /poc/home.html.

8. Material on Richard Feynman was drawn from James Gleick's *Genius : The Life and Science of Richard Feynman*, Pantheon Books, New York, 1992 , pages 3–16, 24–5, 45, 49, 151, 184,190–6, 278, 283–7, 341, 346; the Feynman bio by Mark Martin at www.fotuva.org/online/biography.htm; another by J. J. O'Connor and E.F. Robertson at www.history.mcs.st-andrews.ac.uk/Mathematicians/Feynman.html; the Wikipedia bio at http://en.wikipedia.org/wiki/Richard_Feynman; and http://en.wikiquote.org/wiki/Richard_Feynman; his bio at the Nobel Prize Web site www.nobel.se/physics/ laureates/1965/feynman-bio.htm; and reviews of Feynman's book, *Surely You're Joking Mr. Feynman!* at www.amazon.com.

9. The material on Nobel Prize winners in Physics, Physiology and Medicine, and Chemistry draw on Burton Feldman's *The Nobel Prize*, Arcade Publishing, New York, 2000; Alan Symons' *Nobel Laureates 1901–2000*, Polo Publishing, London 2000; *Encyclopaedia Britannica 2001 Deluxe Edition;* data from the Nobel Web site at www.nobel.se; as well as www.jewishvirtuallibrary.org/jsource/Judaism/ nobels.html; www.Jewhoo.com; www.us-israel.org; www.Yahoodi.com; www.jinfo.org/Nobels, and www.science.co.il/Nobel. Among newspaper and magazine articles used: James Glanz, "Nobel Prize, Robust at 100, Wasn't Always So Healthy," *The New York Times*, Dec 26, 2000; "Scanscam" and interview with Raymond Damadian in *The New York Times Magazine*, Dec. 14, 2003; the March 7, 2005 *Business Week* review of the book *Splendid Solution* about Jonas Salk and Albert Sabin; Sharon Begley, "Nobel Prize Judges Honor Some Greats But Snub Others," *Wall Street Journal*, Oct. 17, 2003.

10. The Albany Medical Center Prize in Medicine is covered at its Web site at www.amc.edu/amcprize_in_medicine.htm; and other pages at that site. Additional material on the recipients came from www.jinfo.org/Biomedical_Research.html; www.chi.org/ers/boyer.html; www.accessexcellence.org/ RC/AB/WYW/ wkbooks/SFTS/biography.html; and www.nellpainter.com/nell/resources/yale_degree.html.

11. Among sources for the Fields Medal section : www.mathunion.org/medals/Fields/Prizewinners.html; www.math.toronto.edu/fields.html; http://db.uwaterloo.ca/~alopez-o/math-faq/mathtext/node19.html; www.faqs.org/faqs/sci-math-feq/fields/; www.icm2002.org.cn/general/prize/fmedal.htm; www.jewhoo.com; www.yahoodi.com; www.ihes.fr?EVENTS/lafforgue/fields.html; www.jinfo.org/Fields_Mathematics.html. In addition, Sylvia Nasar's Book, *A Beautiful Mind, The Life of Mathematical Genius and Nobel Laureate John Nash*, Touchstone, New York, 1998, 2;5-6, Carl Riehm's article "The Early History of the Fields Medal" published in Volume 49, Number 7 *Notices of the AMS*, 778–82; and Florin Diacu's "The Top Mathematics Award" article available at www.pims.math.ca/pi/issue3/page17–18.pdf.

12. Among sources: the American Mathematical Society Web site: www.ams.org/prizes, and www.aquanet.co.il/wolf; www.gap.dcs.st-and.ac.uk/~history/Mathematicians/Cole.html; www.jinfo.org/Mathematics_Com.html; and related pages.

13. Material on Turing Awards is drawn from the Association for Computing Machinery Web site, www.acm.org/awards/taward.html; www.jinfo.org/Computer_Scientists.html; and related pages at that Web site.

14. Material on Edwin Land came from: Victor K. McElheny's biography of Land on the National Academy of Sciences Web site at www.nap.edu/readingroom/books/biomems/eland.html; his May 1999 article, "Brief Life of a Relentless Innovator 1909–1991" for *Harvard* magazine available at www.harvardmagazine.com/issues/ma99/vita.html; a synopsis of his book *Insisting on the Impossible: The Life of Edwin Land* at www.2think.org/land.shtml; reviews of that book at www.amazon.com; Richard L. Garwin's paper "Edwin H. Land: Science and Public Policy" presented at the Nov. 9, 1991 Academy of Arts and Sciences " Light and Life – A Symposium in Honor of Edwin Land," at www.fas.org/rig/land.htm; material on Land, and the history of Polaroid Land from the Web site, www.polaroid.com; *Encyclopædia Britannica 2001, Deluxe Edition*, biographical material on the Land family from http://alvray.com/Family/dag/all-p/p120.htm; an article, "The Glare in the Eyes of Edwin Land" at the Web site www.polarization.com/land/land.html; F.W. Campbell's bio of Land done for the Royal Society as part of its "Biographical Memoirs of Fellows of the Royal Society, 40, pages 195–219 (1994) available at http://www.rowland.org/organization/land/index.php; "Inventor of the Week Archive" at http://web.mit.edu/envent/iow/land.html; www.ideafinder.com/history/inventors/land.htm; www.northstar.k12.ak.us/schools/ryn/projects/inventors/land/land.html; www.nationmaster.com/encyclopedia/Edwin-Land; http://inventors.about.com/library/inventors/blpolaroid.htm; and related pages at that site on instant photography; an article on polarization at www.glenbrook.k12.il.us/gbssci/phys/Class/light/u12l1e.html; and others.

15. Among sources: *Encyclopædia Britannica Almanac 2003;* www.news.harvard.edu/gazette/2001/04.19/ 12-zoll.html; http://corporate.britannica.com/press/ inventions.html; www.Jewhoo.com; and others.

16. Deborah G. Felder and Diana Rosen, *Fifty Jewish Women Who Changed the World*, Citadel Press, Kensington Publishing Corp., New York, 2003, p. 216.

17. Principal sources include: Daniel Golden, "In Effort to Lift Their Rankings, Colleges Recruit Jewish Students," *The Wall Street Journal*, April 29, 2002, available at www.wsj.com; Alexander Nazaryan, "Princeton and Jewish Enrollment," *The Dartmouth Review*, July 22, 1999 available at www.dartreview.com/archives; "Jewish Emory - How Did a Methodist College Become a Hotbed of Jewish Life and Learning" *Jewish Times*, March 5, 1999. available at http://atlanta.jewish.com/ archives/1999/archives199.htm; Stuart Silverstein, "Day of the Jewish Trojan," *Los Angeles Times*, Dec. 11, 2002, available at www.chabadusc.com/latimes; Roger Clegg, "The Chosen" *National Review*, May 1, 2002 available at www.nationalreview.com/clegg/clegg050202.asp; Leon Harris, *Merchant Princes*, Kodansha America, New York, 1994, 31; "Oral Report" available at http://beart.barnard.columbia.edu/students/his3464y/ straus/orept.html; Thomas Sowell, *Ethnic America*, Basic Books, 1981, 69–99, 273–96; Thomas Sowell, *Race and Culture*, Basic Books, New York, 1994, 166–85; Franci Levine Grater, "Ivy League Makeover," *New Voices*, at www.schmoozenet.com/jsps/stories/princeton.shtml; "Harvard's Jewish Problem" at www.us-israel.org/jsource/ anti-semitism/harvard.html; Suzanne Fields, "Anti-Semitism in Harvard" *The Washington Times*, Sept 26, 2002 available at www.washtimes.com/; *American Jewish Desk Reference*, Random House, New York, 1999, 244–5, 254; Harold S. Wechsler, "The Rise and Fall of Discrimination at Columbia" a Nov. 10, 1998 Seminar Talk at Columbia University, available at http://beatl.barnard.columbia.edu/cuhistory/archives/WechslerText.htm; "History of the SAT – A Timeline," part of "Secrets of the SAT: Where Did the Test Come From" a *Frontline* report on public television, available at www.pbs.org/wgbh/pages/frontline/shows/sats/where/timeline.html, and related pages such as www.pbs.org/wgbh/pages/frontline/shows/sats/where/three.html; www.pbs.org/wgbh/pages/ frontline/shows/sats/interviews/lemann.html; and www.pbs.org/wgbh/pages/frontline/shows/sats/test/history.html; Jon Blackwell "1947; "America's Tester-in Chief," *The Trentonian*, available at www.capitalcentury.com/1947/html; James Fallows,

"The Tests and the 'Brightest': How Fair Are the College Boards?" *The Atlantic Monthly*, Feb 1980, Volume 245, No. 2 pages 37–48, available at www.theatlantic.com/issues/95sep/ets/fall.htm; Erik Lords, "Expert: Aptitude Tests Are Biased, He Says U-M's Policy Can Correct Imbalance" Feb. 7, 2001 available at http://aad.englishe.ucsb.edu/docs/lords.html; Thomas Sowell, "Ethnicity and IQ," *American Spectator*, Feb. 1, 1995, Vol. 28, 32, also at www.mugu.com/cgi-bin/Upstream/issues/bell-curve/sowell.html; David Brooks, "The Big Test" *Slate*, Sept. 27, 1999 and Nathan Glazer, "The Meritocratic Revolution" Sept. 27, 1999, an exchange of letters available at http://slate.msn.com/id/2000118/entry/1003687/.; Brian Doherty, "One Track Mind" a book review of Nicholas Lemann's book *The Big Test*, Farrar, Straus and Giroux, in Reason, April 2000 and available at http://reason.com/0004/bk.bd.one.html; Hasia R. Diner, *The Jews of the United States*, University of California Press, Berkeley, 2004; Abraham J. Karp, *A History of the Jews in America*, Schocken, New York, 1985; Stephen Birmingham, *Our Crowd*, Harper & Row, New York, 1967; Lisa Keys, "High (School) Anxiety: The Latest Gift of the Jews", *Forward*, Aug. 9, 2002, available at www.forward.com/issues/2002/02.08.09/education1.html; Justin Shubow, "Jews Should Reject Preferences" Baltimore Sun, July 18,2002, available at www.personal.umich.edu/ ~jshubow/baltsun_oped.html; Herman Green and Dixie Schmittou, "The History and the Mystery of the SAT, available at www.houston.clemson.edu/highlights/history_of_the_sat.pdf; Peter W. Hong, "The Changing Face of Higher Education, *Los Angeles Times*, available at www.jrn.columbia.edu/events/race/ Asians3_LATIMES.html; and Gerald W. Bracey, "The Secret to Those High Asian Test Scores: Affluent, Well Educated Daddies, Mommies, Too: available at www.america-tomorrow.com/ati/gb80211.htm.

18. Jewish population data come from numerous sources and are all subject to some dispute as to which sources are more or less credible. For our purposes, the differences are too small to make a material difference to the clear levels of disproportionate enrollment. Among sources are: A *United Jewish Communities Report* in Cooperation with The Mandell L. Berman Institute – North American Jewish Data Bank, *The National Jewish Populations Survey 2000–01*, and the attendant Power Point Presentation of Findings, September 2003,and available at http://www.ujc.org/content_display.html?ArticleID=83252; it is also summarized on the Jewish Virtual Library site at www.us-israel.org/jsource/US-Israel/ujcpop.html; Dr. Gary Tobin and Sid Groeneman, "Survey of Heritage and Religious Identification 2001–02" available at www.jewishdatabank.org/index.cfm?page=166&disp=p; material on college and university enrollment and Jewish enrollment in those schools come from www.hillel.org; and complemented with material from the Statistical Abstract of the United States: 2000, 157–8, 182, 191; the Jewish Professionals Institute Web site at www.jpi.org/phlsph.htm; Deloris Tarzan Ament, "Touching Lives on College Campuses" written for the Jewish Federation and available at www.jewishinseattle.org/JF/Giving/Annual/Touching_live_on_college_campuses.doc+college+8; Yggdrasil, "Diversity's Losers – Part II – The Universities," at http://home.ddc.net/ygg/ms/ ms-45.htm. Finally, some articles cited in note 1 above provided data used in this section.

19. Among sources: Paul Johnson, *A History of the Jews*, Harper & Row, New York; the Web site, www.jewhoo.com with its lists and bio sketches of prominent Jews in various domains; similar pages from www.jinfo.org which identify Jewish leaders in philosophy, sociology, math, chemistry and many other academic fields; *American Jewish Desk Reference*, pages 244–5; articles from *Encyclopædia Britannica 2001 Deluxe Edition*, including the article on medical education and the role of Abraham Flexner; pages at the Nobel Web site www.nobel.se; James Nestor's article "What's So Funny About Peace, Love and Esperanto, *San Francisco Chronicle Magazine*, June 8, 2003 pages18–20; and a large number of newspaper and web articles on individual Jews whose careers have been academic.

20. Lists of Law professors at Yale, Harvard and Stanford came from the Web sites of those schools; the Princeton Faculty at the Institute for Advance Study came from that Web site. A review of the names on these lists involved the authors judgment; in addition, Chaim Seidler-Feller's article, "Between Assimilation and Identification" at the web site www.shma.com/Dec02/feller.htm. Information on Presidents of Ivy League, Big Ten and Pac Ten schools came from the Web sites of the individual schools; Sten Menashi, "Using His Religion: article in Dartmouth Review, April 8, 1998 also available at www.dartreview.com/issues/4.8.93/religion.html; the article "Universities" at www.jewishtribalreview.org/ coopt.htm;

21. Among sources for the Six Day War section: Michael B. Oren, *Six Days of War*, Oxford University Press, New York, 2002; *Encyclopædia Britannica* 2001; the *Jewish Virtual Library Web* site: www.us-Israel.org/jsource/History/67_War.html; the Norwegian based *LexicOrient* Web site devoted providing information about North Africa and the Middle East at: http://i-cias.com/e.o./sixdaywr.htm; and related pages on Israel, Sinai, Gaza, West Bank and Golan Heights; The *Israeli Defense Force* site www.idf.il/english/history/sixday.stm; The *Peace Encyclopedia* Web pages at www.iaf.org www.workmall.com/wfb2001/egypt/egypt_history_the_june_1967_war.html; www.yahoodi.com/peace/sixdaywar.html; www.jajz-ed.org.il/100/concepts/d3.html, http://members.aol.com/_ht_a/RChera/dist.gif;

22. Among sources: Eli Barnavi, *A Historical Atlas of the Jewish People*, Schocken Books, New York, 2003 52–3, 152–3, 158–9, 175, 210–11, 236–7, 260–61; Hasia R. Diner, *Jews of the United States – 1654 to 2000*, University of California Press, Berkeley, 2004, pages 15, 18, 40, 45–51, 156, 221–2; A. Karp, *A History of Jews in America*, 1997 which provided a table of American Jewish Population 1790 to 1990 shown in Steven Silbiger, *The Jewish Phenomenon*, Longstreet Press, Marietta, Georgia 2000, 8; Seymour "Sy" Brody, Jewish Heroes and Heroines in America and Jewish Recipients of the Medal of Honor, both parts of the *Judaica Collection* of Florida Atlantic University Libraries and available at

www.fau.edu/library/brody6.htm; www.fau.edu/library/cmohtochtm; Seymour "Sy" Brody, "Remembering Those Who Followed Jewish Ideals Into Battle," *New Jersey Jewish News*, Feb. 18, 2005 at www.njjewishnews.com/njjn.com/ 52704/battle.html; The Congressional Medal of Honor Web site: www.cmohs.org; The Canadian Jewish Web site http://collections.ic.gc.ca/heirloom_ series/volume1/chapter5/184–189.htm; The Web site of the *National Museum of American Jewish Military History* at www.nmajmh.org; the *Military Heroes* Section of *Jewhoo.com* at www.jewhoo.com; and others.

23. Among sources: The Space Statistics pages of *CBS News* at www.cbsnews.com/network/news/space/ spacestats.html; The Web site of Kosher Certification and its page on Outer Space at www.okkosher.com/ Content.asp?ID=106; Lisa J. Huriash, "Keeping Kosher to be Out-of-this-world Experience, in *Sun Sentinel*, April 9, 2001 at www.sun-sentinel.com/news/sfl-koshernasa.story; Miryam Z. Wahrman, "'World Jewry' Moves to Outer Space," *Hadassah Magazine*, March 2001 also available at: www.jewishcleveland.org/ content_display.html?print=1&ArticleID=25974;5) The "Adventurers and Discoverers" Web page of *Yahoodi.com* at www.yahoodi.com/famous/adven1.html; Data on flights logged from the Web site: www.astronautix.com/articles/ soyefrom.htm; The *NASA* Web site: www.hq.nasa.gov/office/pao/History/prsnnl.htm; and the pages devoted to Daniel Goldin and Aaron Cohen; "Ben Rich" at www.f-117a.com/Ben.html; and the Web pages devoted to "Astronauts/Aeronautics created by *Jewhoo.com* and available at: www.jewhoo.com/ display_entries.asp?_category_id=90&p_parent_id=38.

24. Among sources for the Milton Friedman bio: Charles K. Rowley and Anne Rathbone, "Milton Friedman, 1912-: Harbinger of the Public Choice Revolution" at www.gmu.edu/departments/economics/bcaplan/rowley.doc; Friedman's autobiography on the Nobel Web site at www.nobel.se/economics/laureates/1976/friedman-autobio.html, and his remarks at the Nobel Memorial Lecture, Dec. 13, 1976 also available on that Web site;; *Encyclopædia Britannica 2001* articles on Friedman and Carpatho-Rutheria, the region where his parents grew up; the Friedman bio on the Web site of *The Concise Encyclopedia of Economics* at www.econlib.org/library/Enc/bios/Friedman.html; Friedman's quotes from www.brainyquote.com/quotes/authors/m/milton_friedman.html;Federal Reserve Governor Ben S. Bernanke's remarks, "Money, Gold and the Great Depression" March 2, 2004, the H. Parker Willis Lecture in Economic Policy at Washington and Lee University, Lexington, Virginia, http://www.federalreserve.gov/boarddocs/speeches/2004/ 200403022/default.htm.

25. Data on the Nobel Prize in Economics was drawn from: Burton Feldman, *The Nobel Prize*, 328–55, 410, 442–7; Alan Symons' *Nobel Laureates;* the Nobel Web site, www.nobel.se/economics; www.jinfo.org.Nobels_Economics.html; www.science.co.il/Nobel.asp?s=ec&sort=y&ord=z&cit=y; www.jewishvirtuallibrary.org/jsource/Judaism/nobels.html; www.yahoodi.com; www.Jewhoo.com.

26. Material on the John Bates Clark Medal comes from: http://jinfo.org/Clark_Economics.html; http://en.wikipedia.org/wiki/John_Bates_Clark_Medal; Daniel Altman, "Provocative Economist at Chicago Awarded Prize" *The New York Times*, April 25, 2003; Jon E. Hilserath, "Deliberations Begin for Economics Prize" *The Wall Street Journal*, April 27, 2001.

27. Material on great economists comes from *Encyclopædia Britannica 2001* articles, Web sites: http://jinfo.org/ economics.html; http://jinfo.org/Economists.html; www.jewhoo.com; *The Concise Encyclopedia of Economics* Web site, www.econlib.org/library/Enc/bios.html; the Web site devoted to the PBS show *Commanding Heights* and its feature on Jeffrey Sachs at www.pbs.org/wgbh/commandingheights/shared/minitextlo/int_jeffreysachs.html; Stephen Moore, "Defusing the Population Bomb" on the Cato Institute Web site, www.cato.org/dailys/10-15-99.html; "Treasury Hall of Fame (and Shame)," *Fortune* magazine, Sept. 29, 2003, p. 206; and others.

28. Federal Reserve material includes: "Federal Reserve System, 1913–2002" at http://;cat4.net/nwo/ fedres.php; "Our History: on the Web site of the Federal Reserve, Chicago at www.chicagofed.org/about_the_fed/ our_history.cfm; "The Founding of the Fed" at www.ny.frb.org/aboutthefed/ history_article.html; "The Fed" at the Trader Talk Web site, www.tradertalk.com/tutorial/fed.html; Michael A. Whitehouse, "Paul Warburg's Crusade to Establish a Central Bank in the United States" at http://minneapolisfed.org/pubs/region/89-05/reg895d.cfm; David Greenberg, "Nixon and the Jews" *Slate*, April 1, 2002, at http://hnn.us/articles/657.html; David Twersky, "Remembering Nixon" *Jewish World Review*, Oct. 14, 1998 at www.jewishworldreview.com/0998/twersky1.asp; an editorial, "Lessons of the Greenspan Era," *Business Week*, Dec. 16, 2002; Seymour "Sy" Brody, "Eugene Isaac Meyer" in the Jewish Virtual Library at at www.us-israel.org/jsource/biography/emeyer.html; Bob Woodward, *Maestro*, Simon & Schuster, New York, 2000; and Ron Chernow, *The Warburgs*, Random House, New York, 1993, 137–40158, 160–2.

29. Among sources: *Encyclopædia Britannica 2001* article on Dianne Feinstein; Darryl Lyman, *Jewish Heroes & Heroines*, Jonathan David Publishers, Inc. Middle Village, New York, 1996; reviews of Jerry Roberts book, *Dianne Feinstein, Never Let Them See You Cry*, at www.Amazon.com; Seymour "Sy" Brody's article "Dianne Feinstein" at www.jewishvirtuallibrary.org/jsource/biography/DFeinstein.html; "Dianne Feinstein" article at http://encyclopedia.thefreedictionary.com/Dianne Feinstein; "Senator Feinstein's Biography" at the official U.S. Senate Web site, http://feinstein.senate.gov/bioprint2.htm; her bios at: the NASA Web site,

http://quest.arc.nasa.gov/women/TODTWD97/feinstein.bio.html; the Info Please site
http://print.infoplease.com/ipa/A0878901.html; the League of Women Voters' site www.smartvoter.org/
2000/11/07/ca/state/vote/feinstein_d/bio.html; and articles on her "Political Philosophy" and her voting record on
different pages at same site; her bio at www.mith2.umd.edu/WomensStudies/GovernmentPolitics/Womenin-
Congress/Biographies/Senate/feinstein-dianne; one at www.wic.org/bio/feinstei.htm; one at
http://members.aol.com/doshishagsas/ dianefeinstein.html; and others; Robert Scheer's interview with her, published
January 31, 1993 in the *Los Angeles Times*, at www.robertscheer.com/_natcolumn/93_columns/013193.htm; Chris
Bull's interview, "Eyewitness to History" at www.findarticles.com/p/articles/mi_m1589/is_1998_Nov_10/
ai_54879377/print; her quote from www.brainyquote.com/quotes/authors/d/dianne_feinstein.html; the article "The
People's Temple" at the Religious Tolerance Web site www.religioustolerance.org/ dc_jones.htm; Howard Nemerov,
"Gun Control: Dianne Feinstein and the 'Assault Weapons' Ban" dated June 21, 2004 on the MichNews Web site at
http://michnews.com/artman/publish/article_3994.shtml; Thomas Sowell's "Senator Feinstein and Property Rights"
article dated Nov 10,2003 at www.townhall.com/columnists/thomassowell/printts20031110.shtm; and others.

30. Data on Jewish population from 1790 to 1990 are from Abraham Karp, *A History of the Jews in America*,
Schocken, New York, 1997; data on Jewish senators and congressmen in the 108th Congress are from the *Jewish Virtual Library* at www.us-israel.org/jsource/US-Israel/jewcong108.html and related pages at that Site; additional information came from http://democrats.senate.gov/senators_alpha.html; the article "David Levy Yulee" at the infoplease Web
site www.infoplease.com/ipa/A0921250.html; one on Judah Benjamin, a controversial figure, at the Jewish Virtual
Library, www.jewishvirtuallibrary.org/ jsource/biography/Benjamin.html. The numbers of Jews in prominent roles in
political history and in recent administrations comes from David G. Dalin & Alfred J. Kolatch, *The Presidents of the
Untied States & the Jews*, Jonathan David Publishers, Inc. Middle Village, New York, 2000; the article "Mr. Bush's
Cabinet Looks Like America—But Without the Jews" Jan. 9, 2001, on the National Jewish Defense Council Web site,
www.njdc.org/read/News.php?shor=119&subcat=3; Jason Keyser, "2 of Kerry's Relatives Died in Holocaust, Historians Find" *San Francisco Chronicle*, March 5, 2004; pages at http://24.202.198.116:8001/facts/fact07.html;
www.jewishtribalreview.org/27govt2.htm; an AOL site http://members.aol.com/_ht_a/gjadoc/page9.html?; pages at
www.jewishtribalreview.org/27govt2.htm; and other sources.

31. The principal source for this section was www.motherjones.com/news/feature/s000/ 10/mojo50.html, and other
pages listing the top 400 donors.

32. Among sources:"The Oyez Project Northwestern University" at http://er.library.northwestern.edu/
detail.asp?id=34363; the "Lawyers, attorneys and Judges" Web at www.yahoodi.com/famous/law1.html; the article on
Justice Benjamin Cardozo in the *American Jewish Historical Society Newsletter*, Spring 2004; Darryl Lyman, *Jewish
Heroes & Heroines*, 34–8, *American Jewish Desk Reference*, 133–75

33. Among sources: Burton Feldman, *The Nobel Prize*, 290 327, 401–2, 410, 441–2; Alan Symons, *Nobel Laureates,
1901–2000*; the Nobel Web site pages including, www.nobel.se/cgi-bin/print; information at www.jchoo.com;
www.jahoodi.com; www.jinfo.org/Nobels_Peace.html; and www.us-israel.org/ jsource/Judaism/nobels.html.

34. Primary sources for the Koufax bio include: Robert Slater, *Great Jews in Sports*, Jonathan David Publishers, Inc.,
Middle Village, New York, 2000, 164–7, Jane Leavy, *Sandy Koufax, A Lefty's Legacy*, Harper Collins, New York, 2002,
reviews of that book at www.amazon.com and at *USA Today*, including Bob Minzesheimer, "'Koufax' Tells of Private
Man Who Throws Celebrity a Curve", Feb 12, 2003 also available at www.usatoday.com/life/books/reviews/ 2003-
02-12-koufax_x.htm, and a Web chat (question and answer session) with Leavy, Feb 20, 2003 posted as
http://cgi1.usatoday.com/mchat/ 20030220001/tscript.htm, the Wikipedia bio at http://en.wikipedia.org/wiki/
Sandy_Koufax, the Seymour "Sy" Brody bio at *Jewish Virtual Library*, www.jewishvirtuallibrary.org/ jsource/
biography/Koufax.html, his bio, Hall of Fame Plaque, and statistics from the National Baseball Hall of Fame, also at
www.baseballhalloffame.org/hofers_and_honorees/hofer_bios/koufax_sandy.htm and related pages, his statistics at
www.baseball-refernce.com/k/koufasa01.html, Sheil Kapadia, "Jewish Baseball Players Have Their Days At Cooper-
stown," *USA Today*, Aug. 18, 2004, and Koufax quotes from www.brainyquote.com/quotes/authors/s/
sandy_koufax.html.

35. Sources for the Professional Football section include the NFL Web site, www.nfl.com and various Hall of Fame
pages at www.profootballhof.com/hof/years.html; football pages at www.jewhoo.com, and at www.yahoodi.com;
"History of Jews in Football," and other articles at www.jewishsports.com, those on football at the American Jewish
Historical Society site, www.ajhs.org; and www.ajhs.org/reference/jew_sport.cfm, which identified Paul Tagliabue, Bud
Selig, Gary Bettman, and Don Garber as 2001 honorees together with Hank Greenberg), lists at www.jewsinsports.org
Peter Ephross's "NFL Quarterback Benny Friedman Finally Reaches Hall of Fame," Feb. 11, 2005 at
www.jewishsf.com/content/2-0-. and Robert Slater, *Great Jews in Sports*, Jonathan David Publishers, Inc. Middle Vil-
lage, New York, 2000; "List of NFL francise owners," at http://en.wikipedia.org/wiki/List_of_NFL_franchise_owners;
"List of Jews in Sports," at http://en.wikipedia.org/List_of_Jews_in_Sports; and others

36. Principal Sources for the baseball material include the Major League Baseball Web site, http://mlb.mlb.com and

later at www.baseballhalloffame.org; with their pages devoted to team rosters, the Hall of Fame, its inductees, all star rosters, and individual active players; numerous player and manager profiles at http://en.wikipedia.org; "National Baseball Hall of Fame and Museum," at http://en.wikipedia.org/wiki/National_Baseball_Hall_of_Fame_and_Museum; the *Jews In Sports* site, www.jewishsports.com and its pages devoted to Jews in baseball, history, and trivia, the Jewhoo site, www.Jewhoo.com, with pages devoted to Jews in baseball, the *Jewish Virtual Library* site, www.us-israel.org/jsource/ Judaism/bball.html, and related pages at that site; Andy Altman,"Opening of New Ballpark Makes Jewish Owners Feel Like They've Hit Home Runs," *Jewish Bulletin*, April 14, 2000, at www.jewishsf.com/bk000414/etballpark.shtml, Todd Wallack, "A's New Era, John Fisher, Son of Gap Founder is the Money Behind the Deal," *San Francisco Chronicle*, March 31, 2005, available at www.sfgate.com/cgi-bin/article.cgi?file=/c/a/2005/03/31/MNGRKC13PD1.dtl; "American Jewish Historical Society Honors Jews in Big League Baseball," *AJHS Newsletter*, Spring 2004, 15–7; Major League Owners," at http://en.wikipedia.org/wiki/List_of_Major_League_Baseball_Principal_Owners; Susan Josephs, "Jamie McCourt" at www.jwmag.org; "Jewish Giants," and "SF Giants Exec Brings Jewish Values to Major Leagues," at www.jewishsf.com; and others.

37. Principal sources for the Basketball section include, Slater, *Great Jews in Sports*, The National Basketball Association Web site, www.nba.com with its pages on teams, rosters, players, great coaches and great players; The Naismith Memorial Hall of Fame Web site at www.hoopball.com; and http://en.wikipedia.org/wiki/List_of_members_of_the_Basketball_Hall_of_Fame; and both sites rosters of Hall of Fame inductees; "Top 10 Coaches in NBA History," at www.nba.com/history/ top_10_coaches.html; *JewishSports.com* at www.jewishsports.com, with its pages on history, lists of Jews in basketball; Profiles of basketball players and coaches at Wikipedia.org and at www.jewhoo.com/ display_entries.asp?p_category_id=68&p_parent_id=39; and at www.jewishsports.org; and www.jewishsports.net/ basketball.html, the team athletes page of www.yahoodi.com, the bio page on David Stern from www.askmen.com, *Encyclopedia Judaica*'s "History of Jews in Basketball" on the CD Rom Edition, Jon Entine, "As the Maccabiah Games Open in Israel, at www.aish.com/societyWork/arts/Jewish_Basketball_Giants.asp; Jon Entine, "The City of Brotherly Love, Hoops and Jews," at www.jewishsports.com; Basketball Hall of Fame information at the Inside Hoops Web site at www.insidehoops.com/basketball-hall-of-fame.shtml. "Basketball Team Owners," at Wikipedia's List of Professional Sports Team Owners" http://en.wikipedia.org/wiki/ List_of_professional_sports_team_owners; and others.

38. "Jews in Sports Journalism" at www.jewishsports.com/jewsin/journalism.htm.

39. Material on boxing came from: "History of Jews in Boxing," Encyclopedia Judaica (CD Rom Edition); "Boxing" at www.jewhoo.com/display_entries.asp?p_category_id=7&p_parent_id=39, "Barney Ross's Greatest Battles," The American Jewish Historical Society at www.ajhs.org/publications/chapters/ chapter.cfm?documentID=258, the International Jewish Sports Hall of Fame at www.jewishsports.net/ BioPages/Tables?Sport/Boxing.htm, Geoffrey Gray, "Jewish Boxers Are Looking to Make a Comeback," *The New York Times*, Dec. 27, 2003, Bert Randolph Sugar, "Punching Through," *The New York Times*, Feb 19, 2006; Joyce Carol Oates, "Beyond Glory: The Good Fight," *The New York Times*, Oct. 2, 2005; Zachary Braziller, "The Tale of the Tape and the Talmud, *The New York Times*, April 3, 2008; and "Boxing: Yuri Foreman Stays Unbeaten, *The New York Times*, Apr. 4, 2008; Alona Wartofsky, "The Ring and a Prayer," Washington Post, Sept. 1, 2002, fighter records at www.boxrec.com, and the Dimitriy Salita Web site, www.dsalita.com/?c=19. Yuri Foreman, Dimitriy Salita, Zab, Daniel, and Josiah Judah, and Roman Greenberg profiles at Wikipedia; Tennis material comes from www.Jewhoo.com, www.jewishsports.com, www.jewsinsports.org, an unattributed story on Boris Becker at http://home.netfront.net/~tennis/usopen.htm., and Lance Gould, "Give Me An 'Oy'!" Salon, Oct 14, 199, available at www.salon.com/people/feature/1999/10/14/jewish/index1.html; player profiles at Wikipedia.org. Golf sources include the golf sections of the web sites cited for tennisMarina Hyde, "What Would Jesus Do? Maybe Take a Few Tips From Tom Lehman," at http://blogs.guardian.com ; Bowler material at www.bowlingmuseum.com/pba.asp; Other sports material included *Encyclopedia Judaica*, www.jewishsports.com, www.jewishsports.net, www.jewhoo.com, www.beliefnet.com, www.jewsinsports.org, www.jewishsports.net, "List of Jewish Americans" at www.spiritus-temporis.com/lis-of-jewish-americans/sports.html; and similar Wikipedia lists. Olympics sources include: Dr. George Eisen, "Jewish Olympic Medalists," at www.jewishsports.net/medalists.htm; the Olympic medals site, http://wos.www8.50megs.com/ogmefen.html, the Olympic site, www.olympic.org/uk/sports, http://cbs.sportsline.com, Lenny Silberman, "Jews in Sports" on the Web site, http://kjc.org/articles/968957389.html, the Jewish Sports Hall of Fame at http://jewishsporthalloffame.com, and the *Jewish Virtual Library* Web site at www.us-israel.org/jsource/history/sportstoc.html; and numerous Wikipedia Web sites which cover medalists at every Olympics since 1896, which profile individual athletes, and which summarize Olympic records of every kind; Karen Crouse, "Torres Opts Out of 100 to Focus on 50 Free," Elizabeth Weil, "A Swimmer of a Certain Age," *The New York Times*, July 8, 2008 and June 29, 2008; and "Franklin, Sidney," at www.jewsinsports.org/profile.asp?sport= bullfighting&ID=1.

40. Chess sources: "Jewish World Chess Champions," at www.jinfo.org/Chess_Champions.html; the chess pages of www.jinfo.org, those of www.jewsinsports.org, www.yahoodi.com, www.jewhoo.com, the Vladimir Kramnik Web site at www.kramnik.com; "World Chess Championship," at http://en.wikipedia.org/wiki/World_Chess_Championship; the RGS Chess Club site, www.rgs.edu.sg/student/cca/chess/greatmasters.html, Gustavo D. Perednik, "Judaism and Chess, at www.gilinski.org/articulo34.htm, Dj100ess?" *The New York Times*, Oct. 4, 2004, the GameKnot Chess Forum at http://gameknot.com/fmsg/chess/1287.shtml, the article, "Hebrews Chess" at www.zalman.org/chess/ history2.htm, the article "Bobby Fischer Spews More anti-Semitism," at http://jewishsf.com/bk990205/ifischer.htm,

and "Who is Bobby Fischer?" at http://bobbyfischer.net/ bobby30.html; Dylan Loeb McClain, "Kramnik Wins Title in Tough Playoff Fight," *The New York Times*, Oct 14, 2006; Brian M. Carney,"Victim of His Own Success: The Tragedy of Bobby Fischer," *The Wall Street Journal*, Jan. 22, 2008; the Kramnik family Web site at www.eilatgordinlevitan.com/ kurenets/k_pages/kramnik.html; and others.

41. Bridge sources: "Emanuel Lasker" at www.geocities.com/TimesSquare/Ring/4860/laker.html, Harris, Merchant Princes, p. 56, Alan Truscott, "Charles Goren, 90, Bridge Expert Dies," *The New York Times*, April 12, 1991; a bio of Goren at www.answers.com/topic/charles-goren, "Famous Players," at www.bridgebum.com/players.php, Alan Truscot, "2 Americans on Winning Team at Fall Bridge Championship," *The New York Times*, Nov. 25, 2003, Ron Klinger, "Its Kosher to Play Bridge in Australia," at www.join.org.au/letters/klinger.html, Fred Gitelman, "Bridge with Gitelman," in *The Canadian Jewish News* at www.cjnews.com/pastissues/02/feb14–02/sports/bridge.htm, reviews of Marc Smith's, *World Class* at the Mind Sports Web site, www.msoworld.com/mindzine/news/bridge/reviews/bridge/ worldclass.html, Matthew Granovetter, "Building Bridges," at www.jewish-holiday.com/build/ bridge.htm; "American Bridge Players at http://en.wikipedia.org/wiki/Category:American_bridge_player; and others.

42. Sources for the Bellow bio include his biography at the Nobel Web site, www.nobel.se/literature/ laureates/1976/bellow-bio.html; his banquet and Nobel lecture on other pages at that site; articles on Bellow, Delmore Schwartz and American Literature at *Encyclopædia Britannica 2001 Deluxe Edition;* a bio at http://en.wikipedia.org/ wiki/Saul_Bellow; others at http://books.guardian.co.uk/authors/ author/0.5917,-20.00.html; www.emanuel/ nyc.org/bulletin/archive/36.html www.bookbrowse.com/index.cfm?page=author&authored=406, www.kirjasto.sci.fi/ bellow.htm; www.todayinliterature.com/stories.asp?Event_Date=12/12/1976; www.litencyc.com/php/ speople.php?rec=true&UID=350; www.csustan.edu/ english/reuben/pal/chap10/bellow.html; and; Robert Fulford, "Saul Bellow, Allan Bloom, and Abe Ravelstein," *Globe and Mail*, Nov. 2, 1999, at www.robertfulford.com/ Bellow.html; reviews of James Atlas book, *Bellow: A Biography*, Random House, New York, 2003 at www.amazon.com; sections from that Book, Joanna Coles, "The Joy of Texts," *Guardian*, Sept. 10, 1997, at http://book.guardian.co.uk/departments/generalfiction/story/ 0,6000,102107,00.html; James Woods, "The Worldly Mystic's Late Bloom," *Guardian*, April 15, 2000, at http://books.guardian.co.uk/departments/generalfiction/ story/0,6000,193628,00.html; Derek Rubin, "Marginality in Saul Bellow's Early Novels," summarizing a Ph.D dissertation at Vrije Universiteit in Amsterdam, Nov. 20, 1995 at www.let.uu.nl/solis/nasa/rubimarg.htm; Mel Gussow and Charles McGrath, "Saul Bellow, Who Breathed Life Into American Novel, Dies at 89," *The New York Times*, April 6, 2005; Edward Rothstein, "Finding Grandeur in the Everyday," October 11, 2003, *The New York Times;* and Edward Rothstein, "Saul Bellow, Saul Bellow, Let Down Your Hair, April 9, 2005, *The New York Times*, as well as other *New York Times* stories in the days immediately following his death. The Bellow quotes came from www.quotationspage.com/quotes.php3?author=Saul+Bellow; and www.yenra.com/quotations/bellow-saul.html. Quotes about Augie March came from www.johnholleman. com/win/augie.html. Data on WWI and WWII casualties came from www.spartacus.schoolnet.co.uk/ FWWdeaths.htm and http://users.erols.com/ mwhite28/ww2stats.htm.

43. Sources include Ellis Rivkin, *The Unity Principle*, Behrman House, Inc. Springfield, New Jersey, 2003, 58–126, Johnson, *History of the Jews*, 152–3. Rabbi Ted Falcon, Ph.D. and David Blatner, *Judaism for Dummies*, 31–42. and Eli Barnavi, Editor, *A Historical Atlas of the Jewish People*, Schocken Books, New York, 2002, 18–63

44. Sources include the Nobel Web site and its pages devoted to the Nobel Prize for Literature, including, http://nobelprize.org/literature/laureates.html; Feldman, *The Nobel Prize*, 55–114, 363–7, 400–1, 407, the Israel Science and Technology Homepage and listing of laureates at www.science.co.il/ Nobel.asp?s=lit&sort=yy&ord=z&cit=y; Asher B. Etkes and Saul Stadtmauer, *Jewish Contributions to the American Way of Life*, Northside Publishing, Inc. Long Island City, New York, 1995; www.science.co.il/Nobel.asp?s=lit&sort=y&ord=z&cit=y; the JInfo web site, www.jinfo.org/Nobels_Literature.html; and www.jinfo.org/Authors.htm; the literature pages at www.jewhoo.com.

45. Sources include the Pulitzer Web site, www.literature-awards.com/pulitzer_prize.htm; the JInfo sites: www.jinfo.org/Authors.htm; and www.jinfo.org/Pulitzer_Fiction.html; the Wikipedia site, http://en.wikipedia.org/ wiki/Pulitzer_Prize_for_Fiction; Etkes, *Jewish Contributions*, and www.miracosta.cc.ca.us/ home/azolynas/ pulitzer.htm, Steven Silbiger, *The Jewish Phenomenon*, Longstreet Press, Marietta Georgia, 2000, 168, and the Jewhoo site.

46. Sources include the Pulitzer Web site at www.literature-awards.com/pulitzer_nonfiction.htm; *Wikipedia*'s http://en.wikipedia.org/wiki/Pulitzer_Prize_for_General_Non-Fiction; the JInfo site www.jinfo.org/Pulitzer_Non-Fiction.html; Etkes, *Jewish Contributions*, the Jewhoo site; Isaac Tarasulo, "Had the Russians Celebrated Christmas on December 25th?" at the Johnson's Russia List site, www.cdi.org/russia/johnson/7003-16.cfm; Peter Myers, "Jared Diamond on the Indo-European Expansion," February 10, 2002; update July 7, 2002 at the Web site, http://users.cyberone.com.au/ myers/diamond.html; the article "Return to NeoEugenics' Home Page," at http://home.comcast.net/ ~neoeugenics/Guns,htm; Seymour "Sy" Brody, "Barbara Tuchman," at www.jewishvirtuallibrary.org/ jsource/biography/tuchman.htm., Gary Kamiya, "Can Israel Be Saved?" at http://fairuse.1accesshost.com/ news2/salon26.htm; Sharon Hartwick, "Role of American Jews in World War II," at www.thevillager.com/ villager_34/ roleofamerican.htm., the interview with David Friendly at http://lukeford.net/profiles/profiles/ david_friendly.htm; the article "Goldberg's Ultimate Hudzpah: Media Not Jewish Enough," Jan. 7, 2002 at

www.nationalist.org/alt/ 2002/jan/bias.html; Nat Hentoff, "Pro-Choice Bigots," July 12, 2004 at http://prolife.
liberals.com/articles/ hentoff.html; "Pulitzer Prize Winners Teach Hillel Students," March 16, 2001 at www.hillel.org;
Patricia Yollin, "Pierre Salinger—Press Secretary to Presidents," *San Francisco Chronicle*, Oct. 17, 2004; "Literary
Luminaries' Receive Koret Awards," at www.jewishsf.com/bk010323/sfkoret.shtml.

47. Sources include the Pulitzer Web site www.pulitzer.org/bycat/drama; the *Wikipedia* site, http://en.wikipedia.org/
wiki/Pulitzer_Prize_for_Drama.html; the JInfo site www.jinfo.org/ Pulitzer_Drama.html; the Tony Web site
www.tonyawards.com/p/tonys_search, Etkes, *Jewish Contributions;* the Jewhoo.com Web site; www.jinfo.org/
Tony_Award_Play.html; http://en.wikipedia.org/wiki/ Tony_Award_for_Best_Play.html; Irene Backalenick, "Nice
Jewish Boys and Girls on Broadway This Season," in the Association for Jewish Theatre site at www.afjt.com/letter3.htm;
Naomi Pfefferman, "Who Exploits Whom?" Aug. 31, 2001 in the *Jewish Journal* at www.jewishjournal.com/home/
preview.php?id=7376, Mike Levy, "Goddess of Shiksa," June 22, 2001 in the *Jewish Journal* at www.jewishjournal.com
home/preview.php?id=7055, and others.

48. For poetry, the Pultizer site, www.literature-awards.com/pulitzer_poetry.html; the Wikipedia sites:
http://en.wikipedia.org/Pulitzer_Prize_for_Poetry.html, & wiki/Category:Jewish_poets.html; the JInfor site:
www.jinfo.org/Pulitzer_Poetry.html; the "Jewish-American" article at www.glbtq.com/literature/jewish_am_lit.html;
Enid Weiss, "Rutgers Professor Builds Lecture Around Jewish Poets and Christian Architecture" at
www.njjewishnews.com/njjn.com/12403/cjrutgers.html; Emma Lazarus, "The New Colossus" at http://xroads.
virginia.edu/~CAP/LIBERTY/lazaruspoem.html; and the back cover of the book, *Voices Within the Ark*, which identifies prominent Jewish poets.

49. Leo Rosten, *The Joys of Yiddish*, Pocket Books, New York, 1970, xxiii; Rabbi Ted Falcon and David Blatner, *Judaism
for Dummies*, 333–6; Etkes, *Jewish Contributions;* Arie Kaplan, "How Jews Created the Comic Book Industry," at
www.ariekaplan.com/kingscomicspart1.html; another by Kaplan at www.myjewishlearning.com/culture/literature/
Overview_Jewish...; "A Comic-Book Response to 9/11 and Its Aftermath," *The New York Times*, Aug. 7, 2004; the
Jewhoo Web site.

50. Among sources: www.jewhoo.com, www.yahoodi.com/famous/authors1.html; and the counterpart pages devoted
to famous journalists and news professionals; the Jewish Authors, Poets and Screenwriters Page at www.jews.net/
jewishauthors.htm; and the article on Jews in the Media at www.hoozajew.org/ reporters7.html.

51. Among sources: Publishing, History of : "Foundations of Modern Journalism," *American Jewish Desk Reference*,
pages 499–571; Darryl Lyman, *Jewish Heroes & Heroines*, Jonathan David Publishers, Inc., Middle Village, New York,
1996, p. 149; Alan Symons, *The Jewish Contribution to the 20th Century*, Polo Publishing, Hampton, Middlesex, 1997.

52. Among sources for *The New York Times* section: "Timeline at www.nytco.com/company-timeline.html; *Encyclopædia Britannica 2001 Deluxe Edition* articles on Adolph Simon Ochs, Arthur Ochs Sulzberger, *The New York Times*.

53. Among sources for *The Washington Post* section: *Encyclopædia Britannica 2001 Deluxe Edition* articles on *Washington Post;* "History & Leadership at www.washpostco.com/history.htm, and other pages at that Web site; "Foundations
of the World Bank: 1944–1948," at http://web.worldbnk.org; Seymour "Sy" Brody, "Eugene Isaac Meyer," at
www.us-israel.org/jsource/biography/emeyer.html; "*The Washington Post*," at www.ketupa.net/wpost.htm; Washington Post Group Proxy Statement concerning "Principal Holders of Stock; Andy Server, "Understated, Underrated, and
One Hell of a CEO," *Fortune*, May 31, 2004.

54. Among sources for *The Wall Street Journal* section: "*The Wall Street Journal*," *Encyclopædia Britannica 2001 Deluxe
Edition;* "Profile of SAJA Guest Speakers Peter Kann & Karen Elliot House," at http://www.saja.org/housekann.html;
Research on Dow Jones & Co. at www.smartmoney.com/wsj/briefingbooks/doPrint.cfm?page=executives&symbol=dj;
Timothy Noah, "Peter Kann Gives Up Publisher's Job, But Not Publisher's Salary!" July 2, 2002, *Slate* at
www.slate.msn.com/id/2067610/; Daniel Gross, "Do as We Say, Not as We Dow," *Slate*, Apr. 20, 2005; Joseph
Nocera, "At Dow Jones It's All About Family," *The New York Times*, Aug 26. 2005 Dean Starkman, "The Tragedy of
Peter Kann," *Columbia Journalism Review* at www.cjr.org/the_audit/the_tragedy_of_peter_kann.php?page=all;.

55. Sources for the *Reuters* section include: *Encyclopædia Britannica 2001 Deluxe Edition* articles "Reuters," "Reuter,
Paul; Julius, Baron (Freiherr) von, on the "About Us" pages at http://about.reuters.com/aboutus/history/
juliusreuter/index.asp; and other pages at that site; "Paul Reuter" at www.fact-index.com/p/pa/paul_reuter.html, and
www.bartleby.com/65/re/Reuter-B.html,

56. Sources for the Pulitzer section include: *Encyclopædia Britannica 2001 Deluxe Edition* articles Joseph Pulitzer, *Saint
Louis Post Dispatch, New York World*, Yellow Journalism, and Pulitzer Prize; Obituary of Joseph Pulitzer, Jr on the
Scripophily.com site; pages on Pulitzer Publishing company at www.scripophily.net/pulpubcom.html; pages at the
Pulitzer, Inc Web site including http://investor.pulitzerinc.com/ireye/ir_site.zhtml?ticker=PTZ&script=2260; the
Corporate Profile on the site, the Pulitzer, Inc.; Proxy Statement for 2003, including its list of "Principal Stockhold-
ers," and the Letter to Shareholders from its *Annual Report*.

57. Source for the *San Francisco Chronicle* section include: Mark Dobbs, "Jewish Community," at www.sfhistoryencyclopedia.com/articles/j/jews.html.

58. Among sources for the Advance Publications, Inc./Newhouse, section: "Newhouse Family," *Encyclopædia Britannica;* "Advance Publications, Inc." at *Hoovers Online;* articles about Advance Publications at www.advance.net; the list of Advance Publications magazines at http://en.wikipedia.org/wiki/ Portland_Business_Journal.html; at the Magazine Publishers of America Web site, http://members.magazine.org/scriptcontent; at the Columbia School of Journalism site, www.cjr.org/ tools/ owners/advance.asp; "Newhouse newspapers" at www.newhouse.com/newspapers.html; Brent Cunningham, "The Newhouse Way," *Columbia Journalism Review,* Jan./Feb. 2000, at http://archives.cjr.org/ year/00/1/newhouse.asp; the article "Samuel Newhouse," from the *Utah History Encyclopedia* at www.media.utah.edu/UHE/n/NEWHOUS,SAMUEL.htm; Richard Perez-Pena, "Can Si Newhouse Keep Conde Nast's Gloss Going?" *The New York Times, Jul. 20, 2008*

59. Among sources for the Triangle/Annenberg section: Annenberg, Walter H." *Encyclopædia Britannica;* "Water Annenberg Dies At 94, at www.forbes.com/2002/10/01/1001annenberg.html; another at www.fact-index.com/ w/wa/walter_annenberg.html, Web pages at The Annenberg Foundation, www.whannenberg.org/

60. Among sources for the Ziff Davis section: "Corporate Timeline" at www.ziffdavis.com/press/timeline; David Armstrong, "Ziff Happens," *Wired,* May 1994 at www.wired.com/wired/archive/ 2.05/ziff_pr.html; a July 20, 1995 Rainforest Alliance press release, "Mrs. William Ziff named Chairman of Rainforest Alliance Board of Directors;" "Ziff-Davis, The Scoop," at www.vault.com/companies/ printsnapshot.jsp?product_id=1181&ch_id=251; Michael J. de la Merced, William B. Ziff Jr., 76, Builder of Magazine Empire Dies," *The New York Times* , Sept. 12, 2006; and other articles on Ziff including a curious reference to a William Ziff who wrote *The Rape of Palestine* in 1938, and who may or may not be the same William Ziff. See www.twf.org/News/1998/JewsArabs.html.

61. Among sources for the Hugo Gernsback section: Sam Mosckowitz, "The Ultimate Hugo Gernsback," at www.twd.net/ird/forecast/1997Auultimate.htm; Ron Miller, "Hugo Gernsback, Skeptical Crusader," *Skeptical Inquirer,* Nov–Dec. 2002, at www.findarticles.com/cf_dls/m2843/ 6_26/94044233/print.jhtml; his Wikipedia bio at http://en.wikipedia.org/wiki/Hugo_Gernsback; and, www.dailyobjectivist.com/Heroes/HugoGernsback.asp.

62. Among sources for the Cahners section: Brendan Jones, "Britons Mapping Publishing Deal," *The New York Times,* Feb. 17, 1966; "Saul Goldweitz of Brookline, 77. (Obituary)," *The Boston Herald,* July 5, 1998; "Norman L. Cahners," *The New York Times,* Mar. 18, 1986; Geraldine Fabrikant, "Publisher To Acquire Variety," *The New York Times,* July 14, 1987; Steven Prokesch, "Britain's Low-Profile Publishing Giant," *The New York Times,* Feb. 9, 1992; "Milton Green, 92; World Record Hurdler Boycotted 1936 Games," *Los Angeles Times,* Aug. 7, 2004;

63. Source for the *Rolling Stone* section: Timothy L. O'Brien, "Rolling Stone's Founder Prepares To Go It Alone 'On the Forward Edge'" *International Herald Tribune,* Dec. 25, 2005.

64. Sources for *The New Yorker* section include: "*The New Yorker,*" and "David Remnick," at http://en.wikipedia.org/ wiki/The_New_Yorker.html; and wiki/David_Remnick.html.

65. Source for the *New York* section: "*New York* (magazine) at http://en.wikipedia.org/wiki/ New_York_(magazine).

66. Among sources for *The New York Review of Books* section: Christopher Lehmann-Haupt, "Elizabeth Hardwick, Writer Dies at 91," *The New York Times,* Dec 4, 2007, "The New York Review of Books," "Robert B. Silvers," "Herbert Croly," and "Barbara Epstein at http://en.wikipedia.org/wiki/ The_New_York_Review_of_Books; wiki/Robert_B._Silvers; and wiki/Barbara_Epstein; and "Robert B. Silvers," at www.nndb.com/people/097/ 000117743/.

67. Among sources for the Random House section: articles on Bennett Cerf and Random House at http://encyclopedia.thefreedictionary.com/Bennett Cerf; the reviews of *At Random: The Reminiscences of Bennett Cerf* at Amazon.com, www.amazon.com/exec/obidos/tg/detail/-/037575976X?v=glance; his bio at www.worldhistory.com/wiki/B/Bennett-Cerf.htm; the Bertelsmann history at www.niulib.niu.edu/publishers/ Bertelsmann.htm; and "About Us," at www.randomhouse.com/about/history.html.

68. Among sources for the Alfred Knopf section: material on Alfred A. Knopf, Inc. at the University of Texas Harry Ransom Humanities Research Center Web site at www.hrc.utexas.edu/research/fa/ aakhist.html; and the bio of Alfred A. Knopf at www.infoplease.com/ipea/A0762606.html

69. Among sources for the Book of the Month Club section: "History of The Book Club," *Encyclopædia Britannica;* Shawn Crawford, "The Business of Reading: The Birth of the Book-of-the-Month Club at www.worldandi.com/specialreport/1999/september/Sa18978.htm; the Bookspan company Overview write up at www.bookspan.com/doc/ cor/TemplateData/aboutUs/aboutUs_theme_2/ AU_CO.jhtml; "Book-of-the-Month Club Reinstates Editorial Judges," *The Write News,* June 29, 2001 at www.writenews.com/2001/062901_bom_panel.htm; the Scherman Foun-

dation, Inc Web site. www.scherman.org/html/policy.html; and other pages at that site; "Maxwell Sackheim" at www.
marketers-hall-of-fame.com/1-maxwell-sackheim.html; another at www.hardtofindseminars.com/
OldMastersMaxwellSackheim.htm; Reminiscences of Harry Scherman and Robert K. Haas at Oral History Online,
www.alexanderstreet6.com/orhi/orhi.detail.interviews.asp?id=1818; Evelyn Harter, "The Life Or the Work," at
www.lib.uiowa.edu/spec-coll/Bai/harter.htm; article on Little Leather Library Books at http://junior.apk.net/
~jamon/MOre_HTML/LLL.html; John S. Major, The Book-of-the-Month Club Welcomes Submissions From Small
Publishers, at www.smallpress.org/articles/bomc.htm; David D. Kirkpatrick, "The Book-of-the-Month Club Tries to
Be More Of-the-Moment" *The New York Times*, June 28, 2001.

70. Among sources for the Simon and Schuster section: the Simon history at www.Simonsays.com; The Simon &
Schuster History page at www.simonsays.com/content/feature.cfm?sid=33&feature_id=1631

71. Among sources for the Farrar, Straus & Giroux section: "Farrar, Straus & Giroux, Lyman," *Encyclopædia Britan-
nica;* Denitia Smith, "Memories of Roger Straus By Writers He Championed," *The New York Times*, Sept. 30, 2004;
Harold Orlans, Farrar, Straus & Giroux – Potpourri – Brief Article at the FindArticles Web site, http://articles.
findarticles.com/p/articles/mi_m1254/is_4_34/ai_87869053/print; the article on the firm at the New York Public
Library Web site, www.nypl.org/research/chss/spe/rbk/faids/fsg/fsginven.html; Maureen O'Brien, "Straus Again
Quits Family Firm Over 'Differences' With Father" *Publishers Weekly*, Sept. 27, 1993; Jack Shafer, "Roger Straus, Inter-
national Man of Mystery," April 9, 2002; *Slate* at http://slate.msn.com/id/2064178/, write up on "Gala for Roger
W. Straus at the Wilhelm Reich Museum" site www.wilhelmreichmuseum.org/new_york_gala.shtml; his obituary in
Economist, June 5, 2004; and the obituary in *The New York Times*, May 27, 2004.

72. Among sources for the Crown Books section: Edwin McDowell, "Nat Wartels, 88, the Chairman of the Crown Publishing Empire," *The New York Times*, Feb 8, 1990; the Random House Web page, www.randomhouse.com/value
publishing/about_us.html; "Crown Publishing Group," at http://en.wikipedia.org/wiki/Crown_Publishing_Group.

73. Among sources for the Viking Press section: "About Us: Viking," at http://us.penguingroup.com/static/html/
aboutus/adult/viking.html; "Viking Sails On" at www.publishersweekly.com/index.asp?layout=articlePrint&artic…;
"Encyclopedia:The Viking Press," at www.nationmaster.com/encyclopedia/The-Viking-Press; The Jewish Committee:
Thirty-Fifth Annual Report, 1943; "Thomas Guinzburg," at www.nndb.com/people/731/000167230; "The Paris
Review," at www.nndb.com/media/963/ 000048819/.

74. Among sources for the Pantheon Books section:; "Pantheon Books," at http://en.wikipedia.org/ wiki/
Pantheon_Books

75. Among sources for the Basic Books section: "Doreen Carvajal, "Harper Collins Selling Basic Books Unit to Venture Capital Firm," *The New York Times*, Aug. 22, 1997; "Basic Books," at http://en.wikipedia.org/wiki/Basic_Books;
About Basic Books," at www.perseusbooksgroup.com/basic/about_us.jsp.

76. Among sources for the Arthur Frommer section: David Butwin, "Travels with Arthur," *Hemispheres Magazine*; articles on Frommer and bios of Arthur Frommer at http://premierspeakers.com/524/ print.cfm; www.frommers.com/
about/; Silbiger, *The Jewish Phenomenon*, 158; an article about J.W. Wiley at www.wiley.com/WileyCDA/Section/
id-144.html; the PR Newswire story "*Newsweek*, Inc. Acquires 'Arthur Frommer's Budget Travel' Magazine from
Group XXVII Communications L.L.C." at www.findarticles.com/cf_dls/m4PRN/1999_Dec_20/ 58316259/
print.jhtml; www.aeispeakers.com/Frommer-Arthur.htm; "*Newsweek* Buys Arthur Frommer's Budget Travel" at
http://foliomag.com/news/ marketing_newsweek_buys_arthur/; and www.allstaragency.com/cgi-bin/speaker/
2001.asp?ID=229.

77. Among sources for the Jacob Kay Lasser section: Mike Smith, "Terese Lasser Reaching For Hope," at www.in.net/
~smith/Lasser.htm; the "Reach to Recovery" description at the American Cancer Society Web site, at www.cancer.org;
J.K. Lasser's Your Income Tax, Macmillan, New York, 1996 and other web sources; J.K. Lasser pages on the Wiley Web
site at www.wiley.com/WileyCDA/Section/id-103272.html; review of *J.K. Lasser's Tax Guide* at www.taxgaga.com/
pages/c-productsreviews/b-jklasseryourincome01.html

78. Among sources for the Streisand bio: her Web site at www.barbrastreisand.com, Liora Moriel, "Barbra Streisand" at
www.jewishvirtuallibrary.org/jsource/biography/streisand.html; Deborah G. Felder and Diana Rosen, *Fifty Jewish
Women Who Changed The World*, Citadel Press, Kensington Publishing Corp, New York, 2003, pages 286–90; "Barbra
Streisand" at http://en.wikipedia.org/wiki/ Barbra_Streisand; the Web pages devoted to Barbra Streisand at
www.divasthesite.com; "Women in Philanthropy" at www.women-philanthropy.umich.edu/donors/donors_nz.html;
and the article Barbra Streisand at www.queeria.org.yu/english/music/barbra-streisand.htm.

79. See the various Web pages at www.kennedy-center.org which detail the honorees, the Board of Trustees and governance, and other articles of interest.

80. See www.albany.edu/~rshaf/conductors.html; the lists of Jewish conductors and "classical" at www.jewhoo.com; at

www.jinfo.org/Conductors.html; and at www.yahoodi.com; as well as, Asher B. Etkes and Saul Stadtmauer, "*Jewish Contributions to the American Way of Life*," Northside Publishing, Long Island City, New York, 1995, pages 10–35; American Jewish Historical Society, *American Jewish Desk Reference*, Random House, New York, 1999, pages 343–431

81. Ibid

82. See the American Symphony Orchestra League Web site at www.symphony.org and its research summary pages as well as the Jewhoo.com and Yahoodi.com Web sites

83. See Knowledge Products Web site at www.audioclassics.net/html/inteli_files/composer.htm; and the Jewhoo and Yahoodi Web sites, Etkes and Stadtmauer, as well as American Jewish Historical Society

84. See the Jinfo.org and Jewhoo.com Web sites, Etkes, and the American Jewish Historical Society.

85. Ibid

86. See the Broadway and Musicals sections of the Jinfo.com and Jewhoo.com Web sites, among others.

87. See write-up on Andrea Most, *Making Americans: Jews and the Broadway Musical*, at www.hup.harvard.edu/catalog/MOSMAD.html, and Michah Rynor, "Broadway Helped Jews Gain Acceptance, Researcher Says" at the University of Toronto Web site www.newsandevents.utoronto.ca/ bin/3/021211e.asp

88. See www.motlc.wiesenthal.com/text/x32/xr3234.html.

89. Neal Gabler, *An Empire of Their Own*, Anchor Books, New York, 1989, pages 139–43

90. See "Longest Running Broadway Shows in History from the League of American Theaters at www.geocities.com/auzziek/broadway_list3 html; the Internet Broadway Database at www.ibdb.com/ production.asp; and the Jinfo.org Web site article "Broadway and Hollywood Musicals Written by Jews," which, in turn cites Jewhoo.com.

91. Tom Williams, "The 25 Broadway Musicals Everyone Should See," at the Chicago Critic.com Web site, www.chicagocritic.com/Feature Articles/Best_Musicals/best_musicals.html.

92. See the Rock 'n' Roll Hall of Fame Web site and its history, inductees and profiles of individuals at www.rockhall.com; Also see the Rock 'n' roll Web pages at www.jewhoo.com; and "Jewish Who's Who of Pop/Rock N'Roll (Foreword Included) at www.sorabji.com/strangle/messages/924/2738.html.

93. The Grammy Web site is at www.grammy.com/awards; and the Big Band and Jazz Hall of Fame site is at www.jazzhall.org/bbjhf.html; It is also available at the *Wikipedia* site http://en.wikipedia.org; the Lincoln Center Ertegun site is www.jalc.org/ejhf_web/i_2005.html; also see the International Academy of Jazz Hall of Fame at www.pitt.edu/ ~pittjazz/academy.html; stories about the American Jazz Hall of Fame at www.allaboutjazz.com; Jewish jazz artists are profiled at the jewhoo.com Web site; also see, Jon Moskowitz, "One of the Nicer Guys': Jazz Legend Riffs on Life," *Forward*, Aug. 22, 2003, a review of George Wein's memoir, *Myself Among Others*; the article, "Harvey Sheldon Jewish American Music Video Research Library at U of Penn Web site, www.library.upenn.edu/cgi-bin/common/pfp.cgi?/ cajs/sheldon; and, Jim Godbolt, "Jews and Jazz," at www.ronniescotts.co.uk/ronnie_scotts/ronniescotts/126/ 126_07.htm.

94. The Country Music Hall of Fame Web site is www.countrymusichalloffame.com; also see, Nate Bloom, "Country Jews," *Jewish Bulletin* at www.jewishsf.com/bk030613/etceleb.shtml; the "Folk/Salsa/Country" Web pages at Jewhoo.com, Kinky Friedman site at www.kinkyfriedman.com; John Dorfman, "Songs of Himself," *Forward*, at www.forward.ocm/issues/1999/99.05.28/arts.html; the Bronco Billy Anderson material from the profile of Leona Anderson at www.spaceagepop.com/ anderson.htm; and, Ralph Blumenthal, "Guess Who Wants To Be Governor," Nov. 29, 2003, *The New York Times*.

95. See www.grammy.com.

96. See the "Comedians" Web pages at www.Jewhoo.com; at www.jews.net; the Rate it All pages at www.rateitall.com; "Televisions Greatest Comedians at www.hellodere.com/dma9aba3bhtml;; the profile of the Joys TV program at www.imdb.com/title/tt0164066/combined.

97. Steve Allen, *Funny People*, p. 30 as reported by Rabbi Joseph Telushkin in his book, *Jewish Humor*, Perennial Imprint of HarperCollins, New York, 2002.

98. See the pages devoted to magic at http://magic.about.com/cs/past/; "Top Magicians" at www.geocities.com/topmagicians/; the "Magicians" pages at www.jewhoo.com; and, "Jews in Magic," at www.jewsinmagic.org/all_mag.asp.

99. Paul Johnson, *History of the Jews,* Harper Perennial, New York, 1987, p. 411.

100. Charles Murray, *Human Accomplishment,* Harper Collins Publishers, New York, 2003, pages 137 497–9, 548–53.

101. *The Holy Bible,* Authorized King James Version (1611), Memorial Bibles International, Inc. Nashville, Tennessee, 1974, p. 67.

102. *Tanakh, The Holy Scriptures,* The Jewish Publication Society, 1985, p. 282.

103. Eli Barnavi, editor, *A Historical Atlas of the Jewish People,* Schocken Books, New York, 2002, pages 12–13, 279.

104. Max Dimont, *Jews, God and History,* New American Library, New York, 1994, pages 116–7.

105. Johnson, p. 411.

106. Ze'ev Weiss, Ehud Netzer, *Promise and Redemption: A Synagogue Mosaic from Sepphoris,* The Israel Museum, Jerusalem, 1998, pages 27 & 43.

107. Dimont, pages 194–5.

108. Dimont, pages 256–7, & Raphael Patai, *The Jewish Mind,* Wayne State University Press, Detroit Michigan, 1996, p. 161.

109. Roza Bieliauskiene, "A Brief History of Jewish Art," on the *Jewish Art Network* Web site at www.jewishartnetwork .com/JewishArt/history.asp.

110. The Al-Tahmazi Web site is at www.fine-art-painting-gallery.com/bahrain-artist-biography.htm.

111. George Gilbert, "Jews in Photography," an article available at www.hebrewhistory.crg/factpapers/photo7.html.

112. Sources for *The Jazz Singer* introduction include: Neal Gabler, *An Empire of Their Own,* First Anchor Books, New York, 1988, pages 120–150; Gabbard, Krin, "*The Jazz Singer,*" *Jammin' at the Margins: Jazz and the American Cinema.* Chicago: Chicago UP, 1996 available at http://xroads.virginia.edu/~ASI/musi212/brandi/jazz.html; Hans J. Wollstein, "*The Jazz Singer*" an AMG Movie Review at http://movies.msn.com/movies/ movie.aspx?m=386679&mp=cr; Sussman's review of *The Jazz Singer* at www.dealtime.com/xPR-The_Jazz-Singer_Neil_Diamond~RD-8070925956; *Wikipedia*'s article "The Jazz Singer" (1927 film) at http://en.wikipedia.org/wiki/ The_Jazz_Singer_(1927_film); and "Al Jolson," at http://en.wikipedia.org/wiki/Al_Jolson; *Encyclopaedia Britannica* articles, "Warner Brothers;" and "History of Motion Picture: The pre-World War II Sound Era – The Introduction of Sound;"and, Herbert G. Goldman, *Jolson: The Legend Comes to Life,* Oxford University Press, 1988, New York and Oxford.

113. Sources for the Studios overview include: *Encyclopaedia Britannica 2001 & 2008* Ultimate Reference Suite, Articles on "Motion Picture History," "Early Growth of the Film Industry," "Edison and the Lumiere Brothers;" *Wikipedia,* "Film History," "Vitagraph Studios," "Essanay Studios," and "List of Hollywood Movie Studios;" *Hollywood Reporter,* "Hollywood Hyperlinks: Major Studios, Mini-Majors, Independent Distributors, Independent Producers" at the Hollywood Reporter Web site: www.hollywoodreporter.com/hollywoodreporter/hyperlink/pd.jsp; and Digital DreamDoor.com, "Academy Award Winning Movies," at www.digitaldreamdoor.com/pages/movie-pages/ movie_acad-awar.php.

114. Sources for Paramount include: Gabler, pages 11–46; *Encyclopaedia Britannica,* "Zukor, Adolph," "Loew, Marcus;" *Wikipedia,* "Paramount Pictures;" Asher B. Etkes and Saul Stadtmauer, *Jewish Contributions to the American Way of Life,* Northside Publishing, Inc., Long Island City, NY, 1995, p. 83; Naomi Pfefferman, "Cocaine, Starlets and Chutzpah: Robert Evans Is Back," *Jewish Bulletin of San Francisco,* at www.jewishsf.com/bk02809/et29.shtml; John Cones, "Who Really Controls Hollywood: Paramount Pictures," at www.mecfilms.com/FIRM/paramount.htm; Viacom's Business Description at Viacom.com; and the "Sumner Redstone bio at www.museum.tv/archives/etv/R/htmlR/redstonesum/restnesum.htm.

115. Sources for Universal include: Gabler, pages 47–64, and 72–78; *Encyclopaedia Britannica,* "Universal Pictures company," *Wikipedia* articles, "Universal Studios," "Music Corporation of America," "Vivendi," and "Vivendi Universal;" the Universal Studios Web site, "Universal Studios Timeline 1867 – 1999," and "History," at www.universalstudios .com; "The Jewish Past of Laupheim," at http://members.aol.com/laupheim/english/laemmle.htm; Cones, "Who Really Controls Hollywood: Universal Pictures;" "Matsushita Sells Stake in Uni Studios to Viveni," *AP,* Feb 3, 2006; and, "Carl Laemmle Jr." at www.imdb.com/name/nm0480673/.

116. Sources for Twentieth Century Fox include: Gabler, pages 64–72 and 109–119; *Encyclopaedia Britannica* articles:

"Twentieth Century–Fox Film Corporation," and "Fox, William;" Wikipedia articles: "20th Century Fox," and "William Fox (producer);" *Internet Movies Data Base* articles, "William Fox," "Awards for William Fox," at www.imdb.com/name/nm0289301/awards; *The German Hollywood Connection* article, "William Fox," and "Fox Film Corporation: 20th Century Fox," at www.germanhollywood.com/fox.html; the article, "Fox Broadcasting company," at the TV Museum Web site at www.museum.tv/archives/etv/F/htmlF/foxbroadcast/foxbroadcast.htm; and Cones, "Who Really Controls Hollywood: 20th Century Fox."

117. Sources for Metro Goldwyn Mayer (MGM) include: Gabler, pages 79–119 and 209–236; *Encyclopaedia Britannica* articles: "Mayer, Louis B(urt)," "Metro-Goldwyn-Mayer, Inc.,""Loew, Marcus," "Goldwyn, Samuel;" *Wikipedia* articles: "Metro-Goldwyn-Mayer," and "Dore Schary," the *MGM* Web site, "History and Timeline," at http://mgm.mediaroom.com/index.php?s=40; and Manohla Dargis, "Mogul of Media Make Believe," a book review of Scott Eyman's *Lion of Hollywood*, Simon & Schuster, appearing in *The New York Times Book Review, Sunday*, July 10, 2005; and Cones, "Who Really Controls Hollywood: MGM;" Marissa Marr and Martin Peers, "Revenge of the B-List: MGM's Library of Old Movies Puts It in Spotlight," *The Wall Street Journal*," July 7, 2004; "Metro-Goldwyn-Mayer." At www.scripophily.net/meinde191.html;

118. Sources for Columbia Pictures include: Gabler, pages 151–183; *Encyclopaedia Britannica* articles: "Cohn, Harry." Columbia Pictures Entertainment, Inc.," and "Capra, Frank;" *Wikipedia* articles: "Columbia Pictures," "Peter Guber," "Jon Peters," "Sony Pictures Entertainment," and "Sony Pictures Classics;" the Internet Movie Database article "Awards for It Happened One Night," at www.imdb.com/title/tt0025316/awards; and Cones, "Who Really Controls Hollywood: Columbia/TriStar;" "Harry Cohn Dead; Movie Executive," *The New York Times*, Feb 28, 1958; Hollis Alpert, "They Ate His Bread and Sang His Song," *The New York Times*, Mar 5, 1967 and "Yes, Sire," *Time*, Apr. 14, 1967, (both are reviews of the book, *King Cohn*, by Bob Thomas);

119. Sources for Warner Brothers include those cited in the above endnote on *The Jazz Singer*, as well as: *Encyclopaedia Britannica* article, "Warner Brothers;" *Wikipedia* articles: "Warner Brothers;" "Steve Ross (Time Warner CEO)," "Kinney National company," "Warner Bros.-Seven Arts," and "Jack Warner;" *Scripophily article*, "Warner Communications Inc. Specimen,: at www.scripophily.net/warcomincspe.html; Jim Hu, "CEO Levin To Retire From AOL Time Warner," at CNet News, www.news.com.com/2102-1023_3-276617.html; *Columbia Journalism Review*, "Who Owns What at Time Warner," at www.cjr.org/tools/owners/timewarner-timeline.asp; Time Warner Web site articles: "Companies," Time Warner Cable," "Turner Broadcasting," and "Warner Brothers Entertainment," at www.timewarner.com; Yahoo! Bio of Terry Semel at http://docs.yahoo.com/docs/pr/executives/semel.html; *TV Museum* articles: "Time Warner," and Levin, Gerald," at www.museum.tv/archives/etv/T/htmlT/timewarner/timewarner.htm (and LhtmlL/levingerald/levingerald.htm); Cones, "Who Really Controls Hollywood: Warner Bros;" and others.

120. Sources for United Artists include: Gabler, p. 41; and *Wikipedia* articles:' "United Artists," and "Arthur B. Krim," Krim's Columbia University obituary at www.columbia.edu/cu/record/archives/vol20/vol20_iss6/record2006.31.html; Michael Aushenker, "The Circuit – The ADL's Kodak Moment," 2001-12-14 at www.jewishjournal.com/home/preview.php?id=7854; and "The Krim Connections," at www.smokershistory.com/AIDSconx.htm; Brooks Barnes and Michael Cieply, "A Studio, A Star, A Fateful Bet," *The New York Times*, Nov. 17, 2008.

121. Sources for Disney include: Gabler, Neal, *Walt Disney: The Triumph of the American Imagination*, Alfred A. Knopf, New York, 2006; Encyclopaedia Britannica article "Disney Company" the Academy of Achievement profile: Michael Eisner at www.achievement.org/autodoc/printmember/eis0pro-1; company Overview of Disney at http://corporate.disney.go.com/corporate/overview.html; and Robert Iger bio on the Disney site; the Michael Eisner profile at www.askmen.com; the *Wikipedia* articles "The Walt Disney company," "Michael Eisner," and "Walt Disney;" the articles "History," and "Latest News," on the Eisner Foundation Web site at www.eisnerfoundation.org/about.html; Marc Gunther, "Is Bob Iger Ready For His Close-up?" *Fortune*, April 4, 2005; Kathryn Harris, "Disney Image Real Loser in Court Case (Walt Disney Co.'s Out-of Court Settlement With Former Disney Executive Jeffrey Katzenberg," *Los Angeles Business Journal*, July 12, 1999 at www.findarticles.com/cf_dis/m5072/28_21/55609908/p1/article.jhtml; and Robert La Franco, "Eisner's Bumpy Ride," *Forbes*, July 5, 1999 at www.forbes.com/forbes/99/0705/6401050a.htm.

122. Sources for Miramax include: the *Cinemablend.com* story, "Weinstein Brother Tell Miramax To **** Off!!!" at www.cinemablend.com/forum/archive/index.php/t-17667.html; *Wikipedia* articles: "Miramax Films," and "The Weinstein company;"; Jonathan Last's review of Peter Biskind's *Down and Dirty Pictures*, Simon & Schuster; *The Wall Street Journal*, January 2004; and Dwight Garner's review of the same book in *The New York Times*, January 14, 2004.

123. Sources for Dreamworks include: *Encyclopaedia Britannica* article, "Year In Review," 1995: biography: Katzenberg, Jeffrey;" *Wikipedia* articles: "Dreamworks;" Sharon Waxman and Geraldine Fabrikant, "Viacom Pounces of Dreamworks," *San Francisco Chronicle*, Dec 10, 2005, p. C1; Peter Kafka and Peter Newcomb, "Cash Me Out If You Can," *Fortune*, March 3, 2003 pages 78–86; Ronald Grover, "Paramount and DreamWorks: Splitsville?" *Business Week* July 19, 2007 available at www.businessweek.com/print/bwdaily/dnflash/content/jul2007/db20070719_311987;

Associated Press, "Dream Appears Over for Spielberg, Paramount," at www.tdn.com/articles/2007/09/23/bi/news01.prt; and David M. Halbfinger, "Next: Spielberg's Biggest Gamble," *The New York Times*, July 1, 2005, Weekend pages 1, 20; "New Deal Frees Spielberg From Paramount," *UPI.com*, Sept 21, 2008; "Steven Spielberg Quits Paramount Pictures For New Venture," DailyStab.com, Oct. 6, 2008.

124. Orion sources include: the prior endnotes covering United Artists; *Wikipedia* articles, "Orion Pictures," and "TriStar Pictures;" Eric Pace, "Arthur B. Krim, 89, Ex-Chief of Movie Studios, *The New York Times*, Sept. 22, 1994; and Andrea Eckert, "I'm About Winning" at www.coop99.atwebsite coop99_05/filme/eric_pleskow_e.htm.

125. Sources for the Coen brothers include: Emanuel Levy, "Profile: Coen, Joel and Ethan: Stylist Filmmakers;" *Wikipedia*, "Coen Brothers."

126. Kubrick sources include: "Biography for Stanley Kubrick" at the Internet Movie Database site, www.imdb.com/name/nm0000040/bio; and Kubrick's *Wikipedia* bio at http://en.wikipedia.org/wiki/Stanley_Kubrick.

127. Selznick sources include: Gabler, *Empire*, pages 93, 108, 147, 226, 244, 245, 284, 342, 393; *Encyclopaedia Britannica*, "Selznick, David;" Wikipedia article, David O. Selznick; and KQED, "American Masters: David O Selznick, at www.pbs.org/wnet/americanmasters/database/selznick_d.html.

128. Spiegel sources include: J.A. Aberdeen, Hollywood Renegades, Excerpt on Sam Spiegel available at www.cobbles.com/simpp_archive/sam_spiegel.htm; Amazon.com's and *Publisher's Weekly* reviews of *Sam Spiegel: The Incredible Life and Times of Hollywood's Most Iconoclastic Producer;* and Yahoo article on Sam Spiegel.

129. Todd sources include: excerpts from Gerald L. Hansen, "Mike Todd — Showman!" at http://my.execpc.com/~ghansen/mtps-ne.txt; David Bennun, Mike Todd, *Stuff Magazine,* UK Edition, 1998; the article, "Mike Todd" at www.cineramaadventure.com/todd.htm; Films In Review interview with Mike Todd, Jr. available at www.in70mm.com/news/2004/todd_jr/interview.htm.

130. Reiner sources include: "Rob Reiner Gets Star on Hollywood Walk of Fame," Oct. 13, 1999 at the Canoe Web site, www.conoe.ca/JamMoviesArtistsR/reiner.html; and Reiner's profile at www.imdb.com/name/mn0001661/.

131. Sources for the "Directors" section include: Wikipedia articles, "Film Director," and "Film Producer;" the Web site of the Academy of Motion Picture Arts and Sciences at, www.oscars.org for its list of Best Directors; the article, "Greatest Film Directors and Their Best Films," at the Web site of *Filmsite.org* www.filmsite.org/directors.html; and Oscar Winning Directors as shown on the Web site, www.pubquizhelp.34sp.com/ent/direct.html; www.filmsite.org/bestdirs.html; the article, "Greatest Directors of the 20th Century," at www.reel.com/reel.asp?node=features/millennium/bestdirectors/01; the list, "Oscar Winning Directors" at www.pubquizhelp.34sp.com/ent/direct.html; the American Film Institute list "100 Greatest American Movies;" Asher B. Etkes, *Jewish Contributions to the American Way of Life*; Lists of Jewish Directors from Wikipedia, Jewhoo.com, Yahoodi.com, www.adherents.com; and, Jews.net.com

132. Sources for the Actors and Actresses section include: "Hollywood Reporter Star Power 2002" at the Web site, www.hollywoodreporter.com/hollywoodreporter/starpower/starpower02.jsp; the identification of Jewish actors and actresses from www.Jewhoo.com; Wikipedia, http://en.wikipedia.org/wiki/List_of_Jewish_actors_and_actresses; "Religious Affiliation of Famous Actors and Actresses" from the Web site, www.adherents.com/movies/adh_actors.html; "Jewish Actors and Directors" from the Web site, www.conerhama.com/jewish/actors.html; "Famous Jews – Jewish Actors/Actresses," at www.jews.net/jewishactors.htm; "The Name Changers," at www.hoozajew.org/hollywoodnamechangers2.html; and Aaron Hale, "Chaplin – An Essay" at www.csse.monash.edu.au/~pringle/ silent/chaplin/aaronhale.html;

133. Sources for Lifetime Awards and Legends include: the American Film Institute lists of Lifetime Achievement Award Winners at www.afi.com/tv/stars.asp; as well as the lists in the prior endnote plus the Jewhoo lists of Screenwriters, Film Crafts, the AOL lists "The Men Who Created Hollywood," at http://members.aol.com/_ht_a/gjadoc/page4.html?.

134. Sources on David Sarnoff include: *Encyclopædia Britannica 2001 Deluxe Edition* article on David Sarnoff, Robert Sobel and David B. Sicilia, *The Entrepreneurs: An American Adventure*, Houghton Mifflin Company, Boston, 1986, pages 253–63; the PBS Web site and its bio of David Sarnoff at www.pbs.org/wgbh/amex/technology/bigdream/masarnoff.html, The *Time* 100 Web site and its bio of Sarnoff at www.time.com/time/time100/builder/profile/sarnoff.html, his bio at the David Sarnoff Library Web site, www.davidsarnoff.org/dsindex.htm, one at Sarnoff Corporation at www.sarnoff.com/ common/print_page/index.asp?pageURL=/about/history/index.asp, one at www.stfrancis.edu/ ba/ghkickul/stuwebs/bbios/biograph/sarnoff.htm, two at the Television Museum archives, one, www.museum.tv/archives/etv/S/htmlS/sarnoffdavi/sarnoffdavi.htm, on Sarnoff, another on NBC at

www.museum.tv/archives/etv/N/htmlN/nationalbroa/nationalbroa.htm, a timeline at http://bnrg.eecs.berkeley.edu/~randy/Courses/CS39C.S97broadcast/broadcast.html and an article "The Dawn of FM Radio" at www.internetcampus.com/frtv/frtv020.htm.

135. Sources of this section's material came from "The History of Radio" at www.tvhandbook.com/History/ History_radio.htm; "The History of the Telegraph" at the About Web site http://inventors.about.com/library/inventors/bltelegraph.htm; the Radio Hall of Fame Web site at www.radiohof.org/inducteesaz.html, and its articles on "Norman Corwin," "Bill Stern," "Rick Sklar," "Martin Block," "John Gambling," "Wolfman Jack," and "Orion Samuelson;" an article on "Karl Haas" at http://nextbook.org/cultural/digest.html?sort=music; "The Jewish Who's Who of Pop/Rock N' Roll" at www.sorabji.com/strangle/messages/942/4738.html?; the article on "Bill Stern" at www.jewishsports.net/BioPages/BillStern.htm; Casey Kasem, "I Want My Son to be Proud," at www.alhewar.com/Casey/Kasem.htm; an article on "Himan Brown" from the *Brooklyn College Magazine*, Fall 2001 Class Notes at www.brooklyn.cuny.edu/bc/text/pubs/bcmag/bcm-fall01/class.htm; one on Susan Stamberg from www.kiallentown.org/events.html; the *Norman Corwin* Web site at http://normancorwin.com; the "Television Hall of Fame" listing at the Web site of *Infoplease* at www.infoplease.com/ipea/AO151618.html; the Web pages of *Jewhoo.com* devoted to Authors, Actors, Directors, Comedians, Actresses; The "Directors and Producers," and "TV and Radio Personalities" articles at www.yahoodi.com; Asher B. Etkes and Saul Stadtmauer, pages 57–98; an article on Charles Cappleman at *looksmart.com;* the "Hillside Cemetery" article at www.seeing-stars.com/Buried2/Hillside2.shtml; "Spiritual Odysseys" at www.aish.com/spirituality/odysseys/ Do_You_Know_Where_Youre_Going_To$.asp; Nate Bloom, "It's a Happy New Year for Mike Nichols . . . " *Jewish Theatre News,* Dec 26, 2003; "About NFJC Donors" at the National Foundation for Jewish Culture, May 24, 2005 also available at www.jewishculture.org/about/about_nfjc_donors.html; the profile of Ethel Winant at www.mtmshow.com/backexecs.shtml; the article on "Herbert Brodkin" at the Academy of Television Arts & Sciences Web site, www.emmys.org/awards/halloffame/herbertbrodkin.php; an article on donations to the Jewish Community Library of Los Angeles at www.jclla.org/onepeople.htm; Nate Bloom, "Celebrity Jews," *Jewish News Weekly,* Oct. 24, 2003 also at www.jewishsf.com; Sandee Brawarsky, "Old Acquaintances, New Love," *The Jewish Week,* July 21, 2004, the *Museum of Broadcast Communications* Web site www.museum.tv/archies articles on "National Broadcasting company," "Columbia Broadcasting System," William S. Paley," "Laurence Tisch," "Leonard Goldenson," "Fred Silverman," "Michael Eisner," "Roone Arledge," and "Mergers and Acquisitions;" *Encyclopædia Britannica Deluxe Edition* articles on "CBS Corporation," and William S. Paley;" a Columbia Broadcasting article at http://encyclopedia.thefreedictionary.com/Columbia Broadcasting System; the article on Otto Klemperer at www.concentric.net/~onk145/Horowitz.htm; an article on Julius Schulman at www.pulpless.com/jneil/memoriam.html; an article on "Eugene Ormandy" at http://home.flash.net/!park29/ormandyap.htm; the obituary of William Paley from *Macleans,* Nov. 5, 1990v103n45p58(1).

136. *Museum of Broadcasting* articles on "Fox Broadcasting," "Barry Diller," "Sumner Redstone," and "Gerald Levin;" the News Corporation Web site at www.newscorp.com; a Peter Chernin article at *BWOnline,* Jan. 12, 2004, at www.businessweek.com; his bio from www.netcaucus.org/speakers/2000/fox.shtml; the Web site of 20th Anniversary Israel Film Festival at www.israelfilmfestival.com; Gaby Wenig, "The Circuit" at *Jewish Journal of Los Angeles* Web site, www.jewishjournal.com/ home/preview.php?id=12187; "Barry Diller," at Forbes Web site www.forbes.com/static/pvp2005/LIRMIIED.htm; the Viacom Web site at www.viacom.com; *American Jewish Desk Reference,* pages 214 & 234; the Comcast 2003 and 2004 *Annual Reports* and *Proxies,* its Web site press room at www.cmcsk.com; the Comcast chronology at the Web site, www.ketupa.net/ comcast2.htm; the article on Comcast at www.morningstar.com; another at www.hoovers.com; Stephanie N. Mehta, "King Comcast" *Fortune,* July 7, 2003 also available at www.fortune.com/fortune/subs/print/ 0,15935,462977,00.html; Dan Ackman, "Bottom-Up Comcast Wants To Go Top Down," *Forbes,* Feb 12, 2004; Christopher Stern, "Shareholders Keep Comcast Voting Structure," *Washington Post;* Parija Bhatnagar, "Comcast's Roberts: Hungary for More," *CNNMoney,* Feb 11, 2004; "UJA Awards Humanitarian Nod," at *Variety,* May 21, 2003; "76 Revolutionary Minds," at www.phillymag.com/Archives/2001Nov/smart_11html; Del Jones, "Comcast CEO Keeps a Pretty Low Profile," *USA Today – Money,* Feb 12, 2004; "America's Most Generous Donors: H.F. (Gerry) Lefest" at http://philanthropy.com; Patricia Horn, "Happy To Give Away Millions," at www.philly.com/mld/inquirer/business/8009153.htm?1c; "The Difference You Make," *Temple Review,* Winter 2003; the article on "Broadcast.com," "Internet radio," :Yahoo!," "Yahoo! Broadcast," at www.answers.com; the Yahoo Web site page dedicated to Yahoo! Plus.

137. Sources include *Museum of Broadcast Communications* articles on the people profiled, an article on Haim Saban at http://saban.com/site/management/hsaban.html; the *Wikipedia* article on Paddy Chayefsky at http://en.wikipedia.org/wiki/Paddy Chayefsky; *TV Tome* profiles of Lorne Michaels, Bud Yorkin, and Tom Werner at www.tvtome.com; obituaries of Ethel Winant at www.emmys.com/news/ 2003/december/winant.php; & www.womenbehindtv.com/news/winant_120303.asp; burial site of Bill Todman from "Cemeteries and Notable Burial Sites in Westchester County," Oct. 2003, *Half Moon Press.*

138. Sources include Jewhoo.com at www.jewhoo.com; Yahoodi.com at www.yahoodi.com; *Museum of Broadcast Communications* articles; Etkes and Stadtmauer, *pages* 57–98, "List of Jews" at http://en.wikipedia.org/wiki/List_of_Jews; Biographies at the *Jewish Virtual Library* at www.jewishvirtuallibrary.org/jsource/bios.html; Silbiger, *The Jewish Phenomenon,* 112–7; *American Jewish Desk Reference,* 431

139. *Encyclopædia Britannica 2001* articles on "Hungary" and "World War II, plus,""Radical Right in Power," at the All Refer Reference Web site at http://reference.allrefer.com/country-guide-study/hungary/hungary47.html. and Joshua Cooper Ramo, "Grove is *Time Magazine's* Man of the Year 1997," *Time* 12/29/97, available at various Web sites including www.heinzawards.net/ articleDetail.asp?articleD=30.

140. Ibid.

141. Ramo, ibid, plus the Amazon reviews of Grove's book, *Swimming Across* at www.amazon.com/exec/obidos/tg/detail/-/0446679704/ref=pd_trkn_qp_b_t/103-1618180-1218263?v=glance .

142. Ibid.

143. Ramo, ibid.

144. Ramo, ibid.

145. Ramo, ibid. plus the article, "Andy Grove," on the Management Giants Web site at www.ultimatebusinessresource.com/downloads/uk/giantsnocigar.pdf.

146. ibid.

147. ibid. plus Bill Rosenblatt's review of Tim Jackson's book, *Inside Intel* at the Sunworld Web site at http://sunsite.uakom.sk/sunworldonline/swol-03-bookshelf.html.

148. Ramo, ibid. and the Andy Grove article on the Management Giants Web site plus, Elmer Epistola, "The Kitchen Aid that Ruled the World," Semicon Fareast.com, March 24, 2003 available at www.semiconfareast.com/article3.htm.

149. Ramo, ibid., the "Andy Grove," article, ibid., the Bill Rosenblatt review, ibid. and Andy Reinhardt, "Intel: Paranoia, Aggression, and Other Strengths," a review of Inside Intel in *Business Week*, Oct. 13, 1997 available at the *Business Week* web site.

150. Ramo, ibid., the Answers.com bio of Grove at www.answers.com/topic/andrew-grove. Jeffrey E. Garten, "Andy Grove Made the Elephant Dance, *Business Week*, April 11, 2005, and Brent Schlender, "Inside Andy Grove's Latest Crusade," *Fortune*, August 23, 2004.

151. Ramo, ibid., Reinhardt ibid., Rosenblatt, ibid., and reviews of *Inside Intel* on the Amazon.com Web site at www.amazon.com/exec/obidos/tg/detail/-/052594141X/qid=1124999335/sr=2-1/ ref=pd_bbs_b_2_1/103-4019570-9417459?v=glance&s=books. Clive Thompson, "The Next Small Thing," *New York Times* book review of *The Man Behind the Microchip*, a biography of Robert Noyce, Aug. 28, 2005

152. Ramo, ibid., Rosenblatt ibid., Garten ibid, David Einstein, "Grove: Author, Leader, Survivor and Innovator," *San Francisco Chronicle*, April 28, 1997 available at the Chronicle's Web site at www.sfgate.com/cgi-bin/chronicle/article.cgi?file=BU20246.DTL&directory=/chronicle/archive/1997/04/28.

153. Ramo, ibid., Einstein, ibid., Reinhardt, ibid.

154. Ramo, ibid.

155. Ramo, ibid., David Lewis, "Living Paranoid After September 11th: The Management Philosophy of Andy Grove," *Financial Times*, available at http://www.ftmastering.com/mmo/mmo11_4.htm

156. Ramo, ibid., Reinhardt, ibid,, Garten ibid., Einstein ibid.

157. Ramo, ibid.

158. Garten, ibid., "Andy Grove" article at the Ultimate Business Resource Web site.

159. Ramo, ibid.

160. Ibid.

161. Schlender, ibid., Garten, ibid.

162. Ramo, ibid., "Andrew Grove to Donate Profits of new Memoir to the IRC," at the International Rescue Commit-

tee Web site at www.theirc.org/index.cfm/wwwID/771, Daniel S. Levine, "UCSF Races Ahead at Mission Bay," *San Francisco Business Times*, Oct. 31, 2003, available at www.bizjournals.com/sanfrancisco/stories/2003/ 11/03/ story3.html, and the Stanford University Web site bio of Grove at http://gobi.stanford.edu/facultybios/bio.asp?ID=54.

163. *National Jewish Population Survey 2000–01: Strength, Challenge and Diversity in the American Jewish Population*, A United Jewish Communities Report, Sept. 2003, Updated Jan 2004, p. 6.

164. Andrew Park and Peter Burrows, "What You Don't Know About Dell," *Business Week*, Nov. 3, 2003; the Michael Dell Bio at the Dell Web site at www.us.dell.com, "Michael Dell," at the *About Men* Web site, www.askmen.com/ men/january00/8_michael_dell.html, the "Michael Dell" profile at www.Forbes.com, William J. Holstein, "Dell: One company, Two CEO's" at the *FindArticles* Web site http://articles.findarticles.com/ p/articles/mi_m4070/is_193/ ai_110811913/print; the "Michael Dell" article at www.zeromillion.com/entre/stories/michael-dell.html; the article on Dell at the *Fortune*, 40 Under 40 site, www.fortune.com/fortune/40under40/snapshot/0,15793,1,00.html; the Michael and Susan Dell Foundation Web site, www.msdf.org/mediacenter/newsarchive.aspx and the company profile on Yahoo.com, http://finance.yahoo.com/q/ks?s=Dell.

165. Google data came from the Google Web site at www.google.com/corporate/facts.html and the profile at http://finance.yahoo.com/q/pr?s=GOOG, Jefferson Graham, "Googley-eyed Over Success," *USA Today*, Aug 27, 2001 at www.usatoday.com/tech/news/2001-08-27-google-profile.htm, Will Smale, "Profile: The Google Founders," *BBC News*, April 30, 2004 at http://news.bbc.co.uk/2/hi/business/3666241.stm, and Mobius, "Google Adds Explanation to 'Jew' Search," at www.jewschool.com/2004/04/google-adds-explanation-to-jew-search.php.

166. "Steve Ballmer" article at the AskMen.com Web site, www.askmen.com/men/business_politics_60/ 68_steve_ballmer.html; "Steve Ballmer," at the Jewish Virtual Library at, www.us-israel.org/jsource/biography/ Ballmer.html, a review of Fredric Alan Maxwell's, "Bad Boy "Ballmer," at www.myshelf.com/biography/04/ badboyballmer.htm.

167. Rich Niemiec, "Retrospective: Still Growing, After All These Years," on the Oracle Web site at http://otn.oracle.com/oramag/oracle/01-nov/o61advice.htm; the *Forbes.com* profile at www.forbes.com, "Larry Ellison," at the *Ask Men* Web site, www.askmen.com/men/may00/24_larry_ellison.htm.; the October 24, 1995 interview of Lawrence Ellison on the Smithsonian Web site at http://americanhistory.si.edu/csr.comphistle/le1.html; the article, "Larry Ellison," at www.zpub.com/un/un-le.html; the review of Mike Wilson's book, *The Difference Between God and Larry Ellison*," at www.Amazon.com; Todd Wallack, "Ellison's Largess to Harvard," *San Francisco Chronicle*, June 4, 2005; Adam Cohen, "Speak, Oracle," *New York Times*, Feb 15, 2004, reviews of the books, *Software* and *Everyone Else Must Fail;* "Larry Ellison Well-Placed In Top Philanthropist List," at http://philanthropy.com; "On the Record: Larry Ellison," Sept. 7, 2003 on the *SFGate.com* Web site at www.sfgate.com/cgi-bin/article.cgi?file=/c/a/2003/ 09/07/BU87317.DTL&type=printable; and others.

168. "Mitchell Kapor Biography at www.kapor.com/homepages/mkapor/bio0701.htm, the article on Visicalc at *About.com*, http://inventors.about.com/library/weekly/aa010199.htm; and at the Dan Briklin site, www.bricklin.com/visicalc.htm; the *Wikipedia* articles on Visicalc and Lotus 123 at http://en.wikipedia.org/wiki/ and "TMF Interview With Onsale President & CEO Jerry Kaplan at www.fool.com/foolaudio/transcripts/1999/ stocktalk990211_Onsale.htm.

169. Adam Cohen, *The Perfect Store: Inside eBay*, Chapter 1 excerpts available at www.businessknowhow.com/man- age/perfectstore.htm; *Forbes.com* profiles of Pierre M. Omidyar and Jeffrey Skoll at www.forbes.com; Michael S. Mal- one, "Good Hard Work," for *ABC News* at http://abcnews.go.com/sections/business/SiliconInsider/ SiliconInsider_021119.html; the "Jeff Skoll" profile and University of Toronto speech available at www.engology.com/eng5skoll.htm; the Annual Report and other materials at the Skoll Foundation Web site, at www.skollfoundation.org; Sally Osberg, "On the Social Edge" *Philanthropy World* magazine, Vol. 9 Issue 1, available at www.philanthropyintexas.com/0901/jeff-skoll-print.htm; and investor information from http://finance.yahoo.com/ q/ks?s=EBAY; and "metrics" from the www.ebay.com Web site.

170. Bethany McLean, "Diller.com," *Fortune*, May 3, 2004, The IAC InterActiveCorp Web site at www.usainterac- tive.com; "Laura Rich, "So That's the Point Of This company," *The New York Times*, Sept. 19, 2004, "Barry Diller," at www.museum.tv/archives/etc/D/htmlD/dillerbarry/dillerbarry.htm; "Celebrity Charity Review" at www.thesmokinggun.com/foundations/list.html; Jennifer Auther, "Gore Campaigns in California, Courts Gay Voters," and other stories at http://members.shaw.ca/libraryan/rainbowthreads/barrydiller.html;

171. "Terry Semel," http://docs.yahoo.com/docs/pr/executives/semel.html; Brian Nelson, "Yahoo Founders Have Something to Whoop About," *CNN*, Sept. 16, 1995 at www.cnn.com/TECH/9509/yahoo/; "Terry Semel, Yahoo!," *Business Week* online, Sept. 29, 2003, at www.businessweek.com/magazine/content/03_39/b3851604.htm; Michael Aushenker, "The Circuit: Film Fest Fun," *The Jewish Journal*, June 6, 2003 available at, www.jewishjournal.com/ home/ preview.php?id=10675; "David Phil, Ph.D." at www.enology.com/eng5filo.htm; Marlene Adler Marks,

"McCain, Jewish Frontrunner?" *Jewish World Review*, June 13, 1999 at www.jewishworldreview.com/Marlene/marks061399.asp; and "Key Statistics," at http://finance.yahoo.com/q/ks?s=YHOO.

172. Among sources were the Qualcomm 10K, copies of mid-2005 presentations made by management, the 2004 Annual Report and other materials available on the Web site at www.qualcomm.com; "Irwin Mark Jacobs" at www.seass.upenn.edu/whatsnew/2000/jacobs-bio.html; Elizabeth Amery, "Wireless Pioneer Jacobs Leads the Way to Philanthropy," *On Philanthropy*, April 2, 2004 available at www.onphilanthropy.com/articles/print.aspx?cid=524; "Executive Profiles: Dr. Irwin M. Jacobs," at www.surferess.com/CEO/html/irwin_m_jacobs.html;
173. RealNetworks' Annual Report, Proxy, Executive Bios, financials and 10K are available at its Web site, www.realnetworks.com; with summary financial information also available at http://finance.yahoo.com/q/ks?s=RNWK; "Rob Glaser Goes After His Next Target," *Fortune*, Sept. 6, 2004; "RealNetworks Changes the Way You Look at Your PC," *CNN.com Transcripts* at www.cnn.com/TRANSCRIPTS/0010/28/cnncom.00html; Maureen O'Gara, "RealNetworks Gives Microsoft a Billion-Dollar Antitrust Suit for Xmas, *NuWorld.com*, Dec 23, 2003 available at www.linuxworld.com/story/38236_p.htm;

174. Xeni Jardin, "I'm a Maverick, Not a Mogul," *Wired*, Dec. 2003 available at www.wired.com/wired/archive/11.12/view.html?pg=3; "Mark Cuban Biography" at the Dallas Maverick's Web site, www.nba.com/mavericks/news/cuban_bio000329.htm; Jeff Heatherington, "The Mav's Money Man: Mark Cuban, *TSN Magazine*, June 30, 2004 available at http://tsn.tsnmax.ca/magazine/feature2.asp; "A Maverick Billionaire," *ABC News.com* at http://abcnew.go.com/onair/2020/2020_000504_billionaire_feature.html; "Mark Cuban," *AskMen.com* article at www.askmen.com/men/business_politics_60/60b_mark_cuban.html; Chuck Finder, "The Big Picture: Cuban's Glory, and Beyond, is a Tough Act," *Post-Gazette.com* Sports at www.post-gazette.com/sports/columnists/s0030417 thebig0417p1.asp; Ginger David, "Mark Cuban Another Business Titan Takes to TV," *Fortune*, Sept. 6, 2004.

175. Ruth Ann Minner, "Statement on the Passing of Irving Shapiro," September 11, 2001, *State of Delaware* Web site, www.state.de.us/governor/news/2001/09september/091301-%irv%

176. Arthur Levitt, "You are the Guardians," *CFO Magazine*, May 2003. Also available at www.cfo.com/article.cfm/3009202/c_3046591?f=magazine_featured

177. Richard L. Zweigenhaft and G. William Domhoff, "The New Power Elite," *Mother Jones.com*, March/April 1998 Issue., also at www.motherjones.com/news/feature/1998/03/zweigenhaft.html

178. Material on Dupont and Shapiro's tenure and role are available at the *Dupont* Web site at http://heritage.dupont.com/touchpoints/tp_1973/depth.shtml, and other pages of the http://heritage.dupont.com site.

179. Zwigenhaft, ibid.

180. Joseph D. Sarna, "A Great Jewish Awakening," an essay delivered April 26, 1995 to a Board Seminar of the Council for Initiatives in Jewish Education available at www.rebooters.net/articles/awakeningEssay.pdf.

181. Zwigenhaft, ibid.

182. Richard Tedlow, Courtney Purrington, Kim Eric Bettcher, "The American CEO in the Twentieth Century: Demography and Career Path," Harvard NOM Research Paper No. 03-21available from http://ssrn.com/abstract=383280.

183. *Encyclopædia Britannica* article on "Guggenheim, Meyer and Daniel, Britannica 2001 edition. And the article on Guggenheim at the Harvard Business School Leadership Web site at www.hbs.edu/leadership/database/leaders/348.

184. From the *Time* magazine archive for April 19, 1937, "Hart, Schaffner, Marx & Hillman," available at http:///time-proxy.yaga.com/time/archive/printout0,23657,757657,00.html and Sandra Dolbow, "The Empire's New Clothes," *Brandweek*, August 21, 2000 available at www.findarticles.com/p/articles/mi_mOBDW/is_33_41/ai_64835597/print.

185. See obituary of Rose Susan (Hirschhorn) Behrend http://legacy.net/Link.asp?ID=LS02906629, the *General Cigar Company* Web site at www.cigarworld.com/history, the article, "Acquisition Strengthens Both Parties" in the *Swedish Match*, July 2000 edition, and the interview of Edgar Cullman, Jr. in the Aug. 9, 2005 issue of *Cigar Aficionado* at www.cigaraficionado.com/Cigar/CA_Profiles?Cigar_Stars_Profile/0,2547,122

186. "Whiskey Archives," August 26, 1935, *Time Magazine* available at the *Time* magazine archive at http://time-proxy.yaga.com/time/archive/printiout/0,23657,748931,00.html.

187. Thomas Sowell, *Ethnic America*, Basic Books, 1981, p. 84

188. See the bio of Rosenwald in a separate chapter of this book which cites many references including Leon Harris, *Merchant Princes – An Intimate History of Jewish Families Who Built Great Department Stores*, Kodansha America, Inc., New York, 1994, pages 280–335.

189. Neal Gabler, *An Empire of Their Own, How the Jews Invented Hollywood*, Anchor Books, 1988, pages 11–47, among many other pages in this comprehensive story of the Jews and Hollywood.

190. Abraham K. Korman, *The Outsiders, Jews and Corporate America*, Lexington Books, Lexington, Mass., 1988.

191. "Fortune 500 Largest U.S. Corporations," *Fortune*, April 5, 2004.

192. Geoffrey Colvin, "Power 25" *Fortune*, August 9, 2005, p. 90, and August 11, 2003.

193. Biography of Sanford Weill from *Academy of Achievement* Web site available at www.achievement.org/autodoc/printmember/wei0bio-1, as well as the bio at *Wikipedia*, http://en.wikipedia.org/wiki/Sanford_I._Weill, and the bibliography at http://wilsontxt2.hwwilson.com/wbd/1983/024/262/abi/00001001.htm.

194. Komansky bio at www.justpeople.com/Content/New/People/Leaders/DB/DavidKomansky.asp, *Merrill Lynch* Web site including www.ml.com/index.asp?id=7695_7696_8149_8688_8588_8178, and the *Vault Career Library* file on Merrill Lynch.

195. Among other sources, see, "Maurice R. Greenberg," *Business Week*, Jan. 14, 2002 available at www.businessweek.com/magazine/content/02_02/b3765033.htm, Noam Scheiber, "Sins of the Son, *New York*, at http://www.newyorkmetro.com/nymetro/news/bizfinance/biz/features/10348/ , The Starr Foundation home page at http://fdncenter.org/grantmaker/starr/; James Bandler, "Hank's Last Stand," *Fortune*, Oct. 13, 2008; Serena Ng and Liam Pleven, "New AIG Rescue Is Bank Blessing," Liam Pleven and Marshall Eckblad, "Under Burden of U.S. Rescue, AIG Chief's Aim IS for a Redo," and, Serena Ng, Carrick Mollenkamp and Michael Siconolfi, "AIG Faces $10 Billion in Losses on Bad Bets," *The Wall Street Journal*, Nov. 12, Dec. 3, and Dec 10, 2008 respectively;and others.

196. Joshua Cooper Ramo, "Grove is Time Magazine's Man of the Year 1997" *Time*, Dec. 29, 1997. available at www.heinzawards.net/articleDetail.asp?articleID=30 and others.

197.Bebeto Matthews, "Former CBS head Tisch dies at 80," *USA Today*, Nov. 15, 2003 available at www.usatoday.com/news/nation/2003-11-15-obit-tisch_x.htm, and the CBS obituary at www.cbsnews.com/stories/2003/11/15/national/main583867.html.

198. "Corporate Governance Case Study – American Express" an article at the Web site, www.cg.org.cn/english/practice/AE.asp, Kenneth Chenault's statement on the Amex Web site at www.onlineproxy.com/amex/2001/ar/sh_shareholder.htm., the American Express material at *Wikipedia*, http://en.wikipedia.org/wiki/American_Express, and others.

199. The Museum of Broadcast Communications has a bio of Levin at www.museum.tv/archives/ etv/L/htmlL/levingerald/levingerald.htm. Mark Lewis, "Levin's Legacy at AOL Time Warner," *Forbes*, May 17, 2002 at www.forbes.com/2002/05/17/0517levin.html., and others.

200. Dell's bio is available at www.askmen.com/men/january00/8_michale_dell.html, Also see the Dell Web site at www1.us.dell.com/content/topics/global.aspx/corp/biographies/en/Michael_dell?

201. Goldstein profile at the *Country Music Hall of Fame* Web site at http://songwritershalloffamc.org//award_recipient_details.asp?ceremonyId=25&aw, the *Aish.com* staff, Profile: Beyond Toys" at www.aish.com/society/Work/work/Profile_Beyond_Toys.asp, the Charles Lazarus profile at www.hbs.edu/leadership/database/leasers/512/ The *About.com* story, "Toys 'R' US Finds New CEO" at http://retailindustry.about.com/library/weekly/aa011200a.htm., and the *Toys 'R' Us* site, www.toysrus.com/about/ourHistory.cfm.

202. "Leslie Wexner" at http://leslie-wexner.biography.ms/, John Kazalia, "Columbus Money Mogul" on the *About* Web site at http://columbusoh.about.com/cs/famouspeople/a/wexner.htm. and the 2004 *Annual Report for Limited Brands*, in particular the letter from the CEO, Les Wexner.

203. Kaufman's bio appears on the *Cyberposium* Web site at www.cyberposium.com/kaufman.asp, Arrow's history and Corporate Overview are available at www.arrow.com/about_arrow/index.html.

204. Platt's bios at the *Wikipedia* site at www.wikipedia.org/wiki/Lewis_Platt, *Forbes* Web site at www.forbes.com/finance/mktguideapps/personinfo/FromMktGuideldPersonTearsheet.jhtml? The *SETI Institute* Web site at http://www.seti.org/site/pp.asp?c=ktj2j9MMlsE&b=279527.

205. "Harry Kamen Profile at *Forbes* Web site, www.forbes.com, and at Met Life, www.metlife.com, and information about Met Life from its own Web site and from the *LookSmart* Web site at www.findarticles.com/p/articles/mi_qa3653/is_199505/ai_n8724093/print, the *NASD* Web site, www.nasd.com, and the *Renaissance Weekend* site, www.renaissanceweekend.org.

206. Bland bios are from the *Zero Million.com* Web site at www.zeromillion.com/entrepreneurship/stories/arthur-blank.html, the *Atlanta Falcons'* Web site at www.atlantafalcons.com/team/frontOfficeBio.jsp?id=87, and from *Answers.com*.

207. Sternberg's bio at www.mccombs.utexas.edu/students/ubc/programs/vip/whitacre.html, is complimented by the *New York Life Annual Report* and *Proxy* statement. See www.newyorklife.com

208. Among others, see, www.museum.tv/archives/etv/R/htmlR/redstonesum/restonesum.htm.

209. Hess is among executives profiled on the www.Forbes.com site, and he and the company are covered on the Buy Blue site at www.buyblue.org/archives/2005/02/prodigy.html, the USLTA site at www.usta.com and the Amerada Hess Web site at http://phx.corporate-ir.net. Additional information is available at www.snopes.com/inboxer/boycotts/hess.asp.

210. Among sources for this material are: Morton, Fredric, *The Rothschilds: A Family Portrait*, Fawcett Publications, Greenwich, Conn. 1961, Wechsberg, Joseph, *The Merchant Bankers*, Pocket Books, New York, 1966, pages 1–14, 196–9 and 262–86, Johnson, *A History of the Jews*, pages 306–10, *Encyclopædia Britannica 2001 Deluxe Edition* articles: "Rothschild Family," " Mayer Amschel Rothschild," "Rothschild Bibliography," "The Second Generation," "Lionel Walter Rothschild," Rishon LeZiyyon," "Bordeaux Wine: Medoc," and "Balfour Declaration," reviews of Niall Ferguson, *The House of Rothschild: Money's Prophets 1798–1848*, Viking, New York, 1998 by Geoffrey Wheatcroft in *The New York Times*, Dec. 20, 1998, Joseph Mandel, *Business Week*, Dec. 7, 1998, Stanley Weintraub, *The Wall Street Journal*, Richard Bernstein's Nov. 4, 1996 *New York Times* review of Amos Elon's book, *Founder: a Portrait of the First Rothschild and His Time*, Viking, New York, 1996, as well as the Rothschild Web site at www.rothschild.info/history/default.asp?doc=articles/chistory1-1,2,3,4,5,6,7, the Wikipedia articles at http://en.wikipedia.org/wiki/Mayer_Amschel_Rothschild_family, and related Wikipedia pages dealing with the family, and the Rothschild articles at www.jewishencyclopedia.com as well as other Web sites.

211. The image is Mayer Amschel's five sons, clockwise from the top: Solomon, Amschel, Karl, James, and Nathan. There is no known likeness of their father.

212. Rabbi Dr. Yitzhak Dov Paris' lecture, "On Taking Interest," May 17, 2003, Bar-Ilan University Parashat Hashavua Study Center, available at www.biu.ac.il/JH/Parasha/eng/bahar/par.html.

213. Johnson, p. 172 and Jewish Encyclopedia.com, article, "Loss on a Debt."

214. *Encyclopædia Britannica 2001*, article "Usury – India: Finance."

215. Johnson, p. 172.

216. Jewish Encyclopedia.com article, "Case of a Gentile."

217. Johnson, pages173–4.

218. Johnson, p. 173.

219. Ibid.

220. Jewish Encyclopedia.com "Case of a Gentile."

221. Johnson, p. 172.

222. Johnson, pages 248 & 251.

223. Rabbi Doniel Neustadt, *Weekly Halacha*, "Interest (Ribbis) With a Corporation," at http://torah.org/advanced/weekly-halach/5758/behar.html.

224. About.com Web site article, "Usury," at http://atheism.about.com/library/glossary/western/bldef_usury.htm.

225. Johnson, p. 174.

226. *Encyclopædia Britannica*, article "Shari'ah: Law of transactions," and "Iran, Finance."

227. Patrick O'Gilfoil Healy, "For Muslims, Loans for the Conscience," *The New York Times*, Aug. 7, 2005, p. 216.

228. Johnson, p. 176.

229. Johnson, pages175–179 & 193–242.

230. Johnson, p. 171.

231. Johnson, p. 178.

232. Johnson, p. 174.

233. Johnson, p. 176.

234. Johnson, p. 253.

235. Johnson, p. 258.

236. Johnson, p. 213.

237. The Medici Archive Project article, "The Jews and the Medici," at www.medici.org/jewish/jewmedici.html.

238. Elliott Horowitz, "Families and Their Fortunes" in David Biale's *Cultures of the Jews*, Schocken Books, New York, 2002 pages 589–622.

239. Eli Barnavi, *A Historical Atlas of the Jewish People*, Schocken Books, 2002, p. 111.

240. *Fortune*, "Most Admired: The List of Industry Champs," Mar. 6, 2006, p. 81.

241. Thompson Financial, Global M&A League Tables as posted to the Rothschild.com Web site at www.rothschild.com/investmentbanking/ibleague.asp?id=ib-regional-manda.

242. "Bloomberg, M&A Financial Advisory League Tables," 1/1/05 – 3/31/05 as provided by the Web site, http://ibcm.sa.utoronto.ca/pdfs/mnaranking.pdf.

243. Goldman Sachs materials come from: American Jewish Historical Society, *American Jewish Desk Reference*, Random House, New York, 1999 pages 214, & 236; Excerpts from *Wall Street Financial Capital* at www.nybookdistributors.com/wall_street/feature/goldman.html; the Goldman Sachs Web site at www.gs.com; Reviews of Lisa Endlich's, *Goldman Sachs: The Culture of Success* at www.Amazon.com and www.Target.com Web sites; Patricia Sellers, "Hank Paulson's Secret Life," *Fortune*, Jan. 12, 2004; "Steven Friedman" at www.whitehouse.gov; Liz Peek, "Goldman Sachs Before the Storm," *The Wall Street Journal*, Oct. 1, 2008; "Goldman Sachs, Into the Whirlwind," *Economist*, Sept. 27, 2008.

244. Lehman materials come from: Stephen Birmingham, *Our Crowd: The Great Jewish Families of New York*, Syracuse University Press, pages 336 & 377, *Wall Street Financial Capital* article "Lehman Brothers;" the Lehman Brothers Web site at www.lehman.com, "Herbert Henry Lehman," at www.jewishvirtuallibrary.org/jsource/biography/lehman.html, Shawn Tully, "The End of Wall Street," *Fortune*, Sept. 21, 2008.

245. Kuhn, Loeb materials com from: Jewish Historical Society, *Desk Reference* pages 214, 238/9; Asher B. Etkes and Saul Stadtmauer, p. 175; Ron Chernow, *The Warburgs*, Random House, New York, 1993, p. 699; and profiles of Jacob Schiff, Otto Kahn, and Paul Warburg from www.spartacus.schoolnet.co.uk/USA.

246. Bear Stearns materials come from: *Wall Street Financial Capital* article "Bear Stearns;" Richard Teitelbaum and Margaret Popper, "Winning Streak at Bear Stearns," Bloomberg Markets, Aug. 2003 at www.bloomberg.com/media/markets/web.aug03.bearst.pdf; C.J. Prince, "In Search of the Bear Market," *The Chief Executive*, Jan. 2002 from www.findarticles.com; Ace Greenberg's bio at the Horatio Alger Awards Web site, www.horatioalger.com; the write up on Bear Stearns on the I won careers Web site at http://www1.iwon.com; the Bear Stearns Web site, www.bearstearns.com; the reviews of his book, *Memos From the Chairman*, at www.amazon.com; Robert Savit, "To the Bear Stearns Minyan, One Last Time," *The Yeshiva World*, May 30, 2008, at http://209.85.173.104/search?q=cache:NPuK_Gt3SOEJ:theyeshivaworld; Duff McDonald, "The Generosity Index," at www.portfolio.com/executive/features/2007/12/17/Top-50-Char...Jan 2008 Issue; "Bear Stearns," at http://en.wikipedia.org/wiki/Bear_Stearns; and others.

247. Lazard materials come from American Jewish Historical Society, p. 218; the Lazard Web site at www.lazard.com; the article on Lazard at Vault, the job search site at www.vault.com; reviews of, *Financier: Biography of Andre Meyer*, at FetchBook.co.uk ; Seymour "Sy" Brody, "Eugene Isaac Meyer" at the Jewish Virtual Library Web site www.jewishvirtuallibrary.org/source/biography/emeyer.html; Sawaya Zina, "Tough Guys With a Genteel Manner: Lazard Freres & Co.," *Forbes*, Jul. 10, 1989 available at www.highbeam.com; the bio of Vernon Jordan at www.thehistorymakers.com Web site and others.

248. Citigroup materials come from the Citigroup Web site at www.citigroup.com; Ari Weinberg, "Weill Leaves Corner Office, Not the Building," *Forbes*, Jul. 16, 2003 at www.forbes.com; Heather Timmons, "Sanford Weill: The Trouble With Sandy," *Business Week*, Nov. 25, 2002 at http://static.elibrary.com; the story, "Sanford Weill to Receive Emma Lazarus Award" at the American Jewish Historical Society Web site www.ajhs.org; Yvette Kantrow, "Spitzer Speaks," *The Deal*, Nov. 15, 2002 at www.thedeal.com; the Citicorp profile at http://wsj.com; Tomas Kellner, "Payback Time," *Forbes* Apr. 12, 2004; "Prince Alwaleed Bin Talal Alsaud," at www.forbes.com/lists/2008/10/billionaires08_Prince-Alwaleed-Bin-Talal-Alsaud_ORDO.html; "Vikram Pandit," and "Gajanan Maharaj," at http://en.wikipedia.org/wiki/Vikram_Pandit; and wiki/Gajanan_Maharaj.

249. Salomon materials come from American Jewish Historical Society, p. 218; Silbiger, p. 77; Michael Lewis, *Liar's Poker*, W. W. Norton, New York, 1989; the corporate time line at www.sbam.com/SBAM /html/history.html; Richard D. Freedman and Velvet V. Mickens, "Salomon Brothers: 'Apologies are Bullshit'" from the NYU Stern School of Business at http://casenet.thomsonlearning.com/casenet/ abstracts/salomon_apologies.html

250. Warburg materials come from Ron Chernow, *The Warburgs*, Random House, New York, 1993, pages 4,5, 13, 508, 699; Etkes, p. 176; American Jewish Historical Society, pages 238–9; *Wall Street Financial Capital* article "Warburg Dillon Read;" the M.M. Warburg Web site at www.mmwarburg.com, the UBS Web site at www.ubs.com; the CSFB Web site at www.credit-suisse.com, and www.csfb.com.

251. Wasserstein materials com from: reviews of Bruce Wasserstein's *Big Deal* at www.amazon.com; and by Leah Nathans Spiro, "Wasserstein's M&A 101," *Business Week*, Apr. 16, 1998; "Will Wasserstein Make It? Wasserstein Choice Stirs Big Questions, *New York Observer*, Dec. 10, 2001; a description of Wasserstein & Co at www.wasserco.com; the i-won career recruiting site write up on Wasserstein Perella at http://www1.iwon.com/home /careers/company_profile/0,15623,803,00.html; "Dresdner, Wasserstein Talk," *CNN Money*, Sep. 12, 2000 at http://money.com/2000/09/12/deals/dresdner; "Masters of the Deal," *Newsday*, Mar. 15, 2002 at www.newsday.com/business/ny-nnymast0315.story; and others.

252. Oppenheimer materials come from: *Wall Street Financial Capital* article "CIBC World Markets;" the Oppenheimer Web site at www.opco.com; "Fahnstock Viner Holdings Inc. to Acquire CIBC Oppenheimer's U.S. Private Client and U.S. Asset Management Business," a press release issued Dec. 10, 2002; the profile of CIBC Oppenheimer Corp. at www.nextwavestocks.com; the CIBC Web site at www.cibc.com; the Oppenheimer Funds site at www.oppenheimerfund.com and the article, "Oppenheimer Capital Names Bruce Koepfgen CEO" on the Pimco Web site, www.pimcoadvisors.com.

253. Cantor Fitzgerald materials come from: the Cantor Web site at www.cantor.com; "Making a Difference in a Difficult Year," *Forward*, Nov. 9, 2000; Maryl Gordon, "Howard Lutnick's Second Life," *New York*, Dec. 10, 2001 and available at www.newyorkmetro.com; "Wall Street Counts the Cost," *BBC News*, Sep. 13, 2001 at http://news.bbc.co.uk/1/hi/business/1542021; Riva D. Atlas, "Firm That Was Hit Hard on 9/11 Grows Anew," *The New York Times*, Sep. 10, 2004, and Charles V. Bagli, "Firm That Lost 658 in Twin Towers Finds a Home on 59th," *The New York Times*, Jul. 27, 2004; and others.

254. Drexel materials come from: *Encyclopædia Britannica* article, "Michael R. Milken;" Jeff Scott, "Drexel Burnham Lambert: A Ten Year Retrospective," a paper delivered to the Austrian Scholar's Conference at Auburn University, Mar. 23–24, 2000; Deirdre Griswold, "From Firestone to Junk Bonds: Capitalist Plunder Lurks Behind Liberia's Chaos," from http://mailman.efn.org; Etkes, p. 168; and others.

255. Allen & Co. materials come from: Ken Auletta, "The Consigliore," *The New Yorker*, May 22, 1995 available at www.kenauletta.com; Alex Gove, "There is no Shortage of Star Power at Mr. Allen's Sun Valley Retreats," *Red Herring*, Oct. 1996 at www.bilderberg.org/sunvalley.htm; Dyan Machan, "Herbert Allen and His Merry Dealsters," *Forbes*, Jul. 1, 1996; Carol Loomis, "Allen & Co.: Inside the Private World of Allen & Co.," *Fortune*, Jun. 14, 2004; the write up on Allen & Co at Vault, the career search firm www.vault.com; and others.

256. Republic Bank/Edmond Safra materials come from: "Celebrities in Switzerland: Edmond Safra" at http://switzerland.isyours.com/d/Beruehmtheiten/bios/76.html; "Fed Approves $9.8 Billion Merger of Republic, HSBC Holdings," *Associated Press*, Dec. 6, 1999; bio of Edmond Safra at www.infoplease.com; "Republic New York Corporation," at www.scripopoly.net/repnewyorcor.html; and others.

257. C.E. Unterberg Towbin materials come from: their Web site www.unterberg.com; and others.

258. Bache materials come from: *Wall Street: Financial Capital* article "Prudential Securities;" Kurt Eichenwald, *Serpent on the Rock*, Harper Business, New York 1995; Etkes, p. 175.

259. J.&W. Seligman materials come from: *Wall Street: Financial Capital* article "J & W Seligman;" and its Web site at www.seligman.com.

260. Inductees, Private Equity Hall of Fame at www.assetnews.com/ped/hall_of_fame/inductees.htm.

261. Material on KKR comes from: the KKR Web site www.kkr.com; Bryan Burrough & John Helyar, *Barbarians at the Gate*, Harper & Row, New York, 1990, pages 131–45; *Desk Reference*, p. 226.

262. Material on Thomas H. Lee company comes from: the speaker biography of Thomas H. Lee at http://ww7.kellogg.nwu.edu/conference/privateequity/2001/speakers.html; Colin C. Haley, "Thomas H. Lee Raises $6 Billion Fund," at http://boston.internet.com/news/article.php/570501; Hoover's profile of Thomas H. Lee company at www.hoovers.com; and at Yahoo, http://biz.yahoo.com/ic/40/40463.html; "Thomas Lee Gives Harvard $22 Million," *Harvard University Gazette*, Sep. 12, 1996 at www.new.harvard.edu/gazette/1996/09.12/ThomasLeeGivesH.html; "Thomas H. Lee," at http://.en.wikipedia.org/wiki/Thomas_H._Lee; and others.

263. Material on Blackstone comes from: Blackstone's Web site at www.blackstone.com; "Biggest Sharks See Market Value Rise," *Challenge*, Aug. 7, 2002 at www.plp.org/cd02/cd0807.html; Michael McKee, "Corporate Bigwigs Can Learn – Ski, Hobnob at Davos Bash," *Seattle Times*, Jan. 21, 2004 at http://seattletimes.nwsource.com; "Blackstone Group," at http://en.wikipedia.org/wiki/ Blackstone_Group.

264. Quantum/Soros material comes from: *Desk Reference* p. 237; the profile of George Soros at Investopedia.com; Jeanne Cummings, "Soros Has a Hunch Bush Can be Beat," *The Wall Street Journal*, Feb. 5, 2004, p. A4.

265. Steinhardt material comes from: NYO Staff, "An Investor's Obsession: Being Right," *New York Observer*, Jan. 14, 2002 at www.findarticles.com; Robert Lenzer, "Michael Steinhardt's Voyage Around His Father," *Forbes*, Nov. 8, 2001; a profile of Steinhardt at www.streetstories.com; his profile at www.investopedia.com; Rabbi Avi Shafran, "Bringing Wall Street Wisdom to the Quest for Jewish Continuity," at www.jewishworldreview.com; "Steinhardt's Make Historic Gift to NYU's School of Education," *NYU Today* Nov. 16, 2000 at www.nyu.edu; "Hillel's New Home," *UPenn Almanac*, Feb. 6, 2004 at www.upen.edu; his "Staff Profile," at www.jewishrenaissancemedia.com/staff.htm; Riva D. Atlas, "A Maverick Investor and Giver," *The New York Times*, Jul. 15, 2005 p. C7; and others.

266. Epstein Material comes from: Landon Thomas, Jr. "Jeffrey Epstein: International Moneyman of Mystery," *New York*, Oct. 28, 2002, at www.newyorkmetro.com; Larry Keller, "Banker Epstein Pleads In Prostitution Case, Gets 18 Months," *Palm Beach Post*, June 30, 2008; "Jeffrey Epstein," at http://en.wikipedia.org/wiki/Jeffrey_Epstein.

267. Caxton/Kovner material comes from: "Bruce Kovner," *Forbes* profile, 2003 and 2008 at www.forbes.com; his profile as Chairman of Julliard at www.julliard.edu/press/kovner.html; Andy Serwer, "The $11 Billion Man," *Fortune*, Sep. 29, 2003 at www.fortune.com; "Caxton Jumps to Top of the Pile," *Hedge Fund Intelligence Press Room* May 19, 2003 at www.hedgefundintelligence.com; "Like Father, Like Sun," *Blog Spot*, Apr. 12, 2002 at http://parsol1789.blogspot.com; "New Daily Newspaper to be Launched in New York City," *The New York Sun*, Jan. 15, 2002; and "Bruce Kovner at http://en.wikipedia.org/wiki/Bruce_Kovner; others.

268. Odyssey/Levy & Nash material comes from: Ian Kaplan, a review of Leon Levy's book, *The Mind of Wall Street*, in *Public Affairs*, Jun. 2003 at www.bearcave.com; Jamie Carr, "Where Have All the Gurus Gone?" *Moneyweb*, Apr. 11, 2003 at http://m1.mny.co.za/; an abstract of Jeff Madrick & Leon Levy's feature article, "Wall Street Blues" from *The New York Review of Books*, Oct. 8, 1998, at www.nybooks.com/articles/729; Robert Lenzner, "Leon Levy Dies at 77," *Forbes*, Apr 7, 2003; Abha Bhattarai, "Jack Nash, Pioneer in Hedge Funds, Dies at 79," *The New York Times*, Aug 2, 2008.

269. Third Avenue/Whitman material comes from: Hillary Rosenberg, *The Vulture Investors*, Harper Business, New York, 1992, pages 9–41; Tom Raynor, "The Worldly Wisdom of Marty Whitman," *Syracuse University Magazine*, Winter 2003–4 at http://sumagazine.syr.edu; the Third Avenue Web site at www.thirdavenuefunds.com; "Focused on Academics, The Lois and Martin Whitman Scholars" at http://sominfo.syr.edu/about/magazine/fall2002/givingreport.pdf.

270. Neuberger & Berman materials some from: the Neuberger Berman Web site at www.nb.com; and "Roy Neuberger," at http://en.Wikipedia.org/wiki/Roy_Neuberger.

271. Appolo/Black materials come from: "Leon D. Black '73," a bio at www.dartmouth.edu; and another at

www.wharton-pec.org/conf2003/keynote_black.asp; the Apollo profile at http://biz.yahoo.com; another at www.hoovers.com; Office of the Attorney General, "Multibillion-Dollar Junk Bond Portfolio Undersold for Major Loss to State," a press release dated Jan. 30, 2002; "Leon Black," and "Apollo Management" at http://en.wikipedia.org/ wiki/Leon_Black and wiki/Appolo_Management; "Ellie Winninghoff, "No Assurances," *Mother Jones*, Jan. 16, 2002 available at www.motherjones.com; and others

272. Hellman materials come from: the Hellman & Friedman LLC Web site at www.hf.com; "A Casual Approach to Success: Warren Hellman," *Harvard Business School Bulletin*, Mar. 2003, at www.alumni.hbs.edu; Doug Robson, "Never Underestimate an Investor Named Warren," *Business Week*, May 7, 2001, at www.businessweek.com; his profile "F. Warren Hellman," at www.forbes.com; bios of Shorenstein company Advisory Board Members at www.shorenstein.com; the Freidman Fleischer & Lowe Web site at www.fflpartners.com; Clifford Carlsen, "Tully Fried-man Steps Out With $800M Buyout Fund," *San Francisco Business Times*, May 1, 1998 at www.bizjournals.com/ sanfrancisco/stories/ 1998; and others.

273. Blum materials come from: the Blum Capital Partners Web site, www.blumcapital.com; Tom Abate, "Profile: Richard Blum, The Man Behind URS, Next to Sen. Feinstein," *San Francisco Chronicle*, May 11, 2003 at www.sfgate.com; Blum's bio on being appointed a University of California regent, Mar. 18, 2002 at www.haas.berkeley.edu: and his later bio at www.universityofcalifornia.edu/regents/regbios/blum.html; others.

274. Rock materials come from: Louis Fabian, "Arthur Rock," *HBS Bulletin*, Dec. 1997, at www.alumni.hbs.edu/ bulletin/1997/december/rock.html; his profile in the Private Equity Hall of Fame at www.assetnews.com/ped/ hall_of_fame/rock.htm; and at www.computerhistory.org; his profile at www.forbes.com; the press release "Arthur Rock Elected to NASD Board of Governors," Jul. 1, 1998 at http://registeredrep.com/mag/ finance_arthur_rock_elected/. "Jewish Giants," Apr. 14, 2000 at www.jewishsf.com; and others.

275. Kleiner materials come from: Matthew Yi, "Fairchild Founder, Engineer to the End," *San Francisco Chronicle*, Nov. 26, 2003; Leslie Goff, "1958: The Birth of Integrated Circuits," *Computerworld*," May 19, 1999 at www.cnn.com/TECH/computing/9905/19/1958.idg; Wally Bock, "Postcards From the Digital Age: Eugene Kleiner and the Making of Silicon Valley," Dec. 8, 2003, at www.bockinfo.com; the KPCB profile at the Private Equity Hall of Fame at www.assetnews.com;

276. Rosen materials come from: "Gentlemen, Start Your Engine," *Fortune*, Sep. 30, 1996, "Ben Rosen," at www.smartcomputing.com; Rosen's *Industry Hall of Fame* bio at www.crn.com/sections/ Special/HOF/ hof00.asp?ArticleID=21433; and others.

277. Moritz materials from: Emily Douglas, "The Golden Google Touch," *Forbes*, Jan. 24, 2008; "Sir Terry Still 'Wales Richest'" at BBC News site, http://newsvote.bbc.co.uk/mpapps/pagetools/print/news.bbc.co.uk/1/hi; Adam Lashinsky, "Google's Banker," *Wall Street Week With Fortune*, at www.pbs.org/wsw/news/ fortunearticle_20040503_01.html;

278. Patricof materials from: Neil Cavuto interview Jan. 19, 2004 at www.foxnews.com; his bio at *Venture Capital Journal* at www.ventureeconomics.com/vcj/protected/ZZZ905OUMYC.html; and another at www.trickleup.org; Peter Gingold, "Private Equity Pioneers Educate Students," *The Bottom Line On Line*, Columbia Business School at http://www3.gsb.columbia.edu/botline/fall02/1010/. His bio in the Private Equity Hall of Fame at www.assetnews.com; "Quotes From Alan Patricof" at www.cis.ohio-state.edu/~kumars/Alan Patricof.html; and, Michael Wolff, "Bonfire of the Securities," *Wired*, Jun. 1998.

279. Perry materials includes Marcia Vickers, "Looking for Trouble," Fortune Sept. 1, 2008 "Richard Perry," at the City File Web site: http://cityfile.com/profiles/richard-perry; and others

280. de Hirsch materials come from *Encyclopædia Britannica* article "Hirsch, Maurice, baron de," Clara de Hirsch, "Baron Maurice de Hirsch," *Jewish Virtual Library* at www.us-israel.org; and others.

281. Baruch materials come from: American Jewish Historical Society, pages 211 & 214.

282. Morgenthau, Jr's material comes from: His bio at *Wikipedia*, http://en.wikipedia.org; "Henry Morgenthau, Jr. (1891–1967)," at www.pbs.org/wgbh/amex/holocaust/peopleevents/pandeAMEX97.html; his U.S. Department of the Treasury bio at www.ustreas.gov; *Encyclopædia Britannica* "Henry Morgenthau, Jr.; and others.

283. Icahn materials come from: American Jewish Historical Society, p. 217; Form 10-K/A for National Energy Group, Inc., on file with the Securities and Exchange Commission an available at http://biz.yahoo.com; Press release, "Phillip Services Corporation Approves Plan Sponsor for Reorganization Plan," Sep. 12, 2003, from http://quickstar.clari.net; "Bankrupt National Airlines is Icahn's Latest Acquisition Target," *World Airline News,* Jun. 8, 2001 at www.findarticles.com; "Comic Wars: How Two Tycoons Battled Over Marvel Comics Empire—and Both Lost," at www.world-literature.com; and others.

284. Perelman materials come from: "Ron Perelman" profile at www.askmen.com; and in *Cigar Aficionado* and at www.cigaraficionado.com; Lloyd Grove with Beth Berselli, "Ron Perelman, Butt of the Funnies," *The Reliable Source,* Oct. 28, 1999 at www.comicscommunity.com; his bio at www.infoplease.com; Larry McShane, "Perelman v. Duff: A Divorce of the Vanities," *The Globe and Mail,* Apr. 19, 1999; Street Life: Andy Serwer, "Rage Against the Ronald Perelman, That Is," *Fortune,* Nov. 26, 2001; and his bio at www.forbes.com.

285. Goldsmith materials come from: "Flamboyant Goldsmith Dies of Heart Attack," *BBC Politics ninety-seven* at www.bbc.co.uk; "Sir James Goldsmith, Tycoon," at www.goodbyemag.com/may97/goldsmith.html; Sir James Goldsmith, "Sleepwalking Into the European Super State," a speech given at the 1996 Referendum Party Conference, also at www.bullen.comon.co.uk; Jorg Zipprick, "Laurent: A Billionaire's Dream," *Paris Pages,* Jun. 1995 at www.paris.org/Jorg/Resto/june95.L.html; John Lloyd, "Will it be Jams Tomorrow?" *New Statesman,* Oct. 18, 1996, at www.findarticles.com; and others.

286. Leucadia/Cumming/Steinberg materials come from: Peter Loftus, "Leucadia Has Kept Low Profile While Expanding Portfolio, *The Wall Street Journal,* Jul. 12, 2004 at www.wsj.com; the Leucadia profiles at: www.forbes.com; www.smartmoney.com/wsj/briefingbooks/, *Morningstar* at http://quicktake.morningstar.com; *Hoovers* at www.hoovers.com; *Reuters* at http://yahoo.investor.reuters.com; bios of Steinberg and Cumming at www.forbes.com; and the Leucadia National Corporation 10K, Dec. 31, 2003.

287. Tisch materials from: American Jewish Historical Society, pages 215, 237–8; "Former CBS Head Tisch Dies at 80," *USA Today,* November 15, 2003, at USATODAY.com; Katrina Brooker, "Like Father, Like Son," *Fortune,* Jun. 28, 2004; "Ex-CBS Head Tisch Dead at 80," *CBSNews.com,* Nov. 15, 2003; "Laurence Tisch," at http://en.wikipedia.org/wiki/Laurence_Tisch; "The Laurence A. Tisch Page and Loews Corporation" at, http://www.smokershistory.com/Tisch.htm.

288. Pritzker material comes from: American Jewish Historical Society, p. 215; Stephanie Fitch, "Shaking the Family Tree," *Forbes,* Sep. 30, 2002 and "Pritzker Vs. Pritzker, *Forbes,* Nov. 24, 2003; Dan Ackman, "Liesel Pritzker, Meet Meadow Soprano," *Forbes,* December 11. 2002, Penelope Patsuris, "A Hyatt IPO? Not So Hot," *Forbes,* Dec. 12, 2002, and bios of Robert A., and Thomas J. Pritzker at www.forbes.com; Shane Tritsch, "Family Circus," *Boston Magazine* at www.bostonmagazine.com; "The House of Pritzker," *Business Week,* Mar. 17, 2003 at www.businessweek.com; "Pritzker Family Donates $30 Million to the University of Chicago, Jun. 5, 2002 at www.uchospitals.edu; and others.

289. Crown materials come from: Silbiger, pages 48,89; "Henry Crown," bios at the Harvard Business School Web site, "20th Century Great American Business Leaders, www.hbs.edu at www.horatioalger.com; at www.forbes.com; at www.engology.com; and at www.aspeninstitute.org; "Henry Crown an company Profile" at http://biz.yahoo.com/ ic/40/40214.html; "$2 Million Gift From Crown Family Creates University Professorship," *Duke News Service* at www.campaign.duke.edu; bio of James S. Crown at http://orgchart.uchicago.edu; www.forbes.com; and others.

290. Bloomberg material from: *Wall Street: Financial Capital* article "Bloomberg L.P.;" various items from the Bloomberg L.P. Web site at www.bloomberg.com; Jim Rutenberg, "Bloomberg, in Israel Trip, Shies Away From Religiosity," *The New York Times,* Mar. 17, 2005 at www.nytimes.com; his bio at http://en.wikipedia.org; and profile, Jan. 1, 2002 at www.BBC.com; and at www.askmen.com; Jill Gardner, "Role of Mayor at Bloomberg LP Is Eyed, *The New York Sun,* Oct 5, 2007; Michael Bloomberg," at www.forbes.com/lists/2008/10/ billionaires08_Michael-Bloomberg; "Bloomberg L.P. at http:en.wikipedia.org/wiki/Bloomberg_L._P.

291. Wolfensohn material from: Etkes, p. 177; Paul Magnusson, a review of Sebastian Mallaby's *The World's Banker,* Penguin Press, 2004, in *Business Week,* Oct. 24, 2004; Wolfensohn's bio at www.oracle.com; at; the World Bank site, http://web.worldbank.org; and a bio and interview at http://abilitymagazine.com.

292. Rukeyser material from www.rukeyser.com; and http://en.wikipedia.org/wiki/Louis_Rukeyser.

293. Salomon materials from: *Encyclopædia Britannica,* "Salomon, Haym," American Jewish Historical Society, p. 213; and "Haym Salomon and the Lost Pages of American History," in *The Jewish Roots of Christianity* pages at www.rbooker.com.

294. Among sources for the Lener section: Hyder Jawad, "The Shaping of the Lerner Legend," *Birmingham Post,* Sep. 9, 2006; "Alfred Lerner," at the Horatio Alger Web site, www.horatioalger.com/ members/ member_info.cfm?memberid=LER98; Tom Withers, "Browns Owner Al Lerner Dies at 69," *AP Sports,* Oct 24, 2002; Richard Goldstein, "Alfred Lerner, 69, Banker; Revived Cleveland Browns," *The New York Times,* Oct 25, 2002; "Al Lerner – Former Marine & Cleveland Brown Owner," at the *Marine Corp Web site,* www.leatherneck.com/forums/ showthread.php?t=1998; "Al Lerner," at www.jewishvirtuallibrary.org/ jsource/biography/AlLerner.html; and others.

295. Among the major sources for this introduction are: Genesis 12–23, *The Jewish Bible – Tanakh – The Holy Scriptures*, The Jewish Publication Society, Philadelphia – Jerusalem, 1985; Eli Barnavi, Editor, *A Historical Atlas of the Jewish People*, Schocken Books, New York 2002; Martin Gilbert, *The Routledge Atlas of Jewish History*, Routledge, London and New York; Paul Johnson, *A History of the Jews*, Harper Perennial, New York, 1988; "Economic History," and "Agriculture," *Encyclopedia Judaica*, CD Rom Edition, Judaica Multimedia (Israel) Ltd.; "Jewish History," the article at http://www.bigpedia.com/encyclopedia/Jewish_history; *Encyclopaedia Britannica*, Ultimate Reference Suite on DVD, Chicago, 2007

296. "The Cave of Machpelah" at http://www.jewishvirtuallibrary.org/jsource/Judaism/machpelah.html.

297. Genesis 12 – 17 and, http://en.wikipedia.org/wiki/Covenant_(biblical).

298. *Historical Atlas*, p. 1.

299. Among other sources, Johnson, pages 152–3; "Ancient History: Creating the Canon," at My Jewish Learning.com http://www.myjewishlearning.com/history_community/Ancient/ReligionandCultureTO/Redaction_.htm; "Biblical Canon," at http://en.wikipedia.org/wiki/Biblical_canon; Rav Adin Steinsaltz interview in Pierre-Henry Salfati's DVD, *Talmud*, Arte Video, Paris, and Facets Video, Chicago, 2007.

300. Johnson pages 162–3 and *Historical Atlas* pages 65, 77; "Sassanian Dynasty" and "History of Mesopotamia." *Encyclopaedia Britannica*; and others.

301. *Historical Atlas* pages 94–5, and Johnson p. 178.

302. Johnson p. 165.

303. Jonathan Ray, The Sephardic Frontier, *The Reconquista and the Jewish Community of Medieval Iberia*, Cornell University Press, 2006, p. 42.

304. Johnson p. 213.

305. *Historical Atlas*, p. 140.

306. *Encyclopedia Judaica* "Economic History" p. 11.

307. Johnson pages 230–1.

308. Johnson p. 226.

309. Johnson p. 229.

310. Ibid.

311. Johnson p. 226.

312. Johnson p. 235 and others.

313. Johnson p. 306, *Historical Atlas*, pages 158–9 and others.

314. Johnson pages 379–402.

315. Ibid.

316. For this paragraph, Johnson pages 304, 358–62 & 365; *Historical Atlas* pages 154–5, 190–1' Yuri Slezkine *The Jewish Century*, Princeton University Press; and others.

317. Johnson pages 321, 396, 401; *Historical Atlas* pages 202–3, 208–9, 220–21; Gilbert, p. 106; "The Jewish People's Land" at http://www.kkl.org.il/kkl/english/main_subject/jewish people land/jewish people land..

318. Ibid., Johnson pages 375–40, *Historical Atlas* pages 202–3, 220–21 and others.

319. *Historical Atlas* pages 180–1, 216–7.

320. "Petaluma's Historic Center Marks its 75th Birthday," at www.jewishsf.com/bk000818/ bnpetaluma.shtml, and

"Chicken Farmers' Chutzpah Intrigues Catholic Dramatist," at www.jewishsf.com/bk030321/sf29.shtml, "When Left Wingers and Chicken Wings Populated Petaluma," at www.jewishsf.com/bk990507/1bchix.shtml, Gaye LeBaron, "Intrigue. Boom, Bust and Ballyhoo in Petaluma's Past," *The Press Democrat*, January 14, 2001; and Ronnie Friedland's reviews of the movies, "A Home on the Range: The Jewish Chicken Ranchers of Petaluma," and "Song of a Jewish Cowboy," www.interfaithfamily.com/article/issue96/friedland1.phtml, and the "Home on the Range" Web site at www.jewishchickenranchers.com/movie, and others.

321. Steven E. Landsburg, "Why Jews Don't Farm," *Slate*, June 13, 2003 at www.slate.msn.com/id/ 2084352; Mark A. Raider, "Jewish Immigrant Farmers in the Connecticut Valley: The Rockville Settlement," *AJA Journal*; Gertrude Harris, "From Shtetl to Prairie," Jewish Agricultural Communities in Frontier Kansas, at www.kancoll.org/books/harris/sod_chap11.htm; Charles Murray, "Jewish Genius," *Commentary*, April 2007; Maristella Botticini and Zvi Eckstein, "From Farmers to Merchants: A Human Capital Interpretation of Jewish Economic History," http://ideas.repec.org/p/cpr/ceprdp/5571.html.

322. Ibid.

323. *Historical Atlas* p. 152–3.

324. *Historical Atlas* pages 196–7, 204–5, 218–19.

325. "To Bigotry No Sanction, to Persecution, No Assistance, George Washington's Letter to the Jews of Newport, Rhode Island," Jewish Virtual Library at www.Jewishvirtuallibrary.org/jsource/US-Israel/ bigotry.html. The quote is taken from David Grubin's television series, *The Jewish Americans*.

326. Among principal sources: Cait Murphy, "A Home of One's Own," *Fortune*, June 12, 2006; Joseph Weber, "A Social Architect," part of the 75th Anniversary Series on The Great Innovators, *Business Week*, May 31, 2004; Charlie Zehren, "The Dream Builder," *Newsday*, undated, but available on line at http://www.newsday.com/community/guide/lihistory/ny-levittown-hslevpro,0,7669595,print.story; Richard Lacayo, "The Time 100 – Most Important People of the Century," December 7, 1998; The Levittown, Pa., Web site operated by the State Museum of Pennsylvania at www.fandm.edu/levittown/ default.html; the Wikipedia article on William Levitt at www.en.wikipedia.org/wiki/William_Levitt; Joel Kotkin, "Suburban Development," *The Wall Street Journal*, November 23, 2007 p. W11; David Streitfeld, "Owned, but Not Occupied," *The New York Times*, January 3, 2008, Business Section, pages 1 & 8; "An Interview with Levitt" *Newsday*, available at www.newsday.com/community /guide /lihistory/ny-levittown-levint,07343038; Levittown real estate guide at www.trulia.com/real_estate/ Levittown-New_York/; Broderick Perkins, "Housing's Historic Levittown Turns 50," in *Realty Times* available at http://realtytimes.com/rtcpages/20020726_levittown.htm; Etkes and Stadtmauer, p. 167; Darryl Lyman, *Jewish Heroes and Heroines*, Jonathan David Publishers, Middle Village, New York, 1996, p. 149, and other sources.

327. Among sources, the bio "Donald Bren," available at www.donald-bren.com/biography.asp; the article, "Donald Bren," from OC Metro, available at http://irvineco.com/aboutus/in_the news/ bren_article/img/bren_home.jpg; "The Irvine company," at www.irvinespectrumfocus.com/" and, "The 50 Most Generous Philanthropists," *Business Week*, Dec 1, 2003.

328. Among Sources: "Broad Builds Up," *Time*, July 17, 1972 on the *Time*.com Web site; Steve Bergsman, *Maverick Real Estate Investing*," John Wiley & Sons, Inc., Hoboken, New Jersey, pages 205–217; Ed Leibowitz, "Committee of One: Eli Broad Built Two Fortune 500 Companies," *Los Angeles Magazine*, Jun 1, 2003; the bio "Eli Broad," on Wikipedia at http://en.wikipedia.org/wiki/Eli_Broad; Peter F. Blackman, "A New Road for Broad," *Los Angeles Business Journal*, May 21, 1990, available at www.highbeam.com/doc/1G1-9224643.html; "Eli Broad: Kaufman Broad," at http://lycos.com/ info/eli-broad-kaufman-broad.html; the historical timeline, company profile, and bios on the KB Home Web site, www.kbhome.com; Michael Corkery, "A Light Goes Out at KB Home," *The Wall Street Journal*, November 14, 2006, p. B6; Christopher Palmeri, "KB Home: Rebuilding Trust," *Business Week*, Sept. 27, 2004, pages 77–8; Maria Bartiromo, "Eli Broad On The Art Bubble," *Business Week*, June 18, 2007; the report "Eli Broad Shares His Philosophy of Business and Leadership with the Anderson Community,: posted on the UCLA Anderson School of Management Web site at www.anderson.ucla.edu/x4518.xml; description of Kaufman Broad on the *Scripophily* Web site at www.scripophily.net/kaandbrinma.html; Peter Woodifield and Simon Packard, Movers: Companies in the News," *International Herald Tribune*, May 24, 2007; and descriptions of the three Broad Foundations and his bio at the Web site, www.broadfoundation.org/ and others

329. Christopher Tkaczyk and Corey Hajim, "All in the Families," *Fortune*, November 26, 2007, p. 126; "Great Real Estate Families," from *Real Estate Weekly*, August 20, 2005. This 48 page story is available at the Web site: www.allbusiness.com/operations/facilities-commercial-real-estate/1187156-1.html.

330. Charles Bagli, "Family Real Estate Empire Expanding to New Shores," *The New York Times*, October 9, 2007, p. A28; The Forbes.com Staff, "The Founders Club Loses Four," posted Sept 18, 2003, and available at

www.forbes.com/2003/09/18/cx_ss_0918400ssansthree.html; Eric Herman, "Bold Builder LeFrak Dead," *New York Daily News,* April 17, 2003 available on the Daily News Web site; the Samuel LeFrak bio on the Songwriters Hall of Fame Web site as recipient of "Patron of the Arts" Award, Samuel LeFrak, "Great Minds, Smart Giving," at the Philanthropy Roundtable Web site www.philanthropyroundtable.org/magazines/1998/may/lefrak.html; the Mann Report article, "The LeFrak Organization—100 years—Four Generations and Still Going Strong," March 2002 at http://lefrak.typepad.com/lefrak_press/FourGenerations.htm; another, The LeFrak Legacy, Multifamily Executive, April 2000 at http://lefrak.typepad.com/lefrak_press/TheLefrakLegacy.htm; Etkes, p. 167, and others.

331. Robert Kolker, "Who Wants to Move to Ground Zero?" New York, April 11, 2005, from the printthis.clickability Web Site; the "Larry Silverstein" article at Wikipedia.org; various articles on the Silverstein Web site: www.silversteinproperties.com; Steve Malaga, "Rebuilding Ground Zero," *The Wall Street Journal,* May 13, 2007, p. A11; Deborah Sontag and others, "Broken Ground 2001–2006," *The New York Times* Feature Section on the 5th Anniversary of 9/11;Andrew Rice, "Silverstein Recovers: Dark Horse May Win World Trade Center," *The New York Observer,* April 8, 2001 available at www.observer.com/node/44259, and others.

332. The "History," "Leadership," "Partner Profiles," "Foundation," "Intrepid," and "Portfolio" articles on the Fisher Brothers web site www.fisherbrother.com; Wolfgang Saxon, "Zachary Fisher, 88, Dies: Helped Alter New York Skyline," *The New York Times,* June 5, 1999; "Paid Notice: Deaths, Fisher, Larry," from *The New York Times,* February 6, 2001; Candace Wu, "Fisher Brothers: A Family Business Grows to a $4 Billion Real Estate Empire," The Stern Opportunity, April 25, 2006 at www.sternopportunity.com; "Arnold Fisher, Intrepid American," *New York Post,* September 19, 2006; "History of the Fisher House Program," at www.fisherhouse.org/aboutUs/history.shtml.

333. The timeline, and profile of properties and personalities on the Durst Organization Web site at www.durst.org; John Salustri, "Up Close, Durst Organization's Douglas Durst," *Globe St,* June 28, 2001, at the *Globe St,* Web site at www.globest.com/upclose062501.html; "A Project 30 Years in the Making: Durst Tries to Revive Fathers Dream, Decades Later," from www.durst.org/press/articles/03_16_99_body.htm; Ilaina Jonas, "Durst, Bank of America Move on New NYC Skyscraper," *Reuters,* Dec 22, 2004; James Traub, "The Dursts Have Odd Properties," *The New York Times,* October 6, 2002; Robin Pogrebin, "High Rises That Have Low Impact on Nature," *The New York Times,* February 2, 2006; Clyde Haberman, "We Will Bury You, in Debt," *The New York Times,* March 24, 2006; Alison Gregor, "Serving Small Tenants With Offices Cut Down to Size," *The New York Times,* July 25, 2007; Matthew Shuerman, "West Side Rail Yards Proposal No. 2: Durst-Vornado Floats, Moves, Relocates People," *The New York Observer,* at www.observer.com/print/60614/full.

334. "Real Estate Leader Lewis Rudin Dead at 74," *Real Estate Weekly,* Sept. 26, 2001, available at www.encyclopedia.com/printable.aspx?id=1G1:79008385; Pranay Gupte, "New York is a Safe Harbor for Investing, It a City on the Rise," the *New York Sun,* March 4, 2005 at the *New York Sun* Web site www.nysun.com/pf.php?id=10086&v=9968778911; the 2006 Form 990PF Tax Filings for The May and Samuel Rudin Family Foundation and The Louis & Rachel Rudin Foundation, Inc.; "Paid Notice: Deaths, Rudin, Lewis" from *The New York Times,* September 23, 2001; Wolfgang Saxon, "May Rudin, 95, a Philanthropist And New York Real-Estate Owner, *The New York Times,* July 24, 1992; The Volozhin - Home Page and Web Site at www.eilatgordinlevitan.com/volozhin and others.

335. Wolfgang Saxon, "Sol Goldman, Major Real-Estate Investor, Dies," *The New York Times,* October 19, 1987; Iver Peterson, "Heirs of Sol Goldman Battle Over Estate," *The New York Times,* September 25, 1988; "Paid Notice: Deaths, Goldman, Lillian, *The New York Times,* August 31, 2002; Ian Fisher, "Waterfront Renewal Turns to Greenpoint," *The New York Times,* June 3, 1990; Richard D. Lyons, "Gotham Restoration Is On Again, *The New York Times,* August 24, 1986; John Altdorfer, "Diamond Lil's Legacy," *Pittsburgh Tribune Review,* April 8, 2003; "Lillian Goldman Law Library: In Memory of Sol Goldman," a *Bulletin of Yale University* at the Yale Web site at www.yale.edu/bulletin/html2003/ law/library.html; "Sol Goldman YM-YWHA of the Educational Alliance" on the "About the 14th Street Y," pdf available at the 14th Street Y Web site; the 2005 990PF Tax Filings for the Sol Goldman Charitable Trust and the Joyce and Irving Goldman Family Foundation, Inc.; Peter Grant and Jim Vandehei, "Towers Developer Makes Some Surprising Strides, *The Wall Street Journal,* March 9, 2004, and others.

336. "Tishman Speyer Properties, L.P., Company History," at the *FindingUniverse*.com Web site; John Holusha, "Commercial Property/666 Fifth Avenue; For Tishman Speyer, a Homecoming of Sorts," *The New York Times,* May 28, 2000; Sabrina Tavernise, "Alan Tishman, 86, Leader in Real Estate Family, Dies," *The New York Times,* January 26, 2004; Wolfgang Saxon, "Margaret Westheimer Tishman, 84, a Leader in Jewish Charities," *The New York Times,* Mar 9, 2004; "About Us," Business Philosophy," "Executive Team," "Portfolio," from the Tishman Speyer Web site at www.tishmanspeyer.com; the description of Tishman Speyer at the Vault.vom Web site; "Speyer, Pincus Lead Trustees," from the Columbia University Web site www.columbia.edu/cu/record/archives/vol21/vol21_iss2; The News Release, "John L. Tishman Honored Among Buildings Magazine's 100 Influences That Have Shaped the Buildings Market," March 24, 2006; the Description of Tishman Realty and Construction on the Yahoo Finance Web site; the "About Us," "Office Locations," Tishman Affiliates," "Executive Bios," "Timeline," from the Tishman Realty and Construction Web site at www.tishmanconstruction.com/; and others.

337. "Philanthropist and Builder Fredrick Rose '44E Dies," Yale Bulletin & Calendar, Sept. 27–Oct 4, 1999; James

Horowitz, "The Rose Family," www.observer.com; Rachelle Garbarine, "Rose Associates Enters the Conversion Market," *The New York Times*, July 11, 1997.

338. The bios, family history and description of the current business are provided on the Hartz Web site at www.hartzmountain.com. Leonard Stern is also profiled on Wikipedia and on Forbes.com.

339. "Towering Vision by Developer Stirs East Side," *The New York Times*, November 15, 2007; Eliot Brown, "The New Gold Coast," the *New York Sun*, September 19, 2007; Carter B. Horsley, "9 West 57th Street," The Midtown Book at the Web site, www.thecityreview.com/57w9.html; Peggy Edersheim Kalb, "Real Estate 2000," New York at http://staging.newyorkmag.com/page.cfm?page_id=2651; *Forbes* 400 list on *Forbes*.com; Forms 990-PF Tax Filings for 2004–5 for The Solow Foundation, The Sheldon Solow Foundation, The Solow Art and Architecture Foundation and the Solow Family Foundation; and others.

340. Michael Specter, "Harold Uris Recollects With Pride," *The New York Times*, July 19, 1981; Glen Collins, "A Foundation Gives Away $30 Million and Calls It Quits," *The New York Times*, June 25, 1998; "The Uris Brothers Foundation Has Awarded $10,000,000 Endowment to Create New Educational Programs at The Metropolitan Museum of Art," at www.tfaoi.com/newsmu/mile1.htm; "Uris Brothers Foundation Gives $3 Million for Childrens' Book Endowment to The New York Public Library," at www.nypl.org/press/uris.html; "Percy Uris (1899–1971) and Harold D. Uris (1905–1982) Descriptions of Papers retained at Columbia University Library" and available at www.columbia.edu/ cu/1web/indiv/avery/da/uris.html.

341. David W. Dunlap, "Dividing Harry Helmsley's Empire," *The New York Times*, November 26, 2000 and the Wikipedia article on "Harry Helmsley."

342. Rhonda Amon, "A Shopping Giant Arrives," *Newsday*.com; the Wikipedia article on "William Zeckendorf."

343. Charles V. Bagli and Terry Pristin, "Harry Macklowe's $6.4 Billion Bill," *The New York Times*, Jan. 6, 2008; John Holusha, "A New Face on Madison Avenue," *The New York Times*, October 26, 2005; Nanette Byrnes, "Leveraging a Landmark," *Business Week*, Oct. 27, 2003; "No.239, Harry Macklowe" *Forbes* 400, Sept 20, 2007 and at www.forbes.com; "Topics of the Times; Chess in Times Square," *The New York Times*, Sept 25, 1990; Joey, "Mack Daddy Sinking Large Fortune Into Plaza," *Curbed*, June 7, 2007 at www.curbed.com/archives/2007/06/07; Andrew Ross Sorkin and Terry Pristin, "Takeover Battle Ends With Sale of Big Landlord," *The New York Times*, Feb. 8, 2007; Terry Pristin, "He'll Take Manhattan (or Chunk of Midtown)," *The New York Times*, Feb 21, 2007; Terry Pristin, "Developer's Big Manhattan Move Faces a Time and Credit Squeeze," *The New York Times*, Aug. 22, 2007; Lingling Wei, "Guarantee Gamble: Developers Dread Return of Recourse," *The Wall Street Journal*, June 18, 2008; Alex Frangos and Jennifer S. Forsyth, "Son Poised to Rise at Macklowe, *The Wall Street Journal*, May 26, 2008; Devin Leonard, "A Real Estate Mogul Risks It All," *The New York Times Sunday Magazine*, March 3, 2008. (All *New York Times* stories are available on their Web site at www.nytimes.com.

344. Sources for the Stephen Ross section include: ""Stephen M. Ross," at http://en.wikipedia.org/wiki/Stephen_M.Ross; and Stephen Ross, bio," on the *Forbes* 400 list at www.forbes.com/lists/ 2007/54/ richlist07_Stephen-Ross_YZL6_.

345. Bill Vlasic, "Pragmatic Partners," *Michigan Today* publication of the University of Michigan from its Web site at www.umich.edu/~newsinfo/MT/97/Spr97/mta1s97.html; Terry Savage, "Terry Savage Talks Money With Sam Zell," from the February 10, 2002 *Chicago Sun Times* and its Web site, www.suntimes.com/savage/talk/ sam_zell_2.thml; Tatiana Serafin, "Invest Like a Billionaire: Sam Zell," *Forbes*, Nov 9, 2006, from the *Forbes* Web site www.forbes.com/2006/11/09/samuel-zell-investments-pf_ii_cz_ts_1109zell_print.html; the Sam Zell article on *Wikipedia*, http://en.wikipedia.org/wiki/ Samuel_Zell; Phil Rosenthal, David Greising and Michael O'Neal, "On the Future, Deal making and Bad Press," *Chicago Tribune*, April 4, 2007 from their Web site www.chicagotribune.com/ business/chi-070409zellinterview,1,393421.story?coll=chi-news-hed; Cheryl Corley, "Sam Zell's Latest Gamble: Tribune Co.," on *NPR's Morning Edition*, April 3, 2007 and their Web site www.npr.org/templates/ story/story.php?storyId=9307849; "$10 Million Gift From Sam Zell, Ann Lurie Creates Major Entrepreneurial Institute at Business School," Shira Ovide, "Tribune Files for Chapter 11," *The Wall Street Journal*, Dec. 9, 2008, p B1; www.umich.edu/~urecord/9399/ Jul19_99.htm; and from a meeting the author had with Zell in the mid '90s.

346. "Company Overview," from The Archstone-Smith Web site at www.archstonesmith.com; and at www.smithapartments.com/abouHistory.asp; the *Reuter's* write-up at www.investor.reuters.com; the Morningstar write-up at http://advqt.morningstar.com; John Frantz, "The High-rise of a REIT Powerhouse," *National Real Estate Investor* at www.nreionline.com/microsites/ magazinearticle.asp?mode=print&magazine dated June 1, 2001; the Charles E. Smith bio at http://psychobiology.org.il/founders/fou_smith.html; and the counterpart biography of David Bruce Smith and Robert H. Smith on the same Web site; Terry Pristin, "Deal For REIT a Surprise to Some Experts." *The New York Times*, May 30, 2007.

347. Terry Pistin, "Vornado Chief Keeps Competitors on Their Toes," *The New York Times*, Feb. 15, 2005; the *Hoovers'* description of Vornado Realty Trust at www.hoovers.com/vornado-realty-trust/; the 2002 Vornado Annual Report to Shareholders; and their Web site at www.vno.com; Peter Grant, "REIT Exec to Pocket $25M Stay Bonus; *The Wall Street Journal*, March 20, 2002; Dan Ackman, "World Trade Center Back On the Block," *Forbes*, March 21, 2001, and at www.forbes.com/2001/03/21/0321worldbust.html; the Steven Roth bio on the Baruch College Web site at www.baruch.cuny.edu/spa; the bio of Daryl Roth at www.newdramatists.org/rothbio.htm; and "Steven Roth: Fanning the Fires of Success," *Columbia Business School Reporter*, Fall 1999;

348. The Mort Zuckerman bio on *The McLaughlin Group* Web site at www.mclaughlin.com/ about/bio.asp?pid=27; and the bio at www.corporate-ir.net/ireye/ ir_site.zhtml?ticker=bxp&script=2220&item_id=3; Tim Boxer, "Praise for Mort Zuckerman Makes Trees Grow in Israel," www.15minutesmagazine.com/archives/issue_23/week; Blair Golson, "Munificent Mortimer.(Financial Observer)," *The New York Observer*, July 1, 2002 also available at www.findarticles.com/cf_dls/m01CQ/2002_July_1/87934795/print.jhtml; and the Boston Properties Web site at www.bostonproperties.com; "Buildings Who's Who – Boston Properties, Boston," at www.buildings.com/Articles;

349. Paul Lukas, "Our Malls, Ourselves," *Fortune*, October 18,2004 p. 243; "Top 25 Shopping Center Owners," on the *National Real Estate Investor* Web site Jul 1, 2007.

350. Robert Sharoff, "Malling the Competition," *Context Magazine*, February/March 2002, available at www.contextmag.com/archives/200002/Feature2MallingTheCompetition.asp; "Mel and Herb Simon," *Indianapolis Star* Web site at www.indystar.com/library/factfiles/people/s/simon/somons.html; the Simon Group 2006 Annual Report Corporate Profile, Board bios, CEO letter and Financial Highlights; the *Forbes* bio of Mel Simon on their Web site at www.forbes.com/lists/2007/10/07billionaires_Melvin-Simon_UIA0.html; the Simon Corporate Profile at www.Morningstar.com; material at the Simon Web site at www.simon.com; "Simon Properties Hikes Taubman Centers Bid," Jan. 13, 2003 at http://phoenix.bizjournals.com/ phoenix/stories/2003/01/13/daily/38.html; the Bren Simon profile at www.motherjones.com/new/ special_reports/mojo_400/75_simon.html; and "Ghermezian Brothers Las Vegas Megamall," at www.canadianencylocpedia.ca/PrinterFriendly.cfm?Params-M1ARTM0012665.

351. "General Growth Properties, Inc," article at www.answers.com/topic/general-growth-properties?cat=biz-fin; and the General Growth Properties article at Wikipedia.com; the Corporate History timeline and Overview at the General Growth Web site, www.ggp.com; the article on General Growth on the *Cranes Chicago Business* Web site www.chicagobusiness.com/cgi-bin/mag/article.pl?article_id24651; the Drake Bucksbaum Lecture Series Web site at www.drake.edu.bucksbaum/; Peter Hochstein, "The Education of Matthew Bucksbaum," *Retail Traffic*, May 1, 2004, at www.retailtrafficmag.com/mag/retail_education_matthew_bucksbaum/index.html; Whitney press release at the Whitney Web site www.whitney.org/information/press/142.html;; Kris Hudson, "General Growth Puts Vegas Malls on Block," *The Wall Street Journal*, Oct. 28, 2008; Kris Hudson and Jeffrey McCracken, "Mall Owner Lines Up Bankruptcy Law Firm," *The Wall Street Journal*, Nov. 20, 2008; Kris Hudson and Robert Frank, "Dark Days for Mall Dynasty," *The Wall Street Journal*, Dec. 9, 2008 the Matthew Bucksbaum bio at *Forbes*. www.forbes.com/lists/2006/10/UAZ3.html.

352. Bergsman, *Maverick Real Estate Investing*, p. 192; the Corporate profile, "Third Quarter 2007 Report to Shareholders and Chairman's Address. May 3, 2007 on the Westfield Group Web site at www.westfield.com/; "Frank Lowy & Family," at www.forbes.com/maserati/billionaires20004; "Like Father, Like Son," at www.icsc.org/srch/sct/current/sct0501/page189.html; the International Council of Shopping Center Web site; Teresa Ooi, "I Earned My $12m Bonus: Lowy," Nov. 15, 2003, at www.fpp.co.uk/online/0311/Lowy_greed.html. the Australian Web site; "Frank Lowy's Big Party," Nov. 28, 2003 and "Frank Lowy: Spin, Philanthropy and AMP, both at www.crickey.com; "Winner Takes Mall," at www.bulletin.ninemsn.com.au/bulletin/EdDesk.nsf/ 0/ 3b9dea9c817885e6ca256abb001a93e1?

353. The Guilford Glazer article at www.forbes.com/lists/2005/54/SNVI.html; Rob Eshman, "Is It Good For Them," *Jewish Journal*, April, 29, 2005 at www.jewishjournal.com/home/preview.php?id=14036; the Wikipedia article on Guilford Glazer at http://en.wikipedia.org/wiki/Guilford_Glazer; various Glazer and affiliate corporate profiles at www.manta.com/coms2/dnB.C.ompany; history of the Del Amo Fashion Center at the Del Amo Web site, and the "Largest Single-Property Real Estate Transactions in 2003" at www.realert.com/Public/MarketPlace/Transactions.

354. The Taubman Centers' 2006 Letter to Shareholders, Portfolio, Business Description and other information from the *Annual Report*; and their Web site at www.taubman.com; the corporate profile at www.morningstar.com; James V. Higgins and Barbara Hoover, "Work, Play Are All One to Taubman," The Detroit News, May 30, 2001 at www.detnews.com/2001/business/0105/03/a04-219877.htm; Francis X. Donnelly, "Taubman's Reputation Goes On Trial," Nov. 5, 2001, *Detroit News*, Donnelly, "Taubman: Meek or Masterful,?" Dec. 3, 2001; Donnelly, "Taubman Case Goes to Jury," Dec. 4, 2001; Donnelly, "Michigan Tycoon Taubman Guilty," Dec 6, 2001, all also on the *Detroit News* Web site; Marion Maneker, "The Secret Life of Alfred Taubman, *New York* magazine Nov. 26, 2001 and available on their Web site at www.newyorkmetro.com/mymetro/new/crimelaw/features/5419/; the Taubman Center Web site at www.ksg.harvard.edu.taubmancenter/; and the A. Alfred Taubman Center for Public Policy and American Institutions at Brown University www.brown.edu/Departments/Taubman_Center; the Taubman College of

Architecture and Urban Planning at the University of Michigan at www.tcaup.unich.edu/; the A. Alfred Taubman Health Care Center at the University of Michigan; the article on Taubman Centers at www.morningstar.com; Alexandra Peers, book review "The Wrong Man," *The Wall Street Journal* May 27, 2004.

355. Description of JMB Realty Corporation on the Hoovers' Web site at www.hoovers.com/jmbrealty/; the bio of Neil G. Bluhm at Forbes.com; "A Very Special Partnership," on the University of Illinois, Urbana-Champaign Web site www.business.uiuc.edu/development/malkinbluhm.html; "Real Estate Top Firms," at www.careers-in-finance.com/retop.htm; and others.

356. "Paul Reichmann," at www.shemayisrael.co.il/orgs/ozar/reichman.htm; Heather Tomlinson, "Canary Wharf Founder Backs Bid, *The Guardian*, Jan. 30, 2004; www.guardian.co.uk/business/story/0.3604.1134697.00.html; Bill Brioux, "The Canary In Their Gold Mine," *Toronto Sun*, May 29, 2000, Mark Tran, "Canary Wharf Still Beckons Reichmann," *The Guardian*, Aug. 27, 2003 and at the *Guardian* Web site, www.guardian.co.uk; Laura Bogormolny, "Real Estate: Lords of Land," part of "The Rich 100," *Canadian Business*.com and available at that Web site.

357. The article on Alan I Casden at the *Forbes* Web site, www.forbes.com; RiShawn Biddle, "Brotherly Feud," *Forbes*, Oct. 14, 2002, and www.forbes.com/forbes/2002/1014/050.html; Vanessa Dodson, "Trustee Alan Casden Makes 'Living Gift,'" and "Beverly Hills Developer Gives $10 million to USC," Luck Center for Real Estate at University of Southern California Web site, www.usc.edu/lusk; and others.

358. Article on Carl Berg on *Forbes*, www.forbes.com/finance/lists/10/2003/LIR.jhtml?; the Mission West profile at Yahoo, http://finance.yahoo.com/q/pr?s=MSW; the *Annual Report*, 10K, and Financial Statements of Mission West Properties, Inc for 2003; Robert Bryce, "Buying Certainty for Stratus," The Austin Chronicle, August 9, 2002 and available at the *Austin Chronicle* Web site, www.austinchronicle.com/issues/dispatch/2002-08-09/pols_feature3.html; Tanya Rutledge, "Berg REIT Purchase is a Rare Deal," *Silicon Valley/San Jose Business Journal*, August 8, 1997, http://sanjose.bizjournals.com/sanjose/stories/1997/08/11/story3.html; Sharon Simonson, "Billionaire Berg Offers Free Rent To Spur Biotech Incubator Deal," *Silicon Valley/San Jose Business Journal*, Oct. 24, 2003; http://sanjose.bizjournals.com/sanjose/stories/2003/10/27/story4.html; and others.

359. Profile of Walter Shorenstein from Shorenstein Properties Web site at www.shorenstein.com; and other sources, including the author's experience.

360. "Ben Swig," Wikipedia article at http://en.wikipedia.org/wiki/Benjamin_Swig; "Melvin Swig, 75, Dies: California Developer," *The New York Times*, March 16, 1993; "Melvin Swig," Wikipedia article; Lois Weiss, "Trizec Makes Splash With Weiler Buy – TrizecHahn Corp," *Real Estate Weekly*, March 5, 1997 at http://findarticles.com; Eric Heimbinder, "Swig Acquires, Renames company; Purchases Weiler Family Interests, Adds New Operating Partner in New York," *Business Wire*, June 5, 1997, also at Find Articles Web site; Adam Feuerstein, "Swig Family Shuffles Billion Dollar Empire," *San Francisco Business Times*, June 2, 1997 a http://sanfrancisco.buzjournals.com; "New Leader for Swig Companies..."*Real Estate Weekly*, July 28, 1993 at www.encyclopedia.com Web site; "Hotel History," at the Fairmont Hotel Web site, www.fairmont.com/sanfrancisco/AboutUs/HotelHistory.htm; Alan Liddle, "Fairmont Vice Chair and Philanthropist Swig Dies..." *Nation's Restaurant News*, Oct. 6, 1997, available at the Find Articles Web site; Leslie Katz, "Patriarch Richard Swig: 'He Was Just Larger Than Life,'" *Jewish Bulletin of Northern California* at www.jewishsf.com; "Paid Notice: Deaths Swig, Richard," *The New York Times*, Sept 28 & 30, 1997; Forbes 400 of 1985; "Kent M. Swig," bio at the Brown Harris Stephens Web site at www.brownharrisstevens.com; "Real Estate Philanthropist, Kent Swig, Is Man of the Year," *Real Estate Weekly*, April 6, 2005 at find articles.com; "Where is Kent M. Swig Today," at www.newyorkbusiness-risingstars.com; "Miss Macklowe Engaged to Kent Swig," *The New York Times*, April 12, 1987; and others.

361. Among sources for the Introductory material are: Leon Harris, *Merchant Princes*, Kodansha International, New York, London, Tokyo, 1994, p. 201; the Henri Pirenne quote comes from Pirenne's book, *Mohammed and Charlemagne*, Dover Publications, 2001; Botticini, Maristella and Eckstein, Zvi, "From Farmers to Merchants, Conversions and Diaspora: Human Capital and Jewish History," in *Journal of the European Economic Association*, Sept. 2007, pages 885–926, including the tally of Jewish casualties from the Jewish Revolts detailed on pages 901 to 903 and the discussion on the premium laced on education of Jews, pages 897 to 900; Thomas Sowell, "History and Culture: Is Anti-Semitism Generic?" *Hoover Digest*, 2005, No. 3; Jonathan Sarna, "Modern History: Peddlers Peddling, Judaism Spreading," from *American Judaism: A History*, Yale University Press 2004, and available at www.myjewishlearning.com/history_community/Modern/ModernSocial/Peddlers.htm; Rabbi MOSHE Fine, "From Shepherding to Banking and Beyond": at the *Cleveland Jewish News*.com Web site at www.clevelandjewishnews.org/articles/2005/01/12/special/family_business/specialIO..Karen Primack, "Jews Have Been in China A Long, Long Time," at www.pass.to/newsletter/jews_have_been_in_china_a_long_long_time.htm; Maria Jose Cano, "Jewish Merchants in the 14th Century," at www.ibnjaldun.com/index.php?id=108&L=7; Shira Schoenberg, "Ashkenazim," at the Jewish Virtual Library at www.jewishvirtuallibrary.org/jsource/Judaism/Ashkenaziam.html.

362. Among sources for this section, some of which are also used in the profiles of specific department stores or chains

are: Leon Harris, *Merchant Princes*, especially pages ix to xxx; Kevin Kingsbury and Gary McWilliams, "Retailers Post Tepid Growth," *The Wall Street Journal*, Jan. 11, 2008 at http://online.wsjcom/article_print/ SB119996760551480659.html; the article, "The Department Store," at the Web site, http://history.sandiego.edu/ gen/soc/shoppingcenter4.html; the Wikipedia article, "Department Store," at http://en.wikipedia.org/wiki/ Department_Store; "Retail-Department Stores: Interesting Dates," at www.kipnotes.come/RetailDepartmentStores.htm; "The retail timeline 1879 to 2003," at www.geocities.com/ zayre88/Timeline.html; Adam Gopnik, "Under One Roof," *The New Yorker*, Sept. 22, 2003 and available at http://newyorker.com/fact/content/?030922fa_fact; and the review of the Exhibition, "Enterprising Emporiums: The Jewish Department Stores of Downtown Baltimore." From *The Journal of American History* Web site at www.historycooperative.org/cgi-bin/ justtop.cgi?act=justtop&url=http://www.historycooperati. .

363. Among sources: Harris, especially pages 36–69; *Encyclopaedia Britannica*, "Macy and Company, Inc.," "Straus, Oscar Solomon," "Straus, Nathan," "Straus Family;" The New York Public Library Manuscripts and Archives Division, "Straus Family Papers 1810–1962, Compiled by Laura K. O'Keefe," June 1994; Wikipedia articles "Macy's," and "Straus Hall," at http://en.wikipedia.org/wiki/Macy's and http://en.wikipedia.org/wiki/Straus_Hall; various articles from *The New York Times* archives including: "Simple Rites Held For Percy Straus," April 11, 1944; Eric Pace, "Jack I. Straus, 85, Macy's Leader Through 4 Decades of Expansion," Sept 20, 1985; "J.I. Straus Made Head of Macy; Percy S. Straus, President Since '33, Elected Chairman…" May 1, 1940; "Paid Notice: Deaths Straus, Robert K." Feb. 26, 1977; Wolfgang Saxon, "Kenneth Straus, Macy's Heir and Philanthropist, Dies at 71," July 26, 1996; and, Isadore Barmash, "A Leveraged Macy's Waits for the Rewards," Jan. 25, 1987, all of which are available at *The New York Times* Web site; the article, "$4,427,608 Estimate of Straus Estate," from the *Encyclopedia Titanica* Web site www.encyclopedia–titanica.org/item/4379/ which quotes an article from *The New York Times*, Aug. 11, 1913; "In Touch With Mrs. Macy," *Time*, Oct. 2, 1964 available at www.time.com/time/printout/0,8816,940535,00.html; the Macy's Web site Timeline at www.macys.com/service/about/timeline/tl. . ; and the profile of Jack I. Straus from the Harvard Business School Leadership Web site at www.hbs.edu/leadership/database/leaders/874.

364. Among sources: Harris, especially pages 1 to 36; *Encyclopaedia Britannica*, "Filene, Lincoln," Filene Edward A." "Filene's" "Lazarus, Fred, Jr.;" Etkes, p. 164; Wikipedia, "Filene's," "A Lincoln Filene," "Edward Filene," and various Web pages of The Century Foundation at www.tcf.org/ American Jewish Historical Society, p. 213.

365. Among sources: Harris, p. 25, 41, 43–4, 50–2; "Abraham Abraham, Merchant, Is Dead," *The New York Times*, June 29, 1911 at *The New York Times* Web site; Wikipedia, "Abraham & Straus," and, "Rothschild Arch, The."

366. Among sources: Harris, esp. pages 44 and 71 to 83; American Jewish Historical Society,pages 213–4; Darryl Lyman, *Jewish Heroes and Heroines*, Jonathan David Publishers, Inc., Middle Village, 1996, p. 145; Wikipedia, "Gimbels," at http://en.wikipedia.org/wiki/Gimbel's and; InfoPlease, "Gimbel" at www.infoplease.com/ce6/people/ A0820846.html.

367. Among sources: Harris, pages 16, 77, 79, 80, 90, 181, 196; Christopher Gray, "Streetscapes/Saks: The Giant Leap From sixth Avenue to Fifth Avenue;" *The New York Times*, April 16, 1995; "Andrew Saks Dead at 65," *The New York Times*, April 9, 1912; "Andrew Saks Will," *The New York Times*, April 13, 1912; Wikipedia, "Saks Fifth Avenue," at http://en.wikipedia.org/wiki/Saks_Fifth_Avenue; and the Saks' Web site at www.saksincorporated.com/aboutus/.

368. Among sources: Harris, pages 10, 181, 185, 191, 196, 249–51; Wikipedia, "Bergdorf Goodman," and "Carter Hawley Hale Stores," at http://en.wikipedia.org/wiki/Bergdorf_Goodman and http://en.wikipedia.org/wiki/ Carter_Hawley_Hale_Stores.

369. Among sources: Harris, pages122, 253, 338–50; Lyman, *Heroes*, p. 144;Mark L. Gardner, "A Brief History of Bloomingdale's Department Stores: A Store Like No Other, Piedmont College; Geoffrey T. Hellman, "Bloomingdale's Bloomingdale," *The New Yorker*, Nov. 7, 1964 at www.newyorker.com/archive/1964/11/07/ 1964_11_07_047_TNY_CARDS_0002745…"Bloomingdales" at www.pdxhistory.com/html/bloomingdales.html; Wikipedia, "Bloomingdale's" and "Alfred S. Bloomingdale," at http://en.wikipedia.org/wiki/Bloomingdales; and wiki/Alfred_S._Bloomingdale; and, David W. Dunlap, "Alfred Bloomingdale, Diners Club Develop Dies," *The New York Times*, August 24, 1982.

370. Among sources: Harris, pages 103, 111, 356; Etkes, p. 162; Murph, "Thingist Department Stores," at http://x-arm.org/hub/liste.php?n=3&body=1164; Wikipedia, "B. Altman and Company" and "Benjamin Altman," at http://en.wikipedia.org/wiki/B._Altman_and_company and wiki/Benjamin_Altman.

371. Among sources: Harris, pages 152,274; American Jewish Historical Society, p. 210; Etkes, p. 162, Wikipedia, "Louis Bamberger," and "Bamberger's" at http://en.wikipedia.org/wiki/Bamberger's; and wiki/Louis_Bamberger.

372. Among sources: "Louis Stern Dies Suddenly in Paris," *The New York Times*, June 23, 1922; "Arthur D. Brandeis Joins Stern Bros." *The New York Times*, May 5, 1914; "A.D. Brandeis Dies; Ill Only a Week," *The New York Times*,

June 11, 1916; "Stern Brothers Department Store," at www.nyu.edu/classes/finearts/nyc/ladies/sterns.html; and Wikipedia, "Stern's," at http://en.wikipedia.org/wiki/Stern's.

373. Among sources: Harris, esp. pages 280–336; Etkes, p. 169; American Jewish Historical Society, Desk Reference, pages 234–5; (also see notes at the end of the Philanthropy Chapter).

374. Among sources: Harris, esp. pages 91–112; Wikipedia, "Kaufmann's," and Edgar J. Kaufmann," at http://en.wikipedia.org/wiki/Kaufmann's; Etkes *Jewish Contributions,* p. 172; and wiki/ Edgar_J._Kaufmann.

375. Among sources: Harris, p. 348; "Department Stores and Downtown Retail – B'More Ghosts," at www.btco.net/ghosts/Buildings/deptstores/deptstores.html; "Enterprising Emporiums: The Jewish Department Stores of Downtown Baltimore," a catalog for the exhibit at the Baltimore Museum at www.historycooperative.org/journals/jah/89.3/exr_5.html; and Wikipedia, "Hecht's," at http://en.wikipedia.org/wiki/Hechts.

376. Among sources: Harris, pages 181, 349; "The Queen of Garfinckel's," an article from *Colliers* magazine, Feb. 10, 1951 and available at www.garfinckels.com/fairall.htm; "Business Spotlight: Brooks Brothers," at www.lowermanhattan.info/assistance/business_spotlight/ business_spotlight_brooks_84281.asp; "Brooks Brothers: A Classically Modern Story," a Columbia Business School Retailing Case; Andrew Ross Sorkin, "Owner of Casual Corner Chain Seen in Deal for Brooks Brothers," *The New York Times,* Nov. 23, 2001; and Wikipedia, "Garfinckel's," "Julius Garfinckel," and "Miller Department Store," at http://en.wikipedia.org/wiki/Garfinckel's; wiki/Julius_Garfinckel; and wiki/Miller's_ Department_Store.

377. Among sources: Harris, pages 112–135; "Goldsmiths," at the Web site of *The Tennessee Encyclopedia of History* and Culture at http://tennesseeencyclopedia.net/imagegallery.php?EntryID-G024; and Wikipedia, "Goldsmith's" at http://en.wikipedia.org/wiki/Goldsmith's

378. Harris, pages 135–156.

379. Among sources: Harris, pages 156–201; Etkes, p. 173; "Mr. Stanley Knows Best," *Time,* Sept. 21, 1963 at www.time.com/time/printout/0,8816,890689,00.html; "Herbert Marcus," at The Internet Accuracy Project Web site, www.accuracyproject.org/cbe-Herber.html; Catherine Zinko, "At 100, Neiman Marcus Keeps Coddling Customers to Sell Luxury," *San Francisco Chronicle,* Sept. 9, 2007; Wikipedia, "Neiman Marcus," and, "Stanley Marcus," at Wikipedia, http://en.wikipedia.org/wiki/ Neiman_Marcus, and wiki/Stanley_Marcus.

380. Among sources: Harris, pages xxii, 28, 56–7, 164, 157–176, 206–7, 248–9, 270 and back cover; Wikipedia, "Sanger-Harris," "Foleys," at http://en.wikipedia.org/wiki/Sanger-Harris; and wiki/Foleys; and "Kirby's Retail Roots," at www.thekirby.net/html/history/history1.htm.

381. Among sources, Harris, pages 217–36; Wikipedia, "Goldwater's" and "Barry Goldwater," at http://en.wikipedia.org/wiki/Goldwater'27s, and wiki/Barry_Goldwater.

382. Among sources: Harris, pages 243–47, 254; " Biography for Richard Gump," at Ask/Art Web site www.askart.com/AskART/artists/biography.aspx?searchtype=BIO&artist=11003966; Jenny Strasburg, "Investors Buying Gump's To Pay $8.5 Million," *San Francisco Chronicle,* Feb. 17, 2005 available at www.sfgate.com/cgi-bin/article.cgi?file=/c/a/2005/02/17/BUG0JBCLE41.DTL&type...; "Macmillan, Inc. – company profile...," at www.referenceforbusiness.com/history2/97/Macmillan-Inc.html.

383. Among sources: Harris, pages 122, 147, 181, 191, 242, 247–254; Katherine Bishop, "Cyril Isaac Magnin, 88, Ex-Head of Store Chain and Patron of the Arts," *The New York Times,* June 9, 1988; Russ Lynch, "Liberty House Prospered With Onasch," *Star Bulletin* at http://starbulletin.com/96/06/24/ community/obits.html; "Joseph Magnin Files for Chapter 11 Protection," *Daily News Record,* Sept. 1984; "Joseph Magnin In Chapter 11," *The New York Times,* Sept. 18, 1984 at http://query.nytimes.com/gst/fullpage.html?res=9D02E0D6163BF93BA2575AC0A962948...; Wikipedia, "I. Magnin," at http://en.wikipedia.org/wiki/I._Magnin;

384. Among sources: Harris, pages 259–80; Wikipedia, "Meier & Frank," http://wikipedia.org/wiki/Meier_&_Frank;

385. Among sources: Harris, pages 109, 110, 278; "David May in Leadville," at www.prinzmetal.net/david_may_i.htm; "Spotlight Leadville," at www.coloradolinks.net/ Colorado_Spotlight/Leadville.htm; "A Boost for Buster," *Time,* June 25, 1951, Time, at www.time.com/time/printout/ 0,8816,806068,00,html; "David May, Store Heir To Wed Doris Zakowski," *The New York Times,* march 28, 1971; Burt A. Folkart, "Obituaries, David May II; Scion Helped Family Store Chain Grow," at www.prinzmetal.net/david_may_ii.htm; Tracie Rozhon, "May Stores Acquiring Marshall Fields," *The New York Times,* June 10, 2004; Wikipedia, "Morton D. May," and "May Department Stores at http://en.wikipedia.org/wiki/May_Department_Stores; and wiki/Morton_May.

386. Among sources: Harris, pages 83–90; "Collection 1959 Albert M. Greenfield Papers, 1921–1967," at the Histori-cal Society of Pennsylvania and available at www.hsp.org/files/ findingaid1959greenfield.pdf; "The company," at www.amgreenfield.com/company.html.

387. Among sources: Harris, pages 20, 25, 21, 88, 122, 133, 154, 196–7, 276, 336–354; "Snapshot," *Fortune,* March 21, 2005; "Shuffling the Lazari," *Time,* Sep. 29.1967 at www.time.com/time/printout/0,8816,899873,00.html; "Many Happy Returns to Lazarus," at www.wosu.org/archive/ lazarus/family.php; "Ralph Lazarus," at www.libraries.uc.edu/research/subject_resources/ business/book_ralph_lazarus.html; Wikipedia, "Simon Lazarus," "Macy's, Inc. at http://en.wikipedia.org/wiki/Federated_Department_Stores; and wiki/Simon_Lazarus; *Encyclopædia Britannica,* "Lazarus, Fred, Jr.; "Macy's History," at www.fds.com/pressroom/about/his_2.asp;

388. Among sources: Jessica Hansen, "Kohl Lived the American Dream," *The Milwaukee Journal Sentinel,* Dec. 30, 2000 at www.highbeam.com/doc/1P2-6843056.html; Kohl's Corporation *FACT BOOK,* Quarter Ended, November 3, 2007 available on the Web site, www.kohlscorporation.com; Kohls' Corporation, "Our Timeline," and "Our Loca-tions," at www.kohlscorporation.com/ AboutKohls/AboutKohls06.htm; and AboutKohls.05asp; "Max Kohl," Univer-sity of Milwaukee Web site at www.uwm.edu/Dept/Business/alumni/gallery/kohl.html; Wikipedia, "Kohl's," and "Herb Kohl," at http://en.wikipedia.org/wiki/Kohl's and wiki/Herb_Kohl; Avrum D. Lank, "In 1972, Kohl's Meant Food Stores," *JSOnline* at www.jsonline.com/bym/your/mar03/122177.asp; Tom Dayton, "Kohl's Food Stores Clos-ing in August," *JSOnline,* June 14,2003 at www.jsonline.com/bym/ News/jun03/147977.asp; David Schuyler, "Local Kohl's Food Stores up for sale: Copps buys Madison stores," at www.bizjournals.com/milwaukee/stories/ 2003/02/24/daily9.html; Pete Millard, "Kohl Brothers Sell Apartments," *The Business Journal,* Oct. 29, 2004, at www.bizjournals.com/milwaukee/ stories/2004/11/01/story2.html?t=printable

389. Among sources: *Alan Symons, Jewish Contribution to the 20th Century,* Polo Publishing, London, 1997; Wikipedia, "Marks & Spencer," "Michael Marks," "Simon Marks, 1st Baron Marks of Broughton," "Israel Sieff, Baron Sieff," "Marcus Sieff, Baron Sieff of Brimpton," "Richard Greenbury," "Paul Myners," "Terrence Burns, Baron Burns," "Stuart Rose," all at http://en.wikipedia.org/wiki/ Marks&Spencer; etc.; Alan Cowell, "Marks & Spencer Rejects a Takeover Offer," *The New York Times,* June 3, 2004, Robert Peston, "Green's Kept His Money, Now Rose Has the Worry," *City Comment, The Telegraph,* July 18, 2004 at www.opinion.telegraph.co.uk/money/main.jhtml?; Michael Carolan, "Marks & Spencer Rejects Bid by Billionaire Retailer Green," *The Wall Street Journal,* June 3, 2004.

390. Among sources: Paul Gallagher, "£500,000 a Day for the 'Wild Man' of the City," *The Scotsman,* May 23, 2002; Kiri Blakeley, "Envy With Green," *Forbes,* March 15, 2004; Leslie Bunder, "M&S Rejects Green Bid," *Something Jew-ish* at www.somethingjewish.com.uk/articles/1023_mands-rejects_green_bi.htm; Erin White, "Wooing A Dowdy Retailer," *The Wall Street Journal,* June 18, 2004, Michael Carolan, "M&S Rejects Offer by Green Raising the Bar for Leadership," *The Wall Street Journal,* July 9, 2004;

391. "Industry: Specialty Retailers," http://money.cnn.com/magazines/fortune/fortune500/industries/ Specialty_Retailers/1.html;

392. Among sources: Dr. Richard E. Hattwick, "Arthur Blank and Bernie Marcus: The Home Depot Story," American *National Business Hall of Fame,* at file:///DI/Hall of Fame ANB/pdf/ htm_files/blank_marcus.htm; "History," "Historical Milestones," at www.homedepot.com?HDUS?EN_US/corporate/about/history.shtml; "The Arthur M. Blank Family Foundation at www.blankfoundation.org; "Arthur Blank Grants $5 Million to Emory's Jewish Studies Institute," at www.emory.edu/WELCOME/journcontents/releases/arthurblank.html; "About Us, The Arthur M. Blank Family Foundation," at www.blankfoundation.org/about/bio_arthurblank.html; Wikipedia, "Arthur Blank," and "Bernard Marcus," at http://en.wikipedia.org/wiki/Arthur_Blank; and wiki/Bernard_Marcus; "Bernie Marcus (b.1929 N)" *The New Georgia Encyclopedia* at www.georgiaencyclopedia.org/nge/ArticlePrintable.jsp?id=h-1920; Mickey Goodman, "Bernie Marcus, Building a Better World," *Points North,* June 2002, at www.ptsnorth.com/ magazine/pn602_bernie_marcus.shtml;

393. Among sources: "Sol Price," Spock at www.spock.com/Sol-Price; Deborah Neville, "Sol Price Part II: The Acci-dental Retailer," Idea Lawyer at www.idealawyerblog.com/2007/06/ sol_price_part_ii_the_accident_1.html; "Archives, Jewish Studies Program," & "JHSSD-Sol Price Collection" at http://jewishstudies.sdsu.edu/archives.htm; and http://jewishstudies.sdsu.edu/archives/ sjssdcollect_price.htm; Wikipedia, "Costco," at http://en.wikipedia.org/ wiki/Costco; "I Was Raised to Lead by Example..." Jewish Federation: Giving Information, at www.jewishinseattle.org/JF/Giving/ Annual/Annual.asp; "Brotman," at www.answers.com/topic/brotman;

394. "Max Feldberg,, Retailer, 90," *The New York Times,* May 2, 1988; "Stanley H. Feldberg, 79, Retailer Who Helped Build Zayre Chain," *The New York Times,* May 16, 2004; "Obituary:Stanley H. Feldberg, 79, Trustee, *The Jus-tice,* May 25, 2004, at www.thejusticeonline.com/home/ index.cfm?event=displayArticlePrinterFriendly&u...; Alison Leigh Cowan, "Ames to Buy Discount Unit From Zayre," *The New York Times,* Sept. 16, 1988; Isadore Barmash, "Company News; Zayre to Take Big Write-Off," *The New York Times,* July 17, 1987; "About Our Company," "The TJX Companies, Inc. Reports Strong Fiscal Year 2008 Results," at TJX Web site, www.tjx.com/about/about.html and

press releases pages; Wikipedia, "TJX Companies," "Zayre," at http://en.wikipedia.org/wiki/TJX_Companies, & wiki/Zayre.

395. Among sources: "The company," "Financial Highlights," "A Message to our Shareholders," "Governance," all at Gap Web site, www.gapinc.com; Wikipedia, "Donald Fisher," "Gap (clothing retailer)," at http://en.wikipedia.org/ wiki/Donald_Fisher; and wiki/Gap_(clothing_retailer); "Mickey Drexler's Redemption," *New York* magazine at http://nymag.com/nymetro/news/bizfinance/biz/features/ 10489/index2.html; Andy Altman-Ohr, Sherith, "Israel's Legacy: Its Outspoken Rabbis," *Jewish News Weekly* at www.jewishsf.com/bk991008/1asherith.shtml; "Leadership Council," at www.jvs.org/ LC_2002.htm; "E-MMIS: March 2001, Local Leaders Named Israel Fellows,"at www.sfjcf.org/ whoweare/news/emmis/emmis030101.shtml.

396. Among sources: "Toys "R" Us" at www.toysrus.com/our/tru; "Toys 'R' Us: Beaten At Its Own Game," *Business Week*, March 29, 2004; David Kiley, "Can Toys 'R' Us Stay in the Game," *Business Week*, Jan. 10, 2005; "Toys "R" Us Sold," at Consumeraffairs.com, March 17, 2005 at www.consumeraffairs.com/new04/2005/toysrus.html; "Charles Lazarus," at Harvard Business School Leadership www.hbs.edu/leadership/database/leaders/512/; Nancy Meyer, "Charles Lazarus Toys "R" Us; He Turned the Baby Boom Into One Booming Business, Baby," *Home Furnishing Network*, at http://findarticles.com/p/articles/mi_hb4360/is_200011/ai_n15213520/print; Stacy Botwinick, "Thinking Outside the Toy Box: Charles Lazarus Raises TRU to be a 'Natural Born Category Killer' (TRU Anniversary Story,) *Playthings*, Jul 1, 2003 at www.accessmylibrary.com/coms2/summary_0286-24295251_ITM; "History," at www.americasgreatestbrands.com/volume3/18402a.htm; "Category Killers (Hardcover)" a book review at www.amazon.ca/Category-Killers-Robert-Spector/ dp/1578519608; Wikipedia, "Toys "R" Us," at http://en.wikipedia.org/wiki/Toys_"R"_us; Mark J. Kay, "Toys "R" Us Japan (A)(B) , Logistics Case Study for Council of Logistics Management, at www.csmp.org/download/public/resourcescasestudy/1996toysruscase.pdf.

397. Among sources: "Leslie H. Wexner," at www.referenceforbusiness.com/biography/S-Z/Wexner-Leslie-H; Kathy Lynn Gray, "Bella Wexner, Noted Philanthropist, 93," at http://slick.org/deathwatch/mailarchive/msg00382.html; "About Our company," at Limited Brands Web site, www.limitedbrands.com/about/index.jsp; Wikipedia, "Limited Brands," and Les Wexner, http://en.wikipedia.org/wiki/Leslie_Wexner; and wiki/Limited_Brands; American Jewish Historical Society, p. 216.

398. Among sources: "About Us," "Mervyns – Past to Present," "Mervyns company Backgrounder," at Mervyn's Web site w www.mervyns.com/corp/about_us.aspx; Wikipedia, "Mervyns," at http://en.wikipedia.org/wiki/Mervyn's; Abby Cohn, "Mervyn's Founder Named to Holocaust Museum Board," www.jewishsf.com/content/2-0-/module/ displaystory/story_id/18374/format/ html/edition_id/368/displaystory.html; Emily Thornton, "What Have You Done To My Company?" *Business Week*, Dec. 8, 2008.

399. Among sources: Maki Shiraki, "Bids Escalate for Barneys New York," *International Herald Tribune*, Aug. 6, 2007, at www.iht.com/bin/print.php?id=6996478; Suzanne Kapner, "Istithmar's Chic Sheiks Eye Barneys Bid," and "Dubai Firm Close to Buying Barneys," *New York Post*, Apr. 13, 2007 and June 13, 2007; Wikipedia, "Barneys New York," http://en.wikipedia.org/wiki/ Barneys_New_York; Sylvia Rubin, "Barneys Prepares to Bow in S.F. With Luxurious New Store," *San Francisco Chronicle*, Sept 18, 2007; Joshua Levine, "The Rise and Fall of the House of Barneys: A Family Tale of Chutzpah, Glory and Greed," *New York Post*, Dec 17. 2008; Troubled company Reporter, "BARNEY'S: The Pressman's Step Down," and "BARNEYS: Sibling Rivalry – The Real Thing," IBL at http://bankrupt.com/TCR_Public/980618.MBX; and http://bankrupt.com/TCR_Public/990813.MBX; Beth Landman Keil & Deborah Mitchell, "Barneys Couple Won't Press On," *New York Post*, Aug 24, 1998; "The Word, Fashion Family Feud," *New York Daily News*, at www.nydailynews.com/news/gossip/stroy/38054p-34911c.html; Beverly Stephen, "Miracle on Madison," *Wine Spectator*, Feb. 28, 1994; Tanya Jensen, "Gene Therapy," *Fashion Wire Daily*, April 21, 2001; Shelly Branch, "Barneys Finds Its Balance," *The Wall Street Journal*, Feb. 11, 2004.

400. Among sources: "Spiffing up Men's Warehouse," *Business Week*, Nov. 1, 2004; "Timeline," "Company Financials" at Men's Warehouse Web site at www.menswearhouse.com; "The Shalom School: A Double Blessing," Lubavitch.com at www.lubavitch.com/Article.asp?Section=60&Article=404; David Scharfenberg, "Latkes, Dancing Rabbis and a Huge Menorah Light Up Union Square," *Jewish News Weekly of Northern California*, Dec. 6, 2002; Wikipedia, "George Zimmer," http://en.wikipedia.org/ wiki/George_Zimmer.

401. Among sources: "Burlington Coat Factory to be Acquired by Bain Capital in $2.06 Billion Transaction," Jan. 18, 2006 at http://corporate.burlingtoncoatfactory.com/corpinfo/financials/jan18release-1.htm; "Corporate Profile" and, "Burlington Coat Factory Honored for its Charitable Efforts With the National Walk Award," Dec. 19, 2002 on www.coat.com/corpinfo/corporate_profile.shtml; www.coat.com/corpinfo/releases/awardrls.shtml; Jordon K. Speer, "Monroe Milstein, the 77-year-old Founder," *Apparel* magazine at http://apparelmag.com/ME2/ dirmod.asp?sid=&nm=&type=Publishing&mod=Publications. . Wikipedia, "Burlington Coat Factory," and "Monroe Milstein, http://en.wikipedia.org/wiki/Burlington_Coat_Factory and wiki/Monroe_Milstein.

402. Among sources: "Who is Sidney Kimmel?" "Sidney Kimmel Foundation," at www.kimmel.org; "Income State-

ment," *Annual Report 2006*,""Form 10-K," "About Us," "History," "Board of Directors," "Jones Apparel Group Brands," all at the Jones Apparel Web site at www.jny.com; Rose DeWolf, "Kimmel's $25M Gets Jewish Museum Rolling, *The Daily News*, Nov. 13, 2002 at www.nmajh.org/ newmuseum/newmuseum1113.htm; "Interview With Sidney Kimmel: at www.philorch.org/styles/ poa02e/www/interviewkimmel.html;

403. Among sources: "Ross Stores, Inc.-Google Finance" at http://finance.google.com/ finance?q=ROST; "Ross Stores, Inc." at Answers.com at www.answers.com/topic/ross-stores-inc?cat=biz-fin; "Stuart Moldav," at www. johnburtonfoundation.org/WhoWeAre.html;

404. Among sources: Silbiger, p. 70; "About Lillian Vernon," "Lillian's Story,"at www.lillianvernon.com/webapp/ wcs/stores/servlet/AboutStaticView?page=a. . ; Chantal Tode, "Lillian Vernon Files for Bankruptcy," *DMNews*, Feb 21, 2008 at www.dmnews.com/Lillian-Vernon-files-for-bankruptcy/PrintArticle/105365; Peter Lattman, "Buyout All-Stars Stumble," *The Wall Street Journal*, Mar 10, 2008; "Many Generations, One People, *Jewish Federation of Palm Beach County Annual Report 2007;"* "Leder Donations – Huffington Post," http://fundrace.huffingtonpost.com/ neighbors.php?type=name&1name=Leder;

405. Among sources: Marlene Adler Marks, "The Meaning of Loehmann's, RIP, *Jewish World Review*," June 8, 1999, at www.jewishworldreview.com/Marlene/marks060899.asp; "About Loehmann's" "Frieda Loehmann," at www.loehmanns.com/?p=about_us; Barney Gimbel, "Loemann's New Owner Keeps the Faith," *Fortune*, Feb. 7, 2005 at http://money.cnn.com/magzines/fortune/ fortune_archive/2005/02/07/3250442/index.htm; Silbiger, p. 81; Korman, p. 22; Wikipedia, "Loehmann's," at http://en.wikipedia.org/wiki/Loehmann's. John Ewoldt, "Loehmann's The forgotten Discounter," *Star Tribune*, Jan. 24, 2002 at www.startribune.com/stories/1229/1115221.html.

406. Among sources: Stephanie Strom, "Milton J. Petrie, Philanthropist, Is Dead at 92," *The New York Times*, Nov. 8, 1994; "Insider Likes Gap," at www.mit.edu/afs/net/user/tytso/usenet/usa-today/ invest/157; "The Raymond Troubh Page," at http://ourworld.compuserve.com/homepages/ CarolASThompson/Troubh.htm; "Form 8-K for Petrie Stores Liquidating Trust," Jan 9, 2004, at http://biz.yahoo.com/e/040109/pstls.ob8-k.html; "Petrie Stores Comments on Bankruptcy Filing," at http://bankrupt.com/TCR_Public/951013.MBX; "Management Buyout Group: Petrie Stores Corporation," at www.financo.com/transations90_94.html; "PBGC to Take Over Petrie Stores Pension Plan," *PBGC News*, July 8, 1998 at www.pbgc.gov.news/press_releases/1998/petric.htm; "10-K405 SEC Filing of Petrie Stores Liquidating Trust," April 2, 2001 at http://sec.edgar-online.com; "Petrie's Dish: A $10.5 Million Sale," *New York Metro*, Apr. 19, 1999 at www.newyorkmetro.com/nymetro/ new/people/columns/intelligencer/ 1126/.

407. Among sources: Ron Russell, "Richard Thalheimer, Founder of Sharper Image, Talks for the First Time About His Ouster," *SF Weekly* Oct 24, 2007 at www.sfweekly.com/2007-10-24/news/ironic-breeze/print; "About Richard Thal-heimer," at www.richardthalheimer.com; "Sharper Image Seeks to Hire a Liquidator,*" The Wall Street Journal*, March 6, 2008; Wikipedia, "Richard Thalheimer," http://en.wikipedia.org/wiki/Richard_Thalheimer; "Sun Capital Takes Bigger Slice of Sharper Image," May 25, 2007 at www.internetretailer.com/printArticle.asp?id-22518; "About Us," "The Sharper Image: A Brief History," at http://shop.store.yahoo.com/sharperimageeurope/about-us.html; Richard Thal-heimer, "How We Got Started," *Fortune*, at www.fortune.com/fortune/fsb/specials/innovators/thalheimer.html.

408. Among sources: "Death of August Brentano,*" The New York Times*, Nov. 3, 1886 at *The New York Times* Web archive; "Brentano's 'Booksellers to the World'" www.brentanos.fr/pages/whoarewe/history/ANG.htm. Wikipedia, "Brentano's," http://en.wikipedia.org/wiki/Brentano's; Etkes, p. 164.

409. Among sources: "Retail-Discount: Interesting Dates," at www.kipnotes.com/RetailDiscount.htm; "The Retail Timeline 1879 to 2003," at www.geocities.com/zayre88/Timeline.html; "Retailing, E-Commerce, Direct Marketing and Wholesaling," at http://academic.brooklyn.cuny.edu/economic/ friedman/mmretailing.htm; Wikipedia, E. J. Korvette, at http://en.wikipedia.org/wiki/E._J._Korvette.

410. Among sources: Caroline Hubbard, "Ritz Comes to Wolf Den," *Atlanta Business Chronicle*, May 7, 1999 at www.bizjournals.com/atlanta/stories/1999/05/10/story1.html; Robert J. Nebel, "A Wolf in Sheep's Clothing," *Atlanta Mag.*, Oct. 1999, at http://bobnebel.tripod.com/chuckwolf.html; David Armstrong, "High Contrast," *Forbes*, Nov. 25, 2002, at www.forbes.com/free_forbes/ 2002/1125/ 192.html; "Growth and Evolution of the Specialty Cam-era Store," at http://photoimagenew.com/history.htm; "Best Camera Stores," *Fairfield County Weekly*, May 13, 2004 at http://westchesterweekly.com/q/base/Guides/content?oid=oid:65616; "Wolf Sells to Ritz," www.vividlight.com/ articles/706.htm; "Wolf Camera Sole to Ritz Camera for $84.7 Million," *Atlanta Business Journal*, Aug. 22, 2001, at http://atlanta.bizjournals.com/atlanta/stories/2001/08/20/ daily28.html; "Generous Capital Campaign Challenge Gift Announced," *Temple Sinai News* at www.templesinai.org/html/news/; "Ritz and Wolf, History in the Making— Relatively Speaking," *Photo Industry Reporter*, June 10, 2004 at www.photoreporter.com/2001/ 09–03/ritz_and_wolf.html; "Wolf Camera Buying Fox Photo Chain," *Atlanta Business Chronicle*, July 1, 1998, www.bizjournals.com/ atlanta/stoies/1998/06/29/daily11.html?jst=s_rs_hl; "Ritz Camera Centers company History," at www.ritzcamera.com/webapp/wcs/stores/servlet/HelpView?storeal=...Julius Bloch—Led Brooks Camera," *San Francisco Chronicle*, July 20, 2004; Wikipedia, "Ritz Camera Centers," http://en.wikpedia.org/wiki/Ritz_Camera.

411. Among Sources: Peter C. Beller, "A Few Easy Payments," *Forbes*, Sept. 17, 2007; "Ron Popiel," The Great Idea Finder, at www.ideafinder.com/history/inventors/popeil.htm; "Annals of Enterprise: The Pitchman," *Gladwell.com*, Oct. 30 2000; at www.gladwell.com/2000/2000_10_30_a_pitchman.htm; "A Brief History of Ron Popeil, Founder of Ronco Inventions, LLC," at www.ronco.com/ history_of_ronco.di4; Wikipedia, "Ron Popeil," and "Veg-O-Matic," at http://en.wikipedia.org/wiki/ Ron_Popeil and wiki/Veg-O-Matic; Dennis McCann, "Chicago Collection Slices and Dices Veg-O-Matic and Ronco Records," *On Wisconsin*, March 19, 2004, at www.jsonline.com/dd/destmid/mar04/215949.asp.

412. Among sources: "King of the Start-Ups At Franklin Mint and QVC - Joseph M. Segel, W'51," Wharton Web site at www.wharton.upenn.edu/alum_mag/issues/125anniversaryissue/segel.html; "QVC Inc.," Funding Universe, at www.fundinguniverse.com/company-histories/QVC-Inc-Company-History.html; Geraldine Fabrikant, "The Media Business: Comcast Gets a Lift In QVC Bid," *The New York Times*, July 22, 1994; Bill Carter, "The Media Business: CBS, QVC and Comcast: A Tale of Personalities," *The New York Times*, July 18, 1994; "Press Release: Comcast Agrees to Sell Its Stake In QVC To Liberty Media, Comcast," July 3, 2003 at Comcast Web site www.comcast.com; "About QVC," " Corporate Facts," "Business Overview," "QVC Milestones," at www.qvc.com; "Financial Statements" from Liberty *Annual Report*, March 2007, pages F-7, 8, 23, 24; Wikipedia, "QVC," "Bud Paxson," "Joseph Segel,"and "Barry Diller," http://en.wikipedia.org/wiki/QVC, wiki/Bud_Paxson, wiki/Joseph_Segel andwiki/Barry_Diller; *Fortune* 5/3/04 p. 91.

413. Among sources: "Company Information," HSN.com at www.hen.som/corp/info/ default.aspx?aid=1870; "Paxson," at www.ketupa.net/paxson2.htm; "Media Mogul of the Month," Kellogg Alumni Media Club at http://kel logggalumni.northwestern.edu/Affinity/media/ additional.asp?id=130; "Bud Paxson," *The Vent*, Sept. 22, 1997, at www.dustbury.com/vent/ vent070.html; "IAC/InteractiveCorp 10-K, February 29, 2008," pages 36, 39, 40; Wikipedia, "Home Shopping Network," at http://en.wikipedia.org/wiki/Home_Shopping_Network.

414. Among sources for the material on Soviet Jewish history include: Yuri Slezkine, *The Jewish Century*, Princeton University Press, Princeton & Oxford, 2004; Martin Gilbert, *The Routledge Atlas of Jewish History*, Routledge, London & New York, 2003; Eli "Barnavi, Editor, *A Historical Atlas of the Jewish People*, Schocken, 2002; "Historical Atlas: Population of Russia" at www.tacitus.nu/historical-atlas/population/russia.htm; "Soviet Union Information Bureau: Area and Population," at www.marxists.org/history/ussr/government/1928/sufds/ch01.htm; "World Jewish Population: Latest Statistics," at www.simpletoremember.com/vitals/world-jewish-population.htm; "Nizar Sakhnini, "Demographic Trends in Palestine," at www.ifamercansknew.org/history/demography.html; "History of the Jews in Russia and the Soviet Union," and "Treaty of Brest-Litovsk," in Wikipedia at http://en.wikipedia.org/wiki/ History_of_the_Jews_in_Russia_and_the_Soviet_Union; and wiki/Treat_of_Brest-Litovsk; "The Doctors' Plot," at www.jewishvirtuallibrary.org/jsource/History/Human_Rights/plot.html; Thomas Sowell, *Ethnic America*, Basic Books, New York, 1981, p. 77–84.
Sources for the material on Lev Leviev include: Zev Chafets, The Missionary Mogul, *The New York Times Magazine*, Sept. 16, 2007; Phyllis Berman and Lea Goldman, "Cracked De Beers," *Forbes*, Sept 15, 2003; "The Discrete Tycoon," *Professional Jeweler*.com, Jan. 2002 at www.professionaljeweler.com/archives/articles/2002/jan02/0102dn2.html; and "Lev Leviev's Angolan Connection," Feb. 2002 at www.professionaljeweler.com/ archives/article/2002/feb02/0202dn1.html; "The Cartel Isn't Forever," *Economist*, July 17, 2004; Chamwe Kaira, "Lev Leviev Squares Up With De Beers," *Namibia Economist*, Feb 2004, at www.economist.com.na/2004/6feb/ 02-06-01.htm; Michael Rochvarger, The Marker, "Lev Leviev, Israel's Richest Man to Leave Country for London," Dec 27, 2007 at www.haaretz.com/hansen/objects/pages/ PrintArticleEn.jhtml?itemNo=939074; "Lev Leviev," "Chabad," "Arcadi Gaydamak," and "Africa Israel Investments," at Wikipedia. http://en.wikipedia.org/wiki/ Lev_Leviev, wiki/Chabad, wiki/Arcadi_Gaydamak, and wiki/Africa_Israel_Investments; Ben Smith, "Meet the Mogul," May 7, 2007, at www.nymag.com; Michael S. Arnold, "Diamond Mogul and Philanthropist Has Ear of Fellow Jews, World Leaders," *The Jewish Telegraphic Agency*, 03.04.2002 available at www.ncsj.org/AuxPages/ 030402Leviev.shtml; "Lev Leviev," The Federation of Jewish Communities of the CIS available at www.fjc.ru/AboutUs/ leader.asp?AID=82007; "Africa Israel Investments March 2007" and "Company Profile," from the Africa Israel Web site at www.africa-asrael.com/eng/inner.asp?id=2100&pext=2100; "Africa Israel's Lev Leviev to Move to London," *Reuters*, Dec. 27, 2007 at http://uk.reuters.com/ articlePrint?articleID=UKL2755912420071227;"Lev Leviev to Launch Russian Property IPO," March 26, 2007 at http://ftalphaville.ft.com/blog/2007/03/26/ 3396/lev-leviev-to-launch-russian-property-ipo/, Guy Chazan, "In Russia, a Top Rabbi Uses Kremlin Ties to Gain Power," *The Wall Street Journal*, May 8, 2007, Lev Gorodetsky, "Competing Chief Rabbis, Arrest, Confuse Russia, *Jewish Telegraphic Agency*, June 16, 2000 at www.ijn.com/archive/s000 arch/061600.htm, and others.

415. Among sources for this section are: "De Beers Consolidated Mines, Ltd.," and "Rhodes, Cecil (John)," *Encyclopaedia Britannica 2001*; Edward Jay Epstein, *The Diamond Invention*, at www.edwardjayepstein.com/diamond; Peter Schmeisser,"Harry Oppenheimer's Empire: going for the Gold," *The New York Times*, March 19, 1989; Alan Cowell, "Mining Giant Steps Out on Its Own," *The New York Times*, April 11, 2001; Alan Cowell with Rachel L. Swarns, "Disentangling a Worldwide Web of Riches," *The New York Times*, Feb 2, 2001; "Weddings: Jennifer Ward, Jonathan Oppenheimer," *The New York Times*, Jun 19, 1994; "De Beers "Profile," De Beers Ownership Structure (Abridged)," "Acquisition of De Beers," "De Beers Societe Anonyme Directors," "HFO Reflects," " Group Struc-

ture/Directorate," "Results For the Year Ended 31 December 2007," and "Nicky Oppenheimer," all from the De Beers' Web site at www.debeersgroup.com; "and "Anglo American Fact Book 2006/07,"and "History," both at the Anglo American Web site at www.angloamerican.co.uk; Terry Macalister, "I am an African," *Guardian*, July 2, 2005; "Is Nicky Oppenheimer an Old-Fashioned Mining Tycoon or a Radical Economic Reformer?" *Economist*, Aug 7, 2003; "Nicky Oppenheimer," *Forbes* March 24, 2008; "Nicky Oppenheimer," "De Beers," "Debswana," all at Wikipedia.org; and John R. Wilke, "De Beers Is in Talks to Settle Price-Fixing Charge," *The Wall Street Journal*, Feb 23, 2004.

416. Among Sources for the Zales sections are: "Our History," on the Zale Web site at www.zalecorp.com/company/company2.aspx; "Zale Corporation," on Morningstar at http://quicktake.morningstar.com/stocknet/IndustryPeers.aspx?Country=USA&Symbol=ZLC; Ann Zimmerman, "Breeden Gets Board Seat at Zale, Aims to Restore Jeweler's Luster," *The Wall Street Journal*, Jan. 19, 2008; and "Zale Corporation," at http://en.wikipedia.org/wiki/Zale_Corporation.

417. Among sources for the Signet section are: Bill Wilson, "Ratner Prepares His Return to the Lions' Den," *BBC News*, Mar 29, 2005, available at http://newsvote.bbc.co.uk/mpapps/pagetools/print/ news.bbc.co.uk/1/hi/business/4314873.stm; "Fact Sheet," "Group History," and "Overview," at the Signet Web site at www.signetgroupplc.com/; "Signet Group," and "British Jews," at http://en.wikipedia.org/wiki/Signet_Group; and http://en.wikipedia.org/w/index.php?title=Category British_Jews; and "Signet Group PLC," at http://quicktake.morningstar.com/StockNet/IndustryPeers. aspx?Country=USA&Symbol=SIG.

418. Among sources for the Borsheim's section are: "Great Plains Store"," March 2007 at www.instoremag.com; "Borsheim's History, " at www.Borsheims.com; "Encyclopedia>Borsheim's Fine Jewelry," at www.nationmaster.com/encyclopedia/Borsheims-Fine-Jewelry; "HDR Designs Renovation for Landmark Jewelry Store," at www.hdrinc.com/8/34/1/default.aspx?entry=290; the Google returns for "Rebecca Friedman" Louis Friedman; and for "Ike Friedman" Rose Blumkin"; and "Borsheim's Fine Jewelry at http://en.wikipedia.org/wiki/Borsheim's_Fine_Jewelry; "Wesley Pruden, "A Modest Proposal for Arkansas Folk," *Jewish World Review*, Jan. 3, 2001 at www.jewishworldreview.com/ cols/pruden010301.asp

419. Among sources for the Helzberg section are: "Our Story," and other parts of the Helzberg Web site at www.helzberg.com and the Berkshire Hathaway, Inc Web site at www.berkshirehathaway.com/subs/sublinks.html; mvan blerk, "Berkshire Companies," at www.marketocracy.com/cgi-bin/WebObjects/Portfolio.woa/ps/ReadTopicPage/source=CdOkFkKIDmEiCnAhMaKiAbBi; .

420. Among sources for the Ben Bridge section are: "About Ben Bridge," "Store Locator," at the Ben Bridge Web site at www.benbridge.com; "Bridge, Herbert "Herb" Marvin (b. 1925)" at www.historylink.org/essays/printer_friendly/index.cfm?file_id=7307; "Interview with Herb Bridge, Arny Robbins, Interviewer," at www.gcl.net/family/scrapbook/Herb-Bridge-Interview.htm; and, "Manny Frishberg, Bridge Works for Kids," March 7, 2008, at www.jtnews.net/index.php?/news/item/4084/C22/.

421. Among sources for the Apparel overview are: Sowell, *Ethnic America*, p. 77–84; Mary Bellis, "Stitches – The History of Sewing Machines at http://inventors.about.com/library/inventors/ blsewing_machine.htm; and "Patent Model of Isaac M. Singer's Sewing Machine 1854," at www.smithsonianlegacies.si.edu/objectdescription.cfm?ID=89.

422. Among sources for the Levi Strauss section are: American Jewish Historical Society, p. 237; "Fact Sheet," and "2007 Annual Report" on the company's Web site at www.levistrauss.com; and "Levi Strauss" at www.emediaplan.com/admunch/Brands/levistrauss.asp; Leon Harris, *Merchant Princes*, Kodansha International, New York, Tokyo, London, pages 68, 185, 194, 220, 239–9, 240, 255.

423. Among sources for the Hattie Carnegie section are various articles from the Web site, www.hattie-carnegie.com; "Hattie Carnegie," at http://en.wikipedia.org/wiki/Hattie_Carnegie.

424. Among sources for the Calvin Klein section are: American Jewish Historical Society, "Klein, Calvin,"pages 216, 226;, 1999; Ingrid Sischy, "Calvin to the Core," *Vanity Fair*, April 2008; "Calvin Klein," at *AskMen*, www.askmen.com/men/business_politics/36_calvin_klein.html; "Calvin Klein," at www.fashion.at/who/calvin1.htm; as well as the Calvin Klein Web site www.calvinklein.com/ sitemap.aspx.

425. Among sources for the Ralph Lauren section are: Suzy Menkes, "Ralph Lauren Returns to his Russian Roots," *International Herald Tribune*, May 14, 2007; "Ralph Lauren Corporation," Google Finance at http://finance.google.com/finance?q=RL; "Genuine Authentic," at the Michael Gross Web site, www.mgross.com/books/genuine-authentic/; Aude Lagorce, "Ralph Lauren Vs. Tommy Hilfiger," *Forbes*, Dec. 1, 2003; "Ralph Lauren – Biography," at http://fashion-forum.org/fashion-designers/ralph-lauren.html; the Ralph Lauren Proxy Statement for the 2007 Annual Meeting; and "Ralph Lauren," at http://en.wikipedia.org/wiki/ Ralph_Lauren.

426. Among sources for the Anne Klein section are: "Anne Klein Dead: Designer Was 51," *The New York Times*,

March 20, 1974, Cathy Horyn, "A Woman in the House: Isabel Toledo," http://runway.blogs.nytimes.com/2007/02/10/a-woman-in-the-house; and "Anne Klein," at http://en.wikipedia.org/wiki/Anne_Klein.

427. Among sources for the Donna Karan section are: "Donna Karan, Times Topics>People" *The New York Times Web site* at http://topics.nytimes.com/top/reference/timestopics/ people/k/donna_karan/ index.html; "Donna Karan Biography," at www.infomat.com/whoswho/donnakaran.html; and "Donna Karan – Biography," at the *Fashion Forum*, available at www.fashion-forum.org/fashion-designers/ donna-karan.html; "Donna Karan," (Her own blog) at www.huffingtonpost.com/donna-karan; "Donna Karan," *St James Encyclopedia of Popular Culture*, 2002 Gale Group; Leslie Kaufman, "LMVH Makes a Two-Part Offer for Donna Karan," Dec. 19, 2000, "company News: LVMH to Acquire Donna Karan International," April 3, 2001, Cathy Horyn, "Stephan Weiss, 62, Fashion Empire's Other Half," June 11, 2001, and "LVMH Completes Donna Karan Deal," Nov. 28, 2001, all in *The New York Times*; and "Donna Karan," and "LVMH" at Wikipedia, http://en.wikipedia.org/wiki/Donna-Karan; and wiki/ LVMH. American Jewish Historical Society, pages 225–6; Etkes, p. 166.

428. Among sources for the section on Liz Claiborne: American Jewish Historical Society, p. 219; "Liz Claiborne" at the Web site: www.distinguishedwomen.com/biographies/claibor.html; Adam Bernstein, "Liz Claiborne, 78; Fashion Industry Icon, *Washington Post*, June 28, 2007; "Liz Claiborne," *Economist*, Jul 5, 2007; and "Liz Claiborne (fashion designer) and Liz Claiborne at Wikipedia Web site, http://en.wikipedia.org/wiki/Liz_Claiborne_(fashion_designer); and wiki/Liz_Claiborne.

429. Among sources for the section on Guess are: "Overview," "The Brothers' Bios," "Timeline,"Letter to Shareholders," "Fundamentals–Snapshot, and "Guess, Inc., *Proxy Statement*," all available at the Guess Web site at www.guess.com; Ingrid Sischy, "The Dreamer (Interview with Paul Marciano)" at www.findarticles.com/cf_dis/m1285/in10_v27/20803791/p1/article.jhtml; and "Who's who Biography of Armand Marciano," at www.infomat.com/whoswho/armandmarciano.html.

430. Among sources for the section on Jordache are: "Jordache Is Not Just Jeans," "The 'Look' For Over 26 Years," "Residential and Commercial Real Estate," from the Jordache Web site at www.jordachecorporate.com/2006 /company.shtml; "Jordache Information Designer History," at www.yournewfragrance.com/Jordache-s/2391.htm; "Jordache," at http://en.wikipedia.org/wiki/Jordache; "Jordache Enterprises, Inc. Company Profile," at http://biz.yahoo.com/ic/44/44247.html; Ji Hyun Lim, "Galloping In From Fashion's Past," at www.asianweek.com/2002 02_15/ cny_jordache.html, and others.

431. Among sources for the Hart, Schaffner & Marx section are "Hart, Schaffner, Marx & Hillman," *Time*, April 19, 1937 available at www.time.com/time/printout/0,8816,757657,00.html; "Hartmarx Brands," "Bringing Luxury to Everyday," "Operating Segment Selected Data," and "Hartmarx Family History," from the Hartmarx Web site at www.hartmarx.com; "Hart, Schaffner & Marx," at www.encyclopedia.chicagohistory.org/pages/2695.html; "Profile Hartmarx Corp" at http://finance.yahoo.com/q/pr?s=HMX, "Hart Schaffner Marx," at www.americasgreatestbrands.com/volume5/pdf/hart-schaffner-marx, and Ross Grossman, "350 Years After First Jewish Settlers, Judaism Thrives in America," at www.jewishworldreview.com/0904/american_Jews.hph3?printer_friendly.

432. Among sources for the section on Phillips-Van Heusen are: "History," at the Phillips Van-Heusen Web site at www.pvh.com; Kathleen Teltsch, "Gift to Beth Israel is Just Part of a Family Tradition," *The New York Times*, April 5, 1994, and "John M. van Heusen Jr., Clothier, 96,"*The New York Times*, November 6, 1993, both from the archives at http://query.nytimes.com; "Collars," *Time*, November 22, 1926 at www.time.com/time/printout/08816,722776,00.html; "Phillips-Van Heusen," from the Wikipedia Web site at www.en.wikipedia.org/wiki/Phillips_Van_Heusen; and "Key Statistics," and "Profile" at http://finance.yahoo.com.

433. Among sources for the section on Warnaco are: "Business Overview" at www.warnaco.com; "Key Statistics," "Competitors," and "Profile," at http://finance.yahoo.com/q/pr?s=WRNC; "Linda Wachner," at www.infoplease.com/ipa/AO776488.html; Diane Brady, "Headliner: Linda Wachner: From Rag Riches to Rags," *Business Week*, June 25, 2001; Michael Gross, "The Word – She's Coming Back," at www.nydailynews.com/new/gossip/story/43481p-40994c.html; Darryl Lyman, *Jewish Heroes and Heroines*, Jonathan David Publishers, Inc., Middle Village, New York, 1996, p. 150; Etkes, p. 171.

434. Among sources for section on Reebok are: LouAnn Lofton, "Rebounding Reebok, "Overview," at the Reebok Web site at www.reebok.com; and www.europe.reebok.com; "Reebok," at http://wikipedia.org.wiki/Reebok, Jenn Abelson, "Fireman Era Ends," at www.boston.com/business/articles/2006/02/01/fireman_era_ends?mode=PF; Silbiger, pages 70, 92.

Among sources for the section on Adidas is Richard Northedge, "Profile: A Shoo-in for Adidas," *Telegraph*.co.uk at www.telegraph.co.uk/money/main.jhtml?xml=/money/2007/09/30/ccprof130.xml; "Alumni Achievement Awards 2000: Robert L. Louis-Dreyfus," at the Harvard Business School Web site http://hsbwk.hbs.edu/archive/1675.html; "Playing to Win Robert L. Louis Dreyfus," at www.alumni.hbs.edu/bulletin/1998/october/global/dreyfus.html; John Tagliabue, "The Media Business: Advertising; Once Behind the Pack, Adidas Vies for the Lead," *The New York*

Times, March 19, 1998; "History," on the Adidas Web site at www.adidas-group.com; "Adidas," and "Robert Louis-Dreyfus," on Wikipedia at http://en.wikipedia.org/wiki/Adidas and wiki/Robert_Louis-Dreyfus.

435. Among sources for the section on Timberland are: "About Timberland," "CSR l Community Engagement," on the Timberland Web site, www.timberland.com; "Timberland Reports Fourth-Quarter and Full Year 2007 Results," at the Money Central Web site at http://news.moneycentral.msn.com/ticker/article.aspx?Feed=BW&Date=20080207&ID=8; "Timberland Co Ownership Breakdown" at http://finance.aol.com/company/the-timberland-company/tbl/ nys/inst; and "The Timberland company," at Wikipedia, http://en.wikipedia.org/wiki/ The_Timberland_Company.

436. Among sources for the section on Florsheim are: "About Us," at www.florsheim.com; "Florsheim Shoe Co." on the Encyclopedia of Chicago Web site at www.encyclopedia.chicagohistory.org/pages/ 2668.html; "Florsheim Shoe Group Inc." at the Answers.com Web site at www.answers.com/ topic/florsheim-shoe-group-inc?cat=biz-fin; "Florsheim Family," at http://loebtree.com/flor.html; Jim Bowman, "The Florsheim Shoe Story," a speech to the Chicago Literary Club, March 29, 2004 available at www.chilit.org/Papers by author/Bowman-Florsheim;

437. Among sources for the section on Dexter Shoe are: "Family Fortunes," *Forbes*, Oct 12, 1998; David R. Holland, "Dexter Players Series Features New Fast Twist," at www.worldgolf.com/ products/dexter-shoes.htm; Sheri Qualters, "Investors Aim To Revive the Etonic Brand," *Boston Business Journal*, Dec.15, 2003 at http://boston.bizjournals.com/boston/stories/2003/12/15/story6.html; "Harold Alfond Keeps on Giving," at www.sjcme.edu/campaign/Recent-CampaignNews_December52003.html; "Dexter Shoes – History," at www.brandnameshoes.com/dexter-shoes.html;

438. Among sources for the section on Maidenform are: "At a Glance, "Our History," "David Kaplan," "Corporate Profile," at the Maidenform Web site, http://ir.maidenform.com/phoenix.zhtml?c=190009&p=irol-IRHome; Erica Copulsky, "Strapped Maidenform Seeks Suitor," *New York Post*, January 15, 2004 at www.nypost.com/seven/01152004/business/15739.htm; "Maidenform Collection, 1922–1997 No.585," at http://americanhistory.si.edu/archives/d7585.htm; and others.

439. Among sources for the Cosmetics overview are: "Beauty and Make-Up History: Make Up Fashion History Before 1950," at http://fashion-era.com/make-up.htm; "Cosmetics," and "History of Cosmetics," at http://en.wikipedia.org/wiki/Cosmetics and wiki/History_of_cosmetics; "Arden, Elizabeth," at *Encyclopædia Britannica 2001*; Linda Woodhead, "Elizabeth Arden and Helena Rubinstein," at www.virago.co.uk/virago/meet/woodhead_extract.asp?TAG=BS2AVX6X4929951X2OUI8T&CID=virago; Suzanne Hoppough, "Father's Past Haunts French Billionaire," *Forbes* March 18, 2005; "Eugene Schueller," at http://in.wikipedia.org/wiki/Eug%C3%A8ne_Schueller"

440. Among sources for the section on Helena Rubinstein are: "Rubinstein, Helena," *Encyclopædia Britannica 2001*; "Seymour "Sy" Brody, Helena Rubinstein," at www.jewishvirtuallibrary.org/jsource/ biography/hrubinstein; "About Helena Rubinstein," "Summary of Grants," "Funding Guidelines," at the Helena Rubinstein Foundation Web site, http://fdncenter.org/grantmaker/rubinstein/guide.html; "Helena Rubinstein," at http://womenshistory.about.com/od/fashion20th/p/helena_rubinste.htm; and "Helena Rubinstein," at the Wikipedia Web site, http://en.wikipedia.org/wiki/Helena_Rubinstein; Lyman, Heroes, p. 147; American Jewish Historical Society, p. 235; Etkes p. 169; Silbiger, pages 70, 186.

441. Among sources for the section on Estée Lauder are: "Officers," "Directors," "Proxy Statement," "Facts at a Glance," at the Estée Lauder Web sites, www.elcompanies.com; Ellen Byron, "Tension Shakes Up Estée Lauder Dynasty," *The Wall Street Journal*, Feb 27, 2008; "Profile Estée Lauder Companies, Inc,' "Major Holders," at http://finance.yahoo.com/q/pr?s=EL; Daniel Roth, "Sweet Smell of Succession," *Fortune*, Sept. 19, 2005; "Estée Lauder—Industry Peers," and "Estée Lauder – Snapshot" at the Morningstar Web site at http://quicktake.morningstar.com/stocknet/IndustryPeers.aspx?Country=USA&Symbol=EL; "Message in a Bottle," April 27, 2004 at www.smh.com.au/articles/2004/04/ 26/1082831_4904480.html?from=storyrhs; Adam Bernstein, "Estée Lauder, Doyenne of Cosmetics Industry She Built Empire Worth Billions From 'Jars of Hope,'" *Washington Post*, April 26, 2004. Lyman, *Heroes*, p. 146; American Jewish Historical Society, pages 214, 232; Silbiger, pages 88, 174–5, 185.

442. Among sources for the section on Revlon are: "Revson, Charles H(askell)," *Encyclopædia Britannica 2001*; "About the Foundation – Charles H. Revson," www.revsonfoundation.org/about_chr.htm; "Charles Revson," at www.infoplease.com/cgi-bin/id/AO771992; "History," "10-K," "Stock Fundamentals," "Corporate Profile," "Proxy Statement," on the Revlon Web site at www.corporate-ir.net/ireye/ir_site.zhtml?ticker=REV&script=950; and "Revlon," at http://en.wikipedia.org/ wiki/Revlon; Etkes, p. 169.

443. Among sources for the section on Max Factor are: "History of Max Factor," on the P&G Web site at www.pg.com; "Descendants of ? Factrowitz, Rabbi," at http://us.geocities.com/gincig/factor/maxfactorfam.htm?200827; "Factor, Max," *Encyclopædia Britannica 2008*, Ultimate Reference Suite; "About Max Factor," on www.maxfactor.com/about/about.jsp; "The Max Factor Beauty Museum," at www.seeing-stars.com/

Museums/MaxFactor;shtml; "Max Factor, Sr," and "Max Factor," at Wikipedia Web sites http://en.wikipedia.org/wiki/Max_Factor, and wiki/Max_Factor,_Sr. Martin Gilbert, *The Jews in the Twentieth Century*, Schocken Books, New York, 2001, p. 49.

444. American Jewish Historical Society, p. 215.

445. Lyman, *Heroes*, p. 149.

446. Allen Symons, "Sassoon, Vidal," *The Jewish Contribution to the 20th Century*, Polo Publishing, London, 1997; Etkes p. 174.

447. Among sources for material on Gottex/Gottliebs are: Bernadine Morris, "For Gottex, Flatter is Step No. 1," *The New York Times*, June 4, 1991; Barbara Rudolph, "Israel's Place in the Sun," *Time*, June 3, 1985; Mari Davis, "Gottex: Celebrating Its 50th Anniversary, *Fashion Windows*, Sept. 9, 2006;Jan Shure, "60 Years of Fashion: Swinging Into the Spotlight," *The Jewish Chronicle* at www.thejc.com/home.aspx?ParentId=m11s19s238&SecId=238&AId=59623&ATyp.

448. Among sources for the material on Häagen-Dazs/Mattus are: Richard D. Lyons, "Reuben Mattus, 81, Founder of Haagen-Dazs (sic)," *The New York Times*, Jan. 29, 1994; Ruth Reichl, "Lives Well Lived: Reuben Mattus; The Vichyssoise of Ice Cream," *The New York Times*, Jan 1, 1995; "Reuben and Rose Mattus," Wikipedia at http://en.wikipedia.org/wiki/Reuben_and_Rose_Mattus; Joel Lipowsky, "Remembering Rose Mattus," *The Jewish Standard*, Dec. 7, 2006; Stephen Miller, "Rose Mattus, 90, Co-Founder of Häagen -Dazs," *The Sun*, Dec. 1, 2006; "A Long and Delicious History! Four Generations!," at the Mattus Ice Cream Web site @ www.mattusicecream.com; "History," on the Häagen-Dazs Web site; "Merger Roulette—Pillsbury and Other Potential Food Industry Takeover Targets," *Prepared Foods*, July 2000; "Nestle Wants to Buy Haagen-Dazs (sic), *Processing Magazine*, Oct. 29, 2001; "Nestle Scoops up Dreyer's Ice Cream," ISA-The Instrument, Systems, and Automation Society, June 17, 2002 at the ISA Web site, www.isa.org/PrinterRemplate.cfm?Section=InTech&template=/ContentManagement/Cont...."Director's Corner," *Dallas Theological Seminary Connection*, Fall, 2001 Vol 9, No. 2; Etkes, p. 173.

449. Among sources for the section on Ben & Jerry's are: "Timeline," at www.benjerry.com; Irina Aleksander, "Peachy Keen: Willie Nelson and a Brief History of Ben & Jerry's Ice Cream," *Rolling Stone*, March 16, 2007; "Ben & Jerry's" at http://en.wikipedia.org/wiki/Ben_&_Jerry's; Ben Fischer and Rick Munarriz, "The Emperors of Ice Cream: Dueling Fools," *The Motley Fool.com*, June 27, 2003 at www.fool.com/specials/2003/03062700ice.htm; "Unilever Scoops Up Ben & Jerry's," BBC News, April 12, 2000 at http://news.bbc.co.uk/1/hi/business/710694.htm; "Unilever Replaces Ben & Jerry's CEO – Unilever Group – Ben & Jerry's Homemade, Inc," *Dairy Foods*, Jan 2001; "Strategies to Expand Trade Opportunities," at www.wia.usda.gov/sessions/TAPE425.htm; and others.

450. Among sources for the Baskin-Robbins section are: Stephen Miller, "He Helped Concoct 31 Flavors Policy and Sold Fun Along With Ice Cream," *The Wall Street Journal*, May 10–11, 2008; Dennis Hevesi, "Irvine Robbins, Ice Cream Entrepreneur And a Maestro of 31 Flavors Dies at 90," *The New York Times*, May 7, 2008; "Baskin-Robbins – Our History," on the company's Web site at www.baskinrobbins.com/About/OurHistory.aspx; "Baskin-Robbins," at http://en.wikipedia.org/wiki/Baskin-Robbins; and others.

451. Among sources for the Dove Bar section are: "Sweet Deal? Selling off Frozen Assets," *University of Chicago Magazine* at http://magazine.uchicago.edu/9812/html/enquirer2.htm; "The Dove Story," at www.dovechocolate.com/Story.aspx; "House Resolution 459," House of Representatives Ninety First General Assembly, Nov. 17, 1999 at www.ilga.gov/house/journals/hdailyjrnls91/hjf91068_r.html; "James Zacharias," on the Illinois Bar Association Web site at www.isba.org/association/12-li.htm; and conversations with Ed Stolman, a friend of the author.

452. Among sources for the Sara Lee/Charles Lubin section are: "Charles W. Lubin, 84, Sara Lee's Founder," *The New York Times*, July 17, 1988; "Sara Lee. Our History," at www.saralee.com.au/special.php?page=history.html; "Sara Lee," at http://en.wikipedia.org/wiki/Sara_Lee_Corporation; "Financial Summary," "Senior Management Team – Brenda Barnes," and "Board of Directors," at www.saralee.com.

453. Among sources for the Starbucks/Howard Schultz section are, Andy Serwer, "Hot Starbucks To Go," *Fortune*, Jan. 26, 2004 pages 60–74; "Financial Highlights," from the Starbuck's *2007 Annual Report*, available on their Web site at www.starbucks.com; "Starbucks," at http://en.wikipedia.org/wiki/Starbucks.

454. Among sources for the Seagrams/Bronfman section are: Frank Prial, "Whiskey Chasers," a review of the Nicholas Faith book, *The Bronfmans*, in *The New York Times*, June 25, 2006; Julie Weiner, "Seagrams Sale Bodes Well," *Jewish Telegraphic Agency* as reproduced in *Jewish News of Greater Phoenix*, June 23, 2000 available at www.jewishaz.com/jewishnews/000623/sale.shtml; "History of the Seagram Plant in Waterloo," on the Waterloo, Ontario Web site at www.city.waterloo.on.ca/SeagramCollection/history/plant_timeline.html; "Seagram Company, Ltd., The," in *Encyclopaedia Britannica 2001*; "*Samuel Bronfman*," a synopsis of the book by the same name by its author, Michael R.

Marrus available on the Brandeis University Press Web site at www.upne.com/JS-0-87451-571-8html; "Samuel Bronf-man," and "Seagram Building," at http://encyclopedia.thefreedictionary.com/Samuel Bronfman; "Edgar M. Bronf-man Honored by UAlbany's Center for Jewish Studies," a May 30, 2003 Press Release issued by the University of Albany at www.albany.edu/news/releases/2003/may2003/bronfman.htm; "Edgar M. Bronfman, Sr. 'Creating a Renaissance in Jewish Life," a biographical write up prepared in conjunction with a lecture to be delivered at the University of California at Santa Barbara, at www.ihc.ucsb.edu/events/past/oldersite/bronfman/; Devin Leonard, "The Bronfman Saga," and "Bronfman: Take Two – What Has the Younger Bronfman Learned From His First Reign?" *Fortune*, Nov. 10, 2002; and May 28, 2003; "Better Luck This Time?" *Economist*, Nov. 27, 2003; "Edgar Bronfman, Jr., at http://en.wikipedia.org/wiki/Edgar_Bronfman_Jr., American Jewish Historical Society, pages 212–6, and others.

455. Among sources for the Welch's/J.M. Kaplan section are: Wolfgang Saxon, "Jacob Kaplan, Philanthropist, Is Dead," *The New York Times*, July 20, 1987; Anthony & Diane Hallett, *Entrepreneur Magazine Encyclopedia of Entrepreneurs*, J. Wiley Publishers, New York, 1997, pages 483–7; "About Welch's Company History," from the Welch's Web site at www.welchs.com; The 2006 Form 990 for the J. M. Kaplan Foundation available at the Web site of *Guidestar* at www.guidestar.org; and at ActivistCash.com; "Raymond T. Ryan Led Welch's, Played Key Role in Grape Industry," a press release at the Welch's Web site. "J.M. Kaplan Fund" Web site at www.jmkfund.org; American Jewish Historical Society, p. 216, and others.

456. Among sources for the Hunt/Norton Simon section are: Eric Pace, "Norton Simon, Businessman and Collector, Dies at 86," *The New York Times*, June 4, 1993; "Norton Simon Biography," on the Web site of the Norton Simon Museum at www.nortonsimon.org/aboutnsm/nsbio.asp; Book review on Amazon.com of Suzanne Muchnic's, *Odd Man in: Norton Simon and the Pursuit of Culture;* Obituary: Simon, Norton, *Encyclopædia Britannica 1994–2001*; "About Hunt's," on the Hunt Food Web site at www.hunts.com/A040Then.jsp?mnav=about; Etkes, p. 170; and, "Norton Simon," at http://en.wikipedia.org/wiki/Norton_Simon; "The David J. Mahoney Page," at www.smokershistory.com/DMahoney.htm; Darryl Lyman, *Jewish Heroes & Heroines*, Jonathan David Publishers, Inc., Middle Village, NY, 1996, p. 150.

457. Among sources for the Slim-Fast/Abraham section are: Lacey Rose, "America's Most Famous Diet Gurus," *Forbes*, April 6, 2005 available at www.forbes.com/2005/04/06/cx_lrlh_0406dietgurus_print.html; "S. Daniel Abraham," at http://en.wikipedia.org/wiki/S._Daniel_Abraham; "Job Board: Slim-Fast – The company (continued)," on the Slim Fast Web site at www.slim-fast.com/jobs/ index.asp?job_continue=cont_next&bhcp=1; "S. Daniel Abraham (with Ewa)," on the *Mother Jones*.com Web site at www.motherjones.com/news/ special_reports/mojo_400/ 1_abraham.html; "S Daniel Abraham," on the Center for Middle East Peace & Economic Cooperation Web site at www.centerpeace.org/bios; David Marino-Nachison, "A Happy Ending for Ben & Jerry's?" on the Motley Fool.com Web site at www.fool.com/news/foolplate/2000/ foolplate000412.htm? "Slim Fast" at http://enwikipedia.org/wiki/ Slim_Fast; and others.

458. Among sources for the Weight Watchers/Nidetch section are: "Jean Nidetch, Benefactor," on the UNLV Web site at http://womenscenter.unlv.edu/benefactor.htm; "Jean Nidetch," at www.horatioalger.com/members/ member_info.cfm? "History & Philosophy: Who We Are," and "A Message From David Kirchhoff, President, Weight Watchers International," at www.weightwatchers.com; "Jean Nidetch," on the Who Made America?" Page at the PBS Web site, www.pbs.org/wgbh/theymadeamerica/ whomade/nidetch_hi.html; "Weight Watchers – How It All Began," at www.handbag.com/healthfit/ wwdiet/wwhistory/; "Jean Nidetch," at http://en.wikipedia.org/wiki/ Jean_Nidetch; "The Weight Watchers Method," on the Israeli Weight Watchers Web site at www.shomreymishkal.co.il/about_e.asp; "Weight Watchers," at http://en.wikipedia.org/wiki/Weight_Watchers; the Weight Watchers Company profile at *WSJ*.com, Etkes, p. 173, and others.

459. Among sources for the NutriSystems/Katz & Satz section are: Lacey Rouse, "America's Most Famous Diet Gurus," *Forbes*, April, 6, 2005 and David Whelan, "Before ...and After," *Forbes*, Oct. 30, 2006; "NutriSystem, Inc.," at The Funding Universe Web site www.fundinguniverse.com/company-histories/NutriSystem-Inc.; "NutriSystems Diet," at http://en.wikipedia.org/wiki/Nutrisystems_Diet; "New Executive Team Takes Leadership of Nutri/System, Inc." a press release issued by Nutrisystem on Dec. 23, 2002; Peter Key, "Back in the Game: Trio Nets Nutri/System," *Philadelphia Business Journal*, Dec 23, 2003; "NutriSystem Inc. Annual Earnings," at *The Wall Street Journal Web* site www.smartmoney.com/wsj/briefingbooks/doPrint.cfm?page= ; "Harold Katz," at www.katzgroup.com/profiles.html; "A Record of Success," at www.la-weightloss.com/about/Franchise/record.aspx; and others.

460. Among sources for the section on Jenny Craig are: Lacey Rouse, "America's Most Famous Diet Gurus," *Forbes*, April 6, 2005; "Jenny Craig Brings 5 Times Its Price in '02," *The New York Times*, June 25, 2007; "ACI Capital, DB Capital Partners Complete Acquisition of Jenny Craig, Inc., 5-14-02," at www.franchisepr.com/jennycraig2.htm; "Jenny Craig, Inc.," at http://en.wikipedia.org/wiki/ Jenny_Craig_Inc. "Jenny Craig Corporate Profile," and other pages at www.jennycraig.com/corporate/ media/profile; "Jenny Craig," at www.hoovers.com/jenny-craig/ -ID_15441-/free-co-factsheet.xhtml; "Sid Craig," and "Jenny Craig," at www.jennycraig.com/corporate/ company/scraig.asp and jcraig.asp; "Jenny Craig," at http://in.wikipedia.org/wiki/Jenny_Craig; "Jenny Craig Life Behind the Scenes," at www.vorhaus.com/new/cbses_jennycraig.html; and others.

461. Among sources for the Lionel/Cowen section are: "Joshua Lionel Cowen," "Lionel Corp," and "Lionel, LLC," at http://en.wikipedia.org/wiki/Lionel_Corporation, wiki/Lionel_LLC, and wiki/ Joshua_Lionel_Cowen; "Lionel History," at www.lionel.com/Central/LionelPastAndPresent/History.cfm; "Lionel Prepares to Exit Bankruptcy," at www.bankruptcy-lawyers-network.com/blog/?p=166; The description, selected pages and reviews of Ronald Hollander's "*All Aboard: The Story of Joshua Lionel Cowen & His Lionel Train Company,*" Workman Publishing Company, New York 1981–2000 pages 1–10 www.Amazon.com; Edward Wyatt, "Martin Davis, 72; Created Modern Paramount," *The New York Times,* Oct. 6, 1999.

462. Among sources for the Mattel/Handler section are: "Paul Lukas and Maggie Overfelt, "Mattel: How a Stylish Doll Became a Head Turning Classic and Put a Pair of Fledgling Entrepreneurs in Play," *Fortune,* April 1, 2003; "History," at the Mattel Web site, www.mattel.com/about_us/history/ default.asp?f=true; Veronica Horwell, "Ruth Handler: Creator of the Doll Whose Changing Style Defined Generations of Young Womanhood," *Guardian Unlimited,* May 2, 2002; Sarah Kershaw, "Ruth Handler, Whose Barbie Gave Dolls Curves, Dies at 85," *The New York Times,* April 29, 2002; Constance L. Hayes, "Chief of Mattel Steps Down After Reporting Loss in 1999," *The New York Times,* February 4, 2000; E. J. Kessler, "Campaign Confidential," *Forward,* April 25, 2003; "Honor Roll – American Jewish University," at www.ajula.edu/Content/ContentUnit.asp?CID=1626&u+53388&t=0; *2007 Mattel Annual Report* and First Quarter 2008 Financial Results available on the Mattel Web site at www.mattel.com; "Mattel," at http://wikipedia.org/wiki/Mattel, Etkes, p. 172; American Jewish Historical Society, pages 216–7; Silbiger, pages 168–9, and others.

463. Among sources for the Hasbro/Hassenfeld section are: "History," "Board of Directors and Executive Officers," and "Consolidated Statement of Operations," on the Hasbro Web site at www.hasbro.com; Silbiger, pages 170–1; "Hasbro," at http://en.wikipedia.org/wiki/Hasbro; and "Company News; Hasbro's Purchase of Coleco Assets," *The New York Times,* July 13, 1989.

464. Among sources for the Grossinger's section are: American Jewish Historical Society, p. 223; Seymour "Sy" Brody, "Jennie Grossinger," *Jewish Virtual Library* at www.jewishvirtuallibrary.org/jsource/ biography/grossinger.html; "Grossinger's Catskill Resort Hotel," at http://en.wikipedia.org/wiki/ Grossinger's_Catskill_Resort_Hotel; "Grossinger's," at www.joe4speed.com/grossingers.htm; "Grossinger's," at www.catskillarchive.com/grossinger/ index.htm; "Catskills," at www.catskills.co.uk/ infopage.htm; and others.

465. Among sources for the Fairmont/Swig section are: "Thomas Storey Appointed President of Fairmont Hotels and Resorts," an April 21, 2008 press release, "Our History," and "Destinations," all at www.fairmont.com; "Kingdom Hotels International and Colony Capital Complete Acquisition of Fairmont. . .," a May 11, 2006 press release available at www.hotel-online.com/News/PR2006_2nd/ May06_ColonyKingdom; "Herman Oelrichs Weds," *The New York Times,* June 4, 1890; "Fact Sheet: New Hotel Management Company "Fairmont Hotels and Resorts, Inc.," at www.hotel-online.com/ News/PressReleases1999 2nd/Apr99_CPFactSheet.html; Christina Valhouli, "Fairmont Hotels & Resorts," at www.forbes.com/lifestyle/travel/2004/02/05/cx_cv_0205feat.html; "1907, Nob Hill, Fairmont Hotel," at www.verlang.com/sfbay0004ref_jm_03.html; "Mark Hopkins Hotel 1930 – San Francisco, California signed by founder George D. Smith as President," at www.scripophily.net/ marhophotco.html; "Virginia Fair Vanderbilt," and "James Graham Fair" at http://en.wikipedia.org/ wiki/Virginia_Fair_Vanderbilt, and wiki/ James_Graham_Fair; and others.

466. Among sources for the Loews/Tisch section are Robert Lenzer, "High on Loews," *Fortune,* Feb. 26, 2007; "Letter To Our Shareholders and Employees," "Financial Highlights," "Results of Operations," "Loews: A Financial Portrait," "Loews Hotels," "About," from the *Annual Report* and Web pages available at http://www.loews.com/ loews.nsf/home.htm; Carl Gutierrez, "Dominion's Sale Makes Waves," *Forbes,* Jun 4, 2007; "Robert Tisch and Laurence Tisch," at the University of Houston Web site, www.hrm.uh.edu/?PageID=200; "Former CBS Head Tisch Dies at 80," *USA Today,* Nov 15, 2003 at www.usatoday.com/news/nation/2003-11-15-obit-tisch_x.htm; "Loews Corporation," on the Wikipedia Web site at http://en.wikipedia.org/wiki/Loews_Corporation.

467. Among sources for the Hyatt/Pritzker section are: "Company Overview: 'Global Hyatt Corporation' and, 'History of Hyatt Corporation," "About Hyatt," at the Hyatt Web site at www.hyatt.com; "Classic Residence: Executive Management," at the web site www.hyattclassic.com/print/company-managment.html; "Hyatt Hotels" and "Global Hyatt," at http://en.wikipedia.org/wiki/Hyatt and wiki/Global_Hyatt_Corporation; *Bloomberg News,* "Investors Buy Stake in Global Hyatt," August 30, 2007, *The New York Times;* "Owners of Hyatt Chain Must Reveal Breakup Plan, Judge Says," April 18, 2003, *The New York Times,* "Hyatt Corporation," at www.fundinguniverse.com/company-histories/ Hyatt-Corporation; and others.

468. Among sources for the Helmsley section are: Enid Nemy, "Leona Helmsley, Hotel 'Queen,' Is Dead at 87," *The New York Times,* August 21, 2007; "Helmsley Enterprises, Inc.," at www.fundinguniverse.com/ company-histories/ Helmsley-Enterprises-Inc.; "Tribute to Leona Helmsley," at www.lastingtribute.co.uk/tribute/ helmsley/2623256; "Leona Helmsley," at http://en.wikipedia.org/ wiki/Leona_Helmsley; Rachel Bell, "Leona Helmsley, the Notorious Queen of Mean," *The Crime Library,* at www.crimelibrary.com/criminal_mind/scams/leona_helmsley/ index?html;

"The Helmsley Collection," at http://www.helmsleyhotels.com/, Stephanie Storm, "Helmsley, Dogs' Best Friend, Left Them Up to $8 Billion," *The New York Times,* July 2, 2008; "The Leona M. and Harry B. Helmsley Charitable Trust," *2006 Form 990-PF* filing at www.guidestar.com; and others.

469. Among sources for the Wynn section are: Joel Stein, "Steve Wynn," *Time,* April 30, 2006; A.D. Hopkins, "Steve Wynn The Winner," *Las Vegas Review-Journal* at www.1st100.com/part3/wynn.html; "Steve Wynn (developer)," and "Wynn Resorts," at http://en.wikipedia.org/wiki/Steve_Wynn_(developer), and wiki/Wynn_Resorts_Limited; Joel Stein, "The Strip Is Back," *Time,* July 26, 2004; Daniel Gross, "Le Reve Gauche," *Slate* at http://slate.msn.com/id/ 2073247/; Julie Creswell, "So What if the Chips Are Down?" *The New York Times,* Aug. 3, 2008; and others.

470. Among sources for the Venetian/Adelson section are: Gary Rivlin, "When 3rd Place on the Rich List Just Isn't Enough," *The New York Times,* Jan. 17, 2008; Matthew Miller, "The Gambler," *Forbes,* March 28, 2005; Mike Langberg, "Tech Show Won't Go On," *The Mercury News,* June 24, 2004; "Sheldon Adelson," "Las Vegas Sands," "The Venetian (Las Vegas)," and "The Venetian Macao," at http://en.wikipedia.org/wiki/Sheldon_Adelson; wiki/ Las_Vegas_Sands; wiki/The_Venetian_(Las_Vegas); wiki/The_Venetian_Macao; No.12 Sheldon Adelson, *Forbes,* March 5, 2008; "Sheldon Adelson," and "Company History at www.venetian.com; and others.

471. Among sources for the Carnival Cruise/Arison section are: "Arison Family," "Ted Arison," "Micky Arison," and "Shari Arison," at http://en.wikipedia.org/wiki/Arison_Family; wiki/Ted_Arison; wiki/Micky_Arison; wiki/ Shari_Arison; "The History of Carnival Cruise Lines," at www.cruiseship-fleets.fsnet.co.uk/The history of Carnival Cruise%; "Carnival Cruise Lines," at http://reviews.iserver.net/carnival/; Amotz Asa-el and Dan Gerstenfeld, "Ted Arison, World's Wealthiest Jew Dies in Tel Aviv," *The Jewish News Weekly,* Oct. 8, 1999 at www.jewishsf.com/content/ 2-0-/module/ displaystory/story_id/12193/edition_id/235/format; "Carnival Corporation: Industry Peers," "Analyst Report," at the Morningstar Web site, http://quicktake.morningstar.com; "Fundamentals-Snapshot," "Corporate Snapshot," "Our Brands," "Historical Background," and "Officers and Directors," at the Carnival Cruise Web site www.carnival.corp; "Micky Arison," at www.Forbes.com; Lea Goldman, "Poor Little Rich Girl," *Forbes,* July 5, 2004, and others.

472. Among sources for the Royal Caribbean/Pritzker section are: "Royal Caribbean – Part 1, 2, 3, & 4," at the Web site, www.shippnostalgia.com/guides/Royal_Caribbean; Ross A. Klein, *Cruise Ship Squeeze,* New Society Publishers, Gabriola Island, B.C., Canada, 2005 p. 25; "Royal Caribbean Cruises, Ltd.," and "Analyst Report," at the *Morningstar* Web site, http://quicktake.morningstar.com/StockNet/MorningstarAnalsys.asp; "Ofer Marks 80th Birthday," at the *S.T.& T. Ltd.,* Web site, www.seatransport.co.il/index.php?&sub=3&nid=17; "Royal Caribbean Founder Edwin W. Stephan Retires From Board After 35 Years With Company," a May 12, 2003 Web site available on the *Royal Caribbean* Web site at www.corporate-ir.net/ireye/ir_site.zhtml?ticker=rcl&script=410&layout=9&item+_id=411073.

473. Among sources for the Hartz Mountain/Stern section are: "About Hartz / Our History" on the *Hartz* Web site at www.hartz.com; Marcia Vickers, "Dynasty in Distress," *Business Week,* Feb. 9, 2004; St. Clair McKelway, "The Sexes Downtown," *The New Yorker,* Dec. 6, 1952; Chacaras And Quintais, "Factory Canaries of Stern Brothers," *Memory,* April 15, 1948, Vol. 77, page 475–76; May 15, 1948, Vol. 77, page 576–78; June 15, 1948, Vol. 77, page 700–03 – translated from Portuguese and available at http://www.ao.com.br/m_stern.htm; "Stern College For Women Launches 50th Anniversary Celebration" *YU News,* Oct. 7, 2003 at www.yu.edu/news_stories/oct2003/jubilee.htm; Lyman, *Heroes,* p. 150; American Jewish Historical Society, p. 216; and others.

474. Please see sources on Land in the endnotes for the Chapter on Invention (endnote 14 on page 534).

475. Among sources for the U.S. Healthcare/Abramson section are: "Madlyn and Leonard Abramson Center For Jewish Life," at www.abramsoncenter.org; "U.S. Healthcare, Inc." at www.fundinguniverse.com/ company-histories/ US-Healthcare; "Leonard Abramson" at http://elitewatch.911review.org/ brookings2.html#_Leonard_Abramson; "Leonard Abramson," at http://en.wikipedia.org/wiki/Leonard_Abramson; "Leonard Abramson," at the *Harvard Business School* Web site at www.hbs.edu/ leadership/database/ leaders/ leonard_abramson.html; "*Republican Jewish Coalition*: at www.nndb.com/ org/258/000118901; "A Big Gift to Cure Cancer," at www.upenn.edu/gazette/ 0298/0298gaz5.html; "Leonard Abramson," at www.forbes.com/finance/ lists/54/1997; and others.

476. Among sources for Ex-Lax/Matz section are: "Israel Matz Dies; Hebrew Scholar," *The New York Times,* Feb. 11, 1950 "Matz, Israel," at www.shtetlinks.jewsihgen.org/Kalvarija/biographies.html; "The Israel Matz Institute for Research in Jewish Law," at http://mishpatim.mscc.huji.ac.il/jewish/ jewres0e.htm; "To Aid Jewish Studies," *The New York Times,* May 11, 1947; Tim Whitmire, "Mayor Ray Nagin: 'We Need to be the Ex-Law'" *Associated Press,* Dec. 9, 2005; "Financial Aid," at www.nyu.edu/gsas/Admissions/Financial_dept.html; "The Sidney Matz Teaching Fellowship," at www.nyu.edu/gsas/dept/hebrew/fellowships.htm; "The Israel Matz Chair of Organic Chemistry," at www.weizmann.ac.il/acadsec/Scientific_Activities/current/Organic_Chemistry.html; "My Home Town, Kalvarija,(Lithuania)," at www.jewishgen.org/Yizkor/lita/lit1499.html; and others.

477. Among sources for the Hertz/Greenbaum/Jacobs section are: Irving Cutler, *The Jews of Chicago,* University of Illinois Press, Chicago, 1955, p. 180; Company News; Ford to Raise Hertz Stake to Total 54%," *The New York Times,*

Feb. 15, 1994; American Jewish Historical Society, p. 217; "Hertz History," at www.hertz.com/about_05/profile/history.jsp; "Hertz Becomes Wholly Owned Subsidiary of Ford Motor Company," Ford Press Release, March 9, 19?? At http://media.ford.com/ print_doc.cfm?article_id7670; "The Hertz Corporation," at http://en.wikipedia.org/wiki/ The_Hertz_Corporation; "The Hertz Corporation," at www.answers.com/topic/the-hertz-corporation?cat=biz-fin; "Ford to Sell The Hertz Corporation to Private Equity Group in $15 Billion Transaction," Ford Press Release dated Sept 12, 2005 at http://media.ford.com/newsroom/release_display.cfm?release=21555.

478. Among sources for the Arthur Murray section are: "Arthur Murray," *Encyclopaedia Britannica 2001*; "History," at the *Arthur Murray* Web site, www.arthurmurray.com/history/asp; "Arthur Murray," at http://en.wikipedia.org/ wiki/Arthur_Murray; Etkes, p. 169; Alan Symons, *The Jewish Contribution to the 20th Century*, Polo Publishing, London, and others.

479. Among sources for the Simplicity/Shapiro section are: Robert MCG. Thomas Jr. "James Shapiro, 85, Innovator In the Home Sewing Industry," *The New York Times*, June 3, 1995; an untitled story about Simplicity and the raiders from *Women's Wear Daily*, Sept. 13, 1983 available at www.jailhurwitz.com/cronies/CAST_of_CRONIES/ AFFINIT;Donald Barlett and James B. Steele, *America, What Went Wrong?* Andrews & McMeel Publishing, Kansas City, MO, pages 143–45; The Simplicity Web site at www.simplicity.com, the *Conso* Web site at www.conso.com and the *Wrights* Web site at www.wrights.com; "Simplicity Pattern," at http://en.wikipedia.org/wiki/Simplicity_Pattern; "Investor Group to Buyout Conso Int'l for 0.55 Times Revenue," at http://findarticles.com/p/articles/ mi_qa3755/is_199910/ai n8861277...; "Conso International Corporation," at www.fundinguniverse.com/company-histories/Conso-International; Etkes, p. 174; and others.

480. Among sources for the Fisher section are: Allan Kozinn, Avery Fisher, Philanthropist, Dies at 87," *The New York Times*, Feb. 27, 1994; "Avery Fisher," at www.ieee-virtual-museum.org/ collection/people.php?taid=&i..., www.geocities.com/fisheramp/index.html?200826, and http://en.wikipedia.org/ wiki/Avery_Fisher; "Avery Fisher Hall," at http://en.wikipedia.org/ wiki/Avery_Fisher_Hall; Etkes, p. 165; and others.

481. Among sources for the H&R Block/Bloch section are: Sabrina Tavernise, "Richard Bloch, 78, Businessman Who Helped Create H&R Block," *The New York Times*, July 22, 2004; "Fast Facts," "Our Company History," "Letter to Shareholders," "Financial Facts," "Henry W. Bloch's Biography," and "Richard Bloch's Biography," from the H&R Block Web site at www.hrblock.com; "H&R Block" at http://en.wikipedia.org/wiki/H&R_Block; "About Henry Bloch," at www.bloch.umkc.edu/about-the-bloch-school/about henry-bloch; Silbiger, p. 70; and others.

482. Among sources for the Jacoby & Meyers section are: Kenneth Noble, "Breakup of a Legal Duo: Jacoby v. Meyers," *The New York Times*, Oct. 21, 1995; Robert Mcg. Thomas Jr., *The New York Times*, April 21, 1996; "Jacoby & Myers" (sic) at www.courttv.com/archive/legaldocs/business/jacoby.html; " "About Southern California Jacoby & Meyers, Personal Injury Lawyers," "New York, New Jersey, Connecticut, and Pennsylvania Office," and "About Personal Injury Attorney Len Jacoby," at www.jacoby-meyers.com; Len Jacoby" at www.laworkshop.com/ admin.drukerschreiber1.lawoffice...; "Unbundle Your Law Practice," at www.zorza.net/resources/Ethics/ most-intro html; and Richard L. Abel, *American Lawyers*, Oxford University Press, New York, Oxford, 1989, p.127–39; Etkes, p. 172.

483. Among sources for the Shell/Marcus section are: Martin Gilbert, *The Jews in the Twentieth Century*, Shocken Books, New York, 2001, p. 81; Lyman, *Jewish Heroes*, p. 149; "Fuel Companies: Royal Dutch Shell," www.grandprix.com/gpe/ fue-011.html; Peerage of the United Kingdom," at www.nationmaster.com/ encyclopedia/ Peerage-of-the-United-Kingdom "Why Shell? The Birth of Shell Tankers," at www.caithness.org/caithnessfieldclub/ bulletins/1996/ how_shell_tankers.htm; "Our International Beginnings," at www.shell.ca/code/who/ about/international.html; and others.

484. Among sources for the Amoco/Blaustein section are: "Louis Blaustein, Oil Leader Dead," *The New York Times*, July 28, 1937; "Jacob Blaustein Is Dead at 78: Founder of the American Oil Co." *The New York Times*, Nov. 16, 1970; American Jewish Historical Society, p. 212; Lyman, Heroes p. 144; Silbiger, p. 187; "Louis Blaustein and the American Oil Company," at www.library.jhu.edu/collections/ specialcollections/manuscripts/...; Terence O'Hara, Blaustein's Split Empire," *Baltimore Business Journal*, Jan. 18, 1999 at www.webshells.com/crown/pages/ blaustein.htm; Martha Hamilton, "A Corporate History Rooted Deeply in Baltimore," *The Washington Post*, Feb. 1, 1999 at www.webshells.com/ crown/pages/history.htm; "Blaustein v. Standard Oil," *Time*, Jun. 17, 1940 at www.time.com; "Family Fortunes," at www.forbes.com; "Blaustein Philanthropic Group," at www.blaufund.org/; "Crown History" at www.crowncentral.com/ourbusiness/history.html; and others.

485. Among sources for the Amerada-Hess/Hess section are: Gerald Eskenazi, "Leon Hess, Who Built a Major Oil Company and Owned the Jets, Is Dead at 85," *The New York Times*, May 8, 1999; "Paid Notice: Deaths Hess, Leon," *The New York Times*, May 9, 1999; "Leon Hess," at http://en.wikipedia.org/Leon_Hess "Hess Oil & Chemical," at the *Scripophily* Web site, www.scripophily.net/hesoilchemco.html; "A Tribute to Leon Hess," at www.hess.com/ financials/ ar99/tribute.html; "Scholarship Funds," at http://law.mc.edu/Students/FinancialAid/funds.htm; "Batteries Included," at http://promomagazine.com/campaigns/marketing_batteries_included/; and others.

486. Among sources for the Occidental/Hammer section are: Eric Pace "Armand Hammer Dies at 92; Executive Forges Soviet Ties," *The New York Times*, Dec. 11, 1990; Lyman, *Heroes*, p. 145; Etkes, p. 166; "Fuel Companies: Occidental Petroleum Corporation," at www.grandprix.com/gpe/fue-007.html; Timothy W. Maier, "Secret FBI File on Albert Gore, Sr." http://findarticles.com/p/articles/ mi_m1571/is_34_17/ai_78334926/pg_1?tag=artBody;col1 (The article summarizes an FBI file on Hammer made available through a public information request.) "*Dossier: The Secret History of Armand Hammer by* Edward Jay Epstein," a book review at www.theforbiddenknowledge.com/ hardtruth/armand_hammer.htm; Ralph Blumenthal, "Armand Hammer's Maze of Skulduggery," *The New York Times*, Oct. 14, 1996; "Armand Hammer," and "Occidental Petroleum," at http:en.wikipedia.org/ wiki/Armand_Hammer; and wiki/Occidental_Petroleum; and others.

487. Among sources for Kaiser-Francis/Kaiser section are: "George Kaiser," at www.Forbes.com/lists; and at http://www.forbes.com/2006/09/20/ent-manage_biz_06rich400_self_made_entrepreneurs_george_kaiser_ print.html; Maricia Shottenkirk, "The Century Club: George B. Kaiser," *The (Oklahoma City) Journal Record* at http://findarticles.com/p/articles/mi_qn4182/is_20070827/ai_n19488741/ print?tag=artBody;col1; "George Kaiser," at http://en.wikipedia.org/wiki/George_Kaiser; "George Kaiser Speech on Childhood Education," *The New York Times*, Feb. 7, 2007, http://www.nytimes.com/ 2007/02/07/education/07economix2.html; "George Kaiser Family Foundation," at Guidestar Web site http://partners.guidestar.org/partners/usnews/ report.jsp?ein=73-1574370; "George Kaiser Family Foundation Announces $50 Million Gift for School of Community Medicine," at www. oufoundation.org/pn/spring/08/; Russell Gold, "A Billionaire Takes a Gamble To Fix Natural-Gas Shortage," *The Wall Street Journal*, July 23, 2004; David Leonhardt, "Bridging Gaps Early On in Oklahoma," *The New York Times*, Feb. 7, 2007; and others.

488. Among sources for the Aurora-Marathon/Fisher section are: Associated Press, "Max Fisher, 96, Philanthropist and Advisor to Presidents, Dies," *The New York Times*, Mar. 4, 2005; "Fisher Gives $20 Million to Business," at www.osu.edu/osu/newsrel/Archives/93–11–15_Fisher_Gives_Millions_to_Business; Jon Pepper, Max Fisher, *The Detroit News*, April 23, 2000 at www.detnews.com/specialreports/2000/michiganians/fisher/fisher.htm; Daniel Howes, "A Life of Power, Compassion," *The Detroit News*, Sept. 26, 2003, at www.detnews.com/2003/business/0309/26/ a01-281889.htm; "Max Fisher," at www.Forbes.com; "Max Fisher," at http://en.wikipedia.org/wiki/ Max_M._Fisher.

489. Among sources for the Davis Petroleum/Davis section are: Patrick Healy, "Marvin Davis, Oil Billionaire Who Bought And Then Sold Fox Studios, Is Dead at 79," *The New York Times*, Sept. 26, 2004; "Marvin H. Davis," *Forbes 400* at www.forbes.com/finance/lists/10/2003/ LIR.jhtml?passListId=10&passYear=2003&pass ListType=Person&datatype=Person&uniqueId=524D; "Marvin Davis," at http://en.wikipedia.org/wiki/ Marvin_Davis; "Marvin Davis," at the *Mother Jones Web site* http://www.motherjones.com/news/special_reports/ mojo_400/63_davis.html; "Davis Petroleum Makes $150 Million Recapitalization Deal," at www.rigzone.com/news/ article.asp?a_id=30102; "Court Confirms Davis Petroleum's Plan of Reorganization," at www.rigzone.com/news/ article.asp?a_id=30229; "Barbara Davis," in "Lists 2005 at www.forbes.com; "Barbara Davis," at http://en.wikipedia.org/ wiki/Barbara_Davis; "Davis Petroleum," at www.businessweek.com; and others.

490. Among sources for the Asarco, et al/Guggenheim section are: "Guggenheim, Meyer and Daniel," *Encyclopaedia Britannica\2001 & 2008;* "Meyer Guggenheim, Smelter King, Dead," *The New York Times*, Mar. 17, 1905; "Guggen-heim, Meyer," at www.*JewishEncyclopedia.com;* "Meyer Guggenheim," at http://en.wikipedia.org/wiki/ Meyer_Guggenheim; "Isaac Guggenheim Dies in England," *The New York Times*, Oct. 11, 1922; "Isaac Guggenheim Left $10,163,113 Net," *The New York Times*, Oct 21, 1932; "Daniel Guggenheim Dies Suddenly At 74 Of Heart Disease," *The New York Times*, Sept. 29, 1930; "S.R. Guggenheim, Mine Owner, Dies," *The New York Times*, Nov. 3, 1949; "$16,557,291 Is Left By S. Guggenheim," *The New York Times*, June 27, 1944; "Daniel Guggenheim," at the Harvard Business School Leadership Web site, www.hbs.edu/leadership/database/leaders/297/; "Guggenheim Left $13,677,133 Estate," *The New York Times*, Feb 1, 1942 "Solomon R. Guggenheim Foundation," at http://en.wikipedia.org/wiki/Solomon_R_Guggenheim/Foundation; "Guggenheim Museum," and "Guggenheim, Peggy," at *Encyclopaedia Britannica 2001& 2008;* "Peggy Guggenheim Is Dead at 81; Known for Modern Art Collec-tion," *The New York Times*, Dec 24, 1979; "Copper Companies in Big Combination," *The New York Times*, Nov 18, 1915; "Back Kennecott With $65,000,000," *The New York Times*, Nov. 25, 1915; Frances Morrone, "Mining a Dynasty for Narrative Riches," a book review of *The Guggenheims: A Family History*, in *The New York Sun*, Jan. 24, 2005; Gary Shapiro, "The Rise of the Guggenheim Family," *The New York Sun*, Feb 18, 2005; Etkes, p. 165; Silbiger, p. 187; Lyman, *Heroes*, p. 148; Symons, *Jewish Contribution;* and others.

491. Among sources for the Hirshhorn section are: :The Hirshhorn Approach," *Time*, Oct. 5, 1962; John Russell, "Joseph Hirschhorn (sic) Dies: Financier; Art Patron," *The New York Times*, Sept. 2, 1981; Les Ledbetter, Joseph H. Hirshhorn, Donor of Art Museum Is Dead At 82," *The New York Times*, Sept. 1, 1981; "Joseph Hirshhorn: The Man Who Heaped the Land with Beauty," *People*, Dec. 30, 1974; "Joseph Hirshhorn," at http://en.wikipedia.org/wiki/ Joseph_H._Hirshhorn; "Record Unit 7449: Joseph H. Hirshhorn Papers, circa 1926–1982 and undated," at the *Smithsonian Archives Web* site at www.si.edu/archives/archives/findingaids/FARU7449.htm; "Hirshhorn Museum and Sculpture Garden," at http://en.wikipedia.org/wiki/Hirshhorn_Museum_and_Sculpture_Garden; "History: Lyndon Johnson," at www.whitehouse.gov/kids/presidents/lyndonjohnson.html; Irvin Molotsky, "Hirshhorn Leaves Art Col-

lection To Museum," *The New York Times*, Sept. 6, 1981; Irvin Molotsky, "Hirshhorn Bequest Adds To Collection," *The New York Times*, May 22, 1983; "The Hirshhorn Story," at http://hirshhorn.si.edu/museum/story_text.html; "Hall of Fame Inductee: Joseph H. Hirshhorn: 1900–1981," at www.halloffame.mining.ca/halloffame/english/bios/hirshhorn.html; Barbara Gamarekian, "At Home With : Olga Hirshhorn; The Thrill of Art, Both Fine and Flea," *The New York Times*, Jan. 18, 1996; Etkes, p. 166; and others.

492. Among sources for the Engelhard section are: "C. Engelhard, 83, Refiner of Metals," *The New York Times*, Dec. 2, 1950; "South African Invader," *Time*, Jan 27, 1961; "Died. Charles W. Engelhard, 54" *Time*, Mar. 15, 1971; "Charles W. Engelhard, Jr." at http://en.wikipedia.org/wiki/ Charles_W._Engelhard%2C_Jr.; "Engelhard Corporation," at www.referenceforbusiness.com/history/ En-Ge/Engelhard-Corporation.html; "The Charles Engelhard Court," at www.sackheritage.com/museums/spotlight.php?museumID=82; "The Charles Engelhard Foundation Form 990 for 2006," at www.Guidestar.com; "Jane Engelhard," at http://en.wikipedia.org/wiki/Jane_Engelhard; "Charlene Engelhard," at www.bostonmagazine.com/ArticleDisplay.php?id=241; Douglas Martin, "Jane Engelhard, 86, Fixture In Society and Philanthropy," *The New York Times*, Mar. 3, 2004; Edward Jay Epstein, "Chapter 18 – The American Conspiracy," at http://edwardjayepstein.com/diamond/ chap18.htm; "The East Room" http://clinton4.nara.gov/WH/Holidays/2000/east.html.

493. Among sources for the Anglo American section are those cited in the description of De Beers and the Oppenheimer family in the chapter featuring Jewelry plus: Phyllis Berman, "Queen Bee," *Forbes*, June 16, 2008; "History," at www.angloamerican.co.uk/article/?afw_source_key19ED07F3-C5AB-427-BACE-...; "Anglo American," at http://en.wikipedia.org/wikiAnglo_American.plc; and *Fact Book 2007* at www.AngloAmerican.co.uk.

494. Among Sources for the Manpower/Winter section are: "Manpower, Inc.," at http://quicktake. morningstar.com; "Manpower, Inc." and Kelly Services, at http://en.wikipedia.org/wiki/ Manpower Inc.; and wiki/Kelly_Services; "Selected Financial Data," "Manpower at a Glance," "Management's Discussion and Analysis," at www.manpower.com; "Manpower Historical Timeline," at http://files.shareholder.com/downloads/MAN/100128166x0x63833/ A80D75D9-95C7-4084-952D-233F94D1005F/Timeline.pdf; "Adecco" synopsis at www.adecco.com; Bill Glauber, "Sculpting Dreams at 95," *Milwaukee Journal Sentinel*, Nov. 24, 2007 at www.jsonline.com/story/ index.aspx?id=689628&format=print; "Elmer Winter," at www.elmerwinter.com; "Fifty Years," at www.kellyservices.com/corpinfo/history/50years.html; American Jewish Historical Society, p. 217; and others.

495. Among sources for the ADP/Taub/Lautenberg section are: George James, "A 'Gentle Presence' Off Court," *The New York Times*, Dec 15, 1996; "Sports People: Pro Basketball; Taub Returns to Nets," *The New York Times*, June 14, 1991; "Automatic Data Processing, Inc., 50th Anniversary: 1949–1999," "Financial Highlights," "2007 Annual Report," at the Company's Web site, www.adp.com; "Lautenberg," at www.cbi.umn.edu/oh/display.phtml?term=lautenberg; "Henry & Marilyn Taub Foundation Form 990 for 2006," at www.Guidestar.com; "The Marilyn and Henry Taub Foundation Gives $10 million to Further Research In Diseases of Aging of the Brain," at www.columbia.edu/cu/new/ 99/12taubGift.html; "Henry Taub," at http://en.wikipedia.org/wiki/Henry_Taub, "Gift From Henry Taub Establishes Center for Israel Studies at NYU," NYU Today, Apr. 1, 2003; "Taub Scholars in Women's Health," http://hora.cpmc.columbia.edu/dept/cwh/gift.html; "Minefields: Bosnia and Herzgovina," at www.landmines.org.uk/ Countries/Minefield_Clearance/Bosnia+and+Herzgovina; American Jewish Historical Society, p. 218; and others.

496. Among sources for the Drucker section are: "Trusting the Teacher in the Grey-flannel Suit," *Economist*, Nov. 19, 2005; John A. Byrne, "The Man Who Invented Management," *Business Week*, Nov. 28, 2005; "Drucker, Peter F(erdinand)," *Encyclopaedia Britannica 2001*; "Pete Drucker," at http://en.wikipedia.org/wiki/Peter_Drucker; "About Peter Drucker," and "Biography," at www.peter-drucker.com; "Peter Drucker's Search for Community," *Business Week*, Dec. 24, 2002; Bruce Rosenstein, "Scandals Nothing New to Business Guru," *Money*, July 5, 2002; Brent Schlender, "Gurus: Peter Drucker Sets Us Straight," *Fortune*, Dec 29, 2003; "About the Drucker School," at http://drucker.cgu.edu/html/ about/index.asp; Etkes, p. 164; Symons, *Jewish Contributions*; and others.

497. Among sources for the Kroll section are: "About Us," and "Jules B.Kroll," at www.kroll.com; Douglas Frantz, "A Midlife Crises at Kroll Associates," *The New York Times*, Sep. 1, 1994; "A Corporate Detective is Saying Farewell," *The New York Times*, July 6, 2008; Neil Weinberg & Michael Maiello, "Insurance Noir," *Forbes*, Nov 29, 2004; "Founder of Marsh & McLennan's Kroll to Retire," *Associated Press*, June 13, 2008; "Kroll Inc." www.answers.com/topic/ kroll-inc?cat=biz-fin; "The Lynn and Jules Kroll Fund for Jewish Documentary Film," at http://jewishculture.org/ ?pid=film; and others.

498. Among sources for the Snyder section are: Harry Jaffe, "The Dan Snyder You Don't Know," *Washingtonian*, Sep. 1, 2006 at www.washingtonian.com/articles/sports/1679.html; "Dan Snyder," "Snyder Communications," "Direct Marketing," "Database Marketing," "Arnold Communications," at http://en.wikipedia.org/wiki/Dan_Snyder; wiki/Direct_Marketing; wiki/Snyder_Communications; wiki/Database_Marketing; and wiki/Arnold_Communications; "Ad Age's Agency Family Trees," at www.flickr.com/photos/seeminglee/2152992109/sizes/o/; "William Bernbach: Early Career," at www.ciadvertising.org/studies/student/98_fall/theory/weirtz/early.htm; "William Bernbach (1911–1982) at www.ciadvertising.org/student_account/spring_02/adv382j/lindloff/2nd/The Paper.htm; Stuart

Elliott, "The Media Business: Advertising; Another Independent Turnover: The Acclaimed Arnold Agency Signs a Deal With Snyder," *The New York Times*, Mar. 27, 1998; "Snyder Communications, Inc." *The Washington Post 200*," at www.washingtonpost.com/wp-srv/business/longterm/ post200/dat. . ; "Havas Advertising Completes Acquisition of Snyder Communications," an Havas press release, Sep. 27, 2000; "Snyder Sold," *Direct Magazine*, Feb. 23, 2000 at http://directmag.com/ news/marketing_snyder_sold; "World Business Briefing: Europe; Advertising Acquisition," *The New York Times*, Feb. 22, 2000; Bruce Schoenfeld, "Crunch Time," *Departures*, Nov.-Dec. 2000; "Snyder Family Foundation," and Michele Snyder Foundation," *Form 990s* for 2006 at www.guidestar.com; and others.

499. Among sources on Chomsky's life are: *Encyclopædia Britannica 2001 Deluxe Edition*, articles on "Chomsky," "linguistics," "B. F. Skinner," "programmed learning," and "behaviorist education;" the bio at his web site, www.chomsky.info/bios/2002-.htm; and other pages at that Web site, including www.chomsky.info/bios/1991-.htm; the MIT site bio http://web.mit.edu/linguistics/www/ biograpy/noambio.html; and the bio timeline at http://cognet.mit.edu/library/books/chomsky/ chomsky/1/index.html; University of Texas journalism class bios at www.utexas.edu/coc/journalism/ SOURCE/j363/chomsky.html; the *Wikipedia* bio at http://en.wikipedia.org/ wiki/Noam_Chomsky; reviews of Robert F. Barsky's *Noam Chomsky: A Life of Dissent*, MIT Press, Cambridge, Mass., 1998 on www.amazon.com; Cecil Adams, "Whatever Became of B.F. Skinner," Aug 15, 2003, at the Web site, www.straightdope.com/columns/0308a5.html; the bio of Aham Ha-Am's (Asher Ginsberg) at www.wzo.org.il/ home/portrait/ahad.htm; and an article on his view of Zionism at www.myjewishlearning.com/history_community/ Modern/ Overview_The_Story_17001914/Zionism/Haam.htm. Articles on linguistics include those on his Web site, the mit.edu site, *Encyclopædia Britannica*, http://fates.cns.muskingum.edu/~psych/psycweb/history/chomsky.htm; and at www.psy.pdx.edu/ PsyCafe/KeyTheorists/Chomsky.htm. Articles on his politics came from his Web site, including his interview by David Barsamian which appeared in *International Socialist Review*, Sept.-Oct, 2004, Issue 37; his interview by Mehr New Agency which appeared in *Tehran Times*, Oct. 11, 2004; his interview by Kevin Doyle, "Noam Chomsky on Anarchism, Marxism & Hope for the Future," May 1995, which appeared in *Red & Black Revolution*, No. 2, and his interview by Heinz Dieterich; "1492: The First Invasion of Globalization," excerpted on his Web site from *Latin America: From Colonization to Globalization*, Ocean Press, 1999 (Oct 1989 and March 1992); reviews of Chomsky's book, *Hegemony or Survival: America's Quest for Global Dominance*, Metropolitan Books, 2003, at www.audible.com; various articles by or about him from www.zmag.org/chomsky/articles.cfm. Comments about him and criticism came from: Nat Hentoff, "The Pariah," *The Washington Post*, June 22, 1985; Christopher Hitchens, "The Chorus and Cassandra," *Grand Street Magazine*, Autumn 1985; an un–attributed article, "The Chorus and the Cassandra: A Response," in the Web Journal, *Cambodia*, at www.mekong.net/cambodia/hitchens.htm; Christopher Hitchens', "A Rejoinder to Noam Chomsky: Minority Report," *The Nation*, 2001, at http://humanities.psydeshow.org/ political/ hitchens-3.htm; Keith Windschuttle, "The Hypocrisy of Noam Chomsky," *The New Criterion*, May 21, 2003, also at www.newcriterion.com/archive/ 21may03/chomsky.htm; Brian Carnell's articles, "Noam Chomsky on David Horowitz," Jan 8, 2002; "Chomsky: Take Bin Laden at His Word," March 4, 2002; "Keith Windschuttle on Noam Chomsky," Sept. 7, 2003; "I Screwed Up On Cuba Crackdown Story," Sept 7, 2003; and "Chomsky Backpedals on Silent Genocide' in Afghanistan;" all five are at various pages on www.leftwatch.com/print/articles.html; Curt Huyette, "Rumble on the Left: Hitchens, Chomsky and Who to Blame," Oct. 3, 2001 at: www.metrotimes.com/editoria/ story.asp?id=2530; David Horowitz, "The Sick Mind of Noam Chomsky," Sept. 26, 2001, *FrontPageMagazine* at www.frontpagemag.com/ Articles/ReadArticle.asp?ID=1020; Alan Dershowitz, "Chomsky's Immoral Divestiture Petition," at www.tech.mit.edu/ V122/N25/col25dersh.25c.html, Noam Chomsky, "Chomsky Replies to Hitchens," and his, "Second Reply to Hitchens…," both at www.zmag.org; an article on Robert Faurisson at www.geocities.com/ onemansmind/hr/revisionist/Faurisson.html; Carol Off, "Re: Counterspin Was the Anathema of Democracy," May 12, 2004 at http://counterspin.tv; Chomsky quotes are from his Web site and from http://en.thinkexist.com/ quotes/noam_chomsky/, www.brainyquote.com/quotes/authors/n/ noam_chomsky.html, and www.quoteworld.org/ author.php?thetext=Noam Chomsky.

500. Sandee Brawarsky and Deborah Mark, *Two Jews, Three Opinions*, Berkley Publishing Group, New York, 1998, p. 10.

501. B'resheet/Genesis 18:23–25.

502. Rabbi Joseph Telushkin, *Jewish Literacy*, William Morrow, New York, 2001, 83–93, 545–615; and Rabbi Ted Falcon, Ph.D. and David Blatner, *Judaism for Dummies*, Hungry Minds, Inc. New York, 2001, pages 22, 29–30, 44–6, 351.

503. Ernest Van den Haag, *The Jewish Mystique*, Stein and Day, New York, 1969, p. 118.

504. Johnson, *History of the Jews*, pages 448–54.

505. Among sources for this section are, *Encyclopædia Britannica Deluxe Edition* articles on "Socialism," "the Bund;" Eli Barnavi, *A Historical Atlas of the Jewish People*, 196–7; the Answers.com Web site bio of "Daniel De Leon;" the Spartacus Web site, www.spartacus.schoolnet.co.uk/GEReisner.htm; Ami Isseroff, "Labor Zionism and Socialist Zionism," at www.mideastweb.org/labor_zionism.htm; and others.

506. Sources include: *Encyclopædia Britannica* articles on "Communism," "Engels," "Mensheviks," "Bund," "Spartacus League," and "The Communist Manifesto;" Arno Lustiger, *Stalin and the Jews*, Enigma Books, New York, 2003, 13–32; Johnson, *History of the Jews*, 448–54; "Communism as Jewish Radical Subculture: The Los Angeles Experi-

ence, 1920–39," part of a doctoral dissertation available at www.world.ryukoku.ac.jp/~michael/docs/oah_paper.html; the article "Communism," at www.faem.com/david/commu-5.htm; and Hank Roth, "The Dream of Equality is the Great Socialist Dream," at http://pnews.org/art/1art/SOCdream.shtml.

507. Sources include: *Encyclopædia Britannica* article on "anarchism;" Wikipedia bios on "Peter Kropotkin," "Mikhail Buakunin," "Jesse Cohn;" "Messianic Troublemakers: The Past and Present Jewish Anarchism" at the *Zeek* Web site, www.zeek.net/politics_0504.shtml; Sabby Sagall, "The Workers' Friend" a review of *East End Jewish Radicals*, at the Socialist Review Web site; "American Experience, Emma Goldman," at www.pbs.org/wgbh/amex/goldman/.

508. Sources include: The Tenant Web site, http://tenant.netCommunity/LES/contents.html and its articles on "Child Labor" and "Women's Working Hours;" *American Jewish Desk Reference*, 206–37; Deborah G. Felder and Diana Rosen, *Fifty Jewish Women Who Changed the World*, Citadel Press, New York, 2003, p. 103–10; the *Answers.com* articles on the "International Ladies Garment Workers' Union (ILGWU)," "Sidney Hillman" and "David Dubinsky" at www.answers.com/; *Encyclopædia Britannica* articles on "Jackie Presser" and "John L. Lewis;" Etckes, pages 180–1; Silbiger, pages 182–3; the *Jewish Currents* interview with Avi Lyon, the director of the Jewish Labor Committee, available at www.jewishcurrents.org/2005-mar-lyon.htm; the Web sites of the labor unions: Unite Here, Communications Workers of America, American Federation of Teachers, United Federation of Teachers, Service Employees International Union, the AFL-CIO, Teamsters, the Retail, Wholesale and Department Store Union; the *eReader.com* article on "Victor Gotbaum;" the ILGWU records at Cornell indexed at http://rmc.library.cornell.edu/EAD/htmldocs/KCL05780.html; the obituary of Murray Finley at www.chicagodsa.org/ngarchive/ng44.html; and others.

509. Sources include the NAACP Web site at www.naacp.org/about/about_history.html; Silbiger, pages 48–9; the Answers.com Web site articles on "Kivie Kaplan" and "Joel Spingarn."

510. See Emily Rosenberg, "The Pursuit of Justice: The Jewish Council on Urban Affairs," *Zeek*, March 2005.

511. See the bio of Winona LaDuke at www.Answers.com.

512. Sources include "Who is Lori Berenson?" at www.freelori.org/whoislori.htm; and the biography of Guzman at www.biography.ms/Abimael_Guzm%E1n.html.

513.Sources include the ACLU Web site, www.aclu.org, *American Jewish Historical Society*,pages 95–6, 143–4, 158; the Norman Siegel Web site, www.norman2005.com; www.holysmoke.org/sdhok/aclu-txt.htm; and www.truthtellers.org/hate crimes/proselyte.html.

514. Sources include, Arthur Liebman, *Jews and the Left (Contemporary Religious Movements)*, John Wiley & Sons, Inc., New York, 1979; Roth, "The Dream of Equality…"; Aviva Kempner, "Important History for Young People, Film Focuses on Radical Jews in Time of Political Turmoil," *Dallas Jewish Week*, Aug. 14, 2003 at www.dallasjewishweek.com/story.html/$rec=9894; the article, "The Weathermen" at www.geocities.com/southernscene/edu3.html?20058; Herb Ford, "Is a Film About '60s Radicals 'Jewish'," *New Jersey Jewish News*, at www.njjewishnews.com/jjjn.com/32504/comradicals.html; Edward Guthman, "The Weather Underground Documentary No Regrets," *San Francisco Chronicle*, July 21, 2003 at www.mindfully.org/Reform/2003/ Weather-Underground-21jul03.htm; "How Jews Controlled the New Left of the 1960s" at www.jewwatch.com/ jew-occupiedgovernments-usa-sds.html; Shmuel Trigano, "Is There a Future for French Jewry?" in the *Free Republic* Web site, April 2005 at www.freerepublic.com/ focus/f-news/1387009/posts; as well as Jodi Peleman, "Transforming the World: The Next Generation of Tikkun Olam Activists," at www.jewishlongbeach.org/ content display html?articleID=9111; and others.

515. Sources include Michael T. Kaufman, "David Dellinger, of Chicago 7, Dies at 88," *The New York Times*, May 27, 2004; Douglas O. Linder, "the Chicago Seven Conspiracy Trial," at the University of Missouri – Kansas City, School of Law Web site www.law.umkc.edu/faculty/projects/ftrials/Chicago7/Account.html.

516. Sources include the Answers.com Web site articles on "Harvey Milk," "Larry Kramer," "Leslie Feinberg," "the Gay and Lesbian Alliance Against Defamation," "John Cloud;," " The *Time* 100 at www.time.com/time/time100/heroes/profile/milk01.html; the Gay and Lesbian Alliance history at www.thetaskforce.org/aboutus/history.cfm; Beth Potier, "Activist Larry Kramer is Not Nice," *Harvard University Gazette*, Oct 2, 2003; and "Keynote: Larry Kramer," at http://tps.studentorg.wisc.edu/ TPS/mblgtcc/headliners/ larry_kramer_bio.html; www.transgenderwarrior.org/writings; www.workers.org/ww/1998/feinberg1224.php; the GLAAD Web site, www.glaad.org; the Human Rights Campaign Web site at www.hrc.org; the *Advocate* Web site, www.advocate.com/staff.asp; the "Twice Blessed," pages at www.oneinstitute.org/~twiceblessed/.

517. Sources include: Answers.com Web site List of Jewish American Political Figures, available at www.answers.com/topic/list-of-jewish-american-political-figures; the List of Jews at Wikipedia at http://en.wikipedia.org/wiki/ List_of_Jews; bios of many women mentioned from the two prior sites; "Jewish H3eroines: Making Their (Post)Mark" at www.goletapublishing.com/jstamps/0202-2.htm; www.wabe.org/history/ Quilt.html; www.frumkin.org.il/ shop-story

.htm; Alessandra Stanley, "A Trip Back in Time, to 1977, in Search of Feminism's Glory Days," *The New York Times*, March 1, 2005, B8; Margalit Fox, "Andrea Dworkin, 58, Writer and Crusading Feminist," *The New York Times*, April 24, 2005; Laura Miller, "Remembering Andrea Dworkin," *San Francisco Chronicle,* April 24, 2005, M2; John Simkin, "Votes for Women: How should it be Taught?" at http://educationforum.ipbhost.com/lofiversion/ index.php/t668.html; Amazon.com's material on the *Ladies Home Journal* Magazine Feature, *100 Most Important Women of the 20th Century;* and bios of various of the women.

518. Sources include the various pages at Greenpeace Web site, www.greenpeace.org/usa/, and at Rex Wyler's site, www.rexweyler.com.

519. Sources include the Amazon.com review of Susan Zaikin's *Coyotes and Town Dogs: Earth First! and the Environmental Movement,* the Earth First! Web site and the Answers.com bio of Judy Bari.

520. Sources include *American Jewish Historical Society*, p. 210; the Answers.com Web pages devoted to "Saul Alinsky," "Karen Ceraso," "Community Action Thirty Years Later;" Shelterforce Online at www.nhi.org/online/issues/ 100/caas.html; and Stephen Valocchi, "A Way of Thinking About the History of Community Organizing," at www.trincoll.edu/depts/tcn/valocchi.htm.

521. Sources include the PBS Frontline Web site devoted to "Israel's Next War" at www.pbs.org/wgbh/pages/ frontline/shows/israel/extreme/nameof.html; Jeffrey Goldberg, "Among the Settlers," *The New Yorker*, May 31, 2004; "Kach, Kahane Chai" at the Council of Foreign Relations Web site, http://cfrterrorism.org/groups/kkc.html; various articles at www.kahane.org/news/ny3.htm; and Tim Wise, "Taliban Jews: Some Extremists are More Equal Than Others," ZNet Web site, May 11, 2002, at www.zmag.org/content/temp/4567693212563.cfm.

522. Sources include Chomsky references above plus the Tom Wise bio on Answers.com.

523. Principal sources for the section on Marxism, Communism and Stalin include: Thomas Sowell, *Ethnic America*, pages 74–5; Lustiger, *Stalin and the Jews*, Enigma Books, New York, 2003, especially, 13–9, 26–32, 307–12; Alan Bullock, *Hitler and Stalin – Parallel Lives*, Vintage Books, New York, 1993, esp. 273, 472–6, 501, 507, 672, 951–3, 983–5; *Encyclopædia Britannica 2001* articles on "Karl Marx" and "Russia" & "The October (November) Revolution;" "Marx After Communism" from *Economist*, Dec. 21, 2002, Geoffrey Wheatcroft, "Still Saluting the Red Flag, After the Flagpole Fell" a review of Eric Hobsbawm's *Interesting Times*, from *The New York Times*, "Books of the Times" section, Sept. 5, 2003; and Richard Rhodes, *Dark Sun – The Making of the Hydrogen Bomb,* Touchstone, New York, 1995, 32 and Rhodes quotes from Victor Kravchenko's, *I Choose Freedom*, Scribner's Sons, 1946, 470.

524. Principal sources for the section on spies and traitors include: Herbert Romerstein and Eric Breindel, *The Venona Secrets*, Regnery Publishing, Inc. 2000, esp. 26–7, 184–6, 234–5, 447–60; Christopher Andrew and Vasili Mitrokhin, *The Sword and the Shield, The Mitrokhin Archive*, Basic Books, New York, 1999, esp. 111–7, 127–34; Rhodes, *Dark Sun*, esp. 49–197; *Court TV's on line Crime Library* at www.crimelibrary.com/terrorists_spies/spies/rosenberg/ 2.html?sect=23; and other pages in this section of the Site; "Obituary, Rem Krasilnikov," *Economist*, April 5, 2003: William J. Broad, "A Spy's Path: Iowa to A-Bomb to Kremlin Honor," *The New York Times*, Nov. 13, 2007; Sam Roberts, "57 Years Later, Figure in Rosenberg Case Says He Spied For Soviets," and "Rosenberg's Sons Sadly Accept That Their Father Was a Spy," *The New York Times*, Sept. 12 and 17, 2008 respectively.

525. Principal sources for the section on Oligarchs include: Yevginia Albats, "Abetting Russia's Oligarchs" *Washington Post*, January 24, 2003, p. A21; Peter Baker, Putin and the Oligarchs at Peace and Profiting," *The International Herald Tribune*, Dec. 16, 2002; Paul Starobin with Catherine Belton, "Open Season on Russia's Oligarchs," *Business Week*, July 10, 2000; reviews of Chrystia Freeland's *Sale of the Century: Russia's Wild Ride from Communism to Capitalism*, at Amazon.com, www.amazon.com/ exec/obidos/tg/detail/-/0812932153/103-1275200-9056; the materials at http://ulfsbo.nu/ussr/ formerussr.html, a Norwegian Web site with an extensive collection on Russia and the Oligarchs; S.A. Greene "Jews Are Fighting and the Whole Country Has To Watch" reviewing David E. Hoffman's *The Oligarchs: Wealth and Power in the New Russia* and Boris Usherenko's *My Jewish Fate*, in *Forward*, Sept 13, 2002 available online at www.forward.com/issues/2002/02.09.13/ arts1.html; Thayer Watkins, "The Russian Oligarchs of the 1990's" on the San Jose State University Economics Department Web site at www.sjsu.edu/faculty/watkins/ oligarchs.htm; Erin E. Arvedlund, "Money, if Not Power," *The New York Times*, Nov 9, 2003; Timothy L. O'Brien, "The Capitalist in the Cage," *The New York Times*, June 20, 2004; Steven Lee Meyers, "Athens Arrests Ex-Media Chief On Charges By Russia," *The New York Times*, Aug. 24, 2003; Nelson D. Schwart, "Russia's Trial of the Century, *Fortune*, Sept 20, 2004; Matthew Brezezinski, *Casino Moscow*, The Free Press, New York, 2001.

526. Principal sources for the section on Mobsters include, Rich Cohen, *Tough Jews*, Vintage Books, New York, esp. 44, 46, 55, 87, and 131, 1999; Sowell, *Ethnic America*, p. 96; John Kalish, Arnold 'The Brain'" a review of David Pietrusza's book *Rothstein: The Life, Times and Murder of the Criminal Genius Who Fixed the 1919 World Series,* in *Forward*, Oct. 31, 2003; multiple articles at *Court TV's Crime Library* sections on "Mob Bosses," "Crime Family Epics," and "Unique Gang Organizations," at www.crimelibrary.com; *Encyclopædia Britannica 2001* article, "Abe Reles," the

"Jewish Gangsters" pages at the Jewish Virtual Library, http://www.jewishvirtuallibrary.org/jsource/US-Israel/gangsters.html, and comparable pages at www.jew.net/jewishcriminals.htm; www.yahoodi.com/famous/crime1.html; and www.zundelsite.org/english/jewish_criminals/.

527. Steven Weinberg, "Member of the Tribe...of Pirates," *San Francisco Chronicle*, Nov. 2, 2008 (a review of Edward Kritzler's *Jewish Pirates of the Caribbean: How a Generation of Swashbuckling Jews Carved Out an Empire in the New World in Their Quest for Treasure, Religious Freedom—and Revenge*, Doubleday).

528. Sources for the section on Violent Crime & Assassins include *Court TV's Crime Library* sections on "Serial Killers," "Notorious Murders," "Gangsters & Outlaws," "Terrorists, Spies & Assassins," "Leopold & Loeb," "Son of Sam," and others available at www.crimelibrary.com; the FBI Web site, www.fbi.gov/mostwant/topten/fugitives/fugitives.htm; and others.

529. Principal sources for the section on Financial Crime, Frauds include: James B. Stewart, *Den of Thieves*, Touchstone, New York, 1992; Brian Burrough & John Helyar, *Barbarians At The Gates*, Harper & Row, New York, 1990; David D. Kirkpartick, "Corporate Scandals: A User's Guide" *The New York Times*, May 11, 2003; Jack Hitt, "Within the Ritual of Scandal" *The New York Times*, July 18, 2004; *Encyclopædia Britannica 2001* articles on the "South Sea Bubble," "Tulip Mania," an other scandals and frauds; The "Scandals & Fraud" Web pages at *Kip Notes*, www.kipnotes.com/ScandalsFraud.htm; "White-Collar Criminals" *Fortune*, Mar. 3, 2002 available at www.fortune.com/fortune/articles/ 0,15114,371011,00.html; Gary McKechnie & Nancy Howell, "Product: Million Dollar Frauds" on the New York Chapter, Institute of Internal Auditors, New York Chapter Web site at www.nyiia.org/newsletter/nov98_prod.htm; Linda Davies, "Classic Financial Scandals," University of Exeter Web site at www.ex.ac.uk/~RDavies/arian/scandals/classic.html; and related pages devoted to money laundering, central banks, mafia, political and similar imbroglios; Penelope Patsuris, "The Corporate Scandal Sheet" *Forbes*, Aug 26, 2002, available at www.forbes.com/home/20002/07/24/accountingtracker.html; various authors, "Wall Street Pays the Price: $1.4 Billion," *The Wall Street Journal*, April 29, 2003; Statement of Carl Levin, Hearing on Private Banking and Money Laundering, Nov. 9, 1999 at http://levin.senate.gov/floor/110999.htm; Robin Pogrebin, "In Madoff Scandal, Jews Feel an Acute Betrayal," *The New York Times*, Dec. 24, 2008; Javier C. Hernandez, "Betrayed by Madoff, Yeshiva U. Adds a Lesson, *The New York Times*, Dec. 23, 2008; Deborah Solomon, "Keeping the Faith," *The New York Times Magazine*, Oct. 5, 2008; Alan Feuer and Christine Haughney, "Standing Accused: A Pillar of Finance," *The New York Times*, Dec. 13, 2008; Eleanor Laise and Dennis K. Berman, "Impact on Jewish Charities is Catastrophic," *The Wall Street Journal*, Dec. 16, 2008; Ronald A. Cass, "Madoff Exploited the Jews," *The Wall Street Journal*, Dec. 18, 2008; "Madoff's Victims," *The Wall Street Journal*, Dec. 22, 2008; and other Web sites, newspaper articles and books.

530. Principal sources for the section on Embarrassments include the "Misfits and Embarrassments" page at Yahoodi.com, www.yahoodi.com/famous/misfits1.html; and "Programmers and Hackers" at www.yahoodi.com/ famous/hack1.html; Rick Lyman, "Winona Ryder Convicted of 2 Counts in Shoplifting," *The New York Times*, Nov. 7, 2002, p. 24, and Nick Madigan, "Actress Sentenced to Probation for Shoplifting," *The New York Times*, Dec. 7, 2002; and related articles from other sites, "Zhirinovsky Admits Jewish Roots," from *BBC News*, July 19, 2001 also at http://news.bbc.co.uk/2/hi/europe/1446759.stm; and the bios of him at www.cs.indiana.edu/~dmiguse/ Russian/vzbio.html, and www.geocities.com/CapitolHill/2768/zhirinoe.html; Shana Alexander, *When She Was Bad*, Random House, New York, 1990; David Reitzes, "In Defense of Jack Ruby," an article at www.jfk-online.com// rubydef.html; Carrie Kirby, "From Hacker to Prisoner, and Now to Celebrity," *San Francisco Chronicle*, April 23, 2003, p. E1.

531. Material on Julius Rosenwald and Sears, Roebuck has been drawn from: Leon Harris, *Merchant Princes*, pages 280–335; American Jewish Historical Society, pages 234–235; Encyclopædia Britannica 2001; the Rosenwald Schools Web site www.rosenwaldplans.org; the article "Rosenwald Schools" on the National Trust for Historic Preservation Web site www.nationaltrust.org; David G. Dalin, "Judaism's War on Poverty" in "*Policy Review* Sept.–Oct. 1997, Number 85," also at www.policyreview.org/sept97/judaism.html ; "Richard Sears" at www.bgsu.edu/departments/acs/1890s/sears/sears2.html; a Rosenwald bio at www.learningtogive.org/papers/people/julius_rosewald.html; "Giving While Living: dated 9/16/02 on the Women's Funding Network Web site: www.wfnet.org/new/story.php?story_id=27; a Rosenwald bio at: www.germanheritage.com; another at: www.acumenfund.org; one at www.myjewishbooks.com; and other Web sites.

532. Daniel J. Boorstin, "From Charity to Philanthropy," 10/25/2001, on the Web at www.acumenfund.org/Acumen/Portal/article/PoCShwArtc.asp?ID=9&IDType=RIP.

533. Daniel J. Boorstin, *Hidden History, Exploring Our Secret Past*, Vintage Books, New York, 1989, pages 193–209.

534. Book review on Web site of *New York Observer*: www.observer.com/pages/story.asp?ID=7834 dated February 12, 2004.

535. Jonathan Freedland "Lessons From America (Citizen Power in the U.S.)" *New Statesman*, July 3, 1998, also available at www.findarticles.com/cf_dls/mOFQP/n4392_v127/20974496/print.jhtml.

536. Material in this paragraph and the one following come from: *The Economist*, "Special Report: Philanthropy" July 31, 2004, 57–59 ; *The 2003 Report of the American Association of Fundraising Council* available at www.aafrc.org/bysourceof.html; "The Reader's Companion to American History—Philanthropy" on the Houghton Mifflin Web site: http://college.hmco.com/history/readerscomp/rcah/html/ah_068500_philanthropy.htm; "Charities Aid Foundation Report" at www.cafonline.org/pdf/International Comparisons of Charitable Giving.pdf; "Americans Give Record $295B To Charity," *USA Today*, Jun. 25, 2007.

537. Among principal sources for this section are: American Jewish Historical Society, p. 515; Telushkin, *Jewish Literacy: The Most Important Things to Know About the Jewish Religion, Its People, and Its History*, William Morrow and Company, Inc., New York, 2001, 118–19, 549, 561, 563–66, 586–88,605–06; Rabbi Ted Falcon, Ph.D. and David Blatner, *Judaism for Dummies*, Hungary Minds, Inc., New York, 2001, pages 30, 46, 74, 351; Johnson, *History of the Jews*, pages 203–04; Lawrence Bush "American Jews and the 'Torah of Money,'" *Tikkun*, July-August 1998, also available at www.findarticles.com; "Tzedakah," at the Jewish Virtual Library Web site www.us-israel.org; "Tzedakah," at www.jewfaq.org; Rabbi Yisrael Rutman, "Generosity & the Jews" at www.aish.com/literacy/mitzvahs/Generosity_and_the_Jews.asp; David G. Dalin, "Judaism's War on Poverty" *"Policy Review,"* September-October 1997, available at www.policyreview.org/sept97/judaism.html; "Tzedaka," at www.tzedaka.org/; "Tikkun Olam: Perfecting the World" at: www.innerfrontier.org/Practices/TikkunOlam.htm; Gary A. Tobin, *"The Transition of Communal Values and Behavior in Jewish Philanthropy 2001,"* Institute for Jewish & Community Research, San Francisco, 8.

538. Sources for this section include: Gary Tobin's comments on the absence of definitive information on rates of Jewish philanthropy in AAFRC Trust for Philanthropy, "Giving USA 2002: The Annual Report on Philanthropy for the Year 2001" Indianapolis, 2002, 102; (This was also the author's experience in researching the question); *"The National Jewish Population Survey 2000–01,* Sept 2003, and updated January 2004," United Jewish Communities in Cooperation with The Mandell L. Berman Institute, pages 6, 13, 14, ; 3) Julia Duin, "Giving in Different Denominations, Religious Giving Has Reached All-time Lows" May June 2001, Philanthropy Roundtable Web site at www.philanthropyroundtable.org/magazines/2001/may/duin.html; Judith Miller, "Israel's Controversy Over Religion Affects Donations by Jews in U.S.," *The New York Times*, Nov. 17, 1997; Julia McCord, "Churches Lagging in Collections," *World-Herald*, April 23, 2000, also reported on www.adherents.com; "Giving Among the World Religions and Cults" at www.generousgiving.org/page.asp?sec=4&page=235; "Statistics" at www.generousgiving.org/page.asp?sec=4&page352; Jack Wertheimer, "A review of "Current Trends in American Jewish Philanthropy" as reviewed by American Jewish Committee, Sept. 3, 1997 at www.charitywire.com/charity11/00342.html; Lawrence Bush and Jeffrey Deko, "Fifteen Years Ago…" *Tikkun*, Sept/Oct 2001, available on www.tikkun.org; Gary A. Tobin, *"The Transition of Communal Values…"* 5; 8; Debra Nussbaum Cohen, "Not Your Parents' Jewish Giving" *The Jewish Week*, also at www.thejewishweek.com/bottom/specialcontent.php3?artid=329; Gary A. Tobin, Ph.D., Jeffrey R. Solomon Ph.D., and, Alexander C. Karp, PH.D. *"Mega-Gifts in American Philanthropy,"* Institute for Jewish & Community Research, San Francisco; and others.

539. Material for this Section comes from: "American Jewish Contributions to Israel (1948–1999)" at www.us-israel.org/jsource/US-Israel/ujatab.html; Gary A. Tobin, Ph.D., et al, *"Mega Gifts in American Philanthropy,"* (see full citation in prior paragraph); 3) Marvin Schotland, "Agenda Fails to Inspire Mega-donors," *Forward*, Nov. 14, 2003 also available at www.forward.com/issues/2003/03.11.14/ giving8.html; Tom Tugend, "Why Aren't Jews Giving to Jews?" *The Jewish Journal*, June 27, 2003, also available at www.jewishjournal.com/home/preview.php?id=10744; Joe Berkofsky, "Jewish Mega-donors Give Little to Jews," *Jewish Community News*, April 2004 also at www.jewishsiliconvalley.org/jcn/04_2004/ jewishmegadonors.html; Judith Milller, "Israel's Controversy (see full citation in prior paragraph).

540. Material for this Section comes from: Julia Goldman, "Moneyed 'Study Group' Is Engine for Charity", *Forward*, Dec. 21, 2001 also at www.forward.com/issues/2001/01.12.21/news7.html; Lisa Miller, "Titans of Industry Join Forces to Work for Jewish Philanthropy," *The Wall Street Journal*, May 4, 1998 also at www.japonica.com/japonical/megagroup.html; Scott Thompson "Who's Who in Mega?," *Executive Intelligence Review*, Nov. 16, 2001 also at www.larouchepub.com/other/2001/ 2844mega_bios.html; Bob Fitraksi, "The Wexner War," *The Free Press*, Aug. 1, 2003, also at www.freepress.org/columns/display/3/2003/725; and many other Web site screeds.

541. Michelle Conlin, Lauren Gard, and Jessi Hempel, "Special Report Philanthropy 2004—The Top Givers," *Business Week*.

542., B'resheet (Genesis) 12:1–2, *Complete Jewish Bible*, Jewish New Testament Publications, Inc.

543. Some would measure the Diaspora from 722 B.C. when the Assyrians conquered and dispersed the ten lost tribes of Israel. Others would start at 586 B.C. when the Babylonians conquered Jerusalem and dispersed the Jews to Babylon. Still others would date the Diaspora from A.D. 70 when the Roman's destroyed the second temple and Jews were dispersed from Palestine. Because the ten tribes disappeared forever, (they died out or were assimilated) this article uses the 586 B.C. dispersal.

544. Raphel Patai, *The Jewish Mind*, Wayne State University Press, Detroit, 1977, p. 317–8.

545. Charles Murray, *Human Accomplishment*, p. 547–53.

546. Michael Barone, *The New Americans*, Regnery Publishing, Washington, D.C., 2001, p. 222.

547. Yuri Slezkine, *The Jewish Century*, pages 90–1, 105, 115–27, 150–2, 158, 169, 175–7, 199, 217–26, 243, 251–5, 301–3, 318, 329–31, 342, 348–9, 358–62, 368–71.

548. Ernst Van Den Haag, *The Jewish Mystique*, Stein and Day Publishers, New York, 1969, pages14–8.

549 William Manchester, *A World Lit Only By Fire: Portrait of an Age*, Little Brown and Company, Boston, Toronto, London, 1992, pages 43, 71, 74, 75–9, 82–6, 125–6 128–9, 130–1, 143, 160.

550. http://www.dangor.com/74029.html, Web site for *The Scribe*, Issue 74, abridging an article from *The Daily Telegraph*.

551. Gregory Cochran, Jason Hardy, Henry Harpending, "Natural History of Ashkenazi Intelligence," available at http://homepage.mac.com/harpend/.Public/AshkenaziIQ.jbiosocsci.pdf, which also appeared in the *Journal of Biosocial Science*, 2006.

552. Nicholas Wade, "In DNA, New Clues to Jewish Roots," *New York Times*, May 14, 2002, (F1, Col 1) "Geneticists Report Finding Central Asian Link to Levites" *New York Times*, Sept. 27, 2003, "Group in Africa Has Jewish Roots, DNA Indicates," *New York Times* May 9, 1999.

553. Nadine Epstein, "Family Matters: Funny, We Don't Look Jewish," *Hadassah Magazine*, January 2001.
554. Belel, Faerman, et al, "Study: North African, Iraqi Jewry Nearly Genetic Twins," *Jerusalem Post*, Nov. 19, 2001.
555. Robert Pollack, "The Fallacy of Biological Judaism," *Forward*, March 7, 2003.

556. Maristella Botticini and Zvi Eckstein, "Jewish Occupational Selection: Education, Restrictions, or Minorities," *Journal of Economic History*, 65, no. 4 (December 2005).

557. Botticini, p.13.

558. Botticini pages 5, 15–17.

559. Corchran, et al, (see above).

560. Nicholas Wade, "Researchers Say Intelligence and Diseases May Be Linked in Ashkenazic Genes," *The New York Times*, June 3, 2005; and "Natural Genius," *Economist*, Jun 2, 2005.

561. Charles Murray, "Jewish Genius," *Commentary*, April 2007.

562. Patai, p. 309.

563. See also David Brooks, "The Luxurious Growth," *The New York Times*, July 15, 2008, p. A-19.

564. Definition of "Culture," *Random House Unabridged Dictionary, Second Edition*, 1993, p. 488.

565. David S. Landes, *The Wealth and Poverty of Nations*, WW Norton & Company, 1998, p. 516.

566. Ibid.

567. David S. Ariel, *What Do Jews Believe?* Schocken Books, New York, 1995, p. 7.

568. Ibid, pages 13, 15 – 16.

569. Ibid, p. 21.

570. B'resheet (Genesis) 1:1.

571. Johnson, p. 2.

572. Thomas Cahill, *The Gifts of the Jews*, Nan A. Talese/Harper Books, New York, 1998, p. 251.

573. Rabbi Falcon, Ph.D., & Blatner, p. 29.

574. Rabbi Morris N. Kertzer, *What Is a Jew?* Macmillan Publishing, New York, 1978, p. 40.

575. Johnson, p. 172.

576. Ibid, p. 585.

577. Daniel J. Boorstin, *Hidden History: Exploring Our Secret Past*, Vintage Books, New York, 1989, pages xv-xvii.

578. Ibid, p.xvi.

579. Thomas Sowell, *Migrations and Cultures*, Basic Books, New York, 1996, p. 246.

580. Sandee Brawarsky and Deborah Mark, editors, *Two Jews, Three Opinions*, A Perigree Book, The Berkeley Publishing Group, New York, 1998.

581. Rabbi Kertzer, p. 5.

582. Rabbi Falcon, Ph.D., & Blatner, p. 38.

583. Cahill, p. 76.

584. B'resheet (Genesis) 18:23-25.

585. This anecdote was related to the author by Rabbi Harold Kushner.

586. Kertzer, p. 141.

587. Ibid, p. 131.

588. Sowell, *Ethnic America*, p. 86.

589. Ibid, p. 280.

590. Ibid, p. 89.

591. Sowell, *Migrations and Cultures*, Basic Books, New York, 1996, 299; Council of Jewish Federations, "Highlights of the CJF 1990 National Jewish Population Survey," 1991, pages 10–12.

592. Sowell, *Ethnic America*, p. 98.

593. Sowell, *Migrations*, p. 305.

594. Ibid, p. 292.

595. Ibid, p. 277.

596. Patai, p. 329.

597. Ariel, p. 68.

598. Sowell, *Ethnic America*, p. 94.

599. Ibid, p. 86.

600. Ariel, p. 69.

601. Rabbi Kertzer, p. 51.

602. Sowell, *Ethnic America*, p. 280.

603. Richard Eder, "Starkly, a Son Revisits His Father's Failures" book review of Sherwin Nuland's book *Lost in America, New York Times*, March 25, 2003.

604. Mark Gribben article on Meyer Lansky, Chapter 2, "A Fortune Found" in Court TV's Crime Library Web site (http://www.crimelibrary.com/gangsters_outlaws/mob_bosses/lansky) .

605. C.M. Pilkington, *Judaism*, Teach Yourself Library, London, 2000, pages 82–88.

606. Ibid, p. 83.

607. David Derbyshire "Gene Helps Jews Resist Alcoholism" *The Daily Telegraph* U.K. Sept. 17, 2002.

608. Michael Barone, *The New Americans*, Regnery Publishing, Washington D.C., 2001, p. 226.

609. Sowell, *Ethnic America*, p. 74.

610. Sowell, *Migrations*, p. 306.

611. Barone, p. 217.

612. Sowell, *Ethnic America*, p. 84.

613. Wikipedia (http://en2.wikipedia.org/wiki/United_Artists describes Charles Chaplin, Douglas Fairbanks, Mary Pickford and D.W. Griffith as the four founders. Chaplin may or may not have some Jewish legacy but the others do not.

614. Sowell, *Ethnic America*, p. 93.

615. Rabbi Kertzer, p. 200.

616. Ibid, p. 131.

617. Johnson, p. 4.

618. Johnson, p. 3.

619. Ibid.

620. B'resheet (Genesis) 12:1-2.

621. Stephen G. Bloom, *Postville: A Clash of Cultures in Heartland America*, A Harvest Book, Harcourt, Inc. San Diego, New York, London, 2000.

622. Burton Feldman, *The Nobel Prize*, Arcade Publishing, New York, 2000, pages 139–149.

623. Sowell, *A Conflict of Visions*, Quill/William Morrow, New York, 1987.

624. Johnson, p. 203–204.

625. "The 50 Most Generous Philanthropists," *Business Week*, Dec. 1, 2003, 81.

626. Johnson, p. 203.

627. Patai, p. 234.

628. Patai, p. 280.

629. Ben Weider, "Napoleon and the Jews," at www.napoleon-series.org/ins/wider/c_jews.html.

630. Eli Barnavi, *A Historical Atlas of the Jewish People,* p. 176.

631. Murray, Human Accomplishment, p. 276.

632. Professor Sergio Della Pergola, "Review of Relevant Demographic Information on World Jewry," a Final Report Presented to The Hon. Secretary Lawrence S. Eagleburger, Chairman, The International Commission on Holocaust Era Insurance Claims.

633. Rabbi Telushkin, Jewish Literacy, p. 482.

634. Among other commentaries, see Ellis Rivkind, *The Unity Principle,* Behrman House, Springfield New Jersey, 2003.

635. Johnson, p. 51.

636. Rivkin, pages 2-5.

637. Rivkin, pages 18-20.

638. Max I. Dimont, *Jews, God and History,* New American Library, New York, 1994 p. 31.

639. Johnson, pages 148-50.

640. Jonathan D. Sarna, "A Great Jewish Awakening," an essay delivered April 26, 1995 to a Board Seminar of the Council for Initiatives in Jewish Education. The essay is available at www.rebooters.net/articles/awakeningEssay.pdf.

641. Roger Kamenetz, *The Jew in the Lotus,* Harper San Francisco, 1994/95.

642. Many articles and editorial opinions were written between mid 2002 and late 2003 regarding the National Jewish Population Survey (NJPS), done by United Jewish Communities. They raised questions about whether or not it accurately portrayed U.S. Jewish demography or was a fraud intended to incite unnecessary worry, increased programming for Jews, and greater donations to Jewish causes. See for example, Daniel J. Wakin, "A Count of U.S. Jews Sees a Dip; Others Demur," *The New York Times,* Oct. 9, 2002, Debra Nussbaum Cohen, "Jewish Population Debate Continues," *Jewish News of Greater Phoenix,* Oct. 4, 2002, and her story, "U.S. Jewry May Be Growing," *The Jewish Week,* not dated, but available at www.beliefnet.com/story/114/story_11418_1.html,.J.J. Goldberg, wrote "A Jewish Recount," *The New York Times,* Sep. 17, 2003. There were many other such stories. The competing study by Gary Tobin's Institute for Jewish Community Research places the 2000 population figure at 6 million, 800,000 more than the NJPS figure of 5.2 million. The principle differences involve Tobin's estimates of Jews who decline to be identified as such, a relative undercount of West Coast Jews, and an undercount of immigrants. For our purposes, however, what matters is not whether the figure should be 5.2 million or 6.0 million. What matters are the trends and the demographic driving forces such as birth rate, intermarriage, etc. With or without the undercount, Tobin's tally does not dispute the forces driving a decline. Presumably the birth rate, high average age, rate of intermarriage and other data are not materially different, or at least if they are, Tobin and his allies did not raise the point in the news coverage. Moreover, DellaPergola uses a 5.3 million figure in his Report to Eagleburger cited above.

643. Rabbi Micah D. Greenstein, "What's Wrong With the 2001 Jewish Population Study," Voice, 1/2/04, at www.uahc.org/tn/ti/Greenstein/BYM.html.

644. Dr. Gary A. Tobin, "A Study of Jewish Culture in the Bay Area," Institute for Jewish & Community Research, p. 6.

645. Douglas Rushkoff, "Don't Judge Judaism By the Numbers," *The New York Times,* Nov. 20, 2002.

646. David Arnow, "Will Judaism Flourish Or Decline in the Next 50 Years?" *Moment Magazine,* at www.moment-mag.com/survey/survey.html.

647. Among other writings on this topic, see Jonathan Rosenblum, "Why Be Jewish?" Baltimore Jewish Times, November 1, 2002 at www.tzemachdovid.org/amechad/why.shtml.

648. Etgar Lefkovits, "Safire: US Jews Should Be More Open To Converts," *Jerusalem Post,* June 16, 2005.

649. Eli Barnavi, Editor, *A Historical Atlas of the Jewish People,* Schocken Books, New York, 2002, p. 1.

650. In significant measure, the post War numbers and high average age have been driven by the loss of an estimated 1.25 million or more children during the Holocaust. Those children, and their offspring might have substantially changed the demographics.

651. Associated Press, "Israel to Have Largest Jewish Population for First Time in 2006, Report," at www.ujc.org/content_display.html?print=1&ArticleID=157836&page=1.

652. U.S. Census Bureau, International Data Base as provided at Infoplease, "Total Population of the World by Decade, 1950-2050" at http://print.infoplease.com/ipa/A0762181.html.

653. DellaPergola, National Jewish Population Survey 2000-01, p. 23.

654. Sowell, *Ethnic America,* p. 94; and Vian Klaff, "The Changing Jewish Population Identity and Structure," *Contact,* Spring, 2003, Vol 5 No. 3.

655. Johnson, p. 341.

656. Charles Murray, *Human Accomplishment,* pages 232-3.

657. Worth reading on this topic is the Yom Kippur Sermon 5764/2003 delivered at the Brooklyn Heights Synagogue, which is available at www.bhsbrooklyn.org/sermonyk03a.htm.

658. Dimont, pages 290-2.

659. Egon Mayor, "The Rise of the Seculars in American Jewish Life," *Contemplate,* Issue Two/2003 available at www.culturaljudaism.org/pdf/ajisbook.pdf; also see the incidence of religious affiliation, synagogue membership and related data in The National Jewish Population Survey 2000-01, pages 7-16; and the Institute for Jewish and Community Research's Survey of Heritage and Religious Identification, 2001-02, pages 1-5.

660. Wikipedia, "Israel," at http://en.wikipedia.org/wiki/Israel

661. Tim Johnson, "An Israeli Icon in Decline," Today, Jan. 23, 2002 at www.cyc-net.org/today2002/today020123.html; and the article, "Kibbutz" at http://en.wikipedia.org.

662. Daniel Boorstin, *Hidden History,* Vintage Books, New York, 1987, p. 224.

663. Michael H. Hart, *The 100: A Ranking of the Most Influential Persons in History,* Citadel Press, Secaucus, New Jersey, 1987

Index